lonely planet

Ireland

Tom Smallman
Fionn Davenport
Dorinda Talbot
Steve Fallon
Pat Yale

LONELY PLANET PUBLICATIONS
Melbourne • Oakland • London • Paris

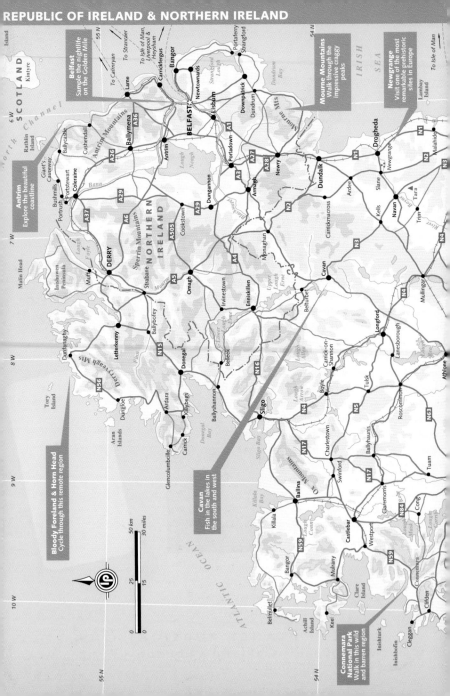

REPUBLIC OF IRELAND & NORTHERN IRELAND

Belfast
Sample the nightlife on the Golden Mile

Antrim
Explore the beautiful coastline

Bloody Foreland & Horn Head
Cycle through this remote region

Cavan
Fish in the lakes in the south and west

Connemara National Park
Walk in this wild and barren region

Mourne Mountains
Walk through the impressive craggy peaks

Newgrange
Visit one of the most remarkable prehistoric sites in Europe

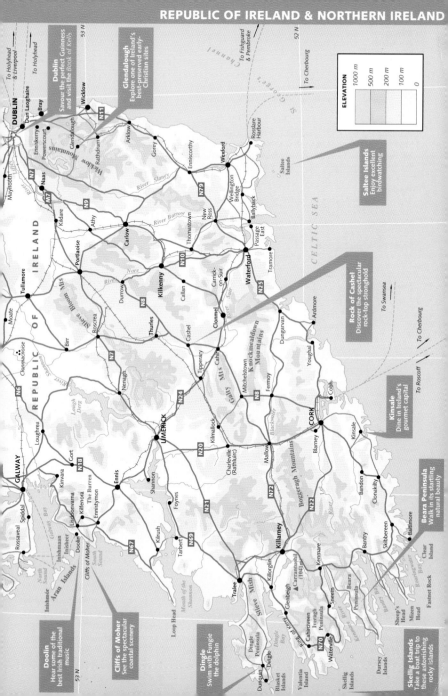

REPUBLIC OF IRELAND & NORTHERN IRELAND

ELEVATION
1000 m
500 m
200 m
100 m
0

St George's Channel

CELTIC SEA

REPUBLIC OF IRELAND

To Holyhead & Liverpool
To Holyhead
To Fishguard & Pembroke
To Cherbourg
To Swansea
To Cherbourg
To Roscoff

Dublin
Savour the perfect Guinness and visit the *Book of Kells*

Glendalough
Explore one of Ireland's best-preserved early-Christian sites

Saltee Islands
Enjoy excellent birdwatching

Rock of Cashel
Discover the spectacular rock-top stronghold

Kinsale
Dine in Ireland's gourmet capital

Beara Peninsula
Walk in its starting natural beauty

Doolin
Hear some of the best Irish traditional music

Cliffs of Moher
See the spectacular coastal scenery

Dingle
Swim with Fungie the dolphin

Skellig Islands
Take a boat trip to these astonishing rocky islands

DUBLIN
Dun Laoghaire
Bray
Enniskerry
Powerscourt
Glendalough
Wicklow
Arklow
Mayooth
Naas
Kildare
Athy
Carlow
Gorey
Enniscorthy
Wexford
Rosslare Harbour
Saltee Islands
Tullamore
Moate
Portlaoise
Kilkenny
Callan
New Ross
Thomastown
Carrick-on-Suir
Waterford
Passage East
Tramore
Clonmap.owen
Clonmacnoise
Birr
Durrow
Roscrea
Thurles
Cashel
Clonmel
Dungarvan
Ardmore
Youghal
Cobh
Nenagh
Tipperary
Cahir
Mitchelstown
Fermoy
Blackwater
CORK
Kinsale
GALWAY
Loughrea
Gort
Kinvara
Ennis
Shannon
Foynes
Limerick
Kilmallock
Charleville (Rathluirc)
Mallow
Blarney
Bandon
Clonakilty
Rosaveal
Spiddal
Lisdoonvarna
The Burren
Kilfenora
Ennistymon
Doolin
Kilrush
Tarbert
Killarney
Kenmare
Bantry
Skibbereen
Baltimore
Clear Island
Tralee
Killorglin
Glenbeigh
Sneem
Cahirciveen
Waterville
Dunquin
Dingle

Wicklow Mountains
Slieve Bloom Mts
Galty Mts
Knockmealdown Mountains
Boggeragh Mountains
Slieve Mish
Dingle Peninsula
Iveragh Peninsula
Beara Peninsula
Caha Mountains

River Slaney
River Barrow
River Nore
River Suir
River Shannon
Lough Derg
Galway Bay
South Sound
North Sound
Aran Islands
Inishmore
Inishmaan
Inisheer
Cliffs of Moher
Mouth of the Shannon
Loop Head
Blasket Islands
Dingle Bay
Valentia Island
Skellig Islands
Dursey Islands
Sheep's Head
Mizen Head
Fastnet Rock
Bantry Bay
Kenmare River
Dingle River

N11
N7
M7
N9
N79
N80
N25
N8
N7
N24
N20
N21
N69
N59
N18
N6
N70
N72
N22

▲ Carrantuohill (1041)

Ireland
4th edition – March 2000
First published – January 1994

Published by
Lonely Planet Publications Pty Ltd A.C.N. 005 607 983
192 Burwood Rd, Hawthorn, Victoria 3122, Australia

Lonely Planet Offices
Australia PO Box 617, Hawthorn, Victoria 3122
USA 150 Linden St, Oakland, CA 94607
UK 10a Spring Place, London NW5 3BH
France 1 rue du Dahomey, 75011 Paris

Photographs
Many of the images in this guide are available for licensing from
Lonely Planet Images.
email: lpi@lonelyplanet.com.au

Front cover photograph
The ruins of an Irish hill farm (Joe Cornish, Tony Stone Images)

ISBN 0 86442 753 0

text & maps © Lonely Planet 2000
photos © photographers as indicated 2000

Printed by Colorcraft Ltd, Hong Kong

Contents – Maps

CENTRAL NORTH

COUNTY DONEGAL

COUNTIES MEATH & LOUTH

BELFAST

COUNTIES DOWN & ARMAGH

COUNTIES DERRY & ANTRIM

COUNTIES TYRONE & FERMANAGH

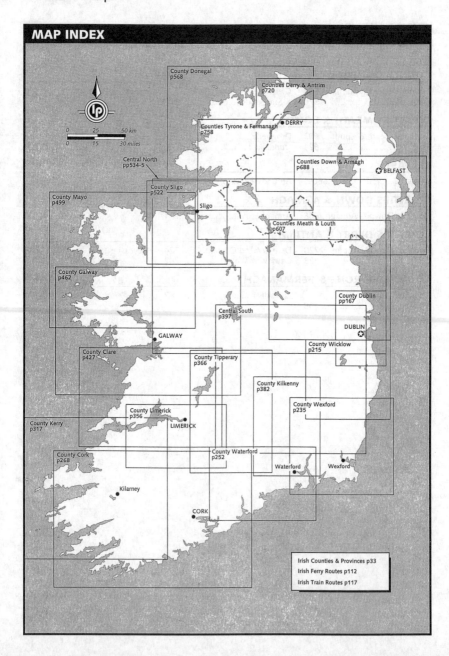

MAP INDEX

County Donegal
p568

Counties Derry & Antrim
p720

Counties Tyrone & Fermanagh
p758

● DERRY

Counties Down & Armagh
p688

✪ BELFAST

Central North
pp534-5

County Sligo
p522

County Mayo
p499

● Sligo

Counties Meath & Louth
p607

County Galway
p462

County Dublin
pp167

Central South
p397

DUBLIN
✪

● GALWAY

County Wicklow
p215

County Clare
p427

County Tipperary
p366

County Kilkenny
p382

County Wexford
p235

County Limerick
p356

LIMERICK ●

County Kerry
p317

County Cork
p268

County Waterford
p252

● Waterford

Wexford ●

● Kilarney

CORK ●

0 25 50 km
0 15 30 miles

Irish Counties & Provinces p33
Irish Ferry Routes p112
Irish Train Routes p117

The Authors

Tom Smallman

Tom lives in Melbourne, Australia, and had a number of jobs before joining Lonely Planet as an editor. He now works full time as an author and has worked on Lonely Planet guides to *Britain*, *Scotland*, *Edinburgh*, *Australia*, *New South Wales*, *Sydney*, *Canada*, *Dublin* and *Pennsylvania*.

Fionn Davenport

Fionn was born in and spent most of his youth in Dublin – that is, when his family wasn't moving him to Buenos Aires or Geneva or New York (all thanks to his Dad, whose job took him far and wide). Infected with the travel disease, he became a nomad in his own right after graduating from Trinity College, moving first to Paris and then to New York, where he spent five years as a travel editor and sometime writer. The call of home was too much to resist, however, so armed with his portable computer, his record collection and an empty wallet he returned to Dublin where he decided to continue where he left off in New York. Only it was quieter, wetter and a hell of a lot smaller. When he's not DJing in pubs and clubs throughout the city he's writing and updating travel guides. He has written about many destinations throughout the world. This is his third book for Lonely Planet, having worked already on *Spain* and *Dublin*.

Dorinda Talbot

Born in Melbourne, she began travelling at the age of five months – to visit her grandparents in Blighty – and has since visited other far-flung corners of the globe. After studying journalism at Deakin University in Geelong, Dorinda worked as a reporter in Alice Springs and a sub-editor in Melbourne before travelling across South-East Asia to London. She worked as a journalist (and sometime fruiterer) in London for several years before hauling on her walking boots to update Lonely Planet's *Canada* (the flat bits as it turned out). Dorinda also updated Lonely Planet's guides to *Morocco* and *Samoa* and has contributed to *Western Europe* and *Africa*.

Steve Fallon

Steve, whose grandparents left counties Roscommon and Cork for America at the beginning of the last century, worked an assortment of menial but character-building – so his parents said – jobs as a youngster to finance trips to Europe and South America. He taught English in Eastern Europe before moving to Asia, where he worked as a journalist and bookseller for 13 years. Steve lived in Budapest for almost three years, from where he wrote Lonely Planet's guides to *Hungary* and *Slovenia* before moving to London in 1994. He has written or contributed to a number of other Lonely Planet titles.

Pat Yale

Pat spent several years selling holidays before throwing off sensible careerdom to head overland from Egypt to Zimbabwe. She then mixed teaching tourism with travel in Europe, Asia, and Central and South America, before becoming a full-time writer. She has worked on Lonely Planet guides to *Dublin*, *Britain*, *London* and *Turkey*, and has contributed to *Walking in Britain*. After stints in London, Cambridge, Cirencester and Bristol, she currently lives in Turkey.

FROM THE AUTHORS

Tom Smallman My eternal gratitude to Sue Graefe for her enduring, patient and tolerant support; to Arthur and Liz who made it all possible; to Lindy Mark for her invaluable information; to Eileen Maguire for the coffee and the *craic* in Dublin; as always to the Ryan Rue family, Kathleen, Christy, Kathleen, Roger and Christy in Tipperary for being such wonderful people; to Tricia and Brian for a great time in spite of the weather; to Bridget, Denis, Tom and Oscar in Cork; to Geraldine at Ionad Árann on Inishmór; to the publican at Ma Murphy's pub in Bantry; to the staff at the Bundoran tourist office, Donegal; to all those other people in the travel industry who patiently answered my questions; to my co-researchers Dorinda and Fionn; and to all those readers who wrote in with comments on the previous edition. My work on this edition is dedicated to the Kelleher family, especially to Pat Kelleher, may he rest in peace.

Fionn Davenport My sincerest thanks to all those working in the different tourist offices, especially the staff in Waterford and Kilkenny – who provided great service with a smile – and more than a couple of invaluable insider tips. A big thank you to everyone who found the time to answer all of my inane questions and multiple non sequitors. All my gratitude to friends who had to put up with my travel neuroses; mumbling about having to huddle in doorways to shield my notebook from the perpetual rain; and general fretting about whether the book was going to get done on time. Thanks to Sorcha for your invaluable knowledge of Wicklow (!).

Dorinda Talbot Many thanks are due to Bernadette and Roisin Meehan for their warm hospitality, practical help and insights into Northern Ireland; to Kenny Doory and Maureen Wheeler for helping to point me in the right direction; to John Tolano and Billy Dixon in Belfast; to Paddy of the Linen House Hostel; to Steve and Yvonne in Derry (and Belfast); to Nigel Glenny and Elaine Cloughan in Armagh City (rhubarb will never be the same again); to Steve at Castle Archdale; to William Gilfillan at Downhill; to

Vivienne Quinn of the Department of Economic Development; to all the helpful NITB staff encountered during research; to the LP faithful who wrote in with invaluable advice and constructive criticism; to all the infinitely polite and patient people of Northern Ireland who helped along the way; and to my great great grandmother Charlotte Templeton for making it from Armagh to Melbourne in 1852.

This Book

The 1st edition of this book was written by John Murray, Sean Sheehan and Tony Wheeler. The 2nd edition was updated by Tom Smallman, Sean Sheehan and Pat Yale. The 3rd edition was updated by Tom Smallman, Pat Yale and Steve Fallon. For this 4th edition, Tom Smallman updated the introductory chapters as well as Counties Cork, Kerry, Limerick & Tipperary, Clare, Galway, Mayo & Sligo and Donegal; he also coordinated the project. Fionn Davenport updated the material on Dublin, Counties Wicklow, Wexford & Waterford, Kilkenny, Meath & Louth, and the Central South and Central North chapters. Dorinda Talbot extensively reworked the Northern Ireland chapters.

From the Publisher

This 4th edition of Ireland was edited and proofed by Claudia Martin, with help from Lynn Bresler, Sam Carew and Anna Jacomb-Hood. Mapping and design was coordinated by Paul Edmunds, with the assistance of Tom Fawcett, Ed Pickard and David Wenk. Nicky Caven and Matt King provided the illustrations. Sam Trafford and Tim Ryder helped with indexing, and Katrina Browning and Marcel Gaston pitched in with final layout corrections. Thanks to Quentin Frayne for compiling the Language chapter and Lonely Planet Images for providing photographs. Thanks to Helena White of the Northern Ireland Statistics & Research Agency for providing population information; this was reproduced from the 1991 Towns and Villages Booklet for Northern Ireland by permission of the Controller of HMSO and the Department of Finance & Personnel. The Guinness poster opposite page 65 is reproduced by permission of Guinness Ireland Archives.

Thanks

Many thanks to the travellers who used the previous editions and wrote to us with helpful hints, useful advice and interesting anecdotes. Your names follow:

A Rozema, A Rzepa, A Zwematra, Al Breddin, Al Bredin, Alain Herman, Alan & Cathie Murdey, Alex Castrodale, Alice McBride, Alison Amdur, Allison Gordon, Andets Dahlsjo, Andrea King, Andrew Auden, Andrew Gregorvich, Andrew Johnson, Ann De Schryver, Anna Crankshaw, Annette de Graaf, Anthony Webb, Baden Brown, Banfshe Hejazi, Barbara Seth, Belinda Brown, Ben Clarke, Ben Pickett, Birgitt Kleimann, Bob Harrison, Bobbi Jo, Boris van der Lee, Brent Pomeroy, Brian & Mary Flynn, Bridget Herold, Bruce Blakemore, C Erica Norum, C Wymberry, Carol Berwick, Caroline Furze, Carsten Boettger, Chris & Linda Perry, Chris Miller, Chris Olsen, Chris Read, Chris Wyatt, Christine Lynn, Christine Murphy, Christopher Romanet, Claire McCombie, Clark Downs,

Claudia Huwald, Cliff Earp, Colin Ogilvy, Corinna Schmolhe, Crystal Hogg, D Fooney, D Smyth, D Tishel , D Valk, Dan Coplan, Daniel Kavanaugh, Daniel Meijer, Daniel Pitts, Danyane Johnston, Daryl Williams, Dave Cedrone, Dave Kernick, David Heffernan, David Ingram, David Monaghan, David Reid, Deborah Bourner, DL & DC Baker, Dominic Goodfellow , Dr & Mrs Jorje Sowers, Dr John Dorling, Dr Madeleine Shataugh, Ed Barbanell, Edmond Hickey, Elaine Crowe, Elinor Drake, Elizabeth Bannear, Emma Dods, Eric Lord, Eric Van Ostol, Eugene Schaefer, Fiona Dodd, Frank Bugeja, Frank J Auriemmo, Frank Jansen, Gary & Jane Martin, Gary Mayne, Genevieve Michael, Geraldine Bailie, Geraldine Exton, Germain Groll, Glenn R Bonkowski, Graham MacLeod, Greg Nedohin, Greg Turley, H Williams, Haatem Reda, Hamish Murray, Han Nabben, Helen Pinoff, Helen Pinoff, Inga Schedlbauer, Ingrid Bjorkman, J Burt , J Clocean, J F Mercille, J Forsberg, J McKenzie , J Smith, J Veenboer, Jacki Hatnett, James Cadman, James Earl, Jan & Marij Krijne, Jane Cosgrave, Janice & Robin Tausig, Janice Teoh, Janine Carter, Jeanne Loughlin, JF Davies, Jill E Bell, Jim Woodfin, Joanne Lafley, Joe Englander, John Bielinski, John Maher, John Murphy, Jolien Ophof, Joram Borenstein, Judith Kiddlo, K Carroll, Karen & Martin Makes, Karen For, Karen Furland, Karin Wedlund, Katherine Cram, Katherine H Schell, Kathleen Madden, Katrina Cartwright, Ken Weilerstein, Kenneth & Barbara Bagnell, Kenneth Folan, Kylie McKernan, Laura McGuinness, Litmari Jurvanen, Liz Burke, Liz Farrell, Liz Schwartz, Lucia Matassoni, Lucy Kelly, Luigi Silvestri, Lynette Eyb, M F Powis, M Rosaria Contestabile, Maeve Tuttle, Malcolm Savage, Marcus Metz, Margaret Fitzherbert, Margaret Pollock, Margaret Powell, Maria Hecht, Marie-Rose Schwizer, Marilyn Doherty, Markus Fussel, Martin Giblin, Martin McKinsey, Martin Sudeberg, Mary C Courtney, Mary Reynolds, Mary Wright-Smith, Mathew Thompson, Megan Roseman, Micaela Nobile , Michael Pantreath, Michael Vielhaber, Michaela Dohnalkova, Michele Sheaff, Michelle Wright, Miraim Lehman, Mr & Mrs R Tocknell, Natalie Thurner, Neil Toyn, Niall Murphy, Nicola White, Nigel Keane, Noreen MacMahon, Oliver Schmidt, Olives Albrecht, Oystein Moen, P Onnekink , P R Birch, Par Longton Collis, Pat de La Chapelle, Pat McLaughlin, Pat O'Shea, Patricia Bernard, Patricia Pyne, Paul Anderson, Paul Hague, Paul Tyler, Pauline Holder, Peter Birch, Peter Ringlever, Peter Stewart, Peter van der Zouwe, Phil Booth, Phil Collins, Phil Waring, Philippa Kay, Polly Ernest, R J Sims, Rachel Kemsley, Rainer Heuck, Rebecca Dengate, Reva B Seybolt, Richard & Dagmar Abbotts, Richard Cole, Richard Parry, Rick Jali, Rob Erickson, Robert Lew , Roberta For, Robin Bar-On, Rod & Jill Hunter, Roy H C Byrne, Rudy Segers, S Watt, Sarah Dewar, Sarah-Jane Hall, Sarajane Marchant, Seamus O'Brien, Sean Kinane, Sebastian Weissberg, Shane Harrison, Shannon Alexander, Shelly Lesher , Shiela Francis, Shlomo M Monnickendam, Shona Nairn, Simon Fitzpatrick, Simone Ostmeier, Sonia Kwiatkowski, Sonia Poljasevic, Sonja Wolf, Stan Bowen, Stephen Brett, Stephen Draper, Stephen Wilson, Sue Magee, Susan Fraiman, Susan Karunaratne, Sylvia Fieres, T Lee, Tanya Lecut, Thea Risby, Thomas Johansson, Tim FitzPatrick, Tom McCluskey, Tomas Homann, Tony Ogilvie, Urs Federer, Wendy Hughes, Wendy Porter, Wendy Wyatt, William Finnerty, Xavier Cattarinich, Yves

Foreword

ABOUT LONELY PLANET GUIDEBOOKS

The story begins with a classic travel adventure: Tony and Maureen Wheeler's 1972 journey across Europe and Asia to Australia. Useful information about the overland trail did not exist at that time, so Tony and Maureen published the first Lonely Planet guidebook to meet a growing need.

From a kitchen table, then from a tiny office in Melbourne (Australia), Lonely Planet has become the largest independent travel publisher in the world, an international company with offices in Melbourne, Oakland (USA), London (UK) and Paris (France).

Today Lonely Planet guidebooks cover the globe. There is an ever-growing list of books and there's information in a variety of forms and media. Some things haven't changed. The main aim is still to help make it possible for adventurous travellers to get out there – to explore and better understand the world.

At Lonely Planet we believe travellers can make a positive contribution to the countries they visit – if they respect their host communities and spend their money wisely. Since 1986 a percentage of the income from each book has been donated to aid projects and human rights campaigns.

Updates Lonely Planet thoroughly updates each guidebook as often as possible. This usually means there are around two years between editions, although for more unusual or more stable destinations the gap can be longer. Check the imprint page (following the colour map at the beginning of the book) for publication dates.

Between editions up-to-date information is available in two free newsletters – the paper *Planet Talk* and email *Comet* (to subscribe, contact any Lonely Planet office) – and on our Web site at www.lonelyplanet.com. The *Upgrades* section of the Web site covers a number of important and volatile destinations and is regularly updated by Lonely Planet authors. *Scoop* covers news and current affairs relevant to travellers. And, lastly, the *Thorn Tree* bulletin board and *Postcards* section of the site carry unverified, but fascinating, reports from travellers.

Correspondence The process of creating new editions begins with the letters, postcards and emails received from travellers. This correspondence often includes suggestions, criticisms and comments about the current editions. Interesting excerpts are immediately passed on via newsletters and the Web site, and everything goes to our authors to be verified when they're researching on the road. We're keen to get more feedback from organisations or individuals who represent communities visited by travellers.

> Lonely Planet gathers information for everyone who's curious about the planet – and especially for those who explore it first-hand. Through guidebooks, phrasebooks, activity guides, maps, literature, newsletters, image library, TV series and Web site we act as an information exchange for a worldwide community of travellers.

Research Authors aim to gather sufficient practical information to enable travellers to make informed choices and to make the mechanics of a journey run smoothly. They also research histori-cal and cultural background to help enrich the travel experience and allow travellers to understand and respond appropriately to cultural and environmental issues.

Authors don't stay in every hotel because that would mean spending a couple of months in each medium-sized city and, no, they don't eat at every restaurant because that would mean stretching belts beyond capacity. They do visit hotels and restaur-ants to check standards and prices, but feedback based on readers' direct experiences can be very helpful.

Many of our authors work undercover, others aren't so secret-ive. None of them accept freebies in exchange for positive write-ups. And none of our guidebooks contain any advertising.

Production Authors submit their raw manuscripts and maps to offices in Australia, USA, UK or France. Editors and cartographers – all experienced travellers themselves – then begin the process of assembling the pieces. When the book finally hits the shops some things are already out of date, we start getting feedback from readers, and the process begins again ...

WARNING & REQUEST

Things change – prices go up, schedules change, good places go bad and bad places go bank-rupt – nothing stays the same. So, if you find things better or worse, recently opened or long since closed, please tell us and help make the next edition even more accurate and useful. We genuinely value all the feedback we receive. Julie Young coordinates a well-travelled team that reads and acknowledges every letter, postcard and email and ensures that every morsel of in-formation finds its way to the appropriate authors, editors and cartographers for verification.

Everyone who writes to us will find their name in the next edition of the appropriate guide-book. They will also receive the latest issue of *Planet Talk*, our quarterly printed newsletter, or *Comet*, our monthly email newsletter. Subscriptions to both newsletters are free. The very best contributions will be rewarded with a free guidebook.

Excerpts from your correspondence may appear in new editions of Lonely Planet guide-books, the Lonely Planet Web site, *Planet Talk* or *Comet*, so please let us know if you *don't* want your letter published or your name acknowledged.

Send all correspondence to the Lonely Planet office closest to you:

Australia: PO Box 617, Hawthorn, Victoria 3122
UK: 10A Spring Place, London NW5 3BH
USA: 150 Linden St, Oakland CA 94607
France: 1 rue du Dahomey, Paris 75011

Or email us at: talk2us@lonelyplanet.com.au

For news, views and updates see our Web site: www.lonelyplanet.com

HOW TO USE A LONELY PLANET GUIDEBOOK

The best way to use a Lonely Planet guidebook is any way you choose. At Lonely Planet we believe the most memorable travel experiences are often those that are unexpected, and the finest discoveries are those you make yourself. Guidebooks are not intended to be used as if they provide a detailed set of infallible instructions!

Contents All Lonely Planet guidebooks follow roughly the same format. The Facts about the Destination chapter or section gives background information ranging from history to weather. Facts for the Visitor gives practical information on issues like visas and health. Getting There & Away gives a brief starting point for researching travel to and from the destination. Getting Around gives an overview of the transport options when you arrive.

The peculiar demands of each destination determine how subsequent chapters are broken up, but some things remain constant. We always start with background, then proceed to sights, places to stay, places to eat, entertainment, getting there and away, and getting around information – in that order.

Heading Hierarchy Lonely Planet headings are used in a strict hierarchical structure that can be visualised as a set of Russian dolls. Each heading (and its following text) is encompassed by any preceding heading that is higher on the hierarchical ladder.

Entry Points We do not assume guidebooks will be read from beginning to end, but that people will dip into them. The traditional entry points are the list of contents and the index. In addition, however, some books have a complete list of maps and an index map illustrating map coverage.

There may also be a colour map that shows highlights. These highlights are dealt with in greater detail in the Facts for the Visitor chapter, along with planning questions and suggested itineraries. Each chapter covering a geographical region usually begins with a locator map and another list of highlights. Once you find something of interest in a list of highlights, turn to the index.

Maps Maps play a crucial role in Lonely Planet guidebooks and include a huge amount of information. A legend is printed on the back page. We seek to have complete consistency between maps and text, and to have every important place in the text captured on a map. Map key numbers usually start in the top left corner.

Although inclusion in a guidebook usually implies a recommendation we cannot list every good place. Exclusion does not necessarily imply criticism. In fact there are a number of reasons why we might exclude a place – sometimes it is simply inappropriate to encourage an influx of travellers.

Introduction

You can almost hear the boom of economic and social change reverberating across the country as Ireland enters the 21st century. In the last decade or so the country has rapidly been transforming itself from a Church-dominated, economically backward nation into a wealthy, near-secular, modern state. Combine these seismic changes with a youthful population and the resurgence of the arts and you have a country almost unrecognisable from that of 20 years ago.

Yet even as it looks forwards, Ireland cannot escape its long, chequered past. The glories of that past are easy to trace, from Stone Age passage tombs and ring forts, through ancient monasteries and castles, down to the great houses and splendid Georgian architecture of the 18th and 19th centuries.

On the tragic side of the ledger, the destruction wrought by the Vikings from the end of the 8th century onwards is still visible in the ruins of once-great monasteries. Following the arrival of the English in the 12th century, the country's history was punctuated by rebellion and repression. Oliver Cromwell's 'visit' between 1649 and 1650 is still remembered with horror. The Famine of the mid-19th century dramatically reduced population levels through mass starvation and emigration – the population began to climb again only as recently as the 1960s. Irish history in the 20th century was no less turbulent, dominated by the Troubles in Northern Ireland.

Yet travellers could be forgiven for forgetting this sad history when facing the peaceful green landscape of the centre with its lakes and mountains, the magnificent cliffs of the wild Atlantic coast, the offshore islands inhabited for millennia, or the friendliness of the people. In spite of the huge recent social changes, many traces of traditional culture survive, especially in remote western areas, and there are still communities in which Irish is the first language.

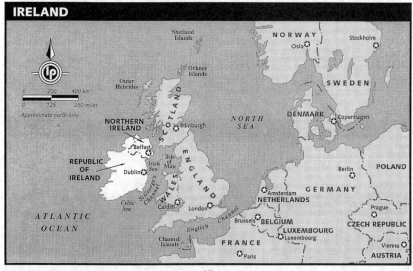

IRELAND

What's in a Name?

When the distinction between Ireland the island and Ireland the state needs to be made in this book, the state is referred to as the Republic of Ireland, the Republic or the South. You may also hear Ireland the state referred to as Éire, Southern Ireland or the Free State. In this book Northern Ireland is either referred to as such or as the North. You may also hear it dubbed the six counties or Ulster, though the latter is technically incorrect. The province of Ulster actually comprises nine counties, but at the time of partition in 1922 six of these (Derry, Antrim, Down, Armagh, Tyrone and Fermanagh) went into Northern Ireland and the other three (Cavan, Donegal and Monaghan) into the Republic of Ireland.

In cities such as Dublin, Cork and Galway, you can still find narrow, medieval streets – a traffic planner's nightmare. Dublin was at its architectural peak in the 18th century and many of its fine Georgian buildings have survived almost unchanged. But these aren't museum cities: they're friendly places with great pubs, a vibrant live-music scene, good theatres and – when it's not raining – cheerful street life. Dublin, in particular, is undergoing an extraordinary programme of urban renewal and the Temple Bar area has been reinvented as the city's 'Left Bank'.

In the North too, in spite of the many false dawns of the peace process, the cities, towns and villages are remarkably welcoming places. Northern Ireland has some beautiful countryside, especially along the Antrim coast. Cities such as Belfast and Derry are experiencing their own economic and cultural resurgence. It's also worth emphasising that they're safer for visitors than most other European cities!

Facts about Ireland

HISTORY
The First Settlers
Ireland was probably first settled by humans about 10,000 years ago, at the end of the last Ice Age. This is relatively late in European prehistory, as Old Stone Age (Palaeolithic) people were living in southern England 400,000 years ago and in Wales 250,000 years ago.

During the last Ice Age, there were land or ice bridges between Ireland and Britain and between Britain and mainland Europe due to low sea levels. However, conditions in Ireland would have been hostile to human migration until the glaciers receded 12,000 to 10,000 years ago. Prey animals such as deer and boar would have been scarce in Ireland until the climate warmed. The Irish giant elk flourished about 12,000 years ago but there were probably no humans around to hunt it.

As the ice caps melted there was an enormous rise in the sea level and, about 9000 years ago, Ireland was cut off from Britain. Around this time the first humans had reached Ireland (arriving in the north-east near the modern-day town of Larne) from Britain, possibly across the land bridge or in small hide-covered boats. These were Middle Stone Age (Mesolithic) hunter-gatherers. They lived in small family or tribal groups, collecting fruit and nuts and hunting any animals they could tackle. Their lifestyle would have been similar to that of the Australian Aborigines or the Kalahari Bushpeople.

Traces of these first Irish people are faint – just a few scattered middens (rubbish dumps) containing shells and the bones of small animals. Their weapons and tools included flint axes and slivers of flint called microliths, which were used as blades and set in a bone or wooden handle. They hunted boar, kept dogs and had a fondness for eels and salmon. The richest concentration of these early sites is in Northern Ireland, including one at Mountsandel Mt near Coleraine; they date from around 8000 to 6000 BC.

The First Farmers
While the first settlers were discovering Ireland, the greatest revolution in human history had already taken place in the fertile crescent of the Middle East. Yet it was another 2000 or 3000 years before farming reached Ireland, around 4000 BC. Farming marked the arrival of New Stone Age (Neolithic) times. Archaeologists can't be certain whether a new wave of farmers colonised Ireland or whether the concept of farming filtered through with just a few immigrants.

A settlement from this era exists at Lough Gur near Grange in County Limerick. The traces of pottery, wooden houses and implements indicate a more prosperous, more settled way of life than before. At Céide Fields, near Ballycastle in northern Mayo, a remarkable complex of intact stone field walls dating from Neolithic times was discovered hidden under a vast blanket of bog. Also around this time one of the first Irish exports was born. Mt Tievebulliagh near Cushendall in County Antrim has an outcrop of remarkably hard stone called porcellanite which formed the basis of a thriving stone-axe industry. Tievebulliagh stone axes have been found as far away as the south of England.

These farmers had enormous respect for the dead and, from about 3000 BC, built the extraordinary passage graves at Newgrange, Knowth and Dowth in the Boyne Valley. Over 1000 megalithic tombs survive from the Neolithic period.

The Bronze Age
The next great human revolution was the ability to work metal and trace the tin and copper ores which could be amalgamated to produce bronze. In Ireland the Bronze Age started around 2500 BC and is characterised by a reduction in the scale and number of

stone tombs but a wonderful legacy of gold and bronze metalwork.

The early prospectors were amazingly astute at finding sources of metal. Almost everywhere that modern geologists have discovered traces of copper and other metals, they have also discovered that someone was there about 4000 years previously, without the help of modern equipment and mapping. Bronze Age mine workings can still be seen on Mt Gabriel near Schull in County Cork. St Kevin's Bed or Cave in Glendalough is thought by many to be an early mine.

Goldworking flourished during the Bronze Age and the quality of the craftwork and the quantity of metal used say something about the wealth of Ireland at that time. The National Museum in Dublin contains the finest collection of prehistoric goldwork in Europe. Some of the gold may have come from the Wicklow Mountains.

During the Bronze Age and the later Iron Age, the tentacles of trade spread out from Ireland. Blue faïence beads manufactured in Egypt were found in graves on the Hill of Tara in County Meath, as was amber from Scandinavia. The skeleton of a Barbary ape from Spain or Portugal was discovered in a site dating from 200 BC on Navan Fort (Emain Macha) in County Armagh.

The Celts

The Celts were Iron Age warrior tribes from Eastern Europe who conquered large sections of central and southern Europe between 800 and 300 BC. The Romans called them 'Galli' (Gauls) and the Greeks used the term 'Keltoi'. Both societies feared the Celts, who plundered Rome in the 4th century AD and were described by contemporary scholars as fierce warriors.

Celtic warriors and adventurers probably reached Ireland around 300 BC, bringing the Iron Age with them, and were certainly well ensconced by 100 BC. They immigrated in relatively small numbers, controlled the country for 1000 years, and left a legacy of language and culture that survives today.

The Celts had a common code of law

called the Brehon Law and their religion was Druidism. They had a distinctive style of design; its swirls and loops are seen on many Irish artefacts from the 2nd and 1st centuries BC. Some good examples are the Broighter Collar in the National Museum in Dublin and the Turoe Stone near Loughrea in County Galway. The Irish language is Celtic in origin.

There are no written records for the early Celtic period but chieftains ensured their immortality through heroic deeds and actions, which were passed down the generations in songs and stories. The epic tales of Cúchulainn and the *Táin Bó Cúailnge* (*Cattle Raid of Cooley*) are believed to have originated in this period. Cúchulainn is the consummate Celtic hero warrior. Similar figures appear in the writings of many cultures, including in Homer's *Iliad* and the *Mahabharata* poem from India. The *Táin Bó Cúailnge* may not be historically accurate but the stories give some idea of Irish society in the first two centuries AD. (See the boxed text 'The Táin Bó Cúailnge' in the Meath & Louth chapter.)

Celtic Ireland was divided into five provinces: Leinster, Meath, Connaught, Ulster and Munster. Meath later merged with Leinster. The principal struggle for power, as reflected in the *Táin Bó Cúailnge*, was between Connaught and Ulster. Within the provinces there were perhaps 100 or more minor kings and chieftains controlling sections (known as *Tuatha*) of the country. Tara in County Meath became the base for some of the most powerful leaders. Navan Fort in County Armagh, which was mentioned in the *Táin Bó Cúailnge*, is recorded on the map of Ireland drawn in the 2nd century AD by the Egyptian scholar Ptolemy. He called it Isamnium.

St Patrick & Christianity

Christianity arrived in Ireland between the 3rd and 5th centuries. Although St Patrick is given the credit for proselytising the native Irish, there were certainly earlier missionaries. Some scholars dispute that there was a St Patrick at all and claim the stories about him are really about these early clerics or are later inventions. However, the evidence suggests that there was a St Patrick who lived in the 5th century and was kidnapped from Britain at the age of 16 by Irish pirates. During six years in Ireland as a slave tending sheep, Patrick found religion.

After escaping back to Britain, he was instructed by powerful visions to return to Ireland. Patrick first went to Europe to train as a cleric, then from around 432 spent his life converting the Irish to Christianity. His base was the town of Armagh, probably chosen because of the symbolic pagan significance of nearby Navan Fort.

Much of our knowledge of Patrick comes from his own writings. St Patrick's *Confession* is a copy of one such account and can be found in the 9th-century *Book of Armagh* (held in Trinity College, Dublin).

The westwards march of the Roman Empire halted in England. As the Empire declined and the Dark Ages engulfed much of the rest of Europe, Ireland in the 7th and 8th centuries became a 'land of saints and scholars', with thriving monasteries where monks wrote in Latin and illuminated manuscripts, including the world-famous *Book of Kells* (also in Trinity College). Outstanding among the monasteries were Clonmacnoise in County Offaly and Glendalough in County Wicklow. Monks such as Colmcille and Columbanus founded monasteries abroad (in Scotland, and in France and Italy respectively).

The Vikings

At the end of the 8th century, Vikings in their slim, powerful boats appeared off the northern and eastern coasts of Ireland and began attacking settlements and plundering monasteries, ushering in a new, more turbulent period of Irish history. In 795 a Viking fleet sailed down the western coast of Scotland, raiding St Colmcille's monastery on Iona before turning its attentions to Ireland's eastern coast. It came ashore either at Rathlin Island off the Antrim coast or Lambay Island near Dublin. Irish weapons and soldiers were no match for the superbly armed, ferocious Norsemen. In passing, it must be said that the local Irish clans were just as fond of raiding the monasteries as the Vikings were: monasteries were places of wealth and power and so were often caught in intertribal squabbles. However, the increasingly frequent Viking raids burned into the consciousness of Irish monks and into their accounts of these times. Round towers were built to act as lookout posts and places of refuge in the event of an attack.

During the 9th century the Vikings started to settle in Ireland and form alliances with native families and chieftains. They established many settlements that bear Viking names today, including Wicklow, Waterford and Wexford. They founded Dublin, which by the 10th century was a small Viking kingdom.

The struggles continued for more than 200 years between the Vikings and the native Irish, who learned many lessons in the art of warfare. The most decisive defeat for Viking ambitions was at the Battle of Clontarf in 1014, by Irish forces led by Brian Ború, king of Munster, who was aided in the fight by Vikings from Waterford and Limerick. The elderly Brian Ború was killed by retreating Vikings and subsequent divisions among his chieftains meant the victory wasn't consolidated, but Viking military power in Ireland had been broken. Large numbers of Vikings, however, remained, marrying with the native Irish, converting to Christianity and joining in the struggle against the next wave of invaders – the Normans.

The Norman Conquest

In 1066 the Normans, under William the Conqueror, invaded and conquered England. They were former Vikings themselves who had settled in northern France 150 years previously, had come to terms with the French king and had adopted the country's language, religion and military technology. After their victory in England they made no immediate effort to involve themselves in Ireland. When they did, they were, ironically, responding to an invitation from an Irish chief.

This came about because the king of

Leinster, Dermot MacMurrough, and the king of Connaught, Tiernan O'Rourke, were arch rivals. Their relationship wasn't improved by MacMurrough's kidnapping of O'Rourke's wife in 1152 (although it appears she went willingly). O'Rourke defeated MacMurrough, who fled abroad in 1166 to search for foreign allies. After arguing his case in France, MacMurrough obtained a hearing with the astute Henry II of England, who at first was too busy to get involved himself but encouraged MacMurrough to seek help elsewhere among his subjects.

MacMurrough went to Wales, where he met Richard FitzGilbert de Clare, earl of Pembroke, better known as Strongbow, who agreed to muster an army to send to Ireland. In return, Strongbow demanded the hand of MacMurrough's daughter in marriage and the inheritance of the kingship of Leinster upon MacMurrough's death. MacMurrough accepted, and the stage was set for more than 800 years of English involvement in Ireland.

In May 1169, the first Anglo-Norman forces arrived in Bannow Bay, County Wexford. MacMurrough joined them and they took Wexford town and Dublin with ease. The next group of Anglo-Normans arrived in Bannow Bay in 1170 led by Strongbow's lieutenant, Raymond le Gros, and defeated a considerably larger Irish and Viking army at Baginbun Head on the Hook Peninsula.

In August 1170, Strongbow himself came and, with le Gros, took Waterford after a fierce battle. A few days later MacMurrough handed his daughter, Aoife, to Strongbow. After MacMurrough's death the following year, Strongbow set about consolidating his new position as king of Leinster.

Meanwhile, Henry II was watching events in Ireland with growing unease. In 1154 he had been recognised by the pope as Lord of Ireland so technically Strongbow was one of his subjects, but Strongbow's independence of mind and action worried him. In 1171 Henry II sailed from England with a huge naval force, landed at Waterford and

declared the place a royal city. He took a semblance of control, but the new Norman lords still did pretty much as they pleased.

Just as the Vikings first settled and were then absorbed, so were the new Anglo-Norman intruders. Barons such as de Courcy and de Lacy set up power bases similar to native Irish kingdoms, outside the control of the English king. Over the next 200 years integration between the Anglo-Normans and native Irish was so successful that in 1366 the English Crown introduced the Statutes of Kilkenny making intermarriage and the use of Irish language and customs illegal. It was too late: assimilation had gone too far. Over the following centuries English control gradually retreated to an area around Dublin known as 'the Pale'. Hence the expression 'beyond the Pale' for an area beyond control.

Henry VIII

In the 16th century Henry VIII moved to reinforce English control of Ireland. He was particularly worried that France or Spain might use Ireland as a base from which to attack England. The principal power brokers in Ireland, the Anglo-Norman Fitzgeralds, earls of Kildare, nominally the representatives of the English Crown in Ireland, were in open rebellion. Henry sought their downfall.

In 1534 Garret Óg, the reigning earl, was meeting with Henry in London. Apparently Óg's 27-year-old son, Silken Thomas, heard rumours that his father had been executed. Silken Thomas gathered his father's forces and attacked Dublin and the English garrisons. In London, Garret Óg was, however, alive and well, and Henry packed off a large army to Ireland which easily crushed Silken Thomas' rebellion. The Fitzgeralds may have been trying to prove they were still a force to be reckoned with in Ireland.

Thomas and his followers surrendered, but were subsequently executed in what became known as the 'pardon of Maynooth'. This pattern of retribution was to become familiar in the following centuries. In 1535, the Fitzgerald estates were divided among

English settlers and an English viceroy was appointed.

Meanwhile, Henry was involved in a separate battle – with the pope, over the difficult matter of his divorce from Catherine of Aragon. In 1532 he broke with the Catholic Church. With the downfall of the earls of Kildare, Henry was able to launch an assault on the property of the Catholic Church in Ireland, which had encouraged rebellion. The wealthy Irish monasteries were dissolved – at considerable profit to the Crown – over the next few years. In 1541 Henry ensured that the Irish Parliament declared him king of Ireland.

Elizabeth I

Under Elizabeth I, the English consolidated their power in Ireland. The forests of Ireland proved invaluable as a source of wood for shipbuilding, and oak was turned into charcoal for smelting ores. Strategically, too, Ireland was important as a possible back door for an invasion from England's enemies in mainland Europe.

English jurisdiction was established in Connaught and Munster despite a number of rebellions by the local ruling families. The success of Elizabeth's policies was borne out when survivors of the 1588 Spanish Armada were washed up on the western coast of Ireland and were mostly massacred by the local sheriffs and their forces.

The thorn in Elizabeth's side was Ulster, the last outpost of the Irish chiefs. Hugh O'Neill, earl of Tyrone, was the prime mover in the last serious assault on English power in Ireland for centuries. O'Neill had been educated in London, and Elizabeth believed that he would be loyal. A story is told of O'Neill's ordering lead from England to reroof his castle; in reality the lead was for bullets. From 1594, O'Neill moved into open conflict with the English and thus began the Nine Years War (1594–1603). He proved a courageous and crafty foe, and the English forces met with little success against him until 1601.

In September of that year, a Spanish force landed in Ireland to join O'Neill. Unfortunately, the Spanish anchored at Kinsale in County Cork, almost 480km from O'Neill's territory. O'Neill was forced to march south to join them and, after an exhausting journey, ended up fighting just outside Kinsale in unfamiliar country. The Irish were defeated by the English forces under Lord Mountjoy while the Spanish army was pinned down in Kinsale.

The Battle of Kinsale was the end for O'Neill and for Ulster. Although O'Neill and his forces made it home, their power was broken. Fifteen months later, in 1603, he surrendered and signed the Treaty of Mellifont, handing power and authority to the English Crown. O'Neill was allowed to stay in Ulster on condition that he pledge allegiance to the Crown, which he did. However, in 1607, after a number of frustrating years of subjugation and harassment, O'Neill and 90 other Ulster chiefs boarded a ship in Lough Swilly for Europe, leaving Ireland for ever. This was known as the Flight of the Earls, and it left Ulster leaderless and open to English rule.

With the native chiefs gone, Elizabeth and her successor, James I, pursued a policy of colonisation known as Plantation – an organised, ambitious expropriation of land that sowed the seeds for the division of Ulster that we see today. Huge swathes of land were confiscated from the Irish and large numbers of new settlers came from Scotland and England. They brought a new way of life and a different religion. Unlike most previous invaders, they didn't intermarry with the native Irish: they kept their culture and religion very much to themselves. Living among these new Protestant landowners was an impoverished, angry population of native Irish and Anglo-Norman Catholics.

Oliver Cromwell

In 1641, worried by developments in England and Ireland and believing Charles I to be pro-Catholic, these Irish and Anglo-Norman Catholics took up arms. What happened subsequently is a matter of debate. Certainly many of the Protestant settlers were killed, but modern historians have revised the likely number of deaths down to perhaps 2000 from earlier wildly exaggerated estimates; many Catholics were also killed in revenge. Stories of the 1641 atrocities have been used in anti-Catholic propaganda ever since.

The English Civil War kept most of the English busy at home for much of the 1640s. In Ireland, the native Irish and Anglo-Norman Catholics, allied under the 1641 Confederation of Kilkenny, supported Charles I against the Protestant parliamentarians in the hope of restoring Catholic power in Ireland. After Charles' execution the victorious Oliver Cromwell, leader of the parliamentarians, decided to go to Ireland and sort it out.

He arrived in 1649 and rampaged through the country, leaving a trail of death behind him and shipping many of the defeated as slaves to the Caribbean. Under the 1652 Act of Settlement others were dispossessed and exiled to the harsh, infertile lands in the west of Ireland, in the province of Connaught. Two million hectares of land were confiscated – more than a quarter of the country – and handed over to Cromwell's supporters, many of whom remained to settle the land. Cromwell's tour of Ireland has never been forgotten.

The Battle of the Boyne

The 1660 Restoration saw Charles II, who kept his Catholic sympathies in check, on the English throne. In 1685 his brother James succeeded him. James II's more open Catholicism raised English ire. He was forced to flee the country for France at the beginning of 1689, intending to raise an army in Ireland and regain his throne from the Protestant William of Orange, who had been invited to sit on the English throne by Parliament.

In late 1688, with rumours spreading among Irish Protestants that Irish Catholics were about to rise in support of James II, the Protestant citizens of Derry had heard that a Catholic regiment was to be stationed in their city. After furious debate among the local worthies, 13 apprentice boys had purloined the keys to the city and slammed the gates in the face of James' soldiers.

In March 1689 James II himself arrived

from France at Kinsale and marched north to Dublin, where the Irish Parliament recognised him as king and began to organise the return of expropriated land to Catholic landowners. The siege of Derry by James' forces began in earnest in April and ended after mass starvation with the arrival of William's ships in July. The Protestant slogan 'No Surrender!' dates from the siege, which acquired mythical status among Irish Protestants over the following centuries.

William of Orange landed in 1690 at Carrickfergus, just north of Belfast, with an army of up to 36,000 men. The Battle of the Boyne took place on 12 July. It was fought between Irish Catholics (led by James II, a Scot) and English Protestants (led by William of Orange, a Dutchman). To make things more complicated, James was William's uncle and his father-in-law. James II's principal supporter was Louis XIV of France, and fear of growing French power led both the Catholic king of Spain and the pope himself to back William and the Protestant side!

William's victory was a turning point and is commemorated to this day by Northern Protestants as a pivotal victory over 'popes and popery'. The final surrender of the Irish came in 1691 when the Catholic leader Patrick Sarsfield signed the Treaty of Limerick. He and thousands of his troops went into exile in France, where they served in the French army.

Penal Times

The 1691 Treaty of Limerick contained quite generous terms of surrender for the Catholics, but these were largely ignored and were replaced by a harsh regime of penal laws a few years later, in 1695. These laws were passed by a Protestant gentry anxious to consolidate its powers and worried that Louis XIV of France might attempt an invasion of Ireland. Also known as a 'popery code', these laws forbade Catholics from buying land, from bringing their children up in their own religion and from entering the army, navy or legal profession. All Irish culture, music and education were banned. Lesser restrictions were also imposed on Presbyterians and other non-conformists.

In response, Catholics organised open-air masses at secret locations usually marked by a 'mass rock'. Illegal outdoor schools known as 'hedge schools' continued to teach the Irish language and culture. Among the educated classes, many Catholics converted to Protestantism to preserve their careers and wealth.

From around 1715, strict enforcement of the religious sections of the penal laws eased off, although many of the restrictions to do with employment and public office still held. A significant majority of the Catholic population were now tenants living in wretched conditions. By the mid-18th century, Catholics held less than 15% of the land in Ireland, and by 1778 barely 5%. Many middle-class Catholics went into trade.

The 18th Century

Meanwhile, Dublin thrived, ranking as Europe's fifth-largest city. The Irish ruling class were members of the established Protestant Episcopalian Church and were descendants of Cromwellian soldiers, Norman nobles and Elizabethan settlers. They formed a new, prosperous upper class known as the Protestant Ascendancy. There was a Protestant-only Parliament, but laws still had to be approved by the British Crown and Parliament. It was from these Protestants that pressure first came for Ireland to be treated on an equal footing with Britain.

A strong Patriot Party calling for independence developed under the leadership of Henry Grattan (1746–1820) and Henry Flood. When the American War of Independence broke out in 1776, Britain was in a difficult position. The majority of her forces were withdrawn from Ireland to fight in the colonies, leaving security in Ireland largely in the hands of Protestant 'volunteer' forces under the control of the landowners and merchant classes. To avoid further clashes with the increasingly independent Irish Parliament, the British government in 1782 allowed the Irish what it considered complete freedom of legislation. The new Irish governing body was known as Grattan's Parliament. However, London still controlled much of what went on in Ireland through royal patronage and favours, and the Crown still had the power of veto.

To achieve prosperity in Ireland, Grattan had espoused improved conditions and rights for Catholics. Henry Flood and the majority of other Protestant members were not as sympathetic and in the life of the Parliament – nearly 20 years – little progress was made.

The French Revolution

With the American War of Independence and – more shocking to Britain – the French Revolution of 1789, the ruling classes could no longer be complacent about the poverty-stricken masses.

In Ireland, an organisation known as the United Irishmen had been formed by Belfast Presbyterians; its most prominent leader was a young Dublin Protestant and republican, Theobald Wolfe Tone (1763–98). The United Irishmen started out with high ideals of bringing together men of all

MATT KING

Theobald Wolfe Tone (1763–98) led a French invasion of Ireland that failed only due to bad weather.

creeds to reform and reduce Britain's power in Ireland, but their attempts to gain power through straightforward politics proved fruitless. When war broke out between Britain and France the United Irishmen found they were no longer tolerated by the establishment. They re-formed themselves as an underground organisation committed to bringing change by any means, violent or otherwise. Tone was keen to enlist the help of the French, who, fresh from their European victories, were easily persuaded.

At the same time, loyalist Protestants were worried by the turn of events and prepared for possible conflict by forming the Protestant Orange Society, which later became known as the Orange Order.

In 1796 a French invasion fleet with thousands of troops approached Bantry Bay in County Cork. On board one of the French ships was Wolfe Tone, decked out in a French uniform. On shore, the local militia were ill equipped to repel them. However, a strong offshore wind frustrated attempts by the fleet to sail up the bay to a safe landing spot. A few ships attempted to drop anchor but, as the wind strengthened into a full gale, they were forced to head for the open Atlantic and back to France. A disappointed Wolfe Tone went back with them.

Saved by the weather, the government in Ireland now realised the serious threat posed by the United Irishmen and similar groups. A nationwide campaign got under way to hunt them out and proved extremely effective. Meanwhile, another group of United Irishmen, led by Lord Edward Fitzgerald, tried to mount a rebellion, but it failed because of informers and poor communication between the rebels. After uncovering yet another attempted rebellion, the government and army intensified their search for arms and rebels. Floggings and indiscriminate torture sent a wave of panic through the population and sparked off the 1798 Rising. Wexford, a county not noted for its rebellious tendencies, saw the fiercest fighting, with Father John Murphy leading the resistance. After a number of minor victories the rebels were finally and decisively defeated at Vinegar Hill just outside Enniscorthy (for more details see the boxed text 'The Battle of Vinegar Hill' in the Counties Wexford & Waterford chapter).

After another failed French invasion, Wolfe Tone himself arrived later in 1798 with a French fleet, but was defeated at sea. Wolfe Tone was captured and taken to Dublin, where he committed suicide in his prison cell. It was the end for the United Irishmen and also, ironically, precipitated the demise of the independent Irish Parliament.

The Protestant gentry, alarmed at the level of unrest, was much inclined to accept the security of British authority. In 1800 the Act of Union, uniting Ireland politically with Britain, was passed, taking effect from 1 January 1801. Many wealthier Irish Catholics supported the Act, especially after the British prime minister, William Pitt, promised to remove the last of the penal laws, most of which had been repealed by 1793. The Irish Parliament voted itself out of existence and around 100 of the members of Parliament (MPs) moved to the House of Commons in London.

As if to remind England of the rebellious nature of Ireland, a tiny and completely ineffectual rebellion was staged in Dublin in 1803, led by a former United Irishman, Robert Emmet (1778–1803). Fewer than 100 men took part and Emmet was caught, tried and executed. He gave a famous speech from the dock which included the oft-quoted words: 'Let no man write my epitaph... When my country takes her place among the nations of the earth, then and not till then let my epitaph be written'.

The Great Liberator
In the meantime, a 28-year-old Catholic Kerry man called Daniel O'Connell (1775–1847) was set on a course that would make him one of Ireland's greatest leaders. The O'Connell family were from Caherdaniel in County Kerry and had made their money from smuggling. Remarkably, the family had managed to hang onto their house and lands through penal times.

In 1823 O'Connell founded the Catholic Association with the aim of achieving political equality for Catholics. The association soon became a vehicle for peaceful mass protest and action. In the 1826 general election it first showed its muscle by backing Protestant candidates who were in favour of Catholic emancipation. In 1828 O'Connell himself stood for a seat in County Clare, even though, being a Catholic, he couldn't take the seat (the remaining penal laws had not been repealed, despite William Pitt's promise). O'Connell won easily, putting the British Parliament in a quandary. If they didn't allow O'Connell to take his seat, there might be a popular uprising. Many in the House of Commons favoured emancipation, and the combination of circumstances led them to pass the 1829 Act of Catholic Emancipation, allowing some well-off Catholics voting rights and the right to be elected as MPs.

After this great victory, O'Connell sought to secure further reforms. Ten years later he turned his attentions to the repeal of the Act of Union and the re-establishment of an Irish Parliament. Now that Catholics could become MPs, such a body would be very different from the old Protestant-dominated Irish Parliaments.

In 1843 the campaign took off, with O'Connell's 'monster meetings' attracting up to half a million supporters and taking place all over Ireland. O'Connell exploited the threat that such gatherings represented to the establishment but he balked at a genuinely radical confrontation with the British. His bluff was called when a monster meeting at Clontarf was prohibited and he called it off.

O'Connell was arrested in 1844 and served a short spell in prison. After that, he quarrelled with the Young Ireland movement (which, having seen pacifism fail, favoured the use of violence) and never again posed a threat to the British. He died in 1847, while his country was being devoured by famine.

The Great Famine

Ireland suffered its greatest tragedy in the years between 1845 and 1851. The potato was the staple food of a rapidly growing but desperately poor population. Between 1800 and 1840 the population had rocketed from four to eight million, putting even greater pressure on the land. Then, between 1845 and 1851, a succession of almost complete failures of the potato crop resulted in mass starvation, emigration and death.

During this time there were excellent harvests of other crops such as wheat, but these were too expensive for the poor to buy. While millions of its citizens were starving, Ireland continued to export food. Some landlords did their best for their tenants, but many others ignored the situation from their homes in Britain.

As a result, about one million people died, many of disease rather than straight starvation, and about another million emigrated. Emigration continued to reduce the population during the next 100 years. Huge numbers of Irish emigrants who found their way abroad, particularly to the USA, carried with them a lasting bitterness. Irish-American wealth would later find its way back to Ireland to finance the independence struggle.

Parnell & the Land League

In spite of the bitterness aroused by the Famine, there was little challenge to

NICKY CAVEN

Daniel O'Connell (1775–1847),
the Great Liberator, fought
for voting rights for Catholics.

Britain's control of Ireland for quite some time. One rebellion was the abortive Fenian (Irish Republican Brotherhood) rising in March 1867. It had its most publicised action in Manchester, England, when 30 Irishmen attempted to free two of their leaders. In so doing they killed an English policeman, either by accident or design. Three of them were executed and became known in nationalist circles as the Manchester Martyrs.

In 1875 Charles Stewart Parnell (1846–91) was elected to Westminster. The son of a Protestant landowner from County Wicklow, he had much in common with other members of the Anglo-Irish Ascendancy. But there were differences. Parnell's mother was American and her father had fought the British in the American War of Independence. Parnell's family supported the principle of Irish independence from Britain. He quickly became noticed in the House of Commons as a passionate, difficult member who asked awkward questions. In 1877 he became leader of the new Home Rule Party, which advocated a limited form of autonomy for Ireland.

In 1879 Ireland appeared to be facing another famine as potato crops were failing once again and evictions were becoming widespread. Cheap corn from America had pushed grain prices down and with that the earnings of the tenants who grew grain on their plots. Michael Davitt, a Fenian, began to organise the tenants, and early on found a sympathetic ear in the unlikely person of Parnell. This odd pair were the brains behind the Land League, which initiated widespread agitation for reduced rents and improved working conditions. The conflict heated up and there was violence on both sides. Parnell instigated the strategy of 'boycotting' tenants, agents and landlords who didn't adhere to the Land League's aims: they were treated like lepers by the local population. Charles Boycott was a land agent in County Mayo and one of the first people the new strategy was used against.

The Land War, as it became known, lasted from 1879 to 1882 and was a momentous period. For the first time, tenants were defying their landlords en masse. An election in 1880 brought William Gladstone to power for the second time in Britain. In the face of the situation in Ireland, he introduced his 1881 Land Act, which improved life immeasurably for tenants, creating fair rents and the possibility of tenants owning their land.

A crisis threatened in 1882 when two of the Crown's leading figures in Ireland were murdered in Phoenix Park, Dublin, and Parnell was tenuously and wrongly implicated. However, reform had been achieved, and Parnell turned his attentions to achieving Home Rule. Parnell had an extraordinary ally in William Gladstone, who was dependent on Parnell for crucial support in Parliament. But Gladstone and Parnell had their Home Rule Bill defeated, partly as a result of defections from Gladstone's own party.

The end was drawing near for Parnell. For 10 years he had been having an affair with Kitty O'Shea, who was married to a member of his own party. When the relationship was exposed in 1890, Parnell refused to resign as party leader and the party split. Parnell was deposed as leader and the Catholic Church in Ireland quickly turned against him. The 'uncrowned king of Ireland' was no longer welcome. Parnell's health deteriorated rapidly and he died less than a year later, aged just 45.

Home Rule Beckons

Gladstone was elected as prime minister for a fourth term in 1892 and this time managed to get his Home Rule for Ireland Bill through the House of Commons, but it was thrown out by the House of Lords.

By now, eastern Ulster was quite prosperous. It had been spared the worst effects of the Famine, and heavy industrialisation meant the Protestant ruling class was doing nicely. While Gladstone had failed for the time being, the Ulster Unionists (the Unionist Party had been formed in 1885) were now acutely aware that Home Rule could surface again. They were determined to resist it, at least as far as Ulster was concerned, and to fight if it became law. The unionists, led by Sir Edward Carson, a Dublin lawyer, formed a Protestant vigilante brigade called the Ulster Volunteer Force (UVF) and it held a series of mass paramilitary rallies.

In Britain a new Liberal government under Prime Minister Asquith had removed the House of Lords' power to veto bills and began to put another Home Rule for Ireland Bill through Parliament – the political price being demanded by Irish Home Rule MPs for their support. The bill was passed (but not enacted) in 1912 against strident union-ist and Conservative British opposition, which mounted in ferocity.

As the UVF grew in strength, a republican group called the Irish Volunteers, led by the academic Eoin MacNeill, was set up in the south to defend Home Rule for the whole of Ireland. They lacked the weapons and organisation of the UVF, however, which succeeded in large-scale gunrunning in 1914. There was also widespread support for the UVF among officers of the British army. Civil war threatened.

However, the Home Rule Act was suspended at the outbreak of WWI in August

Edward Carson

It was Edward Carson (1854–1935), a Protestant lawyer from Dublin, who spearheaded the Ulster opposition to Home Rule and led the movement that eventually resulted in Ireland's partition. Carson's career in law included numerous successful prosecutions of Irish tenants on behalf of British absentee landlords, and he played a leading role in the conviction of Oscar Wilde for homosexuality in 1895.

Carson was elected to the British House of Commons in 1892 and was solicitor general for Britain from 1900 to 1905. He was in line for the leadership of the Conservative Party until, in 1910, his fervent distaste for Home Rule and Irish independence led him to take the leadership of the Ulster Unionists. Carson believed that without Belfast's heavy industries an independent Ireland would be economically unviable and that he could frustrate Irish independence simply by keeping the North separate. The British Liberal government's determination to enact Home Rule was frustrated by Carson's parliamentary manoeuvres in 1912, and a year later he actually established a provisional government for the North in Belfast.

Carson threatened an armed struggle for a separate Northern Ireland if independence was granted to Ireland. By 1913 he had established a private Ulster army. Weapons were landed from Germany at Larne in 1914, shortly before the outbreak of WWI. The British began to bend before this Ulster opposition and, in July 1914, Carson agreed that Home Rule could go through for Ireland, so long as Ulster was kept separate. The events of WWI and the 1916 Easter Rising in Dublin shifted the whole question for Irish nationalists from Home Rule to complete independence. By 1921, however, the Ulster opposition which Carson had nurtured was so strong that the country was carved up.

A statue of Carson fronts Stormont Castle, which was once a symbol of loyalist opposition to a united Ireland but is now home to the Northern Ireland Assembly. Carson himself is buried in St Anne's Cathedral in central Belfast.

MATT KING

1914 and the question of Ulster was left unresolved. Many Irish nationalists believed that Home Rule would come after the war and that by supporting the British war effort they could influence British opinion in their favour. John Redmond, the leader of the Irish Home Rule Party, actively encouraged people to join the British forces to fight Germany.

The Gaelic Revival

While these attempts at Home Rule were being shunted about, something of a revolution was taking place in Irish arts, literature and identity.

The Anglo-Irish literary revival was one aspect of this, championed by the young William Butler Yeats. The poet had a coterie of literary friends such as Lady Gregory, Douglas Hyde, John Millington Synge and George Russell. They unearthed many of the Celtic tales of Cúchulainn and wrote with fresh enthusiasm about a romantic Ireland of epic battles and warrior queens. For a country that had suffered centuries of invasion and deprivation, these images presented a much more attractive version of history. Yeats and his friends were decidedly upper crust themselves and pursued the new literature and poetry primarily through the English language, aiming at the educated classes. A national theatre, later to become the Abbey Theatre, was born in Dublin from their efforts.

At the same time, people such as Douglas Hyde and Eoin MacNeill were doing their best to ensure the survival of the Irish language and the more everyday Irish customs and culture, which they believed to be central to Irish identity. They formed the Gaelic League in 1893, which, among other things, pushed for the teaching of Irish in schools. In the 1890s the Gaelic League was primarily a cultural outfit and assumed a nationalistic aura only later.

The Gaelic Athletic Association (GAA), initially founded in 1884 to promote Irish sport and culture, became, by the turn of the 20th century, a thriving, strongly politicised organisation. A small pressure group called Sinn Féin (We Ourselves) was set up under

the leadership of Arthur Griffith, founder of the *United Irishmen* newspaper. He proposed that all Irish MPs should abandon the House of Commons in London and set up a Parliament in Dublin (a similar strategy to that employed by Hungary in gaining its independence from Austria).

Socialism attracted support in Dublin among the hungry tenement dwellers, who endured some of the worst urban housing conditions in Europe. In 1913 Jim Larkin and James Connolly called the transport workers out on strike. Although the strike ended in a return to work, the employers failed to break the union and Larkin and Connolly had created the Irish Citizens' Army for self-defence. It now joined forces with the newly formed Irish Volunteers.

It must be said, however, that, prior to 1916, the majority of Dubliners were probably more concerned with WWI: while some might have believed that independence from Britain was a good idea, their passions went no further.

The Easter Rising

Many Irishmen with nationalist sympathies went off to the battlefields of Europe believing their sacrifice would ensure that Britain stood by its promise of Home Rule for Ireland. However, a minority of nationalists in Ireland were not so trusting of British resolve. The Irish Volunteers split into two groups: those under John Redmond who adopted a wait-and-see approach and a radical group which believed in a more revolutionary course of action.

Two small groups – a section of the Irish Volunteers under Pádraig Pearse and the Irish Citizens' Army led by James Connolly – staged a rebellion that took the country by surprise. On Easter Monday 1916, they marched into Dublin and took over a number of key positions in the city. Their headquarters was the General Post Office on O'Connell St. From its steps Pearse read out to nonplussed passers-by a declaration that Ireland was now a republic and that his band was the provisional government. Less than a week of fighting ensued before the rebels surrendered in the face of superior

British forces. The rebels weren't popular and had to be protected from angry Dubliners as they were marched to jail.

The rising had been planned by Pearse and others without Eoin MacNeill's (the leader of the Irish Volunteers) knowledge. When he discovered the plans at the last minute, MacNeill attempted to call off the rebellion, resulting in very few turning up on the day. Also, a ship carrying a large consignment of arms from Germany was intercepted by the British navy. So what might have been a real threat to British authority fizzled out completely. Many have said that Pearse knew they didn't stand a chance but was preoccupied with a blood sacrifice, a noble gesture by a few brave souls that would galvanise the nation. Whether he believed this or not, a blood sacrifice was on the way.

The Easter Rising would probably have had little impact on the Irish situation had the British not made martyrs of the leaders of the rebellion. Of the 77 given death sentences, 15 were executed. Pearse was shot three days after the surrender, and nine days later James Connolly was the last to die, shot in a chair because he couldn't stand on a gangrenous ankle. The deaths provoked a sea change in public attitudes to the republicans, for whom support henceforth climbed.

Countess Markievicz was one of those not executed, because she was female and there had been a recent outcry in Britain over the execution by the Germans of Edith Cavell, a British nurse, in Belgium. Countess Markievicz was later to be the first woman elected to the British Parliament (preceding Nancy Astor), but she refused to take up her seat. Eamon de Valera's (1882–1975) death sentence was commuted to life imprisonment because of his US citizenship and he was freed after an amnesty in 1917.

In the 1918 general election, the republicans stood under the banner of Sinn Féin and won a large majority of the Irish seats. Ignoring London's Parliament, where technically they were supposed to sit, the newly elected Sinn Féin deputies – many of them veterans of the 1916 Easter Rising – declared Ireland independent and formed the first Dáil Éireann (Irish assembly or lower house), which sat in Dublin's Mansion House under the leadership of Eamon de Valera. Although the Irish had declared independence, the British had by no means conceded it: a confrontation was imminent.

The Anglo-Irish War
The day the Dáil convened in Dublin in January 1919, two policemen were shot dead in County Tipperary. This was the beginning of the bitter Anglo-Irish War, which lasted from 1919 to the middle of 1921. This was the period when Michael Collins (1890–1922) came to the fore, a charismatic, ruthless leader who masterminded the campaign of violence against the British while at the same time serving as minister for finance in the new Dáil.

The war quickly became entrenched and bloody. On the Irish side was the Irish Republican Army (IRA), successor to the Irish Volunteers, and on the other a coalition of the Royal Irish Constabulary, regular British army soldiers and two groups of quasi-military status who rapidly gained a vicious reputation – the Auxiliaries and the Black and Tans, who were newly demobbed British soldiers. Their use of violence crystallised resentment against British and support for the nationalist cause. The death from hunger strike of Terence MacSwiney, mayor of Cork, further crystallised Irish opinion. The IRA created 'flying columns', small groups of armed volunteers to ambush British forces, and on home ground they operated successfully. A truce was eventually agreed in July 1921.

Then, after months of negotiations in London, the Irish delegation signed the Anglo-Irish Treaty on 6 December 1921. It gave 26 counties of Ireland independence and allowed six largely Protestant Ulster counties the choice of opting out. If they did (a foregone conclusion), a Boundary Commission would decide on the final frontiers between north and south.

The Outbreak of Civil War

The Treaty negotiations had been largely undertaken on the Irish side by Michael Collins and Arthur Griffith. Both knew that many Dáil members wouldn't accept the loss of the north, or the fact that the British monarch would still be head of the new Irish Free State and Irish MPs would still have to swear an oath of allegiance to the Crown. Under pressure from Britain's Lloyd George and after a spell of exhausting negotiations, they signed the Treaty without checking with de Valera in Dublin.

Collins regarded the issue of the monarchy and the oath of allegiance as largely symbolic. He also hoped that the north-eastern six counties wouldn't be a viable entity and would eventually become part of the Free State. During the Treaty negotiations he had been encouraged to think that the Border Commission would decrease the size of that part of Ireland remaining outside the Free State. He hoped that he could convince the rest of his comrades, but he knew the risks and declared, 'I may have signed my death warrant tonight'.

In the end Collins couldn't persuade his colleagues to accept the Treaty. De Valera was furious and it wasn't long before a bitter civil war broke out between comrades who, a year previously, had fought alongside each other.

Ireland Since Partition

For the history of Ireland since partition, see the introductory chapters to the Republic of Ireland and Northern Ireland sections.

GEOGRAPHY & GEOLOGY

Ireland is an island lying off the northwestern edge of the Eurasian landmass, separated from Britain by the Irish Sea and the St George's and North channels. The island's area is 84,421 sq km: 14,139 sq km in the North and 70,282 sq km in the South. It stretches 485km north to south and just over 300km east to west. The convoluted coastline extends for over 5000km.

Political Geography

Ireland is divided into 32 counties. The Republic of Ireland consists of 26 counties, and Northern Ireland of six. The northernmost point in the South (Malin Head in Donegal) is actually farther north than anywhere in the North. To confuse things further, the island has traditionally been divided into four provinces: Leinster, Ulster, Connaught and Munster. The six counties of Northern Ireland are often loosely referred to as Ulster, but three of the Republic's counties – Donegal, Cavan and Monaghan – were also in the old province of Ulster.

Landscape

It can be as little as 50km from the heart of one of Ireland's major cities to an isolated sweep of mountains and bogland. Most of the higher ground is close to the coast, while the central regions are largely flat. Almost the entire western seaboard from Cork to Donegal is a continuous bulwark of cliffs, hills and mountains with few safe anchorages. The only significant breaches in the chain are the Shannon Estuary and Galway Bay.

The western mountain ranges aren't particularly high but they're often beautiful. The highest mountains are in the southwest; the tallest mountain in Ireland is Mt Carrantuohil (1041m) in Kerry's Macgillicuddy's Reeks.

The Shannon is the longest river in Ireland or Britain. It runs for 370km from its source in Cavan's Cuilcagh Mountains down through the midlands before emptying into the wide Shannon Estuary west of Limerick town. Lough Neagh in Northern Ireland is the island's largest lake, covering 396 sq km.

The midlands of Ireland lie above Carboniferous limestone deposited between 300 and 400 million years ago. On the surface, the flat landscape is mostly rich farmland or raised bogs, huge swathes of brown peat rapidly disappearing under the machines of the Bord na Móna (Irish Turf Board).

As you travel west from the midlands, the soil becomes poorer, the fields smaller and stone walls more numerous. The

COUNTIES & PROVINCES

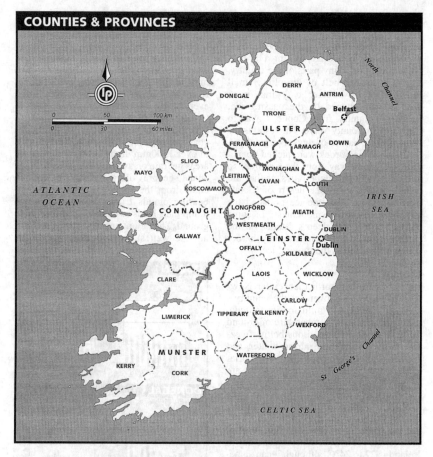

Cromwellian cry 'To hell or to Connaught' wasn't without foundation, as the land west of the Shannon can't compare with fertile counties such as Meath and Tipperary. On the western seaboard, smallhold farmers struggle to make a living by raising sheep, potatoes and some cattle.

Before the Famine, the pressure on land was enormous; eight million people had to be fed and so they farmed in the most inaccessible places. Up the hillsides above today's fields, you may see the faint regular lines of pre-Famine potato ridges called 'lazy beds'.

Ice Age The last Ice Age had a huge impact on the Irish landscape. It lasted from 100,000 to just over 10,000 years ago, during which time most of the country was glaciated. Characteristic U-shaped valleys were carved out by glaciers, as were the small deep-set corrie lakes high on the mountainsides. The receding ice left behind many shallow lakes, mainly in the centre of Ireland. Most of the baked sedimentary rocks covering the Wicklow Mountains were stripped away, exposing the underlying granite. In County Clare, limestone appeared when a layer of waterproof shale and sandstone was removed.

Many of Ireland's mountains and hills have a round, smooth profile, formed by the abrasive effect of moving ice. The ice also deposited soil in its wake, leaving a layer of boulder clay on many parts of the country. There is a large belt of drumlins, small round hills of boulder clay that were dropped and shaped by the passing ice, across the country, from County Cavan to Clew Bay in County Mayo. The result is the characteristic basket-of-eggs topography.

Often pieces of rock were picked up and dropped a long way from their source, so you find granite glacial erratics, as they are called, on the limestone desert of Clare's Burren region. Here the ice polished the limestone to mirror smoothness. In some places you can see deep scratches on the surface of the stone, engraved by harder stones embedded in the moving ice.

CLIMATE

Ireland is farther north than either Newfoundland or Vancouver yet the country's climate is relatively mild for its latitude, with a mean annual temperature of around 10°C. The temperature drops below freezing only intermittently during winter, and snow is scarce – perhaps one or two brief flurries every year. The coldest months are January and February, when daily temperatures range from 4 to 8°C, with 7°C the average. In summer, temperatures during the day are a comfortable 15 to 20°C. During the warmest months, July and August, the average is 16°C. A hot summer's day in Ireland is 22 to 24°C, although it can sometimes reach 30°C. There are about 18 hours of daylight daily during July and August and it's only truly dark after about 11 pm. In May and June, Ireland has an average of five to six hours of sunshine a day, while in the south-east during July and August the average is seven hours.

The reason Ireland has such a mild climate is the moderating effect of the Atlantic Ocean and particularly the Gulf Stream. This is an enormous current which moves clockwise round the Atlantic, bringing warm water up to Western Europe from the Caribbean. Often the Gulf Stream brings

Caribbean sea life with it, washing up turtles and triggerfish on the western coast of Ireland.

One thing you can be sure of about Irish weather is how little you can be sure of. It may be shirtsleeves and sunglasses in February but winter woollies in March and even during the summer.

And then there's the rain. Ireland receives a lot of rain – about 1000mm each year, ranging from 750mm in the midlands to over 1300mm in the south-west. Certain areas get rain on as many as 270 days of the year. The prevailing winds over Ireland come from the south-west, bringing rain-bearing clouds from the Atlantic which dump their loads as soon as they meet high ground. The mountains of south-west Kerry are the wettest part of the country. The

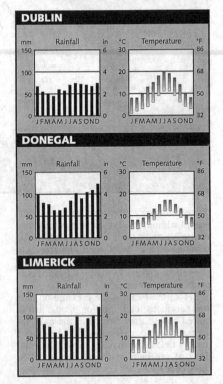

south-east, particularly Counties Wexford and Waterford, is the driest area, enjoying something like a more southern continental climate. If you find the rain getting you down you might find some comfort in the Irish saying: 'It doesn't rain in the pub'!

ECOLOGY & ENVIRONMENT

Ireland has long been associated with the colour green, but the rise in environmental awareness has given this association an added dimension.

Forests

At one time Ireland was largely covered by forests. Then, about 6000 years ago, the first farmers cleared small areas for their crops, the beginning of a long process of deforestation. Substantial tracts of natural oak wood survived until the mid-16th century, but the following 200 years saw the country stripped of its oak for ship timbers, charcoal, tanning and barrels. So extensive was the clearance that by the mid-18th century almost all the country's timber was being imported, right down to the staves for barrels.

In the 20th century, pine plantations were born out of the need for local timber and the desire to do something with what many people considered to be wasteland. There are now state subsidies for plantations, although the most widely used species – sitka spruce and lodgepole pine – are so fast growing and soft as to be unsuitable for high-quality wood products.

Today forests cover about 5.5% of the country and the percentage is slowly increasing, although much of the wood grown is for commercial purposes. Recognition of the need for native forest is found in places such as Glencree in County Wicklow, where there's a project to reforest part of the area with oak trees.

Agriculture

In the past, Ireland experienced limited industrialisation compared to other developed countries, leaving the beautiful Irish countryside mostly untouched. However, in the 1970s, the European Union (EU) encour-

aged intensive, specialised farming and the use of pesticides and chemical fertilisers. These caused serious pollution and land degradation in areas such as the Burren in County Clare. More recently, the EU and the Irish government have promoted environmental protection, less intensive farming methods and the adoption of alternative practices or crops. The result has been a reduction in pollution, though it continues to occur in rivers and lakes.

In the same period the trend towards larger farms led to the destruction of many ring forts and stone walls. Again, the Burren is an example of this.

Water Quality

A 1999 report by the Environmental Protection Agency graded most of Ireland's water supply as satisfactory. Nevertheless, much drinking water in remote rural areas, it said, was unfit for human consumption due to *E. coli* contamination caused by farm slurry pits and run-off from septic tanks. However, this should improve following the introduction of water-management schemes by the Department of the Environment, the National Federation of Group Water Schemes and local authorities.

Beaches

A number of Irish beaches suffer from pollution. As part of a scheme to improve the situation, clean ones are awarded the EU Blue Flag. An Taisce (National Trust for Ireland) keeps a list of these and some are mentioned in the body of this book.

The Urban Environment

Since the mid-1960s most Irish have lived in urban areas. Dublin in particular has grown enormously. Initially, little was done to tackle inner-city decay and population decline, but urban renewal programmes have begun to turn things round. The emergence of Temple Bar as a living cultural and entertainment centre is one example.

To retain Dublin's character much redevelopment is in the form of refurbishment and restoration of existing buildings rather than the construction of new ones. Where

Ireland's Disappearing Bogs

There are three types of bogs (peatland) – raised bogs, fens and blanket bogs.

Raised ones are formed when sphagnum moss gains a foothold in a low-lying, waterlogged area. The moss accumulates as it dies, retaining a lot of water, and the bog starts to form. The centres of these bogs are higher than the edges, hence the term 'raised bog'. These are mostly found in flat areas such as the midlands. The most famous example in Ireland is the Bog of Allen, which once covered as much as 100,000 hectares. The bogs of the midlands have been worked by the Bord na Móna (Irish Turf Board) since 1932. A whole range of enormous machines does the job.

Fens are flat bogs found on the edges of lakes and in waterlogged areas supplied by mineral-rich waters. When that water supply is cut off, raised bogs develop over the top of fens.

The bogs found covering hills and valleys are known as blanket bogs. These develop on acid soil in a very wet climate, which usually means 240 days or more of rain each year. There are good examples of still-surviving blanket bogs in Wicklow, Sligo, Antrim and the Slieve Bloom Mountains.

About 17% of Ireland's landscape was once made up of bogs, but it's now thought that at the present rate of destruction they could all be gone in the very near future, wiping out 10,000 years of accumulation. The phenomenon of bog conservation appeared only towards the end of the 20th century, as previously bogs were seen either as large tracts of potential fuel or as useless and dangerous ground. On top of this, no-one had much affection for them, because they were closely tied to the stereotype of the bog Irishman. Now that so many of these bogs have been almost obliterated, there is an urgent need to conserve some of what's left – it has been suggested that 4% should be earmarked for protection. Some argue that all bogs should be conserved, especially since they are home to their own unique family of plants and insects and provide habitat for bird life.

The preservation properties of bogs are seen as another reason to conserve them. Due to the acidity and lack of oxygen in the peat, fragile organic artefacts that would otherwise have disintegrated long ago are occasionally preserved. The countless relics recovered, some of them 5000 years old, include Iron Age wooden highways, preserved bodies and wooden wheels and buckets. Among more recent items found were 300-year-old packets of cheese and butter.

For more information contact the Irish Peatland Conservation Council (☎ 01-872 2397, email ipcc@indigo.ie), Capel Chambers, Capel St, Dublin 1.

new buildings occur their design is mostly in keeping with the surrounding architecture. Aided by current economic prosperity and finance from the EU and the International Fund for Ireland, this urban renewal is happening in other towns and cities across Ireland.

One consequence of Ireland's affluence is the steep rise in the ownership of private cars, leading to greater traffic congestion in the country's towns and villages. Combine this with tourist traffic during the peak summer season and you have a traffic controller's and town planner's nightmare. To combat this, roads are being upgraded and town bypasses built, but this doesn't please everybody. Kildare town is one of the worst bottlenecks in the country, but construction of a bypass was suspended pending the outcome of a complaint by An Taisce to the European Commission that it threatened flora and fauna on Pollardstown Fen near Newbridge.

Other measures to prevent traffic congestion include higher taxes for large cars and the banning of large, regional car-dependent shopping centres outside urban areas.

Litter
Sadly, in many places, litter, especially plastic, is a common sight. However, awareness of this as a problem (not least for tourism) is growing. Local authorities spend IR£20 million each year on preventing litter pollution and over 700 towns and villages take part in the annual National Tidy Towns competition. April 1999 saw the launch of the inaugural month-long National Spring Clean campaign organised by An Taisce in an attempt to tackle the problem.

Useful Organisations
To find out more about Ireland's environment, a good place to start is ENFO (☎ 01-679 3144, fax 679 5204), 17 St Andrew St, Dublin 2, near the Dublin Tourism Centre. It's a public information service and opens from 10 am to 5 pm Monday to Saturday. Other sources include:

An Taisce (National Trust for Ireland)
  (☎ 01-454 1786) The Tailors Hall, Back Lane, Dublin 8. This nonprofit organisation is dedicated to the preservation of historical buildings and important natural sites.
Conservation Volunteers Ireland
  (☎ 01-668 1844) PO Box 3837, Ballsbridge, Dublin 4. This organisation runs a number of volunteer conservation projects around the country.
Dúchas
  (☎ 01-661 3111) 51 St Stephen's Green, Dublin 2. Dúchas is the government body that oversees many parks, gardens, monuments, inland waterways and sites of natural, historic and cultural importance.
Irish Wildlife Trust
  (☎ 01-676 8588) 107 Lower Baggot St, Dublin 2. The Irish Wildlife Trust is a nongovernment organisation focused on protection of wilderness and the designation of wilderness areas.
National Trust (Northern Ireland)
  (☎ 028-90 510721) Public Affairs Manager, Rowallane, Saintfield BT24 7LH. This organisation performs a similar function to its counterpart in the South.
Voice of Irish Concern for the Environment
  (fax 01-046 22799) 14 Upper Pembroke St,

Dublin 2. This is a nonprofit organisation founded to address local and national environmental issues.

FLORA & FAUNA
Flora
After the end of the last Ice Age about 10,000 years ago, a shrubby flora similar to that found in modern Arctic tundra took hold. This was eventually replaced by oak forest, which established itself on most of the island. In the upland regions and on more exposed hillsides, the oak was mixed with or replaced by birch and pine. In the lower regions where the soil was richer there was also elm, alder, hawthorn and ash. Underneath the oak trees were smaller plants such as holly, hazel, ferns, mosses and brambles, which provided a rich habitat for animals.

Today, however, the Irish landscape and predominant flora are mostly the result of human influence (see Forests and Agriculture in the Ecology & Environment section earlier in this chapter). Only 1% of genuine native oak forest survives. There are remnants in Killarney National Park and in southern Wicklow near Shillelagh, and smaller fragments near Tullamore in County Offaly and Abbeyleix in County Laios. Regimental columns of pine plantations are now a major feature of the Irish countryside and add little in the way of beauty. Pine species include sitka spruce, lodgepole pine, Douglas fir, Norway spruce and Scots pine.

Native plants survive in the hedgerows and in the wilder parts of the country. Because intensive agriculture arrived only comparatively recently, the range of surviving plant species is larger than in many other European countries. Irish hedgerows are a blaze of colour in spring and summer.

The Burren limestone region in Clare was covered in light woodland before the early settlers arrived. Now the area is almost all bare rock, but many of the original plants live on, a remarkable mixture of Mediterranean and alpine species.

The bogs of Ireland are home to a unique flora adapted to wet, acidic, nutrient-poor conditions. Sphagnum moss is the key bog-plant and is joined by plants such as the sundew, which uses its long hairs covered in sweet sticky stuff to catch insects.

Fauna

Mammals The most common native land mammals of any size are foxes and badgers, but although there are plenty about you're unlikely to see any on a casual visit. Smaller mammals include rabbits – introduced by the Normans for food – hares, hedgehogs, red and grey squirrels, shrews and bats. Red deer roam the hillsides in many of the wilder parts of the country, particularly the Wicklow Mountains, and in Killarney National Park, which holds the country's largest herd of native red deer. Other red deer have been introduced from abroad, including the Japanese sika deer.

Less common in Ireland are the elusive otter, stoat and pine marten, which are usually found in remote areas such as the Burren in County Clare or Connemara in County Galway.

Sea mammals include grey and common seals, which are found all around the coastline and can often be seen if you keep quiet and know where to look. There are some substantial colonies of grey seals living on uninhabited islands off County Mayo and around the shores of Strangford Lough in Northern Ireland. Dolphins often swim close to land, particularly in the bays and inlets off the western coast, and for many years Dingle Harbour has had a famous resident bottle-nosed dolphin called Fungie. There are whales in the sea off Ireland, but they tend to be so dispersed and stay so far out from land that they're rarely sighted.

Birds Ireland is home to a wide range of migrating and locally breeding birds. Many birds that breed in the Arctic areas of Canada, Greenland, Iceland and elsewhere fly to Ireland to pass the milder winters there, while others use it as a stopover as they migrate north or south. Brent, barnacle and Greenland white-fronted geese and Bewick's swans are seasonal visitors. They

winter in Ireland in places such as the Wexford North and South Slobs; Dublin's North Bull, Ireland's Eye and Lambay Islands; Tyrone's Lough Neagh; and Down's Strangford Lough. Also found during the winter are teal, redshank and curlew. April to May and September to October are the main migration periods.

The coastlines are home to a huge variety of sea birds – kittiwake, razorbill, puffin, Manx shearwater, storm petrel, cormorants, herons and others – and most breed in the late spring and early summer, the best time to view them. Small Skellig, out in the Atlantic Ocean off Kerry, is the second-largest gannet colony in the world, with some 20,000 pairs breeding annually on the rock. Old Head of Kinsale in County Cork is the nesting place of thousands of fulmars and guillemots. Other good locations for sea birds are Clear Island in Cork; Hook Head and the Saltee Islands in Wexford; the Burren in Clare; Inishbofin Island in Galway; Malin Head, Tory Island and the Inishowen Peninsula in Donegal; and Rathlin Island in Antrim.

Birds of prey include hen harriers, sparrowhawks, falcons (peregrine, merlin and

Puffin colonies can be seen on seaside cliffs.

kestrel) and the odd buzzard. The magnificent peregrine falcon has been making something of a recovery and can be found nesting on cliffs in Wicklow and elsewhere.

Fish The main fish to be found in Ireland are salmon and varieties of trout (brown, rainbow and sea), but there are other species, including mackerel and pollack, off the coast, and pike, bream, perch and roach in lakes and rivers.

Other Fauna The spotted Kerry slug is found, as the name suggests, in Kerry. So is the natterjack toad, Ireland's only species of toad, which lives in sandy areas behind Inch Strand and near Castlegregory on the northern side of the Dingle Peninsula. In the Burren you'll find 28 of Ireland's 33 species of butterfly.

Rare & Endangered Species All species native to Ireland's raised bogs are threatened with extinction if their habitat disappears in the next few years.

One of Ireland's rarest native birds is the corncrake, which used to be common in grasslands and meadows. In recent years there has been a small rise in its numbers. Corncrakes can be found in some remote and undisturbed areas, such as the low-lying flooded grasslands of the Shannon Callows and parts of Donegal (see the boxed text 'The Corncrake Crisis' in the Donegal chapter).

Also rare, the chough – an unusual crow with bright-red feet and beak – can be seen in the west, along coastlines with extensive sand dunes and on Clare Island in Mayo. Other endangered birds are the barn owl, Canadian brent goose, roseate tern, little tern and red-throated diver.

In the Ring of Kerry, the Kerry Bog pony is officially designated a rare breed (see the boxed text 'Kerry Bog Pony' in the Kerry chapter). The Burren is a stronghold of Ireland's most elusive mammal, the weasel-like pine marten. Other endangered mammals are the whiskered bat, hedgehog, Irish hare, badger and otter.

National Parks

Ireland has four national parks – Connemara (Galway), Glenveagh (Donegal), Killarney (Kerry) and Wicklow Mountains (Wicklow). These have been developed to protect, preserve and make accessible areas of significant natural heritage. Camping isn't allowed in the parks, which open year round. Each has its own information office, but for general information contact Dúchas (for details see Useful Organisations in the Ecology & Environment section earlier in this chapter).

Forests & Forest Parks

Coillte Teoranta (Irish Forestry Board) administers about 400,000 hectares of forested land, which includes designated picnic areas and 12 forest parks. These parks open year round and feature a range of wildlife and habitats. Some also have chalets and/or caravan parks, shops, cafés and play areas for children. For further information contact Coillte Teoranta (☎ 01-661 5666), Spruce House, Leeson Lane, Dublin 2.

National Nature Reserves

In Northern Ireland there are over 40 National Nature Reserves (NNRs), which are leased or owned by the Department of the Environment. These reserves are defined as areas of importance for their special flora, fauna or geology and include the Giant's Causeway and Glenariff Glen in Antrim, Marble Arch in County Fermanagh and North Strangford Lough in County Down. More information is available from the Environment and Heritage Service (☎ 028-90 546533), Commonwealth House, 35 Castle St, Belfast BT1 GU.

POPULATION & PEOPLE

The total population of Ireland is around 5.2 million. This figure is actually lower than 160 years ago. Prior to the 1845 to 1851 Potato Famine the population was around eight million. Death and emigration reduced the population to around six million, and emigration continued at a high level for the next 100 years. Not until the

1960s did this haemorrhaging slow down, but economic difficulties meant that even in the 1980s over 200,000 people joined the diaspora.

The Republic's population is 3.6 million. Dublin is the island's largest city and the capital of the Republic, with up to 1.5 million people – about 40% of the population of Éire – living within commuting distance of the city centre. The Republic's next largest cities are Cork with 180,000 inhabitants, Limerick with 79,000 and Galway with 57,000. A high proportion of the population of the Republic – 53.4% – is aged under 25.

Northern Ireland has a population of about 1.6 million, and Belfast, the principal settlement, around 280,000.

Though historically a mixture of many races, genetically the Irish are remarkably homogenous. To generalise, the Irish are a fair-skinned, dark-haired race with quite a number of red-haired, freckled members thrown in. Invaders such as the Vikings, Normans and British added to the gene pool, but their characteristics were diluted through the whole population.

In Northern Ireland, settlers from Scotland and England produced a distinctive Protestant culture which remains separate to this day, but scholars suggest that Catholics and Protestants are genetically almost identical.

Since the early 1990s there has been less emigration than immigration, which mostly consists of returning Irish but also immigrants from Britain, other EU countries and North America. The country has also admitted a small number of refugees from Eastern Europe and Africa.

EDUCATION

Attendance at school is compulsory and free up to and including the age of 15. Most schools at primary and secondary levels are run by religious denominations and receive state aid. Secondary schools are for children aged 12 and over and those who successfully complete their education at this level receive the Leaving Certificate. There are also state-run vocational schools.

At the tertiary level, there are four universities in the Republic. Dublin University is housed in Trinity College; the National University of Ireland (NUI) has colleges in Dublin, Maynooth (Kildare), Cork and Galway; and there are also Dublin City University and the University of Limerick. University College Cork (UCC) is affiliated with the NUI. Regional Institutes of Technology (ITs) provide tertiary vocational training.

Irish is a compulsory subject in primary and secondary schools and the growth of interest in the Irish language and traditional culture has led to a number of Irish-medium schools (*gaelscoileanna*), mostly at the primary level.

In Northern Ireland, education is modelled on the British system, though here, too, many schools are operated by religious denominations. There are two universities: Queen's University in Belfast and the University of Ulster, which has colleges in Belfast, Coleraine, Derry and Jordanstown.

With such a young population it's not surprising that over 25% of Ireland's populace is in full-time education, putting enormous pressure on educators and facilities alike. The competition for tertiary places and jobs also means that there's a lot more pressure to succeed on young people, many of whom take their education far more seriously than their parents ever did.

ARTS
Dance

The most important form of dance in Ireland is traditional Irish dancing, performed communally at *ceilidhs*, often in an impromptu format and always accompanied by an Irish traditional band. Dances include the hornpipe, jig and reel. The west and south-west are strongholds of traditional dance. Irish dancing has received international attention and success through shows such as *Riverdance*, which leaped to fame on the unlikely back of the *Eurovision Song Contest*, and its offshoots *Lord of the Dance* and *Spirit of the Dance*.

Ireland doesn't have a national dance school, but there are a number of schools and companies around the country teaching and performing ballet and modern dance. The Dance Theatre of Ireland and the Irish Modern Dance Theatre are based in Dublin, while the Firkin Crane Centre in Cork is Ireland's only venue devoted solely to dance.

Music

Traditional & Folk The rock band U2 may be Ireland's biggest musical export but when people talk about Irish music they are generally referring to an older, more intimate style of traditional or folk music. For the visitor, the joy of Irish music lies in its sheer accessibility. The biggest names may play the same major venues as the rock stars, but almost every town and village seems to have a pub renowned for its music where you can show up and find a session in progress, or even join in if you feel so inclined.

Most traditional music is performed on the fiddle, the tin whistle, the *bodhrán* (a goatskin drum) and the *uilleann* pipes. Instrumental music fits into five main categories: jigs, reels, hornpipes, polkas and slow airs. There are two main styles of song: *sean nós*, old-style tunes often sung in Gaelic either unaccompanied or with the backing of a bodhrán; and more familiar ballads. Traditional music has its strongest following in the Republic, but that's not to say you can't find it in Northern Ireland. Nor should it be thought of as the 'possession' of one side of the sectarian divide.

Of the Irish music groups, perhaps the best known is the Chieftains, who've been going since the 1960s and have taken their mainly instrumental music as far afield as China and South America. Adding vocals, come bands such as the Clancy Brothers and Tommy Makhem; the Dubliners with their notorious drinking songs (such as 'Seven Drunken Nights'); the Wolfe Tones, who've been described as 'the rabble end of the rebel song tradition'; and the Fureys. Younger groups such as Clannad from Donegal, Altan, Dervish and Nomos espouse a quieter, more mystical style of singing, while the London-Irish band the Pogues, led by Shane MacGowan, helped to keep things wild.

Christy Moore is the most prominent of the contemporary singer-songwriters playing in a broadly traditional idiom. Moore has been performing since the mid-1960s and was a pivotal member of the influential bands Planxty and Moving Hearts. But he's probably best known for solo albums that mix his own songs with renditions of music by everyone from Jackson Browne to Shane MacGowan. Moore's younger brother, Luka Bloom, has carved out a solo career for himself too, as has Andy Irvine, who, like Moore, was once a member of Planxty.

Other male singer-songwriters to listen out for include Finbar Furey, Mick Hanly, Jimmy MacCarthy, Kieran Goss, Strabane-born Paul Brady, Davy Spillane and Christie Hennessy.

Female singer-songwriters have an equally strong following. The mystical voice of Donegal's Enya, formerly of Clannad, has penetrated to a wider audience. Among the best-known contemporary female singers to look out for are sisters Mary and Frances Black, smoky-voiced Mary Coughlan, wild melodion-player Sharon Shannon, Dolores Keane and Eleanor McEvoy.

Stretching the boundaries of Irish music is the band Kíla, who combine traditional music with reggae, Eastern and new age influences.

Rock & Pop Showbands dominated Irish popular music in the 1960s. In the 1970s and 1980s Ireland's rock and pop music scene was exemplified by bands such as Thin Lizzy and the Boomtown Rats and by performers such as Bob Geldof, Rory Gallagher, Gilbert O'Sullivan, Elvis Costello and Chris de Burgh. U2, whose albums include *The Unforgettable Fire*, *The Joshua Tree*, *Rattle and Hum*, *Achtung Baby* and *Zooropa*, are the biggest of them all, but they're now being challenged by Ash from Downpatrick and the hugely internationally successful Limerick-based Cranberries.

Up there too are the Corrs, from Dundalk, who combine a touch of the traditional

New Music from Old Roots

The true origins of traditional Irish music are lost in the proverbial mists of time. However, clues to its humble roots lie in the instruments themselves. The *bodhrán*, the simple drum that resembles a giant cymbal, for example, was originally probably shaken to separate the corn from the chaff, while the small knuckle-ended beater was banged against it to frighten wrens away from the fields.

NICKY CAVEN

Celtic traditional music may have found its way overland from Asia and India some 2000 years ago. The Irish harp may even have been developed in Egypt. Until around 1700, this harp was the most important instrument in Irish music. It was smaller than the version played today, was wooden framed and had wire strings that were sounded with the fingernails rather than the fingertips.

Just as the great painters of the Renaissance in Italy depended on the patronage of wealthy merchants, so the harpists found support and patronage among Ireland's Gaelic chieftains. Consequently, music suffered a serious setback in 1607 when the Flight of the Earls saw the chieftains flee to the Continent, leaving the harpists to teach music to support themselves. The most famous of these itinerant musicians was Turlough O'Carolan (1670–1738), some of whose tunes are still played today. Traditionally, music was performed as a background to dancing, so the 17th-century penal laws did nothing to help by banning all expressions of traditional culture, including dancing. Music was forced underground, which goes some way towards explaining the homely feel of much Irish music today.

Until the late 18th century, Irish music was largely unwritten. In 1762, a book of 49 airs was published in Dublin. Then in 1792 Edward Bunting attended a Belfast harp festival and wrote down the tunes he heard. His manuscripts are still housed in the library of Queen's University in Belfast.

Between 1845 and 1851 the Potato Famine dealt traditional music another blow as musicians either died or emigrated in search of a better life. However, within the Irish diaspora the traditions lived on. To the standard repertoire of songs, new themes were added, as musicians sang nostalgically of the homeland and celebrated their new lives. Piano backing was added to some tunes while others were speeded up.

Eventually the tide turned. Recordings of the music being made in America in the 1920s travelled back across the Atlantic and sparked renewed interest in what had been lost. Copying the Irish-Americans, musicians at home also began to experiment by adding new instruments to the traditional line-up of fiddle, whistle, pipes and drum.

In the 1960s, Seán O'Riada (1931–71) of Cork set up Ceoltóirí Chualann, a band featuring a fiddle, flute, accordion, bodhrán and *uilleann* pipes, and began to perform music to listen to rather than dance to. When his band performed at the Gaiety Theatre in Dublin, it gave a whole new credibility to traditional music. Members of the band went on to form the Chieftains, who still play an important role in introducing Irish music to an international audience. Others who followed and helped develop traditional music into its current forms include Planxty, the Bothy Band (who introduced the bouzouki), Moving Hearts and the Horslips, who added a very 1970s rock twist.

with American pop rhythms and harmonies. With *Talk on Corners* and *Forgiven not Forgotten* they were the first Irish band to hold the top two positions in the UK album charts. Of the so-called 'boy bands', teen idols Boyzone, OTT and Westlife attract crowds of screaming girl fans. The Dublin girl group B*witched were the first band ever to have their first four singles go to number one in the UK.

The controversial Sinéad O'Connor gets headlines these days more for her off-stage activities than for her music (see the boxed text 'Rebel with Several Causes' in the Dublin chapter).

The unique Van Morrison seems to have been going for ever. In the 1960s he was lead singer with Them, whose anthem 'Gloria' was a Beatles-era classic. 'Van the Man' moved on to a solo career in the USA, and his *Astral Weeks* is regularly listed by critics as one of the seminal records of the 1960s. Although he has never generated a mass audience, Van Morrison has always attracted a cult following. His latest album is *Back on Top*.

No account of contemporary Irish music could close without reference to the popularity of country music and to singer Daniel O'Donnell, with millions of album sales (mainly to the over-40s) under his belt. Another perennial over-40s favourite is crooner Joe Dolan.

Literature

English may be an adopted language but the Irish truly have a way with it! If you took all the Irish writers off the university reading lists for English literature the degree courses could probably be shortened by a year!

The first great work of Irish literature was the *Ulaid (Ulster) Cycle*, written down from oral tradition between the 8th and 12th centuries. The chief story is the *Táin Bó Cúailnge*, about a battle between Queen Maeve of Connaught and Cúchulainn, the principle hero of Irish mythology. Cúchulainn appears in the work of Irish writers right up to the present day, from Samuel Beckett (1906–89) to Frank McCourt (born 1930).

Some of the more famous names born before 1900 include: Jonathan Swift (1667–1745), William Congreve (1670–1729), George Farquhar (1678–1707), Laurence Sterne (1713–68), Oliver Goldsmith (1728–74), Richard Sheridan (1751–1816), Bram Stoker (1847–1912), Oscar Wilde (1854–1900), George Bernard Shaw (1856–1950), WB Yeats (1865–1939), John Millington Synge (1871–1909), Sean O'Casey (1880–1964) and James Joyce (1882–1941). And today there are plenty of talented young writers carrying the Irish literary torch into the new millennium.

Ireland can boast four winners of the Nobel Prize for Literature: George Bernard Shaw in 1925, WB Yeats in 1938, Samuel Beckett in 1969 and Seamus Heaney in 1995.

The Ireland Anthology edited by the late Seán Dunne, poet and literary editor of the *Cork Examiner*, is a good introduction to Irish literature, though some might debate its inclusions and omissions. It contains over 200 prose and poetry entries dating from 1220 to the modern day. The *Oxford Companion to Irish Literature*, edited by Robert Welch, is a useful reference.

Fiction & Drama Despite the awesome difficulty of his last work, *Finnegans Wake*, James Joyce (1882–1941) remains accessible as well as rewarding for anyone wanting a window on the Irish soul. *Dubliners* is a collection of remarkable short stories, especially the final story, 'The Dead', which John Huston turned into a memorable film. *A Portrait of the Artist as a Young Man* is, for the most part, a semi-autobiographical tale of a young man coming to realise his artistic vocation.

Ulysses has such topographical realism that it produced a spate of Dublin guides based on the events in the novel. Although much has changed since the time in which it was set, there remains enough to sustain a steady flow of Joyce admirers bent on retracing the events of Bloomsday – 16 June 1904.

Recommended for anyone who wants to know more about Joyce's life (see the

James Joyce

Regarded as probably the most significant Irish writer of the 20th century, James Joyce (1882–1941) had a strange and singular life. He was born into a fairly well-off family and at the age of what he called 'half past six' became the youngest ever pupil at Ireland's most prestigious school – Clongowes Wood School, run by the Jesuits. By the time he entered University College Dublin, at the age of 16, his family had fallen on hard times and Joyce was a brilliant but erratic student. He paid little attention to the formal syllabus and formed few close relationships. He was downright antagonistic to the increasingly popular Irish cultural nationalism and, while WB Yeats was writing books such as *The Cultural Twilight*, Joyce was learning Norwegian so that he could read Henrik Ibsen in the original. He scorned what he later called the 'cultic twalette' of Irish nationalism.

He was determined to become a writer when he graduated in 1902, but then considered studying medicine and wandered between Dublin and Paris for the next couple of years. In 1904 three short stories appeared in an Irish farmers' magazine, written under the pen name Stephen Dedalus; these were later to form part of *Dubliners*.

After leaving Ireland in 1904 with Nora Barnacle, he spent most of the next 10 years in Trieste, Italy, where their two children were born and he reworked *Stephen Hero*, a novel he had started in Dublin, into *A Portrait of the Artist as a Young Man*. He returned to Ireland twice in 1909, but his efforts to find a publisher for *Dubliners* were unsuccessful. It was finally published in 1914. In Trieste Joyce took odd jobs in language schools and gave private lessons when strapped for cash.

The outbreak of WWI forced the family to move to neutral Zürich, Switzerland, in 1915, where Joyce began work on *Ulysses*. In 1918, extracts were published in the US magazine *Little Review*, but notoriety was already pursuing his epic work and censors prevented further episodes from being published after 1920. After a short return to Trieste, from 1920 he spent most of the rest of his life in Paris.

---

boxed text 'James Joyce' above) is *Nora: A Biography of Nora Joyce* by Brenda Maddox. It complements Richard Ellmann's more reverential biography of James Joyce himself.

Samuel Beckett (1906–89) is probably best known for his play *Waiting for Godot* but his unassailable reputation is based on a series of novels and plays. His stark writing doesn't seem as 'Irish' as that of Joyce or Yeats (which can be a help for the reader new to his work) and good places to start are *Murphy* and *Watt*.

A funny, absurdist, post-Joyce novelist was Flann O'Brien (1911–66), real name Brian O'Nuallain and second pseudonym Myles na Gopaleen, whose novels include *The Third Policeman*, *At Swim-Two-Birds* and *The Dalkey Archive*.

Playwright and novelist Brendan Behan (1923–64), expelled from school, a member of the IRA, imprisoned in Britain then deported back to Ireland, and an alcoholic, died in a Dublin hospital at the height of his fame. His most enduring works are *The Quare Fellow*, *Borstal Boy* and *The Hostage*.

John Banville (born 1945) is an important modern writer whose succession of excellent novels, which includes the Booker Prize-winning *Book of Evidence*, are notable for the quality of their prose. His bestseller *The Untouchable* is a fictionalised biography of Cold War British spy Anthony Blunt.

Despite (or maybe because of) Ireland's tragic history, the comic vision has always been a characteristic of Irish writers. Comedy features strongly in the work of Roddy Doyle (born 1958), one of Ireland's most

James Joyce

Joyce constantly spurned the idea of returning to live permanently in Ireland. When asked why he wouldn't return, one of his few recorded replies was 'Have I ever left it?' All his writing bears this out. When he first left, his motives were a mixture of economy and ideology, but his refusal to return was basically ideological. He certainly didn't lack the money now, for Harriet Weaver, editor of the *Egoist* magazine and serial publisher of *A Portrait of the Artist as a Young Man* (1914–15), gave him the equivalent of at least half a million UK pounds in today's money through a series of grants. As well as being an admirer, Weaver also felt sympathetic towards Joyce's problems, which included eye diseases. From 1917 to 1930, Joyce underwent a series of 25 operations for glaucoma, iritis and cataracts, which sometimes left him totally blind for short intervals.

Joyce despised the way the Catholic Church maintained its hold over the hearts and minds of his newly independent country and the thought of returning to that conservatism and repression was anathema to him. Joyce was always political in the broad sense of the word and when he moved to Paris in 1920 he left behind in Trieste a library of books that included classic anarchist texts. His refusal to marry was a political statement and, when he finally agreed to a registry-office marriage in 1931, it was purely to protect his family.

In 1922, Sylvia Beach of the Paris bookshop Shakespeare & Co finally managed to put *Ulysses* into print. Its earlier censorship difficulties, and its genius, made it an instant success. *Finnegans Wake* was published in 1939. When WWII broke out Joyce and his family fled back to Zürich, where he died two years later.

Ireland's treatment of Joyce has been a flagrant case of cultural expropriation, and the benign face that graces the country's £10 note has been craftily doctored to present a kindly old gent, smiling indulgently. It conveys nothing of the man who always refused to change his British passport for an Irish one or the angry young man who left Ireland in 1904 with Nora Barnacle, not to mention the author of a series of thoroughly pornographic letters to his wife.

successful contemporary writers. His stories, set in the working-class world of northern Dublin, won him the Booker Prize in 1993 for *Paddy Clarke Ha Ha Ha*. In 1990, *The Commitments* was made into an internationally successful film. His *The Woman Who Walked into Doors* is about domestic violence.

Christy Brown's (1932–81) marvellous autobiographical novel, *Down all the Days*, summed up Dublin's backstreet energy in the 1940s and 1950s. *The Ginger Man* by JP Donleavy (born 1926) was another high-energy excursion around Dublin, this time from the Trinity College perspective. It received the Church's seal of approval by lingering on the Irish banned list for many years.

Patrick McCabe's (born 1955) gruesome comedy, *The Butcher Boy*, about an orphaned Monaghan boy's descent into madness, received several awards and was made into a successful film. Another novel that made it to the screen was *The Field* by John B Keane (born 1928), about life on the land in the 1920s.

The legacy of history – centuries of fighting the British, the destructive Civil War and the Troubles since the 1960s – has obviously affected Irish writers. *The Informer* by Liam O'Flaherty (1896–1984) is the classic book about the divided sympathies which plagued Ireland throughout its struggle for independence and the ensuing Civil War (he fought on the republican side). John McGahern (born 1935) is worth reading as his fiction is never just narrowly political: *The Barracks* and especially *Amongst Women* are recommended. Gerry Conlon was one of the Guildford Four, who suffered years in prison for IRA bombings in Britain in the 1970s of which they were innocent. His true story, *Proved Innocent*, was made into the film *In the Name of the Father*. Frank McCourt's (born 1930) Pulitzer Prize-winning *Angela's Ashes* is the story of his poverty-stricken Limerick childhood.

One of the most outstanding playwrights of the last two decades is Frank McGuinness (born 1953), whose plays, such as *The Carthaginians*, explore the differing layers of Irish life. The young, prolific Anglo-Irish playwright Martin McDonagh (born 1971) has had his work performed by Britain's National Theatre and on Broadway, where he has won a number of Tony Awards. *The Leenane Trilogy* is set in Leenane in Galway. *Dancing at Lughnasa* by Brian Friel (born 1929) was a great success on Broadway and in London and has been made into a film.

Other talented young playwrights to watch out for in the future include Mark O'Rowe (*Howie the Rookie*) and Enda Walsh (*Misterman*).

The North The Irish way with words is just as obvious north of the border as south – in fact it's astonishing how many good writers a place as small as Northern Ireland manages to turn out. The Troubles feature in much Northern writing.

CS Lewis (1898–1963), from Belfast, is best known for *The Chronicles of Narnia*, a series of allegorical children's stories.

Cal by Bernard MacLaverty (born 1942) traces a life where the choices are miserable and the consequences terrible and inevitable. Those no-win political situations are also seen in *Lies of Silence* by Brian Moore (born 1921), which was shortlisted for the Booker Prize.

In Glenn Patterson's (born 1961) amusing first novel, *Fat Lad*, the political situation is a backdrop to a story that captures the feel of life in Belfast today. And the title? It's an Ulster children's mnemonic for learning the names of the six counties: Fermanagh-Armagh-Tyrone (FAT) and Londonderry-Antrim-Down (LAD).

Call My Brother Back by Michael McLaverty recounts growing up on Rathlin Island and the Falls Rd, Belfast, in the 1920s. Much of the feel of his Belfast survives to this day. From Sinn Féin president Gerry Adams (born 1948), *The Street* is a collection of stories dealing with life in West Belfast, where he grew up.

Belfast-born Robert McLiam Wilson (born 1964) is at the forefront of modern Irish writing. His first novel was the award-winning *Ripley Bogle*, which follows 'the prince of the Pavements... the Parkbench King', a West Belfast tramp, through London, with flashbacks to his youth. His *Eureka Street* is set in Belfast.

The work of playwright and poet Damian Gorman has received considerable praise. *Broken Nails*, his first play, received four Ulster Theatre awards.

Women Ireland has produced its fair share of women writers. Earlier examples, mostly of the Anglo-Irish Ascendancy, were Lady Morgan (1776–1859), Maria Edgeworth (1768–1849), EO Somerville (1858–1949), Violet Martin (1861–1915), who wrote under the pseudonym of Martin Ross, and Elizabeth Bowen (1899–1973).

The work of Edna O'Brien (born 1932) explores the small-minded, hypocritical side of Irish life. In 1960 she enjoyed the accolade of having her *The Country Girls* banned. She's not afraid to confront contemporary issues and in 1997 she wrote *Down by the River*, based on the real-life controversy of the 14-year-old Dublin girl who was raped and went to England for an abortion. O'Brien added incest to the mix by making the girl's father the rapist.

The works of the prolific Iris Murdoch (1919–99) encompass fiction, drama, poetry and philosophy. Her novel *The Sea, The Sea* won the Booker Prize.

The Old Jest by Jennifer Johnston (born 1930) is set in Ireland between the wars. The protagonist is an Anglo-Irish girl growing up in the South at a time when change is about to sweep through the country and the Anglo-Irish Ascendancy is in its final days.

Clare Boylan's (born 1948) books include *Holy Pictures*, *Concerning Virgins* and *Black Baby*. Molly Keane (1904–66) wrote several books in the 1920s and 1930s under the pseudonym MJ Farrell, then had a literary second life in her 70s when *Good Behaviour* and *Time After Time* came out under her real name.

In popular fiction Maeve Binchy (born 1940) is *the* writer of blockbusters that just rise above the sex and shopping genre. *Circle of Friends*, set in Dublin, was made into a film. Her latest novel, *Evening Class*, centres on an Italian evening class in a grim part of Dublin.

Journalist Nuala O'Faolain's (born 1950) *Are You Somebody?* is a memoir of her childhood in Dublin in the 1950s and about coping in a male-dominated world. Mary Costello's (born 1955) *Titanic Town* manages to make growing up in the tough Andersonstown area of West Belfast funny and sad in equal measures.

Young novelists such as Emma Donoghue (born 1969) tackle once-taboo subjects; *Stir-fry* is a lesbian love story.

Poetry WB Yeats (1865–1939) was a playwright and poet, but it's his poetry that has the greatest appeal and, being out of copyright, countless editions are available. His *Love Poems*, edited by Norman Jeffares, makes a suitable introduction for anyone new to his writing. A collected edition, *The Poems*, in the Everyman series edited by Daniel Albright, includes a useful set of notes.

Pádraig Pearse (1879–1916) used the Irish language as his medium and was one of the leaders of the 1916 Easter Rising.

Patrick Kavanagh (1905–67), one of Ireland's most respected poets, was born in Inniskeen, County Monaghan. *The Great Hunger* and *Tarry Flynn* evoke the atmosphere and often grim reality of life for the poor farming community. You'll find a bronze statue of him in Dublin, sitting beside his beloved Grand Canal.

Seamus Heaney (born 1939) was winner of the 1995 Nobel Prize for Literature. In 1997 Heaney added the Whitbread Book of the Year to his accolades for *The Spirit Level*. Some poems reflect the hope, disappointment and disillusionment of the peace process.

Cork-born Irish-language poet Louis de Paor has had two of his collections win Ireland's prestigious Sean O'Riordan Prize. Tom Paulin (born 1949) writes memorable poetry about the North: try *The Strange Museum*.

Other notable contemporary poets are Brendan Kennelly, Eavan Boland, Eiléan Ní Chuilleanáin, Paul Muldoon and Derek Mahon. For a taste of modern Irish poetry try *Contemporary Irish Poetry* edited by Fallon and Mahon. *A Rage for Order* edited by Frank Ormsby is a vibrant collection of the poetry of the North.

Architecture

Ireland is packed with prehistoric graves, ruined monasteries, crumbling fortresses and many other solid reminders of its long, often dramatic, history. The earliest settlers built houses of wood and reeds, of which nothing survives except the faint traces of post holes. The principal surviving structures from Stone Age times are the graves and monuments people built for their dead, usually grouped under the heading of megalithic (great stone) tombs.

Megalithic Tombs Among the most easily recognisable megalithic tombs are dolmens, massive three-legged structures rather like giant stone stools, in which a number of bodies were interred before the whole structure was covered in earth. Most are 4000 to 5000 years old. Usually the earth eroded away leaving the standing stones exposed. Good examples are the Poulnabrone dolmen in the Burren, Clare; Proleek near Dundalk; and at Browne's Hill near Carlow town. The capstone at Browne's Hill weighs more than 100 tonnes.

Court tombs, with a formal forecourt in front of the tomb, are found mostly in Ulster. Ossian's Grave at Cushendall in County Antrim is a good example.

Passage graves such as Newgrange and Knowth in Meath are huge mounds with entrances through narrow stone-walled passages leading to burial chambers. They're surrounded by stone circles of unknown significance. Some passage graves were made from piles of stones erected near or on hilltops, sometimes called cairns. A good example of this is on the Loughcrew Hills in Meath.

A wedge tomb is a stone box tapering in both height and width and about the size of a large double bed. The dead were placed inside and the structure covered in earth and stones. Gleninsheen in the Burren, County Clare, is a good example.

Also plentiful in Ireland are cist graves (chambers excavated in rock or formed of stones or a hollowed tree trunk) and gallery graves (tunnel-shaped tombs).

Ogham Stones These are peculiarly Irish standing stones dating from the 4th to 7th centuries AD. Ogham (pronounced 'o-am') was an early form of Irish script using a variety of notched strokes placed above, below or across a keyline, usually on stones. The stones mainly indicate graves and are inscribed with the name of the deceased. The majority are found in Counties Cork, Kerry and Waterford. Many have been moved: you may find them incorporated in walls, buildings or gateposts.

Forts The Irish names for forts – *dun*, *rath*, *caiseal/cashel* and *caher* – have ended up in the names of countless

towns and villages. The Irish countryside is peppered with the remains of over 30,000 of them. The earliest known examples date from the Bronze Age but they have been built and used for many thousands of years since. Some were lived in as late as the 17th century. Wooden and other types of houses were built within the forts' protective confines.

The most common fort was the ring fort, with circular earth-and-stone banks, topped by a wooden palisade fence to keep out intruders, and surrounded on the outside by a moatlike ditch. Ring forts are found everywhere and were the basic family or tribal enclosure in Ireland for thousands of years. They may have protected anything from one family to the entire court of a tribal chieftain. Ring forts may be surrounded by up to three earthen ramparts; Mooghaun Fort near Dromoland Castle in County Clare is a particularly fine example. Outside Clonakilty in County Cork, the ring fort at Lisnagun (Lios na gCon) has been reconstructed to give some idea of its original appearance.

Some forts were constructed entirely of stone; Staigue Fort in Kerry and Cathair Dhún Iorais on Clare's Black Head are fine examples. Promontory forts were built on headlands or on cliff edges, which gave natural protection on one side. The Iron Age fort of Dún Aengus on

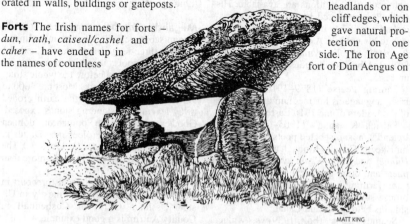

MATT KING

A dolmen, at Kilclooney, north of Ardara in County Donegal, built by Stone Age farmers as a monument to their dead

Inishmór (the largest of the Aran Islands) is a superb example.

The Normans used many ring forts to their full advantage by building inside them. A characteristic early Norman-built fort was the motte and bailey. The motte was a small flat-topped hill surrounded by a ditch and earthen banks at the base for further protection; attached to and surrounding the motte was the bailey, an enclosure for animals and their keepers. These forts were largely military in purpose, built to protect and secure the Normans' newly conquered territory.

Crannógs Artificial islands built in many Irish lakes, crannógs are the equivalent of a ring fort on water. Many were completely constructed by humans: wooden piles were driven into the lake floor and the structure built up with wood, stone, earth and anything else the builders could find. After the island had been completed, the occupants put up wooden fences and a house to live in. Estimates put the number of crannógs in Ireland at over 250. They date back to the Bronze Age and like the ring forts were used by humans right up to the 16th and 17th centuries. The Craggaunowen Project in Clare has a reconstructed example, and the lake near Fair Head in County Antrim has an easily spotted original.

The midland lakes have many crannógs, which today are usually overgrown, with little evidence betraying their artificial origins except perhaps the too-perfect circular outline. Sometimes they were built in bogs, or the original lake has since become a bog, so many are now hidden below the water level. Often there was a secret causeway leading out to the crannóg, just under the surface of the water, and it twisted and turned so that ignorant intruders would have difficulty using it.

Monasteries & Churches After Christianity arrived in Ireland in the 5th century, the first monasteries were built, mainly of perishable materials, particularly wood. Sometimes the central church or chapel was stone – these are often the only structures that survive. The early stone churches were often very simple, some roofed with timber, like 6th-century Teampall Bheanáin (Church of St Benen) on Inishmór of the Aran Islands, or built completely of stone, like the 8th-century Gallarus Oratory on the Dingle Peninsula. Early hermitages include the small beehive huts and buildings on the summit of Skellig Michael off County Kerry.

As the monasteries grew in size and stature, so did the architecture. The cathedrals at Glendalough (12th century) and Clonmacnoise (10th to 15th century) are good examples, although they're tiny compared with modern cathedrals.

Round towers have become symbols of Ireland. These tall, stone needle-like structures were built largely as lookout posts and refuges in the event of Viking attacks. The earliest round towers were built in the late 9th or early 10th centuries.

That other great Irish symbol, the Celtic cross, dates from between the 8th and 12th centuries. Some suggest that the circle imposed on the arms of the cross represents pagan sun worship being incorporated into the new faith. They developed from simple crosses with rough designs to complex works decorated with high-relief scenes, usually of Biblical characters and tales. A fine example of this is Muiredach's Cross at Monasterboice in County Louth.

Ireland's early church architecture developed in isolation, as Europe was experiencing the Dark Ages. However, foreign influences began to appear in the 11th and 12th centuries. The Cistercians, a European order of monks, established their first Irish monastery at Mellifont, County Louth, in 1142. The strict and formal layout of these new establishments was radically different from the simple and relatively random layout of the traditional Irish monastery as exemplified by nearby Monasterboice, Glendalough in Wicklow and Clonmacnoise in Offaly. Cormac's Chapel (1127) at the Rock of Cashel in Tipperary shows strong foreign influence in its European Romanesque design, with its tunnel-vaulted nave and rib-vaulted chancel. Elaborately carved doorways are common in church architecture of the 12th century, with human and animal heads intricately interwoven into the Celtic patterns.

With the Normans in 1169 came the Gothic style of architecture, characterised by tall vaulted windows and soaring V-shaped arches. Fine examples of this can be seen in Christ Church Cathedral (1172) in Dublin, and St Canice's Cathedral (13th century) in Kilkenny.

Castles & Mansions The Normans first built temporary motte-and-bailey forts (see Forts, earlier), but once they had established themselves they built more-permanent stone castles. The great castle at Trim (1172), County Meath, is the best example.

Many castles that you see today are the tall, thin tower houses built between the 14th and 17th centuries for local landlords or chieftains. They're often inside a protective wall called a *bawn*. The earliest of these tower houses are simple, small keeps with few embellishments, such as Bunratty Castle (15th century), while the later forms became more like large, fortified stone houses with sophisticated features, bigger windows and less emphasis on security.

From the 17th century on, as the established landowning families became wealthier and felt more secure, they began to build unfortified houses and classical principles began to emerge, particularly in the less rebellious parts of the country around Counties Kildare, Meath, Dublin and Wicklow.

Cottages Authentic traditional thatched Irish cottages were built of limestone or clay to suit the elements (wooden structures are much less effective at keeping out the rain and cold), but weren't durable and have become rare. They contained an open fireplace for heating and cooking. Some cottages, called longhouses, sheltered animals as well as humans. The building of traditional cottages died out around the middle of the 20th century.

Georgian Houses In Georgian times, Dublin became one of the architectural glories of Europe, with simple, beautifully built Georgian terraces of red brick, with delicate glass fanlights over large, elegant, curved doorways. From the 1960s Dublin's Georgian heritage suffered badly but many buildings, in places such as Mountjoy Square, are being restored. You can see fine examples around Merrion and Fitzwilliam Squares. Georgian urban architecture wasn't confined to Dublin and you'll see other fine examples in places such as Cork and Limerick.

The Anglo-Irish Ascendancy built country houses such as Castletown House (1722) near Celbridge, and Russborough House (1741) near Blessington, which are both excellent examples of the Palladian style, with their regularity and classical correctness.

Modern Architecture Ireland has little modern architecture of note. For much of the 20th century the pace of change was slow and it wasn't until the construction of Dublin's Busáras Station in the 1950s that modernity began to really express itself. It was designed by Michael Scott, who was to have an influence on architects in Ireland for the next two decades. The poorly regulated building boom of the 1960s and 1970s, however, paid little attention to the country's architectural heritage and destroyed more than it created. From that period Paul Koralek's 1967 brutalist-style Berkeley Library in Trinity College, Dublin, has been hailed as Ireland's best example of modern architecture.

Since the 1980s more care has been given to architectural heritage and context, the best example of which has been the redevelopment of Dublin's previously near-derelict Temple Bar area. Among its most interesting buildings is the eco-friendly Green House, which uses only wind and solar power.

Painting Ireland's painting doesn't receive the kind of recognition that its literature and music do. Nevertheless, painting in Ireland has a long tradition dating back to the illuminated manuscripts of the early Christian period, most notably the *Book of Kells*.

The National Gallery has an extensive Irish School collection, much of it chronicling the personages and pursuits of the Anglo-Irish aristocracy. Early noted portrait painters were Garrett Murphy (1680–1716) and James Latham (1696–1747).

In the 18th century, painters began working on landscape and historical themes. Important artists were George Barret, Robert Carver, William Ashford, Roderick O'Connor and Thomas Roberts. James Malton captured 18th-century Dublin in a series of line drawings and on canvas in a series of paintings.

In the 19th century there was still no hint of Ireland's political and social problems in the work of its major artists. The most prominent landscape painter was James Arthur O'Connor, while portrait painters such as Daniel Maclise (1806–70) and William Mulready (1786–1863) had an impact across the Irish Sea in England.

Just as WB Yeats played a seminal role in the Celtic literary revival, his younger brother, Jack Butler Yeats (1871–1957), inspired an artistic surge of creativity in the early 20th century, taking Celtic mythology and Irish life as his subjects. (Their father, John Butler Yeats, had also been a noted portrait painter.) Together with Paul Henry and other painters he formed the Society of Dublin Painters in 1920.

The influence of European cubism and futurism can be seen in the works of Evie Hone (1894–1955) and Mainie Jellett (1897–1944), who helped found the alternative Irish Exhibition of Living Art in 1943. In the post-WWII period, this showcase was a great influence on modernists such as Barrie Cooke (born 1931) and Camille Souter (born 1929). In the 1950s and 1960s, a school of naive artists appeared on Tory Island, off the coast of Donegal; their most accomplished figure was James Dixon. They were inspired by English artist Derek Hill (born 1916), who was made an honorary Irish citizen; he set up the Glebe House and Gallery near Letterkenny, where much of their work is displayed.

Contemporary artists to watch out for include Michael Cullen, Eithne Jordan, Rita Duffy and Patrick Graham.

Cinema

During much of the 20th century Ireland didn't have a particularly active film-making industry, partly because of the small home market and partly because of the moral strictures of the Catholic Church. It was often left to American or British film-makers to represent Ireland to the rest of the world (see Films in the Facts for the Visitor chapter). This began to change in 1981 following the creation of the Irish Film Board and the spending of more money on a home-grown film industry (including tax incentive packages).

Nevertheless, Irish actors do have a long tradition of appearances in film and quite a few have achieved extraordinary international success in the last couple of decades. Liam Neeson (*Schindler's List*) and Daniel Day-Lewis and Brenda Fricker (*My Left Foot*) have won Oscars, Belfast-born Kenneth Branagh's career has invited comparisons with Laurence Olivier's, Gabriel Byrne starred in a series of hits (*The Usual Suspects, Man in the Iron Mask*) and Pierce Brosnan scored the coveted James Bond role. Other actors who achieved success in the same period include Aidan Quinn (*Legends of the Fall*), Stephen Rea (*The Crying Game*), Fionnula Flanagan (*Some Mother's Son*) and Colm Meaney (*The Commitments*). They have followed in the footsteps of the likes of Richard Harris (*The Guns of Navarone, The Field*) and Peter O'Toole (*Lawrence of Arabia, The Last Emperor*), and before them Greer Garson (*Goodbye, Mr Chips*) and Maureen O'Hara (*Jamaica Inn*).

To this crop of acting talent can be added the screenwriter and director Neil Jordan, whose impressive body of work includes *Mona Lisa* (1986), *The Crying Game* (1992), *Interview with the Vampire* (1994), *Michael Collins* (1996) and *The Butcher Boy* (1998). *The Crying Game*, for which Jordan won an Oscar for best screenplay, is perhaps the most intriguing commercial film to feature the IRA. Jordan's powerful *Michael Collins* stars Liam Neeson and Stephen Rea. It follows the life of Collins from the Easter Rising, through the creation of the IRA, to the Anglo-Irish War, Civil War and his death in 1922 at the hands of his former comrades. *The Butcher Boy* was a successful translation of Patrick Mc-Cabe's novel about an orphaned Monaghan boy.

Other important film-makers are producer Noel Pearson and director Jim Sheridan, who worked together on *My Left Foot* (1989) and *The Field* (1990). *My Left Foot* told the true story of Dublin writer Christy Brown, who was crippled with cerebral palsy. Noel Pearson's production of Brian Friel's play *Dancing at Lughnasa* (1998) is set in Ballybegs, Donegal, in the 1930s and stars Meryl Streep. Jim Sheridan's *In the Name of the Father* (1993), filmed in Kilmainham Jail in Dublin, starred Daniel Day-Lewis as Gerry Conlon and Emma Thompson as his lawyer. It tells the story of the arrest and conviction of the Guildford Four for a pub bombing in England, then of the struggle to clear their names. In Sheridan's *The Boxer* (1997) Daniel Day-Lewis plays a Belfast man unable to escape the Troubles. Jim Sheridan also wrote Mike Newell's *Into the West* (1993), a delightful story of two children and a mythical white horse.

Pat O'Connor's credits as film director include Bernard MacLaverty's *Cal* (1984) and Maeve Binchy's *Circle of Friends* (1994), starring Minnie Driver. The latter film changed the book's strong feminist ending into Hollywood schlock!

Theatre

Dublin and Belfast are the main centres, but most sizeable towns, such as Cork, Derry, Donegal, Limerick and Galway, have their own theatres. Ireland has a theatrical history almost as long as its literary one. Dublin's first theatre was founded in Werburgh St in 1637, although it was closed only four years later by the Puritans. Another theatre, named the Smock Alley Playhouse or Theatre Royal, opened in 1661 and continued to stage plays for over a century.

The literary revival of the late 19th century saw the establishment of Dublin's Abbey Theatre, now Ireland's national theatre. Its role is to present works by former greats such as WB Yeats, JM Synge and Sean O'Casey, as well as to promote modern Irish dramatists. Also in Dublin, the Gate Theatre produces classics and comedies, while the Gaiety and Olympia Theatres present a range of productions, as does the Grand Opera House in Belfast.

See the Entertainment section in specific chapters for more information on theatres.

Classic Irish Classics

While films such as *Michael Collins*, *Circle of Friends* and *In the Name of the Father* were box office hits, many Irish films either fail commercially or are unable to secure a distributor. To provide an opportunity for audiences to see more indigenous productions, the Irish Film Board, Clarence Pictures (an independent distributor) and Xtra-Vision (Ireland's biggest video chain) have created Classic Irish Classics, a new video label. On its list are *Dancing at Lughnasa*, *My Left Foot* and *The Field*, as well as lesser-known films. These are all available for purchase.

SOCIETY & CONDUCT

Ireland's recent economic success, social changes and cultural resurgence are rapidly dispelling old stereotypes of the country as a predominantly poor, agrarian backwater stifled by religious strictures and animosities and unable to stop the exodus of its children. In reality, it has a young, expanding population, flourishing arts and a booming economy that has embraced high technology.

Social stratification exists, but movement between classes is fairly fluid and more to do with personal wealth than birth or background. Yet the gap between the 'haves' and 'have nots' has widened alarmingly.

Many people may be enjoying their share of the Celtic Tiger's economic success, but it hasn't reached areas such as the Dublin housing estates, where drugs and crime are a major problem. Booming property prices in Dublin have made housing unaffordable for a large proportion of the city's population. Although unemployment has gone down, the number of Irish living below the poverty line (set at 60% of the national average wage) rose from 31% in 1991 to 38% in 1998.

With the decline in the power of the Church there has been a liberalising of sexual mores. Contraceptive pills and condoms are freely available, though in some areas they're still taboo subjects of discussion. In a 1995 referendum, divorce was narrowly, but finally, accepted.

The thorny abortion issue has been temporarily resolved in a typically Irish compromise. Abortion is still illegal but it's no longer illegal to provide information on abortion, and women who travel to Britain to terminate their pregnancies do so without fear of legal sanction. Still the debate continues: luminaries such as former president Mary Robinson plead for legalisation of abortion, while pro-life activist groups such as Youth Defence organise rallies against it.

Do's & Don'ts

On the whole, Irish of all political or religious persuasions are friendly and accommodating towards foreigners. However, religion and politics are inextricably mixed, especially in the North, and, whenever these subjects come up, as a visitor it's probably a good idea to make this a time to practise your listening skills – at least until you're sure of the situation.

There's a marked difference in opinion and outlook between the older, more 'traditional' generations and young people. While the former may recognise that contraception, divorce, abortion and homosexuality exist in modern Ireland, they are, nevertheless, often wary of entertaining a conversation on such subjects. Religious beliefs among older people, especially in rural areas, are still strong, and they might take offence at a foreigner who doesn't respect their strongly held opinions on these matters.

Younger Irish, on the other hand, have embraced social change as long overdue and are often extremely liberal, sometimes radically so, in their views.

As with any other nation, the Irish don't like to be reminded of their faults by anybody but other Irish. The best policy is to relax and accept the many good things that the people of Ireland have to offer.

RELIGION

The Republic of Ireland is nominally 95% Roman Catholic, but church attendance has fallen, especially among younger people. The rest of the population are 3.4% Protestant and 0.1% Jewish, while 1.5% either have no religious beliefs or belong to other religious groupings, including Islam and Buddhism. In the North the breakdown is about 60% Protestant, 40% Catholic. Most Irish Protestants are members of the Church of Ireland, an offshoot of the Church of England, and the Presbyterian and Methodist Churches.

The Catholic Church has always taken a strong conservative line on abortion, contraception, divorce and censorship, and opposed attempts to liberalise the laws on these matters. But the Church has been weakened by declining attendances, the fall in the number of young men and women entering the religious life and by damaging sex scandals, particularly the abuse of children. The Church is now treated with a curious mixture of respect and derision by various sections of the community.

Despite its declining power, the Catholic Church still wields considerable influence in the South. It retains control of most primary and secondary schools and hospitals (which are funded by the state) and, in rural towns and villages, large numbers attend mass every Sunday as part of the weekly social round.

Oddly enough, the primates of both the Roman Catholic Church and the Church of Ireland sit in Armagh, the traditional base of St Patrick, which is in Northern Ireland. The country's religious history clearly over-rides its current divisions.

LANGUAGE

English is spoken throughout Ireland, but with its own Irish flavour and lilt. There are parts of western and southern Ireland where Irish is the native language; these are known as *Gaeltacht* areas. For more details see the Language chapter at the rear of this book.

Facts for the Visitor

HIGHLIGHTS
Scenery, Beaches & Coastline

The scenery is one of Ireland's major attractions, whether it's those soft green fields, awesome cliffs tumbling into a ferocious Atlantic, or rocky, barren areas in the far west. Highlights include the beautiful scenery around the Ring of Kerry and the Dingle Peninsula, the barren stretches of the Burren, the rocky Aran Islands and the beautiful lake areas south and north.

Favourite stretches of Ireland's coastline include the wildly beautiful Cliffs of Moher, the Connemara and Donegal coasts and the wonderful Antrim coast road, including the Giant's Causeway, of Northern Ireland. There are some fine beaches (and marginally warmer water) around the southeastern coast, and some great surfing around the western and north-western coasts.

The EU Blue Flag flies over Ireland's cleanest and safest beaches. If a beach doesn't have a Blue Flag it's best to inquire locally before venturing out for a swim.

Museums, Castles & Houses

Trinity College Library with the ancient *Book of Kells* is on every visitor's must-see list, but Dublin also has the fine National Museum, National Gallery and the Ceol interactive museum of traditional Irish music. Belfast has the excellent Ulster Museum and, east of the city, in County Down, the extensive Ulster Folk and Transport Museum.

Ireland is littered with castles and forts of various types and sizes and in various stages of ruination. The Stone Age forts on the Aran Islands are of particular interest, but there are other ancient ring forts all over Ireland. Prime examples of castles are Dublin Castle, Charles Fort at Kinsale, and Kilkenny Castle, not forgetting Blarney Castle with its famous stone!

The Anglo-Irish aristocracy left a good selection of fine stately homes, many of which are open to the public, such as Castletown House near Celbridge, Malahide House, Westport House, Bantry House, and Mt Stewart on the Ards Peninsula. The beautiful gardens at Powerscourt Estate are definitely worth a visit.

Religious Sites

Stone rings, dolmens and passage graves are reminders of pre-Christian Ireland (see Architecture in the Arts section of the Facts about Ireland chapter for more information). The massive passage grave at Newgrange is the most impressive of these relics. Early Christian churches, many well over 1000 years old, are scattered throughout Ireland, and ruined monastic sites, many with round towers, are also numerous. Clonmacnoise, Glendalough, Mellifont Abbey, Grey Abbey, Inch Abbey in Downpatrick and Jerpoint Abbey are particularly interesting monastic sites. The rock-top complex at Cashel is one of Ireland's major tourist attractions, and the beehive huts built by monks on Skellig Michael, off the coast of Kerry, are well worth visiting.

Islands

Lying off Ireland's coast are all sorts and shapes of islands, some of them inhabited by humans, others inhabited only by migrating birds, some easily accessible, others requiring the private hire of a boat.

The Aran Islands in County Galway and Achill Island in County Mayo are the most touristy, but it's not difficult to find more isolated ones. A boat trip to the Skelligs is one of the highlights of a visit to Ireland, and their wildlife is fascinating. The Blaskets, off the Dingle Peninsula in County Kerry, are glorious on a fine day. Tory Island, off the Donegal coast, is a wild place and the home of a group of local artists. County Cork has a number of accessible islands, of which Clear Island is famous for its birdlife and scenery and nearby Sherkin Island has sandy, safe beaches.

SUGGESTED ITINERARIES

Any itinerary is very much a matter of personal choice. To do Ireland justice you need at least three to four weeks, but the country is small enough for you to cover a fair bit of territory even in a week. The following suggestions may help:

Three Days
Visit Dublin and, using it as a base, see perhaps a couple of places nearby – Powerscourt Estate and Glendalough monastic site to the south, or Newgrange passage grave, Mellifont Abbey and Monasterboice monastery to the north.

One Week
Visit Dublin, then Newgrange, Mellifont, Kilkenny town, Killarney, Dingle and the Burren.

Two Weeks
As above, plus the Ring of Kerry and some of the sights of County Cork.

One Month
With a car or motorcycle you'd have time to explore all of the above, adding places such as Connemara, Donegal and Antrim to the list, but you'd be moving quite fast. Seeing all of that would be more difficult to achieve within a month on public transport. You could fit in some walking and cycling too.

PLANNING
When to Go

The weather is generally warm in July and August and the daylight hours are long, but the crowds are greater, the costs higher and accommodation harder to come by. If you go in winter there are fewer tourists and accommodation is cheaper, but you may get miserable weather, the daylight hours are short and many tourist facilities are shut. It's worth considering visiting Ireland between April and June or in September, when the weather can be better than in the winter, it's less crowded than in the summer, and most attractions and tourist offices are open. Dublin and Belfast can be visited year round.

Festivals and other events occur throughout the year, with July and August the busiest months. For details see Public Holidays & Special Events later in this chapter.

What Kind of Trip?

Your particular interests will have a large bearing on the kind of trip you choose, as will the amount of time and money at your disposal. The longer you stay, the more likely it is you'll step outside the frequently superficial world of the tourist, and the lower your relative daily expenses will be.

Try to leave enough time to walk one or two waymarked trails (at least part of them, anyway) or to do some cycle touring somewhere off the beaten track. Some visitor attractions have no public transport, so walking or cycling may be your only way to see them.

You may also want to consider hiring a car for part of the trip to visit some out-of-the-way places. However, most attractions can be visited as part of a guided tour. This is often a good way to get a quick overview of areas you're unfamiliar with and allows you to consider your options should you want to return.

Travelling alone is fine, provided you follow the normal precautions, and is a great way to meet new people. Hostels, camp sites and caravan parks are good places to meet fellow travellers, and B&Bs allow you to meet locals, who may offer the kinds of insights unavailable at the local tourist office.

Maps

There are numerous good-quality maps of Ireland. The Michelin *Map of Ireland* No 405 (1:400,000) has most of the scenic roads accurately highlighted in green. The four maps – *North*, *South*, *East* and *West* – that make up the Ordnance Survey Holiday Map series (1:250,000) are useful if you want something more detailed than a whole-of-Ireland map.

For greater detail the Ordnance Survey Discovery series covers the whole island in 89 maps with a 1:50,000 scale (2cm to 1km). They can be obtained from bookshops, including the Government Publications Sales Office bookshop (☎ 01-661 3111), Sun Alliance House, Molesworth St, Dublin 2.

For information on maps suitable for walkers, on and off Ireland's waymarked trails, see Guides & Maps in the Walking section of the Activities chapter.

What to Bring

A travelpack – a combination of backpack and shoulder bag – is the most useful means of carrying gear. A travelpack's straps zip away inside when not needed, making it easy to handle in airports and on crowded public transport. They look better than a backpack and can be made reasonably thief-proof with small combination locks.

A raincoat or an umbrella is a necessity, as are some warm clothes – even during good summer weather it gets chilly in the evenings. Walkers should be well prepared if they're crossing exposed country. Dress is usually casual, and you're unlikely to come across many coat-and-tie-type regulations.

Condoms aren't always easily available in rural areas, though they're becoming more common in pharmacies (you have to be aged over 18 to buy) and pub vending machines in the cities.

A sleeping bag is useful in hostels and when visiting friends; get one that can be used as a quilt. A sleeping sheet with a pillow cover is necessary if you plan to stay in hostels, though you can buy or hire one if you don't bring your own.

Other possible items to bring include a small medical kit (see Medical Kit Check List in the Health section later in this chapter), Swiss Army knife or equivalent, a compass (to help orient yourself on walks), a torch (flashlight), an alarm clock or watch with an alarm function, an adapter plug for electrical appliances, a universal bath/sink plug, sunglasses and an elastic clothesline.

RESPONSIBLE TOURISM

The greater the popularity of a trail or site, the greater the pressure on its ecology. Ireland's system of walking trails, called ways, has been established with the cooperation and good will of various bodies, including private landowners, local authorities and voluntary workers. Walkers therefore need to use the ways sensitively by, for example, minimising disturbance to farm animals and farmland, and by taking home all rubbish, plastics in particular. For information on conservation issues in Ireland have a look at

ENFO's Web site at www.enfo.ie. The Mountaineering Council of Ireland has a very interesting Web site at www.moun taineering.ie that discusses environmental issues such as footpath erosion and litter.

TOURIST OFFICES

Bord Fáilte (Irish Tourist Board) and the Northern Ireland Tourist Board (NITB) operate separate tourist offices but produce some joint brochures and publications.

They also administer a computerised tourist-information and accommodation-reservation service known as Gulliver. It provides information on events, attractions, transport and accommodation and is accessible throughout the world. Call ☎ 1800 668668 in Ireland, ☎ 011 800 66866866 in the US and ☎ 00 800 66866866 in the rest of the world.

Bord Fáilte can be contacted at its Information Service (☎ 1850 230330 in Ireland, 020-7493 3201 in the UK, 212-418 0800 in the US, email info@irishtouristboard.ie), PO Box 273, Dublin 8. Its Web site can be found at www.ireland.travel.ie.

The head office of the NITB (☎ 028-90 246609, fax 90 240960, email info@ nitb.com) is at St Anne's Court, 59 North St, Belfast BT1 1NB. Its Web site is at www.ni-tourism.com.

Local Tourist Offices

Dublin has Bord Fáilte, Dublin Tourism and NITB offices. Belfast has NITB and Bord Fáilte offices. Elsewhere in Ireland and Northern Ireland there's a tourist office in almost every town big enough to have half a dozen pubs (it doesn't take many people in a town to justify half a dozen pubs in Ireland). See under Tourist Offices or Information in specific town sections for addresses.

No doubt as a result of pressures to be self-financing, local Bord Fáilte offices have become almost indistinguishable from souvenir shops. They only book Bord Fáilte-approved accommodation or recommend attractions and services registered with them and often know little about public transport. So it may not always be worth joining queues at busy times. Almost all pamphlets at Bord Fáilte tourist offices have a price tag and there's usually nowhere for local enterprises to advertise their services. Also, some offices open for only very limited periods. As a result, some local communities have set up their own tourist office separate from Bord Fáilte. Often, hostel owners (and some B&B owners) are more useful sources of local information for those on limited budgets.

In the bigger towns and more touristed areas opening hours are usually 9 am to 5 pm Monday to Friday, and 9 am to 1 pm on Saturday, but the hours are often extended in summer. In other areas offices open seasonally only (from April, May or June to August or September) or for much shorter hours from October to April. These offices will find you tourist-board-approved accommodation and book it – for IR£1 if it's local, IR£2 if it's elsewhere.

Tourist Offices Abroad
Offices of Bord Fáilte include:

Australia
    (☎ 02-9299 6177) 5th Floor,
    36 Carrington St, Sydney, NSW 2000 – also
    has information on Northern Ireland
Canada
    (☎ 416-929 2777) Suite 1150,
    160 Bloor St East, Toronto, Ont M4W 1B9
France
    (☎ 01 47 42 03 36) 33 rue de Miromesnil,
    75008 Paris
Germany
    (☎ 069-23 64 92) Untermainanlage 7,
    60329 Frankfurt-am-Main 1
Netherlands
    (☎ 020-622 3101) Leidsestraat 32,
    1017 PB Amsterdam
New Zealand
    (☎ 09-379 3708) Dingwall Building,
    87 Queen St, Auckland 1
Northern Ireland
    (☎ 028-90 327888) 53 Castle St,
    Belfast BT1 1GH
UK
    (☎ 020-7493 3201) Ireland House,
    150 New Bond St, London W1Y 0AQ
USA
    (☎ 212-418 0800) 345 Park Ave,
    New York, NY 10154

Tourist information for Northern Ireland is handled by the British Tourist Authority, but you will also find offices of the Northern Ireland Tourist Board in these locations:

Canada
    (☎ 416-925 6368)
    Suite 450, 111 Avenue Rd, Toronto,
    Ont M5R 3J8
France
    (☎ 01 39 21 93 80)
    3 rue de Pontoise, 78100 St Germain-en-Laye
Germany
    (☎ 069-23 45 04)
    Taunustrasse 52-60,
    60329 Frankfurt-am-Main
Ireland, Republic of
    (☎ 01-679 1977, 1850 230230 within Ireland)
    16 Nassau St, Dublin 2
New Zealand
    (☎ 09-379 3708)
    Dingwall Building, 87 Queen St, Auckland 1
UK
    (☎ 020-7839 8416)
    Britain Visitor Centre, 1 Regent St,
    London SW1Y 4PQ
    (☎ 0141-204 4454)
    7th Floor, 98 West George St,
    Glasgow G2 1PJ
USA
    (☎ 212-922 0101,
    1800 3260036 within the USA)
    Suite 701, 551 5th Ave, New York,
    NY 10176

VISAS & DOCUMENTS
Passport
UK nationals don't need a passport to visit the Republic, but will need some form of identification to prove that they are a UK national if they are stopped at passport control. It's also useful to have a passport or ID when changing travellers cheques or hiring a car. EU nationals can enter Ireland with either a passport or a national ID card.

Visitors from outside the EU will need a passport, which should remain valid for at least six months after their intended stay. If it's about to expire, renew it before you go. This may not be easy to do away from your home country. Applying for or renewing a passport can take from a few days to several months, so don't leave it till the last minute. Things will probably happen faster if you do everything in person, but check first on what you need to take with you. Once you start travelling, carry your passport at all times and guard it carefully.

Visas

For citizens of EU states and most western countries, including Australia, Canada, New Zealand and the USA, no visa is required to visit either the Republic or Northern Ireland. Visas are required from citizens of India, Pakistan and some African states. EU nationals are allowed to stay indefinitely, while other visitors can usually remain for three to six months. If you want to stay longer in the Republic contact the local garda station or the Aliens Registration Office (☎ 01-475 5555), Harcourt St, Dublin 2. To stay longer in Northern Ireland contact the Home Office (☎ 020-8686 0688), Immigration and Nationality Department, Lunar House, Wellesley Rd, Croydon CR9 2BY, England.

Onwards Tickets

Although you don't need an onwards or return ticket to enter Ireland, it could help if there's any doubt that you have sufficient funds to support yourself in Ireland.

Travel Insurance

This not only covers you for medical expenses and luggage theft or loss, but also for cancellations or delays in your travel arrangements under certain circumstances (you might fall seriously ill two days before departure, for example). Ticket loss is also (usually) covered by travel insurance. There's a wide variety of policies and your travel agency will have recommendations. Cover depends on your insurance and type of ticket, so ask both your insurer and your ticket-issuing agency to explain where you stand.

If you're an EU citizen an E111 form covers you for medical care (excluding medications, dental examinations and X-rays etc). In the UK these forms are available from post offices. Otherwise, ask your health authority or travel agency. Other countries, such as Australia, also have reciprocal agreements with Ireland and Britain. Check before you leave home and take along any necessary documentation.

If you do need health insurance, remember that some policies offer lower and higher medical-expense options, but the higher one is chiefly for countries such as the USA that have extremely high medical costs. Everyone should be covered for the worst possible case, such as an accident requiring an ambulance, hospital treatment and an emergency flight home. If you have to stretch out you'll need two seats and somebody has to pay for them! You may prefer a policy that pays doctors or hospitals directly rather than you having to pay on the spot and claim later.

Always check the fine print. Most policies exclude cover for pre-existing illnesses, including AIDS. Make sure the policy includes health care and medication in the countries you may visit to and from Ireland. Some policies exclude 'dangerous activities' such as scuba diving or motorcycling. If such activities are on your agenda, you don't want that policy. Also, a locally acquired motorcycle licence may not be valid under your policy.

Buy travel insurance as early as possible. If you buy it the week before you fly, you may find, for example, that you're not covered for delays to your flight caused by, say, industrial action.

Driving Licence & Permit

Unless you have an EU licence, which is treated like an Irish one, your driving licence is valid for 12 months from the date of entry to Ireland, but you should have held it for two years. If you don't hold an EU licence it's a good idea to obtain an International Driving Permit (IDP) from your home automobile association before you leave. Also ask for a Card of Introduction, which entitles you to services offered by sister organisations (maps and information, help with breakdowns, legal advice etc), usually free of charge. If you take your own vehicle you should always carry a Vehicle Registration Document as proof that it's yours.

Hostel Cards

If you're travelling on a budget, membership of Hostelling International (HI) will give you access to An Óige hostels in the South and YHANI in the North (see Hostels in the Accommodation section later in this chapter). You can become a member (IR£10) by joining your national Youth Hostel Association (YHA). For details look at HI's Web site at www.iyhf.org. Alternatively, once in Ireland you can join by obtaining a guest card from a hostel and paying IR£1 per night for a stamp, on top of the nightly charge. When you have six stamps on your card you are a full HI member. Membership entitles you to a range of discounts on car rental, tours, admission fees and activities in Ireland.

Student & Youth Cards

The most useful is the International Student Identity Card (ISIC), a plastic ID-style card with your photograph. With it you can get discounts on transport, commercial goods and services, and admission to museums and sights. If you're aged under 26 but not a student, you can apply for a Federation of International Youth Travel (FYTO) card or a European Youth Card (EYC), also called a Euro<26 Card, which offer similar discounts to an ISIC. These cards are issued by hostelling organisations, student unions and student travel agencies.

Seniors' Cards

Senior citizens usually need show only proof of age to benefit from the many discounts available to them. These include reductions at museums and galleries and free public transport. The minimum qualifying age is usually 60 to 65 for men, and 55 to 65 for women.

Heritage Discounts

Many parks, monuments and gardens in the South are operated by Dúchas. For IR£15 (children and students IR£6) you can get a Heritage Card permitting free access to these sites for one year. The child/student card in particular can pay for itself in a few visits. For more information contact the Heritage Service (☎ 01-661 3111), Dúchas, 51 St Stephen's Green, Dublin 2.

In Northern Ireland, membership of the National Trust entitles you to free entry to its properties, but there are fewer sites so it makes financial sense only if you're going to tour Britain too. Membership costs UK£28 for adults and UK£14 for those aged under 25 (families UK£54). For more information contact the Public Affairs Manager (☎ 028-97 510721), National Trust, Rowallane, Saintfield BT24 7LH.

You can also join Dúchas or the National Trust at most of their sites.

Photocopies

All important documents (passport data page and visa page, credit cards, travel insurance policy, air/bus/train tickets, driving licence etc) should be photocopied before you leave home. Leave one copy with someone at home and keep another with you, separate from the originals. If your documents are lost or stolen, replacing them will be much easier.

There is another option for storing details of your vital travel documents before you leave – Lonely Planet's on-line Travel Vault. Storing details of your important documents in the vault is safer than carrying photocopies. It's the best option if you're travelling in a country with easy Internet access. Your password-protected Travel Vault is accessible on-line at any time. You can create your own Travel Vault for free at www.ekno.lonelyplanet.com.

EMBASSIES & CONSULATES
Irish & UK Embassies & Consulates Abroad

Irish diplomatic offices overseas include:

Australia
    Embassy:
    (☎ 02-6273 3022, fax 6273 3741)
    20 Arkana St, Yarralumla, Canberra,
    ACT 2600
Canada
    Embassy:
    (☎ 613-233 6281, fax 233 5835)
    130 Albert St, Ottawa,
    Ont K1P 5G4

France
  Embassy:
  (☎ 01 44 17 67 00, fax 01 44 17 67 60)
  4 rue de Paris, 75116 Paris
Germany
  Embassy:
  (☎ 0228-95 92 90, fax 37 35 00)
  Godesberger Allee 119, D-53175 Bonn
Netherlands
  Embassy:
  (☎ 070-363 0993, fax 361 7604)
  Dr Kuyperstraat 9, 2514 BA The Hague
New Zealand
  Embassy:
  (☎ 09-302 2867)
  2nd Floor, Dingwall Building,
  Queen St, Auckland
UK
  Embassy:
  (☎ 020-7235 2171, fax 7245 6961)
  17 Grosvenor Place, London SW1X 7HR
  Consulate:
  (☎ 0131-220 8226)
  City Base, 1 St Colme St,
  Edinburgh EH3 6AA
  Consulate:
  (☎ 029-2023 0709)
  Jury's Hotel, Mary Ann St, Cardiff CF1 2EQ
USA
  Embassy:
  (☎ 202-462 3939, fax 232 5993)
  2234 Massachusetts Ave, NW, Washington,
  DC 20008 – in addition there are consulates
  in Boston, Chicago, New York and San
  Francisco

UK (for Northern Ireland) diplomatic offices abroad include:

Australia
  High Commission:
  (☎ 02-6270 6666, fax 6270 6606)
  Commonwealth Ave, Yarralumla, Canberra,
  ACT 2600
Canada
  High Commission:
  (☎ 613-237 1530, fax 237 7980)
  80 Elgin St, Ottawa, Ont K1P 5K7
France
  Embassy:
  (☎ 01 44 51 31 00, fax 01 47 05 77 02)
  35 rue du Faubourg St Honoré,
  75383 Paris
Germany
  Embassy:
  (☎ 0228-9 16 70, fax 9 16 72 00)
  Friedrich-Ebert-Allee 77, D-53113 Bonn

Netherlands
  Embassy:
  (☎ 070-427 0427, fax 427 0345)
  Lange Voorhout 10, 2514 ED The Hague
New Zealand
  High Commission:
  (☎ 04-472 6049, fax 471 1974)
  44 Hill St, Wellington 1
USA
  Embassy:
  (☎ 202-588 6500, fax 588 7850)
  3100 Massachusetts Ave, NW, Washington,
  DC 20008

Foreign Embassies & Consulates in Ireland

It's important to realise what your own embassy – the embassy of the country of which you are a citizen – can and can't do to help you if you get into trouble.

Generally speaking, it won't be much help if the trouble you're in is remotely your own fault. Remember that you are bound by the laws of the country you are in. Your embassy will not be sympathetic if you end up in jail after committing a crime locally, even if such actions are legal in your own country.

In genuine emergencies you might get some assistance, but only if other channels have been exhausted. For example, if you need to get home urgently, a free ticket is exceedingly unlikely – the embassy would expect you to have insurance. If you have all your money and documents stolen, it might assist with getting a new passport, but a loan for onwards travel is out of the question.

Countries with diplomatic offices in Dublin include:

Australia
  Embassy:
  (☎ 01-676 1517, fax 668 5266)
  2nd Floor, Fitzwilton House,
  Wilton Terrace, Dublin 2
Canada
  Embassy:
  (☎ 01-478 1988)
  4th Floor, 65-68 St Stephen's Green, Dublin 2
France
  Embassy:
  (☎ 01-260 1666)
  36 Ailesbury Rd, Dublin 4

Germany
Embassy:
(☎ 01-269 3011, 269 3123)
31 Trimleston Ave, Booterstown, Dublin 4
Netherlands
Embassy:
(☎ 01-269 3444)
160 Merrion Rd, Dublin 4
New Zealand
Embassy:
(☎ 01-676 2464, fax 676 2489)
46 Upper Mount St, Dublin 2
UK
Embassy:
(☎ 01-205 3742, fax 205 3895,
email bembassy@internet-ireland.ie)
29 Merrion Rd, Dublin 4
USA
Embassy:
(☎ 01-668 7122, fax 668 9946,
email aedublin@indigo.ie)
42 Elgin Rd, Dublin 4

In Northern Ireland the following countries have consular representation:

Netherlands
Consulate:
(☎ 028-28 261300) Old Glenarm Rd, Larne, County Antrim BT42 2ST
USA
Consulate:
(☎ 028-90 328239) Queen's House, 14 Queen St, Belfast BT1 6EQ

CUSTOMS

As of 1 July 1999, duty-free sales within the EU were abolished.

Under the rules of the single market, goods bought in and exported within the EU incur no additional taxes, as long as duty or taxes have been paid somewhere in the EU – provided the goods are for personal consumption.

Over certain limits you may have to show that they are for personal use. There's no customs inspection apart from those concerned with drugs and national security.

Travellers coming from outside the EU are allowed to import, duty free, 200 cigarettes, 1L of spirits, 2L of wine, 60mL of perfume, 250mL of toilet water, and other dutiable goods to the value of IR£73.

MONEY

Currency

In Ireland the Irish pound or punt (IR£) is used, and like the British pound sterling it's divided into 100 pence (p). Irish banknotes come in denominations of IR£100, IR£50, IR£20, IR£10 and IR£5. Coins are IR£1, IR50p, IR20p, IR10p, IR5p, IR2p and IR1p. The EU's single currency, the euro, is legal tender in Ireland (see the boxed text 'Introducing the Euro' on the following page).

The British pound sterling (UK£) is used in Northern Ireland and comes in the same banknote and coin denominations as the Irish punt. Don't confuse Northern Irish pounds (issued by the First Trust Bank, Ulster Bank, Northern Bank and Bank of England) with Republic of Ireland pounds (issued by the Central Bank of Ireland). 'Sterling' or 'Belfast' are giveaway words on the Northern Irish notes. The Northern Irish pound sterling is worth the same as the British variety. Northern Irish notes are not readily accepted in Britain, but British banks will swap them for normal sterling notes. Unlike the Republic, Northern Ireland, as part of the UK, has not adopted the euro.

The Republic's currency is not legal tender in the North and vice versa, though some businesses may accept the other country's notes at the market rate.

In this guide, in the chapters on the Republic the £ symbol denotes the Irish punt, and in the Northern Ireland chapters it denotes the British pound sterling.

Exchange Rates

The Irish punt is worth about 81 UK pence. As this book went to press, exchange rates were:

country	unit		IR£/UK£
Australia	A$	=	£0.48/0.39
Canada	C$1	=	£0.51/0.41
euro	€1	=	£0.79/0.64
France	10FF	=	£1.20/0.90
Germany	DM1	=	£0.40/0.33
Netherlands	NLG1	=	£0.36/0.29
New Zealand	NZ$1	=	£0.38/0.31
USA	US$1	=	£0.75/0.61

Exchanging Money

The best exchange rates are obtained at banks. In the Republic banks normally open 10 am to 4 pm on weekdays, and most stay open till 5 pm on Thursday or Friday (on Thursday in Dublin). In Northern Ireland banks open 9.30 am to 4.30 pm on weekdays, and most stay open till 5 pm on Thursday. The Halifax Bank in Northern Ireland also opens 1 am to noon on Saturday. In remote areas North and South some banks close for lunch from 12.30 to 1.30 pm and some may open only two or three days (or two or three hours) a week, so it's best to change money in larger towns.

Bureaux de change and other exchange facilities usually open for more hours than banks, but the rate and/or commission will be worse. Building societies often handle currency exchange and open more hours than banks. Many post offices in both the Republic and Northern Ireland have a currency-exchange facility and have the advantage of opening on Saturday morning.

If you've not obtained some currency in advance there are unofficial moneychangers near the border between the North and South, often at petrol stations.

Cash & Travellers Cheques Nothing beats cash for convenience – or risk. It's still a good idea, though, to arrive with some local currency in cash, if only to tide you over till you get to an exchange facility.

Most major currencies of travellers cheques are readily accepted in Ireland, but carrying them in pounds sterling has the advantage that in Northern Ireland or Britain you can change them without exchange loss or commission.

American Express (Amex) and Thomas Cook travellers cheques are widely recognised and offices don't charge commission for cashing their own cheques. Eurocheques can also be cashed in Ireland. Keeping a record of the cheque numbers and the cheques you have cashed is vital in case of loss. Keep this list separate from the cheques themselves. Also keep a note of the number to ring in case of loss or theft (you should be given this when you buy the cheques). Travellers cheques are rarely accepted outside banks or used for everyday transactions (as they are in the USA).

Take most cheques in large denominations. It's only towards the end of a stay that

Introducing the Euro

Since 1 January 1999 the Irish punt and the euro – Europe's new currency for 11 European Union (EU) countries – have both been legal tender in the Republic of Ireland. Note that Northern Ireland, as part of the UK, has not adopted the euro. Euro coins and banknotes have not been issued yet but you can already get billed in euros and opt to pay in euros by credit card. Essentially, if there's no hard cash involved, you can deal in euros. Travellers should check bills carefully to make sure that any conversion has been calculated correctly.

The idea behind the current paperless currency is to give euro-fearing punters the chance to limber up arithmetically before euro coins and banknotes are issued on 1 January 2002. The same euro coins (one to 50 cents, €1 and €2) and banknotes (€5 to €500) will then be used in Euroland's 11 countries: Austria, Belgium, Finland, France, Germany, Italy, Luxembourg, the Netherlands, Portugal, the Republic of Ireland and Spain. The Irish punt will remain legal currency alongside the euro until 1 July 2002, when the punt will be hurled on the scrapheap of history.

Until then €1 is 0.788IEP, 13.77ATS, 40.3BEF, 5.95FIM, 6.56FF, 1.96DEM, 1936ITL, 37.5LUF, 2.2NLG, 166.4ESP and 200PTE. The Lonely Planet Web site at www.lonely planet.com has a link to a currency converter and up-to-date news on the integration process. Or have a look at europa.eu.int/euro/html/entry.html.

euro currency converter IR£1 = €1.27

you may want to change a small cheque to make sure you don't get left with too much local currency.

ATMs & Credit/Charge Cards Plastic cards make the perfect travelling companions – they're ideal for major purchases and let you withdraw cash (using a personal identification number or PIN) from selected banks and automatic teller machines (ATMs). ATMs are usually linked to international money systems such as Cirrus, Maestro or Plus, so you can get instant cash from your account back home. Bear in mind, though, that there's a limit on how much you can withdraw and, unless your bank has a direct link with an Irish bank, each transaction incurs an automatic currency conversion fee.

ATMs aren't infallible and they've been known to accidentally swallow cards, which can be a real headache. If you can, withdraw money from a human teller, who'll simply run your card through a magnetic slide to access your account.

Credit cards can be linked to an ATM network: ask your bank for a PIN and which ATMs in Ireland accept your credit card.

Charge cards such as Amex and Diners Club don't have credit limits but may not be accepted in small establishments or off the beaten track. Credit cards such as Visa, MasterCard or Access are more widely accepted, though many B&Bs and some smaller or remote petrol stations take cash only.

Remember to keep a note of the telephone number to ring (your credit card company will supply you with it) if your card is lost or stolen.

International Transfers You, or someone who you've authorised to access your account, can instruct your bank back home to send you a draft. A bank draft is a cheque payable to you, but you won't be able to cash it in Ireland – you will have to pay it into a bank account and then withdraw it only after it has cleared, which may take up to three weeks. Unless you're staying in Ireland for a good while, it won't be practical to open a bank account there.

Two other methods are mail and telegraphic transfers. These are sent by your bank back home to an Irish bank nominated by you in a town or city of your choice. You will be asked for identification, such as a passport, before the money will be paid to you, probably in local currency. Mail transfers take up to two weeks to reach an Irish bank; telegraphic transfers take up to eight days but are more expensive for the sender.

You can also transfer money by Amex, Thomas Cook or Western Union.

Security
Carry your money (and only the money you need for that day) somewhere inside your clothing (in a money belt, a bra or your socks) rather than in a handbag or an outside pocket. You might want to stitch an inside pocket into your skirt or trousers to keep an emergency stash; keep something like IR£50 separate from the rest of your cash in case of emergency. Put your money in several places. Most hotels and hostels provide safekeeping, so you can leave money and other valuables with them. Don't wear, or hide beneath your clothes, any valuable jewellery.

Costs
Ireland is expensive, but costs are lower out of the chief tourist areas.

A bed in a hostel dormitory costs IR£7 to IR£14 a night. A cheap B&B will cost about IR£15 to IR£25 per person, while a more luxurious B&B or guesthouse with attached bathroom would be anything from IR£25 to IR£50 per person. Many places to stay have different high- and low-season prices. In this book, unless it says otherwise, the prices quoted are for the high season. Some places may have not just a high-season but a peak-high-season price. Watch out for the awful practice of charging an extra IR50p or IR£1 for a bath. It's more economical, in terms of accommodation, to travel with another person, since many places charge a single-occupancy supplement. This means that solo travellers often pay more than half the double or twin rate.

Commemoration of Belfast's women

Poet Pádraic O'Conaire, Galway city

Poet WB Yeats contemplates Sligo town.

'Hags with the bags' swap Dublin gossip.

The 'floozy in the Jacuzzi' relaxes in Dublin.

You may find yourself spending a few evenings contemplating the merits of 'the devil's buttermilk' – although you won't feel so philosophical about it the following morning.

A modest meal at lunchtime costs IR£4 to IR£5, while dinner in a reasonable restaurant with a glass of wine or a beer costs from IR£10 to IR£15. A pint of Guinness usually costs about IR£2, and buying a lot of drinks in the pub is a good way of spending a remarkable amount of money in a remarkably short space of time.

Car hire is extremely expensive (see Rental in the Car & Motorcycle section of the Getting Around chapter for details). Petrol prices vary but generally unleaded petrol costs about IR60p a litre, leaded about IR5p extra. In Northern Ireland petrol costs a few pence more than in the South.

Admission prices are often lower for children, seniors and students than for adults. In this book, unless otherwise stated, admission prices to museums and so on are given for adults/children.

If you stay at a hostel, eat a light pub lunch and cook your own meal in the evening, you could get by on IR£20 a day. In practice you usually spend more, and when you move around the country you'll need to allow for the cost of transport.

Tipping

Fancy hotels and restaurants usually add a 10 or 15% service charge and no additional tip is required. Simpler places usually don't add a service charge; if you decide to tip, just round up the bill or add at most 10%. For taxi drivers a tip of 10% is fine, while porters should get IR50p per bag. Tipping in bars isn't expected, but the distinction between pubs and restaurants is blurred by bars becoming more like restaurants at meal times.

Taxes & Refunds

Value-added tax (VAT) is a sales tax on most goods and services in Ireland, excluding books and children's clothing or footwear. Residents of the EU are not entitled to VAT refund. On large purchases that they subsequently export outside the EU, non-EU visitors can claim back the VAT (minus an administration fee). You must be exporting your purchases within three months of the last day of the month in which they were bought.

If you buy something from a store displaying the sign 'Tax Free Shopping' or 'Cashback' you'll be given a voucher which can be cashed at Dublin or Shannon Airports. If the value of the refund is IR£200 or more you'll first need to go to customs in the arrivals hall to have the voucher stamped, before cashing it at the refund desk. If you're not leaving Ireland from those airports, the voucher can be stamped at customs and mailed back for a refund.

In Northern Ireland, shops participating in the refund scheme will give you a form/invoice on request. This must be presented to customs with the goods and receipts when you leave. After customs have certified the form, it will be returned to the shop for a refund.

POST & COMMUNICATIONS
Post

Post offices in the South (run by An Post) open 8.30 am (9.30 am on Wednesday) to 5.30 pm on weekdays, and 9 am to noon on Saturday; smaller offices close for lunch. Postcards cost IR28p to send to EU countries, IR38p outside Europe. Airmail letters cost IR32p to post to EU countries, IR44p to non-EU Europe, IR52p outside Europe. All mail to Britain goes by air so there is no need to use airmail envelopes or stickers.

In the North, Royal Mail post offices open 9 am to 5.30 pm on weekdays, and 9 am to 1 pm on Saturday. Postal rates are as in Britain: UK26/20p for letters by 1st-class/2nd-class mail within the UK, UK30p to European countries, and UK43p for letters and postcards to the Americas and Australasia.

Mail to both the North and the Republic can be addressed to poste restante at post offices but is officially held for only two weeks. Writing 'hold for collection' on the envelope may have some effect.

Over 95% of letters within the country are delivered the next working day. To Britain and the rest of Europe it takes three to five days, to Australasia a week to 10 days, and to North America about 10 days.

Telephone

The international code for the Republic is (00) 353 (knocking off the initial 0 of the area code), and for Northern Ireland it's (00) 44-28. To call Northern Ireland from Britain dial 028 followed by the number.

Éircom, the Republic's main telecommunications company, was privatised in 1999, while in the North most public phones are owned by British Telecom (BT). Other companies compete for their business.

Emergency Numbers The emergency phone number in Northern Ireland is ☎ 999, while in the Republic it's ☎ 999 or ☎ 112. After dialling, specify whether you want the police (garda), fire service, an ambulance or coastal rescue.

Calls from the Republic To call a UK number (except for Northern Ireland) from the South dial 00-44 plus the area code (minus the 0) plus the number. Thus an 020 number in London would start 00-44-20. To call elsewhere overseas dial 00 then the international code for that country (1 for the USA or Canada, 61 for Australia, 64 for New Zealand) then the area code (dropping any leading 0) and then the number.

To call Northern Ireland from the South dial 028 and then the Northern Irish number.

For directory assistance within the Republic and Northern Ireland dial ☎ 1190, for mainland Britain dial ☎ 1197, for elsewhere dial ☎ 1198. For operator-assisted calls dial ☎ 10; for international reverse-charge (collect) calls dial ☎ 114.

Calls from Northern Ireland From Northern Ireland dial 00 for international access followed by the country code. A phone call from Northern Ireland to the South is treated as an international call.

To call the operator dial ☎ 100; for directory assistance within the UK dial ☎ 192. Dial ☎ 155 for the British Telecom (BT) international operator, or ☎ 153 for international directory assistance.

Call Costs for Private Phones In the South the cost of a three-minute local call

from a private phone is IR11.5p. Rates are a little cheaper in the North. Off-peak calls (6 pm to 8 am on weekdays and 24 hours at the weekend) are cheaper in both the South and North. A phone call from a hotel room will cost at least double the standard rate.

The cost of a direct-dial international call in Ireland varies according to the time of day. Reduced rates are available from 6 pm to 8 am. To Australia and New Zealand, reduced rates apply from midnight to 8 am and 2 to 8 pm. Peak charges for one minute from the South (calls from the North are a little cheaper) are:

Australia	IR88p
Canada	IR36p
France	IR39p
German	IR39p
New Zealand	IR88p
UK	IR24p
USA	IR36p

Direct Home Calls Rather than placing reverse-charge (collect) calls through the operator in Ireland you can dial direct to your home-country operator and then reverse charges or charge the call to a local phone credit card. To use the Direct Home service, dial the following codes and then the area code and number you want. Your home-country operator will then come on the line before the call goes through:

Australia	1800 5500 61 + number
France	1800 5500 33 + number
New Zealand	1800 5500 64 + number
UK – BT	1800 5500 44 + number
UK – Mercury	1800 5500 04 + number
USA – AT&T	1800 5500 00 + number
USA – MCI	1800 5510 01 + number
USA – Sprint	1800 5520 01 + number

International Phonecards There's a wide range of international phonecards. Lonely Planet's eKno Communication Card is aimed specifically at independent travellers and provides budget international calls, a range of messaging services, free email and travel information – but for local calls, you're usually better off with a local

New Telephone Numbers

From 1 June 1999, the area code for the whole of Northern Ireland became 028. On top of this, local five- and six-digit numbers became eight-digit local numbers. For example, a five-digit Ballygawley number ☎ 016625-xxxxx became 028-85 5xxxxx, and a six-digit Belfast number ☎ 01232 xxxxxx became 028-90 xxxxxx. You must dial 90 even within Belfast.

Some numbers in the Republic have also changed. As of February 2000 those numbers in the 021 area in Cork had the prefix 4 added to numbers beginning with 2, 3, 5, 6, 7, 8 or 9.

card. You can join on-line at www.ekno .lonelyplanet.com. To join by phone from the South or Northern Ireland, dial the relevant registration number. Once you have joined, to use eKno, dial the access number:

	To join	To access
In the South	1800 554576	1800 554577
In the North	0800 3761704	0800 3761705

Check the eKno Web site for joining and access numbers from other countries and updates on super budget local access numbers and new features.

Payphones Local calls from payphones cost IR30p in the South and UK20p in the North per three-minute unit; long-distance calls cost IR£1.30 for the first three minutes. International calls can be dialled direct from payphones. Direct-dialled international calls cost more from payphones than from private phones. From the Republic, a one-minute peak-rate call to the US costs IR50p, while it costs IR24p to Britain.

Phonecards save fishing for coins and give you a small discount. Éircom's Callcards are available in 10 (IR£2), 20 (IR£3.50), 50 (IR£8) and 100 (IR£16) unit versions in the Republic. Each unit gives you one local phone call. BT phonecards cost UK£2 to UK£20. There are also many other companies selling their own phonecards. Some can be used to phone within Ireland only, so if you want to make an international call using a phonecard check when you're buying it. Bear in mind that you can't make operator-assisted international calls from a card-operated phone.

Fax & Telegram
You can send faxes from post offices, most hotels or other specialist offices. It can be quite expensive, however: about IR£1 per page locally, IR£2 to IR£3 to Europe and approximately IR£4 per page to Australia or the USA. Phone the operator on ☎ 196 in the South to send international telegrams (known as telemessages); in the North call BT on ☎ 0800 190190.

Email & Internet Access
If you plan to carry your notebook or palmtop computer, remember that the power supply voltage (220V) may be different from that at home. The best investment is a universal AC adapter, which will enable you to plug in anywhere without frying the computer's innards. You also need a plug adapter for each country you visit – often it's easiest to buy these before you leave home.

Also, your PC-card modem may or may not work once you leave your home country – and you won't know for sure until you try. The safest option is to buy a reputable 'global' modem before you leave, or buy a local PC-card modem if you're spending an extended time in Ireland. Keep in mind that the telephone socket may be different from home, so ensure that you have at least a US RJ-11 telephone adapter that works with your modem. You can usually find an adapter that will convert from RJ-11 to the local variety. For more information on travelling with a portable computer, see www.teleadapt.com or www.warrior.com.

Major Internet service providers (ISPs) such as AOL (www.aol.com), CompuServe (www.compuserve.com) and IBM Net (www .ibm.net) have dial-in nodes throughout

Europe; it's best to download a list of the dial-in numbers before you leave home. If you access your Internet email account at home through a smaller ISP or your office or school network, it's best either to open an account with a global ISP or to rely on cybercafés and other public access points (post offices, libraries, hostels and universities may have public access) to collect your mail.

To access your Internet mail account from a cybercafé you'll need: your incoming (POP or IMAP) mail server name, your account name and your password. Your ISP or network supervisor will give you these. Another way to collect mail through cybercafés is to open a free Web-based email account such as HotMail (www.hotmail.com) or Yahoo! Mail (mail .yahoo.com).

You'll find cybercafés and/or cyberpubs in most major towns in Ireland. Addresses are listed in specific town sections. The Irish Internet Café Association has a Web site at www.iica.net. You can log on in a cybercafé for about IR£5 an hour.

INTERNET RESOURCES

The World Wide Web is a rich resource for travellers. You can research your trip, hunt down bargain air fares, book hotels, check on weather conditions or chat with locals and other travellers about the best places to visit (or avoid!).

There's no better place to start your Web explorations than the Lonely Planet Web site (www.lonelyplanet.com). Here you'll find succinct summaries on travelling to most places on earth (including Ireland), postcards from other travellers and the Thorn Tree bulletin board, where you can ask questions before you go or dispense advice when you get back. You can also find travel news and updates to many of our most popular guidebooks, and the sub-WWWay section links you to the most useful travel resources elsewhere on the Web.

Bord Fáilte and the NITB have their own Web sites (see Tourist Offices earlier in this chapter); some others are:

Aer Lingus
www.aerlingus.ie
(details of services, flight schedules, special offers and links to related sites)
Blarney Woollen Mills
www.blarney.ie
(lists accommodation options, places to eat and activities throughout North and South)
Dublin Tourism
www.visitdublin.com
(tourist information about Dublin)
Entertainment
www.entertainmentireland.ie
(current information on entertainment around Ireland, including special events and exhibitions)
Geographia
www.interknowledge.com
(government guide to Northern Ireland, with information on accommodation, food, activities etc)
Go Ireland
www.touchtel.ie
(everything from car hire to genealogy, with useful links)
Indigo
www.indigo.ie
(the biggest Irish server, with information on everything from where to eat to what to do with young children)
Ireland Online
www.iol.ie
(general information and useful links)
Irish Food
www.irishfood.com
(restaurants, books and recipes)
Ostlan
www.ostlan.ie
(list of over 270 restaurants in the Dublin area and a comprehensive list of Dublin pubs)
World Wide Web Virtual Library: Ireland
www.itw.ie/wwwlib.html
(information on government, arts, media, education, business, recreation, travel etc)

BOOKS

A glance in almost any bookshop in Ireland will reveal huge Irish-interest sections – fiction, history, current events – and numerous local and regional guidebooks. Many cities have more than one good bookshop, Waterstone's and Eason's being familiar names, and many towns will have a small but well-stocked bookshop.

Most books are published in different editions by different publishers in different countries. As a result, a book might be a hard-cover rarity in one country while it's readily available in paperback in another. Fortunately, bookshops and libraries search by title or author, so they will be able to tell you if they stock the books recommended here.

See Literature in the Arts section of the Facts about Ireland chapter for information on works by Irish writers.

Lonely Planet

Lonely Planet also publishes *Dublin* and *Walking in Ireland*, which provide detailed information for people visiting the capital or walking on Ireland's waymarked trails.

If you're going to be spending time in Britain as well, you may want to look at Lonely Planet's *Britain*, *Walking in Britain*, *Scotland*, *London* or *Edinburgh*. If your travels will be wider, try *Europe on a Shoestring* or *Western Europe*. *Travel with Children* is a guide specifically for those with young children.

Lonely Planet's *World Food Ireland* is a full-colour exploration of the history and culture of Irish food and drink – it's a trustworthy companion for your culinary journey.

Guidebooks

Ireland, and Dublin in particular, has produced so many writers that you could easily plan a literary holiday or just a Dublin literary holiday. The *Oxford Literary Guide to Great Britain and Ireland* details the writers who have immortalised various towns and villages. *A Literary Guide to Dublin* by Vivien Igoe includes detailed route maps, a guide to cemeteries and an eight-page section on literary and historical pubs.

James Joyce groupies can make their own Bloomsday tour of Dublin with a number of books that follow the wanderings of *Ulysses*'s characters in minute detail. *Joyce's Dublin: A Walking Guide to Ulysses* by Jack McCarthy traces the events chapter by chapter with clear maps. *The Ulysses Guide: Tours through Joyce's Dublin* by Robert Nicholson has easy-to-follow maps.

It concentrates on certain areas and follows the events of the various related chapters.

The *Irish Pub Guide* lists and describes a number of pubs across Ireland that are of particular interest. *The Hidden Gardens of Ireland* by Marianne Heron is an informative guide. For all sorts of minutiae about Dublin buildings and streets check the *Encyclopaedia of Dublin* by Douglas Bennett.

See the Activities chapter for details of cycling and walking guidebooks and books on tracing your ancestors. For specialist books on accommodation and food see those sections later in this chapter. For guides to the Aran Islands and Connemara see those sections in the Galway chapter.

Travel

To understand the Anglo-Irish, read *Woodbrook* (1994) by David Thomson, who, when a young man, went to the north-west as tutor to an Anglo-Irish family.

For cycling visitors, Eric Newby's *Round Ireland in Low Gear* (1988) is a Newby classic of travel masochism complete with lousy weather, steep hills, high winds and predatory trucks. *Sealegs: Hitchhiking the Coast of Ireland Alone* (1992) by Rosita Boland tells the tale of an Irish woman's solo exploration of Ireland by thumb. If you think your backpack is heavy, try taking a fridge with you. English comedian Tony Hawks recounts his lunatic journey in *Round Ireland with a Fridge* (1998): he hitched round the country in one month for a bet.

The Crack: A Belfast Year (1987) by Sally Belfrage is a reporter's account of a series of visits to Belfast in the 1980s.

In the mid-1970s Irish travel writer Dervla Murphy jumped on her faithful bicycle Roz, the same one she had taken to India in the 1960s, and rode off to explore Northern Ireland. The result was *A Place Apart* (1978). It's a highly readable book and makes an accessible introduction to things such as Orangeism, Paisleyism and the problems in South Armagh.

US travel writer Paul Theroux included Northern Ireland on his UK itinerary for *Kingdom by the Sea* (1983). Travelling round most of Britain made the famously sour Theroux even more dyspeptic than usual, but he warmed towards the Ulster people. PJ O'Rourke gave Belfast a chapter in his book *Holidays in Hell* (1988) but, like many other visitors, he found Belfast altogether too tame for its reputation. Where are the appalling slums?

History & Politics

For a thorough, detailed account of Irish history there's *The Oxford Companion to Irish History* (1998) edited by SJ Connolly. On the other hand, *Ireland: A Concise History* (1985) by Máire & Conor Cruise O'Brien is a readable and comprehensively illustrated short introduction. *Ireland: A History* (1995) by Robert Kee covers similar ground in a similar format in a book developed from a BBC/RTE TV series. Breandán O'hEithir's *A Pocket History of Ireland* (1989) is a concise account of Irish history.

Focusing on the 19th and 20th centuries, the three volumes of *The Green Flag* (1988) by Robert Kee offer a good introduction, although the emphasis is more on narrative than analysis. A collection of essays make up *The Course of Irish History* (1994) edited by TW Moody & FX Martin.

The classic study of the 1845 to 1851 Famine is *The Great Hunger* (1991) by Cecil Woodham Smith. A more recent analysis is Christine Kinealy's *This Great Calamity* (1994). Liam O'Flaherty's novel *Famine* (1984) was based on the catastrophe, as was *The Hanging Gale* (1995), from a BBC/RTE TV series.

Two useful studies of events surrounding the 1916 Easter Rising are *The Easter Rebellion* (1995) by Max Caulfield, and *Rebels: The Irish Rising of 1916* by Peter de Rosa.

There is a range of books on Michael Collins, including *Michael Collins: The Man Who Won the War* (1990) by T Ryle Dwyer, *The Path to Freedom: Michael Collins* (1995) by Tim Pat Coogan, and *The Troubles* (1989) by Ulick O'Connor about Michael Collins and the Volunteers' struggle for independence.

The Irish Civil War (1998) by Tim Pat Coogan and George Morrison is an illustrated account of the descent into the gruesome civil conflict between former comrades following the signing of the Anglo-Irish Treaty.

The Long War (1999) by Brendan O'Brien traces the evolution of Sinn Féin and the IRA up to the period before the first (1994) IRA ceasefire.

Ireland: Anatomy of a Changing State (1995) by Gemma Hussey is a useful analysis of various social and political issues that bedevilled the country in the mid-1990s. In the same vein are John Ardagh's well-regarded *Ireland and the Irish: Portrait of a Changing Society* (1997) and the excellent *The Lie of the Land: Irish Identities* (1998) by journalist Fintan O'Toole.

Some commentators have talked of a post-Catholic Ireland, but given the crowds that still attend mass it's probably too early to read the last rites over Catholicism. However, journalist Mary Kenny's *Farewell to Catholic Ireland* (1997) traces how attitudes changed during the 20th century. It highlights the shock felt by many ordinary people as one clergy scandal followed another in the 1990s.

If you're heading for the Skelligs, try reading Geoffrey Moorhouse's two-volume *Sun Dancing* (1997), which attempts an imaginative re-creation of medieval monastic life over the centuries, then provides the back-up evidence in a sequence of short essays.

If you need a stout read, *Dark and Light* (1998) by Derek Wilson is a meticulous history of the Guinness-family dynasty, beginning in the 17th century.

The North The problem with books about Northern Ireland's recent confused history is that they're in constant need of updating and it's difficult to find a truly impartial account of what has been happening.

A serious and far-reaching attempt to get to grips with Ulster's story is *A History of Ulster* (1992) by Jonathan Bardon. It's a thorough but readable account stretching from prehistoric Ulster up to the early 1990s. Brian Barton's *A Pocket History of Ulster* (1999) is a concise introduction to the history of the North.

German academic Sabine Wichert, a Belfast resident since the early 1970s, managed to bring an outsider's inside view to the question in *Northern Ireland Since 1945* (1991). J Bowyer-Bell's *The Troubles: A Generation of Violence* (1993) is more recent, as is Tim Pat Coogan's readable *The Troubles: Ireland's Ordeal 1969–1995 and the Search for Peace* (1996). Gerry Adams, the president of Sinn Féin, gave his version of the Troubles in *The Politics of Irish Freedom* (1986) and more recently in *Free Ireland: Towards a Lasting Peace* (1995).

The Dispossessed (1992) investigates the background and reality of poverty in the UK through the 1980s. Writer Robert Wilson and photographer Donovan Wylie are both Belfast-born and the book concentrates on London, Glasgow and Belfast.

Paisley (1986) by Ed Moloney & Andy Pollack is a compelling account by two Irish journalists of the rise to power of the charismatic leader of the Democratic Unionist Party (not the Unionist Party) and the Free Presbyterian Church of Ulster (not the Presbyterian Church). If nothing else, read the introduction with its astonishing Paisley speech.

Despatches from Belfast (1989) by David McKittrick, the Irish correspondent for the UK newspaper the *Independent*, covers 1985 to 1989 with well-informed articles from a liberal point of view.

Two books that get inside the minds of paramilitaries on both sides and try to explain what motivates them are *25 Years of Terror* (1995) by Martin Dillon, and *We Wrecked the Place* (1996) by Jonathan Stevenson. Martin Dillon also wrote *The Shankill Butchers* (1990), a harrowing study of a loyalist gang, led by the psychopathic Lenny Murphy, which terrorised the Catholic community.

Eyewitness Bloody Sunday (1997) edited by Don Mullan contains harrowing accounts by ordinary people caught up in the violent events of 30 January 1972 in Derry/Londonderry.

Based on the BBC TV series, *Loyalists* (1999) by Peter Taylor draws back the veil on the complex story of loyalism, from the 17th century to the 1998 Good Friday Agreement and its aftermath.

General

The *Irish Almanac and Yearbook of Facts* is a good reference, with lots of information on many different aspects of Irish life, on both sides of the border. *May the Lord in His Mercy Be Kind to Belfast* (1994) by Tony Parker is a collection of interviews with Belfast people expressing their point of view about life in the troubled city.

FILMS

If you'd like to get in the mood for your holiday by watching films that are set in Ireland or use Ireland as a backdrop, choose some of the following. For information on films by Irish directors and producers, which generally also have Irish settings, themes and casts, see Cinema in the Arts section of the Facts about Ireland chapter.

Hollywood came to Ireland in 1952 when John Ford filmed John Wayne as *The Quiet Man*, wooing Maureen O'Hara in Cong, County Sligo. You can take Quiet Man tours in Cong today. The 1970 David Lean epic, *Ryan's Daughter*, with Sarah Miles, Robert Mitchum, Trevor Howard and John Mills, was filmed on the Dingle Peninsula in Kerry. The place and the film have been inextricably linked ever since: the Dingle Peninsula has simply become 'Ryan's Daughter country'.

The Tom Cruise and Nicole Kidman vehicle *Far and Away* (1992) provided some picturesque views of the western coast, and Dublin's Temple Bar stood in for late-19th-century Boston! *The Secret of Roan Inish* (1994) is a mystical tale set on the western coast of Ireland. Though filmed on the Isle of Man, *Waking Ned* (1998) is a whimsically humorous, but morally questionable, tale of Irish villagers claiming the lottery money of the deceased winner. *Hear My*

Song (1991), about the Irish tenor Joseph Locke, was a surprise success.

Many films have been set in Dublin. Joseph Strick attempted the seemingly impossible task of putting *Ulysses* on screen in 1967. The film was promptly banned in Ireland. Renowned director John Huston's final film, *The Dead* (1987), was based on a story from James Joyce's *Dubliners*. *The Commitments* (1991), by British director Alan Parker, was a wonderful, bright and energetic hit about a northern Dublin soul band. *The Snapper* (1993) and *The Van* (1995), the other books of Roddy Doyle's trilogy, were also made into films. Following his convincing portrayal of an Irishman in *The Playboys* (1992), Albert Finney played a 1960s Dublin bus conductor who runs an amateur theatre group in *A Man of No Importance* (1994). The city also appeared in John Boorman's *The General* (1997), about the notorious Dublin gangster Martin Cahill, played by Brendan Gleeson.

The Troubles have spawned a number of films. An early one is *Odd Man Out* (1947) starring James Mason. *Some Mother's Son* (1996), starring Helen Mirren, deals with events surrounding the hunger strike of 1981 and the election of Bobby Sands as MP for Tyrone & Fermanagh shortly before his death. Two other films are Channel 4's *A Further Gesture* (1996), about an IRA man (Stephen Rea) escaping to Paris; and *Devil's Own* (1996), with Brad Pitt as an IRA gunrunner unwittingly harboured by New York cop Harrison Ford. Harrison Ford also starred in the thriller *Patriot Games* (1992), the story of a man who thwarts an IRA assassination attempt in London and is then hunted by IRA agents seeking revenge.

Ireland has also been a pure and straightforward backdrop. The Powerscourt Estate near Enniskerry in County Wicklow was the setting for films such as Laurence Olivier's *Henry V* (1943), Stanley Kubrick's *Barry Lyndon* (1975) and John Boorman's *Excalibur* (1980). Youghal in County Cork was Captain Ahab's port in John Huston's *Moby Dick* (1956). The Irish countryside was used for the WWI aerial epic *The Blue Max* (1966), and *Educating Rita* (1982) used Trinity College as its quintessentially English university! Dublin Castle can be spotted in the 1997 version of *Moll Flanders* starring Julia Roberts. Though set in Scotland, Mel Gibson's Oscar-winning *Braveheart* (1994) was mostly filmed in Ireland. The Wexford beaches stood in for the Normandy D-Day landing beaches in Steven Spielberg's *Saving Private Ryan* (1997).

NEWSPAPERS & MAGAZINES

In the South, the daily *Irish Times* is a bastion of liberal opinion and good journalism and is considered by some to be one of the world's best newspapers. The biggest sellers are the *Irish Independent* and its Sunday equivalent, which tend to be lighter in content, with more features and gossip. The *Examiner*, published in Cork, has a good journalistic reputation. The *Star* is the country's daily tabloid. The two main evening papers are the *Evening Herald*, published in Dublin, and Cork's *Evening Echo*. The *Sunday Tribune* has a liberal approach and claims to be good at investigating and breaking stories. One of the biggest sellers on Sunday is *Sunday World*, with plenty of titillation. The *Sunday Business Post* concentrates on financial matters.

In the North you'll find the apolitical evening *Belfast Telegraph*. Morning papers are the tabloid and staunchly Protestant *News Letter* and the pro-nationalist *Irish News*. *An Phoblacht* (Republican News) is published weekly by Sinn Féin.

Ireland has a range of magazines that cater for almost every interest, but the most popular is *RTE Guide*, the weekly radio and TV guide. For serious investigative journalism and opinion there's the current-affairs monthly *Magill*.

British papers and magazines are readily available in both the North and the South. They sell at a slightly higher price in the South than in the North but still undercut the Irish ones. There are sanitised Irish versions of the British daily tabloids in the South. The main European and US newspapers and magazines are sold in the larger newsagents in Dublin, Belfast and Cork.

RADIO & TV

The Republic has four Radion Telefís Éireann (RTE) state-run radio stations. Irish radio, AM or FM, varies in quality. Many of the morning programmes consist of phone-ins. RTE Radio One (88-90 FM or 567/729 MW) has a good mix of documentaries, music and talk shows. Broadcasters such as Pat Kenny, Joe Duffy and Marian Finucane give an insight into the country's foibles. RTE's 2FM (92-93 FM or 612/1278 MW) is the national pop-music station and is a good forum for upcoming Irish rock talent. *The Gerry Ryan Show* in the morning is worth listening to. Lyric FM (96-99 FM) is a 24-hour classical-music and arts service. Radió na Gaeltachta (92.5-96 FM or 540/828/963 MW) is the national Irish-language service. It's possible to tune into British BBC radio and independent channels, though the farther west you go the weaker the signal.

There is a host of regional radio stations offering good local services. The most popular is Highland Radio in Donegal broadcasting on 94.7 FM; others include LM FM in Counties Louth and Meath on 95.8 FM, Radio Kerry on 97.6 FM, and Clare FM on 96.4 FM. In Dublin, 98 FM and FM 104 stations offer a diet of classic international rock and pop tunes.

The state-run TV channels in the Republic are RTE 1 and 2 and the Irish-language Telefís na Ghaelige (TnaG). British BBC and independent TV programmes can be picked up in many parts of the country and offer a welcome substitute for the sometimes dreary Irish programming. In its defence, RTE isn't bad by international standards. It may appear parochial but local topics are always of limited interest to outsiders. TV3, Ireland's first commercial station, began broadcasting in September 1998.

A programme worth watching is *The Late Late Show* (on RTE 1), the longest-running chat show in the world, hosted by Pat Kenny. The show has a good mix of celebrities and current affairs, and is often

Goodbye Gaybo

Until his retirement in 1999, *The Late Late Show* was hosted by Gay Byrne (Gaybo), Ireland's top media personality. As recognition of his services to the country, in the same year he was given the freedom of the city of Dublin. This honour puts him into a small, select group. Previous recipients were US Presidents John F Kennedy and Bill Clinton, Pope John Paul II, Nelson Mandela and Mother Teresa.

an interesting window into Irish life. Current-affairs programmes such as *Prime Time* (on RTE 1) are also worth a look. Watch out for Gaelic football and hurling matches broadcast at the weekend.

In Northern Ireland, there are two TV stations: BBC NI and Ulster TV, which mix their own programming with input from their parent companies in Britain (BBC and ITV respectively). Britain's Channel 4 and Channel 5 also broadcast in Northern Ireland.

Many hotels and pubs, North and South, have Sky satellite TV.

VIDEO SYSTEMS

Overseas visitors thinking of purchasing videos as souvenirs should remember that Ireland, like Britain and much of Europe, uses the Phase Alternative Line (PAL) system, which isn't compatible with other standards unless converted.

PHOTOGRAPHY & VIDEO

Ireland has enough spectacular seascapes, ancient ruins, picturesque villages and interesting faces to keep any photographer or video-camera user happy.

Film & Equipment

If you're keen and using slide film, the slower the film the better, for example Fuji Velvia 50 ASA or Ektachrome 64 or 100 ASA. However, Irish light can be very dull, so to capture the sombre atmosphere you may need faster film, such as 200 or

400 ASA, and a small tripod is useful. In good weather a polariser is terrific for cutting out haze and giving punchy primary-green fields and blue skies with cotton-puff clouds. A plastic bag is handy to stop your camera getting wet.

There are plenty of camera shops in the cities and bigger towns, while in smaller towns and villages chemists (pharmacies) stock film and arrange processing. They'll normally have Fuji or Kodak print film. Slide film is usually Fujichrome or Ektachrome, but don't depend on their being in stock. Kodachrome is scarce and has to be sent to France for processing. Chemists and many smaller camera shops are expensive, so stock up beforehand.

Most towns and cities have good-quality one-hour processing shops. Developing and printing a 24-exposure print film typically costs IR£8.50 for one hour, IR£4 to IR£5 for a slower turnaround. Slide processing costs about IR£6 a roll and takes a few days, though the Film Bank (☎ 01-662 4420), 102 Lower Baggot St, Dublin 2, has a two-hour service. However, it mainly caters to professionals and has prices to match its high quality.

Technical Tips

Almost always it's the mood that makes the shot, and Ireland is noted for its rapidly changing and unusual light. In bright sunlight, western-coast beaches can look like the tropics, and then, a couple of hours and a few clouds later, Arctic Norway. Try to be imaginative with monuments and Celtic crosses: get the sun behind or at the side of your subject, use fill flash, get low with a wide-angle lens and put some plants or other points of interest in the foreground. The best times for pictures are early morning and late evening, when the sunlight is low and warm.

Restrictions

In the North, if you want to take photos of fortified police stations or army posts and other military or quasi-military paraphernalia, ask first to be on the safe side. Some tourist attractions either charge for taking

photos or prohibit it altogether. Use of flash is often forbidden to protect delicate pictures and fabrics. Video cameras are often disallowed because of the inconvenience they can cause other visitors.

Photographing People

You can't generalise about how Irish people will react to having their photograph taken. As always, being courteous and having a chat beforehand will make things easier. It's also courteous to give some money as 'payment' to a street busker or pavement artist for taking their photo.

Airport Security

You'll have to put your camera and film through the X-ray machine at all airports. The machines are supposed to be film-safe, but you may feel happier if you put exposed films in a lead-lined bag to protect them.

TIME

Ireland is on Greenwich Mean Time (GMT), otherwise referred to as Universal Time Coordinated (UTC), the same as Britain. Without making allowances for daylight-saving time changes, when it's 3 am in Los Angeles or Vancouver, it's 7 am in New York, noon in Dublin or London, 8 pm in Singapore and 10 pm in Sydney or Melbourne. As in Britain, clocks are advanced by one hour from late March to the end of October.

ELECTRICITY

Electricity is 220V, 50 cycles AC, and plugs are usually flat three-pins, as in Britain. Some older buildings may still have the older round-pin plugs, but adapters are available from electrical stores. Apart from for shavers, if you have a round two-pin plug bring with you a plastic converter that plugs into the three-pin plug. Many bathrooms have a two-pin 110 to 120V AC source for shavers, which is also useful if you have any 110V gadgets.

WEIGHTS & MEASURES

As in Britain, progress towards metrication is slow and piecemeal. On road signs distances are measured in miles and kilometres; food in shops is priced and weighed in metric; petrol is sold in litres but beer in pubs is served in pints. To help you out of your confusion there's a conversion table on the inside back cover of this book.

LAUNDRY

Most hostels and some cheaper hotels have self-service laundry facilities, while the more expensive hotels will return your clothes washed, dried and neatly folded. Otherwise, there are self-service laundrettes or dry-cleaning places, many of which open daily. Washing a load costs about IR£3 and drying it another IR£1 or so. Laundrettes sometimes have attendants who wash, dry and fold your clothes for IR£5 to IR£6. See Laundry or Information in specific chapters for addresses.

TOILETS

Many Irish restaurants and bars display notices asserting that toilets are reserved for customers only. Given this fact and the money Ireland makes from visitors it wouldn't seem unreasonable to expect that decent facilities would be available elsewhere. Instead, public toilets are often fairly sordid. Even places with a large throughput of visitors seem to regard keeping their facilities clean as a low priority.

Most toilets have signs indicating gender in English and Irish, but some may have a sign in Irish only. To avoid any embarrassment (and any unwanted delay) be warned that the Irish word '*mná*', which looks like the English word 'man', does in fact mean 'women'; the Gaelic word for 'men' is '*fir*'. The Irish word for 'toilet' is '*leithreas*'.

HEALTH

For emergency phone numbers, see Emergency Numbers under Telephone in the Post & Communications section earlier in this chapter.

Apart from cholesterol, Ireland poses no serious threats to health. The Catholic distaste for contraception doesn't prevent condoms being sold, to those aged over 18,

through pharmacies, if the pharmacist isn't personally opposed. Condoms are also available from vending machines in some pubs and nightclubs. The pill is available on prescription only.

There are various regional health boards whose services are listed at the front of the *White Pages* phone book.

Predeparture Planning

Immunisations These aren't necessary for Ireland unless you arrive from an infected area. If you have stopovers in Asia, Africa or Latin America, check with your travel agency and doctor. Don't leave it till the last minute, as the vaccinations may have to be spread out over several weeks. Vaccinations should be recorded on an International Health Certificate, which is available from your physician or government health department.

Health Insurance Citizens of EU countries are eligible for free medical care; other visitors, unless their country has a reciprocal agreement with Ireland or the UK, should have medical insurance or be prepared to pay. See Travel Insurance in the Visas & Documents section earlier in this chapter for more information.

Other Preparations If you wear glasses, take a spare pair and your prescription. Losing your glasses can be a real problem, although in many places you can get new spectacles made up quickly, cheaply and competently. If you require a particular medication or a specific oral contraceptive take note of the generic name rather than the brand name as it may not be available locally. It's wise to have a legible prescription or a letter from your doctor to show that you legally use the medication.

Basic Rules

Care in what you eat and drink and maintenance of personal hygiene are the most important health rules, wherever you travel. Many health problems can be avoided by just taking care of yourself. Wash your hands frequently.

Water Tap water is normally safe but drinking water in remote rural areas has been contaminated by *E. coli*. Don't drink straight from a stream: you can never be certain there are no people or animals upstream.

Water Purification The simplest way of purifying water is to boil it thoroughly. Vigorous boiling for five minutes should be satisfactory; however, at high altitude water boils at a lower temperature, so germs are less likely to be killed.

Filtering won't remove all dangerous organisms, so if you can't boil water it should be treated chemically. Chlorine tablets (Puritabs, Steritabs or other brand names) kill many but not all pathogens. Iodine is very effective in purifying water and is available in tablet form (such as Potable Aqua). Follow the directions carefully and remember that too much iodine can be harmful.

Environmental Hazards

Cold Hypothermia occurs when the body loses heat faster than it can produce it and the core temperature of the body falls. It's easy to progress from very cold to dangerously cold due to a combination of wind, wet clothing, fatigue and hunger, even if the air temperature is above freezing.

Walkers in Ireland should always be prepared for difficult conditions. It's best to dress in layers and a strong, waterproof outer layer is essential. A hat is important, as a lot of heat is lost through the head. Carry basic supplies, including food containing simple sugars to generate heat quickly.

Symptoms of hypothermia are exhaustion, numb skin (particularly toes and fingers), shivering, slurred speech, irrational or violent behaviour, lethargy, stumbling, dizzy spells, muscle cramps and violent bursts of energy.

To treat mild hypothermia, first get the person out of the wind and/or rain, remove their clothing if it's wet and replace it with dry, warm clothing. Give them hot liquids – not alcohol – and some high-calorie, easily digestible food. Do not rub victims: instead, allow them to slowly warm themselves. This should be enough to treat the early stages of hypothermia. The early recogni-

Medical Kit Check List

Following is a list of items you should consider including in your medical kit – consult your pharmacist for brands available in your country.

- ☐ **Aspirin** or **paracetamol** (acetaminophen in the USA) – for pain or fever
- ☐ **Antihistamine** – for allergies such as hay fever, to ease the itch from insect bites or stings, and to prevent motion sickness
- ☐ **Antibiotics** – consider including these if you're travelling well off the beaten track; see your doctor, as they must be prescribed, and carry the prescription with you
- ☐ **Loperamide** or **diphenoxylate** – 'blockers' for diarrhoea
- ☐ **Prochlorperazine** or **metaclopramide** – for nausea and vomiting
- ☐ **Rehydration mixture** – to prevent dehydration such as that due to severe diarrhoea; particularly important when travelling with children
- ☐ **Insect repellent, sunscreen, lip balm** and **eye drops**
- ☐ **Calamine lotion, sting-relief spray** or **aloe vera** – to ease irritation from sunburn and insect bites or stings
- ☐ **Antifungal cream** or **powder** – for fungal skin infections and thrush
- ☐ **Antiseptic** (such as povidone-iodine) – for cuts and grazes
- ☐ **Bandages, Band-Aids (plasters)** and other wound dressings
- ☐ **Water purification tablets** or **iodine**
- ☐ **Scissors, tweezers** and a **thermometer** (note that mercury thermometers are prohibited by airlines)
- ☐ **Cold** and **flu tablets, throat lozenges** and **nasal decongestant**
- ☐ **Multivitamins** – consider for long trips, when dietary vitamin intake may be inadequate

tion and treatment of mild hypothermia is the only way to prevent severe hypothermia, which is a critical condition – sufferers should have urgent medical attention.

Heat Exhaustion Dehydration or salt deficiency can cause heat exhaustion. In hot conditions (they do happen!), or if you're exerting yourself, make sure you get sufficient nonalcoholic liquids. Salt deficiency is characterised by fatigue, lethargy, headaches, giddiness and muscle cramps. Salt tablets may help, but adding salt to your food is better.

Jet Lag Jet lag is experienced when a person travels by air across more than three one-hour time zones. It occurs because many functions of the human body (such as temperature, pulse rate and emptying of the bladder and bowels) are regulated by internal 24-hour cycles called circadian rhythms. When we travel long distances rapidly, our bodies take time to adjust to the 'new time' of our destination, and we may experience fatigue, disorientation, insomnia, anxiety, impaired concentration and loss of appetite.

These effects are usually gone within three days of arrival, but to minimise the impact of jet lag:

- Rest for a couple of days prior to departure
- Try to select flight schedules that minimise sleep deprivation: arriving late in the day means you can sleep soon after you arrive. For long flights, try to organise a stopover
- Avoid excessive eating (which bloats the stomach) and alcohol (which causes dehydration) during the flight. Instead, drink plenty of non-carbonated, nonalcoholic drinks such as fruit juice and water
- Avoid smoking
- To help you sleep on the flight, make yourself comfortable by wearing loose-fitting clothes and perhaps bringing an eye mask and ear plugs
- Try to sleep at the appropriate time for the time zone to which you're travelling

Motion Sickness Eating lightly before and during a trip reduces the chances of motion sickness. If you're prone to motion sickness, try to find a place that minimises movement – near the wing on aircraft, close to midships on boats, near the centre on buses. Fresh air usually helps, while reading or cigarette smoke doesn't. Commercial motion-sickness preparations, some of which can cause drowsiness, have to be taken before the trip begins. Ginger (available in capsule form) and peppermint (including mint-flavoured sweets) are natural preventatives.

Sunburn Even in Ireland, and even through cloud cover, it's possible to get sunburned surprisingly quickly – especially if you're on water, snow or ice. Use a 15+ sunscreen, wear a hat and cover up with a long-sleeved shirt and trousers.

Sexually Transmitted Diseases (STDs)

STDs include gonorrhoea, herpes and syphilis. Sores, blisters or rashes around the genitals, discharges, or pain when urinating are common symptoms. With some STDs, such as wart virus or chlamydia, symptoms may be less marked or not observed at all, especially in women. Chlamydia infection can cause infertility in men and women before any symptoms have been noticed. Syphilis symptoms eventually disappear completely but the disease continues and can cause severe problems in later years.

While abstinence from sexual contact is the only 100% effective prevention, using condoms is also effective. The treatment of gonorrhoea and syphilis is with antibiotics. The different sexually transmitted diseases each require specific antibiotics.

HIV & AIDS Infection with the Human Immunodeficiency Virus (HIV) may develop into Acquired Immune Deficiency Syndrome (AIDS), which is a fatal disease. Exposure to blood, blood products or bodily fluids may put the individual at risk.

Apart from abstinence from sexual contact, the most effective preventative is always to practise safe sex using condoms. It's impossible to detect the HIV-positive status of an otherwise healthy-looking person without a blood test.

HIV/AIDS can also be spread through infected blood transfusions, but in Ireland these are safe. It can be spread by dirty needles: vaccinations, acupuncture, tattooing and ear or nose piercing can potentially be as dangerous as intravenous drug use if the equipment isn't clean. In Ireland, although there may be a risk of infection, it's very small.

Fear of HIV infection should never preclude treatment for serious medical conditions.

WOMEN TRAVELLERS

Women travellers will probably find Ireland a blissfully relaxing experience, with little risk of hassle on the street or anywhere else. Nonetheless, you still need to take elementary safety precautions. Walking alone at night, especially in certain parts of Dublin, is probably unwise. Even though hitching in Ireland is probably safer than hitching pretty well anywhere else in Europe, it is not recommended.

One or two hostel owners let the side down when it comes to bothering female guests. Keep your ears pinned to the ground and heed any warnings that come your way. Should you have any problems, be sure to report them to the local tourist authorities… and to us!

There's little need to worry about what you wear in Ireland, and the climate is hardly conducive to controversial topless sunbathing. Finding contraception is not the problem it once was, although anyone on the pill should bring adequate supplies.

GAY & LESBIAN TRAVELLERS

Gay and lesbian life is simply not acknowledged in most parts of Ireland. Only Dublin and to a certain extent Belfast and Cork have openly gay and lesbian communities. The monthly *Gay Community News* (homepage .tinet.ie/~nlgf) is a free publication with Ireland-wide information on gay and lesbian services, organisations and entertainment. In Dublin it's available through the Temple Bar Information Centre (☎ 01-671 5717), 18

Eustace St, Temple Bar, and from bars and cafés.

Information is also available from the following:

National Lesbian and Gay Federation (NLGF)
 (☎ 01-671 0939) Hirschfield Centre,
 10 Fownes St, Dublin 2
Northern Ireland Gay Rights Association (NIGRA)
 (☎ 028-90 664111) Cathedral Buildings,
 Lower Donegall St, Belfast BT1 1NB
Outhouse
 (☎ 01-670 6377) 6 South William St, Dublin
 2 – a gay, lesbian and transgender community
 centre with a Web site at indigo.ie/~outhouse

The following helplines can be called from anywhere in Ireland:

Gay Switchboard Dublin
 (☎ 01-872 1055) 8 to 10 pm Sunday to
 Friday, and 3.30 to 6 pm on Saturday
Lesbian Line Belfast
 (☎ 028-90 238668) 7.30 to 10 pm on
 Thursday
Lesbian Line Dublin
 (☎ 01-661 3771) 7 to 9 pm on Thursday
Mensline Belfast
 (☎ 028-90 322023) 7.30 to 10.30 pm Monday
 to Wednesday

DISABLED TRAVELLERS

If you have a physical disability, get in touch with your national support organisation (preferably the travel officer if there is one) and ask about your intended visit to Ireland. They often have complete libraries devoted to travel and can put you in touch with travel agencies who specialise in tours for the disabled.

Guesthouses, hotels and sights in Ireland are gradually being adapted for people with disabilities. Bord Fáilte's annual *Accommodation Guide* indicates which places are wheelchair accessible. The NITB publishes *Accessible Accommodation in Northern Ireland*. Your travel agency may have access to the most recent details via Gulliver (see Tourist Offices earlier in this chapter) about facilities available for disabled people.

Alternatively, you can obtain information on individual counties in the Republic by contacting the National Rehabilitation Board (☎ 01-608 0400), 25 Clyde Rd, Dublin 4. In Northern Ireland you can contact Disability Action (☎ 028-90 491011), 2 Annadale Ave, Belfast BT7 3JH, though it is scheduled to move. Travellers to Northern Ireland can also check the Web site of Everybody's Hotel Directory (see Accommodation later in this chapter).

SENIOR TRAVELLERS

Senior citizens are entitled to many discounts in Europe on things such as public transport and museum admission fees, provided they show proof of their age. The minimum qualifying age is usually 60 to 65 for men, and 55 to 65 for women. In your home country, a lower age may already entitle you to all sorts of interesting travel packages and discounts (on car hire, for instance) through organisations and travel agencies that cater to senior travellers. Start hunting at your local senior citizens' advice bureau.

Car rental companies usually won't rent to drivers aged over 70 or 75.

TRAVEL WITH CHILDREN

Successful travel with young children requires effort, but can be done. Try not to overdo things and consider using some sort of self-catering accommodation as a base. This frees you from the limited opening hours of restaurants and hotels, and gives you more flexibility. That said, Ireland is one of the more child-friendly countries in Europe, with provisions often made for children in hotels and restaurants. They're welcome in B&Bs, though you need to check on facilities when you book. Children are allowed in pubs (but not to consume alcohol) until 7 or 8 pm, and in smaller towns this restriction is treated with customary Irish flexibility.

You can often buy a family ticket for admission to attractions, and family passes are available on public transport. Special events occur during the year aimed specifically at children; check in the events guides published by the tourist boards. Include children in the planning process: if they've helped to work out where you'll be going, they'll be more interested when they get there. Include a range of activities – for example, balance a visit to Trinity College, Dublin, with one to the National Wax Museum.

For further general information see Lonely Planet's *Travel with Children* by Maureen Wheeler.

DANGERS & ANNOYANCES

See also Car & Motorcycle in the Getting Around chapter.

Crime

For emergency phone numbers see Emergency Numbers under Telephone in the Post & Communications section earlier in this chapter.

Ireland is safer than most countries in Europe but the usual precautions should be observed. In Dublin, drug-related crime is quite common and the city has its fair share of pickpockets and sneak thieves waiting to relieve the unwary of unwatched bags. See Dangers & Annoyances in the Dublin chapter for more details.

If you're travelling by car don't leave valuables on view inside when the car is parked. Dublin is particularly notorious for car break-ins, and foreign-registered and rental cars are prime targets (though the latter no longer have any markings to identify them as such). Cyclists should lock their bicycles securely and be cautious about leaving bags on the bike, particularly in larger towns or more touristy locations.

The police in the Republic are called by their Irish name of Garda Síochána, or just garda for one police officer and gardaí (pronounced 'gard-ee') for more than one. In Northern Ireland the police are called the Royal Ulster Constabulary (RUC), but at the time of writing the Independent Commission on Policing in Northern Ireland had suggested renaming them the Northern Ireland Police Service and making sweeping reforms in their recruitment and organisation as part of the peace process.

The Troubles

Obviously, there's a certain amount of violence due to the Troubles in Northern Ireland,

euro currency converter IR£1 = €1.27

but it's unusual to come across any personally, and if the peace process continues violence should diminish. That said, it's probably best to make sure your visit to Northern Ireland doesn't coincide with the climax of the Orange marching season on 12 July. Many Northern Irish, both Protestant and Catholic, leave the province for a few days either side of that date.

If you confine yourself to the Antrim coast you may well never see the British army, but in Derry or South Armagh, on the other hand, its presence is more obvious. Tourists are treated with courtesy by the security forces, but you may be asked for some form of identification. Don't leave a bag unattended: apart from the risk of theft it could be the subject of a security alert.

A British accent can be a help or a hindrance, depending on who you're dealing with.

Racism

Racially, the Irish people are very homogeneous and in the past it was mainly the Traveller (Tinker) community that was the butt of intolerance (see the boxed text 'Apartheid Without the Name' in the Kerry chapter). Today, that intolerance extends to other minority groups, especially those with different coloured skin.

In rural areas, where black people are few, they are unlikely to experience anything more than a naive curiosity. In cities, however, especially Dublin with its large concentration of black students and asylum seekers, abuse and physical assault are on the increase (see the boxed text 'Racism' in the Dublin chapter). Refugees from Eastern Europe, particularly if they can't speak English, are also subject to abuse. The widely proclaimed strength of the Irish economy has attracted illegal immigrants, whose presence (though small in number) has fanned racial intolerance.

LEGAL MATTERS

If you need legal assistance contact the Legal Aid Board (☎ 01-661 5811), St Stephen's Green House, Dublin 2. It has a number of local law centres listed in the phone book.

See also Road Rules in the Car & Motorcycle section of the Getting Around chapter.

Drugs

The importation of illegal drugs is prohibited and could result in imprisonment. The possession of small quantities of marijuana attracts a fine or warning, but harder drugs are treated more seriously.

Drinking

The legal drinking age is 18 and you may need a photo ID to prove your age. Although public drunkenness is illegal, the police grant enormous leeway. If matters get a bit rowdy, a police officer will usually give you a verbal caution before sending you on your way. Fighting is treated a little more harshly: if you're involved in a fight you may spend a night in a cell, to 'cool off'.

BUSINESS & PUB HOURS
Business Hours

Offices open 9 am to 5 pm on weekdays. Shops open 9 am to 5.30 or 6 pm, Monday to Saturday. On Thursday and/or Friday shops stay open later. Many also open on Sunday. Tourist offices and attractions often open fewer hours or fewer days per week, or shut completely, October to April.

Outside the cities, shops and businesses often close for one afternoon in the week. It varies from region to region. In small towns most shops are also likely to close for an hour or so at lunchtime.

In Northern Ireland many tourist attractions close on Sunday morning, rarely opening until around 2 pm, well after church finishing time.

For banking hours see Exchanging Money in the Money section earlier in this chapter; for post office hours see Post in the Post & Communications section earlier in this chapter.

Pub Hours

In the Republic pubs open from 10 am to 11.30 pm Monday to Saturday between June and September. The rest of the year closing time is 11 pm. Dublin pubs close for a 'holy hour', which may be one or more hours in the afternoon. On Sunday the opening hours are 12.30 to 2 pm and 4 to 11 pm. At the time of writing a bill was before the Dáil to end the holy hour and extend pub opening times until 1 am throughout the year. The later closing time was proposed to reflect the change in pub-goers' habits and to end the practice of some imbibers of downing 10 pints five minutes before closing time.

The only days when pubs definitely close are Christmas Day and Good Friday.

In the North pubs open 11.30 am to 11 pm Monday to Saturday. On Sunday the hours are 12.30 to 2 pm and 7 to 10 pm, but pubs in Protestant areas often stay closed all day.

PUBLIC HOLIDAYS & SPECIAL EVENTS

Northern and Southern public holidays (bank holidays) don't always coincide, which can have a bearing on the availability of beds in border resorts such as Newcastle.

Public holidays in the Republic of Ireland (IR), Northern Ireland (NI) or both are:

New Year's Day	1 January
St Patrick's Day	17 March
Easter Monday	
May Holiday	First Monday in May
Spring Bank Holiday (NI)	Last Monday in May
June Holiday (IR)	First Monday in June
Orangeman's Day (NI)	12 July
August Holiday (IR)	First Monday in August
August Holiday (NI)	Last Monday in August
October Holiday (IR)	Last Monday in October
Christmas Day	25 December
St Stephen's Day/ Boxing Day	26 December

In 2001 and 2002 the St Patrick's Day holiday will be taken on the following Monday as the 17th falls on a weekend. In the South, banks and many shops, pubs and offices close on Good Friday even though it isn't an official public holiday. In the North,

most shops open on Good Friday but close the following Tuesday.

Following is a list of major annual events and festivals held around the island. For more information on any of them, contact the local tourist office.

January
Horse Racing
There are regular horse races at a number of tracks throughout the country, including Leopardstown near Dublin and Naas in County Kildare.
Rugby
The international rugby season usually begins in January – the matches take place at the Lansdowne Rd Stadium in Dublin.

February
Rugby
International rugby games for the Six Nations Championship (between Ireland, England, Scotland, Wales, France and Italy) take place throughout the month; two are held at Lansdowne Rd, Dublin.

March
Belfast Music Festival
This takes place at Balmoral in Belfast during the first two weeks of the month. It has been going since 1911 and displays the talents of the city's youth in speech, drama and musical events and competitions.
St Patrick's Day
Dublin has a St Patrick's Day parade on March 17 (the following Monday in 2001 and 2002), as do Cork and Armagh; smaller celebrations take place in other cities. Dublin's parade doesn't compare with the razzmatazz in New York, but it's a much bigger celebration than it once was, with an international marching-band competition, fireworks and up to a quarter of a million spectators. The day passes off unostentatiously in the countryside, apart from the traditional wearing of a ribbon or shamrock leaf in one's lapel.

April
Dublin International Film Festival
This celebration of Irish and international film takes place over 10 days – contact Dublin Tourism for exact dates each year.
Gaelic Football League Final
This takes place at Croke Park in Dublin.
Irish Grand National
This horse race takes place at Fairyhouse, County Meath.

World Irish Dancing Championship
At this festival, hosted by a different city each year (contact Bord Fáilte for more information), Irish dancers gather to compete against each other.

May
Dublin Agricultural Spring Show
The Royal Dublin Society Showground in Ballsbridge, Dublin, hosts the Spring Show featuring agricultural and farming pursuits.
Fleadh Nua
Held at Ennis in County Clare in late May, this is a festival of traditional music and dance.
International Choral and Folk Dance Festival
This is held annually in Cork.
Irish Football Association Cup Final
This takes place at Lansdowne Rd Stadium, Dublin.

June
Bloomsday
Bloomsday (16 June) is when Leopold Bloom's journey (in *Ulysses* by James Joyce) around Dublin is re-enacted and various readings and dramatisations take place around the city (see the boxed text 'Bloomsday' in the Dublin chapter).
Fiddler's Stone Festival
This small traditional-music festival is held in Belleek, County Fermanagh.
International Fishing Festival
This takes place at Rathmullen, Donegal.
Irish Derby
Some 48km from the capital this horse race takes place at the Curragh in County Kildare.
Jazz and Blues Festival
This is held in Hollywood (near Belfast) in County Down.
Pettigo Pilgrimage
From 1 June to 15 August pilgrims leave Pettigo in County Donegal for the boat trip across to a small island on Lough Derg to do the penitential Stations of the Cross.
Writers' Week
Listowel in County Cork holds its annual literary festival.

July
Cork Arts Festival
This starts in mid-July.
Fishing
Fishing events get under way in Athlone and Mayo – for details get hold of Bord Fáilte's annual *Angler's Guide to Ireland*.

Galway Arts Festival
This begins in mid-July and features theatre, music, art and a parade.
Galway Film Fleadh
Held in early July, this is one of the country's biggest film festivals.
Reek Sunday
On the last Sunday of the month there's a mass pilgrimage to the top of Mayo's Croagh Patrick.

August
Connemara Pony Show
This is held in Clifden in County Galway.
Dublin Horse Show
The second week of the month sees this annual show at the Royal Dublin Society Showground (Ireland's answer to Wimbledon and Ascot when it comes to showing off one's social status).
Féile
The August bank-holiday weekend (the first Monday in August and the Saturday and Sunday that precede it) is the time for the Republic's major annual rock festival at Thurles in County Tipperary.
Féile an Phobail
Held in West Belfast at the start of the month, this is the largest community arts festival in Ireland.
Kilkenny Arts Week
This takes place in late August, when exhibitions, music and drama take place all over the city.
Oul' Lammas Fair
In Ballycastle in County Antrim this fair occurs over the last weekend of the month and attracts holidaymakers as well as enterprising traders.
Puck Fair
In Killorglin, County Kerry, this ancient festival heralds unrestricted drinking for days and nights.
Tralee
Horse racing takes place in Tralee in County Kerry, and for the last week of the month the town hosts the Rose of Tralee Festival, featuring a beauty contest.

September
All-Ireland Hurling and Football Finals
Both of these take place at Croke Park, Dublin, the hurling on the first Sunday of the month, the football on the third Sunday.
Matchmaking Festival
Lisdoonvarna in County Clare gets down to business.

Sligo Arts Week
This is held annually in Sligo town.
Waterford International Festival of Light Opera
Much of the city takes part and there are singing competitions.

October
Ballinasloe Horse Fair
Ballinasloe in County Galway hosts the Republic's biggest cattle and horse fair.
Cork International Film Festival and International Jazz Festival
The latter takes over the city, with special boat trains bringing audiences from Britain and elsewhere.
Dublin Marathon
This is run on the last Monday of the month.
Dublin Theatre Festival
This takes place over two weeks and features new Irish and top international productions as well as fringe shows.
Gourmet Festival
This is held in Kinsale in County Cork.
Wexford Opera Festival
This is a prestigious event attracting audiences and participants from all over the world.

November
Belfast Festival at Queen's
This three-week festival is the second-largest arts festival in the UK, after Edinburgh.

December
Christmas
This is a quiet affair in the countryside, though on 26 December the ancient practice of Wren Boys is re-enacted: groups of children dress up and expect money after singing a few desultory hymns at your door.

LANGUAGE COURSES
Irish
With the revival of the Irish language there is a growing number of courses in the language and culture, particularly in the Gaeltacht (Irish-speaking) areas.

University College, Galway, runs intensive one/two-week courses costing IR£150/250 plus accommodation; contact the Irish Language Centre (☎ 091-595101) or Áras Mháirtín Uí Chadhain, University College Galway, Galway City. In Glencolumbcille, Donegal, weekend and week-long courses in Irish and Irish culture, combined with outdoor activities, are provided from late March to October by Oideas Gael (☎ 073-30248, fax 30348, email oidsgael@iol.ie) at the Foras Cultúir Uladh (Ulster Cultural Foundation). Language courses cost from IR£50/110 for three-day/week-long courses; week-long cultural courses cost from IR£70 to IR£90. Accommodation can also be arranged costing IR£60 per person per week or IR£125 with breakfast and dinner.

Contact Bord Fáilte for information on other courses.

English
Given Ireland's significant contribution to English literature it's probably not surprising that it has become a centre for the learning of English, particularly for people from other Catholic countries, mainly Spain, Italy, France and Portugal.

Bord Fáilte publishes a list of schools that have been recognised by the Department of Education for the teaching of English as a foreign language. Some schools run summer programmes and provide specialised courses (such as for business people); the schools can arrange accommodation and organise sporting and cultural activities.

There are English-language schools in other parts of the country but most are in and around Dublin. Some of the approved schools in Dublin are:

Centre of English Studies
(☎ 01-671 4233) 31 Dame St, Dublin 2
Dublin School of English
(☎ 01-677 3322) 11 Westmoreland St, Dublin 2
English Language Institute
(☎ 01-475 2965) 99 St Stephen's Green, Dublin 2
Language Centre of Ireland
(☎ 01-671 6266) The Language School, 45 Kildare St, Dublin 2

WORK
Ireland's economic upturn and the fall in unemployment mean that finding casual work has become easier. Lowly paid seasonal work is available in the tourist industry,

usually in restaurants and pubs in cities such as Dublin, Belfast and Cork. Hostel notice boards sometimes advertise casual work and hostels themselves sometimes employ travellers to staff reception or clean rooms.

Without skills, though, it's difficult to find a job that pays sufficiently well to enable you to save money. You're almost certainly better off saving in your country of origin.

Sometimes volunteer work is available in return for bed and board, for example from the Burren Conservation Trust (see Fanore in the County Clare chapter).

Citizens of other EU countries can work legally in Ireland. If you don't come from an EU country but do have an Irish parent or grandparent, it's fairly easy to obtain Irish citizenship without necessarily renouncing your own nationality, and this opens the door to employment throughout the EU. Obtaining citizenship isn't an overnight procedure, so inquire about the process at an Irish embassy or consulate in your own country.

To work in the North, citizens of Commonwealth countries aged 17 to 27 can apply for a Working Holiday Entry Certificate that allows them to spend two years in the UK and to take work that's 'incidental' to a holiday. Commonwealth citizens with a UK-born parent may be eligible for a Certificate of Entitlement to the Right of Abode, which entitles them to live and work in the UK free of immigration control. Commonwealth citizens with a UK-born grandparent, or a grandparent born before 31 March 1922 in what's now the Republic, may qualify for a UK Ancestry-Employment Certificate, allowing them to work full time for up to four years in the UK.

Visiting full-time US students aged 18 and over can get a six-month work permit for Ireland and the UK through the Council on International Educational Exchange (☎ 212-822 2600), 205 East 42nd St, New York, NY 10017. The Web site is at www.ciee.org.

ACCOMMODATION

Bord Fáilte produces a range of annual publications listing B&Bs, hotels, camp sites and other accommodation, but they far from exhaust the possibilities. There are many places that aren't 'tourist board approved' but are in no way inferior to the approved places. The NITB publishes its own *Where to Stay* accommodation guide (UK£4.99). Gulliver (☎ 1800 668668 within Ireland) is the name of their combined computerised accommodation-reservation service. (See Tourist Offices earlier in this chapter.)

Everybody's Hotel Directory (www .everybody.co.uk) is an Internet directory listing accommodation suitable for disabled (and able-bodied) travellers in the UK, including Northern Ireland.

Bord Fáilte and NITB offices book local accommodation for a fee of IR£1, or IR£2 if the accommodation is in another town. All this really involves is their phoning a place on their list; but in high summer, when it may take numerous phone calls to find a free room, that can be money well spent.

Camping & Caravanning

Camping and caravan parks aren't as common as in Britain or on the Continent, but there are still plenty of them around Ireland. Some hostels also have camping space for tents and usually offer the use of the kitchen and shower facilities, which often makes them better value than the main camp sites. At commercial parks, tent sites typically cost IR£4 to IR£9 and many have coin-operated showers. Parks usually have different rates depending on the type of tent (a two-person tent as opposed to a family tent being the usual distinction) and whether you arrive by bike or car. Sites for caravans cost around IR£7 to IR£10.

Free tent camping is often available as long as you ask permission from the farmer. Around the touristy parts of County Kerry and Cork, farmers may ask for a punt or two, but it shouldn't be too difficult to find one who'll let you camp for nothing.

An alternative to normal caravanning is to hire a horse-drawn caravan with which to wander the countryside. In high season you can hire one for around IR£600 a week. Contact Bord Fáilte for a list of operators.

Hostels

The prices quoted in this book for hostel accommodation are for high season and for those aged over 18, or, if two prices are given, for those aged over/under 18. A dorm bed in high season (June to September) generally costs IR£6 to IR£7.50, except for in the more expensive Galway and Dublin hostels.

If you're travelling on a tight budget, the numerous hostels – both official and independent – offer cheap accommodation and are also great centres for meeting fellow travellers. From May to September and on public holidays, hostels can be heavily booked, but so is everything else.

An Óige (Irish Youth Hostel Association) and the Youth Hostel Association of Northern Ireland (YHANI) are the two associations that belong to Hostelling International (HI). You must be a member to stay in one of their hostels. For information on how to join, see Hostel Cards in the Visas & Documents section earlier in this chapter. An Óige and YHANI hostels have changed a lot for the better. They now operate a fax-a-bed-ahead facility. Bookings can be made by credit card at many of the larger hostels. Some hostels have family and smaller rooms. And these days you can take a car to a hostel. An Óige has 36 hostels scattered around the South and YHANI has eight in the North. To use a hostel you must also have or rent a sleeping sheet.

The addresses of the hostel associations are:

An Óige
  (☎ 01-830 4555, fax 830 5808,
  email anoige@iol.ie)
  61 Mountjoy St, Dublin 7
  Web site: www.irelandyha.org
YHANI
  (☎ 028-90 315435, fax 90 439699)
  22-32 Donegall Rd, Belfast BT12 5JN

Ireland has seen independent hostels, with no membership requirements, pop up like toadstools after rain. They emphasise their easy-going ambience and lack of rules but, while most have no curfew, some don't allow you access to your room for part of the day. Not all are of a high standard: some are cold in winter, stuffy in summer and often cramped, with up to 20 people in a room sleeping on flimsy metal bunk beds. Associations with usually reliable accommodation are:

Independent Holiday Hostels (IHH)
  (☎ 01-836 4700, fax 836 4710,
  email ihh@iol.ie)
  57 Lower Gardiner St, Dublin 1 – a
  cooperative group with hostels in both the
  North and the South and a Web site at
  www.hostels-ireland.com
Independent Hostel Owners (IHO)
  (☎ 073-30130, fax 30339)
  Dooey Hostel, Glencolumbcille, County
  Donegal – a 'back to basics' association
  with a Web site at epcmedia.net/ihi

B&Bs

If you're not staying in a hostel you are probably staying in a B&B. It sometimes seems as if every other house in Ireland is a B&B: you'll stumble upon them in the most unusual and remote locations.

The typical cost is IR£15 to IR£25 per person per night, and you rarely pay less or more than that, except in the big towns, where some luxurious B&Bs can cost IR£25 to IR£30 or more per person. Many don't have private bathrooms. In those that do the cost is usually IR£2 or IR£3 higher. Sadly, most B&Bs, like hotels, charge a 'single supplement' for individual travellers. B&Bs are usually small, with two to four rooms, so from April to September they can fill up quickly. Outside big cities, most B&Bs accept cash only.

Hotels

Hotels range from the local pub to medieval castles. It's often possible to negotiate better deals than the published rates, especially out of season. Ask if any discounts are given and try to think of a reason why you merit one. Out of the main holiday season, hotels often have special deals for certain

Breakfast at a B&B

Breakfast at a B&B is almost inevitably cereal followed by 'a fry', which means fried eggs, bacon and sausages, plus toast and brown bread. A week of B&B breakfasts would exceed every known international guideline for cholesterol intake, but if you decline fried food you're left with cereal and toast. If your bloodstream can take the pressure, you'll have eaten enough food to last you almost till dinnertime.

It's a shame, though, that more places don't offer alternatives like fruit, yoghurt or the delicious variety of Irish breads and scones which are widely available.

In Northern Ireland you may meet the awesome Ulster Fry, which adds fried bread, blood sausage, tomatoes and assorted other fried foods to the basic version.

days of the week, but these are usually quite flexible and can often be extended to whatever days you want. Payment for a night's stay usually includes breakfast.

Self-Catering
Self-catering accommodation is often on a weekly basis and usually means an apartment or house where you look after yourself. The rates vary from one region and season to another. A smart cottage in Schull, County Cork, in August can cost IR£620 a week, sleeping six people, while the equivalent in Banagher, County Offaly, in April is about IR£180.

Other Accommodation
During summer, there's accommodation in Dublin at Trinity College and University College (see Student Accommodation in the Places to Stay section of the Dublin chapter), and in Belfast at Queen's University (see Hostels in the Places to Stay section in the Belfast chapter).

Guesthouses are often just like larger and more expensive B&Bs, but sometimes they're more like small hotels, with a restaurant and sitting room, and a telephone and TV in the rooms. Farmhouse accommodation usually means a B&B on a farm; they're sometimes excellent value and you may get a chance to see how the farm works. Country houses are rural B&Bs, usually costing a fair bit more and in a rather grander than usual house.

Another option is to hire a boat, which you can live aboard while cruising Ireland's inland waterways. One company offering boats for hire on the Shannon-Erne Waterway is Emerald Star (☎ 078-20234, fax 21433), The Marina, Carrick-on-Shannon, County Leitrim. Lists of operators are available from the tourist boards.

FOOD
Local Food
Irish cooking once had a poor reputation, but things have improved enormously and now you can generally eat very well. Readily available high-quality produce, the influence of international cuisines brought over by immigrants, a growing awareness of healthy eating, the culinary experiences of the Irish abroad and the higher expectations of Ireland's numerous visitors have combined to produce what is called by some 'new Irish cuisine'. Of course, if you want meat or fish cooked until it's dried and shrivelled and vegetables turned to mush, there are still enough places that can perform the feat.

Irish meals are usually meat based, with beef, lamb and pork common options. Seafood, long neglected, is finding a place on the table in Irish homes. It's widely available in restaurants and is often excellent, especially in the west. Oysters, trout and salmon are delicious, particularly if they're direct from the sea or river rather than a fish farm.

Local cheeses (once mainly limited to an orange version of cheddar) are also widely available. Notable are cheeses from West Cork and Clare, and Tipperary's Cashel Blue and Cooleeny cheeses.

Irish bread has a wonderful reputation and can be very good, particularly in Belfast, but, unfortunately, there's a tendency to rely on the infamous white sliced bread, '*pan*' in Irish. Irish scones are a delight – tea and scones is a great snack at any time of day – that even pubs often offer.

Traditional foods include:

Bacon and Cabbage A stew consisting simply of its two named ingredients
Barm Brack A cakelike bread
Blaa Sausage rolls from Waterford
Boxty Rather like a filled pancake
Carrigeen A seaweed dish
Champ A Northern Irish dish of potatoes mashed with spring onions
Coddle A Dublin dish of semi-thick stew made with sausages, bacon, onions and potatoes
Colcannon Mashed potato, cabbage and onion fried in butter and milk
Crubeens A Cork dish of pigs' trotters
Dulse A dried seaweed that's sold salted and ready to eat, mainly in Ballycastle, County Antrim
Guinness Cake A popular fruitcake flavoured with Guinness
Irish Stew This quintessential Irish dish is a stew of mutton, potatoes and onions, flavoured with parsley and thyme and simmered slowly
Soda Bread This bread, white and brown, is made from flour and buttermilk and found throughout the country
Yellowman A hard, chewy toffee made in County Antrim

Restaurants
It's common for most Irish people to eat their main meal of the day at lunchtime. Every town has at least one hotel, pub or restaurant offering three-course lunches costing around IR£5. A similar meal in the evening may be at least double the cost.

The last decade has seen a huge increase in restaurants of every type and price range. Outside the principal centres the main alternatives to Irish food are provided by Italian and Chinese restaurants. But in cities such as Dublin, Belfast and Cork you'll also find a cosmopolitan range of cuisines, including French, Indian, Middle Eastern and Mexican. The result has been a sea change in attitudes to city dining. What was regarded as a luxury, experienced only on special occasions, is becoming almost a daily habit.

Fast Food
Fast food ranges from traditional fish and chips – fish and chip shops are called 'chippers' – to burgers, pizzas, kebabs and tacos. Pubs are often good places to eat, particularly at lunchtime, when a bowl of the soup of the day (usually vegetable) and some good bread can make a fine, economical meal.

Vegetarian
There are some superb vegetarian places, frequently run by British people or other Europeans who have settled in Ireland. Hotels and restaurants often feature a vegetarian dish on their menus, though they can sometimes be bland and unimaginative. At more expensive restaurants it's a good idea to inform them in advance that you want a vegetarian meal. For vegetarians, staying at a B&B can be a bad deal: the best excuse for the high prices charged by most is the huge breakfast. The vegetarian alternative is usually just cornflakes and toast, but the charge is the same. Some are happy to serve baked beans on toast if you ask.

Publications
There are several specialist food and restaurant guides to Ireland. Bridgestone's *100 Best Restaurants in Ireland* and *Vegetarian's Guide to Ireland*, both by Sally & John McKenna, are practical, independent guides to their subject. Egon Ronay has a guide to Ireland, and recommended restaurants display an Egon Ronay plaque. Bord Fáilte has its own publication, *Dining in Ireland* (IR£3.50), but proprietors simply pay for their entry and submit their own write-up. The NITB publishes *Where to Eat* (IR£2.99), which lists everything from the very expensive to the local Chinese takeaway.

DRINKS
Nonalcoholic Drinks
The Irish drink lots of tea, which is usually served black, in a small teapot, with milk in

a separate jug. Coffee is available in nearly all pubs, costing from IR45p to IR80p usually, but don't expect a smile if you order one at 10.30 pm on a busy night. If you ask for cream with your coffee, cream is what you'll get – a big dollop of it. Other nonalcoholic drinks in pubs and hotels are soft drinks and brand-named fizzy ones (called 'minerals'), but to judge by the prices you might think they were deliberately discouraging customers from drinking them.

Alcoholic Drinks

In Ireland 'a drink' means 'a beer' – either lager or stout. Stout usually means Guinness, the famous black beer of Dublin, although in Cork it can mean a Murphy's or a Beamish. Originating in Britain, stout (also called 'porter' because of its popularity with porters at Covent Garden market, London) was promoted by the Guinness family and soon gained an enduring stranglehold on the Irish tastebuds. Ian Paisley calls draught Guinness 'the Devil's buttermilk'.

If you don't develop a taste for stout (and you should at least try) a wide variety of lager beers are available, including Irish Harp (brewed by Guinness) and many locally brewed 'imports' such as Budweiser, Foster's or Heineken. For British-style bitter try Smithwick's (the 'w' isn't pronounced) or Caffrey's. Simply asking for a Guinness or a Harp will get you a pint (570 ml; IR£1.85 to IR£2.30 in a pub). If you want a half-pint (IR90p to IR£1.35) ask for a 'glass' or a 'half'.

The Irish were pioneers in the development of distilling whiskey (distilled three times and spelled with an 'e' as opposed to the twice-distilled Scotch whisky). Bushmills in County Antrim is the world's oldest (1608) legal distillery. When ordering a whiskey, the Irish never ask for a Scotch (though Scotch whisky is available): they use the brand name of an Irish whiskey instead: Jameson's, Paddy's, Powers, Bushmills or whatever. It may seem expensive but the Irish measure is generous, by law.

Irish coffee is something you'll see on sale in touristy hotels and restaurants, but it's not a traditional drink. It's a modern phenom-enon and was considered novel when served to the first transatlantic passengers arriving at Shannon Airport (though some say it was really invented in San Francisco). It's a mixture of coffee and whiskey served in a heated glass and topped with cream.

ENTERTAINMENT

See Public Holidays & Special Events earlier in this chapter for information on annual festivals and events.

Pubs, Bars & Clubs

Listening to traditional music while nursing a pint of Guinness is the most popular form of entertainment in Ireland. If someone invites you to visit a particular pub for its 'good crack' ('craíc' in Irish), don't think you've just found the local dope dealer. 'Craíc' is Irish for a good time – convivial company, sparkling conversation and rousing music.

In cities such as Dublin, Belfast and Cork old-style pubs are being replaced by sleek, modern bars whose main feature is a 250-watt stereo system. The nightclub scene in Dublin and Belfast is booming, with clubs offering different themes for different nights and partying well into the early morning.

These days many pubs and bars have satellite TV and you can go and watch the latest big – and not so big – sporting events.

Cinemas

Larger towns and cities have multiscreen cinemas, but only Dublin, Belfast and Cork have arthouse cinemas showing alternative or foreign films. Dublin also has an IMAX cinema.

Theatre

Theatre is popular all over Ireland. Dublin, particularly, is renowned for its excellent theatres and there's always a broad range of plays and shows on. Most famous is the Abbey Theatre, founded by WB Yeats, Lady Gregory and other writers and artists behind the Anglo-Irish literary revival. The Gate Theatre is a smaller company but puts on a remarkable variety of new and unusual work. Both the Gaiety and Olympia Theatres are beautifully preserved old showhouses that host a mix of plays, pantomimes and shows. Belfast has a range of theatres, most notably the Grand Opera House. Most major towns have at least one theatre and, in the summer, companies tour the country.

Classical Music & Opera

The majority of classical-music and opera companies are based in Dublin, though Belfast and Cork are also important centres. The main venues for performances are the National Concert Hall, Dublin; Cork Opera House; Belfast Waterfront Hall; and the Grand Opera House, Belfast. The most prestigious operatic event of the year is the Wexford Opera Festival in October.

Medieval Banquets & Irish Cabaret

A 'medieval banquet' finds its way onto many tourist itineraries, with the banquet at Bunratty Castle in County Clare probably the best known. They can be good fun but tend to be expensive and the food is often disappointing.

In Dublin several venues offer Irish cabaret, an evening of Irish music, song and dance with dinner beforehand as an optional extra.

SPECTATOR SPORTS
Gaelic Football & Hurling

Ireland has two native games with a large, enthusiastic following – Gaelic football and hurling.

Gaelic football is a fast and exciting spectacle. The ball is round like a soccer ball and the players can pass it in any direction by kicking or punching it. The goalposts are similar to rugby posts, and a goal, worth three points, is scored by putting the ball below the bar, while a single point is awarded when the ball goes over the bar. Gaelic football is popular in both the South and the North.

Hurling is a ball-and-stick game something like hockey, but much faster and more physical. Visitors are often taken aback by the crash of players wielding what look like ferocious clubs, but injuries are infrequent. The goalposts and scoring method are the same as Gaelic football, but the leather ball or *sliotar* is the size of a baseball. A player can pick up the ball on their stick and run with it for a certain distance. Players can handle the ball briefly and pass it by palming it. The players' broad wooden sticks are called hurleys. Women's hurling is called camogie.

Hurling has an ancient history and is mentioned in many old Irish tales. The mythical Celtic hero Cúchulainn was a legendary exponent of the game. Today hurling is played on a standard field, but in the old days the game might have been played across country between two towns or villages, the aim being to get the ball to a certain spot or goal.

Both Gaelic football and hurling are played nationwide by a network of town and country clubs and under the auspices of the Gaelic Athletic Association (GAA). The most important competitions are played at county level, and the county winners out of each of the four provinces come together in the autumn for the All-Ireland Finals, the climax of Ireland's sporting year. Both finals are played in September at Dublin's Croke Park in front of huge crowds.

Road Bowling

The object of this sport is to throw a cast-iron ball along a public road (normally one with little traffic) for a designated distance, usually one or two kilometres. The person who does it in the least number of throws is the winner. The main centres are Cork and Armagh and competitions take place throughout the year, attracting considerable crowds.

Handball

Handball is another Irish sport with ancient origins and is also governed by the GAA. This handball is different from the Olympic sport – it is played by two individuals or two pairs who use their hands to strike a ball against a forecourt wall, rather like in squash.

euro currency converter IR£1 = €1.27

Soccer & Rugby

Soccer and Rugby Union enjoy considerable support all over the country, particularly around Dublin, and soccer is very popular in Northern Ireland.

The international rugby team consists of players from the North and the Republic and has a tremendous following. The highlights of the rugby year are the international matches played against England, Scotland, Wales, France and Italy in the Six Nations championship between January and March. Home matches are played at Lansdowne Rd Stadium in Dublin.

The North and the Republic field separate international soccer teams and both, though particularly the Republic's, have a good record in competitions. Things look promising for the future too, with the Republic's under-16 and under-18 teams both winning their respective European championships in 1998. International matches are played at Lansdowne Rd Stadium, Dublin, and Windsor Park, Belfast.

Many home players from North and South play professional soccer in Britain and the most successful have the status of pop or movie stars. English clubs Arsenal, Liverpool and Manchester United, and Scottish clubs Celtic and Rangers have strong followings in Ireland.

Both North and South also have a professional soccer league, the Irish League in the North and the League of Ireland in the South.

Athletics, Boxing & Swimming

Athletics is also popular, and the Republic usually has a few international athletes, particularly in middle- and long-distance events. In 1995, Cork athlete Sonia O'Sullivan won the 5000m outdoor final at the World Championships in Gothenberg. After a slump in form she returned to success in 1998 at the European championships, when she won both the 5000m and 10,000m. In that year Catherina McKiernan won the London marathon, having won the Berlin marathon the year before. In Ireland, the main athletic meetings are held at Morton Stadium in Dublin.

Boxing has traditionally had a strong working-class following. Irish boxers have often won Olympic medals or been world champions. Barry McGuigan is a former world featherweight champion, Steve Collins retired as undefeated super middleweight champion in 1997 and Michael Carruth won the world welterweight title in 1998. The principal venue is Dublin's National Stadium.

Ireland hasn't had a strong tradition in swimming, but Michelle Smith (now Michelle de Bruin) raised its profile when she won three gold medals and one bronze at the 1996 Atlanta Olympics. Sadly, she has since been banned for alleged tampering with a urine sample.

Horse Racing

Horses have played a big role in Irish life over the centuries and the country has produced a large number of internationally successful race horses. In 1999, jockey Paul Carberry won the English Grand National on Irish horse Bobbyjo. The previous time an Irish horse won the National was in 1975, when Paul's father, Tommy, rode L'Escargot.

The Irish love of horse racing can be appreciated at various courses around the country, including Leopardstown in County Dublin, Fairyhouse in County Meath, and Naas, Punchestown and the Curragh in County Kildare. Major annual races include the Irish Grand National (Fairyhouse, April), Irish Derby (Curragh, June) and Irish Leger (Curragh, September).

Golf

Golf is enormously popular in Ireland and there are many fine golf courses. If you prefer to spectate rather than participate, the annual Irish Open takes place in June and the Irish Women's Open in September. For details of where they will take place each year, contact the Golfing Union of Ireland (☎ 01-269 4111, email gui@iol.ie), 81 Eglington Rd, Donnybrook, Dublin 4. Players to watch out for are Paul McGinley, Darren Clarke, Pádraig Harrington and Lilian Behan.

Cycling

Cycling is a popular spectator sport and events held annually are the Des Hanlon Memorial Race at Carlow (April), Milk Rás (May), Irish Road Race Championship (June) and Tour of the Mournes (July). In 1998 the first section of the Tour de France was held in Ireland. Sean Kelly was world number one five years in a row in the 1980s and current Irish cyclists include Aidan Duff, Ciaran Power and Tommy Evans.

Snooker

Snooker has a cult following in Ireland. The Irish Masters takes place in March. Three of the top players are Fergal O'Brien, Ronnie O'Sullivan and Ken Doherty. O'Sullivan won the World Snooker Championship in Sheffield, England, in 1997, and O'Brien won it in 1999.

SHOPPING
Clothing

All over the country, but especially in County Galway, it's possible to purchase Aran sweaters. The name comes from the islands where they were first made by women as working garments for their husbands. Hand-knitted ones, not unnaturally, cost a lot more than machine-made ones.

County Donegal is famous for its tweeds and Magee's in Donegal town has a large selection. It can be purchased in lengths or finished as jackets, skirts or caps. Tweed is also produced in County Wicklow and County Dublin.

Irish linen is of high quality and comes in the form of everything from blouses to handkerchiefs, with the main centres in the North. Irish lace is another fine product, at its best in Limerick, or Carrickmacross in County Monaghan. The Irish produce some high-quality outdoor-activities gear – they do have plenty of experience with wet and cold weather after all. Hand-woven shawls and woollen blankets also make lovely presents.

Crystal

Waterford crystal is world famous and is on sale throughout Ireland, although the company has reduced its workforce in Waterford and moved some business overseas. Smaller manufacturers of crystal produce fine work and at more attractive prices. In the North, Tyrone Crystal is based outside Dungannon and the factory can be toured, with no obligation to purchase from the showroom.

Food & Drink

Irish whiskey is not just spelled differently: it also has its own distinctive taste. The big names are Paddy's, Jameson's, Powers, Bushmills and Tullamore Dew, and they're not always readily available in other parts of the world. Two well-established Irish liqueurs are Irish Mist and Bailey's Irish Cream. Some excellent handmade cheeses are worth considering as a gift to take home. Two from West Cork are particularly worth mentioning: Gubbeen is a soft cheese from Schull, while Mileens is more spicy. Tipperary has its own Cashel Blue and Cooleeny cheeses.

Pottery

All over the country there are small potteries turning out unusual and attractive work. The village of Belleek in County Fermanagh, which straddles the Northern Ireland border with Donegal, produces delicate bone china. In the South the area around Dingle in County Kerry has superb pottery. Enniscorthy in County Wexford, and Kilkenny and Thomastown in County Kilkenny also stand out in this regard. Generally, throughout West Cork and Kerry there are countless small workshops that open in the summer with their stocks of pottery and other craftwork.

Other Items

Other possibilities include jewellery, especially Claddagh rings (see the boxed text 'Claddagh' in the Galway chapter), enamel work and baskets woven of willow or rush. Connemara marble is a natural green stone found in the west of Ireland which is often cunningly fashioned into Celtic designs. Plenty of stores sell CDs of Irish music, traditional and modern.

Activities

Although Ireland is expensive to travel in, many activities not only open up some of the most beautiful and fascinating corners of the island but are also within the reach of the tightest budget. In fact, those on a tight budget may find themselves hiking or cycling out of necessity. Fortunately, a walk or ride in the countryside will almost certainly be a highlight – as well as the cheapest part – of an Irish holiday. For those who have the money, other activities such as golf or fishing are available as part of holiday packages that include bed, board and transportation.

Most activities are well organised and have clubs and associations (some of which are listed here) that can give visitors invaluable information and sometimes substantial discounts. Many clubs have national or international affiliations, so check before leaving home.

The tourist boards put out a wide selection of information sheets and brochures which cover just about every activity, and these can be a starting point for further research.

WALKING

There are many superb walks in Ireland and walking has become increasingly popular since the early 1980s, when the Wicklow Way, the country's first waymarked trail, was established. There are now around 30 waymarked trails, varying in length from the 26km Cavan Way to the more than 900km of the Ulster Way. The network of trails is growing all the time and the aim is to link them all up eventually.

The energetic should consider some long-distance walks. Civilisation is never far away so it's generally easy to follow walks that connect with public transport and link hostels, B&Bs and villages. Some walkers might opt to walk the entire length of a way, but others might just choose a section that meets the constraints of ability, time or transport.

In most cases, a tent and cooking equipment aren't necessary. Warm and waterproof clothing (including a hat and gloves), sturdy footwear, lunch and some high-energy food (for emergencies), a water bottle (with purification tablets), first-aid kit, whistle, torch (flashlight), map and compass are all that you need.

The countryside can look deceptively gentle but, especially in the hills or on the open moors, the weather can turn nasty very quickly at any time of year. Although Ireland has a relatively mild climate there is one aspect of the weather that will affect the walker: the rain. As well as getting you wet, it causes the ground underfoot to be slippery, and low clouds in the hills make navigation problematic. It's vital if you're walking in upland areas to be well equipped and to carry (and know how to use) a compass, good maps and/or a walking guidebook. This is important even though at frequent intervals along the ways there are signposts, usually marked with a yellow arrow and walking figure – sometimes the signs are hidden by leafage or simply just missing.

Always leave details of your route with someone trustworthy and let them know when you should be back. Never walk alone in isolated areas.

The ways mainly follow old, disused roads, *'boreens'* (small lanes or roadways) and forest trails. Ireland has a tradition of relatively free access to open country, often through privately owned land, but the growth in the number of walkers and the carelessness of a few have made some farmers less obliging (see Responsible Tourism in the Facts for the Visitor chapter).

Information

The maintenance and development of the ways is administered in the South by the National Waymarked Ways Committee (☎ 01-662 1444, email walsha@entemp .irlgov.ie), Frederick Buildings, South Frederick St, Dublin 2, and in the North by the Sports Council for Northern Ireland (☎ 028-90 381222), House of Sport, Upper Malone Rd, Belfast BT9 5LA.

For Mountain Rescue, ring ☎ 999.

Guides & Maps Lonely Planet's *Walking in Ireland* contains route descriptions and maps of many of the walking trails mentioned later in this chapter, plus lots of practical information on accommodation, food and public transport. Another useful guide is Michael Fewer's *Irish Long-Distance Walks*. *Best Irish Walks* by Joss Lynam is a collection of 76 short walks around the country. There are also regional and individual-trail walking guidebooks available. A visit to a good bookshop such as Eason's in Dublin is recommended.

Bord Fáilte's booklet *Walking Ireland* (IR£1.50) gives a brief description of the waymarked trails in the South. Both tourist boards also have free information and maps on popular walks, but if you're planning more than one day's walking it's worth investing in one of the route maps available. For the Ulster Way, section maps are available from the Sports Council for Northern Ireland (☎ 028-90 381222), House of Sport, Upper Malone Rd, Belfast BT9 5LA. East-West Mapping (☎/fax 054-77835, email eastwest@tinet.ie) has excellent maps of long-distance walks in the Republic and the North.

Tim Robinson of Folding Landscapes, Roundstone, County Galway, produces superbly detailed maps of the Burren, the Aran Islands and Connemara. His and Joss Lynam's *Connemara: A Hill Walker's Guide* contains a useful detailed map.

Ordnance Survey maps cover the whole island in 89 sheets with a 1:50,000 scale (2cm to 1km). They can be obtained directly from:

Ordnance Survey Service
 (☎ 01-820 6100)
 Phoenix Park, Dublin 8
Ordnance Survey of Northern Ireland
 (☎ 028-90 661244)
 Colby House, Stranmillis Court,
 Belfast BT9 5BJ

They can also be obtained from bookshops, including the Government Publications Sales Office bookshop (☎ 01-661 3111), Sun Alliance House, Molesworth St, Dublin 2.

Organised Walks If you don't have a travelling companion one option is to join an organised walking group.

Go Ireland (☎ 066-976 2094, email goireland@fexco.ie), Killorglin, County Kerry, offers walking tours of the west, Donegal, Antrim and Fermanagh. South-West Walks Ireland (☎ 066-28762, email swwi@iol.ie), 40 Ashe St, Tralee, County Kerry, provides a series of guided and self-guided walking programmes around the country, including the North. Hike Those Heights (☎ 087-672841, email hikethos@hikethoseheights.com), 3 Short Quay, Kinsale, County Cork, concentrates on the south-west and has walks lasting from one day to one month.

Joyce's Ireland (☎ 01275-393555, email joyce@linkcheck.co.uk), PO Box 1389, Bristol BS41 9YB, England, offers walking tours for groups of up to 14 people, taking in both the Republic and the North. These tours have the advantage that your luggage (including musical instruments) is carried by minibus. Individual walks take from a couple of hours to a full day, which is perfect for anyone reasonably fit.

Beara Way

This moderately easy, 196km walk forms a loop round the delightful Beara Peninsula in West Cork. The peninsula is relatively unused to mass tourism and makes a pleasant contrast with the Iveragh Peninsula to the north.

Part of the walk, between Castletownbere and Glengarriff, follows the route taken by Donal O'Sullivan and his band after the English took his castle following an 11-day siege in 1602. At Glengarriff, O'Sullivan met up with other families and set out on a journey north, hoping to reunite with other remaining pockets of Gaelic resistance. Of the thousand men who set out that winter, only 30 completed the trek.

The Beara Way mostly follows old roads

ACTIVITIES

and tracks and rarely rises above 340m. There's no official start or finish point and the route can be walked in either direction. It could easily be reduced to seven days by skipping Bere and Dursey Islands, and if you start at Castletownbere you could reach Kenmare in five days or less.

Burren Way

This 35km walk traverses the Burren limestone plateau in County Clare. It presents a strange, unique landscape to the walker. There's very little soil and few trees but a surprising abundance of flora. The way stretches between Ballyvaughan, on the northern coast of County Clare, and Liscannor to the south-west, taking in the village of Doolin, famous as a traditional-music centre. The trail south of Doolin to the dramatic Cliffs of Moher is a highlight of the route. From the cliffs a new path is being developed inland towards Liscannor (though some maps may still show the old route along the cliffs, which has been closed).

The best time for this walk is late spring or early summer. The route is pretty dry, but walking boots are useful as the limestone can be sharp.

Cavan Way

In the north-west of County Cavan the villages of Blacklion and Dowra are the ends of the 26km Cavan Way. The way runs in a north-eastwards or south-westwards direction past a number of Stone Age monuments – court cairns, ring forts, tombs – and this area is said to be one of the last strongholds of Druidism. At the midpoint is the Shannon Pot, a pool on the boulder-strewn slopes of the Cuilcagh Mountains and the source of the River Shannon, which from there flows into Lough Allen. The Shannon Pot divides the walk into two parts: from Blacklion it is mainly hill walking; from Shannon Pot to Dowra it's mainly by road. The highest point on the walk is Giant's Grave (260m).

Dowra links up with the Leitrim Way, which runs between Manorhamilton and Drumshanbo. Blacklion is also on the Ulster Way.

Dingle Way

This 168km walk in County Kerry loops round one of the most beautiful peninsulas in the country. It would take eight days to complete the way, beginning and ending in Tralee, with an average daily distance of 22km. The first three days offer the easiest walk but the first day, from Tralee to Camp, is the least interesting; it could be skipped by taking the bus to Camp and starting from there.

You could also walk 8km from Camp to the Bog View Hostel, and then the next day 15km on to Lispole and on the third day a mere 9km to Dingle. This would also allow for a lovely 15km return trip from the Bog View Hostel to Lough Annascaul.

East Munster Way

This 70km walk travels through forest, open moorland, along small country roads and a river towpath. It's clearly laid out with black markers bearing yellow arrows and could be managed in three days, starting from Carrick-on-Suir in County Tipperary and finishing at Clogheen in County Waterford. The first day takes you to Clonmel, the second to Newcastle and the last to Clogheen (the longest section at 22km).

Kerry Way

The 214km Kerry Way is the Republic's longest waymarked footpath and is usually walked anticlockwise. It starts and ends in Killarney and stays inland for the first three days, winding through the spectacular Macgillycuddy's Reeks and past 1041m Mt Carrantuohil, Ireland's highest mountain, before continuing around the coast through Cahirciveen, Waterville, Caherdaniel, Sneem and Kenmare.

You could complete the walk in about 10 days, provided you're up to walking a good 20km a day. With less time it's worth walking the first three days, as far as Glenbeigh, from where a bus or a lift could return you to Killarney.

Accommodation isn't a problem, but you need to book in July and August. In contrast, places to eat aren't common, so consider carrying your own food.

Kildare Way

The 150km Kildare Way connects a series of canal towpaths in the north of the county. Killed off as transport routes by the advent of the railway, these towpaths were revived by people seeking leisure activities such as walking, cruising, canoeing and fishing. The walk is mainly flat: the highest point is at Glenaree Lock (92m). At the hub of the Kildare Way is Robertstown, from where trails radiate out to Naas, Kildare, Edenderry and Celbridge.

Lough Derg Way

This 52km walking trail begins in Limerick city and ends in County Tipperary at the village of Dromineer on the eastern shore of Lough Derg, one of three lakes along the Shannon and the Republic's largest lake. Eventually the trail will extend as far as Portumna in Galway, north of Lough Derg. The 35km from Limerick to Ballina via O'Brien's Bridge has been fully marked and signposted. It starts outside the Limerick city tourist office and follows the old city canal, the first of the old Shannon navigation canals. One possibility would be to walk part of the trail and then catch a bus back to Limerick city. The only drawback is the lack of accommodation along the route.

Mourne Trail

The Mourne Trail is actually the southeastern section of the Ulster Way, south of Belfast, and runs from Newry, round the Mourne Mountains, to the seaside resort of Newcastle and then on to Strangford, where you can take a ferry across to Portaferry and continue north to Newtownards. From Newry to Strangford is a distance of 106km, which could probably be managed in four days.

There's gorgeous mountain, forest and coastal scenery along the way and, once you've left Newry, not much in the way of built-up towns to spoil the views. Provided you're reasonably fit and well shod, this is not an especially difficult route to walk, although it does climb as high as 559m at Slievemoughanmore, the highest point on the Ulster Way.

Royal Canal Way

It's possible to walk along the towpath of the Royal Canal from Spencer Dock in Dublin to Mullingar, a distance of 77km. Eventually it'll be possible to continue all the way to Shannon and Longford. As it's a towpath there are no hills to slog up.

For the first 6.5km to Reilly's Bridge, the path runs through grotty, run-down urban scenery, but from then on it becomes much more rural and enjoyable (after the interruption of the M50 bridges). There are signposts at every bridge between Clonsilla and Mullingar.

St Declan's Way

This 94km walk, mostly tracing an old pilgrimage way from Ardmore in Waterford to the Rock of Cashel in Tipperary, traverses the Knockmealdown Mountains. Its highest point is the Bearna Cloch an Bhuideal Pass (537m), but for the most part the trail is gently undulating.

The walk can be done in stages and public transport is available from a number of places along the way – Cappoquin, Ardfinnan, Cahir and Newinn. There are B&Bs and hotels along the route. Camping is possible, though you'll need to ask permission from local farmers.

Slieve Bloom Way

Close to the geographical centre of Ireland, the Slieve Bloom Way is a 77km waymarked trail through Counties Offaly and Laois which does a complete circuit of the Slieve Bloom Mountains, taking in most major points of interest. The trail follows tracks, forest firebreaks and old roads, and crosses the Mountrath to Kinnitty and Mountrath to Clonaslee roads. Its highest point is at Glendine Gap (460m). The recommended starting point is the car park at Glenbarrow, 5km from Rosenallis.

Camping in state forests is forbidden, but there's plenty of open space outside the forest for tents; otherwise, accommodation en route is almost nonexistent. Nor is there any public transport to the area, though buses stop in the nearby towns of Mountrath and Rosenallis.

South Leinster Way

The tiny village of Kildavin in County Carlow, just south-west of Clonegal, on the slopes of Mt Leinster, is the northern starting point of the 100km South Leinster Way, which winds through Counties Carlow and Kilkenny. It follows remote mountain roads and river towpaths through the medieval villages of Borris, Graiguenamanagh, Inistioge, Mullinavat and Piltown to the finish post at Carrick-on-Suir just inside the Tipperary border. The southerly section is not as scenic as the rest, but the low hills have their own charm and on a sunny day they offer fine views south over the Suir Valley and Waterford Harbour.

The way leads in a generally southwestwards direction heading from Kildavin to Carrick-on-Suir but could easily be done in the opposite direction. It should take four or five days, depending on whether you stop over in Graiguenamanagh.

The route is marked so you should have no difficulty finding your way. Much of the trail is above 500m and the weather can change quickly. Good hiking boots, outdoor gear and emergency supplies are essential.

Ulster Way: Donegal Section

The main Ulster Way crosses into Donegal at the small pilgrimage town of Pettigo on Lough Erne, but then circles straight back to Rosscor in Northern Ireland. A spur – also confusingly called the Ulster Way – cuts north across the central moorlands of Donegal to Falcarragh on the northern coast. In all, if you follow the spur, this stretch of walk is only 111km long, which means it can be walked in four or five days. Bear in mind, however, that much of central Donegal is bleak, boggy terrain where walking can be tough going, especially if the weather's bad – which it often is! Although the walking-man symbol sometimes appears on markers, in general you'll be looking out for white-painted posts which simply tell you that you're heading in the right general direction.

This stretch of the Ulster Way is intended for wilderness lovers. Some of the scenery en route is truly magnificent, as you pass the Blue Stack and Derryveagh Mountains and Mt Errigal (752m), Donegal's highest peak. The route also skirts the glorious Glenveagh National Park, where you might want to divert and break your journey. There are few dramatic historic remains to distract you, but plenty of minor prehistoric burial sites en route.

Ulster Way: North-Eastern Section

The Ulster Way makes a circuit round the six counties of Northern Ireland and Donegal. In total the footpath covers just over 900km, so walking all of it might take five weeks. However, it can easily be broken down into smaller sections that could more realistically be attempted during a short stay. The scenery along the way varies enormously, encompassing dramatic coastal views, gentler lakeside country and the mountainous inland terrain of the Mourne Mountains.

Some of the most spectacular scenery lies along the north-eastern section, which follows the Glens of Antrim and then the glorious Causeway Coastline, a UNESCO-recognised World Heritage Site. The 165km north-eastern section begins unpromisingly in Belfast's western suburbs, heads north-eastwards to meet the coast at Glenarm then follows the coast round to the Giant's Causeway; this can be completed in six or seven days. The stretch of coast immediately surrounding the Giant's Causeway is likely to be busiest, especially in high summer, when you should book accommodation well ahead.

Walking this stretch of coast shouldn't be beyond most averagely fit and sensibly equipped people, but rockfalls along the coast can occasionally obstruct stretches of it. While some stretches of this walk can seem wonderfully wild, you're never going to be that far from civilisation.

Wexford Coastal Walk

The Wexford Coastal Walk (Slí Charman) follows the county's coastline for 221km from Ballyhack in the south-west on Waterford Harbour to Kilmichael Point in the

There may be quicker means of transport than walking, but you'll never forget getting vertigo on the Carrick-a-rede Rope Bridge, County Antrim (top right), or cursing your 100th stile (bottom right).

EOIN CLARKE

LEE FOSTER

GARETH McCORMACK

LEE FOSTER

DOUG McKINLAY

Climb Fair Head, County Antrim (top left), cycle the Ring of Kerry, County Kerry (bottom), or, if you're feeling less energetic, just wait for a fish to come along, County Galway (middle).

Tracing Your Ancestors

Many visitors, mainly from Canada, the USA and Australia, come to Ireland purely to track down their Irish roots. Success in this activity is more likely if you've conducted some basic research in your home country – in particular, if you've been able to obtain the date, and place, of arrival in your home country of your ancestor(s).

If you have access to the Internet try logging on to www.irelandtoday.ie/business/directory/genealogy, which has lots of links to related sites.

The Genealogical Office (☎ 01-661 8811), 2 Kildare St, Dublin 2, or the Public Record Office of Northern Ireland (PRONI; ☎ 028-90 251318, email proni.nics.gov.uk), 66 Balmoral Ave, Belfast BT9 6NY, are good starting points in Ireland. They can provide you with a list of local research centres, so if you know which county your ancestors came from you can then write to the centres directly. Much of the data of civil and church records is computerised and many local genealogy centres are connected to a computer network.

In Dublin, the Birth, Deaths and Marriages Register of Dublin City (☎ 01-671 1863), the files of the National Library (☎ 01-661 8811) and the National Archives (☎ 01-478 3711) at the Four Courts are all potential sources of genealogical information. The National Archive Records in Dublin Castle are of particular interest to Australians whose ancestors may have arrived in Australia as convicts.

In Northern Ireland the General Register Office (☎ 028-90 252000), 49 Chichester St, Belfast BT1 4HL, houses records of all births and deaths since 1864 and marriage registrations since 1922.

There are numerous commercial agencies that will do the research for you for a fee. For information on these, contact the Association of Professional Genealogists in Ireland (APGI), c/o the Genealogical Office in Dublin, and the Association of Ulster Genealogists and Record Agents (AUGRA), Glen Cottage, Glenmachan Rd, Belfast BT4 2NP.

A huge number of books are available on the subject. *The Irish Roots Guide* by Tony McCarthy serves as a useful introduction. Other publications include *Tracing Your Irish Roots* by Christine Kineally and *Tracing Your Irish Ancestors: A Comprehensive Guide* by John Grenham. All these publications, and other items of genealogical concern, may be obtained from the Genealogy Bookshop (☎ 01-679 5313), 3 Nassau St, Dublin 2; in Belfast the place to go is the Familia bookshop (☎ 028-90 235392), 64 Wellington Place.

north-eastern corner near the border with County Wicklow. As well as passing through the main coastal settlements of Kilmore Quay, Rosslare Harbour and Wexford town, the path takes you past areas of great natural beauty popular with birdwatchers, including the North and South Slobs and Hook Peninsula. The terrain varies from rocky headlands to sandy beaches.

The path is marked by signs showing a man with a walking stick walking on water. For more information contact Wexford town tourist office.

Wicklow Way

Opened in 1982, the popular 132km Wicklow Way was Ireland's first long-distance trail. Despite its name it actually starts in southern Dublin and ends in Clonegal in County Carlow, although most of the way is through County Wicklow. From its beginnings in Marlay Park, Rathfarnham, in southern Dublin, about 13km from the city centre, the trail quickly enters a mountain wilderness (the highest point is White Hill at 633m), though you're never far from a public road. Forest walks, sheep paths, bog roads and mountain passes join up to provide a spectacular walk which passes by Glencree, Powerscourt, Djouce Mountain, Luggala, Lough Dan, Glenmacnass, Glendalough, Glenmalure and Aghavannagh.

Especially south of Laragh, some sections are desolate, with much of the trail above 500m. The weather can change quickly, so good hiking boots, outdoor gear and emergency supplies are essential. There are many worthwhile detours: up Glenmacnass to the waterfall or up to the summit of Lugnaquilla Mountain, for example.

For the entire trail, allow eight to 10 days, plus time for diversions. It's easy to pick up sections and it can be done in either direction, though most walkers start in Dublin. Breaking the journey at Laragh, just under halfway, would let you visit the monastic site at Glendalough and do some local walks. Because of the way's popularity, walking outside the busy June to August period is advisable. Camping is possible along the route, but you'll need to ask permission from local farmers. In peak season you should book accommodation in advance. If you're hostelling you'll need to carry food with you.

If you're a glutton for punishment, the South Leinster Way starts a couple of kilometres south-west of Clonegal in Kildavin.

CYCLING

Many visitors explore Ireland by bicycle. Although the most interesting areas can be hilly, some roads have poor surfaces and the weather is often wet, it's a great place for bicycle touring. The facilities are good, distances are relatively short, roads off the main highways have relatively little traffic, the scenery is beautiful – and you're never too far from a pub. If you intend to cycle in the west, the prevailing winds mean it's easier to cycle from south to north.

You can either bring your own bike or rent one in Ireland. Ferries transport bicycles for free or a small fee and airlines will usually accept them as part of your 20kg luggage allowance. When buying your ticket, check with the ferry company or airline about any regulations or restrictions on the transportation of bicycles.

Bicycles can be transported by bus provided there's enough room in the luggage compartment. With Bus Éireann the charge varies; on Ulsterbus the cost is half the adult one-way fare. By train the cost varies from IR£3 to IR£6 for a one-way journey depending on the distance. Bicycles are not allowed on certain train routes, including the Dublin Area Rapid Transit (DART); you can check with Iarnród Éireann.

Typical rental costs are IR£8 to IR£10 per day or IR£30 to IR£40 per week plus a deposit of around IR£50, which is refunded when the bicycle is returned. Bags and other equipment can also be rented. Several dealers have outlets around the country; the dealers and their head offices are:

Irish Cycle Hire
   (☎ 041-41067, 35369)
   Mayoralty St, Drogheda, County Louth
Raleigh Ireland
   (☎ 01-626 1333, email raleigh@iol.ie)
   Raleigh House, Kylemore Rd, Dublin 10 –
   Ireland's biggest rental dealer, with a Web
   site at ireland.iol.ie/raleigh
Rent-a-Bike Ireland
   (☎ 01-872 5399, 872 5931)
   58 Lower Gardiner St, Dublin 1

There are also many local independent outlets.

Regional and national tour operators organise cycling holidays and the tourist boards can supply you with a list of their names. Irish Cycling Safaris (☎ 01-260 0749, email ics@kerna.ie), 7 Dartry Park, Dublin 6, organises tours for groups of cyclists in the south-west, the south-east and Connemara, with bikes, guides, a van that carries luggage, and B&B accommodation. Their Web site is at www.gorp.com/ics. Go Ireland (see Organised Walks earlier in this chapter) provides cycling tours of the west and Donegal.

Numerous tourist-office publications on cycling exist and there are a number of books and guides. Good maps are also available (see Guides & Maps in the Walking section earlier in this chapter). You might want to get in touch with the Federation of Irish Cyclists (☎ 01-855 1522),

Kelly Roche House, 519 North Circular Rd, Dublin 1, which has information on all aspects of cycling in Ireland. Their Web site is at www.fic.ie.

South-West

Most of West Cork is ideal cycling territory. One recommended route is west from Cork town to Kinsale, then on through Timoleague, Butlerstown, Clonakilty, Rosscarbery and down to Baltimore and Clear Island. Another route is down the Mizen Head Peninsula (starting from Skibbereen, where you can hire bikes), looping around the village of Toormore to take in the southern and northern coasts. A third route would be a circular one of the Sheep's Head Peninsula, starting and finishing in Bantry.

In County Kerry, a wonderful tour would be around the starkly beautiful Beara Peninsula from either Kenmare, Glengarriff or Bantry, taking in the spectacular Healy Pass either down from Lauragh to Adrigole (good brakes are absolutely essential) or with a herculean slog in the other direction. Killarney makes a good base for cycling trips into (but not *around*, unless you want car and coach fumes in your lungs) the Iveragh Peninsula, where many sights are accessible only by bike or on foot. Examples of two such tours are the 30km ride via the Gap of Dunloe and the 80km trip via Lake Acoose and Moll's Gap.

In County Clare the Burren region is good mountain-biking territory.

North-West

The Lough Gill tour in WB Yeats country outside Sligo town lends itself to cycling. There are also many historic and prehistoric sites – and places associated with Yeats – in easy cycling distance of Sligo town, where you can hire bikes.

Achill Island in County Mayo has largely flat roads and so is ideal for cycling. Bikes can be hired at Achill Sound and returned there after cycling west to Keel, turning north up to Dugort and then back south on another road. There are also bikes for hire in Keel.

In County Galway, Clifden is the best base for cycling tours of the superb scenery of Connemara.

In County Donegal you can follow the coast road west of Donegal town via Killybegs to Malinmore. North of Killybegs, past Ardara to Dunfanaghy, the coast is magnificent. There are superb cycling tours around Bloody Foreland and Horn Head. The peninsula that extends west from Ardara and separates Loughros More Bay from Loughros Beg Bay is well worth cycling too. North-east of Donegal town the loop around Lough Eske is a pleasant shorter trip on roads surrounded by the Blue Stack Mountains.

North-East

In County Down, Bangor is a good base from which to cycle the reasonably flat Ards Peninsula: you could follow the coast road south via Donaghadee to Portaferry, from where the A2 heads back north, skirting Strangford Lough. Alternatively, Newcastle is a good spot from which to explore the valley routes through the Mourne Mountains in south County Down.

In Antrim the scenic route along the coast north from Belfast to the Giant's Causeway passes through the foothills of the Antrim Mountains. From Enniskillen in Fermanagh you can hire bikes to visit ancient religious sites and antiquities, following roads along the shores of Lower Lough Erne to Belleek on the Donegal border and back.

South-East

Just south of Dublin, the varied scenery of County Wicklow – moors, bogs, mountains, lakes, valleys and forests – provides some beautiful but strenuous cycling. From Wicklow town south to Wexford town the weather is warmer and the landscape flatter.

In County Wexford the relatively flat Hook Peninsula – out to the lighthouse at the tip of the head and back along the western side to Duncannon – is a good area to explore. Between County Wexford and County Waterford, by taking the Ballyhack to Passage East ferry you avoid the longer route north via New Ross. In the west of

County Waterford the route through the Knockmealdown Mountains offers magnificent views.

Tipperary and Kilkenny have rich, rolling farmland interspersed with ancient monuments, such as the Rock of Cashel, and fine architectural remains. From Kilkenny town there's a beautiful cycling excursion to Kilfane, Jerpoint Abbey, Inistioge and Kells.

Centre
In Westmeath, from Athlone north into County Longford, east of Lough Ree, is Goldsmith country (named after the 18th-century poet, playwright and novelist Oliver Goldsmith), which has gentle terrain ideal for visiting by bike (see the boxed text 'Goldsmith Country Cycling Tour' in the Central North chapter). A cycle tour of the drumlins (rounded hills formed by retreating glaciers) and lakes of Cavan, Monaghan and southern Leitrim along the quiet country roads is very pleasant.

FISHING
Ireland is renowned for its fishing and many visitors come for no other reason. Fishing is divided into several categories, topped by dry-fly fishing, in which an artificial lure, made to imitate a small insect, is gently dropped on the surface in order to deceive and catch the fish. Fish are described as coarse or game fish, the latter because they vigorously struggle against capture.

Bord Fáilte and the Northern Ireland Tourist Board (NITB) produce several information leaflets on fishing. Bord Fáilte also annually publishes *The Angler's Guide*, which lists accommodation, major fishing events and charter boat operators. Three good books are *Game Angling Guide*, *Coarse Angling Guide* and *Sea Angling Guide* from the Central Fisheries Board and published by Gill & Macmillan. They're full of practical information and details of the permits and licences required.

In the South, on private stretches of rivers a permit (costing upwards of IR£15 per day and available from the local tackle shop) is usually necessary. In addition a state national licence is required for salmon and sea-trout fishing. This costs IR£25 annually, IR£10 for three weeks and IR£3 for one day, and can be purchased from a local tackle shop or direct from the Central Fisheries Board (☎ 01-837 9206), Balngowan House, Mobhi Boreen, Glasnevin, Dublin 9.

It's not necessary to have a licence for brown trout, rainbow trout or coarse fish, nor for general sea angling. However, there is a system of share certificates (issued to help raise funds for maintaining stocks and keeping rivers clean) for trout and coarse fishing which you purchase beforehand; in most regions payment is voluntary. The certificates cost IR£12 for a year, IR£5 for three weeks or IR£3 for three days.

In the North, you need a rod licence (coarse/game fishing UK£7.40/9.60 for eight days), which is obtainable from the Foyle Fisheries Commission (☎ 028-71 442100), 8 Victoria Rd, Derry BT47 2AB, for the Foyle area, and from the Fisheries Conservancy Board (☎ 028-38 334666), 1 Mahon Rd, Portadown, Craigavon, County Armagh, for all other regions. You also require a permit from the owner, which is usually the Department of Agriculture, Annexe 5, Castle Grounds, Stormont, Belfast BT4 3PW. Call ☎ 028-90 522157 and ask for the fisheries division. For game fishing it charges UK£11.65/23.50 for one/eight days, coarse fishing UK£6.80/11.90.

WATER SPORTS
Ireland's more than 5630km of coastline, its rivers and its numerous lakes provide plenty of opportunities for a range of water sports.

Swimming & Surfing
The climate and the water temperature are good reasons why Ireland isn't the first place you'd think of for swimming or surfing. On the other hand, it has some magnificent coastline and some great sandy beaches. Sadly, a number of Irish beaches suffer from pollution, but the cleaner, safer ones have been awarded the EU Blue Flag and you can get a list of these from An Taisce (☎ 01-454 1786), The Tailors Hall, Back Lane, Dublin 8.

The Irish Surfing Association (☎ 073-21053, email imagine@indigo.ie), Tirchonaill St, Donegal Town, County Donegal, can supply you with more details. Their Web site is at www.indigo.ie/imagine/irish-surfing.

Following is a selection of Ireland's major surfing spots.

South-West & West Barleycove Beach on the Mizen Head Peninsula is Cork's only surfing beach but it isn't crowded. In Kerry, at Caherdaniel on the Iveragh Peninsula it's possible to hire equipment. The broad, empty beaches around Castlegregory on Castlegregory Peninsula are perfect for surfing. At Inch on the Dingle Peninsula the waves average 1 to 3m. Spanish Point near Miltown Malby and Lahinch in western Clare are also good for surfing.

North-West & North Easky in County Sligo's west is highly regarded by surfers but by international standards it's uncrowded. Achill Island in County Mayo has surfing beaches, as do Bundoran and Rossnowlagh in County Donegal. Portrush to Castlerock on the northern coast in Northern Ireland is a hugely popular surfing area. You can hire equipment in Portrush.

South-East In County Wexford, equipment is available for hire at Rosslare Strand. In County Waterford, Ballinacourty, Dunmore East and Tramore are all worth considering for surfing. Equipment and advice are available in Dunmore East.

Scuba Diving
Ireland has some of the best scuba diving in Europe, almost entirely off the western coast among its offshore islands and rocks. The country's small size makes it easy to visit different sites. The best period for diving is roughly March to October. Visibility averages over 12m but can increase to 30m on good days.

A number of centres around the country offer equipment and training; many of these are listed in the relevant sections in this guide. For more details about scuba diving

in Ireland contact Comhairle Fo-Thuinn (CFT), The Irish Underwater Council (☎ 01-284 4601, email scubairl@indigo.ie), 78A Patrick St, Dun Laoghaire, County Dublin. The council is Ireland's diving regulatory body and publishes the dive magazine *Subsea*. They also have a Web site at www.indigo.ie/scuba-irl.

South-West Bantry Bay and Dunmanus Bay in County Cork are good sites. The area is largely virgin territory – a major draw with divers. In Bantry Bay you can dive to the wreck of the French frigate *La Surveillante*, and lying underwater about 15km from Kinsale is the wreck of the *Lusitania*, sunk in WWI. Other good diving centres in Cork are the waters off Baltimore and Schull, and around Clear and Sherkin Islands.

The Iveragh Peninsula in Kerry has two main bases: Valentia Island and Caherdaniel. Other good Kerry diving spots are the Blasket Islands in Dingle Bay and Ballinskelligs.

West & North In County Clare, Kilkee, Ballyreen (near Lisdoonvarna), Doolin and Fanore are all popular diving centres, as are Achill Island and Clare Island (in Clew Bay) in County Mayo. County Galway offers plenty of opportunities too, particularly along the Connemara coastline and around the Aran Islands. In south-western Donegal, Donegal Bay and the waters off Malinmore are prime sites.

East & South-East From Dun Laoghaire scuba divers head for the waters around Dalkey Island and Muglands. In County Wexford, the waters off Hook Head provide good diving opportunities.

Sailing
Sailing has a long history in Ireland and the country has over 120 yacht and sailing clubs, including the Royal Cork Yacht Club at Crosshaven, which, established in 1720, is the world's oldest. The most popular areas for sailing are the south-western coast, especially between Cork Harbour and

the Dingle Peninsula; the Kerry coastline; the coast of Antrim; along the sheltered coast north and south of Dublin; and some of the larger lakes such as Lough Derg, Lough Erne and Lough Gill.

Ireland has a number of professional training schools catering for people of varying degrees of expertise. They operate under the auspices of the Irish Association for Sail Training (☎ 01-660 1011), Irish Marine Federation, Confederation House, Kildare St, Dublin 2. For more information contact the Irish Yachting Association (☎ 01-280 0239, fax 280 7558), 3 Park Rd, Dun Laoghaire, County Dublin, which is the national body governing the sport. A recommended publication is the *Irish Cruising Club Sailing Directions*, which is available from booksellers. It contains details of port facilities, harbour plans and coast and tidal information.

Windsurfing

The windsurfer has plenty of locations, along the coast and on rivers and lakes, to indulge this popular sport. Even the Grand Canal in Dublin is used by windsurfers. The western coast is the most challenging but is also less crowded. The bay at Rosslare in County Wexford is ideal for windsurfing and you can obtain equipment and tuition there from the Rosslare Windsurfing Centre (☎ 053-32101). The Irish Yachting Association (see the previous Sailing section) is the sport's governing authority and has details of other centres offering tuition.

Canoeing

There are many opportunities for canoeing and it's a great way to travel round the country. Ireland's indented coastline makes it ideal for exploring by canoe. The Liffey Descent in September is a major international competition. The type of canoeing in Ireland and degree of difficulty varies from gentle paddling to white-water canoeing and canoe surfing. The best time for white water is winter, when the heavier rainfall swells the rivers. Adventure centres around the country run courses and organise canoeing trips.

Information on facilities, locations and conditions can be obtained from the Irish Canoe Union (☎ 01-450 9838), House of Sport, Long Mile Rd, Walkinstown, Dublin 12; it also runs training courses on the River Liffey.

Water-Skiing

There are water-ski clubs all over Ireland offering tuition, equipment and boats. Bord Fáilte provides the names of some clubs, but a full list and other details are available from the Irish Water-Ski Federation (☎ 01-624 0526), 29 Hermitage Rd, Lucan, County Dublin.

BIRDWATCHING

The variety and size of the flocks that visit or breed in Ireland make it of particular interest to birdwatchers. It's also home to some rare and endangered species. For a description of some Irish birds and where to find them see Birds in the Flora & Fauna section of the Facts about Ireland chapter.

There are more than 70 reserves and sanctuaries in Ireland, but some aren't open to visitors and others are privately owned so you'll need permission from the proprietors before entering. It's also illegal to interfere with wild birds, their nests and eggs.

Information can be obtained from the tourist boards and the following:

Irish Wildbird Conservancy
    (☎ 01-280 4322)
    Ruttledge House,
    8 Longford Place, Monkstown,
    County Dublin
National Parks and Wildlife Service
    (☎ 01-661 3111)
    Dúchas, 51 St Stephen's Green, Dublin 2
National Trust
    (☎ 028-90 510721)
    Rowallane House, Saintfield, County Down
    BT24 7LH
Royal Society for the Protection of Birds
(RSPB)
    (☎ 028-90 491547)
    Belvoir Park Forest, Belfast BT8 4QT

Some useful publications on birdwatching are *Where to Watch Birds in Ireland* by Clive Hutchinson, *The Birds of Ireland* by G D'Arcy, and *Complete Guide to Ireland's*

Birds by E Dempsey & M O'Cleary. Clive Hutchinson also has a Web site at indigo .ie/~hutch/birdmap.html. Another useful Irish birdwatching Web site is www.geo cities.com/rainforest/2801.

South-West

Clear Island in County Cork is one of the best places in Europe for viewing Manx shearwater and other sea birds. On the Skellig Islands there are colonies of storm petrel, gannet and kittiwake.

North

On the north-eastern cliffs of Tory Island, Donegal, you can see colonies of puffin, and Rathlin Island in Antrim has thousands of sea birds. Birds such as brent goose abound on the shores and mudflats of Strangford Lough in Derry.

East & South-East

There are several birdwatching sites near Dublin. North Bull Island in Clontarf is a wildlife sanctuary where many migratory birds pause in winter. Dalkey Island also has plenty of birdlife, and Ireland's Eye and Lambay Island off Howth are important sea-bird sanctuaries.

County Wexford is one of the main areas in Ireland for birdwatching. As well as the Wexford Wildfowl Reserve on the North Slobs, where thousands of migrating birds make their winter home, there's the Saltee Islands, one of Europe's most important

NICKY CAVEN

The great crested grebe was nearly extinct in Ireland in the 19th century due to its feathers being used in ladies' hats.

bird sanctuaries, plus the Hook Peninsula, Lady's Island and Tacumshin.

Centre

The shores of Lough Erne in Fermanagh and Lough Ree in Westmeath are ideal for birdwatching. Castle Caldwell Forest Park in Fermanagh is the main breeding ground of the common scoter duck.

GOLF

There are nearly 400 golf courses in Ireland, South and North, often in beautiful settings. They range from illustrious, expensive ones at Killarney, Portmarnock near Dublin, and Royal County Down, to more modest places such as the one at Castletownbere on the Beara Peninsula.

Bord Fáilte and the NITB produce information leaflets, plus brochures on customised golfing holidays with descriptions of courses and local accommodation. You could also try contacting the Golfing Union of Ireland (☎ 01-269 4111, email gui@ iol.ie), 81 Eglington Rd, Donnybrook, Dublin 4, or the Irish Ladies Golf Union (☎ 01-269 6244), 1 Clonskeagh Square, Clonskeagh Rd, Dublin 14. The Golfing Union has a Web site at www.gui.ie.

Green fees, usually based on a per-day rather than a per-round basis, start from around IR£15 on weekdays (more at the weekend) but the top-notch places will charge more than three times this. Courses are tested for their level of difficulty and many are playable year round.

It's always advisable to book in advance. Most clubs give members priority in booking tee-off times. It's usually easier to book a tee-off time on a public course, but at the weekend, on public holidays and days when the weather is good it's often busy on all courses. You should also check whether there's a dress code and whether the course has golf clubs for hire (not all do) if you don't have your own.

HANG-GLIDING & PARAGLIDING

Some of the finest hang-gliding and paragliding is found at Mt Leinster in Carlow, Great Sugar Loaf Mountain in Wicklow,

Benone/Magillan Beach in Derry and Achill Island in Mayo. Contact the Irish Hang-Gliding and Paragliding Association (☎ 087-243 3096, email info@newells .com), AFAS House of Sport, Longmile Rd, Dublin 12, for general information. The association's Web site is at www .newells.com. For information on Northern Ireland check the Ulster Hang-Gliding and Paragliding Web site at dnausers.d-n-a .net/dnetszsu.

ROCK CLIMBING

Ireland's mountain ranges aren't high – Mt Carrantuohil in Kerry's Macgillycuddy's Reeks is the tallest mountain in Ireland at only 1041m – but they're often beautiful and offer some excellent climbing possibilities.

Adventure centres around the country run courses and organise climbing trips. For further information contact the Mountaineering Council of Ireland (☎ 01-450 7376, email mciafas@tinet.ie), AFAS House of Sport, Longmile Rd, Dublin 12, which also publishes climbing guides and the magazine *Irish Mountain Log*. Its Web site is at www.mountaineering.ie.

South-West

The highest mountains are in the southwest. County Cork has a number of easy climbs, including Mt Gabriel (407m) on the Mizen Head Peninsula, Seefin (528m) on the Sheep's Head Peninsula and Sugarloaf Mountain (574m) on the Beara Peninsula; Hungry Hill (686m), also on the Beara Peninsula, is more demanding. The Iveragh Peninsula in County Kerry, with the Macgillycuddy's Reeks, has lots of mountains just waiting to be climbed.

West & North-West

In Galway, Clifden makes a good base for climbing in Connemara, and in Clare there's excellent rock climbing at Ballyreen near Fanore. Knocknarea (328m) outside Sligo town is an easy climb, and so, too, is Croagh Patrick (765m) in western Mayo, although it takes a lot longer. On Achill Island in Mayo are some of the highest cliffs in Europe. Mt Errigal (752m) in Donegal

is popular with climbers when the weather allows.

North-East & East

The Mourne Mountains in County Down, Northern Ireland, have steep, craggy granite peaks, including Eagle Mountain, Pigeon Rock Mountain and Slieve Donard, which, at 848m, is the highest peak in the range. You can base yourself in nearby Newcastle. At the northern end of Lough Tay in the Wicklow Mountains are some spectacular cliffs popular with rock climbers. Also popular are the large crags in Glendalough, at the western end of the valley not far from the Upper Lake.

HORSE RIDING

Not surprisingly this is a popular pastime and there are dozens of centres throughout Ireland offering horses or ponies for riding along beaches, country lanes, mountain and forest trails and over farmland. Possibilities range from hiring a horse for an hour (from IR£10) to fully packaged residential equestrian holidays; in some places you can even combine it with English-language tuition. Bord Fáilte and the NITB have full details.

The lovely wooded valleys and heathery mountains of northern County Waterford are good for horse riding, as are the Wicklow Mountains. Kildare is an equestrian paradise. Other areas include the Dingle Peninsula and Killarney National Park in Kerry, Connemara in Galway, around Bundoran and the Finn Valley in Donegal, and near Clonakilty in Cork.

SCENIC ROUTES

If you're visiting Ireland for only a short time, touring by car or motorcycle will help you to fit in a lot more. Following are some scenic routes, though the list is by no means exhaustive. The west of Ireland has the most dramatic scenery, but there are many other parts of the country where the landscape is also stunningly beautiful.

South-West

The main roads that loop round the lush, green peninsulas of Mizen Head and

Sheep's Head and the more desolate Beara in West Cork are all scenic. The northern coast of the Beara, the Healy Pass that cuts through the peninsula, and the Goat's Path along the northern side of the Sheep's Head are the most spectacular parts of these routes.

The road from Bantry to Kenmare and on to Killarney is an attractive drive, as is the one from Bantry east to Macroom. The Ring of Kerry, the road that loops round the Iveragh Peninsula, is justly famous and attracts a lot of vehicles.

From Tralee in County Clare there are two routes into the Dingle Peninsula, but the more beautiful is the one that follows the northern coastline and crosses over the Slieve Mish Mountains via Connor Pass to the town of Dingle and on to the western headlands.

The route that follows Clare's Atlantic coastline offers dramatic views, while the road that follows the south-western shores of Lough Derg passes through gentle countryside and picturesque villages.

West & North-West
In County Mayo the road between Louisburgh and Delphi is one of the most scenic in the west of Ireland. It always works its magic on motorists, who all seem unusually willing to slow down. The route in northern Mayo that passes Ballycastle has magnificent views.

In Galway the road through the Lough Inagh Valley in Connemara between the Maumturk Mountains and the Twelve Bens is one of the most scenic in the country. There are marvellous views along the road between Recess and Clifden to the south of the Twelve Bens.

Donegal has many scenic routes and one of the best is the road from Glencolumbcille to Ardara by way of the visually striking Glengesh Pass. From Ballyliffin to Buncrana on the Inishowen Peninsula there is a scenic coastal road via the Gap of Mamore and Dunree.

North-East
The A2 road east out of Belfast is a pleasant route to Bangor and the eastern coastline of the Ards Peninsula then south to Portavogie and Portaferry. You can return to Belfast north along the A20 following the eastern shoreline of Strangford Lough.

North of Belfast the A2 takes you to the Giant's Causeway following the magnificent Antrim coast, with the Antrim Mountains to the west. Between Cushendun and Ballycastle you can follow an alternative road that loops around the headland and rejoins the A2 at Ballyvoy.

The road that circles Lower Lough Erne from Enniskillen in County Fermanagh takes in many historic sites as well as having beautiful views.

East & South-East
South of Dublin there are several routes into the Wicklow Mountains. The most scenic begins at Glencree, leads south over the Sally Gap to Glendalough, continues to Avoca and then on to Arklow on the coast. The Wicklow coast between Greystones and Rathnew has some lovely countryside, too.

In southern County Carlow quiet roads connect picturesque villages such as Leighlinbridge and Borris with villages in neighbouring Counties Wexford and Kilkenny. Borris is also one starting point for a scenic drive up to nearby Mt Leinster.

In Waterford the coast road between Tramore and Dungarvan has lots of panoramic views and attractive villages. In the west of the county there are signposted scenic drives around the Knockmealdown Mountains with some terrific views.

Getting There & Away

Whichever way you're travelling to Ireland, make sure you take out travel insurance (see Travel Insurance in the Visas & Documents section in the Facts for the Visitor chapter).

AIR
Airports & Airlines

Dublin Airport (☎ 01-844 4900) is the Republic's major international airport, but Cork (☎ 021-313131) and Shannon (☎ 061-471444) also have international airports. You can have a look at their Web sites at www.dublin-airport.com, www.cork-airport .com and www.shannonairport.com. There are flights from these to the UK, Europe and the USA. Some smaller airports, including Galway (☎ 091-755569) and Waterford (☎ 051-875589), also have direct flights to the UK. Aer Lingus is the Irish national airline and Ryanair is the next-largest Irish airline. Both have flights to the UK, Europe and the USA.

Belfast has two airports. Most flights go to the International Airport (☎ 028-94 422888) 30km north of town. Direct flights arrive there from Shannon in the Republic, England, Scotland, Wales, Amsterdam, Brussels and New York. Have a look at the airport Web site at www.bial.co.uk. There's also the more central Belfast City Airport (☎ 028-90 457745), which has flights to London and some regional airports in Britain. City of Derry Airport (☎ 028-71 810784) has flights to Britain, Dublin and Paris. The main carriers to the North are British Airways Express and Jersey European.

Buying Tickets

World aviation has never been so competitive, making air travel better value than ever. But you have to research the options carefully to make sure you get the best deal.

Start early: some of the cheapest tickets must be bought well in advance and some popular flights sell out early. The Internet is a useful resource for checking air fares:

many travel agencies and airlines have a Web site. Talk to recent travellers, look at the ads in newspapers and magazines, including any catering specifically to the Irish community in your country, and watch for special offers. Then phone round travel agencies for bargains. Find out the fare, the route, the duration of the journey and any restrictions on the ticket, then decide which is best for you.

Some airlines now sell discounted tickets direct to the customer. Sometimes, there's nothing to be gained by going direct to the airline – specialist discount agencies often offer fares that are lower and/or carry fewer conditions than the airline's published prices.

The exception to this rule is the new breed of 'no-frills' carriers, which mostly sell direct. Unlike the 'full-service' airlines, the no-frills carriers often make one-way tickets available at half the return fare – meaning that it is easy to stitch together an open-jaw itinerary, where you fly in to one city and out of another.

Round-the-world (RTW) tickets are another possibility and are comparable in price to an ordinary return long-haul ticket. They can be particularly economical if you're flying from Australia or New Zealand. Special conditions might be attached to such tickets (such as you can't backtrack on a route). Also beware of cancellation penalties.

You may find that the cheapest flights are being advertised by obscure agencies. Most such firms are honest and solvent, but there are some rogue fly-by-night outfits around. Paying by credit card generally offers protection since most card issuers will provide refunds if you don't get what you've paid for. Similar protection can be obtained by buying a ticket from a bonded agent, such as one covered by the Air Transport Operators Licence (ATOL) scheme in the UK. If you feel suspicious about a firm it's best to steer clear, or only pay a deposit before you get your ticket, then ring the airline to confirm that you are actually booked on the flight before you pay the balance. Established outfits such as those mentioned in this book offer more security and are about as competitive as you can get.

Once you have your ticket, write down its number, together with the flight number and other details, and keep the information somewhere separate. If the ticket is lost or stolen, this will help you get a replacement.

Student & Youth Fares

Full-time students and people aged under 26 have access to better deals than other travellers. The better deals may not always be cheaper fares but can include more flexibility to change flights and/or routes. You have to show a document proving your date of birth or a valid International Student Identity Card (ISIC) when buying your ticket and boarding the plane.

Union of Students in Ireland Travel (USIT; ☎ 01-602 1600, 677 8117), 19 Aston Quay, O'Connell Bridge, Dublin 2, is the Irish youth and student travel association. It has a Web site at www.usit.ie. The agency offers cheap fares to Ireland for students (see later in this chapter for details of its branches in the UK, France and the USA).

Travellers with Special Needs

If you have special needs of any sort – you've broken a leg, you require a special diet, you're travelling in a wheelchair, taking a baby, terrified of flying, or whatever – let the airline staff know as soon as possible so that they can make the necessary arrangements. Remind them when you reconfirm your booking at least 72 hours before departure, and again when you check in at the airport. It may also be worth ringing round the airlines before you make your booking to find out how they can handle your particular needs.

Guide dogs for the blind will often have to travel in a specially pressurised baggage compartment with other animals, away from their owner; smaller guide dogs may be admitted to the cabin. All guide dogs will be subject to the same quarantine laws (six months in isolation etc) as any other animal when entering, or returning to, countries such as Ireland that are currently free of rabies.

Deaf travellers can ask for airport and inflight announcements to be written down for them.

Children aged under two travel for 10% of the standard fare (or free on some airlines) as long as they don't occupy a seat, but they don't get a baggage allowance. Skycots, baby food and nappies (diapers) should be provided by the airline if requested in advance. Children aged between two and 12 can usually occupy a seat for half to two-thirds of the full fare, and get a baggage allowance.

Britain

Discount air travel is big business in London. Advertisements for many travel agencies appear in the travel pages of the weekend broadsheets, such as the *Independent on*

Saturday and the *Sunday Times*, as well as in publications such as *Time Out* and *Exchange & Mart*. Look out for the free magazines, such as *TNT*, which are available outside the main train and underground stations in London. Those with access to Teletext on television will find a host of travel agencies advertising.

Popular travel agencies in the UK catering mainly, though not exclusively, to students and those aged under 26 include STA Travel (☎ 020-7361 6161), 86 Old Brompton Rd, London SW7 3LQ, which has offices throughout the UK. Visit its Web site at www.statravel.co.uk. USIT Campus Travel (☎ 020-7730 3402, 0870 240 1010), 52 Grosvenor Gardens, London SW1W 0AG, has branches throughout the UK. The Web address is www.usitcampus.com.

Other recommended bucket shops include: Trailfinders (☎ 020-7937 5400), 215 Kensington High St, London W8 6BD, and Flightbookers (☎ 020-7757 2700), 177-178 Tottenham Court Rd, London W1P 0LX.

UK phone numbers and Web sites (where applicable) of airlines flying between Britain and Ireland are:

Aer Lingus
 (☎ 0645 737747)
 www.aerlingus.ie
British Airways
 (☎ 0845 722 2111)
 www.britishairways.com
British Midland
 (☎ 020-8745 7321)
 www.iflybritishmidland.com
Cityjet
 (☎ 00-353-1-844 5566)
EasyJet
 (☎ 0870 600 0000)
 www.easyjet.com
Jersey European
 (☎ 0870 567 6676)
 www.jea.co.uk
Manx Airlines
 (☎ 01624-824313)
 www.manx-airlines.com
Ryanair
 (☎ 0870 333 1250)
 www.ryanair.ie
Virgin Express
 (☎ 020-7744 0004)
 www.virgin-express.com

To/From the Republic of Ireland There are dozens of flights on numerous airlines between Dublin and all the London airports every day. Return fares with British Airways (BA) between London and Dublin range from UK£60 for advance purchase to UK£300 for fully flexible and refundable. Many (cheaper) limited-offer deals become available from time to time and these should be booked well in advance as seats are often limited and snatched up quickly. At the time of writing Ryanair was offering a return fare between London Stansted and Dublin for as low as UK£16.99. No-frills carriers such as EasyJet or Virgin Express offer some of the lowest fares.

Most regional airports in the UK have flights to Dublin. Fares between Manchester and Dublin are similar to London to Dublin fares but other connections can be much more expensive. At the time of writing Cityjet was offering a return between East Midlands Airport and Dublin for as low as UK£80 with certain conditions.

Other cities in Ireland with direct connections to the UK include Cork, Galway, Killarney, Shannon, Sligo and Waterford. At the time of writing Virgin Express was offering a one-way fare between Shannon and London for only UK£40.

To/From Northern Ireland British Airways (BA), British Midland, EasyJet and other airlines fly regularly from the London airports to Belfast International Airport. Return fares range from as low as UK£50 for advance purchase to as high as UK£300 for fully flexible, fully refundable. Jersey European flies from Gatwick to the convenient Belfast City Airport, which is virtually in the centre of the city. BA flies between Glasgow or Edinburgh and Belfast International Airport for as low as UK£120. Ryanair flies twice daily from London Stansted to City of Derry Airport for as low as UK£55 return.

Continental Europe

Dublin is connected with all major centres in Europe. Flights to Belfast go via Amsterdam, Brussels, Shannon in the Republic of Ireland, or Britain.

In France, a branch of the Union of Students in Ireland Travel, USIT Voyages (☎ 01 42 44 14 00), can be found at 12 rue Vivienne, 75002 Paris. From Paris, the standard return fare to Dublin at the time of writing was around 1700FF, to Belfast (via London) 3930FF.

In Germany, try STA Travel (☎ 089-39 90 96), Königstrasse 49, Münich. At the time of writing a return fare between Berlin and Dublin with Air France cost around 500DM; from Berlin to Belfast with Sabena or British Airways cost around 600DM.

In the Netherlands, the student travel agency NBBS Reiswinkels (☎ 020-620 5071), Rokin 38, Amsterdam, offers reliable and reasonably low fares. At the time of writing a return fare between Amsterdam and Dublin cost around 300NLG, while from Amsterdam to Belfast cost 400NLG.

The USA & Canada

In the USA discount travel agencies are known as consolidators. They can be found through the *Yellow Pages* or major newspapers. Check the Sunday travel sections of papers such as the *New York Times*, *Los Angeles Times*, *Chicago Tribune* or *San Francisco Chronicle-Examiner* for the latest fares.

The *Travel Unlimited* newsletter, PO Box 1058, Allston, MA 02134, publishes details of the cheapest air fares and courier possibilities for destinations all over the world from the USA and other countries.

USIT has a branch at New York Student Center (☎ 212-663 5435), 895 Amsterdam Ave (at West 103rd St), New York, NY 10025. Council Travel (☎ 800 2268624), 205 E 42 St, New York, NY 10017, America's largest student travel organisation, has around 60 offices in the USA. Call for the office nearest you or visit the Web site at www.ciee.org. STA Travel (☎ 800 7770112) has offices in Boston, Chicago, Miami, New York, Philadelphia, San Francisco and other major cities. Call the toll-free 800 number for office locations or visit its Web site at www.statravel.com.

Aer Lingus is the chief carrier between the USA and Ireland. It connects Dublin, Belfast, Shannon and other Irish cities with many US cities, including Boston, Chicago, Dallas, Denver, Detroit, Los Angeles, New Orleans, New York, Philadelphia, San Francisco, Seattle and Washington DC. Its New York office (☎ 1800 2236537) is at 538 Broadhollow Rd, Melville.

Delta Airlines (☎ 1800 2414141) operates Atlanta to Shannon to Dublin, linking into its huge US network. Many other airlines fly between the USA and the Republic, including United Airlines (☎ 800 2416522) and Continental Airlines (☎ 800 5250280).

During the summer high season the round trip between New York and Dublin with Aer Lingus costs around US$820 midweek or US$1000 at the weekend. Aer Lingus also offers seasonal discounted specials that are US$150 to US$250 less than the usual fare. Look at their Web site at www.aerlingus.ie/special.html for details. In general, discounted fares between New York and Dublin can start at as low as US$350 in the low season or US$650 in the high season.

Competition on flights to London is so fierce it's generally cheaper to fly to London first then pick up a flight to Dublin, Belfast or other Irish cities. In the low season, discount return fares from New York to London will be in the US$350 to US$600 range, in the high season US$600 to US$800. From the West Coast, fares to London will cost from around US$200 more.

In Canada, check the *Globe and Mail*, *Toronto Star* or *Vancouver Sun* for travel-agency ads. Canada's main student travel organisation is Travel CUTS and it has offices in all major cities. It is known as Voyages Campus in Quebec. Its Web address is www.travelcuts.com.

There are no direct flights from Canada to Ireland – visitors fly to London and get a connection from there. In Canada, Aer Lingus can be contacted by calling ☎ 1800 2236537, although it doesn't actually fly to Canada.

Air Travel Glossary

Baggage Allowance This will be written on your ticket and usually includes one 20kg item to go in the hold, plus one item of hand luggage.

Bucket Shops These are unbonded travel agencies specialising in discounted airline tickets.

Bumped Just because you have a confirmed seat doesn't mean you're going to get on the plane (see Overbooking).

Cancellation Penalties If you have to cancel or change a discounted ticket, there are often heavy penalties involved; insurance can sometimes be taken out against these penalties. Some airlines impose penalties on regular tickets as well, particularly against 'no-show' passengers.

Check-In Airlines ask you to check in a certain time ahead of the flight departure (usually one to two hours on international flights). If you fail to check in on time and the flight is overbooked, the airline can cancel your booking and give your seat to somebody else.

Confirmation Having a ticket written out with the flight and date you want doesn't mean you have a seat. Until the agent has checked with the airline that your status is 'OK' or confirmed, you could just be 'on request'.

Courier Fares Businesses often need to send urgent documents or freight securely and quickly. Courier companies hire people to accompany the package through customs and, in return, offer a discount ticket which is sometimes a phenomenal bargain. In effect, what the companies do is ship their freight as your luggage on regular commercial flights. This is a legitimate operation, but there are two shortcomings – the short turnaround time of the ticket (usually not longer than a month) and the limitation on your luggage allowance. You may have to surrender all your allowance and take only carry-on luggage.

Full Fares Airlines traditionally offer 1st-class (coded F), business-class (coded J) and economy-class (coded Y) tickets. These days there are so many promotional and discounted fares available that few passengers pay full economy fare.

ITX An ITX, or 'independent inclusive tour excursion', is often available on tickets to popular holiday destinations. Officially it's a package deal combined with hotel accommodation, but many agencies will sell you one of these for the flight only and give you phoney hotel vouchers in the unlikely event that you're challenged at the airport.

Lost Tickets If you lose your airline ticket an airline will usually treat it like a travellers cheque and, after inquiries, issue you with another one. Legally, however, an airline is entitled to treat it like cash and if you lose it then it's gone for ever. Take good care of your tickets.

MCO An MCO, or 'miscellaneous charge order', is a voucher that looks like an airline ticket but carries no destination or date. It can be exchanged through any International Association of Travel Agents (IATA) airline for a ticket on a specific flight. It's a useful alternative to an onwards ticket in those countries that demand one, and is more flexible than an ordinary ticket if you're unsure of your route.

No-Shows No-shows are passengers who fail to show up for their flight. Full-fare passengers who fail to turn up are sometimes entitled to travel on a later flight. The rest are penalised (see Cancellation Penalties).

On Request This is an unconfirmed booking for a flight.

Air Travel Glossary

Onwards Tickets An entry requirement for many countries is that you have a ticket out of the country. If you're unsure of your next move, the easiest solution is to buy the cheapest onwards ticket to a neighbouring country or a ticket from a reliable airline that can later be refunded if you do not use it.

Open-Jaw Tickets These are return tickets with which you fly out to one place but return from another. If available, this can save you backtracking to your arrival point.

Overbooking Airlines hate to fly empty seats and, since every flight has some passengers who fail to show up, airlines often book more passengers than they have seats. Usually excess passengers make up for the no-shows, but occasionally somebody gets 'bumped' onto the next available flight. Guess who it is most likely to be? The passengers who check in late.

Point-to-Point Tickets These are discount tickets that can be bought on some routes in return for passengers waiving their rights to a stopover.

Promotional Fares These are officially discounted fares, available from travel agencies or direct from the airline.

Reconfirmation If you don't reconfirm your flight at least 72 hours prior to departure, the airline may delete your name from the passenger list. Ring to find out if your airline requires reconfirmation.

Restrictions Discounted tickets often have various restrictions on them – such as needing to be paid for in advance and incurring a penalty for alteration. Others are restrictions on the minimum and maximum period you must be away, such as a minimum of 14 days or a maximum of one year.

Round-the-World Tickets RTW tickets give you a limited period (usually a year) in which to circumnavigate the globe. You can go anywhere the carrying airlines go, as long as you don't backtrack. The number of stopovers or total number of separate flights is decided before you set off and they usually cost a bit more than a basic return flight.

Stand-By This is a discounted ticket that allows you to fly only if there is a seat free at the last moment. Stand-by fares are usually available only on domestic routes.

Transferred Tickets Airline tickets cannot be transferred from one person to another. Travellers sometimes try to sell the return half of their ticket, but officials can ask you to prove that you are the person named on the ticket. This is less likely to happen on domestic flights, but on an international flight tickets are compared with passports.

Travel Agencies Travel agencies vary widely and you should choose one that suits your needs. Some simply handle tours, while full-service agencies handle everything from tours and tickets to car rental and hotel bookings. If all you want is a ticket at the lowest possible price, then go to an agency specialising in discounted fares.

Travel Periods Ticket prices vary with the time of year. There is a low (off-peak) season and a high (peak) season, and often a low-shoulder season and a high-shoulder season as well. Usually the fare depends on your outward flight – if you depart in the high season and return in the low season, you pay the high-season fare.

Australia & New Zealand

In Australia, STA Travel (☎ 03-9349 2411), 224 Faraday St, Carlton, Melbourne, Victoria 3053, has offices in all major cities and on many university campuses. Call ☎ 131 776 Australia wide for the location of your nearest branch or visit its Web site at www.statravel.com.au. Flight Centre (☎ 131 600 Australia wide), 82 Elizabeth St, Sydney, NSW 2000, has dozens of offices throughout Australia. Its Web address is www.flightcentre.com.au. Shamrock Travel (☎ 03-9602 3700), Level 9, 310 King St, Melbourne, Victoria 3000, specialises in flights to Ireland. Its Web site is at www.irishtravel.com.au.

In New Zealand, Flight Centre (☎ 09-309 6171) has a large central office in Auckland at National Bank Towers (corner of Queen and Darby Sts) and many branches throughout the country. STA Travel (☎ 09-309 0458), 10 High St, Auckland, has other offices in Auckland as well as in Hamilton, Palmerston North, Wellington, Christchurch and Dunedin. The Web address is www.statravel.com.au.

For information about Aer Lingus flights contact World Aviation Systems (☎ 02-9244 2133), 64 York St, Sydney, NSW 2000 (it also has offices in Adelaide, Brisbane, Canberra, Melbourne and Perth). In New Zealand, World Aviation Systems (☎ 09-308 3351) is at Trustbank Building, 229 Queen St, Auckland.

The Saturday travel sections of the *Sydney Morning Herald* and Melbourne *Age* newspapers have many ads offering cheap fares. The *New Zealand Herald* has a travel section in which travel agencies advertise fares. A useful Web site offering discounted fares is www.travel.com.au.

Excursion or Apex fares from Australia or New Zealand to most European destinations can have a return flight to Dublin tagged on at no extra cost. Return fares to Dublin from Australia vary from around A$1450 (low season) to A$2450 (high season) but there are often short-term special deals available.

The cheapest fares from New Zealand will probably take the eastbound route via the USA. An RTW ticket may be cheaper than a return, which in high season costs around NZ$2600.

SEA

There's a great variety of services from France and Britain to Ireland using modern ferries and catamarans. Competition from airlines has helped keep prices down.

Want to travel free? On some routes the cost for a car includes up to four or five passengers. If you can hitch a ride in a less-than-full car, it costs the driver nothing extra.

Throughout this section, the prices quoted are one-way fares for a single adult on foot/up to five adults with a car.

Britain

Numerous services operate from ports in England, Scotland, Wales and the Isle of Man to the Republic and the North. It's wise to plan ahead because fares vary consider-

FERRY ROUTES

ably, depending on the season, time of day, day of the week and length of stay. Some return fares aren't much more than one-way fares. Companies also provide special deals that it's worth keeping an eye out for and offer reductions to ISIC cardholders and Hostelling International (HI) members.

Following is a list of shipping lines.

Irish Ferries
   (☎ 0870 5171717)
   3rd Floor, 35 Dover St, London W1X 3RA
   Web site: www.irishferries.ie
   For services from Holyhead to Dublin, and Pembroke to Rosslare
Isle of Man Steam Packet and SeaCat Services
   (☎ 0870 5523523)
   Room 323, 3rd Floor, India Buildings, Water St, Liverpool L2 0QN
   Web site: www.steam-packet.com
   For catamaran services from Douglas (Isle of Man) to Belfast and Dublin, Liverpool to Dublin, and Heysham, Stranraer and Troon to Belfast
Norse Irish Ferries
   (☎ 0151-944 1010)
   North Brocklebank Dock, Bootle, Merseyside L20 1BY
   Web site: www.norse-irish-ferries.co.uk
   For services from Liverpool to Belfast
P&O European Ferries
   (☎ 0870 2424777)
   Cairnryan, Wigtownshire DG9 8RF
   Web site: www.poef.com
   For services from Cairnryan to Larne
Stena Line
   (☎ 0870 5707070)
   Charter House, Park St, Ashford, Kent TN24 8EX
   Web site: www.stenaline.com
   For services from Holyhead to Dublin and Dun Laoghaire, Fishguard to Rosslare, and Stranraer to Belfast
Swansea Cork Ferries
   (☎ 01792-456116)
   Ferryport, Kings Dock, Swansea, West Glamorgan SA1 1SF
   Web site: www.commerce.ie/cs/scf
   For services from Swansea to Cork

To/From the Republic of Ireland The main routes from Britain to the Republic are:

Fishguard and Pembroke to Rosslare These popular short ferry crossings take 3½ hours (from Fishguard) or 4½ hours (from Pembroke) and cost around UK£20/185 at the weekend during peak season; at other times of year the cost drops to as low as around UK£20/70. The high-speed catamaran crossing from Fishguard takes just over 1½ hours and costs around UK£40/230 at the weekend during peak season.

Holyhead to Dublin and Dun Laoghaire The ferry crossing takes 3½ hours and costs around UK£20/210 at the weekend during peak season. The high-speed catamaran crossing from Holyhead to Dun Laoghaire takes a little over 1½ hours and costs UK£35/250 at the weekend in peak season.

Liverpool to Dublin The catamaran service takes four hours and costs around UK£40/260 at peak times.

Swansea to Cork The 10-hour crossing costs around UK£30/180 at peak times. The ferry doesn't operate in February.

To/From Northern Ireland The main routes from Britain to the North are:

Liverpool to Belfast The trip costs around UK£50/265 on overnight ferries at peak times.

Stranraer to Belfast The SeaCat service races across in just 1½ hours at a cost of around UK£40/220 at peak times. Stena Line also offers a catamaran and ferry service on this route.

Cairnryan to Larne This service takes 2¼ hours on the ferry or one hour on the jetliner and costs UK£25/200 at peak times on the ferry and UK£25/210 on the jetliner.

France

Irish Ferries (☎ 029-861 1717 in Roscoff, 023-323 4444 in Cherbourg, 01-855 2222 in Ireland) operates a service from Roscoff in Brittany to Rosslare during the summer. It takes 16 hours and costs upwards of 360/1000FF. The service from Cherbourg in Normandy to Rosslare runs year round and takes 19 hours but the cost is about the same. InterRail and Eurail passes give reductions on these routes.

From April to August, Britanny Ferries (☎ 021-427 7801 in Ireland, 029-829 2800 in France), 42 Grand Parade, Cork Town, operates a service to Roscoff (14 hours) costing around 570/1710FF.

euro currency converter IR£1 = €1.27

LAND & SEA

The low air fares from Britain make taking the bus or train hardly worth the hassle. On Bus Éireann there are frequent delays, and the train, unless you go from London, often involves horrific connections and hanging around in the dead of night.

Bus Éireann and National Express operate Eurolines services direct from London and other UK centres to Dublin, Belfast and other cities in Ireland. For details in London contact Eurolines (☎ 0870 514 3219), 52 Grosvenor Gardens, Victoria, London SW1W 0AU, or National Express (☎ 0870 580 8080), Victoria Coach Station, Buckingham Palace Rd, London SW1W. Slattery's (☎ 020-7485 1438, email ireland@slatterys.com), 162 Kentish Town Rd, London NW5, is an Irish bus company with routes from Bristol, Leeds, London, Liverpool, Manchester and northern Wales to Dublin, Galway, Limerick, Tipperary, Tralee, Waterford, Ennis and Listowel. It also has an office at Victoria Coach Station for personal callers only. With Bus Éireann, London to Dublin takes about 12 hours and costs around UK£30 to UK£40 return. Bristol to Dublin with Slattery's costs around UK£40 return. London to Belfast via Birmingham and Stranraer takes about 12 hours and costs about UK£50 to UK£60 return.

It's also possible to combine a train and ferry ticket. London to Dublin takes 9½ hours and costs UK£75 return (or UK£65 if you do the overnight crossing) at peak times.

ORGANISED TOURS

Scores of companies offer general- or special-interest tours of Ireland. See your travel agency, check the small ads in newspaper travel pages or contact Bord Fáilte (Irish Tourist Board) and the Northern Ireland Tourist Board (or the British Tourist Authority) for the names of tour operators. (See Tourist Offices in the Facts for the Visitor chapter for contact details of the tourist boards.)

In the USA there are a number of companies offering whirlwind coach tours of Ireland. American Express Vacations (☎ 1800 4466234), Box 1525, Fort Lauderdale, Florida 33302, offers nine-day packages costing US$799. Their Web site is at travel.americanexpress.com/travel. Similar deals can be found with TWA Getaway Vacations (☎ 1800 4382929, fax 1609-985 4125), 28 South 6th St, Philadelphia, Pennsylvania 19106. Have a look at their Web site at www.twa.com/getaway.

More-expensive tours are operated by Abercrombie & Kent International (☎ 1800 3237308, 708-954 2944), Suite 12, 1520 Kensington Rd, Oak Brook, Illinois 60521. Their prices include accommodation in castles and country houses. The company also organises activity-based tours or will help you prepare your own personal tour programme. Their Web site can be found at www.aandktours.com.

From Britain, CIE Tours International (☎ 0870 514 3910, fax 0870 514 3972), 183-185 London Rd, Croydon, London CR0 2RJ, offers a variety of five-day to 14-day coach tours, two of which include the North. Have a look at the Web site at www.cietours.com.

Many of the bus, ferry and airline companies mentioned earlier also offer tour and accommodation packages.

Getting Around

On the map, travelling around Ireland looks simple enough – the distances are short and there's a network of roads and railways – but in practice there are a few problems. In Ireland, from A to B is never a straight line: local towns or villages may not be connected by public transport and there are always a great many intriguing diversions to make. Public transport can be expensive (particularly train services), infrequent or both – and simply doesn't reach many of the interesting places. So having your own transport can be a major advantage and it's worth considering car rental for at least part of your trip. However, the proliferation of cars on the roads, the narrow streets in towns and villages and poor roadsigns in some places create their own difficulties.

Even if you're not driving, with a mix of buses, the occasional taxi, plenty of time, walking and sometimes hiring a bicycle, you can get to just about anywhere.

AIR

Ireland's size makes domestic flying unnecessary, but there are flights between Dublin and Cork, Donegal, Galway, Kerry, Shannon and Sligo. There are also flights between Belfast and Cork and Shannon. Most flights within Ireland take 30 to 40 minutes.

Aer Rianta, the Republic's main airport authority (with responsibility for Dublin, Cork and Shannon Airports) publishes a guide to airport services and flight schedules. Its head office (☎ 01-844 4900) is at Dublin Airport. Its Web site can be found at www.aer-rianta.ie.

As well as handling international flights, Aer Lingus is the main domestic airline. Aer Lingus' head office is at Dublin Airport and it has ticket offices in Dublin, Cork, Belfast and Shannon. For information and bookings call ☎ 01-886 8888 between 7.30 am and 9.30 pm; for flight information call ☎ 01-705 6705. Its Web site is at www.aerlingus.ie.

Another useful air service is the short flight across to the Aran Islands with Aer Árann (☎ 091-593034). See Getting There & Away in the Aran Islands section of the Galway chapter for details of fares and times.

BUS

Bus Éireann (☎ 01-836 6111, email buse@ cie.iol.ie), Busáras, Store St, Dublin 1, is the Republic's bus line, with services throughout the South and to the North. Its Web site can be found at www.info point.ie/buse.

All services are nonsmoking. Fares aren't much more than one-third of the regular train fares, and special deals are often available, for example cheaper midweek return tickets (see the boxed text 'Ferry, Bus & Train Discount Deals' later in this chapter). In winter the bus schedules are often drastically reduced and many routes simply disappear after September. The national timetable (IR£1) is very useful but doesn't list fares.

Private buses compete with Bus Éireann in the Republic and sometimes run where the national buses are irregular or absent. The larger companies usually carry bikes free but you should always check in advance. Most private companies are properly licensed and all passengers are insured, but if this is going to worry you then ask beforehand.

Ulsterbus (☎ 028-90 351201), Milewater Rd, Belfast BT3 9BG, is the service in the North. Call ☎ 028-90 333000 for timetable information 7.30 am to 8 pm Monday to Saturday, and 9 am to 7.30 pm on Sunday. For tickets call ☎ 028-90 320011. There are no private bus companies in the North (partly for fear of possible paramilitary extortion rackets).

Return fares are often the same as, or little more than, a one-way fare. Following are some sample one-way bus fares, travelling times, and their frequency from Monday to Saturday (services are fewer or nonexistent on Sunday):

Dublin to Belfast
   UK£10.50, three hours, seven daily
Dublin to Cork
   IR£12, three hours 30 minutes, five daily
Dublin to Donegal
   IR£10, four hours 15 minutes, five daily
Dublin to Rosslare Harbour
   IR£10, three hours, three daily
Dublin to Tralee
   IR£14, six hours, five daily
Dublin to Waterford
   IR£6, two hours 45 minutes, seven daily
Derry to Belfast
   UK£6.80, one hour 40 minutes, over 20 daily
Derry to Galway
   UK£14, six hours 30 minutes, three daily
Killarney to Cork
   IR£8.80, two hours, five daily
Killarney to Waterford
   IR£13, four hours 30 minutes, three daily

Local country buses can work out quite expensive, and services are usually infrequent. From Bantry in south-western Cork, for example, there's only one bus a week running the 26km journey to Kilcrohane, the last village on the Sheep's Head Peninsula, and the half-hour journey costs over IR£6. Private buses on major routes may be cheaper than Bus Éireann. In County Donegal, Feda Ódonaill buses, for example, charges less than IR£4 for any journey within the county; however, these journeys can be time-consuming.

TRAIN

Iarnród Éireann (Irish Rail; ☎ 01-836 3333), Connolly Station, Amiens St, Dublin 1, operates trains in the Republic on routes which fan out from Dublin. You can also make inquiries at Iarnród Travelcentre (☎ 01-836 6222), 35 Lower Abbey St, Dublin 1. Iarnród Éireann's Web site is at www.irishrail.ie. Although trains get you to the major urban centres faster than buses, the train system is not as extensive: there's no north to south route along the western coast, no network in Donegal, no direct connections from Waterford to Cork or Killarney, and the Dublin to Belfast route is the

only direct train link between North and South. Distances, however, are short: the longest trip you can make by train from Dublin is four hours 30 minutes to Tralee in County Kerry.

Regular one-way fares from Dublin include Belfast IR£14 (two hours 15 minutes, eight daily), Cork IR£32 (three hours 15 minutes, up to eight daily), Galway IR£15 (three hours, four daily) and Limerick IR£27 (two hours 15 minutes, up to 13 daily). Travelling by train on a one-way ticket is expensive, and it's worth considering how to use a return ticket; a midweek return ticket is often about the same as a one-way fare. A same-day return from Dublin to Belfast costs IR£13, a pound less than a one-way ticket! First-class tickets cost IR£4 to IR£8 more than the standard fare for a single journey.

Northern Ireland Railways (NIR; ☎ 028-90 899411), Belfast Central Station, East Bridge St, Belfast BT1 3PB, runs four routes from Belfast. One links with the system in the South via Newry to Dublin; the other three go east to Bangor, north-east to Larne and north-west to Derry/Londonderry via Coleraine.

As with buses, special fares are often available (for more information see the boxed text 'Ferry, Bus & Train Discount Deals' later in this chapter).

CAR & MOTORCYCLE

Ireland's new-found affluence means there are far more cars on the road than ever before, putting a strain on the country's national road system. The building of new roads and the upgrading of existing ones just cannot keep pace. Be prepared for delays, especially in popular tourist towns or busy commercial ones. Unfortunately, there has also been a jump in the number of road accidents, testing the once lenient attitude of authorities to speeding and drink driving.

Although Ireland is gradually shifting to the metric system, the imperial system is still widely used. In the Republic, speed limits are usually shown in miles per hour, though in some areas they are in kilo-

TRAIN ROUTES

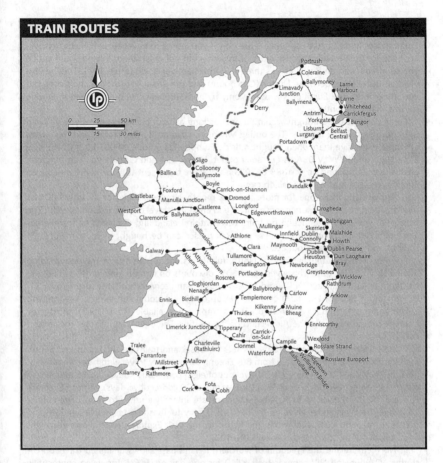

metres, and most car speedometers are in miles. The older white roadsigns give distances in miles, but the newer white ones and the green ones use kilometres. In the North, speed-limit and distance signs are in miles.

On minor roads be prepared for potholes, especially in the South.

Petrol is a few pence cheaper in the South than in the North. Unleaded petrol is available throughout the North and South. Most service stations accept payment by credit card, but some small, remote ones may take cash only.

Road Rules

A copy of the road rules is available from tourist offices . Driving in the Republic and the North is on the left and you should overtake only on the outside (to the right) of the vehicle ahead of you. Safety belts must be worn by the driver and all passengers. Children aged under 12 aren't allowed to sit on the front seats. Motorcyclists and their passengers must wear helmets.

When entering a roundabout, give way to approaching traffic already on the roundabout.

Ferry, Bus & Train Discount Deals

Eurail passes (which make economic sense only if you intend to travel outside Ireland as well) are valid for train travel in the Republic of Ireland – but not in Northern Ireland – and entitle you to a reduction on Bus Éireann's three-day Irish Rambler ticket (see below). They're also valid on Irish Ferries between France (Cherbourg) and the Republic (Rosslare and Cork), but you must book. The Eurail pass is usable only by non-Europeans who have been in Europe for less than six months.

Eurail passes can be bought within Europe, as long as your passport proves you've been there for less than six months. The outlets where you can do this are limited and the passes are more expensive than when bought outside Europe. Rail Europe (☎ 0870 5848848), 179 Piccadilly, London W1V 0BA, is one such outlet. In the USA and Canada you can purchase passes over the phone on ☎ 1888 6679734 and have them sent to your home by courier. Eurail's Web site is at www.eurail.on.ca.

If you've been in Europe for more than six months you're eligible for an **InterRail** pass (which, again, makes economic sense only if you intend to travel outside Ireland as well). The pass gives you a 50% reduction on train travel within Ireland and discounts on Irish Ferries and Stena Sealink connecting ferries. InterRail passes can be bought at most major train stations and student travel outlets.

For IR£8 in the South, UK£6 in the North, full-time students can have a **Travelsave** stamp affixed to their ISIC card. This gives up to 60% discounts on Iarnród Éireann (Irish Rail) and Northern Ireland Railways (NIR), and 15% on Bus Éireann services for fares costing over £1. Holders of an EYC (or Euro<26) card can get up to 50% discounts on Iarnród Éireann with a **Fairstamp** attached to their card. The stamps are available from USIT offices (see Student & Youth Fares in the Air section of the Getting There & Away chapter for contact details).

There's a variety of unlimited-travel tickets for buses and trains, in the North and South. **Irish Rambler** tickets are available from Bus Éireann for bus-only travel within the Republic of Ireland. They cost IR£28 (three days' travel out of eight consecutive days), IR£68 (eight days out of 15 consecutive days) or IR£98 (15 days out of 30 consecutive days). Iarnród Éireann's **Faircard** (IR£8.50) gives up to 50% reductions on any intercity journey to people aged under 26, while the **Weekender** gives up to 30% off (Friday to Tuesday) to people aged 26 and over. For train and bus travel within the Republic, the **Irish Explorer** ticket allows you eight days' travel out of 15 consecutive days (IR£100).

In Northern Ireland the **Freedom of Northern Ireland** pass allows unlimited travel on Ulsterbus, Citybus and NIR services for UK£10 for one day or UK£35 for seven consecutive days.

The **Irish Rover** ticket combines services on Bus Éireann and Ulsterbus. This costs IR£36 for three days, IR£85 for eight days and IR£130 for 15 days. The **Emerald Card** gives you unlimited travel throughout Ireland on all scheduled services of Iarnród Éireann, NIR, Bus Éireann, Dublinbus, Ulsterbus and Citybus. The card costs IR£115 for eight days or IR£200 for 15 days.

Children aged under 16 pay half-price for all these passes and for all normal tickets. Children aged under three travel for free on public transport.

You can buy the above passes after you arrive in Ireland at most major train/bus stations. Although they're good value, many of them make economic sense only if you're planning to travel around Ireland at the speed of light.

Road Distances (km)

	Athlone	Belfast	Cork	Derry	Donegal	Dublin	Galway	Kilkenny	Killarney	Limerick	Rosslare Harbour	Shannon Airport	Sligo	Waterford	Wexford
Athlone	---														
Belfast	227	---													
Cork	219	424	---												
Derry	209	117	428	---											
Donegal	183	180	402	69	---										
Dublin	127	167	256	237	233	---									
Galway	93	306	209	272	204	212	---								
Kilkenny	116	284	148	335	309	114	172	---							
Killarney	232	436	87	441	407	304	193	198	---						
Limerick	121	323	105	328	296	193	104	113	111	---					
Rosslare Harbour	201	330	208	397	391	153	274	98	275	211	---				
Shannon Airport	133	346	128	351	282	218	93	135	135	25	234	---			
Sligo	117	206	336	135	66	214	138	245	343	232	325	218	---		
Waterford	164	333	126	383	357	163	220	48	193	129	82	152	293	---	
Wexford	184	309	187	378	372	135	253	80	254	190	19	213	307	61	---

Speed limits in the North and South are generally the same as in Great Britain: 70mph (112km/h) on motorways, 60mph (96km/h) on other roads, and 30mph (48km/h) or as signposted in towns.

Never drink alcohol if you're planning to drive. Apart from the potential injury and loss of life, stiff fines, jail or other penalties could be incurred if you're caught driving under the influence. In the South the legal limit is 80mg of alcohol per 100ml of blood; in the North it's 35mg/100ml.

Traffic offences (illegal parking, speeding etc) usually incur a fine which you're normally allowed 30 days to pay.

On Ireland's major roads it's a common, but illegal, practice for vehicles to move over to the hard shoulder to allow overtaking (ie speeding) vehicles to pass. On the quiet, narrow, winding rural roads it's advisable to stick to the speed limit, partly because of the danger of head-on collisions and partly because there may be a person walking or an animal grazing beside the road just round the next bend.

Parking

Double yellow lines painted on the kerb-stones usually mean no parking at any time, and single (or broken) yellow lines warn of restrictions on parking times. The only way to establish the exact restrictions is to find the nearby sign that spells them out. Some cities also have red lines, which mean no stopping or parking. In Northern Ireland, kerbstones painted red, white and blue mean you're in a Loyalist area; green, white and orange mean it's Republican.

There are parking meters in Dublin, Belfast and some other cities. Usually parking in car parks or other specified areas is regulated by 'pay and display' tickets or disc parking (you have a disc, available from newsagents, which rotates to display the time you park your car).

In the North, some town centres have Control Zones (though these are gradually being withdrawn), where, for security reasons, cars absolutely must not be left unattended. Again for security reasons, you can be fined for not locking your car.

When parking your car never leave valuables unattended or visible, especially in Dublin (see Dangers & Annoyances in the Dublin chapter for further parking warnings).

Road Signs

When you're travelling around Ireland, particularly the South, you'll need a good road map because, as you'll soon come to realise, roadsigns have to be treated with a certain amount of healthy scepticism – particularly once you get off the motorways and main highways into more remote areas.

In the South there are three main kinds of roadsigns. Those with white lettering on a green background are found on all major routes, with distances given clearly in kilometres. Brown signs with white lettering are used to indicate local tourist offices, sights, accommodation and other facilities. Black-on-white signs are the most problematic for visitors – the older ones give distances in miles, while the newer ones give distances in kilometres; you can usually tell which is which because the newer ones have 'km' after the number, while the older ones just have the number.

Sometimes you'll see a sign for your destination, then, as you travel farther, you'll see signs to other places at road junctions, but not to where you want to go. At some road junctions there may be no sign at all. This is when a good map comes in handy. Assuming you've gone in the right direction, you could arrive at your destination without having seen another sign for it.

Occasionally, when you do find a sign, it could be pointing the wrong way. This is sometimes the work of pranksters, but another explanation is that these signposts are so close to the road that heavy vehicles have hit them as they passed and twisted them round.

Rental

Car rental in Ireland is expensive, so you're often better off making arrangements in your home country with some sort of package deal. In July and August it's wise to book well ahead.

In the Republic typical weekly high-season rental rates with collision-damage waiver (CDW), insurance, value-added tax (VAT) and unlimited distance are around IR£290 for a small car (Ford Fiesta), IR£350 for a medium-sized car (Nissan Almera) and IR£390 for a larger car (Ford Mondeo). In the North, similar cars cost about 10% more. Check that the attractive-looking posted price includes insurance (eg for car theft, windscreen damage), CDW and VAT. If you're travelling from the Republic into Northern Ireland it's important to be sure that your insurance covers journeys to the North. Most cars are manual; automatic ones are available but they're more expensive to hire. There are often special deals and the longer you hire, the lower the relative daily rent. From October to May some companies discount all rates.

People aged under 21 aren't allowed to hire a car; for the majority of rental companies you have to be aged at least 23 and to have had a valid driving licence for a minimum of two years. Your home-country licence is usually enough to hire a car for three months (see Driving Licence & Permit in the Visas & Documents section of the Facts for the Visitor chapter for more information). Some companies won't rent to you if you're aged 70 or over. Conditions for renting a car in the North are similar to those in the South.

The international rental companies Avis, Budget, Hertz and Thrifty, and the major local operators, Argus, Murray's Europcar and Dan Dooley, have offices all over Ireland. There are many smaller, local operators which often offer lower rates than the major companies.

Motorbikes and mopeds are not available for rent.

Automobile Clubs

The Automobile Association (AA) has offices in Belfast (☎ 0870 544 8666 within

Northern Ireland), Dublin (☎ 01-677 9481) and Cork (☎ 021-450 5155). The AA breakdown number in the Republic is ☎ 1800 667788; in the North it's ☎ 0800 887766. In the North, members of the Royal Automobile Club (RAC) can call ☎ 0870 5722722 for information; its breakdown number is ☎ 0800 828282.

WALKING & CYCLING

Walking and cycling are two popular, rewarding ways to explore Ireland, both South and North. For information see the earlier Activities chapter.

HITCHING

Lonely Planet doesn't recommend hitching. It's never entirely safe in any country: the local nutter doesn't carry an identifying badge. Travellers who decide to hitch should understand that they are taking a small but potentially serious risk. People who choose to hitch are safer if they travel in pairs and let someone know where they're planning to go. Women hitching on their own should be extremely careful when choosing lifts – if in doubt, don't. Many local women hitch alone without serious problems, but a tourist is likely to be more at risk.

That said, hitching in Ireland is generally easy. The major exceptions are heavily touristed areas, where the competition from other hitchers is severe and cars are often full with families. In the Republic there are usually large numbers of Irish hitchhikers on the road who use hitching as an everyday means of travel.

The usual hitching rules apply. Carry cardboard and a marker pen so you can make a sign showing where you're going. Try to look like a visitor and put your backpack out on view, ideally with a flag on it. Making yourself an obvious tourist is especially important in the North, and if the subject of the Troubles comes up in conversation it's probably best to exercise a bit of diplomatic caution. Cross-border roads are open and hitching between the Republic and the North presents few, if any, problems.

BOAT

There are many boat services to islands lying off the coast, including to the Aran and Skellig Islands to the west, the Saltee Islands to the south-east, and Tory and Rathlin Islands to the north. Ferries also operate across rivers, inlets and loughs. Some services make useful short cuts, particularly for cyclists. These are the ferry across the River Suir from Ballyhack (County Wexford) to Passage East (County Waterford); from Carrigaloe, near Cobh, to Passage West east of Cork town (both in County Cork); across the Shannon Estuary from Killimer (County Clare) to Tarbert (County Kerry); and in County Down from Strangford across to Portaferry on the Ards Peninsula.

The only ferry between the Republic and the North is the limited service across Carlingford Lough from Omeath on the Cooley Peninsula (County Louth) to Warrenpoint (County Down).

Cruises are very popular on the 258km-long Shannon-Erne Waterway – combining rivers, lakes and canals – from County Leitrim to Lough Erne in Northern Ireland. There are also a variety of cruises on other lakes and loughs.

If you ask at tourist offices about boat trips you won't always get the full information, because the offices don't recommend, or even mention, operators who aren't registered with them. Various boats from Portmagee, Ballinskelligs or Derrynane to the Skellig Islands off the Kerry coast, for instance, don't exist as far as official tourist literature is concerned. Details of non-tourist-board-affiliated boat trips are given under the relevant sections throughout this book.

LOCAL TRANSPORT

There are comprehensive local bus networks in Dublin (Bus Átha Cliath), Belfast (Citybus) and some other larger towns. The Dublin Area Rapid Transport (DART) line in Dublin is the only local train line. A new light rail system is planned to begin operating in Dublin in the winter of 2002.

Taxis in Ireland tend to be expensive.

There are metered taxis in Belfast, Cork, Dublin, Galway and Limerick, but in other places you'll need to agree on the fare beforehand. If you book a taxi by telephone there may be a small pick-up charge. In Belfast and Derry there are share-taxi services operating rather like buses.

See Getting Around in specific chapters for more information.

ORGANISED TOURS

If your time is limited it might be worth considering an organised tour, though it's cheaper to see things independently and Ireland is small enough for you to get to even the most remote places in a few hours. Tours can be booked through travel agencies, tourist offices in the major cities, or directly through the tour companies themselves.

CIE Tours International (☎ 01-703 1888), 35 Lower Abbey St, Dublin 1, runs coach tours of the South and North departing from Dublin. The tours include accommodation, breakfast and dinner. There are discounts for those aged 55 and over. Its five-day Taste of Ireland tour takes in Blarney, the Ring of Kerry, Killarney, the Cliffs of Moher and the region around the River Shannon (IR£373 in the high season). Its other coach tours are from four to 10 days in length. It can also arrange self-drive holidays with pre-booked accommodation.

March to September, Bus Éireann (☎ 01-836 6111), 59 Upper O'Connell St, Dublin, runs day tours to various parts of the South and the North, departing from Dublin's Busáras. Its six-hour trip to Glendalough in Wicklow costs IR£14/7.

Ulsterbus Tours (☎ 028-90 337004) runs a large number of day trips throughout the North. Call for information and bookings or visit the Ulsterbus Travel Centre (open 8.45 am to 5.25 pm on weekdays, 9 am to noon on Saturday) in the Europa Bus Centre, Glengall St, Belfast.

Gray Line Tours (☎ 01-605 7705 in Dublin, ☎ 061-431088 in Limerick) offers half-day, day and extended trips departing from Dublin and Limerick which can be booked through the tourist offices in those cities.

Over the Top and Into the West Tours (☎ 01-838 6128, email info@irishbustours.com) offers minibus budget tours with accommodation in hostels. Its three-day Into the West tour takes in Connemara, the Burren and the Cliffs of Moher for IR£72. Buses leave from outside the tourist office in Dublin. Have a look at the Web site at www.irishbustours.com.

Tir na nÓg (Land of Eternal Youth; ☎ 01-836 4684, fax 836 4710, email tnn@indigo.ie), 57 Lower Gardiner St, Dublin 1, offers three- to six-day backpacker tours to the west and north of Ireland costing upwards of IR£89. Buses take no more than 20 people and fill up fast, so book ahead. Overnights are spent at IHH hostels along the way.

For train enthusiasts, Railtours Ireland (☎ 01-856 0045), 58 Lower Gardiner St, Dublin 1, organises a series of one- and two-day train trips in association with Iarnród Éireann, sometimes combining with coach transport. A day trip from Dublin to Cork, Blarney Castle and Killarney costs IR£59.

See also Organised Walks in the Walking section, and Cycling, both in the Activities chapter.

THE REPUBLIC
OF IRELAND

EOIN CLARKE

The Republic of Ireland

HISTORY
The Irish Free State
The Irish Free State, as it was known until 1949, was established after the signing in December 1921 of the Anglo-Irish Treaty by the British government and an Irish delegation led by Michael Collins. Eamon de Valera had been elected president of the new self-proclaimed republic in August, but he remained in Dublin during negotiations. He wasn't consulted before the signing and was outraged when the delegates returned with what he and many other republicans regarded as a betrayal of the IRA's principles. The treaty was ratified in the Dáil (Irish assembly or lower house) in January 1922. In June the country's first general election resulted in victory for the pro-treaty forces. Fighting broke out two weeks later.

Amazingly, the Civil War was primarily about the oath of allegiance to the Crown, rather than the exclusion of the six counties from the Irish Free State. Of the 400 or more pages of Dáil records on the treaty debate, only seven deal with the issue of Ulster.

During the war Collins was ambushed and shot dead in Cork by anti-treaty forces, and de Valera was imprisoned by the new Free State government, under Prime Minister William Cosgrave, which went so far as to execute 77 of its former comrades. The Civil War ground to an exhausted halt in 1923.

After boycotting the Dáil for a number of years, de Valera founded a new party, called Fianna Fáil (Warriors of Ireland), which won nearly half the seats in the 1927 election. De Valera and the other new teachta Dála (TDs, 'members of the Dáil') managed within weeks to enter the Dáil by the simple expedient of not taking the oath of allegiance to the Crown but signing in as if they had.

Fianna Fáil won a majority in the 1932 election and remained in power for 16 years. De Valera introduced a new constitution in 1937, doing away with the oath and claiming sovereignty over the six counties of the North. In 1938 the UK renounced its right to use certain Irish ports for military purposes, which it had been granted under the treaty. The South was therefore able to remain neutral in WWII. De Valera refused to pay land annuities, which had been agreed upon in the Anglo-Irish Treaty, to the British government. An economic war with Britain ensued, severely crippling Irish agriculture and resolving only shortly before the 1948 general election.

The Republic
Fianna Fáil lost the 1948 general election to Fine Gael – the direct descendants of the first Free State government – in coalition with the new republican Clann an Poblachta. The new government declared the Free State to be a republic at last. Ireland left the British Commonwealth in 1949. In 1955 it became a member of the United Nations.

When Sean Lamass came to power in 1959, as successor to de Valera, he sought to stem the continuing serious emigration by improving the country's economic prospects. By the mid-1960s his policies had been successful enough to reduce emigration to less than half what it had been in the mid-1950s, and many who had left began to return. He also introduced free secondary education.

In 1972 the Republic (along with Northern Ireland) became a member of the European Economic Community (EEC). At first, membership brought some measure of prosperity, but by the early 1980s Ireland was once more in economic difficulties and emigration rose again. By the early 1990s the Irish economy had begun to recover and is now one of the strongest in Europe.

The results of referenda in the 1980s on abortion and divorce left both illegal, but in another referendum on divorce in 1995 it was narrowly accepted, making Ireland the last nation in Europe to legalise it. While single mothers might still have a tough time in remote rural areas, in Dublin they're almost as commonplace as in London and no-one bats an eyelid.

Although the president's power is limited, the election of Mary Robinson to the presidency in 1990 saw her start to wield considerable informal influence over social policies, contributing to a shift away from the traditionally conservative attitudes on issues such as divorce, abortion and gay rights. She was succeeded in 1997 by Mary McAleese from Belfast.

In 1994 Taoiseach (Prime Minister) Albert Reynolds, who had helped negotiate the first IRA ceasefire with Gerry Adams, was forced to resign. His resignation mainly resulted from the appointment of a president to the High Court, Harry Whelehan, who had been criticised for not tackling sexual scandals involving the Catholic Church more vigorously. Reynolds was succeeded by Fine Gael leader John Bruton, who came to power in coalition with the Labour Party and the Democratic Left. Bruton's government was the first to take office without a general election.

When it did face one in 1997 it was ousted by Fianna Fáil under Bertie Ahern, in partnership with the Progressive Democrats and a number of independents. Mary Harney became Ireland's first female tánaiste (deputy prime minister).

Bertie Ahern's government has been closely involved in the peace-making process in Northern Ireland. Among other

Ireland's Female Presidents

The 7th of November 1990 was a red-letter day for Irish women: Mary Robinson, a barrister associated with all sorts of liberal causes (including the rights of single mothers, gays, Travellers and students) was elected president of Ireland.

She had studied at Trinity College, Dublin, and at Harvard University in the USA, later becoming a barrister and Trinity's youngest professor of law. She was elected to the Senate in 1969.

Once appointed to the presidency, Robinson modernised the institution, raising its profile in a relentless tour of the country – there's hardly a tourist attraction in Ireland that doesn't boast a plaque commemorating her visit. Almost single-handedly Robinson dispelled old ideas of a backward Ireland dominated by a reactionary Church that kept women tied to the home. In 1997 she was appointed the United Nations high commissioner for human rights.

Her presidency helped pave the way for her successor, Mary McAleese, a Belfast-born Catholic nationalist and Queen's University law lecturer. Although more conservative than Mary Robinson, she was elected on a platform of continuing Robinson's work and has shown a similarly tolerant attitude to her predecessor's on social issues. This was illustrated in 1999 by her high-profile visit to Outhouse, a gay, lesbian and transgender community centre in southern Dublin.

NICKY CAVEN

Mary Robinson has championed the rights of women, gay people and Travellers.

The Abortion Debate

The issue of abortion continues to tie Ireland in knots.

Prior to 1983, therapeutic abortions were legal, and doctors could use their discretion as to whether or not a pregnancy was 'life-threatening' for the woman. Abortion for any other reason, including severe malformation or pregnancy due to rape, was, and still is, not permitted.

In 1983, the law was tightened and incorporated into the constitution, but in such woolly terms that things went on much as before, with one remarkable exception: women could no longer be given information about seeking abortions abroad. British phone books were duly taken out of libraries, and British women's magazines were impounded or censored at the airports.

While trips to British abortion clinics continued unabated, Ireland held the moral high ground of protecting the unborn child at any cost – until 1992, when parents whose 14-year-old daughter had allegedly been raped by her friend's father took her to England for an abortion. When they contacted the gardai to ask if tissue from the foetus could be collected and used in the prosecution of the alleged rapist they were issued with an injunction ordering them to bring the girl back, foetus intact, or face prosecution. All hell broke loose. The matter went to the High Court, which fudged the issue by saying that the girl could travel to the UK for an abortion since she was suicidal.

Anti-abortion campaigners demanded that the High Court prevent women leaving the country to seek abortions abroad, opening up the prospect of pregnancy tests at airports. Others interpreted the High Court ruling to mean that abortion had become legal if the woman was suicidal.

A referendum on the issue took place in 1992. A clear majority supported the right to travel abroad for an abortion, but the option of making abortion available to all women in Ireland wasn't offered.

Abortion is still illegal, but in 1995 a new law allowed doctors and pregnancy counselling services to give a pregnant woman the names and phone numbers of British abortion clinics, and Irish women who travel to Britain for an abortion do so without fear of any legal reprisals. However, Irish doctors and clinics are barred from making appointments or arrangements in Britain for their patients.

The contentious issue of abortion continues to be debated. Former President Mary Robinson has argued for it to be legalised, while pro-life activist groups such as Youth Defence have organised rallies against it. As Tánaiste (Deputy Prime Minister) Mary Harney once pointed out, although abortion is illegal in Ireland, an Irish woman is more likely to have an abortion than a woman in the Netherlands, where it's freely available.

things the 1998 Good Friday Agreement (see the History section of the introduction to Northern Ireland) made provision for a North-South Ministerial Council, of which the Irish government would be a part, to deal with issues affecting the whole island. Another outcome of the search for a settlement in the North has been improved relations between the Republic and Britain, symbolised by the invitation from Bertie Ahern to British Prime Minister Tony Blair to address the Dáil.

GOVERNMENT & POLITICS

The Republic has a parliamentary system of government loosely based on the British model. The Oireachtas (Parliament) has a lower house known as the Dáil (pronounced 'doyle'), which has 166 elected members who sit in Leinster House on Dublin's Kildare St. Dáil members are known as teachta Dála (TDs), the prime minister as taoiseach (roughly pronounced 'teashock'; the plural is taoisigh) and the deputy prime minister as tánaiste. The Dáil has a relatively high percentage of female members.

The upper house is the Senate, or Seanad, and senators are nominated by the taoiseach or elected by university graduates and councillors from around the country. The Senate's functions are limited – senators debate on and pass legislation framed in the Dáil – but many critics claim it is merely a happy hunting ground for failed TDs.

The country's constitutional head of state is the president (an tuachtaran), who is elected by popular vote for a seven-year term and resides in the Áras an Uachtaráin, in Phoenix Park, Dublin. The president has no executive power but does promulgate bills passed by Parliament, appoint the taoiseach (on nomination from the Dáil) and government ministers (on the advice of the taoiseach), and is head of the defence forces.

The national flag is the tricolour of green, white and orange, the national symbol is the harp and the national anthem is 'Amhrán na bhFiann' (The Soldier's Song).

The Republic's electoral system is proportional representation, a complex but fair system in which voters mark the electoral candidates in order of preference. As the first-preference votes are counted and candidates are elected, the voters' second and third choices are passed on to the various other candidates. Elections are held at least once every five years.

Political Parties

The two principal political parties are Fianna Fáil and Fine Gael, and third is the Labour Party.

Founded by Eamon de Valera and other notables, Fianna Fáil has been the driving force in Irish politics since the early years of the state. Fianna Fáil has normally won the greatest number of seats in general elections and has usually been either in government or barely out of it. It has always been a catch-all party, claiming to be the voice of the rural populace, urban workers and business community alike. Many of Ireland's most notable leaders have come from the party's ranks, including Eamon de

Valera, Sean Lemass, Jack Lynch and more recently the colourful and wily Charles Haughey and Albert Reynolds. The current party leader is Bertie Ahern. Fianna Fáil has in the past usually taken a conservative line on social matters, particularly when it came to divorce, abortion and contraception.

Founded in 1933, Fine Gael, led by John Bruton, is the second-largest party and promotes enterprise. Its image has been clean cut, worthy, middle class and university educated.

Both parties see 'inclusive political talks' as the way forwards in the Republic's relations with the North.

Labour has been on the fringes of power for most of its existence, but has shared in various coalition governments with Fine Gael. The Labour Party, led by Ruairí Quinn, occupies the middle ground and attracts support from all classes of voters.

In 1985 a split in Fianna Fáil resulted in the formation of the Progressive Democrats, which is now led by Mary Harney, currently the tánaiste. Ironically, its two periods of power have been in coalition with Fianna Fáil. The only other party of consequence is the left-wing Democratic Left, led by Proinsias de Rossa, which was part of John Bruton's coalition government.

Coalition has been a feature of most recent governments in the Republic, as the once mighty Fianna Fáil has found itself less able to muster the parliamentary majorities it used to command.

Unfortunately, Irish politics has a reputation for corruption, and it's not just disillusioned voters who say so. When he was ambassador to Ireland, former Israeli Prime Minister Benjamin Netanyahu declared that if Richard Nixon had been president of Ireland he would never have lost office the way he did. In the late 1990s, the Moriarty Tribunal, set up to inquire into payments to politicians, revealed that sformer Taoiseach Charles Haughey may have received as much as UK£2.5 million in cash gifts during his political career. But this was just one of a series of political, financial and judicial scandals that plagued the Ahern government and led to the passing of the Ethics in Public Office Act.

ECONOMY

Ireland is in the middle of the greatest economic boom since independence. Dubbed the Celtic Tiger (an allusion to the once successful 'tiger' economies of Asia), the economy is healthy in almost every capacity, from record low interest rates to a negligible rate of inflation.

This success has been attributed to a variety of factors, including: the intelligent spending of EU funds (of which Ireland has been one of the biggest beneficiaries); the successful promotion of foreign investment through generous tax incentives, which has seen Ireland at the forefront of a number of key industries (such as information technology and pharmaceuticals); the explosion of the tourism industry, which has seen record numbers of visitors in the last decade; the high quality of education; and a reversal in the age-old trend of emigration – since 1995 more people have moved to Ireland than left. Lastly, a new entrepreneurial class has emerged, consisting mostly of young graduates who have taken advantage of the favourable economic atmosphere to start up businesses, many of which have been very successful.

A striking feature of this boom is that the agricultural sector, which once dominated the economy, has had little to do with it. Yet it too is in a healthy state. Ireland has one of the most efficient agricultural industries in the world and the debt burden of Irish farmers is very low.

Doubts persist, however, about the solidity of the economy. Ireland may be in the middle of a boom-and-bust cycle. Some economists argue that Ireland's dependence on transnational corporations, attracted by low corporate tax offered as an incentive, results in a fragile economy at the mercy of world trends. As EU countries get ever closer economically, it seems likely that Europe-wide rules on corporate tax will come into force, eliminating the tax packages that brought those transnational companies to Ireland's shores. The crash of the Asian tiger economies in the late 1990s also serves as a warning of what could happen.

While many have benefited from the economic boom, and unemployment continues to fall, the gap between rich and poor has widened substantially. Property prices, particularly in Dublin, have rocketed, making it increasingly difficult for those with even a decent income to buy property or to rent. The country's wealth (the national income rose by 44% from 1994 to 1999) has yet to trickle down to many wage earners (wages are among the lowest in the EU) or the unemployed who live on inner-city housing estates where drugs and crime are endemic.

Dublin

☎ 01 • pop 952,692

Ireland's capital and its largest, most cosmopolitan city, Dublin is a place of great contrasts. Prosperous Georgian squares can quickly give way to blighted crime-and-drug-ridden housing estates where unemployment is high. Still one of the smallest European Union (EU) capitals, it's growing and modernising fast. In 1998, the city of Dublin was reckoned to be Europe's second-largest building site, after Berlin's Potsdamer Platz. It seems that everywhere you look in the city a new restaurant is opening, a new hotel is being built or a new block of flats has a 'For Sale' sign at the front.

The transformation of the city can be best observed in Temple Bar, which, once decayed and earmarked to be flattened to make way for a bus station, is now one of Dublin's main attractions. Tourism, once a steady trickle of interested visitors, is now proportional to that of any of Europe's most visited cities. In summer, you can hardly walk down Grafton St – Dublin's main drag – for the sheer number of visitors who've come to sample the city's delights.

Inevitably, such dramatic change has also had a negative impact. In its eagerness to capture a larger share of the tourist market, the 'dirty oul' town' of popular song has laid itself open to accusations of kowtowing to the almighty pound, dollar, franc and lira by offering lowest-common-denominator attractions to bring in the unquestioning visitor: this is the other side of areas such as Temple Bar, which, despite its incredible popularity, offers little more than a sanitised, neatly marketed package of the Dublin experience.

Yet Dublin still manages to remain a place with soul: the city's literary history seems to bump against you at every corner and the pubs are always full of life. An evening with a succession of pints of Guinness, that noble black brew, is as much a part of the Dublin experience as the

Highlights

- Take in a Dublin pub crawl
- Explore the Gomorrah that is Temple Bar
- Visit Trinity College and the *Book of Kells*
- See the treasures of the National Museum
- Get to the heart of Irish traditional music at Ceol and then go to a session
- Learn about the tragedy of Irish history in Kilmainham Jail
- Be amused by one man's folly – the Casino at Marino
- Find salvation in St Patrick's Cathedral
- Tour the corridors of power at Dublin Castle
- Taste the 'perfect Guinness' in the Guinness Hop Store

Georgian streets and the fine old buildings. Although there's little modern architecture of note, the city has maintained much of its Georgian character.

It's not only the pubs that are easily accessible. Dublin is a city on a human scale, so it's easy to get around on foot. Accommodation is varied, ranging from cheap and cheerful backpacker hostels to elegant five-star hotels. The food is also surprisingly varied and good, with dishes from every corner of the world as well as down-to-earth local specialities such as Irish stew or Dublin coddle.

Dublin is a curious, colourful place, an easy city to like and a fine introduction to Ireland.

HISTORY

Dublin celebrated its official millennium in 1988 but there were settlements here long before 988. The first early-Celtic habitation was on the banks of the River Liffey, giving rise to the city's Irish name, Baile Átha Cliath (Town of the Hurdle Ford), which comes from the ancient river crossing that can still be pinpointed today. St Patrick's Cathedral is said to be built on the site of a well used by Ireland's patron saint for conversions in the 5th century.

It wasn't until the Vikings turned up that Dublin became a permanent fixture. By the 9th century, raids from the north had become a fact of Irish life and some of the fierce Danes chose to stay rather than simply rape, pillage and depart. They intermarried with the Irish and established a vigorous trading port at the point where the River Poddle joined the Liffey in a black pool, in Irish a '*dubh linn*'. Today there's little trace of the Poddle, which has been channelled underground and flows under St Patrick's Cathedral to dribble into the Liffey by the Capel St (or Grattan) Bridge. Anglo-Norman and then early English Dublin were still centred on the black pool that gave the city its name.

The boom years came with the 18th century, the period of the Protestant Ascendancy, when, for a time, London was the only larger city in the British Empire. As the city expanded, the nouveaux riches abandoned medieval Dublin and moved north across the river to a new Dublin of stately squares surrounded by fine Georgian mansions. The planning of this magnificent Georgian Dublin was assisted by the establishment in 1757 of the Commission for Making Wide and Convenient Streets!

The city's slums soon spread north in pursuit of the rich, who turned back south to new homes in Merrion Square, Fitzwilliam Square and St Stephen's Green. In 1745 when James Fitzgerald, earl of Kildare, began building Leinster House, his magnificent mansion south of the Liffey, he was mocked for this foolish move away from the centre into the wilds. 'Where I go society will follow', he confidently predicted, and was soon proved right. Today Leinster House is home to the Irish Parliament and is right in the centre of modern Dublin.

The Georgian boom years were followed by more trouble and unrest, and the union with Britain in 1801, ending the separate Irish Parliament and returning power to London, spelled the end of Dublin's century of dramatic growth. Dublin entered the 20th century a downtrodden, dispirited place.

NICKY CAVEN

Dublin's coat of arms

The 1916 Easter Rising caused considerable damage to parts of central Dublin, particularly along O'Connell St, where the General Post Office (GPO) was gutted. The continuing struggle between British forces and the IRA led to more damage to Dublin, including the burning of the Custom House in 1921. A year later Ireland was independent, but then tumbled into the Civil War, which inflicted still more damage on the city, including the burning of the Four Courts in 1922 and a further bout of destruction for O'Connell St.

When peace finally came to Ireland, Dublin was exhausted – a shadow of its Georgian self. Until the 1970s it was a city in decay, but Ireland's becoming a member of what was then the European Economic Community (now the European Union) in 1972 held the prospect of better times to come. Today, Ireland's economic turnaround and cultural resurgence has completely transformed the city and gone a long way towards restoring its vitality.

Dublin's expansion has continued south to Dun Laoghaire and beyond, but the River Liffey remains a rough dividing line between southern 'haves' and northern 'have-nots', although that too is beginning to change as rising house prices lead to a gradual gentrification of the entire city centre.

ORIENTATION

Greater Dublin sprawls around the arc of Dublin Bay, bounded to the north by the hills at Howth and to the south by the Dalkey headland.

North of the River Liffey the important streets for visitors are O'Connell St and, just off it, Henry St, the major shopping thoroughfares. Most of the northside's B&Bs are on Gardiner St, which becomes rather rundown as it continues north. At the northern end of O'Connell St is Parnell Square. The main bus station, Busáras, and Connolly Station, one of the city's two main train stations, are near the southern end of Gardiner St.

Immediately south of the river, over O'Connell Bridge, is the Temple Bar area and the expanse of Trinity College. Nassau St, along the southern edge of the campus,

and pedestrianised Grafton St are the main shopping streets. At the southern end of Grafton St is St Stephen's Green. About 2km west, beside the river, is Heuston Station, the city's other main train station.

The postcodes for central Dublin are Dublin 1 immediately north of the river and Dublin 2 immediately south. The posh Ballsbridge area south-east of the centre is Dublin 4. A handy tip for postcodes is to remember that even numbers apply to the southside and odd ones to the north.

Unless stated otherwise, all places mentioned in this chapter are marked on the Dublin map.

Finding Addresses

Finding addresses in Dublin can be complicated by the tendency for street names to change every few blocks and for streets to be subdivided into upper and lower or north and south parts, which in some cases are on two different sides of the city. It doesn't seem to matter if you put the definer in front of or behind the name – thus you can have Lower Baggot St or Baggot St Lower, South Anne St or Anne St South. Street numbering often runs up one side of a street and down the other, rather than having odd numbers on one side and even on the other.

INFORMATION
Tourist Offices

Dublin Tourism is the official tourist-information office for Dublin and the surrounding area. If you arrive by air or sea, you'll find tourist offices at the airport and on the waterfront at Dun Laoghaire. In the city, Dublin Tourism (Around Temple Bar map; ☎ 1850 230330, 8 am to 11 pm on weekdays, and 8 am to 10 pm at the weekend) is in St Andrew's Church, 2 Suffolk St, near Trinity College. It opens 9 am to 6.30 pm Monday to Saturday, and 10.30 am to 2.30 pm on Sunday, July and August; and 9.30 am to 5.30 pm Monday to Saturday, and 10.30 am to 2.30 pm on bank holidays, the rest of the year. As well as information it provides accommodation and tour bookings, car rental and currency exchange facilities, a bookshop and café.

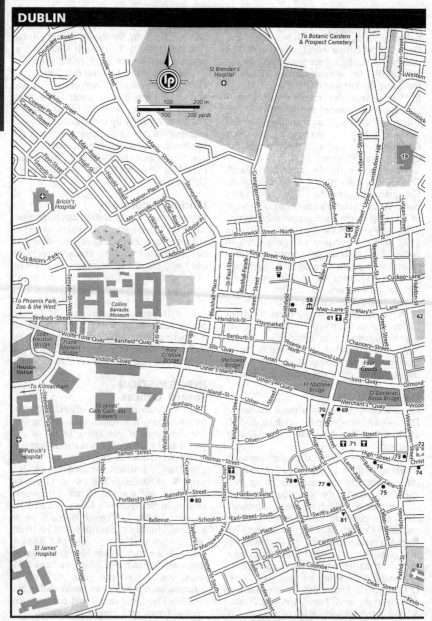

DUBLIN

To Botanic Gardens
& Prospect Cemetery

St Brendan's
Hospital

0   100   200 m
0   100   200 yards

Drumree—Road

Prussia—Street

Aughrin—Street

Cowper—Place

Carnew—Street

Ben—Edar—Road

Finn—Street

Niall—St

Swords—St

Harold—Road

Manor—Place

Mt—Temple—Road

Olaf—Road

Viking—Road

Arbour Pl

Arbour—Hill

Manor—Street

Stoneybatter

Grangegorman—Lower

Morning—star—Ave

Prebend—Street

Constitution—Hill

Church—Street—Upper

Lurgan—Street

Coleraine—St

Beresford—St

Cuckoo—Lane

Halston—St

Auburn—Street

Western

Dominick

19

Bricin's
Hospital

St—Bricin's—Park

20

Brunswick—Street—North

King—Street—North

St—Paul—Street

Blackhall—Parade

Blackhall—Place

Queen—Street

Bow—St

Smithfield

59

58

60

61   21

May—Lane

Mary's—Lane

Greek—St

Church—Street

62

To Phoenix Park,
Zoo & the West

Temple—St—West

Benburb—Street

Collins
Barracks
Museum

Wolfe—Tone—Quay

Liffey—St—W

Ellis—St

Barsfield—Quay

Hendrick—St

Haymarket

Benburb—St

Phoenix—St
North

Hammond—Lane

Chancery—Street

Four
Courts

Sean
Heuston
Bridge

Frank
Sherwin
Bridge

Rory
O'More
Bridge

Victoria—Quay

Ellis—Quay

Mellowes
Bridge

Arran   Quay

Inns—Quay

O'Donovan
Rossa Bridge

Ormond'

Wood

Heuston
Station

To Kilmainham

Steevens's—Lane

St James'
Gate Guinness
Brewery

Usher's—Island

Island—St

Bonham—St

Usher's—Quay

Bridgefoot—Street

Usher   Street

Fr Mathew
Bridge

Merchant's—Quay

70   69

St—Patrick's
Hospital

James'—Street

Echlin—St

Watling—Street

Crane—St

Thomas—Street

Oliver—Bond—Street

Thomas—Court

71   72

Cook—Street

Winetavern—Street

High—Street   J23

76

Christ

74

75

Augustine—Street

Cornmarket

79

78

77

Lamb—Alley

Francis—Street

Nicholas—St

Patrick—St

Portland—St—W

Rainsford—Street

80

Bellevue

School—St

Hanbury—Lane

Earl—Street—South

Vicar—Street

Catherine—Street

Meath—Street

Swift's—Alley

81

John—Dillon—Street

82

St James'
Hospital

Basin—St—Upper

Taylor's—La

Marrowbone—Ln

Summer—St—South

Portland—St

Meath—Place

Gray—Street

Carman—Hall—La

Pimlico—St

Ardee—Street

The—Coombe

Dean—Street

Kevin—

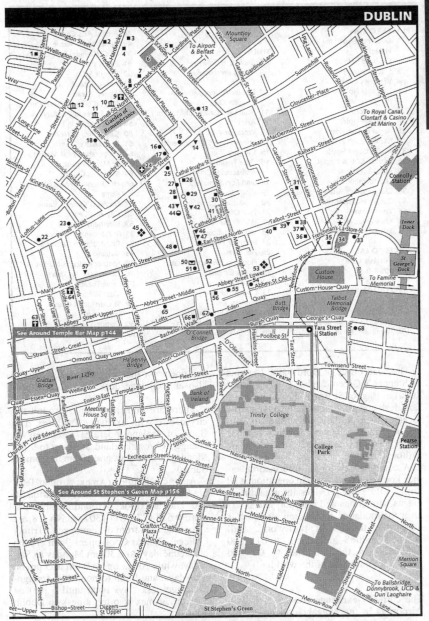

DUBLIN

PLACES TO STAY
1 Dublin International Youth Hostel
2 Caulfield's Hotel
3 Sinclair House
4 Waverley House
5 Dergvale Hotel
7 Barry's Hotel
8 Castle Hotel
26 Gresham Hotel
28 Royal Dublin Hotel
30 Marlborough Hostel
31 Maple Guest House
35 Isaac's Hotel & Hostel
36 Abraham House
37 The Townhouse
38 Globetrotter's Tourist Hostel
40 Cardijn House Hostel
56 Wynn's Hotel
66 Abbey Hostel
74 Jury's Christ Church Inn

PLACES TO EAT
14 Bangkok Café
39 101 Talbot
42 La Pizza
43 McDonald's
46 Beshoff's
47 Café Kylemore
57 Bewley's Oriental Café
70 The Brazen Head

81 Old Dublin

OTHER
6 Belvedere College
9 Abbey Presbyterian Church
10 Dublin Writers' Museum; Chapter One
11 Municipal Gallery of Modern Art
12 World of Wax
13 James Joyce Cultural Centre
15 Laundry Shop
16 Gate Theatre
17 Ambassador Cinema
18 Sinn Féin Bookshop
19 King's Inns
20 Arbour Hill Cemetery
21 Post Office
22 IMAX Cinema
23 Virgin Multiplex
24 Rotunda Hospital
25 Aer Lingus
27 Floozy in the Jacuzzi Statue
29 Savoy Cinema
32 Garda (Police)
33 Eblana Theatre
34 Busáras
41 St Mary's Pro-Cathedral
44 Dublin Bus; Bus Éireann
45 Ilac Centre

48 Project Arts Centre
49 James Joyce Statue
50 GPO (General Post Office)
51 Eason's
52 Clery's & Co.
53 Irish Life Mall
54 Abbey Theatre
55 Iarnród Éireann Travel Centre
58 Old Jameson Distillery
59 Cobblestone Pub
60 Ceol; Chief O'Neills
61 St Michan's Church
62 Corporation Fruit Market
63 St Mary's Abbey
64 St Mary's Church
65 Hot Press Irish Music Hall of Fame
67 Daniel O'Connell Statue
68 City Arts Centre
69 Riverbank Theatre
71 St Audoen's Churches
72 Christ Church Cathedral
73 Dublinia
75 Mother Redcap's Market
76 Tailors Hall; An Taisce
77 Tivoli Theatre
78 Vicar St
79 St Catherine's Church (Protestant)
80 Guinness Hop Store
82 St Patrick's Cathedral

The head office of Bord Fáilte (Around St Stephen's Green map; ☎ 676 5871, 602 4000) at Baggot St Bridge has an information desk and, although it's inconveniently located – well to the south of the city centre, beyond St Stephen's Green – it's also much less crowded. The entrance is on Wilton Terrace.

A computerised tourist-information service known as Gulliver is in operation at all tourist offices. It provides information on events, attractions and transport and offers an accommodation-reservation service. It is accessible throughout the world. Call ☎ 1800 668668 in Ireland, ☎ 011 800 66866866 in the US and ☎ 00 800 66866866 in the rest of the world.

Money

The currency-exchange counter at Dublin Airport is in the baggage-collection area and opens for most flight arrivals; there is also an exchange desk on the departures floor.

There are numerous banks around the city centre with exchange facilities. The Bank of Ireland operates a bureau de change in Westmoreland St, 9 am to 9 pm Monday to Saturday, and 10 am to 7 pm on Sunday.

American Express (Amex; Around Temple Bar map; ☎ 677 2874), 116 Grafton St, and Thomas Cook (Around Temple Bar map; ☎ 677 1721, 677 1307), at No 118, are across the road from the entrance to Trinity College. Thomas Cook opens 9 am (10 am on Wednesday) to 5.30 pm Monday to Saturday, while Amex opens 9 am to 5 pm on weekdays, and 9 am to noon (the foreign-exchange desk stays open until 5 pm) on Saturday. Amex also has a desk in Dublin Tourism.

Post & Communications

Dublin's famed GPO, on O'Connell St, north of the river, opens 8 am to 8 pm Monday to Saturday, and 10.30 am to 6 pm on Sunday and public holidays. Here you'll find the poste restante, a philatelic counter and a bank of telephones. South of the river the handy post office in South Anne St (Around St Stephen's Green map), just off Grafton St, is well patronised by foreign visitors and is used to dealing with their curious requests.

Éircom Telecentre (☎ 661 1111), Findlater House, Upper O'Connell St, has public phones that use cash or phonecards; the staff there will also help with any queries or problems you may have. It opens 9.30 am to 5 pm (4.45 pm on Friday) on weekdays.

Internet Resources

A number of cafés and restaurants offer access to the Internet, including Betacafé (Around Temple Bar map; ☎ 671 5717), in the Arthouse Multimedia Centre for the Arts, on Curved St, which charges £5 per hour. Planet Cyber Café (Around St Stephen's Green map; ☎ 679 0583), 23 South Great George St, in the basement of Laser Video Rentals, has excellent equipment with all the latest accessories and charges the same.

Travel Agencies

Amex and Thomas Cook both have offices in the centre of Dublin (see Money earlier in this section). The office of the Union of Students in Ireland Travel (USIT; Around Temple Bar map; ☎ 679 8833), 19 Aston Quay, south of O'Connell Bridge, opens 9 am to 6 pm (8 pm on Thursday) on weekdays, and 10 am to 5.30 pm on Saturday.

Bookshops

Given Dublin's strong literary tradition it's not surprising that the city has some good bookshops.

Directly opposite Trinity College is the excellent Fred Hanna (Around Temple Bar map; ☎ 677 1255), 27-29 Nassau St. Around the corner is the large, well-stocked Hodges Figgis (Around St Stephen's Green map; ☎ 677 4754), 56-58 Dawson St, with a large selection on things Irish. Facing it is Waterstone's (Around St Stephen's Green map; ☎ 679 1415), 7 Dawson St, which also carries a wide range of books. The Dublin Bookshop (Around St Stephen's Green map; ☎ 677 5568), 24 Grafton St, has a good Irish-interest section.

North of the Liffey, Eason's (☎ 873 3811), 40 O'Connell St, near the GPO, has a wide range of books and one of the biggest selections of magazines in Ireland. The Winding Stair (Around Temple Bar map; ☎ 873 3292), 40 Lower Ormond Quay, does new and second-hand books and has a café upstairs. In the Jervis Street Shopping Centre (Around Temple Bar map), there's a second branch of Waterstone's (☎ 878 1311).

A number of bookshops cater to special interests. Forbidden Planet (Around Temple Bar map; ☎ 671 0688), 5-6 Crampton Quay, Dublin 2, is a wonderful science-fiction and comic-book specialist. The Sinn Féin Bookshop (☎ 872 7096) is at 44 Parnell Square West, Dublin 1. An Siopa Leabhar (☎ 478 3814), Harcourt St, just off St Stephen's Green, has books in Irish. The Irish Museum of Modern Art (IMMA; County Dublin map), at the Royal Hospital Kilmainham, and the National Gallery in Merrion Square both have bookshops offering a good range of art books and books on Ireland generally.

There is an excellent bookshop in the Dublin Writers' Museum, 18 Parnell Square North, Dublin 1. The Library Book Shop at Trinity College has a wide selection of Irish-interest books, including, of course, various titles on the *Book of Kells*. For all kinds of official publications and maps, there's also the Dúchas bookshop (Around St Stephen's Green map; ☎ 661 3111), Sun Alliance House, Molesworth St, Dublin 2.

George Webb (Around Temple Bar map; ☎ 677 7489), 5 Crampton Quay, Dublin 2, has old Irish-interest books, as does Greene's Bookshop (Around St Stephen's Green map; ☎ 873 3149), 16 Clare St, Dublin 2, and Cathach Books (Around St Stephen's Green map; ☎ 671 8676), 10 Duke St, Dublin 2.

DUBLIN

Cultural Centres

Dublin has an international selection of cultural centres. The city is a popular centre for English-language instruction, particularly for students from Spain, Italy and France, who flock to Dublin every summer and have become a colourful part of the city scene. The city's cultural centres, which are marked on the Around St Stephen's Green map unless stated otherwise, include:

Alliance Française
  (☎ 676 1732) 1 Kildare St, Dublin 2
British Council
  (☎ 676 4088) Newmount House,
  22-24 Lower Mount St, Dublin 2
Goethe Institute
  (☎ 661 1155) 37 Merrion Square, Dublin 2
Instituto Cervantes (Spanish Cultural Institute)
  (off Dublin map; ☎ 668 2024) 58 Northumberland Rd, Dublin 4
Italian Cultural Institute
  (☎ 676 6662) 11 Fitzwilliam Square,
  Dublin 2

Useful Organisations

ENFO (☎ 679 3144), opposite Dublin Tourism, is a government body with useful information on the environment. It has videos, brochures and a library and opens 10 am to 5 pm on weekdays.

Travellers with disabilities can get help and advice from the National Rehabilitation Board (off Dublin map; ☎ 668 4181), 25 Clyde Rd, Ballsbridge, Dublin 4, or at 44 North Great George St, Dublin 1 (☎ 874 7503).

The Gay Switchboard (☎ 872 1055) is in Carmichael House, North Brunswick St, Dublin 7.

The Automobile Association (AA; ☎ 677 9481) is at 23 Suffolk St, Dublin 2.

Laundry

Convenient laundries in northern Dublin include Laundry Shop (☎ 872 3541), 191 Parnell St, Dublin 1, off Parnell Square, and Laundrette (☎ 830 0340), 110 Lower Dorset St, near the Dublin International Youth Hostel.

Near Trinity College and Temple Bar is the cheerful All American Laundrette (Around St Stephen's Green map; ☎ 677 2779), 40 South Great George St, which also has a handy notice board. South of the centre and just north of the Grand Canal is Powders Laundrette (Around St Stephen's Green map; ☎ 478 2655), 42A South Richmond St.

If you're staying north-east of the centre at Clontarf there's the Clothes Line (off Dublin map; ☎ 833 8480), 53 Clontarf Rd.

Prices at laundries start at about £4, increasing along with the size of your load.

Medical Services

The Eastern Health Board Dublin Area (☎ 679 0700, 1800 520520), Doctor Steevens Hospital, Dublin 8, has a Choice of Doctor Scheme which can advise you on a suitable doctor from 9 am to 5 pm on weekdays. It also provides services for the physically and mentally handicapped. There are Well Women clinics at 35 Lower Liffey St (☎ 872 8051) and 73 Lower Leeson St (☎ 661 0083). Both can help with female medical problems and can supply contraceptives, including the morning-after pill, which costs about £20.

Emergency

For national emergency numbers see Telephone in the Post & Communications section of the Facts for the Visitor chapter. Other useful numbers include:

Drugs Advisory and Treatment Centre
  (☎ 677 1122)
  Trinity Court, 30-31 Pearse St, Dublin 2
Rape Crisis Centre
  (☎ 1800 778888, 661 4911)
  70 Lower Leeson St, Dublin 2
Samaritans
  (☎ 1850 609090, 872 7700)
  112 Marlborough St, Dublin 1.
  This is the service for people who are
  depressed or suicidal.

Dangers & Annoyances

Dublin was once regarded as a very safe city but, although this is still largely true, a continuing drug problem means there's a fair amount of petty (and not so petty) crime. In 1996 journalist Veronica Guerin was murdered while investigating Dublin's

Racism

In April 1999, a young black man was taunted by a couple of teenagers on busy Dame St, in the heart of Dublin. The taunts soon turned to blows, each one accompanied by a racist epithet. The victim was left badly hurt and bloodied. All the while, not one passer-by saw fit to intervene.

This case is sadly not unique. As the number of Africans increases in Dublin – most are asylum seekers awaiting process of their claim – so do the cases of assault, both verbal and physical. A recent survey suggested that 90% of Africans have been the victim of some kind of racist abuse, and this in a country that prides itself on its spirit of generosity. The truth is that, while Ireland is no more racist than any other European country, it is not less so either. The traditional victims of intolerance are the Travelling communities that reside in temporary halting sites throughout the country (see the boxed text 'Apartheid Without the Name' in the Kerry chapter).

So it's hardly surprising that Africans have been victimised, but their plight is not made any easier by the government, which denies them the right to work during processing, which can take up to two years. A Dublin evening tabloid has done its fair share of fanning the fires of racism, constantly running stories about asylum seekers looking to sponge off the government 'at the expense of the Irish worker'. Such twaddle is rightfully denigrated in more open-minded circles, but the problem of racism remains, and is getting worse.

---

drugs trade. A recent spate of hold-ups by thieves brandishing used syringes seems to have abated, but the drug problem has not, so a certain amount of caution should be exercised – but no more than in any other city.

Notices alert you to the risk of sneak thieves and pickpockets, many of them unusually young. If you have a car, don't leave valuables inside it when it's parked: Dublin is notorious for car break-ins, and foreign-registered and rental cars are a particular target. Cyclists should always lock their bicycles securely and remove anything removable.

A certain amount of caution should be exercised when walking in certain areas of Dublin at night, particularly north of the Liffey: Upper Gardiner St, around Parnell St and poorly lit, secluded areas of Smithfield. South of the Liffey, the Liberties area, near the Guinness brewery, witnesses occasional trouble at night-time, although it is pleasant to stroll around in the daytime. In general, visitors should avoid going to run-down and deserted-looking areas. Camping in Phoenix Park is not only illegal but dangerous as well.

As in other parts of Europe, beggars, some of them alarmingly young, are commonplace. If you don't want to give them money but would like to do something to help the homeless and long-term unemployed, you could buy a copy of the magazine *The Big Issue* (£1.50), some of the proceeds of which go to them.

Like all big cities, Dublin is choking on traffic fumes. Nor has smoking died the social death it has in other western countries: cinemas may be smoke-free zones but not even all the expensive restaurants have designated nonsmoking areas. Consequently, after a few days here you may feel your lungs need a burst of fresh air.

ALONG THE LIFFEY

The River Liffey comes down to Dublin from the Wicklow Mountains, passing the open expanse of Phoenix Park and flowing under 14 city bridges before reaching Dublin Harbour and Dublin Bay. In a straight line it's only about 20km from its source to the sea, but the Liffey meanders for over 100km along its route and changes remarkably in that distance. Well into the city, around Phoenix Park, the Liffey is still rural looking, and if you're waiting for a train at Heuston Station you can wander over to the riverside and watch the fish in the clear water below.

The Liffey isn't a notable river, although Joyce immortalised its spirit in *Ulysses* as Anna Livia, the woman you see lying in sculpted form ('the floozy in the Jacuzzi') in the middle of O'Connell St and on thousands of Dublin doorknockers. The best Liffey views are from O'Connell Bridge or, a little bit upstream, from the pedestrian Ha'penny Bridge of 1816, which leads into the colourful Temple Bar.

Although there have been bridges over the Liffey for nearly 800 years, the oldest existing bridge is Liam Mellowes Bridge, which was originally built as Queen's Bridge in 1768. It's still popularly known as the Queen St Bridge, for the simple reason that Queen St runs down to it.

The River Poddle originally joined the Liffey near Grattan Bridge, better known as Capel St Bridge, which crosses the river from the street of the same name. The '*dubh linn*' (black pool) at this point gave the city its name, but today the miserable Poddle runs its final 5km in an underground channel and trickles into the Liffey through a grating on the southern side of the river just downstream from the channel.

The Liffey does more than divide Dublin into northern and southern halves – it also marks a psychological and social break between north and south.

Although Liffey water was once a vital constituent in Guinness, you'll be relieved to hear that this is no longer the case.

Four Courts

On Inns Quay beside the river the extensive Four Courts with its 130m-long façade was one of James Gandon's (1743–1823) masterpieces. James Gandon was 18th-century Dublin's pre-eminent architect. The Custom House, King's Inns and some elements of the Parliament building (now the Bank of Ireland) are also among his masterpieces. Construction on the Four Courts began in 1786, soon engulfing the Public Offices

(built a short time previously at the western end of the same site), and continued until 1802. By then it included a Corinthian-columned central block connected to flanking wings with enclosed quadrangles. The ensemble is topped by a diverse collection of statuary. The original four courts – Exchequer, Common Pleas, King's Bench and Chancery – branch off the central rotunda.

The 1224 Dominican Convent of St Saviour formerly stood on the site, but was replaced first by the King's Inns and then by the present building. The last Parliament of James II was held here in 1689. The Four Courts played a brief role in the 1916 Easter Rising, without suffering damage, but the events of 1922 were not so kind. When anti-Treaty forces seized the building and refused to leave, it was shelled from across the river. As the occupiers retreated, the building was set on fire and many irreplaceable early records were burned. This event sparked off the Civil War. The building wasn't restored until 1932.

Visitors are allowed to wander through, but not to enter courts or other restricted areas. In the lobby of the central rotunda you'll see bewigged barristers conferring and police officers handcuffed to their charges waiting to enter court.

Custom House

The Custom House, James Gandon's (see the previous section) first great building, was constructed between 1781 and 1791 just past Eden Quay, in spite of opposition from city merchants and dock workers at the original Custom House, upriver in Temple Bar.

In 1921, during the independence struggle, the Custom House was set alight and completely gutted in a fire that burned for five days. The interior was later extensively redesigned, and a further major renovation took place between 1986 and 1988.

The glistening white building stretches for 114m along the Liffey. The best complete view is obtained from across the river, though a close-up inspection of its many fine details is also worthwhile. The building is topped by a copper dome with four clocks. Above that stands a 5m-high statue of Hope.

Famine Memorial

Beside the river, about 200m east of the Custom House, in the old docklands area that's now being redeveloped, is this memorial (off Dublin map) to the people who died or emigrated as a result of the Famine. It was unveiled by Mary Robinson in 1997, 150 years after the Famine began, and consists of seven tall, gaunt, bronze figures 'walking' along the quay towards Dublin Harbour. The memorial was donated by Norma Smurfit, an Englishwoman who has lived in Ireland for more than 30 years and is married to leading entrepreneur Michael Smurfit.

Dublin Harbour

In medieval times the River Liffey spread out into a broad estuary as it flowed into the bay. That estuary has long since been reclaimed (Trinity College has stood on it for 400 years) and the Liffey is embanked as far as the sea.

Dublin Harbour (off Dublin map) first came into existence in 1714, when the Liffey embankments were built. North Wall Quay was then built, and later a 5km breakwater known as the South Wall was added (the chief engineer of the project was Captain Robert Bligh, whose command of HMS *Bounty* resulted in the infamous mutiny), followed by the North and South Bull Walls. The South Wall starts at Ringsend, where Oliver Cromwell first set foot in Ireland in 1649. From there it runs out to the Pigeon House Fort (County Dublin map), built from 1748 and now used as a power station, and from there continues a further 2km out to the 1762 Poolbeg Lighthouse at the end of the breakwater. It's a pleasant, though long, stroll out to the lighthouse.

SOUTH OF THE LIFFEY

Southern Dublin has the fanciest shops, almost all the restaurants of note and a majority of the hotels, as well as most of the reminders of Dublin's early history and the finest Georgian squares and houses.

Trinity College

Ireland's premier university was founded by Elizabeth I in 1592 on grounds confiscated from a monastery. By providing an alternative to education on the Continent, the queen hoped that the students would avoid being 'infected with popery'. The college is in the centre of Dublin, though at the time of its foundation it was outside the city walls. Archbishop Ussher, whose scientific feats included the precise dating of the act of creation to 4004 BC, was one of the college's founders.

Officially, the university's name is the University of Dublin, but Trinity College is the institution's sole college. Until 1793 Trinity College remained completely Protestant apart from one short break. Even when the Protestants allowed Catholics in, the Catholic Church forbade it, a restriction that wasn't completely lifted until 1970. To this day Trinity College is still something of a centre of British and Protestant influence, even though the majority of its 9500 students are Catholic. Women were first admitted to the college in 1903, earlier than at most British universities.

In summer, historical walking tours depart regularly from the main gate on College Green, 9.30 am to 4.30 pm Monday to Saturday, and noon to 4 pm on Sunday. The £5.50 cost of the walking tour is good value since it includes the fee to see the *Book of Kells*.

Main Entrance Facing College Green (the street in front of the college), the Front Gate or Regent House entrance to the college grounds was built between 1752 and 1759 and is guarded by statues of the poet Oliver Goldsmith (1730–74) and the orator Edmund Burke (1729–97).

Around the Campanile The open area reached from Regent House is divided into Front Square, Parliament Square and Library Square. The area is dominated by the 30m-high Campanile, designed by Edward Lanyon and erected between 1852 and 1853 on what was believed to be the centre of the

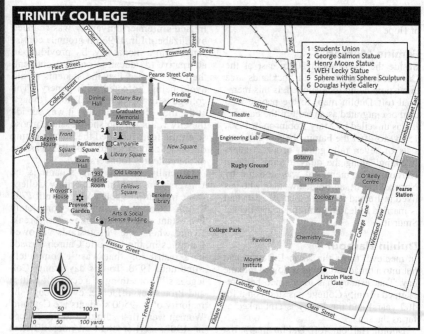

TRINITY COLLEGE

1 Students Union
2 George Salmon Statue
3 Henry Moore Statue
4 WEH Lecky Statue
5 Sphere within Sphere Sculpture
6 Douglas Hyde Gallery

monastery that preceded the college. To the left of the Campanile is a statue of George Salmon, college provost from 1888 to 1904, who fought bitterly to keep women out of the college. He carried out his threat to permit them 'over my dead body' by promptly dropping dead when the worst came to pass.

Chapel & Dining Hall Clockwise round the Front Square from Front Gate, the first building is the chapel, built from 1798 to plans made in 1777 by the architect Sir William Chambers (1723–96) and since 1972 open to all denominations. It's noted for its extremely fine plasterwork by Michael Stapleton, its Ionic columns and its painted, rather than stained-glass, windows. The main one is dedicated to Archbishop Ussher.

Next to the chapel is the dining hall, originally designed in 1743 by Richard Castle, but dismantled only 15 years later because

of problems caused by inadequate foundations. The replacement was completed in 1761 and may have retained elements of the original design. It was extensively restored after a fire in 1984.

Graduates' Memorial Building & the Rubrics The 1892 Graduates' Memorial Building forms the northern side of Library Square. Behind it are the tennis courts in the open area known as Botany Bay. The popular legend behind this name is that the unruly students housed around the square were suitable candidates for the British penal colony at Botany Bay (Sydney) in Australia.

At the eastern side of Library Square, the red-brick Rubrics Building dates from around 1690, making it the oldest building in the college. It was extensively altered in an 1894 restoration and then underwent major structural modifications in the 1970s.

Book of Kells

For visitors, Trinity College's prime attraction is the magnificent *Book of Kells*, an illuminated manuscript dating from around 800, making it one of the oldest books in the world. Although the book was brought to the college for safe-keeping from the monastery at Kells in County Meath in 1654, it undoubtedly predates the monastery itself. It was probably produced by monks at St Colmcille's Monastery on the remote island of Iona, off the western coast of Scotland. When repeated Viking raids made their monastery untenable, the monks moved to the temporary safety of Kells in Ireland in 806, taking their masterpiece with them. In 1007, the book was stolen, then rediscovered three months later, buried in the ground. Some time before the dissolution of the monastery in 1535, the *cumdach* (metal shrine) was lost, possibly taken by looting Vikings who wouldn't have valued the text itself. About 30 of the beginning and ending folios have also disappeared.

MATT KING

St John the Eagle from the beautiful 8th-century *Book of Kells*

The *Book of Kells* contains the four gospels of the New Testament, written in Latin, as well as prefaces, summaries and other text. If it were merely words, the *Book of Kells* would simply be a very old book – it's the extensive and amazingly complex illustrations that make it so wonderful. The superbly decorated opening initials are only part of the story, for the book also has numerous smaller illustrations between the lines.

The 680-page book was rebound in four calfskin volumes in 1953. Two volumes are usually on display, one showing an illuminated page and the other showing text. The pages are turned over regularly, but you can acquire your own reproduction copy for a mere US$19,800. If that's too steep, the library bookshop has various less expensive books, including *The Book of Kells*, a paperback with some attractive colour plates and text costing £10.95.

The *Book of Kells* is usually on display in the East Pavilion of the Library Colonnades, underneath the actual library. As well as the *Book of Kells*, the *Book of Armagh* (807) and the *Book of Durrow* (675) are also on display.

Old Library To the south of the square is the Old Library, which was built in a rather severe style by Thomas Burgh between 1712 and 1732. The Old Library's 65m Long Room contains numerous unique ancient texts, and the *Book of Kells* (see the boxed text) is displayed in the Library Colonnades. Despite Ireland's independence, the Library Act of 1801 still entitles Trinity College Library, along with three libraries in Britain, to a free copy of every book published in the UK. Housing this bounty requires nearly another kilometre of shelving every year and the collection amounts to around three million books. Of course these cannot all be kept at the college library, so there are now additional library storage facilities dotted around Dublin.

The Long Room is mainly used for about 200,000 of the library's oldest volumes. Until 1892 the ground floor Colonnades was an open arcade, but it was enclosed at that time to increase the storage area. A previous attempt to increase the room's storage capacity had been made in 1853, when the Long Room ceiling was raised.

As well as the world-famous *Book of Kells*, on display is the so-called harp of BrianBorú, which was definitely not in use when the army of this early Irish hero defeated the Danes at the Battle of Clontarf in 1014. It does, however, date from around 1400, making it one of the oldest harps in Ireland.

Other exhibits in the Long Room include a rare copy of the Proclamation of the Irish Republic, which was read out by Pádraig Pearse at the beginning of the Easter Rising in 1916. The collection of 18th- and 19th-century marble busts around the walls features Jonathan Swift, Edmund Burke and Wolfe Tone, all former members of Trinity College.

The Long Room and *Book of Kells* exhibition open 9.30 am to 5 pm Monday to Saturday, and noon to 4.30 pm on Sunday. Admission costs £4.50/4 (children aged under 12 free). In high season it gets packed out, so try to come out of season. The Colonnades also houses a busy book and souvenir shop and a temporary exhibition hall.

Reading Room, Exam Hall & Provost's House Continuing clockwise round the Campanile there's the Reading Room and the Public Theatre or Exam Hall, which dates from 1779 to 1791. Like the Chapel building, which it faces and closely resembles, it was the work of William Chambers and also has plasterwork by Michael Stapleton. The Exam Hall has an oak chandelier rescued from the Houses of Parliament (now the Bank of Ireland) across College Green and an organ said to have been salvaged from a Spanish ship in 1702, though the evidence indicates otherwise.

Behind the Exam Hall is the 1760 Provost's House, a particularly fine Georgian

house where the provost, or college head, still resides. The house and its adjacent garden are not open to the public.

Berkeley Library To one side of the Old Library is Paul Koralek's 1967 Berkeley Library. This solid, square brutalist-style building has been hailed as the best example of modern architecture in Ireland, though it has to be admitted the competition isn't great. It's fronted by Arnaldo Pomodoro's 1982 to 1983 sculpture *Sphere within Sphere*. The library isn't open to the public.

George Berkeley was born in Kilkenny in 1685, studied at Trinity when he was only 15 years old and went on to a distinguished career in many fields, but particularly in philosophy. His influence spread to the new English colonies in North America, where, among other things, he helped to found the University of Pennsylvania. Berkeley in California, and its namesake university, are named after him.

Arts & Social Science Building & Douglas Hyde Gallery South of the Old Library is the 1978 Arts and Social Science Building, which backs on to Nassau St and forms the alternative main entrance to the college. Like the Berkeley Library it was designed by Paul Koralek; it also houses the Douglas Hyde Gallery of Modern Art (☎ 608 1116).

The Dublin Experience After the *Book of Kells* the college's other big tourist attraction is the Dublin Experience, a 45-minute audiovisual introduction to the city. Daily shows take place at the back of the Arts and Social Science Building on the hour from 10 am to 5 pm, late May to early October. Admission costs £3/2.75. Combined tickets for the *Book of Kells* and the Dublin Experience are available.

Around New Square Behind the Rubrics Building, at the eastern end of Library Square, is New Square. The highly ornate 1853 to 1857 **Museum Building** (☎ 608 1477) has the skeletons of two enormous giant Irish deer just inside the entrance and the Geological Museum upstairs. It opens by prior arrangement only.

The 1734 **Printing House**, designed by Richard Castle to resemble a Doric temple and now used for the microelectronics and electrical engineering departments, is at the north-western corner of New Square.

At the eastern end of the college grounds are the rugby ground and College Park, where cricket games are often played. There are a number of science buildings at the eastern end of the grounds. The Lincoln Place Gate at this end is usually open and makes a good entrance or exit from the college, especially if you're on a bicycle.

Bank of Ireland

The imposing Bank of Ireland building (Around Temple Bar map; ☎ 671 1488), on College Green directly opposite Trinity College, was originally built in 1729 to house the Irish Parliament. When the Parliament voted itself out of existence by the Act of Union in 1801, it became a building without a role. It was sold in 1803 with instructions that the interior be altered to prevent its being used as a debating chamber in the future. Consequently, the large central House of Commons was remodelled but the smaller chamber of the House of Lords survived. After independence the Irish government chose to make Leinster House the new parliamentary building and ignored the possibility of restoring this fine building to its original use.

Over a long period of time, a string of architects worked on the building, yet it somehow manages to avoid looking like a hotchpotch of styles. Edward Lovett Pearce designed the circular central part, which was constructed between 1729 and 1739, and the eastern front was designed by James Gandon in 1785. Other architects involved in its construction were Robert Park and Francis Johnston, who converted it from a parliament building to a bank.

Inside, the banking mall occupies what was once the House of Commons, but offers little hint of its former role. The Irish House of Lords is much more interesting, with its Irish-oak woodwork, late-18th-century

Dublin crystal chandelier and 10kg silvergilt mace. The tapestries date from the 1730s and depict the Siege of Derry in 1689 and the Battle of the Boyne in 1690, the two great Protestant victories over Catholic Ireland.

The building can be visited during banking hours, 10 am to 4 pm (5 pm on Thursday) on weekdays. Free talks – as much about Ireland and life in general as the bank – take place at 10.30 and 11.30 am and 1.45 pm on Tuesday. The building's role as a tourist attraction isn't pushed very hard, so you'll probably have to ask somebody the way to the House of Lords.

Around the Bank of Ireland

The area (Around Temple Bar map) between the Bank and Trinity College, today a constant tangle of traffic and pedestrians, was once a green swathe and is still known as College Green. In front of the bank stands a **statue of Henry Grattan** (1746–1820), a distinguished parliamentary orator.

The traffic island where College Green, Westmoreland St and College St meet houses public toilets (no longer in use) and a **statue of the poet and composer Thomas Moore** (1779–1852), which is renowned because of James Joyce's comment in *Ulysses* that standing atop a public urinal wasn't a bad place for the man who penned the poem 'The Meeting of the Waters'.

The other end of College St, where it meets Pearse St, has a **1986 sculpture** known as *Steyne*. It's a copy of the *'steyne'* (the Viking word for stone) erected on the riverbank in the 9th century (and not removed until 1720) to stop ships from grounding.

Temple Bar

West of College Green and the Bank of Ireland, the maze of streets that make up Temple Bar (Around Temple Bar map) are sandwiched between Dame St and the river. This is one of the oldest areas of Dublin and has numerous restaurants, pubs and trendy shops. Dame St links new Dublin (centred on Trinity College and Grafton St) and old (stretching from Dublin Castle to encompass

DUBLIN

AROUND TEMPLE BAR

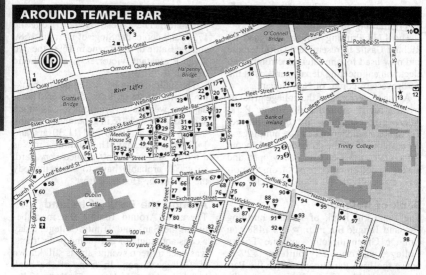

the two cathedrals). Along its route Dame St changes name several times.

Information Temple Bar Information Centre (☎ 671 5717), 18 Eustace St, has information on the area and an exhibition on its development. It publishes the useful *Temple Bar Guide*. It opens 9 am to 6 pm on weekdays, year round, plus 11 am to 4 pm on Saturday, and noon to 4 pm on Sunday, June to August.

The notice board in the Resource Centre/ Well Fed Café on Crow St displays a useful round-up of local goings-on.

History This stretch of riverside land was owned by Augustinian friars from 1282 until Henry VIII's dissolution of the monasteries in 1537, when Sir William Temple (1554–1628) acquired the land that bears his name. The term 'bar' referred to a riverside walkway, so this area was called Temple's Bar. Until 1537, Temple Lane was known as Hogges Lane and gave access to the friars' house. During its monastic era the Temple Bar area was marshy land that had only recently been reclaimed from the river. Much of it was outside the city walls

and the River Poddle flowed through it, connecting the black pool with the Liffey.

The narrow lanes and alleys of Temple Bar started to take form in the early 18th century, when this was a disreputable area of pubs and brothels. Through the 19th century it developed a commercial character, with many small craft and trade businesses, but in the first half of the 20th century it went into decline, along with most of central Dublin.

In the 1960s it was decided that the area should be demolished to build a major bus station, but these plans took a long time to develop and meanwhile the area became a thriving countercultural centre. In the 1980s the bus station plan was abandoned and Temple Bar was encouraged to develop as a centre for arts, restaurants, shops and entertainment instead. The area now boasts two public squares; residential apartments; centres for film, art and photography; a student housing centre; and a Viking museum.

Exploring The western boundary of Temple Bar is formed by **Fishamble St**, the oldest street in Dublin, dating back to Viking

AROUND TEMPLE BAR

PLACES TO STAY
1 Ormond Quay Hotel
2 Morrisson
16 Aston Hotel
19 Gogarty's Hostel
24 Wellington Hotel
25 Clarence Hotel; Kitchen;
   Octagon Bar
30 Temple Bar House
39 Bloom's Hotel; Club M
46 Strollers Budget
   Accommodation
59 Kinlay House
77 Central Hotel

PLACES TO EAT
8 Abrakebabra
9 Chez Jules
14 Beshoff's
15 Bewley's Oriental Café
17 Café Gertrude
18 Elephant & Castle Gallagher's
   Boxty House; Alamo
26 La Med
32 Fitzers
33 Il Pasticcio
35 Bad Ass Café
36 Paddy Garibaldi's
41 Ar Vicoletto
42 Tante Zoe's
43 Well Fed Café;
   Resource Centre
44 Nico's
48 Il Baccaro
49 Eden
50 Fan's Cantonese Restaurant
52 Les Frères Jacques
53 The Mermaid Café

54 Poco Loco
56 Da Pino
60 Lord Edward Restaurant
61 Leo Burdock's
63 Juice
64 The Odessa
65 Stag's Head
68 QV.2
69 Trocadero
75 Old Stand
76 The Cedar Tree
78 Yamamori Noodles
79 Shalimar
80 Good World
82 The Rhino Room;
   Cooke Café
83 Wed Wose Café
84 Munchies
85 La Taverna
86 Aya
87 Alpha
88 Cornucopia
89 Imperial Chinese Restaurant
94 Judge Roy Bean's

OTHER
3 Jervis St Shopping Centre
4 The Winding Stair
5 Hags with the Bags Statue
6 Dublin Woollen Company
7 USIT
10 Tara Street Station
11 Screen
12 Post Office
13 Garda (Police)
20 Rory's Fishing Tackle
21 Forbidden Planet;
   George Webb

22 China Blue
23 Temple Bar Gallery &
   Studios
27 Irish Film Centre
28 Betacafé
29 Temple Bar Information
   Centre
31 Claddagh Records
34 Eager Beaver
37 Eamonn Doran Imbibing
   Emporium
38 Bank of Ireland Arts Centre
40 Flip
45 Condom Power
47 Club Zazu
51 Olympia Theatre
55 Dublin's Viking Adventure
57 City Hall
58 Irish Celtic Craft Shop
62 St Werburgh's Church
66 Rí Rá
67 Andrew's Lane Theatre
70 Dublin Tourism;
   St Andrew's Church
71 Automobile Association
72 Thomas Cook
73 American Express
74 Molly Malone Statue
81 George St Arcade
90 House of Ireland
91 The Sweater Shop
92 Brown Thomas; Switzers
93 Lillie's Bordello
95 Blarney Woollen Mills
96 Fred Hanna
97 Knobs & Knockers
98 Kilkenny Shop;
   Kilkenny Restaurant

times – not that you'd know that to see it now. Christ Church Cathedral (see the entry later in this South of the Liffey section), beside Fishamble St, dates from 1170, but there was an earlier Viking church on this site. Brass symbols in the pavement direct you towards a mosaic laid out to show the ground plan of the sort of Viking dwelling excavated here in 1980 and 1981. Another Viking area is being excavated closer to Parliament St.

Nearby is **Dublin's Viking Adventure** (☎ 679 6040), West Essex St, where there's an entertaining 40-minute tour of Viking Dublin, which was then known as Dyflin.

You take a simulated ride on a Viking ship and land at the village of Dyflin (complete with smells), which you then walk through. Actors play the roles of villagers and tell you about their way of life. It's not often you get to talk to exhibits in a museum. It opens 10 am to 4.30 pm Tuesday to Saturday, and the tour costs £4.95/3.95.

In 1742 Handel conducted the first performance of his *Messiah* in the **Dublin Music Hall**, behind Kinlay House hotel on Lord Edward St, now part of a hotel that bears the composer's name. The Music Hall, which had opened a year earlier, in 1741, was designed by Richard Castle; the only reminder of it today is the entrance and the original door.

Parliament St, which runs straight up from the river to the City Hall and Dublin Castle, has, at No 4, Read's Cutlers, the oldest shop in Dublin, having operated under the same name since 1760. The shop is now closed, but you can still see the sign. At the bottom of the street, beside the river, the Sunlight Chambers has a beautiful frieze running round the façade. Sunlight was a brand of soap manufactured by the Lever Brothers, who built the turn-of-the-century building. The frieze shows the Lever Brothers' view of the world and soap: men make clothes dirty, women wash them! Parliament St was the first of the wide boulevards to be laid out by the Commission for Making Wide and Convenient Streets in 1762.

Eustace St is particularly interesting, with the popular Norseman pub at the river end and the 1715 Presbyterian Meeting House. The Dublin branch of the United Irishmen, who set themselves up to campaign for both parliamentary reform and equality for Catholics, was first convened in 1791 in the Eagle Tavern, now the Friends Meeting House. This should not be confused with the other Eagle Tavern, on Cork St.

Merchant's Arch leads to the **Ha'penny Bridge**. If you cross to the northern side of the Liffey, pause to look at the statue of two stout Dublin matrons sitting on a park bench with their shopping bags, dubbed 'the **hags with the bags**'. The Stock Exchange lives on Anglesea St, in a building dating from 1878.

Dublin Castle

The centre of British power in Ireland and originally built on the orders of King John in 1204, Dublin Castle (Around Temple Bar map; ☎ 677 7129) is more palace than castle. Only the Record Tower, completed in 1258, survives from the original Norman castle. Parts of the castle's foundations remain and a visit to the excavations is the most interesting part of the castle tour. The castle moats, which are now completely covered by more modern developments, were once filled by the River Poddle.

Dublin Castle enjoyed a relatively quiet history despite a siege by Silken Thomas Fitzgerald in 1534, a fire which destroyed much of the castle in 1684, and the events of the 1916 Easter Rising. The castle was used as the official residence of the British viceroys of Ireland until the Viceregal Lodge was built in Phoenix Park. Earlier it had been used as a prison, though not always with great success. Red Hugh O'Donnell, one of the last of the great Gaelic leaders, escaped from the Record Tower in 1591, was recaptured, and escaped again in 1592.

The castle tops Cork Hill, behind the City Hall on Dame St. Tours are held 10 am to 5 pm on weekdays and 2 to 5 pm at the weekend. Tours cost £2.50/1.50. The castle is still used for government business and tours are often tailored round meetings and conferences or sometimes cancelled altogether, so it's wise to phone beforehand.

The visitor centre in the south-eastern corner of the Lower Yard has a gift shop and café.

Tour The main **Upper Yard** of the castle, with an entrance underneath the Throne Room, can also be reached either directly from Cork Hill or via the Lower Yard. From the main entrance, the castle tour takes you round the state chambers, which were developed during Dublin's British heyday and are still used for official state occasions. The sequence of rooms visited on the tour may vary.

From the entrance you ascend the stairs to the **Battle-Axe Landing**, where the viceroy's guards once stood, armed with battle-axes. Turning left, you pass through a series of drawing rooms, formerly used as visitors' bedrooms. One contains a Van Dyck painting of Elizabeth, second Viscountess of Southampton, at the age of 17, another a book painted on vellum between 1989 and 1991 as a sort of latterday *Book of Kells*. The castle gardens, visible from the windows of these rooms, end in a high wall said to have been built for Queen Victoria's visit to block out the distressing sight of the Stephen St slums. James Connolly was detained in the first of these rooms after the siege of the GPO in 1916, before being taken to Kilmainham Jail to face a firing squad.

At the end of this series of rooms you cross the **State Corridor** and enter the **State Drawing Room**, which was seriously damaged by a fire in 1941. It has been restored and contains furniture and paintings dating from 1740. From there you enter the ornate **Throne Room**, built in 1740.

The long **Portrait Gallery** has portraits of some of the British viceroys and ends at an anteroom from which you enter **George's Hall**, added to the castle in 1911 for George V's visit to Ireland. From these rooms you return through the anteroom to the blue **Wedgwood Room** (yes, the whole room does look like Wedgwood china), which in turn leads to the **Bermingham Tower**, originally dating from 1411 but rebuilt between 1775 and 1777. The tower was used as a prison on a number of occasions, particularly during the Anglo-Irish War.

After leaving the tower, you pass through 25m-long **St Patrick's Hall**. The Knights of St Patrick, an order created in 1783, were invested here and their standards are displayed on the walls. These days Irish presidents are inaugurated here and the room is used for receptions. The huge painting on the ceiling shows St Patrick lighting the fire on Slane Hill; the Irish chieftains handing over power to the Anglo-Normans; and the coronation of George III, who created the Order of St Patrick.

St Patrick's Hall ends back on the Battle-Axe Landing but the tour now takes you down to the **Undercroft**, where remnants of the earlier Viking fort, the 13th-century Powder Tower and the city wall can be seen. This excavation of the original moat is now well below street level.

Bedford Tower & Genealogical Office

The Bedford Tower and the Genealogical Office are directly across the Upper Yard from the main entrance. In 1907 the collection known as the Irish Crown Jewels was stolen from the tower and never recovered. The Genealogical Office as an institution

dates from 1552. Its present building dates from the 18th century.

The entranceway to the castle yard, beside the Bedford Tower, is topped by a statue of Justice which has always been a subject of mirth. She faces the castle and has her back to the city – seen as a sure indicator of how much justice the average Irish citizen could expect from the British. The scales of justice also had a distinct tendency to fill with rain and tilt in one direction or the other, rather than assuming the approved level position. Eventually a hole was drilled in the bottom of each pan so the rainwater could drain out.

Royal Chapel

The Church of the Holy Trinity, previously known as the Royal Chapel, built in Gothic style by Francis Johnston between 1807 and 1814, is in the Lower Yard. Decorating the cold grey exterior are over 90 heads of various Irish personages and assorted saints carved out of Tullamore limestone. The interior is wildly exuberant, with fan vaulting alongside quadripartite vaulting, wooden galleries, stained glass and lots of lively-looking sculpted angels.

Record Tower

Rising over the chapel is the Record Tower, which was used as a storage facility for official records from 1579 until they were transferred to the Record Office in the Four Courts building in the early 19th century. (When the Four Courts was burned out at the start of the Civil War in 1922, almost all these priceless records were destroyed.) Although the tower was rebuilt in 1813 it retains much of its original appearance, including the massive 5m-thick walls.

Chester Beatty Library & Gallery of Oriental Art

Reached from a separate entrance on Ship St and housed in the Clock Tower is the castle's newest attraction. The world-famous library and gallery (☎ 269 2386) houses the collection of mining engineer Sir Alfred Chester Beatty (1875–1968). The collection includes over 20,000 manuscripts, some miniature paintings, numerous rare books, clay tablets, costumes and other objects, predominantly from the Middle East and Asia. There are various ancient Bibles and the Arabic collection includes over 270 copies of the Koran. You'll also find texts and books from Tibet, Myanmar (Burma), Thailand and Mongolia and a large collection of Japanese prints. The European collection has fine examples of early books and numerous maps and prints, including a set of Turner's mezzotints.

For many years housed in the fashionable suburb of Ballsbridge, the library was in the process of moving to the Clock Tower at the time of writing – it was due to open in spring 2000. It will open 10 am to 5 pm Tuesday to Friday, and 2 to 5 pm on Saturday. Tours of the library will be available at 2.30 pm on Wednesday and Saturday. Admission will be free.

City Hall & Municipal Buildings

Fronting Dublin Castle on Lord Edward St, the City Hall (Around Temple Bar map) was built by Thomas Cooley between 1769 and 1779 as the Royal Exchange and later became the offices of the Dublin Corporation. It stands on the site of the Lucas Coffee House and The Eagle Tavern, in which Dublin's infamous Hell Fire Club was established in 1735. Founded by Richard Parsons, earl of Rosse, it was one of a number of gentlemen's clubs in Dublin where less-than-gentlemanly conduct took place. It gained a reputation for debauchery and black magic, but there's no evidence that such things took place.

The 1781 Municipal Buildings, immediately west of the City Hall, were built by Thomas Ivory (1720–86), who was also responsible for the Genealogical Office in Dublin Castle.

Christ Church Cathedral

Christ Church Cathedral (Church of the Holy Trinity; ☎ 677 8099) is on Christ Church Place, just south of the river and west of the city centre and Temple Bar. Dublin's original Viking settlement stood between the cathedral and the river. This was also the centre of medieval Dublin, with Dublin Castle, the Tholsel (Town Hall; demolished in 1809) and the original Four Courts (demolished in 1796) all close by. Nearby, on Back Lane, is the only remaining guildhall in Dublin. The 1706 **Tailors Hall** was due for demolition in the 1960s but survived to become the office of An Taisce (National Trust for Ireland).

Originally built in wood by the Danes in 1038, the cathedral was subsequently rebuilt in stone from 1172, by Richard de Clare, earl of Pembroke (better known as Strongbow), the Anglo-Norman noble who invaded Ireland in 1170. The archbishop of Dublin at that time, Laurence (Lorcan in Irish) O'Toole, later became St Laurence, the patron saint of Dublin. Strongbow died in 1176 and Laurence O'Toole in 1180, before the church was destined to have a long life: the foundations were essentially a peat bog and the southern wall collapsed in 1562, though it was soon rebuilt. Most of what you see from the outside dates from architect GE Street's major 1871 to 1878 restoration. Above ground, the northern wall, the transepts and the western part of the choir are almost all that remain from the original.

Through much of its history, Christ Church vied for supremacy with nearby St Patrick's Cathedral, but, like its neighbour, it fell on hard times in the 18th and 19th centuries and was virtually derelict by the time restoration took place. Earlier, the nave had been used as a market and the crypt had housed taverns. Today both Church of Ireland cathedrals are outsiders in a Catholic nation.

From the south-eastern entrance to the churchyard you walk past ruins of the chapter house, which dates from 1230. The entrance to the cathedral is at the south-western corner and as you enter you face the northern wall. This survived the collapse of its southern counterpart but has also suffered from subsiding foundations: from the eastern end it leans visibly.

The south aisle has a monument to the legendary Strongbow. The armoured figure on the tomb is unlikely to be of Strongbow (it's more probably the earl of Drogheda) but his internal organs may have been buried here. A popular legend relates that the half-figure beside the tomb is of Strongbow's son, who was cut in two by his father when his bravery in battle was suspect.

The south transept contains the superb Baroque tomb of the 19th earl of Kildare (died 1734). His grandson, Lord Edward Fitzgerald, was a member of the United Irishmen and died in the abortive 1798 Rising. The entrance to the Chapel of St Laurence is off the south transept and contains two effigies, one of them reputed to be that of either Strongbow's wife or sister. Laurence O'Toole's embalmed heart was placed in the Chapel of St Laud.

At the eastern end of the cathedral is the Lady Chapel or Chapel of the Blessed Virgin Mary. Also at the eastern end is the Chapel of St Edmund and the chapter house, the latter closed to visitors. Parts of the choir, in the centre of the church, and the north transept are original, but the baptistry was added during the 1871 to 1878 restoration.

An entrance just by the south transept descends to the unusually large arched crypt, which dates back to the original Viking church. Curiosities in the crypt include a glass display case housing a mummified cat chasing a mummified mouse that were trapped inside an organ pipe in the 1860s! From the main entrance, a bridge, part of the 1871 to 1878 restoration, leads to Dublinia (see the following section).

The cathedral opens 10 am to 5.30 pm daily and a donation of £2/1 is requested.

Dublinia

Inside what was once the Synod Hall attached to Christ Church Cathedral, the Medieval Trust has created Dublinia, a lively attempt to bring medieval Dublin to life. The ground floor has models of 10 episodes in Dublin's history that are explained through headsets as you walk around. On the 1st floor, finds from medieval excavations are displayed alongside a large model of the city. There are also models of the medieval quayside and of a cob-

bler's shop. On the top floor is the Medieval Fayre, a replica of a 12th-century fair outside the city gates. The displays include merchants' wares, a medicine stall, an armourer's pavilion, a medieval confessional booth and a bank. Finally you can climb neighbouring St Michael's Tower for views over the city to the Dublin Hills.

Dublinia opens 10 am to 5 pm daily, April to September; and 11 am to 4 pm Monday to Saturday, and 10 am to 4.30 pm on Sunday, the rest of the year. Admission costs £3.95/2.90, which gets you into Christ Church Cathedral free (via the link bridge).

St Patrick's Cathedral

St Patrick himself is said to have baptised converts at a well within the cathedral grounds, so the cathedral (☎ 475 4817) stands on one of the earliest Christian sites in the city. Like Christ Church Cathedral it was built on unstable ground, with the subterranean River Poddle flowing under its foundations. Because of the high water table St Patrick's doesn't have a crypt.

Although a church stood on the Patrick St site from as early as the 5th century, the present building dates from 1190 or 1225 – opinions differ. Its current form dates mainly from some rather overenthusiastic restoration in 1864 which included the addition of the flying buttresses. St Patrick's Park, the expanse of green beside the cathedral, was a crowded slum until it was cleared and its residents evicted in the early years of the 20th century.

Like Christ Church Cathedral, the building has suffered a rather dramatic history. A storm brought down the spire in 1316 and, soon after, the building was badly damaged in a fire. Another, more disastrous, fire followed in 1362. This resulted in the addition of Archbishop Minot's west tower in 1370. For some reason it was built at a slight angle to the rest of the cathedral. In 1560 one of the first clocks in Dublin was added to the 43m tower, and a 31m spire in 1749. Oliver Cromwell, during his 1649 visit to Ireland, converted St Patrick's to a stable for his army's horses, an indignity to which he also subjected numerous other Irish

Chancing One's Arm

Leaning against a column at the western end of the cathedral is an old door which was once the entry to the chapter house and has a rectangular hole cut through it. In 1492 a furious argument took place within the cathedral between the earl of Kildare and the earl of Ormond. When strong words were about to lead to heavy blows, the earl of Ormond retreated to the chapter house. The earl of Kildare, realising that the dispute was pointless, wanted to end it but Ormond didn't respond. Using a spear, Kildare cut a hole in the door and thrust his hand through to show his good faith. It was clasped by another hand, the door was opened and the two men embraced, thereby ending the dispute.

In extending his arm through the door, the earl of Kildare added the phrase 'chancing one's arm' to the English language.

churches. Jonathan Swift was the dean of the cathedral from 1713 to 1745, but prior to its 1864 restoration it became very neglected.

Entering the cathedral from the south-western porch you come almost immediately, on your right, to the graves of Swift and Esther Johnson, or Stella, Swift's long-term companion. On the wall nearby are Swift's own Latin epitaphs to the two of them, and a bust of him.

The huge, dusty Boyle Monument to the left was erected in 1632 by Richard Boyle, the earl of Cork, and is decorated with numerous painted figures of members of his family. It stood beside the altar until, in 1633, Dublin's viceroy, Thomas Wentworth, the future earl of Strafford, had it shifted. Wentworth won this round in his bitter conflict with the earl of Cork, but the latter had the final say when he contributed to Wentworth's impeachment and execution. The figure in the centre on the bottom

level is of the earl's five-year-old son, Robert Boyle (1627–91), who became a noted scientist. His contributions to physics include Boyle's Law, which relates the pressure and volume of gases.

In the north-western corner of the church is a cross on a stone slab, which once marked the position of St Patrick's original well. The south transept was formerly a separate chapter house.

During the cathedral's decay in the 18th and 19th centuries the north transept was virtually a separate church. It now contains memorials to the Royal Irish Regiments. The Swift corner, in the north transept, features Swift's pulpit, his chair and a book-filled glass cabinet containing his death mask.

The Guinness family were noted contributors to the cathedral's restoration and a monument to Sir Benjamin Guinness's daughter stands in the Chapel of St Stephen beneath a window bearing the words 'I was thirsty and ye gave me drink'! The chapel also has a chair used by William of Orange at a service in the cathedral after his victory at the Boyne.

The cathedral opens 9 am to 6 pm on weekdays, 9 am to 5 pm (4 pm from November to April) on Saturday, and 10 (9.30 am from May to October) to 11 am and 12.45 to 3 pm (plus 4.15 to 5.30 pm from May to October) on Sunday. Admission costs £2/1.50. The cathedral's choir school dates back to 1432 and the choir took part in the first performance of Handel's *Messiah* in 1742. You can hear the choir sing at 5.35 pm Monday to Thursday (times may vary at Christmas).

Bus Nos 50, 50A and 56A from Aston Quay and Nos 54 and 54A from Burgh Quay run to the cathedral.

Marsh's Library

In St Patrick's Close, beside St Patrick's Cathedral, is Marsh's Library (☎ 454 3511), founded in 1701 by Archbishop Narcissus Marsh (1638–1713) and opened in 1707. It was designed by Sir William Robinson, who was also responsible for the Royal Hospital, Kilmainham. The oldest public library in the country, it contains 25,000 books dating from the 16th to the early 18th centuries, as well as maps, numerous manuscripts and a collection of incunabula, the technical term for books printed before 1500. One of the oldest and finest books in the collection is a volume of Cicero's *Letters to his Friends* printed in Milan in 1472. The manuscript collection includes one in Latin dating back to 1400.

The three alcoves where scholars were once locked in to peruse rare volumes still stand in the virtually unchanged interior. The skull lurking in the farthest one doesn't, however, belong to some poor forgotten scholar. Instead it's a cast taken of Swift's Stella's head. A bindery to repair and restore rare old books operates from the library, which makes an appearance in Joyce's *Ulysses*.

The library has regular exhibitions and opens 10 am to 12.45 pm and 2 to 5 pm Monday and Wednesday to Friday, and 10.30 am to 12.45 pm on Saturday. An admission donation of £2 is requested. You can reach the library by taking bus Nos 50, 50A or 56A from Aston Quay or bus Nos 54 or 54A from Burgh Quay.

St Werburgh's Church

In Werburgh St, just south of Christ Church Cathedral and beside Dublin Castle, St Werburgh's (Around Temple Bar map) stands on ancient foundations. Its early history, however, is unknown. It was rebuilt in 1662, in 1715 and again in 1759 (with some elegance) after a fire in 1754. It is linked with the Fitzgerald family; Lord Edward Fitzgerald, a member of the United Irishmen who was a leader of the 1798 Rising, is interred in the vault. In what was an unfortunately frequent theme of Irish uprisings, compatriots betrayed him and he died from wounds received while being captured. Major Henry Sirr, his captor, is buried in the graveyard.

Despite its long history, fine design and interesting interior, the church is run-down and rarely used except for Sunday-morning mass. A note at the front directs you round the corner to 8 Castle St if you want to have

a look inside (between 10 am and 4 pm). If you can't raise anybody, try phoning ☎ 478 3710.

Werburgh St was also the location of Dublin's first theatre and Jonathan Swift was born just off the street in Hoey's Court in 1667.

St Audoen's Churches

Lucky St Audoen has two churches to his name, both just west of Christ Church Cathedral. The Church of Ireland church is the older and smaller building, and is the only surviving medieval parish church in the city. Its tower and door date from the 12th century and the aisle from the 15th century, but the church today is mainly a 19th-century restoration. Parts of an even earlier Viking church of St Colmcille may be included in the later constructions. The tower's bells include the three oldest bells in Ireland, all dating from 1423.

There are several entries to the church grounds including via an arch beside Cook St, to the north of the church. Part of the old city wall, this arch was built in 1240 and is the only surviving reminder of the city gates.

Joined onto the older Protestant St Audoen's is the newer and larger Catholic St Audoen's, which was completed in 1846. The dome was replaced in 1884 after it collapsed, and the front, with its imposing Corinthian columns, was added in 1899. Unfortunately, you're unlikely to find either church open, except during weekend services.

National Museum

On Kildare St, the National Museum (Around St Stephen's Green map; ☎ 677 7444) was designed by Sir Thomas Newenham Deane and completed in 1890. The star attraction is the Treasury, which has two superb collections and an accompanying audiovisual display.

One of the collections is of Bronze and Iron Age gold objects, including a magnificent gold collar and a delicate little gold model of a galley, both from the Broighter Hoard (1st century BC). Most of the hoards displayed were discovered by railway workers, ploughmen and peat cutters – rarely by archaeologists.

The other Treasury collection is from medieval times. Outstanding among the objects on display are the 8th-century silver Ardagh Chalice, the 12th-century Cross of Cong, which once enshrined a supposed fragment of the True Cross, and the beautiful 8th-century Tara Brooch, made of gold, enamel and amber.

Upstairs, Viking Age Dublin tells the story of Dublin's Viking era, with exhibits from the excavations at Wood Quay – the area between Christ Church Cathedral and the river, where Dublin City Council plonked its new headquarters. Other exhibits focus on the 1916 Easter Rising and the independence struggle between 1900 and 1921. Frequent short-term exhibitions are also held.

The museum's collections of Irish decorative arts, ceramics and musical instruments and of Japanese decorative arts are housed in the annexe at Collins Barracks in Benburb St, off Ellis Quay.

The museum opens 10 am to 5 pm Tuesday to Saturday, and 2 to 5 pm on Sunday. Admission is free. Guided tours are available daily, June to September, for £1. There's a good café on the ground floor.

National Gallery

Opened in 1864, the National Gallery (Around St Stephen's Green map; ☎ 661 5133) looks out on Merrion Square. Its excellent collection is strong in Irish art, but there are also high-quality collections of every major school of European painting.

On the lawn in front of the gallery is a statue of the Irish railway magnate William Dargan, who organised the 1853 Dublin Industrial Exhibition at this spot; the profits from the exhibition were used to found the gallery. Nearby is a statue of George Bernard Shaw, a major benefactor of the gallery.

The gallery has three wings: the original Dargan Wing, the Milltown Rooms and the North Wing. The Dargan Wing's ground floor has the imposing Shaw Room, lined with full-length portraits and illuminated by a series of spectacular Waterford crystal chandeliers. Upstairs, a series of rooms is dedicated to the Italian early and high Renaissance, 16th-century northern Italian art and 17th- and 18th-century Italian art. Fra Angelico, Titian and Tintoretto are among the artists represented, but the highlight is undoubtedly Caravaggio's *The Taking of Christ,* which lay undiscovered for over 60 years in a Jesuit house in Leeson St and was accidentally discovered by chief curator Sergio Benedetti.

The central Milltown Rooms were added between 1899 and 1903 to hold Russborough House's art collection, which was presented to the gallery in 1902. The ground floor displays the gallery's fine Irish collection plus a smaller British collection, with works by Reynolds, Hogarth, Gainsborough, Landseer and Turner. One highlight is the room at the back of the gallery displaying works by Jack B Yeats (1871–1957), younger brother of WB Yeats. Other rooms display specific periods and styles of Irish art, including one room of works by Irish artists painting in France.

Upstairs are works from Germany, the Netherlands and Spain. There are rooms full of works by Rembrandt and his circle and by the Spanish artists of Seville. The Spanish collection features works by El Greco, Goya and Picasso.

The North Wing was added only between 1964 and 1968 but has already undergone extensive refurbishment. It houses works by British and European artists.

The gallery also has an art reference library, a lecture theatre, a good bookshop and the deservedly popular Fitzers café. The gallery opens 10 am to 5.30 pm (8.30 pm on Thursday), Monday to Saturday, and 2 to 5 pm on Sunday. There are guided tours at 3 pm on Saturday and at 2.30, 3.15 and 4 pm on Sunday. Admission is free.

Leinster House – Irish Parliament

The Dáil (Lower House) and Seanad (Upper House) of the Oireachtas na hÉireann

(Irish Parliament) meet in Leinster House (Around St Stephen's Green map) on Kildare St. The entrance to Leinster House from Kildare St is flanked by the National Library and the National Museum. Originally built as Kildare House between 1745 and 1748 for the earl of Kildare, the building had its name changed when the earl also assumed the title of duke of Leinster in 1766. One of the members of the Fitzgerald family who held the title was Lord Edward Fitzgerald, who died of wounds he received in the abortive 1798 Rising.

Leinster House's Kildare St frontage was designed by Richard Castle to look like a town house, whereas the Merrion Square frontage was made to look like a country house. The lawn in front of the Merrion Square frontage was the site for railway pioneer William Dargan's 1853 Dublin Industrial Exhibition, which in turn led to the creation of the National Gallery. There's a statue of him at the National Gallery end of the lawn. At the other end of the lawn is a statue of Prince Albert, Queen Victoria's consort. Queen Victoria herself was commemorated in massive form on the Kildare St side from 1908 until the statue was removed in 1948. The obelisk in front of the building is dedicated to Arthur Griffith, Michael Collins and Kevin O'Higgins, architects of independent Ireland.

The Dublin Society, later named the Royal Dublin Society, bought the building in 1814 but moved out in stages between 1922 and 1925, when the first government of independent Ireland decided to establish Parliament there.

The Seanad meets in the north-wing saloon, while the Dáil meets in a less interesting room that was originally a lecture theatre added to the original building in 1897. When Parliament is sitting, visitors are admitted to an observation gallery. You get an entry ticket from the Kildare St entrance on production of some identification. Bags can't be taken in, or notes or photographs taken. Parliament sits for 90 days a year, usually November to May, 2.30 to 8.30 pm on Tuesday, 10.30 am to 8.30 pm on Wednesday, and 10.30 am to 5.30 pm on Thursday. When the Dáil is not in session, guided tours of the Parliament are available on weekdays. Call ☎ 618 3000 for details.

Government Buildings
On Upper Merrion St, the domed Government Buildings (Around St Stephen's Green map) were opened in 1911, in a rather heavy-handed Edwardian interpretation of the Georgian style. Forty-minute tours are conducted from 10.30 am to 3.30 pm on Saturday. Tickets are available free from the National Gallery ticket office. Only 16 people can join each tour, so if a group has just arrived you may have to wait. Although you can't book in advance, you can go along in the morning and put your name down for later in the day. You get to see the Taoiseach's office, the ceremonial staircase with stunning stained-glass window, the cabinet room and innumerable fine examples of Irish arts and crafts on loan from the Arts Council. Bags can't be taken into the building.

Across the road at 24 Upper Merrion St, **Mornington House** is a Georgian mansion thought to be the birthplace of the duke of Wellington, who was somewhat ashamed of his Irish origins. It's possible that his actual birthplace was Trim in County Meath. The mansion is now part of Dublin's latest posh hotel, Merrion Hotel.

National Library
Flanking the Kildare St entrance to Leinster House is the National Library (Around St Stephen's Green map), which was built between 1884 and 1890, at the same time and to a similar design as the National Museum, by Sir Thomas Newenham Deane and his son Sir Thomas Manly Deane. Leinster House, the library and museum were all part of the Royal Dublin Society (formed in 1731), which aimed to improve conditions for poor people and to promote the arts and sciences. The library's extensive collection has many valuable early manuscripts, first editions, maps and other items. The library's reading room featured in James Joyce's *Ulysses*. Temporary displays are

often held in the entrance area. The library opens 10 am to 9 pm on Monday, 2 to 9 pm Tuesday and Wednesday, 10 am to 5 pm Thursday and Friday, and 10 am to 1 pm on Saturday.

Heraldic Museum & Genealogical Office

On the corner of Kildare and Nassau Sts, the former home of the Kildare St Club (an important right-wing institution during Dublin's Anglo-Irish heyday) is shared by the Heraldic Museum and Genealogical Office and the Alliance Française (Around St Stephen's Green map). It's a popular destination for visitors intent on tracing their Irish roots. A session with a genealogical expert costs £25 per hour, so you're better off attempting the trace yourself. Note the whimsical though rather worn stone carvings of animals, including monkeys playing billiards, that decorate the building's windows.

The Heraldic Museum's displays follow the story of heraldry in Ireland and Europe. It opens 10.30 am to 12.30 pm and 2 to 4.30 pm on weekdays. Admission is free.

Natural History Museum

The Natural History Museum (Around St Stephen's Green map; ☎ 677 7444) has scarcely changed since 1857 when Scottish explorer Dr David Livingstone delivered the opening lecture. It's known as the 'dead zoo', but despite that disheartening appellation it's well worth a visit: its collection is huge and well kept. The moth-eaten look that afflicts neglected collections of stuffed animals has been kept at bay and children in particular are likely to find it fascinating.

On the ground floor, the collection of skeletons, stuffed animals and the like covers the full range of Irish fauna. It includes three skeletons of the Irish giant deer, which became extinct about 10,000 years ago. On the 1st and 2nd floors are fauna from around the world.

The museum opens 10 am to 5 pm Tuesday to Saturday, and 2 to 5 pm on Sunday. Admission is free.

Grafton St & Around

Grafton St was the major traffic artery of southern Dublin until it was turned into a pedestrian precinct in 1982. It's now Dublin's fanciest and most colourful shopping centre, with plenty of street life and the city's most entertaining buskers. The street is equally lively after dark, as some of Dublin's most interesting pubs are clustered around it.

Apart from fine shops, such as the Brown Thomas department store (Around Temple Bar map; opened in 1848 and now teamed up with Switzers), Grafton St also boasts **Bewley's Oriental Café** (Around St Stephen's Green map). This branch of the chain has memorabilia upstairs relating to the company's history.

Johnson's Court leads off Grafton St to the elegantly converted **Powerscourt Townhouse Shopping Centre** (Around St Stephen's Green map) on South William St. Built between 1771 and 1774, this grand house has a balconied courtyard and, following its conversion in 1981, now shelters three levels of shops and restaurants. It was extensively restored in 1998. The Powerscourt family's principal residence was Powerscourt House in County Wicklow and this city mansion was soon sold for commercial use. It survived that period in remarkably good condition and in its present incarnation forms a convenient link from Grafton St to the South City Market on South Great George St. The building features plasterwork by Michael Stapleton, who worked on many Dublin buildings.

At the College Green end of Grafton St is the modern **statue of Molly Malone** (Around Temple Bar map) of song fame, rendered in such extreme *déshabillée* that she's nicknamed 'the tart with the cart'.

Dublin Civic Museum

Located in the 18th-century Assembly House beside Powerscourt Townhouse Shopping Centre, Dublin Civic Museum (Around St Stephen's Green map; ☎ 679 4260), 58 South William St, is a stone's throw from Grafton St. It has changing exhibitions relating to the history of the city.

In particular, look out for the head from Nelson's Pillar on O'Connell St which was toppled by the IRA in 1966. It's worth popping in just to see the architecture.

The small museum opens 10 am to 6 pm Tuesday to Saturday, and 11 am to 2 pm on Sunday. Admission is free.

Mansion House

The Mansion House (Around St Stephen's Green map) on Dawson St was built in 1710 by Joshua Dawson, after whom the street is named. Only five years later the house was bought as a residence for the Lord Mayor of Dublin. The building's original brick Queen Anne style has all but disappeared behind a stucco façade tacked on in the Victorian era. The building was the site for the 1919 Declaration of Independence. It isn't generally open to the public.

Next door is the **Royal Irish Academy**, whose 18th-century library houses many important documents, including an extensive collection of manuscripts such as the *Táin Bó Cúailnge*. Also held there is the entire library of 18th-century poet Sir Thomas Moore. The academy opens 10.30 am to 5 pm on weekdays. Admission is free.

St Stephen's Green & Around

On warm summer days the nine hectares of St Stephen's Green (Around St Stephen's Green map) provide a popular lunchtime escape for office workers. The green was originally an expanse of open common land where public whippings, burnings and hangings took place. The green was enclosed by a fence in 1664 when Dublin Corporation sold off the surrounding land for buildings. A stone wall replaced the fence in 1669 and trees and gravel paths soon followed within the park. By the end of that century restrictions were in force prohibiting buildings of less than two storeys or those constructed of mud and wattle around the green. At the same time, Grafton St, the main route to the green from what was then central Dublin, was upgraded from a 'foule and out of repaire' lane to a Crown causeway.

The fine Georgian buildings round the square date mainly from Dublin's mid-to-

late-18th-century Georgian prime. At that time the northern side was known as the Beaux Walk and it's still one of Dublin society's most esteemed meeting places. Some further improvements were made in 1753, with seats being put in place, but in 1814 railings and locked gates were added and an annual fee of one guinea was charged to use the green. This private use continued until 1877 when Sir Arthur Edward Guinness, later Lord Ardilaun, pushed an act through Parliament to once again open the green to the public. He also financed the central park's gardens and ponds, which date from 1880.

The main entrance to the green is through **Fusiliers' Arch** at the north-western corner. Modelled on the Arch of Titus in Rome, the arch commemorates the 212 soldiers of the Royal Dublin Fusiliers who died in the Boer War (1899–1902).

Around the fountain in the centre of the green are a number of statues, including a **bust of Countess Markievicz**. The centre of the park also has a **garden for the blind**, complete with signs in Braille and plants that can be handled. To the south is a fine old **bandstand**, erected for Queen Victoria's jubilee in 1887. Concerts often take place here in the summer. On the eastern side of the green there's a children's play park.

Just inside the green at the south-eastern corner, near Leeson St, is a **statue of the Three Fates**, presented to Dublin in 1956 by West Germany in gratitude for Irish aid immediately after WWII. The north-eastern corner, opposite the Shelbourne Hotel and Merrion Row, is marked by the **Wolfe Tone Monument** to the leader of the abortive 1796 invasion. The vertical slabs that serve as a backdrop for Wolfe Tone's statue have been dubbed 'Tonehenge'. Just inside the park at this entrance is a **memorial to the victims of the Famine**.

Across the road from the western side of the green are the 1863 **Unitarian Church** and the **Royal College of Surgeons**, the latter with one of the finest façades round St Stephen's Green. It was built in 1806 and extended from 1825 to 1827 to the design of William Murray. In the 1916 Easter Rising,

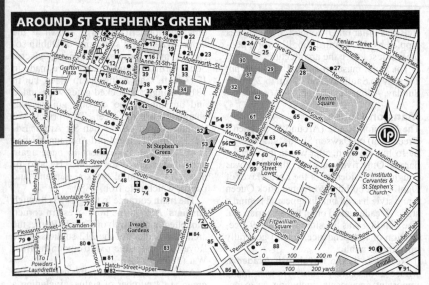

AROUND ST STEPHEN'S GREEN

the building was occupied by the colourful Countess Markievicz (1868–1927), an Irish nationalist married to a Polish count. The columns still bear bullet marks.

Other notable buildings round the green include the imposing 1867 **Shelbourne Hotel** on the northern side, with statues of Nubian princesses and their ankle-fettered slave girls decorating the front. Just beyond the Shelbourne is a small **Huguenot cemetery** dating from 1693, when many French Huguenots fled here from persecution under Louis XIV.

At No 80-81 on the southern side of the green is **Iveagh House**, where the Guinness family once lived; today it is home to the Department of Foreign Affairs, the Irish Foreign Office. Designed by Richard Castle in 1730, this was his first project in Dublin. He went on to create many more buildings, including Leinster House and the Rotunda Hospital.

At 85-86 St Stephen's Green on the southern side is **Newman House** (☎ 475 7255), now part of University College, Dublin. These buildings have some of the finest plasterwork in the city. No 85 was built between 1736 and 1738 by Richard

Castle for Hugh Montgomery MP. The particularly fine plasterwork was by the Swiss stuccodores Paul and Philip Francini (also known as Paolo and Filippo Lafranchini) and can be best appreciated in the wonderfully detailed Apollo Room on the ground floor.

Richard Chapel Whaley MP took possession of No 85 in 1765 but decided to display his wealth by constructing a much grander home next door at No 86. Whaley's son Buck contrived to become an MP while still a teenager and also one of the more notorious members of Dublin's Hell Fire Club. He was also a noted gambler, once walking all the way to Jerusalem to win a bet.

The Catholic University of Ireland, predecessor of University College, Dublin, acquired the building in 1865, and then passed it to the Jesuits. Some of the plasterwork was a little too detailed for Jesuit tastes, however, so cover-ups were prescribed. On the ceiling of the upstairs saloon, previously naked female figures were clothed in what can best be described as furry swimsuits. One survived the restoration process.

AROUND ST STEPHEN'S GREEN

PLACES TO STAY
2 Avalon House
3 Horse & Carriage
6 Brooks Hotel
11 Westbury Hotel
26 Davenport Hotel
48 Staunton's on the Green
54 Shelbourne Hotel
63 Merrion Hotel; Restaurant Patrick Guilbaud; Lloyd's Brasserie
66 Georgian House; Ante Room
68 Longfield's
71 Fitzwilliam
76 Albany House
77 Russell Court Hotel; The Vatican
78 Frankies
81 Harcourt Hotel
84 Hotel Conrad
85 Stephen's Hall
86 Leeson Court Hotel
89 Latchford's

PLACES TO EAT
8 Velure
12 Pasta Fresca
13 Kaffe Moka
15 Bewley's Oriental Café
16 Eddie Rocket's; Café Java; Gotham Café
19 Fitzers
35 La Stampa
37 La Pizza
38 Captain America

43 Peacock Alley
44 Chicago Pizza Pie Factory
57 Pierre Victoire
60 Georgian Fare
64 Miller's Pizza Kitchen
91 Fitzers Take-Out

OTHER
1 Whitefriars Carmelite Church
4 All American Laundrette
5 Planet Cyber Café
7 Break for the Border
9 Dublin Civic Museum
10 Powerscourt Townhouse Shopping Centre
14 HMV
17 Dublin Bookshop
18 Cathach Books
20 Hodges Figgis
21 Dúchas Bookshop
22 Waterstone's
23 Renard's
24 Heraldic Museum; Genealogical Office; Alliance Française
25 Greene's Bookshop
27 Goethe Institute
28 Oscar Wilde Statue
29 National Gallery
30 National Library
31 Leinster House (Irish Parliament)
32 National Museum
33 St Anne's Church
34 Mansion House
36 Aer Lingus

39 Post Office
40 Gaiety Theatre
41 St Stephen's Green Shopping Centre
42 Fusiliers' Arch
45 Royal College of Surgeons
46 Unitarian Church
47 An Siopa Leabhar
49 Bandstand
50 Countess Markievicz Bust
51 Three Fates Statue
52 Famine Victims Memorial
53 Wolfe Tone Memorial
55 Huguenot Cemetery
56 Post Office
58 Irish Ferries
59 Shaft
61 Government Buildings
62 Natural History Museum
65 Irish Architectural Archive
67 Irish Traditional Music Archive
69 No 29 Lower Fitzwilliam St
70 British Council
72 Post Office
73 Iveagh House
74 Newman House; The Commons
75 Catholic University Church
79 George Bernard Shaw House
80 Copper Face Jack's
82 PoD; Odeon
83 National Concert Hall
87 Focus Theatre
88 Italian Cultural Institute
90 Bord Fáilte

The Catholic University named Newman House after its first rector, John Henry Newman. Gerard Manley Hopkins, professor of classics at the college from 1884 until his death in 1889, lived upstairs at No 86. It wasn't until some time after his death that his innovative, if rather depressing, poetry was published. His room is now preserved as it was during his residence. Among former students of the college are James Joyce; Pádraig Pearse, leader of the 1916 Easter Rising; and Eamon de Valera.

The house opens fromJune to August and can be visited only as part of an organised tour. Tours run at noon and 2, 3 and 4 pm Tuesday to Friday, on the hour from 11 am to 1 pm on Saturday, and on the hour from 2 to 4 pm on Sunday. Each tour lasts about 40 minutes. Tours can also be organised at other times of year; call ☎ 475 7255 for details. Admission costs £2/1.

Next to Newman House is the **Catholic University Church**, or Newman Chapel, built between 1854 and 1856 with a colourful neo-Byzantine interior that attracted a great deal of criticism at the time. Today this is one of the most fashionable churches in Dublin for weddings.

One of Dublin's best-kept secrets is landscaped **Iveagh Gardens**, directly behind Newman House and reached via Earlsfort Terrace or Clonmel St, just off Harcourt St. The imposing walls give the impression that they are private gardens, but they are one of the nicest places to relax on a summer's day or before a show in the National Concert Hall. They open dawn till dusk year round.

Harcourt St, running from the south-western corner of the green, was laid out in 1775. Well-known names associated with the street include Edward Carson, who was born at No 4 in 1854. As the architect of Northern Irish unionism, he makes an easy scapegoat for many of the problems caused by Ireland's division. Bram Stoker, author of *Dracula*, lived at No 16, and George Bernard Shaw at No 61. For 99 years from 1859 to 1958 the Dublin to Bray train line used to terminate at Harcourt St Station, which is at the bottom of the road and now a giant bar called Odeon.

Merrion Square

Merrion Square (Around St Stephen's Green map), with its well-kept Archbishop Ryan Park and elegant Georgian buildings, dates back to 1762. Round this square you can find some of the best of Dublin's Georgian entrances, with fine doors, peacock fanlights, ornate door knockers and more than a few foot scrapers where gentlemen removed mud from their shoes before venturing indoors.

Oscar Wilde's parents, the surgeon Sir William Wilde and the poet Lady Wilde, who wrote under the pseudonym Speranza, lived at 1 Merrion Square North. Oscar was born in 1854 at 21 Westland Row, just north of the square. Enthusiasts should check out the **Oscar Wilde statue** at the north-western corner of the square, as it is adorned with the witty one-liners for which Wilde became famous.

WB Yeats (1865–1939) lived at 52 Merrion Square East and later, between 1922 and 1928, at 82 Merrion Square South. George (AE) Russell (1867–1935), the 'poet, mystic, painter and co-operator', worked at No 84. Daniel O'Connell (1775–1847) was a resident of No 58 in his later years. The Austrian Erwin Schrödinger (1887–1961), co-winner of the 1933 Nobel Prize for physics, lived at No 65 between 1940 and 1956. Dublin seems to attract the writers of horror stories: Joseph Sheridan Le Fanu (1814–73), who penned the vam-

pire classic *Carmilla*, was a resident of No 70.

The UK Embassy was at 39 Merrion Square East until it was burned out in 1972 in protest against Bloody Sunday in Derry, Northern Ireland. The Architectural Association is at 8 Merrion Square North, a few doors down from the Wilde residence.

The Leinster Lawn at the western end of the square has the 1791 **Rutland Fountain** and an 18m obelisk honouring the founders of independent Ireland.

Merrion Square hasn't always been merely graceful and affluent, however. During the Famine, soup kitchens were set up in the gardens, which were crowded with starving rural refugees.

Damage to fine Dublin buildings hasn't always been the prerogative of vandals, terrorists or protesters. Merrion Square East once continued into Lower Fitzwilliam St in the longest unbroken series of Georgian houses anywhere in Europe. In 1961 the Electricity Supply Board (ESB) knocked down 26 of the houses to build an office block.

At the south-eastern corner of Merrion Square the ESB had the decency to preserve one of the fine old Georgian houses at **No 29 Lower Fitzwilliam St**. It has been restored to give a good impression of genteel home life in Dublin between 1790 and 1820. The house opens 10 am to 5 pm Tuesday to Saturday, and 2 to 5 pm on Sunday. A short film on its history is followed by a 30-minute guided tour in groups of nine or less. Admission costs £2.50/1.

Upper Merrion St & Ely Place

Upper Merrion St (Around St Stephen's Green map), which runs south from Merrion Square to St Stephen's Green, was built around 1770. The duke of Wellington was probably born at 24 Upper Merrion St. On the other side of Baggot St, Merrion St becomes Ely (pronounced 'e-lie') Place.

John Philpot Curran (1750–1817), a great advocate of Irish liberty, once lived at No 4, as did the novelist George Moore (1852–1933). The house at No 6 was the residence of the earl of Clare. Better known as Black

Jack Fitzgibbon (1749–1802), he was a bitter opponent of Irish political aspirations, and in 1794 a mob attempted to storm the house. Ely House at No 8 is one of the city's best examples of a Georgian mansion. At one time the surgeon Sir Thornley Stoker (whose brother Bram Stoker wrote *Dracula*) lived here. Oliver St John Gogarty (1878–1957) lived for a time at No 25, but the art gallery of the Royal Hibernian Academy now occupies that position.

Fitzwilliam Square

South of Merrion Square and east of St Stephen's Green, the original and well-kept Fitzwilliam Square (Around St Stephen's Green map) is a centre for the Dublin medical profession. Built between 1791 and 1825, it was the smallest and the last of Dublin's great Georgian squares. It's also the only square where the central garden is still the private domain of residents of the square. William Dargan (1799–1861), railway pioneer and founder of the National Gallery, lived at No 2, and Jack B Yeats (1871–1957) at No 18. Look out for the attractive 18th- and 19th-century coal-hole covers. The square is a night-time favourite for women practising the world's oldest profession.

Other Southern Dublin Churches

St Andrew's Church The Protestant St Andrew's Church (Around Temple Bar map), on St Andrew's St near Trinity College, is now the home of Dublin Tourism. Designed by Charles Lanyon, the Gothic church was built between 1860 and 1873 on the site of an ancient nunnery. Across the street, on the corner of Church Lane and Suffolk St, there once stood a huge Viking '*thingmote*' (ceremonial mound). It was levelled in 1661 and used to raise the level of Nassau St, which had previously been subject to flooding.

Whitefriars Carmelite Church Next to the popular Avalon House backpackers hostel on Aungier St, the Carmelite Church (Around St Stephen's Green map) stands on the site of the Whitefriars Carmelite

monastery. The monastery was founded in 1278 but, like other monasteries, was suppressed by Henry VIII in 1537 and had all its lands and wealth seized by the Crown. Eventually the Carmelites returned to their former church and re-established it, dedicating the new building in 1827.

In the north-eastern corner of the church, the 16th-century Flemish oak statue of the Virgin and Child escaped destruction during the Reformation; it probably once belonged to St Mary's Abbey in northern Dublin. The church's altar contains the remains of St Valentine, of St Valentine's Day fame, donated to the church in 1836 by the pope.

St Anne's Church St Anne's (Around St Stephen's Green map), on Dawson St near Mansion House, was built in 1720 but is now lost behind an 1868 neo-Romanesque façade. There's a fine view of it looking down South Anne St from Grafton St, and it is noted for its lunchtime recitals.

St Stephen's Church Built in 1824 in Greek Revival style, St Stephen's (off Around St Stephen's Green map), complete with cupola, is at the far end of Upper Mount St from Merrion Square and has been converted into business units. Because of its appearance, it was nicknamed the 'Peppercanister Church'. You can visit inside 12.30 to 3.20 pm on weekdays.

Other Southern Dublin Museums

George Bernard Shaw House (Around St Stephen's Green map; ☎ 872 2077), 33 Synge St, Dublin 2, opens 10 am to 6 pm Monday to Saturday, and 11.30 am to 6 pm on Sunday and public holidays, May to October. Admission costs £2.40/1.15 (students £2).

The **Irish Traditional Music Archive** (Around St Stephen's Green map; ☎ 661 9699), 63 Merrion Square South, collects, preserves and organises traditional Irish music. The archive opens to the public by appointment.

The **Irish Architectural Archive and Architecture Centre** (Around St Stephen's Green map; ☎ 676 3430), 73 Merrion

Square South, traces Dublin's architectural history from 1560 to the present day. The archive is housed in a fine 1793 town house. The Royal Institute of the Architects of Ireland (☎ 676 1703) has its headquarters across the square at 8 Merrion Square North, and exhibitions and displays are also held there.

Other Southern Dublin Galleries

City Arts Centre (☎ 677 0643), 23-25 Moss St, has changing exhibitions in its two galleries, which open 11 am to 5.30 pm on weekdays, and noon to 4 pm on Saturday. Admission is free.

In the **Bank of Ireland Arts Centre** (Around Temple Bar map; ☎ 661 5255), in Foster Place, behind the actual bank, there are usually changing displays of contemporary Irish art.

Temple Bar Gallery (Around Temple Bar map; ☎ 671 0073), 5 Temple Bar, is an important exhibition space for contemporary artists from both Ireland and abroad.

NORTH OF THE LIFFEY

Though southern Dublin has the lion's share of the city's tourist attractions, there are still many reasons to head across the Liffey, starting with Dublin's grandest avenue.

O'Connell St

O'Connell St is the major thoroughfare of northern Dublin and probably the most important and imposing street in the city. Its earlier glory has gone, but city authorities have earmarked it for rejuvenation. It started life in the early 18th century as Drogheda St, named after Viscount Henry Moore, earl of Drogheda. There are still a Henry St, a Moore St and an Earl St nearby. The earl even managed to squeeze in an Of Lane! At that time, Capel St, farther to the west, was the main traffic route, and Drogheda St, lacking a bridge to connect it with southern Dublin, was of little importance.

In the 1740s, Luke Gardiner, later Viscount Mountjoy, widened the street to 45m to turn it into an elongated promenade bearing his name. However, it was the completion of Carlisle Bridge across the Liffey in 1794 that quickly made it the city's most important street. In 1880, Carlisle Bridge was replaced by the much wider O'Connell Bridge, which stands today. Gardiner's Mall soon became Sackville St, but was renamed again, in 1924, after Daniel O'Connell, the Irish nationalist leader. An 1854 bronze **statue of Daniel O'Connell** surveys the avenue from the river end.

O'Connell St has certainly had its share of drama; its high-speed redevelopment began during the 1916 Easter Rising when the GPO building (see the following entry) became the starting point for, and main centre of, the abortive revolt. Only six years later, in 1922, the unfortunate avenue suffered another bout of destruction when it became the scene of a Civil War clash that burned down most of the eastern side of the street. The bullet marks on the GPO and O'Connell's statue are a legacy of this period.

The street's once most famous monument, Nelson's Pillar, was a victim of 'explosive' redesign. In 1815 O'Connell St was graced with a Doric column topped by a statue of Nelson, the British naval captain who defeated the French at Trafalgar. It predated his column in Trafalgar Square, London, by 32 years. In 1966, however, to mark the 50th anniversary of the 1916 Easter Rising, this symbol of British imperialism was damaged by an IRA explosion and subsequently demolished. One aspect of the demolition that never fails to amuse Dubliners is that, while the original explosion caused no damage to anything other than poor Nelson, the charges set by the Irish army to demolish the remaining pedestal blew out virtually every window in O'Connell St! Nelson's head can be seen in the Dublin Civic Museum. Nelson's demise put an end to the quip that the main street of the capital city of this most piously Catholic of countries had statues honouring three noted adulterers: O'Connell at the bottom of the street, Parnell at the top and Nelson in the middle.

Poor O'Connell St suffered more damage in the 1960s and 1970s, when parts of

Dublin went through a period of rampant redevelopment under lax government controls. Today's tacky fast-food and cheap-office-block atmosphere is a legacy of that era.

The site of Nelson's demolished column is halfway up the street, between Henry and Earl Sts, opposite the GPO. To celebrate the millennium, a 160m-high spire was set to go up on the spot once occupied by Nelson. Nothing had been done at the time of writing, but authorities were predicting a grand unveiling in time for New Year's Eve 1999. Nearby, a **James Joyce statue** stands nonchalantly outside Café Kylemore on the corner of pedestrianised North Earl St. South of the former site of the column is a **fountain statue of Anna Livia**, Joyce's spirit of the Liffey – a 1988 addition to the streetscape. It was almost immediately dubbed 'the floozy in the Jacuzzi'.

Farther north is the **statue of Father Theobald Mathew** (1790–1856), the 'apostle of temperance' – a hopeless role in Ireland. This quixotic task, however, also resulted in a Liffey bridge bearing his name. The northern end of the street is completed by the imposing **statue of Charles Stewart Parnell** (1846–91), Home Rule advocate and victim of Irish morality. Just to the west of O'Connell St, on Moore St, is an energetic and colourful **open-air market**.

General Post Office

The GPO building on O'Connell St is an important landmark physically and historically. The building, designed by Francis Johnston and opened in 1818, was the focus for the 1916 Easter Rising when Pádraig Pearse, James Connolly and the other leaders read their proclamation from the front steps. In the subsequent siege the building was burned out. The façade with its Ionic portico is still pockmarked from the 1916 clash and from further damage wrought at the start of the Civil War in 1922. The GPO wasn't reopened until 1929. Its central role in the history of independent Ireland has made it a prime site for everything from official parades to personal protests.

Abbey Theatre

Opened in 1904, Abbey Theatre (☎ 878 7222), on the corner of Marlborough and

Rebel with Several Causes

For some years it looked as if motherhood had tamed the bad girl of Irish pop. But Sinéad O'Connor was destined for a life of dogged controversy, ever since she burst into the world's consciousness as the shaven-headed, doe-eyed singer of 'Nothing Compares 2 U'. At a New Jersey concert she refused to have the US flag flown; she has confessed to an abortion; she took out a full-page ad in a national daily to detail her abused childhood (provoking fury from her novelist brother Joseph, who claimed it was all a lie); and she has even admitted IRA sympathies (since retracted).

Quiet for a few years, Sinéad was once again in the limelight in 1998 as the result of a messy paternity suit with the father of her second child, *Irish Times* journalist John Waters (who retained custody).

Then, in April 1999, the biggest bombshell of all: the woman who ripped up the pope's picture on the US TV show *Saturday Night Live* was ordained by the rebel Catholic order of the Latinate TKTK as Mother Bernadette Mary and was devoting the rest of her life to serving God. Predictably, Ireland reacted with a mixture of shock, dismay and humour, especially when it emerged that she had paid £350,000 for the ordination, ostensibly to pay for a priest's operation (which she then took back). Will a priest's collar make her immune to controversy? Not likely, especially if she signs her name 'Saint Mother Bernadette Mary', which she did on the door of a Dublin restaurant in 1999.

Lower Abbey Sts, is just north of the Liffey. Here the Irish National Theatre Society soon became a name not only for playwrights such as JM Synge and Sean O'Casey but also for Irish acting ability and theatrical presentation. The 1907 premiere of JM Synge's *The Playboy of the Western World* brought a storm of protest from theatre-goers, and Sean O'Casey's *The Plough and the Stars* prompted a similar reaction in 1926. On the latter occasion WB Yeats himself came on stage after the performance to tick the audience off!

The original theatre burned down in 1951. It took 15 years to come up with a replacement and this dull building fails to live up to its famous name or the company's continuing reputation. The smaller Peacock Theatre at the same location presents new and experimental works.

Hot Press Irish Music Hall of Fame

Dublin's newest museum, at 57 Middle Abbey St, is a celebration of Ireland's key role in popular music. From 1960s legend Van Morrisson to current girl band B*witched, they're all here, or at least some of their memorabilia is. You can see U2 drummer Larry Mullen's first drum kit, the original Live Aid contract received by Bob Geldof, and plenty of other bits and bobs, some of which are more interesting than others. There's also the embarrassingly named Jam restaurant and a 500-seat venue (see HQ under Concerts in the Entertainment section later in this chapter).

The Hall of Fame (☎ 878 3345) opens 10 am to 7 pm daily. Admission costs a whopping £6/4 but includes a headset for the audiovisual tour. If you're a big fan of Irish rock and pop acts, you'll enjoy it. If not, give it a miss.

St Mary's Pro-Cathedral

On the corner of Marlborough and Cathedral Sts, just east of O'Connell St, is Dublin's most important Catholic church, built between 1816 and 1825. Unfortunately, the cramped Marlborough St location makes it difficult to stand back far enough to admire the front with its six Doric columns, modelled on the Temple of Theseus in Athens.

The 1814 competition for the church's design was won by John Sweetman, a former owner of Sweetman's Brewery. And who organised the competition? Why William Sweetman, John Sweetman's brother. And did John Sweetman design it himself? Well, possibly not. He was living in Paris at the time and may have bought the plans from a French architect who designed the remarkably similar Notre Dame de Lorette in northern France. The only clue as to the church's architect is in the ledger, which lists the builder as 'Mr P'. And what does 'pro' mean? It's not clear, but it implies something like 'unofficial cathedral'. The cathedral opens 8 am to 6 pm daily. Admission is free.

You wouldn't know it now, but this area was once a busy red-light district known as Monto which featured in Joyce's *Ulysses* as Nighttown.

Parnell Square

The principal squares of northern Dublin are poor relations of the great squares south of the Liffey, though they do have their points of interest. Parnell Square's northern side was built on lands acquired in the mid-18th century by Dr Bartholomew Mosse, founder of the Rotunda Hospital, and was originally named Palace Row. The terrace was laid out in 1755 and Lord Charlemont bought the land for his home at No 22 in 1762. Charlemont's home was designed by Sir William Chambers, who also designed Lord Charlemont's extraordinary Casino at Marino. Today, the building houses the Municipal Gallery of Modern Art. The street was completed in 1769 and the gardens were renamed Rutland Square in 1786, before acquiring their current name.

In 1966 the northern slice of the square was turned into a **Garden of Remembrance** for the 50th anniversary of the 1916 Easter Rising. Its centrepiece is a sculpture by Oisin Kelly depicting the myth of the children of Lir, who were turned into swans by their wicked stepmother.

There are some fine, though rather run-down, Georgian houses on the eastern side of the square. Oliver St John Gogarty, immortalised as Buck Mulligan in Joyce's *Ulysses*, was born at No 5 in 1878.

Rotunda Hospital In 1757, Dr Bartholomew Mosse opened the Rotunda Hospital, the first maternity hospital in Ireland or Britain. It was built at a time when Dublin's burgeoning urban population suffered horrific levels of infant mortality. The hospital shares its basic design with Leinster House because Richard Castle reused the floorplan as an economy measure. To his Leinster House design Castle added a three-storey tower which Mosse had intended to use as a lookout to raise funds for the hospital's operation. The Rotunda Assembly Hall, now occupied by the Ambassador Cinema, was built as an adjunct to the hospital as another fundraiser. The Rotunda Chapel is over the main entrance of the hospital and was built in 1758 with superb coloured plasterwork by Bartholomew Cramillion.

The Rotunda Hospital still functions as a maternity hospital. The **Patrick Conway pub** opposite the hospital dates from 1745 and has been hosting expectant fathers since the day the hospital opened.

Gate Theatre In the south-eastern corner of Parnell Square is the Gate Theatre, opened in 1929 by Micheál MacLiammóir and Hilton Edwards (the actual building dates from 1784 to 1786, when it was constructed as part of the Rotunda Hospital complex). MacLiammóir continued to act at his theatre until 1975, when he retired at the age of 76 after making his 1384th performance of the one-man show *The Importance of Being Oscar* (Oscar being Oscar Wilde, of course). The Gate Theatre was the stage for Orson Welles' first professional appearance and also featured James Mason early in his career.

Today it features a more exciting brand of theatre than its longtime rival, the Abbey, with a worthwhile mix of classic plays from Ireland and abroad, and more modern, experimental work.

Municipal Gallery of Modern Art The Municipal Gallery of Modern Art or Hugh Lane Gallery (☎ 874 1903), 22 Parnell Square North, has a fine collection of work by French Impressionists and by 20th-century Irish artists.

The gallery was founded in 1908 and moved to its present location in Charlemont House in 1933. The gallery was established by wealthy Sir Hugh Lane with no help from the government. He died in the 1915 sinking of the *Lusitania*, which was torpedoed off the southern coast of Ireland by a German U-boat. The lack of official funding was the subject of one of WB Yeats' most vitriolic poems, *September 1913*. The Lane Bequest pictures, which formed the nucleus of the gallery, were the subject of a dispute over Lane's will between the gallery and the National Gallery in London. A settlement was finally reached in 1959, splitting the collection. From November 1999 the gallery has displayed Manet's *Eva Gonzales*, Pissarro's *Printemps*, Berthe Morisot's *Jour d'Eté* and the most important painting of the collection, Renoir's *Les Parapluies*.

The gallery has a shop and the Gallery Restaurant. It opens 9.30 am to 6 pm (8 pm on Thursday from April to August) Tuesday to Thursday, 9.30 am to 5 pm Friday and Saturday, and 11 am to 5 pm on Sunday. Admission is free.

Dublin Writers' Museum This museum (☎ 872 2077), 18 Parnell Square North, celebrates the city's long and continuing history as a literary centre. The Gallery of Writers upstairs houses busts and portraits of some of Ireland's most famous writers; their letters, photographs and first editions are downstairs. The museum also has a bookshop and the Chapter One restaurant.

The museum opens 10 am to 5 pm (6 pm on weekdays from June to August) Monday to Saturday, and 11 am to 5 pm on Sunday. Admission costs £3/2.55, which includes taped guides with readings from relevant texts in English and other languages. If you plan to visit the James Joyce Museum (see Sandycove in the Around Dublin section) and George Bernard Shaw House (see Other Southern Dublin Museums in the earlier South of the Liffey section), bear in mind that a combined ticket is cheaper than three separate ones.

While the museum concerns itself primarily with dead authors, next door at No 19 the **Irish Writers' Centre** provides a meeting and working place for their living successors.

Abbey Presbyterian Church The soaring spire of this church, at the corner of Frederick St and Parnell Square North, is a convenient landmark. Dating from 1864, the church was financed by the Scottish grocery and brewery magnate Alex Findlater and is often referred to as Findlater's Church.

World of Wax

Every city worth its tourist traps has a wax museum. Dublin's National Wax Museum (☎ 872 6340) is on Granby Row, north of Parnell Square. Along with the usual fantasy and fairy-tale offerings, the inevitable Chamber of Horrors and a rock music 'megastars' area, there are also figures of Irish heroes such as Wolfe Tone, Robert Emmet and Charles Parnell; the leaders of the 1916 Easter Rising; and taoisigh (prime ministers, plural of taoiseach). Prominent literary and political figures also get a look in, including John Hume, Ian Paisley, David Trimble and Gerry Adams. Recorded commentaries help to explain each individual's role in Irish history. The museum opens 10 am to 6 pm Monday to Saturday, and noon to 6 pm on Sunday. Admission costs £3.50/2.50 (families £10).

Great Denmark St

From the north-eastern corner of Parnell Square, Great Denmark St runs eastwards to Mountjoy Square, passing the 1775 Belvedere House, which has been used since 1841 as the Jesuit **Belvedere College**. James Joyce was a student here between 1893 and 1898 and describes it in *A Portrait of the Artist as a Young Man*. The building

is renowned for its magnificent plasterwork by the master stuccodore Michael Stapleton and for its fireplaces by the Venetian artisan Bossi. It's not open to the public.

Mountjoy Square

Built between 1792 and 1818, Mountjoy Square was a fashionable and affluent centre at the height of the Protestant Ascendancy. Today it's a run-down symbol of northern Dublin's urban decay, though redevelopment is beginning to happen. Viscount Mountjoy, after whom the square was named, was that energetic developer Luke Gardiner, who briefly gave his name to Gardiner Mall before it became Sackville St and then O'Connell St. The square was in fact named after him twice, as it started life as Gardiner Square.

Legends relate that this was where Brian Ború pitched his tent at the Battle of Clontarf in 1014. Residents of the square have included Sean O'Casey, who set his play *The Shadow of a Gunman* here, though he referred to it as Hilljoy Square. As a child James Joyce lived just off the square at 14 Fitzgibbon St.

St George's Church

St George's Church, on Hardwicke Place off North Temple St, was built by Francis Johnston from 1802 in Greek Ionic style and has a 60m-high steeple modelled after that of St Martin-in-the-Fields in London. The church's bells were added in 1836. The duke of Wellington was married here. Although this was one of Johnston's finest works, the church is no longer in use.

St Mary's Church

On Mary St, between Wolfe Tone and Jervis Sts, St Mary's was designed in 1697 (and completed in 1702) by Sir William Robinson, who was also responsible for the Royal Hospital at Kilmainham. The church was a popular one among the social elite of the period: many famous Dubliners were baptised and married here, including Arthur Guinness, who tied the knot in 1793. In 1747 John Wesley, the founder of Methodism, preached here for the first time in

Ireland. Sadly, the most important church of the 18th century barely survives today and is no longer in use. Irish patriot Wolfe Tone was born in the adjacent street now bearing his name.

St Mary's Abbey

Despite the intriguing history of St Mary's Abbey, there's little to see, and even finding the abbey is tricky: it's just west of Capel St in Meetinghouse Lane, which runs off a street named Mary's Abbey.

When the abbey was founded in 1139 by Benedictine monks this was a rural location, far from the temptations of city life. In 1147, it was taken over by the Cistercians. Until its suppression in the mid-16th century this was the most important monastery within English-controlled Ireland. The monastery's property was confiscated by Henry VIII in 1537; it turned out to be the most valuable in all of Ireland, at a total of £537 sterling. Mellifont Abbey, north of Dublin, came in second at £352 sterling, but no other Irish monastery was worth over £100 sterling.

By the end of the 16th century the abbey was virtually derelict. In 1676, stones from the abbey were used to construct Essex Bridge. Using it as a quarry soon removed all visible traces of the monastery and not until comparatively recently were the remaining fragments rediscovered.

The chapter house (☎ 872 1490), where monks gathered after morning mass, is the only surviving part of the abbey, which, in its prime, covered land stretching as far east as Marino. The floor level in the abbey is 2m below street level – a clear indication of the changes wrought over eight centuries. The chapter house opens 10 am to 5 pm on Wednesday, mid-June to mid-September. Admission costs £1/40p.

James Joyce Cultural Centre

No 35 North Great George St (☎ 878 8547) was were Denis Maginni taught dance in the front room early this century. Hardly remarkable, but the fact that he and his home featured several times in *Ulysses* led Joycean scholar and leading gay activist Senator David Norris to take over the house in 1982. He proceeded to restore the house and convert it into a centre for the study of Joyce and his books.

Visitors see the room were Maginni taught and a collection of pictures of the 17 different Dublin homes occupied by the nomadic Joyce family and the real individuals fictionalised in the books. Some of the fine plaster ceilings are restored originals, others careful reproductions of Michael Stapleton's designs.

The house opens 9.30 am to 5 pm on weekdays, and 12.30 to 5 pm at the weekend. Admission costs £2.75/2. For information on James Joyce-related walking tours departing from the centre, see Walking Tours in the Organised Tours section later in this chapter.

St Michan's Church

Named after a Danish saint, St Michan's Church on Lower Church St, near the Four Courts, was founded by Danes in 1095, though there's little trace of the original. The battlement tower dates from the 15th century, but otherwise the church was rebuilt in the late 17th century and considerably restored in the early 19th century and again after the Civil War, during which it had been damaged.

The church contains a 1724 organ which Handel may have played for the first performance of his *Messiah*. The organ case is distinguished by a fine oak carving of 17 entwined musical instruments on its front. A skull on the floor on one side of the altar is said to represent Oliver Cromwell. On the opposite side, a penitent's chair was where 'open and notoriously naughty livers' did public penance. But the church's main 'attraction' lies in the subterranean crypt, where bodies have been preserved to varying degrees, not by mummification but by the constant dry atmosphere. You can visit the church any time during opening hours, but you can see the crypt only as part of a tour.

Tours of the church and crypt are conducted 10 am to 12.45 pm and 2 to 4.45 pm on weekdays, and 10 am to 12.45 pm on

Saturday. The tour costs £2/50p and lasts about 15 minutes.

Old Jameson Distillery

Where does Irish whiskey get its particular colour and smooth bouquet from? While most people have heard the term 'single malt', how many can actually tell what it is? These are just some of the secrets you can learn at the Old Jameson Distillery (☎ 807 2355), a museum devoted to Irish whiskey just north of St Michan's Church. It opened in 1997 after a £7 million renovation of the old Jameson distillery, which produced Ireland's best-loved whiskey from 1791 until its closure in 1966 (when Jameson, along with the other main Irish producers, united to form Irish Distillers, with an ultra-modern distillery in Midleton, County Cork).

The museum can be visited only by guided tour, but it's well worth it. A short film kicks off the tour, after which visitors are led through a re-creation of the old factory, where the guide explains the entire process of whiskey distilling from grain to bottle. Visitors are then invited into the Jameson Bar, where they are offered a complimentary glass of 'the hard stuff' (as it is referred to in Dublin vernacular). The tour finishes with a surprise competition, but you'll have to visit to find out what it is! There's also a restaurant on the premises. The museum opens 10 am to 5 pm daily; tours depart every 30 minutes. Admission costs £3.50.

Ceol

Dublin's newest attraction is an ultra-modern, interactive museum in the Chief O'Neills complex that is devoted entirely to *ceol* (music). The music in question is the Irish traditional kind. If that sounds a little limited, it is anything but.

The museum's interactive displays cover virtually every aspect of the entire tradition of Irish music both sung and instrumental from the Middle Ages, through the early attempts to catalogue the thousands of jigs, reels and hornpipes in the 18th century, and on to the explosion of the distinctly Irish sound on the international stage after WWII.

The wonderful audiovisuals detail the music's unique characteristics and sounds, with particular emphasis on the four main instruments: *uilleann* (elbow) pipes, fiddle, flute and button accordion. Of particular interest is the room devoted to song, especially the *sean nós* style, an ancient form that involves the telling of a story through song punctuated by plenty of grace notes. There are plenty of video performances by some of Ireland's best players. Kids will enjoy the game of musical twister, in which floor pads light up as a tune is played and the listener is invited to re-create the tune by standing on the pads.

The complex also includes a bar and a hotel (see North of the Liffey under Top End – Hotels in the Places to Stay section, and Trendy under Pubs in the Entertainment section, later in this chapter). The museum opens 9.30 am to 6 pm Monday to Saturday. Admission costs £3.95/2.50.

King's Inns & Henrietta St

King's Inns, home of the Dublin legal profession, is on Constitution Hill and Henrietta St. This classical building by James Gandon suffered many delays between its design in 1795 and its completion in 1817. Several other architects lent a hand along the way, including Francis Johnston, who added the cupola. The building is normally open only to members of the Inns.

Henrietta St, along the southern side of the building, was Dublin's first Georgian street and has buildings dating from 1720 but is unfortunately now in a state of disrepair. These early Georgian mansions were large and varied in style. For a time Henrietta St rejoiced in the name Primate's Hill, as the archbishop of Armagh and other high church officials lived there. Luke Gardiner, who was responsible for so much of the early development of Georgian northern Dublin, lived at 10 Henrietta St.

Arbour Hill Cemetery

West of the Old Jameson Distillery at Arbour Hill is a small cemetery that is the final

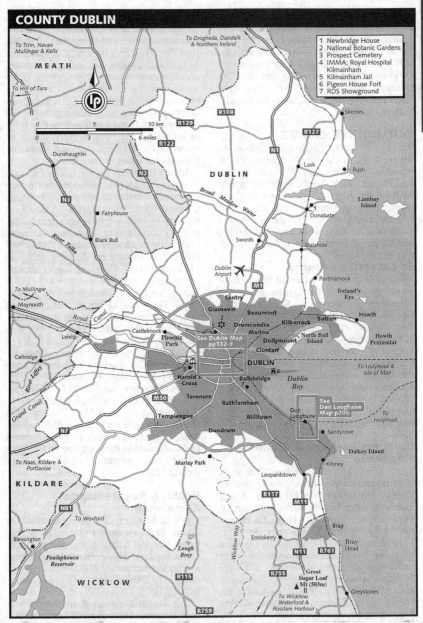

COUNTY DUBLIN

1 Newbridge House
2 National Botanic Gardens
3 Prospect Cemetery
4 IMMA; Royal Hospital Kilmainham
5 Kilmainham Jail
6 Pigeon House Fort
7 RDS Showground

To Trim, Navan Mullingar & Kells

MEATH

To Hill of Tara

0   5   10 km
0   3   6 miles

To Drogheda, Dundalk & Northern Ireland

R129

R108

R127

Skerries

Dunshaughlin

R122

N1

Lusk

Rush

N2

DUBLIN

River Tolka

Fairyhouse

Black Bull

Broad Meadow Water

Lambay Island

Donabate

Swords

Malahide

To Mullingar

Royal Canal

Dublin Airport

Santry

M1

Portmarnock

Ireland's Eye

Maynooth

Castleknock

Glasnevin

Beaumont

Drumcondra

Kilbarrack

Sutton

Howth

Leixlip

Phoenix Park

Marino

North Bull Island

Howth Peninsular

Celbridge

River Liffey

See Dublin Map pp132-3

Dollymount

Clontarf

DUBLIN

To Holyhead & Isle of Man

Harold's Cross

Ballsbridge

Dublin Bay

Grand Canal

M50

Terenure

Rathfarnham

See Dun Laoghaire Map p205

To Holyhead

N7

Templeogue

Milltown

Dun Laoghaire

Sandycove

Dundrum

Dalkey Island

To Naas, Kildare & Portlaoise

Marlay Park

Killiney

KILDARE

Leopardstown

R117

M11

N81

To Wexford

Bray

Blessington

Enniskerry

N11

R761

Bray Head

Poulaphouca Reservoir

Lough Bray

Wicklow Way

Great Sugar Loaf Mt (503m)

Greystones

WICKLOW

R115

R755

R759

To Wicklow, Waterford & Rosslare Harbour

resting place of all 14 of the executed leaders of the 1916 Easter Rising, including Pádraig Pearse and James Connolly. The burial ground is plain, with the 14 names inscribed in stone. Beside the graves is a cenotaph with the Easter Proclamation. The cemetery opens 9 am to 4.30 pm Monday to Saturday, and 9.30 am to noon on Sunday. Admission is free.

OUTSIDE THE CENTRE

There's still much more to see in Dublin. To the west are the Guinness Brewery in the colourful Liberties area, Kilmainham Jail and Phoenix Park. To the north and northeast are the Royal Canal, Prospect Cemetery, Botanic Gardens, the Casino at Marino and Clontarf. To the south and south-east are the Grand Canal, Ballsbridge and the Royal Dublin Society Showground.

St Catherine's Church

Westwards from St Audoen's Churches, towards that more recent Dublin shrine, the Guinness Brewery, is St Catherine's Church, whose huge front faces Thomas St. The church was built on the site of St Thomas Abbey, which Henry II built in honour of Thomas à Becket, archbishop of Canterbury, after having him killed. The church was completed in 1769 and is now used as a community centre. After his being hanged, the corpse of patriot Robert Emmet was put to the further indignity of being beheaded outside the church in 1803.

Guinness Brewery & Guinness Hop Store

West of St Audoen's churches, Thomas St metamorphoses into James' St in the area of Dublin known as the Liberties. Along James' St stretches the historic St James' Gate Guinness Brewery, where 2.5 million pints of stout are brewed daily. From its foundation by Arthur Guinness in 1759, the operation has expanded down to the Liffey and across both sides of the street. It covers 26 hectares and for a time was the largest brewery in the world. The oldest parts of the site are south of James' St; at one time there was a gate spanning the street.

In the Guinness Hop Store (☎ 453 3645), on the corner of Sugar House Lane (the southern extension of Crane St) and Rainsford St, visitors can watch a Guinness audiovisual display and inspect an extensive Guinness museum. Upstairs, the Guinness Zone is an interactive exhibition highlighting the history of Guinness advertising: postwar posters bearing the legend 'Guinness Is Good For You' have become *objets d'art* in their own right. It may not be a tour of the brewery, but your admission fee includes a pint of the black stuff.

In its early years Guinness was only one of dozens of Dublin breweries, but it outgrew and outlasted all of them. At one time a Grand Canal tributary was cut into the brewery to enable special Guinness barges to carry consignments onto the Irish canal system or to Dublin Harbour. When the brewery extensions reached the Liffey in 1872, the fleet of Guinness barges became a familiar sight. There was also a Guinness railway on the site, complete with a spiral tunnel. Guinness still operates its own ships to convey the vital fluid to the British market. Over 50% of all the beer consumed in Ireland is brewed here. The upper floors of the building house temporary art exhibitions.

The Hop Store opens 9.30 am to 5 pm Monday to Saturday. Admission costs £4/3. To get there take bus Nos 21A, 78 or 78A from Fleet St near the Bank of Ireland.

Round the corner at No 1 Thomas St, a plaque marks the house where Arthur Guinness (1725–1803) lived. In a yard across the road stands **St Patrick's Tower**, Europe's tallest smock windmill, which was built around 1757.

IMMA & Royal Hospital Kilmainham

The Irish Museum of Modern Art (IMMA; County Dublin map; ☎ 612 9900) at the old Royal Hospital Kilmainham is close to Kilmainham Jail. The permanent collection and regular temporary exhibitions display a range of 20th-century Irish and international art.

The Royal Hospital Kilmainham was built between 1680 and 1687 but not as a hospital. It was in fact a home for retired soldiers and continued to fill that role until after Irish independence. It preceded the similar Chelsea Hospital in London and inmates were often referred to as 'Chelsea Pensioners', although there was no connection. At the time of its construction, it was one of the finest buildings in Ireland and there was considerable muttering that it was altogether too good a place for its residents. The building was designed by William Robinson, whose other work included Marsh's Library near St Patrick's Cathedral.

There's a good café and bookshop. The IMMA opens 9.30 am to 5 pm (4.30 pm from October to March) Tuesday to Saturday, and 10.30 am (noon from October to March) to 4.30 pm on Sunday. Admission is free and there are guided tours of the museum at 2.30 pm on Wednesday and Friday and at 12.15 pm on Sunday. Heritage tours, which discuss the historical significance of the building, run at 2.30 and 3.30 pm on Sunday (£1). You can get there on bus Nos 24, 79 or 90 from Aston Quay outside the Virgin Megastore.

Kilmainham Jail

Built between 1792 and 1795, Kilmainham Jail (County Dublin map; ☎ 453 5984) on Inchicore Rd, Dublin 8, is a solid, grey, threatening building. During each act of Ireland's long, painful path to independence, at least one part of the performance took place at the jail.

The uprisings of 1798, 1803, 1848, 1867 and 1916 ended with the leaders' confinement here. Robert Emmet, Thomas Francis Meagher, Charles Stewart Parnell and the 1916 Easter Rising leaders were all visitors, but it was the executions in 1916 that most deeply etched the jail's name into the Irish consciousness. Of the 15 executions that took place between 3 and 12 May after the rising, 14 were conducted here. As a finale, prisoners from the Civil War struggles were held here from 1922. The jail closed in 1924.

An excellent audiovisual introduction to the building is followed by a thought-provoking tour. Incongruously sitting outside in the yard is the *Asgard*, the ship that successfully ran the British blockade to deliver arms to nationalist forces in 1914. The tour finishes in the gloomy yard where the 1916 executions took place. There's also an exhibition area on the history of the jail.

The museum opens 10 am to 6 pm daily, May to September; and 1 to 4 pm on weekdays, and 1 to 6 pm on Sunday, October to April. Admission costs £3/1.25. You can get there by bus Nos 23, 51, 51A, 78 or 79 from the city centre.

Phoenix Park

The 700-plus hectares of Phoenix Park (County Dublin map) make it one of the world's largest city parks, dwarfing Central Park in New York (a mere 337 hectares) and all the London parks – Hampstead Heath is only 324 hectares. There are gardens and lakes, a host of sporting facilities, the second-oldest public zoo in Europe, a visitor centre, a castle, the Garda Síochána (Police) Headquarters, various government offices, the residences of the US ambassador and the Irish president, and even a herd of deer.

Lord Ormond turned this land into a park in 1671 but it wasn't opened to the public until 1747 by Lord Chesterfield. 'Phoenix' is actually a corruption of the Irish words for 'clear water', *fionn uisce*. The park played a crucial role in Irish history, as Lord Cavendish, the British chief secretary for Ireland, and his assistant were murdered here in 1882 by an Irish nationalist group called the National Invincibles. Lord Cavendish's home is now Deerfield, the US ambassador's residence, and the murder took place outside what is now the Irish president's residence.

Near the Parkgate St entrance to the park is the 63m-high **Wellington Monument** obelisk. This took from 1817 to 1861 to build, mainly because the duke of Wellington fell from public favour during its construction. Nearby are the **People's Garden**, dating from 1864, and the bandstand in the **Hollow**. Behind the zoo, on the edge of the park, the Garda Síochána Headquarters has a small **police museum**.

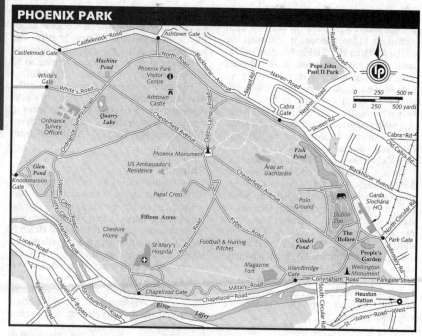

PHOENIX PARK

In the centre of the park, the **Papal Cross** marks the site where Pope John Paul II preached to 1.25 million people in 1979. **Phoenix Monument**, erected by Lord Chesterfield in 1747, looks very unphoenix-like and is often referred to as the Eagle Monument. The southern part of the park is given over to a large number of football and hurling pitches and, though they occupy about 200 acres, the area is known as Fifteen Acres. To the west, the rural-looking **Glen Pond** corner of the park is extremely attractive.

Back towards the Parkgate entrance is **Magazine Fort**, on Thomas' Hill. The fort took from 1734 to 1801 to build and never served any discernible purpose, although it was a target in the 1916 Easter Rising.

Dublin Zoo Established in 1830, 12-hectare Dublin Zoo (☎ 677 1425) is one of the oldest in the world, but is mainly of interest to children. The lion-breeding pro-

gramme dates back to 1857 and includes among its offspring the lion that roars at the start of MGM films.

It opens 9.30 am to 6 pm Monday to Saturday, and 10.30 am to 6 pm on Sunday, March to October; and 9.30 am to 4.30 pm Monday to Saturday, and 10.30 am to 4.30 pm on Sunday, November to February. Admission costs £5.80/3.10. The zoo can be reached by bus No 10 from O'Connell St or bus Nos 25 or 26 from Middle Abbey St.

Áras an Uachtaráin The residence of the Irish president was built in 1751 and enlarged in 1782 then again in 1816, on the latter occasion by noted Irish architect Francis Johnston, who added the Ionic portico. From 1782 to 1922 it was the residence of the British viceroys or lord lieutenants. After independence it became the home of Ireland's governor-general until Ireland cut ties with the British Crown and created the office of president in 1937.

Phoenix Park Visitor Centre & Ashtown Castle Phoenix Park Visitor Centre (☎ 821 3021) is in what were the stables of the Papal Nuncio. A video outlines the history of the park and there are two floors of exhibits. Visitors are taken on a tour of neighbouring Ashtown Castle, a 17th-century tower house which had been concealed inside the Papal Nuncio until its demolition in 1986; box hedges pick out the ground plan of the old building. The visitor centre is open 9.30 am to 5.30 pm daily, April to May; 9.30 am to 6.30 pm daily, June to September; 9.30 am to 5 pm daily, late March and in October; and 9.30 am to 4.30 pm at the weekend, November to mid-March. Admission costs £2/1.50.

The Royal Canal

Constructed from 1790, by which time the older Grand Canal was already past its prime, the Royal Canal (off Dublin map), which encircles Dublin to the north, was a commercial failure – but its story is certainly colourful. It was founded by Long John Binns, a Grand Canal director who quit the board because of a supposed insult over his being a shoemaker. He established the Royal Canal principally for revenge but it never made money and actually became known as the Shoemaker's Canal. In 1840 the canal was sold to a railway company and tracks still run alongside much of the canal's route through the city.

The Royal Canal towpath makes a relaxing walk through the heart of the city. You can join it beside Newcomen Bridge at North Strand Rd, just north of Connolly Station, and follow it to the suburb of Clonsilla and beyond, over 10km away. The walk is particularly pleasant beyond Binns Bridge in Drumcondra. At the top of Blessington St, near the Dublin International Youth Hostel, a large pond, used when the canal also supplied drinking water to the city, attracts water birds.

National Botanic Gardens

Founded in 1795, the National Botanic Gardens (County Dublin map), directly north of the centre on Botanic Rd in Glasnevin, were used as a garden before that time, but only the Yew Walk, also known as Addison's Walk, has trees dating back to the first half of the 18th century.

The 19.5-hectare gardens are flanked to the north by the River Tolka. In the gardens is a series of curvilinear glasshouses dating from 1843 to 1869. The glasshouses were created by Richard Turner, who was also responsible for the glasshouse at Belfast Botanic Gardens and the Palm House in London's Kew Gardens. Within these Victorian masterpieces you will find the latest in botanical technology, including a series of computer-controlled climates reproducing environments in different parts of the world. The gardens also have a palm house, built in 1884. Among the pioneering botanical work conducted here was the first attempt to raise orchids from seed, back in 1844. Pampas grass and the giant lily were first grown in Europe in these gardens.

The gardens open 9 am to 6 pm Monday to Saturday, and 11 am to 6 pm on Sunday, March to October; and 10 am to 4.30 pm, Monday to Saturday, and 11 am to 4.30 pm on Sunday, November to February. The conservatories have shorter opening hours; in particular, on Sunday they open only 2 to 4.15 pm. Admission is free. You can get there on bus Nos 13 or 19 from O'Connell St or Nos 34 or 34A from Middle Abbey St.

Prospect Cemetery

Prospect or Glasnevin Cemetery (County Dublin map), Finglas Rd, north-west of the city centre, is the largest in Ireland. It was established in 1832 as a cemetery for Roman Catholics, who faced opposition when they conducted burials in the city's Protestant cemeteries. Many monuments and memorials have staunchly patriotic overtones, with numerous high crosses, shamrocks, harps and other Irish symbols. The single most imposing memorial is the colossal monument to Cardinal McCabe (1837–1921), archbishop of Dublin and primate of Ireland.

A modern replica of a round tower acts as a handy landmark for locating the tomb of Daniel O'Connell, who died in 1847 and was reinterred here in 1869, when the tower was completed. Charles Stewart Parnell's tomb is topped with a huge granite rock. Other notable people buried here include Sir Roger Casement, who was executed for treason by the British in 1916 and whose remains weren't returned to Ireland until 1964; the republican leader Michael Collins, who died in the Civil War; the docker and trade unionist Jim Larkin, a prime force in the 1913 general strike; and the poet Gerard Manley Hopkins.

There's also a poignant 'class' memorial to the men who have starved themselves to death for the cause of Irish freedom over the century, including 10 men in the 1981 H Block hunger strikes.

The most interesting parts of the cemetery are at the south-eastern Prospect Square end. The watchtowers were once used to keep watch for body snatchers. The cemetery is mentioned in *Ulysses* and there are several clues for Joyce enthusiasts to follow.

Bus No 40 from Parnell St stops outside the cemetery gates.

Casino at Marino

The Casino at Marino (off Dublin map; ☎ 833 1618), just off Malahide Rd, north of the junction with Howth Rd in Clontarf, about 5km north-east of the city centre, is a casino only in the original Italian sense of the word. It's a pleasure house built for the earl of Charlemont in the grounds of Marino House in the mid-18th century. Although Marino House itself was demolished in the 1920s the casino survives as a wonderful folly.

Externally, the building, with its 12 Tuscan columns forming a temple-like façade and its huge entrance doorway, creates the expectation that inside it will be a simple single open space. But the interior is an extravagant convoluted maze: flights of fancy include chimneys for the central heating which are disguised as roof urns, downpipes hidden in columns, carved draperies, ornate fireplaces, beautiful parquet floors constructed of rare woods, and a spacious wine cellar. A variety of statuary adorns the outside but it's the amusing fakes that are

The Earl & the Casino

The somewhat eccentric James Caulfield (1728–99), later to become the earl of Charlemont, set out on a European grand tour in 1746 at the age of 18. The visit lasted nine years, including a four-year spell in Italy. He returned to Ireland with a huge art collection and a burning ambition to bring Italian style to the estate he acquired in 1756. He commissioned Sir William Chambers to design the casino, a process that started in the late 1750s, continued into the 1770s, and never really came to a conclusion, in part because Lord Charlemont frittered away his fortune. When Lord Charlemont married, the casino became a garden retreat rather than a bachelor's quarters. It's said that a visit from Charlemont's mother-in-law would send him scuttling down a 400m-long underground tunnel that joined the main house to the casino.

Another building housed the art and antiquities he had acquired during his European tour, so it's fitting that his town house on Parnell Square, also designed by Sir William Chambers, is now the Municipal Gallery of Modern Art. Despite his wealth, Charlemont was a comparatively liberal and free-thinking aristocrat. He never fenced in his demesne and allowed the public to use it as an open park. After Charlemont's death, his estate, crippled by his debts, collapsed and the art collection was dispersed.

Charlemont wasn't the only local eccentric: in 1792 a painter named Folliot took a dislike to the lord and built Marino Crescent at the bottom of Malahide Rd purely to block Charlemont's view of the sea. Bram Stoker (1847–1912), author of *Dracula*, was born at 15 Marino Crescent.

most enjoyable. The towering front door is a sham and a much smaller panel opens to reveal the secret interior. The windows have blacked-out panels to hide the fact that the interior is a complex of rooms, not a single chamber.

In 1870 Marino House was sold to the government. The Marino estate followed in 1881 and the casino in 1930, though it was decrepit by then. Restoration is continuing and new planting helps to hide the surrounding houses.

The casino opens 9.30 am to 6 pm daily, June to September; 10 am to 5 pm daily, May and October; and noon to 4 pm Sunday and Wednesday, November, February and March. At other times of year call ☎ 833 1618 for details of opening hours. You can visit the building only on a guided tour. Admission costs £2/1. Bus Nos 20A, 20B, 27, 27A, 27B, 32A, 42 and 42B will take you there from the city centre.

Clontarf & North Bull Island

Clontarf, a bayside suburb 5km north-east of the centre, takes its name from '*cluain tarbh*' (bull's meadow). In 1014, Brian Ború defeated the Danes at the Battle of Clontarf, though the Irish hero was killed along with his son and grandson. The Normans later erected a castle here which was handed on to the Knights Templar in 1179, rebuilt in 1835 and later converted into a hotel.

The North Bull Wall, extending from Clontarf about 1km into Dublin Bay, was built in 1820 at the suggestion of Captain William Bligh of HMS *Bounty* mutiny fame, in order to stop Dublin Harbour from silting up. Many birds migrate to North Bull Island from the Arctic in winter, and at times the bird population can reach 40,000. You reach the interpretive centre on the island via the northern causeway, which is a good 1.5km to walk across. Bus Nos 30 and 32X run to the start of the causeway on James Larkin Rd. The Royal Dublin and St Anne's golf courses are also on the island.

The Grand Canal

Built to connect Dublin with the River Shannon, the Grand Canal (off Dublin map)

makes a graceful 6km loop round southern Dublin. At its eastern end the canal forms a harbour connected with the Liffey at Ringsend. True Dubliners, it's said, are born within the confines of the Grand and Royal Canals.

History Although Parliament proposed the canal in 1715, work didn't begin until 1756. Construction was slow, but by 1779 the first cargo barges started to operate to Sallins, about 35km west of Dublin. Passenger services began a year later, when the terminus of the canal was St James' St Harbour, near the Guinness Brewery. By 1796 it was the longest canal in Britain or Ireland. It extended for 550km, of which about 250km were along the Shannon and Barrow Rivers.

Railways started to spread across Ireland from the mid-19th century and the canal went into decline. WWII provided a temporary respite, but the private canal company folded in 1950 and the last barge carried a cargo of Guinness from Dublin in 1960.

The canal fell into disrepair and, in the early 1970s, St James' St Harbour and the stretch of canal back from there to the Circular Line (the stretch of canal round southern Dublin) were filled in. The canal is now enjoying a modest revival as a tourist attraction. Despite the limited number of boats that ply the canal, all the locks are in working order.

Along the Canal The Grand Canal enters the Liffey at **Ringsend**, through locks that were built in 1796. The large **Grand Canal Dock**, flanked by Hanover and Charlotte Quays, is now used by windsurfers and canoeists. At the north-western corner of the dock is **Misery Hill**, once the site for the public execution of criminals. It was once the practice to bring the corpses of those already hung at Gallows Hill, near Upper Baggot St, to this spot, to be strung up for public display for anything from six to 12 months.

Upstream from the Grand Canal Dock is the **Waterways Visitor Centre** (☎ 677 7510). It's run by Dúchas and houses an exhibition and interpretive centre on the construction and operation of Irish canals and waterways. From its roof you can get your bearings and try to imagine what the grim surroundings will look like when/if re-development plans get into their stride. The centre opens 9.30 am to 6.30 pm daily, June to September; and 12.30 to 5 pm Wednesday to Sunday, October to May. The last admission is one hour before closing. Admission costs £2/1.

A memorial to the 1916 Easter Rising can be seen on the **Mount St Bridge**. A little farther along, Baggot St crosses the canal on the 1791 **Macartney Bridge**. The main office of Bord Fáilte is on the northern side of the canal, and Bridge House and Parson's newsagency are on the southern side.

This lovely stretch of the canal with its grassy, tree-lined banks was a favourite haunt of the poet Patrick Kavanagh. Among his compositions is the hauntingly beautiful 'On Raglan Road', which Van Morrison put to music; fans can find it on the album *Irish Heartbeat* featuring the Chieftains. One Kavanagh poem requested that he be commemorated by 'a canal bank seat for passers-by' and Kavanagh's friends obliged with a seat beside the lock on the southern side of the canal. A little farther along on the northern side you can sit down by Kavanagh himself, cast in bronze, comfortably lounging on a bench and watching his beloved canal.

The next stretch of the canal has some fine pubs, such as the *Barge* and the *Portobello*, both right by the canal. The Portobello is a fine old-fashioned place with music on weekend evenings and Sunday morning. *Lower Deck*, on Richmond St, is also near the canal. You could also pause for a meal at *Locks Restaurant*, on Windsor Terrace. The Institute of Education Business College by the Portobello was built in 1807 as Portobello House; as the Grand Canal Hotel, it was the Dublin terminus for passenger traffic on the canal. The artist Jack B Yeats, brother of WB Yeats, lived there for seven years until his death in 1957.

Farther west from here, the Circular Line isn't as interesting and is better appreciated by bicycle than on foot. The spur running off the Circular Line alongside Grand Canal Bank to the old St James' St Harbour is filled in and is now a park and bicycle path.

Ballsbridge & Donnybrook

South-east of central Dublin, the suburb of Ballsbridge (off Dublin map) was principally laid out between 1830 and 1860. Many streets have British names with a distinctly military flavour. Many embassies, including the US embassy, are in Ballsbridge. It also has some mid-range B&Bs and several top-end hotels. The main attractions are the Royal Dublin Society Showground and the Lansdowne Rd rugby stadium.

To the south of Ballsbridge is Donnybrook, at one time a village on the banks of the River Dodder. For centuries it was famous for the Donnybrook Fair, which was first held in 1204. By the 19th century it had become a 15-day event centred on horse dealing and was such a scene of drunkenness and sexual debauchery that the increasingly sedate residents of Donnybrook had it banned in 1855.

Royal Dublin Society (RDS) Showground On Merrion Rd in Ballsbridge, the Royal Dublin Society Showground (County Dublin map) is used for various exhibitions throughout the year. The society was founded in 1731 and had its headquarters in a number of well-known Dublin buildings, including, from 1814 to 1925, Leinster House. The society was involved in the foundation of the National Museum, Library, Gallery and Botanic Gardens. The most important annual event at the showground is the August Dublin Horse Show, which includes an international showjumping contest.

You can book tickets for the Horse Show from the Ticket Office (☎ 668 0866), Royal Dublin Society, Box 121, Ballsbridge, Dublin 4. Ask at the tourist office or consult a listings magazine for other events. To get to the showground, take bus No 7 from Trinity College.

Pearse Museum

Pádraig Pearse was a leader of the 1916 Easter Rising and one of the first to be executed at Kilmainham Jail. St Enda's, the school he established with his brother Willie to further his ideas of Irish language and culture, is now a museum and memorial to the brothers.

The Pearse Museum (off Dublin map; ☎ 493 4208) is at the junction of Grange Rd and Taylor's Lane in Rathfarnham, southwest of the city centre. It opens 10 am to 1 pm and 2 to 5.30 pm (5 pm from February to April and in September and October, and 4 pm from November to January) daily. Admission is free. You can get there on bus Nos 16 or 47A from the city centre.

Other Museums Outside the Centre

The main display at the **Museum of Childhood** (off Dublin map; ☎ 497 8696), The Palms, 20 Palmerston Park, Rathmines, Dublin 6, south of the centre, is a collection of dolls, some nearly 300 years old. It opens 2 to 5.30 pm on Sunday. Admission costs £1/75p.

The **Geological Survey of Ireland** (off Dublin map; ☎ 670 7444), Beggars Bush, Haddington Rd, Dublin 4, has exhibits on the geology and mineral resources of Ireland. It opens 2.30 to 4.30 pm on weekdays.

The **Irish Jewish Museum** (off Dublin map; ☎ 453 1797), 3-4 Walworth Rd, off Victoria St, Portobello, Dublin 8, is housed in what was once a synagogue and relates the history of Ireland's Jewish community. It opens 11 am to 3 pm Tuesday, Thursday and Sunday, May to September; and 10.30 am to 2.30 pm on Sunday, October to April.

ACTIVITIES

Dublin offers plenty of sporting opportunities. See the County Dublin map for all locations mentioned in this section.

Beaches & Swimming

Dublin is hardly the sort of place to work on your suntan and even a hot Irish summer day is unlikely to raise the water temperature much above freezing. However, there are some pleasant beaches. Many Joyce fans feel compelled to take a dip in Forty Foot Pool at Dun Laoghaire (see Dun Laoghaire in the Around Dublin section later in this chapter). Sandy beaches near the centre of Dublin include Sutton (11km), Portmarnock (11km), Malahide (11km), Claremount (14km) and Donabate (21km). Although the beach at Sandymount is nothing special, it is only 5km south-east of central Dublin. There are outdoor public pools at Blackrock, Clontarf and Dun Laoghaire.

Fishing

Fishing-tackle shops in Dublin can supply permits, equipment, bait and advice. In the city centre, Rory's Fishing Tackle (Around Temple Bar map; ☎ 677 2351), 17a Temple Bar, is a good shop for gear and tackle. Sea fishing is popular at Howth, Dun Laoghaire and Greystones. The River Liffey has salmon fishing (only fair) and trout fishing (good). Brown trout are found between Celbridge and Millicent Bridge, near Clane in County Kildare, 20km west of the city centre. The Dublin Trout Anglers' Association has fishing rights along parts of this stretch of the Liffey and on the River Tolka, to the north-west.

Golf

Public courses include Corballis (☎ 843 6583) at Donabate (24km north), Deer Park (☎ 832 2624) at Howth (15km north) and, closer to the city centre, the relatively new Elmgreen (☎ 820 0797) at Castleknock (10km north-west). There are more than 20 private nine-hole and 18-hole courses in and around Dublin as well as a great many short pitch-and-putt courses, a particularly Irish version of par-3 golf.

Hang-Gliding & Paragliding

In County Wicklow, south of Dublin, Great Sugar Loaf Mountain and Mt Leinster are popular locations for these sports, though you need to bring your own equipment. Phone ☎ 831 4551 for information or contact the Irish Hang-Gliding Association (☎ 450 9845), AFAS House of Sport, Longmile Rd, Dublin 12.

Jogging & Cycling

Away from the traffic fumes, large Phoenix Park offers the best opportunity for jogging or cycling.

Sailing, Windsurfing & Canoeing

Howth, Malahide and Dun Laoghaire are the major sailing centres in the Dublin area, but you can also go sailing at Clontarf, Kilbarrack, Rush, Skerries, Sutton and Swords. See the Dun Laoghaire section later in this chapter for details of the sailing clubs there. The Irish Sailing Association (☎ 280 0239) is at 3 Park Rd, Dun Laoghaire.

Dinghy sailing courses are offered by the Irish National Sailing School (☎ 284 4195), Marine Activity Centre, West Pier, Dun Laoghaire, and by the Fingall Sailing School (☎ 845 1979), Upper Strand Rd, Broadmeadow Estuary, Malahide. In Dublin itself, the Surfdock Centre (☎ 668 3945), Grand Canal Dock, Dock Rd South, Ringsend, runs sailing, windsurfing and canoeing courses. Windsurfing courses cost £90 for four three-hour sessions. You can also rent sailboards for £10 per hour, canoes for £5 and boats for £10.

Scuba Diving

The Irish Underwater Council (☎ 284 4601), 78A Patrick St, Dun Laoghaire, publishes the quarterly magazine *Subsea*. Oceantec Adventures (☎ 280 1083) is a dive shop in Dun Laoghaire that organises local dives and runs courses. See the Dun Laoghaire section later in this chapter for more information.

ORGANISED TOURS

Many Dublin tours operate only during the summer months, but at that time you can take bus and walking tours. You can book these tours directly with the operators or through your hotel front desk, at the various city tourist offices or with a travel agency or Amex.

Bus Tours

Gray Line (☎ 670 8822) runs tours around Dublin and farther afield via Dublin Tourism (☎ 605 7777), Suffolk St, but only from March to November. There are half-day tours to Glendalough (£15.50), the Boyne Valley and Newgrange (£15.50), and a longer tour to Glendalough (£27) that also includes Powerscourt and Russborough House on the itinerary. All prices include admissions.

Gray Line also offers nightlife tours to Jury's Irish Cabaret (see Irish Cabaret in the Entertainment section later in this chapter) or to Doyle's Irish Cabaret (£18.90 with two drinks or £29.90 with dinner).

Dublin Bus (☎ 872 0000, 873 4222) tours can be booked at its office, 59 Upper O'Connell St, or at Dublin Tourism. The three-hour Grand Dublin Tour uses an open-top double-decker bus (weather permitting) and operates twice daily throughout the year. The tour costs £7/4. Dublin Bus also operates a hop-on hop-off service which does a one hour 15 minutes city tour, with commentary, 11 times daily, mid-April to late September. From June to August there are eight additional daily circuits. The £5/2.50 ticket lets you travel all day, getting on or off at the eight stops.

Old Dublin Tour/Gray Line (☎ 458 0808) offers similar city sightseeing tours.

Bus Éireann tours can be booked directly at Busáras (☎ 836 6111), or through the Bus Éireann desk at the Dublin Bus office, 59 Upper O'Connell St, or at Dublin Tourism. It runs a day tour to Glendalough and Wicklow which operates Saturday to Thursday, April to September, and costs £14/7. It offers a similar tour of the Hill of Tara, Newgrange and the Boyne Valley costing £17/9. In the summer months there are also day tours farther afield to places such as Kilkenny, the River Shannon, Waterford, Armagh and Navan, the Mourne Mountains and Lough Erne.

Mary Gibbons Tours (☎ 283 9973) offers half-day Dublin city tours (£12) and tours to the Boyne Valley (£15) or Powerscourt and Glendalough (£16).

Walking Tours

Walking tours are a great way to explore this very walkable city. A historical walking tour of **Trinity College** departs frequently from Front Gate just inside the college and costs £5.50 including admission to the *Book of Kells*. See Trinity College in the South of the Liffey section earlier in this chapter for more details.

Dublin Footsteps Walking Tours (☎ 496 0641) operates two-hour walks at 11 am and 2.30 pm daily. The tours start from Bewley's Oriental Café, on Grafton St, and explore medieval Dublin or Georgian and literary Dublin. The tour costs £6, which includes a coffee or tea.

One-hour walking tours of northern Dublin, focusing on sites associated with James Joyce, depart from the **James Joyce Cultural Centre**, 35 North Great George St, at 2.30 pm Monday to Saturday; phone ☎ 873 1984 to check for tours outside the summer months. A tour of the cultural centre and a walk costs £3.

Historical Walking Tours (☎ 845 0241) are conducted by Trinity College history graduates, take two hours and depart from the front gates of Trinity College. The walks take place several times daily, mid-May to September; and at the weekend only the rest of the year. A tour costs £5/4.

The **Dublin Literary Pub Crawl** (☎ 454 0228) starts at 7.30 pm daily from The Duke on Duke St, just off Grafton St. May to September there are also tours at 3 pm and at noon on Sunday. The walk is great fun and costs £6.50/5, though Guinness consumption can quickly add a few pounds to the figure. Indeed, the emphasis seems more on drinking than literature. The actors leading the tour put on a theatrical performance appropriate to the various places and pubs along the way. The particular pubs chosen vary each night.

The **Dublin Musical Pub Crawl** (☎ 478 0191) leaves from upstairs in the Oliver St John Gogarty pub (Dublin's Pubs & Bars map) in Temple Bar at 7.30 pm Saturday to Thursday. Two musicians take you to McDaids and The Clarendon and put on sample traditional-music sessions with a commentary. You wind up in O'Donoghue's for a final session around 10 pm. Once again this is great fun and a good intro

to traditional music if you're interested but ignorant. Tours cost £7.

The **Zozimus Experience** (☎ 661 8646) leaves from the gates of Dublin Castle at 6.45 pm daily on a tour of the city's superstitious and seedy medieval past. The tour finishes with a macabre surprise. Tours must be booked and cost £5.

Carriage Tours
You can pick up a horse and carriage with a driver/commentator at the junction of Grafton St and St Stephen's Green. Half-hour tours cost £25 and the carriages can take four or five people. Tours of different lengths can be negotiated with the drivers.

Tour Guides
The Federation of Irish Guiding Interests (FIGI; ☎ 278 1626), 24 Main St, Blackrock, can put you in touch with approved guides. The recommended fees for a full-day guide in Dublin are £45 to £65 in English, £80 in a foreign language.

SPECIAL EVENTS
For information on Dublin's special events, see Public Holidays & Special Events in the Facts for the Visitor chapter. For information on Bloomsday, 16 June, see the boxed text on the following page.

PLACES TO STAY
Dublin's increased popularity as a tourist destination has meant a massive increase in the number of hotels, and plans are afoot to build even more over the next few years. At the lower end of the accommodation scale, the number of hostels and cheaper hotels has increased, but the real change has been in the number of top-end hotels. Mid-range and cheaper hotels, due to the ever-rising demand for quality service, have upgraded and refurbished existing properties. Consequently, prices have soared. In some cases, prices now rank alongside those in the world's most expensive cities. It seems that the days of cheap accommodation are gone.

Another consequence of Dublin's popularity is that finding a bed can be tricky in anything from the cheapest hostel to the

DUBLIN

Bloomsday

Six days after meeting her, the writer James Joyce had his first date with Nora Barnacle, the woman he was to marry, on 16 June 1904. Later, when he came to write his masterpiece *Ulysses*, which describes a single day in the life of Dubliner Leopold Bloom, the date he chose for this latter-day odyssey was 16 June 1904. Now Dublin duly celebrates Bloomsday on 16 June each year, with a range of entertainment, some serious, some less so, at venues all around the city. Serious Bloomsdayers don Edwardian costume for the day.

In general, events are designed to follow Bloom's progress round town. You can kick things off with breakfast either at the *James Joyce Centre* (☎ *878 8547, 35 North Great George St*) or at *South Bank Restaurant* (☎ *280 8788, 1 Martello Terrace, Dun Laoghaire*). In both cases, the 'inner organs of beast and fowl' come accompanied by celebratory readings, a fact reflected in the prices.

NICKY CAVEN

**James Joyce, one of Ireland's
most revered authors**

In the morning, guided tours of Joycean sites usually leave from the GPO, on O'Connell St, and the James Joyce Centre. Lunchtime activity focuses on *Davy Byrne's* (*Dublin's Pubs & Bars map; Duke St*), Joyce's 'moral pub', where Bloom paused to dine on a glass of Burgundy and a slice of Gorgonzola (£4 at today's prices). Street entertainers are likely to keep you amused as you eat.

In the afternoon, the guided walks are topped up with animated readings from *Ulysses* and Joyce's other books at appropriate sites and times: *Ormond Quay Hotel* (*Around Temple Bar map; Ormond Quay*) at 4 pm and *Harrison's* restaurant (*Westmoreland St*) later in the day.

Should you have any energy left, you can spin things out to the early hours, perhaps in *Bewley's* (*Around Temple Bar map; Grafton St*), where animated performances of Molly Bloom's closing (and at one time controversial) soliloquy take place.

Events also take place in the days leading up to and following Bloomsday. The best source of information about what's on in any particular year is likely to be the James Joyce Centre, although the free *Event Guide* also publishes outline details in advance. Popular events sell out quickly: advance booking, especially for the breakfasts, is essential.

You don't have to know anything about Joyce or his books to enjoy the day, although it certainly helps!

most expensive five-star hotel, especially in summer. If you can plan ahead and book your room, it will make life easier.

The alternative is to go to one of the Dublin Tourism offices and ask them to book you a room. For £1 plus a 10% deposit on the cost of the first night, they'll find you somewhere to stay, and will do so efficiently and with a smile. Sometimes booking may require a great deal of phoning round, so it can be a pound well spent. Another option is Bed Finders (☎ 670 4704), 8

Dawson St, next to Waterstone's, a private company offering a computerised accommodation-reservation service.

Accommodation in central Dublin can be neatly divided into areas north and south of the River Liffey. The southern side is generally neater, cleaner and more expensive than the northern side. Prices drop as you move away from the centre. The seaside suburbs of Dun Laoghaire and Howth (see Around Dublin later in this chapter) and Bray (see the County Wicklow chapter) are within easy commuting distance of central Dublin on the convenient DART train service.

Camping

There's no convenient central camp site in Dublin. *Do not* try to camp in Phoenix Park: a German cyclist camping there was murdered in 1991. At *Shankill Caravan and Camping Park* (☎ 282 0011), 16km south of the centre on the N11 Wexford road, a site for two people costs £6 in summer. You can get there on bus Nos 45 or 46 from Eden Quay or bus No 45A from Dun Laoghaire. Another site is *Donabate Caravan Park* (☎ 843 6008), near Swords, 16km north of Dublin. Sites cost £4 per person (motorists £6); bus No 33B runs there from Eden Quay.

Hostels

Since there are no conveniently central camp sites in Dublin, budget travellers usually head for one of Dublin's numerous hostels, one operated by An Óige, the others independently. Hostels offer the cheapest accommodation and are also great for meeting other travellers and exchanging information. Late April to late September, they can be heavily booked, but then so is everything else.

North of the Liffey The An Óige *Dublin International Youth Hostel* (☎ 830 1766, 61 Mountjoy St) is a big, well-equipped, 460-bed hostel in a restored and converted old convent. From Dublin Airport, bus No 41A drops you in Upper Dorset St, a few minutes' walk away. It's a longer walk from the bus and train stations but it's signposted.

The hostel is in the run-down northern area of the city centre; security at the hostel is good but keep an eye on your bags in adjacent streets. The nightly cost for Hostelling International (HI) members is £9, non-members £9.50.

The IHH *Cardijn House Hostel* (☎ 878 8091, 15 Talbot St), aka 'Goin' My Way', is a smaller, older hostel east of O'Connell St. It charges £8 per night plus 50p for a shower. Breakfast is included and there are good, clean cooking facilities. The IHH *Marlborough Hostel* (☎ 878 7629, 81-82 Marlborough St), next to St Mary's Pro-Cathedral, charges £7.50 for beds in four-to 10-bed dorms and £13 per person for doubles. Rates include breakfast and cooking facilities are available.

For convenience you can't beat the new *Abbey Hostel* (☎ 878 0700, 29 Bachelor's Walk) just next to O'Connell Bridge. Prices range from £14 for beds in 12-bed dorms to £30 per person for doubles (less in low season). All rooms are furnished handsomely and the facilities are excellent. It's a little pricey, but its location and amenities have made it a stand-out favourite among travellers: book early.

Also convenient is the big IHH *Isaac's Hostel* (☎ 836 3877, 2-5 Frenchman's Lane), a stone's throw from the Busáras and not far from popular restaurants and pubs on either side of the Liffey. The downers are that dorms are closed between 11 am and 5 pm, and baggage in the basement locker can be retrieved only on the hour and half-hour; light sleepers should also take note that trains rumble close by. Still, the low prices (£7 to £8.50 for dorm beds, £19/32 for singles/doubles) make it a pretty good option.

Nearby, the much more relaxed and welcoming IHH *Globetrotter's Tourist Hostel* (☎ 873 5893, 46-48 Lower Gardiner St) offers dorm beds costing £10 including continental breakfast. With 10 people to a dorm there's bound to be some disturbance, but this is a clean, modern place with good security. Breakfasts are in a pleasant dining room overlooking a small garden. At the IHH *Abraham House* (☎ 855 0600, 82-83

Lower Gardiner St) dorm beds cost £7.50/9.50 in the low/high season.

South of the Liffey Beside Christ Church Cathedral, the big, well-equipped IHH *Kinlay House (Around Temple Bar map; ☎ 679 6644, 2-12 Lord Edward St)* is central, but some rooms can suffer from traffic noise. It charges upwards of £11 for beds in four-bed dorms, £11.50 to £13 for beds in dorms with bathrooms, and £18/28 for singles/doubles. Continental breakfast is included and cooking facilities are available. Bus Nos 54A, 68A, 78A and 123 (which stop down O'Connell St and around Trinity College) stop outside.

The IHH *Avalon House (Around St Stephen's Green map; ☎ 475 0001, 55 Aungier St)*, in a comprehensively renovated old building, is nicely positioned just west of St Stephen's Green. It's well equipped and some of the cleverly designed rooms have mezzanine levels, which are great for families. There have been complaints about the service, however. The basic nightly cost for dorm beds is £10.50 including a continental breakfast. Beds in four-bed dorms with attached bathroom cost £12, doubles £14 per person. Take bus No 16, 16A, 19 or

NICKY CAVEN

Georgian doorknocker, a reminder of Dublin's heyday

22 to the door or bus No 11, 13 or 46A to nearby St Stephen's Green. From the Dun Laoghaire ferry terminal you can take bus No 46A to St Stephen's Green or the DART to Pearse Station.

Right in the lively (and noisy) Temple Bar area is *Strollers Budget Accommodation (Around Temple Bar map; ☎ 677 5614, 29 Eustace St)*, costing £10.50 to £14.50 per person including breakfast. There's no common room or cooking facilities, but there are a couple of public car parks nearby.

Nearby is the newish *Temple Bar House (Around Temple Bar map; ☎ 671 6277, 1 Cecilia St)*, with prices ranging from £10 for dorm beds to £18 per person for doubles. The more expensive rooms have en suite facilities and there are self-catering facilities. If you're driving, the hostel has a discount deal with a nearby covered car park.

At the back of the Oliver St John Gogarty pub is *Gogarty's Hostel (Around Temple Bar map; ☎ 671 1822, 18-21 Anglesea St)*, which has dorm beds costing £12 to £17 (depending on the season and the day) and doubles from £16 to £21 per person. All rooms are en suite. There is a good common area and laundry facilities.

Farther out but with a good range of sleeping set-ups is *Morehampton House (off Dublin map; ☎ 668 8866, 78 Morehampton Rd, Donnybrook, Dublin 4)*. The cheapest beds, at £7.95, are in 10-bed basement dorms. In bigger, lighter eight- and four-bed rooms you pay £11.95, and £15 per person in twins and triples (cheaper in low season). Breakfast costs another £1, but there are clean, spacious cooking facilities and a garden for alfresco picnics. Bus Nos 10, 46A and 46B (which stop down O'Connell St and Around St Stephen's Green) pass by.

Student Accommodation
In the summer months you can stay at *Trinity Hall (off Dublin map; ☎ 497 1772, Dartry Rd, Rathmines, Dublin 6)*, which charges £15 to £25 for singles or £14 to £25 per person for doubles. There are some fam-

Some B&Bs for Gay & Lesbian Travellers

Dublin has several central gay B&Bs catering to the pink punt. The largest is the none-too-salubrious **Horse and Carriage** (Around St Stephen's Green map; ☎ 478 3537, fax 478 4010, 15 Aungier St), where singles/doubles (none with bathroom) cost from £38/57; single-room bookings aren't accepted at the weekend.

Frankies (Around St Stephen's Green map; ☎ 478 3087), a friendly place on narrow Camden Place between Camden and Harcourt Sts, has a dozen smallish rooms (three with showers) costing £32 per person. **Inn on the Liffey** (☎ 677 0828, 21 Upper Ormond Quay), convenient for the Out on the Liffey pub, charges the same.

ily rooms where children aged under 10 can stay for £3 with two adults. To get there, take bus Nos 14 or 14A from D'Olier St beside the O'Connell Bridge. It's substantially cheaper than staying at **Trinity College** (☎ 608 1177), where sometimes wonderfully positioned rooms cost a minimum of £28 per person for B&B.

University College Dublin's **UCD Village** (off Dublin map; ☎ 706 7777) is 6km south of the centre, en route to Dun Laoghaire. Accommodation here is in apartments, with three single rooms sharing a bathroom and a kitchen/living area. It's modern and well appointed but way out from the centre and, at £24 per person, rather expensive. For a family a three-room apartment at £350 per week (minimum stay) could be good value. If you have a car, the ease of parking may compensate for the distance and the soulless surroundings; if you don't, bus No 10 departs every 10 minutes from O'Connell St or St Stephen's Green and goes direct to the campus (one way £1.10).

B&Bs

B&Bs, the backbone of cheap accommodation in Ireland, are well represented in Dublin and typically cost £15 to £30 per person per night. The cheaper B&Bs usually don't have private bathrooms, but those that do generally charge just a pound or two more. More-expensive B&Bs are listed in the following Mid-Range – Guesthouses & Hotels section.

If you arrive when accommodation is tight and don't like the location offered, the best advice is to take it and then try to book something better for subsequent nights. Booking just one or two days ahead can often turn up a much better choice.

If you want something cheap but close to the city, Upper and Lower Gardiner St in Dublin 1 on the northern side of the Liffey is the place to look. It's a rather grubby, run-down area, but is cheap and convenient.

Farther out, you can find a better price-and-quality combination north of the centre at Clontarf, or in the seaside suburbs of Dun Laoghaire or Howth. The Ballsbridge embassy zone, south of the centre, offers convenience and quality but you pay more for the combination. Other suburbs to try are Sandymount (immediately east of Ballsbridge) and Drumcondra (north of the centre en route to the airport).

Gardiner St There's a large collection of places on Lower Gardiner St, near the bus and train stations, and another, cheaper, group on Upper Gardiner St, north past Mountjoy Square. The B&Bs on Upper Gardiner St are respectable if rather basic.

North of Mountjoy Square (off Dublin map) at the renovated, friendly **Harvey's Guesthouse** (☎ 874 8384, 11 Upper Gardiner St), singles with shared facilities cost £18, doubles with bath £22.50 per person. There are several more B&Bs nearby, including **Stella Maris** (☎ 874 0835), next door at No 13, **Flynn's B&B** (☎ 874 1702), at No 15, **Carmel House** (☎ 874 1639), at No 16 and **Fatima House** (☎ 874 5410), at No 17. The cheapest is **Marian Guest House** (☎ 874 4129), at No 21, offering rooms costing £15 per person, though the plumbing can be a little loud sometimes.

Just off Upper Gardiner St from Mountjoy Square is **Dergvale Hotel** (☎ 874 4753, 4 Gardiner Place), where singles/doubles with bathroom cost £26/50.

Hardwicke St, only a short walk from Upper Gardiner St, has a couple of B&Bs that will do at a pinch: **Waverley House** (☎ 874 6132), at No 4, and **Sinclair House** (☎ 855 0792), next door at No 3. At these places singles cost £20 to £22 and doubles £30 to £34.

Clontarf There are numerous places along Clontarf Rd (off Dublin map), about 5km from the city centre.

One of these is the friendly **Ferryview** (☎ 833 5893) at No 96. Farther along there's the slightly more expensive **White House** (☎ 833 3196) at No 125, **San Vista** (☎ 833 9582) at No 237, **Bayview** (☎ 833 9870) at No 265 and **Sea Breeze** (☎ 833 2787) at No 312. These Clontarf Rd B&Bs typically cost £20 to £28 for singles, £30 to £45 for doubles.

Bus No 130 from Abbey St will get you there for £1.10.

Ballsbridge & Donnybrook These B&Bs south-east of the centre are off the Dublin map. To get there by public transport take bus Nos 46 or 46A from Trinity College or St Stephen's Green or bus No 10 from O'Connell St.

Farther south at No 113, traditional **Morehampton Lodge** (☎ 283 7499) has rooms costing £44/60.

Just past the suburb of Ranelagh is the excellent **Ashfield House** (☎ 260 3680, 5 Clonskeagh Rd, Milltown), which has seven beautifully appointed rooms costing £35 per person, rising to £50 in the summer. The breakfast alone is worth the stay.

Mid-Range – Guesthouses & Hotels

The line dividing B&Bs from guesthouses and cheaper hotels is often a hazy one.

Places listed in this mid-range bracket usually cost from £30 to £60 per night per person. Some of the small, central hotels in this category are among the most enjoyable places to stay in Dublin.

These mid-range places are a big jump up from the cheaper B&Bs in facilities and price but still cost a lot less than Dublin's expensive hotels.

Breakfast is usually provided (it usually isn't in the top-end hotels) and it's very good (unlike that offered by some cheap B&Bs). Many of these hotels offer fruit, a choice of cereals, croissants, scones and other morning delights to supplement the inevitable bacon and eggs. Add 12.5% tax to all prices.

North of the Liffey Just north of the Liffey is **Wynn's Hotel** (☎ 874 5131, 35-39 Lower Abbey St). Only a few steps from the Abbey Theatre, this older hotel offers 66 rooms, all with attached bathroom, which cost £60/90 for singles/doubles with reductions at weekends.

Right by the river, the **Ormond Quay Hotel** (Around Temple Bar map; ☎ 872 1811, Upper Ormond Quay) offers 55 rooms with attached bathroom costing £55/100. A plaque outside notes the hotel's role in 'The Sirens' episode of Ulysses.

The Townhouse (☎ 878 8808, 47-48 Lower Gardiner St), next to the Globetrotter's Tourist Hostel and sharing a breakfast room with it, offers singles/doubles with bathroom costing £37.50/60, including a good breakfast. This is a pleasingly decorated and furnished and safety-conscious guesthouse with a small Japanese garden and a car park – an excellent choice.

Across the road at No 75 is family-run **Maple Guest House** (☎ 874 0225, 874 5239), which offers singles/doubles costing £40/60 with attached bathroom.

On Frenchman's Lane next to Isaac's Hostel is **Isaac's Hotel** (☎ 855 0667), with an Italian restaurant and en suite rooms costing £50/70.

Farther from the river is **Castle Hotel**

(☎ 874 6949, 34 Gardiner Row), with 35 rooms. It's just off Parnell Square, only a few minutes' walk from O'Connell St but on the edge of the better part of northern Dublin, before the decline sets in. Rooms cost £45/82/105 for singles/doubles/triples including breakfast. Farther along on the same side of the road is *Barry's Hotel* (☎ 874 9407, 1-2 Great Denmark St). The hotel's 29 rooms cost £30/51, or £33/54 with attached bathroom. Slightly farther afield is *Caulfield's Hotel* (☎ 878 0643, fax 872 7674, 18-19 Dorset St), with 20 rooms costing £35/60. Weekend rates are slightly more expensive, but still a bargain. A full Irish breakfast is included.

South of the Liffey Just off O'Connell Bridge, *Aston Hotel* (Around Temple Bar map; ☎ 677 9300, fax 677 9007, 7-9 Aston Quay) is a comfortable new hotel with 27 rooms and all mod cons, including cable TV and attached bathroom. For its location, prices are reasonable at £50/70 for singles/doubles. The central *Fitzwilliam* (Around St Stephen's Green map; ☎ 662 5155, fax 676 7488, 41 Upper Fitzwilliam St) is on the corner of Lower Baggot St but is still quiet at night. The 12 en suite rooms in this small hotel cost £45/70 in the summer.

Staunton's on the Green (Around St Stephen's Green map; ☎ 478 2133, fax 478 2263, 83 St Stephen's Green South) is in a Georgian house in an excellent position. Rooms cost £53/88 including breakfast.

Close to the green, in another magnificent Georgian building, is *Russell Court Hotel* (Around St Stephen's Green map; ☎ 478 4991, fax 478 4066, 21-25 Harcourt St), with 42 rooms, all with attached bathroom and costing £65/87. Across the road at No 84, elegant *Albany House* (Around St Stephen's Green map; ☎ 475 1092, fax 475 1093) charges £60/100. Farther down at No 60-61, in another Georgian building, where George Bernard Shaw lived from 1874 to 1876, is *Harcourt Hotel* (Around St Stephen's Green map; ☎ 478 3677, fax 475 2013), with 40 rooms costing £35/60, or £56/100 with bathroom.

Leeson Court Hotel (Around St Stephen's Green map; ☎ 676 3380, fax 661 8273, 26-27 Lower Leeson St) has a warm open fire in the lobby, and its 20 en suite rooms cost £55/85. *Latchford's* (Around St Stephen's Green map; ☎ 676 0784, 99-100 Lower Baggot St) offers serviced rooms with self-catering facilities in an impressive Georgian house with fine plaster ceilings in some bedrooms. It charges £52/79, with reductions for week-long stays. There's an excellent bistro attached.

Immediately opposite Christ Church Cathedral, in Christ Church Place, big *Jury's Christ Church Inn* (☎ 475 0111, fax 454 0012) offers rooms costing £59 per person. Overlooking the River Liffey and backing on to the fascinating Temple Bar area, renovated *Wellington Hotel* (Around Temple Bar map; ☎ 677 9315, fax 677 9387, 21-22 Wellington Quay) charges £65/75. Nearby, *Bloom's Hotel* (Around Temple Bar map; ☎ 671 5622, fax 671 5997), on Anglesea St behind the Central Bank, offers 86 rooms costing £65/75.

Outside the Centre All of the following hotels are off the Dublin map.

Friendly *Ariel Guesthouse* (☎ 668 5512, fax 668 5845, 52 Lansdowne Rd) is 2km south-east of the centre in the Ballsbridge area. It's conveniently close to Lansdowne Rd Station and the big Berkeley Court Hotel. The 28 en suite rooms cost £50/100 for singles/doubles, with breakfast extra; out of season you may be able to negotiate a discount.

Farther down, Lansdowne Rd changes its name to Herbert Rd, where you'll find *Mt Herbert* (☎ 668 4321, fax 660 7077, 7 Herbert Rd), about 3km from the centre. This larger hotel was once the Dublin residence of an English lord. The 155 en suite rooms cost £43.50/63; breakfast costs extra.

The well-equipped *Ashling Hotel* (☎ 677 2324, 677 2783, Parkgate St) is 2.5km west of the centre and directly across the river from Heuston Station. Its 54 rooms cost £56.50/86 including breakfast. The philosopher Ludwig Wittgenstein stayed here in 1948 en route to the Aran Islands.

Top End – Hotels

North of the Liffey At the top end of O'Connell St is *Royal Dublin Hotel* (☎ 873 3666, fax 873 3120), with 117 rooms costing £99/126 for singles/doubles.

The new *Chief O'Neills* hotel (☎ 817 3838, fax 817 3839), part of the Smithfield Village complex that is home to Ceol, near the Old Jameson Distillery, has smallish but elegant rooms replete with minimalist furnishings. Singles or doubles cost £125 (£98 at weekends); there are three very nice suites at £160. Be warned that at the time of writing the hotel had just opened and these prices will go up.

The £100 million *Morrisson* (Around Temple Bar map; ☎ 878 2999, fax 878 3185, Lower Ormond Quay) opened in June 1999 with a view to rivalling Clarence Hotel as Dublin's coolest top-end hotel. It's an extraordinary place. Rooms cost upwards of £155; the penthouse costs a modest £750.

South of the Liffey All of the following hotels are marked on the Around St Stephen's Green map unless stated otherwise.

The small *Longfield's* (☎ 676 1367, fax 676 1542, 9-10 Lower Fitzwilliam St), between Merrion and Fitzwilliam Squares, offers 26 rooms costing £90/140. Just south of Dame St is *Central Hotel* (Around Temple Bar map; ☎ 679 7302, fax 679 7303, 1-5 Exchequer St), which has 70 rooms starting at £95/140 without breakfast. Though the rooms are rather small it's well located.

Brooks Hotel (☎ 670 4000, fax 670 4455, 59-62 Drury St) has 75 comfortable and modern rooms starting at £110/150 without breakfast. *Stephen's Hall* (☎ 661 0585, fax 661 0606, 14-17 Lower Leeson St) is just a stone's throw from the south-eastern corner of St Stephen's Green. The 37 rooms, all with attached bathroom, cost £95/134.

Also central is *Georgian House* (☎ 661 8832, 20-21 Lower Baggot St), equally close to St Stephen's Green and Merrion Square. Once again this is a fine old Georgian building that has recently been refurbished. Its 47 rooms have bathrooms and

cost £95/137 in summer. The breakfast is excellent and there's a car park.

Davenport Hotel (☎ 661 6800, fax 661 5663, Lower Merrion St) offers 120 rooms in what was once Merrion Hall, built in 1863 for the Plymouth Brethren (a puritanical religious sect). All rooms cost £200.

Prices and quality start their rapid ascension at *Hotel Conrad* (☎ 676 5555, fax 676 5424, Earlsfort Terrace), south of St Stephen's Green. This is a popular business and showbusiness hotel run by the Hilton group. Its 191 rooms start at £160.

Also close to St Stephen's Green, modern 203-room *Westbury Hotel* (☎ 679 1122, fax 679 7078) is in narrow Balfe St just off Grafton St, Dublin's pedestrianised main shopping street. Rooms on the upper floors offer views of the Dublin Hills. Rooms start at £200. This is a surprisingly popular hotel with showbiz names.

The city's best-known (and still most elegant) hotel is the 160-room *Shelbourne Hotel* (☎ 676 6471, fax 661 6006, 27 St Stephen's Green), indubitably the best address in Dublin to meet. Despite the prices (singles start at £170), many rooms are a little cramped, but afternoon tea (£7.50, 3 to 5.30 pm) at the hotel is something all Dublin visitors should experience, regardless of whether they stay there.

In time, *Merrion Hotel* (☎ 603 0600, fax 676 5424, Upper Merrion St) may come to rival Shelbourne Hotel as the city's most elegant lodgings. Occupying four Georgian town houses (one of which is the birthplace of Arthur Wellesley, duke of Wellington), this hotel is strictly for those who can afford the best. Singles start at £200 and doubles at £220. If you stay here, go the whole hog and ask for a room in the main house (those in the annexe are smaller and less classy): doubles start at £265.

Dublin's most '-est' (nicest, trendiest, chicest and dearest) hotel is *Clarence Hotel* (Around Temple Bar map; ☎ 670 9000, fax 670 7800, 6-8 Wellington Quay). Bought by rock band U2 in 1992, it underwent a three-year facelift and is now a luxury hotel *par excellence*, with a large clientele among the cultural and showbiz elite. Prices range from £180 for a simple single to £540 for a double suite. The penthouse suite costs a nifty £1500 per night, and breakfast *isn't* included!

Outside the Centre The following hotels are all off the Dublin map.

Ireland's largest hotel (451 rooms) is the *Burlington* (☎ 660 5222, fax 660 8496, Upper Leeson St). It is 2km south of the centre on the edge of Ballsbridge, overlooking the Grand Canal. Singles/doubles cost £123/139 without breakfast. In Ballsbridge, *Jury's Hotel and Towers* (☎ 660 5000, fax 660 5540, Pembroke Rd) charges £129/150. It has a swimming pool and in summer the Irish cabaret here is very popular (see Entertainment later in this chapter). Nearby, *Sachs Hotel* (☎ 668 0995, fax 668 6147, 19-29 Morehampton Rd) is a small but elegant and expensive place with 20 rooms, all en suite, costing £140 per person (with lower off-season rates).

Also in Ballsbridge, *Berkeley Court Hotel* (☎ 660 1711, fax 661 7238, Lansdowne Rd) offers 187 spacious rooms costing £200 and has a fitness centre. It also has an extraordinary penthouse suite that is a favourite with visiting dignitaries.

Around the Airport There are several hotels near Dublin Airport (County Dublin map), including the large *Forte Posthouse Hotel* (☎ 844 4211, fax 842 5874), off the M1 motorway beside the airport. It offers 188 singles/doubles costing £89/105. Airport hotels are subject to a 15% tax on top of the price.

PLACES TO EAT

There are limited restaurant possibilities north of the Liffey, but the trendy Temple Bar enclave, south of the river, is packed with restaurants of all types. There are also numerous restaurants on both sides of busy Grafton St and along Merrion Row and Baggot St.

North of the Liffey

Dining possibilities north of the Liffey essentially consist of fast food, cheap eats or chains – which isn't to say that you'll eat badly here.

Restaurants Below the Dublin Writers' Museum on the northern side of Parnell Square, *Chapter One* (☎ 873 2266, 873 2281) is worth a look even though the food is resolutely conservative (but it is delicious). It serves lunch (weekdays only) and dinner, and features a pre- and post-theatre menu for literary-minded theatregoers who might be attending a play at the nearby Gate.

Nearby is *Bangkok Café* (☎ 878 6618, 106 Parnell St), which is one of the city's best Thai restaurants, despite its rather shabby exterior.

Closer to the river, *101 Talbot* (☎ 874 5011), at, funnily enough, 101 Talbot St, opens for lunch Monday to Saturday and dinner Tuesday to Saturday in an attempt to bring good food north of the river. The prices are reasonable, the food moderately adventurous and well prepared. Filling pasta dishes cost upwards of £4.95.

Il Vignardo (☎ 855 2798), in Isaac's Hotel on Frenchman's Lane, serves Italian food from noon onwards.

Fast Food & Cafés O'Connell St is the fast-food centre of Dublin; most outlets are clustered towards the bridge. *La Pizza* (☎ 878 8010, 14 O'Connell St) is a local chain; it also offers home delivery.

Café Kylemore (1-2 O'Connell St) is a big, somewhat impersonal but always busy fast-food place; it's good for a cup of tea or coffee or a snack any time of day.

Alternatively, on the 1st floor of *Clery's & Co* department store, you can get afternoon tea (£4.25) complete with cucumber sandwiches in stylish surroundings.

Ireland's most famous purveyor of fish and chips, costing upwards of £3, *Beshoff's*, has a branch on O'Connell St with great views from the upstairs windows.

There's a branch of *Bewley's Oriental Café* at 40 Mary St. In the Corporation Fruit Market, between Chancery St and Mary's Lane, is *Paddy's Place* (☎ 873 5130), where the food is as staunchly Irish as the name. It opens 7.30 am to 3 pm on weekdays, so you can go there for an early breakfast (£2 to £3.50, served all day) or a filling lunchtime Irish stew or Dublin coddle.

For good coffee visit *Ernest's Coffee House* (☎ 878 1143), on the ground floor of the Jervis St Shopping Centre on Mary St.

Isaac's Hostel and *Dublin International Youth Hostel* (see North of the Liffey, Hostels in the Places to Stay section earlier in this chapter) have good cafeteria-style facilities.

Temple Bar
Temple Bar is bounded by the river to the north, Westmoreland St to the east and Christ Church Cathedral to the west. The southern boundary is Dame St and its extension, Lord Edward St. All of the following places are on the Around Temple Bar map.

Restaurants For burgers and steaks try *Paddy Garibaldi's* (☎ 671 7288, 15-16 Crown Alley). It also offers a range of pizzas and pastas.

Nico's (☎ 677 3062, 53 Dame St), on the corner of Temple Lane, offers conservative Italian food with a strong Irish influence. It's solidly popular and has a piano player. It opens for dinner Monday to Saturday, and also for lunch on weekdays. Pastas cost £6.50, fish mains £11.50 to £12.

Il Pasticcio (☎ 677 6111, 12 Fownes St) serves wood-baked pizzas and good pasta in a rather cramped setting, with paintings on the walls by up-and-coming artists. Pasta main dishes cost £4.50 to £6.95, pizzas £4.50 to £7.

At the Diceman's Corner of Meeting House Square is *Il Baccaro* (☎ 671 4597), an Italian trattoria whose rustic cuisine is very popular with Dublin's Italian community. It opens only in the evenings.

For a truly excellent Italian meal costing less than £15, *Ar Vicoletto* (☎ 670 8662, 5 Crow St) is hard to beat. The warm gorgonzola salad is sublime, and the spaghetti carbonara is as authentic as it gets.

Just down the street at No 1 is *Tante Zoe's* (☎ 679 4407). It opens for lunch

Monday to Saturday and dinner Monday to Sunday, and is further proof of how cosmopolitan Dublin dining is: Cajun and Creole food is the speciality, with starters costing £2.75 and main dishes starting at £7. While there are virtually no cheap restaurants in Temple Bar, *Da Pino* (☎ 671 9308, 38-40 Parliament St), on the corner of Dame St, is the exception. The £4.40 lunch menu – offering a selection of delicious pizzas or a minute steak – is hard to beat. The à la carte menu is more expensive, but still great value.

Omelettes (starting at £5.75) are a speciality at the popular and bustling, but somewhat overpriced, *Elephant and Castle* (☎ 679 3121, 18 Temple Bar). How 'free' are coffee fill-ups when the first cup costs £1.50? It stays open until midnight on Friday and Saturday, until 11.30 pm on other days. Right next door is the equally popular *Gallagher's Boxty House* (☎ 677 2762, 20-21 Temple Bar). A boxty is rather like a stuffed pancake and tastes like a bland Indian masala dosa. Real Irish food isn't something that's widely available in Dublin so it's worth trying. Main dishes cost £6 to £9. Next to that is *Alamo* (☎ 677 6546), where you can get good, reasonably priced Mexican dishes. *La Med* (☎ 670 7358, 22 Temple Bar) has a choice of Mediterranean dishes costing about £7.

Poco Loco (☎ 679 1950, 32 Parliament St) offers straightforward Tex-Mex interpretations of Mexican food, but they do serve Corona beer and their combination plates are great value at £6 to £9. It opens for dinner daily.

Dame St's international mix of restaurants includes Chinese possibilities such as *Fan's Cantonese Restaurant* (☎ 679 4263, 679 4273) at No 60. However, the best Chinese food in the area is at *Good World* (☎ 677 5373, 18 South Great George St), a favourite among Dublin's Chinese community; they choose their dishes from a Chinese menu rather than the one presented to locals. Needless to say, the former has more exciting selections than the latter. Still, the £6 or £7.50 lunch special is very good. Across the street at No 71, *Yamamori*

Noodles is one of the most popular and trendy restaurants in the city centre. The large sushi platter costs £11 but you can eat well for about £8. The £5 lunch special is available until 5.30 pm and is a bargain. Just down the street in Castle House is *Juice* (☎ 475 5001), a super-trendy vegetarian restaurant that puts an imaginative, California-type spin on all kinds of dishes. Try a fruit smoothie!

Les Frères Jacques (☎ 679 4555, 74 Dame St) is one of Temple Bar's fancier places, with set meals costing £22. The food is as French as the name would indicate, the mood is slightly serious, and the bill can make quite a dent in your budget. It opens for lunch on weekdays, for dinner Monday to Saturday.

The Mermaid Café (☎ 670 8236, 22 Dame St) is fast earning a reputation as one of the better seafood restaurants in the city. An average evening meal costs about £30 per person. Just down the road in Meeting House Square, *Eden* (☎ 670 5372) is the epitome of Temple Bar chic, with good, solid dishes served in minimalist surroundings. You can eat for about £20, but it'll cost you more to eat well.

The cream of Temple Bar's restaurants is *The Tea Rooms* (☎ 670 7766, Clarence Hotel, 6-8 Wellington Quay). It's pricey, but the food is very good. It opens for dinner daily, but serves lunch on weekdays only.

Fast Food & Cafés Near O'Connell Bridge there is a branch of *Abrakebabra* (☎ 671 9248, Westmoreland St). *Beshoff's* has a branch (☎ 677 8026, 14 Westmoreland St) with waiter service upstairs, also just south of O'Connell Bridge.

The vegetarian *Well Fed Café* (☎ 677 2234, 6 Crow St) is a big, busy, alternative-style place, great for lunch or a snack with large servings. Mexican taco costs £2.60. It opens noon to 8 pm Monday to Saturday.

Café Gertrude (☎ 677 9043, 3-4 Bedford Row), down a side turning and therefore likely to have tables when other places are full, serves pizza at reasonable prices (£4.25 to £5.50).

Round the corner from Dublin Castle, *Leo Burdock's* (☎ 454 0306, 2 Werburgh St), next to the Lord Edward pub, is said to dole out the best fish and chips in Dublin. You can eat them down the road in the park beside St Patrick's Cathedral.

There are two branches of *Bewley's Oriental Café* on the edges of Temple Bar. These huge cafeteria-style places offer good-quality food, especially the all-day special of bacon, egg, sausages, beans and chips costing £3.50, including coffee, tea or a soft drink. They're equally good for a quick cup of tea or coffee and offer a variety of teas, a pleasant surprise in a country where tea often comes strong and stewed. Watch the cake prices though. The branch at 11-12 Westmoreland St opens 7.30 am to 9 pm Monday to Saturday, and 9.30 am to 8 pm on Sunday. Another branch is at 13 South Great George St, although at the time of writing it was closed and it is unclear when (or if) it will reopen.

The newest branch of local chain *Fitzers* (*Upper Fownes St*), beside Temple Bar Square, serves BLT sandwiches with fries and salad (£6.25) and mains costing £8 to £15.

The popular *Bad Ass Café* (☎ 671 2596, 9-11 Crown Alley) is a cheerful, bright, warehouse-style place that offers reasonable pizzas costing about £7.50. Sinéad O'Connor once worked here as a waitress.

Around Grafton St

Pedestrianised Grafton St is the No 1 shopping street in southern Dublin and notably lacking in restaurants and pubs. The streets to the east and west are more promising. Dame St restaurants are covered in the previous Temple Bar section.

Restaurants Apart from fast-food joints, the only place to eat on Grafton St proper is at *Bewley's Oriental Café* (*Around St Stephen's Green map*; ☎ 677 6761), about halfway up at No 78. This is the flagship branch of the chain, and a recent renovation has converted it from an old-style café to a restaurant proper, with table service and fancier dishes than the other branches, though you can still get a lovely cup of coffee and a bun. It opens 7.30 am to 1 am Monday to Thursday, 24 hours Friday and Saturday, and 9.30 am to 7 pm on Sunday.

St Andrew's St, just west of Grafton St's northern end, is packed with good restaurant possibilities. The excellent *Trocadero* (*Around Temple Bar map;* ☎ *677 5545, 679 9772, 3 St Andrew's St*) offers no culinary surprises, which is why it's so popular. Simple food, straightforward preparation, large helpings and late opening hours are the selling points. Main courses cost around £10. The Troc, as it's locally known, opens past midnight every night except Sunday, when it closes just a little earlier.

Across the road, *QV.2* (*Around Temple Bar map;* ☎ *677 3363, 14-15 St Andrew's St*) manages to look more expensive than it is. There are good pasta dishes costing upwards of £6 and main courses costing £7.25 to £12.50, but vegetables cost extra. It offers good, mildly adventurous food, pleasant surroundings and a dessert called Eton mess (£3.95) which shouldn't be missed. It opens for lunch and dinner until after midnight Monday to Saturday.

Still on St Andrew's St, *The Cedar Tree* (*Around Temple Bar map;* ☎ *677 2121*) at No 11A is a Lebanese restaurant with a good selection of vegetarian dishes. Or turn left at the corner to excellent *La Taverna* (*Around Temple Bar map;* ☎ *677 3665, 33 Wicklow St*). Open for lunch and dinner daily, it combines sunny Greek food with an equally sunny atmosphere. A three-course meal costs about £15. It has a good vegetarian selection. Opposite at No 12A, *Imperial Chinese Restaurant* (*Around Temple Bar map;* ☎ *677 2580*) opens daily and is notable for its lunchtime dim sums. Most mains cost £8.50 to £9.50.

Modern, cheerful *Pasta Fresca* (*Around St Stephen's Green map;* ☎ *679 2402, 679 8965, 3-4 Chatham St*), just off Grafton St's southern end, proves once again that the Irish really like their Italian food. It serves authentic pasta dishes costing £4.95 to £8.50 and opens from 8 am until reasonably late Monday to Saturday, and noon to 8.30 pm on Sunday. Just off Exchequer St

is *The Odessa* (*Around Temple Bar map;* ☎ *670 7634, 13 Dame Lane*), where you can eat well in comfort and style for £10 to £17; Sunday brunch is a favourite with the city's trendy crowd.

Tex-Mex *Judge Roy Bean's* (*Around Temple Bar map;* ☎ *679 7539, 45-47 Nassau St*), on the corner of Grafton St, serves whopping helpings of tacos (£7.95) and has a popular bar with music. *Eddie Rocket's* (*Around St Stephen's Green map;* ☎ *679 7340, 7 South Anne St*) is a 1950s-style American diner ready to dish out anything from breakfast at 7.30 am to a late-night hot dog (£3.25). Friday and Saturday nights it opens until 4 am. Next door is the trendy, popular *Gotham Café* (☎ *679 5266, 8 South Anne St*), with pizzas prepared with some pizzazz. If you can stand the smell, *Periwinkle Seafood Bar* (*Around St Stephen's Green map;* ☎ *679 4203*), in the Powerscourt Townhouse Shopping Centre, serves economically priced seafood lunches with the accent on shellfish.

Visitors to India may remember Rajdoot as a popular brand of Indian motorcycle. Those in search of Indian food in Dublin can scoot down to *Rajdoot Tandoori* (*Around St Stephen's Green map;* ☎ *679 4274, 26-28 Clarendon St*) in the Westbury Centre, behind the Westbury Hotel, for superb North Indian tandoori dishes. Set 'executive lunches' cost £7.50. Nearby, and with similarly Mogul-style Indian cuisine, is the large *Shalimar* (*Around Temple Bar map;* ☎ *671 0738, 17 South Great George St*), on the corner of Exchequer St, which offers a wide variety of delectable Indian breads and baltis (£7.50 to £8.50).

Dublin's first fully fledged sushi bar, *Aya* (*Around Temple Bar map; Clarendon St*), hadn't opened at the time of writing, but it's recommended on the basis that it is being opened by the same family that have successfully run Baggot St's and Foxrock's Ayumi-Ya restaurants, the latter renowned as Dublin's best Japanese eatery. The Baggot St branch closed down in anticipation of Aya's opening.

La Stampa (*Around St Stephen's Green map;* ☎ *677 8611, 35 Dawson St*) is

Dublin's upmarket Italian restaurant with a large and very attractive Georgian dining area, liberally festooned with colourful paintings. It opens lunchtime until late daily and main courses cost £10.50 to £15.

For a French restaurant without the pretentiousness that sometimes implies, try *Chez Jules* (☎ 677 0499), tucked away at 16A D'Olier St, just north-west of Trinity College. You eat at long benches with red-and-white check cloths. The food is well cooked and not extortionately priced: mains start at £9.

The Rhino Room (*Around Temple Bar map;* ☎ 670 5260, 14 South William St), just beside Powerscourt Townhouse Shopping Centre, is a trendy-cum-casual spot where you can eat extremely well for less than £20, excluding wine (and there are plenty to choose from). The fresh raspberry dessert is divine. It opens for lunch and dinner Monday to Saturday. Downstairs is *Cooke's Café* (*Around Temple Bar map;* ☎ 679 0536), more expensive than its sister restaurant upstairs but without food good enough to justify the extra expense. The socially aware love it, though. Reservations are essential for dinner.

Velure (*Around St Stephen's Green map;* ☎ 670 5585, 47 South William St) opened in June 1999 with a menu (and prices) fit to match those of the Clarence Hotel's Tea Rooms. A three-course meal will cost you about £30 (without wine) but, if you plan on splashing out during your trip to Dublin, this is the place to do it. Reservations are advisable.

On St Stephen's Green, Fitzwilliam Hotel at No 109 is home to *Peacock Alley* (*Around St Stephen's Green map;* ☎ 478 7015), owned by super-chef Conrad Gallagher, whose speciality is French provincial cuisine. A dinner will set you back about £40, but you can have lunch for about half that amount.

In the basement of Newman House, at 85-86 St Stephen's Green, is *The Commons* (*Around St Stephen's Green map;* ☎ 475 2597), one of Dublin's Michelin-starred restaurants. As you'd expect, the food here is pricey and it would be as well to book

ahead, especially for weekends. The six-course 'tasting menu' of seven courses costs £45.

Fast Food, Cafés & Pubs Grafton St is the fast-food centre south of the Liffey. The area has office workers, Trinity College students and tourists to feed and there are plenty of cafés and restaurants to keep them happy at lunchtime.

Captain America (*Around St Stephen's Green map;* ☎ 671 5266, 44 Grafton St) serves burgers until midnight every night; last food orders are about 11.30 pm. The singer Chris de Burgh performed here in his post-student days. Round the corner is a branch of *La Pizza* (*Around St Stephen's Green map;* ☎ 671 7175, 1 St Stephen's Green North*).

Backpackers staying at *Avalon House* (*Around St Stephen's Green map*), on Aungier St, can take advantage of the most stylish hostel café in town.

Café Java (*Around St Stephen's Green map;* ☎ 670 7239, 5 South Anne St) serves excellent three-course weekday lunches of soup, a sandwich and tea or coffee costing £3.95. There's a second branch (*off Dublin map;* ☎ 660 0675) at 145 Upper Leeson St.

Munchies (*Around Temple Bar map*), on the corner of Exchequer and South William Sts, just west of Grafton St, claims to produce the best sandwiches in Ireland. For £2 to £2.40 you can check if it's true. Head along Exchequer St to try *Wed Wose Café* (*Around Temple Bar map*) at No 18, which has sandwiches and burgers (upwards of £1.60) and an all-day breakfast costing £3.95.

A little closer to Grafton St is *Cornucopia* (*Around Temple Bar map;* ☎ 677 7583, 19 Wicklow St*), a popular wholefood café turning out all sorts of goodies for those trying to escape the Irish cholesterol habit. There's even a hot vegetarian breakfast (£2.65) as an alternative to muesli. It opens for breakfast and lunch Monday to Saturday and until 8 pm on weekday evenings, 9 pm on Thursday.

The Powerscourt Townhouse Shopping Centre (Around St Stephen's Green map) is stuffed with eating places and makes a great place for lunch. Cafés include *Blazing Salads II* (☎ 671 9552), a popular vegetarian restaurant on the top level, with a variety of salads costing 80p each. It opens 9.30 am to 6 pm Monday to Saturday. *La Piazza*, next door, serves pizzas costing £4.75. On the 1st floor, *Chompy's* (☎ 679 4552) boasts a Grand Slam breakfast (£5), salads (£4) and lunches (£4.50 to £5.50). On the ground floor you'll find the *Whistlestop Café* and *Fair City Sandwich Bar*, serving everything from soups to burgers.

A café that has been entirely unaffected by the dining revolution is *Alpha* (*Around Temple Bar map;* ☎ 677 0213, 37 Wicklow St). For nearly 35 years this hard-to-find café (the entrance is actually on Clarendon St and it is upstairs) has been serving solid lunches and dinners to Dublin's working community at prices that you won't see beaten anywhere in the city.

On the 1st floor of St Stephen's Green Shopping Centre (Around St Stephen's Green map) is a branch of *O'Brien's*, serving sizeable sandwiches costing under £3. Other places to eat in the shopping centre include a branch of *Café Kylemore* on the 1st floor and *Pavlova Pantry* on the 2nd, which serves sandwiches and snacks as well as the Australian-invented cake.

Just beside the Centre is a branch of *Chicago Pizza Pie Factory* (*Around St Stephen's Green map;* ☎ 478 1233), where pizzas cost £7.25 to £13.95. Nearby, in Clarendon Market, the new *Kaffe Moka* serves large, delicious sandwiches (£2.30 to £3.75), and has a variety of good coffees and teas. It opens late every night.

The large *Kilkenny Restaurant* (*Around Temple Bar map;* ☎ 677 7066, 6 Nassau St) is on the 1st floor of the Kilkenny Shop. The generally excellent food is served cafeteria-style and at times the queues can be discouragingly long. There's a simpler food counter which can be faster. It opens 9 am to 5 pm Monday to Saturday, and noon to 5 pm on Sunday.

There's a large cafeteria at the *Alliance Française* (*Around St Stephen's Green map*) on the corner of Kildare and Nassau

Sts, also opposite Trinity. From the windows you can gaze across to the college grounds.

Fitzers' slick outlets are great places for lunch or early-evening meals on weekdays, and there's a branch (*Around St Stephen's Green map;* ☎ 677 1155, 51 Dawson St) with outside tables.

There are several pubs with good food close to Grafton St. *Stag's Head* (*Dublin's Pubs & Bars map;* ☎ 679 3701) is on Dame Court and, apart from being an extremely popular drinking spot during summer (see Traditional under Pubs in the Entertainment section later in this chapter), turns out simple, well-prepared, economical meals. On the corner of St Andrew's and Wicklow Sts is the *Old Stand* (*Around Temple Bar map; 37 Exchequer St*), another popular place for pub food, with meals costing upwards of £5.

Davy Byrne's (*Dublin's Pubs & Bars map; 21 Duke St*) has been famous for its food ever since Leopold Bloom dropped in for a sandwich. It's now a swish watering hole but you can still eat there, as you can across the road at *The Bailey.* Farther west, *Lord Edward Restaurant* (*Around Temple Bar map;* ☎ 454 2420, 23 Christ Church Place), upstairs in the Lord Edward pub, opposite Christ Church Cathedral, is Dublin's oldest seafood restaurant. It opens for lunch on weekdays and for dinner Monday to Saturday. Even farther west, *The Brazen Head* in Bridge St is always packed at lunchtime. It has a variety of menus offering everything from sandwiches to a carvery.

Merrion Row, Baggot St & Beyond

Merrion Row, leading south-east from St Stephen's Green, and its extension, Baggot St, have an eclectic selection of pubs and restaurants.

Restaurants The *Ante Room* (*Around St Stephen's Green map;* ☎ 660 4716, 20 Lower Baggot St*), underneath the Georgian House guesthouse, is a seafood specialist with main courses costing around £10 and traditional Irish music on most summer nights.

The best restaurant in Dublin is the elegant, Michelin-starred **Restaurant Patrick Guilbaud** (Around St Stephen's Green map; ☎ 676 4192, The Merrion Hotel, Upper Merrion St). Don't come here unless your credit card is in A1 condition. The smooth décor and service is backed up by delicious food. There's nothing overpoweringly fancy about anything: it's just good food, beautifully prepared and elegantly presented. There's a table d'hôte lunch menu costing £20, but dinner is à la carte. It opens for lunch on weekdays and for dinner Monday to Saturday. Also in the hotel is **Lloyd's Brasserie** (☎ 662 7240), a large French brasserie owned by Peacock Alley's Conrad Gallagher.

Out from the centre is **Lobster Pot Restaurant** (off Dublin map; ☎ 668 0025, 9 Ballsbridge Terrace). It's a staunchly old-fashioned place offering substantial and solid dishes in an equally substantial atmosphere. As the name indicates, seafood is the speciality. Prices are fairly high. Next door is **Roly's Bistro** (☎ 668 2611), at No 7, which receives rave write-ups for its food; advance booking is advisable. Close by is **Kites Chinese Restaurant** (off Dublin map; ☎ 660 7415, 15-17 Ballsbridge Terrace), which serves Chinese food with style and moderate to high prices.

Old Dublin (☎ 454 2028, 90 Francis St), not far from St Patrick's Cathedral, makes an interesting departure from most menus, as it specialises in Russian and Scandinavian food. Dinner costs around £20, but it's worth the splash.

Fast Food & Cafés All of the following places to eat are marked on the Around St Stephen's Green map.

Fitzers (☎ 668 6481), inside the National Gallery on Merrion Square, is well worth a detour, particularly at lunchtime. The artistic interlude as you walk through makes a pleasant introduction to this slightly pricey but popular restaurant. It opens the same hours as the gallery and has varied meals costing £5.25 to £6.25, as well as salads,

cakes and wine. **Pierre Victoire** (☎ 678 5412, 11 Merrion Row) serves set lunches costing £4.90 and set dinners costing £7.90.

Farther to the south-east, **Georgian Fare** (☎ 676 7736, 14 Lower Baggot St) offers good sandwiches, while **Miller's Pizza Kitchen** (☎ 676 6098, 9-10 Lower Baggot St) has a full range of pizzas and pastas.

ENTERTAINMENT

Dublin is undoubtedly one of Europe's most vibrant entertainment capitals, with a plethora of options to satisfy (nearly) every desire. It has theatres, cinemas, nightclubs, concert halls, stadiums and horse and dog tracks, but the real centre of activity is still the pub – and in Dublin there are about 700 of them to suit every taste, fashion and trend. A thriving nightlife – bars, cafés and clubs are packed virtually every night of the week – has made the city one of the most popular getaway destinations in Europe.

Dublin's 'party district' is undoubtedly Temple Bar, although its designation as the city's cultural quarter is somewhat of a misnomer, at least after sundown, when it turns into a northern Gomorrah with few rivals in Europe. The pubs and clubs are crammed, the music is loud, and the party goes on till the wee hours.

If 'Ibiza in the rain' isn't to your taste, do not despair: there's still plenty to do outside the confines of Temple Bar's cobbled streets. Most of the best old-fashioned pubs are outside the district, and in recent times Dubliners looking to discover a new trendy area have begun exploring the hitherto untapped resources of the northern side of the river, especially in and around the Smithfield area west of Capel St. Its cobbled streets and big, unused spaces have virtually guaranteed its role as the Temple Bar of the new millennium. It is hoped that in exploiting the area developers will bear in mind what went wrong in Temple Bar and avoid making the same mistakes.

For what's-on information get the fortnightly magazines In Dublin or Hot Press (both £1.95), or the bimonthly giveaway Event Guide, an excellent resource for up-to-date information on everything from

DUBLIN

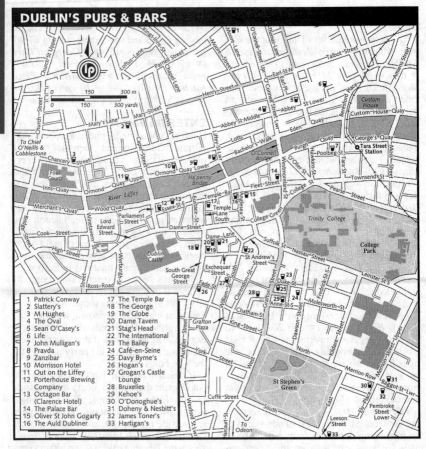

DUBLIN'S PUBS & BARS

1 Patrick Conway	17 The Temple Bar
2 Slattery's	18 The George
3 M Hughes	19 The Globe
4 The Oval	20 Dame Tavern
5 Sean O'Casey's	21 Stag's Head
6 Life	22 The International
7 John Mulligan's	23 The Bailey
8 Pravda	24 Café-en-Seine
9 Zanzibar	25 Davy Byrne's
10 Morrisson Hotel	26 Hogan's
11 Out on the Liffey	27 Grogan's Castle
12 Porterhouse Brewing	Lounge
Company	28 Bruxelles
13 Octagon Bar	29 Kehoe's
(Clarence Hotel)	30 O'Donoghue's
14 The Palace Bar	31 Doheny & Nesbitt's
15 Oliver St John Gogarty	32 James Toner's
16 The Auld Dubliner	33 Hartigan's

clubs and concerts to plays, movies and art exhibitions. It's available almost everywhere around the city centre.

Pubs

Since Irish life is closely tied up with pub culture, a visit to one of the many pubs spread throughout the city is an absolute must. Despite the challenges of 'Europeanisation' – the increase in cafés, clubs, restaurants and so on – pubs are still the hub of virtually all social activity in the city, a meeting point for friends and strangers alike, and where Dubliners are at their friendly and convivial best (and, it must be said, sometimes their drunken and incoherent worst!).

There are all kinds of pubs (over 700 in the city alone): from old-style, traditional establishments that date from centuries past (like some of the clientele, it would seem!) to ultra-sleek new bars where chilled wine and cappuccinos seem more popular than the ubiquitous pint of Guinness (but not quite!). And, of course, there's music – from live traditional *seisúns* (sessions) or jamming rock bands to the latest sounds from commercial and

You will find more suitable souvenirs in Dublin.

Dublin street entertainment

While away a cold evening listening to traditional Irish music in a Dublin pub.

Shopping on Grafton St

Dublin's Temple Bar is a maze of pubs, restaurants and shops.

Bedford Tower, Dublin Castle

The 1816 Ha'penny Bridge spans the River Liffey, Dublin.

Howth, County Dublin

Custom House, Dublin

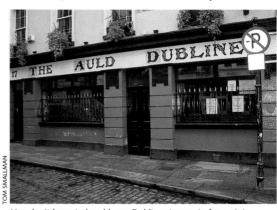

You don't have to be old or a Dubliner to pop in for a pint.

Gay & Lesbian Nightspots

Nightly gay venues in Dublin include the multilevel, ever-throbbing *The George (Dublin's Pubs & Bars map; 89 South Great George St)*, the most popular place in town for drinking and cruising, especially when it hosts the Block disco on Friday and Saturday nights or bingo on Sunday night; and *Out on the Liffey (Dublin's Pubs & Bars map; 27 Upper Ormond Quay)*, a 'harder' pub popular with the biker or butch set of both sexes.

Other places (including most dance clubs) are gay, lesbian and/or mixed on certain nights of the week. Consult the *Gay Community News* monthly freebie – available through coffee shops around the city centre, Temple Bar Information Centre on Eustace St, or Condom Power (Around Temple Bar map) on Dame St – or the 'Queer' pages of the fortnightly what's-on magazine *In Dublin*, for specific days and times.

Such 'one-off' venues included, at the time of writing (bear in mind that venues change constantly): Mildred at *Da Club* next to Break for the Border *(Around St Stephen's Green map; Lower Stephen St)* on Tuesday; HAM at *PoD (Around St Stephen's Green map; Old Harcourt St Station)* on Friday; Playground at *Republica (Earl of Kildare Hotel, corner of Nassau and Kildare Sts)*; Tag and Shag at *Republica* on Tuesday; Freedom at *Club Zazu (Around Temple Bar map; Eustace St)* on Monday; Flirt at *Tivoli Theatre (Francis St)* on Saturday night; Fruit Factory at *Velvet Nightclub (Around St Stephen's Green map; Harcourt Hotel)*; and the women-only *Stonewallz* at Griffith College *(off Dublin map; South Circular Rd)* on Saturday.

underground dance charts. Whatever your fancy, there's bound to be something that will appeal. We have selected only some of the best. For some information on gay and lesbian pubs, see the boxed text 'Gay & Lesbian Nightspots'.

Most pubs close by 11.30 pm (11 pm in winter), but an increasing number have late licences which permit them to serve until 1.30 am on Thursday and Friday and until midnight on Saturday. At the time of writing a deregulation bill was being considered in the Dáil to extend pub opening times until 1 am throughout the year. If it does happen, it will be long overdue.

The listed pubs can be found on the Dublin's Pubs & Bars map.

Traditional North of the Liffey just off O'Connell St, *The Oval (Middle Abbey St)* is a popular journalists' hangout. Farther north is *Patrick Conway (70 Parnell St)*. Although slightly out of the way, this is a true gem of a pub. It has been operating since 1745, so, no doubt, new fathers have been stopping in here for a celebratory pint from the day the Rotunda Maternity Hospital opened across the road in 1757.

In Temple Bar, *The Palace Bar (Fleet St)*, with its wooden niches and mirrors, is often said to be the perfect example of an old Dublin pub. It's popular with journalists from the nearby *Irish Times*. *John Mulligan's (Poolbeg St)* is another pub that has scarcely changed over the years. It featured as the local in the film *My Left Foot* and is also popular with journalists from the nearby newspaper offices. Mulligan's was established in 1782 and has long been reputed to have the best Guinness in Ireland, as well as a wonderfully varied collection of 'regulars'.

Dame Tavern and *Stag's Head* face each other from opposite corners of the intersection of Dame Court and Dame Lane, just off Dame Street. A street party takes place between the pubs on summer evenings. Stag's Head was built in 1770 then remodelled in 1895, and is sufficiently picturesque to have featured on a postage-stamp series of Irish pubs.

Just off Grafton St, be sure to pop your head into *Kehoe's (9 South Anne St)*, one of the only city-centre bars to have recently passed into new ownership without losing any of its traditional appeal. Its snug is still

DUBLIN

The Perfect Pint of Guinness

What makes a perfect pint of Guinness? This much debated question has no complete, definitive answer, but we can offer a few indications, as gleaned from the experts themselves: Dubliners.

Everyone agrees that proximity to the St James' Gate Brewery is one requirement, for although a pint in Kuala Lumpur can still be a fine thing, Guinness at its best can be found only in Ireland. But not even that is a guarantee, for there are still some substandard pints to be had in Dublin. So, what is a good test?

The proper pour is an essential. First, you need a good, experienced bartender (preferably one who has served the required apprenticeship) who has ensured that the pipes are clean and free-flowing (there's nothing worse than dirty pipes). Once everything is in place, the pour can begin. The glass is tilted to about 45 degrees, then the tap is pulled forwards so that the liquid is poured against the back of the glass. When it is about three-quarters full, the glass is left to 'settle', which means that the heavier black liquid settles underneath the lighter, creamy head. After a few minutes, the pint is topped up by pushing the tap backwards, allowing only the black beer into the glass. When the pint is full, it is left to settle a second time, and then it's ready to drink. It isn't that difficult, but it takes time: as Guinness' advertising will tell you, 'It's worth waiting for'.

Now it is time to test the quality of the pint. When you're about halfway through, look at the sides of the glass: if there are rings of white foam round the inside (the thicker the better), you can be sure that the pint is a good one. First-time stout drinkers usually have difficulty with the bitter, heavy taste. If that is the case, have no fear: Guinness is most definitely an acquired taste. Practice does indeed make perfect!

---

intact, while upstairs drinks are served in what was once the publican's living room. And it looks it!

Grogan's Castle Lounge (South William St), known simply as Grogan's (after the original owner), is a city-centre institution. It has long been a favourite haunt of Dublin's writers, painters and others of the drop-out alternative set, most of whom seem to be waiting for the 'inevitable' moment when they are finally recognised as geniuses-in-waiting. An odd quirk of the pub is that drinks are marginally cheaper in the stone-floor bar than the carpeted lounge, even though they're served by the same bar!

Facing each other across Lower Baggot St are two traditional pubs, *James Toner's* at No 139 and *Doheny & Nesbitt's* at No 5. James Toner's, with its stone floor, is almost a country pub in the heart of the city, and the shelves and drawers are reminders that it once doubled as a grocery store. Doheny & Nesbitt's is equipped with antique snugs and is a favourite place for political gossip among politicians and journalists: Leinster House is only a short stroll away.

Just off St Stephen's Green, *Hartigan's (100 Lower Leeson St)* is about as spartan a bar as you'll find in the city, and the daytime home to some serious drinkers, who go about their business in the quiet, no-frills, no-fuss surroundings. In the evening it is popular with students from the nearby medical faculty of University College, Dublin.

Music North of the Liffey, *Slattery's* (☎ 872 7971, 129 Capel St), on the corner of Mary's Lane, is considered by many to be the home of Dublin pub rock. Brian Downey, the former drummer with 1970s group Thin Lizzy, plays a regular weekly session with his band. *Sean O'Casey's* (☎ 874 8675, 105 Marlborough St) has a weekly menu of live rock and some Irish traditional-music sessions.

The Perfect Pint of Guinness

A new system known as 'cold flow' was recently introduced by Guinness to standardise the taste of the drink, making it colder and easier to pour. While this has been welcomed in the Irish bars of New York or Melbourne, Dublin traditionalists have reacted with deep suspicion of anything that may change their beloved pint. Consequently, you won't find the system in operation anywhere Guinness is given the respect and adoration its drinkers feel it deserves. What you might see more of in the future, however, is a particular brand of Guinness known as Extra Cold: this is the company's reaction to the American and Australian tradition of serving their beers ice cold.

Now that you know what to look for, where will you find the perfect pint of the 'black stuff', as it is referred to in Dublin? Most Dubliners agree that the pint served in the **Guinness Hop Store** is among the best served anywhere, despite Guinness' assurances that it is no different from that found in any pub.

Few will argue with the quality of the pint served in **John Mulligan's** of Poolbeg St, where the assorted regulars are considered experts on the subject. **Grogan's Castle Lounge** on South William St is another spot where the Guinness is top notch. **Kehoe's** of South Anne St has a lovely snug where you can enjoy the excellent pint. **Hartigan's**, just off St Stephen's Green on Lower Leeson St, might not look like much, but the Guinness is beyond reproach. All the above pubs are marked on the Dublin Pubs & Bars map.

A Guinness pilgrimage to **Kavanagh's** (off Dublin map), just behind the Glasnevin cemetery off DeCourcey Square, will be rewarded with a pint that is truly exceptional. The pub is commonly referred to as 'The Gravediggers' because it is the traditional drinking hole of the cemetery employees.

For the best Irish traditional sessions in Dublin, two northside pubs are a must. *M Hughes* (☎ 872 6540, 19 Chancery St) is directly behind the Four Courts and has nightly, if impromptu, sessions which often result in a closed door – that is, they go on long past official closing time. The pub is also a popular lunchtime spot with barristers working nearby. *Cobblestone* (Dublin map; ☎ 872 1799, North King St) is on the main square in Smithfield, the future hot spot of Dublin. The music sessions here are superb.

Temple Bar has plenty of pubs where you'll find music. The traditional-music sessions at *Oliver St John Gogarty* (☎ 671 1822) are extremely popular with tourists, most of whom couldn't care less if the music is less than authentic.

The International (☎ 677 9250, 23 Wicklow St) does live jazz and blues most nights except Wednesday, when it hosts a comedy night. *Bruxelles* (☎ 677 5362,

Harry St) has weekly live rock music, perhaps the only link the now-trendy pub has to its heavy-metal past.

The most famous traditional-music bar in Dublin is *O'Donoghue's* (☎ 661 4303, Lower Baggot St), where world-famous folk group the Dubliners started off in the 1960s. On summer evenings a young, international crowd spills out into the courtyard beside the pub.

Serious aficionados of traditional music should make the trip to *Comhaltas Ceoltóiri Éireann* (off Dublin map; ☎ 280 0295, 35 Belgrave Square, Monkstown), towards Dun Laoghaire. The name, pronounced 'keol-tas quail-tori Erin', means 'Fraternity of Traditional Musicians of Ireland'. It's here that you'll find the best Irish music and dancing in Dublin, with some of the country's top players. To get there, take bus Nos 7, 7A or 8 from Trinity College, get off before Monkstown village and follow the blue signs. Alternatively, you can take the

DART; it's a five-minute walk inland (westwards, following the signs) from Seapoint Station.

Trendy The northside of Dublin is fast becoming a trendy spot for pubs. *Pravda*, just north of Ha'penny Bridge; *Life (Irish Life Mall)*, off Lower Abbey St; and *Zanzibar (Ormond Quay)* opened in 1998 and firmly established themselves on the city's 'in' scene. In Smithfield, *Chief O'Neills (Dublin map)*, part of the complex that is home to Ceol, is a great place for a drink and, as the area is developed, is sure to do well with the cool set. The basement bar in the new *Morrisson Hotel* is the new northside trendsetter, with a strict door policy that declares trainers a sin and allows entry only to those who've stepped (in leather shoes, of course) out of the pages of a fashion magazine.

The trendiest bar in Temple Bar is easily *Octagon Bar (6-8 Wellington Quay)* in Clarence Hotel. Drinks are marginally more expensive than elsewhere but, judging by the clientele who have passed the bouncer's strict entry test, this is hardly a concern.

The Globe (11 South Great George St) was one of the first of the new breed of trendy pubs to open in the city. Farther up the street at No 35 is *Hogan's*, a gigantic boozer spread across two floors. A popular hangout for young professionals, it gets full at weekends with folks eager to take advantage of its late licence.

Just off Grafton St is *The Bailey (2 Duke St)*, an ultra-chic reincarnation of the pub that featured in *Ulysses*. Across the street is another Joycean favourite, *Davy Byrne's*, which is now popular with the 'raised collars' set.

Parallel to Grafton St, *Café-en-Seine (40 Dawson St)* is an überbar that looks more like a giant Parisian bistro than an Irish pub. Its super-hip clientele may have moved on to fresher pastures, but it's still a big hit with the 'in' crowd.

South of the city centre, *Odeon (Around St Stephen's Green map)*, in Old Harcourt St Station at the top of the street of the same name, is a new, trendy spot with a 50m-long bar and ample space for the hundreds of punters to show off their designer gear.

Popular rather than trendy, in Temple Bar is *The Auld Dubliner*, whose unashamed pursuit of the tourist punt has led to it being jokingly referred to as 'The Auld Foreigner'. *The Temple Bar (Temple Lane)* is incredibly popular, especially in summer. *Porterhouse Brewing Company (Parliament St)* is a microbrewery that has dared challenge the supremacy of Guinness. Its Wrassler XXXX is an excellent stout.

Nightclubs

Visiting Dublin today, it's hard to imagine that the nightclub scene was once confined to a grim strip of basement clubs along Lower Leeson St. The last decade has seen a revolution in nightlife, with late-night venues springing up all over the city, both north and south of the Liffey. The seemingly endless list of 'what's on' is constantly changing, so check out the listings in *In Dublin* and *Event Guide*. Most clubs open just after pubs close (11 to 11.30 pm) and close at 2 or 2.30 am. Admission to most costs £4 to £6 on weekdays, going up to £8 at weekends. For gay and lesbian clubs, see the boxed text 'Gay & Lesbian Nightspots' earlier in this Entertainment section.

Dublin's most renowned nightclub is still *PoD ('Place of Dance'; Around St Stephen's Green map; ☎ 478 0166, 35 Harcourt Street)*, a futuristic, metal-gothic cathedral of dance that attracts large weekend crowds of mostly twenty-somethings. It's not nearly as popular as it used to be, which may have less to do with fickle trends and more to do with the somewhat negative reputation of its bouncers, who are notoriously difficult to get past.

In Temple Bar, the U2-owned *Kitchen (Around Temple Bar map; ☎ 677 6635, Clarence Hotel, 6-8 Wellington Quay)* is surprisingly laid back, considering its far-flung fame. The music is hard and fast (currently a mix of techno and house) and the back bar is usually patronised by celebrities and those eager to see and be seen.

Formerly the Mission, *Club Zazu* *(Around Temple Bar map; Eustace St)* is a little hard to handle unless your idea of a good time is drinking yourself into a near-coma. *Club M (Around Temple Bar map; ☎ 671 5485, Anglesea St)*, at Bloom's Hotel, offers a mix of 90s Ibiza-style dance music and 80s tunes to a dancefloor of kids convinced that an 80s revival is long overdue.

Eamonn Doran Imbibing Emporium (Around Temple Bar map; ☎ 679 9773, 3A Crown Alley) offers food, drink and music every night. Monday night is great for hip-hop. *Rí Rá (Around Temple Bar map; ☎ 677 4835, 1 Exchequer St)* is one of the more people-friendly clubs in the city centre, which is handy considering it's full nearly seven nights a week. Doors open at 11.30 pm.

Lillie's Bordello (Around Temple Bar map; ☎ 679 9204, Adam Court), off Grafton St, is strictly for the well-heeled and fat-walleted, except on Sunday night, when the atmosphere is more relaxed for Lost in Music, which features live soul and salsa as well as some excellent DJs. Like Lillie's, *Renard's (Around St Stephen's Green map; ☎ 677 5876, South Frederick St)* is upmarket and more than a little snobby. Strictly for the wannabe set.

Gaiety Theatre (Around St Stephen's Green map; ☎ 677 1717, South King St) is no longer home to Mambo! and Velure, but their replacements offer the same mix of soul and salsa that made their predecessors the most successful Friday and Saturday nights in Dublin. Doors open at 11.30 pm.

Break for the Border (Around St Stephen's Green map; ☎ 478 0300, Lower Stephen St) is an enormous country-and-western-style eatery that reverts to a night-club once pubs close. It's good fun if a little cheesy, and is renowned in Dublin as one of the biggest pick-up joints around.

Columbia Mills (off Dublin map; ☎ 677 8466, Sir John Rogerson's Quay), about 1km east of Tara St Station, is a great club, with a good mix of music from techno to 80s chart hits. It opens from Thursday to Saturday.

Copper Face Jack's (Around St Stephen's Green map; ☎ 475 8777, 29 Harcourt St) is popular with an older crowd and lacks much of the pizzazz found in other night-clubs. This may have something to do with its popularity with off-duty police officers!

The Vatican (Around St Stephen's Green map; ☎ 478 4066, Russell Court Hotel) offers precious little in terms of décor, but that doesn't seem to stop the droves of young people that flock here from Tuesday to Saturday nights. It is very popular with weekenders from Britain.

If none of the above is to your satisfaction, you'll hardly console yourself with the basement clubs along Lower Leeson St. They are more or less all the same, and the only advantage they have over other clubs in the city is that for some bizarre reason they are allowed to keep their doors open until 4 am. There are no admission charges, but the price of drinks certainly makes up for that: count on paying at least £18 for a bottle of basic wine.

Irish Cabaret

Although strictly aimed at tourists, there are several places in Dublin where you can go for an evening of Irish entertainment with Irish songs, Irish dancing and probably a few jokes thrown in along the way. All venues are outside the area shown on the Dublin map.

Jury's Irish Cabaret (☎ 660 5000, Jury's Hotel, Pembroke Rd, Ballsbridge) features 2½ hours of Irish music, song and dance. This is a tourist favourite and has been for over 30 years. You can either come for dinner and the show from 7.30 pm (£36.50) or just for the show from 8 pm (£22, including two drinks). It operates Tuesday to Sunday nights from early May to mid-October. To get there, take bus Nos 7, 46 or 46A.

Similar performances are put on at *Burlington Hotel (☎ 660 5222, Leeson St)*. The two-hour performances take place from 8 pm nightly May to October. Dinner starts an hour earlier and the cost for a four-course dinner and the show is £36.50. Mock-medieval *Clontarf Castle (☎ 833 2321, Castle Ave, Clontarf)* has shows from 7.30 pm Monday to Saturday. Bus No 44A passes nearby.

Concerts

Bookings can be made either directly at the concert venue or through HMV (Around St Stephen's Green map; ☎ 679 5334, 24-hour credit card bookings 456 9569), 65 Grafton St.

Classical concerts are performed at the *National Concert Hall (Around St Stephen's Green map; ☎ 671 1888, Earlsfort Terrace)*. There are lunchtime concerts (from 1.05 to 2 pm) on Friday from May to September with admission costing £4. Classical performances may also take place at the *Bank of Ireland Arts Centre (Around Temple Bar map; Foster Place)*, *Municipal Gallery of Modern Art (Parnell Square)* or *Royal Dublin Society Showground Concert Hall (County Dublin map)*.

Big rock concerts are held at the *Point Depot (off Dublin map; ☎ 836 3633, East Link Bridge, North Wall Quay)*, by the river and originally constructed as a train terminus in 1878. *Lansdowne Rd Stadium (off Dublin map)*, a mecca for rugby enthusiasts, is also used for big rock performances. The castle grounds in *Slane*, 46km north-west of Dublin, play host to the yearly Slane Festival, a one-day summer extravaganza featuring the biggest names in rock.

Smaller performances take place at the new all-seater *Vicar Street (☎ 454 5533, Thomas St)* near Christ Church Cathedral. Dublin's latest venue is *HQ (☎ 878 3345, 57 Middle Abbey St)*, which so far has featured acts who made their fame in the 1970s and 1980s.

Buskers

Dublin is well set up for free entertainment in the form of buskers, but contributions are always gratefully accepted. The best of the city's plentiful supply work busy Grafton St, where they're occasionally hassled by shopkeepers (for blocking access to their concerns) and the police, but are mainly left to get on with it. You're likely to meet crooning folk singers, raucous rock bands or classical string quartets. At the Trinity College end of Grafton St, you'll usually trip over pavement artists, some of them distressingly young, busily chalking pictures around the statue of Molly Malone.

Cinemas

Dublin's cinemas are more heavily concentrated on the northern side of the Liffey. The mainstream cinemas are the *Ambassador (☎ 872 7000, Parnell St)*, the five-screen *Savoy (☎ 874 6000, Upper O'Connell St)*, and the 12-screen *Virgin Multiplex (☎ 872 8400, Parnell Centre, Parnell St)*. Next door is the *IMAX Cinema (☎ 817 4222)*, with its giant 25m-wide screen showing documentaries made with IMAX cameras.

The three-screen *Screen (Around Temple Bar map; ☎ 671 4988, 872 3922, 2 Townsend St)*, south of the river, is more arthouse, less big release. The *Irish Film Centre (Around Temple Bar map; ☎ 679 5744, 6 Eustace St)* has two screens. The complex also has a bar, a café and a bookshop; comedy shows are sometimes staged in the atrium.

Admission prices are generally about £3.50 for afternoon shows, rising to £5 for evening shows. The IMAX is more expensive, with prices between £5 and £7.50, depending on the feature. The Savoy has late-night shows at the weekend.

Theatre

Dublin's theatre scene is small but busy. Bookings can usually be made by quoting a credit card number over the phone, and the tickets can then be collected just before the performance.

The famous *Abbey Theatre (☎ 878 7222, Lower Abbey St)*, near the river, puts on new Irish works as well as revivals of classic Irish works by WB Yeats, JM Synge, Sean O'Casey, Brendan Behan, Samuel Beckett and others. Performances are at 8 pm, with Saturday matinées at 2.30 pm. Tickets cost £10 to £12.50, but student discounts are available, and all seats cost £8 on Monday. The smaller *Peacock Theatre* is part of the same complex but ticket prices are lower. Together, the two theatres make up Ireland's National Theatre.

Also north of the Liffey is the *Gate Theatre* (☎ *874 4045*), on the south-eastern corner of Parnell Square, at the top of O'Connell St. It specialises in international classics and older Irish works with a touch of comedy by playwrights such as Oscar Wilde, George Bernard Shaw and Oliver Goldsmith, although newer plays are sometimes staged.

South of the river, the *Gaiety Theatre* (*Around St Stephen's Green map;* ☎ *677 1717, South King St*), off Grafton St, was built in 1871 and is Dublin's oldest theatre. It hosts a variety of performances, including modern plays and TV-show recordings.

Olympia Theatre (*Around Temple Bar map;* ☎ *677 7744, Dame St*) is the city's largest and second-oldest theatre. Performances include rock concerts as well as plays. Over in the Liberties, experimental performances take place at *Tivoli Theatre* (☎ *454 4472, 135 Francis St*), opposite the now closed Iveagh Market.

Andrew's Lane Theatre (*Around Temple Bar map;* ☎ *679 5720, 9-17 St Andrew's Lane*) is a well-established fringe theatre, while the *Project Arts Centre* (☎ *671 2321, Henry Lane*), just off Henry St, produces excellent productions of experimental plays by up-and-coming Irish and international writers. Trinity College *Players' Theatre* (☎ *677 2941, ext 1239*), on the campus, hosts student theatre throughout the academic year as well as the main plays of the Dublin Theatre Festival in October.

The International bar (*Dublin's Pubs & Bars map;* ☎ *677 9250, 23 Wicklow St*) sometimes hosts theatrical performances. Puppet performances are put on at *Lambert Puppet Theatre and Museum* (*off Dublin map;* ☎ *280 0974, Clifton Lane, Monkstown*). To get there, take the DART to Salthill & Monkstown Station, turn right, walk about 200m and then follow the signs.

Theatrical performances also take place at:

City Arts Centre
  (☎ 677 0643) 23-25 Moss St, Dublin 2
Eblana Theatre
  (☎ 679 8404) Busáras, Dublin 1

Focus Theatre
  (Around St Stephen's Green map;
  ☎ 676 3071) 6 Pembroke Place, Dublin 2
Riverbank Theatre
  (☎ 677 3370) 10 Merchant's Quay,
  Dublin 8

SPECTATOR SPORTS

All venues mentioned here are outside the area shown on the Dublin map. The Irish love of horse racing can be observed at Leopardstown Race Course (☎ 289 3607), about 10km south of the city centre in Foxrock. Special buses depart the city centre on race days: ring the race course for details. Greyhound racing takes place at Harold's Cross Park (☎ 497 1081), 151 Harold's Cross Rd, near Rathmines (take bus Nos 16 or 16A), and Shelbourne Park (☎ 668 3502), Bridge Town Rd, Ringsend (take bus No 3 from D'Olier St). For current information on horse and greyhound meetings call ☎ 1550 112218 (24 hours).

The rugby season is from September to April and the soccer season from August to May; rugby and soccer international matches take place at Lansdowne Rd Stadium (☎ 668 9300) near Ballsbridge (take the DART to Lansdowne Rd Station).

Hurling and Gaelic football games are held February to November at Croke Park (☎ 836 3222), headquarters of the Gaelic Athletic Association, north of the Royal Canal in Drumcondra. To get there, take bus Nos 19 or 19A. Call ☎ 1550 112215 (24 hours) for the latest details.

SHOPPING

If it's made in Ireland, you can probably buy it in Dublin. Popular purchases include fine Irish knitwear such as the renowned Aran sweaters; jewellery with a Celtic influence, including Claddagh rings with two hands clasping a heart; books on Irish topics; crystal from Waterford, Galway, Tyrone and Tipperary; Irish coats of arms; china from Beleek; Royal Tara chinaware; and linen from Donegal. Citizens of non-EU countries can reclaim the VAT (sales tax) paid on purchases made at stores displaying a Cashback sticker; ask for details. For information on bookshops, see that entry in the Information section earlier in this chapter.

Shopping Centres & Department Stores

Dublin's main shopping street is pedestrianised Grafton St, where you'll find the big department stores: long-established Brown Thomas (Around Temple Bar map), which has now teamed up with Switzers, and the newer Marks & Spencer. At the southern end of Grafton St is the striking white-balconied St Stephen's Green Shopping Centre, but more interesting is Powerscourt Townhouse Shopping Centre, a converted 18th-century building, between South William St and Clarendon St, worth visiting for the architecture even if you can't afford the designer wedding dresses.

Grafton St has most of the international-name stores, but Temple Bar is the area to head for if you want to find some interesting one-offs. All of the following places are on the Around Temple Bar map. China Blue (☎ 671 8785), Merchant's Arch; Eager Beaver (☎ 677 3342), Crown Alley; and Flip (☎ 671 4249), 4 Upper Fownes St, are just a few of the designer clothes shops. Giving the lie to Dublin's squeaky-clean image is Condom Power (☎ 677 8963), a sex shop by any other name, in the basement of 57 Dame St.

North of the river, Jervis St Shopping Centre (Around Temple Bar map), 125 Upper Abbey St, is a huge mall with department stores, a food court and the Republic's first branch of the English Boot's the chemist.

Irish Crafts & Souvenirs

The following places appear on the Around Temple Bar map unless stated otherwise. At the Trinity College end of Grafton St is Nassau St, with the House of Ireland (☎ 671 6133), at No 38, and the Kilkenny Shop (☎ 677 7066), at No 6, both selling a variety of Irish crafts. This is also where you'll find Knobs and Knockers (☎ 671 0288), at No 19, if you fancy a Dublin doorknocker to grace your front door. The Colonnades

shop in Trinity College has a range of merchandise linked to the *Book of Kells*, while the Guinness Hop Store (Dublin map), in the Liberties area, can kit you (and your fridge) out in Guinness advertising material. Also worth trying for small gifts and souvenirs is the Irish Celtic Craft Shop (☎ 679 9912), 10-12 Lord Edward St.

For woollens, head for the Dublin Woollen Company (☎ 677 5014), 41 Ormond Quay; The Sweater Shop (☎ 671 3270), 9 Wicklow St; or Blarney Woollen Mills (☎ 677 7066), 21-23 Nassau St.

Celtic Note (☎ 670 4157), 12 Nassau St, near the Kilkenny Shop, stocks CDs and tapes of traditional and modern Irish music. Claddagh Records (☎ 677 0262), 2 Cecilia St, sells a wide range of Irish traditional and folk music.

If you're interested in antiques, Francis St (Dublin map; south of Tivoli Theatre), in the Liberties area, is the place to go.

Markets

Of Dublin's markets, probably the most promising for visitors, with a good selection of second-hand books, crafts, pictures, jewellery and records, is Mother Redcap's (☎ 454 0652) in Back Lane, near Christ Church Cathedral. It opens 10 am to 5.30 pm Friday to Sunday. Also worth checking out is George Street Arcade (Around Temple Bar map), between South Great George St and Drury St, an excellent covered market with some great second-hand-clothes stores.

GETTING THERE & AWAY
Air

Dublin is Ireland's major international gateway airport, with direct flights from Europe, North America and Asia. See the Getting There & Away chapter for details on flights and fares.

Airline offices in Dublin include:

Aer Lingus
   (☎ 705 3333 for reservations, 705 6705 for
   arrival and departure inquiries)
   40-41 Upper O'Connell St, Dublin 1:
   13 St Stephen's Green (on the corner of

Dawson St); Jury's Hotel, Ballsbridge;
12 Upper George's St, Dun Laoghaire
Air France
  (☎ 677 8899) 29-30 Dawson St, Dublin 2
Alitalia
  (☎ 677 5171) 4-5 Dawson St, Dublin 2
British Airways Express
  (☎ 1800 626747)
British Midland
  (☎ 283 8833) Nutley, Merrion Rd, Dublin 4
Delta Air Lines
  (☎ 676 8080) 24 Merrion Square, Dublin 2
Iberia
  (☎ 677 9846) 54 Dawson St, Dublin 2
Lufthansa Airlines
  (☎ 844 5544) Dublin Airport
Manx Airlines
  c/o (☎ 260 1588) British Midland
  (phone reservations only)
Qantas Airways
  (☎ 874 7747) Dublin Airport
Ryanair
  (☎ 677 4422) 3 Dawson St, Dublin 2;
  (☎ 609 7800) Dublin Airport
Sabena
  (☎ 844 5454) Dublin Airport
Scandinavian Airlines (SAS)
  (☎ 844 5440) Dublin Airport
Singapore Airlines (SIS)
  (☎ 671 0722) 3rd Floor, 29 Dawson St,
  Dublin 2
TAP Air Portugal
  (☎ 679 8844) 54 Dawson St, Dublin 2
Virgin Atlantic
  (☎ 873 3388) 30 Lower Abbey St,
  Dublin 1; (☎ 844 5566) Cityjet to London

Bus

Busáras, at Store St, just north of the Custom House and the River Liffey, is Bus Éireann's central bus station. Information on buses is available there from the Travel Centre (☎ 836 6111), 8.30 am to 7 pm Monday to Saturday, and 9 am to 7 pm on Sunday and public holidays.

For information on fares, frequencies and durations to various destinations in Éire and Northern Ireland, see Bus in the Getting Around chapter.

Train

For general information contact Iarnród Éireann Travel Centre (☎ 836 6222), 35 Lower Abbey St, which opens 9 am to 5 pm on weekdays, and 9 am to 1 pm on Saturday.

Connolly Station (☎ 836 3333), just north of the Liffey and the city centre, is the station for Belfast, Derry, Sligo and other points north. Heuston Station (☎ 836 5421), just south of the Liffey and well west of the centre, is the station for Cork, Galway, Killarney, Limerick, Wexford, Waterford and other points west, south and south-west. See Train in the Getting Around chapter for more information.

Ferry

There are two direct services from Holyhead on the north-western tip of Wales: one to Dublin and the other to Dun Laoghaire, the port on the southern side of Dublin Bay. There are also services from Liverpool. A new terminal is being built in Dublin and should be operating by the time you read this. See Sea in the Getting There & Away chapter for more information.

Bus & Ferry

There are coaches direct from London and other British centres to Dublin. See Land & Sea in the Getting There & Away chapter for more information.

GETTING AROUND
To/From Dublin Airport

Dublin Airport (County Dublin map; ☎ 844 4900) has a currency-exchange counter in the baggage arrivals area, a branch of the Bank of Ireland on level 2 which keeps regular banking hours and also offers currency exchange, an Aer Rianta (Irish Airport Authority) desk (☎ 704 4222) with information about the airport's facilities, a Bord Fáilte office that books accommodation, and a CIE (Córas Iompair Éireann; Transport Service of Ireland) desk with information on trains and buses. It also has shops, restaurants, bars, a hairdresser, a nursery, a church and car-hire counters. There's a post office in the car park atrium, which opens 9 am to 5 pm on weekdays, and 9 am to 12.30 pm on Saturday, and a left-luggage office (☎ 704 4633), which opens 6 am to 10 pm daily.

The airport is 10km north of the centre and can be reached by bus or taxi.

Airport Bus Services The Airlink Express Coach (☎ 872 0000, 873 4222), operated by Dublin Bus, runs to/from Busáras (the central bus station north of the River Liffey in central Dublin) costing £3/1.50. It also runs to/from Heuston Station for the same price. Both journeys take about half an hour. Timetables are available at the airport or in the city. Monday to Saturday, Busáras to Dublin Airport services go about every 20 to 30 minutes from 7.30 am to 10.40 pm. On Sunday they operate less frequently from 7.35 am to 12.10 am. Monday to Saturday, airport to Busáras services operate 6.40 am to 11 pm. On Sunday they run 7.10 am to 10.55 pm. The demand for seats sometimes exceeds the capacity of the bus, in which case it's worth getting a group together and sharing a taxi.

The alternative service is on the slower bus Nos 41 and 41A, which make a number of useful stops on the way, terminate on Eden Quay near O'Connell St and cost £1.10. The trip can take up to one hour, but they run more frequently than the express bus.

There are direct buses between Dublin Airport and Belfast.

Airport Taxi Services Taxis are subject to additional charges for baggage, extra passengers and 'unsocial hours'. However, a taxi usually costs about £12 between the airport and the centre, so between four people it's unlikely to be more expensive than the express bus. There's a supplementary charge of 80p from the airport to the city, but this charge doesn't apply from the city to the airport. Make sure the meter is switched on, as some Dublin Airport taxi drivers can be as unscrupulous as their brethren anywhere else in the world.

To/From the Ferry Terminals

Buses go to Busáras from the Dublin Ferryport terminal (off Dublin map; ☎ 855 2222), Alexandra Rd, east of the city centre, after all ferry arrivals. Buses also run from Busáras to meet ferry departures. For the 9.45 am ferry departure from Dublin, buses leave Busáras at 8.45 am. For the 9.45 pm departure, buses leave Heuston Station at 8.15 pm and Busáras at 8.15 pm.

To travel between Dun Laoghaire's Carlisle Terminal (☎ 280 1905) and Dublin, take bus No 46A to Fleet St in Temple Bar, bus No 7 to Eden Quay, or bus Nos 7A or 8 to Burgh Quay. Alternatively, take the DART (see Train later in this section) to Pearse Station (for southern Dublin) or Connolly Station (for northern Dublin).

Between Connolly & Heuston Stations

The bus No 90 Rail Link runs between the two stations up to six times an hour at peak periods and costs 60p. Connolly Station is a short walk north of Busáras.

Bus

Dublin Bus (Bus Átha Cliath) information office (☎ 873 4222), 59 Upper O'Connell St, opens 8.30 am to 5.30 pm on Monday, 9 am to 5.30 pm Tuesday to Friday, and 9 am to 1 pm on Saturday. The central bus station, or Busáras, is just north of the river, behind the Custom House, and has a left-luggage facility (£1.50 per day).

The Dublin Bus Citizone stretches from Swords in the north to Ballybrack in the south. Fares range from 55p to £1.10. Those aged under 16 pay reduced fares. Outside the Citizone the maximum fare is £1.25. Ten-ride tickets offer discounts of between 50p and £1.50. One-day passes cost £3.30 for the bus, or £4.50 for bus and train. Other passes include a one-week Citizone bus pass costing £11 (students £9), or a bus and train pass costing £15.50 (plus £2 for a photo).

Nitelink late-night buses run from the College St, Westmoreland St, D'Olier St triangle hourly, midnight to 3 am, Thursday, Friday and Saturday nights. They go as far north as Howth and Swords, and as far south as Dun Laoghaire and Rathfarnham.

Train

The Dublin Area Rapid Transport (DART) provides quick train access to the coast as far north as Howth and as far south as Bray. Pearse Station is convenient for central

Dublin south of the Liffey, and Connolly Station for north of the Liffey. Monday to Saturday there are services every 10 to 20 minutes, sometimes even more frequently, from around 6.30 am to midnight. Services are less frequent on Sunday. It takes about 30 minutes from Dublin to Bray to the south, or to Howth to the north. Dublin to Dun Laoghaire takes about 15 to 20 minutes. There are also Suburban Rail services north as far as Dundalk, inland to Mullingar and south past Bray to Arklow.

A one-way DART ticket from Dublin costs £1.10 to Dun Laoghaire or Howth, £1.30 to Bray. Within the DART region, a one-day, unlimited-travel ticket costs £3.50. A ticket combining DART and Dublin Bus services costs £4/2 (families £6), but you can't use this ticket during weekday peak hours (7 to 9.45 am, 4.30 to 6.30 pm). A weekly DART and bus ticket costs £15.50 but requires an ID photo. A Dublin Explorer ticket allows you four days' DART and bus travel for £11.50, but you can't use it until after 9.45 am on weekdays.

Bicycles can't be taken on DART services, but they can be taken on the less frequent suburban train services, either in the guard's van or in a special compartment at the opposite end of the train from the engine. There's a £2 charge for transporting a bicycle up to 56km.

There are left-luggage lockers at Heuston Station which cost £1.50 (or £4 in the large ones) per day. There's a left-luggage office at Connolly Station which charges £1 per day, or £2 for backpacks.

Car

As in most big cities, having a car in Dublin is as much a millstone as a convenience, though it can be useful for day trips outside the city limits.

There are parking meters around central Dublin and a large number of open and sheltered car parks. Parking illegally is not advised, especially as Dublin has introduced a clamping system, with a £65 charge for removal. However, you don't have to go far from the centre to find free roadside parking, especially in northern Dublin.

However, the gardaí warn visitors that it's safer to park in a supervised car park, since cars are often broken into even in broad daylight. Cars with foreign number plates, which may contain valuable personal effects, are a prime target. Rental cars are also targeted, but nowadays most have no external indication that they're owned by a rental company.

When you're booking accommodation check on parking facilities. Some B&Bs that claim to offer private parking, especially in the centre, may have a sharing arrangement with a nearby hotel to use its car park – provided the car park hasn't been filled by the hotel patrons' cars.

Rental See Car & Motorcycle in the Getting Around chapter for information on car rental. A number of rental companies have desks at the airport, and other operators are based close to the airport and deliver cars for airport collection. Some of the main rental companies in Dublin are:

Avis Rent-a-Car
  (☎ 677 5204) 1 East Hanover St, Dublin 2
  (☎ 844 5204) Dublin Airport
Budget Rent-a-Car
  (☎ 837 9802) 1 Lower Drumcondra Rd, Dublin 9
  (☎ 844 5919) Dublin Airport
Dan Dooley Car and Van Rentals
  (☎ 677 2723) 42-43 Westland Row, Dublin 2
  (☎ 844 5156) Dublin Airport
Hertz Rent-a-Car
  (☎ 660 2255) 149 Upper Leeson St, Dublin 2
  (☎ 844 5466) Dublin Airport
Murrays Europcar Car Rental
  (☎ 668 1777) Baggot St Bridge, Dublin 4;
  (☎ 844 4179) Dublin Airport
Payless Car Rentals
  (☎ 844 4092) Dublin Airport
Sixt Rent-a-Car
  (☎ 862 2715) Old Airport Rd, Santry, Dublin 9
  (☎ 844 4199) Dublin Airport
Windsor Motors
  (☎ 454 0800) Rialto, South Circular Rd, Dublin 8
  (☎ 840 0800) Dublin Airport

Taxi

Taxis in Dublin are expensive, with a £1.90 minimum price for the first half-mile or four minutes, then 80p for every half-mile thereafter. In addition, there are a number of extra charges: 40p for each extra passenger, 40p for each piece of luggage, £1.20 for telephone bookings and 40p for 'unsocial hours', which means 8 pm to 8 am and all day Sunday. Public holidays are even more unsocial and require a higher supplement.

Taxis can be hailed on the street and are found at taxi ranks around the city, including on O'Connell St in northern Dublin, College Green in front of Trinity College and St Stephen's Green at the end of Grafton St. There are numerous taxi companies that will dispatch taxis by radio. Try City Cabs (☎ 872 2688) or National Radio Cabs (☎ 677 2222). There aren't nearly enough taxis, however: queues at ranks can be frustratingly long, and even calling one by phone is often met with a negative response at busy times. Phone the Garda Carriage Office on ☎ 475 5888 for complaints about taxis and queries regarding lost property.

Bicycle
Dublin isn't a bad place to get around by bicycle, as it is fairly small and flat. However, the absence of cycle lanes is a source of considerable local grievance. Many visitors explore farther afield by bicycle, a popular activity in Ireland despite the often less-than-encouraging weather.

All the hostels seem to offer secure bicycle parking areas but, if you're going to have a bike stolen anywhere in Ireland, Dublin is where it will happen. Lock your bike up well. Surprisingly, considering how popular bicycles are in Dublin, there's a scarcity of suitable bicycle parking facilities. Grafton St and Temple Bar are virtually devoid of places to lock a bike. Elsewhere, there are signs on many likely stretches of railing announcing that bikes must not be parked there. Nevertheless, there are places where you can park your bike, such as the Grafton St corner of St Stephen's Green and in Trinity College.

Rental Typical rental costs are £7 to £10 per day or £32 to £38 per week. Some hostels offer bike rental.

Rent-a-Bike Ireland has a number of offices around the country, including Belfast, and offers one-way rentals between its outlets for an extra £5. The head office is at Bike Store (☎ 872 5399), 58 Lower Gardiner St, Dublin 1, round the corner from Isaac's Hostel and a stone's throw from Busáras. It can arrange cycling tours staying in either B&Bs or hostels.

Raleigh Rent-a-Bike agencies can be found all over Ireland, north and south of the border. Contact them at Raleigh Ireland (☎ 626 1333), Raleigh House, Kylemore Rd, Dublin 10. Raleigh agencies in Dublin include:

C Harding for Bikes
 (☎ 873 2455) 30 Bachelor's Walk,
 Dublin 1
Joe Daly
 (☎ 298 1485) Lower Main St, Dundrum,
 Dublin 14
Hollingsworth Cycle
 (☎ 490 5094) 14/54 Templeogue Rd,
 Templeogue, Dublin 6

Around Dublin

There are a number of seaside suburbs round the curve of Dublin Bay. Dun Laoghaire to the south and Howth to the north are historic ports and popular day trips from the city. Connected to central Dublin by the convenient DART train service, they also make interesting alternatives to staying in the city. Malahide with its castle, the imposing Anglo-Irish mansion of Newbridge House, and the village of Swords are other Dublin-area attractions.

DUN LAOGHAIRE
Dun Laoghaire (pronounced 'dun leary'), only 13km south-east of central Dublin, is both a busy harbour with ferry connections to Britain and a popular resort. From 1821, when King George IV departed from here after a visit to Ireland, until Irish independence in 1922, the port was known as Kingstown. The fact that there are many B&Bs in Dun Laoghaire that are a bit cheaper than those in central Dublin, combined with the

DUN LAOGHAIRE

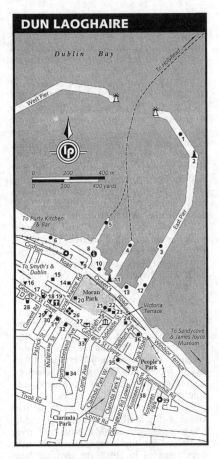

DUN LAOGHAIRE

PLACES TO STAY
14 Port View Hotel
15 Old School House Hostel
20 Royal Marine Hotel
22 Kingston Hotel
23 Bayside B&B
24 Hotel Pierre
34 Innisfree
38 Rosmeen Gardens B&Bs

PLACES TO EAT
9   Brasserie Na Mara
16 The Black Tulip
18 Ann's Bakery
29 Lal Qila
30 Ritz Café
33 The Coffee Bean
37 Outlaws

PUBS
17 Cooney's
28 Dunphy's

OTHER
1   Anemometer
2   Lifeboat Memorial
3   Bandstand
4   Carlisle Pier
5   St Michael's Pier
6   Royal Irish Yacht Club
7   Dun Laoghaire DART Station
8   Ferry Terminal; Dublin Tourism Office
10 Royal St George Yacht Club
11 King George IV Monument
12 Compass Pointer
13 National Yacht Club
19 St Michael's Church
21 Christ the King Sculpture
25 National Maritime Museum
26 Dun Laoghaire Shopping Centre
27 Post Office
31 Eason's
32 Aer Lingus
35 Star Laundry
36 Oceantec Adventures
39 Sandycove & Glasthule DART Station

fast and frequent DART train connections, makes it easy to stay out here.

History

There was a coastal settlement on the site of Dun Laoghaire over 1000 years ago, but it was little more than a small fishing village until 1767, when the first pier was constructed. Dun Laoghaire grew more rapidly after that, and the Sandycove Martello Tower was erected in the early 19th century, as there was great fear of an invasion from Napoleonic France.

Construction of the harbour was proposed in 1815 to provide a refuge for ships unable to reach the safety of Dublin Harbour in inclement weather. Originally, a single pier was proposed, but engineer John Rennie decided to build two massive piers enclosing a huge 100-hectare artificial harbour. Work began in 1817 and by 1823 the workforce comprised 1000 men. However, despite huge expenditure, the harbour wasn't completed until 1842, Carlisle Pier wasn't added until 1859 and parts of the West Pier stonework have never been finished. The total cost approached £1 million sterling, an astronomical figure in the mid-19th century.

Shipping services began to and from Liverpool in England, and Holyhead in Wales in the mid-19th century, and the completion of a train link to Dublin in 1834 made this a state-of-the-art transport centre. The line from Dublin was the first railway anywhere in Ireland. The first mail steamers took nearly six hours to make the 100km crossing to Holyhead, but by 1860 the crossing time was reduced to less than four hours and, on one occasion in 1887, the paddle steamer *Ireland* made the crossing in less than three hours. Car ferries were introduced in the early 1960s. During WWI RMS *Leinster* was torpedoed by a German U-boat 25km from Dun Laoghaire and over 500 lives were lost.

Orientation & Information

Upper and Lower George's St, which runs parallel to the coast, is the main shopping street through Dun Laoghaire. The huge harbour is sheltered by the encircling arms of the East and West Piers. Sandycove with the James Joyce Museum and Forty Foot Pool is about 1km east of central Dun Laoghaire.

The Dublin Tourism office, in the Carlisle Ferry Terminal, opens 10 am to 9 pm daily. A bureau de change, also in the terminal, opens for ferry arrivals and departures. The post office, on Upper George's St, opens 9 am (9.30 am on Tuesday) to 6 pm on weekdays, and 9 am to 5.30 pm on Saturday. At 5 Upper George's St is a branch of Eason's (☎ 280 5528), the newsagent and bookshop chain.

The Harbour

The 1290m East and 1548m West Piers, each ending in a lighthouse dating from the 1850s, have always been popular for walking (especially the East Pier), birdwatching and fishing (particularly from the end of the West Pier). You can also ride a bicycle out along the piers (bottom level only). In the 19th century the practice of 'scorching' – riding out along the pier at breakneck speed – became so prevalent that bicycles were banned for some time.

The East Pier has an 1890s bandstand and a memorial to Captain Boyd and the crew of the Dun Laoghaire lifeboat who were drowned in a rescue attempt. Near the end of the pier is the 1852 anemometer, one of the first of these wind-speed measuring devices to be installed anywhere in the world. The East Pier ends at the East Pier Battery with a lighthouse and a gun saluting station, which is useful when visiting VIPs arrive by sea (which rarely happens nowadays, thanks to the aeroplane!).

The harbour has long been a popular yachting centre and the Royal Irish Yacht Club's building, dating from around 1850, was the first purpose-built yacht club in Ireland. The Royal St George Yacht Club's building dates from 1863 and that of the National Yacht Club from 1876. The world's first one-design sailing-boat class (a race in which all boats taking part are the same type, so there's no need for handicaps) started life at Dun Laoghaire with a dinghy design known as Water Wag. A variety of specifically Dublin Bay one-design classes still race here, as do Mirrors and other popular small sailing boats.

Carlisle Pier, opened in 1859, is also known as the Mailboat Pier and was modified to handle drive-on/drive-off car ferries in 1970. With the completion of the new ferry terminal in 1995, the terminal here closed. St Michael's Pier, also known as the Car Ferry, was added in 1969. Over on the West Pier side of the harbour are two anchored lightships which have now been replaced by automatic buoys.

National Maritime Museum

Between Haigh Terrace and Adelaide St, the museum (☎ 280 0969) is housed in the Mariner's Church, built in 1837 'for the benefit of sailors in men-of-war, merchant ships, fishing boats and yachts'. The window in the chancel is a replica of the Five Sisters window at York Minster in England.

Exhibits include a French ship's longboat captured at Bantry in 1796 during Wolfe Tone's abortive invasion. The huge Great Baily Light Optic, driven by clockwork, came from the Baily Lighthouse on Howth Peninsula. It operated from 1902 until 1972, when it was replaced with an electrically powered lens. There's a model of the *Great Eastern* (1858), the early steam-powered vessel built by English engineer Isambard Kingdom Brunel. The boat proved a commercial failure as a passenger ship but successfully laid the first transatlantic telegraph cable between Ireland and North America. There are various items from the German submarine *U19*, which landed Sir Roger Casement in Kerry in 1916 (see Sandycove later in this section). These were donated 50 years after the event by the U-boat's captain, Raimund Weisbach.

The museum opens 1 to 5 pm Tuesday to Sunday, May to September. Admission costs £1.50/75p.

Around the Town

Nothing remains of the *dún* (fort) that gave Dun Laoghaire its name, as it was totally destroyed during the construction of the train line. The train line from Dun Laoghaire to Dalkey was built along the route of an earlier line known as the Metals, which was used to bring stone for the harbour construction from the quarries at Dalkey Hill. By means of a pulley system, the laden trucks trundling down to the harbour pulled the empty ones back up to the quarry.

On the waterfront is a curious monument to King George IV to commemorate his visit in 1821. It consists of an obelisk balanced on four stone balls, one of which is missing as a result of an IRA bomb attack.

On the other side of Queen's Rd is the *Christ the King* sculpture, which was created in Paris in 1926, bought in 1949 and then put in storage until 1978 because the religious authorities decided they didn't really like it all that much.

Sandycove

Only 1km south of Dun Laoghaire is Sandycove, with a pretty little beach and the Martello tower that houses the James Joyce Museum. Sir Roger Casement, who attempted to organise a German-backed Irish freedom force during WWI, was born here in 1864. He was captured after being landed in County Kerry from a German U-boat and executed by the British as a traitor in 1916.

James Joyce Museum The Martello tower, which houses the museum (☎ 280 9265, 280 8571), is where the action begins in James Joyce's epic novel *Ulysses*. The museum was opened in 1962 by Sylvia Beach, the Paris-based publisher who first dared to put *Ulysses* into print, and has photographs, letters, documents, various editions of Joyce's work and two death masks of Joyce on display.

A string of Martello towers was built around the coast of Ireland between 1804 and 1815 in case of invasion by Napoleon's forces. The granite tower stands 12m high with walls 2.5m thick and was copied from a tower at Cape Mortella in Corsica. Originally, the entrance to the tower led straight into what is now the 'upstairs'. Other tower sites included Dalkey Island, Killiney and Bray, to the south of Dun Laoghaire; and to the north, Howth and Ireland's Eye, the island off Howth. There are fine views from the tower. To the south-east you can see Dalkey Island with its signal tower and Killiney Hill with its obelisk. Howth Head is visible on the northern side of Dublin Bay. There's another Martello tower not far to the south near Bullock Harbour.

The tower opens 10 am to 1 pm and 2 to 5 pm Monday to Saturday, and 2 to 6 pm on Sunday, April to October. Admission costs £2.50/1.50 (students £1.80). At other times of the year the tower opens only on weekdays and then only to groups for a flat fee of £55.

You can get to the tower by a 30-minute walk along the seafront from Dun Laoghaire Harbour, a 15-minute walk from Sandycove & Glasthule DART station or a five-minute walk from Sandycove Ave West, served by bus No 8 which runs from Dublin through Dun Laoghaire.

Forty Foot Pool Below the Martello tower is Forty Foot Pool, an open-air sea-water bathing pool that took its name from the army regiment, the Fortieth Foot, that was stationed at the tower until the regiment was disbanded in 1904. At the close of the first chapter of *Ulysses*, Buck Mulligan heads off to the Forty Foot Pool for a morning swim. A morning wake-up here is still a Dun Laoghaire tradition, winter or summer. In fact, a winter dip isn't much braver than a summer one since the water temperature varies by only about 5°C, winter or summer. Basically, it's always bloody cold.

Originally nudist and for men only, pressure from female bathers eventually opened this public stretch of water to both sexes, despite strong opposition from the 'forty foot gentlemen'. They eventually compromised with the ruling that a 'togs must be worn' sign would now apply after 9 am. Prior to that time nudity prevails and swimmers are still predominantly 'forty foot gentlemen'.

Activities
A series of walks in the Dun Laoghaire area make up the signposted Dun Laoghaire Way. The *Heritage Map of Dun Laoghaire* includes a map and notes on the seven separate walks.

Scuba divers head for the waters around Dalkey Island and to Muglands, a small rocky island farther out. Oceantec Adventures (☎ 280 1083, fax 284 3885) is a dive shop at 10-11 Marine Terrace. It rents diving equipment at £22.50 per day; local dives cost £12.50. It's also a fully accredited PADI centre and runs courses year round.

Places to Stay
As a major ferry port, Dun Laoghaire has plenty of accommodation, especially in the form of B&Bs.

Hostels Not far from the ferry terminal, the IHH *Old School House Hostel* (☎ 280 8777) is off Eblana Ave. It has a large kitchen area and lounge, opens year round and charges £7.95 to £10 for dorm beds, £14 per person in private rooms.

B&Bs Rosmeen Gardens is packed with B&Bs. To get there, just walk south along George's St, the main shopping street; Rosmeen Gardens is the first street after Lower Glenageary Rd, directly opposite People's Park. *Mrs Callanan* (☎ 280 6083) is at No 1, *Rathoe* (☎ 280 8070) is at No 12, *Rosmeen House* (☎ 280 7613) is at No 13, *Mrs McGloughlin* (☎ 280 4333) is at No 27, *Annesgrove* (☎ 280 9801) is at No 28 and *Mrs Dunne* (☎ 280 3360) is at No 30. Prices here are £22 to £30 for singles, £35 to £45 for doubles.

There are also B&Bs on Northumberland Ave, such as *Innisfree* (☎ 280 5598) at No 31. With views of the harbour, *Bayside B&B* (☎ 280 4660, Seafront, 5 Haddington Terrace) is slightly more expensive, with singles/doubles costing £27/40. Others can be found on Mellifont and Corrig Aves.

Hotels Dun Laoghaire has a number of attractively situated seaside hotels.

In small *Port View Hotel* (☎ 280 1663, fax 280 0447, Royal Marine Rd) half of the 20 rooms are en suite, and these better rooms cost £40/60 for singles/doubles. The larger *Hotel Pierre* (☎ 280 0291, fax 284 3332, 3 Victoria Terrace) is also close to the waterfront. There are 36 rooms, almost all of them with en suite bathroom, costing £50/65 including breakfast. Close by is *Kingston Hotel* (☎ 280 1810, fax 280 1237, Haddington Terrace), with 24 en suite rooms costing £39/63 with breakfast.

The port's premier hotel is *Royal Marine Hotel* (☎ 280 1911, fax 280 1089, Royal Marine Rd), only a few minutes' walk from Dun Laoghaire's Carlisle Terminal. There are 104 en suite rooms costing upwards of £70/89.

Places to Eat
Restaurants Open from 5.30 pm, *Outlaws* (☎ 284 2817, 62 Upper George's St) offers steak, burgers (including a vege-burger) and Tex-Mex fare; fajitas cost £6.95. *Lal Qila* (☎ 280 5623, Convent Rd), just off Lower George's St, has a standard Indian menu, with main courses costing £7 to £8.

Near the harbour, *Brasserie na Mara* (☎ 280 6787), in what used to be the train station, is more expensive but offers a four-course dinner for around £20; the emphasis is on seafood. Open for lunch and dinner, *The Black Tulip* (☎ 280 5318, 107 Lower George's St) is another fancier restaurant which offers excellent seafood; baked salmon costs £12.95.

Fast Food & Cafés Fast-food outlets, including branches of *La Pizza* and *Abrakebabra*, can be found on George's St. Just off George's St on Patrick St is *Ritz Café*, serving traditional fish and chips.

Everything is baked on the premises at *Ann's Bakery*, which has good tea and snacks during the day. *The Coffee Bean (Upper George's St)*, near the corner of Corrig Ave, is popular at lunchtime, with good coffee and snacks, such as baked potatoes and quiche, costing £3 to £4.

Entertainment
Popular pubs include *Cooney's (88 Lower George's St)*, and *Dunphy's*, right across the road at No 41. Farther out along George's St is *Smyth's*, with a seafaring interior and music five nights a week. *Hotel Pierre* is noted for its jazz performances, and *Purty Kitchen and Bar* on the Old Dunleary Rd often has traditional Irish music, rock, country and comedy.

Getting There & Away
See the introductory Getting There & Away chapter for details of the ferries between Dun Laoghaire and Holyhead in the UK.

Bus Nos 7, 7A, 8, and 46A or the DART train service take you from Dublin to Dun Laoghaire. It takes only 15 to 20 minutes to cover the 12km by DART (day return £2.20).

DALKEY
One kilometre south of Sandycove is Dalkey (Deilginis), which has the remains of a number of old castles. On Castle St, the main street, two 16th-century castles face each other: **Goat Castle** and **Archbold's Castle**. On the same street is the ancient **St Begnet's Church**, dating from the 9th century. **Bulloch Castle** overlooking Bulloch Harbour, north of town, was built by the monks of St Mary's Abbey in Dublin in the 12th century.

To the south there are good **views** from the small park at Sorrento Point and from Killiney Hill.

Dalkey Quarry is a popular site for rock climbers, and originally provided most of the granite for the gigantic piers at Dun Laoghaire Harbour.

Dalkey has several holy wells, including **St Begnet's Holy Well** (the waters of which are reputed to cure rheumatism) on nine-hectare Dalkey Island, which lies a few hundred metres offshore. There's plenty of birdlife here and the waters around the island are popular with scuba divers.

A number of rocky swimming pools are found along the Dalkey coast.

Dalkey is on the DART suburban train line, or, for a probably slower journey, you can catch bus No 8 from Burgh Quay in Dublin. Both cost £1.10.

HOWTH
The bulbous Howth Peninsula forms the northern end of Dublin Bay. Howth (Binn Éadair) town is only 15km from central Dublin and is easily reached by DART train or by simply following the Clontarf Rd out around the northern bay shoreline. En route you pass Clontarf, site of the pivotal clash between Celtic and Viking forces at the Battle of Clontarf in 1014. Farther along is North Bull Island, a wildlife sanctuary where many migratory birds pause in winter. Howth is a popular excursion from Dublin and has developed as a residential suburb.

History
Howth's name (which rhymes with 'both') has Viking origins and comes from the Danish word 'hoved' (head). Howth Harbour dates from 1807 to 1809 and was at that time the main Dublin harbour for the packet boats from England. Howth Rd was built to ensure rapid transfer of incoming mail and dispatches from the harbour to the city. The

replacement of sailing packets with steam packets in 1818 reduced the transit time from Holyhead to seven hours, but Howth's period of importance was short because, by 1813, the harbour was already showing signs of silting up. It was superseded by Dun Laoghaire in 1833. The most famous arrival to Howth was King George IV, who visited Ireland in 1821 and is chiefly remembered because he staggered off the boat in a highly inebriated state. He did manage to leave his footprint at the point where he stepped ashore on the West Pier.

In 1914 Robert Erskine Childers' yacht, *Asgard*, brought a cargo of 900 rifles into the port to arm the nationalists. During the Civil War, Childers was court-martialled by his former comrades and executed by firing squad for illegal possession of a revolver. The *Asgard* is now on display at Kilmainham Jail in Dublin.

Around the Town

Howth is a pretty little town built on steep streets running down to the waterfront. Although the harbour's role as a shipping port has long gone, Howth is now a major fishing centre and yachting harbour.

St Mary's Abbey stands in ruins near the centre and was originally founded in 1042, supposedly by the Viking King Sitric, who also founded the original church on the site of Christ Church Cathedral in Dublin. St Mary's was amalgamated with the monastery on Ireland's Eye in 1235. Some parts of the ruins date from that time, but most of it was built in the 15th and 16th centuries. The tomb of Christopher St Lawrence (Lord Howth), in the south-eastern corner, dates from around 1470. You can walk around the abbey grounds, but to enter the abbey itself you need to obtain the key (instructions on where to get it are on the inside gate) from the caretaker.

Howth Castle & Demesne

Howth Castle's demesne was acquired by the Norman noble Sir Almeric Tristram in 1177 and has remained in the family ever since, though the unbroken chain of male succession finally came to an end in 1909.

The family name was changed to St Lawrence when Sir Almeric won a battle at St Lawrence's behest (or so he believed).

Originally built in 1564, the St Lawrence family's Howth Castle has been much restored and rebuilt over the years, most recently in 1910 by the British architect Sir Edwin Lutyens.

A legend relates that in 1575 Grace O'Malley, the 'queen' of western Ireland, dropped by the castle on her way back from a visit to England's Queen Elizabeth I. When the family claimed they were busy having dinner and refused her entry, she kidnapped the son and returned him only when Lord Howth promised that in future his doors would always be open at meal times. As a result, so it's claimed, for many years the castle extended an open invitation to hungry passers-by.

Despite Grace O'Malley's demands, the castle is no longer open, but you can visit the gardens in spring and summer and there's a popular golf course beyond the castle.

The castle gardens are noted for their rhododendrons, which bloom in May and June, for their azaleas and for a long stretch of 10m-high beech hedges planted back in 1710. The castle grounds also have the ruins of 16th-century **Corr Castle** and an ancient dolmen known as **Aideen's Grave**. It's said that Aideen died of a broken heart after her husband was killed at the Battle of Gavra near Tara in 184, but that's probably mere legend as the dolmen is thought to be much older.

To get to the castle, turn right out of the station, follow the road round then turn left at the sign for the Deer Park Hotel and National Transport Museum.

National Transport Museum

In a green, corrugated-iron, barnlike building, the National Transport Museum (☎ 847 5623) has a variety of exhibits. These include double-decker buses, fire engines and trams, including a Hill of Howth tram which operated from 1901 to 1959. It opens 10 am to 6 pm daily, June to August; and 2 to 5 pm at the weekend, the rest of the year.

Admission costs £1.50/50p. You can reach the museum by entering Howth Castle gates and turning right just before the castle.

Around the Peninsula

The **Summit** (171m), to the south-east of the town, offers views across Dublin Bay to the Wicklow Mountains. From the Summit you can walk to the top of the Ben of Howth, which has a cairn said to mark a 2000-year-old Celtic royal grave. The 1814 **Baily Lighthouse** at the south-eastern corner is on the site of an old stone fort and can be reached by a dramatic clifftop walk. There was an earlier hilltop beacon here in 1670.

Ireland's Eye

A short distance offshore from Howth is Ireland's Eye, a rocky sea-bird sanctuary with the ruins of a 6th-century monastery. There's a **Martello tower** at the north-western end of the island, where boats from Howth land, while the eastern end plummets into the sea in a spectacularly sheer rock face. As well as the sea birds overhead, you can see young birds on the ground during the nesting season. Seals can also be spotted around the island.

Doyle & Sons (☎ 831 4200) take boats to the island from the East Pier of Howth Harbour during the summer, from 11 am daily if there are enough people. The cost is £4/2 return. Don't wear shorts if you're planning to visit the monastery ruins, as they're surrounded by a thicket of stinging nettles. And take your garbage away with you – too many island visitors don't.

Farther north from Ireland's Eye is **Lambay Island**, an important sea-bird sanctuary that cannot be landed on.

Places to Stay

There are several B&Bs along Thormanby and Nashville Rds, which are about 1km south-east of the DART station, along Church St and over Main St, with typical overnight costs of £15 to £22 per person. *Gleann-na-Smol* (☎ 832 2936) is on Nashville Rd, while *Hazelwood* (☎ 839 1391) and *Highfield* (☎ 832 3936) are both on Thormanby Rd.

St Lawrence Hotel (☎ 832 2643, Harbour Rd), directly overlooking the harbour, has 11 en suite rooms costing £30 per person including breakfast.

By the golf course in the grounds of Howth Castle is the larger *Deer Park Hotel* (☎ 832 2624), which charges £62/90 for singles/doubles. On the Dublin side of Howth village there are good views of Ireland's Eye from the more upmarket *Howth Lodge Hotel* (☎ 832 1010), where en suite rooms cost £70 per person.

Places to Eat

If you want to buy food and prepare it yourself, Howth has fine seafood that you can buy fresh from the string of *seafood shops* on West Pier. *Pizza Milano* (☎ 839 3045, 53 Harbour Rd) serves pizzas costing £3.95 to £7.95 during the day; upstairs, *Porto Fino's Ristorante* (☎ 839 3054) serves Italian food in the evenings, with pasta costing £6.50 to £9.50. Other economical alternatives include Howth's plentiful supply of pubs, such as *Pier House* (☎ 832 4510) on East Pier, and *Ye Old Abbey Tavern* (☎ 839 0307) near St Mary's Abbey. *St Lawrence Hotel* (☎ 832 2643) by the harbour has a carvery restaurant that opens daily.

The King Sitric (☎ 832 5235), near East Pier, is known for its fine seafood and opens for lunch and dinner Monday to Saturday. Most mains cost £18 to £25; wild Irish salmon costs £19.50

Entertainment

Howth's pubs are noted for their jazz performances and some also provide traditional Irish music. You can try *The Cock Tavern*, near the entrance to the abbey grounds; *Baily Court Hotel*, on Thormanby Rd, to the south-east; *Waterside Inn* and *Pier House*, both on Harbour Rd; *Ye Old Abbey Tavern*, on Main St, which runs north to south from near East Pier; and others – they're all likely to have something on and are all in the centre.

Getting There & Away

The easiest, quickest way to Howth from Dublin is by the DART, which whisks you there in just over 20 minutes for £2.20 return.

SWORDS

The village of Swords (Sord) is 16km north of Dublin and 5km west of Malahide. The Archbishop of Dublin built a **fortified palace** here in the 12th century, but the castellated walls date from the 15th century and numerous other modifications were made over the centuries. The windows to the right of the main entrance date from around 1250.

Swords also had an ancient monastery, but today only its 23m-high **round tower** remains, and that was rebuilt several times between 1400 and 1700. It stands in the grounds of the Church of Ireland. The body of Brian Ború was kept overnight in the monastery after his death in 1014 at the Battle of Clontarf, when his forces defeated the Vikings.

Bus Nos 33 and 33B depart from Dublin's Eden Quay every half-hour or so and take less than an hour to get to Swords.

MALAHIDE

Malahide (Mullach Ide) is 13km north of Dublin on the coast beyond Howth. It has virtually been swallowed by Dublin's northwards expansion, although it still has its own pretty marina. The well-kept 101 hectares of the Malahide Demesne, which contains Malahide Castle, is the town's principal attraction. Talbot Botanic Gardens are next to the castle and the extensive Fry Model Railway is in the castle grounds.

Malahide Castle

Despite the vicissitudes of Irish history, the Talbot family managed to keep Malahide Castle (☎ 846 2184) under their control from 1185 to 1976, apart from a short interlude while Cromwell was around from 1649 to 1660. The oldest part of the castle is a three-storey, 12th-century tower house; otherwise it's the usual hotchpotch of additions and renovations. The façade is flanked by circular towers added in 1765.

The castle is packed with furniture and paintings, and Puck, the family ghost, is

still in residence. Highlights include the 16th-century oak room with its decorative carvings, and the medieval Great Hall with family portraits, a minstrel's gallery and a gigantic painting of the Battle of the Boyne.

The castle opens 10 am to 12.45 pm and 2 to 5 pm on weekdays, and 11.30 am to 6 pm at the weekend (2 to 5 pm at the weekend and public holidays, November to March), year round. Admission costs £3/1.65 (students £2.50). Combined tickets are available for the castle and Fry Model Railway (see the following section) and for the castle and Newbridge House (see Newbridge House later in this chapter).

Fry Model Railway

Ireland's biggest model railway layout covers 240 sq metres and authentically displays much of Dublin and Ireland's train and public transport system, including the DART line and Irish Sea ferry services in O-gauge (track width of 32mm). There's also a separate room exhibiting railway models and other memorabilia.

It opens 10 am to 1 pm and 2 to 6 pm Monday to Thursday (also on Friday, June to September), 11 am to 1 pm and 2 to 6 pm on Saturday, and 2 to 6 pm on Sunday, April to September; and 2 to 5 pm at the weekend, the rest of the year. Admission costs £2.75/1.60 (students £2.10). You can get combined castle and railway tickets costing £4.65/2.60 (students £3.60).

Getting There & Away

Bus No 42 from Beresford Place, near Busáras, takes about 45 minutes to Malahide. Alternatively, take a Drogheda suburban train to Malahide station, only 10 minutes' walk from the park.

NEWBRIDGE HOUSE

North of Malahide at Donabate is Newbridge House (☎ 843 6534), a historic 1737 Georgian mansion with fine plasterwork, a private museum, an impressive kitchen and a large traditional farm with cows, pigs and exotic chickens. In the stables look out for the Lord Chancellor's elaborate coach, built in 1790. It was painted black for Queen

Victoria's funeral and it wasn't until 1982 that the paint was scraped off to reveal the glittering masterpiece underneath.

Newbridge House opens 10 am to 1 pm and 2 to 5 pm daily, April to September; and 2 to 5 pm at the weekend and public holidays the rest of the year. Admission costs £2.95/1.60 (students £2.55). Combined Newbridge House and Malahide Castle tickets cost £4.85/2.45 (students £3.30).

Donabate is 19km north of Dublin. Bus no 33B runs from Eden Quay to Donabate village. You can also get there on the suburban train service from Connolly or Pearse Stations.

LUSK HERITAGE CENTRE
On the way to Skerries you'll spot the turrets of Lusk (Lusca) Church, where a 10th-century round tower stands beside and joined to a medieval tower. The various floors of the tower are now used to display a selection of medieval and later effigies from churches in County Dublin. The much duller 19th-century nave contains Willie Monks' dusty, somewhat forlorn collection of household and other items.

The heritage centre (☎ 843 7683) opens 2 to 5 pm on Wednesday and Sunday (last admission 4.15 pm), mid-June to mid-September. Admission costs £1.50/50p. Bus No 33 from Eden Quay in Dublin takes just under an hour to get here.

SKERRIES
The sleepy seaside resort of Skerries (Na Sceiri) is 30km north of Dublin. St Patrick is said to have made his arrival in Ireland here at what is now called St Patrick's Island, which has an old church ruin. He also apparently visited Red Island, now attached to the mainland. There's a good cliff walk south from Skerries to the bay of Loughshinny. At low tide you can walk to Shenick's, a small island off Skerries. Farther offshore is Rockabill, with a lighthouse. The 7th-century oratory and holy well of St Moibhi and the ruins of Baldongan Castle are all near Skerries.

Bus No 33 departs from Dublin's Eden Quay about every hour and takes just over an hour to reach Skerries. Trains from Connolly Station are less frequent but slightly faster.

County Wicklow

Not all of Ireland's impressive landscapes are in the west of the country. Barely 16km south of Dublin, you can drive for an hour through wild and desolate scenery without seeing more than a handful of houses or people. The most beautiful parts of County Wicklow (Cill Mhantáin) fall within a broad north-south swathe running down the centre of the mountains, beginning at Glencree close to Dublin and ending near Avoca. The county's rolling granite hills are the source of Dublin's River Liffey. Glendalough has some of the country's best-preserved early-Christian remains.

Southern Wicklow was one of the last outposts of the Gaelic Irish: using remote valleys such as Glenmalure and the Glen of Imaal as hide-outs, families such as the O'Tooles and the O'Byrnes would sally forth to attack the English. Such was the Crown's concern that they built an access road from Dublin through the heart of the mountains to the bandits. Thanks to their efforts, the Military Rd still takes you through the finest Wicklow scenery.

In northern Wicklow, the Anglo-Irish gentry felt close enough to the safety of Dublin to build magnificent mansions such as those at Russborough near Blessington and Powerscourt near Enniskerry. The exquisite formal gardens of the latter are one of the county's biggest draws.

Wicklow is particularly known for its beautiful gardens, and during the Wicklow Gardens Festival in May and June many gardens not normally open to the public welcome visitors. For details contact Wicklow County Tourism (☎ 0404-66058), St Manntan's House, Kilmantin Hill, Wicklow.

Wicklow's highways and main towns, many of them dormitories for Dublin, lie along the relatively narrow coastal strip leading south to Wexford. Heading south, there are pleasant seaside resorts and some fine beaches along the way, especially at Brittas Bay.

For information on walking or cycling

Highlights

- Explore the many good beaches, especially those at Brittas Bay
- Travel along Military Rd, going through the finest Wicklow scenery
- Visit Russborough House near Blessington, one of the most magnificent stately homes in Ireland
- Walk along the Wicklow Way, the longest hiking trail in the country
- Wander around Glendalough, the site of some of the best-preserved early-Christian remains in Ireland
- Enjoy Powerscourt Estate near Enniskerry, with its fine formal gardens

the 132km Wicklow Way, see Walking in the Activities chapter.

As well as the usual bus and train connections around County Wicklow, the much praised Wild Wicklow Tour (☎ 01-280 1899), complete with storytelling guide, covers the Wicklow Mountains and Glen-

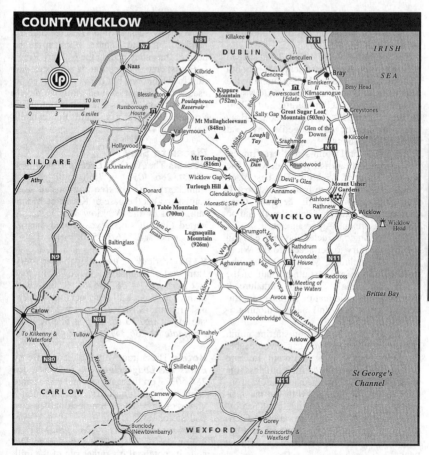

COUNTY WICKLOW

dalough (£22). Tours depart the Dublin Tourism office at 9.10 am Thursday to Sunday, April to October. Over the Top and Into the West (see Organised Tours in the Getting Around chapter for details) operates tours of the county costing £15/13. These depart from outside the Dublin Tourism office at 9.45 am daily.

Wicklow Mountains

From Killakee, a few kilometres north of Glencree, you can turn your back on Dublin's sprawl and travel south for 30km across vast sweeps of heather-clad moors, bogs and mountains dotted with small corrie lakes along the Military Rd.

The Wicklow Mountains are a vast granite intrusion, or batholith, a welling-up of hot igneous rock that consolidated some 400 million years ago. The heat baked the overlying clays and sedimentary rocks, producing shiny mica schists which can be seen across the county but particularly in the rivers and streams around Glenmalure. The soft metamorphosed rocks have weathered away over the millennia, exposing the granite, but significant traces remain, such as the cap of schist on top of Lugnaquilla Mountain (926m).

The mountains were rounded and shaped during the Ice Ages, producing the smooth profiles you see today. While flattening the peaks, the ice also created deep valleys such as Glenmacnass, Glenmalure and Glendalough. Corrie lakes such as Lough Bray Upper and Lower were gouged out by ice at the head of glaciers.

Beginning on Dublin's southern fringes, the narrow Military Rd winds down to the remotest parts of Wicklow. The best place to join it is at Glencree from Enniskerry. It then runs south through the Sally Gap, Glenmacnass, Laragh, Glendalough and on to Glenmalure and Aghavannagh.

The British constructed the road early in the 19th century to get access to the Wicklow rebels, including Michael Dwyer, who were holed up in the southern half of the county, particularly around Glenmalure. It was a considerable feat of engineering, traversing open bog and barren mountain-scapes for 50km.

Enniskerry makes a good starting point, and on the trip south you can divert east at the Sally Gap to look at Lough Tay and Lough Dan. Farther south you pass the great waterfall at Glenmacnass before dropping down into Laragh, with the magnificent monastic ruins of Glendalough nearby. Continue south through the valley of Glenmalure and, if you're fit enough, climb Lugnaquilla Mountain, Wicklow's highest peak.

ENNISKERRY
☎ 01 • pop 1275

Enniskerry, south of Dublin on the R117, owes its beginnings to the adjoining Powerscourt Estate. The landlord built this elegant, picturesque little village to accompany his impressive manor, the entrance to which is just south of the village square. Set round a small triangular green, the rows of cottages ooze quiet charm. A number of pleasant cafés make great places to unwind after a foray into the mountains, for which Enniskerry is an excellent base.

Heading west up the hill takes you through some lovely scenery into Glencree and the hamlet of the same name, 10km up at the head of the valley and on the Military Rd.

Enniskerry is a popular day-trip destination for Dubliners, but the village has so far escaped the blight of modern urban development. Don't miss the small detour to Powerscourt Waterfall and the estate's gardens.

Places to Stay

Hostels The An Óige *Lackan House* hostel (☎ 286 4036) is 7km south-west of Enniskerry, in Knockree (signposted from Enniskerry) at the base of Knockree Mountain, right by the Wicklow Way in a converted farm. It's open year round, has 42 beds and charges £6.50/5 for members.

B&Bs Overlooking the valley in Monastery, 1km west of Enniskerry on the Dublin road is *Cherbury* (☎ 282 8679). Rooms with bathroom cost £20 per person. In Enniskerry are *Corner House* (☎ 286 0149), starting at £20/30 for singles/doubles, and *Ferndale* (☎ 286 3518), starting at £24/35.

Hotels The attractively isolated and cosy *Enniscree Lodge Hotel* (☎ 286 3542, fax 286 6037), on the right as you head up into Glencree from Enniskerry, offers wonderful views of the valley. Singles/doubles cost £60/85 for B&B.

Powerscourt Arms (☎ 282 8903) is right in Enniskerry village facing the square. Despite its potential it's rather run of the mill, although renovation is pending. Singles/doubles cost £37/50 with bathroom and breakfast.

Places to Eat

Up the hill past the post office is *Buttercups*, a small deli and bread shop serving delicious takeaway food. Readers have also enjoyed eating at the very cosy *Poppies Country Cooking*, on the square, which offers an inviting selection of pies, quiches, cakes and main courses costing from £3.50 to £5. The homemade desserts are fantastic. Also reasonably priced is *Harvest Home*, up the hill past the Glenwood Inn, where meals cost around £6. A fourth choice is **Stepping Stones**, which does breakfast for £3.99.

For more luxurious surroundings, you have a couple of choices on the road west leading to Glencree. The first is **Curtlestown House Restaurant** (☎ *282 5803*), an upmarket restaurant in a farmhouse about 5km along. Its set menu costs £20. At **Enniscree Lodge Hotel** (☎ *286 3542*) a four-course dinner costs £27.

Five kilometres north-west of Enniskerry in Glencullen is **Johnnie Fox's** (☎ *295 5647*), which is renowned throughout the region for its superb seafood. There is a great traditional-music session nightly throughout the summer. Daniel O'Connell was a regular here and today it's a very popular tourist destination.

Getting There & Away

Enniskerry is just 3km west of the N11, the main Dublin to Wexford road. Bus Éireann (☎ 836 6111) express buses from the Busáras in Dublin will drop you at the turn-off for Enniskerry. Dublin area bus No 44 goes to Enniskerry from Hawkins St in Dublin, or you can take the DART train to Bray and get bus No 85 from the station.

POWERSCOURT ESTATE

This 64 sq km estate near Enniskerry, with its magnificent formal gardens, is a major tourist attraction. The main entrance to the house and estate is 500m south of the square in Enniskerry.

Powerscourt House (1743) was designed by Richard Castle, who also designed Dublin's Leinster House and Russborough House near Blessington. Unfortunately, a disastrous fire gutted the interior in 1974 just before the house was to be opened to the public. Today it's owned by the Slazenger family. At the time of writing a new visitor centre, restaurant and Avoca Handweavers shop were due to open.

The 20-hectare formal gardens were created in the 19th century, with Great Sugar Loaf Mountain providing a magnificent natural backdrop to the east. Five terraces drop more than 500m to the lovely Triton Lake. The Italian Gardens alone took 100 men 12 years to complete.

The wilder parts of the estate provided the setting for such films as John Boorman's *Excalibur* (1980), Stanley Kubrick's *Barry Lyndon* (1975) and Laurence Olivier's *Henry V* (1943).

The estate opens 9.30 am to 5.30 pm daily, year round. Tickets come with a map laying out 40-minute and hour-long tours of the gardens. Don't miss the Japanese Gardens or the Pepperpot Tower, supposedly modelled on a three-inch version inside the house. Admission to the gardens and visitor centre costs £4/3; to the gardens alone costs £3/2.

A 6km walk takes you to a separate part of the estate and a lovely ramble down to the **Powerscourt Waterfall**, at 130m the highest in Britain or Ireland and most impressive after heavy rain. You can also get to the falls by road (5km), following the signs from the estate entrance. The waterfall is accessible from 10.30 am to 7 pm (dusk in winter) daily year round, and admission costs £1.50/80p. The waterfall road continues along the southern slopes of Glencree and joins up with the Military Rd.

There's an excellent Bus Éireann tour that includes Powerscourt Gardens (for details see Russborough House in the Western Wicklow section later in this chapter).

GLENCREE
☎ 01

Just south of the border with Dublin and 10km west of Enniskerry is Glencree, a leafy hamlet set into the side of the valley of the same name which opens east to give a magnificent view down to Great Sugar Loaf Mountain and the sea.

The valley floor is home to the Glencree Oak Project, an ambitious plan to reforest part of Glencree with the native oak vegetation which once covered most of the country.

The village, such as it is, has a tiny shop and a hostel but no pub. A small grotto to the Virgin Mary, who is said to have appeared here in the 1980s, is set into the

WICKLOW

hillside. There's also a poignant German cemetery dedicated to servicemen who died in Ireland during WWI and WWII, mostly after shipwrecks or plane crashes. Just south of the village, the former military barracks are now a retreat house and reconciliation centre for people of different religions from the Republic and the North.

Places to Stay

The An Óige **Stone House** hostel (☎ 286 4037), just up from the German cemetery, has 40 beds costing £6.50. It gets busy in summer so be sure to book ahead.

SALLY GAP

The Sally Gap is one of the two main east-west passes across the Wicklow Mountains. From the turn-off on the lower road (R755) between Roundwood and Kilmacanogue near Bray, the narrow road (R759) passes above the dark waters of Lough Tay and Lough Dan and the Luggala Estate. It then heads up to the Sally Gap crossroads, where it cuts across the Military Rd and heads north-west for Kilbride and the N81, following the young River Liffey, still only a stream. Just north of the Sally Gap crossroads is Kippure Mountain (752m) with its TV transmitter. The surrounding bogs have dark lines cut into them by turfcutters.

Midway along the R759 from the Gap to Sraghmore you'll find **McGuirk's Tearoom** hiding in a clump of rhododendrons. It's been there since 1989 and is still churning out pleasant cakes and scones.

LOUGH TAY & LOUGH DAN

Lough Tay lies like a spilled pint of Guinness at the bottom of a spectacular gash in the mountains 5km south-east of the Sally Gap crossroads. The lake is part of Luggala, a private estate owned by Garech de Brun, a member of the Guinness family and the founder of Celtic Records. The estate featured in John Boorman's film *Excalibur*. At the northern end of the lough above a creamy brown beach sits Luggala House, overlooked by spectacular cliffs popular with rock climbers.

Luggala Estate covers almost all of the valley, as far down as Lough Dan, which nestles among lower hills to the south. The road to the Sally Gap skirts the top of the valley on the eastern side and is crossed by the Wicklow Way walking trail, which continues south past Lough Dan. A good option is to walk part of the Wicklow Way to Lough Dan; from the highest point on the road this is about 4km. There's a lovely view of the cliffs and Lough Tay from among the trees on the valley floor. If you look carefully, you can make out traces of old potato furrows (or 'lazy beds') dating back to Famine times on the hills.

ROUNDWOOD

☎ 01 • pop 440

At 238m above sea level, Roundwood is widely touted as Ireland's highest village, though it's hardly Mont Blanc. The village is essentially one long main street, which leads south to Glendalough and southern Wicklow. Otherwise, there isn't really much to the place. Turn-offs lead to Ashford to the east and the southern shore of Lough Dan to the west. Unfortunately, almost all Lough Dan's southern shoreline is private property and you can't get to the lake on this side. To the north is the turn-off to Bray.

Roundwood's pubs are usually packed with tired walkers on weekend afternoons. There are shops, a post office and a thriving market selling cakes, breads, flowers etc, held every Sunday afternoon, March to December, in the small hall on Main St.

North-west of the village you'll find some of the county's best scenery on the road to the Sally Gap, with a tremendous panorama over Lough Tay and the Luggala Estate.

Places to Stay

Roundwood Caravan and Camping Park (☎ 281 8163), within walking distance of the village pubs, has good facilities; tent pitches for hikers and cyclists cost £9. It opens from Easter to September. The many-gabled **Coach House Inn** (Main St) has comfortable if unspectacular rooms costing £20/40 for singles/doubles including breakfast. ***Tochar House*** *(☎ 281 8247)* at the southern end of Main St has better rooms for £25/40. ***Roundwood Inn*** does food, as does the Coach House Inn. The latter has been recommended by readers; all main courses cost £8 to £9.

Getting There & Away
St Kevin's Bus Service (☎ 281 8119) passes through Roundwood on its twice-daily run between Dublin and Glendalough (see Getting There & Away in the Glendalough section for more details).

GLENMACNASS
The most desolate section of the Military Rd runs through wild bogland between the Sally Gap crossroads and Laragh. Along the way you may catch glimpses of Lough Dan to the east and, until you reach the top of Glenmacnass Valley, not a single building breaks the sense of isolation.

The highest mountain to the west is Mt Mullaghcleevaun (848m), and River Glenmacnass flows south and tumbles over the edge of the mountain plateau in a great foaming cascade. The drop marks a boundary between granite and metamorphosed schist.

There's a car park near the top of the waterfall. Be careful when walking on rocks near Glenmacnass Waterfall as a few people have slipped to their deaths. There are fine walks up Mt Mullaghcleevaun or in the hills to the east of the waterfall car park.

WICKLOW GAP
Between Mt Tonelagee (816m) to the north and Table Mountain (700m) to the southwest, the Wicklow Gap is the second major pass over the mountains. The eastern end of the road begins just to the north of Glendalough and climbs through some lovely scenery north-westwards up along the Glendassan Valley. It passes the remains of some old lead and zinc workings before meeting a side road which leads south and up Turlough Hill, the location of Ireland's only pumped storage power station.

A lake was created on the summit and a tunnel was bored down through the hill to

the other lake at its base. The water is pumped to the top reservoir at times of low electricity demand and sent down through the turbines in the tunnel at times of high demand. You can walk up the hill to have a look over the top lake.

The gap was part of the second stage of the 1998 Tour de France. Despite being labelled a fairly easy climb, the exposed road and hard wind made it a far more difficult challenge than expected. In tribute to their efforts, you can still see the names of competitors, including Jan Ullrich and the eventual winner, Marco Pantani, painted in large letters on the tarmac.

GLENDALOUGH
☎ 0404
Glendalough (Gleann dá Loch, 'Glen of the Two Lakes') is a magical place – an ancient monastic settlement tucked beside two dark lakes and overshadowed by the sheer walls of a deep valley. It's one of the most picturesque settings in the Wicklow Mountains or, for that matter, in Ireland, and the site of one of the most significant ancient monastic settlements in the country.

Barely an hour away from Dublin, Glendalough is extremely popular. Visit early or late in the day or out of season to avoid the coach-tour crowds and atmosphere-shattering school parties.

History
Glendalough's past and present status are thanks to St Kevin, an early-Christian bishop who established a monastery here in the 6th century. From rough beginnings as a hermitage on the southern side of the Upper Lake, accessible only by boat, his monastery began to attract followers. In time it became a monastic city catering to thousands of students and teachers. During the Dark Ages, Glendalough was one of the places that gave Ireland its reputation as the island of saints and scholars.

The main sections of the monastery are thought to have been a few hundred metres west of the round tower, and it must have spread over a considerable area. Most of the present buildings date from between the

10th and 12th centuries. A famous son of Glendalough was St Laurence O'Toole, who studied here and then became abbot of Glendalough in 1117 and archbishop of Dublin in 1161. Glendalough's remote location was still within reach of the Vikings, who sacked the monastery at least four times between 775 and 1071. The final blow came in 1398, when English forces from Dublin almost completely destroyed it. Efforts were made to rebuild and some life lingered on here as late as the 17th century, when, under renewed repression, the monastery finally died.

Geography

Glendalough Valley was carved out by a series of glaciers, the last one retreating around 12,000 years ago. There was once one long deep lake which was later divided into the two you see today by the delta of the River Poulanass from the southern slopes. The larger Upper Lake is about 35m deep. The surrounding mountains are formed mostly of 400-million-year-old granite and schist, the remains of earlier sediments cooked by the welling-up granite. The granite has a number of mineral veins in it containing white quartz and ores of lead,

silver and zinc. There were extensive mining operations here between 1800 and 1920, with as many as 2000 miners working the mines, some of which became known as Van Diemen's Mines because of their remote location (a reference to Van Diemen's Land, the original name for Tasmania, Australia, one of Britain's former penal colonies).

The remains of the mine buildings and poisonous grey tailings are clearly visible at the far end of the Upper Lake and on the surrounding slopes. Some of the shafts extended north for nearly 2km through the mountain into the Glendassan Valley, and you can see the remains while driving through the Wicklow Gap.

Orientation & Information

At the valley entrance just before the Glendalough Hotel is the Glendalough Visitor Centre (☎ 45325), which has a good 20-minute audiovisual presentation on the Irish monasteries. It opens 9.30 am to 6 pm daily, and admission costs £2/1.

At the Upper Lake a small information office (☎ 45425) has details of activities in the Wicklow Mountains National Park. It opens 10 am to 6.30 pm daily, late April to

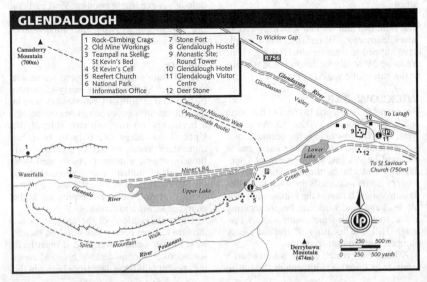

late August, but if you find it closed the staff may be out running guided walks. *Exploring the Glendalough Valley* (Dúchas) is a good booklet on the trails in the area.

It's important to get your bearings in Glendalough as the ruins and sites are spread out all over the valley. Coming from Laragh you first see the visitor centre, then the Glendalough Hotel, which is beside the entrance to the main group of ruins and the round tower. The Lower Lake is a small dark lake to the west, while farther west up the valley is the much bigger and more impressive Upper Lake, with a large car park (car £1.50, motorbike 50p) and more ruins nearby. Be sure to visit the Upper Lake and take one of the surrounding walks.

A model in the visitor centre should help you fix where everything is in relation to everything else.

Upper Lake Sites

The original site of St Kevin's settlement, **Teampall na Skellig**, is at the base of the cliffs towering over the southern side of the Upper Lake and accessible only by boat; unfortunately, there's no regular boat service to the site. The terraced shelf has the reconstructed ruins of a church and early graveyard. Rough wattle huts once stood on the raised ground nearby. Scattered around are some early grave slabs and simple stone crosses.

Just east of here and 10m above the lake waters is a little 2m-deep cave called **St Kevin's Bed**, said to be where Kevin lived. A local story relates how a woman appeared in the cave to tempt Kevin. The earliest human habitation of the cave was long before St Kevin's era. It may have been the burial chamber of a Bronze Age chief or perhaps even a prehistoric mine – there's evidence that people lived in the valley for thousands of years before the monks arrived. In the green area just south of the car park is a large circular wall thought to be the remains of an early-Christian *caher* or **stone fort**.

Follow the lakeshore path south-west of the car park until you find the considerable remains of **Reefert Church** above the tiny

River Poulanass. This is a small, rather plain, 11th-century, Romanesque nave-and-chancel church with some reassembled arches and walls. Traditionally, Reefert (King's Burial Place) was the burial site of the chiefs of the local O'Toole family, and they probably built the church on the site of an earlier one. The surrounding graveyard contains a number of rough stone crosses and slabs, most made of shiny mica schist.

If you climb the steps at the back of the churchyard and follow the path to the west, you'll find, at the top of a rise overlooking the lake, the scant remains of **St Kevin's Cell**, a small beehive hut.

For the millennium, Church authorities are hoping to build (depending on planning permission) five individual hermitages, or retreats, around the lake, each equipped with a bed, table and fireplace: visitors will be able to stay for a day or two in contemplative tranquillity, St Kevin's very reason for coming here in the first place.

Lower Lake Sites

While the Upper Lake has the best scenery, the most fascinating buildings lie in the lower part of the valley east of the Lower Lake.

Just round the bend from the Glendalough Hotel is the stone arch of the monastery **gatehouse**, the only surviving example of a monastic entranceway in the country. There used to be another storey and a containing wall. Just inside the entrance is a large slab with an incised cross.

Beyond that lies a graveyard which is still in use. The 10th-century **round tower** is 33m tall and 16m in circumference at the base. The upper storeys and conical roof were reconstructed in 1876. Near the tower, to the south-east, is the **Cathedral of St Peter and St Paul**, with a 10th-century nave. The chancel and sacristy date from the 12th century. Inside are some good carvings and early gravestones.

At the centre of the graveyard to the south of the round tower is the **Priest's House**. This odd building dates from 1170 but has been heavily reconstructed. It may have been the location of shrines of St

The Saint Who Lived in a Tree

Born around 498, St Kevin was a member of the royal house of Leinster and his name is derived from Cóemgen, meaning 'fair one' or 'well featured'. As a child he studied under the three holy men Énna, Eoghan and Lochan and supposedly went to Glendalough and lived in a tree. His closeness to animals became legendary: one story tells of a bird that trusted him so much she laid an egg in his hand! Later he lived as a hermit in the cave that became known as St Kevin's Bed. It was, however, impossible for him to escape the world completely: knowledge of his piety spread and people flocked to Glendalough to share his isolated existence. His monastic settlement spread from the Upper Lake to the site of the town whose remains we see today. St Kevin became abbot of the monastery in 570 and died in 617 or 618 – which would have made him around 120 years old! In the Middle Ages his shrine was so revered that seven pilgrimages to Glendalough were said to equal one to Rome.

Kevin. Later, during penal times it became a burial site for local priests – hence the name. The 10th-century **St Mary's Church**, 140m south-west of the round tower, probably originally stood outside the walls of the monastery and belonged to local nuns. It has a lovely western doorway. A little to the east are the scant remains of **St Kieran's Church**, the smallest at Glendalough.

Glendalough's trademark is **St Kevin's Church** or **Kitchen** at the southern edge of the enclosure. This church, with miniature round-tower-like belfry, protruding sacristy and steep stone roof, is a stone masterpiece. How it came to be known as a kitchen is a mystery as there's no indication that it was anything other than a church. The oldest parts of the building and the belfry date from the 11th century – the structure has been remodelled since but it's still a classic early Irish church. It was used by Catholics up to 1850 and now stores miscellaneous carvings and slabs.

At the junction with Green Rd as you cross the river just south of these two churches is the **Deer Stone** in the middle of a group of rocks. Legend claims that, when St Kevin needed milk for two orphaned babies, a doe stood here waiting to be milked. The stone is actually a *bullaun*, used as a grinding stone for medicines or food. Many are thought to be prehistoric and they were widely regarded as having supernatural properties: women who bathed their faces with water from the hollow were supposed

to keep their looks for ever. The early churchmen brought them into their monasteries, perhaps hoping to inherit some of the stones' powers.

The road east leads to **St Saviour's Church**, with its detailed Romanesque carvings. To the west a nice woodland trail leads up the valley past the Lower Lake to the Upper Lake.

Walks

Numerous fine walks fan out from Glendalough. The first, easiest and most popular is the gentle but delightful half-hour walk along the north shore of the Upper Lake to the lead and zinc mine workings, which date from 1800. The better route is along the lake shore rather than on the road, which runs 30m in from the shore. Continue on up the head of the valley if you wish.

Alternatively, you can go up **Spink Mountain**, the steep ridge with vertical cliffs running along the southern flanks of the Upper Lake. You can go part of the way and turn back, or complete a circuit of the Upper Lake by following the top of the cliff, eventually coming down by the mine workings and going back along the northern shore. The circuit takes about three hours.

The third option is a hike up **Camaderry Mountain** (700m), hidden behind the hills that flank the northern side of the valley. It starts on the road just 50m back towards Glendalough from the entrance to the Upper Lake car park. Head straight up the steep hill to the north and you come out on open mountains with sweeping views in all directions. You can then continue up Camaderry to the north-west or just follow the ridge west looking over the Upper Lake. To the top of Camaderry and back takes about four hours.

If you're intending to go on a serious hike, make sure you take all the usual precautions, have the right equipment and tell someone where you're going and when you should be back. For Mountain Rescue, ring ☎ 999. For more detailed information on walking in the area, check *Hill Walker's Wicklow* or *New Irish Walk Guides, East and South East*, both by David Herman. For walking partners check at the hostels or go on an organised walk with the National Park information office (☎ 45425) or Tiglin Adventure Centre (☎ 40169) near Ashford.

Other Activities

At the western end of the valley beyond the Upper Lake and mine workings are a couple of large crags popular with rock climbers. The Mountaineering Council of Ireland publishes a guide to the routes which is available from Joss Lynam (☎ 01-288 4672). Laragh Trekking Centre (see Places to Stay later in this section) runs horse-riding excursions.

Organised Tours

Bus Éireann (☎ 01-836 6111) runs tours to Glendalough leaving at 10.30 am and returning at 4.30 pm on Wednesday, Saturday and Sunday, January to March (£14/7); and leaving at 10.30 am and returning at 5.45 pm daily, April to October (£17/9). Aran Tours (☎ 01-280 1899) does a Wicklow tour which includes Glendalough (£22, including admission to the visitor centre) from Friday to Sunday, April to September. It picks up at four points in Dublin (Dublin Tourism office, Shelbourne Hotel, Gresham Hotel and Jury's in Ballsbridge), beginning at 8.50 am and returning between 4 and 4.30 pm.

Places to Stay

Camping No camping is allowed within the National Park. The nearest official camping spot is in Roundwood (see that section earlier in this chapter).

Hostels There are several hostels near Glendalough. The recently refurbished An Óige *Glendalough Hostel* (☎ 45342) is about 300m west of the round tower. The pleasant garden comes in for particular praise. Beds cost £10. Another An Óige hostel, *Tiglin Hostel* (☎ 49049), in Devil's Glen about 10km north-east of Laragh via Annamoe, has hostel accommodation for £6.50. To book, call the hostel before 9 am or after 5 pm to catch the warden; otherwise, call the An Óige office (☎ 01-830 1766) in Dublin.

In the village of Laragh, *Wicklow Way Hostel* (☎ 45398), beside Lynham's Bar, charges £7 for a dorm bed and opens year round.

B&Bs Most B&Bs are in or around Laragh, the village 3km east of Glendalough, or on the way there from Glendalough. *Lilac Cottage* (☎ 45574) in Laragh is run by an expat New Zealander and has simple but adequate rooms with separate bathroom costing £15 per person. Farther down towards Glendalough opposite the Trinity Church, *Valeview* (☎ 45292) has well-kept rooms, a great view of the valley and, as well as the normal cooked breakfast, provides the option of yoghurt and fruit. It charges upwards of £17 per person.

Housed in attractive farm buildings 1km south of Laragh on the road to Rathdrum is the *Riverhouse B&B* (☎ 45156), formerly the IHO Old Mill Hostel. Two-bed rooms cost £16.50 per person with a continental breakfast (£18.50 with a full Irish fry); there are other singles/doubles with better views that cost a hefty £25/50.

Laragh Trekking Centre (☎ 45282) charges £34/48 for singles/doubles with bathroom. The house is in Glenmacnass: turn north at the shop-cum-petrol-station in Laragh, on the Dublin side of the bridge, and keep going for almost 4km. Five kilometres north-east of Glendalough in Annamoe, on the main road to Roundwood, is *Carmel's* (☎ 45297), which charges £18/36

Wicklow Mountains National Park

Most of Glendalough is contained within two nature reserves, owned and managed by Dúchas and legally protected by the Wildlife Act. The larger reserve, west of the visitor centre, conserves the extensive heath and bog of the Glenealo Valley, an important habitat for moorland birds and deer, plus the Upper Lake and valley slopes on either side. The second reserve, Glendalough Wood Nature Reserve, conserves oak woods stretching from the Upper Lake as far as the Rathdrum road to the east.

Together with other state-owned land, the two reserves form the heart of the 12,700-hectare Wicklow Mountains National Park. At Liffey Head, north-east of Sally Gap, 2500 hectares of mountain blanket bog will eventually form part of the National Park too. The aim is ultimately to have a park of up to 30,000 hectares of mostly higher ground stretching the length of the Wicklow Mountains.

for singles/doubles with bathroom. It opens March to October.

Derrybawn House (☎ *45134*) stands in wooded grounds just south of Laragh on the road to Rathdrum. Singles/doubles start at £28/65 for B&B.

Hotels Close to the ruins and with the river running under the restaurant, *Glendalough Hotel* (☎ *45135, fax 45142*) has one of the country's best locations. It's gradually being extended and modernised. Singles/doubles cost £60/94 for B&B.

Places to Eat

At Glendalough itself there are surprisingly few places to eat. *Glendalough Hotel* has a huge restaurant that serves a very good three-course lunch for £11.95; there's also a limited bar menu, or a scone and tea for £1.80. Otherwise, there's a takeaway booth in the Upper Lake car park.

For anything else, you need to go into Laragh. About the best place for anything substantial is *Wicklow Heather Restaurant* (☎ *45157*), beside Lilac Cottage. Main courses cost around £6.50 and it's open for dinner until 8.30 pm; the trout (farmed locally) is excellent. During summer, villagers put out signs and serve tea and scones on the village green.

Getting There & Away

St Kevin's Bus Service (☎ 01-281 8119) runs to Glendalough from outside the Royal College of Surgeons, west of St Stephen's Green in Dublin at 11.30 am and 6 pm daily year round. Monday to Saturday the buses return to Dublin at 4.15 pm (Sunday 5.30 pm), leaving you just three hours at the site; it's much better to stay the night and return on the 7.15 am service (Saturday and Sunday 9.45 am). The one-way/return fare is £6/10. From Bray there are services at 12.10 and 6.40 pm (return £6).

GLENMALURE

Deep in the mountains, near the southern end of the Military Rd, is Glenmalure, a sombre and majestic blind valley overlooked on its western side by Lugnaquilla Mountain, Wicklow's highest peak at 926m, and flanked farther up by classic scree slopes of loose boulders. After coming over the mountains into Glenmalure you turn north-west at the Drumgoft bridge. From there it's about 6km up the road beside the Avonbeg River to a car park where trails lead off in various directions.

For a long time, Glenmalure was a stronghold of resistance to the English. Various clans, particularly the O'Byrnes, made forays up into the Pale, harassing the Crown's forces and loyal subjects. The most famous clan leader was Fiach MacHugh O'Byrne. In 1580 he defeated an army of 1000 English soldiers led by the lord deputy, Lord Grey de Wilton, at Glenmalure; over 800 men died in the battle and English control over Ireland was set back

Peaceful Glenmalure Valley, County Wicklow, was once a stronghold of rebel Irish clans.

Round tower, Glendalough, County Wicklow

Ancient ruins surround Glendalough's lakes.

COLIN SHAW

You don't have to go far off the beaten track in County Waterford to find unspoiled, sleepy villages.

DOUG McKINLAY

Hook Head Lighthouse, County Wexford

DOUG McKINLAY

Etching crystal at the Waterford Crystal Factory

COLIN SHAW

Stout by the pint or gallon in County Waterford

for decades. Fiach was captured in 1597 and his head impaled on the gates of Dublin Castle.

Near Drumgoft is Dwyer's or Cullen's Rock, which commemorates both the Glenmalure battle and Michael Dwyer, a 1798 Rising rebel who holed up here. Men were hanged from the rock during the Rising. For information about Dwyer's life, see Glen of Imaal in the Western Wicklow section later in this chapter.

Walks

You can walk up Lugnaquilla Mountain or head up the blind Fraughan Rock Glen east of the car park. Alternatively, you can go straight up Glenmalure Valley passing the small, seasonal An Óige Glenmalure Hostel, after which the trail divides – heading north-east, the trail takes you over the hills to Glendalough, while going north-west brings you into the Glen of Imaal.

The head of Glenmalure and parts of the neighbouring Glen of Imaal are off-limits – it's military land, well-posted with warning signs.

Places to Stay

About 1km up from the car park in Glenmalure is the small 36-bed An Óige *Glenmalure Hostel*. It opens daily in July and August and at the weekend the rest of the year. It has no phone or electricity and dorm beds cost £6.50 in high season. Much bigger is the An Óige *Aghavannagh House* hostel (☎ 0402-36366), 14km south-west in a former barracks built at the time of the 1798 Rising; it was at one time used as a shooting lodge by Charles Stewart Parnell. Beds cost £8 in high season. Both hostels make good bases for walking up Lugnaquilla.

Western Wicklow

The western slopes of the Wicklow Mountains were less deeply glaciated than the eastern ones, and the landscape isn't as spectacular. From the Sally Gap crossroads to Kilbride, however, you pass the upper reaches of the River Liffey and some lovely wild scenery. Another picturesque trip passes over the Wicklow Gap from Glendalough.

Western Wicklow's most interesting features are the Poulaphouca Reservoir (also known as Blessington Lakes), nearby Russborough House and, farther south, the lovely Glen of Imaal.

BLESSINGTON
☎ 045 • pop 1860

Once an important stop on the stage-coach run between Dublin, Carlow, Kilkenny and Waterford, Blessington is 35km south-west of Dublin on the N81. Its main street is lined with solid 17th- and 18th-century town houses. There isn't much in town to detain the visitor, but it makes a good base for exploring the surrounding area.

Blessington owes its beginnings to an archbishop of Dublin, Michael Boyle, who designed it in the 1670s. Boyle's manor, Downshire House, was destroyed by fire in 1760, and the village was all but destroyed by rebels in 1798.

Blessington is near the shores of Poulaphouca Reservoir, created in 1940 to drive the turbines of the local Electricity Supply Board (ESB) power station to the east of town and to supply Dublin with water.

Information

The tourist office (☎ 865850) is in the Blessington Business Centre, across the road from the Downshire House Hotel. It's *usually* open 10 am to 6 pm Monday to Saturday, June to August, but it basically depends on whether someone is there or not!

Places to Stay

Hostels Five kilometres from Blessington, the An Óige *Baltyboys Hostel* (☎ 867266), on the peninsula opposite Russborough House, opens March to November and has beds for £6.50/5. Take the road south to Poulaphouca and turn east at Burgage Cross towards Valleymount. Dublin bus No 65 passes by.

euro currency converter IR£1 = €1.27

B&Bs Overlooking the reservoir in Poulaphouca, *Heathers* (☎ 864554) is 7km south along the Baltinglass road and only 3km from Russborough House. Singles/doubles cost £22/36 for B&B. Also in Poulaphouca is the similarly priced *The Conifers* (☎ 864298).

Hotels The prominent *Downshire House Hotel* (☎ 865199, Main St) charges £50/88 for singles/doubles including breakfast.

The early-19th-century *Manor* (☎ 01-458 2105, fax 458 2607) has 18 hectares of gardens with views over the Wicklow Mountains. It's about 10km north-east of Blessington, just south of Kilbride, and opens April to September. B&B starts at £50 per person. Even more expensive is the rambling *Rathsallagh House* (☎ 403112, fax 403343), 20km south of Blessington in Dunlavin. For £105 you get a single or double room, plus breakfast and dinner; smaller rooms without any view cost £85, breakfast and dinner included.

Places to Eat
Next to the tourist office, *The Courtyard Restaurant* stays open until 9 pm from Easter to September, serving a range of basic meals. The smoked-salmon-and-brown-bread platter is lovely for £5.95. For somewhere to drink, *Hennessy's Lounge*, also on Main St, deserves credit for its pretty hanging baskets.

Getting There & Away
Blessington has regular daily services by Dublin suburban bus No 65 from Eden Quay in Dublin. Bus Éireann (☎ 01-836 3111) express bus No 005 to and from Waterford stops in Blessington two or three times daily; from Dublin it's pick-up only, from Waterford drop-off only.

RUSSBOROUGH HOUSE
Five kilometres south-west of Blessington is one of Ireland's finest stately homes, built for Joseph Leeson, later Lord Russborough, whose family were major players in Ireland's 18th-century brewing industry.

A truly magnificent Palladian villa, Russborough House was built between 1741 and 1751. It was designed by Richard Castle, at the height of his fame and ability, with the help of another architect, Francis Bindon from County Clare. At the front, the granite central building is flanked by two elegant wings connected to the main block by curving, pillared colonnades. This 275m frontage is further extended by granite walls and Baroque gates, and topped off with urns and heraldic lions. The interior has many impressive state rooms and remarkable plasterwork by the Francini brothers, Paul and Philip, whose work can also be seen in Castletown House in Celbridge, County Kildare.

Joseph Leeson filled the house with treasures and it stayed in the family until 1931. In 1952 it was sold to Sir Alfred Beit, nephew of another Sir Alfred Beit who was co-founder, with Cecil Rhodes, of de Beers. The older Sir Alfred had used the wealth from the diamonds to purchase important works of art. The nephew inherited the lot, and paintings by Velasquez, Vermeer, Goya and Rubens now slot comfortably into their grand surroundings. Unfortunately, they've attracted some unwanted attention. In 1974 an Englishwoman, Rose Dugdale, stole 16 of the paintings to help fund the IRA, but the paintings were recovered.

The house was closed to the public until 1976, when Sir Alfred established the Beit Foundation, making the house a centre for the arts. However, a second robbery in 1986, masterminded by crime baron Martin Cahill (aka The General), resulted in the recovery of only part of the haul of stolen paintings; some of those recovered were badly damaged (Cahill may have been a master criminal but he didn't have a clue about handling priceless works of art) while others were recovered only recently in the Netherlands. The robbery is central to *The General*, John Boorman's 1997 film about Cahill.

In 1988 the most valuable works of the collection were donated to the National Gallery in Dublin, but considering what still remains it was hardly an idle boast that at one time the collection was among the finest in private hands in Europe. In return for the gift of the paintings, the National Gallery often lends paintings to the collection as temporary exhibits. Needless to say, security is quite tight and the possibility of a third robbery is less than remote!

The house opens 10.30 am to 5.30 pm (closing at 2.30 pm, except on Sunday, May and September) daily, May to September. It opens on Sunday and bank holidays only, April and October. The main 45-minute tour of the house including all the important paintings costs £3/1 (students £2). An additional 30-minute tour of the bedrooms upstairs containing more silver and furniture costs £1.50 (children free).

June to September, Bus Éireann runs an excellent day trip to Russborough House and Powerscourt Gardens leaving the Búsaras in Dublin at 10 am. The £17 cost includes admission fees, and the tour takes in Lough Tay and the Sally Gap as well.

GLEN OF IMAAL

Seven kilometres south-east of Donard, the lovely Glen of Imaal, overlooked by Lugnaquilla Mountain, is about the only scenery of consequence on the western flanks of the Wicklow Mountains. It's named after Mal, a brother of the 2nd-century king of Ireland Cathal Mór. Unfortunately the glen's north-eastern slopes are mostly cordoned off as an army firing range and for manoeuvres. Look out for red danger signs.

The area's most famous son was Michael Dwyer, who led rebel forces during the 1798 Rising and held out for five years in the local hills and glens. On the south-eastern side of the glen at Derrynamuck is a small whitewashed, thatched cottage where Dwyer and three friends were surrounded by 100 English soldiers. One of his companions, Samuel McAllister, ran out the front, drawing fire and meeting his death, while Dwyer escaped into the night. He was eventually deported in 1803 and jailed on Norfolk Island, off the east coast of Australia, but became chief constable of Liverpool near Sydney before he died in 1825. The cottage is now a small folk museum.

The 40-bed An Óige **Ballinclea Hostel** (☎ 045-404657), 5km south-east of Donard on the road to Knockanarrigan, opens March to November. Beds cost £6.50/5.

BALTINGLASS
☎ 0508 • pop 1065

In the far western corner of Wicklow, 27km south-west of Blessington along the N81, is Baltinglass on the banks of the River Slaney. This small town grew up around the Cistercian **Abbey of Vallis Salutis**, founded in 1148 by Dermot MacMurrough as a satellite to Mellifont Monastery in County Louth. It was MacMurrough, as king of Leinster, who 'invited' the Anglo-Normans to Ireland, an offer they gratefully accepted. The rest, as they say, is history. Some locals suggest MacMurrough was laid to rest here in 1171, though he is more probably buried near his base in Ferns, County Wexford. Records suggest that the Irish Parliament met in the abbey for three days in 1397.

The ruined nave, with several simple Gothic arches and scant remnants of a cloister, lies 350m north of the town centre. The eastern section of the structure was used as a Protestant church long after the dissolution of the monasteries in 1541. A Gothic bell tower was added in 1815.

A stiff climb to the summit of Baltinglass Hill to the north-east brings you to **athcoran**, a large hill fort, and a Bronze Age cairn with several passage graves.

The IHH **Rathcoran House** hostel (☎ 81073), in Baltinglass, offers dorm beds costing £8.50 and twins costing £10; it opens mid-June to August.

At least two buses daily pass through Baltinglass between Dublin and Waterford and vice versa.

The Coast

The main N11 from Dublin to Wexford passes to the west of Bray and then south through Wicklow, keeping a few kilometres inland from the sea. South of Kilmacanogue you see Great Sugar Loaf Mountain (503m) to the west and pass through a great glacial rift, the Glen of the Downs, carved out of an Ice Age lake by floodwaters and with its slopes covered in native oak and beech. There's a forest walk up to a ruined tea house on top of the ridge to the east.

If you're travelling farther south, the coastal route through Greystones, Kilcoole and then along country lanes to Rathnew is preferable.

Worth seeing around Wicklow town are the Mt Usher Gardens near Ashford and the fine beaches of Brittas Bay, which stretch south into County Wexford.

BRAY
☎ 01 • pop 25,252
Bray is a run-down dormitory town on the coast 19km south of Dublin. In 1854 the railway's arrival turned it into the 'Brighton' of Ireland, a bustling seaside resort with a long promenade fronted by a beach and backed by hotels and lodging houses, all nicely overshadowed by Bray Head to the south. Unfortunately the seafront, which should be modern Bray's glory, is now home to cheap hotels, fast-food places, amusement arcades and endless parking space for DART train commuters. In short, Bray isn't a very appealing town. The other focal point is Main St, lined with shops and pubs.

Information
The tourist office (☎ 286 6796) is in the 19th-century courthouse beside the Royal Hotel at the bottom of Main St. It opens 9.30 am to 5 pm (4.30 pm October to May) Monday to Saturday, year round. Inquire here about Finnegan Bray's (☎ 286 0061) half-day and full-day tours to Glendalough, Dublin and the 'Ballykissangel' of the popular TV soap, aka Avoca.

The excellent Dubray Books, on Main St, sells maps and Wicklow walking guides.

Things to See & Do
A fine 8km cliff walk winds around Bray Head to Greystones from the southern end of the promenade, offering good views south to Great Sugar Loaf Mountain. Bray Head has many old smuggling caves and railway tunnels, including one that's 1.5km long, the second longest in Ireland, built by the engineer Isambard Kingdom Brunel in 1856. The inland rail route was an easier and more obvious choice, but the local earl didn't want the railway cutting through his land. James Joyce lived in Bray from 1889 to 1891 and, as in Sandycove near Dun Laoghaire, there is a **Martello tower**.

The tourist office houses a **heritage centre** which opens 9 am to 1 pm and 2 to 5 pm on weekdays, and 10 am to 1 pm and 2 to 4 pm on Saturday. As well as an exhibition on the town's history, there is a room devoted to folklore and an exhibit about engineer William Dargan (1799–1867), the man who brought the railway to Bray.

National Sealife (formerly the National Aquarium; ☎ 286 6939) on the seafront is the other main attraction in town. It has 30 displays, with around 2000 different fish representing 50 species. It opens 11 am to 5 pm daily, April to September; off-season times vary so call ahead. Admission costs £5.50/3.95.

Kilruddery House and Gardens, about 3km south of Bray, has been home to the Brabazon family since 1618 and has one of Ireland's oldest gardens. The house (☎ 286 3405) opens 1 to 5 pm daily, May, June and September. The gardens are open for the same times, April to September. Admission to the house and gardens costs £4/2.50; to the gardens only costs £2/1.50.

Places to Stay
If Dublin is full (not impossible over summer weekends) there are many B&Bs along Bray's sea-facing Strand Rd, just minutes from the DART station. At the northern end they tend to overlook parking lots so it's worth continuing south towards Bray Head. Try **Strand House** (☎ 286 8920), right at the end, where singles/doubles cost £25/40, or more central **Ulysses** (☎ 286 3860) charging £24/45. Otherwise, **Crofton Bray Head Inn** (☎ 286 7182) is a 130-year-old building right on the seafront under Bray Head Mountain. B&B rates start at £22 per person.

Modern **Royal Hotel** (☎ 286 2935, fax

286 7373, *Main St)* charges an acceptable £35/60. It has a leisure centre with a pool, sauna and other watery amenities. *The Westbourne (☎ 286 2362, fax 8530, Quinsboro Rd)* is a smaller hotel that charges upwards of £30 per person. The best hotel in town (although it is being rivaled by the Royal) is the *Esplanade (☎ 286 2056)*, which charges £60/90.

Places to Eat
The delightful *Escape (☎ 286 6755, Albert Ave)* is a good vegetarian restaurant just off Strand Rd. Main courses cost £7.95 and booking is advisable. *The Tree of Idleness (☎ 286 3498, Strand Rd)* serves delicious Greek-Cypriot food; main courses start at £12.95. The nearby *Porter House* does pub food but its main attraction is the wide variety of beers from around the world.

Getting There & Away
Bus Dublin suburban bus Nos 45 (from Hawkins St) and 84 (from Eden Quay) run every 45 minutes or so between Dublin and Bray. You can also catch them outside Trinity College on Nassau St. Both go past Bray train station. Bus Nos 84 and 84A run on to Greystones and Kilcoole. Bus No 85 runs from the train station to Enniskerry every 25 to 45 minutes.

On its Dublin to Rosslare Harbour route Bus Éireann (☎ 836 6111) picks up passengers in Bray for destinations south to Rosslare Harbour and drops them off in the reverse direction. You'll be dropped on the highway, 15 minutes' walk from the B&Bs.

St Kevin's Bus Service (☎ 281 8119) runs buses daily from the town hall to Dublin at 8 am and 5 pm (one way £1.20).

Train Bray train station (☎ 236 3333) is 500m east of Main St just before the seafront. There are DART trains into Dublin and farther north to Howth every five minutes at peak times and every 20 or 30 minutes at quiet times.

The station is also on the mainline from Dublin to Wexford and Rosslare Harbour, with up to five trains daily in each direction Monday to Saturday, four on Sunday.

Getting Around
Bray Sports Centre (☎ 286 3046), 8 Main St, is the Raleigh Rent-a-Bike dealer, with bikes costing £10/56 per day/week.

KILMACANOGUE
The biggest and best local craft shop is **Avoca Handweavers** (☎ 286 7466), set in a 19th-century arboretum in Kilmacanogue, 4km south of Bray on the N11. The showroom has a huge array of handmade crafts and garments, and a *café* serves snacks and lunches.

Bray tourist office's *Wicklow Trail Sheet No 4* (£1) details a three-hour exploration of Great Sugar Loaf Mountain starting from Kilmacanogue.

To drive to Kilmacanogue from Bray, take the right fork up by the town hall, continue for 3km until you come to the N11 then turn left (south) for 1km. Local bus No 145 from Bray sometimes stops in Kilmacanogue; check with the driver.

GREYSTONES TO WICKLOW
Eight kilometres south of Bray, the resort of **Greystones** was once a charming fishing village, and the seafront around the little harbour is idyllic, with a broad bay and beach sweeping north to Bray Head. In summer, the bay is dotted with dinghies and windsurfers. Sadly, the surrounding countryside is vanishing beneath housing developments.

Kilcoole, 3km south of Greystones, is noteworthy as the setting for Ireland's leading TV soap, *Glenroe*, based on a farm. Bus Éireann runs a couch-potato tour taking in 'Glenroe' and 'Ballykissangel' (Avoca) which leaves the Búsaras in Dublin at 10 am on Saturday, June to September. It costs £17/9.

South of Kilcoole, in Ashford, are the eight-hectare **Mt Usher Gardens** (☎ 0404-40205), informally laid out around the River Vartry with rare plants from around the world. The gardens were first designed in 1868 by Dublin textile magnate Edward Walpole, with succeeding generations of the Walpole family working to maintain and expand the grounds. At the entrance you'll find craft shops, a bookshop and café. The

WICKLOW

WICKLOW

gardens open 10.30 am to 6 pm daily, mid-March to October. Admission costs £3.50/2.50. There are guided tours of the gardens (for groups only) costing £20. Bus Éireann (☎ 01-836 6111) buses stop outside Ashford House on the three-times-daily Dublin to Rosslare Harbour route.

West of Ashford the road leads into the Wicklow Mountains through **Devil's Glen** (beginning 3km from Ashford), a beautiful wooded glen with a fine walking trail. **Tiglin Adventure Centre** (☎ 0404-40169), 3km farther west, runs courses in rock climbing and canoeing and also organises treks.

Places to Stay & Eat
The absolutely gorgeous *Tinakilly Country House* (☎ 0404-69274, fax 67806) is a Victorian Italianate manor house just outside Rathnew, on the road towards Wicklow. It was built for Captain Robert Halpin (1836–94), who commanded the *Great Eastern*, which was famous for being the largest ship in the world and participated in the laying of the first transatlantic cable. B&B rates start at £65 per person, and there is a very good restaurant too; prices are high but the food is excellent.

WICKLOW & AROUND
☎ 0404 • pop 6416

Wicklow town, 27km south of Bray, is not an exciting county town but does boast a fine big harbour which hosts the start of the biennial Round Ireland Yacht Race. The sweep of beach and bay to the north and the bulge of Wicklow Head to the south are the area's best features.

There's not much to see here, although Wicklow makes a good base for exploring the surrounding area. Unfortunately, the layout is not very backpacker-friendly, with the bus stop and train station some distance from the hostel and the B&Bs, and from each other.

The helpful tourist office (☎ 69117) on Fitzwilliam Square opens 9.30 am to 6 pm Monday to Saturday, June to September; and 9 am to 1 pm and 2 to 5 pm on weekdays, October to May.

Wicklow's Historic Jail
The history of Wicklow's infamous jail is told through audiovisuals, figures, graphics and even actors at this new heritage centre housed in the prison where thousands of convicts were kept in inhumane conditions, and that was after the prison reforms of the late 18th century! The 1st floor has exhibits detailing the 1798 Rebellion in Wicklow (which didn't actually end until the surrender of Michael Dwyer in 1803) and the consequences of the prison reforms, which for many prisoners resulted in transportation to the penal colonies in New South Wales. Their gruelling journey is outlined on a model of a convict ship, the HMS *Hercules*, on the 2nd floor. The top floor is devoted to the story of prisoners once they arrived in Australia and how they made a life for themselves in a new country thousands of miles from home.

The jail (☎ 61599) opens 10 am to 6 pm daily (last admission at 5 pm); tours take place every 10 minutes except between 1 and 2 pm. Admission (and tour) costs £3.75/2.

Other Things to See & Do
The few remaining fragments of the **Black Castle** are on the shore at the southern end of town, with pleasant views up and down the coast. The castle was built by the Fitzgeralds from Wales in 1169 after they were granted lands in the area by Strongbow. It used to be linked to the mainland by a drawbridge, and rumour has it that an escape tunnel ran from the sea cave underneath up into the town. At low tide you can swim or snorkel into the cave.

The walk along the cliffs to **Wicklow Head** offers great views of the Wicklow Mountains. A string of **beaches** – Silver Strand, Brittas Bay and Maheramore – start 16km south of Wicklow; with high dunes, safe bathing and powdery sand, the beaches attract droves of Dubliners in good weather. Caravan parks lurk behind the dunes.

Places to Stay
The very welcoming *Wicklow Bay Hostel* (☎ 69213) may not boast the most scenic

surroundings but there are fine sea views from the dorms. The building itself has had an unusually chequered history as, in turn, school, hotel, barracks, orphanage and bottling plant. There's a big, clean kitchen. Dorm beds cost £9 in high season and there are some family rooms too.

There's a clutch of B&Bs in and around Dunbur Hill and a few more uphill along St Patrick's Rd. In the town centre *Bayview Hotel* (☎ 67383) has singles/doubles costing £25/50. *Bridge Tavern* does B&B in a building famed as the birthplace of Captain Halpin (commander of the *Great Eastern*) and for its live music sessions.

Places to Eat

Hannah's (Main St) will sort you out for breakfast, light lunches or afternoon tea. *The Old Forge* has a good choice of bar meals. *The Opera House (Market Square)* offers pasta and pizza costing upwards of £6. *The Bakery Café and Restaurant* (☎ 66770, Church St) is good for vegetarians, with dishes such as apple and Camembert strudel (£7.95).

Getting There & Away

Up to two Bus Éireann (☎ 01-836 6111) buses daily leave from the Grand Hotel on Main St for Dublin and for Rosslare Harbour. Trains (☎ 01-836 3333) stop at Wicklow at least four times daily in each direction between Dublin and Rosslare Harbour. The station is 10 minutes' walk north of the town centre.

Getting Around

Wicklow Cabs (☎ 66888), Main St, picks up passengers from the 6.30 and 7.30 pm Dublin trains. The fare to anywhere in town is £3. The same company organises tours to local beauty spots, nightclubs and music pubs.

Southern Wicklow

RATHDRUM

☎ 0404 • pop 1234

These days Rathdrum is little more than a few old houses and shops to the south of Glendalough and the Vale of Clara, the pleasant valley leading north to Laragh, but in the late 19th century it could have claimed to be the unofficial capital of Wicklow, with a healthy flannel industry and a poorhouse. The railway and fine aqueduct were built in 1861. More recently, Rathdrum provided a setting for parts of the Neil Jordan film *Michael Collins*.

Avondale House

In 1846 the great Irish politician Charles Stewart Parnell was born in Avondale House (☎ 46111), which was designed by James Wyatt in 1779. The house was recently restored to its 1850s splendour and a 20-minute audiovisual presentation tells the story of Parnell.

The house is signposted 1.5km south of Rathdrum and opens to the public 10 am to 6 pm daily, May to September; 11 am to 5 pm the rest of the year. Admission costs £3/2.50.

The 209 hectares of woodland incorporate an arboretum and nature walks. You can visit during daylight hours year round. Parking costs £3.

Places to Stay

The IHH *Old Presbytery* hostel (☎ 46930) in Rathdrum offers dorm beds costing £9 and private rooms for £20. You can camp in the grounds and there's a laundry.

Most of Rathdrum's B&Bs are actually in Corballis, 1km along the road south to Avoca and Arklow. *Beechlawn* (☎ 46474), 500m south on the Avoca road, charges upwards of £22/38 for singles/doubles. Nearby, *Avonbrae House* (☎ 46198) costs £24 per person. At *The Hawthorns* (☎ 46217), also in Corballis, singles/doubles cost upwards of £25/36 for B&B.

Getting There & Away

The Bus Éireann (☎ 01-836 6111) Dublin to Wexford and Rosslare Harbour bus stops at Rathdrum twice daily in each direction. Three trains (☎ 01-836 3333) stop at Rathdrum daily in each direction between Dublin and Rosslare Harbour.

WICKLOW

WICKLOW

VALE OF AVOCA

The Avonbeg and Avonmore Rivers come together to form the River Avoca at Meeting of the Waters, a lovely spot made famous by Thomas Moore's poem of the same name:

There is not in this wide world a valley so sweet
As that vale in whose bosom the bright waters meet;
Oh! the last rays of feeling and life must depart,
'Ere the bloom of that valley shall fade from my heart.

The Vale of Avoca is a gentle, darkly wooded valley which is charming if hardly awe-inspiring. Unfortunately there's some badly scarred landscape north-west of Avoca village, the legacy of centuries of copper mining, which also polluted the river. The last mine closed in 1982. In the 18th century the valley was cut off from the outside world and had its own coinage, the cronbane.

Meeting of the Waters is marked by a pub called *The Meetings* (☎ 0402-35226), which serves food all day and has music at the weekend year round. There are ceilidhs between 4 and 6 pm on Sunday, April to October. Buses to Avoca from Dublin stop at The Meetings, or you can walk from Avoca.

Avoca

☎ 0402 • pop 490

The tiny village of Avoca (Abhóca) shot to fame in 1996 when it was chosen as the location for the unexpectedly popular BBC TV series *Ballykissangel*. The focal point of the town and the series is *Fitzgerald's*, a suitably olde-worlde pub by the river. While tucking into pub food here you can admire snapshots of the former stars, Stephen Tompkinson and Dervla Kirwan, on the walls. There's a seasonal tourist office in the library.

Also in the village is **Avoca Handweavers** (☎ 35105), which has been in business since 1723 and claims to be Ireland's oldest surviving business. You can look around the weaving sheds and then admire the pricey tweeds, throws and other fabrics in their shop. The excellent café opens for lunches and teas.

Places to Stay

Camping There are two well-equipped camp sites near the village of Redcross, about 7km north-east of Avoca on the R754 country road. *Johnson's* (☎ 0404-48133), just north of Redcross, charges £9 per tent, as does *River Valley Park* (☎ 0404-41647), just south of Redcross.

B&Bs The Georgian *Riverview House* (☎ 35181), by the bus stop in Avoca, is

---

The Village of Make Believe

The post office is really a teashop, the National School a community centre. O'Reilly's provisions shop may say it's open but never actually is. The pub offers accommodation – until you try to book a room. This is *Ballykissangel*, the fictional TV village so popular that it has virtually eclipsed Avoca, the real-life village where much of the filming takes place.

When the BBC started to film a TV series about an English priest washed up in a small Irish village, they were not to know they had a smash hit on their hands. But with *Ballykissangel* sold to Australia, the USA and Ireland itself, Avoca has rocketed to the top of the tourism pops, so much so, in fact, that the tiny library has had to turn itself into a tourist office to cope with the 70,000 people streaming off the tour buses annually.

Not everyone is thrilled about this, and the good news for them is that no further episodes of *Ballykissangel* will be made after the fifth series. Perhaps Avoca can return to a semblance of normality but, considering the magic (dreaded) word 'rerun', you wouldn't bet on it.

highly recommended. It opens Easter to September and offers singles/doubles with separate bathroom costing £22/34. *Arbours* (☎ 35294) has great breakfasts and rooms with separate bathroom costing £23/37.

Ashdene (☎ 35327), 2km north-west of Avoca in Knockanree Lower, on the road to Redcross, and open mid-March to October, offers B&B starting at £23.50/36. *Greenhills* (☎ 35197), also in Knockanree Lower, charges £25/40 for singles/doubles with bathroom and opens May to September.

Hotels One and a half kilometres south of Avoca on the R752, *Valley Hotel* (☎ 35200, fax 35542) is nestled in a scenic valley. Rooms start at £29 including breakfast. Four kilometres south of Avoca, overlooking Woodenbridge Golf Course, is *Woodenbridge Hotel* (☎ 35146, fax 35573), which dates from 1608 and is held to be Ireland's oldest hotel. Luckily, it has undergone several refurbishments since it first opened. Rates range from £30/60 to £45/90, depending on the season.

Getting There & Away
Bus No 133 from Dublin to Arklow via Bray, Wicklow and Rathdrum stops in Avoca twice daily (once on Sunday). A day return from Dublin costs £6... and you get a free cup of tea and a scone at Avoca Handweavers thrown in.

ARKLOW
☎ 0402 • pop 8519
Besides Bray, Arklow is probably County Wicklow's busiest town. A thriving commercial shopping centre with some light industry, it makes a reasonable base for exploring the Wicklow Mountains but is not particularly attractive in its own right.

Once a minor fishing village, Arklow became one of the country's busiest ports and a well-known boat-building centre. Sir Francis Chichester's *Gypsy Moth IV* (now in Greenwich, London) and the Irish training vessel *Asgard II* were built here. In 1841 the port had 80 schooners working out of the harbour.

During the 1798 Rising, Arklow saw fierce fighting when some 20,000 of the rebels led by Father Michael Murphy tried to storm the town and were defeated by the better-equipped and better-trained British army. Murphy and 700 men died in the battle. A monument to them sits in front of St Mary and St Peter's church today.

The tourist office (☎ 32484), in a Portakabin beside the courthouse, theoretically opens 9.30 am to 1 pm Monday to Saturday.

The small **maritime museum** in St Mary's Rd traces the town's sea-going past. It opens 10 am to 1 pm and 2 to 5 pm daily. Admission costs £2.

Places to Stay & Eat
There are plenty of B&Bs, especially on the southern side of town. You could try *Tara* (☎ 39333), about 1km south of the town centre on the Gorey road, with singles/doubles costing £22/32 with shared bathroom. On Main St *Óstán Beag* (☎ 33044) charges £31 per person.

Riverwalk Restaurant by the river offers kippers and smoked haddock to ring the breakfast changes. On Main St *Kitty's* pub-restaurant serves main courses for around £5, while *Christy's* also does good food, including vegetarian options. Lunch specials cost £5.95.

Getting There & Away
Bus Bus Éireann (☎ 01-836 6111) operates regular services from Busáras in Dublin to Arklow via Wicklow town. They stop outside the Chocolate Shop.

Train DART trains run to Dublin via Rathdrum, Wicklow town, Greystones and Bray six times daily (three times on Sunday). One early-morning service continues to Drogheda via Malahide, Rush, Lusk and Skerries. There are five trains daily to Rosslare (three on Sunday) and two to Gorey.

WICKLOW

Counties Wexford & Waterford

The ferries arriving in Rosslare Harbour bring to the counties of Wexford and Waterford lots of visitors who are on their way to destinations farther afield, but there are places here to enjoy in their own right. The coastline offers superb beaches and possibilities for water sports, and Wexford town and, particularly, Waterford city make good bases for exploring the area. Both counties are rich in history, and the countryside, while lacking the rugged splendour of the island's west and south-west, has a beauty that surprises many visitors.

There's a short cut between Counties Wexford and Waterford by taking the Ballyhack to Passage East ferry, avoiding the longer route via New Ross.

County Wexford

County Wexford occupies the south-eastern corner of Ireland. Although it hasn't a huge amount to divert visitors, there are a few spots worth pausing for. The county is almost entirely flat, except near its western borders with Kilkenny and Carlow, where the Blackstairs Mountains rise to 796m at their highest point, Mt Leinster. There are some pleasant routes through these little-explored hills, particularly to the west of Enniscorthy and over the Scullogue Gap.

Wexford town is pleasant enough but retains few traces of its Viking past. To its north, a string of fine beaches runs along the coast towards County Wicklow. In the centre of County Wexford, Enniscorthy is an attractive hilly town on the banks of the River Slaney. Farther west, the River Barrow runs through New Ross, a good base for exploring the river's lovely upper reaches.

On the southern coast is the fishing village of Kilmore Quay and, farther west, the flat and lonely Hook Peninsula, home to one of the world's oldest lighthouses.

Highlights

- Walk, cycle or drive along the lovely Hook Peninsula in County Wexford
- Learn about Wexford's rebel history at the National 1798 Visitor Centre in Enniscorthy
- Watch the birds on the Saltee Islands
- Explore the historic sights of Waterford city

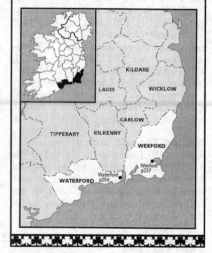

WEXFORD
☎ 053 • pop 9533

Wexford (Loch Garman) vies with Waterford city for the position of principal settlement in the south-east. It was once a thriving port but over the centuries the slow-moving River Slaney has deposited so much silt and mud in the estuary that the channel has become almost unusable. Now most commercial sea traffic goes through Waterford and all passenger traffic through Rosslare Harbour, which is 20km to the south-east.

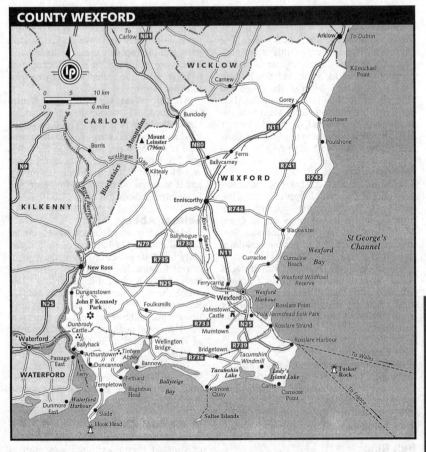

COUNTY WEXFORD

The Vikings arrived in the region around 850, attracted by its handy location near the mouth of the River Slaney. The Viking name Waesfjord means 'harbour of mud flats' or 'sandy harbour'. The Normans captured the town just after their first landings in 1169, and traces of their fort can still be seen in the grounds of the Irish National Heritage Park north-west of town at Ferrycarrig.

Cromwell included Wexford in his Irish tour from 1649 to 1650. Three-quarters of the town's 2000 inhabitants were put to the sword, including all of the town's Francis-can friars – the standard treatment for towns that refused to surrender. After the massacre at Wexford, surrender became increasingly popular. During the 1798 Rising, rebels made a determined stand in Wexford town before they were defeated.

Modern Wexford is renowned for its opera festival, a good time to visit provided you plan well ahead (see Special Events later in this section for details).

Orientation

From Wexford Bridge at the northern end of the town, the quays (Commercial Quay,

Custom House Quay and Paul Quay) lead south-east along the waterfront, with the tourist office in the small kink called The Crescent. The quays are of little interest except as places for an evening stroll but run roughly parallel to North and South Main St, a block inland. Most of the shops and other commercial outlets are along the Main Sts. There's a bank on North Main St to the south-east of Common Quay St and another at the corner of Common Quay St and Custom House Quay; both have ATMs.

Information

The tourist office (☎ 23111) is on the waterfront on The Crescent. It opens 9 am to 6 pm Monday to Saturday, and 9 am to 5 pm on Sunday, July and August; 9 am to 6 pm Monday to Saturday, May, June and September; and 9 am to 5.15 pm on weekdays, the rest of the year.

The Book Centre on North Main St stocks books on Irish topics as well as a limited selection of foreign newspapers and magazines. Readers Paradise, which is farther north on North Main St, stocks second-hand paperbacks.

The Crescent

As well as the Chamber of Commerce building which houses the tourist office, The Crescent is home to a statue of Commodore John Barry. A local seaman born in 1745, he emigrated to America and founded the US navy during the American Revolution.

Bull Ring

At the intersection of Common Quay St and North Main St is the Bull Ring, at one time a centre for bull-baiting but also the site of Cromwell's long-remembered massacre. The Lone Pikeman statue commemorates the participants in the 1798 Fenian rebellion.

Market stalls are usually set up in the New Market beside the Bull Ring on Friday and Saturday mornings.

Westgate

Some stretches of the town wall remain intact, including a fine section near Cornmarket. Of the six original town gates only the

14th-century West Gate survives, at the northern end of town on Westgate opposite the end of Slaney St. It was originally a toll gate, and the recesses used by the toll collectors are still intact, as is the lockup used to incarcerate 'runagates' – those who tried to avoid paying.

At the **Westgate Heritage Centre** (☎ 46506, 42611), beside the gate, an audiovisual display – *In Selskar's Shadow* – tells the history of Wexford. The centre opens 9.30 am to 5.30 pm Monday to Saturday, and 2 to 6 pm on Sunday, July and August; and 11 am to 5.30 pm Monday to Friday, and 2 to 6 pm on Sunday, May, June and September. Admission costs £1.50/1.

Selskar Abbey

Selskar Abbey was founded by Alexander de la Roche in 1190 after a crusade to the Holy Land. Its present ruinous state is a result of Cromwell's visit in 1649. Bascilla, the sister of Richard FitzGilbert de Clare (Strongbow), is supposed to have married Raymond le Gros, one of Henry II's brave lieutenants, in the abbey, and it is rumoured that Henry did penance here for the murder of Thomas à Becket (as depicted in the film *A Man for All Seasons*).

The ruins should be unlocked when the Westgate Heritage Centre is open. At other times, a key is available from the guardian at 9 Abbey St.

St Iberius' Church

South of the Bull Ring on North Main St the existing St Iberius' Church was built in 1760 on the site of several previous churches (including one reputed to have been founded by St Patrick). The graceful 18th-century interior is worth a look, the most noteworthy features being the altar rails from a Dublin church and a set of 18th-century monuments in the gallery. The church opens 10 am to 5 pm daily. A guided tour costs £1.

Organised Tours

Tynan Tours (☎ 65929) runs walking tours that depart from the tourist office from 9.15 am to 4.30 pm Monday to Saturday

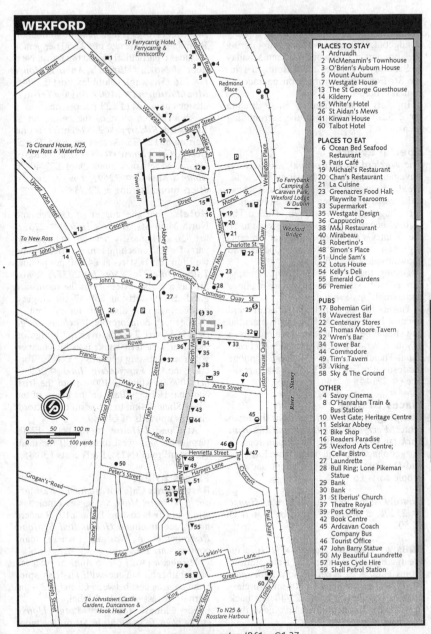

WEXFORD

To Ferrycarrig Hotel,
Ferrycarrig &
Enniscorthy

To Clonard House, N25,
New Ross & Waterford

To New Ross

To Ferrybank
Camping &
Caravan Park,
Wexford Lodge
& Dublin

Wexford
Bridge

River Slaney

To Johnstown Castle
Gardens, Duncannon &
Hook Head

To N25 &
Rosslare Harbour

0   50   100 m
0   50   100 yards

PLACES TO STAY
1 Ardruadh
2 McMenamin's Townhouse
3 O'Brien's Auburn House
5 Mount Auburn
7 Westgate House
13 The St George Guesthouse
14 Kilderry
15 White's Hotel
26 St Aidan's Mews
41 Kirwan House
60 Talbot Hotel

PLACES TO EAT
6 Ocean Bed Seafood
   Restaurant
9 Paris Café
19 Michael's Restaurant
20 Chan's Restaurant
21 La Cuisine
23 Greenacres Food Hall;
   Playwrite Tearooms
33 Supermarket
35 Westgate Design
36 Cappuccino
38 M&J Restaurant
40 Mirabeau
43 Robertino's
48 Simon's Place
51 Uncle Sam's
52 Lotus House
54 Kelly's Deli
55 Emerald Gardens
56 Premier

PUBS
17 Bohemian Girl
18 Wavecrest Bar
22 Centenary Stores
24 Thomas Moore Tavern
32 Wren's Bar
34 Tower Bar
49 Commodore
49 Tim's Tavern
53 Viking
58 Sky & The Ground

OTHER
4 Savoy Cinema
8 O'Hanrahan Train &
   Bus Station
10 West Gate; Heritage Centre
11 Selskar Abbey
12 Bike Shop
16 Readers Paradise
25 Wexford Arts Centre;
   Cellar Bistro
27 Laundrette
28 Bull Ring; Lone Pikeman
   Statue
29 Bank
30 Bank
31 St Iberius' Church
37 Theatre Royal
39 Post Office
42 Book Centre
45 Ardcavan Coach
   Company Bus
46 Tourist Office
47 John Barry Statue
50 My Beautiful Laundrette
57 Hayes Cycle Hire
59 Shell Petrol Station

WEXFORD & WATERFORD

euro currency converter IR£1 = €1.27

(from 11 am on Sunday) between June and August. The Wexford Historical Society conducts free guided walking tours during the summer, at 11 am and 2.30 pm Monday to Saturday, from the Talbot Hotel on Trinity St. For more information contact the tourist office.

In July and August, Bus Éireann (☎ 22522) runs tours of the surrounding areas.

Special Events
The **Wexford Opera Festival**, a 17-day extravaganza held in October, is an excuse for Wexford townsfolk to shake out their cocktail dresses and dinner jackets and prepare for a huge influx of cultured visitors. The festival began in 1951 and has grown to be the country's premier opera event, presenting many rarely performed operas and shows to packed audiences.

During the festival the town is transformed, with street theatre, poetry readings and exhibitions every day.

Tickets for the principal operas are hard to come by and pricey. Booking is essential and should be done at least three months in advance. Write to the Wexford Opera Festival at Theatre Royal, 27 High St, or phone the festival office (☎ 22240) or the box office (☎ 22144).

Places to Stay
Camping Across the river from the town centre, *Ferrybank Camping and Caravan Park* (☎ 44378) is off the Dublin road. It has good facilities and opens from Easter to mid-October. A pitch for a tent and two people costs £6.

Hostels At the comfortable *Kirwan House* (☎ 21208, 3 Mary St) dorm beds start at £7.50.

B&Bs At *Westgate House* (☎ 22167) on Westgate, not far from the train station, rooms start at £23 per person. *Ardruadh* (☎ 23194) is on Spawell Rd and singles/doubles cost upwards of £25/40; set back from the road, it could be a bit quieter than Westgate House.

McMenamin's Townhouse (☎ 46442, 3 Auburn Terrace) is also near the station, off Redmond Rd. The rate of £22.50 per person includes a particularly good breakfast. Next door at No 2, *O'Brien's Auburn House* (☎ 23605), singles/doubles cost £25/45. *Mount Auburn* (☎ 24609, Auburn Terrace) charges upwards of £22 per person.

About 500m west of the centre on St John's Rd, *Kilderry* (☎ 23848) offers rooms starting at £25/35. Across the road *The St George Guesthouse* (☎ 43474), at the top of George St, charges upwards of £27/40. *St Aidan's Mews* (☎ 22691, Lower John St) offers rooms starting at £22/38.

Hotels Near the corner of George and North Main Sts, *White's Hotel* (☎ 22311, fax 45000) is mostly new but incorporates part of an old coaching inn. It's friendly and well run; B&B starts at £41.50 per person. *Talbot Hotel* (☎ 22566, fax 23377, Trinity St) has a garish exterior but the rooms are good. B&B starts at £50/87 for singles/doubles, with big discounts for children.

The very comfortable *Wexford Lodge* (☎ 23611, fax 23342), over the bridge on the river's eastern bank, is a bit cheaper, with rooms costing upwards of £40/70. Top-class, modern *Ferrycarrig Hotel* (☎ 20999, fax 20982), which is 100m from the Irish National Heritage Park on the banks of the River Slaney, 4km to the north of Wexford, charges upwards of £40/80.

At *Clonard House* (☎ 43141), a 1780s farmhouse 3km west of town off the main Waterford road (N25), B&B costs £30/45.

Places to Eat
Restaurants Café-ish *Michael's Restaurant* (94 North Main St) serves omelettes, steak and fish costing £4 to £10. Readers have recommended *Ocean Bed Seafood Restaurant* on Westgate, where main courses start at £9.

Mirabeau (☎ 21777, 6 Anne St) focuses on continental cuisine with an Irish spin; main courses cost between £9 and £13 – the Barbary breast of duck is delicious.

For Chinese food, try *Lotus House* (☎ 24273, 70 South Main St) or, for more upmarket European and Chinese food, **Chan's Restaurant** (☎ *22356, 90 North Main St*). There's also **Emerald Gardens** (☎ *24856*) farther down South Main St.

Fast Food & Cafés Downstairs in the marvellous **Westgate Design** shop, on North Main St, a café serves breakfast (£3.95) until 4 pm.

Kelly's Deli (80 South Main St) serves sandwiches and lunches including some vegetarian choices. Similarly, **La Cuisine** *(80 North Main St)* offers soups and toasted sandwiches costing around £2.50. Other possible lunch stops include **Cappuccino**, on the corner of North Main and Rowe Sts, **Simon's Place** *(37 South Main St)* and **Paris Café** at the northern end of Selskar St. The **Cellar Bistro**, in the Wexford Arts Centre, Cornmarket, is another popular lunch venue.

North and South Main Sts cater for most tastes, with fish and chips on offer at the **Premier** *(104 South Main St)* or fast food at **Uncle Sam's** *(53 South Main St)*. At **Robertino's** *(19 North Main St)*, pizzas start at £3.90 and pasta costs upwards of £4.95. Also on North Main St is the **M&J Restaurant**, a cafeteria-style place with an extensive menu and a takeaway service. It closes at 6 pm Monday to Thursday, and 7.30 pm Friday and Saturday.

There's a good **supermarket** just up from Wren's Bar. You can put together a picnic at **Greenacres Food Hall** *(North Main St)* or sit down for a bite and a drink at **Playwrite Tearooms** at the back.

Entertainment

Pubs Even by Irish standards, Wexford has plenty of pubs, many of them strung along North and South Main Sts, where you'll find **Tim's Tavern**, **Commodore**, **Viking** and **Bohemian Girl**.

The trendiest pub in town is **The Sky and the Ground** *(South Main St)*, with old-style décor and a jukebox popular with young people.

On Cornmarket is the atmospheric old **Thomas Moore Tavern**. Music often features at **Wren's Bar** on the quay and **Tower**

Bar just up the street. For the 20s to 30s age group, the in pub is the **Centenary Stores** *(Charlotte St)*, just off North Main St, which features Irish music on Wednesday night. At the **Wavecrest Bar** *(Commercial Quay)* there is Irish music almost every night during the summer.

Theatre & Cinemas The **Theatre Royal** (☎ *22144, 27 High St*) stages drama and opera. **Wexford Arts Centre** (☎ *23764*), in the 18th-century Market House and Assembly Room on Cornmarket, caters for exhibitions, theatre, dance and music performances.

The three-screen **Savoy** cineplex is near the train station on Redmond Rd. Artier films are shown at the Arts Centre at 8 pm on Tuesday night.

Getting There & Away

The N25 leads south-east from the quays and Trinity St to Rosslare Harbour. For Duncannon or Hook Head, turn west either at The Crescent along Harpers Lane or from Paul Quay along King St.

Bus Bus Éireann (☎ *22522*) is based at the O'Hanrahan train station on Redmond Place at the northern end of town. Buses run from Wexford to Rosslare Harbour (£2.50, 20 minutes, six daily), Dublin (£7, two hours 30 minutes, six daily), Killarney (£15, five hours 30 minutes, two daily) and all stops en route. Twice-weekly services also run to Gorey via Courtown Harbour.

JJ Kavanagh (☎ *0503-43081*) operates a twice-daily service to Carlow via Enniscorthy from Redmond Place. Ardcavan Coach Company (☎ *22561*) operates daily services between Wexford and Dublin. Buses leave from outside Asple's Irish pub on The Crescent at 8 am. The one-way fare is £5.

Train O'Hanrahan Station (☎ *22522*) is at the northern end of town on Redmond Place. Wexford is on the Dublin (£10, two hours 30 minutes) to Rosslare Harbour (£3.50, 25 minutes) line and is serviced by three trains daily in each direction. There are also two trains daily to Wicklow (£8)

WEXFORD & WATERFORD

and frequent services to Enniscorthy (£4.50, two hours).

Getting Around

At the Bike Shop (☎ 22514), 9 Selskar St, and Hayes (☎ 22462), 108 South Main St, bikes cost £8/30 per day/week.

Parking discs (30p per hour) for street parking can be bought in most newsagents.

AROUND WEXFORD TOWN
Irish National Heritage Park

Four kilometres north-west of Wexford town, at Ferrycarrig on the Dublin to Rosslare N11 road, the Irish National Heritage Park (☎ 053-20733) is an outdoor theme park which attempts to condense the country's entire history on one site.

A visit takes in re-creations of a Mesolithic camp site, a Neolithic farmstead, a dolmen, a cist burial tomb, a stone circle, a rath or ring fort, a monastery, a *crannóg* or lake settlement, a Viking shipyard, a motte and bailey, a Norman castle, a round tower and a couple of other smaller displays. A replica Viking longship is anchored on the River Slaney outside the park.

The park opens 9.30 am to 6.30 pm daily, March to November, with last admissions at 5 pm. Admission costs £5/4.50 and includes an informative guided tour. A bus runs to the park from Wexford town; phone Westgate Minitours (☎ 24655) for details.

Johnstown Castle & Gardens

Seven kilometres south-west of Wexford town on the way to Murntown, the former home of the Fitzgerald and Esmonde families is a splendid 19th-century Gothic-style castellated house overlooking a small lake and surrounded by 20 hectares of thickly wooded gardens.

The castle and its outbuildings now house an agricultural research centre, the headquarters of the Irish Environmental Protection Agency and an agricultural **museum**, in which the main attraction is the collection of Irish country furniture. There is also a small Famine exhibition detailing life before, during and after the potato blight.

The castle itself isn't open to the public, but the gardens open 9 am to 5.30 pm daily, year round. The museum opens 9 am to 5 pm on weekdays, and 2 to 5 pm at the weekend, June to August; 9 am to 12.30 pm and 1.30 to 5 pm on weekdays, and 1.30 to 5 pm at the weekend, April, May and September to 2 November; and 9 am to 12.30 pm and 1.30 to 5 pm on weekdays, 3 November to March. Admission to the gardens costs £1.50/50p; admission to the museum costs £2.50/1.50.

Wexford Wildfowl Reserve

Five kilometres north-east of Wexford town are the North Slobs, a swathe of low-lying land reclaimed from the sea. In winter, the Slobs are home to half the world's population of the Greenland white-fronted goose, numbering some 10,000 birds. It's a great sight to stand on the sea wall and watch the V-shaped formations of geese flying into the darkness of the bay, where they pass the night on sandbanks and islands.

Winter is also a good time to spot the brent goose from Arctic Canada, and throughout the year you'll see mallard, pochard, godwit, mute and Bewick's swans, redshank, tern, coot, oystercatchers and many other species.

Wexford Wildfowl Reserve was set up to protect the birds' feeding grounds. Alongside the usual visitor centre there's an observation tower and assorted hides. It opens 9 am to 6 pm daily, mid-April to September; and 10 am to 5 pm daily, the rest of the year. Admission is free.

The reserve is on the Wexford to Dublin road; head north for 3.5km from Wexford until you see a signpost pointing to the right.

Yola Farmstead Folk Park

Nine kilometres south of Wexford town on the road to Rosslare Harbour is this pretty, interesting folk park (☎ 053-31177), a reconstructed village from the 19th century. There are thatched cottages, a working windmill (one of the few left in the country) and a tiny church, all intended to give visitors an impression of what life was like in

Forth & Bargy Is Yola to Me

Faint remnants of a dialect called Yola, sometimes called 'Forth and Bargy', still survive in south-eastern County Wexford. Yola stands for 'ye olde language' and is a mixture of old French, English, Irish, Welsh and Flemish. Examples of the language would be to *curk*, meaning to sit on your thighs, or to be *hachee* or bad-tempered. A *chi o' whate* means a small amount of straw, while a *stouk* is a truculent woman. There is a story told of a local Yola speaker who had never left the valley where she was born. In the late 1960s she was brought to the top of the valley so that she could take a peek at the world beyond. She took one look and turned to go home, muttering that she didn't like what she saw!

rural Ireland (although one can't help feeling that this is the sanitised version). There's the ubiquitous craft shop and a Heritage and Genealogy Centre where visitors can trace their roots. It opens 10 am to 6 pm daily, May to October; and 10 am to 4.30 pm on weekdays, March, April and November. Admission costs £3.50/2.50.

Curracloe Beach

Over 11km long, Curracloe is one of a string of magnificent beaches that line the coast north of Wexford town. Extensive dunes behind the beach provide some shelter, and you can pitch a tent if you're discreet. Curracloe Beach is 15km north-east of Wexford off the Dublin road.

The Raven

At this lovely nature reserve, near Curracloe, a long walk through forest brings you out on dunes where you may see Greenland white-fronted goose and various waders. From Wexford town, follow the signposts for Curracloe Beach and watch for signs for the Raven off to the right.

ROSSLARE STRAND
☎ 053

Rosslare Strand is about 8km north-west of Rosslare Harbour and 15km south-east of Wexford town. The long, golden beaches attract huge crowds in summer and there are also good walks north to Rosslare Point. The long, shallow bay is ideal for windsurfing. Boards, wetsuits and tuition are available from Kieran Lambert at the Rosslare Windsurfing Centre (☎ 32101).

Places to Stay

Camping Just south of the village, *Burrow Camping and Caravan Park* (☎ 32190) has excellent facilities, including a laundry, games room and tennis courts. It charges £8 to £14 per tent depending on the season, regardless of tent size or number of people. *Rosslare Holiday Park* (☎ 32291) has more basic facilities and charges £9 per tent (for two people).

B&Bs At *Decca House* (☎ 32410), 1km from Rosslare Strand, singles/doubles start at £20/28. The *Coral Gables Guesthouse* (☎ 31213), just outside Tagoat, has comfortable rooms costing £25/40. Breakfast is £5 extra.

Hotel With every sports and leisure facility in the book, *Kelly's Resort Hotel* (☎ 32114, fax 32222) is popular with families. B&B starts at £53/100 for singles/doubles.

Getting There & Away

Only the 11 am bus from Rosslare Harbour and the 11 pm from Wexford to Rosslare Harbour stop at Rosslare Strand. Trains on the mainline between Dublin, Wexford and Rosslare Harbour stop at Rosslare Strand.

ROSSLARE HARBOUR
☎ 053 • pop 1023

In the south-eastern corner of the country, Rosslare Harbour (Ros Láir) is 20km south-east of Wexford town and is a busy port with ferry connections to Wales and France. The harbour's surroundings are not particularly pretty or pedestrian-friendly and you

WEXFORD & WATERFORD

might prefer to head straight on to Wexford. If you do need to stay there is plenty of accommodation in what is really a large village.

Information
The tourist office (☎ 33622) in the ferry terminal building opens 10 am to 5.30 pm, June to September. The office (☎ 33232) by the main Wexford road in Kilrane, north of town, opens 11 am to around 2 pm daily, year round.

Places to Stay
Camping You might be able to pitch a tent for £4 per person at *Foley* (see B&Bs). The nearest official camp sites are 8km to the north in Rosslare Strand (see Rosslare Strand earlier in this chapter for details).

Hostels The An Óige *Rosslare Harbour Hostel* (☎ 33399, Goulding St) is up the hill from the ferry terminal; take the flight of steps on the left as you leave the harbour and cut down beside Hotel Rosslare. It opens early or late for ferry arrivals and departures. Beds in 19-bed dorms cost £7.50 (£6.50 in low season). Sleeping bags and sheets can be hired for £1.50 per night.

B&Bs The cheapest place to stay is the basic *Foley* (☎ 33522, 3 St Martin's Rd), where beds cost £9. Otherwise, one of the cheapest B&Bs is the welcoming *Glenville* (☎ 33142), on the N25 Wexford road, where singles/doubles cost £17/32. At *Carragh Lodge* (☎ 33492) in quieter Station Rd, rooms cost £22.50/34. Overlooking the harbour, the big *Ailsa Lodge* (☎ 33230) charges £27/40. *St Anthony's* (☎ 33599, St Martin's Rd) is a comfortable and laid-back B&B that costs £20/34. If these are full there are lots of other B&Bs overlooking the harbour and about 1km farther inland along the Wexford road in Kilrane.

Hotels There are several smart hotels on St Martin's Rd overlooking the ferry port. The bright-pink *Hotel Rosslare* (☎ 33110) sits on top of the cliff and offers plenty of facilities costing £40/70 in singles/doubles; ask

about special deals for longer stays. The nearby *Tuskar House Hotel* (☎ 33363) charges £42/74 in high season. Plushest of all is the *Great Southern Hotel* (☎ 33233), which has an indoor pool and costs £55 (low season) to £70 (high season) per room. It also provides a good weekend rate of £82 to £110, depending on the time of year.

Places to Eat
One burger bar aside, there are few places to eat except in the hotels. *Hotel Rosslare* serves excellent lunches starting at £7.50. Its attractive *Portholes Bar* also serves hefty portions of bar food; main courses start at around £5.

Getting There & Away
Bus Bus Éireann runs services to Wexford (£2.50, 20 minutes, six daily) and Dublin (£9, three hours, six daily), and a single daily service to Galway via Kilkenny in July and August (£16, six hours 30 minutes). Buses leave from Rosslare Europort station.

Ardcavan Coach Company (☎ 22561) operates one service daily between Rosslare Harbour (beside the church) and Dublin via Wexford, Enniscorthy, Ferns, Gorey and Arklow. It leaves Rosslare at 7.30 am, returning at 9 pm.

Train Trains (☎ 33114) depart from Rosslare Europort station, at the ferry terminal, for Wexford (£3.50, three daily), Dublin (£10.50, three hours, three daily), Waterford (£6, one hour 20 minutes, two daily except Sunday) and Limerick (£12, three hours 30 minutes, one daily except Sunday).

Car Rental Budget (☎ 33318), Hertz (☎ 23511) and Murrays (☎ 33634) share a desk in the ferry terminal.

Boat Two ferry companies operate services to and from Rosslare Harbour and there's a convenient train and bus station by the ferry terminal.

Stena Line (☎ 33115) has day and night crossings to Fishguard in Wales taking three hours 30 minutes, while Irish Ferries

(☎ 33158) has two daily sailings to Pembroke in Wales, taking four hours 30 minutes. They also operate the Lynx catamaran service, which takes two hours 30 minutes but is more expensive than the ferry. Irish Ferries also has one or two sailings a week to Cherbourg, and one or two to Roscoff in France from late May to mid-September. The journeys take between 19 and 24 hours.

For more information see Sea in the Getting There & Away chapter.

SOUTH OF ROSSLARE HARBOUR

Nine kilometres south of Rosslare Harbour is **Carnsore Point**, where Ireland's first nuclear power station was to be built, had cost not killed it off. Carnsore Point was noted as the country's south-easternmost point on the map drawn by Ptolemy in the 2nd century. Offshore to the east is Tuskar Rock Lighthouse.

Carne has a fine beach, and *Carne Beach Caravan and Camping Park* (☎ 053-31131) is near Carnsore Point. There's excellent pub food and seafood in the *Lobster Pot* (☎ 053-31110) bar and restaurant in Carne. A reader rated the mussels but warned that you need to grab a seat by 6.30 pm.

Turning west brings you to **Tacumshin**, where in 1840 Nicholas Moran built the Tacumshin Windmill, one of Ireland's few thatched windmills. The key can be picked up from the shop where you park but you'll probably be charged to visit the windmill.

To the east of the windmill is **Lady's Island**, site of an early Augustinian priory and still a centre of devotion. Both Tacumshin and Lady's Island have small brackish **lakes** which are home to migrating and breeding birds. Lady's Island is best from autumn to spring, when you may see brent goose, shelduck, redshank, godwit, mute swans, teal and various terns.

Bridgetown, 12km south-west of Wexford town off the road to lovely Kilmore Quay, was the first part of Ireland to be colonised by the Anglo-Normans. To the west, en route to Hook Head, the Irish chapter of the Hell's Angels meet at **Wellington Bridge** over the June bank-holiday weekend! **Hook Head** is well worth a detour if

you are en route to Waterford and you can save yourself a circuitous trip north by taking a ferry from Ballyhack across to Passage East in Waterford (for details see Passage East in the Waterford section later in this chapter). There's no public transport to this area.

KILMORE QUAY
☎ 053 • pop 406

A small fishing village on the eastern side of Ballyteige Bay, peaceful Kilmore Quay is noted for its lobsters and deep-sea fishing. The **Seafood Festival** in the second week of July involves all types of seafood tastings, music and dancing.

Lining the attractive main street up from the harbour are a fair number of whitewashed thatched cottages. The harbour is the jumping-off point for the Saltee Islands, clearly visible out to sea. In the harbour the Guillemot Lightship houses a small **maritime museum**, open during the summer. To the north-west quite a good **sandy beach** stretches towards Cullenstown.

Places to Stay & Eat
Killturk Hostel (☎ 29883), 2km out of Kilmore Quay in Grange, along the R739, is a good place to stay. Dorm beds cost £7.50, private rooms cost £9, and there is a low-priced café.

At *Coral House* (☎ 29640), in Grange, singles/doubles start at £21/32.

Dining possibilities include *Wooden House Restaurant and Bar*, *Silver Fox Restaurant* and *Hotel Saltees* (☎ 29601). The last mentioned offers a good-value tourist menu and B&B costing £32/50.

Getting There & Away
Public transport to Kilmore Quay is very limited. On Wednesday and Saturday only there are two Bus Éireann services daily from Wexford town. There's also a private bus every Friday from Kilmore Quay to Wexford. For details, ask at the post office.

SALTEE ISLANDS
The Saltee Islands are 4km offshore from Kilmore Quay and feature some of the

oldest rocks in Europe, dating back 2000 million years or more. Findings also suggest that the islands were inhabited by the pre-Celts as long ago as 3500 to 2000 BC.

In more recent times the haunt of privateers and smugglers, the Saltees now constitute one of Europe's most important bird sanctuaries, home to over 375 recorded species, principally gannet, guillemot, cormorant, kittiwake, puffin and the Manx shearwater. The best time to visit is the spring and early-summer nesting season; once the chicks can fly, the birds leave. By early August it's eerily quiet.

The Saltees – nicknamed the 'graveyard of a thousand ships' – were touched by the 1798 Rising: it was here that two of the Wexford rebel leaders, Bagenal Harvey and Dr John Colclough, were found hiding before they were both brought to Wexford, hanged and beheaded. The Saltees were bought in 1943 by Michael Neale, who then crowned himself Prince Michael, the 'First Prince of the Saltees'. He even erected a throne and obelisk in his own honour on the Great Saltee.

To book a crossing to the Saltees try local boatmen such as Declan Bates (☎ 053-29684) or Tom O'Brien (☎ 053-29727). Boats leave from the harbour at Kilmore Quay most days in summer at 11 am and return at about 3 or 4 pm, with more crossings according to numbers. Docking on the islands depends on the direction of the winds, and the operators will know the night before whether a landing is possible or not. It's a 30-minute crossing and the return fare is £12. For more on the islands read *The Saltees, Islands of Birds and Legends* by Richard Roche & Oscar Merne (O'Brien Press).

HOOK PENINSULA
☎ 051

The south-west of the county is dominated by the long, tapering finger of the Hook Peninsula, terminating at Hook Head. Cromwell's statement that Waterford town would fall 'by Hook or by Crooke' referred to the two possible landing points from which to take the area: here or at Crooke in

County Waterford. In good weather, it's a fine journey out to the lighthouse at the tip of the head and back along the western side to Duncannon.

On the way out to Hook, **Tintern Abbey** is a 12th-century Cistercian abbey in a lovely rural setting near the village of Saltmills. It was founded by William Marshall, earl of Pembroke, after he nearly perished at sea. At the time of writing it was still closed for renovation. Continuing south towards the head, **Fethard-on-Sea** is the largest village in the area.

Just south of Fethard, near Bannow Bay, is **Baginbun Head**. This is where the Anglo-Normans made their first landings in Ireland in 1169. Joining forces with the far larger army of Dermot MacMurrough, they captured Wexford in the same year. Ramparts were built to fortify the headland at Baginbun until more Normans arrived in 1170 under Raymond le Gros. Shortly after he landed, 3000 Irish-Norse soldiers set out from Waterford city and attacked Baginbun, outnumbering the defenders seven to one.

Le Gros stampeded a herd of cattle onto them and then taught them a lesson in organised warfare. Seventy of Waterford's citizens and soldiers were captured, had their legs broken and were thrown over the cliffs to their death. So it was to be that:

At the creek of Baginbun,
Ireland was lost and won.

After the Norman leader Strongbow had landed at Passage East with another 1200 men, the Anglo-Normans gathered their forces and marched on to Waterford city, marking the start of more than 800 years of English involvement in Ireland.

Today a small road leads down to a rather battered memorial overlooking Baginbun Beach. If you look carefully at the headland on the right, you can just make out the overgrown earthen ramparts built by the Normans when they first arrived. The stone **Martello tower** dates back to the early 1800s.

The journey out to **Hook Head** is lovely, the land extremely flat with few houses interrupting the open space. About 2km from the head, turning left at a T-junction brings you down to the village of **Slade**, where a ruined castle dominates the harbour.

Farther south, Hook Head is crowned by Europe's, and possibly the world's, oldest **lighthouse**. It's said that monks lit a beacon on the head from the 5th century and that the first Viking invaders were so happy to have a guiding light that they left the monks alone. In the 12th century a more solid beacon was erected by Raymond le Gros; 800 years later it's largely the same structure you see today.

There are fine **walks** both sides of the head, a haunting and beautiful place in the evening. Be careful of the numerous blowholes on the western side of the peninsula. The rocks around the lighthouse are Carboniferous limestone, rich in fossil remains. If you search carefully, you may find 350-million-year-old shells and tiny disc-like pieces of crinoids, a type of starfish. Hook Head is also a good vantage point for **birdwatching**; over 200 species have been recorded passing through.

The village of **Duncannon** is a small holiday resort with a lovely sandy beach and a good view over Waterford Harbour. To the west is **Duncannon Fort**, one of many structures built on this site since pre-Norman times. Admission costs £1.50/50p.

Four kilometres to the north of Duncannon is **Ballyhack**, from where a ferry sails year round to Passage East in County Waterford (see the Passage East section later in this chapter). There's also a 15th-century **Knights Templar castle** overlooking the estuary. It opens 10 am to 6 pm daily, July and August; and noon to 6 pm Wednesday to Sunday, September and April to June. Admission costs £1/50p.

Dunbrody Abbey is a beautiful ruin on the western side of Hook Head, near the village of Campile and about 9km north of Duncannon. It was built around 1170 by Cistercian monks from Buildwas in Shropshire, England. Most of the structure survives to make a fine sight among the fields. Nearby are the ruins of **Dunbrody Castle**, with a craft shop and small museum. The site opens 10 am to 7 pm daily, July and August; and 10 am to 6 pm daily, April to June and in September. Admission costs £2/1.50, with an additional charge to visit the maze.

Scuba Diving

Hook Head is popular with divers. The best spots are out from the inlet under the lighthouse or from the rocks at the southwestern corner of the head. The underwater scenery is pleasant, with lots of caves, crevasses and gullies. It's a maximum of 15m deep. If it's too rough, try Churchtown, about 1km back from the point just before the road goes inland by the ruined church. Follow the path west to some gullies and coves. Otherwise, try the rocks south of Slade Harbour, a popular area. Tanks can be filled at Hotel Naomh Seosamh in Fethard, and in summer local dive groups often meet here.

The Hook Sub-Aqua Club (☎ 388302) in Slade provides dive-site information and a full range of facilities, including a compressor and storage. Wexford Diving Centre and Dive Charters (☎ 053-39373), at Riverstown Farm, Murrintown, has similar facilities and offers diving charters.

Places to Stay

Most of the accommodation is in Fethard-on-Sea, but there are a few places to stay on the western side of the peninsula around Duncannon and Ballyhack.

Camping At the northern end of Fethard-on-Sea is *Fethard Camping and Caravan Park* (☎ 397123), while the *Ocean Island Caravan Park* (☎ 397148) is about 1km farther north. At both a tent for two costs around £9. Your best bet is to stock up and head 12km south out to Hook Head, where you can camp along the shore. There's a small petrol station and shop about 5km from the headland which is useful for replenishing supplies.

Hostels The only hostel in the region is the An Óige *Arthurstown Hostel* (☎ 389411), 1km south of Ballyhack on the western side of the peninsula. Dorm beds cost £7.

euro currency converter IR£1 = €1.27

B&Bs In Fethard *Hotel Naomh Seosamh* (☎ 397129), on the main street, is popular and good fun at the weekend; B&B starts at £20 per person. The *Bore-a-Trae House* (☎ 397102), 3km south-west of Fethard on the way to Templetown Head, is a good B&B where singles/doubles cost £21/34. Near the Arthurstown Hostel, *Marsh Mere Lodge* (☎ 389186) charges £25/40.

Places to Eat

Fethard's hotels and pubs are the peninsula's principal eating spots, but nowhere particularly stands out. On the western side of the peninsula, the *Neptune Bar and Seafood Restaurant* (☎ 389284) in Ballyhack is a terrific place serving simple but delicious seafood. A la carte dinners cost around £18 but you can bring your own bottles (£3 corkage charge).

At the *Cellar Restaurant* (☎ 565771, *Hopetown House*), in Foulksmills, dinner starts at £21.95. Early-bird midweek specials, served until 8 pm, cost £16.95.

Moorings Seafood Bar and Restaurant (☎ 389242), in Duncannon, serves very good seafood, while *Templar's Inn*, in Templetown, also specialises in seafood.

Shopping

The peninsula is renowned for its craft shops and local craft workers, who specialise in such diverse activities as rugmaking, pottery, woodturning and embroidery. Kelly Krafts (☎ 397240) in Fethard is one of the better shops.

Getting There & Away

Particularly if you're travelling by bike, it's well worth taking the 10-minute crossing between County Wexford and County Waterford on the Ballyhack to Passage East ferry. For details on fares and times see Passage East in the County Waterford section later in this chapter. Bus services are virtually nonexistent; on Monday and Thursday, Bus Éireann buses running from Wexford to Waterford will drop you in Fethard. They leave Wexford town at 2.50 pm; return services leave Fethard at 11.26 am. At least one bus daily runs from New Ross to Duncannon.

NEW ROSS
☎ 051 • pop 5012

New Ross (Rhos Mhic Triúin), 34km west of Wexford town, is a sizeable settlement astride the River Barrow. It advertises itself as the 'Norman gateway to the Barrow Valley', but you'd have to look fairly hard to find any trace of its Norman past. It's not an especially pretty town, with large oil-storage tanks and old warehouses looming over the riverbanks, but the eastern bank is better than the western one, with some steep, narrow streets and St Mary's Church.

New Ross was the scene of fierce fighting during the 1798 Rising when a group of rebels under Bagenal Harvey and John Kelly tried to take the town. They were repelled by the defending garrison, leaving 3000 people dead and much of the town in ruins.

Information

A tourist office (☎ 421857) operates from the refurbished grain-store building at 22 The Quay. It opens 9 am to 1 pm and 2 to 6 pm Monday to Saturday, and 11 am to 4 pm on Sunday, June to August; and 9 am to 1 pm and 2 to 6 pm on weekdays, May and September.

St Mary's Church

A roofless ruin on Church Lane, St Mary's Church was founded by Isabella of Leinster and her husband, William, in the 13th century. Inside is a rough slab with some barely decipherable words: 'Isabel... Laegn', which translates roughly as 'Isabel of Leinster'. She died around 1220 and was buried in England so this is probably a memorial to her. The church key is available from the caretaker across the road.

SS Dunbrody Famine Ship

On the river just outside town is a full-scale reconstruction of SS *Dunbrody* (☎ 425239), built in 1845 and used to ferry emigrants escaping the ravages of the Famine to the USA. Partially funded by the JFK Trust, the project has suffered delays and, at the time of writing, was still under construction, but should be completed by the end of 1999, when it will make its maiden voyage to Boston before returning permanently to New Ross.

A short film details the history of the original ship as well as the construction of the new one. When the ship is completed, it will include an interactive visitor centre on board and a database of Irish emigration to America from 1820 to 1920, which will give the lie to the commonly held assumption that these ships were death traps for passengers (hence the term 'coffin ship'): 97% of all those who embarked on the voyage to the USA made it across safely. As the schedule for the ship's construction and eventual sailing is less than secure, call ahead before visiting.

Cruises

The Galley Cruising Restaurant (☎ 421723) operates a lunchtime cruise which sails at 12.30 pm May to October and costs £16. A two-hour cruise including afternoon tea leaves at 3 pm from June to August and costs £7.50. Dinner cruises from May to September start at £20 and depart at 5.30 or 7 pm.

Places to Stay & Eat

The IHH *MacMurrough Farm Hostel* (☎ 421383) is a well-thought-of place sleeping 17, 3km north-east of town. A bed costs £7. At the top end of the scale, *Brandon House Hotel* (☎ 421703, fax 421567) provides comfort and elegance for £60/90 for singles/doubles.

Katie Pat's (☎ 22404), on the quay, is good for cheap sandwiches and lunches. It also has a restaurant upstairs where dinner is served from 5 to 9 pm; main courses cost £6 to £12. Across the road from Katie Pat's is *John V's* pub, which does a good bar lunch and has a seafood restaurant upstairs. *The Sweeney* (1 Mary St), just off the quay, offers an all-day Irish breakfast (£5.45) and a grilled sirloin steak (£6.45) as well as assorted salads and sandwiches.

Getting There & Away

Bus Éireann (☎ 053-22522) runs a twice-daily service to Dublin. It departs from outside Ryan's on the quay. There are also at least three daily services to Wexford and Rosslare Harbour, and to Waterford. At least one bus daily goes to Duncannon on the Hook Peninsula.

AROUND NEW ROSS

Five kilometres south of New Ross, **Dunganstown** was the birthplace of Patrick Kennedy, grandfather of John F Kennedy. Patrick left Ireland for the USA in 1858 and JFK visited the town during his presidency. The original Kennedy house no longer exists, but there's a small cottage belonging to the Ryan family, who are direct descendants, and a small plaque marks the spot. Nearby, **Kennedy Homestead** (☎ 051-388264) is a visitor centre celebrating five generations of the Irish-American dynasty. Admission costs £2.50/1.

A couple of kilometres to the south, the **John F Kennedy Park and Arboretum** (☎ 051-388171) covers 252 hectares of woodlands and gardens with more than 4500 species of trees and shrubs. The park was opened in 1968 in memory of the late US president, funded by some prominent Irish-Americans. It opens 10 am to 5 pm daily, October to March; 10 am to 6.30 pm daily, April and September; and 10 am to 8 pm, May to August. Admission costs £2/1.

Slieve Coillte hill, opposite the park entrance, offers a splendid view of the surrounding countryside and the Saltee Islands.

ENNISCORTHY

☎ 054 • pop 3788

Enniscorthy (Inis Coirthaidh) is an attractive hilly little town on the banks of the River Slaney in the heart of County Wexford, 20km north-west of Wexford town. It was the site of some of the fiercest fighting of the 1798 Rising.

Information

The tourist office (☎ 34699) in the town centre opens 10 am to 6 pm Monday to Saturday, mid-June to August. The main post office is at the bottom of Castle Hill on Abbey Square.

WEXFORD & WATERFORD

A Fierce Wallop

The rise of Enniscorthy is in large part due to the efforts of Sir Henry Wallop, who bought the castle in 1580 with a view to exploiting the agricultural potential of the land around it. Consequently, labourers were hired from all over the county to farm the land, and the modern town was born. However, Sir Henry was an exacting and dictatorial landlord. His tendency to upbraid his workers with a fierce beating if they displeased him hardly endeared him to the local populace; it also introduced a new verb to the English language, a synonym for hitting someone hard: to wallop.

Wallop's descendants were later made the earls of Portsmouth, and they continue to collect ground rents on the land around the castle up to the present day; indeed, the local garda station paid ground rents until 1996, when they moved location. Luckily for Wallop's descendants, they seem not to have inherited his bad temper – they would have had difficulty dealing with their police tenants as their ancestor had done with his!

A good time to visit is late June or early July, when Enniscorthy holds its Strawberry Fair, a harvest festival with longer pub opening hours, strawberries and cream, and the crowning of a 'Strawberry Queen'. For exact dates and details phone ☎ 21688.

Enniscorthy Castle & Wexford County Museum

A fine stout building with drum towers at the corners, Enniscorthy's impressive Norman castle dates back to 1205 and was a private residence until 1951. Queen Elizabeth I rewarded the poet Edmund Spenser for the many flattering things he said about her in his epic *The Faerie Queene* by awarding him the lease on the castle, but he sold it on to a local landlord, Edward Sinnott, whose grandson then sold it on to Sir Henry Wallop in 1580.

It was the site of a fierce battle in 1649, and during the 1798 Rising the rebels took control of the town and used the castle as a prison. Today it houses Wexford County Museum (☎ 35926), a mish-mash of bits and pieces which is sorely in need of an overhaul but which includes artefacts from the 1798 Rising and the 1916 Easter Rising. The castle and museum open 10 am to 1 pm and 2 to 6 pm Monday to Saturday, and 2 to 5.30 pm on Sunday, June to September; 2 to 5.30 pm daily, October, November and February to May; and 2 to

5.30 pm on Sunday, December and January. Admission costs £3/2.

National 1798 Visitor Centre

The castle was overtaken as the town's most important attraction in 1998 by the opening of this interpretive centre commemorating the bicentennial of Wexford's abortive uprising against British rule in Ireland. Little is left to the imagination, with rich interactive displays and audiovisuals highlighting the circumstances and events surrounding the rebellion, as well as the fate of the rebels, most of whom were butchered with impunity by Crown forces. There's a clever and fascinating audiovisual dramatisation of a debate between the pro-rebellion radical Thomas Paine and the loyalist Anglo-Irish conservative Edmund Burke. It is an excellent museum – it has been heralded as Ireland's best – and well worth the admission cost of £4/2.50. It opens 9.30 am to 6 pm Monday to Saturday, and 11 am to 6 pm on Sunday, year round.

Places to Stay

Hostels The only hostel in town is *Platform 1* (☎ 37766, *Railway Square*), where dorm beds start at £8 in low season, rising to £12 between June and September.

B&Bs At *Murphy's* (☎ 33522, *9 Main St*), above a bar and shop, singles/doubles start at £17/30. Also central is *Old Bridge House* (☎ 34222, Slaney Place). *Murphy Flood's Hotel* (☎/fax 33413, Main St) is conveniently close to Market Square; B&B starts at £32/50.

Woodville House (☎ 47810), with comfortable rooms starting at £21/32, is 8km to the south on the minor Ballyhogue road, along the western side of the River Slaney. *Oakville Lodge* (☎ 88626) and its fine gardens overlook the Slaney Valley; B&B starts at £22/34. The house is 9km from Ballycarney, signposted off the N80 road north to Bunclody. A lovely mansion dating from 1840, *Ballinkeele House* (☎ 38105) lies 10km to the south-east of Enniscorthy in Ballymurn. The four elegant rooms cost £48/80 but are let between March and October only.

Hotels Just over Enniscorthy Bridge from the town centre, *Treacy's* (☎ 37798, fax 37733) is a new hotel with comfortable, elegant singles/doubles starting at £40/70.

Places to Eat

Concorde, at the top of Rafter St, serves set lunches costing £4.25. At *Waffle's Bistro* on Castle Hill, lunch specials cost £6.95. *Rackard's* on Rafter St is also extremely popular at lunchtime.

At the monument end of Rafter St try *Paris Café* or *The Baked Potato* for tea and cakes.

China China dishes up Chinese meals at the top of Rafter St, while *Malocca's* on Slaney St offers rather overpriced pizzas as well as full Irish breakfasts (£3.95). The restaurant at *Murphy Flood's Hotel* serves early-evening bar specials costing £6.50.

Antique Tavern, at the bottom of Slaney St, offers good and affordable lunches (but not to 'footpads, thimblemen or three-card tricksters'), as does the *Tavern* in Templeshannon, on the eastern bank of the river, which hosts live music on Sunday night.

Shopping

If you fancy buying a clay plant pot, there are numerous potteries around town, including the Hillview and Carley's Bridge

The Battle of Vinegar Hill

A memorial to Father John Murphy and the band of rebels who stormed Enniscorthy and captured the castle in May 1798 dominates the Market Square. One faction marched under the banner MWS (Murder Without Sin). The last major battle of the rising took place on Vinegar Hill, to the east of town, where the rebels had set up their headquarters. On 9 June, a force of 20,000 troops led by Generals Lake and Johnson almost completely surrounded the rebels, who held out against huge odds for 30 days before being defeated. The ruined windmill on the hill was once the rebel command post.

The road to Vinegar Hill is signposted from the train station. It's a half-hour walk, and you'll be rewarded by panoramic views of Enniscorthy.

potteries (the latter dating back to 1694), both on the road to New Ross; Badger's Hill Pottery, farther along the same road; and Kiltrea Bridge Pottery, north-west of the town centre.

Getting There & Away

Bus Bus Éireann buses stop on the eastern bank of the river outside the Bus Stop Shop. There are six daily buses (five on Sunday) to Dublin, as well as to Rosslare Harbour (£5, one hour) and Wexford town (£3, one hour).

Train Enniscorthy is on the Dublin to Rosslare Harbour line; three trains run daily in each direction. The train station (☎ 33488) is on the eastern bank of the river.

FERNS

☎ 054 • pop 915

Ferns is 17km south-west of Gorey. Most traffic whizzes south for Wexford and Rosslare Harbour, but this sleepy little village was once the administrative capital of Leinster and an important diocese for several hundred years. It was the base of the Mac-Murrough kings of Leinster, in particular Dermot MacMurrough, who brought the Normans to Ireland and died here in 1171 (see The Norman Conquest in the History section of the Facts about Ireland chapter).

Ferns Castle

Dating back to around 1220, the remains of this castle at the north-western end of the village are thought to stand on the site of Dermot MacMurrough's old fortress. A couple of walls and part of the moat survive, with good views available from the top of the one complete tower. To the left of the door at the top is a murder hole through which oil or arrows could be dropped onto attackers below. Parliamentarians under Sir Charles Coote destroyed the castle and put most of the local population to death in 1649. The castle is open year round and admission is free.

Other Things to See

Other antiquities include fragments of the 13th-century **Cathedral of St Aidan** (now part of the modern Church of Ireland cathedral), which has a graveyard and the remains of a high cross used to mark the grave of Dermot MacMurrough. Father Redmond, who is buried in the graveyard, is said to have saved the life of a young French student, one Napoleon Bonaparte. Also in the grounds are the remains of a 6th-century abbey.

Outside the graveyard is **St Moling's Well**. Look also for the remains of an **Augustinian monastery**, founded by Dermot MacMurrough in the 1150s.

Places to Stay & Eat

The friendly *Clone House* (☎ 66113) is a 350-year-old farmhouse 3km south-west of Ferns on the Enniscorthy road. It has five bedrooms, four with private bathroom, starting at £30/50 for singles/doubles (the smaller room costs £20).

The *Courtyard* (☎ 66531), at the southern end of Main St, is a bar with its own restaurant (Dandy Pat's). It's pretty fancy: main courses cost around £10.

Getting There & Away

Bus Éireann buses on the main Dublin to Wexford route stop in Ferns; there are six buses daily in both directions. Contact Wexford bus station (☎ 053-22522) for details.

GOREY

☎ 055 • pop 2150

Gorey is a small, grim, traffic bottleneck of a town 20km south of Arklow on the main Dublin to Wexford road, below the foothills of the Wicklow Mountains.

The tourist office (☎ 21248), on Lower Main St, opens 9 am to 5 pm Monday to Saturday, year round.

During the 1798 Rising the town was attacked by rebels trying to reach the coast road to Dublin. They camped on Gorey Hill just south-west of the town and there's a memorial to their efforts at one end of Main St. The Church of Ireland parish **church** has some fine stained glass by Michael Healy, created around 1904. There's a good ramble out to **Tara Hill**, which is 7km north-east of town.

Places to Stay & Eat

Gorey isn't a great place to stay, but one reason to do so is to spend a night at *Marlfield House* (☎ 21124, fax 21572), 2km east of town, off the Courtown road in a beautifully wooded setting. A firm favourite of such Irish luminaries as the retired Gay Byrne (the 'uncrowned king' of Irish broadcasting) and former Taoiseach (Prime Minister) Charles Haughey, it charges kingly rates for a kingly service: a standard double room costs £155 in the low season.

The Country Kitchen, opposite the tourist office on Lower Main St, is a bit ramshackle, but it serves lovely salads and filling sandwiches costing less than £4.

COURTOWN

☎ 055 • pop 364

Seven kilometres south-east of Gorey along the L31 is the small seaside resort of Courtown, at the mouth of the River Ounavarra. It boasts Ireland's lowest rainfall. The beach to the north of the village is popular with Dublin holidaymakers and has the usual amusement arcades, takeaways and seaside caravan parks and guesthouses. Out of high season, though, it is a ghost town. The Bayview Hotel dominates the beachfront (which isn't much to look at anyway). In summer, visitors can dance the night away at the Beacon, a large, ugly disco on the edge of town.

Places to Stay

Camping Just south of Courtown, *Parklands Holiday Park* (☎ 25202) has only 10 tent pitches and charges £12/14 for a family tent or £6.50/7.50 for a hiker or cyclist in low/high season. Otherwise you could find a quiet spot among the dunes and pitch your tent for free.

Hostels IHO *Anchorage Hostel* (☎ 25335) is a small place some 5km south of Courtown at Poulshone. Dorm beds cost £7, doubles £16.

B&Bs At *Riverchapel House* (☎ 25120), 1km inland from the harbour, doubles start at £30. At *Seamount House* (☎ 25128), in the village, singles/doubles start at £19/30.

Hotels The best address in town is the *Bayview Hotel* (☎ 25307, fax 25576), right on the harbour. Rooms start at £25 per person without breakfast.

Places to Eat

Good restaurants include *Bosun's Chair* (☎ 25198), in Ardmine, 2km south of Courtown along the coast, and *Cowhouse Bistro* (☎ 25219), at Tomsilla Farm, outside town on the Gorey road, where a set five-course dinner costs £18.

MT LEINSTER

Bunclody, on the border with County Carlow 16km north-west of Ferns, is a good base from which to climb Mt Leinster, at 796m the highest mountain in the Blackstairs. If you want to drive to the top, take the Borris road out of Ferns for 8km, turn right at the sign for the South Leinster Scenic Drive, and continue to the radio

mast at the top. The last few kilometres are on narrow, exposed roads with steep falloffs, so drive slowly and watch out for sheep. Mt Leinster provides some of Ireland's best **hang-gliding**.

At *Bunclody Holiday Hostel* (☎ 054-76076), in the old schoolhouse on the Ryland Road in Bunclody, dorm beds cost £6. It opens from 15 March to September.

WEXFORD COASTAL WALK

The Wexford Coastal Walk (Slí Charman) follows the county's coastline for 221km from Ballyhack to Kilmichael Point. See Walking in the Activities chapter for more details.

County Waterford

Wedged into Ireland's south-eastern corner, County Waterford combines the low farmland and sandy coastlines typical of County Wexford with the more rugged landscape common in County Cork.

WATERFORD

☎ 051 • pop 42,540

Like Kilkenny, Waterford (Port Láirge) feels almost medieval, with narrow alleyways leading off many of the larger streets. Reginald's Tower marks the city's Viking heart and the surrounding area is particularly attractive. Georgian times left a legacy of fine houses and commercial buildings, particularly around The Mall, George's St and O'Connell St.

But Waterford is first and foremost a commercial city and port. The River Suir's estuary is deep enough to allow large modern ships right up to the city's quays and the port is still one of Ireland's busiest. Sadly, this means the northern bank of the river is marred by industrial development. The Quays Committee is fighting a valiant battle to brighten up the southern side, at present little more than a parking lot with bus stops (for private buses). Bus Éireann buses may eventually be allowed to drop off and pick up passengers here instead of across the river.

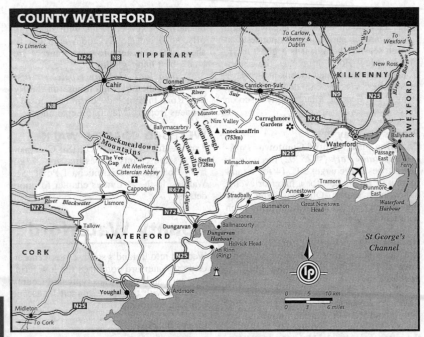

COUNTY WATERFORD

The hand-blown Waterford crystal made here is one of Ireland's most famous exports.

History

In the 8th century Vikings settled at a riverside site called Port Láirge which they renamed Vadrafjord. Recent excavations suggest the city was founded in 914 and quickly became a booming trading post. In their efforts to consolidate their presence, the Vikings adopted a ferocity in dealing with the natives which made them the most powerful – and feared – settlement in the country. All the local tribes paid them a tribute, known in Irish as the Airgead Sróine (Nose Money): if you didn't pay it, they cut your nose off!

Waterford's strategic importance ensured that its fortunes were closely linked to those of the island as a whole. In 1170 an Irish-Viking army was defeated in battle by the newly arrived Anglo-Normans: 70 prominent citizens were thrown to their deaths off Baginbun Head. Later that year the city was besieged by Strongbow, who overcame a desperate defence.

In 1210 King John extended the original Viking city walls and Waterford became Ireland's most powerful city and an important trading centre. In the 15th century it resisted the forces of two pretenders to the English Crown, Lambert Simnel and Perkin Warbeck, thus earning the motto *Urbs intacta manet Waterfordia* (Waterford city remains unconquered).

The town defied Cromwell in 1649 but in 1650 his forces returned and the city finally surrendered. Although it escaped the customary slaughter, much damage was done and the population declined: Catholics were either exiled to the west or shipped as slaves to the Caribbean.

Orientation

Waterford lies on the tidal reach of the River Suir, 16km from the coast. The main shopping street runs directly south from the River Suir, beginning as Barronstrand St and changing names as it runs south to become Broad St, Michael St and John St before intersecting with Parnell St. This runs north-east back up to the river, becoming The Mall on the way. Most of the sights and shopping areas lie within this triangle.

Reginald's Tower at the northern end of The Mall and the Clocktower at the northern end of Barronstrand St make good landmarks.

Information

The tourist office (☎ 875788) is in The Granary on Merchants Quay. It opens 9 am to 6 pm daily, June to August; 9 am to 5 pm Monday to Saturday, April, May, September and October; and 9 am to 5 pm on weekdays, the rest of the year.

In Parnell Court, off Parnell St, you can send and receive email messages at Voyager Internet Café (☎ 843843) from 11 am to 11 pm daily. At the time of writing, this was the only Internet café in the region.

USIT Travel (☎ 872601) is at 36-37 George's St.

The excellent Book Centre on Barronstrand St has three floors and sells books (including some foreign papers and magazines) and records; there's also a café. Gladstone's on Gladstone St sells second-hand paperbacks.

Duds 'n' Suds, 6 Parnell St, is a laundrette with a rudimentary café. It opens 7.30 am to 9 pm daily.

City Walls

Waterford's city walls were originally built by the Vikings around 1000, and extended by King John two centuries later. After Derry's, these are Ireland's best-surviving city walls.

Near the Theatre Royal in the Palace Garden some remnants stretch out near the houses in Spring Gardens Alley. Several towers also remain, including the Half Moon Tower on Patrick St, the Watch Tower near Railway Square, the French and Double Towers on Castle St and Reginald's Tower on The Mall.

Reginald's Tower

The most interesting relic of the walls is Reginald's Tower (☎ 873501) at the northern end of the Mall, built by the Normans in the 12th century on the site of a Viking wooden tower. With walls 3 to 4m thick, it was the city's key fortification.

Over the years the tower has served as a mint, an arsenal and a prison. Many of Waterford's royal visitors stayed in this 'safe house', including Richard II, Henry II and James II, who took a last look at Ireland from the tower before departing to exile in France.

The tower museum has several exhibits, including artefacts connected to one of Waterford's most famous sons, Thomas Francis Meagher (1823–67). Meagher was a Young Ireland leader captured for his part in the 1848 Rising and shipped to a penal colony in Australia. From there he escaped to the USA, where he eventually became governor of Montana. He died in 1867, having tripped on a coil of rope and fallen overboard while on a Missouri paddle steamer. His body was never recovered. The museum opens 10 am to 5 pm on weekdays, and 2 to 6 pm at the weekend, Easter to October. Admission costs £1.50/1.

Behind the tower a section of the **old wall** is incorporated into Reginald's bar and restaurant. The two arches were sallyports, to let boats 'sally forth' onto the inlet which used to flow right by the wall.

The Mall

The Mall is a wide 18th-century street running back from the river and built on reclaimed land which, until 1735, was a tidal inlet running alongside the walls. The **City Hall** was built in 1788 by local architect John Roberts. A remarkable Waterford glass chandelier hangs in the council's meeting room (there's a replica in Philadelphia's Independence Hall in the USA). The City Hall houses Waterford's Municipal Art Gallery but access is only via sporadic guided tours; for details phone ☎ 873501 ext 489.

Also built by John Roberts, the **Theatre Royal** is Ireland's finest intact 18th-century theatre.

WEXFORD & WATERFORD

WATERFORD

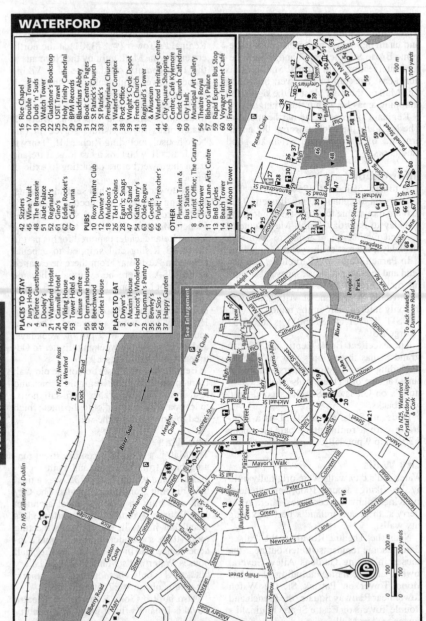

PLACES TO STAY
2   Jurys Hotel
4   Portree Guesthouse
5   Dooley's
21 Waterford Hostel
24 Granville Hotel
40 Viking House
53 Tower Hotel &
    Leisure Centre
55 Derrynane House
58 Beechwood
64 Corlea House

PLACES TO EAT
3   Dwyer's
6   Maxim House
7   Haricot's Wholefood
23 Chapman's Pantry
35 Bewley's
36 Suí Síos
37 Happy Garden

16 Rice Chapel
17 Double Tower
19 Duds 'n' Suds
20 Watch Tower
22 Gladstone's Bookshop
25 USIT Travel
27 Holy Trinity Cathedral
29 BPM Records
30 Blackfriars Abbey
31 Book Centre; Pages
32 St Patrick's Church
33 St Patrick's
    Presbyterian Church
34 Waterford Complex
38 Post Office
39 Wright's Cycle Depot
41 French Church
43 Reginald's Tower
    & Museum
44 Waterford Heritage Centre
46 City Square Shopping
    Centre; Café Kylemore
49 Christ Church Cathedral
50 City Hall;
    Municipal Art Gallery
56 Theatre Royal
57 Bishop's Palace
59 Rapid Express Bus Stop
60 Voyager Internet Café
68 French Tower

42 Sizzlers
45 Wine Vault
48 The Brasserie
51 Jade Palace
52 Reginald's
61 Gino's
62 Eddie Rocket's
67 Café Luna

PUBS
10 Roxy Theatre Club
15 Downe's
18 Muldoon's
26 T&H Doolans
28 Egan's; Snags
47 Olde Stand
54 Katty Barry's
63 Olde Rogue
65 Geoff's
66 Pulpit; Preacher's

OTHER
1   Plunkett Train &
    Bus Station
8   Tourist Office; The Granary
9   Clocktower
11 Garter Lane Arts Centre
12 BnB Cycles
14 Beach Tower
15 Half Moon Tower

The austere **Bishop's Palace** was begun in 1741 after a stretch of the wall was demolished. One of Ireland's finest town houses, it was designed by Richard Castle (or Cassels), who was also responsible for Powerscourt House in County Wicklow, Westport House in County Mayo, and Dublin's Leinster House and Rotunda Hospital. It now acts as the city engineering offices.

The Granary

Waterford's newest (from May 1999) attraction is the fine collection of treasures housed in The Granary (☎ 304500), which is also the new home of the tourist office. Formerly a grain store, it has been superbly converted into a museum, with plenty of sleek metal and glass to give it a futuristic look. The exhibits are equally fascinating, with a comprehensive collection of local treasures from the last 1000 years. Audiovisual displays and interactive presentations are expertly put together.

The museum opens 9.30 am to 9 pm daily, June to August; and 10 am to 5 pm daily, September to May. Admission costs £3/2.50.

Christ Church Cathedral

Behind City Hall is Christ Church Cathedral (☎ 396270), in Cathedral Square; it is Europe's only neo-classical Georgian cathedral. It was designed by John Roberts and stands on the site of an 11th-century Viking church. While the medieval cathedral was being demolished, a remarkable collection of 15th-century Italian priests' vestments was uncovered.

Don't miss the tomb of James Rice, seven times lord mayor of Waterford, who died in 1469 and is depicted in a state of decay with worms and frogs crawling out of his body. The cathedral also houses several bibles written in Irish.

A recorded presentation on the city's history takes place at 9.30 and 11.30 am, 2.40 and 4 pm Monday to Saturday (afternoons only on Sunday), between June and September. In April, May and October performances are at 11.30 am and 2.40 and 4 pm on weekdays. Admission costs £3/2.50. At

45 minutes, it will be about 15 minutes too long for many attention spans.

French Church

The ruins of a French Church built in 1240 by Franciscan monks ('Grey Friars') are on Greyfriars St. It became a hospital after the dissolution of the monasteries and was then occupied by French Huguenot refugees between 1693 and 1815. One of its last leading doctors was TF Meagher's father, Thomas Meagher Senior, mayor of Waterford. You can pick up the church key across the road at 5 Greyfriars St.

Waterford Heritage Centre

Next to the ruins of the French Church is the small, uninspiring Waterford Heritage Centre (☎ 871277), which exhibits royal charters dating back to 1215 and local Viking artefacts. It opens 10 am to 8.30 pm on weekdays, and 2 to 8.30 pm on Saturday, June to August; and 10 am to 5 pm on weekdays, and 2 to 5 pm on Saturday, the rest of the year. Admission costs £2/1.

Other Buildings

The ruins and square tower of the Dominican **Blackfriars Abbey** on Arundel Square date back to 1226. Nearby on Barronstrand St the Catholic **Holy Trinity Cathedral** was built between 1792 and 1796 by John Roberts, who also designed the Protestant Christ Church Cathedral. The sumptuous interior boasts a fine carved pulpit, painted pillars with Corinthian capitals and lovely Waterford crystal chandeliers.

Near Ballybricken Green is the old city wall's **Half Moon Tower** near Patrick St. **St Patrick's Church** on Jenkins' Lane is an 18th-century Catholic chapel which managed to survive the savage suppression of Catholicism at that time. At the top of Jenkins Lane is the **Beach Tower**, another remnant of the old city wall.

The **Chamber of Commerce** building on George's St was originally built as a town house by John Roberts and has a magnificent staircase.

Edmund Ignatius Rice, founder of the Christian Brothers, established his first

WEXFORD & WATERFORD

school at Mt Sion on Barrack St, where the **Rice Chapel** is a delightful combination of red brick and stained glass, with Rice's tomb in pride of place awaiting the likely canonisation of its occupant. If you phone ☎ 874390 you can also arrange to see an audiovisual presentation on Rice's life and works. See also the boxed text 'A Saint in the Making'.

Waterford Crystal Factory

The first Waterford glass factory was established at the western end of the riverside quays in 1783, but closed in 1851 as a result of punitive taxes imposed on the raw materials by the British government. The business wasn't revived until 1947, and the existing factory opened in 1971. Today, it employs 1600 people, among them highly skilled glass blowers, cutters and engravers who take from eight to 10 years to learn their craft. The glass is a heavy lead (over 30%) crystal made from red lead, silica sand and potash.

The visitor centre (☎ 373311) is 2km south on the Cork road. Between April and October you can guide yourself around the plant, with staff on hand to explain things; the site opens 8.30 am to 4 pm daily. During the rest of the year there are guided tours from 9 am to 3.15 pm on weekdays. They're worth it if only to see the fountain designed for Harrods in London in 1971. It's made up of 3034 pieces of glass, weighs 360kg and cost £110,000.

A visit costs £3.50/1.75. In summer you can buy a ticket in advance from the tourist office to avoid long queues at the factory. Afterwards you can part with large amounts of money in the Crystal Gallery and then have lunch or tea in the café. Yellow 'Imp' buses run to the factory from Shop 'Round the Clock opposite the clocktower on the quays every 10 minutes (return £1.40).

Organised Tours

Walking Tours One-hour historical walking tours (☎ 873711) depart from the Granville Hotel on Meagher Quay at noon and 2 pm daily, March to October (£3.50).

Cruises The Galley Cruising Restaurant (☎ 421723) operates between June and August. Morning cruises leaving Meagher

A Saint in the Making

Born at Westcourt near Callan in County Kilkenny in 1762, Edmund Rice had a rudimentary education, like most Catholics of that era. At 17 he was apprenticed to his uncle in Waterford, later inheriting his business.

On the surface Rice appeared a conventional businessman, but behind the scenes he was already helping the poor. In 1802 he established his first school before quitting ship chandlery to become a full-time teacher. In 1804 he opened a new classroom at Mount Sion in Waterford. New schools in Clonmel and Dungarvan soon followed.

In 1820 the pope approved the Institute of the Brothers of the Christian Schools of Ireland, and Rice remained the 'superior general' until his death in 1838. By then the Christian Brothers had schools in Britain, Gibraltar, Australia, the USA and South Africa.

The Brothers have played an important role in educating Catholic youngsters throughout the 20th century. Among those to have received their tutelage were broadcaster Gay Byrne, actor Gabriel Byrne, writer Brendan Behan and politicians Pádraig Pearse, Eamon de Valera, Gerry Adams and Bertie Ahern.

Then in the 1990s scandal rocked the movement after men claimed they had been physically and sexually abused by their teachers. Despite the inevitable cloud cast over the movement, Rice himself is still revered and has been beatified by the pope, the first step towards attaining sainthood.

Quay at 10.30 am cost £6. Two-hour cruises including afternoon tea leave at 3 pm and cost £7. Evening cruises leaving at 7 or 8 pm cost £6.

Special Events

Waterford's Light Opera Festival takes place in September and October. It's cheaper and more easily accessible than the more famous Wexford Opera Festival but booking is still advisable. Much of the city takes part, and there are pub singing competitions and longer pub opening hours. For more details contact the Theatre Royal (☎ 874402), The Mall, Waterford.

Places to Stay

The frequency of buses to Tramore (see later in this chapter) means you can stay there and commute into Waterford if you can't find anything that takes your fancy here.

Hostels The IHH's clean, modern *Barnacles Viking House* (☎ 853827) is tucked behind the quayside on Coffee House Lane in the city's old quarter. Dorm beds start at £7.50 (£8.50 in high season); good doubles cost £13.50 to £15.50. Breakfast is included in the price. On the down side the door is locked from noon to 3 pm.

Waterford Hostel (☎ 850163, 70 The Manor St) opens between June and September. At the time of writing it was closed for extensive renovations, but should have reopened by the time you read this.

B&Bs Waterford is disappointingly lacking in good, central, tourist-board-approved B&Bs. The Mall and Parnell St have several relatively cheap B&Bs, but traffic noise can be a problem. You could try *Derrynane House* (☎ 875179, 19 The Mall), but for a quiet night ask for a room at the back. Singles/doubles cost £16/32. The attractively positioned *Beechwood* (☎ 876677, 7 Cathedral Square) charges £17/30. At *Portree Guesthouse* (☎ 874574, Mary St) rooms start at £18/27. Also worth trying is *Corlea House* (☎ 875764, 2 New St), where B&B costs £17/29.

Almost 5km from Waterford on the Dunmore East road, the *Knockboy House* (☎ 873484) offers rooms starting at £19/28.

Hotels At the classy *Granville Hotel* (☎ 305555, fax 305566, Meagher Quay), B&B starts at £50/100 in singles/doubles. For a bedside view of Reginald's Tower try the modern *Tower Hotel and Leisure Centre* (☎ 875801, fax 870129), at the northern end of The Mall, which has an indoor pool, sauna and gymnasium. B&B costs £56/89. Across the river, *Jurys Hotel* (☎ 832111, fax 832863, Dock Rd) offers much the same facilities for £55/75.

Newly restored *Dooley's* (☎ 873531, Merchants Quay) offers good value for money: spacious rooms cost £60/100 from June to September.

Most exclusive of all of Waterford's hotels is *Waterford Castle* (☎ 878203, fax 879316), 5km east of town in Ballinakill and accessible by ferry just off the Passage East road. If you need to ask about the prices you probably can't afford it!

Places to Eat

Restaurants At *Gino's (Applemarket)*, just off Michael St, delicious pizzas are served, including a masterpiece of a vegetarian special (£3.75).

For Chinese meals and takeaways, try *Maxim House (O'Connell St)* or *Happy Garden* (☎ 855640, High St), where main courses cost under £10. More upmarket is *Jade Palace* (☎ 855611, The Mall), said to be one of Ireland's best (and most expensive) Chinese restaurants.

Behind Reginald's Tower, *Reginald's* bar and restaurant (☎ 855087) serves bar meals and a set dinner (£14.95). Late-night burger-hunters should head for *Eddie Rocket's (John St)*, open until 4 am at the weekend.

One of the best places in town is *Dwyer's* (☎ 877478, 5 Mary St), in an old barracks near the bridge. Sophisticated food comes in generous helpings and an early-bird menu (£15) is available between 6 and 7.30 pm; later, a full dinner costs more like £28. It is closed on Sunday and bank

WEXFORD & WATERFORD

holidays. Also good is the *Wine Vault* (☎ *853444, High St)*, where the dinner bill, and the quality of the food, will be about the same.

If you're feeling flush you could head 5km east to Ballinakill and the *Waterford Castle* restaurant (☎ *878203)*. Dinner will cost at least £35 per person.

Fast Food, Cafés & Pubs Near Reginald's Tower, *Sizzlers* opens 24 hours at the weekend and serves some cheapish burger-style meals. *Chapman's Pantry* is a terrific coffee-shop-cum-restaurant next to the Granville Hotel on Meagher Quay. It opens 8 am to 6 pm and the deli in front is good too. *Haricot's Wholefood (11 O'Connell St)* serves vegetarian and non-vegetarian dishes costing around £5 (lunch specials £4.50). It opens 10 am to 8 pm on weekdays, and 10 am to 5.45 pm on Saturday. *Suí Síos (55 High St)* is a pleasant little café serving salads and sandwiches costing £4 to £5.

Bewley's has a coffee house upstairs in the Broad St mall. In the City Square shopping centre there's a branch of *Café Kylemore* for quick coffee fixes. *Pages*, in the Book Centre on Barronstrand St, is also good for teas and light lunches.

For coffee and all sorts of sandwiches, *Café Luna (John St)* provides a cool setting with artwork on the walls and sounds from soul to latin in the background. This is the trendiest café in Waterford, with the city's hip young things passing through for caffeine infusions. At the time of writing it was expected to get a wine licence. It opens until 4 am on Friday and Saturday and to 3.30 am on Wednesday, Thursday and Sunday.

The Brasserie, at the edge of the City Square shopping centre, serves moderately priced pizzas and toasted sandwiches.

The Barronstrand St pubs are locked in healthy competition for lunch trade: specials cost around £3 to £5. *Egan's* serves the food cafeteria-style in a separate area at the back.

T&H Doolan *(George's St)* is good for lunches (roast beef £5.45), as is *Olde Stand*

(Michael St), which serves bar food downstairs and seafood and steaks upstairs (around £10).

Entertainment

Pubs & Nightclubs Waterford's nightlife relies heavily on the presence of students from all over the country who attend the local technical college. There's a youthful feel around town, particularly at the weekend (going out during the week can prove to be a lonely experience!). Many pubs feature live music. The venerable *T&H Doolan (George's St)* incorporates a remnant of the 1000-year-old city wall. Sinead O'Connor played here before she hit the big time.

Where John St becomes Michael St is *Geoff's*, easily the city's hippest bar. Next door is the *Pulpit*, which also attracts a lively young crowd. Upstairs in the nightclub, *Preacher's*, there is a good, old-fashioned disco in a weird Gothic setting at the weekend. Across the road is the *Olde Rogue*, while just up the road at the junction with Manor St there's *Muldoon's*, featuring regular live-music sessions.

Egan's (Barronstrand St) has the odd karaoke night and a fully fledged nightclub, *Snags*, upstairs. *Reginald's*, near the tower, has a nightclub and occasional jazz sessions (though it's strictly for the over-30s and off-duty police). Nearby, *Katty Barry's (Mall Lane)* is rumoured to serve the best Guinness. *Downe's (Thomas St)* is a beautiful bar where the only noise you'll hear is bar-room chat – not a loudspeaker in sight. *Roxy Theatre Club (O'Connell St)* is a pretty-good nightclub which features DJs from all over Ireland.

About 7km out on the Dunmore road is *Jack Meade's*, a gigantic beer garden open from June to September only. It has a capacity of 3000, with picnicking tables and even a small pet zoo. There's live music on Sunday.

Theatre & Cinemas The *Garter Lane Arts Centre* (☎ *855038, 22A O'Connell St)* stages films, exhibitions, poetry readings and theatre. It opens 10 am to 6 pm Monday to Saturday.

The 90-minute Waterford Show in the *City Hall* (☎ 875788), on The Mall, combines music, dancing and wine in a programme about the city's history. Between May and September it takes place at 8.45 pm on Thursday, Friday and Sunday. Tickets cost £7 and can be booked at the tourist office, Waterford Crystal Factory or City Hall.

The five-screen *Waterford Cineplex* (☎ 74595, Patrick St) shows first-run movies.

Shopping

BPM Records, on the corner of Barronstrand and High Sts, is a good record shop.

Getting There & Away

Air Waterford Airport (☎ 875589) is 6km south of the city. The daily British Airways Express flight to Stansted can cost as little as £79 return. Suckling Airways (☎ 01223-292524) runs three daily flights to Luton. There is no bus service to the airport. A taxi (☎ 877773) will cost around £12.

Bus The Bus Éireann station (☎ 873401) is at Plunkett train station across the bridge to the north of the river. There are plenty of buses daily to Dublin (£6), Cork (£8), Limerick (£8), Rosslare and Tramore.

Rapid Express Coaches (☎ 872149), at Parnell Court on Parnell St, runs a service between Waterford and Dublin via Dungarvan, Carlow and Naas (£5, at least seven daily); this bus also serves Tramore.

Suirway (☎ 382422) runs services to Dunmore East (£1.80, 30 minutes, at least three daily) and Passage East (£1.50, 30 minutes, two daily). They depart from near the Maxol petrol station and opposite Shop 'Round the Clock on Meagher Quay.

Train From Plunkett Station (☎ 873401) on the northern side of the river, there are regular services to Dublin (£11, two hours 30 minutes, four daily), Limerick (£10, two hours 30 minutes, one daily) and Rosslare Harbour (£6, one hour 20 minutes, two daily).

Getting Around

Wright's Cycle Depot (☎ 874411), on Henrietta St, is a Raleigh Rent-a-Bike outlet. Bike hire costs £10/40 per day/week. BnB Cycles (☎ 870356), 22 Ballybricken Green, also hires out bikes.

There are taxi ranks at Plunkett train station and outside Penney's department store; fares start at £2.70.

PASSAGE EAST

Eleven kilometres east of Waterford city on the coast road is Passage East, with its little harbour and thatched cottages at the foot of low hills. The Passage East to Ballyhack ferry makes a useful short cut between Counties Waterford and Wexford.

Just south of the village is **Crooke**, with the remains of the Geneva Barracks nearby. Built in the 18th century as part of a settlement for Swiss refugees, the buildings were turned into barracks after the plan fell through. It was here that a young rebel of the 1798 Rising came to confess his sins to a priest who turned out to be an army officer in disguise. The lad was arrested and subsequently hanged, a story immortalised in the song 'Croppy Boy'.

There are a couple of cheap B&Bs, *Cois Abhann* and *Harbour Lights*.

Getting There & Away

Bus Suirway (☎ 051-382422) runs two buses daily from Waterford city to Passage East (£1.50, 30 minutes).

Boat If you're heading to or from Wexford, the car ferry across the estuary from Passage East to Ballyhack in County Wexford can save you an hour's drive compared with the route via New Ross to the north. The ferry company (☎ 051-382488) is on Barrack St in Passage East and the ferry operates a continuous service from 7.20 am to 10 pm, April to September; and 7.20 am to 8 pm, the rest of the year. On Sunday, the first sailings are at 9.30 am. The 10-minute crossing costs £4/6 one-way/return for a car, 80p/£1 for pedestrians, and £1/1.50 for cyclists. Return tickets are valid for an unlimited time.

WEXFORD & WATERFORD

DUNMORE EAST
☎ 051 • pop 1430

Dunmore East (Dún Mór) is a pretty fishing village strung out along a coastline of low, red sandstone cliffs and discreet coves. Many of the thatched cottages are summer homes. Most of the accommodation clusters around Ladies Cove, although the hostel, Dunmore Harbour House, is by the busy harbour, which is overlooked by an unusual **Doric lighthouse** built in 1823. There's a good view of Hook Head lighthouse across the water in County Wexford. The noisy birds nesting in the cliffs around the harbour are kittiwakes. The most popular **beaches** are Counsellor's Beach, facing south and set among the cliffs, and Ladies Cove, right in the village.

The **Dunmore East Adventure Centre** (☎ 383783) hires out equipment for windsurfing, canoeing, surfing and snorkelling. Short courses in most of these sports are also available.

If you're interested in going **fishing** for sharks or in exploring old wrecks off the coast contact Dunmore East Angling Charters (☎ 383397).

Places to Stay

Camping Just south of the village, *Dunmore East Caravan and Camping Park* (☎ 383816) charges £10 per tent.

Hostels At the *Dunmore Harbour House* (☎ 383218), overlooking the harbour, dorm beds cost £9 and singles/doubles start at £13.50/17 without breakfast. There's a good restaurant as well as the usual kitchen. The hostel was once a hotel servicing passengers travelling on the mail boats between Dunmore East and Milford Haven in Wales.

B&Bs The *Church Villa* (☎ 383390) is one of a row of cottages in the town opposite the Protestant church and near Ship Inn. Its cosy doubles, most with shower, cost £36. Elegant *Carraig Laith* (☎ 383273), on the main Harbour Rd, offers singles/doubles with great sea views costing £24/36. Next to the post office, *Creaden View* (☎ 383339, Harbour Rd) charges the same prices.

Hotels There are three hotels on Harbour Rd. *Candlelight Inn* (☎ 383215, fax 383289) has doubles starting at £27.50, while the *Haven Hotel* (☎ 383150, fax 383488) is a black and white Victorian mansion in extensive grounds where B&B starts at £38/62 in singles/doubles. At the less attractive *Ocean Hotel* (☎ 383136, fax 383576) rooms start at £55.

Places to Eat

Candlelight Inn has a good restaurant where main courses start at £6. *Ship Inn* also serves good food, particularly seafood, both in the bar and the restaurant.

Strand Inn (☎ 383174), overlooking Ladies Cove, specialises in seafood. A full dinner will cost you around £20 but the bar food is more than adequate. It opens for lunch from 12.30 to 2.30 pm and for dinner from 7 to 10 pm. The nearby *Anchor Bar* also serves bar meals and sometimes hosts live music.

At the *Dunmore Harbour House* hostel (☎ 383218), the restaurant specialises in seafood. The set dinner costs £18 but you can get by for less if you eat à la carte.

Getting There & Away

Suirway (☎ 382422) runs four daily buses from Waterford to Dunmore East (£1.80, 30 minutes) in July and August (three daily the rest of the year).

TRAMORE
☎ 051 • pop 6536

The busiest of County Waterford's seaside resorts, Tramore (Trá Mhór) is 12km south of Waterford. A delightful 5km beach is backed with 30m-high dunes at its eastern end. Tramore itself is fairly tacky, with amusement arcades and fast-food outlets running down to the seafront.

Standing on the shore, the bay is hemmed in by **Great Newtown Head** to the southwest and **Brownstown Head** to the northeast, with their standing pillars and the **Iron Man**, a huge painted iron figure of an 18th-century sailor in white breeches and blue jacket with his arm pointing seawards as a warning to approaching ships. The pillars were erected by Lloyds of London in 1816 after 360 lives were lost when a boat mistook Tramore Bay for Waterford Harbour and was wrecked.

The beach aside, Tramore's biggest attraction used to be the Celtworld heritage ride close to the bus stop. At the time of writing this was closed, although new owners may yet revive it. Instead you can entertain yourself at the adjacent **Splashworld** (☎ 390176), an outsize swimming pool; phone for details of classes and activities.

Places to Stay
Camping There are three caravan and camp sites near Tramore. The best facilities are at *Newtown Cove Caravan and Camping Park* (☎ 381979) on the R675 to Dungarvan. It opens April to September and costs £10 for a car or a caravan, or £5 per person for hikers and cyclists. The other sites are *Atlantic View Caravan and Camping* (☎ 381610), on the seafront, which charges £9.50 for a two-person tent or caravan, and *Fitzmaurice's Caravan Park* (☎ 381968), near the Atlantic View on the inland side of the road, with similar facilities and rates.

Hostels Not far from the tourist office is *The Monkey Puzzle* (☎ 386754, *Upper Branch Rd*). Beds cost £7.50 and there are two doubles for £19. To reach it, go up the steep street more or less opposite the bus stop and turn right. It might be wise to phone before arriving.

B&Bs Cliff Rd is lined with B&Bs offering great sea views. *The Cliff* (☎ 381497) and *Ard Mor* (☎ 381716) are promising, or, just about 1km from the bus stop, there's *Cliff House* (☎ 381497), where singles/doubles start at £22/34. At *Oban* (☎ 381537, *1 Eastlands, Pond Rd*), to the north-east of town, doubles cost £34.

In Fenor, just 7km west of Tramore on the way to Dungarvan, *Mountain View* (☎ 396107) is one of Ireland's few thatched B&Bs. Prices start at £23/34.

Hotels For something grander there's the *Majestic Hotel* (☎ 381761) immediately

opposite the bus stop. Singles/doubles cost £52.50/75. A bit cheaper and less overwhelming is *O'Shea's Hotel* (☎ 381246, *Strand St*), where rooms cost £34/65.

Places to Eat
Pub food is available at *The Victoria* (*Queen St*) or at *The Seahorse* (*Main St*).

For something more formal try *Hartley's Bistro* (☎ 390888, *21 Queen St*). Early-bird menus cost £11.50. Expect modern Irish cuisine.

Getting There & Away
Bus Éireann (☎ 873401) runs more than 15 buses daily from Waterford to Tramore.

TRAMORE TO DUNGARVAN
The road between Tramore and Dungarvan, 41km to the west along the coast, is punctuated by numerous small villages set in tidy coves. **Annestown**, **Bunmahon** and the picturesque **Stradbally** come in quick succession along a winding road. The *Cove Bar* in Stradbally serves reasonable pub food, or there's *Ye Olde Bank Restaurant*, 5km north of Stradbally in Kilmacthomas.

Eight kilometres to the west of Stradbally is the popular Blue Flag beach at **Clonea**, where the *Clonea Strand Hotel* (☎ 058-42416) has a 10-pin bowling alley and Turkish baths. There's also a camp site here, *Casey's* (☎ 058-41919), where a family tent costs £10, £4.75 for hikers or cyclists. There's a surfing beach to the south-west in **Ballinacourty**.

DUNGARVAN
☎ 058 • pop 7175
The small port and market town of Dungarvan (Dún Garbhán), 48km west of Waterford city, grew up in the shelter of an Anglo-Norman castle.

Modern Dungarvan has a lovely setting at the foot of forested hills on the wide bay where the River Colligan meets the sea. Until the river was bridged in the last century this shallow crossing was known as Dungarvan's Prospects: women had to raise their skirts to wade across and the sight was famous among local men. The view aside,

WEXFORD & WATERFORD

The Barber of Kilmacthomas

In 1650, when Oliver Cromwell and his army prepared to take Waterford city, they were delayed by flooding of the River Mahon and were forced to camp outside the town of Kilmacthomas. Ever conscious of his appearance, Cromwell ordered that the local barber be brought to him so that he could get a decent shave. The barber duly arrived and was preparing his razor when Cromwell warned him that a cut would cost the barber his life. Undeterred, he proceeded to shave his belligerent customer cleanly and without drawing blood.

Later, when recounting the story to the locals, the barber was asked whether Cromwell's threat had made him nervous. 'Well, look at it this way', he is said to have answered, 'I was holding the razor to *his* neck!' Apocryphal or not, the story guaranteed the barber a free pint in his local pub for the rest of his days.

Dungarvan can hardly be described as a picturesque town. The harbour is filthy, and on grey days it can be downright grim. Still, it is the administrative centre for County Waterford. The large Harbour Bay complex developing beside the castle ruins could liven things up a bit.

Abbeyside, in the north-east of town, was the birthplace of Ernest Walton, whose work on nuclear fission won the Nobel Prize for physics in 1951.

Dungarvan makes a convenient base for exploring western County Waterford and the Monavullagh, Comeragh and Knockmealdown Mountains to the north.

Orientation & Information

The town's main shopping area is centred on the neatly laid-out Grattan Square on the southern side of the river. Main St (also called O'Connell St) runs along one side of it.

The tourist office (☎ 41741) on Grattan Square opens April to August but has little useful information.

Things to See & Do

By the quays, **King John's Castle** (1185) is just a collection of rotting walls. The 17th-century **Old Market House** houses a small museum (admission free), open 11 am to 1 pm and 2 to 5 pm on weekdays. As you leave Dungarvan to travel west, you'll pass a **monument** to the greyhound Master McGrath which won the Waterloo Cup three times in the 1860s.

Special Events

Over the early-May bank-holiday weekend 17 Dungarvan pubs and two hotels play host to the Féile na nDéise, a lively and fun traditional-music festival which attracts around 200 musicians. For more information, phone ☎ 42998.

Places to Stay

The IHH *Dungarvan Holiday Hostel* (☎ 44340) is opposite the garda station on the N25 Youghal road and costs £7.50 for dorm beds and £17 for doubles.

At the friendly *Abbey House* (☎ 41669, Friars Walk, Abbeyside), near the church, doubles cost £36. *Fáilte House* (☎ 43216) overlooks the sea from the Youghal road; singles/doubles cost £22/36.

At the *Old Rectory* (☎ 41394), just out of town on the Waterford road, rooms cost around £22/36. Almost 8km south-west of Dungarvan on the Youghal road, *Seaview* (☎ 41583) offers sweeping views over Dungarvan and the sea. Rooms cost £21/32.

At *Lawlor's Hotel* (☎ 41122, TF Meagher St), just off Grattan Square, B&B costs £33 per person.

Places to Eat

An Bialann (*Grattan Square*) serves popular lunch specials costing £4.50. *Flanagan's* (*Main St*) also packs them in at lunchtime. For teas and snacks the upstairs *Koffee Korner*, just off Grattan Square opposite the Lady Belle pub, is comfortable. For reasonably priced pub food, cosy

Merry's (☎ *41974*), at the Old Market House end of Main St, is a good choice. Dungarvan's newest eatery is *The Mill* (☎ *45488, Davitt's Quay*). It has a reasonable menu with main courses costing £8 to £12, and the emphasis is – naturally – on fish. It closes on Monday evening.

Entertainment
Molly Molone's and *Downey's* on Main St attract a young crowd, as does the *Buttery Bar* in Lawlor's Hotel. The *Moorings* and the *Anchor* on the quay have a good atmosphere at the weekend; the latter hosts local bands and traditional Irish music. *Bean a'Leanna* offers live music on Thursday, Friday and Saturday. For a particularly Irish music scene head out to *Tigh an Cheoil* at Helvick, towards An Rinn, or to *Seanachie*, a few kilometres out on the Cork road.

Getting There & Away
Bus Éireann (☎ 051-873401) services run to Dublin, Waterford (return £6), Killarney and Cork from the stop on Davitt's Quay.

Getting Around
Murphy Cycles (☎ 41376), the Raleigh Rent-a-Bike dealer on Main St, hires bikes costing £10/40 per day/week.

AN RINN (RING)
An Rinn, 12km south of Dungarvan on Helvick Head, is one of the most famous Gaeltachts – Irish-speaking areas, with their own special heritage and culture – in Ireland. Many an Irish teenager has studied the language in Ring College on the Helvick Head road. The school runs *ceilidhs*, *seisúns* (sessions) of traditional music and dance, most nights during the summer, and there are also evening seisúns in the *Tigh an Cheoil* (☎ 058-46209) bar in an old cottage in Baile na nGall on the way to Helvick Head. On the road to Youghal, the *Seanchaí* pub, beside the road in the middle of nowhere, also has frequent music sessions. *Mooney's* pub in An Rinn has excellent sessions every night during the summer.

Aisling B&B (☎ 058-46134) charges £16 per person for B&B, as does *Failoeán*

(☎ *058-46127*), which overlooks Helvick Head pier. All households speak Irish and English.

Getting There & Away
The very limited bus service runs from Waterford at 1.45 pm on Saturday. This becomes a daily service during July and August.

ARDMORE
☎ 024 • pop 436
South of Helvick Head the coast road veers inland and after 23km brings you back to the sea at Ardmore. A popular seaside resort with a Blue Flag beach, Ardmore has a main street of pretty, pastel-coloured buildings. Don't be put off by the ugly sprawl of caravan parks that spoils the coastal view to the east: this is a nice little place and the beach is lovely.

It is claimed locally that St Declan set up shop here between 350 and 420 well before St Patrick arrived from Britain to convert the heathens.

Information
The locally run tourist office (☎ 94444) is in a white sandcastle-shaped building on the seafront. It opens daily May to September and you can change money here.

St Declan's Church & Oratory
In a striking position on a hill above the town the ruins of St Declan's Church and a fine slender round tower stand on the site of St Declan's original monastery. The 30m-high tower dates back to the 12th century.

The outer western gable wall of the 13th-century church features some stone carvings retrieved from an older 9th-century church and placed here. They show the Archangel Michael weighing souls, the adoration of the Magi, Adam and Eve, and a clear depiction of the judgement of Solomon. Inside the church are two Ogham stones, one of them particularly fine. Look out for the tombstone of a women called Pigeon in the nave.

The smaller building in the compound is the 8th-century St Declan's Oratory, or

WEXFORD & WATERFORD

Beannachán. It was restored in the 18th century and is traditionally said to be the resting place of St Declan. The depression in the floor is due to worshippers removing earth from the grave site – it was supposed to protect from disease.

St Declan's Well
Overlooking the sea, St Declan's Well is beyond the Cliff House hotel to the south of town. Pilgrims once washed in it. Beside it are the ruins of Dysert Church. A fine 5km **cliff walk** leads from the well; a free map is available from the tourist office. At the southern end of the beach is **St Declan's Stone**, said to have arrived on the waves from Wales following St Declan. Crawling under it on St Declan's Day (24 July) is said to cure rheumatism and bring spiritual benefits.

St Declan's Way
This 94km walk mostly traces an old pilgrimage way from Ardmore to the Rock of Cashel in Tipperary. A map guide (£4.50), which also shows circular routes taking in parts of the Way, is available from the tourist office. See Walking in the Activities chapter for more details.

Places to Stay
Hostels The *Ardmore Beach Hostel* (☎ 94501), in an old stone house near the seafront, offers dorm beds costing £8.50 and family rooms at a discount. Ask at the Cup and Saucer Restaurant opposite.

B&Bs The *Byron Lodge* (☎ 94157) is a Georgian house on the edge of town, with singles/doubles starting at £21/32. To get there find the second thatched cottage on the main street and turn up the road beside it, passing over a crossroads. Byron Lodge is on your right.

Hotels In the village, *Round Tower Hotel* (☎ 94494) charges £25/44 in singles/doubles for B&B. The big, white *Cliff House* (☎ 94106), on the low cliffs overlooking the bay, offers rooms costing £25/62 without breakfast.

Places to Eat
Paddy Mac's pub on Main St offers good pub snacks and lunches; jacket potatoes start at £2.80. Beside the pub the small *Beachcombers Restaurant* serves snacks, soups and spaghetti costing £1.50 to £5. Across the road *Cup and Saucer Restaurant* offers middle-of-the-road quiche, jacket potatoes and lasagne.

Getting There & Away
Buses stop outside O'Reilly's pub on Main St. There are three services daily (one on Sunday) to Cork year round, and two daily to Waterford via Dungarvan in July and August (otherwise it's a Friday and Saturday only service).

NORTHERN COUNTY WATERFORD
Some of the most scenic parts of County Waterford are in the north of the county around **Ballymacarbry** and in the **Nire Valley**, which runs through the heart of the Comeragh Mountains. While not as rugged as the west of Ireland, the mountain scenery has a beauty of its own. The hills form the easternmost extension of a great mass of red sandstone from the Devonian period, some 370 million years ago, which underlies most of the Cork and Kerry scenery.

The lovely wooded valleys and heathery mountains are good for **pony trekking**. Melody's Riding Stables (☎ 052-36147) in Ballymacarbry hires horses for half-day (£22) or full-day (from £50) outings between Easter and October.

The **East Munster Way** walking trail covers near 70km between Carrick-on-Suir in County Tipperary and the northern slopes of the Knockmealdown Mountains. East of the Vee Gap the East Munster Way becomes the Blackwater Way and crosses a path which marks the ancient Rían Bó Phádraig (Track of St Patrick's Cow), a highway and pilgrimage route connecting Lismore with Ardfinnan and Cashel. Nearby is a modern memorial to Liam Lynch, who was killed during the Irish Civil War of 1922–3. See Walking in the Activities chapter for more details of this walk.

Touraneena Heritage Centre, 15km to the north of Dungarvan on the R672, focuses on a lost way of life, with displays on bread and butter making, and home-curing bacon. There's also a working forge. It opens 10 am to 6 pm daily, mid-May to October. Admission costs £3/1.50.

Driving from Waterford to Ballymacarbry you can take in **Curraghmore Gardens**, 14km north-west of Waterford city. The fine house dates from the 18th century and is home to the marquess of Waterford. Although the house is open only to groups by prior arrangement (☎ 051-387102), you can visit the gardens and the 18th-century shell grotto from 2 to 5 pm on Thursday and bank holidays, Easter to mid-October. Admission costs £2.

Places to Stay & Eat
At *Hanoras Cottage* (☎ 052-36134), in the Nire Valley, singles/doubles cost £45/70 for B&B; the tearoom-cum-restaurant provides excellent snacks and lunches. From the main Dungarvan to Clonmel road (R672), head to Ballymacarbry then turn east off the N72 to Nire Church.

At *Nire Valley Farmhouse* (☎ 052-36149), just north-west of Ballymacarbry, B&B costs around £20/32. Farther north on the same road is *Clonanay Guesthouse* (☎ 052-36141), where rooms start at £30/53.

Getting There & Away
There's a Tuesday only bus service from Dungarvan at 2 pm, and two buses from Clonmel on Friday at 1.20 and 5.35 pm.

CAPPOQUIN
☎ 058
The small market town of Cappoquin is overlooked by the Knockmealdown Mountains. The River Blackwater takes an abrupt turn southwards near the town and the Blackwater Valley to the west is picturesque. There's excellent coarse and game **fishing** locally, and **Glenshelane Park**, just outside the town, offers some lovely forest walks and picnic spots. Salmon-fishing permits are available from the Toby Jug Guesthouse (☎ 54317). The Blackwater

Valley is also where traces of the earliest Irish peoples have been found – Mesolithic microliths (small stone blades) from around 9000 years ago have been discovered.

Mt Melleray Cistercian Abbey (☎ 54404) is just over 6km to the north of town. The abbey was founded in 1832 by a group of Irish monks who had been expelled from a monastery near Melleray in Brittany, France. A fully functioning monastery, Mt Melleray is open to visitors seeking quiet reflection and to those who want to see something of the daily routine. There's no charge for a bed in the guesthouse, but it would be bad manners not to make a donation.

Getting There & Away
Twice weekly a bus leaves Waterford for Cappoquin travelling via Dungarvan; it leaves at 8.30 am on Friday and at 5.30 pm on Sunday (this service doesn't operate in July and August). On Friday a bus also leaves Cork for Cappoquin at 4.30 pm, travelling via Midleton and Tallow.

LISMORE
☎ 058 • pop 729
Lismore is a small town beautifully situated on the River Blackwater at the foot of the Knockmealdown Mountains. The river rolls on east and then south to Youghal and the sea.

Lismore was the location of a great monastic university first founded by St Cartach, or Carthage, in the 7th century. In the 8th century the monastery became a famous centre of learning under St Colman. From the 10th century on it was sacked many times by the Vikings but hung on as the religious capital of Deise (Deices). Until the 17th century, the remains of eight churches could still be seen.

Information
Lismore has a tourist office (☎ 54975), with a bureau de change, in Lismore Heritage Centre, in the old courthouse in the town centre. It opens daily April to October and stocks a free town-walk map. Ask about guided tours of the town which cost £1.50

WEXFORD & WA

(children free). Alternatively, for £1 you can buy *A Walking Tour of Lismore*, which describes all the local sights.

St Carthage's Cathedral

The striking cathedral (1633) sits among peaceful gardens. Inside are some noteworthy tombs, including a MacGrath family crypt dating from 1557, and the small chapel of St Colmcille.

Lismore Castle

From the Cappoquin road there are fine glimpses of majestic Lismore Castle overlooking the river. In the 12th century Henry II chose this site for a castle, which was eventually erected by Prince John, lord of Ireland, in 1185. The castle was the local bishop's residence until 1589, when it was presented to Sir Walter Raleigh along with around 200 sq km of the surrounding countryside.

Raleigh, a famous soldier and favourite of Queen Elizabeth I, later sold it to the earl of Cork, Richard Boyle. His 14th child, Robert Boyle (1627–91), was born here and is credited with being the first methodical modern scientist; Boyle's Law is the principle that the pressure of a gas varies with its volume at a constant temperature, a discovery fundamental to modern physics.

Lismore Castle passed to the duke of Devonshire in 1753 and his descendants still own it. The present castle mostly dates from the 19th century, but incorporates small sections of the earlier buildings. During rebuilding, the 15th-century *Book of Lismore* and the Lismore Crozier (both now in the National Museum in Dublin) were discovered. The book documents the lives of a number of Irish saints, but also holds an account of the voyages of Marco Polo. A more recent castle occupant was Adele Astaire, sister of the famous Fred.

The castle is closed to day-trippers but can be rented by seriously rich groups. The gardens (☎ 54424) open 1.45 to 4.45 pm daily, May to September. Admission costs £3/2.

Lismore Heritage Centre

Lismore Heritage Centre (☎ 54975) is in the old courthouse. It opens 9.30 am to 6 pm Monday to Saturday, and 10 am to 5.30 pm on Sunday, June to August; 9.30 am to 5.30 pm Monday to Saturday, and 10 am to 5 pm on Sunday, April, May, September and October; and 9 am to 5.30 pm on weekdays, the rest of the year. There is an audiovisual presentation on local history and attractions, legends, follies and walks along the River Blackwater. There are shows every half-hour. Admission costs £2.50/1.50.

Places to Stay & Eat

There's no official camp site nearby but you could ask local farmers if you can camp in their fields. At the IHO *Kilmorna Farm Hostel* (☎ 54315) dorm beds cost £8.

Beechcroft (☎ 54273, Deerpark Rd) is about 1km from the town centre; singles/doubles start at £19/28. *Lismore Hotel* (☎ 54555) is a straightforward place where B&B costs £27 per person. *Ballyrafter House* (☎ 54002), 1km north of town, offers rooms starting at £37.50/60; an excellent set dinner costs £24.

Rafters (East Main St), above Roche's supermarket, serves middle-of-the-road lunches and dinners costing £5 to £10. *Rose's West End* pub on Main St offers soup and toasted sandwiches. Two good pubs that serve food are *Eamon's* and *Madden's*.

Getting There & Away

Buses stop outside O'Dowd's pub on West St. A bus leaves Waterford city for Lismore via Dungarvan at 8.40 pm Monday to Saturday. On Friday there's also a bus at 8.30 am, and on Sunday (except in July and August) there's a bus at 5.30 pm. For details contact Waterford bus station (☎ 051-873401).

County Cork

Ireland's biggest county, County Cork (Corcaigh) has everything that makes Ireland so attractive – a case could be made for arriving here before Dublin. Though growing, Cork city is still engagingly small and relatively free of urban stress. The northern part of the county is renowned for fishing, while the main tourist trail heads down to Kinsale, Ireland's gourmet capital, and west through the historic towns of Clonakilty and Skibbereen to the peninsulas jutting into the Atlantic. These underpopulated extremities are rich in history and nature, and offer wonderful scenery for walkers, climbers and cyclists. The county's best-known attraction is the Blarney Stone, but you'll probably remember for far longer just drifting through West Cork.

Cork

☎ 021 • pop 180,000

Although hardly exciting, the Irish Republic's second-largest city is a pleasant place in which to while away a day or so, with a considerable French input as a result of the ferry connections. The city has some fine Georgian buildings; Grand Parade and South Mall boast the finest architecture. The pubs are as lively as anywhere and Cork City Jail makes an interesting visit.

The city's population is growing rapidly as people take up employment in the new industries of computing and call centres. Cork's roads endure much traffic but the new Lee Tunnel, joining eastern and West Cork without going through the centre, should ease things.

HISTORY

The city dates back to the 7th century, surviving Cromwell's visit only to fall to William of Orange in 1690. In the 18th century it was an important commercial centre with a major butter market. A century later the Potato Famine reduced Cork to a sorry

Highlights

- Taste the gastronomic treats of Kinsale
- Take the scenic route to West Cork from Kinsale, through Clonakilty and Skibbereen to Mizen Head
- Go walking and birdwatching on Clear Island
- Hike or cycle round the desolate Beara Peninsula to experience its natural beauty
- Climb Hungry Hill on the Beara Peninsula for some great views
- Visit Bantry House for its eclectic collection of art and beautiful gardens

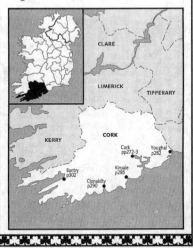

place from where many disillusioned, dispossessed emigrants bade farewell to their homeland. The nearby port of Cobh remained the major departure point until 1970; between 1815 and 1970 over three million people are thought to have emigrated from there.

CORK

COUNTY CORK

Cork played a key role in Ireland's struggle for independence. Thomas MacCurtain, a mayor of the city, was killed by the Black and Tans in 1920. His successor, Terence MacSwiney, died in London's Brixton Prison after 75 days on hunger strike. The Black and Tans were at their most brutal in Cork and much of the town was burned down during the Anglo-Irish War. Cork was also a centre for the Civil War that followed independence, and the pro-Treaty leader Michael Collins was ambushed and killed nearby.

ORIENTATION

The city centre is an island between two channels of the River Lee. The bridges – and the river smell – are vaguely reminiscent of Amsterdam. The curve of St Patrick's St is the centre of the main shopping precinct, with restaurants and trendy shops crammed into the pedestrianised streets of the Huguenot Quarter to the north. From the centre, Washington St (which becomes Lancaster Quay and Western Rd) leads south-west to the university, Killarney and West Cork, passing B&Bs and two hostels along the way.

Over the river and to the north-east are Kent Train Station and several hostels. In this district MacCurtain St is the main thoroughfare. West of here, the Shandon area, up on a hillside, cherishes some interesting old buildings but is otherwise rather rundown.

INFORMATION
Tourist Offices

The tourist office (☎ 427 3251), Grand Parade, opens 9 am to 1 pm and 2.15 to 5.15 pm Monday to Saturday, with extended hours from June to August. The information desk is to the rear. The staff are helpful but there's little information about Cork city itself, and what's on display you have to pay for.

From June to September you'll be better off visiting the Cork City Information Booth in St Patrick's St; it has a lot of city information, and its leaflets and maps are free.

Money

The Bank of Ireland and Allied Irish Bank (AIB), both on St Patrick's St, have ATMs and currency-exchange facilities.

Post

The main post office is on Pembroke St, just off Oliver Plunkett St.

Travel Agencies

The USIT office (☎ 427 0900), 66-70 Oliver Plunkett St, opens 9.30 am to 5.30 pm on weekdays, and 10 am to 4 pm on Saturday.

Bookshops

Waterstone's runs between St Patrick's and Paul Sts. Eason's on St Patrick's St has a wide, less academic stock, including French newspapers and magazines. Connolly's, on Rory Gallagher Place next to the Paul St Shopping Centre, has a second-hand selection, as do Vibes & Scribes, 3 Bridge St, and The Shelf on George's Quay. For lovers of blood-and-gore literature there's also Mainly Murder at 2A Paul St.

Laundry

The Laundrette, 14 MacCurtain St, is next to the Everyman Palace Theatre, and Clifton Laundrette, Western Rd, is opposite the gates of University College Cork (UCC).

ST FINBARR'S CATHEDRAL

Dramatically lit at night, this imposing Protestant cathedral was designed by the Victorian architect William Burges, who was also responsible for Cardiff Castle and Castell Coch in Wales. He beat 67 other entrants in a competition to design a new cathedral to replace the crumbling old one. Work was completed in 1879. The finished building has three spires and a High Victorian interior. Particularly impressive are the huge pulpit and the colourful chancel ceiling.

SHANDON

The northern side of Cork is dominated by the curious stepped tower of 18th-century **St Anne's Church**, of which two walls are

CORK

Walking Tour of Cork

This tour starts at the eastern end of South Mall, across the river from the grey **City Hall**. On a visit to Ireland in 1963, President John F Kennedy gave an address from the steps of the City Hall. He had returned as a conquering hero to the land his great-grandfather had left, and the city came to a standstill as a massive crowd turned out to welcome him.

Walk west along the river until you reach **Holy Trinity Church**, designed by the Pain brothers in 1834 for Father Theobald Matthew, the 'Apostle of Temperance'. He led an effective, but short-lived, crusade against 'the demon drink' which resulted in a reduction in the production of whiskey by more than half in the early 1840s.

Take the turning to the right just before the church, which brings you out on South Mall. Across the road to the right you'll see the **Imperial Hotel**, dating back to 1816, where Michael Collins, commander-in-chief of the Irish Free State army, slept before setting out on a journey that would end in ambush and his death on 22 August 1922. When he arrived at the Imperial the two sentries in the lobby were asleep and Collins knocked their heads together in irritation.

Walk west along South Mall until you reach a small monument to the victims of the Hiroshima and Nagasaki atomic bombs on your left. A few steps farther and you'll reach the ornate **Nationalist Monument**, erected in memory of Irish patriots who died between the 1798 and 1867 risings.

Turn right along Grand Parade, with the tourist office on your right and three 18th-century bow-fronted houses on your left. Between Oliver Plunkett and Washington Sts is the small Bishop Lucey Park on the Washington St side of Grand Parade. Cross the park to the old church in the right, end corner which now houses the Cork Archive Centre. Adjoining it is the **Triskel Arts Centre**, an important arts venue (for more details see Entertainment in the Cork city section).

Turn left down South Main St. Just before the Tudor-style Beamish & Crawford brewery turn left again down Tuckey St and go to the end, where, on the left, a bollard bears testimony to the days when Grand Parade was an open canal and boats moored by the quayside.

On your right you'll again see the Nationalist Monument. From there, turn left along South Mall then right onto the single-arched **Parliament Bridge**, built by the British in 1806 to commemorate the union of the British and Irish Parliaments five years previously. Cross the bridge and turn right along Sullivan's Quay. To your right you'll see **South Gate Bridge** (1713), which marks the site of the medieval entrance to the city.

Continue straight ahead along Bishop St to **St Finbarr's Cathedral**. From there it's a short walk west to the entrance to **University College Cork** (UCC), where a collection of Ogham stones is housed in the corridor of the north wing (the one with a tower), directly behind you as you face the main entrance to the Boole Library.

If you face the front of the Boole Library and walk to the left, you'll see the Department of Plant Science. Behind it is the gorgeous **Honan Chapel**, built in 1915. The stained-glass windows and elaborate mosaic floors are well worth a look.

Return to the quadrangle and follow the path by the tower through the north wing. Follow the road down to the main gate, noting the **Greek Revival portico** originally built for Cork County Jail on your left. As you emerge onto Western Rd the **Cork Public Museum** is close by, on the other side of Mardyke Walk in Fitzgerald Park.

Bus No 8 will ferry you back into the town centre from the main gate of UCC.

faced with limestone and two with sand-stone, on Eason's Hill. The salmon-shaped weathervane was apparently chosen because the local monks reserved for themselves the right to fish for salmon in the river. The church opens 10 am to 5 pm Monday to Saturday. It costs £3 to climb the tower and ring its bells, but it's free to view the interior; its small collection of 17th-century Bibles and other books includes the letters of poet John Donne.

Nearby is the expensive **Shandon Craft Centre** in what was once the Cork Butter Exchange. Opposite it is the circular **Firkin Crane Centre**, which used to house the weighing scales for the butter-casks (firkins) and is now home to a dance company (for details see the Entertainment section later).

CORK PUBLIC MUSEUM

The ground floor of this small, rather old-fashioned museum is mostly devoted to Cork's role in the fight for independence, while the 1st floor features archaeological displays. The museum is in pretty Fitzgerald Park north of Western Rd. The museum opens 11 am to 1 pm and 2.15 to 5 pm on weekdays, and 3 to 5 pm on Sunday (except bank-holiday weekends). Admission is free except on Sunday, when it costs 75p.

Take bus No 8 to the main gates of UCC and follow the brown sign pointing to the museum.

CRAWFORD MUNICIPAL ART GALLERY

Crawford Municipal Art Gallery (☎ 427 3377), on Emmet Place, is in a building that was built in 1724 as the Customs House and became the Cork School of Art in 1884. It now houses an excellent permanent collection, featuring works by Irish artists such as Jack Yeats and Seán Keating, as well as works of the British Newlyn and St Ives' schools. It is currently in the process of being extended, which affects access to some galleries.

There's an excellent café. The gallery opens 10 am to 5 pm Monday to Saturday. Admission is free.

CORK CITY JAIL

The jail (☎ 430 5022), on Convent Ave west of the city, received its first prisoners in 1824 and its last in 1923. The 35-minute taped tour, which guides you around the restored and refurnished cells, is very moving and probably more interesting than the 20-minute audiovisual display on the prison's history. Upstairs is the **National Radio Museum** where, alongside collections of beautiful old radios, you can hear the story of Marconi's conquest of the airwaves. In the high season there are storytelling sessions two evenings each week.

The jail opens 9.30 am to 6 pm daily, March to October; and 10 am to 5 pm daily, November to February. Last admission is one hour before closing. Admission costs £3.50/2.

Take bus No 8 from the bus station to the stop outside UCC, then walk north across Fitzgerald Park and over Daly Bridge. Turn right up the hill along Sunday's Well Rd, left along Convent Ave and you'll see the brown signpost to the jail.

CORK HERITAGE PARK

Cork Heritage Park (☎ 435 8854) is a collection of maritime and other exhibits in landscaped gardens 5km east of the city in Bessberro, Blackrock. You can walk or take bus No 2. The park opens 10.30 am to 5.30 pm daily, April to September (by appointment only from October to March). Admission costs £3.50/1.50.

ORGANISED TOURS

Between June and September, Discover Cork (☎ 429 3873) organises free walking tours on Tuesday and Thursday at 7.30 pm, departing from outside the tourist office.

Walking tours of UCC start at the main gates on Western Rd. Call the UCC information office (☎ 490 2731) for details.

Bus Éireann (☎ 450 8188) operates a three-hour open-top-bus tour of Cork city and Blarney between mid-June and early September (£6/3), departing from the bus station at 10.15 am and 2.45 pm Monday to Saturday.

Between late May and September, Guide

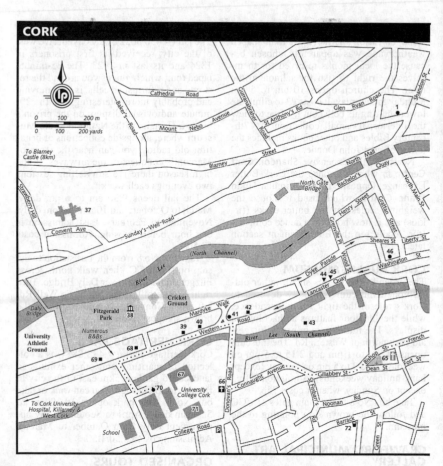

CORK

Friday (☎ 01-676 5377) runs open-top hop-on, hop-off daily bus tours around Cork city from Grand Parade opposite the tourist office. Tickets cost £7.50/2.50.

SPECIAL EVENTS

The Cork International Jazz Festival and the International Film Festival both take place in October. Tickets for both can sell out quickly. Programmes are available from Cork Opera House (☎ 427 0022), Emmet Place. The International Choral and Folk Dance Festival runs from late April to early May in the City Hall and other venues.

PLACES TO STAY

Camping

Bienvenue Ferry Caravan and Camping Park (☎ 431 2711) is on a slip road opposite the entrance to Cork Airport off the N27. The airport bus stops about half a kilometre away. A tent site for two adults costs £8.

Hostels

Three hostels are quite close together, north of the river from the bus station. Just off Wellington Rd is the clean, friendly *Sheila's* (☎ 450 5562, 4 Belgrave Place),

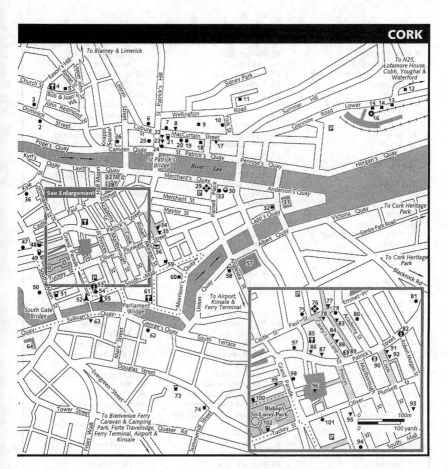

which has bags of facilities: a laundry, a café, a foreign exchange, a Western Union link, bike hire, Internet access, and even a sauna. Dorm beds start at £7; doubles cost £18 (£22 with bathroom).

Bigger and more easily found is the IHH *Isaac's* (☎ *450 0011, 48 MacCurtain St*), where dorm beds start at £7.95. It's a rather impersonal place and residents can collect their baggage from the security room only on the hour and half-hour, but it does have 24-hour dorm access.

The friendly IHH *Kinlay House Shandon* (☎ *450 8966, Bob and Joan's Walk*) is

in the old Shandon district immediately behind St Anne's Church. Beds in four-bed dorms cost £7.50 and twin rooms cost £22, all including a light breakfast. Internet access costs £1.50 for 15 minutes.

Other fairly central possibilities include: *Cork City Independent Hostel* (☎ *450 9089, 100 Glanmire Rd Lower*), just east of Kent Train Station, where dorm beds cost £6 and doubles £17; *Kelly's* (☎ *431 5612, 25 Summerhill St*), in a terraced house near the corner of Douglas St south of the river, where beds start at £7.50; and the modern *Island House* (☎ *427 1716, Morrison's*

CORK

PLACES TO STAY
5   Kinlay House Shandon
9   Isaac's Hostel; Hotel Isaac's & Restaurant
11 Sheila's
12 Cork City Independent Tourist Hostel
13 Kent House
14 Oakland
15 Tara House
18 Metropole
32 Jury's Cork Inn
39 Antoine House
40 St Kilda's
42 Garnish House
43 Jury's Hotel
59 Imperial Hotel
60 Island House
68 Cork International Youth Hostel
69 Campus House
74 Kelly's

PLACES TO EAT
8   O'Briens
17 Luciano's
22 Pico's Bistro
23 Taste of Thailand
34 Gino's
35 The Long Valley
44 Reidy's Vault Bar
45 Café Paradiso
63 Quay Co-Op
77 Bully's
78 Gingerbread House Café
83 Meadows & Byrne
84 Paddy Garibaldi; Gambieni's
86 Abrakebabra
87 Gloria Jeans
88 Café Mexicana
91 Ambassador Chinese Restaurant

92 Bewley's Café
93 Java Joe's
95 The Ivory Tower
96 English Market
99 O'Briens

PUBS
21 Gallagher's
48 Washington Inn
49 John Rearden & Son
51 An Spailpín Fánac
58 The Lobby; Charlie's; An Phoenix; Donkey's Ears
72 Nancy Spain's
73 Loafers
102 Mollies

OTHER
1   Cycle Scene
2   Shandon Craft Centre (Cork Butter Exchange)
3   Firkin Crane Centre
4   St Anne's Church, Shandon
6   City Limits
7   The Living Tradition
10 Tents & Leisure
16 Kent Train Station
19 The Laundrette
20 Everyman Palace Theatre
24 Irish Ferries Office
25 Vibes & Scribes
26 Cork Arts Theatre
27 Cork Opera House
28 Crawford Municipal Art Gallery & Gallery Café
29 Merchant's Quay Shopping Centre
30 Bus Station
31 Customs House
33 The Tent Shop
36 Kilgrew's Cycles

37 Cork City Jail; National Radio Museum
38 Cork Public Museum
41 Clifton Laundrette
46 Kino
47 Courthouse
50 Beamish & Crawford Brewery
52 Nationalist Monument
53 Tourist Office; Stena Line Office
54 Brittany Ferries Office
55 Hiroshima & Nagasaki Monument
56 Post Office
57 City Hall
61 Holy Trinity Church
62 The Shelf
64 Elizabeth Fort
65 St Finbarr's Cathedral
66 Honan Chapel
67 North Wing of University College Cork
70 Greek Revival Portico
71 Boole Library
75 Connolly's
76 Paul St Shopping Centre
79 Mainly Murder
80 Aer Lingus Office
81 Eason's Bookshop
82 Cork City Information Booth
85 Church of St Peter & St Paul
89 AIB
90 Bank of Ireland
94 Swansea Cork Ferries Office
97 Waterstone's Bookshop
98 Capitol Cineplex
100 Triskel Arts Centre & Café; Cork Archive Centre
101 USIT Office

Quay), where dorm beds cost £10.50 and singles/doubles £27/38.

Out by UCC is the big An Óige *Cork International Youth Hostel* (☎ 454 3289, 1-2 *Western Rd*), in a renovated red-brick Victorian house. It's good value at £8 per night in a dorm; the kitchen, lounge and dining room are all immaculate.

Should it be full, the much smaller IHH *Campus House* (☎ 434 3531, 3 *Woodland View, Western Rd*), just a few doors farther west, has beds costing £7.50. Bus No 8

from the bus station stops outside UCC nearby.

B&Bs
Glanmire Rd Lower near Kent Train Station is lined with cheapish B&Bs. At *Kent House* (☎ 450 4260), No 47, singles/doubles cost £23.50/34; *Oakland* (☎ 450 0578), at No 51, costs £25/36; and *Tara House* (☎ 450 0294), at No 52, has rooms with shared bathroom costing £21.50/32.

On the opposite side of town, along

CORK

Western Rd near UCC, there are plenty of B&Bs. At *Garnish House* (☎ 427 5111) the breakfasts are great, offering a wide choice which includes homemade breads and yoghurt. Singles/doubles cost £60/72 in the high season, but are much cheaper during the rest of the year. A few doors along is the less expensive *Antoine House* (☎ 427 3494) charging £25/40. Pricier is *St Kilda's* (☎ 427 3095), a big blue house, where rooms cost £50/70. All of these places have their own car park.

If you're coming into Cork from the west, some of these B&Bs can be reached from the roundabout at Cork University Hospital; east of the UCC gates, Western Rd is one way so B&Bs along this section can be approached by westbound traffic only.

Hotels

Attached to the hostel of the same name, *Hotel Isaac's* (☎ 450 0011, 48 MacCurtain St) is central. Singles/doubles cost £49/70, and self-catering apartments are available, starting at £70. The biggest place in the city is *Jury's Hotel* (☎ 427 6622, fax 427 6144, Lancaster Quay), to the west of the city, with an ugly exterior. Singles/doubles cost an absurd £120/142, excluding tax and breakfast, although there's a small outdoor swimming pool. *Imperial Hotel* (☎ 427 4040, fax 427 5375, South Mall) is more central and more attractive, if somewhat faded. It's being renovated and at the time of writing only a limited number of rooms were available, at a room rate of £49. Prices will rise when renovations are finished.

Originally a temperance hotel, rooms at the somewhat drab *Metropole* (☎ 450 8122, fax 450 6450, MacCurtain St) start at £65/98.

Good value, especially for families, are two hotels with fixed room rates for up to three adults and two children. *Jury's Cork Inn* (☎ 427 6444, fax 427 6144, Anderson's Quay), in the city centre opposite Customs House, charges £57, while *Forte Travelodge* (☎ 1800 709709, fax 431 0707), near the airport at the Kinsale Rd roundabout, charges £49.95.

At Tivoli, on the Waterford road, the *Lotamore House* (☎ 482 2344) stands in delightful grounds. Singles/doubles cost £45/64.

PLACES TO EAT
Restaurants

In the pedestrian area between St Patrick's and Paul Sts, *Bully's* (☎ 427 3555, 40 Paul St) serves pizza starting at £4.99 and pasta costing upwards of £3.99. A block to the south, *Café Mexicana* (☎ 427 6433, Carey's Lane) offers enchiladas and tacos costing £7.50, while the stylish *Paddy Garibaldi* serves up pizzas and pastas (£4.95) plus fish and burgers. Next door the more traditional *Gambieni's* offers lunchtime pasta starting at £4.50.

Gino's (☎ 427 4485, 7 Winthrop St), off Oliver Plunkett St, and *Luciano's* (MacCurtain St) are two good pizzerias. Gino's also serves good ice cream. Luciano's opens only in the evening.

Ambassador Chinese Restaurant (Cook St) is a comfortable little place where most main courses cost around £13. It opens only for dinner.

For vegetarians, *Café Paradiso* (Lancaster Quay), near Jury's Hotel, offers delicious dishes such as baked crêpe of leeks (£13). It closes on Sunday and Monday. Also catering for vegetarians, the upstairs *Quay Co-Op* (☎ 431 7026, 24 Sullivan's Quay) serves soups starting at £1.75 as well as more elaborate evening menus. Organic food is sold in its shop next door.

Isaac's Restaurant (☎ 450 3805), not run by the MacCurtain St hostel to which it's attached, is deservedly popular and offers some of the best-value meals around; menus feature dishes such as salmon and potato cakes for £4.45 and a number of vegetarian options. At *Taste of Thailand* (8 Bridge St) a three-course dinner costs £10.95 between 6 and 7.30 pm. *Pico's Bistro* (4 Bridge St) uses mostly organic food and also offers a three-course 'early diner' meal costing £10.25.

The Ivory Tower (☎ 427 4665, 35 Princes St) serves interesting world food; seafood and vegetarian dishes are always

CORK

available. A set dinner costs £25, but lunch, costing around £9 to £12, is better value.

Fast Food, Cafés & Pubs

If you're self-catering or want to put together a picnic, head straight for the *English Market* off the western end of St Patrick's St (but with access from other streets too). It sells all manner of fruit, fish, meat, homemade cakes, bagels and West Cork cheeses. Along St Patrick's St is the usual collection of fast-food outlets, including a branch of *Abrakebabra* where the service is indifferent and not necessarily fast.

Two of the nicest places for a light lunch or afternoon tea are *Gallery Café* in Crawford Municipal Art Gallery, Emmet Place, and the renovated upstairs café at *Triskel Arts Centre (Tobin St)*. Alternatively, *O'Briens (39 MacCurtain St)*, near Isaac's Hostel, is good for tea, sandwiches, light meals and ice cream. Lasagne costs £3.70. It's also one of the few places open early for Sunday breakfasts. There's another branch on Washington St.

On Cook St, *Bewley's Café* is a good place for breakfast or a light meal at other times, as is *Java Joe's (14-15 Cook St)*, where scrambled eggs costs £1.80. *The Long Valley (Winthrop St)*, a low-key pub near the post office, is famous for its giant lunchtime sandwiches (£2.15).

Between St Patrick's St and pedestrianised Paul St are a couple of narrow lanes with good places for a sandwich or meal. On French Church St try the *Gingerbread House Café* or *Meadows and Byrne* for lunch, or just a coffee or tea. At *Gloria Jeans (84 St Patrick's St)* great coffee starts at £1; it also serves pastries. It opens at noon on Sunday, when a lot of other places are closed.

Reidy's Vault Bar (Western Rd), near Jury's Hotel, is a comfortable pub serving seafood all day; dishes cost £6 to £11. Smoked salmon costs £8.95.

ENTERTAINMENT
Pubs

Cork's cultural rivalry with Dublin extends to drink. Locally brewed Murphy's is the stout of choice here, or there's Beamish, which is often cheaper.

On the corner of Union Quay and Anglesea St, *The Lobby*, *Charlie's*, *An Phoenix* and the *Donkey's Ears* pubs are side by side, and one or other has music on most nights.

The Beamish ought to be good at *An Spailpín Fánac (South Main St)* since it's opposite the Beamish & Crawford Brewery; it's 'probably the oldest pub in Ireland' according to the tourist-board pub guide. To the south, the arty *Nancy Spain's (48 Barrack St)* offers good music and attracts a young crowd. *Mollies (Tuckey St)* also has music – and televised football, if that's your scene – and packs them in on weekend nights.

Washington St has a cluster of popular student pubs with music; two of them are near the imposing Courthouse – *Washington Inn* and *John Rearden & Son*.

Loafers (26 Douglas St) is essentially a lesbian pub that attracts male gays at the weekend.

Gallagher's (MacCurtain St) has a backpackers' night on Tuesdays, when pitchers of beer cost £6 and there's traditional music.

Theatre & Cinemas

Cork prides itself on its cultural pursuits. The top mainstream theatre is *Cork Opera House (☎ 427 0022, Emmet Place)*. The *Cork Arts Theatre (☎ 450 8398, Knapps Square)*, north of the river, is more adventurous, as is the *Triskel Arts Centre (☎ 427 2022, Tobin St)*, off South Main St, which also shows arthouse films. The restored *Everyman Palace Theatre (☎ 450 1673, MacCurtain St)* stages a range of theatrical productions.

Firkin Crane Centre (☎ 450 7487), near St Anne's Church, Shandon, has mid-week sessions of traditional dancing in summer and is a venue for national and international dance companies.

Capitol Cineplex (☎ 427 8777, Grand Parade) shows mainstream films, while the downbeat *Kino (☎ 427 1571, Washington St West)* is more arthouse.

Comedy
The comedy club at *City Limits* (*Coburg St*) boasts top comedy acts from 8.45 pm on Friday and Saturday.

SHOPPING
If you're keen on traditional music look in at The Living Tradition (☎ 450 2025), 40 MacCurtain St, which sells a wide range of tapes, CDs and music publications. It opens 9.30 am to 5.30 pm Monday to Saturday.

You can hire camping equipment from The Tent Shop (☎ 427 8833), 7 Parnell Place, near the bus station, or, just round the corner from Isaac's Hostel in York St, Tents and Leisure (☎ 450 0702) sells and hires out tents.

GETTING THERE & AWAY
Air
There are direct flights to Dublin, London, Manchester, Exeter, Jersey, Paris, Rennes and Amsterdam from Cork Airport. Other overseas flights go via Dublin. For flight information ☎ 313131 or contact the Aer Lingus office (☎ 432 7155) on Academy St.

Bus
Bus Éireann operates from the bus station (☎ 450 8188) on the corner of Merchant's Quay and Parnell Place. You can get to most places from Cork, including Dublin (£12, 4¼ hours, four daily), Killarney (£8.80, two hours, five daily), Waterford (£8, 2¼ hours, six to eight daily) and Wexford (£12, 3¾ hours, two daily). Fares listed are all one way.

Train
Kent Train Station (☎ 450 4777) is north of the Lee River on Glanmire Rd Lower. There's a direct train connection to Dublin (£32, 2½ hours, eight daily) and indirect routes to other towns such as Killarney (£13.50, two hours, four daily) and Waterford (£17, three to five hours, four daily).

An hourly service south-west to Cobh stops at Fota, enabling you to take in the Fota Wildlife Park and Cobh Heritage Centre (see the following Around Cork City section) on a round trip.

Boat
Regular ferries link Cork with the UK and France. A number of companies have offices in Cork city:

Brittany Ferries
    (☎ 427 7801) 42 Grand Parade
Irish Ferries
    (☎ 455 1995) 9 Bridge St, at the corner of St Patrick's Quay
Stena Line
    (☎ 427 2965) in the Tourist Office, Grand Parade
Swansea Cork Ferries
    (☎ 427 1166) 52 South Mall (also an office at the ferry terminal)

For more details see Sea in the Getting There & Away chapter.

GETTING AROUND
To/From the Airport
Between April and September four buses daily run from the bus terminal to the airport (£2.50). The airport is about 8km south of the city centre on the South City Link Rd. It takes about 20 minutes to get there by car.

To/From the Ferry Terminal
The ferry terminal is at Ringaskiddy, about 15 minutes by car south-east from the city centre along the N28. Bus Éireann runs a fairly frequent daily service to the terminal; the journey takes 45 minutes.

Bus
Most places you'll need to get to are within easy walking distance of the centre. If you're staying at Cork International Youth Hostel, however, the bus fare from the bus station is 70p; if you're staying a long time it might be worth considering a weekly ticket for £9. You'll need a photo to obtain it.

Car
Budget (☎ 427 4755) has a desk at the tourist office as well as at the airport. Car rental starts at £33 per day including insurance and unlimited mileage.

Parking Parking coupons (50p per hour) are obtainable from the tourist office and

CORK

some newsagents. They must be displayed inside the car window to park virtually anywhere in the city centre. Alternatively, use the big car park behind Merchant's Quay Shopping Centre, or park for free in the Shandon area, north of Pope's Quay.

Bicycle
Bike hire costs £10/40 per day/week. Cycle Scene (☎ 430 1183), 396 Blarney St, and Kilgrew's Cycles (☎ 427 6255), 6-7 Kyle St, handle the Raleigh Rent-a-Bike scheme.

Around Cork City

BLARNEY
☎ 021 • pop 1950
Just north-west of Cork, the village of Blarney (An Bhlarna) has one overwhelming drawcard – Blarney Castle. The tourist office (☎ 438 1624), near the bus stop, opens 9 am to 7 pm daily, June to September; 9 am to 5 pm daily, March and April; and 9 am to 4 pm daily, the rest of the year. Behind it is **Blarney Woollen Mills**, a giant tourist shop selling everything from quality garments to tacky Ireland-shaped green telephones accompanied by a 'no blarney' guarantee.

Blarney Castle
Even the most untouristy visitor will probably feel compelled to kiss the Blarney Stone and get the gift of the gab or, as an 18th-century French consul put it, 'gain the privilege of telling lies for seven years'. It was Queen Elizabeth I, exasperated with Lord Blarney's ability to talk endlessly without ever actually agreeing to her demands, who invented the term.

Dating from 1446, the castle is a tower house built on solid limestone in wonderful grounds; remember to pack a picnic.

Bending over backwards to kiss the sacred rock requires a head for heights. You're unlikely to fall since there's a grill and someone there to hold you but a word of warning about general safety is in order. The sacred rock is at the top of the castle and the long spiral staircases are narrow and steep.

The castle (☎ 438 5252) opens 9 am to 6.30 pm Monday to Saturday, and 9.30 am to 5.30 pm on Sunday, May and September; 9 am to 7 pm Monday to Saturday, and 9.30 am to 5.30 pm on Sunday, June to August; and 9 am to 6 pm (or sundown) Monday to Saturday, and 9.30 am to 5 pm (or sundown) on Sunday, October to April. Admission costs £3.50/1. Your enjoyment of your visit to Blarney will probably be in inverse proportion to the number of coach tours there at the time. Getting there at opening time is one way of beating the crowds.

Places to Stay
Camping & Hostels The *Blarney Caravan and Camping Park* (☎ 438 5167), 2.5km from town on the R617, is signposted from Blarney. A tent site costs £3.50 for hikers and cyclists, £4 for motorcyclists, and £5 with a car. Three kilometres west of Blarney, on the road to Killarney, is a very basic unaffiliated *hostel* (☎ 438 5580), where dorm beds cost £7, doubles £16.

B&Bs Blarney has a host of B&Bs, most of them open only from April or May to October or November. Two that are open year round are *Buena Vista* (☎ 438 5035) and *Killarney House* (☎ 438 1841), both on Station Rd; singles/doubles cost £25/36. More central is *Rosemount* (☎ 438 5584), where singles/doubles start at £24.50/36; to get there take the first right past the Blarney Park Hotel off the Killarney road.

Hotels There are two big hotels, *Blarney Park* (☎ 438 5281, fax 438 1506) and *Christys* (☎ 438 5011, fax 438 5350), where doubles cost £118 and £98 respectively. The smaller *Blarney Castle* (☎ 438 5116, The Square) is cheaper: a single without bathroom costs £22, a double with bathroom £52.

Places to Eat
Blarney has several restaurants as well as pubs serving food. At *Blarney Stone Restaurant* lunch dishes start at £3.50. *Mackey's*, next door, serves Irish stew cost-

ing £6 and has several vegetarian options plus a set menu costing £10. Bar food at the *Muskerry Arms* opposite is also reasonably priced. The huge *Mill Restaurant*, next to Blarney Woollen Mills, is popular and has long queues; a roast dinner here costs £5.50.

Getting There & Away
Blarney is 8km north-west of Cork and buses run regularly from the Cork bus station (£2.50 return, 30 minutes).

BALLINCOLLIG
The village of Ballincollig, 8km west of Cork on the main Killarney road, is home to the **Royal Gunpowder Mills**. Throughout the 19th century this was one of Europe's largest gunpowder manufacturing plants. It opens 10 am to 6 pm daily, April to September. Admission costs £2.50/1.50. Regular buses run to the village from Cork city bus station (£2.50 return, 15 minutes).

PASSAGE WEST
If you're travelling from West to eastern Cork and want to avoid going through Cork city it's worth knowing about the Ferry Link (☎ 021-481 1223), which connects Passage West with Carrigaloe daily between 7.15 am and 12.30 am the following morning. One-way fares are £2.50 for a car, £1.30 for a motorcycle and 60p for pedestrians.

CROSSHAVEN
☎ 021 • pop 1360
The R612 south-west from Cork brings you to pretty little Crosshaven on the River Owenboy. The **marina** can look delightful when the sun shines, but otherwise the only sights are Georgian **Crosshaven House**, which is not open to the public, and the scant remains of the 16th-century **Fort Camden**. You could also have a meal and a drink in one of the pubs that line the harbour.

Grand Hotel (☎ 483 2270) was being totally renovated at the time of writing. If it reopens as a hotel, expect prices to reflect its striking architecture and views which take in the river.

There are regular buses to and from Cork.

FOTA WILDLIFE PARK
To the east of Cork, Fota Wildlife Park (☎ 021-481 2678), a kind of zoo without bars, is ideal for children of all ages. Giraffes, ostriches, monkeys, kangaroos and penguins wander freely, and lemurs invade the coffee shop. Cheetahs may not have space to hit full speed here but they're bred and exported to countries from where they originated. Look out in particular for the glorious white and brown scimitar-horned onyx, believed to be extinct in the wild.

The *Coffee Shop* is pretty ordinary so it might be worth bringing a picnic. A 'gravy train' runs a circuit round the park every 15 minutes (50p). The park opens 10 am (11 am on Sunday) to 5 pm daily, Easter to October. Admission costs £3.80/2.30.

With time on your hands it's worth strolling down to look at the graceful exterior of the 18th-century **Fota House**, once one of Ireland's grandest houses but now sadly neglected, and the 150-year-old **arboretum**, both towards the station end of the park.

Getting There & Away
Fota is 16km from Cork. Since cars must be left outside (parking fee £1) and visitors walk around the park, it's probably easier to take the hourly Cork to Cobh train which stops here (£1.80 return, 15 minutes).

COBH
☎ 021 • pop 6230
Picturesque Cobh (pronounced 'cove') was for many years the port of Cork, and has always had a strong connection with Atlantic crossings. In 1838 the *Sirius* was the first steamship to cross the Atlantic, sailing from Cobh. The *Titanic* made its last stop here before its fateful Atlantic crossing in 1912, and it was near Cobh that the *Lusitania* was torpedoed in 1915. The world's first yacht club, the Royal Cork Yacht Club, was founded here in 1720, but now operates from Crosshaven on the other side of Cork Harbour. The old Yacht Club building now

CORK

The Irish Diaspora

About half the people born in Ireland since 1820 have emigrated, but the story of Irish emigration goes back much further than that, and continued, albeit on a smaller scale, until very recently.

Between 1652 and 1653, Oliver Cromwell expelled around 30,000 soldiers and had thousands of civilians transported. The West Indies was a favourite destination because once there they could be sold as slaves. After the Treaty of Limerick was signed in 1691, another 20,000 men and their families fled to France.

NICKY CAVEN

Oliver Cromwell

In the 18th century emigration to North America began, especially from Ulster, where Presbyterians were weary of being treated as second-class citizens. Between 1791 and 1853, 39,000 convicts were transported from Cobh to Australia for crimes ranging from theft to murder. Between 1848 and 1850, 4000 orphaned girls were sent to Australia from the workhouses to provide mates for the men.

The most dramatic and tragic period of emigration was precipitated by the Potato Famine of 1845 to 1851, which accelerated an already well-established process. During that period more than a million people left and, between 1855 and 1914, another four million Irish people emigrated for a new life, mostly in the USA and Britain.

Once a man or woman – and women often outnumbered men in their determination to leave – had decided to book their transatlantic passage it was understood that they were unlikely ever to return; hence the 'American Wake', a farewell party recognised as marking a final parting between emigrants and their families and friends.

Accurate figures are difficult to come by but today tens of millions of people around the world are of Irish origin. In North America approximately 40 million claim an Irish connection, with the biggest concentration of those with Irish roots being in New York, Boston and Philadelphia. Some of these people feel their roots strongly, a few even contributing financially to the nationalist paramilitaries in Northern Ireland. About one-third of Australia's 19 million or so people also have an Irish connection.

Ireland's improved economic circumstances have staunched the flow of emigrants, and since the early 1990s there has been net immigration. Many of these immigrants have been the returning children of the diaspora.

---

houses a small tourist office (☎ 481 3301) and arts centre, open 9.30 am to 5.30 pm on weekdays, and 11.30 am to 5.30 pm at the weekend, March to September; and 2.30 to 5.30 pm daily, October to February.

Cobh is on Great Island, which fills much of Cork Harbour and is joined to the mainland by a causeway. In the British era it was known as Queenstown because it was where Queen Victoria arrived in 1849 on her first visit to Ireland.

St Colman's Cathedral

Cobh is dominated by this massive but comparatively new cathedral standing on a huge platform above the town. Construction of the French-Gothic-style cathedral began in 1868 but it wasn't completed until 1915. The Irish communities in Australia and the USA contributed much of the construction cost. The cathedral is noted for its 47-bell carillon, the largest in Ireland; the biggest bell weighs 3440kg. St Colman (522–604) is the patron saint of the local diocese of Cloyne.

Cobh Heritage Centre

Part of Cobh train station has been converted to house the impressive Cobh Heritage Centre. It tells the 'Queenstown Story' with interesting displays on the mass emigrations following the Famine, the era of the great liners, and the tragedies of the *Titanic* and *Lusitania*.

The heritage centre (☎ 481 3591) opens 10 am to 6 pm daily. Admission costs £3.50/2. There's also a craft and coffee shop.

Cobh Museum

A small history museum is housed in the 19th-century Scots Presbyterian church which overlooks the train station. It opens 11 am to 1 pm and 2 to 6 pm Monday to Saturday, and 3 to 6 pm on Sunday, April to September.

Harbour Cruises

Early June to September, Marine Transport Services (☎ 481 1485) organises one-hour cruises of the harbour costing £3.50/2.50. The tourist office also has details.

Places to Stay & Eat

If you don't care for big towns, Cobh makes a pleasant alternative to Cork. The cheapest and one of the best B&Bs is *Westbourne House* (☎ 481 1391), which charges £12 per person. It's on the left as you walk up from the train station and has views of the harbour. If that's full, try *Bellavista* (☎ 481 2450, Bishop's Rd), where singles/doubles cost £25/40.

Commodore (☎ 481 1277) is the premier hotel and has a heated indoor pool. Singles/doubles cost £48/80 in July and August. It's also the most reliable place for a decent meal, offering set lunches, bar meals and dinner (£20).

A couple of *cafés* in town serve quick meals, as do some of the many *pubs*. The menu at the *River Room* is a little more interesting than in most cafés; large vegetarian samosas cost £1.75.

Getting There & Away

Cobh is 24km south-east of Cork, off the main N25 Cork to Rosslare road. Hourly trains connect Cobh with Cork (£2.50 return, 30 minutes). Alternatively, between June and September you can take a passenger cruiser which leaves Cobh at 3.15 pm and costs £5.50/3.50.

MIDLETON
☎ 021 • pop 3000

Midleton (Mainistir na Corann) is about 20km east of Cork. There's a tourist office (☎ 461 3702) at the Jameson Heritage Centre which opens 9.30 am (11.30 am on Sunday) to 1 pm and 2.15 to 5.30 pm daily.

Whiskey has been distilled here since the early 19th century, and the old works were opened to the public as the Jameson Heritage Centre (☎ 461 3594) after a new distillery was opened. Twenty-four million bottles of whiskey are produced at this new plant each year.

Forty-five-minute guided tours start with a film show and continue with a walkabout that reveals the whole whiskey-making process. You see the storeroom where local farmers had their barley weighed and deposited, have the malting process explained to you and then see the huge water wheel that used to power the plant. Don't miss the world's largest copper. The tour ends in the bar, where two lucky volunteers get to compare assorted Irish whiskeys with Scotch and Bourbon. Everyone gets a free tipple and there's a café for snacks and lunches.

Between March and October there are regular daily tours from 10 am to 6 pm. During the rest of the year there are tours at noon and 3 pm on weekdays. Admission costs £3.95/1.50.

If you want to stay overnight, the IHH *An Stor Midleton Tourist Hostel* (☎ 463 3106,

CORK

Drury's Ave) has dorm beds costing £8, doubles £20.

Getting There & Away

There are regular buses from Cork to Midleton, some of which continue to Waterford.

YOUGHAL

☎ 024 • pop 5530

Youghal (pronounced 'yawl'; Eochaill) is an interesting little town where the River Blackwater meets the sea. Safe beaches stretch away south of town. Sir Walter Raleigh was town mayor from 1588 to 1589 and, tradition has it, he planted the first potatoes here after bringing them back from the New World.

Orientation & Information

Youghal is little more than one long street, appropriately called North Main St and South Main St and carrying traffic one way only for most of its length. Come through

Youghal in the wrong direction (from Waterford to Cork) and you could miss the lot.

The old Clock Gate at the southern end of North Main St is Youghal's major landmark. Nearby is the tourist office (☎ 92390), in Market House, Market Square. It opens 9 am to 7 pm daily, May to September; and 9.30 am to 5.30 pm Monday to Saturday, the rest of the year. A small heritage centre here (admission £1), open the same hours, explains the town's history, or you can buy the *Story of Youghal* (£1.95), which incorporates a town-trail map.

Things to See & Do

Heading from south to north, some of the town's sights are detailed here.

The elegant red-brick **Town Hall** on the seafront south of the tourist office was once Mall House, built in 1789 as a place of entertainment, with a ballroom, tearooms, and space for gambling and reading.

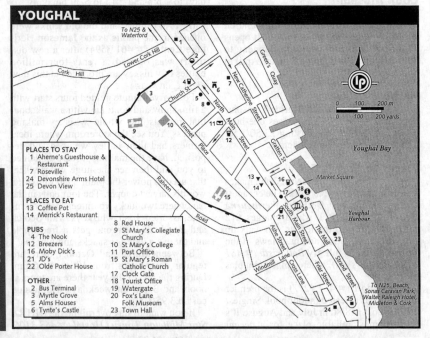

YOUGHAL

To N25 & Waterford

To N25, Beach, Sonas Caravan Park, Walter Raleigh Hotel, Midleton & Cork

Youghal Bay

Youghal Harbour

Market Square

PLACES TO STAY
1 Aherne's Guesthouse & Restaurant
7 Roseville
24 Devonshire Arms Hotel
25 Devon View

PLACES TO EAT
13 Coffee Pot
14 Merrick's Restaurant

PUBS
4 The Nook
12 Breezers
16 Moby Dick's
21 JD's
22 Olde Porter House

OTHER
2 Bus Terminal
3 Myrtle Grove
5 Alms Houses
6 Tynte's Castle

8 Red House
9 St Mary's Collegiate Church
10 St Mary's College
11 Post Office
15 St Mary's Roman Catholic Church
17 Clock Gate
18 Tourist Office
19 Watergate
20 Fox's Lane Folk Museum
23 Town Hall

CORK

Fox's Lane Folk Museum, signposted down an alley between The Mall and South Main St, displays over 400 bygones and a Victorian kitchen. It opens 10 am to 1 pm and 2 to 6 pm, Tuesday to Saturday, July and August, or you can make an appointment through the tourist office. Admission costs £2/1.

The curious **Clock Gate** bridges Main St. In 1777 the present building, a combination of clock tower and jail, replaced the medieval Trinity Gate, a key part of the town's fortifications. In 1798 several members of the rebellious United Irishmen were hanged from its walls.

The **Red House**, on North Main St, was designed in 1706 by the Dutch architect Leuventhen, with typically Dutch characteristics, such as the cornerstones positioned under the triangular gable. Its name comes from its red bricks. A few doors farther up the street are **Alms Houses** built in 1610 by Richard Boyle, the local lord, to house ex-soldiers.

Across the road stands the 15th-century **Tynte's Castle**. Originally it had a defensive riverfront position but as the River Blackwater silted up and changed course it was left high and dry. In 1584 the castle was confiscated and given to Sir Robert Tynte, who married the widow of the poet Edmund Spenser. Today it's semi-derelict.

Built in 1220, **St Mary's Collegiate Church** (covered in scaffolding for restoration work at the time of research) incorporates elements of an earlier Danish church dating back to the 11th century. In the late 16th century the earl of Desmond housed his troops here, leading to the destruction of the old chancel roof. Inside there's a monument to Richard Boyle, who bought Raleigh's Irish estates and became the first earl of Cork. It shows him with his wife and all 16 of his children, those who died as infants shown lying down. Look out, too, for a monument to Catherine, widow of the 11th earl of Desmond, who supposedly died in 1614, aged 140! There are also interesting gravestones to look at, some with Norman-French inscriptions. This is one of the oldest churches still in use

in Ireland, with Sunday services at 11 am. At other times it's usually locked; phone ☎ 91076 for the key. The churchyard is bounded by a fine stretch of the old town wall and one of the remaining turrets. The walls date back at least as far as the 13th century and remained in use until the 17th century.

Beside the church, **Myrtle Grove** is an interesting house which retains some 16th-century features. Local history relates that it was home to Sir Walter Raleigh, who made the mistake of smoking tobacco in front of a servant who had never seen such a thing and, accordingly, threw a bucket of water over him to douse the fire. The weather vane depicts the famous story of Raleigh, Queen Elizabeth, the puddle and the cloak.

St Mary's Roman Catholic Church, dating from 1796, is south of Myrtle Grove on Emmet Place.

Organised Tours

Between June and August, 90-minute walking tours costing £2.75/1.75 leave the tourist office at 11 am and 3 pm Monday to Saturday.

Special Events

The late-August holiday weekend is the occasion for a busking (street music) festival when the pubs are particularly lively.

Places to Stay

Camping The *Sonas Caravan Park* (☎ 98132), in Ballymacoda, is about 15km to the south of Youghal, on the seashore. To get there, take the road off the N25 (west of town) to the village of Ballymacoda, then head west through the village. A tent site for two people with a car costs £8.

B&Bs & Hotels Coming into town from Waterford, welcoming *Roseville* (☎ 92571, New Catherine St) is near the beginning of the one-way part of the street. All rooms have a bathroom and cost £20 per person.

The elegant Georgian *Devon View* (☎ 92298) is at the Cork end of town, opposite the Devonshire Arms Hotel; singles/doubles cost £20/32.

CORK

At the Georgian *Devonshire Arms Hotel* (☎ *92018, Pearse Square)* rooms start at £38 per person. The large *Walter Raleigh Hotel* (☎ *92011, O'Brien's Place),* at the Cork end of town, costs £40 per person. *Aherne's Guesthouse and Restaurant* (☎ *92424, 163 North Main St)* offers 12 spacious en suite rooms starting at £60 per person.

Places to Eat

For light lunches costing £3 to £6 try the *Coffee Pot* in the middle of town or the cafeteria-style *Merrick's Restaurant* next door.

The *Devonshire Arms Hotel* has a reasonable bar menu and specialises in seafood; barbecued salmon costs £7.95. Award-winning *Aherne's Guesthouse and Restaurant* serves tasty seafood pies, pizzas and pasta costing around £7.50.

Entertainment

On Main St *Olde Porter House, JD's, Breezers* and *The Nook* often have traditional music. *Moby Dick's* near the tourist office has little to recommend it beyond being John Huston's port of call during the filming of *Moby Dick* (1954) starring Gregory Peck.

Getting There & Away

There are frequent Bus Éireann buses to Cork (£3, 1¼ hours) and Waterford.

West Cork

KINSALE & AROUND
☎ 021 • pop 1785

Kinsale (Cionn tSáile) has a picture-postcard prettiness reminiscent of Cornwall in England and, like Cornwall, it's blighted by traffic jams in summer (as well as on Sunday and public holidays throughout the year). The crowds are drawn not just by the scenery and historic buildings but by the fact that Kinsale is the undisputed gourmet capital of Ireland. It's easily reached by car from Cork by taking the route south past the airport.

History

In September 1601, a Spanish fleet anchored at Kinsale was besieged by the English. The Irish army marched the length of the country to attack the English but were defeated in battle outside Kinsale on Christmas Eve. For the Catholics of Kinsale, the immediate consequence was that they were banned from the town. It was another 100 years before they were allowed to return. Historians now cite 1601 as the beginning of the end of Gaelic Ireland.

After 1601 the town developed as a ship-building port. In the early 18th century Alexander Selkirk left Kinsale Harbour on a voyage that left him stranded on a desert island, providing Daniel Defoe with the idea for *Robinson Crusoe*.

Orientation & Information

Most of the hotels and restaurants ring the harbour, but some are out at Scilly, a peninsula to the south-east. A path continues from there south-east to Summer Cove and the Charles Fort. To the south-west, Duggan Bridge links Castlepark Marina and the scant ruins of James Fort to The Pier Rd.

The tourist office (☎ 477 2234), on the harbourfront close to the bus stop, opens 9.15 am to 1 pm and 2.15 to 5.30 pm Monday to Saturday, March to October, plus on Sunday in July and August.

Kinsale Laundrette is on Main St.

Museum

The small museum in the 17th-century courthouse on Market Square displays exhibits relating to the 1915 sinking of the *Lusitania*, but at the time of writing was closed for repairs.

Desmond Castle

This 16th-century tower house on Cork St was occupied by the Spanish in 1601. Since then it has served as a prison for French and American captives and as a workhouse during the Great Famine. In the care of Dúchas, it now houses a small museum on the history of wine. It opens 9.30 am to 6.30 pm daily, mid-June to mid-September. Admission costs £1.50/60p.

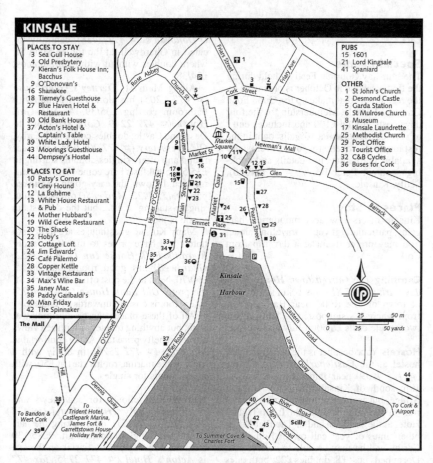

KINSALE

PLACES TO STAY
3 Sea Gull House
4 Old Presbytery
7 Kieran's Folk House Inn;
   Bacchus
9 O'Donovan's
16 Shanakee
18 Tierney's Guesthouse
27 Blue Haven Hotel &
   Restaurant
30 Old Bank House
37 Acton's Hotel &
   Captain's Table
39 White Lady Hotel
43 Moorings Guesthouse
44 Dempsey's Hostel

PLACES TO EAT
10 Patsy's Corner
11 Grey Hound
12 La Bohème
13 White House Restaurant
   & Pub
14 Mother Hubbard's
19 Wild Geese Restaurant
20 The Shack
22 Hoby's
23 Cottage Loft
24 Jim Edwards'
26 Café Palermo
28 Copper Kettle
33 Vintage Restaurant
34 Max's Wine Bar
35 Janey Mac
38 Paddy Garibaldi's
40 Man Friday
42 The Spinnaker

PUBS
15 1601
21 Lord Kingsale
41 Spaniard

OTHER
1 St John's Church
2 Desmond Castle
5 Garda Station
6 St Mulrose Church
8 Museum
17 Kinsale Laundrette
25 Methodist Church
29 Post Office
31 Tourist Office
32 C&B Cycles
36 Buses for Cork

Charles Fort

In Summer Cove, 3km east of Kinsale, stand the huge ruins of 17th-century Charles Fort (☎ 477 2263), one of the best-preserved star forts in Europe. Now a Dúchas site, it was built in the 1670s and remained in use until 1921, when much of the fort was destroyed as the British withdrew. Most of the ruins you see inside date from the 18th and 19th centuries. It opens 9 am to 6 pm daily, mid-March to October; and 9 am to 5 pm daily, the rest of the year. Admission costs £2/1.

Even those not enthralled by military history will enjoy the harbour views from the massive walls. If you follow the signposted Scilly Walk you'll have similar views all the way.

Activities

Castlepark Marina Centre (☎ 477 4959) organises deep-sea fishing and scuba-diving trips and hires out equipment; hostel accommodation is also available (see Places to Stay later in this section).

Organised Tours

Between June and August, one-hour walking tours leave from outside the tourist office at 11.15 am and 2.30 pm. They cost £3/1.

Special Events
The four-day Gourmet Festival held during the first weekend in October is organised by the restaurants that make up the Good Food Circle of Kinsale. Membership for the four days costs around £100 and includes entry to various events and a 10% discount in the restaurants. Tickets to some events are available on the day. For details and bookings contact Peter Barry (☎ 477 4026), Scilly, Kinsale.

Places to Stay
Kinsale offers few accommodation bargains, particularly if you're travelling alone. You may prefer to make a day trip from Cork.

Camping The *Garrettstown House Holiday Park* (☎ 477 8156) is 10km south-west of town on the R600 near Ballinspittle, from where it's signposted. A tent site for two people costs £6.50 in July and August.

Hostels Your best bet is the clean, modern hostel at the *Castlepark Marina Centre* (☎ 477 4959) near James Fort. It's about 1km south of Kinsale then over Duggan Bridge, but from June to September ferries run on the hour after 8 am from Trident Hotel at the southern end of The Pier Rd; at other times of year call owner Eddie McCarthy and he may be able to collect you. Dorm beds cost £8, doubles £22; both rates include breakfast. There's a small beach immediately behind the hostel, an on-site café and The Dock pub next door.

Dempsey's Hostel (☎ 477 2124) is an uphill walk from the centre and closer to town than Castlepark Marina Centre. Its location, behind the Texaco garage on the Cork road, is nothing to write home about, but the traffic noise is muted inside. Dorm beds cost £6. The seven double rooms cost £16 each.

B&Bs There are lots of B&Bs in and around Kinsale, but many close from November to March and some have doubles only.

One of the few less-expensive places is *O'Donovan's* (☎ 477 2428), centrally located in Guardwell, at the top of Main St, where doubles without/with bathroom cost £34/38.

Along Main St, *Tierney's Guesthouse* (☎ 477 2205) has doubles without/with bathroom costing £35/39. At *Sea Gull House* (☎ 477 2240, Cork St), close to Desmond Castle, doubles cost £40. Nearby, *Old Presbytery* (☎ 477 2027) is open year round and offers singles/doubles starting at £35/50; breakfasts here come highly recommended. In town, the easy-going *Shanakee* pub (☎ 477 4422, Market St) offers en suite singles starting at £22, but the downstairs music is loud.

Many Kinsale guesthouses are more like hotels and have prices to match. Friendly *Kieran's Folk House Inn* (☎ 477 2382, Guardwell) has good rooms starting at £60/70. Next to the post office on Pearse St, the pretty *Old Bank House* (☎ 477 4075) offers rooms costing upwards of £45/85.

All of these places can be a bit noisy at night but anything quieter or with sea views attracts a hefty price tag. At the comfortable *Moorings* (☎ 477 2376), in Scilly with a view of the marina, rooms start at £50, with no discounts for singles.

Hotels First choice for sea views and amenities is ugly *Trident Hotel* (☎ 477 2301, fax 477 4173), overlooking the harbour, where singles/doubles start at £85/130 from June to September. Easier on the eye is *Acton's Hotel* (☎ 477 2135, fax 477 2231), with singles/doubles costing upwards of £95/130 in July and August. More central is the even pricier *Blue Haven* (☎ 477 2209, fax 477 4268, Pearse St), though it does have special deals throughout the year. A bit cheaper is the *White Lady Hotel* (☎ 477 2737, fax 477 4641, Lower O'Connell St), which charges £40/70.

Places to Eat
Restaurants Some of the more upmarket places serve affordable lunches and early-evening meals. *Cottage Loft* (☎ 477 2803,

Main St) serves three-course dinners costing £17.50. *Janey Mac (☎ 477 4860, Main St)* serves meat and fish dishes costing £12 to £15, while vegetarian dishes start at £10.50. *Hoby's (☎ 477 2200, Main St)* is small and unpretentious; three-course dinners cost £14.50. *Max's Wine Bar (☎ 477 2443, Main St)* offers poached salmon (£10.50) and has some cheaper vegetarian options.

You'll pay around £25 to £30 for an à la carte dinner at the more expensive places. *Blue Haven (☎ 477 2209, Pearse St)*, *Vintage Restaurant (☎ 477 2502, Main St)*, *Captain's Table*, at Acton's Hotel, and *Savannah Waterfront* restaurant, at the Trident Hotel, all have good reputations.

One of the best things about *Man Friday (☎ 477 2260)* is its location off the beaten track at Scilly. It's on a hill overlooking the harbour and there are good views of Kinsale. Turbot costs £14.75.

Cafés & Pubs Good places for breakfast and inexpensive meals are *Mother Hubbard's*, on the corner of Pearse St, and *Patsy's Corner (Market Square)*. *Copper Kettle (Pearse St)* serves meals all day; breakfasts cost £3.25, roast beef £4.50.

Café Palermo (Pearse St) offers gourmet pizzas costing £7.50 and pasta costing £5.50. *Wild Geese Restaurant (Main St)* offers four-course lunch specials (£7.50) and breakfasts (£3.25). *The Shack*, just across the road, serves tasty prawns with pasta (£7.25), as well as steak, chicken and vegetarian dishes. Tucked away on Lower O'Connell St, *Paddy Garibaldi's* serves pizzas and pasta costing £7.50 and under.

In central Kinsale the rather functional *White House* pub is the oldest in town and offers good-value bar food; Irish stew costs £4.50. Other pubs worth frequenting for a drink and a bite are the *1601 (Pearse St)*, where bacon and cabbage in Irish-whiskey sauce costs £5.95, and the noisy *Grey Hound*, which dates from 1690, near Market Square.

Jim Edwards' (☎ 477 2541, Market Quay) is probably the best pub for seafood; sole fillet costs £13.95. *La Bohème (☎ 477 4109)* also has a reputation for good seafood but was closed for renovations at the time of writing. Out at Scilly, *The Spinnaker* pub *(☎ 477 2098)* serves Irish stew (£6) and fresh wild salmon (£9.15).

Entertainment

Kinsale has a lively pub scene and music is easy to find in summer. The *1601 (Pearse St)* is always crowded and you can read up on the finer details of the battle while you wait to be served.

Also popular for Irish music are *Lord Kingsale (Main St)* and the *Shanakee* (An Seanachai) round the corner. Just across the road, *Kieran's Folk House Inn* has a popular bar. Out at Scilly, the cosy *Spaniard* has traditional music on Wednesday night.

The nightclub at *White Lady Hotel* (see Places to Stay, earlier) is popular with the younger crowd at the weekend. *Bacchus*,

---

Road Bowling

You're likely to encounter this rare sport only on a quiet road on a Sunday afternoon in West Cork or in County Armagh in Northern Ireland – it's not played anywhere else in either the Republic or the North. The object of the game is to cover a set distance of winding road in as few hurls of the ball as possible. The rules allow for the ball to be lofted over a stretch of field hoping to shortcross a bend. Bets are laid on teams and even individual bowls of the 18cm, 794g steel ball. A giveaway sign of a game in progress is small groups of mostly men waiting at the roadside for your vehicle to pass so that the game can resume. Some distance ahead of the main group will be a smaller group, whose task is to chart the distance that a ball has been thrown by the two competing sides.

CORK

attached to Kieran's Folk House Inn, opens on Thursday and Saturday nights.

Getting There & Away
Bus Éireann buses connect Kinsale with Cork three or four times daily (£5.80 return, 45 minutes). The bus stops at the Esso garage on The Pier Rd near the tourist office.

Getting Around
You can hire bikes from C&B Cycles (☎ 477 4884) on Main St. Taxis can be hired locally (☎ 477 4900, 477 2642). The fare to the Castlepark Marina Centre is about £3.

KINSALE TO CLONAKILTY
Following the quays west out of Kinsale the main R600 road passes through Ballinspittle and Timoleague before joining the main road from Bandon to reach Clonakilty. Once you're in Timoleague you can detour south to Courtmacsherry and along a small coastal road that goes through Butlerstown to Clonakilty.

Old Head of Kinsale
If you have time, it's worth diverting along the R604 coast road to Ballinspittle via the Old Head of Kinsale.

Although the headland is given over to a golf course, paths on either side before the entrance lead down to viewpoints overlooking spectacular rocky coastline, the nesting place of thousands of fulmar and penguin-like guillemot. From the entrance you can take the main path through the golf links to the lighthouse; this is private land and the golf club charges a small fee (for insurance liability in case you have an accident) to do this.

On the way to the headland *Speckled Door* (An Doras Breac) serves pub food.

Ballinspittle
If you've visited Knock in Mayo you'll appreciate knowing that this village narrowly avoided a similar fate. In the summer of 1985 a grotto outside town with a statue of the Virgin Mary began to attract worshippers after it was reported that the statue had moved. Tens of thousands of people claimed to have seen the same phenomenon, thereby putting Ballinspittle (Béal Átha an Spidéil) on the map. Similar reports came in from other parts of the country but then the whole thing came to a sudden end. The grotto is on the left-hand side of the main road before you enter Ballinspittle from Kinsale.

Timoleague
☎ 023 • pop 305
Once a thriving port, Timoleague is now a sleepy village approached via a causeway across an inlet in Courtmacsherry Bay. The waters and mudflats attract migratory birds from Iceland, Greenland, and the Russian and Canadian Arctic. Most of the time you should be able to see cormorant and heron fishing here, but from September to May you may also spot golden plover and rare white egret.

Timoleague Friary This Franciscan friary was probably founded in the 13th century but the buildings date from various periods, with some alterations dating back to the early 17th century. In 1642 the English vandalised the friary and smashed the stained glass, but the remains are quite impressive and clearly visible as you approach Timoleague from Kinsale. Today it serves as the village cemetery.

Timoleague Castle Gardens Little remains of the 13th-century Ballymore Castle that once stood here. However, the attractive gardens are worth visiting. The palm trees, in particular, are a reminder of the mild climate, and there's a superb *Callistemon linearis* (bottlebrush) tree. The gardens open 11 am to 5.30 pm Monday to Saturday, and 2 to 5 pm on Sunday, June to August. Admission costs £2.50/1.

Places to Stay The *Sexton's Caravan and Camping Park* (☎ 46347) is signposted off the main road (R600) to Clonakilty. A hiker or cyclist pays £4.50 for a pitch, a car driver £7 and a motorcyclist £5.

Picturesque Cobh Harbour, County Cork

Rock formations at Mizen Head, County Cork

What better prize at the end of the rainbow than the Jameson whiskey distillery in Midleton?

The problem is deciding which colour to go for next in the pretty village of Eyeries, County Cork.

Ruined church, County Cork

The Beacon stands sentinel at Baltimore.

Kinsale, gourmet capital of Ireland

High on a hill outside Timoleague on the right-hand side of the road to Clonakilty is beautiful *Lettercollum House* (☎ 46251). It was once a convent but is now a restaurant with rooms with spectacular views. Singles/doubles start at £22/30. The décor is wonderfully arty and there are interesting residential courses on everything from Pacific Rim cookery to birdwatching.

In nearby Courtmacsherry, *Travara Lodge* (☎ 46493) is a Georgian house with views of the bay. Singles/doubles start at £27/42. It opens mid-March to October.

Building construction is going on around the once-isolated *Courtmacsherry Hotel* (☎ 46198). It's on a cul-de-sac and is comfortable and friendly; singles/doubles start at £40/70.

Places to Eat In Timoleague village, *Dillon's Bar and Café* serves the likes of pizza and seafood chowder in pleasant surroundings at lunch and dinner. Next door, *Gráinne's* pub offers soup and sandwiches for lunch and steak-style meals in the evening. The restaurant at *Lettercollum House* (see Places to Stay) is housed in what was once a convent chapel and serves easily the best food in the area. Three-course set lunches cost £12, set dinners £21; booking is essential.

Getting There & Away The only bus service to Timoleague from Cork leaves at 5.45 pm on weekdays. Going back to Cork, the bus leaves from outside Pat Joe's pub at 8 am.

CLONAKILTY
☎ 023 • pop 2445

This small, pretty town received its first charter in 1292 but was refounded in the early 17th century by the 1st earl of Cork. He settled it with 100 English families and planned a Protestant town from which Catholics would be excluded. His plan failed: Clonakilty is now very Irish and very Catholic – witness the Presbyterian chapel that has been turned into a post office.

From the mid-18th until the mid-19th century over 10,000 people worked in the town's linen industry. Houlihan & Sons bakery by the public water pump was once a linen hall, and the fire station stands on the site of the old linen market. What was once a corn mill driven by the nearby river has been pleasingly converted into a library.

Michael Collins was born nearby and went to school in Clonakilty, a fact of which the community is very proud.

Orientation & Information
Roads converge on Asna Square, dominated by a statue commemorating local men who died at the Battle of Big Cross during the 1798 Rising. Also in the square is the small Kilty Stone which gave Clonakilty its name.

The tourist office (☎ 33226), 9 Rossa St, opens 9 am to 6 pm on weekdays, and 9 am to 1 pm on Saturday, June to September. The *Historical Walk of Clonakilty and its Sea-Front* booklet (£2.50) includes a clear illustrated map of the town and is available from Kerr's Bookshop on Ashe St. Book Fayre on Pearse St stocks second-hand books. Spiller's Lane, off Bridge St, shelters a cluster of craft shops.

West Cork Regional Museum
This small, rather sad museum is, nonetheless, the best Cork has to offer when it comes to material relating to local industrial and social history. It opens 10.30 am to 6 pm Monday to Saturday, and 2.30 to 6 pm on Sunday, May to October. Admission costs £1/50p.

Places to Stay
Camping The *Desert House Caravan and Camping Park* (☎ 33331) is 500m east of town on the road to Ring and overlooking the river. You can camp at Easter and from May to September; a tent site for two costs £5.

Hostels The brightly painted *Old Brewery Hostel* (☎ 33525) is in a quiet cul-de-sac off Emmet Square. Beds in six-bed dorms cost £8, and there are two doubles for £20. There is a small kitchen and dining room, and the hostel offers access for disabled people.

CORK

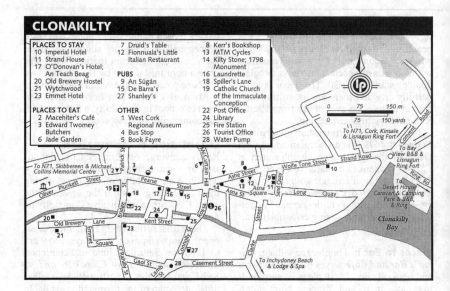

CLONAKILTY

PLACES TO STAY	7 Druid's Table	8 Kerr's Bookshop
10 Imperial Hotel	12 Fionnuala's Little	13 MTM Cycles
11 Strand House	Italian Restaurant	14 Kilty Stone; 1798
17 O'Donovan's Hotel;		Monument
An Teach Beag	PUBS	16 Laundrette
20 Old Brewery Hostel	9 An Súgán	18 Spiller's Lane
21 Wytchwood	15 De Barra's	19 Catholic Church
23 Emmet Hotel	27 Shanley's	of the Immaculate
		Conception
PLACES TO EAT	OTHER	22 Post Office
2 Macehiter's Café	1 West Cork	24 Library
3 Edward Twomey	Regional Museum	25 Fire Station
Butchers	4 Bus Stop	26 Tourist Office
6 Jade Garden	5 Book Fayre	28 Water Pump

B&Bs Opposite the Old Brewery Hostel is the pleasingly decorated *Wytchwood* (☎ 33525), where spacious singles/doubles start at £24.50/40. Inquire at the An Súgán pub on Sand Quay about rooms in *Strand House* next door, once home to the poetess Mary Jane Irwin, who married O'Donovan Rossa, the founder of the Fenians. Just outside town past the roundabout, *Bay View* (☎ 33539) offers rooms starting at £23/36. On the Ring road, with views overlooking the river, *Desert House* (☎ 33331) is attached to the camp site; singles/doubles cost £23/38.

Hotels The *Imperial Hotel* (☎ 34185), at the Cork end of Wolfe Tone St, offers beds in well-equipped rooms; prices start at £20. A little pricier, but more central and with more facilities, is *O'Donovan's Hotel* (*Óstan uí Dhonnabhán;* ☎ 33250, *Pearse St*), where B&B costs upwards of £25. Charles Stewart Parnell and Michael Collins stayed here. Georgian *Emmet Hotel* (☎ 33394), on picturesque Emmet Square, charges £25/45 for singles/doubles. If you want to stay in luxury the *Lodge and Spa* (☎ 33143), at Inchydoney, is a modern hotel

with rooms from £79 and a thalassotherapy (seawater) spa.

Places to Eat

Black pudding, made from the blood of pigs (and a common ingredient in the full Irish breakfast), is found throughout Ireland, but Clonakilty black pudding is particularly renowned. *Edward Twomey Butchers* (*16 Pearse St*) is reputed to make the best black pudding in Cork.

Even if you're not into black pudding you can eat well in Clonakilty. At the Rosscarbery end of the main street, *Macehiter's Café*, at the junction of Oliver Plunkett and Patrick Sts, serves avocado salad costing £4.25 and fresh salmon for £8.50. It opens Wednesday to Sunday.

O'Donovan's Hotel has a café-style restaurant serving mostly standard meals during the day; roast chicken costs £4.75. The evening menu is a little more adventurous; lasagne costs £7.80.

At *Fionnuala's Little Italian Restaurant* (☎ 34355, *Ashe St*) there's pizza starting at £5.50 and pasta from £6.95; it also serves good coffee. Out of season it closes on Monday and Tuesday. Across the road

Druid's Table opens for a druid's breakfast (including black pudding) costing £3.50. In the evening you can bring your own bottle.

An Súgán (Wolfe Tone St) serves popular pub lunches; baked lasagne costs £6.90. Set dinners at the upstairs restaurant are pricey unless you catch the early-bird tourist menu before 8 pm. *Jade Garden (☎ 34576, MacCurtain Hill)* offers Chinese meals for middle-of-the-road prices; king prawns with green pepper costs £6.

The bistro at the *Emmet Hotel* has a good reputation, uses organic produce and serves moderately priced lunches: seafood pancake costs £4.25.

Entertainment

Clonakilty has a lively pub scene, especially during its 10-day festival in July. *An Súgán (Wolfe Tone St)* and *De Barra's (Pearse St)* are crowded at the weekend, but also have music during the week. Another place to try is *Shanley's (Connolly St)*, which offers live music nightly. *O'Donovan's Hotel* has music in its lounge bar on Tuesday and Saturday nights, while there's traditional music on Saturday from 9.30 pm at *An Teach Beag* in Recorder's Alley, leading through to the hotel car park.

Getting There & Away

At least three Cork (☎ 021-450 8188) buses stop daily in Clonakilty on Pearse St. The journey takes 1¼ hours and costs £5.90/ 8.50 one-way/return. Westbound buses continue to Skibbereen and Schull twice daily. From late May to mid-September you can get from Clonakilty to Killarney via Schull daily.

Getting Around

MTM Cycles (☎ 33584), 33 Ashe St, hires out bikes for £8/40 per day/week.

AROUND CLONAKILTY

One of Cork's best beaches is **Inchydoney**, 5km south of Clonakilty, but watch for the dangerous riptide; when lifeguards are on duty a red warning flag indicates danger. Deep-sea fishing and shore angling are possible at **Ring**.

Lisnagun (Lios na gCon) Ring Fort

Of over 30,000 ring forts scattered across Ireland, this is the only one that has been reconstructed to give some impression of life in a 10th-century defended farmstead. It is complete with a *souterrain* (underground chamber) and a central hut thatched by someone who would have been paid only in food for his months' labours.

In theory the fort opens 9 am to 5 pm on weekdays, and 10 am to 5 pm at the weekend. In practice if there's no-one there to collect the £2/1 admission fee you'll get to see only the circular ditch and the encircling wooden palisade. If you're driving, follow the sign to Lios na gCon Animal Park off the N71 outside Clonakilty on the Cork road opposite Mount Carmel Hospital. Take that turning and keep going until you come to another on the right. The fort/farmstead is on the left, just past Clonakilty Agricultural College.

If you're walking from Clonakilty and want to avoid traffic, take the turning at the Fax Bridge roundabout at the end of Strand Rd signposted to Bay View B&B. Follow this road uphill for about 1.5km until you reach a T-junction. Turn right and almost immediately you'll see metal farm gates on your right. Go through the gates and keep walking straight ahead until you come to a crossroads with a cowshed. Take the track to the left and walk downhill until you reach a minor road. Turn right and the fort is on the left, near the Clonakilty Agricultural College.

Michael Collins Memorial Centre

Dúchas manages a small memorial centre to Michael Collins, who was born near Clonakilty in 1890. The old house where he was born and lived for about 10 years has been repaired but little remains of the newer house his family later built beside it, where Collins lived until he emigrated to London in 1906. This was burned down by the Black and Tans in 1921. Despite the meagre remains, the place generates a sense of respect for a man who would have been

CORK

heartbroken at the consequences of the treaty he signed in 1921.

The birthplace site is signposted on the N71, 5km west of Clonakilty.

ROSSCARBERY TO SKIBBEREEN

You can get from Rosscarbery to Skibbereen along the main N71 via Leap, but far more enjoyable is the longer route that winds south-west from the end of the causeway at Rosscarbery, taking in the picturesque villages of Glandore and Union Hall as well as some stunning coastal scenery.

Rosscarbery
☎ 023 • pop 455

Set back from the main N71, Rosscarbery (Ros O'gCairbre) is little more than a village at the head of a landlocked inlet of Rosscarbery Bay with a quiet central square. O'Donovan Rossa, founder of the Fenians, was born here in 1831. To reach Rosscarbery when coming from Clonakilty, turn right at the end of the causeway just before the unmissable Celtic Ross Hotel.

St Fachtna's Cathedral dates back to the 12th century and has an elaborately carved western doorway as well as an impressive statue of Lord Carbery (1763–1842) in slashed doublet and hose. The shallow estuary beside the causeway is wonderful for watching wading birds, especially golden plover, in winter. Rosscarbery Riding Centre (☎ 48232) organises **horse trekking**. It's signposted opposite the turn-off for Owinhincha Beach.

Places to Stay & Eat The *Carbery Arms* (☎ *48101*), in the square, offers B&B costing £17.50 per person and serves pub food during the day, as does nearby *Nolan's*. *O'Callaghan Walshe's Seafood Restaurant* (☎ *48125*) opens 6.30 to 9.15 pm Wednesday to Sunday (Friday and Saturday only in winter) and serves dishes such as seafood tagliatelle (£9.50).

Getting There & Away Buses from Clonakilty to Goleen stop in Rosscarbery at least twice daily (15 minutes).

Castle Salem

The most surprising aspect of this 15th-century castle, originally called Benduff Castle, is the entrance. In the 17th century, a house was built onto one of the 3m-thick castle walls, and at the top of its carpeted staircase an ordinary-looking door opens onto the 1st floor of the castle. Otherwise the castle is slowly crumbling away.

Cromwell gave it to an English soldier, Major Apollo Morris, who later became a Quaker. He renamed it Shalom, Hebrew for peace, which was corrupted into Salem. An old Quaker churchyard is behind the wall on the right immediately after entering the grounds. William Penn (founder of Pennsylvania) is said to have visited Morris in the house.

Castle Salem is signposted off the N71 Skibbereen road west of Rosscarbery. Admission is through a farmyard and costs £2/1. You can stay in the 17th-century *house* (☎ *48381*) attached to the castle. B&B costs £15; ask for the bed that Penn slept in.

Drombeg Stone Circle

Of the many stone circles in West Cork, this particular group of 17 stones dating from around 100 BC is particularly impressive, not least because of its stunning setting. On the south-western side a horizontal stone (the axial stone) faces two taller stones (portal stones) on the north-eastern side. The axis of these two stones and the recumbent one is aligned to sunset on the winter solstice (21 December).

Nearby is a cooking area with a stone trough in which hot stones can bring 318.5 litres of water to the boil in 18 minutes and keep it hot for roughly three hours afterwards.

Travelling from Clonakilty, the N71 crosses a causeway at Rosscarbery. Just past the end of the causeway, beside the Orchard B&B, a road is signposted off to the left for Glandore, Coppinger's Court and assorted B&Bs. Some way along this road the stones are signposted to the left and a rough road continues to a small car park; from there a path leads to the circle.

Glandore
☎ 028

The exquisite fishing village of Glandore (Cuan Dor) bursts into life in summer when well-off boating folk arrive, something that would surely have dismayed William Thompson (1785–1833), who established a commune here as a model for his socialist philosophy. Marx refers to him in *Das Kapital*.

Meadow Camping Park (☎ *33280*) is 2km east of the village on the Rosscarbery road. From mid-March to September a small tent site costs £8. The *Marine Hotel* (☎ *33366*) charges £43/76 for singles/doubles so you'll probably prefer just to use its bar. Three kilometres east of Glandore *Kilfinnan Farm* (☎ *33233*) charges upwards of £20/30 for B&B.

Union Hall & Around
☎ 028

Disappointingly, there's no union hall in this small village, accessible via a narrow road bridge over the estuary. Instead it was named after the 1800 Act of Union, which abolished the separate Irish Parliament. Its equally unfortunate Irish name, Bréantrá, means 'foul beach'. Jonathan Swift came here in 1723 to grieve over the death of his friend Vanessa.

Farther along the road to Castletownshend is the small **Ceim Hill Museum** (☎ 36280) run by Teresa O'Mahony, who practises folk medicine in her ancient farmhouse. It's recommended for its wonderful mixture of eccentricity and genuine artefacts, not to mention the spectacular views from the winding track. It opens 10 am to 7 pm and admission costs £2/1. From Maria's Schoolhouse (see the next paragraph) follow the road up the hill and watch for a narrow lane leading uphill off to your right. The museum is about 2km from this turn-off.

If prizes were being handed out for hostels then the IHH *Maria's Schoolhouse* (☎ *33002*) would have to be the front-runner. A stunning conversion of a 19th-century National School building on the Castletownshend side of Union Hall, it has a bright, cheerful 10-bed dorm with beds costing the usual £8, together with private rooms with en suite facilities costing £12 to £17. The sitting and dining area is a delight, and Maria cooks dinners on request for £15 per person (vegetarians catered for). Her breakfasts, if you don't want to rustle up your own, cost £3.50 and include local fish and cheese. The hostel also organises sea-kayaking trips exploring the coastline close by.

SKIBBEREEN & AROUND
☎ 028 • pop 1890

Traffic-blighted Skibbereen (Sciobairín) owes its existence to Algerians who raided nearby Baltimore in 1631. The frightened English settlers moved north-east, establishing two settlements which grew into Skibbereen. For a long time the town was associated with its Protestant founders but during the Famine years it became known for the sufferings of the local Catholic peasantry. The repercussions were long-lasting: nearly half the local population emigrated in the first half of the 20th century. The newsagents sell *The Skibbereen Trail* (£1), which guides you around local sites with links to the Famine. Today the town prospers from its Friday market (12.30 to 2.30 pm) and a steady influx of tourists on the West Cork trail.

Orientation & Information

The main landmark is a statue, dedicated to the heroes of the many Irish rebellions against the British, which stands at the junction of three roads. Market St heads south past the post office to Lough Ine and Baltimore. The main shopping street, Main St, leads to a junction with Ilen St, which heads west over the river to Ballydehob and Bantry. North St heads towards the main Cork road and houses the tourist office (☎ 21766), which opens 9.15 am to 5.30 pm on weekdays, September to May; and 9 am to 7 pm Monday to Saturday, and 10 am to 1 pm and 2.15 to 6 pm on Sunday, June to August.

Hourihane's Laundrette is on Bridge St behind the Busy Bee fast-food outlet.

CORK

Liss Ard Experience

One kilometre east of Skibbereen on the Castletownshend road, the Liss Ard Experience (☎ 22368) is a 16-hectare expanse of woodland, wild-flower meadows and small lakes on the banks of Lough Abisdeasly. It's the work of German Veith Turske, who searched Europe for somewhere suitable to create a magical, natural garden. One- and two-hour walks are clearly marked out. Don't miss the Irish Sky Garden where you walk across a crater and then into a mound and up steps like a Mayan pyramid to emerge in an amphitheatre with nothing to focus on except the sky. It also hosts concerts featuring international names.

The gardens open 9.30 am to 5 pm on weekdays, May to September. Admission costs £5/2.

Other Things to See & Do

Along North St, next to the church, the **West Cork Arts Centre** (☎ 22090) opens 10 am to 6 pm Monday to Saturday. It hosts regular art exhibitions and in summer it often stages something theatrical or musical, too. The notice board provides useful information about what's happening locally.

On the Baltimore road (R595) 6km out of town you can bathe at tiny **Tragumna**, little more than a pub, a beach and a knitwear shop.

Continuing south towards Baltimore you'll come to the eight-hectare organically managed **Creagh Gardens** on the right. These gardens, set around Creagh House, have a lovely riverside setting and are spectacular in April and May, when the rhododendrons are in bloom, and in August and September, when the fuchsias and blue hydrangeas are flowering. The gardens open 10 am to 6 pm daily, March to October, and admission costs £3/1.50.

A little farther back towards Skibbereen off the Baltimore road is **Lough Ine** (or Lough Hyne), a saltwater lake connected to the sea by a narrow channel which is now a nature reserve. Lough Ine is 6km due south of Skibbereen and well signposted from the town statue. **Knockomagh Wood**, an attractive mixture of deciduous and evergreen

trees, is to the right of the road approaching the lough from Skibbereen. You can get to Baltimore by diverting along the seldom-used minor road around the lough.

Boat trips to **Heir Island** in Roaring Water Bay are run by John O'Neill (☎ 38144) and cost £5 return.

Places to Stay

Camping One kilometre east of town on the Castletownshend road is **Hideaway Camping and Caravan Park** (☎ 33280), open May to mid-September. It costs £8 to pitch a small tent You can also camp at **Russagh Mill Hostel** for £4 per person.

Hostels One and a half kilometres east of town on the Castletownshend road is the **Russagh Mill Hostel and Adventure Centre** (☎ 22451), an old corn mill with much of its machinery still in place. Beds in relatively spacious dorms cost £8 and there are eight private rooms for £20. Owner Mick Murphy is an experienced mountaineer and canoeist. For between £8 and £10 you can join in a day's canoeing, rock climbing or whatever may be going on. A path leads back to town from behind the hostel, avoiding the main road.

B&Bs Easily the best place to stay in town is **Bridge House** (☎ 21273, Bridge St), which has wonderfully opulent Victorian-style décor; rooms start at £17.50 per person and the breakfasts are very good. Alternatively, the plainer **Ivanhoe B&B** (☎ 21749, 67 North St) costs £22/36 for singles/doubles with shower.

The Baltimore road is lined with B&Bs. **Marguerites** (☎ 21166) is about 1km out of town and charges £22.50/32 with shared facilities or £24.50/36 en suite.

Six kilometres east of Skibbereen near Adrigole, **Mont Bretia** (☎ 33663, Drinagh Rd) is worth seeking out for its relaxed atmosphere and wholefood meals. B&B costs £18 per person, and dinner costs £8. It's out of the way so you'll need your own transport. Coming from Skibbereen on the N71, take a left turn signposted for Drinagh off the main road. After the Adrigole creamery, take the second left at the fork just past it (signposted for another B&B called Sprucedale). Mont Bretia is on the left.

Hotels On Bridge St (the continuation of Main St in the direction of Schull) the refurbished *Eldon Hotel* (☎ 21300) has a quiet charm; singles/doubles cost £25/35. The pleasantly balconied *West Cork Hotel* (☎ 21277, Ilen St), opposite the river, charges upwards of £60 a night for two. *Liss Ard Lake Lodge* (☎ 40000) is a small, beautifully located, luxury hotel; rooms start at £110.

Places to Eat

Eldon Hotel offers good bar meals, such as baked fisherman's pie costing around £4.50, until 9 pm. Also on Bridge St, at No 11, *Annie May's* pub serves above-average bar food costing around £4 or £5.

For coffee and snacks, try *O'Donovan's* next door, or *The Stove*, which also serves breakfast all day (full Irish breakfast £3.50). *Fields Coffee Shop*, near the monument, is popular with shoppers at the adjoining supermarket.

Kalbo's Bistro (*North St*) serves steaks and other fairly standard dishes; sirloin steak costs £11.75. Its menu also includes a couple of vegetarian dishes costing £6.95. Farther along towards the arts centre, the cheaper *Ivanhoe Restaurant* serves lunches costing around £3.95; in the evening poached salmon costs £8.95.

For pub food, *Bernard's Bar* (*Main St*), set back from the road, is particularly popular; lasagne costs £5.95.

Good value and good fun is the £19 set dinner at *Island Cottage* (☎ 38102) on Heir Island. For transport details, see Other Things to See & Do earlier in this section.

Entertainment

Wine Vaults (*Bridge St*) is a particularly popular pub with live music on Friday and a disco on Saturday night. *Seán Óg's* (*Market St*), near the square, *Kearney's Well* (*North St*) and *Baby Hannah's* (*Bridge St*) also have music most weekends. *Annie May's* (*Bridge St*) hosts some interesting

traditional-music evenings. *Cellar Bar* (*Bridge St*) has a nightclub upstairs.

Getting There & Away

Bus Éireann buses run at least daily to Cork, Baltimore, Schull, Drimoleague and Killarney from outside the Eldon Hotel on Main St. Skibbereen to Schull takes just 30 minutes (return £3.20).

Getting Around

Bicycles can be hired from Roycroft's Cycles (☎ 21235) on Ilen St opposite the West Cork Hotel; this building acted as a soup kitchen during the Famine.

BALTIMORE

☎ 028 • pop 220

Just 13km down the River Ilen from Skibbereen, sleepy Baltimore has a population of 220 which swells enormously during the summer months, as sailing folk, divers and visitors to Sherkin and Clear Islands flock in. The harbour is dominated by the remains of the Dún na Sead (Fort of the Jewels), one of nine castles built in the area by the O'Driscoll clan.

Information

The small tourist office (☎ 21766) at the harbour opens only in the high season but lots of useful information is pinned up on a board outside when it's closed. Staff can also arrange accommodation on both Clear and Sherkin Islands.

Activities

The Baltimore Diving Watersports Centre (☎ 20300) arranges diving expeditions around Baltimore and off Clear and Sherkin Islands for everyone from beginners to the more experienced.

The Baltimore Sailing School (☎ 20141) provides sailing courses from May to September for both beginners and advanced sailors.

Special Events

Over the third weekend of May, Baltimore stages a seafood festival: jazz bands perform and mussels and prawns are on offer

CORK

in the pubs. Contact the tourist office for more details.

Places to Stay

In a garden on the edge of Baltimore, pleasant and friendly *Rolf's Hostel* (☎ 20289) has dorm beds, some of them in a loft, costing £9; doubles cost £25. *Algiers Inn* (☎ 20145) is open year round; beds cost £16. Next door, *The Old Post House* (☎ 29155) also charges £16 per person. At *Corner House* (☎ 20143), on the other side of the pub, doubles cost £32.

Places to Eat

One of the best places to eat without busting the budget is *Café Art*, attached to Rolf's Hostel. Salads and more-substantial meals are served in a restaurant that doubles as an art gallery; delicious baguettes cost £3.

For light meals try the inexpensive *Lifeboat Restaurant* attached to the post office and bureau de change. *Algiers Inn* and *Declan McCarthy's Bar* both serve reasonably priced pub meals; fish and chips costs £4.95.

La Jolie Brise, facing the harbour, offers good pizzas and pastas; spaghetti bolognese costs £5. Moving up in price, *Chez Youen* (☎ 20136), overlooking the harbour, serves good French-style seafood. Most main courses cost £10 to £15.

Entertainment

There are regular traditional-music nights at *Declan McCarthy's Bar* in the square, although an admission charge of £4 to £6 can seem a tad steep.

Getting There & Away

On weekdays, at least four buses daily connect Skibbereen with Baltimore. There's a limited Saturday service from late May to mid-September. Since Baltimore is only 13km from Skibbereen, you could also cycle between the two.

From June to mid-September a boat leaves Baltimore for Schull via Heir Island at 10 am and 1.45 and 4.40 pm, returning from Schull at 11.30 am and 3 and 5.40 pm;

call ☎ 39153 for details. A single crossing costs £6 and bikes are free.

CLEAR ISLAND

☎ 028 • pop 150

Rugged Clear Island (Oileán Cléire), also called Cape Clear Island, is the second-most-southerly point of Ireland, after the Fastnet Rock, 6km to the south-west. Clear Island is also an Irish-speaking (Gaeltacht) area, with one shop, lots of B&Bs and three pubs. It's a place for walking and birdwatching: the island is probably the best place in Europe for viewing Manx shearwater and other sea birds.

Orientation & Information

The island is 5km long and just over 1.5km wide at its broadest point but narrows in the middle where an isthmus divides the northern and southern harbours. There's a tourist information post beyond the pier, open 4 to 6 pm daily, July and August. If it's closed the nearby coffee shop stocks a useful *Walkers' Guide* (£2).

Heritage Centre

A small heritage centre has exhibits on the island's history and culture. It opens 2.30 to 5.30 pm daily, June to August. There are fine views looking north across the water to the Mizen Head Peninsula. From the heritage centre it's a short walk downhill to the shop and pubs.

Birdwatching

The white-fronted, two-storey Bird Observatory is by the harbour. Turn right at the end of the pier and it's 100m along. It's worth calling in to ask about any planned birdwatching trips.

Clear Island is famous for large movements of sea birds, especially in July and August, when Manx shearwater, gannet, fulmar and kittiwake regularly fly past the island's southern end. The guillemot is the only notable sea bird that breeds on the island; the others live on the westerly Kerry rocks and fly past each morning heading for the Celtic and Irish Seas. In the evening they return and the sight is equally amazing:

in summer up to 35,000 shearwater can fly past in an hour, just skimming the surface of the water.

The best place from which to view the birds is Blananarragaun, the south-western tip of the island. To reach it from the pier, head up to the shop and turn right, following the sign for the camp site. When the road ends, head due south to the end of the spur of land.

Other Activities
Cape Clear Island Hostel (see Places to Stay, next) houses an adventure centre which arranges a number of outdoor activities, including kayaking and whale or dolphin watching.

Places to Stay
Signposted from the shop, the *camp site* (☎ 39136) costs £3 per person and opens June to September.

A short walk from the pier, An Óige's fairly basic *Cape Clear Island Hostel* (☎ 39198) charges £7 and opens March to October. *The Glen* hostel (☎ 39121), in a traditional cottage, is open year round and costs £7 per person; remember to bring your own food.

The *Bird Observatory* (no telephone; see the earlier Birdwatching entry) has limited hostel accommodation; just turn up and see if a bed is available – least likely at the beginning of October.

B&B is available year round at *Cluain Mara* (☎ 39153), costing £15 to £18 per person; evening meals cost £10. It is signposted behind the last of the three pubs.

Self-catering cottages are available, starting at £150 per week from October to March and rising to £380 in July and August. Two places to try are *Ciarán O'Driscoll* (☎ 39153) and *Chuck and Nell Kruger* (☎ 39157).

Places to Eat
For self-caterers the *shop* near the pier has some limited stock. *Chistin Cléire*, near the pier, is the only restaurant and serves light meals. *Ciarán Danny Mike's* serves pub food.

Entertainment
The island's three pubs, *Ciarán Danny Mike's*, *The Club* and *Cotters Bar* are within staggering distance of each other and at night drinking-up time is generous.

Getting There & Away
In June and September, boats leave Schull pier at 2.30 pm, returning at 5.30 pm, daily. In July and August they leave at 10 am and 2.30 and 4.30 pm, returning at 11 am and 3.30 and 5.30 pm, daily. The return fare is £9/4. Call ☎ 28278 or ☎ 28138 for more details.

The boat from Baltimore takes 45 minutes to cover the 11km journey and it's a stunning trip on a clear day, retracing the route Algerians took through the harbour when they launched their attack in 1631. From Baltimore boats leave at 2.15 and 7 pm daily (plus noon and 5 pm on Sunday in June), June to September. Coming back they leave Clear Island at 9 am and 6 pm Monday to Saturday, and 11 am and 1, 4 and 6 pm on Sunday (noon and 6 pm only in September); bikes travel free. The return fare is £8/4; bikes travel free.

SHERKIN ISLAND
☎ 028 • pop 70
People visit this minuscule island – 5km long and about the same wide – for the beaches and the two pubs. The three sandy areas – Trabawn, Cow and Silver Strands – are all on the far side of the island from the pier and reached by road. All are safe for swimming and suitable for children. During the annual regatta in late August the pubs stay open even longer than usual. The best place for general information is the post office (☎ 20181), which is beside the road running across the island from the pier to the beaches.

Places to Stay & Eat
Camping is free; ask permission from the farmer first.

B&Bs include *Island House* (☎ 20314), *Cuina House* (☎ 20384) and *Jolly Roger Tavern* (☎ 20379), all charging about £15 per person.

CORK

Murphy's Bar, on the site of the old O'Driscoll Castle, and the older *Jolly Roger Tavern* opposite, both serve bar food. To get to either pub from the pier, turn right just before the post office.

Getting There & Away

Boats leave Baltimore seven times daily from 10.30 am to 8.30 pm for the 10-minute crossing. The return fare is £4. June and September, boats to Sherkin also depart from Schull at 1.45 pm, and in July and August at 10.30 am and 1.45 and 4.15 pm (return £8); call ☎ 20125 for details.

Mizen Head Peninsula

From Skibbereen the road winds west to Ballydehob. Expatriates from Britain and northern Europe are scattered across West Cork. While Kinsale attracts the well-heeled, the less economically advantaged – or blow-ins as they are semi-affectionately called – have discovered the land around Ballydehob. They help breathe new life into the area, as many local young people leave to look for work elsewhere.

From Ballydehob the road goes west to Schull, with Mt Gabriel (407m) identifiable by the two tracking spheres, part of an air-and-sea monitoring system, perched on the summit.

From the top of Mt Gabriel (which can be reached by road) and most high ground on the peninsula, there are views of the Fastnet Lighthouse on a rock 11km off the coast. The first lighthouse was built in 1854 but was replaced in 1906 by a sturdier one which is now fully automated.

The next stop west is Goleen, a small village on the way to Crookhaven, Barleycove and Three Castle Head. Returning from Mizen Head you can take the spectacular coastal road that traces Dunmanus Bay on the left for most of the way to Durrus. At Durrus, one road heads for Bantry while the other turns west to the Sheep's Head Peninsula.

BALLYDEHOB
☎ 028 • pop 260

This tiny village takes its name from the Irish *Béal an dhá Chab* (Ford at the Mouth of Two Rivers). Approaching from the east, watch for the old 12-arched tramway viaduct. Limited tourist information is available from Shepherd's supermarket on the main street.

Special Events

Ballydehob stages a procession; villagers decorate their houses, and place religious statuary in their windows and flowers on the pavement. Schull and Ballydehob host the procession in late May of alternate years. It's Ballydehob's turn in 2001.

Places to Stay

At the small but cosy *Ballydehob Hostel* (☎ 37232), on the Durrus road, dorm beds cost £7; from June to September camping is also available. Call for directions. B&B is available at *The Woodcock* (☎ 37139), on the corner of the road to Durrus, costing upwards of £15 per person. On the Schull road, *Lynwood* (☎ 37124) has three rooms costing £24.50/36 for one/two people.

Places to Eat

Clara Bookshop has a small café serving soup and sandwiches (£1.70). *Hudson's Wholefoods* nearby sells takeaways, local West Cork cheeses and organic fruit and vegetables. *Annie's* is renowned for its seafood and steak dinners (£25), while *The Woodcock*, opposite, serves bar food and has a restaurant offering grilled meals, which start at £8.

Getting There & Away

The twice-daily Clonakilty to Schull bus stops in Ballydehob, only 8km from Schull.

SCHULL
☎ 028 • pop 580

A small, laid-back village at the foot of Mt Gabriel, Schull (pronounced 'skull') gets as touristy as anywhere on the Ring of Kerry from June to September, but relapses into tranquillity during the rest of the year. For some Irish people, civilised Ireland ends here and they are surprised that people want to venture into or live in the wilds farther south.

For good views of Schull Harbour and the Fastnet Lighthouse, take the road from Ballydehob to Durrus and Goleen, and turn off for Schull after 5km.

Information

The AIB branch at the top of Main St has an ATM and bureau de change. Fuschia Books, also on Main St, sells second-hand books.

Schull Planetarium

In the grounds of Schull Community College, the Republic's only planetarium (☎ 28552) has an 8m dome and a video and slide show. It opens 3 to 5 pm on Sunday in April and May, with its Star Show at 4 pm; 3 to 5 pm Tuesday, Thursday and Saturday, in June; and 2 to 5 pm Tuesday to Saturday, and 7 to 9 pm Monday and Thursday, July and August, with Star Shows at 4 pm on Wednesday and Saturday, and at 8 pm Monday and Thursday. Admission, including the Star Show, costs £3/2.

The planetarium is at the Goleen end of the village on the Colla road, just past the Schull Backpackers' Lodge. You can also reach it by walking along the Foreshore Path from the pier.

Other Things to See & Do

There's a challenging walk up Mt Gabriel from Schull, making a round trip of about 14km. The mountain was once mined for copper and there are Bronze Age remains as well as 19th-century mine shafts and chimneys.

Schull Watersports Centre (☎ 28554) by the pier offers sailing, windsurfing, diving and other activities.

If you would like to visit a local cheese-making farm, contact either Gubbeen House (☎ 28231) or West Cork Natural Cheeses (☎ 28593) for directions.

For details of Schull's biannual procession, see Special Events in the Ballydehob section earlier in this chapter.

Places to Stay

Camping & Hostels The excellent IHH *Schull Backpackers' Lodge* (☎ 28681) is off the Colla road, in a quiet, forested location a little before the planetarium. Beds in spotless, spacious dorms start at £9, while doubles cost upwards of £24. Camping is sometimes possible.

B&Bs Friendly *Schull Central* (☎ 28227, *Main St)* has comfortable clean rooms costing £16 per person. *Adele's* (see Places to Eat, later) also has a few rooms; if you're having trouble finding a single room it's worth asking here. At the top of Main St on the corner of the Goleen road *Old Bank House* (☎ 28306) has four doubles costing £36.

Hotels The *East End Hotel* (☎ 28101), at the Ballydehob end of Main St, is a pub with open fires; singles/doubles cost £35/50. At the *Colla House Hotel* (☎ 28105), 2km west of Schull in the hamlet of Colla, B&B costs £27/48. The hotel can also arrange horse riding excursions.

Places to Eat

If you're planning a picnic, stock up at *Courtyard* on Main St: it sells a wide range of West Cork cheeses. There's a small coffee shop at the back and, down an alley beside it, a bar that serves tasty seafood starting at £8.50. To sample locally baked bread with coffee there's nowhere better than *Adele's* across the road. At night it reopens as a restaurant *(☎ 28459)*; main dishes such as tagliatelle cost around £8.50. *Cotter's Yard* opposite will rustle up tea and scones or sandwiches (£1.85) if Adele's is full, which it often is.

The longest bar menu is to be found at the popular *Bunratty Inn* at the Goleen end of the village; garlic mussels cost £5.90. It doesn't serve lunch on Sunday, when *Waterside Inn* at the other end of Main St fills the gap.

Getting There & Away

Buses leave Cork (☎ 021-450 8188) at 11.20 am and 6 pm and travel to Schull via

CORK

Clonakilty, Skibbereen and Ballydehob. In the other direction, they leave Schull at 8.05 am and 5.50 pm from near the AIB bank, Main St.

Boats for Clear Island and Sherkin Island leave from the pier (see the Clear Island and Sherkin Island Getting There & Away sections for details). See the Baltimore Getting There & Away section for details of the Schull to Baltimore boat service.

Getting Around

Bikes can be hired from the Schull Backpackers' Lodge or from Cotter's Yard (☎ 28165), Main St, for £8 per day.

WEST OF SCHULL TO MIZEN HEAD

The road west from Schull leads 14km through a rocky landscape to the small village of Goleen. From Goleen, one road runs out to Mizen Head and the other to Crookhaven.

Goleen & Around
☎ 028

Mizen Tourism (☎ 35591, 35253) maintains a small year-round tourist office and foreign exchange just off the main square in Goleen (An Góilín).

If you hanker after artistic creativity it's worth coming to Goleen just to visit *The Ewe* (☎ 35492), a magical artists' hideaway with pretty gardens and stunning views. From Easter to October, Sheena and Kurt offer one-week creative escapes to let you try your hand at pottery and other handicrafts; accommodation and tuition costs £195 per person. Shorter courses are also available as well as non-residential ones. Non-artists may be content to check out the small shop where Sheena's colourful work is on display.

The Ewe, the blue house tucked into the hillside, is signposted to the right as you enter Goleen from Schull.

Places to Stay & Eat If you're driving from Schull to Goleen, after 8km you'll come to the pleasant, slate-floored *Altar Restaurant* (☎ 35254) just before the right

turn-off to Durrus. At lunchtime you can sample dishes such as oysters in stout for around £5 to £6.50. In the evening a set seafood dinner costs £20. The Altar also has a couple of well-equipped rooms where B&B costs £20 per person. There are remains of a megalithic tomb on the hillside beside the restaurant.

Heron's Cove Restaurant (☎ 35225) in Goleen opens year round for B&B (£20 per person) and dinner. Non-residents must make a reservation for dinner.

Getting There & Away The Clonakilty to Goleen bus leaves Clonakilty at 7.05 pm (12.25 pm on Sunday) and stops in Rosscarbery, Leap, Skibbereen, Ballydehob and Schull. Returning from Goleen, there are buses at 7.45 am and 5.30 pm Monday to Saturday, and at 5.30 pm on Sunday.

Crookhaven
☎ 028 • pop 40

Crookhaven was built on the far side of a spur of land that runs eastwards from the mainland, enclosing a harbour. The road from Goleen comes down to the northern side of the harbour, passing the remains of a once-thriving stone quarry. Crookhaven was once very important as the most westerly harbour along the coast. Mail from America was collected here and it was a busy port for sailing and fishing ships from all over the world.

Today the village still attracts sailors and there are a couple of B&Bs, pubs and seafood restaurants.

Places to Stay & Eat The *Marconi House* (☎ 35168), on the right when entering the village, was where Guglielmo Marconi (1874–1937), the Italian physicist who developed radiotelegraphy, erected a radio mast in 1902. Singles/doubles cost £20/36. It also has a small restaurant open for all meals.

The refurbished *Crookhaven Inn* serves dishes such as steak-and-stout pie (£6.50), while *O'Sullivan's Bar* offers meals such as good, moderately priced homemade soup and chowder.

Barleycove
☎ 028
This is West Cork's most splendid beach and, because a smaller beach nearer the camp site attracts holidaymakers, Barleycove itself is never crowded. It's a great place for children, with long stretches of sand and a safe sandy area where a stream flows down to the sea.

The popular *Barleycove Holiday Park* (*☎ 35302*) is open over Easter and from May to mid-September. Family tent sites cost £12 and bikes can be hired here.

At *Barley Cove Beach Hotel* (*☎ 35234*) B&B costs £43/66 for singles/doubles in July and August. The restaurant serves bar food, afternoon tea and dinner; roast of the day costs £7.50 and a set dinner is £15.

Mizen Head
Mizen Head Signal Station (☎ 028-35115) was completed in 1910, complementing Fastnet Lighthouse and giving extra protection to Atlantic-bound ships. It's on a small island connected to the mainland by a superb suspension bridge that gives exciting views of the nearby rock formations. The bridge was built in its entirety elsewhere and lifted into position here by cables.

The Mizen Vision is an exhibition on how the lighthouse operated before it was automated in 1993. It opens 10 am to 6 pm daily, June to September; 10.30 am to 5 pm daily, mid-March to May and in October; and 11 am to 4 pm at the weekend, November to mid-March. Admission costs £2.50/1.25.

Although it's interesting to see how the lighthouse keeper would have lived, on a clear day it's the vision out of the windows that will enthral you. Look out for gannets swirling and diving above the rocks.

In July and August you can see whales from Mizen Head, and seals can often be seen from the bridge throughout the year, when the waters are calm.

Three Castle Head
A prime reason for making the journey to Three Castle Head is to visit 13th-century Mizen Castle on the headland. According to

the *Annals of Innisfallen* it was built in 1217 and was once a stronghold of the O'Mahoney clan. Today it's a lonely ruin by the side of a supposedly haunted lake, with a sheer drop to the sea behind it.

At the time of writing the castle was closed for repairs and there was no public right of way from the farm gate (see the following paragraph). If you'd like to see if it has reopened, the following directions will help you get there.

Leaving the Barley Cove Beach Hotel car park, don't turn left for Mizen Head but go right and then left at the first T-junction. This quickly leads to another T-junction. Go right, follow the road to its end, and go through the farm gate on the right. Take the path to the house, follow the sign to the left and walk north for 10 minutes.

Dunmanus & Durrus
☎ 027
The coast road from Mizen Head to Durrus is spectacularly beautiful and takes you past the ruins of another medieval castle at Dunmanus.

In Durrus (Dúras) you could drop into **Kilvarock Garden** (☎ 61111), which opens 2.30 to 5.30 pm at the weekend, and at other times by appointment. *Dunbeacon Caravan and Camping Park* (*☎ 61246*), about 5km from Durrus on the Goleen road, charges £3 per person for camping plus another 50p for a shower.

On the main road *The Long Boat Bar* and *Ivo's* both serve bar meals; salmon steak costs £7.50. Opposite the post office, where the road turns west for Kilcrohane, *Suzanne's* is open for dinner from 7 to 9 pm Tuesday to Sunday. Just outside Durrus, on the cross-peninsula road to Goleen, the remote *Blair's Cove* (*☎ 61127*) serves reputedly wonderful seafood and meat dishes. Dinner costs £29.

BANTRY
☎ 027 • pop 2810
Bantry (Beanntraí) narrowly missed fame in the late 18th century thanks to storms that prevented a French fleet landing to join the United Irishmen's rebellion. A local

CORK

Englishman, Richard White, was rewarded with a peerage for trying to alert the British military in Cork. His grand home is open to the public and this, along with an exhibition devoted to the events of 1796, is now the town's main attraction.

Before Irish independence, Bantry Bay was a major anchorage for the British navy, and after WWII Spanish trawlers were regular visitors. The bay's deep waters were also exploited by Gulf Oil, who built an oil terminal on Whiddy Island, bringing unexpected prosperity.

The island is close to Bantry Harbour and can be seen from the Cork road when entering town. In 1979, 51 lives were lost when fire broke out at the terminal. The disused storage tanks are still visible from the Bantry to Glengarriff road.

Orientation & Information

The two main roads into Bantry converge on the large Wolfe Tone Square, now mostly a free car park. A small market is held here on Friday and some of the region's many expatriates, who are known as 'blow-ins' or 'hippies' to the locals, come in to sell their wares.

The tourist office (☎ 50229), in the old courthouse at the eastern end of Wolf Tone Square, opens 9.15 am to 5.30 pm Monday to Saturday, May to September, plus 10 am to 6 pm on Sunday, July and August. There's a laundrette next door but the entrance is round the corner on New St. Nearby on New St is Bantry Bookstore, which has a stock of some general and local-interest books.

Bantry Museum

Tiny, dejected Bantry Museum, lurking behind the fire station, is in need of better premises. It contains a collection of local historical artefacts and opens 10.30 am to 1 pm Tuesday and Thursday, and 2.30 to 5 pm Wednesday and Friday, June to September. Admission costs 50p.

Bantry House & Gardens

Bantry House is superbly situated overlooking the bay. Parts of the house date back to the mid-18th century, but the fine sea-facing northern front was added in 1840.

Despite its air of fading gentility, the interior is noted for its French and Flemish

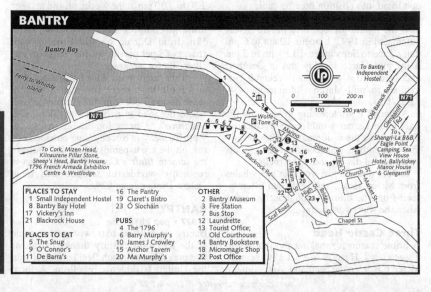

tapestries and the eclectic collection of art assembled by the 2nd earl of Bantry during his overseas peregrinations between 1820 and 1850. The old kitchen, with range intact, is now a tearoom serving excellent cakes and light lunches, and a craft shop.

But the gardens of Bantry House are its greatest glory and feature in the closing scenes of the film *Moll Flanders*. In front of the house, a well-kept lawn sweeps down towards the sea. Even better is the formal Italian garden at the back with a 'stairway to heaven' offering spectacular views over the bay. Come in May to see the ring of wisteria beautifully in bloom around a fountain.

The house and gardens open 9 am to 6 pm daily (extended hours in July and August) and admission costs £6 (children free). Admission to the gardens costs only £2. See Special Events, later in this Bantry section, for details of the West Cork Chamber Music Festival held at Bantry House.

1796 French Armada Exhibition Centre
Considering how Lord Bantry obtained his title it's ironic that the grounds of the house now harbour an exhibition recording the sorry saga of the attempted French landing of 1796. The exhibition includes a few artefacts rescued from the scuttled French frigate *La Surveillante*, together with a 30-minute video about diving on wrecks. The centre (☎ 51796) is run independently of Bantry House even though it's close by in the house's former stables. It opens 10 am to 6 pm daily, April to October. Admission costs £3/1.25.

Kilnaurane Pillar Stone
This isolated stone is worth seeking out because of its rare depiction of the kind of boat St Brendan is assumed to have used to reach America. To find it, leave Bantry on the N71 Cork road. When you reach the Westlodge Hotel, 2km out of town, take the turning on the left. After 800m a sign points towards a gate on the right. Go through the gate and walk straight ahead until you spot the stone just over the brow of the hill. On the way back you'll have fine views of Bantry Bay ahead of you.

Whiddy Island
You can reach Whiddy Island by boat (☎ 50310), which leaves from the pier daily between May and September (return £4).

Special Events
In the second week of May, Bantry holds a Mussel Fair with various musical events and free mussels distributed around the pubs.

The week-long West Cork Chamber Music Festival is held at Bantry House at the end of June and beginning of July. The house closes to the public during this time, although the garden, craft shop and tearoom remain open.

Places to Stay
Camping The nearest camp site is *Eagle Point Camping* (☎ 50630) in Ballylickey, 6km from town on Glengarriff Rd. A tent site for two with a car costs £10.50. It opens late April to September.

Hostels The IHH *Bantry Independent Hostel* (☎ 51050) is off the Glengarriff Rd at Bishop Lucey Place; coming from the town centre, take the left fork by the Micromagic shop and continue about 600m along the rough Old Barrack Rd to the top of the hill. Dorm beds cost £6.50, doubles £18. There's a small kitchen, a cosy sitting room with lots of walking information and a pleasant garden.

Small Independent Hostel (☎ 51140) is beside the harbour on the northern bank of the bay. Dorm beds cost £7, doubles £14.

B&Bs In New St near the square, the venerable, old, musty *Vickery's Inn* (☎ 50006) was once the town's coaching inn; beds start at £16 per person with shared bathroom. For solo travellers this is a good bet. There's even an Internet connection (email costs £1).

Also central is *Blackrock House* (☎ 50432, *Blackrock Terrace*), on William

CORK

St beside the post office; singles/doubles cost £25/36.

B&Bs are strung out along the Glengarriff Rd. *Shangri-La* (☎ *50244*) has a good reputation but fills up quickly; singles/doubles start at £24/36.

Hotels At refurbished *Bantry Bay Hotel* (☎ *50062, fax 50261, Wolfe Tone Square*) singles/doubles cost £37/60. The charmless *Westlodge* (☎ *50360, fax 50438*) is about 2km outside town on the Cork road. It's beautifully situated and boasts an indoor swimming pool. Singles/doubles start at £55/75.

Sea View House Hotel (☎ *50073, fax 51555*), in Ballylickey, is a superior country house and is a bit more expensive at £62/90. To get there follow Glengarriff Rd a few kilometres and you'll see it on the right. If you reach a sharp bend where the road to Macroom is signposted, you've passed it.

Romantics will jump at the chance to stay at *Bantry House* (☎ *50047*). From May to September beds cost £75; in March, April and October they're £65. Dinner costs another £25 per person but you get the gardens to yourself after the crowds have gone home. Another pricey but interesting option is the 17th-century *Ballylickey Manor House* (☎ *50071, fax 50124*), which charges upwards of £132 for doubles. It opens April to October.

Places to Eat

Best of the few cafés is *The Pantry* (*New St*), up a flight of stairs near Vickery's Inn. Alongside the usual salads, soups and sandwiches you can get chicken burritos (£4.95). Also on New St, *De Barra's* opens for breakfast and serves tasty snacks, rolls and sandwiches (£1.75).

Ó Síocháin (*Bridge St*) has a standard café-style menu with specials such as roast and three veg (£3.95). *Vickery's Inn* (see Places to Stay) serves unadventurous but filling three-course lunches costing around £8.50; dinner costs £15.

Lunch, served until 4 pm, at the convivial *Claret's Bistro* (☎ *52187, Barrack St*) costs around £5, and dinner main courses, served from 6 to 9.30 pm, cost upwards of £10.50.

Several pubs serve bar lunches, including *Barry Murphy's* and *The Snug*, both just off the square. At the latter the menu is in French, German and Spanish as well as English; fried plaice costs £6.20.

O'Connor's (☎ *50221, Wolfe Tone Square*) is an acclaimed seafood restaurant. Lunch costs around £6 to £9, dinner from £11 to £15, and mussels are a speciality. *Bantry Bay Hotel* (see Places to Stay) also has a good, if pricey, menu; vegetarians might fancy the exotic pineapple pilaff with saffron rice (£6). Bar meals are good value; sandwiches (£1.85) are served on a plate with several accompanying salads.

On Whiddy Island, the pub and restaurant *Bank House* (☎ *51739*) serves bar food and meals, mostly seafood.

Entertainment

When the British navy was here there were more than 50 pubs; now 'only' 17 or so serve the town. *Barry Murphy's* has traditional-music sessions, as does *James J Crowley*, where the emphasis is on ballads and ceilí bands. *Bantry Bay Hotel* is also worth checking out.

Even without music, *Anchor Tavern* is an interesting old pub. Look out, too, for *Ma Murphy's*, an old-style walk-through shop with a pub out the back. Both places are on New St.

The 1796, off the square next to The Snug, is a reliable music and comedy venue.

Getting There & Away

Throughout the year there are three buses daily between Cork and Bantry. During summer the express bus service between Cork and Killarney also stops outside Barry Murphy's in Bantry. It leaves for Glengarriff, Kenmare and Killarney at 11.45 am and 3 pm and departs for Skibbereen, Clonakilty and Cork at 12.05 and 6.10 pm. For details phone Bus Éireann (☎ *021-508188*).

The private Berehaven bus (☎ *70007*) links Castletownbere with Bantry via Glengarriff (one way £3). It leaves from the fire station in Wolfe Tone Square at noon and 5.50 pm on Monday, and 3.45 pm on Tuesday, Friday and Saturday.

Sheep's Head Peninsula

The least visited of Cork's three peninsulas, Sheep's Head Peninsula nevertheless has a charm of its own. There are no substantial antiquities but a loop road runs close to the sea along most of the length; there are wonderful seascapes to appreciate and country walks where other visitors will be few.

The second turning on the right after leaving Bantry southwards for Cork is the beginning of **Goat's Path Scenic Route**, which runs along the northern side of the peninsula. The southern part of the loop road begins farther along the main Cork road, just past the Esso garage. This road also follows in part the 88km **Sheep's Head Way**, a trail that traces the peninsula's coastline from Bantry to the lighthouse at Sheep's Head.

The only bus services to Ahakista and Kilcrohane leave Bantry at 10 am and 2.30 pm on Saturday and return from Kilcrohane at 10.40 am and 3.15 pm.

WALKING

A walk to the summit of **Seefin** (334m) begins at the top of Goat's Path, about 2km north of Kilcrohane village. Across the road from the walk's start is a rather forlorn imitation of Michelangelo's *Pietà*, erected by an American with local family roots. Although there's no obvious path, it isn't difficult to aim for the summit and reach it in less than 45 minutes. There are fine views from the top, and not many people make the climb.

There's also a good three-hour walk from the top of the Goat's Path. Standing near the *Pietà* and facing Bantry Bay, locate an old road about 100m to the right, recognisable by a low slate wall on the sea-facing side. Follow this remote track until it joins a

surfaced road that heads out farther west along the peninsula and eventually crosses to the southern side where the main road leads back to Kilcrohane. A left turn at the village church would bring you back to the start of the walk at the top of the Goat's Path.

You can also walk part or all of the 88km **Sheep Head's Way**, which begins at Turning Table, Tooreen, near Kilcrohane, and circles the peninsula via Sheep's Head, Bantry and Durrus.

AHAKISTA
☎ 027

Calling Ahakista (Atha an Chiste) a village is stretching the meaning of the word: there are two unprepossessing pubs, one shop and an expensive Japanese restaurant.

The first B&B west of Ahakista is the friendly *Grove House* (☎ 67060), where rooms with bathroom cost £19 per person. A little farther west a sign points to *Hillcrest* B&B (☎ 67045), which charges the same. Other B&Bs are dotted along the road, and cost much the same, so it's just a matter of picking one that takes your fancy.

If you're looking for something special and don't mind the cost, *Shiro* (☎ 67030), in beautiful grounds across the road from the Ahakista Bar, serves Japanese meals in a delightfully intimate setting. With just four tables, booking is essential despite the £41-per-head price tag.

Ahakista Bar has a surprisingly delightful garden at the back and music on Friday night; otherwise it opens sporadically.

KILCROHANE
☎ 027

The village of Kilcrohane lies about 6km south-west of Ahakista beside a fine beach. *Carbery View Hostel* (☎ 67035) is a basic bunkhouse with just eight beds costing £7 each. Follow the 'Hostel' sign from the western end of the village.

Of Kilcrohane's two pubs, *Fitzpatrick's*, just north of the church, serves tea, coffee and sandwiches, while both it and *Bay View Inn*, on the main road, host live-music sessions.

CORK

Beara Peninsula (Ring of Beara)

The appeal of the Beara Peninsula (Mor Choaird Bheara) lies in its startling natural beauty, best experienced by climbing the hills and cycling the roads. It's a lot bigger and much wilder than Sheep's Head Peninsula to the south and occupies part of both Cork and Kerry. While there is lush greenery (reminiscent of the Ireland imagined by long-departed emigrants) amid the rocky scenery on the Mizen Head and Sheep's Head Peninsulas, the Beara is a desolate, harsh, rocky landscape. It makes wonderful walking country and is littered with prehistoric rocks, stone circles and old tombs.

The 197km **Beara Way** is a well-signposted long-distance walk linking Glengarriff with Kenmare (in Kerry) via Castletownbere, Bere Island, Dursey Island and the northern side of the peninsula. Much of the route is along green roads. For more details see Walking in the Activities chapter.

ORIENTATION & INFORMATION

A small northern part of the peninsula lies in Kerry but is dealt with here for the convenience of people travelling the Ring of Beara. Castletownbere in Cork or Kenmare in Kerry would make good bases for exploring the peninsula. Small official tourist offices are open in Castletownbere and Glengarriff in July and August.

In theory you could drive the 137km around the coast in one day, but at the price of missing a great deal. In particular you would miss the spectacular **Healy Pass**, which cuts across the peninsula to join Adrigole in Cork with Lauragh in Kerry.

The route described below assumes you are starting out from Glengarriff and working your way round the peninsula clockwise to Kenmare.

GLENGARRIFF
☎ 027 • pop 245

A long, thin village, Glengarriff (An Gleann Garbh) is strung out along the main West Cork to Killarney road with the Eccles Hotel at one end. At the other end the road divides, with one branch leading to Kenmare and the other to the Beara Peninsula. Its sheltered position at the head of Bantry Bay, together with the influence of the Gulf Stream, gives it a particularly mild climate, and the local flora is lush and sometimes exotic.

During the second half of the 19th century, Glengarriff became a popular retreat for prosperous Victorians, who would sail from England to Ireland then take the train to Bantry, from where a paddle steamer chugged over to Glengarriff. By 1850 the road to Kenmare had been blasted through the mountains and the link with Killarney was established.

A major attraction is the Italianate garden on nearby Garinish Island, although it's pleasant just walking in the crassly named Blue Pool Amenity Area which rings the coast in the middle of the village.

Information

The Bord Fáilte tourist office (☎ 63084) opens only in July and August and is inconveniently positioned in the Eccles Hotel car park. You'd do better to call into the privately run version in the shop in the village centre beside the Blue Pool Ferries terminal. This opens 10 am to 1 pm and 2 to 6 pm Monday to Saturday, June to August. The small AIB on the main street has a bureau de change but no ATM.

Garinish Island (Ilnacullin)

In the early 20th century the English architect Harold Peto created an Italianate garden on this 15-hectare island. He planted exotic plants never before seen in Ireland, and they continue to flourish, providing a blaze of colour in a landscape usually dominated by greens and browns. There are panoramic views from the top of the 19th-century Martello tower, built to watch out for a possible Napoleonic invasion.

The Dúchas-run gardens open 9.30 am to 6.30 pm Monday to Saturday, and 11 am to 7 pm on Sunday, July and August; 10 am to 6.30 pm Monday to Saturday, and 1 to 7 pm on Sunday, April to June and September; and 10 am to 4.30 pm Monday to Saturday, and 1 to 5 pm on Sunday, March and October. Admission costs £3/1.25.

Two ferry companies serve the island. Harbour Queen Ferryboats (☎ 63116) leave from a pier on the other side of the road from the Eccles Hotel, while the Blue Pool Ferries (☎ 63333) terminal is in the centre of the village, near the Quills Woollen Market. Both charge £5 return for the 10-minute crossing, during which you'll probably see colonies of seals basking on rocks.

Glengarriff Woods

These 300-hectare oak and pine woods were owned by the White family of Bantry House in the 18th century. After the government took over in the 1950s the range of trees was expanded. The thick tree cover maintains humid conditions that allow ferns and mosses to flourish. Look out especially for tiny white flowers on red stems rising from rosettes of leaves: these are kidney saxifrage, rare elsewhere.

The woodlands and bogs are also home to the Kerry slug, the 'aristocrat of slugs', found only here and in parts of Kerry and the Iberian Peninsula. It's coffee-coloured with cream spots.

To get to the woods, leave Glengarriff on the N71 Kenmare road. The entrance is about 1km along on the left. A sign, just inside the gate, points across a footbridge to **Lady Bantry's Lookout**. It's a short, steep climb which brings you out seemingly on top of the world.

Scuba Diving

Both Bantry and Dunmanus Bay boast exciting sites for scuba diving. Bantry Bay Divers (☎ 51310) is recommended for both dedicated and occasional divers. Package trips are arranged and other water activities can be organised. At the time of writing it was trying to set up a new centre from which to base operations. Call for details.

Places to Stay

Camping Two kilometres west of Glengarriff on the Castletownbere road, *Dowlings*

Caravan and Camping Park (☎ 63154) is open from Easter to October. It has a licensed bar and music in the summer. A tent site for two costs £8. *O'Shea's Caravan and Camping Park* (☎ 63140), close by, charges similar rates.

Hostels In the centre of Glengarriff, between the Blue Pool Ferries terminal and Casey's Hotel, *Murphy's Village Hostel* (☎ 63555) offers dorm beds costing £8.50, doubles £22. There's a small café on the ground floor to supplement the 1st-floor cooking facilities. If this is full, about 1km from the village and signposted along the Kenmare road, *Glengarriff Independent Hostel* (☎ 63211) is an isolated but hardly picturesque bungalow charging £6 for dorm beds and £3 for tent sites.

B&Bs Bungalow B&Bs line the road out to Bantry. At *Sea Front* (☎ 63079), near Eccles Hotel, singles/doubles with shared bathroom cost £22.50/32. *Island View House* (☎ 63081) has singles/doubles at the same rate plus rooms with bathroom costing £24.50/36. In the village centre, where some of the shops double as B&Bs, there are cheaper alternatives; rates are around £12 to £15 per person.

Hotels Grand but fading *Eccles Hotel* (☎ 63003, fax 63319) boasts past literary guests such as Thackeray, Yeats and Shaw but is very much a coach-tour stop-off now. Facing the sea on the main road at the Bantry end of the village, it offers singles/doubles starting at £40/60. *Casey's Hotel* (☎ 63010, fax 63072), in the village centre, charges £30/50 in peak season.

Places to Eat

John Barry's pub near the post office offers open fish sandwiches costing £6.50. For simpler, cheaper sandwiches (£1.45) during the day try *Blue Loo* pub on the other side of the road. John Barry's also boasts a seafood restaurant where main dishes cost £10 to £12. *Rainbow Restaurant* next door serves beef curry costing £6.50. *Eccles Hotel* serves pub food all day, as does

CORK

Casey's Hotel, where fish and chips costs £5.60.

For coffee and delicious homemade cakes, try *Café de la Paix* opposite John Barry's.

Getting There & Away

An express bus travels daily between Cork and Glengarriff (2½ hours) via Bantry (£1.50, 15 minutes). Coming from Bantry it stops outside the post office; going back to Bantry it stops by the phone boxes across the road.

Late May to mid-September, buses from Cork to Killarney also pass through Bantry and Glengarriff daily; phone ☎ 021-508188 for details.

The private Berehaven bus (☎ 70007) departs for Bantry at 7.30 am daily and returns at 7.45 pm. This service continues on to Cork.

Getting Around

Jem Creations (☎ 63113), where the road divides for Castletownbere, is the Raleigh Rent-a-Bike agent; hire costs £10/40 per day/week.

SUGARLOAF MOUNTAIN

Eight kilometres south-west of Glengarriff towards Castletownbere look out for a turning on the right; it's 500m after a disused school on the right of the road, opposite a blue Community Alert Area sign in the middle of nowhere. Follow this road for 1.5km and leave your bicycle or car near the single two-storey house (with pine trees behind it) or near the bungalow just past it.

Sugarloaf Mountain (575m) is best approached by walking up behind the houses and crossing an old road. A steady approach up the side of the mountain would bring you to the triangulation point at the summit in about an hour.

There are excellent views from the top: the Caha Mountains to the north, Hungry Hill to the west, Garinish Island to the east and Bantry Bay spread out to the south. On the way up, look out for the insectivorous great butterwort around the old road, in May and June.

ADRIGOLE

☎ 027

Twenty-four kilometres south-west of Glengarriff, the first village you come to on the peninsula is Adrigole (Eadargóil), where not a lot happens. It's mainly a string of scattered buildings along the coast with no real centre. The small, simple *Adrigole Hostel* (☎ 60228), about 150m after the T-junction on the Castletownbere road west of the village, charges £7.50 for dorm beds and has space for tents.

HUNGRY HILL

Hungry Hill (686m) is the highest point on the peninsula. A sign points to one route to the top, 7km west of Adrigole. A longer but more comfortable ascent begins by ignoring this sign, carrying along the road, and turning right just past a church on the right side of the road. This road goes north until blocked by a wire sheep gate. A vehicle could be left just before this or taken past for another kilometre or so. The overgrown road eventually stops near some lakes, and from here, keeping the lakes to the left, you head up the eastern ridge and climb the summit from the northern side.

A quicker descent can be made by following the stream down the south-western side to some farmhouses and a road that connects with the one where you began. The whole journey will take at least five hours but the rockscapes are fabulous and the views of West Cork from the top are tremendous. Less arduous would be a walk to the end of the road and a picnic by the lakes.

CASTLETOWNBERE

☎ 027 • pop 920

Castletownbere (Baile Chais Bhéara) is Ireland's largest whitefish port and when its full name – Castletownberehaven – is used it shares with Newtownmountkennedy, in County Wicklow, the proud claim of having the country's longest place name. The main town on the peninsula, it originally developed out of the copper-mining industry at Allihies and remains little touched by tourism.

CORK

Castletownbere is little more than one traffic-choked street with the Bere Island ferry and the harbour at the east and the main square given over to a fire station, garage, car park and fishing suppliers. Tourist information (☎ 70344) is available in July and August from what amounts to a garden shed squeezed in next to the fire station. Otherwise there are supermarkets, a post office with a limited bureau de change, an AIB branch with an ATM, a couple of laundrettes and a string of pubs.

Places to Stay

Camping The *Berehaven Camper and Amenity Park* (☎ 70700) is 1.5km east of town overlooking the bay. You can also camp at *Beara Hostel* (see Hostels) on the Dursey side of town for £4, which allows use of the hostel's facilities.

Hostels About 3km west of Castletownbere, on the main road just past the sign for Dunboy Castle, *Beara Hostel* (☎ 70184) has dorm beds costing £7, or doubles, some of them in pleasant wooden chalets, for £17. *Garranes Farmhouse Hostel* (☎ 73147), between Castletownbere and Allihies, has a superb location overlooking Bantry Bay, about 2km off the road. It's owned by the Dzogchen Buddhist retreat centre next door and guests have the option of joining in daily meditation sessions, based on Tibetan Buddhist principles. Dorm beds cost £6.50.

B&Bs The half-dozen B&Bs include *Bay View House* (☎ 70099, *West End*), where singles/doubles with shared facilities cost £17/30. *The Old Bank Seafood Restaurant* (☎ 70252), right in the town centre, offers B&B throughout the year; it charges £16 per person. At *Ford Rí Hotel* (☎ 70379), along the waterfront, singles/doubles start at £40/60.

Places to Eat

Niki's, in the town centre, serves breakfast (£4.95) and seafood dinners costing around £16.50. Across the road, *Jack Patrick's* has good lunch specials; shepherd's pie costs £3.50.

Old Bank Seafood Restaurant, just west of the main square, opens Easter to September. Dinner costs around £12. Even farther west the relaxed *Old Bakery Café and Restaurant*, with paintings on the wall and a varied menu, is good value. Daily specials, such as Mexican pancake, cost £3.50, while soup with soda bread costs £2.30.

Entertainment

Some pubs host traditional live music at night. Try *Twomey's* on a Friday.

Getting There & Away

Express buses run from Cork (☎ 021-450 8188) twice daily. In July and August there's also one bus daily, Monday to Saturday, to Killarney via Eyeries, Ardgroom, Lauragh and Kenmare.

Getting Around

Bikes can be hired from the SuperValu supermarket (☎ 70020) on the eastern side of town near the ferry; hire costs £7.50/35 per day/week.

BERE ISLAND

☎ 027 • pop 40

This island may be about the same size as Manhattan but it has a very different kind of appeal. The deep anchorage helped make it the base for the British navy and the whole Allied fleet spent some time here before the Battle of Jutland in WWI. At the outbreak of WWII, Winston Churchill wanted to continue using it, and a deal for the return of the six northern counties was in the air. However, it wasn't to be.

The 21km section of **Beara Way** is the best reason for visiting the island. There are a couple of pubs and small shops but tourist accommodation is limited to four beds at *Harbour View* (☎ 75011), available from April to October only; singles/doubles cost £16/28 with shared bathroom, £18/32 en suite. It's best to book in advance.

A ferry (☎ 75009) to Bere Island runs daily year round from Castletownbere quay. It costs £15 return for a car and driver, £4/2 for passengers. In July and August there

CORK

are seven boats daily between 10.30 am and 6 pm.

DUNBOY CASTLE & PUXLEY MANSION

About 3km south-west of Castletownbere you come to a sign to Dunboy Castle (☎ 027-70044), which is in a beautiful setting. Little now remains of the castle, the fortress of the O'Sullivan clan, who ruled supreme for three centuries before succumbing to the English, armed with cannons and 4000 men, in 1602.

Don't make the mistake of thinking the grand ruins you come to first are the magnificent remains of a Gaelic stronghold. This is Puxley Mansion, bearing testimony to the vast wealth generated by the copper mined on the Puxley family estate. It was built in the 19th century and burned down by the old IRA in 1921, but enough remains to show the extravagance of its style. Check out the Italian marble of the columns still standing in what was once the grand hallway.

If you don't mind roughing it, it's possible to camp in the grounds of Dunboy Castle for £2 per person. Ask at the house on the right after passing the main gate.

Admission to the castle grounds costs 50p per person or £2 for a car. On a good day you're much better off walking down. The grounds are open Easter to mid-October; when the gate's not staffed put the admission fee in the box.

DURSEY ISLAND

☎ 027 • pop 50

At the end of the peninsula is Dursey Island, just 6.5km long by 1.5km wide and 250m offshore. Ireland's only cable car connects the inhabitants and their cattle with the mainland. Three hundred people sought refuge here in 1602, when Dunboy Castle was under siege by the English; they were slaughtered and thrown into the sea. Dursey Island is a wild-bird and whale sanctuary, and dolphins can sometimes be seen swimming in the waters around it.

The cable car (return £2.50) crosses between 9 and 11 am, 2.30 and 5 pm and 7 and 8 pm, Monday to Saturday. Note that cattle get precedence over humans in the queue for the ride! The two Sunday-morning crossings are timed to get people to mass at Cahermore or Allihies, but there are also crossings at 7 pm and 11 pm. From June to August there are also Sunday crossings between 4 and 5 pm.

Although there's no accommodation on the island it's easy to find somewhere to camp. The **Beara Way** loops round the island for 11km, and the signal tower is an obvious destination for a shorter walk. Bikes are not allowed on the cable car.

Just before the cable-car terminus, *Windy Point House* (☎ 73017) offers B&B costing £22/34 in singles/doubles and serves tea, coffee and light meals.

ALLIHIES & THE COPPER MINES

☎ 027

Copper was discovered in 1810. While mining quickly brought wealth to the Puxley family, who owned the land, it brought low wages and dangerous, unhealthy working conditions for the workforce, which at one time numbered 1300 men, women and children. Experienced Cornish miners were brought into the area, and the ruins of their stone cottages remain. As late as the 1930s, over 30,000 tonnes of pure copper were being exported annually, but by 1962 the last mine was closed. Characters in Daphne du Maurier's novel *Hungry Hill* are based on the Puxley family.

In Allihies (Na hAilichí), a small tourist information kiosk, beside the church, is open in the peak season. There's no bank but the small post office has a bureau de change.

Walking

The copper mines are just north of Allihies village and 19km west of Castletownbere; signs point the way to the remains of a quarry. An old road leads to the ruins of a chimney stack, where you can follow a road up, passing an old reservoir on the right. Mine shafts are scattered around but they're fenced off and you can approach the main chimney stack in relative safety. The track eventually leads to Eyeries and can be followed for as long as you wish. Half an hour's walk leads to a lookout with a view of Coulagh Bay and Kenmare Bay beyond. You can climb the hills by cutting over the moor to the right, but it's best to consult a local walking guide such as *West Cork Walks* by Kevin Corcoran.

Places to Stay & Eat
In Allihies village is the IHH *The Village Hostel (Bonnie Braes;* ☎ *73107)*; dorm beds cost £8 and private rooms £18. There's limited camping space in the garden costing £4 per person. In among the surrounding copper mines is the An Óige *Allihies Hostel (*☎ *73014)*, where beds cost £6.50/5.

In the village, B&B is available at the *Sea View Guest House (*☎ *73004)* starting at £19.50 per person, or at *Tig Seán Máire (*☎ *73076)*, Killaugh East, for £16.

O'Neil's pub and *Lighthouse Bar* are good for some pub grub or a drink.

Getting There & Away
Allihies is served by the privately run Berehaven bus company. Call ☎ 70007 for information.

EYERIES & ARDGROOM
☎ 027
Heading north and east from Allihies, a 23km coastal road with hedges of fuchsia and rhododendron twists and turns all the way to Eyeries. If you're driving or cycling watch out for grazing sheep wandering onto the road. Look back almost immediately after leaving Allihies and you'll be able to see the Bull, Cow and Calf Rocks off Dursey Head.

Eyeries (Na hAoraí) is a village of brightly coloured houses with three pubs, a post office and a church. Singles/doubles cost £15/26 at *The Shamrock (*☎ *74058)*, on Strand Rd.

The coast road eventually rejoins the main road at Ardgroom (Ard Dhór), a small village where food is available at *Village Inn* and *The Holly Bar*.

As you head east towards Lauragh look for signs pointing right to the Ardgroom

stone circle, a beautifully located Bronze Age monument, the most striking in a valley littered with reminders of prehistory. The ground can be boggy so be careful after rain.

LAURAGH (COUNTY KERRY)
☎ 064
Although Lauragh (Laith Reach), north-east of Ardgroom, is actually in Kerry, it's included here for the convenience of people travelling the Ring of Beara.

From Lauragh, a serpentine road travels 11km south across Healy Pass, offering spectacular views of the rocky inland scenery.

Lauragh is also home to the century-old **Derreen Gardens**, planted by the 5th Lord Lansdowne. An abundance of interesting plants thrive here, including spectacular New Zealand tree ferns and red cedars normally found in rainforests. The gardens open 11 am to 6 pm daily, April to September. Admission costs £2.50/1.50.

Walking
About 1km west of Lauragh along the R572, a road to the left is marked for Glanmore Lake. Follow this road then take the first turning to the right and stay on it until it ends by a couple of farms, the first of which has a stone circle in its back yard. From the end of the road, a path continues across a stream and into the valley until it reaches the remains of some stone dwellings. This undemanding walk will take you less than an hour from the stone circle.

A more exhilarating walk is to head up behind the house with the stone circle, crossing a sheep fence and keeping to the right of the stream. A stiff climb leads to a hanging valley with mountains on both sides. Head right to climb the shorter summit of **Cummeennahillan** (361m), which affords tremendous views. From there you can walk along the mountain ridge then down through holly woods and invasive rhododendrons through another farm to the Glanmore Lake road. This longer trek takes at least a couple of hours.

CORK

Places to Stay

Creveen Lodge Caravan and Camping Park (☎ *83131*), 1.5km south-east of Lauragh on the Healy Pass road, opens from Easter to the end of October; a small tent site costs £7 to £8. The An Óige *Glanmore Lake Hostel* (☎ *83181*), in an old lakeside schoolhouse 5km from Lauragh, opens Easter to September; beds cost £6.50/5. At *Mountain View* (☎ *83143*), distinctively located near the Healy Pass, B&B starts at £21/32 in singles/doubles, and dinner costs £13.

Getting There & Away

The bus service is very limited. Running between Killarney and Castletownbere, it operates only in July and August, and stops in Lauragh once daily, Monday to Saturday.

Northern Cork

The chief reasons for visiting northern Cork are the fishing and the golf. A few distinguished country houses with fine gardens are open to the public for evening meals and short stays, but this is hardly budget travellers' territory: permission to fish for a day on the River Blackwater could cost £35; a night for two in a country house with dinner could easily approach £200. There are no hostels or official camp sites, but B&Bs are never far away.

FERMOY
☎ 025 • pop 2300

Fermoy (Mainistir Fhear Muighe) is a small town on the River Blackwater at the point where the cross-country roads from Dublin to Cork and from Rosslare to Killarney intersect. There's not a great deal to do here unless you're into fishing, but the number of teashops makes it a good place to break your journey.

The town hosts a Fishing Festival in the week straddling May and June, in an attempt to lure visitors from England during their bank-holiday weekend and then Irish anglers for their bank-holiday weekend the week after.

Information

The tourist office (☎ 31811) is in the Fermoy Community Resource Centre, a white building on MacCurtain St, but it may move. It opens 9 am to 6 pm on weekdays. The post office is on Patrick St.

Any fishing inquiries should be made to Brian Toomey Sports (☎ 31101), 18 MacCurtain St.

Places to Stay & Eat

If you need a bed for the night, B&B at *St Anne's* (☎ *31205*), on the Cahir side of the bridge, costs £16 per person.

Beside the bus stops on MacCurtain St, *Mary's* and *Partners* both serve all-day breakfasts costing £3.50. For an unexpectedly interesting dinner try *La Bigoudenne* (☎ *32832, 28 MacCurtain St*), a Breton crêperie which opens for lunch and again for dinner. Savoury crêpes start at just £1.85, and a more conventional seven-course set dinner costs £18.

Getting There & Away

Fermoy is on the main Dublin to Cork bus route, with three daily services from Monday to Saturday, and two on Sunday. There are also direct buses to Cahir and Waterford.

MALLOW & AROUND
☎ 022 • pop 6245

Much bigger than Fermoy, Mallow (Mala) is a prosperous, picturesque town in the Blackwater Valley that caters for fishing, golfing and horse racing. Nineteenth-century visitors to its spa christened it the 'Bath of Ireland', although these days the comparison would seem pretty far-fetched.

The tourist office (☎ 42222), on Bridge St near the castle, opens 9.30 am to 1 pm and 2 to 5 pm on weekdays, March to October, plus on Saturday and at lunchtime, June to August.

From Mallow to Killarney the landscape is fairly nondescript, although you might want to divert to see the well-preserved remains of 17th-century **Kanturk Castle** – it's said that the mortar was mixed with the blood of the builders who were forced to work on its construction. The English, however, objected to an Irish chief building such a massive mansion and didn't allow it to be roofed.

Kanturk, 15km west of Mallow, offers fishing (☎ 029-50257) and the superior, peaceful, 17th-century *Assolas Country House* (☎ 029-50015, fax 50795), where B&B costs £78/126 for singles/doubles in the high season. It opens April to October.

There are regular buses between Mallow and Cork, but for Kanturk you really need your own transport.

Inland Cork

The most popular westwards route from Cork heads south to Kinsale and then along the N71 through Clonakilty and Skibbereen. An alternative route from Cork to Bantry cuts inland via Macroom, and takes in the Gougane Barra Forest Park. The quickest route between Killarney and Cork is also via Macroom.

A quicker inland route to Bantry takes the main road to Bandon and Dunmanway, but there are few attractions along the way except the pleasant IHH *Shiplake Mountain Hostel* (☎ 023-45750), where you can hire bikes and find out about local cycling trips. Dorm beds cost £9.75.

BANDON
☎ 023 • pop 1945
Twenty kilometres north-east of Clonakilty on the river of the same name, Bandon (Droichead na Banndan) was a major Protestant settlement in the 17th century, infamous for excluding Catholics. **West Cork Heritage Centre**, in an old church, features various exhibits relating to local life through the ages, the most successful being the re-created country shop and bar. It opens 10 am to 6 pm Monday to Saturday, and 2 to 6 pm on Sunday, April to October. Admission costs £3.

Getting There & Away
Bus Éireann runs at least four express buses daily between Cork (☎ 021-450 8188) and

Bandon, some of which continue to Bantry and Glengarriff. Some also go on to Schull and Skibbereen.

MICHAEL COLLINS AMBUSH SITE
In 1922 Michael Collins (see the boxed text 'Michael Collins... The Big Fella' on the following page), commander-in-chief of the army of the new Provisional Government that had just won independence from Britain, was assassinated at Beal-na-Blath, near Macroom. He was on a tour of West Cork and was recognised by anti-Treaty forces, who were meeting secretly nearby. In the evening they ambushed his car and Collins was shot dead. Apparently, Collins ignored advice to drive on after the first shots were fired, choosing instead to make a fight of it.

The site of the ambush is marked by a stone memorial with a Gaelic inscription. Each year, a commemorative service is held on the anniversary of the killing (22 August).

Getting There & Away
Follow the N22 west from Cork then after about 20km take the left turn (R590) to Crookstown. From there turn right onto the R585 to Beal-na-Blath. The ambush site is on the left after 4km.

GOUGANE BARRA FOREST PARK
This is the most picturesque part of inland Cork. The source of the River Lee is a mountain lake fed by numerous silver streams. St Finbarr, the founder and patron saint of Cork, came here in the 6th century and established a monastery. He had a hermitage on the island in Gougane Barra Lake (Lough an Ghugain), which is now approached by a short causeway. The small modern chapel on the island has fine stained-glass representations of obscure Celtic saints.

A road runs through the park in a loop and a signboard map shows the meandering paths and nature trails leading off it. It's worth heading for Bealick's summit for the fine views.

CORK

Michael Collins... The Big Fella

NICKY CAVEN

Michael Collins

Michael Collins was born on 16 October 1889 and reared in West Cork. As a young man he left Ireland to work as a civil servant in London. At the age of 26 he returned to take part in the 1916 Easter Rising and became committed to the continued armed struggle against the British. During the War of Independence (1919–21), he earned a reputation as a ruthless organiser of guerilla warfare.

Collins inspired tremendous respect among the Irish and fear among the British, who offered a large reward for his capture. He became a living legend, not least for the ease with which he evaded arrest, seldom bothering to disguise himself and riding freely around Dublin on his bicycle.

Collins infiltrated the British civil and military presence in Ireland, frustrating their efforts to maintain control. His 'flying columns' and assassination squads were clinical and helped to drive the British to the negotiating table in 1921.

Eamon de Valera sent Collins to Downing St, London, to negotiate a truce. Collins resisted the order, but to no avail. In going to London, he was forced to give up his most important weapon – his anonymity. Reluctantly, Collins signed a treaty which partitioned Ireland, leaving the six counties of the North under British rule. He considered the partition a stepping stone to a completely independent Ireland and believed it was the best deal that could be secured at the time, while prophetically declaring, 'I may have signed my death warrant tonight'.

The treaty split the Irish people and a brutal civil war followed its acceptance, with de Valera heading the anti-treaty faction. Collins was killed on 22 August 1922 in an ambush near Macroom in Cork.

Much of Neil Jordan's film *Michael Collins* (1996) was shot in West Cork. Despite some inevitable 'Hollywoodising' of the story, it remains a worthwhile, accessible introduction to the 'Big Fella', played by Liam Neeson.

Places to Stay & Eat

Seven hundred metres before the main park entrance, *Gougane Barra Hotel* (☎ 026-47069) overlooks the Gougane Barra Lake; singles/doubles start at £40/68. There's a small gift shop in the hotel grounds and nearby *Cronin's* bar serves light meals.

Three kilometres before the turn-off to Gougane Barra, to the right of the main road from Macroom, the IHH *Tig Barra Hostel*

(☎ 026-47016) has dorm beds costing £6 and two doubles for £18.

B&B, costing £22/34 for singles/doubles with shared bathroom, is available at *Cois na Coille* (☎ 026-47172), which is 1km from Ballingeary. As the name might suggest, this is a Gaeltacht area.

Opposite the junction of the N71 and R584 is *Ouvane Falls Hotel*, where it's worth stopping for a pub meal or a drink to

CORK

appreciate the lovely lake views from the garden at the back.

Getting There & Away
In July and August there's a Saturday-only bus service that leaves Macroom at 8 am and passes by the Gougane Barra Forest park.

Driving from Cork to Bantry along the N22 and R584 you'll see a signpost for the park after Ballingeary. Returning to the main road afterwards and continuing west, you'll pass over the Pass of Keimaneigh and emerge on the N71 at Ballylickey, midway between the Beara Peninsula and the Sheep's Head Peninsula.

County Kerry

The town of Killarney bursts at the seams and the Ring of Kerry is chock-a-block with tour coaches throughout summer, but the rest of the county is big enough for visitors to escape the crowds. The tourist hype detracts little from the landscape's wild splendour. Countless opportunities exist for long and short walks, easy and hard climbs and bike rides where your only companions will be the birds, the odd sheep and a few like-minded travellers. Especially beautiful is Dingle Peninsula, but the Iveragh Peninsula to the south has even more opportunities for open-air activities. There's the usual quota of pubs with lively music at night and several small towns of historic interest.

Killarney & Around

KILLARNEY
☎ 064 • pop 7250

As tourist towns go Killarney (Cill Airne) is Numero Uno. There's more registered accommodation here than anywhere else outside Dublin and the shops around the tourist office do a fine line in leprechaun-adorned T-shirts, mugs, towels – you name it. Killarney has been doing well economically and High St's pricey restaurants are testimony to this prosperity. Still, with a National Park and three lakes on its doorstep, Killarney offers easy escape from commercial excesses for walkers and cyclists. The town also has its own form of environmentally friendly transport – the horse-drawn jaunting car – which also gives it its distinctive aroma of dung. These carriages have been in use for well over a hundred years, but the tail bag hasn't yet caught on. Allow two or three days to do justice to Killarney and the National Park.

Orientation & Information

The centre of Killarney is focused on the T-junction where New St meets High and Main Sts. The National Park is to the south,

Highlights

- Walk or cycle in beautiful Killarney National Park

- Enjoy the boat trip from Ross Castle to Lord Brandon's Cottage in Killarney National Park

- Walk all or part of the Kerry Way

- Cycle or drive through stunning Ballaghbeama Pass, avoiding the ritualised Ring of Kerry

- Take a boat trip to the island of Skellig Michael, with its astonishing 7th-century monastery perched on top

- Swim with Fungie the dolphin at Dingle

- Visit 9th-century Gallarus Oratory on Dingle Peninsula

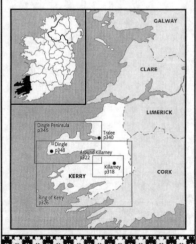

while the bus and train stations are to the east.

Killarney's busy but efficient tourist office (☎ 31633), in a new building on the

316

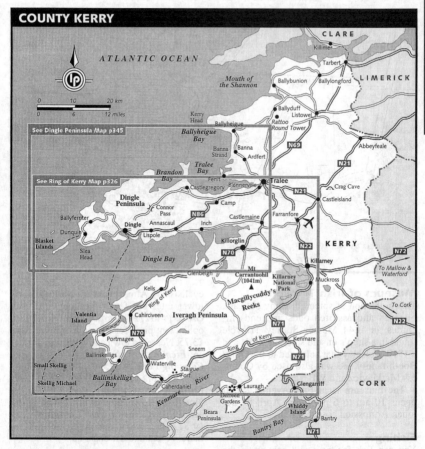

COUNTY KERRY

corner of Beech Rd (which runs south of New St), opens 9.15 am to 5.30 pm (later in July and August) Monday to Saturday, year round.

Many banks have either a bureau de change or an ATM or both and there's also a branch of American Express (Amex; ☎ 35722) on East Avenue Rd.

J Gleeson's Laundrette lurks behind the Spar supermarket at the Plunkett St end of College St.

Killarney Bookshop (☎ 34108), 32 Main St, has a selection of maps and guidebooks upstairs.

Internet access is available at Kerry Telephone Directory (☎ 36711, email ktd@ tinet.ie), 49 Lower New St.

St Mary's Cathedral

Built between 1842 and 1855, this cruciform cathedral, at the western end of New St in Cathedral Place and facing the pedestrian entrance to Killarney National Park, was designed by the architect Augustus Pugin. During the Famine it acted as a refuge for the destitute and the huge tree on the front lawn marks the mass grave of women and children who died.

KERRY

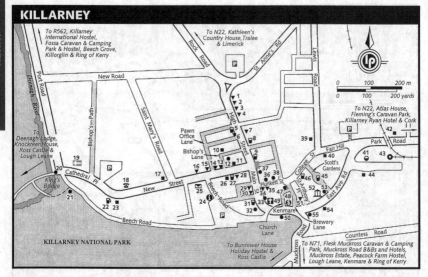

KILLARNEY

To R562, Killarney
International Hostel,
Fossa Caravan & Camping
Park & Hostel, Beech Grove,
Killorglin & Ring of Kerry

To N22, Kathleen's
Country House, Tralee
& Limerick

To N22, Atlas House,
Fleming's Caravan Park,
Killarney Ryan Hotel & Cork

New Road

Deenagh River

Port Road

Bishop's Path

Saint Mary's Road

To Deenagh Lodge,
Knockreer House,
Ross Castle &
Lough Leane

Cathedral Pl

King's
Bridge

New Street

Beech Road

Beech Road

High Street

Main St

College St

St Anthony's Pl

East Ave Rd

Fair Hill

Scott's
Gardens

Park Road

Plunkett St

Kenmare

Church
Lane

Brewery
Lane

Countess Road

Muckross Road

Rock Road

St Anne's Rd

Lewis Road

KILLARNEY NATIONAL PARK

To Bunrower House
Holiday Hostel &
Ross Castle

To N71, Flesk Muckross Caravan & Camping
Park, Muckross Road B&Bs and Hotels,
Muckross Estate, Peacock Farm Hostel,
Lough Leane, Kenmare & Ring of Kerry

0   100   200 m
0   100   200 yards

Museum of Irish Transport

This collection of splendid, shiny old cars, bicycles and assorted odds and ends includes an 1844 Meteor Starley Tricycle found in a shop's unsold stock in 1961, and a 1910 Wolseley that belonged to the Gore-Booth family and was also used by Countess Markievicz and WB Yeats.

The museum is in East Avenue Rd. It opens 10 am to 6 pm daily, April to October. Admission costs £3/1.50.

Fishing

You can fish for trout and salmon in the Rivers Flesk and Laune and in the lakes in Killarney National Park. The small lakes around the southern side of Killarney towards Kenmare also have brown and rainbow trout, although there's no coarse fishing locally. Permits, licences, equipment and information are available from O'Neill's (☎ 31970), 6 Plunkett St.

Places to Stay

Camping The *Fossa Caravan and Camping Park* (☎ 31497) is 5.6km west of town on the Killorglin road. A tent pitch costs £6.50 for a car and two people (hikers and cyclists £4). Almost next door, with slightly lower rates but fewer facilities, is *Beech Grove* (☎ 31727), across from Hotel Europe; a tent pitch for a cyclist or hiker costs £3.75. Nearer to town and with similar rates are *Fleming's White Bridge Caravan and Camping Park* (☎ 31590), 1.6km out along the N22 Cork road, and *White Villa Farm Caravan and Camping Park* (☎ 32456), 3km from town on the N22. The *Flesk Muckross Caravan and Camping Park* (☎ 31704) is 1.5km out on the N71 to Kenmare. A tent and car costs £5.

Hostels Killarney's many hostels mostly charge around £8 for a dorm bed. Some will pick you up from the bus or train stations. Even though there are so many hostels, you'd be well advised to book ahead in July and August.

Just off Park Rd and closest to the bus and train stations, the well-equipped IHH *Killarney Railway Hostel* (☎ 35299) offers dorm beds costing £7 to £9 and doubles costing £17.

Off New St in the town centre a lane leads to the large, friendly IHH *Neptune's Town Hostel* (☎ 35255), with some en suite

KILLARNEY

PLACES TO STAY	16 Grunts Café	21 Pedestrian Entrance to
10 Neptune's Town Hostel	28 Caragh Restaurant	Killarney National Park
11 Belvedere Hotel	29 Stella Restaurant	22 Shell Petrol Station
17 Killarney Townhouse	30 Flesk	24 Tourist Office
23 West End House	34 The Celtic Cauldron	25 Post Office
26 Eviston House Hotel	35 Strawberry Tree	32 Town Hall
39 Súgán Hostel	51 Taste of India	33 Dero's Tours
40 Arbutus Hotel		36 O'Neill's Fishing Tackle
42 Killarney Railway Hostel	PUBS	& Bike Hire
44 Great Southern Hotel	5 Courtney's	37 Killarney Bookshop
54 Killarney Park	8 O'Connor's	38 Music Kingdom
	9 Laurels	41 Bus Station
PLACES TO EAT	27 Charlie Foley's	43 Train Station
1 Gaby's Restaurant	31 McSorley's	47 J Gleeson's Laundrette
2 Bricín Restaurant	45 Scott's Gardens Hotel	48 American Express
3 Foley's	46 Killarney Grand	49 St Mary's Church
4 Swiss Barn		50 Jaunting Cars Pick-Up
6 Abrakebabra;	OTHER	Point
Sceilig	12 O'Sullivan's Bike Hire	52 Museum of Irish Transport
7 Allegro	18 Kerry Telephone Directory	53 Destination Killarney Lake
13 Den Joe's	19 St Mary's Cathedral	Tours
14 Busy B's Bistro	20 Pedestrian Entrance to	55 Killarney Cineplex
15 Country Kitchen	Killarney National Park	Cinema

doubles costing £22, dorm beds costing £8, and a good, big kitchen. You can get your laundry washed for £4.50. The central, IHO *Súgán Hostel* (☎ 33104, Lewis Rd) is small but friendly with lots of info on what to see and do. Dorm beds cost £8.

A little out of town in a quiet setting, the IHH *Bunrower House Holiday Hostel* (☎ 33104) is owned by the same people as the Súgán. Dorm beds are OK but, although the showers are hot, the washing facilities are fairly basic. Heading towards Kenmare, turn right at the Esso garage onto the road signposted for Ross Castle. From the hostel, it's a pleasant 20-minute walk across the park to town (at Cathedral Place) but there's also free transport between Bunrower and Súgán. You can camp here for £4 per person. Note that there are no restaurants or pubs in the vicinity.

An Óige's large *Killarney International Hostel* (☎ 31240), 2km west of the centre at Aghadoe House, costs £8/6.50 per night. A hostel bus meets trains from Dublin and Cork. The IHH *Fossa Holiday Hostel* (☎ 31497), slightly farther out, has dorm beds costing £6 and a camp site.

The comfortable, clean, well-equipped

Atlas House (☎ 36144) is 1km from the station off the Cork road; turn left at the Texaco garage. A dorm bed costs £10 but includes continental breakfast. There are doubles costing £28 and en suite doubles/ triples costing £35/37.50.

The *Peacock Farm Hostel* (☎ 33557), an IHH hostel, is in Gortdromakiery, Muckross. Take a left turn on to the Lough Guitane road just after the jaunting-car entrance at Muckross House. The hostel offers free pick-ups from town.

B&Bs There are plenty in the town centre and along the Cork, Kenmare (Muckross Rd) and Tralee roads, but finding a room can be tricky in high season; then, it's worth paying the £1 fee to let the tourist office do the hunting.

In town on New St *West End House* (☎ 32271), beside the Shell garage, and the friendly *Killarney Townhouse* (☎ 35388), at No 31, offer singles/doubles costing £30/45.

On Muckross Rd less than 1km from the town centre *Fuchsia House* (☎ 33743) offers singles/doubles starting at £38/50. One kilometre out on Muckross Rd *Tower*

KERRY

House (☎ 33884) offers doubles costing £38. Two kilometres out *Carriglea Farmhouse (☎ 31116)* is an elegant house in a quiet location with doubles costing £35.

Expect to pay up to £80 for doubles in smarter guesthouses such as *Kathleen's Country House (☎ 32810)*, 3km out of town on the Tralee road.

Hotels Hotels costing £60 to £100 for doubles include *Eviston House Hotel (☎ 31640, fax 33685)* and *Belvedere Hotel (☎ 31133)*, both in New St. Also central is the *Arbutus Hotel (☎ 31307, fax 34033, College St)*, with a friendly atmosphere. The imposing *Great Southern Hotel (☎ 31611, fax 31642)*, built for the convenience of Victorian travellers, is opposite the train station.

Charging £100-plus for doubles, there's *Killarney Ryan Hotel (☎ 31555, fax 32438)*, on the Cork road, or the even more posh and more plush *Killarney Park (☎ 35555, fax 35266, Kenmare Place)*. *Gleneagle Hotel (☎ 31870, fax 32646, Muckross Rd)* has all sorts of facilities: squash, tennis, pitch and putt, and a range of eateries. Closer to town the sedate *Cahernane Hotel (☎ 31895, fax 34340, Muckross Rd)* was built in 1877 for the earl of Pembroke. *Lake Hotel (☎ 31035, fax 31902, Muckross Rd)* has a stunning lakeside setting and its own Victorian jaunting car. Singles/doubles cost £66/100 in high season.

Places to Eat

More-expensive restaurants tend to hug the northern end of High St. For cheaper eats, head down to Main St or turn down New St.

Restaurants The *Allegro (High St)* serves basic pizza (£5.95), pasta (£5.50) and burgers. Near the town hall *Stella Restaurant (Main St)* is a straightforward 'and chips' type place with main courses costing £5.90 to £9.35. Around the corner, *Caragh Restaurant (New St)* is similar; steak and chips costs £9.80. Back on High St, *Sceilig* is more upmarket, with pizza, pasta and specials costing £6 to £9.

The inviting *Bricín (High St)*, above a craft shop, serves boxties costing £9 and several vegetarian options. *Swiss Barn (☎ 36044, High St)* serves good Swiss specialities costing £13.50 to £15.50; there's a three-course tourist menu costing £14.50.

Killarney has several Indian restaurants. At *Taste of India (☎ 34694, St Anthony's Place)*, in the lane that joins East Avenue Rd with College St, you can enjoy balti and tandoori dishes; it has a three-course lunch special costing £7.95.

Almost next door to the Strawberry Tree, *The Celtic Cauldron (☎ 36821, Plunkett St)* serves a variety of items taken from the culinary traditions of Scotland, Ireland, Wales and Brittany. Haggis, neeps and tatties (turnips and potatoes) costs £5.95.

The popular *Flesk (☎ 31128, High St)* has an impressively lengthy menu concentrating on seafood; salmon costs £12.95. The delightful *Strawberry Tree (☎ 32688, Plunkett St)* serves promising organic and wholefood dishes costing around £16. It's closed Sunday and Monday.

At the top end of High St, *Foley's (☎ 31217)* offers mostly seafood; main courses cost under £16. At nearby *Gaby's (☎ 32519)* a Kerry shellfish platter of oysters, crab claws, lobster and other delicacies costs £25.

Fast Food & Cafés For breakfast, lunchtime sandwiches or a salad try *Grunts Café (New St)* or *Country Kitchen*, almost next door, where filling meals cost £4.

Near Neptune's Town Hostel in New St, *Den Joe's* is a US-style fast-food eatery good for soup and burgers, while *Busy B's Bistro*, above Pat Sheahan supermarket, has a long list of cheap dishes, such as shepherd's pie and vegetable lasagne, costing under £5; it opens until midnight Monday to Wednesday, and until 2.30 am the rest of the week. On High St is a branch of *Abrakebabra*.

Entertainment

Many Killarney pubs have live music. At some it's traditional and often impromptu while at others it's very tourist oriented.

The 8th-century dry-stone Gallarus Oratory, County Kerry

Clockwatching, Kerry-style

Sea birds are the only inhabitants of bleak Great Blasket Island, County Kerry.

Who needs TV when there are tourists around?

Monday-morning rush, Dingle, County Kerry

The Rock of Cashel, County Tipperary, was the Munster seat of power for over a thousand years.

The fantastic view from the Rock of Cashel was a great defensive weapon for its kings.

Some pubs don't admit anyone aged under 21.

If you can't bear entertainment of the 'And this is for all the Canadians/Scots/ Germans/Australians in the audience' variety, *The Laurels (Main St)* won't be for you. Still, if the mood takes you, follow the coach parties and expect to pay a £4 cover charge. *Scott's Gardens Hotel*, between College St and East Avenue Rd, also has music nightly (from 9 pm), as does the *Danny Mann Lounge (New St)* in Eviston House Hotel.

For something a bit more authentic you could try *O'Connor's (High St)* or *Courtney's*, across the road. Other pubs worth trying include *Charlie Foley's (New St)*, *McSorley's (College St)* and the *Killarney Grand (Main St)*. There's no scheduled music at the tiny *Strawberry Tree (Plunkett St)* but its spit-and-sawdust appearance makes a pleasant backdrop for a few pints.

Mid-April to October *Killarney Manor Banquet (☎ 31551, Loreto Rd)*, off Muckross Rd, offers a five-course dinner and musical entertainment (£28); reservation is advisable as coach parties often fill the place.

Killarney Cineplex (☎ 37007, East Avenue Rd) has four screens.

Shopping

Irish-music CDs and tapes are sold at Music Kingdom (☎ 36522), 9 Plunkett St.

Getting There & Away

Air Kerry Airport (☎ 066-64644) is at Farranfore, about 15km north of Killarney off the N22. There are direct Aer Lingus flights to Dublin, and Manx Airlines flights to Luton and Manchester. It's also possible to fly direct from London Stansted to Kerry Airport. Call Ryanair in Dublin (☎ 01-609 7800) for details.

Bus Bus Éireann (☎ 34777) operates from next to the train station, with regular links to Tralee (£4.40), Cork (£8.80), Dublin (£14), Galway (£13), Limerick (£9.30), Waterford (£13) and Rosslare Harbour (£15). There's also a service to London via Cork and Waterford, leaving at 2.35 pm daily.

From late May to mid-September, the Ring of Kerry has its own service, departing Killarney at 8.30 am and 1.30 pm for Killorglin, Cahirciveen, Waterville, Caherdaniel, Sneem and back to Killarney.

Train Travelling by train to Cork (one way £13.50) involves changing at Mallow, but there's a direct route to Dublin via Limerick Junction. Phone ☎ 31067 for details.

Getting Around

Bicycles are ideal for exploring the scattered sights of the Killarney area, many of which are accessible only by bike or on foot. Several places hire bikes at around £6 per day. There's O'Sullivan's Bike Hire (☎ 31282), near Neptune's Town Hostel off New St, and Killarney Rent-a-Bike (☎ 32578), in Old Market Lane alongside the Laurels pub. O'Neill's (☎ 31970), on Plunkett St, has children's bikes and will deliver free to your accommodation. Most hostels also offer bike hire.

If you're not on two wheels, Killarney's traditional transport is the horse-drawn jaunting car, which comes with a driver known as a *jarvey*. The pick-up point is on Kenmare Place just past the town hall but they also congregate in the N71 car park opposite Muckross House and at the Gap of Dunloe. Trips cost £12 to £32, depending on distance, and the traps officially carry four people.

AROUND KILLARNEY
Organised Tours

Dero's Tours (☎ 31251), 22 Main St, across the road from Killarney's town hall, organises coach day trips around the Ring of Kerry (£10) and Dingle Peninsula (£12). However, unless you're really pushed for time these are too rushed a way to do justice to the scenery. For information on tours within Killarney National Park, see the following sections.

For organised horse-riding trips contact Killarney Riding Stables (☎ 31686), in Ballydowney 1km from Killarney on the R562,

KERRY

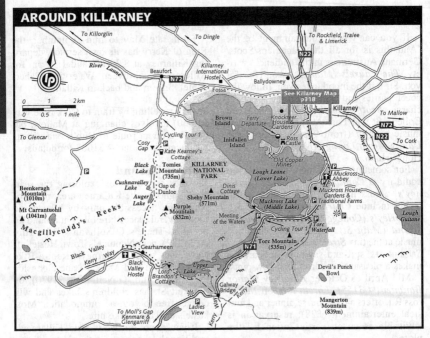

AROUND KILLARNEY

or Rockland's Stables (☎ 32592), in Rockfield 3km from town on the Tralee road.

Killarney National Park

Killarney's 10,236-hectare National Park extends to the south-west of town, with two pedestrian entrances immediately opposite St Mary's Cathedral and others (for drivers) off the N71.

Enclosed within the park are beautiful Lough Leane (the Lower Lake or 'Lake of Learning'), Muckross Lake and the Upper Lake, as well as the Mangerton, Torc, Shehy and Purple Mountains. This is wonderful walking and biking country, although there are also specific sights, including the restored Ross Castle, the monastic ruins on Inisfallen Island, and Knockreer and Muckross Houses with their fine gardens. A herd of deer lives in the park and many species of birds can be spotted. In 1981 the park was designated a UNESCO Biosphere Reserve.

In season, lunches and teas are available at thatched 19th-century **Deenagh Lodge** just inside the gate opposite St Mary's Cathedral.

Knockreer House & Gardens Near the St Mary's Cathedral entrance to the park stands Knockreer House, surrounded by lovely gardens. The original 19th-century building burned down and the present incarnation dates from the 1950s. The house isn't open to the public, but you can walk around the gardens and there are great views across the valley and lakes to the mountains. With these views you can understand why they built the house here. To get to the house, from the St Mary's Cathedral entrance, follow the path immediately to your right uphill for about 500m (even though the sign near the gate says it's only 250m).

Ross Castle Restored by Dúchas, Ross Castle (☎ 35851) dates back to the 14th century, when it was a residence of the O'Donoghues. It was the last place in Munster to succumb to Cromwell's forces under the command of Ludlow.

According to prophecy, the castle would be captured only from the water, so in 1652 Ludlow had floating batteries brought upriver from Castlemaine, then transported overland before being launched onto the lake. Seeing the prophecy about to be fulfilled, the defenders, having resisted the English siege from the land for months, surrendered promptly.

The castle opens 10 am to 6.30 pm daily, June to August; 10 am to 6 pm daily, May and September; 11 am to 6 pm daily, March and April; and 11 am to 5 pm Monday to Saturday, the rest of the year. Admission costs £2.50/1.

It's a 2.4km walk from the St Mary's Cathedral pedestrian park entrance to Ross Castle. If you're driving from Killarney, turn right opposite the Esso garage at the start of Muckross Rd, just past the roundabout. The castle is at the end of the road near the car park.

Hour-long **lake cruises** depart from Ross Castle 10.30 am to 5.45 pm daily. Bookings can be made at the tourist office or with Destination Killarney (☎ 32638), at Scott's Gardens, or Killarney Watercoach Cruises (☎ 31068), 3 High St. Out of season you can buy the ticket on the boat.

Inisfallen Island The first monastery on the island is said to have been founded by St Finian the Leper in the 7th century. The island's fame dates from the early 13th century when the *Annals of Inisfallen* were written here. The annals, now in the Bodleian Library, Oxford, England, remain a vital source of information on early Munster history. On the island, there are ruins of a 12th-century oratory with a carved Romanesque doorway and of a later monastery built on the site.

You can hire boats from Ross Castle to row to the island. Alternatively, boatmen charge passengers £4 each for the crossing. Some Gap of Dunloe boat and bus tours also stop at the island.

Muckross House, Gardens & Traditional Farms The core of Killarney National Park is the Muckross Estate, which was donated to the state by Arthur Bourn Vincent in 1932. Muckross House (☎ 31440) opens to the public and, unusually, you can walk around the rooms, with their faded 19th-century fittings, free of guided tours or overintrusive custodians. Some of the rooms contain exhibits on 19th-century Kerry housing, the Vincent family and once-fashionable bog-oak jewellery. You can inspect a variety of crafts, including bookbinding and stone-cutting, in the basement. It opens 9 am to 6 pm daily, year round. Admission costs £3.80/1.60.

The beautiful gardens laid out by Arthur Bourn Vincent slope down to the lake and include an arboretum. A block behind the house contains a restaurant and craft shop. Jaunting cars wait outside to run you around the park.

Immediately east of Muckross House are the **Muckross Traditional Farms**, reproduction Kerry farmhouses of the 1930s complete with chickens, pigs, cattle and horses. You can walk round the circuit or save your legs and use the 'vintage coach' that shuttles between the buildings. The site opens 1 to 6 pm daily, May; and 10 am to 7 pm daily, June to October. Admission costs the same as for Muckross House but combined tickets for the two properties work out cheaper at £5.50/2.75.

Muckross House is 5km from town on the N71 Kenmare road. Vehicle access is about 1km beyond the Muckross Park Hotel. During the summer a tourist bus leaves for the house at 1.45 pm from outside O'Connor's pub, returning at 5.15 pm (£5 return). The house is also included in some day tours of Killarney.

If you're walking or cycling to Muckross there's a cycle track alongside the Kenmare road for most of the first 2km. A path then turns right into Killarney National Park. Following this path, after 1km you'll come to **Muckross Abbey**, which was founded in 1448 and torched by Cromwell's troops in 1652. Look out for fine black Kerry cattle with white horns in fields nearby. Muckross

House is another 1.5km from the abbey ruins.

A day trip around Killarney National Park involving a woodland walk and a boat trip on Muckross Lake and Lough Leane leaves from Muckross House at 10.30 am.

From Muckross House, there's a 3.7km walkable or cyclable track round the northern shore of Muckross Lake to the **Meeting of the Waters**, where it joins the Upper Lake. Nearby *Dinis Cottage* serves teas in a 200-year-old hunting lodge. Check the graffiti etched in the window: the oldest dates back to 1816. From the Meeting of the Waters it's another 1.5km back onto the N71 Kenmare road.

Warning for Cyclists If you're planning to cycle round Muckross Lake, note that you should do so only in an anticlockwise direction (from Muckross House towards Meeting of the Waters and not vice versa). Nasty accidents involving broken limbs have occurred when two cyclists travelling at speed in opposite directions have collided on corners.

Gap of Dunloe Technically the Gap of Dunloe is outside the National Park but, as most people start or end their visit to it in the park, details are included here. In high summer, the Gap is Killarney tourism at its worst. Every day cars and buses disgorge countless visitors at Kate Kearney's Cottage. They then proceed to pay £32 for a one-hour horse-and-trap ride through the Gap (no cars allowed in summer). You could also walk through the narrow gorge to the Black Valley Hostel at the other end, but don't do this in summer if you want to be alone.

The best way to see the Gap is to hire a bike from Killarney and cycle to Ross Castle, then take the boat across the lakes to Lord Brandon's Cottage and cycle through the Gap and back into town via the N72 and a path through the golf course. Including bike hire, this should cost you about £14.

The boat ride alone justifies the trip. It lasts 1½ hours and passes through all three lakes, with lovely views of the surrounding

mountains and of the Meeting of the Waters and Ladies View, which was much enjoyed by Queen Victoria's ladies-in-waiting, who gave it its name. Lunches and teas are available at *Kate Kearney's Cottage* and *Lord Brandon's Cottage*.

Organised Gap of Dunloe tours – by bus to Kate Kearney's Cottage, then by horse, bike or jaunting car through the Gap, finishing with a boat trip back to Killarney – can be booked through the tourist office, Castlelough Tours at O'Connor's pub (☎ 32496), Dero's Tours (☎ 31251) or Killarney Boating Centre (☎ 31068). The basic trip costs £13 return, plus another £12 for a seat in a jaunting car.

Cycling Tours
One possible cycle tour is an adventurous 30km ride via the Gap of Dunloe and Black Valley Hostel, the last third of this journey best undertaken on a dry day. The route is marked on the Around Killarney map. A longer trip is an 80km journey via Lough Acoose and Moll's Gap. Its route is marked on the Ring of Kerry map.

Killarney to Kenmare
The N71 links Killarney to Kenmare, with spectacular lake and mountain scenery along the way. Two kilometres south of the entrance to Muckross House a path leads 200m to the pretty **Torc Waterfall**. After another 8km on the N71 you come to **Ladies View**, with fine views along Upper Lake. There's another good viewpoint 5km farther along at **Moll's Gap**, with a branch of Avoca Handweavers (see Avoca in the Southern Wicklow section in the County Wicklow chapter). The inviting café *Moll's Country Kitchen* buys spectacular views for its diners at the price of inflicting a bit of an eyesore on those outside.

Ring of Kerry

The Ring of Kerry, the 179km road circuit round the Iveragh Peninsula, is one of Ireland's premier tourist attractions, partly because its width makes it more accessible to coaches than the narrower peninsulas to the north and south. Although it can be 'done' in a day by car or bus, or three days by bike, the more time you take the more you'll enjoy it. Getting off the beaten tourist track is also worthwhile. The Ballaghbeama Pass cuts across the peninsula's central highlands with some spectacular views and remarkably little traffic: it's perfect for a long cycle.

See Walking in the Activities chapter for details of the 215km Kerry Way, which starts and ends in Killarney. It is marked on the Ring of Kerry map.

Tour buses approach the Ring in an anti-clockwise direction. In high season it's hard to know which is more unpleasant – driving round behind them or travelling in the opposite direction and coming up against them on blind corners. Note that petrol gets more expensive the farther west you go: fill up before setting out.

Although the scenery on the Ring is beautiful, some visitors will prefer the Beara or Mizen Head Peninsulas, partly because the views are even more striking, partly because they're so much less touristy, with classier hotels and places to eat. It's worth noting that things get much quieter at the western end of the Iveragh Peninsula, when you leave the Ring of Kerry for the Skellig Ring.

GETTING AROUND

Late May to mid-September Bus Éireann operates a Ring of Kerry bus service. Buses leave Killarney at 8.30 am and 1.30 pm Monday to Saturday, 9.40 am (July and August only) and 12.45 pm (May to September only) on Sunday. They stop at Killorglin, Glenbeigh, Kells, Cahirciveen, Waterville, Caherdaniel and Sneem before returning to Killarney via Moll's Gap. For more details ring Killarney bus station (☎ 064-34777).

KILLORGLIN
☎ 066 • pop 1300
Travelling anticlockwise from Killarney, the first town on the Ring is Killorglin (Cill Orglan), which is famed for its annual Puck Fair Festival.

There's a summer (exact dates depend on the number of visitors) tourist office in a stone booth beside the unclearly marked roundabout from which one of the roads leads to Glenbeigh. The AIB, Bridge St, and the Super Valu supermarket have ATMs.

Puck Fair Festival
This rumbustious three-day celebration takes place during the second weekend in August. It is based round the custom of installing a billy goat (a puck), horns festooned in ribbons, on a pedestal in the town centre and leaving it there while everyone takes advantage of the special licensing hours. Pubs stay open till 3 am, although it often seems that they simply serve for three days nonstop. Accommodation is hard to come by if you haven't planned ahead and booked in advance.

Places to Stay
Camping Just under 2km from the bridge in Killorglin, on the road to Killarney, is the small family-oriented *West's Holiday Park* (☎ 976 1240), open Easter to October. It costs £3.50 for a cyclist or hiker to pitch a tent.

Hostels About 2km from the bridge, on the Tralee road, the IHH *Laune Valley Farm Hostel* (☎ 976 1488) comes complete with satellite TV. Beds cost £8/9 in a six/four-bed dorm, doubles upwards of £20.

B&Bs On the Killarney road, *Riverside House* (☎ 976 1184) charges upwards of £16 for a bed. You could also try *Hillcrest* (☎ 976 1552), where singles/doubles cost £24.50/36. Two kilometres out on the Tralee road *Hillview Farm* (☎ 976 7117) charges upwards of £23.50/36.

Hotels At the central *Bianconi* (☎ 976 1146, Lower Bridge St) rooms are perhaps overpriced considering their condition and lack of tea/coffee-making facilities. But the hotel is being refurbished so things may improve. Singles/doubles with bath cost £35/54.

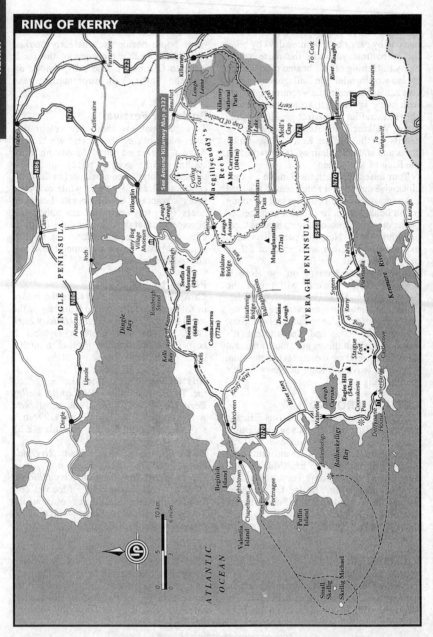

RING OF KERRY

See Around Killarney Map p322

Cycling Tour 2

DINGLE PENINSULA

IVERAGH PENINSULA

ATLANTIC OCEAN

Macgillycuddy's Reeks
▲ Mt Carrauntoohil (1041m)

Killarney National Park

Gap of Dunloe

Lough Leane

Upper Lake

Killarney

Beaufort

To Cork

River Roughty

Moll's Gap

Kenmare

To Killabunane

To Glengariff

Kenmare River

Farranfore

Tralee

Castlemaine

Camp

Inch

Anascaul

Lispole

Dingle

Killorglin

Kerry Bog Village Museum

Lough Caragh

Glencar

Glenbeigh

Rossbeigh Strand

Kells Bay

Ring of Kerry

Seefin Mountain (494m) ▲

Been Hill (668m) ▲

Coomacarrea (772m) ▲

Kells

Kerry Way

Cahirciveen

Waterville

River Inny

Lissatinnig Bridge

Ballaghbeama Pass

Ballaghisheen Pass

Ballaghbeama Pass

Bealalaw Bridge

Lough Acoose

Mullaghanattin (772m) ▲

Derriana Lough

Lough Cloonaghlin

Ballaghbeama

Sneem

Tahilla

Parknasilla

Ring of Kerry

Caherdaniel

Derrynane House

Staigue Fort

Eagles Hill (543m) ▲

Coomakesta Pass

Lough Currane

Ballinskelligs Bay

Beginish Island

Knightstown

Chapeltown

Valentia Island

Portmagee

Puffin Island

Small Skellig

Skellig Michael

0   10 km
0   6 miles
0   5
0   3

Dingle Bay

Places to Eat

Overlooking the roundabout from which one of the roads leads to Glenbeigh, *Bunkers*, a combined pub-restaurant-take-away, serves meals such as chicken curry (£4.50). Less expensive is *Starlite Diner* in the town centre, which offers a mixed grill costing £4.

Nick's Restaurant and Bar (☎ 976 1219, *Main St*) serves seafood and steaks costing £12 to £18; dover sole costs £16.50. A more interesting menu is at *Bianconi* (☎ 976 1146), which offers seafood or meat dinners costing upwards of £11 and serves bar food until 9.30 pm.

Entertainment

Old Forge, at the top of Bridge St, has traditional music every night.

Getting Around

Bikes can be hired from O'Shea's Cycle Centre (☎ 976 1919), Lower Bridge St, for £7.50/40 per day/week.

KERRY BOG VILLAGE MUSEUM

On the N70 between Killorglin and Glenbeigh, Kerry Bog Village Museum (☎ 066-976 9184), beside the Red Fox pub, re-creates the homes and other buildings of 19th-century turfcutters. Admission costs £2.50/1.50, which includes a free cup of coffee or tea at the Red Fox pub. The museum opens 9 am to 7 pm daily, year round. Some Kerry Bog ponies are in a field behind the museum.

The *Red Fox* pub is a real tourist trap but serves good pub food (turfcutter's delight is a steak burger costing £4.95) and puts on live-music weekends. There's a useful notice board just inside the porch, where there's a phone to follow up interesting leads.

GLENBEIGH

☎ 066 • pop 185

Glenbeigh (Gleann Beithe), 10km west of Killorglin, nestles at the foot of **Seefin Mountain** (494m) and has the attraction of a superb Blue Flag beach (unpolluted and safe for swimming, with lifeguards on duty during the day). The 5km of **Rossbeigh Strand** look across to the Dingle Peninsula and even with a camp site in the vicinity it's easy to find a quiet spot. Swimming is safe and the mud flats off the eastern spit of land make good birdwatching territory. To get to Rossbeigh Strand, bear right at the Y-junction at the Cahirciveen end of town and continue for 3km.

The Kerry Bog Pony

This unique breed of pony has existed in Kerry since before the 17th century. Its ancestor was probably originally imported from Asturias, Spain. There were once large herds of these small ponies, then known as Hobbies, which, because of their strength, toughness and easy maintenance, were used to bring turf from the bogs and seaweed to farms.

However, their numbers declined rapidly when many were taken (back) to Spain to serve as pack animals, and food, for the British army during the Peninsular Wars against Napoleon at the start of the 19th century. This decline was accelerated by changes in agricultural equipment and practices that necessitated the use of stronger, taller ponies and horses. By the early 20th century they were thought to be extinct.

Enter John Mulvihill, who runs the Kerry Bog Village Museum and is a breeder of ponies and horses. He discovered a small group of ponies but, although he recognised their rare quality, didn't know that they were Kerry Bog ponies until they had undergone blood typing and DNA testing. Following an intensive breeding programme and the creation of the Kerry Bog Pony Society to protect them, there are now about 180. They were designated a rare breed in 1994 and today are used for riding and trekking.

KERRY

Places to Stay

Camping The *Glenross Caravan and Camping Park* (☎ 976 8451) is in town next to the Glenbeigh Hotel. Two people with a tent and car will be charged £9.50 (cyclists and hikers £7.50).

B&Bs The *Village House* (☎ 976 8128) has comfortable rooms costing upwards of £20 per person, while *Ocean Wave* (☎ 976 8249), a few doors away, open March to October, offers singles/doubles costing upwards of £25/36. *Hillcrest House* (☎ 976 9165), 4km out at Ballycleave, west on the N70, charges £22.50/32 and opens April to October.

Hotels The *Towers Hotel* (☎ 976 8212), in the town centre, is cosy, relaxed and well used to families. Singles/doubles cost upwards of £47/68. *Falcon Inn* (☎ 976 8215), about 1km from the centre at the Cahirciveen end of town, charges upwards of £25 per person, while *Olde Glenbeigh* (☎ 976 8333), by the side of the N70 to Killarney, charges the same.

Places to Eat

There's very little inexpensive food other than in the pubs. Out at Rossbeigh Strand *Ross Inn* is worth a try. The three hotels do bar food and have restaurants for dinner. The fresh seafood at the *Olde Glenbeigh*, with a slightly quieter atmosphere than the others, is excellent, as is the chicken curry (£5.50). At *Falcon Inn* a two-course meal costs around £6, while at *Towers Hotel* set dinners cost £20.

Entertainment

On Sunday, *Towers Hotel* has live music, *Olde Glenbeigh* offers set dancing and *Ross Inn* has bands.

KELLS

☎ 066

Kells is a district of scattered buildings with no real centre. There's a pub at one end and a craft shop/post office/garage at the other.

Near Kells the route of the old **Great Southern and Western Railway** (a branch

line that ran from Killorglin to Valentia Harbour Station, west of Cahirciveen, and closed in 1960) can be seen on the hillside, with its tunnels and retaining walls. The small beach at **Kells Bay**, 4km from Kells on a minor road, doesn't look too clean, but there are good views of Dingle Peninsula.

Places to Stay & Eat

Kells Bay Caravan and Camping Park (☎ 947 7647) is signposted off the road before you get to Kells from Glenbeigh. Nearby, *Seaview* (☎ 947 7610) offers B&B costing £16 per person.

Thatched *Caitin Beatear's* (☎ 947 7614) is a roadside pub and restaurant at the Glenbeigh end of town that draws in the coach parties. It has a hostel at the back with dorm beds costing £7 and doubles £18. Year round it serves soup-and-sandwich lunches but in July and August Irish stew and seafood are on the menu. Music sessions are held throughout the summer. At the other (Cahirciveen) end of Kells, snacks and tourist information are available at *Pat's* rather touristy craft shop.

CAHIRCIVEEN

☎ 066 • pop 1300

As late as 1815, Cahirciveen (Cathair Saidhthin), also spelled Cahersiveen, had only five houses, but it's now one of the larger settlements along the Ring, even if it remains more or less one long street.

Daniel O'Connell, 'The Great Liberator', was born near here. The ruins of his home can be seen left of the new bridge as you come into town from Kells, and the large church in the town centre is called the O'Connell Memorial Holy Cross Church.

The tourist office (☎ 947 2589), in The Barracks, opens 10 am to 6 pm Monday to Saturday, and 1 to 6 pm on Sunday, May to September; and 9.30 am to 5.30 pm on weekdays, the rest of the year. It sells an *O'Connell Heritage Trail* leaflet (£1). The 6.5km trail takes about 2½ hours.

The Barracks

This heritage centre is superbly situated in what was once an intimidating Royal Irish

Constabulary (RIC) barracks. The building was burned down in 1922 by anti-Treaty forces, but was reconstructed to its present remarkable state, looking not unlike some kind of fairy-tale castle. The story goes that the plans for this building got mixed up with ones intended for India; when you see the place you might believe this particular piece of blarney.

The exhibits feature information on Daniel O'Connell, the Fenian Rising and other subjects of local and national interest. The centre opens the same hours as the tourist office and admission costs £3/1.50. To get there, coming from the Kells end of town, turn right at the junction of Bridge and Church Sts.

White Strand

If you go past The Barracks and across the bridge, after 5km you come to White Strand, a beach that's safe for swimming.

Places to Stay

Camping The *Mannix Point Camping and Caravan Park* (☎ 947 2806), a 15-minute walk west of town and signposted off the N70, is well run and charges a flat rate of £3.40 per person, including showers.

Hostels The IHH *Sive Hostel* (☎ 947 2717) is at the eastern end of the long main street. Beds cost £7.50 and there are three doubles costing £18 each. Boat trips to the Skellig Islands can be arranged here. There's also the IHO *Mortimer's* (☎ 947 2338), in the centre of town, with beds costing £7.

B&Bs The *Mount Rivers* (☎ 947 2509, Carhan Rd), a striking old house on the N70 to Killarney, charges upwards of £25/36 for singles/doubles. Close to each other at the Valentia end of town are *Castleview* (☎ 947 2252) and *San Antoine* (☎ 947 2521), which charge £22/32 and £24.50/36 respectively.

Hotels Two-star *Cahirciveen Park Hotel* (☎ 947 2543, Valentia Rd) offers singles/

doubles costing £35/58 (in peak season) including breakfast.

Places to Eat

Opposite O'Connell Memorial Holy Cross Church, popular, small but cosy *Grudles* café specialises in Mediterranean-style food; pizzas/pastas cost upwards of £4.95/5.50. Nearby, *Red Rose Restaurant* serves a salmon sandwich and salad costing £4.50. *Sceilig Rock Bar* (☎ 947 2426) offers good lunch specials such as roast beef (£5).

Well regarded is the 1st-floor *Brennan's Restaurant* (☎ 947 2021), which offers gourmet food such as fillet of ostrich (£18.70). Vegetarian meals are cooked on request.

Entertainment

At the Glenbeigh end of town *Shebeen* has live Irish music nightly. You might prefer the less touristy *Mike Murt's* a couple of doors away. *Sceilig Rock Bar* has traditional music, while *The Harp* has Saturday-night discos. Even without music *The Anchor* is quite atmospheric. *Craineen's*, next to The Anchor, has traditional-music sessions. If you don't like any of these, there are almost 50 more to choose from!

Getting There & Away

As well as the regular Ring of Kerry bus service, from April to September there is a ferry service (☎ 947 6141) to Knightstown on Valentia Island from Reenard Point, 5km west of Cahirciveen. The 10-minute crossing costs £4 for a car (pedestrians and cyclists £3). It operates 7.30 am to 10.30 pm Monday to Saturday, 8.30 am to 10.30 pm on Sunday.

PORTMAGEE
☎ 066

Portmagee (Port Mhic Aoidh) is a string of houses, restaurants and pubs overlooking the Maurice O'Neill Bridge to Valentia Island. Fishing is still an important activity, but just as important is the business of ferrying tourists out to the Skellig Islands, with roughly half the licensed boats leaving from here.

If you have to wait around for good enough weather to make the crossing *The Moorings* (☎ 77108) offers B&B costing £30/50 for singles/doubles. The attached *Bridge Bar* serves food from 12.30 to 3 pm and 6 to 8 pm; it specialises, not surprisingly, in seafood. *The Fisherman's Bar* is a popular lunch spot.

Bridge Bar is worth checking out for its Friday-night free set-dancing lessons.

VALENTIA ISLAND
☎ 066

Valentia Island (Oileán Dairbhru) may be only 11km long and 3km wide but it doesn't feel like an island, especially if you come by road. It's a low-key place: unless you're into scuba diving, the Skellig Experience is about the only real distraction.

Valentia was chosen as the site for the first transatlantic telegraph cable, and when the connection was made in 1858 it put Cahirciveen in direct contact with New York even though it had no connection with Dublin! The link worked for 27 days before failing, but went back into action some years later. The telegraph station was in operation until 1966.

Most visitors reach the island via the long bridge from Portmagee, turning right for Chapeltown and Knightstown when they get to the island.

The Skellig Experience

Immediately across the bridge you'll see The Skellig Experience (☎ 947 6306) on the left of the road. It contains exhibitions on the life and times of the Skellig Michael monks, the history of the lighthouses on Skellig Michael, and the wildlife. An interesting 15-minute audiovisual show describes the monastery's history. If you're planning a trip to the Skelligs it's worth coming here for background info. If the weather's bad this may be as close as you get to the islands.

The Skellig Experience opens 9.30 am to 7 pm daily, March to October. Admission costs £3/1.50. Teas and some light meals are available in *Fionan's Kitchen* at the back.

Chapeltown

Chapeltown (An Caol) is just a small scattering of houses with a hostel and garage. *Ring Lyne Hostel* (☎ 947 6103) offers dorm beds costing £8 and three doubles costing £17. Meals are available in the attached bar and restaurant; mussels in garlic butter costs £5.50. The Ring Lyne puts on music sessions after 9.30 pm most evenings.

Knightstown & Around

Valentia's main population centre is Knightstown (Baile an Ridire), accessible by ferry from Reenard Point west of Cahirciveen. It's named after the Knights of Kerry, who once owned it. The small seasonal tourist office on the waterfront has a bureau de change.

Glenleam Gardens If you head out towards the quarry (see Quarry & Grotto later in this section) then turn right and go downhill for 500m, you'll come to these gardens of non-native plants, open 11 am to 5 pm daily. Admission costs £2.50/1.

Angling & Diving For sea angling trips contact Dan McCrohan (☎ 947 6142). There are three reliable diving centres: Lavelle's Valentia Island Diving Centre (☎ 947 6124), Valentia Hyperbaric Diving Centre (☎ 947 6225) and Valentia Island Seasports (☎ 947 6204) at the Dive Centre.

Places to Stay The huge, dilapidated *Royal Pier Hostel* (☎ 947 6174), overlooking the harbour, offers dorm beds costing £8.50. You can book Skellig Islands boat trips here. The An Óige *Valentia Island Hostel* (☎ 947 6154) occupies three of the former coastguard station cottages. Beds cost £6.50/5. It opens June to September.

Two kilometres out of Knightstown towards Chapeltown, *Glenreen Heights* (☎ 947 6241) offers singles/doubles costing upwards of £22.50/32. It opens March to October. On Jane St up from the waterfront, *Altazamuth House* (☎ 947 6300) opens April to October and charges upwards of £21/32.

Places to Eat At the western end of Knightstown the inviting *Gallery Kitchen* (☎ *947 6105)* is a combined restaurant, wine bar and sculpture gallery; pastas in interesting sauces cost around £7.50. Next door, *O'Conaill's* pub serves popular home-cooked dishes and is especially lively on Friday and Sunday. On the waterfront, *Moriarty's* specialises in seafood and steaks.

Quarry & Grotto
In the 19th century, slate quarrying was an important Valentia industry, with boats from the nearby harbour carrying away the roofing slates and flagstones. If you ever wondered what Charing Cross Station in London and San Salvador Station in El Salvador have in common, the answer is that they were both roofed with Valentia slate. A disused quarry tunnel was converted into a religious grotto in 1954, but despite this the place retains a sense of history. The quarry is at the northern end of the island, signposted from the Maurice O'Neill Bridge.

Getting There & Away
The ugly Maurice O'Neill Bridge at Portmagee links Valentia Island to the mainland. April to September, pedestrians, cyclists and motorists can also cross by ferry from Reenard Point near Cahirciveen to the pier at Knightstown (see Getting There & Away in the Cahirciveen section earlier in this chapter).

SKELLIG ISLANDS
A boat trip to the Skellig Islands (Oileáin na Scealaga), 12km out in the Atlantic Ocean, is one of the highlights of a trip to Ireland. The crossing can be rough and there are no toilets or shelter on the islands. Bring stout shoes, something to eat and drink, warm clothing and something waterproof to protect you and your bag from the boat's spray.

Birdlife
If you can't get to the Galapagos then a trip to the Skelligs offers a taster of the peculiar pleasure of spying on nesting sea birds. From the boat, look out for diminutive storm petrel, black birds that dart over the water like swallows, and for yellow-headed gannet with a wingspan of 107cm. Kittiwake – lemon-beaked sea gulls with black-tipped wings – are easy to see and hear around the covered walkway of Skellig Michael just after stepping off the boat. They winter at sea but then come in their thousands to breed between March and August. Farther up the rock you'll see snub-nosed fulmar and black-and-white guillemot and razorbill. Look out, also, for the delightful puffins with their multicoloured beaks and waddling gait. Puffins lay one egg in May at the end of a burrow and parent birds can be seen guarding their nests. Puffins stay only until the first week or two of August.

Skellig Michael
The 217m-high jagged rock of Skellig Michael (Archangel Michael's Rock), the larger of the two islands and a UNESCO World Heritage Site, looks like the last place on earth that anyone would try to land, let alone establish a community. Yet early-Christian monks survived here from the 6th until the 12th or 13th century. They were influenced by the Coptic Church founded by St Anthony in the deserts of Egypt and Libya, and their desire for solitude led them to this remote, westernmost corner of Europe.

The monastic buildings are perched on a saddle in the rock, some 150m above sea level. The astounding 6th-century oratories and beehive cells vary in size, the largest cell having a floor space of 4.5m by 3.6m. The projecting stones on the outside have more than one possible explanation: steps to reach the top and release chimney stones, or maybe holding places for turf that covered the exterior. Some cells have interior rows of stones, and the guides who live on the rock from mid-May to September will provide a possible explanation for these as well. They'll also point out the cistern in the rock for storing rainwater.

Little is known about the life of the monastery, but there are records of Viking raids in 812 and 823. Monks were killed or taken away but the community recovered and carried on. In the 11th century a rectangular oratory was added to the site, but although it was expanded in the 12th century the monks abandoned the rock around this time, perhaps because of more than usually ferocious Atlantic storms.

After the introduction of the Gregorian calendar in 1582, Skellig Michael became a popular spot for weddings. Marriages were forbidden during Lent, but since Skellig used the old Julian calendar a trip over to the islands allowed those unable to wait for Easter to tie the knot. Crates of alcohol were hauled over to facilitate the merrymaking.

In the 1820s two lighthouses were built on Skellig Michael, together with the road that runs round the base.

You're asked to do your picnicking on the way up to the monastery, or at Christ's Saddle just before the last flight of steps, rather than among the ruins. This is to keep sandwich-loving birds and their droppings away from the monument.

Small Skellig

Small Skellig is a bird sanctuary and you cannot land on it. While Skellig Michael looks like two triangles linked by a spur, Small Skellig is longer, lower and much craggier. From a distance it looks as if someone had battered it with a feather pillow that burst. Close up you realise you're looking at a colony of 20,000 pairs of breeding gannets. Most boats circle the island so you can see them. Check beforehand if the boat will pause to look for basking seals.

Getting There & Away

Because of concerns for the fragility of Skellig Michael there are limits on how many people can visit on the same day. Nineteen boats are licensed to carry no more than 12 passengers each, so there should never be more than 250 people there at any one time. Because of these limits it's wise to book ahead in July and August, always bearing in mind that if the weather's bad the boats may not be able to sail.

You can depart from either Portmagee (and even Cahirciveen), Ballinskelligs or

Derrynane and the crossing usually costs £20 return. The boat owners try to restrict you to two hours on the island, which is the bare minimum, on a good day, to see the monastery, look at the birds and have a picnic. The crossing from Portmagee takes about 90 minutes.

Some operators to try include: Joe Roddy (☎ 066-947 4268), Sean Feehan (☎ 066-947 9182) and JB Walsh (☎ 066-947 9147) at Ballinskelligs; Brendan O'Keefe (☎ 066-947 77103), Michael O'Sullivan (☎ 066-947 4255), Murphy's (☎ 066-947 7156) and Casey's (☎ 066-947 7125) at Portmagee; and Sean O'Shea (☎ 066-947 5129) at Derrynane, near Caherdaniel. Most pubs and B&Bs in the area will point you in the right direction.

Warning A notice on the island warns of 'an element of danger' in visiting Skellig Michael. Although you could fall on the rocks or stone steps, the biggest element of danger seems attached to getting off the boat at the island. Make sure your shoes have a good grip.

WATERVILLE
☎ 066 • pop 475

The popular resort of Waterville (An Coireán) is a triangle of fairly tacky pubs, restaurants and B&Bs on a narrow bit of land between Ballinskelligs Bay and Lough Currane. Charlie Chaplin was probably the town's most famous visitor; there's a statue of him on the foreshore and photographs of him in the Butler Arms pub.

Fishing

There are lots of angling possibilities around Waterville. Lough Currane has free fishing for sea trout while the Inny River is a breeding ground for wild salmon and trout. Sea angling takes in mackerel, pollack and shark. For information ask at Tadhg O'Sullivan (☎ 947 4433), a tackle shop on Main St.

Places to Stay

Waterville Caravan and Camping Park (☎ 947 4191), 1km north of town off the

N70, opens April to mid-September. A hiker or cyclist pays £4 for their tent. The small IHO *Peter's Place Hostel* (☎ 947 4608), at the Caherdaniel end of town, offers dorm beds for £7 and doubles for £17.

For B&B you'd be better off stopping about 5km south of Waterville on the N70 at the *Scariff Inn* (☎ 947 5143) on the Coomakesta Pass. It boasts 'Ireland's best-known view' (fog permitting) from its Vista Bar. B&B costs £24/40 for singles/doubles and the restaurant serves dishes such as Irish stew and seafood. Alternatively, *The Old Cable House* (☎ 947 4233), 1km north of Waterville on the N70, charges £30/40.

Places to Eat

Most of Waterville's eating places are fairly indifferent, but worth giving a whirl is *An Corcán (Main St)*, which opens 8.30 am to 10 pm daily and serves seafood and vegetarian dishes; plaice and chips costs £4.95.

Beachcove Café beside the post office will do if you just want tea or coffee. *Sheilin Restaurant* (☎ 947 4237), round the corner from An Corcán, opens for dinner only; fresh salmon costs £12.

SKELLIG RING

The Skellig Ring is a scenic route that links Waterville with Portmagee via Ballinskelligs (Baile an Sceilg). Leaving Waterville, it begins with a turn to the left, signposted after the church and a small bridge, and goes down to an unmarked junction: the short potholed road to the left goes to Ballinskelligs Bay, the road straight on goes to the Ballinskelligs departure point for the Skelligs, and a right turn eventually leads to Portmagee and more departures for the Skelligs. It's an enjoyable cycle route, but there are lots of small unmarked roads, making it easy to get lost.

Ballinskelligs Monastery & Bay

The exact relationship between this monastery and the one on Skellig Michael isn't clear. It was probably founded after the monks left Skellig in the 12th or 13th century. The sea is gradually wearing away the ruins and it's the sort of place that children like to explore. Take the road down to Ballinskelligs Bay and walk to the remains from there. At the western end of this beautiful Blue Flag beach are the last remnants of a 16th-century castle stronghold of the McCarthys.

Places to Stay & Eat

The An Oíge *Ballinskelligs Hostel* (☎ 066-947 9229), with its bright external mural, is reached by turning right at the small junction after passing the post office in Ballinskelligs; beds here cost £6.50/5. *Island View* (☎ 066-947 9128), in Ballinskelligs, offers B&B costing upwards of £21.50/30 for singles/doubles. The *Ballinskelligs Inn*, behind the post office, serves food Easter to September.

CAHERDANIEL

☎ 066

Caherdaniel is just a couple of streets but boasts a particularly important historic house, a couple of sandy beaches by the harbour and a choice of hostels.

Derrynane National Historic Park

Having grown rich on smuggling with France and Spain, the O'Connells bought **Derrynane House** (☎ 947 5113) and the surrounding parkland, evading official restrictions on the purchase of land by Catholics with the help of a cooperative Protestant.

Two kilometres off the main Ring road, the house is largely furnished with items relating to Daniel O'Connell, the campaigner for Catholic emancipation. The dining room is full of early-19th-century furniture and silver given to O'Connell by grateful Catholics. The drawing room is renowned for a table carved over a period of four years by two men. Upstairs you can view O'Connell's deathbed. Most amazing of all is the restored triumphal chariot in which O'Connell rode around Dublin after his release from prison in 1844.

The surrounding parkland includes a sandy beach and **Abbey Island**, which can usually be reached on foot across the sand.

KERRY

The **chapel** which O'Connell had added to Derrynane House in 1844 is a copy of the ruined one on Abbey Island.

The house opens 9 am to 6 pm Monday to Saturday, and 11 am to 7 pm on Sunday, May to September; 1 to 5 pm Tuesday to Sunday, April and October; and 1 to 5 pm at the weekend, November to March. Admission costs £2/1. There's an excellent café serving scrumptious cakes.

Look out for an **ogham stone** to the left of the road leading down to the house.

Activities

Caherdaniel competes with Valentia Island as the diving base for the Iveragh Peninsula. Two companies offer courses and equipment hire. Derrynane Diving School (☎ 947 5110) offers a half-day discovery course for those without certificates. Skellig Aquatics Dive Centre (☎ 947 5277), opposite the Caherdaniel Village Hostel, organises a variety of outdoor courses, including diving trips off the Skellig Islands, abseiling, rock climbing and hill walking. Contact Derrynane Sea Sports (☎ 947 5266) for canoeing, windsurfing and water-skiing.

Places to Stay

Camping The *Wave Crest Caravan Park* (☎ 947 5188) has lots of facilities but only 10 tent pitches. With a car you'll pay £7.50; without, just £3.25.

Hostels In the congested main street the IHH *Caherdaniel Village Hostel* (☎ 947 5227) offers dorm beds costing £8. On the main Ring road, *Traveller's Rest* (☎ 947 5175) offers dorm beds costing £8 and private rooms costing £18. The IHH *Carrigbeg Country Hostel* (☎ 947 5229), 1km to the west and signposted, has the same rates.

B&Bs & Hotels For B&B try *Mrs O'Sullivan* (☎ 947 5124) or *The Olde Forge* (☎ 947 5140), both with en suite singles/ doubles costing £24.50/36. Mrs O'Sullivan also has rooms without bathroom costing £22.50/32.

The smartest place around is *Derrynane Hotel* (☎ 947 5136, fax 947 5160), with

B&B costing £60/90 (July and August prices).

Places to Eat

Across the road from Caherdaniel Village Hostel *Courthouse Restaurant* serves standard fry-ups, and ice cream. *Stepping-Stone Restaurant* (☎ 947 5444), next door, offers more-formal dinners, such as rack of lamb, costing around £14. *The Blind Piper* and *Freddie's* serve pub food.

STAIGUE FORT

This 2000-year-old fort is one of Ireland's finest dry-stone buildings. Its 5m-high circular wall up to 4m thick is surrounded by a large bank and ditch, rather like at Grianán of Aileách in County Donegal, although this fort hasn't been so thoroughly restored.

The fort probably dates from the 3rd or 4th century. Despite having sweeping views down to the coast it can't be seen from the sea. It may have been a communal place of refuge, or a royal residence as the sophisticated staircases incorporated into the walls suggest.

It's about 4km off the main road, reached by a partly potholed country lane which narrows as it climbs to the site. In summer the road and car park become the scene of absurd traffic jams! A sign by the gate demands 50p for access to the land (for what it calls 'trespass') even though the fort is owned by Dúchas. A small metal honesty box is nearby to put the money in.

SNEEM

☎ 064 • pop 310

Visitors have differing reactions to the oddly named town of Sneem (pronounced 'shneem'; An tSnaidhm). The Irish word means 'knot' or 'twist'. It's an hourglass-shaped village, with two greens joined by a small bridge, and sits in an open valley surrounded by mountains. With its brightly coloured, picturesque buildings, it's found quaint by some, while others think it has sold its soul to tourism.

The small **Sneem Museum** in the old courthouse west of the bridge looks like a cluttered antique shop inside. It opens 10 am to 1 pm and 2 to 5.30 pm daily, May to September. Admission costs £1.

Places to Stay

Camping Turn down past the bridge, near the church, for the small *Goosey Island Campsite* (☎ 45181). Campers can fish in the Sneem River nearby. It opens April to October and a tent site costs £4 per person.

Hostels A three-minute walk from the village at the Kenmare end is the *Harbour View Hostel* (☎ 45276). Dorm beds cost £7.50 and en suite doubles in chalets cost £20. The décor of the chalets is nothing special but they do boast extras such as kettles – something that not all B&Bs manage.

B&Bs The imposing *Old Convent House* (☎ 45181) is owned by the same family as the next-door camp site and has a fine riverside setting. Singles/doubles cost £24.50/ 36. *Derry East Farmhouse* (☎ 45193), 1km out of town on the road to Waterville, charges upwards of £26.50/36 and offers an evening meal costing £14.50.

Hotels A few kilometres out on the Kenmare road at Parknasilla, the *Great Southern Hotel* (☎ 45122, fax 45323) charges at least £146 for doubles. Past guests include Charles de Gaulle, Princess Grace of Monaco and Bernard Shaw (who wrote most of *St Joan* here).

Places to Eat

West of the bridge *Riverside Coffee Shop* and *Village Kitchen* compete for the lunch trade with home-baked, simple meals such as steak-and-kidney pie (£2.50). *The Hungry Knight* (☎ 45237) is said to do fish and chips good enough to draw some French customers back year after year.

At the western end of the village *O'Sullivan's Sacre Coeur Restaurant* (☎ 45186) opens April to October and serves seafood meals at lunch and dinner, with main courses costing £9 or more.

East of the bridge *The Green House* serves up moderately priced soup and sand-

wiches. *The Blue Bull* (☎ 45382), facing the eastern green, dispenses pub food costing upwards of £4, including fresh crab and smoked salmon.

Pygmalion Restaurant (☎ 31262), at Great Southern Hotel, is the most prestigious restaurant on the Ring of Kerry. It serves a surprisingly reasonable four-course dinner costing £18 (plus service charge and drinks).

Getting There & Away

As well as the regular Ring of Kerry bus service, in July and August a bus links Kenmare to Sneem (35 minutes) twice daily Monday to Saturday.

Getting Around

West of the bridge, Burns Bike Hire (☎ 45140) hires out bikes for £8 per day.

KENMARE

☎ 064 • pop 1130

At the point where the Finnihy, Roughty and Sheen Rivers empty into Kenmare River, the pocket-sized town of Kenmare (Neidín) is ablaze with vivid yellow, green, red and blue buildings. Outside July and August it's a sleepy place, its many restaurants and pubs waiting for the tourist onslaught. For those with their own transport, Kenmare makes a pleasant alternative to Killarney as a base for visiting the Rings of Kerry and Beara.

Orientation & Information

In the 18th century Kenmare was laid out on an X-plan, with a triangular market square in the centre and Fair Green nestling in its upper V. To the south, Henry and Main Sts are the primary shopping and eating/ drinking thoroughfares, with Shelbourne St joining them up at the south end. Kenmare River stretches out to the south-west, with glorious views in both directions.

The tourist office (☎ 41233), on The Square, opens 9.15 am to 7 pm daily, July and August; and 9.15 am to 5.30 pm Monday to Saturday, the rest of the year. Pick up a free heritage-trail leaflet showing places of historic interest.

KERRY

The AIB, on the corner of Main and Henry Sts, has an ATM and bureau de change. Kenmare Bookshop, on Shelbourne St, stocks *A Guide to Kenmare: Tuosist –Sneem* (£2), which details sights and possible walks in the area.

Kenmare Heritage Centre

Behind the tourist office and open the same hours, Kenmare Heritage Centre (☎ 41491) recounts the history of the town from its founding as Neidín by William Petty-Fitzmaurice in 1670. Particularly interesting is the information about the Kenmare Poor Clare Convent (still standing behind Holy Cross Church), which was founded in 1862 and provided local women with work as needlepoint lacemakers. Samples of their work are on display here and more can be seen upstairs in **Kenmare Lace and Design Centre**. Also interesting in the heritage centre is the story of Margaret Anna Cusack (1829–99), the Nun of Kenmare, an early advocate of women's rights who was eventually hounded out of Kenmare as a polit ical agitator, then renounced Catholicism in favour of Protestantism and died, embittered, in Leamington, England.

Admission costs £2/1.

Other Things to See & Do

South-west along Market St and Pound Lane is the Bronze Age **Druid Circle**, the largest stone circle in south-west Ireland, with 15 stones ringing a boulder dolmen. Sadly the land nearby has been used to dump garbage.

Our Lady's Well is a holy well in a small, pretty flower garden. To find it walk down Bridge St beside the tourist office and through the car park. Turn left and, just past the first house, on the right is a sign and path to the well.

Holy Cross Church in Old Killarney Rd was built in 1864 and boasts a splendid wooden roof with 14 angels carved from Bavarian wood.

Seafari River Cruises (☎ 83171) depart from the pier across from Our Lady's Bridge to the south beyond Henry St. Two-hour cruises around Upper Kenmare Bay

cost £10/5. Four-hour cruises to Sneem Harbour or full-day cruises of Kilmakilloge Harbour are also possible. The company rents out sailing, canoeing and windsurfing equipment.

Kenmare is ringed with lovely scenery and short **walks** can be made along the river or into the hills. The Kerry Way passes through Kenmare (see Walking in the Activities chapter for more details).

Walking Festival

During the last week of May, Kenmare hosts a Walking Festival in which people can undertake a series of walks of varying difficulty around town. To join in you must pay £10 and register at a booth in the square 30 minutes before the walk departs. For more information phone ☎ 41682. During the festival two-day classes in mountain skills, costing £45, are also organised. If you want to take part call ☎ 066-69244. Accommodation in town is hard to come by during the festival, so be sure to book ahead.

Places to Stay

Camping The *Ring of Kerry Caravan and Camping Park* (☎ 41648), 5km west of town on the Sneem road, opens May to September. For a car and tent, pitches cost £7.50 plus £1.50 per adult.

Hostels The pleasant IHH *Fáilte Hostel* (☎ 42333), at the junction of Henry and Shelbourne Sts, has a good kitchen and sitting room. Dorm beds cost £9, private rooms £10.50 per person. On the opposite corner above Kenmare Cycle Centre, *Finnegan's Corner Hostel* (☎ 41083) has a laundry and kitchen, plus a car park at the back; dorm beds cost £7.50.

B&Bs The Kenmare area has lots of B&Bs. Beside Fair Green, *Rose Cottage* (☎ 41330) was where the original Poor Clare nuns stayed when they arrived in Kenmare in 1861. Singles/doubles cost £30/40. *Greenville* (☎ 41769), overlooking Kenmare Golf Club, offers doubles costing £20 per person.

South of Kenmare a couple of B&Bs overlook Kenmare River. *Sallyport House*

(☎ 42066) offers doubles costing £90 and some delightful river views. *Ard Na Mara* (☎ 41399), on Pier Rd, has similarly good views but is much cheaper at £22/34 for singles/doubles.

Hotels The handily positioned *Wander Inn* (☎ 41038, Henry St) charges upwards of £20 per person. Across the road *Foley's Shamrock Hotel* (☎ 41379) offers singles/doubles costing £25.50/38.

Apartheid Without the Name

As you travel around Ireland, you'll notice huddles of caravans in lay-bys on the outskirts of towns. These are home to many of the country's estimated 30,000 Tinkers (or Travellers, as many prefer to be called these days), a group so unpopular with Irish society at large that they might as well be lepers.

There are many theories about Travellers' origins. Some suggest that they're descendants of children left orphaned by the Famine of the mid-19th century; others say that they're descendants of families driven westwards by Oliver Cromwell in the 17th century. However, study of their language suggests that the Travellers have been around for much longer and that they may be descendants of Bronze Age tinsmiths and related to Europe's other gypsy and nomadic groups.

Until relatively recently, they had a distinct place in society. Before the days of Tupperware, their tin receptacles had a real value, as did their donkeys and mules before the advent of tractors. Until radio and TV came along, villagers also saw their arrival in the district as a way of keeping in touch with the world outside. Now, however, all these roles have vanished.

Despite the apparent poverty of the families you see in the lay-bys and of the beggars on the streets, some actually make a good living from the scrap business or from dealing in second-hand cars. Others sell copper or the lead from old car batteries. A few have even grown wealthy trading in antiques. But even when they own fine houses, most still keep their caravans and spend part of every year on the road.

Community ties remain very strong, families of 12 children are still common and single parents are almost unheard of – perhaps unsurprisingly, since many girls are married as soon as they turn 16.

But the Travellers face an uphill struggle to be accepted and lead worthy lives. They have a dismal reputation for drinking and fighting (although they would argue that this is a fine case of the pot and the kettle), and inevitably there are complaints that they leave sites dirty and strewn with litter. Pubs often refuse to serve them and hotels turn away bookings for wedding receptions if it's suspected that the happy couple are actually

MATT KING

Travellers. When families find permanent housing, neighbours sometimes make it known that they're not wanted. When their children are admitted to mainstream schools, most other parents forbid their offspring to mix with them, thus depriving them of the social benefits of education. As a result, special schools are sometimes set up for Traveller children, guaranteeing that integration doesn't take place.

Lansdowne Arms Hotel (☎ *41368)*, at the junction of Main and Shelbourne Sts, dates back to the 18th century. It's not the most welcoming place but it has singles/doubles starting at £40/60.

Two of Ireland's most expensive hotels compete for business in Kenmare. *Park Hotel* (☎ *41200, fax 41402)* is the oldest, with a superb interior full of antiques. Its singles/doubles start at £166. *Sheen Falls Lodge* (☎ *41600, fax 41386)* is next to the old Kenmare cemetery, with the remains of a 7th-century church and a walk down to the sea. Here a room costs a whopping £258.

Places to Eat
Most of Kenmare's eating places serve lunch and dinner, with prices rising considerably in the evening.

Restaurants The *Purple Heather Bistro* (☎ *41016, Henry St)* serves meals such as open crab sandwiches (£5.95). At its partner restaurant, *Packie's* (☎ *41508, Henry St)*, open 5.30 to 10 pm, most main courses cost £8 to £10.

Virginia's (☎ *41021)*, near the Fáilte Hostel, serves tasty meals costing under £10; pasta in basil-and-pesto sauce costs £8.95.

An Leath Phingin (☎ *41559, Main St)* serves handmade pasta costing upwards of £6.50. Arty *Giuliano's*, at the top of Main St, has pizzas costing £8.85 or more (try the excellent Florence) and pasta costing £8.95 and over; there's even something for vegans here. Next door, *D'Arcy's* (☎ *41589)* has main dishes such as fillet of plaice costing £13 to £17.

The Lime Tree (☎ *41225)* is a delightful place in Shelbourne St with main dishes costing £9.50 and over. The building housing it was once the Lansdowne Estate office. Here 4616 people were given free passage to North America in the 1840s. It later became a school, hence the desks displaying the menus.

The restaurant at *Riversdale House* (☎ *41299)* hotel overlooks Kenmare River. A set dinner will set you back £15.95 without wine. Follow Henry St south and the hotel is just over the river on the left.

Cafés & Pubs In Henry St, moderately priced *La Brasserie* opens for breakfast, lunch and dinner and has an interesting menu; spiced lentil in pitta bread costs £3.50. *The New Delight* farther south is a vegetarian café that opens only until 5.30 pm, except in June, July and August, when it reopens from 6.30 to 9.30 pm for dinner. Sandwiches cost £2.50.

In Henry St *Foley's* and *The Coachman* serves pub lunches and pricier dinners. A seafood pancake at the former costs £6.95.

Shopping
This is a good place to shop for real Irish crafts as opposed to the usual leprechaunery. Shops in Main, Henry and Shelbourne Sts sell fine knitwear, lace, linen and pottery, often at alarming prices. Sounds of Music in Henry St has a good range of Irish tapes and CDs.

Getting There & Away
As well as the main Ring of Kerry bus service and a daily bus to Cork there's a July and August service between Sneem and Kenmare (see the Sneem section earlier in this chapter) and another to Castletownbere. Buses stop outside Brennan's pub on Main St.

Getting Around
Kenmare Cycle Centre (☎ 41083), below Finnegan's Corner Hostel, is the Raleigh Rent-a-Bike dealer, with bikes costing £8/50 per day/week.

Tralee & Northern Kerry

The northern Kerry landscape is somewhat ordinary and many travellers rush through to County Clare via the Tarbert ferry. However, there are some places of historic interest and the coastal strip is popular with Irish holidaymakers.

TRALEE
☎ 066 • pop 20,000

Tralee (Trá Lí) has enough attractions to occupy a day or so but is also a useful stopover en route to the Dingle Peninsula as it's well stocked with hostels, restaurants and lively music pubs.

In the last week of August the Rose of Tralee festival centres on a beauty contest and most B&Bs raise their prices by £4 or £5 for its duration.

Founded by the Normans in 1216, Tralee has a long history of rebellion. In the 16th century the last ruling earl of the Desmonds was captured and executed. His head was sent to Elizabeth I, who had it displayed on London Bridge. His property was given to Sir Edward Denny. The Desmond castle once stood at the junction of Denny St and The Mall. Any trace of medieval Tralee that survived the Desmond Wars was razed in the Cromwellian period.

Orientation & Information

Tralee is a fairly small town and you'll find most things you need along The Mall and its continuation, Castle St, and in wide, elegant Denny St, with the tourist office at its southern end. The bus and train stations are a 10-minute walk north-east from the town centre.

The tourist office (☎ 712 1288) is at the back of Ashe Memorial Hall. The hall is named after Thomas Ashe, a Kerryman who led the largest Easter Rising action outside Dublin in 1916. He went on a hunger strike in prison but died from medical neglect in 1917 after being forcibly fed. The tourist office opens 9 am to 7 pm Monday to Saturday, and 9 am to 6 pm on Sunday, July and August; 9 am to 1 pm and 2 to 6 pm Monday to Saturday, May, June and September; and 9 am to 1 pm and 2 to 5 pm on weekdays, October to April.

On Castle St you'll find banks with ATMs and bureaux de change.

The Walk Information Centre (☎ 712 8733), 40 Ashe St, is the HQ of South-West Walks Ireland and has a lot of useful maps and walking guides. It opens 9 am to 5.30 pm on weekdays.

Kerry the Kingdom Museum

Also in the Ashe Memorial Hall but entered round the corner from the tourist office, the museum (☎ 712 7777) gives a concise history of Ireland – with the emphasis on Kerry. Downstairs, visitors ride around a recreation of the walled town of Tralee in 1450 in time cars. Children love it and a commentary in eight languages is available.

The exhibition opens 10 am to 6 pm daily, March to October; and noon to 4.30 pm, November and December. Admission costs £5.50/3.

Tralee & Dingle Steam Railway

Between 1891 and 1953 a narrow-gauge railway connected Tralee with Dingle. The first short leg of the journey, from Tralee to Blennerville, was reopened and now operates May to September. The train leaves Ballyard Steam Railway Station (☎ 712 1064) on the hour, 11 am to 5.30 pm, and the 20-minute journey costs £4/2.

Blennerville Windmill

About 1km south-west of town, Blennerville used to be the chief port of Tralee, although it has long since silted up. A flour mill was built here in 1800 but fell into disuse by 1880. It has been restored and is the largest working mill in Ireland or Britain. A short video tells its story and there are 40-minute guided tours.

The modern visitor centre (☎ 712 1064) detracts from views of the mill but houses an exhibition about the thousands of emigrants who boarded 'coffin ships' for a new life in the USA from what was then Kerry's largest embarkation point. The windmill opens 10 am to 6 pm daily, April to October. Admission costs £3/1.75. To get there you can take the steam train (combined fare and windmill entry £5.50/2.75) or follow the canalside path, looking out for birds as you go.

Close by, over the next few years visitors will be able to watch the building of a replica of the **Jeannie Johnston** (☎ 712 9999), a ship that ferried several thousand emigrants to Baltimore, New York and Quebec in the mid-19th century without

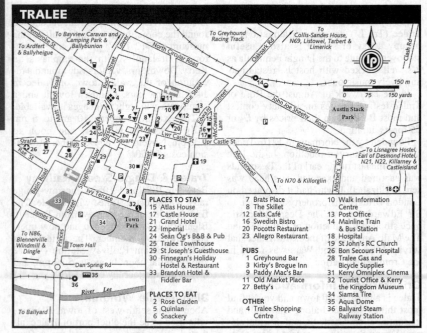

TRALEE

0   75   150 m
0   75   150 yards

PLACES TO STAY
15 Atlas House
17 Castle House
21 Grand Hotel
22 Imperial
24 Seán Óg's B&B & Pub
25 Tralee Townhouse
29 St Joseph's Guesthouse
30 Finnegan's Holiday
   Hostel & Restaurant
33 Brandon Hotel &
   Fiddler Bar

PLACES TO EAT
2 Rose Garden
5 Quinlan
6 Snackery

7 Brats Place
8 The Skillet
12 Eats Café
16 Swedish Bistro
20 Pocotts Restaurant
23 Allegro Restaurant

PUBS
1 Greyhound Bar
3 Kirby's Brogue Inn
9 Paddy Mac's Bar
11 Old Market Place
27 Betty's

OTHER
4 Tralee Shopping
  Centre

10 Walk Information
   Centre
13 Post Office
14 Mainline Train
   & Bus Station
18 Hospital
19 St John's RC Church
26 Bon Secours Hospital
28 Tralee Gas and
   Bicycle Supplies
31 Kerry Omniplex Cinema
32 Tourist Office & Kerry
   the Kingdom Museum
34 Siamsa Tíre
35 Aqua Dome
36 Ballyard Steam
   Railway Station

ever losing a single passenger to disease. There's a visitor centre and guided tours of the workshops and shipyard. It opens 9 am to 6 pm daily (except 23 December to 3 January). Admission costs £4/2.

Aqua Dome

The Aqua Dome, in an impressive building on the south-western outskirts, has water slides, wave pools, saunas, the lot, but you pay through the nose (£5/3) to use them. It opens 10 am to 10 pm on weekdays, and 11 am to 8 pm at the weekend, April to September. For other times of year phone ☎ 712 9150.

Places to Stay

Camping The *Bayview Caravan and Camping Park* (☎ 712 6140), 1.6km from town on the Ballybunion road, charges £5 for a tent and two people. You can also camp at *Collis-Sandes House* hostel (see the following section).

Hostels Attractively positioned, the Georgian *Finnegan's Holiday Hostel* (☎ 712 7610, 17 Denny St) offers dorm beds costing £10 and doubles costing £25. Cooking and lounge facilities here are exceptionally good. The modern *Atlas House* (☎ 20722, McCowans Lane), off Castle St, offers dorm beds costing £9 with breakfast.

Collis-Sandes House (☎ 28658), a Georgian house in Oakpark, is the longest walk from the centre and charges £9 for dorm beds, £28 for private rooms. *Lisnagree Hostel* (☎ 27133, Ballinorig Rd), east of the town centre at Clash Cross, charges £8.50 for dorm beds and £22 for private rooms.

B&Bs Centrally placed B&Bs include *Castle House* (☎ 712 5167, 27 Upper Castle St) and *Seán Óg's* (☎ 712 8822, 41 Bridge St). The latter is over a pub so it could be noisy. Elegant *St Joseph's Guesthouse* (☎ 712 1174, 2 Staughton's Row) offers singles/

doubles costing £19/36. Nearby, in High St, the large, modern, purpose-built *Tralee Townhouse* (☎ 718 1111) charges £22.50/40 for clean rooms.

Hotels In Denny St *Grand Hotel* (☎ 712 1499, fax 712 2877) charges £70 for doubles, while *Imperial* (☎ 712 7755, fax 712 7800) charges upwards of £45. Four kilometres out on the Killarney road, *Earl of Desmond Hotel* (☎ 712 1299, fax 712 1976), offering singles/doubles costing £45/70, is good value; book early in summer. The large, central, modern *Brandon Hotel* (☎ 23333, Princes St) doesn't look too out of place between the older buildings and charges upwards of £56/80.

Places to Eat

During the day it's not hard finding somewhere reasonable for lunch or a snack. In the evening, however, there are few alternatives to the pubs.

Pocotts Restaurant (☎ 712 9500, Ashe St) serves a full breakfast (£3.50) and has a set dinner menu (£8.50). It also has a bakery across the road. At *The Skillet* (☎ 712 4561, Barrack Lane) most meat and vegetarian dishes cost under £5 during the day. The Chinese *Rose Garden* (Rock St Lower) charges £7.50 to £10 for main dishes, and much less at the takeaway next door. Popular *Brats Place* (18 Milk Market Lane) opens for tasty vegetarian lunches but not for dinners; soup and bread costs £2.

At *Allegro Restaurant*, on the corner of Denny St and The Mall, the food's OK and the service friendly, but the lack of alternatives guarantees queues for tables. Pizzas cost £4.95.

The basement restaurant at *Finnegan's Holiday Hostel* (☎ 712 7610, 17 Denny St) brings good food to what can seem like a culinary desert. Tasty continental cuisine is served in cosy surroundings; roast lamb costs £12.95. *Swedish Bistro* (☎ 712 1711, McCowans Lane), off Castle St, offers herrings and other delicacies, such as pasta costing £6.95.

Inexpensive daytime meals can be had at the small *Eats Café* (Ashe St), where

lasagne and salad costs £4.25, or *O'Brien's* in Tralee Shopping Centre, off Russell St. The *Snackery* (The Mall) serves a mini-breakfast (£2.35) and fried food costing under £5.

Nearby, *Quinlan* calls itself a 'select luncheon bar' and is good for light meals until 6 pm (vegetarian special £3.50), when it becomes a conventional bar.

Entertainment

Castle St is thick with pubs, many of them with live entertainment of one kind or another. *Kirby's Brogue Inn* (Rock St), *Greyhound Bar* (Pembroke St) and *Fiddler Bar*, in Brandon Hotel on Princes St, have something most nights.

Betty's (Strand St) is recommended for traditional music at the weekend. *Paddy Mac's Bar* (The Mall) has music on Tuesday night.

The popular *Old Market Place*, attached to the Abbey Gate Hotel, has pavement tables in summer.

At *Siamsa Tíre* (pronounced 'shee-am-sah-tee-reh'; ☎ 712 3055) the National Folk Theatre of Ireland re-creates aspects of Gaelic culture through song, dance and mime. Events take place at 8.30 pm, May to September. The theatre is close to the tourist office and tickets cost around £10.

Kerry Omniplex Cinema (☎ 712 3944, Ivy Terrace) has four screens.

Getting There & Away

Bus Bus Éireann (☎ 712 3566) express bus No 13 daily connects Dublin and Tralee, via Limerick and Listowel. Bus No 40 runs daily to Rosslare via Killarney, Cork and Waterford. Other services connect Tralee with Clifden, Ennis, Kenmare, Shannon, Westport and Derry, and locally with Dingle and Dunquin.

Bus Éireann also runs regularly to London via Limerick, Tipperary and Waterford, departing at 2.15 pm (one way from £35).

Train There are regular daily trains between Tralee (☎ 712 3522) and Dublin (4 hours 15 minutes).

KERRY

Getting Around

Bikes can be hired from Tralee Gas and Bicycle Supplies (☎ 712 2018), High St, for £6/30 per day/week.

AROUND TRALEE
Crag Cave

Crag Cave was discovered only in 1983 when problems with water pollution led to a search for the source of the local river. Although the cave entrance had been known for years the system had never been explored until then.

The cave opens 10 am to 6 pm (6.30 pm in July and August) daily, March to November. Guided tours cost £4/2. Coffee and snacks are available.

To get to the cave, head for Castleisland on the N21 and, when you get there, look for the signs at the Limerick end of town. In July and August there's at least one bus daily (except Sunday) between Tralee and Castlemaine that stops in Castleisland.

Ardfert

☎ 066 • pop 675

Ardfert (Ard Fhearta) lies about 7km northwest of Tralee on the Ballyheigue road. Most of **Ardfert Cathedral** (☎ 713 4711), which is owned by Dúchas, dates back to the 13th century, but the Romanesque doorway is 12th century. Set into one of the interior walls is an effigy popularly said to be of St Brendan the Navigator, who was educated in Ardfert and founded a monastery here. There are ruins of two other churches – 12th-century Templenahoe and the 15th-century Templenagriffin – in the grounds.

The continuing work on shoring up the cathedral will take many years and access to the interior is by guided tour only. It opens 9.30 am to 6 pm daily, early May to late September. Admission costs £1.50/60p.

Turning right in front of the cathedral and going down the road for 500m brings you to the extensive remains of a **Franciscan friary**, dating from the 13th century but with 15th-century cloisters. Many will find this the more romantic of the two sites, mainly because it's in semi-isolated farmland.

O'Sullivan's Cottage Bar and *Kate Browne's* pub serve food and there's a Spar supermarket so you can stock up on groceries if you're camping on the coast to the north or south.

July and August, Bus Éireann bus No 274 between Tralee and Ballyheigue stops at least once daily in Ardfert.

FENIT

☎ 066

Eight kilometres south-west of Ardfert is the small resort of Fenit (An Fhianait), with an offshore lighthouse and a pier running out to an unpromising shed which turns out to contain the rather good **Fenit Seaworld** (☎ 713 6554). This is one of a new generation of aquaria that uses wave machines and touch pools to make the underwater world more exciting. For the sake of youngsters a story of piracy, complete with sometimes bloodied models, is woven around the fish. It opens 10 am to 5.30 pm (8.30 pm in July and August) daily. Admission costs £4/2. There's also a café.

Friday only, a Bus Éireann bus leaves Tralee for Fenit at 9.45 am and 1.45 pm, returning at 10.15 am and 2.15 pm.

BANNA STRAND & BALLYHEIGUE

☎ 066

Banna Strand, an 8km stretch of sandy beach, is better known for its history than for its recreational qualities. Attempting to bring in rifles for the Easter Rising, Sir Roger Casement (1864–1916) was arrested as soon as he landed here in April 1916 from a German submarine. He was tried for treason and executed in London but many years later his body was returned to Ireland. As you approach the beach, a sign points left to the Casement memorial. It's 1km, past the caravan park.

The beach itself is safe for swimming. You can camp free on the sand dunes at Banna and there are public toilets, but no showers, at the main entrance to the beach. A couple of caravan parks stretched along the beach attract mainly Irish holidaymakers.

To the north of Banna Strand is the smaller but equally sandy beach at otherwise uninspiring Ballyheigue (Baile Uí Thaidg). Camping is possible at *Casey's Caravan and Camping Park* (☎ 33195), where hikers and cyclists pay £3.50 each. The *Wave Crest* (☎ 713 3177, Cliff Rd) offers singles/doubles costing upwards of £22.50/32.

Bus Éireann bus No 274 runs once daily between Tralee and Ballyheigue.

RATTOO ROUND TOWER

Kerry's only complete round tower has six floors and is in fine condition. The top windows face the four points of the compass to act as lookouts for raiders, suggesting that this was a wealthy monastic site in the 9th and 10th centuries. Nothing else remains from that era on this site. To the east are the ruins of a 15th-century church.

The tower is visible from the main road before entering the small town of Ballyduff from the south. The turning is signposted. There's no access to the tower, only to the graveyard next door.

BALLYBUNION

☎ 068 • pop 1450

In June 1834 a longstanding feud between two Ballybunion (Baile an Bhuinneánaigh) families culminated in a brawl on the beach involving over 3000 combatants. During the summer the beach is still crowded, but mainly with Irish holidaymakers, who have made Ballybunion a popular seaside resort. Tourist information is available from a small seasonal tourist office on the main street.

There's little to see except the ruins of **Ballybunion Castle** overlooking the beach, where there are opportunities for both **swimming** and **surfing**.

Many tourists come here to play **golf**, and in 1998 US President Bill Clinton visited Ballybunion to do just that. To commemorate this historic event, a statue of the president in full swing has been erected in front of the Garda station.

Regular Bus Éireann buses connect Ballybunion with Tralee and Listowel.

LISTOWEL

☎ 068 • pop 3325

Listowel (Lios Tuathail) is 15km south of Tarbert, from where a ferry crosses the Shannon Estuary to County Clare. The main attraction in Listowel is the annual Writers' Week, although there are some places of interest in the vicinity. The tourist office (☎ 22590), in St John's Church in the town square, opens 10 am to 1 pm and 2 to 6 pm Monday to Saturday, May to September; and 9.30 am to 1 pm and 2 to 6 pm on weekdays, October to April.

Surprisingly for a town credited with spawning 360 books by more than 60 writers, Peter J McGuire's, at the top of Church St, is the only bookshop.

Special Events

John B Keane is probably the most famous writer associated with Listowel, especially since the filming of *The Field*, and usually features in Writers' Week. Bryan Mac-Mahon, a short-story writer, is another local literary talent. The festival takes place each May. Details are available from Writers' Week, PO Box 147, Listowel. Many events are held in St John's Arts Centre (☎ 22566) in St John's Church.

The other big event of the year is the Listowel horse races in late September.

Getting There & Away

There are up to four Bus Éireann express buses daily between Tralee (30 minutes) and Limerick (one hour 40 minutes). In July and August there are three buses daily to Ballybunion.

AROUND LISTOWEL
Carrigafoyle Castle

The peaceful location of this five-storey castle, perched above the Shannon Estuary, is very attractive. Its name comes from *Carragain Phoill* (Rock of the Hole). It was probably built at the end of the 15th century by the O'Connors, who ruled most of northern Kerry. It was besieged by the English in 1580, was retaken by O'Connor but fell again to the English under George Carew in 1600, during the suppression of O'Neill's rebellion, and was finally destroyed by Cromwell's forces in 1649. You can climb the spiral staircase 29m (108 steps) to the top for a good view of the estuary.

The castle is 2km west of the village of Ballylongford (Bea Atha Longphuirb), which is infrequently accessible by bus from Listowel, Ballybunion or Tarbert.

Lislaughtin Abbey

This Franciscan friary was also founded by the O'Connors in the late 15th century. When Carrigafoyle Castle was attacked in 1580, the friary was also raided and three elderly friars were murdered in front of the altar. The National Museum in Dublin contains a processional cross (the Ballylongford Cross) from the abbey.

Take the small road to Saleen from Ballylongford and the abbey ruins soon come into view.

Tarbert

☎ 065 • pop 680

A 20-minute car ferry (☎ 905 3124) runs between Tarbert and Killimer in County Clare every hour on the half-hour year round. It's useful if you want to avoid travelling through Limerick city. (See under Killimer in the County Clare chapter for more details.)

The IHH *Ferry House Hostel* (☎ *903 6555, The Square*) opens year round and charges £9 for dorm beds, £20 and upwards for doubles.

May to September there are up to three Bus Éireann buses daily from Tralee and Listowel.

Dingle Peninsula

Less touristy and even more beautiful than the Ring of Kerry, the Dingle Peninsula is the Ireland of *Ryan's Daughter* and *Far and Away*, with an extraordinary number of ring forts, high crosses and other ancient monuments.

Dingle is the main town. Ferries run from Dunquin to the bleak Blasket Islands, off the tip of the peninsula.

A touring route, the Slea Head Drive, heads west from Dingle to Slea Head, Dunquin, Ballyferriter, Brandon Creek and back to Dingle. You could drive it in a day but it's more fun to spin it out.

The 178km circular Dingle Way walking trail could be started in Tralee. It passes through Dingle and Dunquin, returning to Tralee via Castlegregory. The whole walk takes eight days but the last four days, from Dunquin to Tralee, are by far the best in terms of scenery. See Walking in the Activities chapter for further details.

TRALEE TO DINGLE VIA CONNOR PASS

There are two routes from Tralee to Dingle, though they both follow the same road out of Tralee past the Blennerville Windmill. Near the village of Camp a right fork heads off to the Connor Pass, while the N86 via Annascaul takes you to Dingle more quickly. The Connor Pass route is much more beautiful and panoramic, and goes past Castlegregory Peninsula, which divides Brandon and Tralee Bays. The broad, empty beaches around Castlegregory are perfect for surfing and those close to Sandy Bay Caravan Park near Castlegregory have been particularly recommended. Bring your own gear.

Castlegregory

☎ 066

A small, traffic-congested village, Castlegregory (Caislean an Ghriare) has a seasonal visitor centre and a couple of hostels. A sand-strewn road heads north on a spit of land between Tralee and Brandon Bays to Rough Point. It's very pretty and would be more so were it not for the caravans and bungalows marring the views.

Places to Stay The *Anchor Caravan Park* (☎ *713 9157*), 3km before Castlegregory, coming from Tralee, is signposted on the main road and opens Easter to September. There are 30 pitches and a tent and car cost £10 for two people (hikers and cyclists £7). *Seaside Caravan and Camping Park* (☎ *713 0161*) is also on the beach.

KERRY

DINGLE PENINSULA

Euro Hostel (☎ 713 9133) is above Fitzgerald's pub as you join the road to Rough Point in town. Beds in six-bed dorms cost £7 and doubles cost £14.

Lynches Hostel (☎ 713 9128, Main St), attached to a funeral parlour of all things, charges £7 for dorm beds and £20 for doubles.

Griffins Tip Top Farmhouse (☎ 713 9147), on the main road about 1km north of Castlegregory, charges £23/36 for B&B in singles/doubles.

Getting There & Away A year-round bus service leaves Tralee for Castlegregory on Friday only at 8.55 am and 2 pm and returns at 10.35 am only. In July and early August there are also two services daily on Wednesday, leaving Tralee at 10.20 am and 4.15 pm, and returning at 11.05 am and 5 pm.

Cloghane & Brandon
☎ 066

At Kilcummin a road cuts south-west over the Connor Pass to Dingle. A fork to the right heads to the relatively little-visited villages of Cloghane (An Clochán) and Brandon (Cé Bhréannain) and on to Brandon

Point, with fine views of Brandon Bay. The area is one of only three in Ireland that is working towards acquiring an EU 'eco-label', the environmental equivalent of a Blue Flag beach and indicating an area of pristine natural quality.

Cloghane has a helpful information centre (☎ 713 8277) where you can buy the *Cloghane and Brandon Walking Guide* (£3), with details of all the trails you'll see signposted. Those interested in the region's many archaeological sites should ask about guided walks or buy *Loch a'Dúin Archaeological and Nature Trail* (£3).

Immediately opposite the information centre, **St Brendan's Church** has a stained-glass window showing the Gallarus Oratory and Ardfert Cathedral.

Mt Brandon At 951m, Mt Brandon (Cnoc Bhréannain) is Ireland's second-highest mountain. There are two main walking routes up: a gradual one from the west and a more exciting one from the east; allow at least five hours for the climb. If you want to climb, make sure there's no danger of a mist descending, as the top is frequently shrouded in cloud. If you do get caught, you may need a compass to make your way down. The traditional way up the mountain is by way of the Saint's Rd, which starts at Kilmalkedar Church (see that entry in the West of Dingle section later in this chapter). The eastern, more demanding, approach starts just beyond Cloghane and is clearly signposted.

The ruins of St Brendan's Oratory mark the summit. The legend is that the navigator saint climbed the mountain with his seafaring monks before they set out in their curraghs for the journey to Greenland and America.

Places to Stay The *Green Acres Caravan and Camping Park* (☎ 713 9158), close to Crutchs Hillville House Hotel, charges £9 for a tent and two adults. The inviting *Crutchs Hillville House Hotel* (☎ 713 8118, Connor Pass Rd) is tucked away on the left (if you're heading north) just south of Cloghane. It provides B&B costing £38.50 to £47 per person. *Fermoyle Room Restaurant* here serves dinner costing £25, but bar food is also available.

Getting There & Away Friday only, bus No 273 leaves Tralee at 8.55 am and 2 pm for Cloghane (one hour 10 minutes). Returning, it leaves at 10.05 am and 3.10 pm.

Connor Pass & Around

At 456m, the Connor (or Conor) Pass is the highest in Ireland and offers spectacular views of Dingle Harbour to the south and Mt Brandon to the north. There's a car park near the summit. Take the path up behind it to see the peninsula spread out below you.

Connor Pass Hostel (☎ 713 9179) is by the main road at Stradbally (An Sráid Bhaile). The proprietor also runs the pub opposite. Dorm beds cost £7. *Beenoskee* (☎ 713 9263), at Cappateigue, just west of Stradbally, charges upwards of £22.50/32 for B&B in singles/doubles.

TRALEE TO DINGLE VIA ANNASCAUL

For drivers this route has little to recommend it other than being faster than the Connor Pass route. By bike it's less demanding. On foot the journey constitutes the first three days of the Dingle Way.

The friendly IHH *Bog View Hostel* (☎ 066-915 8125) is a converted school halfway between Tralee and Dingle at Lougher. Dorm beds cost £7, while private rooms cost £18. Meals are available, bikes can be hired and there's a free pick-up service.

A few kilometres past Bog View Hostel the well-equipped IHH *Fuschia Lodge Hostel* (☎ 066-915 7150) charges upwards of £7.50 for dorm beds, £18 for doubles, and has camping space.

Annascaul
☎ 066

The main reason to pause in Annascaul (Abhainn an Scáil), also spelled Anascaul, is to visit the *South Pole Inn* by the river. It commemorates villager Tom Crean (1877–1938), who went to the South Pole with Scott and Shackleton. You can study the memorabilia and read up on his expeditions while tucking into your lunch. A **walking trail** begins at the South Pole Inn and heads 14km north to Ballyduff Bridge near Brandon Bay.

Other eateries in Annascaul include the *Anchor Restaurant* (☎ 915 7382), where main courses cost around £10, and, next door, *Dan Foley's*, which serves up bar food.

There are three buses daily (two on Sunday) from Tralee.

CASTLEMAINE TO DINGLE

The quickest route between Killarney and Dingle is by way of Killorglin and Castlemaine. At Castlemaine a road heads west to Dingle, soon meeting the coast and passing Inch on the way to joining the main Tralee road to Dingle. Apart from the odd pub or two there's little provision for food, so bring your own.

At least two Bus Éireann buses between Tralee and Dingle stop at Lispole daily. Late May to mid-September they also stop at Castlemaine and Inch and continue to Killarney.

Inch
☎ 066

The main attraction at Inch (Inse) is the 6km-long **sand spit** that runs into Dingle Bay – a location for the film of *The Playboy of the Western World*. The sand dunes were once home to Iron Age settlements. Cars are allowed on the beach, but be very careful because vehicles regularly get stuck in the wet sand. Bring your gear for **surfing** waves which average 1 to 3m.

Lispole
☎ 066

The road from Inch to tiny Lispole (Lios Póil) passes through Annascaul (see Tralee to Dingle via Annascaul earlier in this section). Between Annascaul junction and Lispole look out for a turning on the left to the 15th-century **Minard Castle**, a single keep on a low cliff looking out to sea. It has been in a dangerous condition since its destruction by Cromwellian forces in the 17th century. Children should not be left unsupervised.

Places to Stay & Eat

About six kilometres west of Castlemaine (Caisleán na Mainge) you'll see the *Phoenix Café and Vegetarian Hostel* (☎ 976 6284) beside the road. Beautiful ethnic fabrics and artefacts decorate a hostel with simple dorm beds on the floor costing £8.50, doubles costing £24/28 without/with bath. There's a wide choice of books in the lounge. Even self-caterers must stick with the no-meat rule. You can camp in the adjoining field for £3.50. Lorna and Bill, the owners, will pick you up from Castlemaine. The café uses mostly organic food, much of which is grown in the adjoining garden. Dishes include cyclists' dream, a thick stew with homemade bread. Breakfast and lunch cost £3.50, dinner £7.50. If you wish to eat at the café only, it's advisable to book.

In Inch, up a lane leading off the main road at the Castlemaine end, *Inch Farm Hostel* (☎ 915 8181) offers simple dorm beds costing £7, doubles costing £16; the price includes linen. You can also camp here. *Waterside* (☎ 915 8129) offers ocean

views from some rooms and B&B costing £20/34 in singles/doubles. Dinner is available costing £15.

The remote, clifftop *Seacrest Hostel* (☎ 51390) near Lispole offers dorm beds costing £7 and doubles costing £16. It's signposted just over 1km west of the village, from where it's another 2km uphill. There's a free pick-up service.

DINGLE
☎ 066 • pop 1270

The attractive little port of Dingle (An Daingean) makes a good base for exploring the Dingle Peninsula and has a famous resident dolphin. What saves it from complete surrender to tourism is the continued existence of a large resident fishing fleet. At the time of writing, tempers were running high over whether to replace the old boat yard on the quay with a tourism complex complete with large hotel, restaurant and 'theme' bar.

Information

The tourist office (☎ 915 1188), by the pier, opens 9 am to 6 pm (7 pm in July and August) daily, April to September; and 9.15 am to 1 pm and 2.15 to 5.30 pm Monday to Saturday, March and October.

The banks on Main St have ATMs and bureaux de change. Dingleweb (☎ 915 2477), Lower Main St, offers Internet access costing £1.15 for 15 minutes, £5 for an hour. Mountain Man (☎ 915 1868), Strand St, sells outdoor equipment and maps and hires out bikes. Níolann Laundrette is off Green St.

Fungie the Dolphin

In the winter of 1984 fisherfolk began to notice a solitary bottlenose dolphin that followed their vessels, jumped about in the water and sometimes leaped over their boats. Fungie the dolphin is now an international celebrity.

During the summer, regular boats leave the pier for a one-hour dolphin-spotting trip. This costs £6/3 (it's free if Fungie doesn't show, but he usually does). A daily boat also leaves at 8 am for those who want to swim with Fungie. The trip lasts two

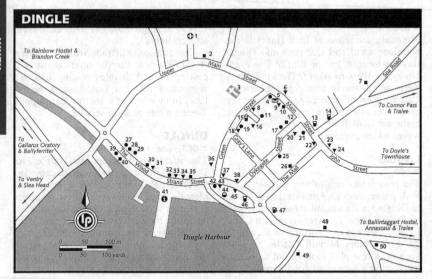

DINGLE

To Rainbow Hostel &
Brandon Creek

To Gallarus Oratory
& Ballyferriter

To Ventry
& Slea Head

To Connor Pass
& Tralee

To Doyle's
Townhouse

To Ballintaggart Hostel,
Annascaul & Tralee

Dingle Harbour

0   50   100 m
0   50   100 yards

hours and costs £10/5 (plus £14 to hire a wetsuit if necessary). Wetsuits can also be hired from Flannery's (☎ 915 1337), in a house near the Esso garage. Ballintaggart Hostel also has wetsuits for hire, mainly for residents. As well as Fungie, you'll get the chance to watch cormorant, guillemot, razorbill and shearwater.

You can watch Fungie from the shore, although without getting nearly so close. From Dingle take the Tralee road and turn right down a lane about 1.5km from the Esso garage. The turning is easy to miss so look for a set of whitish gateposts beside the lane. At the end of the lane is a tiny parking space (remember that the farmer needs access to his fields). Walk along the sea wall towards the old tower and you'll come to the harbour mouth.

Dingle Oceanworld

This aquarium (☎ 915 2111), opposite Dingle Harbour, concentrates on showing off the fish and other sealife from the local area. Most of the specimens were caught by the local fisherfolk. There's a walk-through tunnel, a touch pool and a shark tank. It opens 9 am to 9 pm daily, July and August;

and 9 am to 5 pm Monday to Saturday, and 9.30 am to 5 pm on Sunday, the rest of the year. Admission costs £4.50/2.75. The café has fine harbour views.

Activities

Hidden Ireland Tours (☎ 087-255 0334) provides organised walking programmes including half-day walks in the beautiful countryside west of Dingle and full-day hikes up Mt Brandon.

Snorkelling and scuba diving in Dingle Bay and around the Blasket Islands can be arranged at Dingle Marina Diving Centre (☎ 915 2422), near the harbour.

Ask at the tourist office for details of sea fishing trips, or call ☎ 915 1163.

Places to Stay

Camping Three hostels provide for campers: *Seacrest* (see Places to Stay & Eat in the Castlemaine to Dingle section earlier in this chapter), *Ballintaggart Hostel* and *Rainbow Hostel* (see the following section); sites cost £3.50 per person.

Hostels Dingle has lots of hostel accommodation, with the going rate for dorm beds

DINGLE

PLACES TO STAY	18 Beginish Restaurant	OTHER
2 Boland's	20 An Café Liteártha	1 Hospital
7 Hillgrove Hotel	22 Old Smokehouse	3 St Mary's Church
10 Benner's Hotel	23 Half Door	4 Foxy John's
12 Grapevine Hostel	24 Doyle's Seafood Bar	5 Post Office
26 Captain's House	31 Waterside	11 Níolann Laundrette
28 An Caladh Spáinneach	33 Danno's Restaurant	17 Paddy's Bike Hire
30 Marina Hostel	Bar	19 Lisbeth Mulcahy
32 Marina Inn	34 Armada	Shop
35 Murphy's B&B & Pub	36 Fenton's Restaurant	21 Dingleweb
40 Ocean View	37 Oven Doors	25 Phoenix Cinema
48 Alpine House	38 Forge Restaurant	27 Craft Village
49 Lovett's	43 Nell's Coffee Shop	29 Dingle Oceanworld
50 Dingle Skellig Hotel	45 Greany's	39 Brian De Staic
		Jewellery
PLACES TO EAT	PUBS	41 Tourist Office; Dolphin's
6 Adams Restaurant & Bar	13 An Droisead Beag	Boat Office & Pier
8 El Toro	14 An Conair	42 Mountain Man
9 Lord Baker's	15 Dick Mack's	44 Bus Stop
16 Loft Café	46 O'Flaherty's	47 Esso Petrol Station

being £7 to £8. The inviting *Grapevine Hostel* (☎ 915 1434, Dykegate St) offers beds in dorms and four-bed rooms. *Lovett's* (☎ 915 1903) is a small family house down the road from the Esso garage, about 150m from the main roundabout. The IHO *An Caladh Spáinneach* (☎ 915 8181, Strand St), across from the marina, opens June to October and as well as dorm beds offers one private room costing £20.

For a more rural setting try the deservedly popular *Rainbow Hostel* (☎ 915 1044), about 700m north-west of town (free pick-ups from the bus stop), with a good, big kitchen. East along the Tralee road the equally popular IHH *Ballintaggart Hostel* (☎ 915 1454), in a spacious early-19th-century house, also has a free shuttle service to and from town, plus bike hire, a bureau de change and pony trekking.

If these are full, in town the basic *Marina Hostel* (☎ 915 1065, The Wood), near the pier, offers 20 dorm beds costing £7, plus private rooms costing £15.

B&Bs A few pubs on Strand St offer B&B: *Marina Inn* (☎ 915 1660) provides B&B costing £12 per person, while *Murphy's* (☎ 915 1450) offers rooms with separate bathroom costing £16 per person.

On The Mall, *Captain's House* (☎ 915 1531), charging from £25/46 for singles/doubles, overlooks a beautiful stream and garden.

Main St has several B&Bs, including *Boland's* (☎ 915 1426), with good views and singles/doubles costing £18/30 or more. The comfortable *Doyle's Townhouse* (☎ 51174), at the bottom of John St, costs £45/76. In a terraced house by the harbour, *Ocean View* (☎ 915 1659, The Wood) opens March to November and charges £15/26.

On the Tralee road, just east of the roundabout, big *Alpine House* (☎ 915 1250) charges upwards of £34/50. The sea views are terrific.

Hotels The *Benners Hotel* (☎ 915 1638, fax 915 1412, Main St), in a Georgian house, is attractively furnished and charges upwards of £40/60 for B&B in singles/doubles. Bigger and pricier is unattractive *Dingle Skellig Hotel* (☎ 915 1144, fax 915 1501), a 10-minute walk from town, south-east of the roundabout. Doubles cost £70 to £160.

The less expensive but not much prettier *Hillgrove Hotel* (☎/fax 915 1131) is a five-minute walk from town on Spa Rd; it charges upwards of £30 per person.

euro currency converter IR£1 = €1.27

KERRY

Places to Eat

Restaurants The *Forge Restaurant* (☎ *915 1209, Strand St*) offers standard meals, including vegetarian choices, costing £7 to £13. *Armada*, opposite the pier, serves seafood and grills costing between £8.75 and £12.95; a four-course set dinner between 6 and 9 pm costs £15.95. *Waterside*, also near the pier, is a French restaurant offering mostly seafood; scallops sautéed in saffron and cream sauce costs £14.

The unpretentious *Old Smokehouse* (☎ *915 1149*), on the corner of The Mall and Main St, specialises in seafood; scampi costs £8.50.

Opposite St Mary's Church *El Toro* (☎ *915 1820, Green St*) serves pizzas costing £5.75 or more and seafood costing upwards of £11.95. Farther down the road *Fenton's Restaurant* (*Green St*) offers a set dinner costing £18.95. Excellent value for money is the award-winning *Beginish Restaurant* (☎ *915 1588, Green St*), which can always be relied on for a good seafood or vegetarian meal; john dory costs £15.50.

On Main St, *Adams* has a bar on one side and a small restaurant on the other side serving vegetarian and fish dishes costing £4 to £8; it closes on Sunday. *Lord Baker's* (☎ *915 1277*) is a seafood restaurant; grilled plaice costs £9.90. *Doyle's Seafood Bar* (☎ *915 1174, 4 John St*) serves dinner only; most main courses cost £12.50 to £17. *Half Door* (☎ *915 7600*), next door, is similar but a bit cheaper; seafood pancake costs £6.

Cafés & Pubs The excellent *An Café Liteártha* (*Dykegate St*) is a bookshop with a small, quiet and inexpensive café, with a handy notice board, at the back.

Pleasant *Oven Doors*, on the corner of Green and Strand Sts, serves pizzas costing upwards of £3.65 until 10.30 pm. *Greany's* (*Strand St*) opens for lunch, serves a set dinner (£12.95) and has a selection of vegetarian dishes (£5.95). It closes on Thursday. *Nell's Coffee Shop* (*Strand St*) opens daily and can fix you a smoked-salmon sandwich costing £4.

Loft Café, at the end of the lane opposite St Mary's Church in Green St, offers snacks during the day and meals such as baked hake (£8.50) in the evening.

Most of the pubs opposite the pier serve bar food all day. *Murphy's* offers a traditional bacon-and-cabbage meal costing £5.75 until 9 pm. *Danno's Restaurant Bar* stands on the site of the old Dingle Station and offers a menu of fish (upwards of £6.50), burgers and pasta.

Entertainment

Many pubs have live music, but three in town are particularly worth checking out: *O'Flaherty's* near the roundabout, *Murphy's* by the pier, and *An Droisead Beag* (Small Bridge Bar) at the end of Main St by the bridge. The An Droisead Beag has traditional music from 9 pm nightly. *An Conair* (*Spa Rd*) has set dancing on Monday night. In Green St, *Dick Mack's* is a marvellous old-style pub with a shop on one side and a drinks counter on the other.

Phoenix Cinema is on Dykegate St.

Shopping

The Craft Village on The Wood has several workshops specialising in leatherware and garments. Go to Brian de Staic nearby to have your name inscribed in ogham script on a piece of jewellery.

Green St is packed with craft shops. Look out for Lisbeth Mulcahy, where you'll find lovely, if pricey, pottery and woven garments. She and her husband have a workshop west of Dingle near Ballyferriter (see Louis Mulcahy Pottery in the Dunquin & Around section later in this chapter).

Getting There & Away

Bus Éireann buses stop outside the car park behind the Super Valu store. Buses leave Tralee (☎ 712 3566) at 11 am and 2, 4.15 and 6 pm Monday to Saturday, plus 9 am from late May to mid-September and 8.10 pm from June to September. At least five buses daily depart Killarney Monday to Saturday for Dingle. From Dingle, the earliest daily bus to Tralee leaves at 7.25 am; from Tralee there are onwards connections to Killarney. There are fewer services on Sunday. An infrequent bus service links

Dingle to Ventry, Slea Head, Dunquin and Ballyferriter.

Getting Around

There are several bike rental places, including Paddy's Bike Hire, which charges £5/25 per day/week. Foxy John's (☎ 915 1316), Main St, does the Raleigh Rent-a-Bike scheme.

WEST OF DINGLE

The area west of Dingle has the greatest concentration of ancient sites in Kerry, if not in the whole of Ireland. To do them justice you should use one of the specialist guides on sale in the An Café Liteártha café/bookshop or the tourist office in Dingle town. The sites listed in this book are among the most interesting and easiest to find.

The land west of Dingle has some other attractions. It is a Gaeltacht, or Irish-speaking, area. The landscape is dramatic, except when it's hidden in mist, and there are striking views of the Blasket Islands from Slea Head. The sandy beach nearby, Coumenole, is lovely to walk along but, like most in the area, is treacherous for swimming.

Tourism came late to Dingle but the area is handling it well, avoiding the tackiness of Killarney and the Ring of Kerry. In 1971, David Lean filmed *Ryan's Daughter* here. Much of it was shot near Dunquin, and the ruins of the film's schoolhouse can still be found. Film buffs should inquire at Kruger's pub in Dunquin.

Orientation

If you cross the bridge west of Dingle and take the first right, where there's a clutter of signs (mostly in Gaelic), you come to a Y-junction after 5km. To the right are Kilmalkedar Church and Brandon Creek, from where you could return to Dingle on a circular route. To the left are the Gallarus Oratory and the Riasc site, from which you can reach Ballyferriter and Dunquin, for boats to the Blasket Islands. This road continues down the coast and back to Dingle, via Ventry.

Kilmalkedar Church

This 12th-century church was once part of a complex of religious buildings. The characteristic Romanesque doorway has a tympanum with a head on one side and a mythical beast on the other. There is an ogham stone, pierced by a hole, in the grounds. About 50m away is a two-storey building known as St Brendan's House which is believed to have been the residence of the medieval clergy. The road connecting these two ruins is the beginning of the Saint's Rd, the traditional approach to Mt Brandon (see Cloghane & Brandon earlier in this Dingle Peninsula section).

Brandon Creek

Tradition has it that St Brendan set off from this inlet and sailed to America in the 5th century. As Tim Severin shows in *The Brendan Voyage*, this voyage could indeed have been done hundreds of years before Columbus. The fishing boats add to the creek's atmosphere, and on a warm day the water is inviting.

To get there, carry on along the road that you turned off to reach Kilmalkedar Church. After a few kilometres turn right at the junction where Tigh A'Phoist Hostel is signposted, then right at the unmarked T-junction. Carry on along this road for nearly 2km until you reach the tiny village of Bothar Bui and the hostel. Carry straight on to the next junction and turn left (signposted the Slea Head Drive) at the unnamed pub for Brandon Creek. A right turn at this junction returns to Dingle.

The basic IHH *Tigh A'Phoist Hostel* (☎ *066-915 5109*) in Bothar Bui village is attached to a shop and offers beds in four-bed dorms costing £9.50 (in the high season) and doubles costing £19. It opens April to October. On Tuesday and Friday the Dingle to Ballydavid bus goes close to the hostel – ask to be dropped off at the Caragh church.

The friendly *An Bothar* (☎ *066-915 5342)* pub offers B&B costing £15 per person and is ideally located if you want to climb Mt Brandon. To get there, continue past the hostel for half a kilometre.

Gallarus Oratory

Simple but stunning, this superb dry-stone oratory is reason enough for visiting the Dingle Peninsula. It's in perfect condition, apart from a slight sagging in the roof, and has withstood the assault of the elements for some 1200 years. Traces of mortar suggest that the interior and exterior walls may have been plastered. Shaped like an upturned boat, it has a doorway on the western side and a small round-headed window on the eastern side. Inside the doorway are two projecting stones with holes which once supported the door.

Bear left at the Y-junction after leaving Dingle via the bridge (see Orientation earlier in this section) and after 2km turn left at the sign. The oratory is half a kilometre down the road on the left.

Europe's westernmost camp site is *Teach an Aragail* (*'Oratory House Camp'*; ☎ 066-915 5143), near the oratory. A tent site for a car with two occupants costs £9 (hikers and cyclists £6).

Tuesday and Friday only, a bus leaves Dingle at 9 am and drops off at Gallarus 10 minutes later. From Gallarus it picks up for Dingle at 1.25 pm.

Riasc Monastic Settlement

The remains of this 5th- or 6th-century monastic settlement are impressive. Excavations have revealed, among other finds, the foundations of an oratory first built with wood and later stone, a kiln for drying corn and a cemetery. Most interesting is a pillar with beautiful Celtic designs.

From Dingle a sign points the way from the Y-junction (see Orientation earlier in this section). Follow the road for 4km until you see a sign on the left to Reask View B&B and the monastic settlement. The site is 500m up this road.

BALLYFERRITER

☎ 066

Heading north on the R559 road out of Dingle and following the Slea Head Drive signs, you'll eventually come to the small village of Ballyferriter (Baile an Fheirtearaigh), named after Piaras Ferriter, a poet and soldier who emerged as a local leader in the 1641 rebellion and was the last Kerry commander to submit to Cromwell's army. Near the village are the Three Sisters hills, Smerwick Harbour and the remains of Dún an Óir Fort.

Ballyferriter Museum

Social, cultural and historical aspects of life on the Dingle Peninsula and the Blasket Islands are the focus of the small Ballyferriter Museum (☎ 915 6100). It opens 9.30 am to 5 pm daily, over Easter and June to September. Admission costs £1.50/75p.

Dún an Óir Fort

During the 1580 rebellion in Munster, the 'Fort of Gold' was held by an international brigade of Italians, Spaniards and Basques. On 17 November, English troops under Lord Grey attacked the fort and the people inside surrendered. 'Then putt I in certeyn bandes who streight fell to execution. There were 600 slayne', said the poet Edmund Spenser, who was secretary to Lord Grey.

To get to Dún an Óir, head west from Ballyferriter. After 1km turn right at a brown sign to Dún an Óir Hotel. After a further 1.5km, take the right fork at a Y-junction. Go straight on, ignoring side tracks, until you come to a T-junction. Turn right and after roughly 300m you'll see a signpost to the fort along a wretchedly surfaced road; do your suspension a favour and walk it. The views alone justify the effort of finding the scant remains of the fort.

Places to Stay & Eat

Free camping is possible near Ferriter's Cove but there are no facilities. The IHO *An Cat Dubh Hostel* (☎ 915 6286), on the Dunquin road in an ordinary house attached to a shop, opens May to September and offers dorm beds costing £7. Dotted around are a few good B&Bs, such as *Mrs Ferris* (☎ 915 6282), 3km west, charging £19/28 for singles/doubles.

To get to *Óstan Dún an Óir* (☎ 915 6133) look for a sign on the right after leaving Ballyferriter heading west. Singles/doubles cost £35/55 and there's an outdoor heated swimming pool. The hotel also serves food. Nearby, *Tigh Pheig* serves bar food such as bacon and cabbage costing under £5 and often puts on traditional-music sessions.

DUNQUIN & AROUND
☎ 066

If Ballyferriter is small, it does at least have a centre, unlike scattered Dunquin (Dún Chaoin), from where you catch a boat to the Blasket Islands. It's on the Slea Head Drive out of Dingle, roughly the same distance whether you set out north via Ballyferriter or west via Ventry.

Blasket Centre (Ionad an Bhlascaoid Mhóir)
The wonderful heritage centre (☎ 915 6444) at Dunquin celebrates the lost lifestyle of the Blasket Islanders, and the Irish language and culture. The 20-minute audiovisual presentation can be seen in French and German as well as English. The centre cost £4 million to build, most of it provided by the EU, and the building provides an incidental showcase for marvellous stained glass, ceramics and weaving. There's a café with Blasket Island views and a small bookshop selling the various books written by and about the islanders. This Dúchas-operated centre opens 10 am to 6 pm (7 pm in July and August) daily, April to October. Admission costs £2.50/1.

Louis Mulcahy Pottery
This is certainly one of the most interesting potteries on the peninsula. Visitors can see the potters at work and the two floors of the shop display a variety of tea sets, bowls, lamps, vases and platters; most items cost under £100, but some go up to £400 or £500. Purchases can be mailed overseas from the shop (☎ 915 6229), which opens 10 am to 5.30 pm Monday to Saturday, and 11 am to 5.30 pm on Sunday. The pottery is on the road just north of Dunquin.

Beehive Huts & Dunbeg Fort
The road between Dunquin and Slea Head is dotted with beehive huts, forts and church sites. The Fahan huts are accessible from two points and you'll see signs pointing the way from the road.

Prehistoric Dunbeg Fort, on a clifftop promontory, has a sheer drop to the Atlantic and four outer walls of stone. Inside are the remains of a house and a beehive hut as well as an underground passage. The fort is 8km from Dunquin heading towards Dingle.

To visit any of these sights you'll be charged £1, pretty steep given that there's no 'presentation' (they just sit and take your money) and other sites on the peninsula are free.

Slea Head
Slea Head offers some of the Dingle Peninsula's best views, good walks and fine beaches and is thoroughly popular with coach parties. *Bearfoot Café*, across the road from the car park, serves sandwiches costing around £3.50, while upstairs is the **Enchanted Forest Museum** of toys. It isn't perhaps the most obvious, or appropriate, development for a beauty spot, but parents with children who've had enough of beehive huts may be grateful for the break. It opens noon to 5 pm daily, Easter to June and September; and 11 am to 6 pm daily, July and August. Admission costs £2.50/1.50 (families £7).

Ventry
The small village of Ventry (Ceann Trá) is next to a wide sandy bay and has a marvellous post-office-cum-delicatessen-cum-wineshop. For sit-down dinners there's also the cheerful *Skipper Restaurant* (☎ 915 9858), which serves good seafood; black sole costs £10.50.

Places to Stay
The year-round An Oíge *Dunquin Hostel* (*☎ 915 6121*) is conveniently close to the Blasket Centre and not too far from the ferry departure point for Great Blasket Island. Beds cost £6.50/5.

The old-fashioned *Krugers Guesthouse* (*☎ 915 6127*), in a pleasant setting, is within walking distance of the ferry to the Blasket Islands. Beds cost £16.

KERRY

Places to Eat

Despite its dreary décor, *Kruger's Pub*, next to the guesthouse, is Dunquin's social centre and one of the few places to get an evening meal. After you've seen photos in the Blasket Centre of people dancing here in its heyday you may feel slightly less inclined to turn up your nose at it. There are more photos inside the pub.

A better choice is the *Café-Gallery Tig Aine*, tucked away on the coast side of the road north of Dunquin, near the Louis Mulcahy Pottery. From April to September it opens for breakfast, lunch and tea and from 7pm for dinner (main courses cost around £6).

On the road to Slea Head *Dunquin Pottery Café* provides meals and snacks; soup and bread costs £1.85. The unpromising exterior conceals a thoughtful interior decorated with a fine Irish dresser and old editions of Blasket Island books. Note an upturned Blasket Island boat in the garden.

Getting There & Away

Year round, Monday and Thursday only, a bus operates from Dingle to Dunquin via Ventry, Slea Head and Ballyferriter. Late June to mid-September a bus leaves Dingle at 12.30 and 3.10 pm Monday to Saturday. Late May to mid-September, a Monday to Saturday service leaves Tralee at 9.45 am and Killarney at 10.30 am. For more details phone Bus Éireann in Tralee (☎ 066-712 3566).

BLASKET ISLANDS

The Blasket Islands (Na Blascaodaí), 5km out into the Atlantic, are a group of four big and two smaller islands, the most westerly islands in Europe. At 6km by 1.2km, Great Blasket (An Blascaod Mór) is the largest and most visited and is mountainous enough for strenuous walks, including a good one detailed in Kevin Corcoran's *Kerry Walks*.

The last islanders left for the mainland in 1953 but lyrical stories of their lives survive. Three books in particular are usually available at the Blasket Centre or An Café Liteártha in Dingle. The best is the English translation of Thomas O'Crohan's *The Islandman*; the other two are Maurice O'Sullivan's *Twenty Years A-Growing* and the translation of Peig Sayers' *Peig*.

Places to Stay & Eat

There's no accommodation on the island but camping is free. A *café* serves snacks and campers can arrange for meals to be cooked.

Getting There & Away

Weather permitting, boats (☎ 066-915 6533) operate May to September; the 20-minute crossing costs £10/5 return. Boats leave Dunquin on the hour 10 am to 3 pm and return on the half-hour. The last boat from Great Blasket leaves at 3.30 pm.

Monday and Thursday, the first bus for Dunquin leaves Dingle at 8.50 am, giving you 40 minutes in Dunquin before the first boat leaves.

Counties Limerick & Tipperary

While these counties are outshone by neighbouring Cork, Kerry, Clare and Galway, both County Limerick and County Tipperary have places of interest that invite you to pause rather than merely pass through. Limerick city makes an obvious base for visiting Lough Gur and the village of Adare, while County Tipperary boasts the Rock of Cashel as well as the pleasant towns of Cahir, Carrick-on-Suir and smaller Fethard.

County Limerick

In 1690, the Siege of Limerick played centre stage in the struggle between Ireland and England, to which the imposing remains of the city's castle bear testimony. As well as the historic interest and amenities of Limerick city itself, the fascinating historic and prehistoric sites south of the city make ideal bicycle excursions. The nearby village of Adare is one of the prettiest in Ireland, in striking contrast with proletarian Limerick city.

LIMERICK
☎ 061 • pop 79,000
Despite being one of Ireland's largest cities, being set on the River Shannon and having a name to put pens in motion, Limerick (Luimneach) used to be regarded as pretty dismal. Fortunately, it is shedding its old, grim 'Stab City' image – it once had a reputation for violence – and things are improving. With redevelopment continuing apace and a number of attractions, including the excellent Hunt Museum and some fine Georgian architecture to match Dublin's, Limerick is a place of interest in its own right. There are plenty of places to eat and the city has a lively music scene.

History
The Vikings first reached Limerick in the 10th century. From then on they fought over

Highlights

- Explore Lough Gur and its remarkable Stone Age remains, south of Limerick city
- Visit the Hunt Museum, with its excellent collection of Irish art and antiquities, in Limerick city
- Discover the spectacular Rock of Cashel in County Tipperary, best visited early in the morning before the tour buses arrive

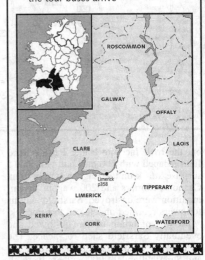

ROSCOMMON

GALWAY

OFFALY

CLARE

LAOIS

Limerick
p358

LIMERICK

TIPPERARY

KERRY

CORK

WATERFORD

the town with the native Irish until Brian Ború's forces defeated the Norsemen at the Battle of Clontarf in 1014. Throughout the Middle Ages the Irish clustered to the south of the Abbey River in Irishtown and the English to the north in Englishtown.

In 1690, Limerick acquired heroic status in the ongoing saga of the English occupation of Ireland. After the Battle of the Boyne, the defeated Jacobite forces withdrew west behind the famously strong walls of Limerick. Surrender seemed inevitable,

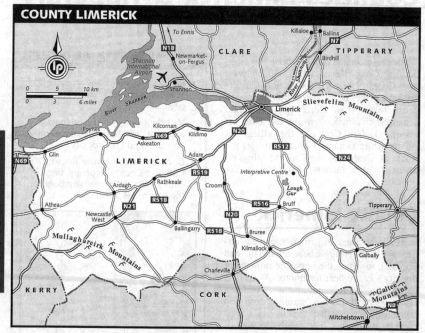

COUNTY LIMERICK

but the Irish Jacobite leader Patrick Sarsfield escaped with 600 men and launched a surprise attack on the English supply train. Cannons, mortars and 200 wagons of ammunition were destroyed. Sarsfield and his followers returned undetected to Limerick.

Months of bombardment followed and eventually Sarsfield sued for peace. The terms of the Treaty of Limerick were agreed and Sarsfield and 14,000 soldiers were allowed to leave the city for France. The treaty guaranteed religious freedom for Catholics, but the English reneged on it and enforced fierce anti-Catholic legislation, an act of betrayal that came to symbolise the injustice of British rule.

The new town of Limerick developed and prospered in the 18th century after the old town walls were demolished. However, by the early 20th century that prosperity had passed and in 1919 there was a general strike in protest against British military rule. A Strike Committee took charge of running essential services and for one week the city of Limerick operated outside all legal structures. The Strike Committee even issued its own banknotes, becoming known as the Limerick Soviet.

Limerick has revived considerably in recent years and, although there are still pockets of poverty, a lot of redevelopment is taking place and many of the old Georgian houses to the south are being restored.

Orientation & Information

The main street through town changes name from Rutland St to Patrick St, O'Connell St, The Crescent and Quinlan St as it runs south. Most things of interest are clustered to the north on King's Island, to the south around The Crescent and Pery Square, and along the riverbanks.

The tourist office (☎ 317522), on Arthur's Quay near the river, opens 9 am to 7 pm (6 pm at the weekend) daily, July and August; 9.30 am to 1 pm and 2 to 5.30 pm

Monday to Saturday, May, June, September and October; and 9.30 am to 1 pm and 2 to 5.30 pm on weekdays, and 9.30 am to 1 pm on Saturday, November to April.

The train and bus station lies south-east, off Parnell St. The banks on O'Connell St have ATMs and bureaux de change. The post office is on Lower Cecil St.

Eason's Bookshop is at 9 O'Connell St, but for books on all things Irish try Celtic Bookshop (☎ 401155), 2 Rutland St.

For walking gear and maps River Deep, Mountain High (☎ 400944) is at 7 Rutland St. Union of Students in Ireland Travel (USIT; ☎ 415064) is at 55 O'Connell St. Parking discs are available from most newsagents.

There are laundrettes on Ellen St, Broad St and Cecil St.

St Mary's Cathedral

The oldest building in the city but now restored, the cathedral was founded in 1172 by Donal Mór O'Brien, king of Munster. The original Romanesque west doorway and clerestory survive, but the chancel and chapels were added in the 15th century. There are grand tombs, memorial stones and splendid black-oak misericords (support ledges for choristers) dating from around 1489, carved with pictures of animals and other figures. The graveyard boasts many 18th-century tombstones.

Visitors are asked to donate £1 towards the cathedral's upkeep.

King John's Castle

King John of England had this castle built between 1200 and 1212, on the site of an earlier fortification, to guard and administer the rich Shannon region. The new cannon technology necessitated stronger defences than ever before and the castle became the most formidable bastion of English power in the west of Ireland.

But whoever described the modern interpretive centre in the middle as a 'cross-barred horror' hit the nail square on the head – interesting it may be, beautiful it isn't. After watching a 20-minute presentation on the castle's history you can descend to inspect the remains of mines and countermines dug by besiegers and besieged. In the courtyard stand replicas of three engines of early castle warfare: two catapults – a mangonel and a trebuchet, used to hurl weights, burning material and dead animals at the enemy – and a battering ram.

The castle opens 9.30 am to 5.30 pm (last admission 4.30 pm) daily, April to October. Admission costs £4/2.50.

Opposite the castle on the other side of the river, the **Treaty Stone** marks the spot on the riverbank where the Treaty of Limerick was signed. But before you cross the bridge look out for the 18th-century **Bishop's Palace** and the ancient **tollgate**.

Limerick Museum

At the time of writing, this history museum (☎ 417826) was due to open in purpose-designed premises near King John's Castle. Its collection includes Bronze and Stone Age artefacts, the civic sword and the city charters of Charles I. It will open 10 am to 1 pm and 2.15 to 5 pm Tuesday to Saturday. Admission will be free.

Hunt Museum

This wonderful museum (☎ 731 2833), the private collection of John and Gertrude Hunt, is housed in the Palladian Custom House on the banks of the river on Rutland St. It contains probably the finest collection of Bronze Age, Celtic and medieval treasures outside Dublin. Look out in particular for a marvellous 17th-century statue of Apollo draped with the tools of assorted trades; for an extraordinary self-portrait of the artist Robert Fagan and his half-naked wife; and for a Syracusan coin thought to have been one of the '30 pieces of silver' paid to Judas to betray Christ.

It opens 10 am to 5 pm Monday to Saturday, and 2 to 5pm on Sunday. Admision costs £4/2.

Limerick City Gallery of Art

At the time of writing this gallery was being set up in the Civic Centre at Merchant's Quay. It's hoped it will have more space (and labelling) for its excellent permanent

LIMERICK

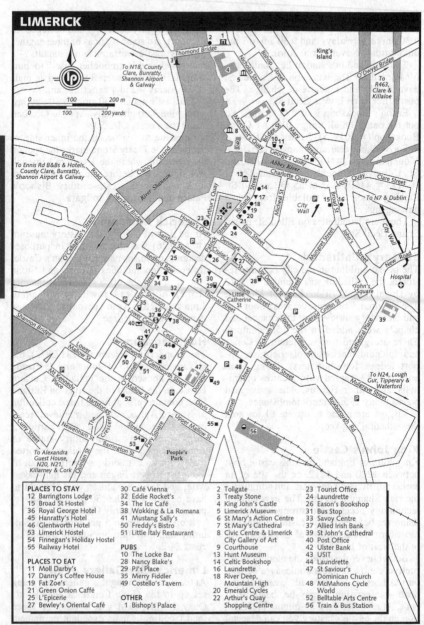

To N18, County
Clare, Bunratty,
Shannon Airport
& Galway

To Ennis Rd B&Bs & Hotels,
County Clare, Bunratty,
Shannon Airport & Galway

To R463,
Clare &
Killaloe

To N7 & Dublin

To N24, Lough
Gur, Tipperary &
Waterford

To Alexandra
Guest House,
N20, N21,
Killarney & Cork

PLACES TO STAY			
12 Barringtons Lodge	30 Café Vienna	2 Tollgate	23 Tourist Office
15 Broad St Hostel	32 Eddie Rocket's	3 Treaty Stone	24 Laundrette
36 Royal George Hotel	34 The Ice Café	4 King John's Castle	26 Eason's Bookshop
45 Hanratty's Hotel	38 Wokking & La Romana	5 Limerick Museum	31 Bus Stop
46 Glentworth Hotel	41 Mustang Sally's	6 St Mary's Action Centre	33 Savoy Centre
53 Limerick Hostel	50 Freddy's Bistro	7 St Mary's Cathedral	37 Allied Irish Bank
54 Finnegan's Holiday Hostel	51 Little Italy Restaurant	8 Civic Centre & Limerick	39 St John's Cathedral
55 Railway Hotel		City Gallery of Art	40 Post Office
	PUBS	9 Courthouse	42 Ulster Bank
PLACES TO EAT	10 The Locke Bar	13 Hunt Museum	43 USIT
11 Moll Darby's	28 Nancy Blake's	14 Celtic Bookshop	44 Laundrette
17 Danny's Coffee House	29 PJ's Place	16 Laundrette	47 St Saviour's
19 Fat Zoe's	35 Merry Fiddler	18 River Deep,	Dominican Church
21 Green Onion Caffé	49 Costello's Tavern	Mountain High	48 McMahons Cycle
25 L'Epicerie		20 Emerald Cycles	World
27 Bewley's Oriental Café	OTHER	22 Arthur's Quay	52 Belltable Arts Centre
	1 Bishop's Palace	Shopping Centre	56 Train & Bus Station

LIMERICK & TIPPERARY

collection, which includes work by artists such as Jack B Yeats and Sean Keating. It'll open 10 am to 1 pm and 2 to 6 pm on weekdays, and 10 am to 1 pm on Saturday. Admission will be free.

St Saviour's Dominican Church

This well-kept 19th-century church in Glentworth St contains a statue of Our Lady given to the Dominicans in 1640 by a rich Limerick citizen who wanted to atone for the fact that his uncle had sentenced a man to death for letting a priest say mass in his house. There's also some striking modern stained glass.

Organised Tours

June to August walking tours depart from St Mary's Action Centre (☎ 318106), 44 Nicholas St. There's both a historical tour and one of Limerick locations mentioned in Frank McCourt's *Angela's Ashes*. They cost £4/2.

May to September, Bus Éireann operates open-top-bus tours of the city costing £5/2.50 per person.

Places to Stay

Camping The *Shannon Cottage Caravan and Camping Park* (☎ 377118) is about 12km from Limerick in County Clare. It's reached by turning left at Birdhill – the signpost is easily missed – on the N7 road to Dublin. After Birdhill follow signs to O'Brien's Bridge and turn sharp right after crossing the bridge. A pitch for a small tent with a car costs £9 (motorcyclists £4, hikers or cyclists £3.50).

Hostels The An Oíge *Limerick Hostel* (☎ 314672, 1 Pery Square) is a short walk across People's Park from the bus and train station. Beds cost £7.50/6. The IHH *Finnegan's Holiday Hostel* (☎ 310308, 6 Pery Square) is in a fine Georgian house, but we've had some negative feedback from travellers about facilities. Dorm beds cost £7.50, doubles £10 per person. The large IHH *Barringtons Lodge* (☎ 415222, George's Quay) charges £7.50 per person in two- to four-bed dorms. The bigger single

rooms are good value at £11 and the riverside situation close to the castle is a distinct plus. However, some rooms need a little maintenance and the hostel's size makes it a bit impersonal. South across the river is the modern and clean *Broad St Hostel* (☎ 317222, Broad St), with dorm beds costing £9 and singles/doubles costing upwards of £13/18 including continental breakfast and bed linen. There's a convenient laundrette opposite.

B&Bs The *Alexandra Guest House* (☎ 318472, 6 Alexandra Terrace, O'Connell Ave) is fairly close to the centre and charges upwards of £18 per person. Otherwise, Ennis Rd, to the north-west, is lined with B&Bs for several kilometres, including, 1km out, *Clifton House* (☎ 451166), charging upwards of £20 per person, and *Curraghgower House* (☎ 454716), with good singles/doubles costing upwards of £22.50/32.

Hotels Cheapest is the *Railway Hotel* (☎ 413653, 419762, Parnell St), opposite the station, with singles/doubles costing upwards of £18/36. The comfortable, central *Royal George Hotel* (☎ 414566, fax 317171, O'Connell St) can be noisy at night. Rooms (sleeping up to three people) cost £59 excluding breakfast. Pleasantly furnished *Glentworth Hotel* (☎ 413822, fax 413073, Glentworth St) costs upwards of £40/70. *Hanratty's Hotel* (☎ 410999, fax 411077, Glentworth St), near by, has an olde-worlde feel and costs upwards of £29/50.

Most of the big hotels along Ennis Rd are unnecessarily expensive for the average traveller. Just 1km from town *Woodfield House Hotel* (☎ 453022, fax 326755) offers B&B from £39.50 per person. Going upmarket, the four-star *Limerick Inn Hotel* (☎ 326666, fax 326281) charges upwards of £63 per person for B&B.

Places to Eat

Restaurants From 5.30 pm Tuesday to Sunday, *Freddy's Bistro* (☎ 418749), tucked away down Theatre Lane between

Lower Mallow and Lower Glentworth Sts, serves decent meals such as steaks (£13.95) and chicken (£9.95). *L'Epicerie*, at the corner of Henry and Sarsfield Sts, is a small French restaurant serving dishes such as rib of lamb (£9.30) and lunchtime specials costing £3.80.

Opposite Royal George Hotel, *La Romana (O'Connell St)* serves mostly pasta dishes costing £5 to £7. Opposite the Hunt Museum, *Fat Zoe's*, in the 19th-century Commercial Buildings, is similar; most pastas cost £4.95. The more upmarket *Little Italy Restaurant* (☎ 315844, 55 O'Connell St), aka La Piccola Italia, serves pasta costing upwards of £5.25.

The classy *Hunt Museum Restaurant* is a popular lunch stop, but does get smoky; arrive early for the tables with river views. Poached mussels cost £2.90, grilled goat's cheese £3.80.

The laid-back, refurbished *Green Onion Caffé* (☎ 400710, 3 Ellen St) serves pasta and pitta dishes costing £6 to £14 after 6 pm; it has a particularly good wine list. *Mustang Sally's* (103 O'Connell St), a bright Tex-Mex joint open from 5 pm, serves burritos costing upwards of £7.50. Just up from Barringtons Lodge Hostel, *Moll Darby's* (☎ 417270, George's Quay) serves tasty, crispy pizzas costing £7.95.

Fast Food & Cafés For cheap eats try *Sails* on the 1st floor of the modern Arthur's Quay Shopping Centre beside the tourist office; fish, chips, peas, bread and tea costs £4.50. *Wokking (O'Connell St)*, opposite Royal George Hotel, is a Chinese-food place with a sit-in counter and takeaway service; meals cost upwards of £3.50. On the other side of the road, *Eddie Rocket's* is a US-style diner serving good hamburgers costing upwards of £3.50. *The Ice Café (Henry St)* also serves burgers, plus pizzas (£4.55).

At stylish *Danny's Coffee House (Rutland St)* breakfast costs £2.95 and tea comes in big mugs. Popular at lunchtime, *Café Vienna (William St)* is OK for soups (£1.20), sandwiches and salads. *Chimes*, in the basement at Belltable Arts Centre, serves good quiche (£3.50). *Bewley's Oriental Café*, on pedestrianised Cruise's St, serves good tea and coffee; sandwiches cost £2.25.

Entertainment

The music scene varies depending on the night, but there's often something at the popular *Nancy Blake's (Upper Denmark St)*. You could also try *Costello's Tavern (Dominic St)* or *Merry Fiddler (Lower Cecil St)*. *The Locke Bar (George's Quay)* has outdoor tables beside the river and is immensely popular on mild evenings. *PJ's Place (Little Catherine St)* has a mock thatched roof and traditional music.

Belltable Arts Centre (☎ 319866, 69 O'Connell St) hosts travelling theatre companies and has a small gallery.

Savoy Centre, off Henry St and Bedford Row, houses an eight-screen cinema; also here is *Termites* nightclub, where you can dance Saturday night away from 11 pm.

Getting There & Away

Air Shannon Airport (☎ 471444), in County Clare, handles both domestic and international flights.

Bus Bus Éireann services operate from the train and bus station (☎ 313333), a short walk south of the centre. There are regular connections to Dublin (£10, one hour 15 minutes), Tralee (£9, two hours), Cork (£9, one hour 50 minutes), Galway, Killarney, Rosslare, Donegal, Sligo, Shannon, Derry and most other centres. You can often be dropped at the bus stop on O'Connell St.

Train There are regular trains to all the main towns: eight trains daily to Dublin; two daily to Rosslare Harbour, Cahir and Tipperary; and one to Cork. Other routes involve changing at Limerick Junction, 20km south-east of Limerick. Phone Colbert station (☎ 315555) for details.

Getting Around

Regular buses connect Limerick train and bus station with Shannon Airport (one way £3.50). The airport is 24km north-west of Limerick, about 30 minutes by car.

As Limerick is quite small you can easily get around on foot or by bike. To walk across town from St Mary's Cathedral to the train station takes about 15 minutes.

Bikes can be hired at Emerald Cycles (☎ 416983), 1 Patrick St, and McMahons Cycle World (☎ 415202), 30 Roches St. Both are part of the national Raleigh Rent-a-Bike scheme; rates are £10/40 per day/week, plus £15 if returning outside Limerick.

AROUND LIMERICK

A few places south of Limerick could be taken in by car in a day or covered by bike over a few days. The R512 road to Lough Gur continues through the village of Bruff to the historic town of Kilmallock. From there, it's a short journey to the pretty village of Bruree, former home of Eamon de Valera. From Bruree a country road leads to Bruff and the R512 back to Limerick.

Lough Gur

The area around this small horseshoe-shaped lake is of great archaeological significance. There are a number of Stone Age sites and, coming from the city on the R512, the first is the 4000-year-old **Grange Stone Circle**, just past the village of Grange to the left of the road. With its 113 stones it's the largest in Ireland. One kilometre farther along the road a left turn goes up towards Lough Gur. Farther down the R512, 100m past a ruined 15th-century church, there's a **wedge tomb** on the other side of the road.

Another 2km along the R512 is an **interpretive centre** (☎ 061-360788), in a thatched replica of a Neolithic hut, where you can see a 12-minute slide presentation on the prehistoric remains. There's also a small **museum** with a few Neolithic artefacts and a replica of the Lough Gur shield that's now in the National Museum in Dublin (although the Lough Gur finds in the Hunt Museum in Limerick are more impressive). The 700 BC shield is 72cm in diameter with six circles of raised bosses designed to weaken the impact of an enemy's sword. The centre opens 10 am to 6 pm daily, early May to late September. Admission costs £2.10/1.20.

The lake, to which you can walk from the centre, is set in pleasant parkland, perfect for picnics; look out for the burial mounds, standing stones, ancient enclosures and other remains dotted around. To get there, leave Limerick on the N24 road south to Waterford. Look for a sign to Lough Gur indicating a right turn at the roundabout outside town. This takes you onto the R512.

Kilmallock
☎ 063 • pop 1500

On the River Lubach 26km south of Limerick, Kilmallock was Ireland's third-largest town in the Middle Ages, after Dublin and Kilkenny. It developed around an abbey founded in the 7th century by St Mochealllóg. From the 14th to the 17th centuries it was the seat of the earls of Desmond, in an important defensive position. In the mid-18th century it had a brief flurry of renewed importance with the coming of the railway, then sank back into the sleepy state it's in today.

Coming into Kilmallock from Limerick, the first place to see is the four-storey **King's Castle**, a 15th-century tower house with the street pavement running through it. On the other side of the road a lane leads down to the tiny **Kilmallock Museum**, which houses a ramshackle local collection and a model of the town in 1597. It opens 1.30 to 5.30 pm on weekdays, and 2 to 5 pm at the weekend. Admission is free.

Beyond the museum and across the River Lubach are the ruins of the 13th-century **Dominican priory**, with an attractive 13th-century east window and a tower and south window added in the 15th century. Kilmallock surrendered to Cromwell's forces in 1648 and the priory was sacked and partly destroyed.

Returning to the main street, you'll see a **medieval stone mansion** – one of the 30 or so that once housed the town's prosperous merchants and landowners.

Continue along the main street and take the turning on the left that goes down to the 13th-century **Collegiate Church**. This has a round tower, which probably belonged to an earlier, pre-Norman monastery on the site.

LIMERICK & TIPPERARY

The impressively carved door on the southern side of the nave dates from the 15th century.

Farther along the main street, turn left into Wolfe Tone St. Just before the bridge you'll see a plaque marking the house where the Irish poet Aindrias Mac Craith died in 1795. Across the road one of the pretty single-storey **cottages** (the yellow and white one) leaves its door open so you can peek in and see what a three-roomed dwelling used to look like.

Near the junction of Sarsfield and Lord Edward Sts is **Blossom Gate**, the one surviving gate of the original medieval town wall, traces of which can be seen nearby.

If you want to spend a night here, *Deebert House* (☎ 98106) is a good B&B in a fine old house. It offers singles/doubles costing upwards of £20/30 with shared facilities. To find it go down Wolfe Tone St, turn right after the bridge and head up the hill.

There are up to four Bus Éireann buses daily Monday to Saturday to Limerick.

Bruree
☎ 063 • pop 265
As a child, Eamon de Valera lived in a small cottage in Bruree (Brú Rí) and attended a Christian Brothers school in the nearby town of Charleville. The **cottage** where he spent his formative years is open to the public, although there's little in it apart from some period furnishing and fittings. At the Kilmallock end of the village a sign points to the cottage, just over 1km down the road. The key to the house is available from the next house, 250m farther up the road on the right-hand side.

De Valera Museum and Bruree Heritage Centre (☎ 91300) is in the National School attended by de Valera by the bridge at the Limerick end of the village. It contains items associated with his life, as well as information on local history. It opens 10 am to 5 pm Tuesday to Friday, 2 to 5 pm at the weekend. Admission costs £3/1.

Buses between Limerick and Charleville stop in Bruree twice daily Monday to Saturday. Bruree is off the N20 road connect-

ing Limerick and Cork and on the R518 from Kilmallock.

ADARE & AROUND
☎ 061 • pop 900
This pretty village 16km south-west of Limerick is tourist Ireland at its most sanitised. The charming thatched cottages that comprise part of the village were created by the 3rd earl of Dunraven in the 1820s; nowadays they're mostly craft shops or restaurants. Coach tours generally stop in Adare (Áth Dara), which means high prices for food and accommodation.

Information
The helpful tourist office (☎ 396255) is in the Adare Heritage Centre on the main street. Opening hours are fluid and depend on the level of demand. Its core hours are 9 am (8.30 am in July and August) to 7 pm (6 pm in October) on weekdays, and 9 am to 6 pm at the weekend, June to October; and 9 am to 1 pm and 2 to 5 pm Monday to Saturday, March to May and in November and December.

Traffic congestion can get quite bad at times. There's a free car park behind the heritage centre. The AIB near the centre has an ATM and bureau de change.

Adare Heritage Centre
In the centre of the village, this surprisingly good heritage centre (☎ 396666) uses models and a short audiovisual presentation to help you make sense of the ruins scattered about; the model showing the village in 1500 is particularly worth a look. It opens 9 am to 5 pm daily, St Patrick's Day to October. The rest of the year it opens on request. Admission costs £3/2.

Desmond Castle
Dating back to around 1200, this photogenically ruined castle was partly rebuilt in the following century and besieged by English forces in 1580. When Cromwell's army took possession in 1657, it had already lost its strategic importance. Restoration work is due to be completed in the year 2000, from which time you should be able to view the

Eamon de Valera

Eamon de Valera was born in New York in 1882 to an Irish mother and Spanish father. His father died when de Valera was two, and his mother sent the young Eamon to Ireland in 1885 with his uncle.

As a young mathematics teacher, he attended a meeting organised to protest at the 1911 visit to Ireland of the British monarch. Enthused by the idea of an independent Irish republic, he quickly joined the new Irish Volunteers. During the 1916 Easter Rising he ambushed British reinforcements travelling to Dublin, securing the greatest military success of the rebellion.

Like the other leaders, he was sentenced to death for his role in the uprising, but his US citizenship helped secure his escape from the firing squad with life imprisonment. After the amnesty of June 1917, he was let out of prison and elected Sinn Féin MP for East Clare, becoming Sinn Féin president from 1917 to 1926. In 1918 he was imprisoned in Lincoln Prison, England, but escaped using a duplicate key.

MATT KING

When the IRA split in 1921 over the Anglo-Irish Treaty, 'Dev' led the anti-Treaty forces in a bitter civil war. Following defeat in the war, in 1926 he formed a new party, Fianna Fáil (Soldiers of Destiny), and in the subsequent election was elected to the Irish Parliament (the Dáil), but refused to swear the contentious oath of allegiance to the British king. Eventually he entered the Dáil, skirting round the oath by not taking it but signing in as if he had, and claiming he was entering to ensure its abolition.

In 1932 Fianna Fáil established a government for the first time and retained power for the next 16 years. In 1937 the new constitution abolished the oath of allegiance and included a claim to sovereignty over the six Northern counties. He also refused to pay land annuities, which were agreed upon in the Anglo-Irish Treaty, to the British government. This led to an economic war with Britain which severely crippled Irish agriculture and was resolved only in 1948 shortly before de Valera's government was defeated in elections. The defeat didn't end de Valera's role in public life: he subsequently served two terms as president of the Republic, which was declared in 1949.

De Valera was the dominant figure of 20th-century Irish politics, but there has been much recent revision of his reputation. During his lifetime he was unable to achieve his three main aims: a united Ireland, an end to emigration and a revival of the Gaelic language. However, the fact that two of these aims have since been achieved is in no small measure due to him.

castle, in the grounds of Adare Manor golf course, without risking your life on the busy main road.

Adare Manor

When the earl of Dunraven decided to create a new mansion in 1832 he enlisted the architectural help of James Pain and AC Pugin, who came up with quirky details such as 52 chimneys and 365 windows. The building work it offered is said to have helped the village survive the Famine rather better than some others. Nowadays the house is an exclusive hotel surrounded by golf courses. Most of the year you can walk around its lovely grounds, but in summer there is usually someone at the gate to control the number of visitors.

Religious Houses

At the time of the dissolution of the monasteries in 1539, Adare had three flourishing religious houses, the remains of which can still be seen. In the village itself the dramatic tower and south wall of the **Church of the Most Holy Trinity** are the remains of a 13th-century Trinitarian monastery (the only one in Ireland) which was restored by the 1st earl of Dunraven and is now the Catholic church. There's a restored 14th-century **dovecot** which used to belong to the monastery down the side turning next to the church.

The ruins of a **Franciscan friary** founded by the earl of Kildare in 1464 stand in the middle of the Adare Manor golf course beside the River Maigue south of the village. Ask at the clubhouse for permission to visit but you'll have to walk all the way to the 15th tee. Look out for a well-preserved sedilia (set of seats for priests) in the south wall of the chancel.

Also south of the village, on the N21 north of Adare Manor, the Church of Ireland parish church was once the **Augustinian friary**, founded in 1316. The tower was added in the 15th century and the church was restored in 1807 by the 1st earl of Dunraven.

Celtic Park & Gardens

In Kilcornan, 7km north-west of Adare, the Celtic Park (☎ 394243) is a collection of recreated 'Celtic' structures (plus a few originals) on a site known to have been inhabited in Celtic times. There's also an extensive rose garden and tearooms. The site opens 9 am to 7 pm daily, March to November. Admission costs £3 (children free).

Matrix Castle

This carefully preserved and still-lived-in 15th-century Norman tower (☎ 069-64284) is full of artefacts and objets d'art. Tours start at 10.30 am and continue until 6.30 pm daily. Admission costs £3/1. The castle is 13km south-west of Adare on the N21, near Rathkeale.

Organised Tours

May to September a costumed guide leads daily walking tours of Adare; contact the tourist office for details.

Special Events

The International Music Festival takes place over St Patrick's weekend in March; phone the tourist office for details.

Places to Stay

There are several B&Bs in the village but single travellers are in for an expensive time: better to stay in Limerick and commute. *Elm House* (☎ 396306, Mondellihy), 1km north of town, charging £22.50/32 for singles/doubles, is recommended. Or you could try *Riversdale* (☎ 396751, Station Rd), which charges the same rates.

At *Adare Manor* (☎ 396566, fax 396124) a double can cost up to £355. Compared with that, *Dunraven Arms* (☎ 396633, fax 396541) on the main street sounds a positive snip at £90/120 for singles/doubles without breakfast.

Places to Eat

For reasonable pub lunches try *Lena's Bar* or *O'Coileain (Collins)* in the main street. Alternatively there's *Dovecot* in the heritage centre; soup costs £1.55, sandwiches £1.75. Roast beef costs £3.95 at the *Blue Door* opposite the Church of the Most Holy Trinity; it's open for dinner too. A few doors away at award-winning *Wild Geese* (☎ 396451) main dishes such as grilled seabass cost £7.95; it's closed Sunday and Monday. Dinner at *Adare Manor* will set you back £34.50, plus service charge.

Entertainment

There's traditional music at *Bill Chawke Lounge Bar* on Thursday and a singalong on Friday night. The *Sean Collins* pub has Irish music on Tuesday and Sunday.

Getting There & Away

The five daily Dublin to Tralee buses call at Limerick and then Adare (return to Limerick £2.50). For times contact Limerick bus station (☎ 061-313333).

County Tipperary

County Tipperary occupies a fair chunk of Ireland's southern midlands and boasts the sort of limey, fertile soil that farmers dream of. Consequently, Tipperary is at the heart of Irish farming. The county is mostly flat in the centre, with hills intruding over the borders from other counties. The River Suir cuts through the county's heart and every major town lies on the banks of the Suir or one of its tributaries. Some towns have active animal fairs or marts, especially Tipperary town, which, incidentally, isn't the major settlement: Clonmel is far larger, while Carrick-on-Suir, Thurles and Nenagh also have bigger populations.

TIPPERARY
☎ 062 • pop 4772

Originally an Anglo-Norman settlement, Tipperary town (Tiobrad Árann) is a working town consisting essentially of long Main St.

The tourist office (☎ 51457) is off the western end of Main St on James St. It opens 10 am to 6 pm Monday to Saturday, mid-March to October. The rest of the year you can get information from the helpful Clann na hÉireann shop (☎ 33188) round the corner at 45 Main St. The post office is on Davis St off Main St.

Things to See & Do

In the middle of Main St is a **statue of Charles T Kickham** (1828–82), a local novelist (author of *Knocknagow*) and Young Irelander. **Sean Treacy Memorial Swimming Pool** at the eastern end of Main St houses two display cabinets, with letters, photographs and artefacts relating to the War of Independence (1919–21), which had its very first engagement in a quarry a few kilometres north of the town. It's free, but for diehard enthusiasts only.

Tipperary Racecourse is 3km out on the Limerick road and has regular meetings during the year. See the local press for details or phone ☎ 51357. A lively **cattle mart** is held at the eastern end of Main St on Wednesday and Friday.

Places to Stay & Eat

Ach na Sheen (☎ 51298, Bansha Rd) charges £19 per person. The *Royal Hotel* (☎ 51204, Bridge St) charges £25 per person for B&B with shared bathroom. B&Bs can also be found either side of town on the N24.

Most of the pubs along Main St serve breakfast, tea and coffee, and lunch. In peak season they also do evening meals. In Kickham Place behind the statue *The Basement Restaurant* (☎ 33867) is particularly popular for snacks and light lunches. It's open 8 am to 5 pm and serves Irish breakfasts costing £3.25. Hidden in St Michael's St, just off Main St, *Cranley's* (☎ 33917) is an excellent small restaurant serving things such as mixed grills for £5.50.

Getting There & Away

Rafferty Travel (☎ 51555), Main St, handles bookings for Bus Éireann and Iarnród Éireann and opens 9 am to 6 pm Monday to Saturday.

Bus Most buses stop near the Brown Trout on Abbey St, except for the Rosslare Harbour service, which stops outside Rafferty Travel. There are regular buses on the Limerick to Waterford express route. There's also one daily on weekdays in each direction between Tipperary and Shannon in County Clare.

On weekdays Kavanagh's (☎ 51563) buses travel daily from Tipperary to Dublin

It's a Long Way...

No WWI movie would be complete without some British private singing:

> It's a long way to Tipperary,
> It's a long way to go.
> It's a long way to Tipperary,
> To the sweetest girl I know...

It was written as a marching song by Englishman Jack Judge in 1912. He had never set foot in Ireland and the word 'Tipperary' was chosen only for its sound.

LIMERICK & TIPPERARY

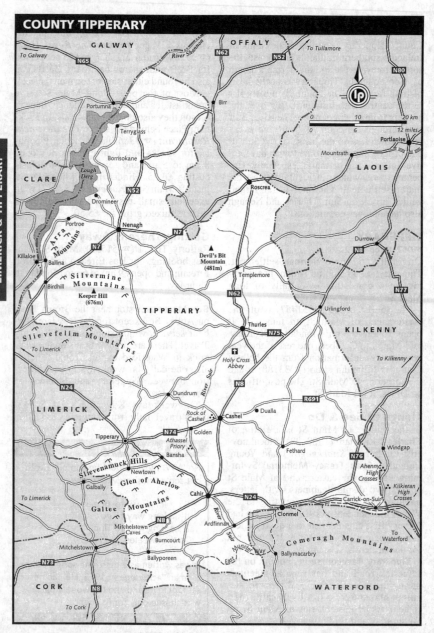

COUNTY TIPPERARY

via Cahir and Cashel. They leave at 7.45 am from outside the Marian Hall at the end of St Michael's St farthest from Main St.

Train Tipperary is on the Waterford to Limerick Junction line. There's one daily service to Cahir, Clonmel, Carrick-on-Suir, Waterford and Rosslare Harbour, and multiple connections from Limerick Junction (☎ 51406), barely 3km from Tipperary along the Limerick road, to Cork, Kerry, Waterford, Rosslare Harbour and Dublin.

GLEN OF AHERLOW & GALTEE MOUNTAINS

South of Tipperary are the Slievenamuck Hills and the Galtee Mountains, separated by the gently beautiful Glen of Aherlow. Between Tipperary and Cahir is Bansha (An Bháinseach), at the eastern end of the glen. The village marks the start of a 20km trip west to Galbally, an easy **bike ride**. It's a pleasant area for low-key **hiking**, with plenty of country accommodation. Cahir is a good base from which to explore the Galtees. The **scenic drive** through the Glen of Aherlow is signposted from Tipperary town.

Places to Stay

Ballinacourty House Caravan and Camping Park (☎ 062-56230) has excellent caravan and camping facilities, as well as a fine garden, restaurant, wine bar and tennis court. This oasis is 10km from Bansha on the R663 to Galbally and opens from late March to late October. A pitch for a tent with car costs £8 (hikers and cyclists £4) plus £1 per adult.

An Óige's *Ballydavid Wood House* (☎ 062-54148) is an old hunting lodge in the south-eastern corner of the glen 3km off the Tipperary to Cahir road, from which it's signposted, on the northern slopes of the Galtees. Beds cost £7/5.50.

Georgian *Bansha House* (☎ 062-54194) is only 200m from Bansha village and charges £28/46 for singles/doubles with breakfast.

Close by Bansha House is *Bansha Castle* (☎ 062-54187), a lovely castellated

19th-century house and former residence of some of the Butlers of Ormond. B&B costs £25 per person, dinner from £16.

Getting There & Away

Bus Éireann express bus No 55 from Limerick to Waterford via Tipperary town stops at Bansha five times daily. For details, contact Rafferty Travel (☎ 062-51555) in Tipperary town.

CASHEL

☎ 062 • pop 2475

Cashel (Caiseal Mumhan) is a prosperous market town with a staggering tourist drawcard in the Rock of Cashel. Unfortunately it's right on the main Dublin to Cork road and traffic thunders through at all hours. The good news is that the ruins you've come to admire are well away from the main road and that the high street doesn't feel quite as swamped by tourism as, say, Killarney's.

Information

The town hall in the main street contains Cashel's tourist office (☎ 61333), which opens 9.30 am to 5.30 pm on weekdays, with extended hours and weekend opening from Easter to September. The post office is at the bottom of Main St.

Rock of Cashel

The Rock of Cashel (☎ 61437) is one of Ireland's most spectacular archaeological sites. In the middle of a grassy plain, on the outskirts of Cashel a huge lump of limestone bristling with ancient fortifications rises up. Mighty stone walls encircle a complete round tower, a roofless abbey and the finest 12th-century Romanesque chapel in the country. For over a thousand years, the Rock of Cashel was a symbol of power, the base of kings and churchmen who ruled over the region and large swathes of the country.

The word 'cashel' is an anglicised version of the Irish word *'caiseal'*, meaning 'fortress', and it's easy to imagine that the site developed in territory hostile to the Church. From the Dublin road, the Rock is concealed by smaller hills until the last minute. The site is busy, especially in July and August, so go first thing in the morning or in late afternoon.

History In the 4th century, the Rock of Cashel was chosen as a base by the Eóghanachta clan from Wales, who went on to conquer much of Munster and become kings of the region. For some 400 years it rivalled Tara as a centre of power in Ireland.

The clan's links with the Church started early: St Patrick converted its leader in the 5th century in a ceremony in which he accidentally stabbed him in the foot with his crozier. Thinking this a painful initiation rite, the king bore the pain with fortitude. Possibly he was afraid to react, considering how St Patrick had reacted to unbelievers on previous occasions.

In the 10th century the clan lost possession of the Rock to the O'Brien, or Dál gCais, tribe under Brian Ború's leadership. In 1101, King Muircheartach O'Brien presented the Rock to the Church, a move designed to curry favour with the powerful bishops and to stop the Eóghanachta ever regaining the Rock, as they could never ask the Church to return such a present. So the Eóghanachta, by now the MacCarthys, moved to Cork. As a sign of goodwill Cormac MacCarthy built Cormac's Chapel in 1127 before leaving. This chapel proved to be too small. A new cathedral was built in 1169 but was replaced in the 13th century.

In 1647, the Rock fell to a Cromwellian army under Lord Inchiquin which sacked and burned its way to the top. Early in the 18th century the Protestant Church took it over for 20 years, but this was the last time the Rock was officially used as a place of worship. The abbey roof collapsed only in the late 18th or early 19th century.

Information The Rock of Cashel opens from 9 am to 7.30 pm daily, from June to mid-September; and 9.30 am to 4.30 pm (5.30 pm mid-March to June) daily, mid-September to June. Admission costs £3/1.25 and final admission is 40 minutes before closing. There are two parking spaces for disabled visitors on the Rock itself; everyone else should use the car park at the foot (£1).

Hall of the Vicars Choral The entrance to the Rock is through this 15th-century house, which contains the ticket office. A 20-minute audiovisual presentation runs every half-hour, detailing the Rock's history (there are French, German and Italian showings as well as English). The exhibits downstairs include some very rare silverware, Bronze Age axes and **St Patrick's Cross**, a badly worn 12th-century crutched cross with a crucifixion scene on one face, animals on the other. Tradition held that the kings of Cashel and Munster – including Brian Ború – were inaugurated at the base of the cross. A replica stands outside. The kitchen and dining hall upstairs contain period furniture, tapestries and paintings.

The Cathedral This 13th-century Gothic structure overshadows the other ruins. Entry is through a small porch facing the Hall of the Vicars Choral. The cathedral's western end is formed by the **Archbishop's Residence**, a 15th-century, four-storey castle which had its great hall built over the nave. Soaring above the centre of the cathedral is a huge, square tower with a turret on the south-western corner.

Scattered throughout are monuments, panels from 16th-century altar tombs and coats of arms of the Butlers. On the northern side of the choir is the recess tomb of Archbishop Hamilton. Opposite this is the tomb of Miler Mac Grath, who died in 1621. Miler was Catholic bishop of Down and Connor until 1569, when he switched to the Protestant faith and ordained himself Protestant archbishop of Cashel with Elizabeth I's blessing. Her forces were busy at the time torturing and executing his rival, the Catholic Archbishop Dermot O'Hurley.

Round Tower On the north-eastern corner of the cathedral is the sandstone 11th- or 12th-century round tower, the earliest building on the Rock. It's 28m tall and the doorway is 3.5m above the ground – perhaps for structural rather than defensive reasons.

Cormac's Chapel

Cormac's Chapel This is the Rock of Cashel's *pièce de résistance*, standing completely intact to the south of the cathedral. Built from 1127, Cormac's Chapel is small, solid, stone roofed and cruciform shaped, with an unusual square tower on either side. Compared with other churches of the same era, the chapel is sophisticated in design and displays influences from Britain and the Continent – including the square towers.

Outside are impressive Romanesque arches, richly carved. Above the north door (opposite the entrance) in the minute courtyard adjoining the cathedral is a carving of a Norman helmeted figure firing an arrow at a huge lion which has just killed two animals.

The chapel's interior is dark, its windows either blocked up – perhaps to shield the murals from light – or in the constant shadow of the cathedral. The barrel-vaulted nave is only 12m long, with a fine archway into the east chancel boasting many finely carved heads and capitals. The southern tower leads to a stone-roofed vault or croft above the nave. Inside the main door to the chapel, on the left, is the sarcophagus said to house King Cormac, dating from between 1125 and 1150. The deeply cut, interlacing design is highly developed, with motifs more commonly found on metalwork from earlier centuries.

Outside is scaffolding for restoration work on the external masonry. Inside, in the chancel, the carvings and ancient frescoes have been restored as much as possible, though not a lot remains of the frescoes.

Hore Abbey

The extensive ruins of 13th-century Hore Abbey are set in farmland less than 1km north of the base of the Rock. It was the last daughter house – a religious house affiliated to the main monastery – of the Mellifont Cistercians and was a gift from a 13th-century archbishop who expelled the Benedictine monks after dreaming that they planned to murder him. A pleasant walk (signposted) from the Rock leads to Hore Abbey, passing the O'Brien's Farmhouse Hostel.

Cashel Folk Village

A thatched blue building in Dominic St houses this small but interesting museum, which incorporates old buildings and shop fronts from around the town. Of particular interest are the model penal chapel where priests might have said mass in the days when to do so put them at risk of imprisonment, the slate-fronted republican museum room, and a traditional caravan which was home to a family of 16 until 1986. Read some of the folk remedies, such as a shamrock and dogfern paste to cure lumbago, and garlic in the shoe to ward off rheumatism.

The museum opens 9.30 am to 7.30 pm daily and admission costs £2/50p.

Other Things to See

Around town there are a number of ruins which are sometimes overlooked. To get your bearings it's worth calling into the small **heritage centre** attached to the tourist office where a model shows what Cashel looked like in the 1640s. It opens the same hours as the tourist office and admission costs £1/50p.

The first right-hand turn after leaving the Rock leads onto Dominic St, with its small **St Dominic's Friary** ruin from 1243. Unlike Hore Abbey, it has been engulfed by the town. Up John St directly opposite the Cashel Palace Hotel is **GPA Bolton Library** (GPA stands for Guinness Peat Aviation). This small building, once a chapter house in the grounds of the graceful 18th-century Protestant cathedral, is now home to valuable manuscripts and first editions. It opens 9.30 am to 5.30 pm on weekdays, year round, with extended opening hours April to September, funding permitting. Admission costs £1.50/50p.

Cashel Palace Hotel, in the main street, is a lovely Queen Anne residence built by Edward Lovett Pearce (architect of the Bank of Ireland in College Green, Dublin) for Archbishop Bolton in 1730.

Places to Stay

Hostels The IHH *O'Brien's Farmhouse Hostel* (☎ 61003), in a converted coach

LIMERICK & TIPPERARY

house on the Dundrum road, north-west of town, is friendly and well equipped, with views of the Rock and Hore Abbey to die for. Beds in reasonably spacious dorms cost £8, doubles £20. The IHH *Cashel Holiday Hostel* (☎ *62330, 6 John St*), in a quiet turning off Main St, also gets good reports. Dorm beds cost £7 to £8, the two double rooms £20 each.

B&Bs Dominic St, on the way from Main St to the Rock, has several quiet B&Bs with views of the Rock. The first you'll come to is *Abbey House* (☎ *61104*), with good facilities costing upwards of £16 per person. *Maryville* (☎ *61098*), a little farther along (it also has an entrance on Main St), charges £24/32 for singles/doubles without bath. Farther still, *Rockville House* (☎ *61760*) charges £24.50/36 for en suite rooms.

In peaceful John St, *Ashmore House* (☎ *61286*) offers rooms for £18/22.50 without bath. On Main St, *Bailey's* (☎ *61937*) is a fine Georgian town house charging £21 per person for B&B. Front rooms give good Rock views but traffic noise can be irksome. There's a restaurant in the basement. *Rosguill House* (☎ *62699*), 1km out on the Dualla road (R691), also has Rock views, plus exceptionally good breakfasts. Rooms cost upwards of £26/37 and it's open May to late October.

Hotels *Kearney's Castle Hotel* (☎ *61044, Main St*) is a 15th-century square tower once known as Quirke's Castle with singles/doubles costing upwards of £25/40. *Cashel Palace Hotel* (☎ *62707, fax 61521, Main St*) is exquisite, with an unbeatable view of the Rock; a private footpath joins the two. The bad news is that at £175 (from April to October) per double you're talking dreamland for most travellers.

Places to Eat
Despite the number of tourists flowing through, the Cashel eating scene is, with a few exceptions, fairly basic. Cashel Blue cheese is actually made at Beechmount in Fethard, but you can still buy chunks of it in the tourist office.

The Spearman Restaurant, at the Dublin end of Main St, serves meals such as lamb burgers for £7.50. *Pasta Milano*, on the terrace in Ladyswell St, serves pizzas/pastas costing upwards of £4.95/5.95; it's open until midnight at the weekend.

The best restaurant in town is *Chez Hans* (☎ *61177*), inside a converted church to the right at the end of Dominic St. A terrific dinner is likely to set you back a good £25 per person, but there's nothing for vegetarians unless they've asked in advance.

For tea and coffee, breakfast or a light lunch the best place on Main St is the *Coffee Shop* above the Bakehouse Bakery across the road from the tourist office. Just down from the Rock near Brú Ború, similar fare is available from the pink-coloured, flower-bedecked *Granny's Kitchen*, which sells cottage pie for £4.95. *O'Dowd's (Main St)* does takeaways but doesn't open till 11 am.

For good pub food try *Hannigan's*, opposite Pasta Milano, or *Dowling's* at the bottom of Main St.

Entertainment
Down the hill past the Rock car park is *Brú Ború* (☎ *61122*), a centre for traditional Irish music that serves it up Tuesday to Saturday, mid-June to mid-September. Starting at 9 pm there's music, song, dance, storytelling and *crack* galore. Admission costs £6 for the night, and there's an optional pre-show banquet.

For pub music try *Con Gleeson's*, *John Feehan's* or *Alexander Knox & Co*, all along Main St, or *Moor Lane Tavern*, behind the tourist office.

Getting There & Away
Bus Éireann runs three express buses daily between Dublin and Cork via Cahir and Fermoy, and vice versa (two on Sunday). Late June to August there are an extra four buses daily to Cahir. There's also one bus daily each way on the Cork to Athlone via Thurles, Roscrea and Birr route. Rafferty Travel (☎ *62121*), Main St, handles Bus Éireann tickets and inquiries.

Kavanagh's (☎ *51563*) has three buses daily to Dublin, the first leaving Cashel at

9.35 am. Coming back, they leave Dublin from George's Quay near Tara St Station. It also does a twice-daily run between Cashel and Clonmel, departing from Cashel at noon and 6.35 pm. Buses also go to Thurles, from where you can take a train.

Getting Around

June to September the Cashel Heritage Tram trundles around town linking up the places of interest. While this is obviously good for people who have trouble walking, it will seem disappointingly Disneyish to others. Tickets cost £3.50/1.75 from the tourist office.

The hostels hire out bicycles, as does Cashel Cycle Centre at McInerney's on Main St. Cahir and Fethard are both within cycling distance.

ATHASSEL PRIORY

Eight kilometres south-west of Cashel is Athassel Priory. This extensive and long-abandoned Norman monastery sits peacefully on the western bank of the River Suir. It was built around 1200 by William de Burgh, who wanted it to be one of the richest and most important in the country. The native Irish, in the guise of the earl of Desmond and the O'Briens, burned the priory and its accompanying town in 1319 and again in 1329. What's left today are the remains of a gatehouse, gateway, surrounding walls and the cloisters or arched passageways where monks would walk in prayer, as well as some foundations of various other monastic buildings, including the chapter house.

To get there take the N74 to the village of Golden and then head south for 2km to the priory.

CAHIR

☎ 052 • pop 2120

Cahir (pronounced 'Care', An Cathair) is 15km south of Cashel, at the eastern tip of the Galtees and on the banks of the River Suir. Dominated by its spectacular castle, Cahir is on the main Dublin to Cork road, which ensures constant heavy traffic. St Declan's Way passes through town.

Orientation & Information

Buses stop in Castle St near a large car park (50p) between the tourist office and the castle. East of Castle St, the square is ringed with shops, pubs and cafés. The post office is north of the square on Church St.

The tourist office (☎ 41453) opens 9.30 am to 1 pm and 2 to 6 pm Monday to Saturday, April to September, and also 11 am to 5 pm on Sunday, July and August. Ask for its free leaflet showing walking routes around Cahir Park.

Cahir Castle

Cahir's most noteworthy feature is the great 13th- and 15th-century castle in the town centre. One of Ireland's largest, the castle was founded by Conor O'Brien in 1142 and passed to the Butler family in 1375. Its occupants surrendered to Cromwell in 1650 without a struggle – memories of the battering the place had suffered at the hands of the earl of Essex and his meagre two cannons in 1599 were still fresh. Consequently the castle is remarkably intact. It was also extensively restored in the 1840s and again in the 1960s, when it came into state ownership. Some of John Boorman's *Excalibur* was filmed here.

The castle sits on a rocky island in the River Suir. It consists of three wards (yards) surrounded by a thick fortifying curtain wall, with the main structural towers and halls around the innermost ward. Entry is along the sloping barbican running parallel to the inner-ward wall, and then through the reception area. This opens into the small middle ward, overshadowed by the large gatehouse and keep to the right. Go through this gatehouse, under the reconstructed and fully functioning portcullis, to reach the inner ward. Its buildings are sparsely furnished, although there are small exhibitions on arms, Irish castles and Irish women in Tudor times. Don't miss the 10,000-year-old antlers of a giant Irish deer in the banqueting hall.

Beside the north-eastern tower, the small **well tower** offers the best vantage point over the river (marred, unfortunately, by a hideous grain silo with bright-red shutters).

The tower spirals down to the river and once provided a vital water supply for any extended siege.

The large garden-like outer ward has a **19th-century cottage** at the far end. This houses a short audiovisual show on other local sites of historic interest.

Cahir Castle, run by Dúchas, opens from 9 am to 7.30 pm daily, mid-June to mid-September; 9.30 am to 5.30 pm daily, April to mid-June and mid-September to mid-October; and 9.30 am to 4.30 pm daily, mid-October to March. Admission costs £2/1.

Afterwards, cross the bridge beside the castle and follow the road for five minutes until you come to the ruins of 13th-century **Cahir Abbey** on the right.

Swiss Cottage

A pleasant riverside path from behind the car park wanders 2km south to Cahir Park and the Swiss Cottage, also run by Dúchas. The Swiss Cottage is an exquisite thatched *cottage ornée*, the best in Ireland, surrounded by roses, lavender and honeysuckle. It was designed by Regency architect John Nash as a place of retreat for Richard Butler, 12th Baron Caher, and his wife. In accordance with contemporary French ideas, the cottage was supposed to look as if it had sprung fully formed from the earth; straight lines and symmetry were abhorred and your guide will point out all the tricks used to make it seem more 'natural'. The 30-minute (compulsory) guided tours are thoroughly enjoyable.

The cottage opens 10 am to 6 pm daily, May to September; and 10 am to 1 pm and 2 to 4.30 pm (5 pm in April) Tuesday to Sunday, late March to April and in October and November. Admission costs £2/1.

John Nash was also responsible for **St Paul's Church** (1820), whose graceful spire is visible from Cahir Bridge in the town centre.

Places to Stay

Camping At Moorstown on the N24 between Cahir (6km) and Clonmel (9km) you can camp at *The Apple Caravan and Camping Park* (☎ 41459), on a fruit farm.

The charge is £3.75 per adult and £1.75 per child. It's open early January to November.

Hostels Near Cahir there are two independent hostels. The run-of-the-mill IHH *Lisakyle Hostel* (☎ 41963) is 2km south of town on a back road to Ardfinnan past the Swiss Cottage. Dorm beds cost £8 and there's one double costing £18. Maurice Condon's shop opposite the post office in Church St handles inquiries and arranges lifts to the hostel.

The remote IHO *Kilcoran Farm Hostel* (☎ 41288), on an organic farm, is 6km west of Cahir, signposted off the N8 Mitchelstown road at the Top petrol station, from which it's 1km. It has free showers, kitchen facilities and donkey rides for kids. Beds cost £7.50 per person.

The nearest An Óige hostel is *Ballydavid Wood House*, 10km away (see Glen of Aherlow & Galtee Mountains earlier in this chapter).

B&Bs & Hotels One kilometre along the Cashel road, *The Rectory* (☎ 41406) is a lovely Georgian house with rooms costing upwards of £17 per person. It opens May to October. Close by is *Ashling* (☎ 41601), charging £25/33 for singles/doubles for B&B.

At Cahir you can stay the night in a castle as well as simply view one. The 16th-century *Carrigeen Castle* (☎ 41370), 1km out on the Cork road (N8), is often mistaken for Cahir Castle. It's actually a B&B, with singles/doubles costing upwards of £28/36 without breakfast.

In the town centre, *Castle Court Hotel* (☎ 41210, fax 42333, Church St) is a pleasant family-run hotel costing £25/40. Six kilometres along the Cork road, busy *Kilcoran Lodge Hotel* (☎ 41288, fax 41994) has a pool and health club. B&B costs upwards of £38.50/70.

Places to Eat

Opposite Cahir Castle car park and above a craft shop is *Crock of Gold*, a self-service restaurant offering breakfasts (£3.75) and light meals until 8 pm. Frillier and more inviting is **Kay's Coffee Shop** *(The Square)*, where cottage pie costs £3.99. Also in The Square, **Galtee Inn** serves soup and a roll (£1.60) and main courses (£4.95). **Italian Connection** *(Castle St)* offers pizzas/pastas costing upwards of £3.95/5.35. **Roma Café**, just off The Square, serves burgers and sandwiches.

Getting There & Away
Bus Cahir is on several Bus Éireann (☎ 062-51555) express bus routes, including Dublin to Cork, Limerick to Waterford, Galway to Waterford, Kilkenny to Cork and Cork to Athlone. There are frequent daily buses to Cashel. Buses stop near the Crock of Gold restaurant.

Kavanagh's (☎ 062-51563) buses travel Monday to Saturday via Cahir between Tipperary town, Cashel and Dublin.

Train Monday to Saturday, one train daily on the Waterford to Limerick Junction line stops at Cahir, with connections to Cork, Rosslare and Tralee. For details, contact Thurles train station (☎ 0504-21733).

MITCHELSTOWN CAVES
The Galtee Mountains are sandstone, but along the southern side runs a narrow band of limestone which is home to the Mitchelstown Caves. They're near Burncourt, 16km south-west of Cahir and signposted on the road to Mitchelstown (Baile Mhistéala). Far superior to Kilkenny's Dunmore Caves and yet less developed for tourists, these caves are among the most extensive in the country.

In 1833, Michael Condon was quarrying limestone when he lost his crowbar down a crack in the rock. His efforts to retrieve it opened up the system now called the New Caves. Another cave system nearby – now called the Old Caves – was already known to have been used in prehistoric times. Although the Old Caves contain the system's largest chamber, the New Caves form the basis of the tour. Exploration begins through Condon's original opening. Internal temperatures are pretty constant at around 13°C. Underground, there are nearly 2km of passages and spectacular chambers full of textbook formations, inventively labelled from classical and biblical sources.

The caves (☎ 052-67246) open 10 am to 6 pm daily. Call at English's farmhouse opposite the car park for tickets and a tour guide (a tour requires a minimum of two people). Admission costs £3/1.

Places to Stay
Six kilometres due north of the caves on the slopes of the Galtees is the An Óige **Mountain Lodge Hostel** *(☎ 052-67277)*, north off the main Mitchelstown to Cahir road. It's open March to September and is a handy base for exploring the Galtees. Beds cost £6.50/5.

Getting There & Away
Daily Bus Éireann (☎ 062-51555) express buses from Dublin to Cork or Athlone will drop you at the Mountain Lodge Hostel gate.

CLONMEL
☎ 052 • pop 16,000
Clonmel (Cluain Meala, 'Meadows of Honey') is Tipperary's largest, liveliest, most cosmopolitan town. If you're coming from Carrick-on-Suir watch out for Bulmer's cider orchards alongside the road.

Orientation & Information
Clonmel's heart lies on the northern bank of the River Suir. Set back from the quays and running parallel to the river, the main street runs from east to west, starting off as Parnell St and becoming Mitchel St and O'Connell St before passing under West Gate and becoming Irishtown and Abbey Rd. Running north off this long thoroughfare is Gladstone St, with lots of shops and pubs.

The tourist office (☎ 22960), opposite Clonmel Arms Hotel, opens 9.30 am to 5.30 pm on weekdays. The post office is in a courtyard of the one-time county jail at the northern end of Emmet St, which runs north off Mitchel St.

Walking Tour
A good starting point for a whip round town is **Hearn's Hotel**, the former headquarters of

LIMERICK & TIPPERARY

LIMERICK & TIPPERARY

Charles Bianconi

Over the centuries Clonmel's wealth has attracted many businesspeople, one of whom is now synonymous with Clonmel. Charles Bianconi (1786–1875) arrived in Ireland from northern Italy, aged 16 and sent by his father in an attempt to break a liaison with a young lady who was already spoken for. In 1815, he set up a coach service between Clonmel and Cahir, and the company quickly grew, becoming a nationwide passenger and mail carrier. For putting Clonmel on the map, Bianconi was twice elected mayor. The company's former headquarters is now Hearn's Hotel on Parnell St – Hearn was an assistant to Bianconi.

Bianconi's coach business. South of Parnell St in Nelson St is the **County Courthouse** designed by Richard Morrison in 1802. It was here that the Young Irelanders of 1848, including Thomas Francis Meagher, were tried and sentenced to be transported to Australia. In July and August it's possible to see some of the most famous trials recreated; phone Molly Daly on ☎ 23903 for details.

Back on Parnell St the faded **County Museum** exhibits the shirt worn by Michael Hogan, who was captain of the Tipperary Gaelic Football team in Croke Park when they played Dublin in November 1920. In retaliation for the deaths of 14 British army intelligence officers, the British police auxiliaries (Black and Tans) opened fire on the crowd and players during a match, killing Hogan and 13 others. This was the first of several Bloody Sundays. The museum opens 10 am to 1 pm and 2 to 5 pm Tuesday to Saturday. Admission is free.

West along Mitchel St (past the pistachio-coloured town hall with its statue commemorating the 1798 Rising) and south down Abbey St is the **Franciscan friary**. The 15th-century tower is surrounded by newer work dating only from 1848 and 1884. Inside, near the door, is a 1533 Butler tomb depicting a knight and his lady. There's some fine modern stained glass, especially in St Anthony's Chapel to the north.

Back up on Mitchel St at the junction with Sarsfield St is the **Main Guard**, a Butler courthouse from 1674, based on a design by Christopher Wren. It's undergoing major restoration. Turn south down Bridge St and cross the river, following the road round

until it opens out at **Lady Blessington's Bath**, a picturesque stretch of the river, excellent for picnicking.

Return to O'Connell St. Spanning the far end is the **West Gate**, an 1831 reconstruction of an earlier town gate. On the eastern side is a plaque commemorating Laurence Sterne (1713–68), a native of the town and author of *A Sentimental Journey* and *Tristram Shandy*.

Just before the arch is Wolfe Tone St, which heads north past **White Memorial Theatre**, once the Wesleyan chapel, to **Old St Mary's Church**, built in 1204 by William de Burgh and boasting a fine octagonal tower. To the northern and western sides are overgrown stretches of the 14th-century town wall.

On the other side of West Gate is **Irishtown**, named after those native Irish who worked inside the town but were forbidden to live within its walls.

Places to Stay

Camping The *Power's the Pot Caravan and Camping Park* (☎ 23085) has a Clonmel address even though it's 9km to the south-east on the northern slopes of the Comeragh Mountains, well inside County Waterford. To get there, cross south over the river in Clonmel and then follow the road to Rathgormuck. The park has a good restaurant and 'beds are available in bad weather'. A pitch for a tent for two and a car costs £7 (hikers and cyclists £4).

B&Bs & Hotels Many B&Bs are on Marlfield Rd, due west of Irishtown and Abbey Rd. *Benuala* (☎ 22158) charges upwards of

£17/30 for singles/doubles, while *Hillcourt* (☎ 21029) costs from £16/30. *Amberville* (☎ 21470), on Glenconnor Rd, north off Western Rd beside St Luke's Hospital, is within walking distance of the centre. B&B costs upwards of £22.50/32.

Hearn's Hotel (☎ 21611, fax 21135), right in the town centre, offers singles/doubles costing £42/72.50. The fine *Clonmel Arms Hotel* (☎ 211233, fax 21526) is down from the main street towards the river on Sarsfield St and costs from £38 per person for B&B.

South of the River Suir, *Hotel Minella* (☎ 22388, fax 24381) is a three-star hotel with four hectares of gardens, almost 2km east of town on the Coleville road (follow the South Quays east). B&B costs upwards of £55/70.

A good choice, 6km from Clonmel, is 16th-century *Knocklofty Country House Hotel* (☎ 38222, fax 38300) set in 42 hectares of parkland beside the River Suir. Rooms cost £45 to £55 per person.

Places to Eat
Cosy *Niamh's (Mitchel St)* is a coffee shop offering dishes such as coronation-chicken pitta (£2.95), while *Angela's (Abbey St)* is good for light lunches and snacks, with baguettes costing £3.50. In Marystone Centre off Gladstone St, *Coyle's Coffee House* is open until 5.30 pm, serving snacks such as beans on toast (£1.60).

Bar food is available in *Tierney's Pub (O'Connell St)*, with seafood pancake costing £5.75 and vegetarian dishes £4.25. *Barry's*, close by, serves Tex-Mex meals; beef tacos cost £6.95. *Mulcahy's (Gladstone St)*, a vast pub and restaurant, opens 10 am to 10 pm and serves standard meals such as sirloin steak (£10) or roast beef and Yorkshire pudding (£4.75). *Clonmel Arms Hotel (Sarsfield St)* is one of the best places in town for reasonably priced bar lunches; Singapore chow mein costs £4.30.

Emerald Garden (☎ 24270, *O'Connell St)* is a Chinese restaurant that's cheaper for lunch than dinner; its takeaway offshoot is across the road near the West Gate. *La Scala* (☎ 24147, *Market St)*, off Gladstone

St, is an Italian restaurant with pastas costing £5.50 and fish dishes upwards of £7.50. Another Italian place is *Catalpa (Sarsfield St)*, where pizzas/pastas cost upwards of £4.20/4.75.

Entertainment
Lonergan's (O'Connell St) has music on Monday night. Many other bars, such as *Coachman (Parnell St)* and *Mulcahy's (Gladstone St)*, have local bands and Irish music in the summer.

Blue Anchor Lane in Clonmel Arms Hotel is a Friday and Saturday nightclub.

South Tipperary Arts Centre (☎ 27877, *Nelson St)*, off Parnell St, has temporary art exhibitions.

Spectator Sports
Clonmel is the heartland of Irish greyhound racing and coursing. At the eastern end of Parnell St on Davis St is the greyhound track, which has dog racing at 8 pm Monday and Thursday. Powerstown Park Racecourse is north of town and has 11 meetings a year. For details of fixtures call ☎ 21422.

Getting There & Away
Bus Bus Éireann (☎ 051-79000) has two buses daily each way between Dublin and Cork, with more-numerous services to Waterford, Limerick and Kilkenny. Rafferty Travel (☎ 22622) acts as Bus Éireann's ticket agency and the bus stop is at the train station. Kavanagh's (☎ 062-51563) has twice-daily buses between Cashel and Clonmel.

Train The train station (☎ 21982) is north of Gladstone St on Prior Park Rd, within walking distance of the town centre. Clonmel is on the Cork to Limerick to Rosslare Harbour line, with one train each way daily Monday to Saturday. There's no direct train link to Dublin, but there are connections from Waterford or Limerick Junction.

AROUND CLONMEL
Directly south of Clonmel are the Comeragh Mountains over the border in County Waterford. There's a fine scenic route south

to Ballymacarbry and the Nire Valley. Instead of coming back the same way you can do a circle, heading down to Ballymacarbry from the east and heading back up to Clonmel from the western side. For more details, see Northern County Waterford in County Waterford.

The **East Munster Way** (see Walking in the Activities chapter) passes through Clonmel following the old towpath along the River Suir. At Sir Thomas Bridge the trail cuts south away from the river and into the Comeraghs to Harney's Crossroads before rejoining the River Suir again at Kilsheelan Bridge, from where it follows the towpath all the way to Carrick-on-Suir. From Clonmel, you can take shorter walks along parts of the trail using the same towpath.

The main road between Clonmel and Carrick-on-Suir follows the river through some lovely countryside dotted with ruined 16th- and 17th-century tower houses and roofless medieval churches.

FETHARD
☎ 052 • pop 980
Fethard, 14km north of Clonmel on the River Clashawley, is a sleepy community grown rich from the proceeds of the local stud farm. Fethard is sprinkled with medieval ruins but hasn't really caught on to the potential of tourism, making it a pleasant place for those seeking peace and quiet.

Things to See
The single most striking survivor from medieval times is **Holy Trinity Church**, off Main St through a cast-iron gateway. The church dates from the 13th century and boasts a sturdy tower that looks as if it was built to defend the church, although the clergy probably lived in it. Surrounding the churchyard is a stretch of reconstructed **medieval wall** complete with 15th-century turrets. Unfortunately, to get into the churchyard you must collect a key from Whyte's supermarket in Main St, while to get into the church you must collect a separate key from Dr Stoke's surgery at the eastern end of Main St. Almost next to the church in Main St is

the 17th-century **town hall**, with some fine coats of arms mounted on the façade.

The greatest concentration of medieval remains can be found south of the church at the end of Watergate St. Beside the Castle Inn are the ruins of several fortified **tower houses** dating from the 17th century. Better still you can see the entire length of the **town wall** dating from the 15th or 16th centuries, although parts are even older. Near Watergate Bridge a **sheila-na-gig** is set into a section of the wall. East along Abbey St is the 14th-century **Augustinian friary**, now in use as the Catholic church and with some fine medieval stained glass.

Fethard's only signposted attraction is the small **Folk Museum** in the old train station on the Cashel road. It houses a collection of agricultural appliances and hosts a Sunday market. It opens 10.30 am to 5 pm daily, June to August; and 12.45 to 5 pm on Sunday only, the rest of the year. Admission costs £2/1.

Places to Stay & Eat
The Gateway (☎ 31701, Rocklow Rd) is a small B&B near the ruined 15th-century North Gate with singles/doubles costing £22.50/32.

G&T's, at the western end of Main St, will do you sandwiches (£1.50) and burgers costing upwards of £5. For something a little bit more formal there's *J's Restaurant* (☎ 31176) next door. It opens for dinner 6 to 10 pm Wednesday to Sunday and for lunch 12.30 to 2.30 pm on Sunday.

Getting There & Away
There's no public transport to Fethard but it would make a pleasant cycle ride from Cashel, 15km to the west.

CARRICK-ON-SUIR
☎ 051 • pop 5145
The market town of Carrick-on-Suir (Carraig na Siúire), 20km east of Clonmel, grew to considerable importance through the brewing and wool industries during the Middle Ages. For a long time, the seven-arched 15th-century bridge was the first crossing point on the river for the 40km

from the Suir's mouth at Waterford Harbour. In the 18th century, the population was 11,000, almost twice what it is today. Compared to Clonmel, Carrick-on-Suir is quiet and unsophisticated, perhaps because the N24 bypasses the town centre. The town is surrounded by rich green farmland, with the Comeragh Mountains in the distance.

Most places make a fuss of their famous inhabitants only after their demise, but Carrick-on-Suir was quick to honour Sean Kelly, one of the world's greatest cyclists of the late 1980s. The town square now bears his name, as does the sports centre.

From Carrick-on-Suir the East Munster Way winds its way west to Clonmel before heading south into Waterford. For more details see Walking in the Activities chapter.

Information

Off Main St through a cast-iron gate, an old church houses the tourist office (☎ 640200), which opens 9 am to 1 pm and 2 to 5 pm Monday to Saturday, and 2 to 5 pm on Sunday, March to October. There's also a small **heritage centre** here but it makes little attempt to provide a narrative or explain its ragbag of exhibits. Consequently the £1/50p charge isn't really worth it.

Ormond Castle

Carrick-on-Suir was once the property of the Butlers, the earls of Ormond, who built the castle on the banks of the river at the eastern end of Castle St in the 14th century. Anne Boleyn, the second of Henry VIII's six wives, is rumoured to have been born here, though many other castles claim this distinction. She was the great-granddaughter of the 7th earl of Ormond. The Elizabethan mansion next to the castle was built by the 10th earl of Ormond, Black Tom Butler, in anticipation of a visit by his cousin, Queen Elizabeth I, who unfortunately never got round to seeing the result of all his efforts.

Some of the rooms have fine 16th-century stuccowork, especially the Long Gallery with its depictions of Elizabeth and the Butler coat of arms. Considering the turmoil of the period, it's interesting to note

the house's almost complete lack of defences. Indeed this is Ireland's only example of the sort of Tudor manor house common in more settled England. Unfortunately, the Dúchas-owned castle opens only 9.30 am to 6.30 pm daily, mid-June to September. Admission costs £2/1.

Places to Stay

Camping The small *Carrick-on-Suir Caravan and Camping Park* (☎ 640461) is at Ballyrichard off the Kilkenny road (N76). A tent site plus car costs £7 (hikers and cyclists £3.50).

B&Bs & Hotels On John St, nor far from the Greenside bus stop, *Fatima House* (☎ 640298) offers singles/doubles costing £20/38.

The large *Carraig Hotel* (☎ 641455, fax 641604, Main St) charges upwards of £40 per person for B&B. Spacious and more modern is *The Bell and Salmon Arms* (☎ 645555, 95-97 Main St) with singles/doubles costing £33/55.

Places to Eat

At the Sean Kelly Square end of Main St, *The Weir* is a pleasant teashop which serves soup and good brown bread costing £1.60 and lunch specials costing £4.50. Most of the Main St pubs do lunches. *Europa*, also on Main St, does takeaways; fish and chips costs £3.

Weavers Restaurant in the Carraig Hotel is probably the best place to eat. Steak costs upwards of £9.35 and there's a good vegetarian selection; the three-course dinner will set you back £12.95.

Entertainment

On Main St, *N Cooney* is an atmospheric old bar. *The Bell and Salmon Arms* puts on traditional music from around 9 pm on Wednesday. There's line dancing at *Carraig Hotel* from 8 to 11 pm on Wednesday. The drab *Strand Theatre*, by the new bridge, doubles as a cinema.

Getting There & Away

Bus Bus Éireann (☎ 79000) has extensive

LIMERICK & TIPPERARY

buses to Carrick-on-Suir. The bus No 55 between Limerick and Waterford serves Tipperary town, Cahir, Clonmel and Carrick-on-Suir five to six times daily, with connections to Galway and Rosslare Harbour. Bus No 7 from Clonmel to Dublin via Carrick-on-Suir and Kilkenny stops up to four times daily, with connections to Cork. Buses stop at Greenside, the park beside the N24 road.

Train There's one train daily Monday to Saturday on the Cork to Rosslare Harbour line via Limerick Junction and Waterford. For information contact Thurles train station (☎ 0504-21733).

AHENNY & KILKIERAN HIGH CROSSES

Roughly 5km and 8km north of Carrick-on-Suir and signposted off the road to Windgap are the two groups of high crosses at Ahenny and Kilkieran.

At Ahenny the two impressive crosses are both 4m tall and date from the 8th century. Unusually, they're almost exclusively covered in an interlacing design in high relief. The more typical religious scenes appear only on the base. The crosses are said to represent the transition from the older abstract designs of high crosses to the pictorial scenes found on many later crosses.

Another odd feature is the removable capstones, sometimes known as mitres (bishops' hats). Legend has it that these caps can cure migraine headaches if placed on the sufferer's head. Given the size of the stones, the victim would have more than migraine to worry about!

About 2km nearer Carrick-on-Suir are the three Kilkieran crosses. The western cross is similar to those in Ahenny: 4m tall, richly decorated and with mitre intact. The second is extremely plain.

The most interesting is the needle-like Long Shaft Cross, in a shape unique in Ireland. At the far end of the cemetery is **St Kieran's Well**, whose waters are said to cure headaches. There must have been a plague of headaches, given the plethora of cures to be found locally.

THURLES

☎ 0504 • pop 6685

Thurles (Durlas), a large market town 22km north of Cashel, was founded by the Butlers in the 13th century. Little of note has been built since and, Liberty Square, the town square, is little more than an ugly car park.

The tourist information desk (☎ 23579) is in the same building as the Lár na Páirce museum on the Cashel road south off Liberty Square. It opens 9.30 am to 1 pm and 2 to 5 pm on weekdays, May to September; it also opens at the weekend if there's a Gaelic football or hurling match on.

Things to See

The ruins of two square tower houses survive: 15th-century **Barry's Castle** by the bridge and **Black Castle** at the opposite end of Liberty Square, behind the shops. An incongruous **bird sanctuary** sits on an island in the middle of the River Suir. About 200m farther on is the Catholic **Cathedral of the Assumption**, built in the 1860s in the Italian Romanesque style.

In Liberty Square is **Hayes Hotel** (now being refurbished). Here, as every Irish schoolchild learns, the Gaelic Athletic Association (GAA) was founded in 1884 to foster the pursuit of Irish sports and pastimes, particularly Gaelic football and hurling, which it continues to oversee. Over the years, the GAA has been the most successful of the Gaelic revivalist groups. **Lár na Páirce** (☎ 23579), on the Cashel road, is a museum of Gaelic games, with a 20-minute video of game highlights. It opens the same hours as the tourist information desk and admission costs £2.50/1.50.

Getting There & Away

Bus Éireann (☎ 061-418855) bus No 71 stops at Thurles once daily between Cork and Athlone, with connections to Cahir, Roscrea and Birr. There are frequent trains to Thurles (☎ 21733) on the Dublin to Limerick and Dublin to Cork lines.

HOLY CROSS ABBEY

The picturesque Cistercian Holy Cross Abbey is 6km south-west of Thurles beside the River Suir. The abbey was in ruins until the early 1970s, but the cloisters and chapels were restored and now form a living church again. Though founded in 1168, the buildings you see today date from the 15th century, when the abbey was largely remodelled. The ground plan is typically Cistercian: a fine cruciform church with a square tower and cloisters to the east. Inside the church, look out for the small fleurs-de-lis and other symbols carved on the old stone pillars, the individual trademarks of the stonemasons. There's also a fine medieval fresco showing a hunting scene.

The abbey complex includes a tourist information office and café. Holy Cross Abbey is signposted from Thurles and Cashel.

ROSCREA
☎ 0505 • pop 4380
For somewhere to break your journey between Dublin and Limerick, the medium-sized town of Roscrea (Ros Cré) is more inviting than Nenagh. On the eastern edge of the county, Roscrea, like Mountrath in County Laois, can be used as a base for exploring the Slieve Bloom Mountains to the north-east. Although the main Limerick to Dublin road cuts through the town, the wide streets are better able than those in smaller towns to cope with the traffic.

Roscrea owes its beginnings to a 5th-century monk, St Crónán, who set up a way station for the travelling poor. Most of the historical structures are on or near the main street, Castle St.

Things to See
Coming into the town centre from the Dublin side, you see a truncated **round tower** on one side of the road. On the other side are the remains of St Crónán's second monastery: the gable end of **St Crónán's Church** with its finely worked stone Romanesque doorway. The rest of the church was torn down in 1812.

A **high cross** dating from the 12th century normally stands in the churchyard but has been removed for restoration. The site of St Crónán's first monastery is almost

A Relic of the True Cross

Holy Cross Abbey was once home to a relic of the True Cross, a splinter of wood said to be from Jesus' cross. It was kept in a golden shrine and attracted pilgrims to the abbey from its foundation in 1168. The splinter was said to have been presented by Pope Pascal II to the king of Munster, Murtagh O'Brien, in the early 12th century. It was the only cross relic in the country and was passed on to the nuns of the Ursuline Convent in Blackrock, Cork, in the 19th century, where it remains.

2km east of town and south of the main Dublin road.

The Book of Dímma, a 7th-century illuminated manuscript that originated here, can now be seen in Trinity College, Dublin.

In the centre of town is the Dúchas-restored 13th-century **castle**, with the substantial remains of a gatehouse, walls and towers. Inside the courtyard stands austere **Damer House**, the Queen Anne-style residence of the Damer family, which houses **Roscrea Heritage Centre** (☎ 21850). This contains several interesting exhibitions, including one on the medieval monasteries of the midlands and another on early-20th-century farming life. It opens 9.30 am to 5.45 pm daily, June to September, and admission costs £2.50/1.

Abbey St has considerable remains of a 15th-century **Franciscan friary**. Nearby, in Rosemary Square, is Roscrea's answer to Brussels' Mannequin Pis, a fountain with four cherubs pouring water out of urns.

Places to Stay & Eat
If you want to stay here, *Grant's Hotel* (☎ 23300, fax 23209), opposite the castle, offers B&B costing £40/70 for singles/doubles. *Waterfront Coffee Shop and Gallery*, signposted as you walk from the castle to the round tower, serves soup (£1.70), sandwiches (£1.50) or light lunches such as seafood tagliatelli (£5.50).

Getting There & Away

Frequent Bus Éireann (☎ 01-836 6111) express buses stop at Roscrea between Dublin (two hours) and Limerick (one hour). There are also daily buses to Athlone, Carrick-on-Shannon, Roscommon, Sligo, Thurles, Cahir and Cork.

Two Dublin to Limerick trains stop at Roscrea daily. For details ring Thurles train station (☎ 0504-21733).

LOUGH DERG

The 130 sq km Lough Derg, a popular boating and fishing area, marks the border between Counties Tipperary and Clare and extends north to County Galway. The **Lough Derg Way** begins in Limerick city and ends at the village of Dromineer in Tipperary (see Walking in the Activities chapter).

If you're heading north-east from Limerick city towards Nenagh it's more enjoyable to take the scenic route from Birdhill along the River Shannon to Ballina and then follow the road between the eastern edge of Lough Derg and the Arra Mountains rather than to follow the N7 all the way. Ballina is joined by the Shannon Bridge to the heritage town of **Killaloe** in County Clare (see Killaloe & Around in the County Clare chapter).

NENAGH & AROUND

☎ 067 • pop 5530

Nenagh (An tAonach) is a busy, rather dreary town on the main Dublin to Limerick road and blighted by heavy traffic. Most street names are in Gaelic.

The tourist office (☎ 31610), on Connolly St (Sraid ui Chonghaile), opens 9.30 am to 1 pm and 2 to 5.30 pm Monday to Saturday, May to September, and stocks a good free town-trail map.

Things to See

In the early 13th century **Nenagh Castle** was the seat of the first butler of Ireland, Theobald fitzWalter, and it remained in the family's possession for 400 years. The fitzWalters changed their name to Butler and in the late 14th century moved their principal seat of power to Kilkenny Castle. All that remains of their castle at Nenagh is a striking circular donjon, or tower, dating from 1217. It's over 30m tall; the final 8m was added by the bishop of Killaloe in 1860.

Across the road is a Doric courthouse and beside it a convent, originally a prison. Some of the buildings now house **Nenagh Heritage Centre** (☎ 32633), which is in two parts. The first, and most interesting, is the Gatehouse Gaol, where 17 men were hanged between 1842 and 1858. You can inspect the cells of the condemned and read about their crimes, before gazing on their last drop. Along the driveway is the octagonal Governor's House, which contains good mock-ups of an old country schoolroom, a pub/shop, a kitchen and a dairy.

The centre opens 9.30 am to 5 pm on weekdays, March to late September. Admission costs £2/1.

Getting There & Away

Bus Buses to Nenagh stop in Banba Square in the town centre; some also stop at the train station. Frequent Bus Éireann express buses between Dublin and Limerick stop in Nenagh. A less frequent daily service runs from Tralee to Roscrea, Birr and Athlone via Nenagh. A Monday to Saturday service runs between Nenagh and Limerick via Killaloe. In July and August, the Galway to Rosslare Harbour bus also stops at Nenagh.

Rapid Express Coaches (☎ 26266) runs up to four buses daily to Dublin via Roscrea, Portlaoise and Kildare, leaving from near Slattery's clothing store in Pearse St.

Train The station is on the Thurles side of town. Twice-daily Dublin to Limerick trains stop here Monday to Saturday (one on Sunday). For details ring Thurles train station (☎ 0504-21733).

County Kilkenny

The verdant farming county of Kilkenny is peppered with solid stone walls and medieval ruins. The Normans liked this part of Ireland and settled here in large numbers, leaving their stamp on Kilkenny town, Ireland's most enchanting medieval settlement. The county's most attractive areas are along the Rivers Nore and Barrow, on which there are some charming villages such as Inistioge and Graiguenamanagh. Jerpoint Abbey and Kells Priory are two of the country's finest medieval monastic settlements.

Since medieval times, Kilkenny's history has been inextricably linked with the fortunes of one Anglo-Norman family, the Butlers, earls of Ormond. After arriving in 1171, they made the region their own, promoting first the Norman cause and then that of the English royal household. They were based in Kilkenny town.

Walking the stretch of the South Leinster Way that crosses southern Kilkenny offers an opportunity to see rural Ireland at its prettiest.

Kilkenny

☎ 056 • pop 18,696

Kilkenny is perhaps the most attractive large town in the country, although, with less than 20,000 inhabitants, it's far from being the largest; its status has more to do with its role in the past than in the present. Still, modern Kilkenny is a vibrant cultural centre, renowned throughout Ireland for its devotion to the visual and musical arts.

Despite being ransacked by Cromwell during his 1650 visit, Kilkenny retains some of its medieval ground plan, particularly the narrow streets, which can lead to nasty traffic jams. The town's Irish name is Cill Chainnigh after the monastery of St Canice (Cainneach) which existed here in the 6th century. The saint's name is also attached to the town's splendid medieval

Highlights

- Visit Jerpoint Abbey and Kells Priory, two of the finest medieval monastic settlements in Ireland

- Explore the Rivers Nore and Barrow, by which you'll find charming villages such as Inistioge with its 10-arched stone bridge

- Spend time in Kilkenny town, perhaps the most attractive large town in Ireland

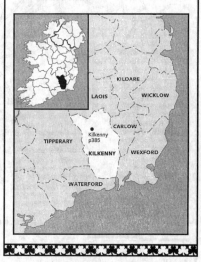

cathedral. Overlooking a sweeping bend in the River Nore, Kilkenny Castle is the other 'must' for visitors. Kilkenny is sometimes called the 'Marble City' because of the local black limestone seen to most striking effect in the cathedral.

HISTORY

In the 5th century, St Kieran is said to have visited Kilkenny and, on the site of the present Kilkenny Castle, challenged the chieftains of Ossory to accept the Christian faith.

KILKENNY

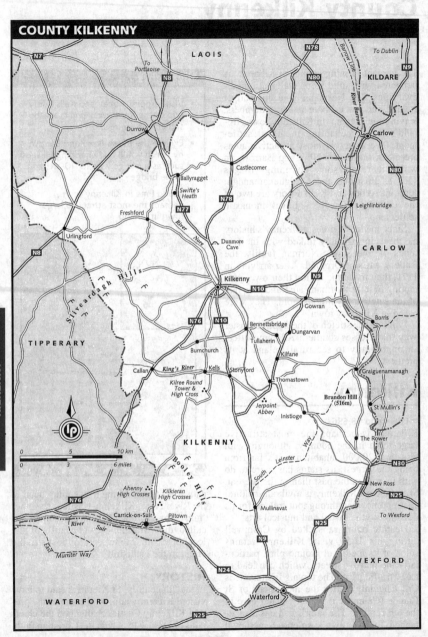

COUNTY KILKENNY

LAOIS

N7

To Portlaoise

N8

N78

Barrow Line

To Dublin

KILDARE

N9

River Barrow

Durrow

Carlow

N80

Castlecomer

Ballyragget

Swifte's Heath

N78

Leighlinbridge

Freshford

N77

River Nore

CARLOW

Urlingford

N8

Dunmore Cave

Kilkenny

N9

Slieveardagh Hills

Gowran

Borris

N76

N10

Bennettsbridge

Dungarvan

TIPPERARY

Burnchurch

Tullaherin

Kilfane

Callan

King's River

Kells

Stonyford

Graiguenamanagh

Kilree Round Tower & High Cross

Thomastown

Brandon Hill (516m)

St Mullin's

Jerpoint Abbey

Inistioge

KILKENNY

The Rower

Booley Hills

South Leinster Way

N30

Ahenny High Crosses

Kilkieran High Crosses

New Ross

N76

N25

Carrick-on-Suir

Piltown

Mullinavat

To Wexford

River Suir

N9

Munster Way

N24

WEXFORD

WATERFORD

Waterford

N25

0   5   10 km
0   3   6 miles

The Butler Family

Kilkenny town and Castle are intimately associated with the Butler family, the earls of Ormond. This Anglo-Norman clan were originally known as the Walters but changed their name after Theobald fitzWalter was given the title of chief butler of Ireland by Henry II in 1185. With the title came the butlerage, or duty, charged on all wine imported into Ireland and England. When Walter Butler was strapped for cash in 1811, he sold the right for nearly £216,000, an extraordinary sum in those days. The three wine glasses on the family shield commemorate this important source of family wealth.

The Butlers owned vast tracts of land in Tipperary and Kilkenny. During Henry VIII's reign, their power extended across much of southern Ireland, but they lost out under Cromwell when the earl was exiled. Even so, his wife, Lady Ormond, managed to hang on to the estates: because her treacherous husband wasn't in control, Cromwell didn't take away the family's positions or titles.

The Butlers bounced back with the accession of Charles II in 1660 (James Butler was a great friend of the monarch) and picked the victorious side at the Battle of the Boyne in 1690, only to go down in flames when they backed a planned Spanish invasion of England in 1714. Although they later reclaimed some of their influence, they never again reached their earlier importance. Both Tipperary and Kilkenny have numerous castles built by the family, including Carrick-on-Suir Castle (in Tipperary), Ireland's finest Elizabethan mansion.

St Canice established his monastery here in the 6th century. Kilkenny consolidated its importance in the 13th century under William Marshall, the earl of Pembroke and son-in-law of the Norman conqueror Strongbow. Kilkenny Castle was built to secure a crossing point on the Nore.

During the Middle Ages, Kilkenny was intermittently the unofficial capital of Ireland, with its own Anglo-Norman Parliament. In 1366 the Parliament passed the so-called Statutes of Kilkenny, a set of draconian laws aimed at preventing the assimilation of the increasingly assertive Anglo-Normans into Irish society. Anglo-Normans were prohibited from marrying the native Irish, taking part in Irish sports, speaking or dressing like the Irish or playing any Irish music. Any breach of the law resulted in the confiscation of Anglo-Norman property and death to the native Irish: Ireland's own version of apartheid.

Although the laws remained theoretically in force for over 200 years, they were never enforced with any great effectiveness and did little to halt the absorption of the Anglo-Normans into Irish culture.

During the 1640s, Kilkenny sided with the Catholic royalists in the English Civil War. The 1641 Confederation of Kilkenny, an uneasy alliance of native Irish and Anglo-Normans, aimed to bring about the return of land and power to Catholics. After Charles I's execution, Cromwell besieged Kilkenny for five days, destroying much of the southern wall of the castle before Ormond surrendered. The defeat signalled a permanent end to Kilkenny's political influence over the affairs of Ireland.

ORIENTATION

At the junction of several major highways, Kilkenny straddles the River Nore, which flows through much of the county. St Canice's Cathedral sits on the northern bank of the River Bregagh (a tributary of the Nore) to the north of the town centre outside the town walls. Kilkenny's main thoroughfare runs south-east from the cathedral, past St Canice's Place to Irishtown (where the common folk were once concentrated, outside the town walls) then over the bridge, eventually becoming Parliament St, which then splits in two. Kilkenny Castle is

KILKENNY

on the banks of the River Nore and dominates the town's southern side.

INFORMATION

The tourist office (☎ 51500) is in the lovely stone Shee Alms House on Rose Inn St. There were plans to move it to a larger building on the quays but a bureaucratic foul-up meant that planning permission wasn't applied for in time and the tourist authority lost its £40,000 deposit! The office sells excellent guides to the town and walking maps of the county for 40p per sheet. It also runs an efficient accommodation booking system costing £2 plus 10% of the cost of the accommodation, which is deducted when you pay the hotel or B&B. You can also get information on the tourist office's Web site at www.kilkennycats .ie/kilkenny-tourism.

For information on local events, check out the weekly *Kilkenny People* newspaper or tune into Radio Kilkenny, which broadcasts from 7 to 2 am on 96.6FM. The Kilkenny Tourist Hostel has an excellent notice board for events around town which is updated daily.

Book Centre, 10 High St, stocks a range of books and maps on Ireland, while farther north, at 67 High St, Ossory Bookshop also sells second-hand books.

KILKENNY CASTLE

The first structure on this strategic site overlooking the River Nore was a wooden tower built in 1172 by Richard de Clare, the Anglo-Norman conqueror of Ireland better known as Strongbow. Twenty years later, his son-in-law, William Marshall, erected a stone castle with four towers, three of which still survive. The castle was bought by the powerful Butler family in 1391 and their descendants continued to live there until 1935. Maintaining such a structure became an enormous financial strain and most of the furnishings were finally sold at auction. The castle was handed over to the city in 1967 for the princely sum of £50 and is now administered by Dúchas.

Work continues to restore the castle to its Victorian splendour and many of the rooms have only recently been opened to the public. The **Long Gallery** (the wing of the castle nearest the river), with its vividly painted ceiling mixing Celtic and Pre-Raphaelite motifs with portraits of the Butler family members over the centuries, is particularly splendid and forms the focus of the 40-minute guided tour.

The castle (☎ 21450) opens 10 am to 7 pm daily, June to September; 10.30 am (11 am on Sunday) to 12.45 pm and 2 to 5 pm Tuesday to Sunday, October to March; and 10 am to 5 pm daily, April and May. Admission costs £3/1.25.

The castle is also home to the **Butler Gallery**, one of the country's most important art galleries outside Dublin. There are art exhibitions throughout the year. In the basement, the castle kitchen houses a popular summertime restaurant (see Places to Eat later in this section).

Twenty hectares of **parkland** extend to the south-east, with a Celtic-cross-shaped rose garden, a fountain to the northern end and a children's playground to the south. Admission to the grounds is free and they're open 10 am to 8.30 pm daily in summer.

ST CANICE'S CATHEDRAL

The approach to the cathedral on foot from Parliament St leads you over Irishtown Bridge and up St Canice's Steps, which date from 1614; the wall at the top contains fragmentary medieval carvings. Around the cathedral are a graveyard, a round tower and an 18th-century bishop's palace. Although the present cathedral was built between 1202 and 1285, it has a much longer history.

This site may well have pre-Christian significance. Legend has it that the first monastery was built here by St Canice (Cainneach or Kenneth), Kilkenny's patron saint, who moved here from Aghaboe, County Laois, in the 6th century. There are records of a wooden church on the site which was burned down in 1087. The 30m-high **round tower**, which is beside the church, is the oldest structure within the cathedral grounds and was built somewhere

KILKENNY

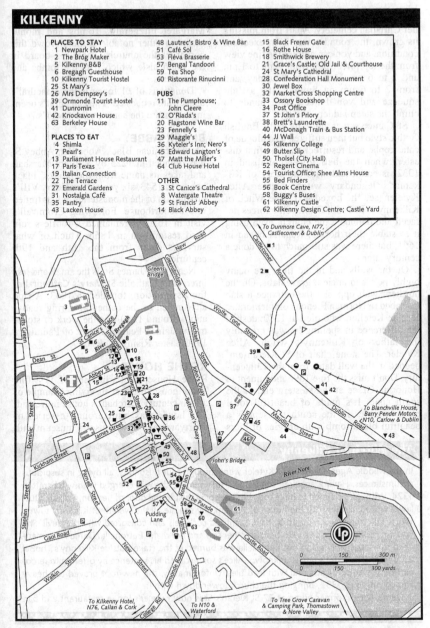

PLACES TO STAY
1 Newpark Hotel
2 The Bróg Maker
5 Kilkenny B&B
8 Bregagh Guesthouse
10 Kilkenny Tourist Hostel
25 St Mary's
26 Mrs Dempsey's
39 Ormonde Tourist Hostel
41 Dunromin
42 Knockavon House
63 Berkeley House

PLACES TO EAT
4 Shimla
7 Pearl's
13 Parliament House Restaurant
17 Paris Texas
19 Italian Connection
22 The Terrace
27 Emerald Gardens
31 Nostalgia Café
35 Pantry
43 Lacken House

48 Lautrec's Bistro & Wine Bar
51 Café Sol
53 Fléva Brasserie
57 Bengal Tandoori
59 Tea Shop
60 Ristorante Rinucinni

PUBS
11 The Pumphouse;
   John Cleere
12 O'Riada's
20 Flagstone Wine Bar
23 Fennelly's
29 Maggie's
36 Kyteler's Inn; Nero's
45 Edward Langton's
47 Matt the Miller's
64 Club House Hotel

OTHER
3 St Canice's Cathedral
8 Watergate Theatre
9 St Francis' Abbey
14 Black Abbey

15 Black Freren Gate
16 Rothe House
18 Smithwick Brewery
21 Grace's Castle; Old Jail & Courthouse
24 St Mary's Cathedral
28 Confederation Hall Monument
30 Jewel Box
32 Market Cross Shopping Centre
33 Ossory Bookshop
34 Post Office
37 St John's Priory
38 Brett's Laundrette
40 McDonagh Train & Bus Station
44 JJ Wall
46 Kilkenny College
49 Butter Slip
50 Tholsel (City Hall)
52 Regent Cinema
54 Tourist Office; Shee Alms House
55 Bed Finders
56 Book Centre
61 Kilkenny Castle
62 Kilkenny Design Centre; Castle Yard

KILKENNY

between 700 and 1000 on the site of an earlier Christian cemetery. Apart from missing its crown, the round tower is in excellent condition, and you can admire the fine view from the top for £1/50p from 9 am to 1 pm and 2 to 6 pm Monday to Saturday, and from 2 to 6 pm on Sunday. It's a tight squeeze and you'll need both hands to climb the steep ladders.

St Canice's was built in early English Gothic style but then suffered a catalogue of catastrophe and resurrection. The first disaster, when the bell tower collapsed in 1332, is connected with the story of Kilkenny's legendary witch, Dame Alice Kyteler (see the boxed text 'The Witch of Kilkenny'). In 1650, Cromwell's forces defaced and damaged the church, even using it to stable their horses. Repairs began in 1661, but there was still much to be done a century later.

On the walls and in the floor are many highly polished ancient **graveslabs**. On the northern wall opposite the entrance a slab inscribed in Norman French commemorates Jose de Keteller, who died in 1280; despite the difference in spelling he was probably the father of Kilkenny's witch, Alice Kyteler. The stone chair of St Kieran embedded in the wall dates from the 13th century. Don't miss the fine 1596 monument to Honorina Grace at the western end of the south aisle. It's made of beautiful local black marble. In the south transept is a beautiful **black tomb** with effigies of Piers Butler, who died in 1539, and his wife, Margaret Fitzgerald. Tombs and monuments to other notable Butlers crowd this corner of the church. There's a board in the south aisle which lists the tombs and monuments.

Donations of £1 towards the cathedral's upkeep are requested. The cathedral's opening hours are the same as the tower's.

BLACK ABBEY

The Dominican Black Abbey on Abbey St was founded in 1225 by William Marshall and takes its name from the monks' black habits. In 1543, six years after Henry VIII's dissolution of the monasteries, it was turned into a courthouse. Following Cromwell's visit in 1650, it remained a roofless ruin until restoration in 1866. Much of what survives dates from the 18th and 19th centuries.

Nearby, off James St, is the small and less interesting Catholic **St Mary's Cathedral of the Assumption**, founded in 1843. A side altar added to the cathedral during renovations around 1890 was the work of stonemason James Pearse (father of Pádraig, a 1916 Easter Rising leader).

ROTHE HOUSE

Rothe House, on Parliament St, is a fine Tudor house, the best surviving example of a 16th-century merchant's house in Ireland. The house was built around a series of courtyards and now houses a museum with

---

The Witch of Kilkenny

In the Middle Ages, Dame Alice Kyteler went through four husbands, all dying in suspicious circumstances. Having acquired some powerful enemies, she was charged with witchcraft in 1324. Witnesses claimed to have seen her sweeping dust to the door of her son, William Outlawe, while chanting, 'To the house of William, my son, lie all the wealth of Kilkenny town'. Worse still, she was supposed to have sacrificed cockerels and consorted with the devil. She was duly convicted, along with her sister, her son and her maid, Petronella. Dame Alice managed to escape to England but Petronella was burned at the stake outside Kilkenny's Tholsel (City Hall). The sister's fate is unknown. Alice's son escaped his sentence by offering to reroof part of St Canice's Cathedral with lead tiles. Unfortunately, the new roof proved too heavy and collapsed in 1332, bringing the church tower down with it.

Dame Alice's former home at 27 St Kieran's St is now Kyteler's Inn, a restaurant and bar.

a sparse collection of local items and costumes from various periods displayed in its old timber-vaulted rooms. The fine king-post roof of the 2nd floor is a meticulous and impressive reconstruction. A 20-minute audiovisual presentation sets the scene for your visit.

In the 1640s, the wealthy Rothe family played a part in the Confederation of Kilkenny, and Peter Rothe, son of the original builder, had all his property confiscated. His sister was able to reclaim it, but just before the Battle of the Boyne (1690) the family supported James II and so lost the house permanently. In 1850 a Confederation banner was discovered in the house. It's now in the National Museum, Dublin.

Rothe House opens 10.30 am to 5 pm Monday to Saturday and 3 to 5 pm on Sunday, April to October. The rest of the year it opens only 3 to 5 pm on Saturday and Sunday. Admission costs £2/1.

SMITHWICK BREWERY

Founded in 1710 on the site of a Franciscan monastery, the Smithwick Brewery, on Parliament St, is now owned by Guinness and brews Budweiser under licence as well as Smithwick's own brands. From June to August the brewery shows a short video on the production process, more or less as an excuse for the beer tastings that follow. Shows take place at 3 pm on weekdays and although they're free you have to collect a ticket from the tourist office first.

St Francis' Abbey, behind the brewery, was founded by William Marshall in 1232 but desecrated by Cromwell in 1650. The monks were reputed to be expert brewers.

OTHER THINGS TO SEE

Stretches of the old Norman city walls can still be traced, but Black Freren Gate, on Abbey St, is the only gate still standing.

Shee Alms House, on Rose Inn St, was built in 1582 by local benefactor Sir Richard Shee and his wife to provide help for the poor. It continued as a hospital until 1740 but now houses the tourist office. The Tholsel, or city hall, on High St was built in 1761 on the spot where Dame Alice

Kyteler's maid, Petronella, was burned at the stake in 1324 (see the boxed text 'The Witch of Kilkenny'). Just north of the Tholsel is the Butter Slip, a narrow alleyway built in 1616 to connect High St with Low Lane (now St Kieran's St) and once lined with the stalls of butter sellers.

On the corner of Parliament St and the road leading down to Bateman's Quay, a monument beside the Bank of Ireland marks the site of the Confederation Hall, where the national Parliament met from 1642 to 1649. Nearby is Grace's Castle, originally built in 1210 but lost to the family and converted into a prison in 1568 and then in 1794 into a courthouse, which it remains today. Rebels from the 1798 Rising were executed here. People taking part in one of Tynan's Tours (see Organised Tours) get to see inside the cells.

Across the river stand the ruins of St John's Priory, which was founded in 1200 and was noted for its many beautiful windows until Cromwell's visit. Nearby, Kilkenny College, John St, dates from 1666. Its students included Jonathan Swift and the philosopher George Berkeley, but it now houses Kilkenny's county hall.

ORGANISED TOURS

Tynan Tours (☎ 65929) conducts hour-long walking tours of the town six times daily (four on Sunday), April to October, starting from the tourist office. They cost £3/2. The rest of the year, three tours daily are scheduled for Tuesday to Saturday.

The Old Kilkenny Tour is a hop-on, hop-off open-top-bus tour of the town that departs from Kilkenny Castle every half-hour between 10 am and 5 pm. Tickets cost £6/2.50.

SPECIAL EVENTS

The Confederation of Kilkenny Festival, which commemorates Kilkenny's days as the Irish capital, takes place in June, bringing the streets to life with parades and historic pageantry.

Over the June bank-holiday weekend the Cat Laughs Comedy Festival is an increasingly important crowd-puller, attracting

KILKENNY

some of the best talent from the country and abroad. New York comedian Dave Attell was the star of the 1998 show. Its popularity means that beds can be almost impossible to find. For details phone ☎ 63207.

The highlight of the year is the Kilkenny Arts Week Festival in late August, when exhibitions, music, and theatrical events take place all over town. Beds will be like gold dust, so book well ahead. Phone ☎ 52175 or email kaw@iol.ie for details.

PLACES TO STAY
Camping
The small *Tree Grove Caravan and Camping Park* (☎ 70302) is 1.5km south of Kilkenny on the New Ross road. A tent site for two costs £6.50. Otherwise, *Nore Valley Caravan and Camping Park* is about 11km away, near Bennettsbridge; see that section later in this chapter for details.

Hostels
The IHH *Kilkenny Tourist Hostel* (☎ 63541, 35 Parliament St) is friendly, clean and central. It has a kitchen and laundry (£3), and charges £7 in dorms or £9 in private rooms. The one family room costs £40. All prices go up by £1 between May and September. Guests can get a shiatsu massage (£12) on Sunday and Monday mornings.

Ormonde Tourist Hostel (☎ 52733, John's Green) is close to the train and bus station and has dorm beds costing £7.50, doubles at £10 per person. Good facilities include a kitchen, laundry, TV room and plentiful parking space, although it can't quite shake off an institutional air – it was once the county council offices.

The An Óige hostel is beautifully sited in *Foulksrath Castle* (☎ 67144), a 16th-century Norman castle 13km north of Kilkenny in Jenkinstown near Ballyragget. Beds cost £6/4.50. June to September, it serves reasonably priced meals. For details of how to get there by bus, see Getting There & Away later in this section.

B&Bs
There are plenty of B&Bs, especially south of the city along Patrick St and north of the

city on Castlecomer Rd, but accommodation can still be hard to find at the weekend and especially during festival times. Bed Finders (☎ 70088), 23 Rose Inn St, can help you find somewhere to stay without charging a booking fee, a service that could come in handy at busy times.

In the centre, *Mrs Dempsey's* (☎ 21954) and *St Mary's* (☎ 22091) are two small town houses side by side on James St. Mrs Dempsey charges £15/34 for singles/doubles with bathroom. St Mary's charges £16/36 and serves big breakfasts.

Also central is *Bregagh Guesthouse* (☎ 22315, Dean St), near St Canice's Cathedral, starting at £20/36. A few doors down is *Kilkenny B&B* (☎ 64040), with a wide variety of rooms costing upwards of £18 per person.

Knockavon House (☎ 64294, Dublin Rd), quite near the train station, charges £22/36 with bathroom, while nearby *Dunromin* (☎ 61387) charges £20/34 including a top-notch breakfast. *The Bróg Maker* (☎ 52900, Castlecomer Rd) is a cheerful pub/guesthouse offering B&B for £24 per person.

Hotels
Georgian *Berkeley House* (☎ 64848, fax 64829, 5 Lower Patrick St) charges from £25/45 for singles/doubles. Modern *Newpark Hotel* (☎ 22122, fax 61111), north of the train station on Castlecomer Rd, has swimming pools, saunas, a gym and 20 hectares of parkland. Singles/doubles start at £67/88. *Kilkenny Hotel* (☎ 62000, fax 65984), about a 10-minute walk from the town centre on College Rd, has excellent facilities and costs from £55 per person depending on the season.

Blanchville House (☎ 27197, fax 27636, Maddoxtown) is a lovely 19th-century house on its own farm about 8km east of the town. B&B starts at £35/60 for singles/doubles and it's open from March to October. To get there, go along the N10 Carlow road and take the first right after the Pike pub. After 3km turn left at a crossroads near Connolly's pub. It's almost 2km down the road on the left.

Highly rated *Lacken House* (☎ *61085, fax 62435)*, just out of town on Dublin Rd, costs from £55 (April to October) per person including breakfast and a four-course evening meal in its excellent restaurant.

PLACES TO EAT
Restaurants

The popular *Italian Connection* (☎ *64225, 38 Parliament St)* serves delicious spaghetti in pesto sauce for £7.50. More upmarket is *Ristorante Rinucinni* (☎ *61575, The Parade)*, a cellar restaurant with delicious pastas, all freshly prepared. Near Kyteler's Inn on St Kieran's St is the late-night *Lautrec's Bistro and Wine Bar* (☎ *62720)*, which serves an eclectic range of Italian and Mexican dishes (starting at £3.95) until 1 am.

Parliament House Restaurant (*Parliament St)*, opposite Kilkenny Tourist Hostel, serves traditional food but is quite expensive; a set lunch costs £12.95.

At the Chinese restaurant *Emerald Gardens* (☎ *61812, High St)* main courses start at £7. *Pearl's* (☎ *23322, 10 Irishtown)* serves excellent dishes that are marginally more expensive (all main courses cost around £10), but it's worth it. *Bengal Tandoori* (☎ *64722, Pudding Lane)* offers eat-as-much-as-you-like Sunday lunch from 1 to 5 pm for £7.95. Opposite Bregagh Guesthouse, *Shimla* was due to open at the time of writing, promising to serve good-quality Indian cuisine for less than £10.

North-east of the river, *Edward Langton's* (☎ *21728, 69 John St)* pub has an award-winning restaurant. Lunches such as roast beef will cost a reasonable £5, and sandwiches start at £3.50 including chips. Set dinners, served until 11 pm, cost £18.50; à la carte dishes range from £12.50 to £14.

Widely regarded as the best local restaurant is *Lacken House* (☎ *61085)*, just out of town on Dublin Rd. Dinner will cost you £22 or more.

Fast Food, Cafés & Pubs

In summer, *Kilkenny Castle Kitchen* is a good place for lunch or for delicious, if pricey, cakes; you don't have to pay the castle admission charge to eat there. Across the road, the restaurant upstairs in the *Kilkenny Design Centre* (open 9 am to 5 pm daily) is excellent for snacks or lunch but attracts coach parties.

An excellent choice for lunch is *Café Sol* (☎ *64987)*, tucked away down William St and with the sort of colour scheme to evoke the sunny Med rather than wet and windy Kilkenny. Lunch costs around £6, dinner more like £22 a head. The menu here is very Modern Irish, as it is at *Fléva Brasserie* (☎ *70021, 84 High St)*, near the Tholsel; a baguette filled with hot chicken, dill and lemon costs £4.25, Kilkenny meatloaf with potatoes £5. *Paris Texas* (*High St)* comes highly recommended by the folks at the nearby hostel; its Mexican and Cajun dishes are big favourites. *The Terrace* (*High St)* offers an all-day menu for around £5.

Nostalgia Café (*High St)* favours over-the-top kitsch décor as a backing for a good choice of lunch and dinner dishes; roast chicken costs £4.25, vegetarian pasta £3.55. It stays open until 10 pm. The *Pantry*, a small self-service coffee shop on St Kieran's St, carries things to the other extreme, with rather austere décor. Still, it's very popular with the locals for lunch. At the unpretentious *Tea Shop* (*Patrick St)* sandwiches start at £1.50. There's also a branch of *Bewley's* on the ground floor of the Market Cross Shopping Centre.

Kilkenny has plenty of pubs serving reasonable food. On St Kieran's St, *Kyteler's Inn* (☎ *21604)* has a rustic restaurant downstairs. While the food isn't brilliant, it's certainly popular. A mixed grill costs £6.75, breaded chicken £5.25. *John Cleere* and *The Pumphouse*, both on Parliament St, are also well worth trying.

ENTERTAINMENT
Pubs

There's no shortage of pubs in Kilkenny and there's often live music in several at the same time. A string of pubs line the northern end of Parliament St opposite the Kilkenny Tourist Hostel. *The Pumphouse* offers rock and pop, as well as traditional music on Tuesday and Wednesday. Next

KILKENNY

door, *O'Riada's* is a great old bar whose only acknowledgement of the 20th century is in the use of electricity. *John Cleere* stages regular, year-round productions of plays, revues, poetry readings and anything else that's going. Monday night is traditional Irish music and folk night. Spontaneous sessions can happen any time. Other places to try include *Fennelly's* on Monday and Friday nights and *Maggie's*, on St Kieran's St, on Tuesday and Thursday nights. *Matt the Miller's*, just across the river, is another popular pub in which to hang out.

Flagstone Wine Bar, in a basement a few doors up from Kilkenny Tourist Hostel, has weekend discos from 11.30 pm until 2 am. The music is alternative and the dress code is very relaxed. Next door to Kyteler's Inn, *Nero's* is a big and popular dance club spread across two floors featuring the latest dance music until 2 am Thursday to Sunday. Over the river, *Edward Langton's (John St)* has discos on Tuesday and Saturday nights.

On Tuesday night in July and August there's live musical entertainment of the more touristy type at *Club House Hotel* (☎ 21994, Patrick St). It kicks off around 8.30 pm and admission costs £5.

Theatre & Cinemas

Watergate Theatre (☎ 61674, Parliament St) hosts drama, comedy and musical performances by both professional and amateur groups. The *John Cleere* stages various productions (for details see the previous Pubs section).

The single-screen *Regent* cinema is at the end of William St, a cul-de-sac opposite the Tholsel.

SHOPPING

All shops open 9 am to 6 pm Monday to Saturday; some stay open until 9 pm on Thursday. Across The Parade from Kilkenny Castle are the elegant former Castle Stables (1760), which have been tastefully converted into the Kilkenny Design Centre, where there's an outstanding collection of Irish goods and crafts for sale. Behind the shop through the arched gateway is Castle

Yard, lined with the studios of various local craftspeople. For locally made jewellery – from the traditional to the more way-out kind – check out the Jewel Box on High St.

GETTING THERE & AWAY
Bus

Bus Éireann (☎ 64933) operates out of McDonagh train station and provides seven services daily to and from Dublin, Monday to Saturday, with four on Sunday. There are three buses daily to and from Cork town (two on Sunday). Two buses daily (except Sunday) also pass through Kilkenny en route from Dublin to Waterford.

On the Waterford to Longford route, one bus daily passes through in each direction. In July and August one bus daily (except Sunday) links Kilkenny with Galway and Waterford. On Thursday there's also a bus from New Ross to Kilkenny, leaving at 10 am and returning at 1.15 pm.

JJ Kavanagh & Sons (☎ 31106) runs daily buses between Kilkenny and Cashel via Kells and Fethard, and buses to Carlow, Portlaoise and Thurles. These buses stop on The Parade.

Buggy's Buses (☎ 41264) runs a daily service Monday to Saturday to Foulksrath Castle (and the An Óige hostel), Ballyragget, Dunmore Cave and Castlecomer. Buses leave The Parade at 11.30 am and 5.30 pm; from the hostel they leave at 8.25 am and 3 pm. The fare is £1 and the journey takes about 20 minutes. Some JJ Kavanagh buses also pass near the hostel.

Train

McDonagh train station (☎ 22024) is on Dublin Rd, north-east of the town centre via John St. Four trains daily (five on Friday, three on Sunday) link Dublin (Heuston Station) with Waterford via Kilkenny; the journey takes just under two hours. For details phone ☎ 01-836 6222.

GETTING AROUND

JJ Wall (☎ 21236), 86 Maudlin St, rents bikes at £10 per day, plus a deposit of £30. The circuit round Kells, Inistioge, Jerpoint Abbey and Kilfane makes a fine day's ride.

Barry Pender Motors (☎ 65777), 1.5km out on Dublin Rd, offers car rental for a steep £55 per day (cheaper in the off-season, when some cars are available for £35).

Central Kilkenny

The most scenic parts of this area, taking in some of the Nore and Barrow Valleys, are from Graiguenamanagh in the east, down to The Rower and then north-west on the road to Inistioge, Thomastown, Kells and Callan near the Tipperary border.

BENNETTSBRIDGE
☎ 056 • pop 601

Bennettsbridge, a village south of Kilkenny on the River Nore, has two of Ireland's most renowned potteries and an official camping ground. In a big mill by the river, **Nicholas Mosse Pottery** (☎ 27105) turns out handmade spongewear – creamy-brown pottery covered with sponged patterns. The factory shop opens 10 am to 6 pm Monday to Saturday year round, and 2 to 6 pm on Sunday in July and August. There's a café opposite.

Almost 2km north of Bennettsbridge on the R700 road to Kilkenny, **Stoneware Jackson Pottery** (☎ 27175) produces a wide variety of chunky pottery. It opens 10 am to 6 pm Monday to Saturday.

Two kilometres south of Bennettsbridge on the Waterford road is **Nore Valley Park** (☎ 27229), an open farm aimed at kids: they can bottle feed lambs and goats, cuddle rabbits, play in a fort and jump on a straw bounce. There's a tearoom and picnic area. The park opens 9 am to 8 pm Monday to Saturday, Easter to mid-September.

Nore Valley Camping and Caravan Park (☎ 27229) is on a farm and charges hikers and cyclists £4 per person to camp. If you're coming into Bennettsbridge from Kilkenny along the R700, turn right just before the bridge and the park is signposted. It opens from Easter to October.

KELLS

Only 13km south of Kilkenny, Kells is not to be confused with its namesake in County Meath. This is a treat of a hamlet, nestling beside a fine stone bridge on the King's River, a tributary of the Nore. In Kells Priory, the village has one of Ireland's most impressive and romantic monastic sites.

Kells Priory

The earliest remains of the magnificent Kells Priory date from the late 12th century, while the bulk of the present ruins date from the 15th century. In a sea of rich farmland, a protective wall, carefully restored, connects seven dwelling towers. Inside the walls are the remains of an Augustinian abbey and the foundations of some chapels and houses. It's unusually well fortified for a monastery and the heavy curtain walls hint at a troubled history. Indeed, within a single century from 1250, the abbey was twice fought over and burned down by squabbling warlords.

Extraordinarily there's no charge for visiting and no set opening hours, provided you don't mind braving the sheep in the surrounding fields. The ruins are 800m east of Kells on the Stonyford road.

Kilree Round Tower & High Cross

Two kilometres south of Kells (signposted from the priory car park) there's a 29m-high round tower and a simple early high cross, which is said to mark the grave of a 9th-century Irish high king, Niall Caille. He's supposed to have drowned in the King's River at Callan some time in the 840s while attempting to save a servant, and his body washed up near Kells. His final resting place lies beyond the church grounds because he wasn't a Christian.

Callan Famine Graveyard

Ten kilometres west of Kilree, and signposted off the main road 2km south of Callan, is a cemetery where the local victims of the Great Famine lie buried. It isn't much to look at, but it is a poignant reminder of the anonymity of starvation: the victims here have no names and the only plaque serves to maintain a link between those who died in Ireland and the victims of more recent famines, such as Bangladesh in 1974 and Angola in 1994.

THOMASTOWN & AROUND
☎ 056 • pop 1581

Thomastown is a small market town nicely situated by the River Nore. Unfortunately it's also on the main Dublin to Waterford road (N9) and the traffic can be horrific. However, most people ignore this aspect of the town and concentrate on its many drinking establishments, some with live music, others with reasonable food.

Named after a Welsh mercenary in 1169, Thomastown has some fragments of a medieval wall and the partly ruined 13th-century **Church of St Mary**. **Mullin's Castle** down by the bridge is the sole survivor of the 14 castles that were originally here. On the outskirts of Thomastown is *Mount Juliet* (☎ *24455, fax 24766*), a stately home turned hotel with a riverside park and lovely walled gardens. Visits to the grounds are possible at any time but to stay you're looking at more than £120 per person to stay.

At the edge of town on the Waterford road, **Grennan Mill Craft School** (☎ 24557) has a craft shop open 9 am to 5 pm Monday to Saturday.

Jerpoint Abbey

One and a half kilometres south-west of Thomastown on the Waterford road, Jerpoint Abbey was established by a king of Ossory in the 12th century. One of Ireland's finest Cistercian ruins, it has been partially restored. The fine tower and cloister are late 14th or early 15th century. Fragments of the cloister are particularly interesting, with a series of often amusing figures carved on the pillars. There are also stone carvings on the church walls and in the tombs of members of the Butler and Walshe families. Faint traces of a 15th- or 16th-century painting remain on the northern wall of the church. This chancel area also contains a tomb thought to be that of Felix O'Dullany, Jerpoint's first abbot and bishop of Ossory, who died in 1202.

According to local legend, St Nicholas (or Santa Claus) is buried near the abbey.

While retreating in the Crusades, the Knights of Jerpoint removed his body from Myra in modern-day Turkey and reburied him in the Church of St Nicholas to the west of the abbey. The grave is marked by a broken slab decorated with a carving of a monk.

Jerpoint Abbey (☎ 24623) opens 9.30 am to 6.30 pm daily, June to mid-September; and 10 am to 1 pm and 2 to 5 pm (4 pm in the second half of November) Wednesday to Monday, mid-September to November and March to May. Admission costs £2/1.

A few kilometres from Jerpoint Abbey, in the town of Stonyford, the nationally renowned **Jerpoint Glass Studio** (☎ 24350) is housed in an old stone-walled farm building. Many of the pieces produced here are extremely beautiful.

If you want to stay at Jerpoint Abbey, the attractive Georgian *Abbey House* (☎ *24166*), opposite the entrance, has singles/doubles starting at £29/40.

Kilfane

Three kilometres north of Thomastown on the Dublin road, the village of Kilfane has a small ruined 13th-century **church and Norman tower**, 50m off the road and signposted. The church has a remarkable stone carving of Thomas de Cantwell called the Cantwell Fada or Long Cantwell. It depicts a tall, thin knight in detailed chain-mail armour brandishing a shield decorated with the Cantwell coat of arms.

Another 2km north along the N9 brings you to the **Kilfane Glen and Waterfall**, a Romantic-period garden with a *cottage ornée* (an elaborately decorated cottage). The top part of the garden is replete with works of art by Irish artists. It opens 11 am to 6 pm daily, July and August; and 2 to 6 pm on Sunday, April, June and September. Admission costs £3/2.

Getting There & Away

Bus Bus Éireann (☎ 64933) operates up to seven buses daily between Dublin and Waterford with stops at Gowran, Thomastown and Mullinavat. One service daily links Waterford with Longford via Thomastown,

Kilkenny, Carlow, Tullamore and Athlone. On Thursday there's also one service from New Ross, leaving at 10 am. Buses stop outside O'Keeffe's supermarket on Main St.

Train The town is on the main Dublin to Waterford train line with the same service as Kilkenny. It's about 15 minutes to Kilkenny, 25 minutes to Waterford and two hours to Dublin. The train station is 1km west of town past Kavanagh's supermarket.

INISTIOGE
☎ 056 • pop 270

Inistioge (pronounced 'Inishteeg') is a delightful little village with a 10-arched stone bridge spanning the River Nore and a picturesque tree-lined square with many of its original shop and pub fronts. Somewhere so inviting could hardly hope to escape the Hollywood sleuths: Inistioge's film credits include *Widow's Peak* (1993), *Circle of Friends* (1994) and *Where the Sun Is King* (1996). Inistioge is also on the South Leinster Way.

One kilometre south, on Mt Alto, is **Woodstock Park**. The hike up is well worth the effort for the panorama of the valley below and the demesne itself. The 18th-century house was one of the finest in the county but was destroyed during the Civil War in 1922. The elevated garden and forest are now a state park with picnic areas and trails. For another fine walk, follow the river bank and climb any of the surrounding hills. At the bottom of the hill that leads to Woodstock Park is a **pottery** which produces lovely work in light pastel colours.

School House Café, by the river, is a good, if unsophisticated, place to stop for tea, sandwiches and cakes.

Getting There & Away
On Thursday only, a single bus runs between New Ross and Kilkenny, calling at Inistioge on the way. It leaves New Ross at 10 am and comes back from Inistioge at 1.50 pm.

GRAIGUENAMANAGH
☎ 056 • pop 1374

Graiguenamanagh (pronounced 'Greg-na-mana') is a small market town on a lovely stretch of the River Barrow, 23km southeast of Kilkenny at the foot of Brandon Hill (516m). There's no public transport but it is on the South Leinster Way (see Walking in the Activities chapter for more details).

KILKENNY

Michelle de Bruin's Fall from Grace

When the Court of Arbitration for Sport decided on 9 June 1999 to reject Michelle Smith de Bruin's appeal against a four-year ban imposed on her for tampering with a urine sample, the fall from grace of Kilkenny's favourite daughter was complete.

The cloud of suspicion fell on her almost immediately after her record-breaking swims at Atlanta in 1996 (where she won three golds, the first Irish athlete ever to do so): the improvements in her times were too miraculous to be the result of intensive training alone. In one event – the 400m freestyle – it had taken 18 years to reduce the record by 20 seconds but de Bruin improved her personal best by 18 seconds in just over 18 months. Furthermore, she was not helped by the public image of her husband, Erik de Bruin, a former Olympian banned from competition for drug use.

She was banned from competition for four years in 1998 when a urine sample was found to have a lethal level of whiskey in it. Her appeal received little more than lukewarm support from an Irish public that only three years earlier had rejoiced in her victories as a great moment in Irish sporting history. The day after her appeal was rejected de Bruin retired from swimming, a sad end to the tragic tale of an athlete who had to win at all costs but ended up paying too high a price for success.

DUISKE ABBEY

Dating back to 1204, Duiske Abbey was once Ireland's largest Cistercian abbey. Today it has been completely restored and its pleasantly simple, whitewashed interior is in everyday use. Its name comes from the Irish Dubh Uisce (Black Water), a tributary of the River Barrow.

Inside the abbey to the right of the main entrance is the Knight of Duiske, a 14th-century high-relief carving of a knight in chain mail who's reaching for his sword. On the floor nearby a glass panel reveals some of the original 13th-century floor tiles, which are now 2m below the present floor level.

To the left of the entrance is the 18th-century painted reredos taken from an old mass house which was attached to the ruins before they were restored. The nave has been reroofed in medieval style, without the use of nails.

In the grounds stand two early high crosses, brought here for protection in the last century. The smaller Ballyogan Cross has panels on the eastern side depicting the crucifixion, Adam and Eve, Abraham's sacrifice of Isaac, and David playing the harp. The western side shows the massacre of the innocents.

Round the corner the **Abbey Centre** houses a small exhibition of Christian art, plus pictures of the abbey in its unrestored state.

Opposite the abbey *Café Duiske* serves meals such as lasagne (£3.95).

GOWRAN
☎ 056 • pop 476

The village of Gowran, 12km east of Kilkenny, is famous for its **racecourse** and 13th-century **St Mary's Church**, which has some fine carvings and Butler-family tombs.

Whitethorns (☎ *26102*), 300m off the main Dublin to Kilkenny road, is a pleasant guesthouse offering B&B from £22/34 for singles/doubles.

Gowran is on the Dublin to Waterford express bus route, with up to five services daily in each direction.

Southern Kilkenny

Much of southern Kilkenny is sparsely populated, with gentle hills separating the valleys of the Nore, Barrow and Suir Rivers. Carrick-on-Suir in Tipperary and Waterford town are within easy reach. Both towns have a wide choice of accommodation and restaurants.

Southern Kilkenny is crossed by the **South Leinster Way**, which runs from Carrick-on-Suir, through Piltown, Mullinavat, Inistioge, Graiguenamanagh and on to Borris in County Carlow. See Walking in the Activities chapter for more details.

MULLINAVAT
☎ 051 • pop 275

Twelve kilometres north of Waterford on the Kilkenny road (N9), Mullinavat makes an agreeable spot to spend a relaxing day or two.

Two kilometres south of the village, *Tory View* (☎ *85513*) offers B&B in smallish rooms for £13.50/16 per person without/with bathroom, and evening meals are available. Alternatively, there's the 17th-century *Rising Sun* (☎ *898173*), on Main St, a beautiful old stone building with an upstairs restaurant. All rooms have bathroom, phone and TV but at £28/46 a single/double for B&B it's a bit pricey.

Express buses between Dublin and Waterford call at Mullinavat up to five times daily, stopping outside Mulhearn's on Main St. One service daily links Mullinavat with Longford via Thomastown, Carlow, Tullamore and Athlone. In July and August there's also one request service daily linking Mullinavat with Galway via Kilkenny, Thurles and Nenagh.

Northern Kilkenny

CASTLECOMER & AROUND
☎ 056 • pop 1380

An attractive town 18km north of Kilkenny, Castlecomer is on the River Dinin, which flows across the Castlecomer Plateau. The town became a centre for anthracite mining after the fuel was discovered nearby in 1636; the mines closed for good only in the mid-1960s. The anthracite was widely regarded as being Europe's best, containing very little sulphur and producing almost no smoke.

Castlecomer saw action in the 1798 Rising when the Fenian rebels, led by Father John Murphy, captured it en route from Wexford to the midlands. There's little to do here, but the tree-lined square and neat town houses are thoroughly pleasing.

Things to See
Eight kilometres west of Castlecomer is **Ballyragget**, with an almost intact square tower in the 16th-century Butler Castle.

Almost 2km south of Ballyragget is **Swifte's Heath**, home to Jonathan Swift during his school years in Kilkenny and now offering B&B accommodation.

Places to Stay & Eat
Foulksrath Castle (☎ 67144), near Ballyragget, is now a busy An Óige hostel with a superb setting. For more details see Places to Stay in the Kilkenny section earlier in this chapter.

In Castlecomer, *Avalon* pub/guesthouse (☎ 41302), on the square near the bridge, is in the old mine offices; B&B costs £27/40 for singles/doubles. Alternatively, 19th-century *Wandesforde House* (☎ 42441) has six rooms, all with a bathroom; B&B costs £21/36 and dinner is £15.

Getting There & Away
Castlecomer is on Bus Éireann's (☎ 64933) route between Cork, Kilkenny and Dublin and is served by up to four buses daily Monday to Saturday (three on Sunday). Buses stop outside Houlihan's. JJ Kavanagh (☎ 31555) runs buses twice daily between Clonmel, Kilkenny, Castlecomer, Athy and Dublin (Gresham Hotel); from Castlecomer the journey to Dublin takes 75 minutes. Buggy's Buses (☎ 41264) runs a Monday to Saturday service from Kilkenny to Castlecomer.

DUNMORE CAVE
Dunmore Cave, 10km north of Kilkenny on the Castlecomer road (N78), is a large cave divided into three parts, with many limestone formations. According to sources, marauding Vikings killed 1000 people at two ring forts near Dunmore Cave in 928. When survivors hid in the caverns the Vikings tried to smoke them out by lighting fires at the entrance. It's thought that they then dragged off the men as slaves and left the women and children to suffocate. Excavations in 1973 uncovered the skeletons of at least 44 people, mostly women and children. They also found coins dating from the 920s but none from a later date. One theory suggests that the coins were dropped by the Vikings (who often carried them in their armpits, secured with wax) while enthusiastically engaged in the slaughter. However, there are few marks of violence on the skeletons, which lends weight to the theory that suffocation was the cause of death.

The limestone cave is well lit and spacious. After a steep descent through the large entrance, you enter imaginatively nicknamed caverns full of stalactites, stalagmites and columns, including the 7m Market Cross, Europe's largest freestanding stalagmite. It's damp and cold, so a sweater or coat is advised. The compulsory guided tours are very worthwhile.

The cave opens 10 am to 7 pm daily, mid-June to mid-September; 10 am to 5 pm daily, mid-March to mid-June and mid-September to October; and 10 am to 5 pm at the weekend only, November to mid-March. Admission costs £2/1.

Buggy's Buses (☎ 056-41264) runs a Monday to Saturday bus from The Parade in Kilkenny that drops you off 1km from the cave. It leaves Kilkenny at 12.30 pm and returns at 4.15 pm (£2 return), giving you more than three hours at the cave, where there's not even a café. However, one of the visitors is bound to be able to run you back to town. On Saturday there's a bus back at 2.30 pm, leaving a much more reasonable 1½ hours to inspect the cave.

KILKENNY

Central South

The four counties of Carlow, Kildare, Laois and Offaly make up a large portion of the Irish midlands. Sites of interest include the Rock of Dunamase near Portlaoise, Moone High Cross in Kildare, Kildare town's cathedral, Browne's Hill Dolmen just outside Carlow town, Rosse Estate and Observatory in Birr and, most impressive of all, Clonmacnoise on the banks of the River Shannon, probably Ireland's most important monastic site.

County Kildare

Kildare (Cill Dara), to the west and south-west of Dublin, is mostly rich green farmland in the south, with the extensive Bog of Allen peatland hogging the north-western corner. A limestone plain underlies the pasture and bog.

The main towns are dominated by traffic, a problem that should be alleviated as the local councils finish building bypasses round them. Nearly all the country's main road and train arteries cross the county, as do the 18th-century Grand and Royal Canals, which are now enjoying a new lease of life. The River Barrow marks the county's western border, while the Curragh forms a great sweep of unfenced countryside to the south.

GRAND & ROYAL CANALS

The Grand and Royal Canals were built in the 18th century to revolutionise goods and passenger transport but, as the railways superseded them during the 19th century, the canals fell into disuse. Today they're owned by Dúchas and offer a pleasant way of drifting across the country.

Grand Canal

The Grand Canal was first commissioned in 1715 by an Act of Parliament, but a lack of funds delayed its construction and the first cargo barges started to operate between

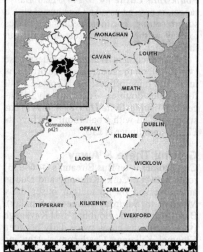

Dublin and Sallins in 1779. It carried passengers until 1852 and goods until 1960. The canal threads its way from Dublin through County Kildare to Robertstown. From there one branch heads west through

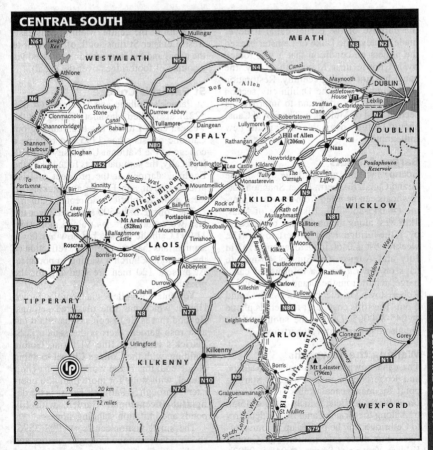

CENTRAL SOUTH

Tullamore to join the River Shannon at Shannon Harbour in County Offaly, while the other turns south to join the River Barrow at Athy, providing passage to New Ross in County Wexford and to Waterford town.

Besides the many finely crafted locks and tiny lock cottages, you will come across treasures such as the seven-arched Leinster Aqueduct, 5km north of Naas near the village of Sallins, where the canal crosses the River Liffey. Farther south of Robertstown, sections of the River Barrow are particularly lovely.

Royal Canal

The Royal Canal follows Kildare's northern border and also wends its way to the River Shannon, joining it farther north at Cloondara (or Clondra) in County Longford above Lough Ree. However, it's only navigable between Blanchardstown in County Dublin and Mullingar in County Westmeath. It was never a profitable enterprise, but its history is a colourful one. It was founded by Long John Binns, a director of the Grand Canal Company who quit the board over a supposed insult about him being a shoemaker. He established the

Royal Canal in 1790 but since it duplicated the purpose of the earlier canal it never made money. The Duke of Leinster backed the project on condition that it was routed by his house near Maynooth. Sadly, the canal has not aged gracefully. Restoration work aims to link the Dublin-city section with the River Liffey and to improve the section west of Mullingar. The Royal Canal should be fully navigable early in the new millennium.

Barges & Boats

Boating facilities are available only on the Grand Canal. Six-berth River Shannon narrowboats can be hired from Lowtown Marine (☎ 045-860427), 13km west of Naas, 1km west along the north bank of the canal over the bridge from Robertstown. The weekly cost is £460 in October and £747 in July and August. On Sunday 45-minute trips on the *Eustace*, a refurbished canal barge, depart from the Grand Canal Hotel in Robertstown on the hour between 2 and 6 pm. The trips cost £3/2; for details phone ☎ 045-870005. During the summer there are also day trips from Robertstown.

Walking the Towpaths

The canal towpaths are ideal for walkers, and Robertstown makes a good starting point for many canal walks. Three *Canal Bank Walks* leaflets, which detail a 45km trail along the Grand Canal from Edenderry to Celbridge, can be picked up at tourist offices. For more information call County Kildare Youth and Sports (☎ 045-879502).

Robertstown is also at the hub of the Kildare Way and River Barrow towpath trails, the latter stretching all the way to St Mullins, 95km south in County Carlow. From there it's possible to connect with the South Leinster Way at Graiguenamanagh or the southern end of the Wicklow Way at Clonegal, north of Mt Leinster.

MAYNOOTH & AROUND
☎ 01 • pop 8528

Twenty-four kilometres west of Dublin on the N4, Maynooth (Maigh Nuad) has a tree-lined main street with stone-fronted houses

and shops and the Royal Canal passing to the south of the centre. Main St runs east-west. Leinster St runs south off Main St to the canal and the train station (accessed via a couple of footbridges over the canal).

St Patrick's College

St Patrick's College and Seminary (☎ 628 5222), also called Maynooth College, at the western end of town, has been turning out Catholic priests since 1795 and became a college of the National University in 1910. Ironically, the seminary was founded by the English, alarmed at the prospect of Irish priests studying in France and picking up ideas about revolution and republicanism.

The college has 4500 students. Over the last two centuries it has trained more than 11,000 Catholic priests, but now has fewer seminarians than ever before, a reflection of the Catholic Church's waning importance. At present 120 men are studying for the priesthood.

You enter the college via Georgian Stoyte House, which has fine plastered ceilings. Beyond that is St Joseph's Square laid out as a rose garden. Across the square is St Patrick's House, a fine Victorian Gothic building, with the College Chapel looming at one end; this is the world's largest choir chapel, with stalls for more than 450 choristers. Through St Patrick's House is the delightful Bicentennial Garden, with lily ponds and imitation standing stones.

The small visitor centre (☎ 708 3576) shows a video on the College's history and stocks a leaflet for guiding yourself around the buildings. Guided tours cost £2/1.50. It opens 11 am to 5 pm on weekdays, and 2 to 6 pm on Sunday. The small science museum, open on request, costs £1/50p.

Maynooth Castle

The ruined gatehouse, keep and great hall of the 13th-century castle stand by the entrance to St Patrick's College. The key can be picked up from 1 Parsons St in return for a deposit.

The castle was one of the homes of the Fitzgeralds (the other was at Kilkea; see Naas to Carlow later in this section). After the 1536 rebellion led by Silken Thomas Fitzgerald, the English besieged the castle, whose garrison surrendered after being promised leniency. Then, in what became ironically known as the Pardon of Maynooth, Thomas and his men were summarily executed. The castle was dismantled in Cromwellian times when the Fitzgeralds moved to Kilkea Castle.

Canoeing

The town of **Leixlip** on the River Liffey between Maynooth and Dublin is an important canoeing centre. It's the starting point of the Irish Sprint Canoe Championships and annual 28km International Liffey Descent Race, when the Electricity Supply Board (ESB) releases 30 million tonnes of water from the Poulaphouca Reservoir in County Wicklow to bring the river up to flood level. Canoes can be hired from Kilcullen Canoe and Outdoor Pursuits Club (☎ 045-812408), 10km south-west of Naas.

Places to Stay

B&Bs *Park Lodge* (☎ 628 6002, 201 Railpark), 1km south of Maynooth near the bridge, charges £18 per person, while *Windgate Lodge* (☎ 627 3415), 2km farther south in Barberstown, costs upwards of £22/36 for singles/doubles.

Hotels The attractive old *Leinster Arms* (☎ 628 6323, Main St) has rooms with shower costing £30 per person. Breakfast is an extra £4.50. If your trunkload of cash is weighing you down, the lovely Georgian *Moyglare Manor* (☎ 628 6351, fax 628 5405) is 3.5km to the north. One of Ireland's best country houses, it charges £95/150 for singles/doubles with breakfast.

Places to Eat

For light lunches *Kehoe's Coffee Shop* (Main St) is very popular for snacks such as soup and toasted sandwiches. For more substantial meals *Orange Tree Restaurant* (Mill St), behind the Mill pub, does an early-bird two-course dinner which costs £10.95.

Leinster Arms has a carvery restaurant serving food from 12.30 to 9.30 pm; prices are reasonable at £4.50 to £7 for a main course.

Getting There & Away

Bus From Middle Abbey St in Dublin, suburban bus Nos 66 and 67 go to Maynooth (one hour). Numerous long-distance buses also pass through en route to Galway and Sligo. For information ring ☎ 873 4222. Bus No 66 stops outside Brady's pub on Main St, while No 67 stops on Leinster St, near the train station.

Train Maynooth is linked to Dublin by the Western Suburban line and is on the main Dublin to Sligo line, with four to five trains daily in each direction. Call ☎ 836 6222 for details.

CELBRIDGE

☎ 01 • pop 12,289

Celbridge, 6.5km south-east of Maynooth on the River Liffey, wouldn't have a lot going for it were it not home to the magnificent Palladian Castletown House.

Castletown House

This huge Irish mansion, with its tree-lined avenue from the village (continue straight ahead after entering the gate), is said to be Ireland's largest private house. It was built between 1722 and 1732 for William Conolly, who started life as the son of a pub owner and rose to become speaker of the Irish House of Commons. He financed Castletown House from a fortune amassed as a land agent in the chaotic aftermath of the Battle of the Boyne.

Castletown was designed by Alessandro Galilei, and continued by Edward Lovett Pearce (creator of the Bank of Ireland building on College Green, Dublin), who oversaw the building of the two sweeping columned wings. The style is, inevitably, Palladian: there is hardly a big house built in Ireland in the 18th century that wasn't influenced by the style of Italian architect Andrea Palladio (1508–80), though the Irish version was certainly added to by the likes of Richard Castle, James Gandon and

CENTRAL SOUTH

Lovett Pearce. The house remained with the Conolly family until 1965, when it was bought by the Guinness family, who ran it in conjunction with the Irish Georgian Society. In 1979 the Castletown Federation took it over and it is now cared for by Dúchas, who have just finished a £4.9 million restoration of the property.

Many of the magnificent rooms were decorated well after the building had been finished. The Italian Francini brothers did the plasterwork in the hall and above the main staircase.

Castletown has two follies, commissioned by William Conolly's wife, Lady Louisa, to provide employment for the poor. The **obelisk**, designed by Richard Castle, can be seen from the Long Gallery at the back of the house. Completed in 1740, it consists of a series of arches piled one upon another and topped by a 40m-high obelisk.

The even more curious **Wonderful Barn**, lying north-east on private property just outside Leixlip, dates from 1743. It consists of four domes one on top of another and scaled by a spiral staircase. It too has recently been renovated.

The house (☎ 628 8252) opens 10 am to 6 pm on weekdays, and 1 to 6 pm at the weekend, June to September; 10 am to 5 pm on weekdays, and 1 to 5 pm on Sunday, in October; and 2 to 5 pm (6 pm in April and May) on Sunday only, November to May. Admission costs £2.50/1.

Dublin bus Nos 67 or 67A to Celbridge will drop you at the gate. The fare is £2.50 from Dublin, and the trip takes about an hour.

Celbridge Abbey

At the other end of Main St from Castletown House, and beside the River Liffey, is Celbridge Abbey, built in the 1690s by Bartholomew van Homrigh, a Dutch merchant who became Lord Mayor of Dublin. His daughter, Vanessa, was a close friend of Jonathan Swift, whose visits to her at the abbey she marked by preparing a bower and planting laurel trees.

The abbey is now owned by the St John of God Brothers but the picturesque grounds

are open to the public 10 am to 6 pm Monday to Saturday, and noon to 6 pm on Sunday. Admission costs £2.50/1.50. Facilities include a model railway, river walks, picnic areas and a café.

Places to Stay

One kilometre out of town on the Dublin road is **Green Acre** (☎ 627 1163), a B&B with beds costing upwards of £18. **Mt Carmel** (☎ 627 3461), a little farther out, has very similar facilities and singles/doubles costing £22/34; it opens mid-March to October.

More expensive is **Setanta House** (☎ 627 1111, fax 627 3387, Clane Rd), an elegant family-run hotel, with singles/doubles costing £65/85 with breakfast.

Places to Eat

For tea, coffee or a light meal, head for **Gulliver's** just inside the entrance to the abbey. **Castletown Inn** has things such as burgers costing upwards of £3.25.

Getting There & Away

Bus Nos 67 and 67A go from Middle Abbey St in Dublin to Celbridge, departing every 40 minutes.

STRAFFAN

South-west of Celbridge on the road to Clane, in the village of Straffan, is the **Straffan Steam Museum**, housed in the former church of St Jude in Lodge Park. The museum contains several working steam engines and displays on the history of steam power. It opens 2 to 6 pm Tuesday to Saturday, June to August; and 2.30 to 5.30 pm on Sunday only, April, May and September. Admission costs £3/2.

At the **Straffan Butterfly Farm** in Ovidstown, you can see butterflies flying freely in a tropical greenhouse, as well as stick insects, bird-eating spiders and reptiles safely behind glass. The farm opens noon to 5.30 pm daily, May to late August. Admission costs £2.50/1.50.

Bus Éireann (☎ 01-836 6111) runs five services daily (one on Sunday) from Dublin to Straffan.

BOG OF ALLEN

The Bog of Allen is Ireland's best-known raised bog, a huge expanse of peat that once covered much of the midlands. The bog stretches like a brown desert through Offaly, Laois and Kildare, but like other raised bogs it's rapidly being reduced to potting compost and fuel. For details of the Bord na Móna Bog Rail Tour, see Shannonbridge in the County Offaly section later in this chapter. (See also the boxed text 'Ireland's Disappearing Bogs' in the Facts about Ireland chapter.)

RATHANGAN

☎ 045 • pop 1190

The sleepy Victorian village of Rathangan, surrounded by the Bog of Allen, is on the Grand Canal 20km west of Naas but well off the beaten track. For information on coarse fishing and boat hire contact John Conway (☎ 524331) at the Carasli Caravan and Camping Park.

Peatland World

In a converted farm in Lullymore on the R414 9km north-east of Rathangan is Peatland World, an interpretive centre with displays covering flora, fauna, fuel, conservation and archaeological finds, as well as a video presentation and trails through parts of the bog.

It opens 9.30 am to 5 pm on weekdays, and 2 to 6 pm at the weekend. Admission costs £2/1 (students £1.50).

Places to Stay

Carasli Caravan and Camping Park (☎ 524331), on the outskirts of Rathangan, charges £8 per tent plus £1 for power. The entrance is beside the Jet service station.

Milorka (☎ 524544) is 1km along the Portarlington road in Kilnantogue. B&B in excellent rooms costs £18 per person, and evening meals are available.

Places to Eat

Tommies, on the main street, serves reliable burgers, fish and chips, and other meals costing around £3.50. *Dillon's Bar* and *Village Pump* are worth trying for pub food.

HILL OF ALLEN

The Hill of Allen rises above the flatlands of Kildare, which gradually change from green to the desolate brown of the Bog of Allen. Nine kilometres north-west of Newbridge and marked today by a folly, the hill has been a strategic spot through the centuries due to its commanding views in all directions.

The Iron Age fortifications are said to mark the home of Fionn McCumhaill, the leader of the Fianna, a mythical band of warriors who feature in many tales of ancient Ireland (see also the boxed text 'Fionn McCumhaill & the Salmon of Knowledge' in the Counties Meath & Louth chapter).

ROBERTSTOWN

Tiny Robertstown might have had all passing traffic diverted for the past 100 years. It's 12km north-west of Naas, and its old buildings overlook the Grand Canal, which is spanned by a stone bridge. On summer Sundays, the refurbished barge, *Eustace*, offers short cruises (☎ 045-870005). (See Barges & Boats in the Grand & Royal Canals section earlier in this chapter.)

NAAS

☎ 045 • pop 14,074

Kildare's uninspiring county town of Naas (pronounced 'Nace') is about 27km south-west of Dublin. You're probably unlikely to want to linger unless you're visiting the Naas, Punchestown or Curragh racecourses, although Naas (An Nás) does have a cinema, reasonable shops and an array of pubs boasting the Sky sports channel so no-one need miss the racing.

Tourist information is available from the Apollo Travel Agency (☎ 876934), 19 North Main St.

One kilometre south on the N7 to Kildare town is **Jigginstown House**, Naas' only notable ruin, which was begun by Thomas Wentworth, earl of Strafford and lord deputy of Ireland from 1632 to 1641. It would have been one of Ireland's largest brick buildings if he hadn't been executed before it was finished.

CENTRAL SOUTH

Places to Stay

B&B is available at *Avondale* (☎ 876254) on the Dublin road for £40 for doubles, or at *Lucerne* (☎ 897533), farther along the Dublin road, for £28/42 for singles/doubles. If you want to splash out, a good place to stay is *Naas Court Hotel* (☎ 866073, Main St), where rooms cost £52.50/80.

Places to Eat

Opposite the bus stop on Main St, *Hanra-han's* serves snacks such as chicken vol-au-vents (£1.95), while *Alice's Restaurant* offers big breakfasts, and tea and cakes. *Five Lamps* (Main St) serves pub lunches round a roaring fire.

In Kilcullen Rd, the southerly extension of Main St, *Finan's Restaurant and Pizzeria* serves up set lunches costing £4.95 and Punchestown Special set dinners costing £15.95. A very good place for a quick burger is *Jailhouse Diner* in the Naas Court Hotel.

Getting There & Away

Bus Éireann (☎ 01-836 6111) runs hourly services to Dublin, as well as services to Limerick, Kilkenny, Waterford, Clonmel, Portlaoise, Kildare, Carlow and Newbridge. New Princess Coaches (☎ 01-679 1549) offers two services daily from Dublin to Kilkenny and Clonmel via Naas. The bus stop is along Main St opposite the post office.

NEWBRIDGE & THE CURRAGH
☎ 045 • pop 12,970

The town of Newbridge (Droichead Nua) is the gateway to the Curragh. At around 20 sq km, it is one of the country's largest pieces of unfenced fertile land and is home to the Curragh Racecourse (☎ 41205) and a large military training barracks. Horse trainers use the Curragh's wide open spaces to exercise their thoroughbred charges.

The N7 highway runs through the Curragh between Newbridge and Kildare town. The No 126 Dublin to Kildare bus service stops in Newbridge and at Curragh Camp. You might want to pause to visit the **Newbridge Cutlery Visitor Centre**.

KILDARE
☎ 045 • pop 4278

Kildare is a small cathedral and market town 24km south-west of Naas. Its busy triangular square with pubs on each side makes a pleasant change from the county's other nondescript urban centres, although when it's wet it is an awfully dreary place.

In Market House in the centre of the square, the county's main tourist office (☎ 522696) is, unfortunately, a bit of a disaster. Nominally open from June to September, it suffers from lack of funding and staffing. At the time of writing it was closed; whether this sorry state of affairs will be remedied is anyone's guess.

St Brigid's Cathedral

One of the country's best-loved saints, St Brigid is remembered by St Brigid's Cross, a simply constructed four-pointed cross woven from reeds and found in many homes and gift shops. In the 5th century she founded a religious centre, unusual in that it was shared by nuns and monks, who were separated by screens in church. A fire, tended only by virgins over the age of 30, was kept burning perpetually in a fire temple, out of bounds to males. It survived until the dissolution of the monasteries in 1537. The restored fire pit can be seen in the grounds of the 13th-century Protestant St Brigid's Cathedral, whose solid presence looms over Kildare square.

Inside the cathedral, there is a fine stained-glass window facing west that depicts the three main saints of Ireland: Patrick, Brigid and Colmcille. The most important monument in the church is the tomb of Walter Wellesley, bishop of Kildare from 1529 to his death 10 years later. The tomb disappeared soon after his death and was found again only in 1971, when it was restored and placed in the cathedral.

The 10th-century round tower in the grounds is Ireland's second highest at 32.9m. Its original conical top has been replaced with an unusual Norman battlement. In the graveyard are buried members of the Fitzgerald family, earls and dukes of Kildare.

The cathedral and round tower open 10 am to 1 pm and 2 to 5 pm Monday to Saturday, and 2 to 5 pm on Sunday, May to October. Provided the guardian is around, you can also climb to the top of the round tower on payment of £2. To see the cathedral, a donation of 50p for the upkeep is requested.

Irish National Stud & Japanese Gardens

More than any other county, Kildare is synonymous with the multi-million-pound bloodstock industry. Kildare town is twinned with another famous horse-breeding centre, Lexington-Fayette in Kentucky, USA.

The Irish National Stud (☎ 521251), 1km south of the centre in Tully, was set up in 1900 by Colonel Hall Walker (of Johnnie Walker whiskey fame, later Lord Wavertree), who gave it to the Crown in 1915. The site was chosen because the mineral-rich River Tully is especially good for bone formation. Walker was remarkably successful with his horses, although his breeding techniques were notably eccentric: when a foal was born, he drew up its horoscope and used this to decide whether to keep it. The stallion boxes were built with lantern roofs that were opened to reveal the moon and the stars, thus influencing the horses' fortunes. In the hands of the Irish government since 1943, the stud's purpose is to breed high-quality stallions to mate with mares from all over the world.

On the hour every hour there are guided tours of the stud which let you see the intensive-care unit for newborn foals and learn about the horse that likes to listen to the radio and the horse with the straw allergy. Afterwards you can walk through the various stables, paddocks and meadows, or pop into the foaling unit and watch a 10-minute video on the birth of a foal. Better still, if you visit in spring or early summer, you might be able to watch a foal being born. Look out for Vintage Crop, the horse who won the Melbourne Cup in 1993 and earned over £1 million before coming here to retire.

The small but interesting **Irish Horse Museum** examines the role horses have played in Irish life over the centuries and includes the skeleton of Arkle, who won the prestigious Cheltenham Gold Cup race in Britain three years running in the 1960s. There's also a lengthy video on Arkle's life. Arkle was the object of national adoration and after his death in 1968 the country went into mourning.

Next door are the delightful Japanese Gardens (☎ 521617), created between 1906 and 1910 by Colonel Hall Walker. Laid out by master gardeners Tassa Eida and his son Minoru (and 40 other nameless workers!), they are considered by experts to be the best of their kind in Europe. Although not entirely oriental in style (they include such western trees as Scots pine), they were created in accordance with the strict rules of Japanese gardening.

The gardens chart the journey from birth to death through 20 landmarks, including the Tunnel of Ignorance (No 3, which represents a child's lack of knowledge), the Hill of Ambition (No 13) and a series of bridges signifying – among other things – engagement (No 8) and marriage (No 9). Finally, you pass through the Gateway to Eternity (No 20), beyond which lies not everlasting life but a Buddhist sand garden. Despite the incongruity of its setting, the garden is a wonderful place to go for a stroll, provided it isn't raining!

The National Stud and Japanese Gardens open 9.30 am to 6 pm daily, February to November. The large visitor centre houses a café, a shop and a children's play area. Admission is with a combined ticket costing £6/4.50, with a £1 discount for Bus Éireann ticket holders.

If you walk from Kildare look out for the ruins of the 12th-century **Black Abbey** on the left. Shortly afterwards a turn on the right leads to **St Brigid's Well**. It's probably sacrilegious to say so but this quiet spot would make a great place for a picnic.

Places to Stay

In town, *Fremont (☎ 521604)*, just south of the town square on the Tully road, charges

A Day at the Races

Kildare has more horseflesh per square kilometre than any other Irish county, and the race-courses are home to some of the biggest meetings of the year. The calcium-rich grass breeds strong-boned horses, while excellent stud facilities and generous tax concessions attract many foreign horse owners.

Travelling through Kildare you'll see plenty of studs, most of them private and not too keen on visitors. You can, however, visit the state-owned National Stud just outside Kildare town. You could also check out a thoroughbred auction at Goff's Sales (☎ 045-877211), Kildare Paddocks, a huge complex beside the main Dublin road (N7) near Kill, north-east of Naas. There you'll see spindly thoroughbred foals and yearlings change hands for astronomical sums.

Almost everyone in Ireland goes to the races. At meetings you'll see all of Irish society at play: the glitterati swilling champagne in their private boxes and the ordinary punters oblivious to everything except their bets – and, between races, their drink.

With three of Ireland's most famous tracks, Kildare has racing year round. Best known is the Curragh Racecourse (☎ 045-441205), over 2km south-west of Newbridge on the road to Kildare town. The March to November Curragh Racecourse season boasts some of the biggest meetings of the country's racing calendar, including the 1000 and 2000 Guineas in May, the Irish Derby in June, the Irish Oaks in July, and the St Leger in September. Expect to pay around £10 for a ticket.

Four kilometres south of Naas is Punchestown (☎ 045-897704), a top-notch steeplechase course where the Irish National Hunt Festival is held every April; a ticket will cost around £10. Finally, just to the north, Naas has its own racetrack (☎ 045-897391), which holds well-attended meetings every two weeks or so.

Special bus services operate from Dublin's Busáras to the Curragh, Naas and Punchestown on race days; phone Bus Éireann (☎ 01-873 4222) for details. There are also special train services to Curragh on race days; phone ☎ 01-836 6222 for details.

£18/36 for singles/doubles. *Catherine Singleton's* (☎ *521964, 1 Dara Park*), off Station Rd, has three en suite doubles costing £35.

Lord Edward Guesthouse (☎ *522389*), behind the Silken Thomas pub on the square, charges £18/30. On the Dublin road, *Curragh Lodge Hotel* (☎ *522144*) charges £35 per person for B&B.

In Maddenstown, near the Irish National Stud, *St Mary's* (☎ *521243*) offers B&B costing £16 per person.

Places to Eat

You needn't move far from the main square for a meal. For fast food there's a branch of *Abrakebabra* on the corner of Market Square and Station Rd. Just down Station Rd is *The Country Kitchen*, which does a full Irish breakfast costing £3.20 and other

hearty dishes for around the same price. *Simply Gourmet* serves everything from breakfasts through to full dinners, although it can't quite live up to the promise of its name. Nearby *George's* (☎ *521984*) offers pasta costing upwards of £5.95 and pizza from £4.95.

Silken Thomas (☎ *522232*), partly converted out of a cinema, has an unusually impressive, popular menu costing around £10. Upstairs is the Geraldine Hall, which puts on local plays. *Boland's Pub* across the square serves dishes such as steak-and-mushroom pie (£2.50).

Getting There & Away

Bus The main N7 highway from Dublin to western Ireland passes through Kildare. Bus Éireann runs numerous coaches from the Busáras (☎ 01-836 6111) which take about

1½ hours. One bus daily (two on Sunday) stops at the Irish National Stud; a day return costs £5/2.75.

Train Kildare is on the Dublin to Limerick to Ennis, Dublin to Galway and Dublin to Kilkenny to Waterford train lines. It's 30 minutes from Dublin (£7.50). For other details ring ☎ 01-836 6222.

NAAS TO CARLOW

The 48km stretch of the N9 between Naas and Carlow town offers several interesting side trips.

Kilcullen

The tiny village of Kilcullen is on the River Liffey, 12km east of Kildare town. Nearby at **Old Kilcullen**, the scant remains of a high cross and round tower are all that remain of an early-Christian settlement.

On the edge of the Curragh, 4km north-west of Kilcullen on the western side of the L19, **Donnelly's Hollow** was the scene of numerous victories of Dan Donnelly (1788–1820), Ireland's greatest bare-knuckle fighter of the 19th century. It's said he had a reach so long that he could touch his knees without having to stoop, and that a fight here attracted about 20,000 spectators. An obelisk at the centre of the hollow details his glorious career.

Back in Kilcullen his mummified arm can be seen in **The Hideout** (☎ 045-81232), a famous and wildly eccentric pub.

Ballitore & Timolin

During the 18th and 19th centuries, Ballitore was a Quaker settlement. One of the settlers was Abraham Shackleton, an ancestor of the Antarctic explorer Ernest, who was born nearby in Kilkea House.

The **Quaker Museum** (☎ 0507-431109) is housed in an old schoolhouse; its most famous student was political philosopher Edmund Burke (1729–97). Burke later studied at Trinity College, Dublin, and had one of the libraries there named after him. The museum opens 11 am to 6 pm Tuesday to Friday, and 11 am to 1 pm on Saturday, year round, depending on the presence of the

caretaker. A small donation is requested but not required.

Crookstown Mill and Heritage Centre (☎ 0507-23222) has a functioning water mill and a display covering the history of milling and baking. It also has a coffee shop and a new craft shop. It opens 10 am to 7 or 8 pm daily, April to September. Admission costs £2.50/1.50.

Two kilometres west is the **Rath of Mullaghmast**, an Iron Age hill fort where Daniel O'Connell, champion of Catholic emancipation, held one of his 'monster rallies' in 1843.

Three kilometres south of Ballitore and just north of Moone, the village of Timolin is home to the **Irish Pewter Mill and Craft Centre** (☎ 0507-24164).

Woodcourte House (☎ *0507-24167*), in Timolin, has a tennis court, runs arts-and-crafts weekends and offers B&B costing upwards of £17.50 per person with bathroom. Take the turn beside the Sportsman Inn and the house is about 200m on the right past the Irish Pewter Mill.

Moone

The barely noticeable village of Moone is just south of Timolin. One kilometre west in an early-Christian monastic churchyard is the magnificent **Moone High Cross**. This 8th- or 9th-century masterpiece is slender and, at 6m, remarkably tall. The numerous crisply carved panels display biblical scenes including the loaves and fishes, the flight into Egypt and a wonderful representation of the 12 apostles.

The 18th-century *Moone High Cross Inn* (☎ *0502-24112*) is a delightful bar and guesthouse about 100m west of the N9, 1km south of Moone village. It does hefty pub food including a great Irish stew. B&B costs £25 per person. It is closed in January.

Kilkea Castle

This 12th-century castle, completely restored in the 19th century, is 5km north-west of Castledermot on the Athy road and was once the second home of the Maynooth Fitzgeralds. The castle grounds are supposed to be haunted by the son of Silken

Thomas, Gerald the Wizard Earl, who rises every seven years from the Rath of Mullaghmast to free Ireland from its enemies, a neat trick given that the Wizard Earl was buried in London.

Although the castle is now an exclusive hotel (☎ 0503-45156, fax 45187) you can still have a drink in the bar and pick up a booklet on the building's history. Among its oddities is an **Evil Eye Stone** set high up on the exterior wall at the back of the castle. Thought to date from the 13th or 14th century, this is a depiction of various animal, half-human and birdlike figures erotically entwined. The castle has formal gardens and a forest park.

In case you're interested, accommodation starts at £100/140 for singles/doubles.

Castledermot

Castledermot's ruined **Franciscan friary** is right by the road at the southern end of town on Abbey St. It dates from the mid-13th century and the key is available from the adjacent cottage.

A little farther north on Main St and back from the road is a **churchyard**, the site of a monastery founded originally by St Diarmuid in 812. Two fine 9th- or 10th-century granite high crosses stand beside the remains of a round tower 20m high and topped with a medieval battlement, and a 12th-century Romanesque church doorway.

Places to Stay & Eat The old stone *Kilkea Lodge* (☎ 0503-45112) has big open fires and is more expensive than most B&Bs at £30 a bed. The small, intimate *Doyle's Schoolhouse Inn* (☎ 0503-44282) is consistently rated as one of Ireland's best restaurants. Dinner will cost around £27 and reservations are essential. It also offers B&B at £28 per person.

ATHY

☎ 0507 • pop 5306

Founded in the 12th century, Athy (pronounced 'A-thigh') sits at the junction of the River Barrow and the Grand Canal near the County Laois border. Athy (Áth Í) has the feel of a genuine country town, with a pleasant if somewhat dilapidated old square. The 16th-century tower of **White Castle**, built by the earls of Kildare, who once owned the town, is now a private house. The modern Catholic church is unremarkable but for the interior, which has Stations of the Cross by noted Irish artist George Campbell and a crucifix designed by local artist Brid Ní Rinn.

The tourist office (☎ 31859), in the town hall building on Emily Square, opens year round. The town hall also houses a local museum and library.

There's coarse, salmon and trout fishing on the Grand Canal and the River Barrow. For information check with Kane's pub (☎ 31434).

Places to Stay & Eat

There are several B&Bs in and around Athy. *Forest Farm* (☎ 31231), a small country farmhouse 5km out of Athy on the Dublin road, and the *Ballindrum Farm* (☎ 26294), a few kilometres farther out in Ballindrum, both charge around £22/34 for singles/doubles without bath.

For cheap-and-cheerful pub food, try *Castle Inn (Leinster St)*, or the *Leinster Arms* on the corner of Emily Square. *Duck Press Restaurant* (☎ 38952), at the southern end of Leinster St over the river, is good for lunch or dinner.

The excellent *Tonlegee House* (☎/fax 31473), in a beautiful setting beside the remains of an old church south of town on the Kilkenny road, is expensive at about £28 for dinner. It also has guest rooms upstairs costing £55/75 for singles/doubles.

Getting There & Away

Buses from Dublin to Clonmel stop at Athy and provide connections to Naas, Kilkenny and Carrick-on-Suir. Contact Bus Éireann (☎ 01-836 6111) or JJ Kavanagh (☎ 056-31106) for details.

County Carlow

Carlow (Ceatharlach), Ireland's second-smallest county, has the scenic Blackstairs

Mountains to the east, the Killeshin Hills to the west, and sections of the Rivers Barrow and Slaney, with quietly picturesque villages such as Rathvilly, Leighlinbridge and Borris. The Dublin to Carlow town route via south-western Wicklow runs through some wild and lightly populated country. The rest of Carlow is mainly undulating farmland where you will quite often see sugar beet awaiting collection by the roadside. Browne's Hill Dolmen, the county's most interesting archaeological feature, is just outside Carlow town.

CARLOW
☎ 0503 • pop 11,721
Its strategic location on the River Barrow, on the border with the Pale, made Carlow a frontier town for many centuries. Today, it's a busy market and industrial centre serving a large rural area. Carlow was the first town outside Dublin to have electric street lighting, from power generated downstream at Milford. Railway pioneer William Dargan, who founded the National Gallery in Dublin, was born here. Perhaps the main reason for pausing is to inspect Browne's Hill Dolmen on the outskirts.

Orientation & Information
Dublin St is the city's principal north-south axis, with Tullow St, the main shopping street, running off it at a right angle. The tourist office (☎ 31554), in Kennedy Ave, is theoretically open year round. The post office is on the corner of Kennedy Ave and Dublin St.

Things to See
In Castle St, Carlow Castle was built by William Marshall in the 12th century on the site of an earlier Norman motte-and-bailey fort. Officials once had to be paid danger money to live here among the native Irish. The castle survived Cromwell's attentions and would be largely intact if a Dr Middleton hadn't decided to turn it into an asylum and blow it up in 1814; the mighty castle was reduced to a single wall flanked by two towers.

It's said that the plans for Carlow and

Cork courthouses got mixed up, so this little town ended up with Richard Morrison's splendid 1830 building, based on the Parthenon in Athens, while Cork had to make do with a less impressive design. The cannon beside the steps was taken from the Russians during the Crimean War. The **courthouse** is at the northern end of Dublin St.

Down College St from the courthouse, the 1833 **Cathedral of the Assumption** has an elaborate pulpit and some fine stained-glass windows. John Hogan's statue of Bishop Doyle, better known as JKL (James of Kildare and Leighin) for his work as a supporter of Catholic emancipation, includes a woman who represents Ireland rising up against her oppressors.

The small **Carlow County Museum** is housed in the town hall, on Centaur St off the Haymarket. It has some interesting displays on the town's history. It opens 11 am to 5 pm Tuesday to Friday, and 2 to 5 pm at the weekend. Admission costs £1/50p.

In 1798, 640 United Irish rebels were killed in the bloodiest fighting of the rising around what is now Tullow St. A Celtic **high cross** marks the Croppie Grave, across the river, where most of the bodies were buried.

Activities
The River Barrow is popular with canoeists, kayakers and rowers (Carlow Rowing Club has been going since 1859). Otterholt Riverside Lodge (see Places to Stay) can arrange canoeing for around £14 for a half-day. Alternatively, phone Adventure Canoeing Days on ☎ 0509-31307.

Places to Stay
The IHH *Otterholt Riverside Lodge* (☎ 30404, Kilkenny Rd) has delightful gardens and charges £9 in a 10-bed dorm. *Red Setter House* (☎ 41848, 14 Dublin St) is a spotless, central B&B with a range of rooms, some with shower, some without. Prices start at £16/32 for singles/doubles. *Barrow Lodge* (☎ 41173) has a pleasant riverside setting and beds costing £18 per person.

CENTRAL SOUTH

Royal Hotel (☎ *31621, 8 Dublin St*) has rooms costing £38/65. The modern *Óstan Dinn Rí* (☎ *43311, Tullow St*) has singles/doubles for £35/57 in a complex with bar, restaurant and nightclub.

Places to Eat

Muffins (*Tullow St*) serves 'healthy' breakfasts (£1.95). Also on Tullow St, *Bradbury's Coffee Shop* is good for light lunches (soup and a roll £1.20) and is one of the few places other than pubs open on Sunday.

Teach Dolmain (*Tullow St*) has a lengthy bar-meals menu; seafood chowder costs £2.75, and a thoroughly unhealthy vegetarian mix of french fries, onion rings and battered mushrooms in mayonnaise costs £3.95.

Beams Restaurant (☎ *31824, Dublin St*) opens Tuesday to Saturday for meals costing £10 to £13. Nearby *The Owl* does a range of 'roast beef and shepherd's pie' style meals. Across the road in the *Royal Hotel Restaurant*, pasta in an asparagus sauce costs £5.50.

Entertainment

Carlow has wall-to-wall pubs, with something to suit most tastes. The triangular Haymarket is very typical, with *Tormey's*, *Ewing's* and *The Market House Bar* facing each other along the sides. *The Plough* (*Tullow St*) has a few outdoor tables, chickens and a dovecote. Farther up the road *Teach Dolmain* makes much of its dolmen décor. *The Castle Inn* has traditional music on Friday night.

Óstan Dinn Rí has a Thursday nightclub with free admission until 2 am. When bands play there's a variable admission charge, but it's usually no more than £5.

Getting There & Away

Bus Bus Éireann (☎ *01-836 6111*) has regular services to Dublin (1½ hours, at least five daily), Kilkenny (30 minutes, three daily except Sunday) and Waterford (1½ hours, at least five daily). Rapid Express Coaches (☎ *43081*) has at least seven buses daily to Dublin and Waterford. JJ Kavanagh

(☎ 43081) has a twice-daily service to Athy, Monasterevin, the Curragh and Kildare; a daily service to Portlaoise; a service to Wexford; a Friday and Sunday service to Cork via Kilkenny, Cashel and Cahir; and a Friday and Sunday service to Limerick. All these buses leave from near the Rapid Express office on Barrack St south of the post office.

Train The station (☎ 31633) is on Railway St to the north-east of town. Carlow is on the Dublin to Kilkenny and Waterford line with at least four trains daily in each direction (three on Sunday). A day return to Dublin or Waterford costs £5.50.

AROUND CARLOW TOWN

There's no public transport to the following sights, but they are within easy cycling distance of Carlow town.

Browne's Hill Dolmen

This 5000-year-old granite monster is believed to have the largest capstone in Europe, weighing well over 100 tonnes. When complete, the structure would have been covered with a mound of earth. The dolmen is 3km east of town on the R726 Hacketstown road; a path leads round the field to the dolmen.

Milford

One of the nicer drives to the south is via Milford on the minor road that follows the River Barrow valley. The village lies midway between Carlow town and Leighlinbridge. The old mill at Milford was the site of the turbine that first powered Carlow town's electric street lighting in the 1890s. John Alexander, the present owner, still runs a turbine and supplies electricity to the Electricity Supply Board (ESB). There's good salmon and trout fishing here.

TULLOW

☎ 0503 • pop 2244

Tullow is a well-known angling town on the River Slaney in the north of the county. Father John Murphy, a local leader of the 1798 Rising, was captured and executed in the market square in July 1798; a memorial stands in the town centre. **Tullow Museum**, beside the town bridge, opens on Sunday and Wednesday afternoons.

Five kilometres due east of Tullow on Shillelagh Rd is the Iron Age ring fort of **Rathgall**, dating from the 8th century BC and protected by three overgrown outer ring walls. The final wall is still in good condition, though somewhat lower nowadays. Rathgall is said to be the burial site of the kings of Leinster.

Eleven kilometres south-west of Tullow near Ballon are the beautiful **Altamont Gardens**, with a lake, bog garden and arboretum. Unfortunately they're only open from 2 to 6 pm on Sunday and bank holidays, April to October. Admission costs £2.50.

Places to Stay
The early-Georgian *Sherwood Park House* (☎ 59117) is south of Tullow in Kilbride just off the N80 between Ballon and Kildavin. B&B costs £28/44 for singles/doubles with bathroom.

Getting There & Away
Tullow is on Bus Éireann's (☎ 01-836 6111) Dublin to Waterford route, which also stops at Enniscorthy and New Ross. There are three buses daily in each direction (two on Sunday).

BORRIS
☎ 0503 • pop 584
Sixteen kilometres south of Leighlinbridge, the Georgian village of Borris is overlooked by a disused railway viaduct with 16 arches. **Borris House** is the residence of the MacMurrough Kavanaghs, descendants of the ancient kings of Leinster, and is still in the family's possession, Andrew MacMurrough Kavanagh being the present occupant.

A most remarkable MacMurrough Kavanagh was Arthur (1831–89), who was born with only rudimentary limbs yet learned to ride and shoot and later became an MP. Visits to the castle are by appointment only. The entrance is at the northern end of town near the White House pub.

Borris is a starting point for the Mt Lein-

ster Scenic Drive (which can also be walked) and is also on the South Leinster Way. Alternatively, there's a lovely 10km walk along a towpath beside the River Barrow to picturesque Graiguenamanagh, just inside County Kilkenny.

Places to Stay & Eat
Breen's (☎ 732318, Church St) offers B&B costing £15/30 for singles/doubles. Halfway between Borris and Bagenalstown, *Lorum Old Rectory* (☎ 735282) is overlooked by the Blackstairs Mountains and charges upwards of £31.50/52, with good dinners costing £22.

Getting There & Away
Foley's (☎ 24641) operates one bus daily (except Sunday) to Borris from Kilkenny, leaving at 5.30 pm.

MT LEINSTER
At 796m, Mt Leinster offers some of Ireland's finest hang-gliding. It's also worth the hike up for the panoramic views over Counties Carlow, Wexford and Wicklow. To get there from Borris, follow the Mt Leinster Scenic Drive signposts 13km towards Bunclody in County Wexford (see Mt Leinster in the Counties Wexford & Waterford chapter for details). It takes a good two hours on foot or 20 minutes by car.

SOUTH LEINSTER WAY
South-west of Clonegal, on the northern slopes of Mt Leinster, is the tiny village of **Kildavin**, the starting point of the South Leinster Way. See Walking in the Activities chapter for details.

County Laois

Laois (pronounced 'Leash') is a 1½ hour drive south-west of Dublin and is the only inland county surrounded on all sides by counties that do not touch the coast. For most visitors it's somewhere to whip through en route to Limerick or Cork, with a fairly uninteresting landscape of raised bogs and poor farms. Yet with time to linger

CENTRAL SOUTH

you'll find some pleasant country towns and the unspoiled Slieve Bloom Mountains.

PORTLAOISE
☎ 0502 • pop 3531
Although founded by the O'Mores just before the 16th-century Plantations, Portlaoise is mostly modern, and only the courthouse by Richard Morrison on the corner of Main and Church Sts is notable. Bristling with wire fencing at the eastern end of town is a maximum-security prison, Portlaoise's main claim to fame for many people. Even before the bypass was built there was little to linger for. Once it's completed you'll probably sweep straight past.

To the west lie the Slieve Bloom Mountains, while to the east is the one historic site worth a special detour, the impressive Rock of Dunamase on the Stradbally road (see the following section).

Information
The tourist office (☎ 21178), in the shopping-centre car park beside the bypass on James Fintan Lawlor Ave, has lots of information on the county. To get there from Main St, cut through the lane beside Dowling's café. It opens 10 am to 6 pm Monday to Saturday, May to September.

Places to Stay & Eat
If you need a hotel, *O'Loughlin's* (☎ *21305, Main St*) offers singles/doubles costing £27.50/43. There's a bar and restaurant downstairs.

Dowling's, also on Main St, serves good hot food (upwards of £4) and sandwiches during the day.

Getting There & Away
Bus Portlaoise is on one of the busiest main roads in the country, at the junction of the N8 and N7, with frequent Bus Éireann (☎ 01-836 6111) buses passing between Dublin and Cashel, Cork, Limerick and Kerry. It is also on the Waterford, Kilkenny, Carlow, Athlone and Longford route.

JJ Kavanagh's private bus company (☎ 056-31106) runs two buses daily to Carlow.

Train Just one hour from Dublin on the main line to Tipperary, Cork, Limerick and Tralee, Portlaoise is serviced by numerous daily trains. The station (☎ 21303), on Railway St, is a five-minute walk north of the town centre.

ROCK OF DUNAMASE
Six kilometres east of Portlaoise along the Stradbally road is a dramatic fractured limestone hill covered with the remains of fortifications. It may not be Cashel, but the surrounding countryside is so flat that the summit offers fine views of the Timahoe round tower to the south, the Slieve Blooms to the north and – on a clear day – the Wicklow Mountains to the east.

It seems that the site was known outside Ireland as long ago as 500 BC. The Egyptian astronomer Ptolemy wrote of a place called Dunum, and it is held here that what he was writing of was Dun Masc, the Celtic name for Dunamase. Little was left of the original fortifications after a sacking by the Vikings in 845. The slopes of Dunamase can be treacherous, particularly on the northern side, and these natural barriers would have complicated any assault on its defenders.

Dunamase was later given away by Dermot MacMurrough, king of Leinster, as part of his daughter Aoife's dowry when in 1170 she married Strongbow, the Norman invader of Ireland. Dunamase was then reinforced by William Marshall, Strongbow's successor, who built three baileys on the spot.

The local clan, the O'Mores, captured the rock from the English near the end of the 14th century and held it until it was retaken by Charles Coote in 1641. He was a leading Parliamentarian and one of Cromwell's most able leaders in Ireland. Recaptured five years later by Catholic forces, it was finally wrecked by Cromwell's henchmen Reynolds and Hewson in 1650. Hewson gave his name to the hill to the south-west, which has the ruined 9th-century church of Dysert.

The earth embankments 500m to the east of the rock are known as Cromwell's lines, although they're actually the remains of an Iron Age two-ringed fort. The main ruins consist of a badly shattered 12- or 13th-century castle on the summit (best seen from the northern side) surrounded by an outer wall of which little remains. You enter the complex through the twin-towered gateway, which leads to the outer bailey and fortified courtyard to the south-east.

JJ Kavanagh's (☎ 056-31106) two daily Portlaoise to Carlow buses pass by the rock. Otherwise, it's a good hour's walk from Portlaoise town centre.

EMO COURT & DEMESNE

Thirteen kilometres north-east of Portlaoise and signposted off the main road to Dublin, Emo Court was the country seat of the 1st earl of Portarlington. The rather unusual house with its prominent green dome was designed by James Gandon (architect of Dublin's Customs House) in 1790 and served as a Jesuit novitiate for many years. The estate offers long walks through forests and by Emo Lake, and is littered with Greek statues. From the Emo village gate it's a 2km walk along the drive to the house.

Restored by Dúchas, the house (☎ 0502-26573) is open to the public for guided tours from 10 am to 6 pm daily, mid-June to mid-September. Admission costs £2/1. The grounds are open free during daylight hours.

South of Emo village off the main Portlaoise road is the elegantly simple **St John's Church**, in Coolbanagher, also designed by Gandon in 1786 as a replacement for a thatched church which was destroyed in 1779.

Emo is just off the main Portlaoise to Dublin road, and has daily buses in both directions.

STRADBALLY

The village of Stradbally (or Strathbally), 10km south-east of Portlaoise, was once a seat of the mighty O'More clan. Most of the present buildings date from the 17th century.

The O'Mores were the force behind the Franciscan friary established here in 1447.

The family were the holders of the *Book of Leinster*, a manuscript compiled between 1151 and 1224 to record all the knowledge of Aéd Crúamthainn, scribe to the high kings of Ireland. This book contained, among other things, vivid descriptions of the banqueting hall at Tara, the seat of the high kings, and is now to be found in Trinity College Library, Dublin.

Stradbally Steam Museum

At the southern end of town, this museum has a collection of fire engines, steam tractors and steamrollers, lovingly restored by the Irish Steam Preservation Society. Housed in a tightly packed warehouse, the prize exhibits include a Merryweather horse-drawn fire engine from 1880.

The 1895 Guinness Brewery steam locomotive in the village is used six times annually for a day trip to Dublin. During the three-day Steam Rally in early August the 40 hectares of Cosby Hall are taken over by steam-operated machines and vintage cars.

The museum opens 11 am to 1 pm and 2 to 4 pm on weekdays. Admission costs £1.50 (children free).

Getting There & Away

JJ Kavanagh (☎ 056-31106) runs two daily buses from Portlaoise to Carlow via Stradbally. Stradbally is also on Bus Éireann's (☎ 01-836 6111) twice-daily Waterford to Longford service, which also passes through Kilkenny, Carlow, Portlaoise and Athlone.

PORTARLINGTON
☎ 0502 • pop 3320

Portarlington (Cúil an tSúdaire) grew up under the influence of French Huguenot and German settlers introduced by Lord Arlington, who was granted land here after the Cromwellian wars. Some of the finer 18th-century buildings are a result of the efforts of Henry Dawson, earl of Portarlington, to improve the town. Unfortunately, many are terribly neglected.

The 1851 **St Paul's Church**, on the site of the original 17th-century French church, was built for the Huguenots, some of whose

CENTRAL SOUTH

tombstones stand in a corner of the churchyard. The power station's large **cooling tower** is a local landmark. Built in 1936, it was the first in Ireland to use peat to generate electricity.

Getting There & Away
Portarlington is on the main train lines between Dublin and Galway, Limerick, Tralee and Cork, with numerous daily trains in both directions. For details contact Portlaoise train station (☎ 0502-21303). There are no bus services.

LEA CASTLE
On the banks of the River Barrow 4km east of Portarlington, this ivy-clad 13th-century ruin was the stronghold of Maurice Fitzgerald, 2nd baron of Offaly. It consists of a fairly intact towered keep with two outer walls running down to the Barrow and a twin-towered gatehouse. It was burned in 1315 by Edward Bruce, the brother of King Robert Bruce of Scotland, when he came to Ireland at the invitation of Irish chieftains to create trouble for the Anglo-Normans. He hoped this would distract the English and lessen their pressure on his brother in Scotland. Crowned high king of Ireland, Edward Bruce hassled the forces loyal to England until he was killed in 1318 at the Battle of Faughart near Dundalk. His remains are said to be buried in a churchyard at Faughart 4km from Castleroche.

In the 16th century Silken Thomas sought refuge here after his failed 1534 rebellion against Henry VIII. In 1650 the castle was blown up by Cromwell's forces, fresh from their success at Dunamase. The castle stairways were filled with explosives to maximise the damage.

In early morning and evening the ruins can be tranquil and evocative. Access is through a farmyard half a kilometre to the north off the main Monasterevin road (R420).

MOUNTMELLICK
☎ 0502 • pop 2325
Mountmellick is a faded market town with many Georgian houses, 10km north of Port-

laoise on the River Owenass. Its fortunes rose with Quaker settlers who produced linen, which was exported by barge on a branch of the Grand Canal, which runs away to the east. Something of a boom town in the late 18th and early 19th centuries, it was home to Ireland's first sugar-beet factory, built in 1851. The small **visitor centre** (☎ 24525), with a display on Quaker life and Mountmellick embroidery, opens 10 am to 5 pm on weekdays year round; plus 2 to 6 pm at the weekend, June to September.

Getting There & Away
Mountmellick is on Bus Éireann's (☎ 01-836 6111) twice-daily Waterford to Longford route, which passes through Kilkenny, Carlow, Stradbally, Portlaoise and Athlone. There's also a daily service to and from Dublin via Naas, Newbridge and Kildare.

MOUNTRATH & AROUND
☎ 0502 • pop 1298
Like so many other Irish settlements, Mountrath is associated with St Patrick and St Brigid, who are supposed to have established religious houses here, although no trace of either remains. Much of the town and surrounding land belonged to Sir Charles Coote, an ardent supporter of Cromwell during and after the wars of the 1640s. Mountrath's glory days were in the 17th and 18th centuries, when it prospered from the linen industry.

St Fintan's Tree
Three kilometres east on the Portlaoise road, there are scant remains of the 6th-century monastery of St Fintan at Clonenagh. St Fintan's Tree is a large sycamore with a water-filled groove in one of its lower branches. Supposedly this never dries out, and the tree has long been a place of pilgrimage. The coins embedded in the trunk are offerings by pilgrims who attribute healing powers to the water.

Ballyfin House
Eight kilometres north of Mountrath off the Mountmellick road is Ballyfin House, built

by Sir Charles Henry Coote in 1850 to the designs of Richard Morrison (better known for his courthouses). Overlooking a small lake in quiet, rolling countryside, it has been described as Ireland's finest 19th-century house. Inside, some of the ornamentation is completely over the top: in the dining room, or 'gold room', someone ran amok with plaster and gold paint, creating something that would look at home in Versailles. Sir Charles reckoned all good houses should have a lake, and the one in front is artificial.

An intriguing piece of contemporary aristocratic eccentricity was megalithomania, or a passion for building imitation Stone Age monuments. Ballyfin has an excellent example in the form of a rough stone shelter hidden among the trees on the far side of the fence to the right of the avenue, about 200m short of the house. Such extravagances were still being built just years after the Potato Famine decimated the population. An unattractive modern wing now houses a school.

Places to Stay & Eat
The Lodge (☎ 32756, Coote Terrace) has four rooms with separate bathroom costing £19 per person. *Phelan's Restaurant*, on Main St by the square, serves reasonable burgers and chips.

One of the finest country houses in Ireland, *Roundwood House (☎ 32120)* is 5km outside Mountrath on the Slieve Blooms road. This Palladian mansion has wonderful original furnishings and superb service without a hint of pretension. For the quality of the place, the prices are decent at £51/82 for singles/doubles for B&B. The excellent dinner costs £23.

Getting There & Away
Mountrath is on the main Bus Éireann (☎ 01-836 6111) Dublin to Limerick route, with up to four buses daily in each direction. Buses stop in front of Darcy's.

SLIEVE BLOOM MOUNTAINS
One of the best reasons for visiting Laois is to explore the Slieve Bloom Mountains

(Slieve is pronounced 'Shleeve'). Their name means Mountains of Bladhma, after a Celtic warrior who used the mountains as a refuge. Though nowhere near as splendid as their cousins in Wicklow and the west, the Slieve Blooms win out for their relative absence of visitors. You can't miss the brown signs on almost every road into the hills.

The highest point is Mt Arderin (528m) south of the Glendine Gap on the Offaly border. On a clear day it's possible to see the highest points of all four of the ancient provinces of Ireland. East is Lugnaquilla in Leinster, west is Nephin in Connaught, north is Slieve Donard in Ulster, and south-west is Carrantuohil in Munster.

Mountrath to the south and lovely **Kinnitty** to the north of the hills make good bases. **Glenbarrow**, south-west of Rosenallis, has a gentle walk by the River Barrow, which has its source just a few kilometres farther up in the hills. There are some waterfalls, a large moraine on the northern side of the river and unusual local plants, including orchids, butterwort and blue fleabane. Other spots worth checking out are **Glendine Park** near the Glendine Gap, and the **Cut** mountain pass. The road north of the mountains from Mountmellick to Birr via Clonaslee and Kinnitty is particularly scenic.

Slieve Bloom Way
The Slieve Bloom Way is a 77km signposted trail which does a complete circuit of the mountains, taking in most major points of interest. See Walking in the Activities chapter for more details.

WESTERN LAOIS
South of the Slieve Bloom Mountains, **Borris-in-Ossory** on the N7, once known as the Gate of Munster, was a major coaching stop in the 18th century before the railways developed. It's on the Bus Éireann express Dublin to Limerick route, with four buses daily in each direction (three on Sunday).

About 3km farther west on the same road, **Ballaghmore Castle** (☎ 0505-21453) controlled the edges of the Fitzpatrick family lands and is one of several small castles

CENTRAL SOUTH

414 County Laois – Abbeyleix

open to the public. The square tower fortress dating from 1480 has been faithfully restored. Those with good eyesight might spot the **sheila-na-gig** in the southern wall. Ballaghmore Castle opens 9.30 am to 5.30 pm daily. Admission costs £2.50/1.50.

ABBEYLEIX

☎ 0502 • pop 1259

Abbeyleix, 14km south of Portlaoise, is as well tended a country town as you will find. It grew up around a 12th-century Cistercian monastery in nearby Old Town, though the only traces of this are two ancient monuments. In the 18th century the local landowner, Viscount de Vesci, moved the town centre to its present location and supervised the layout of tree-lined streets and neat town houses. During the Famine, de Vesci proved a kinder landlord than many and the fountain obelisk in the square was erected as a thank-you from his tenants.

De Vesci's mansion, **Abbeyleix House**, was erected in 1773 from a design by James Wyatt. It's 2km south-west of town on the Rathdowney road, but is not open to the public.

The old National School building at the Portlaoise end of town is now the **Heritage House**, which details the town's history and contains some examples of the Turkish-influenced carpets woven in Abbeyleix from 1904 to 1913. It opens 9 am to 5 pm on weekdays, and 1 to 5 pm at the weekend. Admission costs £2/1. A coffee shop in the basement serves breakfast until noon and light lunches.

Places to Stay & Eat

Creeper-clad *Preston House* (☎ *31432*) offers B&B in what were once the assembly rooms; a double costs £50. There's a café here too.

The striking greystone *Hibernian Hotel* (☎ *31252*) charges £34/54.50 for singles/doubles without breakfast.

Entertainment

Morrissey's in the high street is a marvellous old pub-shop which used to act as a travel agency and undertaker's as well.

Drinkers down their pints around an old-fashioned stovepipe, or perch on stools at a sloping counter gazing on packets of soap powder.

Getting There & Away

Abbeyleix is on an express Bus Éireann (☎ 01-836 6111) route between Dublin and Cork, with three buses daily (two on Sunday). JJ Kavanagh's private bus service (☎ 056-31106) runs a daily Portlaoise, Abbeyleix, Durrow, Cullahill and Urlingford bus, and a Friday-only service between Carlow and Limerick.

TIMAHOE

Tiny Timahoe is just a handful of houses around a grassy square, 10km north-east of Abbeyleix on a minor road (R426). South of the village seven roads converge on a 30m-tall **round tower** with a slight tilt, all that remains of a 12th-century monastery. The tower has a beautifully worked Romanesque entrance with carved human faces.

DURROW

In Durrow, about 10km south of Abbeyleix at the junction of the N77 and N8, neat rows of houses surround a manicured green with the imposing gateway to the 1716 **Castle Durrow**, a large Palladian villa, on the western side. The castle is privately owned and not open to the public.

The *Castle Arms Hotel* (☎ *0502-36117*), on the square, charges £25 per person for B&B and provides entertainment on most weekends.

KILLESHIN CHURCH

Killeshin Church is a mere 5km from Carlow town. Killeshin used to be one of the biggest towns in Laois and had one of the finest round towers in the country. A local farmer is said to have destroyed it in the 18th century in case it collapsed and killed his livestock.

The shattered 11th-century church has a steeply arched Romanesque doorway bearing intricately carved patterns and human heads.

County Offaly

Offaly has the typical flat, boggy landscape of central Ireland, exemplified by the extensive Bog of Allen and Boora Bog between Ferbane and Kilcormac. The Bog of Allen is an enormous brown expanse that stretches over into Kildare and which – along with many other bogs – is being mined by the huge machines of the Bord na Móna (Irish Turf Board) for potting compost and fuel briquettes (for details of the Bord na Móna Bog Rail Tour see Shannonbridge later in this chapter). However, some of Offaly's bogs, such as Clara Bog, are remarkably untouched and are recognised internationally for their plant and animal life. (See also the boxed text 'Ireland's Disappearing Bogs' in the Facts about Ireland chapter.)

The mighty River Shannon forms part of Offaly's border with Galway, while the Grand Canal also threads its way through the county. Offaly shares the Slieve Bloom Mountains with County Laois. The county is also home to Clonmacnoise, one of Ireland's most extensive and attractive monastic sites.

BIRR

☎ 0509 • pop 3355

On the River Camcor, a small tributary of the River Shannon in the south-west of the county, Birr is Offaly's most attractive town. With formal tree-lined avenues and Georgian terraces, Birr retains much of its 18th- and 19th-century character.

Many traditional shopfronts survive along Connaught and Main Sts, and all the main roads converge on Emmet Square, where a statue of the duke of Cumberland (victor of the Battle of Culloden) stood on the central column until 1925. In one corner, Dooly's Hotel, dating from 1747, was once a coaching inn on the busy route to the west.

History

After starting out as a 6th-century monastic site founded by St Brendan of Birr, the town acquired an Anglo-Norman castle in 1208.

During the Plantation of 1620, the castle and estate were given to Sir Laurence Parsons, who laid out streets, established a glass factory and issued decrees that anyone who 'cast dunge rubbidge filth or sweepings in the forestreet' was to be fined four pennies. Any woman caught working as a barmaid was to 'be set in the stocks by the constable for three whole market days'.

Later, the Parsons became earls of Rosse. The present earl and his wife still live on the estate, which has remained in the family for 14 generations.

Orientation & Information

The centre of town is Emmet Square, with the post office in the north-western corner.

The tourist office (☎ 20110) is on Rosse Row, almost directly opposite the castle gates, and opens 10 am to 5.30 pm daily, May to September. At the time of writing there were plans for it to move, either to Crotty's Church on Castle St or to the Birr Heritage Centre in John's Mall, but they had not been finalised.

The two finest streets of Georgian houses are tree-lined Oxmantown Mall, connecting Rosse Row and Emmet Square, and John's Mall.

Birr Castle & Demesne

Most visitors to Birr come to see the castle and grounds, which are among the finest in Ireland. Most of the present structure dates from around 1620, when Sir Laurence Parsons was granted the estate. A later Laurence presided over alterations in the early 19th century, which left the castle almost exactly as you see it today. In 1820 the castle was fortified again after a local Protestant woman, Mrs Legge, convinced her brethren that the Catholics were going to rise up and kill them in their beds.

The demesne, which runs north from the castle, consists of 50 hectares of magnificent gardens set round a large artificial lake. The gardens hold over 1000 species of shrubs and trees from all over the world, including a collection from the Himalayas and China, brought back from the 6th earl's 1935 honeymoon in Peking. The world's

CENTRAL SOUTH

tallest box hedges, planted in the 1780s, now stand some 12m high.

Hidden in one of them is a wicker sculpture known as the Sweeney. Legend has it that a Celtic king called Sweeney insulted a woman who turned out to have magical powers and duly transformed the king into a creature that was half-man, half-bird. Ashamed of his new appearance, Sweeney took to hiding in trees until he disappeared altogether, never to be seen again. Since the sculpture is almost impossible to find, the castle's owners have created a Sweeney Trail which gives clues as to the whereabouts of the elusive king, and it is up to visitors to find him.

Today the castle is the home of Lord and Lady Rosse. Group visits are possible if arranged well in advance through the Estate Office (☎ 20056), Rosse Row, Birr, County Offaly. The demesne opens 9 am to 6 pm daily, year round, but the exhibitions associated with the telescope open only 2.30 to 5.30 pm daily, May to mid-September. Admission costs £4/2.50.

Other Things to See & Do

The tourist office has a free leaflet covering a town trail with 10 stops at Birr's most important landmarks. **John's Mall** has John Henry Foley's statue of the 3rd earl of Rosse and a Russian cannon from the Crimean War. Nearby is the **Birr Stone**, a megalithic stone found in an early-Christian monastery and said to have marked the centre of Ireland. Some fine Victorian houses built between 1870 and 1878 are on the side of the square opposite the Birr Heritage Centre. This was closed at the time of writing but the Civic Trust was hoping to reopen it.

South-west of Emmet Square are the remains of **Old St Brendan's Church**, reputedly the site of St Brendan's 6th-century settlement.

A fine **riverside walk** runs east along the River Camcor from Oxmantown Bridge near the Catholic church to Elmgrove Bridge.

Birr Outdoor Education Centre (☎ 20029), Roscrea Rd, offers courses in walking, sail-

ing, canoeing and rock-climbing in the nearby Slieve Blooms.

Places to Stay

Hostels The nearest hostel is *Crank House Hostel* in Banagher, 13km north. (See Places to Stay & Eat in the Banagher & Around section later in this chapter.)

B&Bs B&Bs in town are not particularly cheap. *The Chains* (☎ 21687, John's Mall) offers singles/doubles costing upwards of £22.50/33. *Ard na Gréine* (☎ 20256), in Hillside 1km from Birr along the Roscrea road, is cheaper, with rooms costing £19/28. The Georgian *Ormond House* (☎ 20291, Emmet Square) and *The Green House* (☎ 21214), also on the square, charge upwards of £20 for a bed. *The Stables* (☎ 20263, Oxmantown Mall) offers rooms costing £25/40.

Hotels The best place in town is the charming *Spinner's Townhouse and Bistro* (☎/fax 21345, Castle St), a stone's throw from the castle gates. It has 10 rooms, all carefully decorated with locally made furniture and woven linen, set round a fabulous courtyard garden that is great for reading and relaxing. It opens 17 March to November only, though groups are welcome throughout the year. Singles/doubles cost £25/40, which includes an excellent breakfast.

The friendly *County Arms Hotel* (☎ 20791, fax 21234) is within walking distance of the centre on Railway Rd, which becomes the road to Roscrea. Rooms are well equipped and B&B starts at £36 per person.

Built in 1747 as a coaching lodge, *Dooly's Hotel* (☎ 20032, fax 21332, Emmet Square) has 18 comfortable rooms costing upwards of £35/60 for B&B.

An interesting alternative is *The Ring* (☎/fax 20976), a working farm just outside town. All rooms are en suite and prices start at £17 per person.

The 18th-century *Tullanisk House* (☎ 20572, fax 21783), 2km out towards Banagher up a long avenue on the right, has

Birr Observatory & Telescope

Birr Castle grounds hold one of Ireland's most extraordinary scientific structures. The 3rd earl of Rosse, William Parsons (1800–67), wanted to build the world's biggest telescope. The resulting 'leviathan of Parsonstown', a 72-inch (183cm) reflector telescope completed in 1845, remained the largest in existence for 75 years, attracting astronomers and scientists from all over the world. The instrument was used to map the moon's surface, and made innumerable discoveries, including the spiral galaxies. The telescope was built using local engineering and materials.

The telescope is slowly being restored and three times daily there are demonstrations of how it works.

The remarkable Rosse family were not just stargazers. The next earl of Rosse, Laurence Parsons, built a device to measure the heat given off by the moon. Charles Algernon Parsons, Laurence's brother, invented the steam turbine for the earliest British iron battleships, while their mother, Mary Rosse, the 3rd earl's wife, was a pioneer in 19th-century photography.

delightful rooms on the Birr Estate. B&B costs £35 to £45 per person, with a single-room supplement of £7.

Places to Eat
The pleasant *Castle Kitchen* in the same building as the tourist office serves vegetarian dishes as well as the regular food. *Dooly's Hotel* has an excellent cafeteria-style coffee shop (open 8.30 am to 10 pm); lunch is available at the bar from 12.30 to 2.30 pm, while the restaurant in the front of the hotel serves dinner. *Spinner's Bistro* serves a simple but lovely dinner (no lunch) for around £10.

North of the square and near the castle walls is *The Stables Restaurant* (see B&Bs in Places to Stay earlier), in a converted mews. It serves good four-course dinners Tuesday to Saturday costing £17 and lunch on Sunday. *County Arms Hotel* (see Hotels in Places to Stay earlier) serves good bar lunches and more-than-acceptable dinners in the evenings costing around £20.

Tullanisk House (see Hotels in Places to Stay earlier) blends old-English and Asian influences in a £25.50 set dinner.

Entertainment
Foster's (Connaught St), at the back of Dooly's Hotel, is an old-style pub which gets a good crowd at the weekend and usually has music. On the same street is *Whel-*

ehan's, popular with the town's younger population. *Palace Bar (O'Connell St)* often has live bands at the weekend. *Craughwell's (Castle St)* is great for impromptu sing-a-long sessions. *Kelly's* is a locals' haunt, just off the square towards the castle. *Mary Walshe's Bar* has Irish music on Friday and Saturday nights. In Dooly's Hotel *Melba's Nite Club* opens Friday, Saturday and Sunday nights.

Getting There & Away
A single daily bus passes through on the Dublin to Portumna route, as does another heading from Athlone to Cork. Call Athlone bus station (☎ 0902-72651) for times.

Kearn's Coaches (☎ 22244) runs services from Dublin and Tullamore through Birr to Portumna. Three daily buses pass through Birr on Sunday, Monday and Friday, two daily on Saturday and one daily Tuesday to Thursday. Up to two buses daily go from Portumna to Birr and Dublin. A one-way ticket from Birr to Dublin costs £5. All buses stop in Emmet Square.

LEAP CASTLE
South-east of Birr between Kinnitty and Roscrea (in Tipperary) are the remains of Leap Castle, in one of the few areas of Offaly rich in pre-Christian ring forts and burial mounds. It was originally an O'Carroll

CENTRAL SOUTH

family residence, keeping guard over a crucial route between Munster and Leinster, and was renowned for a 'smelly ghost'; indeed it was said by locals to be one of the most haunted castles in Europe. It was destroyed in 1922 during the Civil War. Today it hosts occasional Irish music sessions with Sean Ryan, arguably the best tin-whistle player in Ireland. The site offers good views of the Slieve Bloom Mountains.

SLIEVE BLOOM MOUNTAINS

It's a bit of an exaggeration to call them mountains, but the Slieve Blooms in the south-east of the county are little visited and yet boast moorlands, pine forests and hidden river valleys. It's a lovely journey from Birr to the hamlet of **Kinnitty**, the jumping-off point for the mountains. There's also a good trip over the hills to Mountrath (County Laois), and a pleasant drive around the northern flanks of the hills between Kinnitty and Mountmellick (also in County Laois).

For more details see Slieve Bloom Mountains in the County Laois section earlier in this chapter.

Places to Stay

Kinnitty has a few B&Bs to choose from. On a small road north-west of town is *Roselawn* (☎ 0509-37040), which has three rooms for £15 per person. Three kilometres south-east of town is one of Ireland's most

---

The Ely O'Carroll

The Ely O'Carroll territory covered some 500 sq km in present-day Offaly and northern Tipperary. The *eile* (sept) was originally founded by Cian, son of the king of Munster, in the 3rd century, and its borders were marked by 40 castles belonging to different branches of the family. These fortifications began at Cadamstown and Kinnitty in the north-east and continued southwards through the foothills of the Slieve Blooms to Leap, Ballybritt, Dungar, Clonlisk, Clashagad, Dunkerrin, Castleroan and Clonymohan. Swinging northwards at Cullenwaine, O'Carroll castles stood at Rathenny, Cloughjordan, Modreeny and Banagher... and there were more. The dynasty's principal stronghold, however, was the castle in Birr, and from there they ruled all-powerful. O'Heerin, a 15th-century bard, wrote:

Lords to who the hazlenuts stoop,
are the O'Carrolls of the Plain of Birr.
Fearless in enforcing their tributes
are the forces of the flaxen hair.

All good things must come to an end, but this is where the O'Carroll story gets interesting. Cromwell's policy of Surrender and Regrant resulted in the confiscation of the O'Carroll lands by the Jacobean and Cromwellian Plantations, reducing many of them to the status of tenants on lands they had formerly owned.

The institution of the Penal Laws pushed one member of the clan, Charles O'Carroll (1661–1720), to emigrate to the American colony of Maryland in 1688, where he was granted 60,000 acres of land and founded a new dynasty of Carrolls (the 'O' was dropped). His grandson Charles was known as 'the Signer' because he was the only Catholic signatory of the Declaration of Independence, while his cousin Daniel served in the 1787 Convention that produced the US Constitution. His brother John was made Bishop of Baltimore, and later became the first Catholic archbishop of the USA. And it didn't end there. When the US government decided to build a permanent capital, they turned to Daniel Carroll of Duddington, Maryland, a first cousin of Daniel and John, who sold the government the land upon which now stands Washington, DC.

renowned castle hotels, *Kinnitty Castle* (☎ *0509-37318, fax 37284*). This former O'Carroll residence is now a luxury hotel that is popular for celebrity weddings, especially from Britain. Singles/doubles start at £100/200.

BANAGHER & AROUND
☎ 0509 • pop 1414

While a post office clerk in the quiet riverside town of Banagher in 1841, Anthony Trollope (1815–82) wrote his first novel, *The Macdermots of Ballycloran*. Charlotte Brontë (1816–55) honeymooned here, and her husband, the Reverend Arthur Bell Nicholls, stayed on after she died in England. Cuba Ave is named after local boy George Frazer, who became governor of that island.

There is a tourist information desk (☎ 51458) in Crank House on Main St, and some pleasant pubs and restaurants.

Things to See & Do
About 3km south of Banagher and 10km north-west of Birr, in Lusmagh near the confluence of the Rivers Little Brosna and Shannon, is Cloghan Castle. The well-preserved Norman keep has an adjoining 19th-century house and protective walls. Cloghan Castle has been in use for nearly 800 years. It's built on the site of a 7th-century monastery founded by St Cronan. The first castle was a McCoghlan stronghold, which was later taken over by the mighty O'Carroll clan, and over the course of its history the castle has seen more than its fair share of bloodshed. The present owner, Brian Thompson, has brought together a very interesting and varied assortment of antiques. Pride of place in the main hall goes to the enormous antlers of an Irish elk. At the end of the 45-minute tour, the visitor can examine Cromwellian armaments in the rustic dining room and marvel at just how heavy the breastplates were.

The castle (☎ 51650) opens 2 to 7 pm Wednesday to Saturday, May to September. Admission costs £4/2.50. There's no bus service, but the owners will collect people from Crank House by arrangement.

Twenty kilometres south of the castle is Emmell Castle, also owned by the Thompsons, which can be rented by the week.

Seven kilometres north-east of Banagher is Cloghan, where all six roads out of town lead into wide tracts of peat. Five kilometres from Cloghan, on the road northwestwards to Shannonbridge, 16th-century Clonony Castle's four-storey square tower is enclosed by an overgrown castellated wall. Stories that Henry VIII's second wife, Anne Boleyn, was born here are unlikely to be true, but her cousins Elizabeth and Mary Boleyn are buried beside the ruins.

Eight kilometres south of Banagher on the County Galway side of the border is the delightful Meelick Church, one of the oldest still in use in Ireland.

You can hire canoes for trips on the River Shannon or Grand Canal from Shannon Adventure Canoeing Holidays (☎ 51411), 21 Cuba Ave.

Places to Stay & Eat
The only hostel in the region is the excellent IHH *Crank House Hostel* (☎ *51458, Main St*), which charges £8 per person in two- and four-bed rooms, and opens year round. Crank House also contains the tourist information desk, an exhibition room for local artists and the office of Crann (☎ 51718), set up to restore some of the deciduous trees that once covered much of Ireland. At the back is *Alma's Traditional Irish Coffee Shop*, open until 6 pm daily.

The cheapest B&B is *Ashling* (☎ *51228, Cuba Ave*), which has singles/doubles with bath costing £14.50/29. The *Hayes B&B* (☎ *51360, Main St*) has rooms costing upwards of £15/30.

Cloghan Castle (☎ *51650*) offers B&B costing £40 per person.

Entertainment
In the evening you could do worse than head for pretty, vine-draped *JJ Hough's*, the 'singing pub' on Main St.

Getting There & Away
Kearn's Coaches (☎ 22244) includes Banagher on its daily Portumna to Dublin

CENTRAL SOUTH

service. Bus Éireann has one Saturday service to Banagher, leaving Dublin's Busáras (☎ 01-836 6111) at 9.30 am.

SHANNONBRIDGE
☎ 0905 • pop 266

At otherwise unremarkable Shannonbridge a narrow bridge crosses the river into County Roscommon. Look for the 19th-century **fort**, on the western bank just up from the bridge, where heavy artillery was placed to bombard Napoleon lest he was cheeky enough to try to invade via the river. Part of the road north towards Clonmacnoise runs along the top of the esker on which Clonmacnoise is also built.

Just south of Shannonbridge, a 45-minute **Bord na Móna Bog Rail Tour** on the Clonmacnoise and West Offaly Railway/Blackwater Railway (☎ 74114) takes you through the Blackwater section of the Bog of Allen on the narrow-gauge line which used to transport the peat. A green-and-yellow diesel locomotive pulls one carriage at an average speed of 24km/h across 9km of bog rail (only a tiny section of the nearly 1200km of railway in the area). During the trip, you'll be told about the bog landscape and its special flora, which has remained unchanged for thousands of years.

The journey begins near the Bord na Móna Blackwater (Uisce Dubh in Irish) peat-fired power station, which is visible for miles around. Trips leave on the hour from 10 am to 5 pm daily, April to October, and cost £4/2.50. Tickets are available from the coffee shop.

CLONMACNOISE
Ireland's most important monastic site is superbly placed, overlooking the River Shannon from a ridge. It consists of a walled field containing numerous early churches, high crosses, round towers and graves in remarkably good condition. The site is surrounded by marshy ground and fields known as the Shannon Callows. These are home to many wild plants and are one of the last refuges of the seriously endangered corncrake (see the boxed text 'The Corncrake Crisis' in the Donegal chapter).

History
Of the several monastic sites that dot the edges of this section of the Shannon, this is by far the most spectacular, ranking alongside Glendalough in Wicklow as the country's most important. Roughly translated, Clonmacnoise (Cluain Mhic Nóis) means 'Meadow of the Sons of Nós'. The glacial ridge called the Esker Riada (Highway of the Kings) on which it stands was once one of the principal cross-country routes between Leinster and Connaught. St Ciarán, the son of a chariot maker, is said to have founded the monastery in 548 and died only seven months later after building the first church with the assistance of Diarmuid, the high king of Tara.

The monastery's beginning was humble as only eight followers of Ciarán had set out with him, but it soon became an unrivalled bastion of Irish religion, literature and art. Between the 7th and 12th centuries monks from all over Europe came to study and

---

Eskers & Highway of the Kings

Western Offaly's flat boglands are often prevented from draining into the River Shannon by eskers, long, winding, glacial ridges made up of fossilised coarse sand and gravel deposits from meltwater rivers that ran underneath glaciers. Over time the water-logged vegetation built layers of peat up to 10m deep. The best-known esker is Esker Riada (Highway of the Kings), which ran across much of the country, forming the principal highway between Leinster and Connaught. You can still see parts of it near the main road to Dublin. Clonmacnoise sits on part of this esker in the north-western corner of Offaly.

Esker is one of the few Irish words that has entered the English language.

pray here. Clonmacnoise was one of the reasons Ireland became known as the 'island of saints and scholars' while much of Europe languished in the Dark Ages. Such was its importance that the high kings of Connaught and Tara were brought here for burial; many lie in the cathedral, or the Church of Kings, among them the last high king of Tara, Rory O'Connor, who died in 1198.

Most of the remains date from the 10th to 12th centuries; earlier buildings of wood, clay and wattle have long since disappeared. The monks would have lived in small huts scattered in and around the monastery, which would probably have been surrounded by a ditch or rampart of earth. It was recorded that there were 106 houses and 13 churches here in 1179, when the site was ravaged by fire. These scattered Irish sites contrast with the strict layout and planning of monasteries elsewhere in Europe.

The river became a deadly conduit when Viking raiders used it to penetrate into the heart of Ireland. Clonmacnoise was pillaged repeatedly between 830 and 1165 (records

suggest on at least eight occasions). The Vikings were not the only ones guilty of attacks: the monastery was burned at least 12 times between 720 and 1205, and attacked 27 times by native Irish forces between 830 and 1165. After the 12th century, it fell into decline and by the 15th century it was home to a bishop of only minor importance. The end came in 1552 when it was plundered by the English regiment based in Athlone: 'Not a bell, large or small, or an image, or an altar, or a book, or a gem, or even glass in a window, was left which was not carried away'.

Among the treasures that survived the continued onslaught are the crozier of the abbots of Clonmacnoise in the National Museum, Dublin, and the 12th-century *Leabhar na hUidhre* (*The Book of the Dun Cow*), now in the Royal Irish Academy in Dublin.

Information

Dúchas provides a museum, an on-site interpretive centre and coffee shop. The tourist office (☎ 0905-74134) in the car park opens April to September.

CENTRAL SOUTH

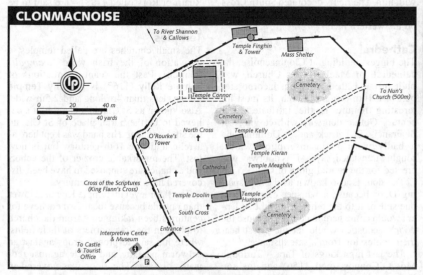

CLONMACNOISE

To River Shannon & Callows

Temple Finghin & Tower   Mass Shelter

Temple Connor

Cemetery

To Nun's Church (500m)

Cemetery

North Cross   Temple Kelly

O'Rourke's Tower

Temple Kieran

Cathedral   Temple Meaghlin

Cross of the Scriptures (King Flann's Cross)

Temple Doolin   Temple Hurpan

South Cross

Cemetery

Entrance

Interpretive Centre & Museum

To Castle & Tourist Office

0   20   40 m
0   20   40 yards

Clonmacnoise opens 9 am to 6 pm daily, mid-March to mid-September; and 10 am to 5 pm daily, mid-September to mid-March. Visiting early or late will help you avoid the crowds. Admission costs £3/1.50. The 20-minute audiovisual show provides a good introduction to the site.

High Crosses

In the compound are three replicas of 9th-century high crosses (the originals are now in the museum for protection). The sandstone **Cross of the Scriptures** is the most richly decorated and has unique upwards-tilted arms. Its western face depicts the crucifixion, soldiers guarding Jesus' tomb and the arrest of Jesus. On the eastern face are scenes of St Ciarán and King Diarmuid placing the corner stone of the cathedral. It's also known as King Flann's Cross because a rough inscription on the base is said to attribute it to him. He died in 916.

Nearer the river the **North Cross** dates from around 800. Only the shaft remains, with lions, rich spirals and a single figure, thought to be the Celtic god Cerrunnos or Carnunas, who sits in a Buddha-like position. The two-headed snake is associated with him. The richly decorated **South Cross** has more carvings, including the crucifixion on the western face.

Cathedral

The biggest building at Clonmacnoise, the cathedral, or MacDermot's Church, was built in the 12th century but incorporates part of a 10th-century church. Its most interesting feature is the intricate 15th-century Gothic doorway with carvings of St Francis, St Patrick and St Dominic and a badly worn Latin inscription which, roughly translated, says: 'This doorway was erected for the eternal glory of God'.

The door is also known as the Whispering Door because a whisper carries from one side of it to the other. It's said that lepers would come here to confess because the door's acoustics would let the priest hear their confession from a safe distance.

The last high kings of Tara – Turlough Mór O'Connor (died 1156) and his son

MATT KING

The 9th-century Cross of the Scriptures

Ruairí or Rory (died 1198) – are said to be buried near the altar.

Temples

The small churches are called temples, a derivation of the Irish word '*teampall*' (church). Past the scant foundations of **Temple Kelly** (1167) is the tiny **Temple Kieran**, less than 4m long and 2.5m wide. Also known as St Ciarán's Church, it's believed to be the burial place of St Ciarán, the site's founder. His hand was kept here as a relic until the 16th century, but is now lost. The remarkable crozier of the abbots and a chalice are supposed to have been discovered here in the 19th century.

The floor level in Temple Kieran is lower than outside because local farmers have for centuries been taking clay from the church to place in the four corners of their fields, where it's said to protect crops against an eelworm parasite and cattle against redwater disease. The floor was covered in slabs to stop further digging but even today handfuls of clay are removed from outside the church in the early spring.

Near the temple's south-western corner is a '*bullaun*' (an ancient grinding stone), supposedly used for making medicines for the monastery's hospital. Today the rainwater that collects in it is supposed to cure warts.

Continuing round the compound you come to the 12th-century **Temple Meaghlin**, with its attractive windows, and the twin structures of **Temple Hurpan** and **Temple Doolin**. Doolin is named after Edmund Dowling, who repaired it in 1689 and made it the family crypt. At the same time he may have restored Temple Hurpan, which is also known as Claffey's Church.

Round Towers

Overlooking the River Shannon is the truncated O'Rourke's Tower, a 20m-high tower named after the high king of Connaught, Fergal O'Rourke (died 964). The top of the tower is said to have been blown apart by lightning in 1135, but the tower was used until 1552.

Temple Finghin and its round tower are on the northern boundary of the site, also overlooking the Shannon. The quaint building, also known as MacCarthy's Church and Tower, appears in most photographs of Clonmacnoise and dates from around 1160 to 1170. It has some fine Romanesque carvings and the unusual miniature tower's cone roof has stones set in a herringbone pattern. This is the only Irish round tower roof that has never been altered. Most such towers were used by monks for protection when their monasteries were attacked, but this one was probably used as a bell tower as the doorway is at ground level.

Other Remains

Still used by Church of Ireland parishioners on the last Sunday of the summer months, **Temple Connor** is a little, roofed church. Beyond the boundary wall, 500m east through the modern graveyard, is the secluded **Nun's Church** with wonderful Romanesque arches; it's well worth seeking

out. West of the church is a **cairn** said to mark the burial place of a servant of St Ciarán who was supposedly refused burial in the monastery graveyard after losing the saint's dun cow.

On the ridge near the car park is a motte with the oddly shaped ruins of a 13th-century **castle**. John de Grey, bishop of Norwich, is said to have had it built to watch over the Shannon.

Museum

The three beehive-like structures near the entrance are a museum echoing the design of the early monastic dwellings. It contains the originals of the three principal high crosses and various artefacts uncovered during excavation, including silver pins, beaded glass and an ogham stone.

The museum also contains many of Clonmacnoise's 8th- to 12th-century graveslabs, the largest collection of early-Christian graveslabs in Europe. Many are in remarkable condition with inscriptions clearly visible, often starting with '*oroit do*' or '*ar*', meaning 'a prayer for'.

Places to Stay

If you want to stay the night close to the ruins try *Kajon House* (☎ 0905-74191), with singles/doubles costing upwards of £20/30. It's on the road signposted to Tullamore. Alternatively, a more picturesque option is the restored 19th-century *Cottage* (☎ 0905-74149), where rooms cost upwards of £12 per person.

Getting There & Away

Clonmacnoise is 7km north of Shannonbridge and about 24km south of Athlone. Paddy Kavanagh (☎ 0902-74839) runs a minibus to Clonmacnoise from Athlone, departing the castle at 11 am and returning at 4 pm. A ticket costs £7. To visit both Clonmacnoise and the West Offaly Railway (see Shannonbridge earlier in this chapter) costs £16.50.

There are river cruises to Clonmacnoise from Athlone in County Westmeath; see River Cruises in the Athlone section of the Central North chapter for details.

CENTRAL SOUTH

TULLAMORE
☎ 0506 • pop 9221

Tullamore (Tulach Mór), Offaly's county town 80km due west of Dublin on the Grand Canal, is pleasant enough to while away a few hours, with Charleville Forest Castle the main attraction. The market square and some of the old houses are attractive.

Founded in 1750 by the Bury family of Limerick, Tullamore soon superseded Philipstown (now Daingean) as the county capital. In 1785 a hot-air balloon crashed and started a fire that consumed hundreds of homes!

Information

The tourist office (☎ 52617), open on weekdays, June to September, is on Bury Quay between the defunct Irish Mist factory and the canal. In the same building is the Offaly Historical Archaeological Society (open 9.30 am to 4 pm on weekdays), which may be able to help when the tourist office is closed. The post office faces O'Connor Square, which is little more than a parking lot.

Charleville Forest Castle

The great Gothic structure of Charleville Forest Castle (☎ 21279) sits in a large estate to the west of the town centre. What some call a 'Gothic fantasy castle', due to its spires and turrets, was the family seat of the Burys, who in 1798 commissioned the design from Francis Johnston, one of Ireland's most famous architects.

From the entrance on Charleville Rd, south of town on the road to Limerick, there's a rough 1.5km lane (take the right fork after you enter the gate) to the castle itself which is popular with joggers. (Tullamore Harriers is one of Ireland's premier running clubs.) The present owners of the castle, the Hutton-Burys, intend to restore the property and turn it into a classy hotel.

Thirty-minute tours must be booked in advance and cost £3.50/2. If you haven't booked, your best hope of tagging onto a tour is 11 am to 5 pm, Wednesday to Sunday, June to September, or at the weekend only, April and May. The castle grounds are also worth exploring.

Tullamore Dew Heritage Centre

Since Irish Mist and Tullamore Dew relocated to Clonmel, Tullamore has lost its other main focus. However, a new heritage centre attached to the tourist office on Bury Quay should have opened by the time you read this. It will concentrate on the history of the Irish Mist and Tullamore Dew whiskeys, on the vital link created by the Grand Canal between the town and the rest of the country, and on Tullamore local history. It will open 9 am to 6 pm Monday to Saturday, and noon to 5 pm on Sunday, March to September; and 10 am to 5 pm Monday to Saturday, the rest of the year. Admission will cost £3.50/2.25.

Cruises

Celtic Canal Cruisers (☎ 21861) has boats available by the week costing £320 for two people in the low season up to £1220 for nine people in July. You can cruise west to the River Shannon, joining it at Shannon Harbour, or east to Edenderry, Laytown and down into the Grand Canal and River Barrow systems.

Places to Stay & Eat

Of the two hotels on the main street, *High House* (☎ 51358) is preferable to *Phoenix Arms Hotel* (☎ 21066), with beds in comfortable rooms costing £26.50 per person. Neither is ideal because of the noise of traffic roaring through.

The most popular place to eat seems to be *Bridge House Inn* on Bridge St, which has a familiar mix of grills and steaks. Of the fast-food places, the best is the spanking-new *Abrakebabra (Church St)*.

Getting There & Away

Bus The Bus Éireann (☎ 21431) stop is at the train station, south of town on Western Relief Rd off Charleville Rd. From Tullamore there is one bus daily each way on the Dublin (1¾ hours) to Portumna (one hour) route, and one daily on the Waterford (3½ hours) to Longford (1½ hours) route.

Kearn's Coaches (☎ 0509-22244) runs three buses daily from Tullamore on Monday, Friday and Sunday, two on Saturday and one daily Tuesday and Wednesday on its Dublin to Portumna route.

Train There are at least seven trains daily to Dublin (one hour) and Galway (2½ hours) on weekdays, and five at the weekend.

DURROW ABBEY

St Colmcille (also known as St Columba) founded a monastery at Durrow Abbey in the 6th century, and the monastery's scriptorium later produced the *Book of Durrow*, a Latin gospel. The book was kept here for over 800 years until the dissolution of the monasteries, when it fell into the hands of a local farmer. The book's bright illustrations survived being immersed in his cattle's drinking water to ward off evil spirits. In 1661 the local bishop gave it to Trinity College, Dublin, where it can be seen today.

The *Book of Durrow* fared better than the rest of the monastery. The monastery was damaged in 1186 by Hugh de Lacy, who literally lost his head in the process when a local man took exception to his using the monastery stones to build a castle on the mound nearby.

Today, the site's only prominent structures are a Georgian mansion and a derelict 19th-century Protestant church. Some high kings of Tara are said to have been buried here, including Donal (died 758) and a grandson of Brian Ború, Murcadh (died 1068).

The remains include St Colmcille's Well to the north-east of the church and a 10th-century high cross. The eastern face of the cross shows King David, Abraham's sacrifice of Isaac and the Last Judgment, while the western face shows soldiers guarding Jesus' tomb and the crucifixion.

Durrow Abbey is 7km north of Tullamore down a long lane west off the N52 Kilbeggan road.

EDENDERRY
☎ 0405 • pop 3591

On the River Boyne bordering County Kildare and the Bog of Allen, Edenderry is 16km north-east of Daingean. Although it sprang to life with the arrival of the Grand Canal in 1802, Edenberry goes back to the 14th century and the de Berminghams, whose ruined **Carrickoris Castle** is 7km north of town on Carrick Hill. The name Edenderry came from the oak woods that once blanketed the hills around the town. The local O'Connor family used to harry the English and retreat into the bogs that cover the region. The post office is on the oddly named JKL St.

Three kilometres to the north-west on the Rhode road is the scanty monastic site of **Monasteroris**. It was built for the Franciscans by John de Bermingham in 1325 to ease his conscience over his father's massacre of 32 local chieftains 20 years before in Carrickoris Castle.

There's a pleasant **walk** from the imposing Georgian town hall along the canal towpath out to the Downshire Bridge.

Places to Stay & Eat

Bellavista (☎ 31179, St Mary's Rd) offers B&B costing £14 per person (shared bathroom). There isn't much choice for dining but *Eden Restaurant* and *The Coffee Shop (O'Connell Square)* serve plain, dependable food; the latter serves breakfast (£2.95).

Getting There & Away

Bus Éireann (☎ 01-836 6111) has up to six buses daily to Dublin (three on Sunday). A single daily bus goes to and from Tullamore, Banagher and Birr.

CENTRAL SOUTH

County Clare

Clare (An Clár) doesn't get the attention of Kerry or Galway, although it has its own special charms. It's almost a peninsula, with the Shannon Estuary cutting deep into its southern border and Galway Bay on its northern side. Wedged between Kerry and Galway, Clare's land is mostly poor, with a large sweep of limestone rock in the north of the county forming the unique, fascinating Burren region. The landscape of the Burren contains countless monuments, castles and rare flowers, and there are some wonderful walks. The county has some spectacular scenery, particularly around the Cliffs of Moher.

Many of Clare's towns and villages have resisted the commercialisation and 'prettification' of more heavily touristed places in Ireland. Ennis, Clare's county town, retains its charming narrow streets, while villages such as Ennistymon have many old shops, and pubs that host traditional-music sessions on summer evenings. Two villages have become magnets for particular types of visitors. Doolin attracts music lovers and backpackers, while genteel Ballyvaughan has become a weekend seaside retreat for the more well heeled.

The county has some 250 castles in various stages of preservation: Knappogue near Quin and the famous tower house at Bunratty are fine examples. As for activities, there's scuba diving at Kilkee, Doolin and Fanore, excellent rock climbing at Ballyreen near Fanore, and caving is possible all over the Burren.

The shortest route to Clare if you're travelling north up the coast is via the car ferry from Tarbert in County Kerry to Killimer.

Ennis & Around

ENNIS
☎ 065 • pop 18,000
Ennis (Inis), Clare's principal town, is a busy market centre and one of the Repub-

Highlights

- Visit 15th-century Bunratty Castle – worthwhile despite the kitsch

- Discover the spectacular Cliffs of Moher and make the three-hour trek to Hag's Head

- Enjoy traditional Irish music in the village of Doolin

- Go walking, cycling or spelunking in the Burren

- Walk all or part of the 45km Burren Way

- See the 5000-year-old Poulnabrone Dolmen in the Burren, especially at sunset or early in the morning

lic's larger towns. It lies on the banks of the River Fergus, which runs east and then south into the Shannon Estuary. The town's medieval origins are visible in its narrow streets, and there are many old shops and pubs. The friary, founded in the 13th century, is Ennis' most important historical site.

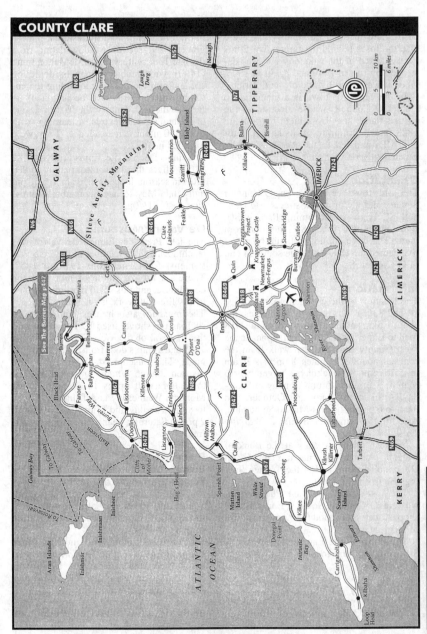

COUNTY CLARE

GALWAY

TIPPERARY

LIMERICK

KERRY

CLARE

ATLANTIC OCEAN

Galway Bay

Lough Derg

Slieve Aughty Mountains

The Burren

Aran Islands
Inishmaan
Inisheer
Inishmór

To Rossaveal
To Galway

Black Head
Fanore
Ballyvaughan
Burren
Kinvara
Carron
Corofin
Belharbour
Kilfenora
Kilnaboy
Lisdoonvarna
Doolin
Liscannor
Lahinch
Ennistymon
Dysert O'Dea

Burren Way
Ballyreen

Cliffs of Moher
Hag's Head

Portumna
Nenagh
Mountshannon
Scarriff
Feakle
Clare Lakelands
Tuamgraney
Holy Island
Killaloe
Ballina
Birdhill

Quin
Craggaunowen Project
Knappogue Castle
Newmarket-on-Fergus
Dromoland Castle
Ennis
Shannon Airport
Shannon
Kilmurry
Sixmilebridge
Cratloe
Bunratty
LIMERICK

River Shannon

Corofin

Milltown Malbay
Quilty
Spanish Point
Mutton Island
White Strand
Doonbeg
Donegal Point
Intrinsic Bay
Kilkee
Carrigaholt
Kilbaha
Loop Head
Killrush
Killimer
Scattery Island
Tarbert
Labasheeda
Knockalough

Shannon Estuary

See The Burren Map p447

Roads (labels): N52, N65, R352, N6, N63, N65, N6, N18, R460, N67, R478, R461, R463, R469, R474, N85, N68, N7, N24, N20, N21, N9, N69, N67

0 5 10 km
0 3 6 miles

CLARE

The O'Briens, kings of Thomond, built a castle here in the 13th century and were also the force behind the impressive Ennis Friary. Much of the wooden town was destroyed by fire in 1249 and again in 1306, when it was razed by one of the O'Briens.

In the centre of town is a memorial to Daniel O'Connell, whose election to the British Parliament by a huge majority in 1828 forced Britain to lift its bar on Catholic MPs and led to the Act of Catholic Emancipation a year later.

Orientation
The old town centre is on O'Connell Square, and the principal streets – O'Connell St, High St (becoming Parnell St), Bank Place and Abbey St – fan out from there. The large but not particularly attractive cathedral (1843) is at the southern end of O'Connell St.

Information
The location of the excellent tourist office (☎ 682 8366) suits those with vehicles: it's about 1.5km south of the centre, on the N18 road to Limerick and Shannon, opposite the West County Inn. You can walk from the centre in about 20 minutes. It opens 9.30 am to 5.15 pm on weekdays, November to March; 9 am to 5.45 pm Monday to Saturday, April to mid-May and October; and 9 am to 6 pm daily, mid-May to September. Ask for the pamphlet *Ennis: A Walking Trail.*

You can change money at the Bank of Ireland (which also has an ATM) on O'Connell Square and at the Trustee Savings Bank on Abbey St.

The post office is on Bank Place, northwest of O'Connell Square. Ennis Bookshop, Abbey St, is good for maps and books of local interest.

The Snow White Laundrette, on Abbey St, opens 8.30 am to 6.30 pm Monday to Saturday.

Ennis Friary
Ennis Friary was founded by Donnchadh Cairbreach O'Brien, king of Thomond, some time between 1240 and 1249, though a lot of the present structure was completed in the 14th century. Partly restored, it has a graceful five-section window dating from the late 13th century and a McMahon tomb (1460) with alabaster panels depicting scenes from the Passion, including the entombment of Christ. At the height of its fame in the 15th century, the friary was one of Ireland's great centres of learning, with over 300 monks in residence. They were expelled in 1692.

Being a Dúchas site, Ennis Friary (☎ 682 9100) offers the usual informative guided tours in season. It opens 9.30 am to 6.30 pm daily, late May to late September. Admission costs £1/40p.

De Valera Museum
The late President Eamon de Valera was teachta Dála (TD, member of the Irish Parliament) for Clare from 1917 to 1959. There's a bronze statue of him near the courthouse, and this small museum devoted to his life and work is on Harmony Row. The museum also houses random items such as the shovel used by Parnell to turn the first sod of the West Clare Railway in 1885 and a ship's door from the Spanish Armada. The museum (☎ 682 1616) is in a disused church which you enter via the town library. It opens 10 am to 5.30 pm Monday, Wednesday and Thursday, 10 am to 8 pm Tuesday and Friday, and 10 am to 2 pm on Saturday, year round. Admission is free.

Places to Stay
Hostels The rule-ridden but friendly *Abbey Tourist Hostel* (☎ *682 2620, Harmony Row*), in an old hotel up from O'Connell Square, has 80 beds (£7.50) and opens year round. The five private rooms, none with en suite bathrooms, cost £17.

Open year round, the modern *Clare Lodge Hostel* (☎ *682 9370, Cornmarket St*) has 50 beds and a restaurant. Dorm beds cost £12.50, private rooms £18.50 per person; rates include bed linen.

B&Bs Ennis isn't short of guesthouses. South of the centre on Clare Rd, *Ardlea*

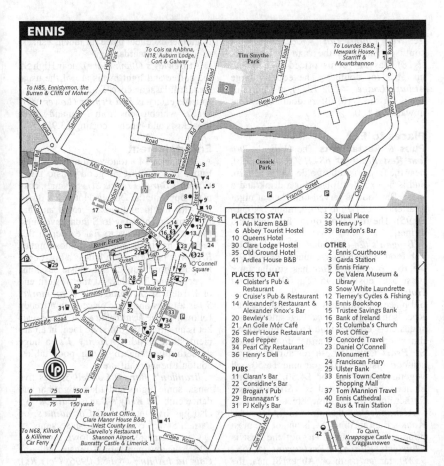

ENNIS

To Cois na hAbhna,
N18, Auburn Lodge,
Gort & Galway

Tim Smythe
Park

To Lourdes B&B,
Newpark House,
Scarriff &
Mountshannon

To N85, Ennistymon, the
Burren & Cliffs of Moher

Cusack
Park

Cusack Road

Highfield Park

Sandfield Park

College Road

Gort Road

New Road

Lifford Road

Clon Road

Tulla Road

Will Rd

Mill Road

Harmony Row

Bindon St

Newbridge Rd

Francis Street

Clon Road

★ 3
▼ 4
6 ▼
7 ■
▲∴ 5
8 ●
▼ 9
▼ 10

17
18 ✉
River Fergus
▲ 14
15 $ ●
16 ● $
19 ●
20 ●
22 ▲ 21
▲ 23
24
▲ 12
13 ▲
$ 25
O'Connell Square
26 ▼
27 ▼
28 ●
29 ●
30
31 ●
32
33 ●
34 ▼
35 ▼
36 ▼
37 ●
38 ▼
39 ▼
40

Cusack Road
Cornmarket Street
Bank Place
Abbey Street
Francis Street
Parnell Street
High St
Chapel Lane
Summerhill
Market Place
O'Connell Street
Lwr Market St
Old Barrack St
Station Road
Carmody Street
Kilrush Road
Dumbiggle Road
Clare Road

0   75   150 m
0   75   150 yards

To Tourist Office,
Clare Manor House B&B,
West County Inn,
Garvello's Restaurant,
Shannon Airport,
Bunratty Castle & Limerick

To N68, Kilrush,
& Killimer
Car Ferry

Ardlee Road

Clon Road Mor

■ 41

42

To Quin,
Knappogue Castle
& Craggaunowen

PLACES TO STAY		OTHER	
1	Aín Karem B&B	2	Ennis Courthouse
6	Abbey Tourist Hostel	3	Garda Station
10	Queens Hotel	5	Ennis Friary
30	Clare Lodge Hostel	7	De Valera Museum &
35	Old Ground Hotel		Library
41	Ardlea House B&B	8	Snow White Laundrette
		12	Tierney's Cycles & Fishing
PLACES TO EAT		13	Ennis Bookshop
4	Cloister's Pub &	15	Trustee Savings Bank
	Restaurant	16	Bank of Ireland
9	Cruise's Pub & Restaurant	17	St Columba's Church
14	Alexander's Restaurant &	18	Post Office
	Alexander Knox's Bar	19	Concorde Travel
20	Bewley's	23	Daniel O'Connell
21	An Goile Mór Café		Monument
26	Silver House Restaurant	24	Franciscan Friary
28	Red Pepper	25	Ulster Bank
34	Pearl City Restaurant	33	Ennis Town Centre
36	Henry's Deli		Shopping Mall
		37	Tom Mannion Travel
PUBS		40	Ennis Cathedral
11	Ciaran's Bar	42	Bus & Train Station
22	Considine's Bar		
27	Brogan's Pub		
29	Brannagan's		
31	PJ Kelly's Bar		

32	Usual Place		
38	Henry J's		
39	Brandon's Bar		

House (☎ 682 0256) offers singles/doubles costing £25/35.

North of the centre *Aín Karem* (☎ 682 0024, 7 Tulla Rd) has rooms costing £20/33 with shared bathroom. Round the next corner heading north, *Lourdes* (☎ 682 2578, Lifford Rd) has similar rooms at the same rates.

At *Clare Manor House* (☎ 682 0701, Clare Rd), about 2km south, the six rooms, all with en suite bathroom, cost £24.50/39 for singles/doubles.

Two kilometres north of Ennis on Tulla Rd, the continuation of Clon Rd, is *Newpark*

House (☎ 682 1233), a 300-year-old country manor with excellent breakfasts and rooms costing upwards of £30/50. To get there go along the Scarriff road and turn right at the Roslevan Arms Travel Lodge. It opens April to October.

Hotels The lovely *Old Ground Hotel* (☎ 682 8127) is on the corner of O'Connell St and Station Rd near the town centre, and its 58 singles/doubles cost upwards of £60/85. The comfortable 30-room *Queens Hotel* (☎ 682 8963, Abbey St) is a little cheaper at £45/80.

CLARE

Two other good hotels are out of the centre. **West County Inn** (☎ *682 8421*), just south of Ennis on the road to Limerick (N18), has 98 rooms priced at £75 and upwards for doubles. The equally large **Auburn Lodge** (☎ *682 1247*), just north of Ennis on the N18, offers doubles costing upwards of £60.

Places to Eat

Pubs & Restaurants The *Cruise's Pub and Restaurant* (☎ *684 1800, Abbey St*), near the friary, is full of olde-worlde charm and is an excellent place for a drink and a meal. Bar food is served until late at night (starters cost £1.25 to £2.60, mains £4.95 to £6.95). The restaurant opens for lunch and dinner.

Brogan's (24 O'Connell St) serves good pub food; a three-course lunch costs £5.95. Nearby, **Brandon's Bar** has similar fare; roast beef costs £4.95. The **Old Ground Hotel** (see Places to Stay earlier) is a huge old place with lunches at tables in the bar. Rock-solid Irish fare – cabbage and piles of spuds etc – costs around £6. A four-course dinner costs £17.95. Farther up O'Connell St, **Pearl City** Chinese restaurant serves seafood dishes costing around £6.50 and vegetarian choices for £4.50. A second choice for rice and noodles is **Silver House**, farther north on the same street.

Alexander's, upstairs in Alexander Knox's Bar on Abbey St, is one of the most popular eateries in town, but the best is **Cloister's Pub and Restaurant** (☎ *682 9521*), farther north on Abbey St near the friary. It's also the most expensive, charging upwards of £25 (including service) per person for a four-course dinner. It also does excellent meals in the bar from noon to 10 pm, with main courses costing from £6.50. If you don't mind travelling, **Garvello's** (☎ *684 0011*), about 1km past the tourist office on the N18 to Limerick, serves superb seafood and Mediterranean specialities.

Fast Food & Cafés An excellent new café-delicatessen is **Henry's** (*Old Barrack St*); try the local cheeses or the homemade ice cream. **An Goile Mór** (*'The Big Ap-*

petite'; 17 Salthouse Lane), off Parnell St, is another excellent place for lunch, a snack, or to write postcards.

At **Bewley's** (*Bank Place*), near High St, the coffee and light meals are of the usual standard; lasagne costs £4.25. Another reasonable eatery is **Red Pepper** (*Lower Market St*), which opens from 7 am and serves breakfasts and lunches costing £3.95.

Entertainment

As the capital of a renowned music county, Ennis is not short of good music pubs. **Cíaran's Bar** (*1 Francis St*) is a small, cosy place opposite the Queens Hotel. It's popular with the local football crowd and has Irish music Thursday to Sunday evenings. **Cruise's** (see Places to Eat earlier in this section) has traditional music most nights. **Brogan's** (see Places to Eat) is a big, popular pub with frequent live-music sessions, especially on Tuesday. At the western end of Parnell St, **Brannagan's** (*Cornmarket St*) is a blues and rock place with a trendy following. The **Usual Place** pub in the market is an attractive, old-style local in an ancient stone building. **Henry J's**, a huge modern place nearby with pool tables, couldn't be more different.

Brandon's Bar (*O'Connell St*) has live music some nights and a late-night bar and dance club. **PJ Kelly's Bar** (*5 Carmody St*) also has live music, and **Considine's**, on Parnell St, has occasional Irish sessions.

One kilometre north of town along the N18 is a low pentagonal music hall, the **Cois na hAbhna** (☎ *682 0996, Gort Rd*), where a céilí, a session of traditional music and dancing, is held from 8.30 to 11 pm Wednesday night, year round (£1.50). There's an *'oíche céilí'* (music night) from 9.30 to 11.30 pm most Saturdays (£4.50). Its shop has a good selection of tapes, books and records for sale.

Shopping

On Saturdays, there is a market at the Old Market Place. For general shopping, use the huge Ennis town centre shopping mall, which contains Dunnes supermarket and can be entered halfway down O'Connell St.

Getting There & Away
Bus The Bus Éireann depot (☎ 682 4177) is at the train station. Buses run from Ennis to Limerick (40 minutes) up to 15 times daily from Monday to Saturday (seven on Sunday). There's a frequent direct service to Dublin (four hours) from Monday to Saturday (six on Sunday), five buses daily to Galway (two hours) and Cork (three hours), and up to seven daily (four on Sunday) to Shannon Airport (30 minutes).

Train From Ennis train station (☎ 684 0444) direct trains leave twice daily Monday to Saturday (once on Sunday) for Dublin (three hours) via Limerick. There are frequent trains between Dublin and Limerick, 37km south-east of Ennis; check with Limerick train station (☎ 061-315555) for times.

Getting Around
You can order a taxi on ☎ 682 3456 or ☎ 682 4759.

Tierney's Cycles and Fishing (☎ 682 9433), 17 Abbey St, has well-maintained mountain bikes costing £10/40 per day/week plus deposit. Tom Mannion Travel (☎ 682 4211), 71 O'Connell St, can fix you up with anything from a car to a motor home. King Car Rentals at Concorde Travel (☎ 682 9989), on Bank Place, is another place to try.

AROUND ENNIS
North of Ennis is the early-Christian site of Dysert O'Dea; to the south-east are several fine castles.

Getting Around
There are local and express buses covering most areas around Ennis, but the frequency of service varies; many buses run only May to September (some only July and August) and on certain days. Before making plans confirm times and destinations with Ennis bus station (☎ 065-682 4177).

You can pick up the express bus service between Limerick and Galway in Ennis (up to seven times daily) to get to Clarecastle, Newmarket-on-Fergus and Bunratty, but many of the stops on the route are 'request only'. Bus No 334 also operates regularly to Limerick via Clarecastle, Newmarket-on-Fergus and sometimes Bunratty.

An infrequent weekday service goes north-west to Ennistymon, then south along the coast to Kilkee.

Dysert O'Dea
On the Corofin road (R476) 9km north of Ennis is Dysert O'Dea, the site where St Tola founded a monastery in the 8th century. The church and high cross, the White Cross of St Tola, date from the 12th or 13th centuries. The cross depicts Daniel in the lions' den on one side and a crucified Christ above a bishop carved in relief. Look for carvings of animal and human heads in a semicircle on the southern doorway of the Romanesque church. There are also the remains of a 12m-high round tower.

In 1318, the O'Briens, who were kings of Thomond, and the Norman de Clares of Bunratty fought a pitched battle nearby, which the O'Briens won, thus postponing the Anglo-Norman conquest of Clare for some two centuries. The 15th-century O'Dea Castle nearby houses **Clare Archaeology Centre** (☎ 065-683 7401), which opens 10 am to 6 pm daily, May to September. Admission costs £2.50/1. A 3km history trail around the castle passes some two dozen ancient monuments – from ring forts and high crosses to an ancient cooking site.

South of Dysert O'Dea off the N18 is **Dromore Wood** (☎ 065-683 7166), a Dúchas nature reserve encompassing some 400 hectares as well as the ruins of the 17th-century O'Brien Castle, two ring forts and the site of Kilakee church. The wood opens 10 am to 6 pm daily, mid-June to mid-September.

Getting There & Away In July and August, there's a daily Bus Éireann (☎ 065-682 4177) bus on weekdays from Limerick, which leaves Ennis for Corofin and Ennistymon at 2.10 pm, passing Dysert O'Dea en route. The rest of the year, a bus departs Ennis on the same route at 3 pm on weekdays and at 3.50 pm on Saturday.

CLARE

Quin
☎ 065

Quin (Chuinche), a tiny village 10km south-east of Ennis, was the site of the Great Clare Find of 1854, the most important discovery of prehistoric goldwork in Ireland. Sadly, few of the several hundred torcs, gorgets and other pieces, discovered by labourers working on the Limerick to Ennis railway, made it to the National Museum in Dublin: most were sold and melted down. The source of this and much of ancient Ireland's gold may have been the Wicklow Mountains.

Quin Abbey This Franciscan friary was founded in 1433 using part of the walls of an older de Clare castle built in 1280. Despite many periods of persecution, Franciscan monks lived here until the 19th century. The last friar, Father Hogan, who died in 1820, is buried in one corner. The impressively named Fireballs McNamara, a notorious duellist and member of the region's ruling family, is also buried here. An elegant belfry rises above the main body of the abbey, and you can climb the narrow spiral staircase and look down on the fine cloister and surrounding countryside.

The abbey opens 10.30 am to 6 pm on weekdays, and 11.30 am to 5 pm at the weekend, May to October. Call ☎ 684 4084 for viewing at other times.

Beside the friary is the 13th-century Gothic **Church of St Finghin**.

Knappogue Castle

Knappogue Castle (☎ 061-368103), 3km south-east of Quin, was built in 1467 by the McNamaras. They held sway over a large part of Clare from the 5th to mid-15th centuries and built 42 castles in the region. Knappogue's huge walls are intact, and it has a fine collection of period furniture and fireplaces.

When Oliver Cromwell came to Ireland from England in 1649, he used Knappogue as a base while in the area, which is one of the reasons it was spared from destruction. The McNamara family regained the castle after the Restoration in 1660.

Knappogue Castle opens 9.30 am to 5 pm daily, May to October. Admission costs £2.75/1.55. There is a small souvenir shop in the courtyard. Knappogue also hosts medieval banquets (☎ 061-360788); see Medieval Banquets under Bunratty in the Eastern and South-Eastern Clare section later in this chapter. Knappogue, unlike Bunratty, lays on knives and forks.

Craggaunowen Project

To give a sense of Irish history, the Craggaunowen Project, 6km south-east of Quin, includes re-created ancient farms, dwellings such as a crannóg and a ring fort, plus real artefacts like a 2000-year-old oak road, and related items such as Tim Severin's leather boat the *Brendan*, in which he crossed the Atlantic between 1976 and 77. Craggaunowen Castle is a small, well-preserved McNamara fortified house. With lots of animals, some rare, this is a good place to bring kids.

The Craggaunowen Project (☎ 061-367178) opens 10 am to 6 pm daily, Easter to mid-May and October; and 9 am to 6 pm daily, mid-May to September. Last admission is at 5 pm. Admission costs £4.20/2.60; a family ticket costs £11 (for up to six children!). It also has a nice little café. Cullaun Lake nearby is a popular boating and picnic spot with forest trails.

Dromoland Castle

North of Newmarket-on-Fergus is Dromoland Castle (☎ 061-368144), a magnificent building constructed in 1826 and today one of Ireland's finest hotels. It sits in 220 hectares of vast, beautiful gardens by the River Fergus and has an 18-hole golf course. Inside, oak panels and silken fabrics adorn virtually every bit of wall space. A room in the hotel costs from £133 to £297 and is beyond most travellers' budgets, but you can venture in for a drink at the bar.

Mooghaun Ring Fort In Dromoland demesne are the remains of one of Europe's largest Iron Age hill forts: three circular earthen banks enclosing some 13 hectares. The fort's occupants may have been the owners of the huge gold hoard uncovered nearby in Quin in 1854. Access to the fort is through Dromoland Forest, which is signposted off the Newmarket to Dromoland road (N18).

Eastern & South-Eastern Clare

Clare's eastern boundary is formed by the River Shannon and long, narrow Lough Derg, which stretches some 48km from Portumna in County Galway, to just south of Killaloe. The road between the two towns swings west of the lake through some gentle countryside and picturesque hamlets, such as Mountshannon. From high ground, there are panoramic views across the lake to the Silvermine Mountains in Tipperary. Eastern Clare is fishing and shooting country, and the villages on the western shores of Lough Derg are favoured by hunters.

South-eastern Clare is visually unremarkable compared with the county's Atlantic coastline or the lakeside scenery north of Killaloe. Most people pass through quickly, taking in diversions such as Bunratty Castle or Cratloe's ancient oak woods. Some 24km west of Limerick is Shannon Airport.

SHANNON AIRPORT
☎ 061

Shannon, Ireland's second-largest airport, sits in the apparent wilderness of southeastern Clare. Like Gander Airport in Newfoundland, Shannon Airport used to be a vital fuelling stop on the transatlantic air route, as piston-engined planes barely had enough range to make it across the ocean. If you fly into Shannon, the extensive runways and numerous departure gates will remind you of its successful past. Large-scale redevelopment work to upgrade the airport is now under way.

It's said that Irish coffee (a healthy slug of whiskey in a strong coffee topped with cream) was invented at Shannon Airport for early transatlantic passengers.

The world's first duty-free shop opened at Shannon in 1947 but, since the end of duty free in the European Union (EU) in June 1999, duty free is only available to those who are flying to destinations outside the EU.

Information
There's a none-too-helpful tourist office (☎ 471664) in the arrivals hall, open 6 am (6.30 am in winter) to 6 pm daily. For flight information, phone ☎ 471444.

The Bank of Ireland counter opens from the first flight (about 6.30 am) to 5.30 pm; there's an ATM here. In Shannon town centre, an enclosed shopping mall, in the dreary town of Shannon, there are three banks (Bank of Ireland, Ulster Bank, AIB) and a post office.

Places to Stay
Hostels The closest hostels are in Ennis (see earlier in this chapter) and Limerick (see the Counties Limerick & Tipperary chapter).

B&Bs There are plenty of B&Bs 5km from the airport in Shannon, Ireland's only 'new town'. Only 400m from Shannon town centre down a quiet cul-de-sac is *Moloney's B&B* (☎ 364185, 21 Coill Mhara St). Singles/doubles cost upwards of £21/32. The *Estuary View* (☎ 364602, 20 Coill Mhara St)* has the same rates.

Hotels On the road into Shannon town is the 75-room *Oak Wood Arms Hotel* (☎ 361500), with B&B costing upwards of £38 per person. The comfortable *Shannon Great Southern Hotel* (☎ 471122), directly in front of the airport terminal, charges £100 for one of its 115 rooms.

Places to Eat
The airport departure hall has the self-service *Courtyard* and the upmarket *Lindbergh Room* (set lunches £11), but it's worth going to Shannon town centre, where the *Rineanna Bar* in the Shannon Knights Inn serves reasonable bar food. *Café 2000* offers coffee and snacks.

CLARE

Getting There & Away

Air For general inquiries, call the airport authority, Aer Rianta (☎ 471444). Aer Lingus (☎ 471666), Delta Air Lines (☎ 471200), Aeroflot (☎ 472299), AB Shannon (☎ 363636), the French carrier Corsair (☎ 01-679 1233) and Virgin Atlantic (☎ 1800 331188) fly to and from Shannon.

Bus There are up to seven Bus Éireann buses daily to Ennis (four on Sunday). The ticket office (☎ 474311) in the airport opens at 7 am, the first bus leaves at 8 am and the one-way fare is £2.50. There are also services to Limerick (40 minutes, nine daily, seven on Sunday), Galway (two hours, up to four daily, one on Sunday) and Dublin (three hours 20 minutes, up to eight daily, six on Sunday).

Taxi A taxi to the centre of Limerick or Ennis costs about £16, with possible extra charges for luggage or 'unsocial hours'.

BUNRATTY
☎ 061

The castle at Bunratty (Bun Raite), which overlooks the Shannon Estuary, is in excellent condition and well worth a look, but it's a prime tourist attraction and is besieged by coach tours in summer. With an attached folk park and Durty Nelly's 'auld Oirish' pub nearby, the area is as close as you'll get to a medieval Irish Disneyland. Go early in the day.

A small visitor information office in Bunratty Village Mills, opposite the castle, opens 9 am to 5 pm on weekdays, year round; plus 9 am to 5 pm at the weekend, mid-May to September. It has a bureau de change and beside it is an ATM.

Bunratty Castle

The Vikings built a fortified settlement at this spot, a former island surrounded by a moat. Then came the Normans; Thomas de Clare built the first stone structure on the site in the 1270s.

The present castle, the fourth or fifth incarnation to occupy the location beside the River Ratty, was built in the early 1400s by the energetic McNamara family. It fell shortly thereafter to the O'Briens, kings of Thomond, in whose possession it remained until the 17th century. Admiral Penn, father of William Penn, the Quaker founder of the US state of Pennsylvania and the city of Philadelphia, resided here for a short time.

A complete restoration was carried out in modern times, and today the castle's magnificent Great Hall holds a fine collection of 14th- to 18th-century furniture, paintings and wall hangings. Combined admission to the castle (☎ 361511) and Bunratty Folk Park costs £5/2.50 (families £12). It opens 9 am to 4.45 pm daily, June to August; and 9.30 am to 4.15 pm the rest of the year.

Medieval Banquets The Great Hall hosts 'medieval banquets' (☎ 360788), replete with comely maidens playing the harp, court jesters cracking corny jokes, and food à la Middle Ages (a pale imitation) served by wenches and washed down with mead, a kind of honey wine. You eat with your fingers. A seat at the banquet table will set you back £32, and they're heavily booked with coach parties. The whole thing is stage Irish but taken in spirit can be quite fun.

The banquets at Knappogue and Dunguaire castles (the latter in Galway) are generally smaller, quieter and often more pleasant. All run two banquets at 5.30 pm and 8.45 pm daily subject to demand. Bunratty's runs year round, Knappogue's from May to October and Dunguaire's from May to September.

Bunratty Folk Park

Bunratty Folk Park is a reconstructed traditional Irish village, with cottages, a forge and working blacksmith, weavers weaving and buttermakers making butter. There's a complete village street with post office, pub and small café, some of them transplanted from the site of Shannon Airport. Agricultural-machinery buffs will find a good collection here in Bunratty House overlooking the Folk Park.

Admission to just the Bunratty Folk Park (not including Bunratty Castle) costs £3.70/2.

Every evening from May to October a **Shannon Céilí** is held in the folk park, serving up music, dancing, Irish stew, apple pie and soda bread. It's meant to demonstrate how the peasants passed their time while the gentry gorged themselves in the safety of their castles. It costs £26.50 per person, and there are céilís at 5.30 and 8.45 pm daily. For bookings ring ☎ 360788.

Places to Eat

Durty Nelly's (☎ 364861), the olde-worlde pub beside the castle, serves fairly good bar food and also houses two restaurants: *Oyster* downstairs, open noon to 10.30 pm, and *Loft* upstairs, open 6 to 10.30 pm (closed Sunday). Both are fine, with main courses costing £12 to £17. *Kathleen's Irish Bar*, attached to Bunratty Castle Hotel, serves good bar food, with burgers and pizzas costing £6.

In Bunratty Folk Park, *Mac's Bar* serves light meals, as does *Avoca Cottage Café* across the river from Durty Nelly's. *Bunratty Cottage*, opposite the castle, has a café for snacks and a cafeteria-style restaurant for meals; smoked haddock costs £3.95. *PJ's Restaurant (☎ 361177)* in the Fitzpatrick Bunratty Shamrock Hotel is a good hotel restaurant, with a three-course lunch costing £11.50, dinner £21. It opens until 10 pm daily.

MacCloskey's (☎ 364082), in the cellars of Bunratty House Mews, a fine Georgian house up a quiet country lane past Fitzpatrick Bunratty Shamrock Hotel, is the best and most expensive restaurant in the area. Dinner costs £30 (or more), but the food, with mostly Irish ingredients, is top class.

Entertainment

Durty Nelly's was built in 1620, and the atmosphere is laid on by the shovel load. A peat fire burns in front of rough wooden chairs and benches. But it can be good fun, and the pub does attract a local crowd as well as tourists. There's music most evenings.

Mac's Bar, in the folk park, has Irish music on Wednesday, Friday, Saturday and Sunday evenings, June to September; and at the weekend only the rest of the year. It's accessible even after the park is closed. *Kathleen's Irish Bar* has traditional music on weekend nights.

Shopping

Avoca Cottage, across the river from Durty Nelly's, has a good selection of tweeds, crafts and woollen suits, plus Waterford crystal and Belleek pottery. In Bunratty Village Mills, opposite the castle, Bunratty Cottage stocks every conceivable Irish jumper (sweater), and Tipperary crystal.

Mike McGlynn Antiques and Fine Art shop, opposite the Fitzpatrick Bunratty Shamrock Hotel, is also worth a look. Along the Limerick to Shannon road is Ballycasey Craft and Design Centre, home to weavers, silversmiths, leatherworkers and potters.

Getting There & Away

Four Bus Éireann buses daily (three on Sunday) between Limerick and Galway stop at Bunratty outside the Fitzpatrick Bunratty Shamrock Hotel; the first leaves Limerick bus station (☎ 061-313333) at 11.35 am.

Buses travelling south through Bunratty leave Ennis daily from 10.12 am onwards. Bunratty is also served by up to 17 (10 on Sunday) daily buses on the Shannon Airport to Limerick route.

Getting Around

You can hire bikes at the Shannon Cycle Centre (☎ 364696), 12 Firgrove, Hurlers Cross, almost 4km north of Bunratty on the main road to Ennis.

CRATLOE
☎ 061

Cratloe, 3km east of Bunratty just north of the main Limerick road (N18), is a picturesque village overlooking the Shannon Estuary. Nearby are hills covered in oak trees – a rare sight in Ireland today, although such forests once blanketed the island. The oak roof beams of Westminster Hall in London are said to be from Cratloe. To reach the woods, go along the Kilmurry road from Cratloe, under a railway bridge

CLARE

and turn right. There are some fine **walks** in the area and views over the estuary from Gallows Hill and Woodcock Hill.

A rare 17th-century longhouse called **Cratloe Wood House** (☎ 327028), off the N18, opens to the public 2 to 6 pm Monday to Saturday, June to mid-September. Admission costs £2.50/1.50, which includes an excellent guided tour.

Places to Stay

Cratloe has a fair selection of guesthouses. *Cratloe Heights (☎ 357253)*, Ballymorris, charges upwards of £20/30 for singles/doubles. *Cratloe Lodge (☎ 357168)*, just off the N18, is similarly priced, and Maura and Tom will give you a warm welcome.

Getting There & Away

While there is no bus service directly to Cratloe, plenty of buses pass through Bunratty nearby. Visitors can hire a bike in Hurlers Cross (see Getting Around in the Bunratty section earlier in this chapter) or walk out to Cratloe.

KILLALOE & AROUND
☎ 061 • pop 1030

Killaloe (Cill Dalua) is one of the principal crossings on the River Shannon, and a fine old 13-arched bridge spans the river. Across the river and in County Tipperary, **Ballina** is Killaloe's other half and some of the better pubs and restaurants are found there. From Killaloe, the Shannon is navigable all the way north to Lough Key in County Sligo, and in summer the town is jammed with weekend sailors.

The town has a fine setting, with the Slieve Bernagh Hills rising abruptly to the west, the Arra Mountains to the east and Lough Derg at its doorstep. Plus, it's on the 180km East Clare Way.

Orientation & Information

The narrow street running from the river on the Killaloe side is Bridge St, which turns right, becoming Main St. The tourist office (☎ 376866), in the Killaloe Heritage Centre building beside Shannon Bridge, opens 10 am to 6 pm daily, May to mid-September. It stocks a free walking-tour leaflet that covers Ballina as well.

Things to See & Do

Also known as St Flannan's Cathedral, **Killaloe Cathedral** dates from the early 13th century and was built by the O'Brien family on top of an earlier 6th-century church. Take a look at the carvings inside around the Romanesque southern doorway, which dates from an older chapel; the carvings are among the finest in the country.

Next to the doorway is early-Christian **Thorgrim's Stone**, unusual in that it bears both the old Scandinavian runic and Irish ogham scripts. It's the shaft of a stone cross and could have been carved by a converted Viking doing penance for his past sins. The runic script reads: 'Thórgrímr carved this cross'. The translation of the ogham is: 'A blessing on Thórgrímr'. In the cathedral grounds is **St Flannan's Oratory**, of 12th-century Romanesque design.

The modern Church of St Flannan up the hill to the west of the river is without interest except for 9th-century **St Lua's Oratory** in the churchyard. It was moved here from Friars Island in the Shannon when the island was flooded by a hydroelectric scheme.

Killaloe Heritage Centre, in the same building as the tourist office and open the same hours, has exhibits dealing with local history and the cathedral. Admission costs £1.50/1.

In Ballina over the bridge, TJ's Angling Centre (☎ 376009) sells **fishing** tackle and has equipment and boats for hire.

Places to Stay & Eat

In Ballina, the comfortable *Kincora House (☎ 376149, Church St)* offers singles/doubles with shared bathroom costing £25/44 and opens year round. *Simply Delicious*, a coffee shop on the main street near the bridge, opens for breakfast and serves snacks and lunches costing under £5. The thatched *Gooser's Pub and Restaurant (☎ 376792)* has some of the best food in town; its restaurant at the back is fine but expensive, with mains costing £13.50 to £23. *Anchor Inn* in Killaloe serves decent bar food.

Entertainment

Good pubs in Killaloe/Ballina are *Molly's*, *Gooser's*, *Crotty's Courtyard* and *Anchor Inn*; most have traditional music at the weekend.

Getting There & Away

There are regular Bus Éireann (☎ 061-313333) buses Monday to Saturday from Limerick to Killaloe. The bus stop is outside the cathedral.

KILLALOE TO MOUNTSHANNON

The journey north on either side of Lough Derg to Mountshannon, or Portroe in Tipperary, is very scenic. To get to Mountshannon from Killaloe take the Scarriff (An Scairbh) road.

About 1.5km north of Killaloe, **Beal Ború** is an earthen mound or fort said to have been Kincora, the palace of the famous Irish King Brian Ború, who defeated the Vikings at the Battle of Clontarf in 1014. Traces of Bronze Age settlement have been found. With its commanding view over Lough Derg, this was obviously a site of strategic importance.

About 3km north of Killaloe is the **University of Limerick Activity Centre** (☎ 061-376622, Two Mile Gate), where individuals and groups can learn kayaking, canoeing, sailing and windsurfing; a private lesson costs £25 for two hours. Check the Web site at www.ul.ie/~sports/activity.html.

About 4.5km north of Killaloe is Cragliath Hill, which has another fort, **Grianamlaghna**, named after Brian Ború's great grandfather, King Lachtna.

Shannonside Activity Centre (☎ 061-376622) is an approved sailing centre offering sailing, windsurfing, canoeing, pony trekking, hill walking and biking. It's 3km south-west of Mountshannon on the Scarriff road (R352).

Also nearby is **Mountshannon Pony Centre** (☎ 061-921428), with ponies for hire and riding lessons.

Places to Stay & Eat

Kincora Hall (☎ *061-376000*), a lovely 25-room hotel about 500m north of Killaloe on the Scarriff road, costs £60/72 or £65/90 for singles/doubles.

Lough Derg Holiday Park (☎ *061-376329*) is a camp site 5km north of Killaloe along the Scarriff road (R463) on the lake shore. It charges £7.50 for a tent and £2.50/1 per adult/child. Hikers and cyclists pay £4.

Nearby in Ogonnelloe (Tuath Ó gConnaille), *Lantern House* serves simple, wholesome food.

MOUNTSHANNON & AROUND
☎ 061

Mountshannon (Baile Uí Bheoláin), on the south-western shores of Lough Derg, is an attractive 18th-century village. The small stone harbour is usually busy with fishing boats and is the main port for trips to Holy Island, one of Clare's finest early-Christian settlements.

There's a small seasonal tourist office (☎ 927300) next to Hickey's post-office-cum-shop on the main street.

Holy Island

Lying 2km offshore from Mountshannon, Holy Island (Inis Cealtra) is the site of a monastic settlement thought to have been founded by St Cáimín in the 7th century. On the island you'll see a round tower which is over 27m tall (though missing its top storey). You'll also find four old chapels, a hermit's cell and some early-Christian gravestones dating from the 7th to 13th centuries. One of the chapels has an elegant Romanesque arch. Inside the chapel is an inscription in old Irish, which translates as 'Pray for Tornog, who made this cross'.

The Vikings treated this monastery roughly in the 9th century, but under the subsequent protection of Brian Ború and others it flourished. The Holy Well was once the focus for a lively festival that was banned in the 1830s because a lot of, well, nonreligious behaviour was creeping in.

R&B Marine Services (☎ 375011) has trips aboard the *Derg Princess* from Mountshannon to Holy Island costing £4/2, May to October. Trips can also be arranged from Mountshannon through the East Clare

CLARE

Heritage Centre (☎ 061-921351, 921615), based in Tuamgraney about 10km south-west on the R352.

Activities
Hickey's (☎ 927255), on the main street, has fishing tackle and equipment as well as boats for hire. The Lakeside Caravan and Camping Park (see Places to Stay next) hires out boats and equipment for windsurfing, rowing and sailing.

Places to Stay
The *Lakeside Caravan and Camping Park* (☎ 927225), open May to September, charges car drivers £5 for a tent plus £1/50p per adult/child; hikers or cyclists pay £3.50. Hostel accommodation may be available on the grounds in mobile homes or chalets. To get there, go north along the Portumna road (R352) from Mountshannon and take the first turn right.

Derg Lodge (☎ 927180), in the village, offers singles/doubles costing £21/30 for B&B and opens year round.

Oak House (☎ 927185), a country house overlooking the lake 6km north of the village, costs upwards of £22.50/32. In the village, the delightful 14-room *Mountshannon Hotel* (☎ 927162) charges £35 per person.

Places to Eat
An Cupán Caife (The Coffee Cup), on the main street, is a licensed (and BYO wine) bistro that opens 10 am to 9 pm daily, March to November. *Cois na hAbhna*, also on the main street, serves pub grub and has traditional Irish music at the weekend in summer.

Getting There & Away
Weekday Bus Éireann bus No 345 from Limerick to Killaloe continues to Scarriff (8km south-west of Mountshannon). On Saturday only, bus No 346 from Limerick (at 1.15 pm) to Whitegate via Scarriff runs to Mountshannon (one hour 25 minutes); from Mountshannon the bus leaves at 8.50 am. The bus stop is outside Keane's on the main street.

NORTH TO GALWAY
North of Mountshannon, the R352 follows Lough Derg to Portumna in Galway. Inland is an area known as the **Clare Lakelands**, based around Feakle, where numerous lakes offer good coarse fishing.

South-Western & Western Clare

Loop Head at the county's south-western tip is a big wedge splitting the mighty waves of the Atlantic Ocean. The coast between Loop Head and Kilkee has some outstanding cliff scenery. North of Kilkee, a popular seaside resort, the road (N67) moves inland, but there are some worthwhile detours to the lonely coast and beaches where Spanish Armada ships were wrecked over 400 years ago. Kilkee, White Strand, Spanish Point and Lahinch all have good beaches.

North and north-west of Ennis are a number of small villages, including Corofin and Ennistymon. These are both at the very southern limits of the outstanding Burren region (see that section later in this chapter), and nearby are Hag's Head (a superb walk with excellent views) and the Cliffs of Moher, one of Ireland's most spectacular natural features. From there the road dips downhill towards Doolin, a well-known rest stop for backpackers and a centre of Irish music.

GETTING THERE & AWAY
This region has infrequent local bus services to the coastal towns and villages; some buses run from Limerick, while others are on express routes from Galway or Tralee. Services are more frequent from May to September. Phone Ennis bus station (☎ 065-682 4177) for exact times and fares.

Bus Éireann express bus No 15 terminates in Ennis or Ennistymon. It runs through Lahinch, Miltown Malbay, Lisdoonvarna, Doolin, Kilrush and Kilkee. Bus No 50 goes to Galway, Kilcolgan and Kinvara (both in County Galway), Ballyvaughan, Lisdoonvarna, Doolin, the Cliffs of Moher, Lahinch,

Miltown Malbay, Doonbeg, Kilkee, Kilrush and on to Killarney in County Kerry. Local bus No 333 travels between Limerick, Ennis, Ennistymon, Lahinch, Quilty, Doonbeg, Kilkee and Kilrush.

In summer, bus No 337 runs three times daily (once on Sunday) between Limerick and Lisdoonvarna, passing through Ennis, Ennistymon, Lahinch, Liscannor, the Cliffs of Moher and Doolin en route. The rest of the year it goes once daily only.

KILLIMER
☎ 065

Killimer is a nondescript village, close to the Shannon Estuary and Moneypoint, Ireland's largest power station. At 915 megawatts, Moneypoint is capable of supplying 40% of the country's needs and burns two million tonnes of coal a year. (You can see another power station across the estuary in Tarbert.)

The Colleen Bawn (White Girl) was a woman called Eileen Hanly who was murdered in 1819 and thrown into the River Shannon by her husband, John Scanlon. Her body washed ashore and was buried in Killimer graveyard. Scanlon was hanged. The story has inspired novels, plays, songs and operas. Unfortunately, her tombstone has been carried away by souvenir hunters.

Getting There & Away

A 20-minute car ferry (☎ 905 3124) runs from Killimer, across the Shannon Estuary, to Tarbert in County Kerry, on the hour, year round (every half-hour in peak season). April to September, the schedule is from 7 am (9 am on Sunday) to 9 pm; during the rest of the year sailings are 7 am (10 am on Sunday) to 7 pm. From Tarbert schedules begin and finish 30 minutes later. The one-way/return fares are £2/3 for bikes and foot passengers, £8/12 for cars and £4/6 for motorcyclists. You pay on board.

KILRUSH
☎ 065 • pop 2750

This small town overlooks the Shannon Estuary and the hills of Kerry to the south, but it isn't particularly attractive. Kilrush (Cill

Rois) has the western coast's biggest marina, the 120-berth Kilrush Creek.

Kilrush's tourist office (☎ 905 1577), in the town hall on Market Square, opens 10 am to 1 pm and 2 to 6 pm Monday to Saturday, late May to August. On Frances St, the main street, you'll find a Bank of Ireland and an AIB (the latter has an ATM) and the post office. The Internet Bureau (☎ 905 1061), at the bottom of Frances St, offers Internet access costing £3 per 30 minutes.

Things to See & Do

Kilrush Heritage Centre (☎ 905 1596), in the town hall, has an exhibition entitled Kilrush in Landlord Times. It opens 10 am to 6 pm Monday to Saturday, and noon to 4 pm on Sunday, late May to August; and 10 am to 4 pm on weekdays, September to April. Admission costs £2/1.

If you're interested in stained glass, **St Senan's Catholic church** contains some attractive examples by well-known artisan Harry Clarke. East of town is **Kilrush Wood**, which has some fine old trees and a picnic area.

An exhibition on the history and wildlife of Scattery Island is housed in the Dúchas-run **Scattery Island Centre** (☎ 905 2144), on Merchant's Quay. It's free and open 9.30 am to 6.30 pm daily, mid-June to mid-September.

Kilrush Creek Adventure Centre (☎ 905 2855, fax 905 2597), near the marina, offers a range of activities, including archery, windsurfing, kayaking, sailing and dolphin watching, plus accommodation (see Kilrush Creek Lodge in the following section).

Places to Stay & Eat

The IHH *Katie O'Connors Holiday Hostel* (☎ 905 1133, 49-50 Frances St), just off the square and open year round, offers dorm beds costing £7.50; doubles cost £18. Modern *Kilrush Creek Lodge* (☎ 905 2595) charges £10 per person for dorm beds or £15 to £20 for private rooms.

There are plenty of B&Bs in the Kilrush area, including *Ferry Lodge* (☎ 905 1291, Cappa Rd), which opens May to September

CLARE

and offers singles/doubles with bathroom costing £20/34.

Central Restaurant and *Coffey's*, both on Market Square, are inexpensive places for a meal. Coffey's serves pizzas costing upwards of £3.50.

Getting There & Away

For information on buses to and from Kilrush, see the introductory Getting There & Away entry to this South-Western & Western Clare section.

Getting Around

You can hire bikes at Gleeson's Cycles (☎ 905 1127), Henry St, for £10/40 per day/week plus deposit.

SCATTERY ISLAND
☎ 065

This windswept, treeless island, 2.5km south-west of Cappa pier, is the site of a Christian settlement founded by St Senan in the 6th century. It has one of the tallest, best-preserved round towers in Ireland. It's 36m high, and the entrance is at ground level instead of the usual position high above the foundation. There are remains of five medieval churches, including a 9th-century cathedral.

To build his monastery, St Senan had to rid the island of a monster. The Irish name for the island is Inis Cathaigh, Cathach being the sea serpent who had made his lair on the island. With the help of the archangel Raphael, Senan banished the monster and also excluded all women. A local, apparently very friendly, virgin named Cannera wanted to join Senan, provoking much speculation about how he withstood the temptation.

> Legend hints that had the maid,
> Until morning's light delayed,
> And given the saint one rosy smile,
> She'd ne'er have left his lonely isle.

Scattery was a beautiful but unfortunate site for a monastery, as it was all too easy for the Vikings to sail up the estuary and pillage the place, which they did repeatedly in the 9th

and 10th centuries. They occupied the island for 100 years until 970, when they were dislodged by Brian Ború.

See the previous Kilrush section for information on the island's history and wildlife exhibition.

Getting There & Away

The harbour at Cappa village near Kilrush is where you catch the boat to Scattery Island. To get there turn left at the bottom of Frances St in Kilrush and follow the road for 2km.

During the summer, Scattery Island Ferries (☎ 905 1237) runs boats from Cappa pier to the island costing £4.50 return. There's no strict timetable as the trips are subject to demand and weather conditions. You can buy tickets at the small kiosk on Merchant's Quay. The ferry company can also take you to see bottle-nose dolphins in the Shannon Estuary.

KILKEE
☎ 065 • pop 1300

During the summer, Kilkee's wide bay is thronged with day-trippers and holiday-makers from all over Clare and Limerick. Kilkee (Cill Chaoi) first became popular in Victorian times when rich Limerick families built seaside retreats here. Today, Kilkee is a little too fat with guesthouses, amusement arcades and takeaways.

Information

The seasonal tourist office (☎ 905 6112), on O'Connell St, is just up to the left from the seafront. It opens 10 am to 1 pm and 2 to 6 pm daily, late May to August. On O'Curry St, the Bank of Ireland has a bureau de change, and the AIB has an ATM.

Things to See & Do

Many visitors come for the fine sheltered **beach** and the **Pollock Holes**, natural swimming pools in the Duggerna Rocks to the south of the beach. **St George's Head** to the north has good cliff walks and scenery, while south of the bay the **Duggerna Rocks** form an unusual natural amphitheatre. Farther south is a huge **sea cave**. These sights can be reached by driving to Kilkee's West End area and following the coastal path.

Kilkee is a well-known **diving** centre. There are shore dives from the Duggerna Rocks fringing the western side of the bay, or boat dives on the Black Rocks farther out. Right at the tip of the Duggerna Rocks is the small inlet of Myles Creek, and there is excellent underwater scenery out from it. Kilkee Diving and Watersports Centre (☎ 905 6707) by the harbour has tanks and other equipment for hire and runs five-day PADI courses costing £270 to £350.

Places to Stay

Camping There are plenty of camp sites. *Cunningham's Holiday Park* (☎ 905 6430) opens late May to late September and charges drivers £8 to £11 for a tent plus £1/50p per adult/child (hikers and cyclists £3.50). From the N67 on the Kilrush side of town, turn left, go through the roundabout and take the first left.

Green Acres Caravan and Camping Park (☎ 905 7011), with a flat £8 charge (cyclists and hikers £3), is 6km south of Kilkee on the R487.

Hostels The IHH *Kilkee Hostel* (☎ 905 6209) is clean, well run and open February to October. It's 50m from the seafront on O'Curry St, and charges £8 for dorm beds (no private rooms). It rents bicycles and has a well-equipped kitchen, a laundry room and a small coffee shop.

B&Bs There are countless guesthouses in Kilkee, usually a little more expensive than in other areas. There are some good ones at West End, including *Dunearn* (☎ 905 6545), charging £24.50/40 for singles/doubles, and *Harbour Lodge* (☎ 905 6090, 6 Marine Parade), with doubles costing upwards of £32. At busy times you may have to take whatever the tourist office can get you.

Hotels There are plenty of hotels in Kilkee, but for the extra money you don't get much extra luxury. *Halpin's Hotel* (☎ 905 6032, 2 Erin St), past the tourist office, is a pleasant, friendly family-run hotel. B&B costs upwards of £40/65 in singles/doubles.

Places to Eat

There are plenty of fast-food joints. For good home cooking at reasonable prices try *Pantry* (☎ 905 6576), halfway along O'Curry St from the seafront, on the left, or *Old Bistro*, next to Myle's Creek pub, where mains cost £9.50 to £12. *Michael Martin's* pub, on Erin St next to Halpin's Hotel, and the *Strand* pub, on the seafront, are worth trying for good meals costing around £5.

Almost 2km north of Kilkee, signposted from the seafront, is the popular *Manuel's Seafood Restaurant* (☎ 905 6211). It opens for dinner only, Easter to September; steamed or grilled turbot costs £18.75.

Entertainment

Opposite the hostel on O'Curry St is the *Myle's Creek* pub, Kilkee's trendiest spot. The pub is on the band circuit and attracts many of Ireland's best young rock groups. *M O'Mara*, also on O'Curry St, and the popular *Strand*, on the seafront, have a range of musical evenings during the week.

Getting There & Away

For information on buses to and from Kilkee, see the introductory Getting There & Away entry in this South-Western & Western Clare section.

Getting Around

Bicycles can be hired at Williams (☎ 905 6141), on Circular Rd near the Catholic church, for £10/40 per day/week.

KILKEE TO LOOP HEAD

The land from Kilkee south to Loop Head is poor and flat, but the cliff scenery is spectacular: the coast is peppered with sea stacks, arches and wave-sculpted rocks. It's a glorious day's bike ride down to the head and back. Better still, if you have the energy, is the 24km cliff walk between Loop Head and Kilkee. The cliffs compare with the more famous Cliffs of Moher to the north and are much less visited.

CLARE

Intrinsic Bay

About 3km south of Kilkee is Intrinsic Bay, named after the ship wrecked here in 1856 en route to America. The summit shadowing the bay is Lookout Hill. To the north are Diamond Rock and **Bishop's Island**, the latter a remarkable pillar of rock with a medieval oratory perched on the summit. The oratory is attributed to the 6th-century St Senan, who also built the settlement on Scattery Island (see earlier in this chapter). Later, a selfish bishop supposedly lived here while his people starved in a famine; when the gap to the mainland widened in a storm, the bishop himself starved to death.

Kilbaha

At the end of the R487, 7km east of Loop Head, Kilbaha's tiny church contains an unusual relic of more repressive times. The **Little Ark** is a small wooden altar used by Catholics in the 1850s. In order for the priest to celebrate mass, the altar was wheeled below the high-tide mark, where it was outside the jurisdiction of the local Protestant landlord. A stained-glass window above the church door depicts the ark in use. Father Michael Meehan, the courageous local priest who had the ark built, is buried in the church.

There's a **Submerged Forest**, a collection of 5000-year-old tree stumps (probably pine) on the shore east of Rinvella Bay, near Kilbaha. They were originally preserved in peat bog, which was washed away as the sea level rose, leaving the stumps visible.

Keating's claims to be the closest pub on the Irish mainland to New York city.

Carrigaholt

☎ 065

On 15 September 1588, seven tattered ships of the Spanish Armada took shelter off Carrigaholt (Carraig an Chabaltaigh), a tiny village inside the mouth of the Shannon Estuary. One, probably the *Annunciada*, was torched and abandoned, sinking somewhere out in the estuary. Today, Carrigaholt has a safe beach and the substantial remains of a 15th-century McMahon castle with a square keep overlooking the water. From May to October, Dolphinwatch (☎ 905 8156, 088-258 4711), with an office opposite the post office, runs two-hour trips (£10/6) in the estuary to view some resident bottle-nose dolphins (there are about 100 pods in the Shannon Estuary).

The best place to eat is the *Long Dock* *(☎ 905 8106, West St)*, open Easter to September. It's a cosy pub-cum-restaurant with bar food (chicken curry £4.95), seafood dinners and Irish music three times a week. *Morrissey's Village Pub* nearby has traditional music and set dancing at the weekend. You might also try *Fennell's*, a dumpy little pub, or *Keane's Bar*, both with music on some nights.

Loop Head

On a clear day, Loop Head (Ceann Léime), Clare's southernmost point, has magnificent views south to the Dingle Peninsula crowned by Mt Brandon (953m), and north to the Aran Islands and Galway Bay. There are bracing walks in the area and a long hike running along the cliffs to Kilkee.

KILKEE TO ENNISTYMON

North of Kilkee, the 'real' west of Ireland begins to assert itself. The N67 runs inland for some 32km until it reaches Quilty. Take the occasional lane to the west and search out unfrequented places such as White Strand, north of Doonbeg. **Ballard Bay** is 8km north of Doonbeg, where an old telegraph tower looks over some fine cliffs. **Donegal Point** has the remains of a promontory fort.

There's good fishing for bass, pollock and mackerel all along the coast, and safe beaches at Seafield, Lough Donnell and Quilty.

Getting There & Away

From May to September Bus Éireann express bus No 50 between Killarney and Galway stops three times daily (twice on Sunday) at Doonbeg, Miltown Malbay and Lahinch. Monday to Saturday, the rest of the year, bus No 333 connects Doonbeg, Quilty, Spanish Point, Miltown Malbay and Lahinch. Contact Ennis bus station (☎ 065-682 4177) for times and fares.

CLARE

Doonbeg
☎ 065

Doonbeg (An Dún Beag) is a tiny fishing village about halfway between Kilkee and Quilty. Near the mouth of the River Doonbeg, another Armada ship, the *San Esteban*, was wrecked on 20 September 1588. The survivors were later executed at Spanish Point. **White Strand** (Trá Ban) is a quiet beach, 2km long and backed by dunes. There are two **ruined castles** nearby, Doonbeg and Doonmore.

Places to Stay & Eat For campers the side roads around Doonbeg are good places to pitch a tent and watch the sun go down. *An Tinteán* (*'The Hearth'*; ☎ 905 5036) is a seafood restaurant and guesthouse with turf fires and good rooms with bathrooms. B&B costs upwards of £15 per person. Igoe Inn has *Olde Kitchen Restaurant* (☎ 905 5039), which does steak and seafood costing £12 to £15. It opens for dinner only most of the year, but for lunch too in the peak tourist season. *San Esteban* (☎ 905 5105), signposted from the north of the village, is 1km from Doonbeg in Rhynagonaught. B&B costs upwards of £23/36 in singles/doubles.

Entertainment For music try *Morrissey's* pub, on Main St, or visit the shocking-pink *Tubridy's* pub, next to the cemetery, on Thursday.

Quilty
☎ 065

The small village of Quilty, on a particularly bleak stretch of coast, is a centre for seaweed production. Kelp and other plants are collected, dried on the stone walls and sent for processing. The resulting alginates are used in toothpaste, beer, agar and certain cosmetics. Quilty has a good **beach**, and boats are available for **deep-sea angling**.

One of the most powerful ships of the Spanish Armada, the *San Marcos*, was wrecked off nearby Mutton Island in September 1588. It had taken a terrible battering, and only four of its 1000 crew survived.

Cúchulainn's Leap

The 'Loop' in Loop Head is a corruption of the word 'leap'. Legend has it that the Celtic warrior Cúchulainn was being chased all over Ireland by the formidable Mal. Cornered on this headland, he leapt onto a sea stack and, when she tried to follow him, Mal fell to her death. The sea turned crimson and her body washed ashore at various points along the coast, giving Hag's Head and Malbay their names. Some say the headland looks like a seated woman looking out over the Atlantic. West of the lighthouse you'll find the sea stack in question; the gap is known as Cúchulainn's Leap.

Local guesthouses include *Clonmore Lodge* (☎ 708 7020), some 3km from the village. B&B costs £23/36 for singles/doubles, dinner £12, and it opens April to October.

Miltown Malbay
☎ 065 • pop 615

Like Kilkee, Miltown Malbay was a resort favoured by well-to-do Victorians, though the town isn't actually on the sea: the beach is 3km away at Spanish Point. Miltown Malbay has a thriving music scene and every year hosts a **Willie Clancy Irish Music Festival** as a tribute to one of Ireland's greatest pipers. The festival usually runs during the first week in July, when the town is overrun with wandering minstrels, and Guinness is consumed by the bucket. You can also find music in the surrounding villages.

Excellent pubs here include *Clancy's*, on the main street, and *Queally's*, just off the southern end of the main street. The reasonably priced *Ocean View Restaurant*, on the main street, opens daily and offers beef in Guinness stew (£4.50).

Spanish Point
There's a great beach at Spanish Point (Rinn na Spáinneach), and when the waves are running there's good **surfing**.

CLARE

The beach gets its name from the execution of 60 Spanish Armada survivors on Cnoc na Crocaire (Hill of the Gallows) nearby. They had swum ashore, only to be executed by Boetius Clancy, the sheriff of Clare, and Turlough O'Brien, the local chief loyal to the English Crown.

Lahinch

☎ 065 • pop 550

Lahinch (Leacht Uí Chonchubhair) is the archetypal seaside resort, full of fast-food joints, amusement arcades and places to stay. The town sits on a protected bay with a fine beach. In 1943, a US bomber flying off course landed on the beach, and the 12 airmen were repatriated to Allied forces through Northern Ireland. Lahinch is very busy in the summer: you may prefer to move on to Ennistymon, Liscannor or Doolin. Surprisingly, there are no banks, though you can change money at the post office.

The **surfing** can be good any time of year and surfboards and wet suits can be rented on the seafront from the Surf Shop. For those who like to swim in warmer water there's the **Lahinch Seaworld Leisure Centre** (☎ 708 1900) on the Promenade. The **Willie Daly Riding Centre** (☎ 707 1385), between Lahinch and Ennistymon, has pony trekking and is signposted from the north of the town.

Places to Stay & Eat The IHH *Lahinch Hostel* (☎ 708 1040, Church St) has dorm beds costing £8 and doubles costing £24 to £28, and there's a laundry.

An excellent restaurant is *Mr Eamon's* (☎ 708 1050, Kettle St). It opens for lunch and dinner (costing £18 or more), March to November. Simpler, filling fare is to be had at *Coffee Dock (Main St)*, where soup and bread costs under £2, chicken with veg £4.50.

ENNISTYMON

☎ 065 • pop 1040

Ennistymon (Inis Díomáin), a moderately attractive little town with essentially one long main street called Church St, is 3km inland from Lahinch on the banks of the River Inagh. The town started out as a settlement round a castle built by Turlough O'Brien in 1588. The town's appearance has scarcely changed over the past few decades, and its charm derives primarily from its well-maintained shops and old pubs. The River Inagh runs directly below and parallel to Church St.

In a street uphill off the centre of Church St there's a branch of the AIB with a bureau de change and an ATM.

Things to See & Do

The bridge over the River Inagh is just above the 200m rapids known as the **Cascades**, which can be impressive if the river is high. There's trout and salmon fishing here. The Cascades are just down the lane beside the Arch Café Bar. It's a pleasant stroll around here in the evening. When the Inagh is in flood, though, the waters can rise almost to the houses. Down river, **Falls Hotel** is a former residence of the McNamara family and has its own water-powered generator.

Places to Stay

Station House (☎ 707 1149), about half a kilometre south on the Ennis road (N85), offers en suite rooms costing £18 per person.

Falls Hotel (☎ 707 1004) is a comfortable old country house in 20 hectares of wooded gardens with singles/doubles costing upwards of £35/60 and self-catering apartments.

Places to Eat

Franco's Fast Foods, on Church St, is one of the few decent low-priced eateries in Ennistymon, with pizza (upwards of £2.70) and other takeaways. Also on Church St, *Sugan Chair* is a large restaurant good for snacks and light meals. *Cooley's House* pub on Church St serves reasonable bar food, as does *Arch Café Bar*.

For something more substantial – and upmarket – try *Falls Hotel* (see Places to Stay earlier), where a set dinner costs £18.

CLARE

Entertainment

On Church St, *Cooley's House* pub has music at the weekend and most evenings during the summer. *Carrigg's* is also worth a look. *Eugene's* is a cosy place for a drink.

Getting There & Away

Bus Éireann bus No 15 between Limerick and Lisdoonvarna stops at Ennistymon in front of Aherne's on Church St. Contact Ennis bus station (☎ 065-682 4177) for times and fares.

LISCANNOR & AROUND

☎ 065

This small fishing village offers a fine view over Liscannor Bay and Lahinch as the road (R478) heads for the Cliffs of Moher and Doolin. Liscannor (Lios Ceannúir) has given its name to a paving stone with ripples on the surface. The stone is widely used locally for floors, walls and even roofs.

John Philip Holland (1840–1914), the inventor of the submarine, was born in Liscannor. He emigrated to the USA in 1873, and he hoped his invention would be used to sink British warships.

Things to See & Do

On the way north to the Cliffs of Moher and close to Murphy's Arch Bar and Considine's pub is the **Holy Well of St Brigid**, marked by a tall stone column topped with an urn. The well's significance probably predates Christian times, as its Irish name suggests a connection with a pre-Christian god, Crom Dubh.

People from all over Clare and the Aran Islands, with all sorts of physical problems, come to pray and drink the healing waters. There is a collection of discarded religious memorabilia nearby. The pilgrimage to the well takes place in July, particularly on the last weekend of the month, and there can be up to 400 people there on the Sunday.

Clahane Beach to the west of Liscannor is good and safe. A 'lost city' and church known as Kilstephen are supposed to sit on an underwater reef in Liscannor Bay. The Celtic hero Conan is buried on **Slieve** Callan to the south. He is said to lie with the key to the lost church.

The ruined square **castle** on the point just outside Liscannor was built by the O'Connor family.

The Liscannor-based **Cliffs of Moher Pony Trekking and Riding Centre** (☎ 708 1283) has ponies for hire.

Places to Stay

The IHH *Liscannor Village Hostel* (☎ 708 1550) is at the eastern end of the village behind the Captain's Deck craft shop and restaurant. It's a big, well-run place but could be cleaner. Dormitory beds cost £8, doubles £18. It opens March to October.

Coming from Lahinch, just before the village, on the right, is *Sea Haven* (☎ 708 1385), with B&B costing £23.50/34 for singles/doubles and good, hard beds.

Three kilometres north-west of Liscannor you'll find the closest B&B to the Cliffs of Moher – friendly *Moher Lodge* (☎ 708 1269). It charges £25/38 and is open April to October.

Places to Eat

For cheap meals try the pubs on the main street such as *Vaughan's Anchor Inn*, where most mains cost between £4.50 and £10.50. There's good fresh seafood at *Captain's Deck* (☎ 708 1666) in front of the hostel. It opens Monday to Saturday for dinner, with main courses costing £7.50 to £11.50.

Cottage Restaurant is a small seafood restaurant tucked away in a tiny cottage above the Holy Well of St Brigid (see Things to See & Do earlier).

Entertainment

There is a string of pubs in Liscannor on the main street, most with music. *Joseph McHugh's* is the best known and is as genuine an old Irish pub as you'll find anywhere, down to the groceries and other oddments piled on the shelves. For music, try Joseph McHugh's on Tuesday or the equally good *Egan's*, two doors along. *Vaughan's Anchor Inn* has music almost every night during the summer.

CLARE

Getting There & Away

From May to September, Bus Éireann express bus No 50 between Killarney and Galway stops at Liscannor. Bus No 337 between Limerick and Lisdoonvarna stops daily year round. Contact Ennis bus station (☎ 065-682 4177) for times and fares.

HAG'S HEAD

Hag's Head forms the southern end of the touristy but magnificent Cliffs of Moher and is an excellent place from which to view the cliffs. The **Hag's Head Walk** is superb and well worth the effort. The return trip takes about three hours.

To get to the head, go just over 5km out of Liscannor towards the Cliffs of Moher until, just past the Moher Lodge, you spot a rough track turning to the left. You can drive only a short distance, and then you'll have to walk along the path out towards the point. There's a huge sea arch at the tip and another visible to the north. At the head a signal tower was erected in case Napoleon tried to attack on the western coast. The tower is built on the site of an ancient promontory fort called Mothair, which has given its name to the famous cliffs to the north.

CLIFFS OF MOHER

One of Ireland's most spectacular sights, the Cliffs of Moher (Aillte an Mothair) rise from Hag's Head and reach their highest point (203m) just north of O'Brien's Tower, before slowly descending farther north again. On a clear day, the views are tremendous: the Aran Islands stand etched on the waters of Galway Bay, and beyond lie the hills of Connemara in western Galway.

From the cliff edge you can just hear the booming far below as the waves eat into the soft shale and sandstone. Sections of the cliff often give way, and they're generally so unstable that few birds or plants make them their home. With a due-west exposure, sunset is the best time to visit, and there is a bracing 8km walk along the cliff edge down to Hag's Head. Part of the walk was walled off with Liscannor stone by the eccentric local landlord Cornelius O'Brien

(1801–57), who built the lookout tower, **O'Brien's Tower**, to impress lady visitors. It opens daily and it costs £1/60p to climb up and use the telescope.

The sea stack – covered with seabirds and their guano – just below the tower is called Breanan Mór and is itself over 70m high.

Information

The visitor centre (☎ 065-708 1171) opens 9 am to 8 pm daily, July and August; 9 am to 7 pm, June; 9 am to 6.30 pm, May and September; and 9.30 am to 5 pm (6 pm in April), the rest of the year. There's a bureau de change, a small café and a gift shop full of souvenirs. Be warned: the cliffs are one of the most popular attractions in Ireland, and coaches roll up ceaselessly during the day. The car park costs £1.

A Risky Route

The cliffs just north of Moher are known as Aill na Searrach (Cliff of the Foals) because a group of young fairy horses are supposed to have leapt into the sea at this point. There's a precipitous and dangerous path to the base of these cliffs, suitable only for the fittest of walkers and in dry weather.

The beginning of the path is about 2km north of the Cliffs of Moher car park. Where the road comes off the mountain, there is a small bridge and a rough track leading to a galvanised gate. Cross the field to the dip on the left, where the path begins. At the bottom, massive boulders have been worn smooth and piled high by the Atlantic rollers.

You can also reach this path by following the clifftop path north from O'Brien's Tower, as if walking to Doolin. You can clearly see the path, which zigzags down to the rocky beach.

Getting There & Away

Bus Éireann's Limerick to Lisdoonvarna bus stops daily at the Cliffs of Moher, as does the express bus from Galway to Kilrush. Contact Ennis bus station (☎ 065-682 4177) for times and fares. See also Organised Tours in the Galway city section of the Galway chapter.

The Burren

Between Corofin in northern Clare and Kinvara in County Galway, and stretching to the Atlantic coast, is the Burren region, an extraordinary, unique place.

Boireann is the Irish for 'rocky country' or 'karst', and when you see the kilometres of polished limestone stretching in every direction you'll know why one of Cromwell's generals was moved to exclaim that there was 'neither water enough to drown a man, nor a tree to hang him, nor soil enough to bury him'.

Along the coast are a few settlements, including Doolin, a popular Irish-music centre with some wonderful caves nearby, and Ballyvaughan, an attractive little village on the southern coast of Galway Bay. This area has a lot of historical sites, notably Corcomroe Abbey and the churches of Oughtmama near Bellharbour. The deeply indented coastline has plenty of wildlife and some fine walks.

INFORMATION

The nearest information point is the Cliffs of Moher Visitor Centre (☎ 065-708 1171). A must if you intend spending some time in the Burren is Tim Robinson's *Burren Map and Guide* (£4.50), available in many shops, which shows almost every object and place of interest. *Book of the Burren* (£11.95), published by Tír Eolas, is a delightful introduction to its ecosystems, history and folklore.

ARCHAEOLOGY

The Burren's bare limestone hills were once lightly wooded and covered in soil. Towards the end of the Stone Age, about 6000 years ago, the first farmers arrived in the area. They began to clear the woodlands and use the upland regions for grazing.

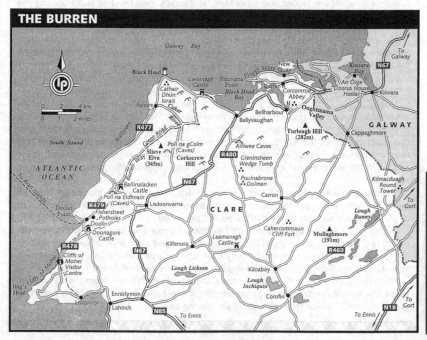

Over the centuries, the soil was eroded and the huge mass of limestone we see today began to emerge.

Despite its desolation, the Burren supported quite large numbers of people in ancient times and has over 2500 historic sites. Chief among them is the 5000-year-old Poulnabrone Dolmen, one of Ireland's finest ancient monuments.

There are at least 65 megalithic tombs erected by the Burren's first settlers. Many of these tombs are wedge-shaped graves, stone boxes tapering both in height and width and about the size of a large double bed. The dead were placed inside, and the whole structure was covered in earth and stones. Gleninsheen, south of Aillwee Caves, is a good example.

Ring forts dot the Burren in prodigious numbers. There are almost 500, including Iron Age stone forts such as Cahercommaun near Carron.

Geology of the Burren

The Burren is the most extensive limestone region, or karst (after the original Karst in Slovenia), in Ireland or Britain. It consists almost entirely of limestone, except for a cap of mud and shale that sits on the higher regions, from Lisdoonvarna north to Slieve Elva.

During the Carboniferous period 350 million years ago, this whole area was the bottom of a warm and shallow sea. The remains of coral and shells fell to the seabed, and coastal rivers dumped sand and silt on top of these lime deposits. Time and pressure turned the layers to stone, with limestone below and shale and sandstone above.

Massive rumblings in the earth's crust some 270 million years ago buckled the edges of Europe and forced the seabed above sea level, at the same time bending and fracturing the stone sheets to form long, deep cracks. Wind, rain and ice have since removed most of the overlying shale, leaving these mountains of limestone.

The difference between the areas of porous limestone and nonporous shale is acute. Shale country is a depressing dull green, covered in acid bogs, marshes and reeds. On limestone the soil is sparse, water disappears and grey rock predominates.

Being slightly acidic, rainwater dissolves the limestone, widening the vertical cracks known as grikes. (The horizontal slabs are called clints.) Springs, rivers and even lakes (such as the turloughs around Corofin) appear and disappear. The water follows weak points (sinkholes) in the rock, carving out underground rivers and caverns. The calcium bicarbonate from the dripping water below creates stalactites (the ones that hang down) and stalagmites (the ones that shoot up). When these underground caverns collapse – which they do periodically – they form a depression. Rainwater is caught on top of the shale and eventually drains off at the edges into the limestone, which it erodes. A ring of caves appears along the shale-limestone boundary.

The southern boundary of the Burren is roughly where the limestone dips under the shale between Doolin and Lough Inchiquin. Underneath the limestone of the Burren is a huge mass of granite, which surfaces to the north-west in Connemara.

During numerous ice ages, glaciers scoured the hills, rounding the edges and sometimes polishing the rock to a shiny finish. The glaciers also dumped a thin layer of rock and soil over the region. Huge boulders were carried by the ice, incongruous aliens on a sea of flat rock. Seen all over the Burren, these 'glacial erratics' are often a visibly different type of rock.

The only surface river in the Burren is the Caher River, which flows down the Caher River Valley (the so-called Khyber Pass) before meeting the sea at Fanore. The valley is lined with glacial sediments, which stop the water from leaking away.

Did someone call a taxi?

Early-Christian ruins, Clonmacnoise

High cross, Clonmacnoise, County Offaly

The limestone Burren region, County Clare

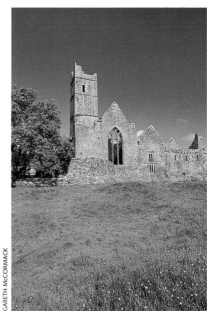
Fifteenth-century Quin Abbey, County Clare

The breathtakingly spectacular Cliffs of Moher, County Clare, are a highlight of any trip to Ireland.

In later times, many castles in the area were built by the region's ruling families, and these include Leamanegh Castle near Kilfenora, Ballinalacken Castle near Doolin and Gleninagh Castle on the Black Head road.

Unfortunately many ring forts and stone walls have been bulldozed into extinction.

FLORA & FAUNA

Soil may be scarce here, but the small amount that gathers in the cracks is limey, well drained and rich in nutrients. This, together with the soft Atlantic climate, supports an extraordinary mix of Mediterranean, Arctic and Alpine plants.

The Burren is a stronghold of Ireland's most elusive mammal, the weasel-like pine marten. They are rarely seen, although there are certainly some living near Gleninagh Castle and up the Caher Valley. Badgers, foxes and even stoats are common throughout the region. Otters and seals live along the shores around Bellharbour, New Quay and Finavarra Point.

The estuaries along this northern coast are rich in birdlife and frequently attract brent geese during the winter. More than 28 of Ireland's 33 species of butterfly are found here, including one endemic species, the Burren green.

Unfortunately, modern farming and EU 'land-improvement' grants have had their effect on the Burren. Weedkillers and fertilisers encourage grass and little else.

WALKING

'Green roads' are the old highways of the Burren, crossing hills and valleys to some of the remotest corners of the region. Unpaved and possibly dating back thousands of years, they're now used mostly by hikers and the occasional farmer. Many are signposted.

Particularly good walks are the green road from Ballinalacken Castle to Fanore, which forms part of the Burren Way, and the climb up Black Head to the Iron Age fort called Cathair Dhún Iorais. The Burren Way (see Walking in the Activities chapter) runs down through the Burren from Bally-

vaughan to Doolin and then south to the Cliffs of Moher. The section from the cliffs to Liscannor has been closed, though you may still see it marked on some maps; a new route running inland from the cliffs is being developed.

Guided nature, history, archaeology and wilderness walks are available through Burren Hill Walks (☎ 065-707 7168) based at Corkscrew Hill, Ballyvaughan, or South-West Walks Ireland (☎ 066-712 8733) in Tralee, County Kerry.

CAVING

Serious caving is not for the faint-hearted. If you fancy trying it, take a course or at least find an experienced guide.

Tim Robinson's *Burren Map and Guide* has most of the cave entrances marked on it. Serious spelunkers should consult *The Caves of Northwest Clare* by Tratman.

GETTING THERE & AWAY

For precise times and other details of the buses to the Burren area, ring the bus stations in Ennis (☎ 065-682 4177), Limerick (☎ 061-313333) or Galway (☎ 091-562000).

Various buses pass through the Burren. From Limerick bus No 337 runs three times daily (once on Sunday) from late May to September, once daily the rest of the year. It connects with Ennis, Ennistymon, Lahinch, Liscannor, the Cliffs of Moher, Doolin and Lisdoonvarna. Express bus No 50 connects Galway with Ballyvaughan, Lisdoonvarna, Lahinch, Kilkee and Tralee. It runs three times daily (once on Sunday) from late May to late September. From Galway to Kinvara, Ballyvaughan, Black Head, Fanore, Lisdoonvarna and Doolin, bus No 423 runs three times daily (once on Sunday) from late May to late September. During the rest of the year it runs once daily, Monday to Saturday.

See also Organised Tours in the Galway city section of the Galway chapter.

GETTING AROUND

The best way to see the Burren is on foot (see Walking earlier in this section) or by cycling, and good mountain bikes are available from Paddy's Doolin Hostel (☎ 065-707 4006), Doolin, or Burke's Garage (☎ 065-707 4022), Lisdoonvarna. You can easily ride a mountain bike along the green roads.

DOOLIN
☎ 065 • pop 200

Doolin – or Fisherstreet on some maps – stretches for several kilometres along the road, but despite appearances it has some of the best music pubs in the west, a couple of decent restaurants, and plenty of good cafés, hostels and guesthouses. It's also an excellent base for the Burren, which lies just to the north. There are ferries to the Aran Islands (for information on the islands, see the Aran Islands section in the County Galway chapter), and the Cliffs of Moher begin a few kilometres south.

Doolin is extremely popular among backpackers and music lovers, and at night the pubs are filled with a cosmopolitan crowd. In high season it can be difficult to get a bed, so try to book ahead. The place is particularly popular with German aficionados of traditional Irish music, who flock with all the zeal of medieval pilgrims to visit what was once the base of the Kellys, a popular German-Irish music family.

Orientation & Information

Doolin is made up of three parts. Coming from the north along the R479 you first hit the Catholic church on the left, then after less than 1km the upper village of the Roadford area, with a shop, restaurant and cafés, hostels, two pubs and the Doolin post office. Then there's a slightly bigger gap before reaching Fisherstreet, the lower village, which has the popular Paddy's Doolin Hostel, more shops and O'Connor's pub. It's another 1.5km to the harbour and the ferry to the Aran Islands.

There are no banks in Doolin, but a mobile bank visits on Thursday. You can change money and travellers cheques in Roadford at the post office, and in Fisherstreet at Paddy's Doolin Hostel and O'Connor's pub just over the bridge.

Activities

For walking tours of the Burren, see Walking earlier. Doolin Pitch and Putt, halfway between Fisherstreet and the harbour, is bigger than your average putting green.

Places to Stay

Camping Down by the harbour two people can pitch a small tent at *Nagles Doolin Caravan and Camping Park* (☎ 707 4458) for £4 plus £1.50/50p per adult/child. It opens April to September. *O'Connors Riverside Camping and Caravan Park* (☎ 707 4314) nearby charges £4 to £6 for a tent and £1.50/50p per adult/child. It too opens April to September.

Hostels Budget travellers are well catered for. All but the Aille River Hostel remain open year round, and they're all IHH. *Paddy's Doolin Hostel* (☎ 707 4006), more commonly known as Paddy Moloney's, is in the lower village, Fisherstreet. Dorm beds in this friendly place cost £8.50, doubles £20. Paddy's can get busy, so book ahead. Across the road, *Fisherstreet House* (same telephone number and ownership) is usually reserved for groups.

In Roadford, the upper village, the *Rainbow Hostel* (☎ 707 4415) is near McGann's pub. It's smaller (only 16 beds) and older than Paddy's Doolin Hostel, and its front room has an open turf fire. Dorm beds cost £7.50, doubles £20. Also here is *Flanagan's Village Hostel* (☎ 707 4564), with dorm beds costing £7.50, doubles £17.

Off the road on the way down to O'Connor's pub from the upper village is *Aille River Hostel* (☎ 707 4260) in a converted farmhouse with turf fires. Dorms cost £7.50, its three doubles £18. Aille River opens mid-March to December.

B&Bs In the upper village past the post office and McGann's pub and round the bend on the left is the excellent *Doolin House* (☎ 707 4259), charging £34 for doubles.

Between Roadford and Fisherstreet and fronting the little River Aille, *Cullinan's* (☎ 707 4183) has excellent rooms costing £17 to £22.50 per person. Another good place nearby is **Doonmacfelim House** (☎ 707 4503), with rooms costing £16 to £20 per person.

In Fisherstreet, **Moloney's Horseshoe Farmhouse** (☎ 707 4006), near Paddy's Doolin Hostel and owned by the same family, charges £36 to £40 for doubles only. The nearby **Sancta Maria** (☎ 707 4124) charges upwards of £26 for a double. **Atlantic View** (☎ 707 4189), offering singles/doubles costing £18/27, is closer to the harbour.

A good B&B outside Doolin is **Island View House** (☎ 707 4346), 3km from Doolin on the Lisdoonvarna road via Garrahy's Cross. It charges £22.50/32.

Hotels The **Aran View House** (☎ 707 4061), with 19 rooms, is a comfortable, friendly country-house hotel 1km north of town past the turning for Lisdoonvarna and the Catholic church. Singles/doubles here cost £45/70 or, June to September, £50/90.

Places to Eat

Both **O'Connor's** in the lower village and **McGann's** in the upper village serve decent pub food all day; the latter offers Irish stew costing £5.50 – and photographs of the singing Kellys on the walls.

Doolin Café, opposite the post office, serves excellent food, including vegetarian dishes, in large portions. Breakfast costs £3.95. Nearby is **Big Mac's Doolin Chipper** next to MacDiarmada's pub. **Flagship Restaurant** at Doolin Crafts Gallery, 1km from the upper village along the Lisdoonvarna road (turn just before the church), serves delicious snacks and light meals as well as dinner. **Cullinan's** B&B (see Places to Stay earlier) also has an excellent restaurant; main dishes cost £9.50 to £16, and its desserts, including homemade ice cream, are £3.95.

If you feel like splashing out, there are several very good restaurants, including **Bruach na hAille** (☎ 707 4120), in the upper village next to McGann's; it opens for dinner 6.30 to 9 pm daily, and mains cost under £13. The **Lazy Lobster** (☎ 707 4390), opposite MacDiarmada's and back from the

main road, specialises in seafood; salmon costs £12. The French-influenced restaurant at **Aran View House** (see Places to Stay earlier) serves an excellent dinner costing £15.

Entertainment

Doolin is renowned for Irish music, and you can hear it almost every night in summer and occasionally in winter. **O'Connor's** pub in Fisherstreet is the best known (note the international collection of police badges behind the bar), but the staff at **McGann's** in Roadford can be friendlier. On a good night, the atmosphere in either pub is hard to beat. **MacDiarmada's**, also in Roadford near the post office, is frequented by locals and reportedly has some of the best traditional music in town. Watch out for music sessions in nearby Lisdoonvarna or Kilfenora. Even if you're not staying at **Aran View House**, its bar provides a pleasant way to escape the tumult in the village.

Getting There & Away

Bus The Bus Éireann stop is outside Fisherstreet House opposite Paddy's Doolin Hostel. There are buses between Doolin and Ennis, Galway, Limerick and Dublin. For contact details, see the introductory Getting There & Away section to the Burren.

Boat Doolin is the departure point for ferries to the Aran Islands (see the Aran Islands section in the County Galway chapter). These are operated by Doolin Ferries (☎ 707 4189, 707 4455 at the pier kiosk) daily, April to September.

It takes around 30 minutes to cross the 8km to Inisheer, the smallest and the easternmost of the three Aran Islands, and the return fare is £15. June to August there are around seven sailings daily, beginning at 10 am. The last ferry returns from Inisheer at 6 pm.

From June to August the first ferry to Inishmór, the largest island, leaves Doolin Harbour at 10 am and the last ferry from Inishmór departs at 4 pm. The trip takes 50 minutes, and the return fare is £20.

From June to August, the first ferry to

CLARE

Inishmaan leaves at 10 am and the last ferry back to Doolin leaves at 4.30 pm. The journey takes about 40 minutes and costs £18.

Getting Around

The Paddy's Doolin and Aille River Hostels have bikes costing around £8/40 per day/week plus deposit.

AROUND DOOLIN
Caves

Doolin is very popular with spelunkers. The British seem particularly fond of this sport and use Doolin as a base, spending their days crawling blindly through dirty holes and their nights crawling blindly through Doolin's pubs. The Fisherstreet Potholes are nearby, and **Poll na gColm**, 5km northeast of Lisdoonvarna, is Ireland's longest cave, with over 12km of mapped passageways.

A few hundred metres south of Ballinalacken Castle, you'll see some low cliffs on the eastern (or inland) side across a field. These hide the entrance to **Poll an Eidhnain** (or Poll an Ionáin), a cave which, after a difficult and mucky passage, widens to a chamber containing a 6m stalactite said to be the longest in Western Europe. The cavern is difficult to get to, and the farmer is not keen on trespassers, so ask permission first.

The rocks to the north of Doolin Harbour are honeycombed with an unusual system of undersea caves called the **Green Holes of Doolin**. They are the longest known undersea caves in temperate waters – one of them has been explored inland for 1km. Nondivers can look into Hell, a large gash in the rocks, north of the harbour and about 50m from the sea. The gash is about 6m wide, and the heaving water at the bottom leads to a maze of submarine passages.

Doonagore Castle

If you follow the coastal road (R478) for about 3km south of Doolin you'll come to Doonagore Castle, a restored 15th-century tower with a surrounding walled enclosure (or *bawn*). There's a lovely view from here over Doolin and the Aran Islands, especially at sunset.

Ballinalacken Castle

Five kilometres north of Doolin en route to Fanore is Ballinalacken Castle. Sitting astride a small cliff, this 15th-century O'Brien tower house is in excellent repair. The stairway is intact and there are good views of the Burren from the top. Look out for an original fireplace perched halfway up the interior with the date 1679 carved on it. Access to the castle is via the Ballinalacken Castle Hotel, which was closed at the time of research.

Just beside the gateway to the castle and hotel, a minor road leads inland up into the Burren. After about 1km, it meets one of the Burren's ancient green roads, and in good weather this route up to Fanore makes for a lovely walk. It also forms part of the Burren Way (see Walking in the Activities chapter).

LISDOONVARNA
☎ 065 • pop 650

Lisdoon, as the town is generally called (its Irish name is Lios Dún Bhearna), is well known for its mineral springs, which people have been visiting for centuries to drink and to bathe in. The town also used to be the centre for '*basadóiri*' (matchmakers) who, for the appropriate fee, would fix you up with a mate. Most aspiring swains would hit town in September, after the hay was in.

Today, genuine matchmaking is a little thin on the ground, but the Matchmaking Festival is still a great excuse for drinking, merrymaking and music in the pubs. And with all those singles events, a few romances must blossom.

Orientation & Information

Lisdoonvarna is essentially a one-street town with a square in the centre from where you turn west for Doolin and the coast. The town has plenty of shops, B&Bs, pubs and smart hotels with good restaurants. There's a Bank of Ireland branch behind the Ritz Restaurant on the square, but it opens only 11 am to 1 pm Monday and Thursday, July to September; and Thursday only the rest of the year. The post office is on Main St to the north. Lisdoonvarna Laundrette is at the rear of the car park facing the Imperial Hotel.

Spa Wells Health Centre

At the southern end of town, the health centre (☎ 707 4023), the only working spa in Ireland, has a sulphur spring, a Victorian pump house, massage room, sauna and mineral baths, all in an agreeable, wooded setting. The iron, sulphur, magnesium and iodine in the water are supposed to be good for rheumatic and glandular complaints, so if you have a spot of hyperthyroidism or ankylotic spondylitis, this is the place for you. You can drink the water, but it's not a pleasant experience. A sulphur bath costs £8. The centre opens 10 am to 6 pm daily, June to mid-October.

Burren Smokehouse Visitor Centre

If you've ever wanted to know more about the 'ancient Irish tradition of oak-smoking Atlantic salmon', The Salmon of Knowledge Experience audiovisual display at the visitor centre (☎ 707 4432) will answer all your questions – and then some. Smoked salmon in all its guises is on sale, and there's local tourist information available. The centre, open 10 am to 6 pm (extended hours in summer) daily year round, is just west of Lisdoonvarna on the Doolin road (N67).

Places to Stay

There are lots of B&Bs and some of the cheaper ones are in the centre. *O'Loughlin's* (☎ 707 4038, Main St) has plain but clean singles/doubles costing £17.50/30. There are about a dozen hotels in Lisdoonvarna, all charging around £35 to £50 for singles and £40 to £75 for doubles, depending on the season. Among the best is the 84-room, yellow and blue *Imperial Hotel* (☎ 707 4042), charging upwards of £37.50/55. Opposite Burren Smokehouse, the smaller *Carrigan Hotel* (☎ 707 4036), with 20 rooms, charges £37/58.

Places to Eat

In town, *Irish Arms* and *Meg Maguire's* are popular pubs offering food and music at the weekend. *Matchmaker Bar* at the Imperial Hotel has music and two-course meals costing £6. Bar meals at the *Royal Spa Hotel* cost £3.50 to £6.50; mushroom tagliatelle costs £6.25.

Orchid Restaurant at Sheedy's Spa View Hotel, on the Liscannor road, has been recommended; fish mains cost around £10 to £15.

Getting There & Around

For bus services, see the introductory Getting There & Away entry to the Burren section earlier. Burke's Garage (☎ 707 4022) on the square has bikes for hire costing £5/30 per day/week.

BALLYREEN

Ballyreen is no more than a deserted stretch of rocky coast about 6km south of Fanore, but it's a lovely spot and a good place to camp. There's a cliff called **Ailladie**, which boasts some of Ireland's finest rock climbing. For scuba divers, a barely visible track leads to a small inlet that has some excellent underwater scenery on the left, dropping quickly to a depth of about 20m, with vertical walls and gullies covered in jewel anemones.

Offshore after heavy rain you may see currents of brown water coming through the clear surface water. These are resurgences: fresh water flooding from an undersea cave. On land, Ice Age glaciers have polished the limestone to a gloss. The incongruous stones and boulders were dumped here by glaciers.

There's no bus to Ballyreen.

FANORE
☎ 065

Fanore (Fanóir), 5km south of Black Head, is less a village and more a stretch of coast, with a shop, a pub, and a few houses scattered along the main road (R477). It has a fine sandy beach with an extensive backdrop of dunes. It's the only **safe beach** between Lahinch and Ballyvaughan. The remains of a Stone Age settlement were discovered near the small river that runs down through the dunes. Along the road south of

CLARE

the beach are a scattering of 10th- and 11th-century **church ruins**.

Fitzpatrick's, the only shop in the area, 4km south of the beach on the ocean side of the road, is a small grocery-store/post-office/newsagent/fishing-tackle-shop.

Things to See & Do

Just behind Fanore Beach, a road goes inland and up the **Khyber Pass**, or Caher River Valley. This is the only surface river in the Burren. The first few kilometres are very pleasant, and there is a village up on the left that has been deserted since the Famine. There are foxes, badgers and pine martens in the area, though you'll be lucky to spot any.

John McNamara at the Admiral's Rest Restaurant (☎ 707 6105, email jdmna@iol.ie), which is the home of the Burren Conservation Trust, organises a Burren Wildlife Weekend twice a year, in May and October. The trust has also created a **nature reserve** about 5km south of Fanore in the Caher River Valley. Volunteers are given accommodation and food at the Admiral's Rest in exchange for working at the reserve. Contact John for details.

Fanore has a couple of lovely **walks**. On the coast road about 400m south of the beach, a small road goes inland. After about 1km, it meets an old green road that can be followed south to Ballinalacken Castle and is part of the Burren Way. Alternatively, you can park at the Admiral's Rest Restaurant and go straight up through the fields to the green road. On top of this hill are two caves. **Poll Dubh** is a relatively easy cave for amateurs to explore, with delicate stalactites on view. The other, **Poll Mor**, is home to badgers, foxes, hares and rabbits.

There's a well-preserved **ring fort** and souterrain on top of a hill at the southern end of Fanore and about 1km inland.

Places to Stay & Eat

At the northern end of Fanore, a few hundred metres inland from where the river crosses the road, is the IHO *Bridge Hostel* (☎ 707 6134). It's in an old police station, with 20 dorm beds costing £6 or three

doubles costing £8.50 per person. The hostel opens March to October.

At the southern end of Fanore is the *Admiral's Rest Seafood Restaurant* (☎ 707 6105) run by John McNamara, which also does B&B. Clean, tidy rooms cost £15 per person; there are also family rooms costing £40. Dinner at the restaurant costs £8 to £18. Those staying at the Admiral's Rest for a week get a free boat ride on Galway Bay.

Entertainment

O'Donohue's pub almost opposite Fitzpatrick's shop (see Information earlier) is a friendly place, with music on Saturday night. There are no other bars along this stretch of coast.

Getting There & Away

For information on bus services, see the introductory Getting There & Away entry to this Burren section earlier.

BLACK HEAD & CATHAIR DHÚN IORAIS

Black Head, Clare's north-westernmost point, is a bleak but imposing mountain of limestone dropping swiftly into the sea. The head has an unstaffed lighthouse and good shore **angling** for sea bass and cod. If you're lucky, you may see dolphins.

There's a great hike up the head to the large Iron Age stone fort, Cathair Dhún Iorais (Fort of Irghus). The views across Galway Bay and the Aran Islands are exceptional, especially with the steep walls of the fort as a backdrop. Inland, the hills rise to 318m and farther back is Slieve Elva (345m), capped with shale. Some of the intervening summits are marked with Bronze Age cairns. On your way up to the fort you cross an old green road.

BALLYVAUGHAN & AROUND
☎ 065

Ballyvaughan (Baile Uí Bheacháin) is a small, pretty fishing village on a quiet corner of Galway Bay that attracts well-heeled visitors. Its attractive pubs, restaurants and places to stay make it a good base for visiting the northern part of the Burren.

Just west of the village, past the holiday cottages and the Tea Rooms restaurant, is the quay and Monk's Bar. The harbour was built in 1829 at a time when boats traded with the Aran Islands and Galway, often bringing in turf – a scarce commodity in this area.

Ballyvaughan is a T-junction. Going south and inland on the N67 brings you to the centre of the Burren, Aillwee Caves, Poulnabrone Dolmen and Lisdoonvarna. Turning west leads you to the magnificent coast road (R477), Black Head and south towards Doolin. Going north-east on the N67, you reach Kinvara and County Galway.

Information

There are no banks in Ballyvaughan, but you can change money on Main St in the post office or Walsh's Craft Shop, or at the Whitethorn Craft and Visitor Centre, north-east of Ballyvaughan on the way to Kinvara. Alternatively, try Hyland's Hotel (see Places to Stay later).

Burren Exposure

The Burren Exposure (☎ 707 7277), at the Whitethorn Craft and Visitor Centre 3km north-east of town on the Kinvara road, is an interesting audiovisual presentation on the history, geology, flora and fauna of the region. It opens 10 am to 5 pm daily. Admission costs £3.50.

Corkscrew Hill

Six kilometres south of Ballyvaughan on the Lisdoonvarna road is a series of severe bends up Corkscrew Hill. The road was built as part of a Famine-relief scheme in the 1840s. From the top there are spectacular views of the northern Burren and Galway Bay, with Aillwee Mountain and the caves on the right and Cappanawalla Hill on the left, with the partially restored 16th-century Newtown Castle, erstwhile residence of the O'Lochlains, at its base. From here, the route to Lisdoonvarna is through boggy and fairly boring countryside.

Gleninagh Castle

Down a narrow leafy lane and just off the coast road about 6km west of Ballyvaughan is Gleninagh, another 16th-century O'Lochlain castle (the O'Lochlains were chieftains in this region). The castle was inhabited as late as 1840. In front of the castle is a holy well still in use, and the ruins of a medieval church. To the east you may find a small horseshoe-shaped mound of earth: a '*fulacht fiadh*' (cooking place) dating from the Bronze Age.

Places to Stay

You can *camp* in many of the fields around Ballyvaughan or along the coast just beyond the harbour. There are no hostels in Ballyvaughan. The closest ones are the *Bridge Hostel* to the west in Fanore (see the Fanore section earlier) or *Johnston's Hostel* in Kinvara, County Galway (see the County Galway chapter).

For B&B, *Micko's Place* (☎ 707 7060) is a bungalow in the centre with singles/doubles costing £19/28. *Stonepark House* (☎ 707 7056, Bishops Quarter), just over 1km along the Kinvara road, costs upwards of £18/28. There are many more guesthouses out around Doorus and New Quay, and they all get busy in season, so book ahead.

A particularly good B&B is *Rusheen Lodge* (☎ 707 7092), a little over 1km out on the inland road to Lisdoonvarna. At £40/60 from May to October, it's not cheap, but the rooms and breakfasts are top class. *Hyland's Hotel* (☎ 707 7037), in the middle of Ballyvaughan, is a 19-room, family-run hotel with a cosy atmosphere, costing £47 per person in the high season. It opens April to December.

Places to Eat

Tea Rooms, in an old cottage down towards the harbour near Monk's Bar, has top-notch soups, salads and home-cooked desserts. It opens till 6 pm. The *Tea Junction Café* in the village centre serves a good breakfast (£3.50) and good snacks and meals (including vegetarian) all day.

Most bars in town serve pub food. *Monk's Bar*, a popular place on the harbour, has melt-in-your-mouth mussels in

CLARE

garlic butter (£6.50), seafood chowder and brown bread.

Whitethorn Craft and Visitor Centre (see the Burren Exposure earlier) has a good coffee-shop-cum-restaurant; potato-and-onion tart costs £5.95.

The restaurant at ***Hyland's Hotel*** specialises in seafood; fried crab claws in garlic costs £7.95. Dinner costs £18.

Entertainment

Monk's Bar has traditional-music sessions on Tuesday and from Friday to Sunday in summer. ***Hyland's Hotel*** has music at the weekend, while, a few doors down, ***O'Brien's*** has music Thursday to Sunday nights. Tiny ***Óloćlainn***, on the left as you head down to the harbour, is a lovely old country pub, much less touristy than Monk's Bar.

Getting There & Away

For information on bus services see the introductory Getting There & Away entry to the Burren section earlier.

CENTRAL BURREN

The road through the heart of the Burren – the R480 and R476 – runs between Ballyvaughan and Corofin via Leamanegh Castle. Travelling south from Ballyvaughan, turn east before Corkscrew Hill at the sign for the Aillwee Caves. The road goes past Gleninsheen Wedge Tomb, Poulnabrone Dolmen and into some really desolate scenery.

Aillwee Caves

The extensive limestone Aillwee Cave system (☎ 065-707 7036) is a good place to spend a rainy afternoon or to take children. The main passage penetrates for 600m into the mountain, widening into larger caverns, one with its own waterfall. The caves were carved out by water some two million years ago. Near the entrance are the remains of a brown bear, extinct in Ireland for over 10,000 years.

Aillwee was discovered in 1944 by a local farmer, and today has a discreetly designed outer building with an excellent

café. The delicatessen here makes its own cheese. Behind the cave entrance there is a relatively easy scramble up 300m Aillwee Mountain, with fine views from the summit.

You can go into the cave only as part of a guided group; tours cost £4.50/2.50 (families from £13.50). Aillwee opens 10 am to 6 pm (to 7pm in summer) daily, mid-March to November. The last tour departs at 5.30 pm (6.30 pm in summer). Try to visit early in the day before the crowds arrive.

Gleninsheen Wedge Tomb

This tomb is known in folklore as the Druid's Altar, though the druids lived a long time after this was built. The tomb is beside the R480 just south of Aillwee Caves. It's thought to date from 4000 to 5000 years ago and, like most of the other tombs in the Burren, it's on high ground.

A magnificent gold torc was found nearby in 1930 by a boy hunting rabbits. It was in a crack in the limestone and at first the boy thought it was part of a coffin. Dating from around 700 BC, the torc is reckoned to be one of the finest pieces of prehistoric Irish craftwork and is now on display at the National Museum in Dublin.

Poulnabrone Dolmen

Poulnabrone Dolmen is one of Ireland's most photographed ancient monuments, the one you see on all the postcards with the sun setting behind it. The dolmen is a three-legged tomb, sitting in a sea of limestone without a house in sight. At quiet times of day, this is a truly lovely place. It's 8km south from Aillwee and signposted from the R480.

Poulnabrone was built over 5000 years ago. It was excavated in 1989, and the remains of more than 25 people were found among pieces of pottery and jewellery. Radiocarbon dating suggests that they were buried between 3800 and 3200 BC. When the dead were originally entombed here, the whole structure was covered in a mound of earth, which has since worn away. The Irish 'poll na bró' means 'hole of the grinding stone', and the capstone weighs five tonnes. Try to visit early in the morning or at sunset for good photographs. Better still, try a moonlit night.

Carron & Cahercommaun Cliff Fort

The remote **Burren Perfumery and Floral Centre** (☎ 065-708 9102) near the tiny village of Carron (or Carran on some maps), a few kilometres east of the R480, uses wildflowers of the Burren to produce its scents, and it's the only handicraft perfumery in Ireland. There's a free audiovisual presentation and the centre opens 9 am to 6 pm daily.

Three kilometres south of Carron and perched on the edge of an inland cliff is the great stone fort of Cahercommaun. It was inhabited in the 8th and 9th centuries by people who hunted deer and grew a small amount of grain. There are the remains of a souterrain leading from the fort to the outer cliff face. To get there, go south from Carron and take a left turn for Kilnaboy. After 1.5km a path on the left leads up to the fort.

East of Carron

If you turn east at Carron, you have two options. The first is to turn north after about 3km, which takes you on a magnificent drive through a valley to Cappaghmore in County Galway. If you continue east from Carron you come close to the lovely **Mt Mullaghmore** (191m). Later, just over the Galway border on the main road to Gort (R460), is **Kilmacduagh**, a monastic site with a splendid round tower.

KILFENORA

☎ 065

The tiny, windswept village of Kilfenora (Cill Fhionnúrach) lies on the southern fringes of the Burren, 8km south-east of Lisdoonvarna. Most visitors come to see the monastic remains, five high crosses and a tiny 12th-century cathedral. The village itself is a touch forlorn, but has some attractive shopfronts and pubs.

Burren Centre

The centre (☎ 708 8030) was built by the local community and has a fair amount of information on the Burren as well as maps and guidebooks for sale. There's a display, a video presentation and a decent café attached. The centre opens 9.30 am to 6 pm daily, June to September; and 10 am to 5 pm daily, March to May and October. Admission costs £2.50/1.50.

Kilfenora Cathedral

The pope has the honour of also being the bishop of the diocese of Kilfenora and Killaloe; in the past the ruined 12th-century cathedral was an important place of pilgrimage. St Fachan (or Fachtna) founded the monastery here in the 6th century, and it later became the seat of Kilfenora diocese, the smallest in the country.

The cathedral is the smallest you are ever likely to see. Only the ruined structure and nave of the more recent Protestant church are actually part of the cathedral. The chancel has two primitive carved figures on top of two tombs. One is a bishop (note the mitre), and it must be said that neither was a very handsome gentlemen. The theory goes that after the Black Death in the 14th century there was a general decline in craft skills across the continent, and these poor carvings may be examples of this.

High Crosses

Kilfenora is best known for its high crosses, three in the churchyard and a large 12th-century example in the field about 100m to the west.

The most interesting one is the 800-year-old **Doorty Cross**, standing prominently to the west of the church's front door. It differs significantly from the standard Irish high cross in that it's without the usual pierced disc or wheel. It was lying broken in two until the 1950s, when it was re-erected.

The eastern face of the cross is the better preserved. One interpretation of the carvings has Christ on top ordering two figures in the middle to destroy the devil/bird at the bottom, which is misbehaving; another is that it portrays St Patrick. The western face is much less clear. Christ still appears to be on top, this time surrounded by birds. Directly underneath are delicate designs and a

CLARE

man on horseback holding the ends of the patterns. Some say it's Christ's entry into Jerusalem. One theory suggests the cross may commemorate Kilfenora being made the diocesan seat in the 12th century.

Places to Stay
One kilometre along the Lisdoonvarna road is the welcoming *Mrs Geraldine Howley's* B&B (☎ 708 8075), charging £22.50/32 for singles/doubles. The *Burren Farmhouse* (☎ 707 1363), 2km along the Ennistymon road, is equally pleasant and charges £16 per person for its three rooms (with shared bathroom).

Places to Eat
Burren Centre has a reasonable tea room next door, open 9.30 am to 6 pm. It serves lunch specials costing £4. The *Parlour Restaurant* at Vaughan's pub on the green offers bar food, as does *Linnane's* nearby.

Entertainment
Several pubs put on traditional music throughout the year. *Vaughan's* has regular Irish-music sessions on weeknights and Saturday. *Nagle's Lounge Bar* and *Linnane's* have music at the weekend.

COROFIN & AROUND
☎ 065
Corofin (Cora Finne), also spelled Corrofin, is a small village on the southern fringes of the Burren. Commonly found in the area are turloughs (from the Irish '*turlach*'), small lakes that often disappear during dry summers. O'Brien castles abound in this boggy countryside: two of them are on the shores of nearby Lough Inchiquin.

Corofin is home to the interesting **Clare Heritage and Genealogical Centre** (☎ 683 7955), which has a display covering the period around the Potato Famine. Over 250,000 people lived in Clare before the Potato Famine; today the county's population stands at about 91,000 – a drop of some 64%. The heritage centre opens 10 am to 6 pm daily, May to September. Admission costs £2/1. In a separate building nearby the genealogical centre has facilities for people

researching their Clare ancestry and can be contacted year round.

About 4km north-west of Corofin, on the road to Leamanegh Castle and Kilfenora (R476), look for the small town of **Kilnaboy**. The ruined church here is worth seeking out for the sheila-na-gig over the doorway.

Places to Stay
Open February to October, the IHH *Corofin Village Hostel* (☎ 683 7683), on Main St, is a fine hostel with good facilities. Dorm beds cost £7.50, and the three doubles cost £18. At the rear is a camp ground with powered sites, shower and laundry.

There are plenty of B&Bs in the area, many of them in Kilnaboy along the road to Kilfenora and Lisdoonvarna. Good ones include *Cottage View* (☎ 683 7662), 2km from Corofin, charging £22.50/32 for singles/doubles and open April to early October; and *Shamrock and Heather* (☎ 683 7061), with en suite doubles costing £32, and singles without bathroom costing £14.

Places to Eat
For pub food, on Main St try *Corofin Arms* or *Bofey Quinn's*, where simple delicious meals such as Irish stew cost £5.35. Bofey Quinn's has a popular seafood restaurant open in the evening, Easter to September.

Getting There & Away
Bus Éireann bus No 333 from Kilkee or Doonbeg to Ennis and Limerick stops in Corofin on Monday only. Check with the Ennis bus station (☎ 065-682 4177) or Corofin Village Hostel for times.

LEAMANEGH CASTLE
Leamanegh is a well-preserved castle-cum-fortified-house 8km north-west of Corofin on the Kilfenora road. The castle's name is pronounced 'lay-um-on-ay' and is from the Irish for 'deer's leap' or 'horse's leap'. If you look carefully, you will see that there are two parts joined together. The five-storey tower house on the right was built around 1480 by the O'Briens and is much more solid and better defended than the

main house, which Conor O'Brien added in 1640. This has four storeys, and its most appealing features are the largely intact stone window frames. The whole building was originally surrounded by a high wall.

Just above the tower-house entrance is a vertical shaft or 'murder hole'. If this was the 15th century and you were an uninvited guest, all manner of unspeakable things could be dropped on top of you from here, including boiling oil, tar, arrows, dead animals – or anything else that came to hand.

There's a fine view from the top of the tower, but the castle is on private property and no access is allowed.

NORTHERN BURREN

Low farmland stretches south from County Galway until it meets the bluff limestone hills of the Burren. The Burren begins just west of Kinvara and Doorus in County Galway, where the road forks, going inland to Carron or along the coast to Ballyvaughan.

From Oranmore in County Galway to Ballyvaughan, the coastline wriggles along small inlets and peninsulas; some such as Finavarra Point and New Quay are worth a detour.

Just inland near Bellharbour is the largely intact Corcomroe Abbey, and the three ancient churches of Oughtmama lie up a quiet side valley. Galway Bay forms the backdrop to some outstanding scenery: bare stone hills shining in the sun, with small hamlets and rich patches of green wherever there is soil.

Getting There & Away

Late May to late September, Bus Éireann bus No 50 between Galway and Cork passes through Kinvara and Ballyvaughan up to four times daily. Bus No 423 between Galway and Doolin also stops in those two places; there are up to three buses daily May to September, one bus daily Monday to Saturday the rest of the year. Check the details with Galway bus station (☎ 091-562000) or Ennis bus station (☎ 065-682 4177).

New Quay & the Flaggy Shore

New Quay (Ceibh Nua), on the Finavarra Peninsula, is about 2km off the main Kin-

Maire Rua McMahon

Conor O'Brien was killed in 1651 while fighting for the royalists against Cromwell. His wife, the infamous Maire Rua McMahon, reportedly refused to take his body back into Leamanegh Castle. After his death, she offered to marry one of Cromwell's soldiers to ensure that her son Donough didn't lose his inheritance. Marry Maire did, but they still lost the estate. Despite this setback, she and her new husband, John Cooper, stayed together. They regained their property in 1675, but later records show she was tried – and acquitted – for Cooper's subsequent murder. She died in 1686.

vara to Ballyvaughan road (N67). There are a few thatched cottages on the peninsula and the ruins of a 17th-century mansion.

Linnane's pub in New Quay serves seafood and is next to Ireland's largest oyster farm.

The Flaggy Shore, west of New Quay, is a particularly fine stretch of coastline. Layers of limestone march boldly into the sea and, behind the coastal path, swans parade gently on Lough Muirí. There are otters in the area. On the way out to Finavarra Point (continue on the road past Linnane's) is Mt Vernon Lodge, the summer home of Lady Gregory, playwright and friend of WB Yeats. She was prominent in the Anglo-Irish literary revival.

On Finavarra Point is one of the western coast's few **Martello towers**, built in the early 1800s to warn Galway in case Napoleon came sailing by and sneaked into Ireland through the back door. The road loops back and joins the main road beside a small lake, which is rich in birdlife, including ducks, moorhens and herons.

Bellharbour

Bellharbour is no more than a crossroads with some thatched holiday cottages and a pub, about 8km east of Ballyvaughan.

CLARE

The Legend of Corcomroe

In 1317, the Battle of Corcomroe was fought very near the abbey between two O'Brien clans trying to win control of Clare. Legend has it that one of the chieftains, Donough, was passing by Lough Rask on his way to battle when he saw a witch washing a pile of bleeding limbs in the water. The witch told Donough that her name was Bronach Boirne and that the corpses would be those of his soldiers if he insisted on going into battle. To make matters worse, Donough's own head was in the pile.

Donough's men tried to capture the elusive witch, but she flew up in the air and rained curses on them. To reassure his men, Donough told them that Bronach was the lover of his arch rival, Dermot O'Brien, and her warnings merely a ploy to frighten them off. Unfortunately for Donough, by that night he and most of his army were lying dead in the abbey.

Incidentally, on nearby Moneen Mountain is a pass called Mam Catha (Pass of the Battle), which could refer to the route taken by Donough and his army. Dermot, the victor, later defeated de Clare of Bunratty, halting the spread of Anglo-Norman influence in Clare for a couple of hundred years.

There's an excellent **walk** along an old green road that begins behind the modern Church of St Patrick, 1km north up the hill from the Y-junction at Bellharbour, and threads north along Abbey Hill.

Inland from here is Corcomroe Abbey, the valley and churches of Oughtmama, and the interior road that takes you right through the heart of the Burren.

Wildlife You can almost be guaranteed a sighting of seals along the coast west of Bellharbour. Go about 1km along the Ballyvaughan road until you spot a large dark-green farm shed on the right. Follow the path down to the shore, and you may see seals. This inlet is also thick with birds, and winter visitors include brent geese from northern Canada.

Corcomroe Abbey Corcomroe, a former Cistercian abbey 1km inland from Bellharbour, lies in its own small valley surrounded by low hills and is a very peaceful place.

It was founded in 1194 by Donal Mór O'Brien. His grandson, Conor O'Brien (died 1267), king of Thomond, occupies the tomb in the northern wall, and there is a crude carving of him below an effigy of a staring bishop armed with a crozier. Some fine Romanesque carvings are scattered throughout the abbey.

Oughtmama Valley Oughtmama is a lonely, deserted valley hiding some small, ancient churches. To get there turn inland at Bellharbour, left at the Y-junction, and go up to a clump of trees and a house on the right. A rough track from here leads east up a blind valley to the churches. St Colman MacDuagh, who also built churches on the Aran Islands, founded the monastery here in the 6th century. The three churches were built in the 12th century by monks in search of solitude. It's a hardy walk up **Turlough Hill** behind the chapels, but the views are tremendous. Near the summit are the remains of an Iron Age hill fort.

County Galway

County Galway is one of the highlights of any visit to Ireland. Stretching westwards from Ballinasloe in the midlands, through the wilds of Connemara, to the craggy Atlantic coastline beyond Clifden, Galway has just about everything packed into its 5940 sq km. It's the second-largest county in Ireland, after Cork, and the city of Galway is the western coast's liveliest, most populous settlement.

Galway's neighbour to the south is County Clare, and the Burren limestone region peters out near Kinvara, a picturesque little coastal town just within the Galway border. The limestone emerges out to sea in a long, grey reef that forms the three Aran Islands. These are famous for their folklore, bleak but evocative scenery, Irish speakers and woollen sweaters.

Galway's landscape is extremely varied. Lough Corrib cuts off the rugged coastal region from the largely flat interior that makes up the bulk of the county.

Galway

☎ 091 • pop 57,000

Galway city is a delight, with its narrow streets, old stone and wooden shopfronts, good restaurants and bustling pubs. It's also the administrative capital of the county, and home to the local government, University College Galway and a regional college east of town. There's a ferry to the Aran Islands from the docks, although you're better off travelling farther west along the Connemara coast and taking a boat from Rossaveal.

In marked contrast to most of the depopulated western coast, Galway is one of Europe's fastest-growing cities and ranks fourth in size in Ireland, after Dublin, Cork and Limerick. Large factories and a bustling energy underlie its relative economic security.

Galway is a gateway to Connemara and the west, as it sits at the southern tip of

Highlights

- Enjoy the pubs, theatres and festivals of Galway city
- Get in touch with nature by walking in Connemara National Park
- Take the scenic route through the Lough Inagh Valley in Connemara
- Walk or cycle the ruggedly beautiful Sky Road near Clifden in Connemara
- Visit Inishmór (one of the Aran Islands) and explore Dún Aengus stone fort perched on its southern cliffs
- Cycle or walk on the timeless Inishmaan and Inisheer (Aran Islands)
- Explore tranquil Inishbofin Island

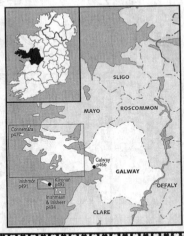

Lough Corrib, which forms a natural border to the region. The city is also a handy base for exploring the Burren in County Clare, which begins some 30km south.

Galway has always attracted a bohemian crowd of musicians, artists, intellectuals and young people – a mix that's partly due

GALWAY

COUNTY GALWAY

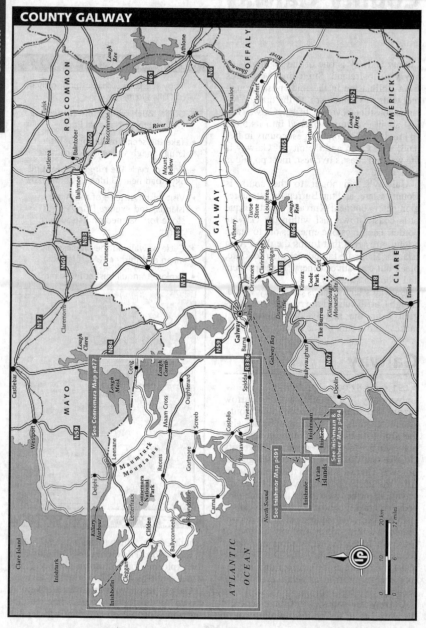

to the presence of the university. The main attractions for the traveller are the nightlife and pubs, where talk and drink flow with equal force. The city is a major Gaelic centre, and Irish is widely understood. The Druid Theatre is one of the best in Ireland, and the city hosts a hugely popular arts festival every summer. The place goes wild during Galway Race Week in the last week of July. If you haven't booked, accommodation is going to be very difficult to find at these times.

While the city centre deserves its accolades, the approaches and suburbs don't. Coming from the east, you pass huge modern hotels, barren housing developments and the ugly regional college. The coast road west through the beach resort of Salthill and on to Spiddal is one of the worst examples of ribbon development in the country. Only after Spiddal do the bungalows start to thin out.

HISTORY
Galway grew from a small fishing village in the Claddagh area at the mouth of the River Corrib to become an important walled town when the Anglo-Normans under Richard de Burgo (also spelled de Burgh or Burke) captured territory from the local O'Flahertys in 1232. The Irish word for 'outsiders' or 'foreigners' is *gaill*, which may be the origin of the city's name in Irish, Gaillimh. The town walls were built by the Anglo-Normans from around 1270.

Galway became something of an outpost in the 'wild west'. In 1396, Richard II granted a charter to the city, which effectively transferred power from the de Burgos to 14 merchant families or 'tribes'. This led to the name 'City of the Tribes', by which Galway is still known. These powerful families were mostly English or Norman in origin, and clashes with the leading Irish families of Connemara were frequent. At one time the city's western gate bore the prayer and warning: 'From the fury of the O'Flahertys, good Lord deliver us'. To ensure the ferocity was kept on the outside, the city fathers warned in the

early 16th century that no uninvited 'O' or 'Mac' should show his face on Galway's streets.

English power throughout the region waxed and waned, but the city maintained its independent status under the ruling merchant families, who were mostly loyal to the English Crown. Galway's relative isolation encouraged a huge trade in wine, spices, fish and salt with Portugal and Spain. At one point, the city rivalled Bristol and London in the volume of goods passing through its docks.

For a long while Galway prospered. A massive fire in 1473 destroyed much of the town but created space for a new street layout, and many solid stone buildings were erected in the 15th and 16th centuries.

It is said that Christopher Columbus tarried in Galway to hear Mass and pray at the Collegiate Church of St Nicholas of Myra. This Galway side-trip supposedly occurred either because one of the crew was a Galway man or because Columbus wished to investigate tales of St Brendan's earlier voyage to the Americas from here.

Galway's faithful support of the English Crown led to its downfall with the arrival of Cromwell. The city was besieged in 1651 and fell in April 1652 after nine months of resistance. Cromwell's forces under Charles Coote wreaked their usual havoc, and Galway's long period of decline began. In 1691 the city chose the wrong side again, and William of Orange's forces added to the destruction. The important trade with Spain was almost at an end and, with Dublin and Waterford taking most of the sea traffic, Galway stagnated until its revival in modern times.

In 1992, the city's Catholic faithful learned that their bishop, Dr Eamon Casey, a conservative on matters of celibacy, contraception, abortion and other sex-related issues, had as a priest fathered a son (who was by then 18 years old). The Church's damage-control efforts provided the city with some high drama and serious debate for the next few weeks but – this being Ireland – the humour behind the hypocrisy won out. Jokes about the bishop and the bishopric (as it were) were the order of the day.

ORIENTATION

Galway's tightly packed town centre lies on both sides of the River Corrib, which connects Lough Corrib with the sea, though Eyre Square and most of the main shopping areas are on the river's eastern (left) bank. There are three main bridges; the northernmost, Salmon Weir Bridge, looks over a salmon trap and is overshadowed by St Nicholas' Cathedral.

From Eyre Square, the meandering main shopping street starts as Williamsgate St, becomes William St and then Shop St, before splitting into Mainguard St and High St. The combined bus and train station are just east of Eyre Square, while the tourist office is close to its south-eastern corner.

South and east of Wolfe Tone Bridge is the historic, but totally redeveloped, district of Claddagh; to the west is the beach resort of Salthill, a fairly popular area for accommodation and restaurants.

Medieval Galway: A Rambler's Guide and Map, published by Tír Eolas, is available in most bookshops (and at the tourist office).

INFORMATION
Tourist Offices

The big Ireland West Tourism office (☎ 563081), east of Eyre Square on the corner of Victoria Place and Merchants Rd, opens 9 am to 5.45 pm Monday to Saturday, May; 9 am to 6.45pm Monday to Saturday, June; 8.30 am to 7.45 pm daily, July and August; and 9 am to 5.45 pm on weekdays, and 9 am to 12.45 pm on Saturday, the rest of the year. At the height of the season it's busy, and there may be delays of an hour or more in making accommodation bookings.

There's a seasonal (open July and August) tourist office branch (☎ 563081) in Salthill in an ugly UFO-like building. Head towards the seafront along Salthill Rd until you come to a roundabout at the promenade. Turn left and you'll see the office on the left.

Money

Irish banks all have branches in the city centre. There's a Bank of Ireland at 43 Eyre Square, another one on the square's western side, and an Allied Irish Bank (AIB) in Lynch's Castle on Shop St; all open 10 am to 4 pm on weekdays (5 pm on Thursday) and have ATMs. The building societies in Eyre Square have bureaux de change open 9.30 am to 5 pm on weekdays, and sometimes 10 am to 1 pm on Saturday. The main tourist office also changes money, as does the post office. The bureau de change, beside the entrance to Eyre Square Centre on the south-eastern corner of Eyre Square, opens 8 am to 10 pm daily, in summer; and 9 am to 5 pm Monday to Saturday, the rest of the year. American Express (Amex; ☎ 562316), on the northern side of Eyre Square, opens 9 am to 1 pm and 2 to 5 pm on weekdays.

Post & Communications

The post office, on Eglinton St off William St, opens 9 am to 6 pm Monday to Saturday.

Cyberzone (☎ 561415), above Supermac's on Eyre Square, offers Internet access 10 am to midnight daily. It costs £2/3.50 per half-hour/hour. South of the river, Jamie Starlight's Internet Café, Upper Dominick St, costs £2.50/5 per half-hour/hour.

Travel Agencies

USIT's travel office (☎ 565177) is at the Kinlay House Hostel, Victoria Place, Eyre Square.

Bookshops

Hawkins House, 14 Churchyard St, opposite the Collegiate Church of St Nicholas of Myra, and Charlie Byrne's (☎ 561766) in the Cornstore on Middle St are good bookshops. There's also Eason's (☎ 562284) on Shop St. Kenny's Bookshop (☎ 562739), High St, is one of the leading antiquarian bookshops in Ireland.

Laundry

There's The Laundrette on Sea Rd, the continuation of West William St just off Upper Dominick St, and Bubbles Laundrette on

Mary St. The more central Olde Malt Laundrette can be found in the Malt House shopping arcade, off High St; it opens 8.30 am to 6 pm Monday to Saturday.

EYRE SQUARE

The square is the focal point for the eastern part of the city centre, though it shows no great imagination in its design and layout. The eastern side of the square is taken up almost entirely by the Great Southern Hotel, a large grey limestone pile. In the centre of the square is **Kennedy Park**. US President John F Kennedy visited Galway in 1963, and a stone tablet in the square marks the occasion.

On the western side of the square is **Browne's Doorway** of 1627, a fragment from the home of one of the city's merchant rulers. Behind Browne's Doorway there's a curious object that is supposed to evoke the sails of a '*húicéir*' (hooker), a traditional Galway vessel. It was designed by Eamon O'Doherty and erected during the city's quincentennial in 1984. To the north is a controversial statue to the Galway-born writer Pádraic O'Conaire (1883–1928), a noted hell-raiser.

COLLEGIATE CHURCH OF ST NICHOLAS OF MYRA

This Protestant church on Shop St with its curious pyramidal spire dates from 1320. Not only is it Galway's most important monument but also the largest medieval parish church in Ireland still in use. Although it has been rebuilt and enlarged over the centuries, much of the original form has been retained. After Cromwell's victory, the church suffered the usual indignity of being used as a stable. Much damage was done – look for the damaged stonework – but at least it survived; 14 other Galway churches were simply razed to the ground. The church has numerous finely worked stone tombs and memorials. The two church bells date from 1590 and 1630.

Parts of the floor are paved with gravestones from the 16th to 18th centuries, and the Lynch Aisle holds the tombs of the powerful Lynch family. A large block tomb in one corner is said to be the grave of James Lynch, a mayor of Galway in the late 15th century who condemned his son, Walter, to death for killing a young Spanish visitor. None of the townsfolk would act as executioner, and the mayor was so dedicated to upholding justice that he personally acted as hangman, after which he went into seclusion – or so the story goes. A stone plaque, complete with skull and crossbones beneath it, on the **Lynch Memorial Window**, outside on Market St north of the church, tells the tale and claims to be the spot where the gallows stood.

At the end of the south transept is the empty frame which once held an icon of the Virgin Mary. It was supposedly taken to Gyor in western Hungary in the 17th century by an Irish bishop sent packing by Cromwell, and is still an object of veneration there.

It opens 9 am to 5.45 pm, mid-April to September; and 9.30 am to 4.30 pm, the rest of the year. A £1.50 donation is requested.

BOWLING GREEN

Across the road from Lynch's Memorial Window is Bowling Green. No 8 Bowling Green was once the **home of Nora Barnacle** (1884–1951), companion and, later, wife to James Joyce. He first visited the house in 1909 and again several times during the summer of 1912. The house, now a small museum (☎ 564743) dedicated to the couple, opens 10 am to 5 pm daily, May to September. Admission costs £1.

LYNCH'S CASTLE

On the corner of Shop and Upper Abbeygate Sts, parts of the old stone town house called Lynch's Castle (now a branch of the AIB) date back to the 14th century. Most of the present building, said to be the finest town castle in Ireland, dates from around 1600, however. The Lynch family were the most powerful of the 14 ruling Galway 'tribes', and members of the family held the position of mayor no less than 80 times between 1480 and 1650 – including the son-slayer James Lynch (see Collegiate Church of St Nicholas of Myra earlier on this page).

GALWAY

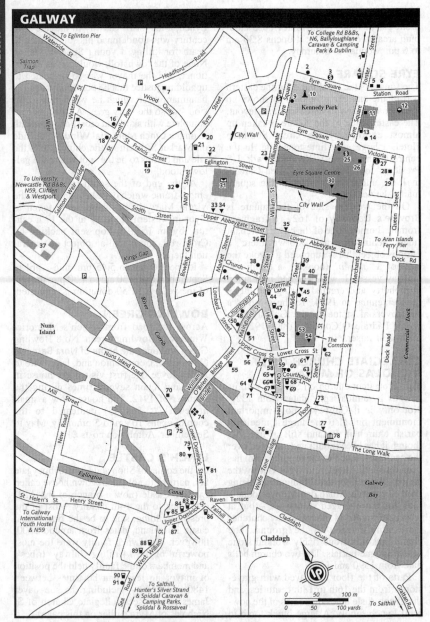

To Eglinton Pier
Waterside St
Salmon Trap
Weir
Waterside St
St Vincent's Ave
St Francis Street
To University, Newcastle Rd B&Bs, N59, Clifden & Westport
Salmon Weir Bridge
Nuns Island
Corrib
Nuns Island Road
River
Kings Gap
Bowling Green
Mill Street
New Road
William O'Brien Bridge
Lower Dominick Street
Eglington
Canal
St Helen's St
Henry Street
To Galway International Youth Hostel & N59
Upper Dominick St
West William St
Seat Road
To Salthill, Hunter's Silver Strand & Spiddal Caravan & Camping Parks, Spiddal & Rossaveal
Headford Road
Wood Quay
Eyre Street
City Wall
St Francis Street
Eglinton Street
Mary Street
Smith Street
Upper Abbeygate Street
Market Street
Church Lane
Lombard Street
Churchyard St
Mainguard St
High Street
Upper Cross St
Lower Cross St
Cross Street
Bridge Street
Raven Terrace
Fairhill St
To Eglinton Pier
Eyre Square
Williamgate St
William St
Shop Street
Lower Abbeygate St
Buttermilk Lane
Middle Street
St Augustine Street
Merchants Road
The Cornstore
Courthouse Ln
Aero
Flood Street
Wolfe Tone Bridge
Claddagh Quay
Claddagh
To College Rd B&Bs, N6, Ballyloughlane Caravan & Camping Park & Dublin
Forster Street
Station Road
Eyre Square
Kennedy Park
Eyre Square Centre
City Wall
Victoria Pl
Queen Street
To Aran Islands Ferry Pier
Dock Rd
Dock Road
Commercial Dock
The Long Walk
Galway Bay
To Salthill
Grattan Rd

0   50   100 m
0   50   100 yards

GALWAY

PLACES TO STAY
5 Galway International Youth Hostel
6 Great Western House
7 Woodquay Hostel
11 Great Southern Hotel
15 Salmon Weir Hostel
17 Corrib Villa
26 Kinlay House & USIT Office
28 Celtic Tourist Hostel
66 Barnacle's Quay St House
67 Spanish Arch Hotel
70 St Martin's B&B
76 Jury's Galway Inn
82 Arch View Hostel

PLACES TO EAT
22 Conlon's Restaurant
30 Sails
33 Couch Potatoes
34 Brannagan's
35 Food for Thought
45 Brasserie Eleven
54 Le Café de Paris
56 Busker Brownes
57 Hungry Grass
59 Quay West
61 Mocha Beans
63 Sev'nth Heav'n
65 Pierre's
69 Fat Freddy's
71 Kirwan's Lane Creative Cuisine
72 McDonagh's Restaurant
73 Shama

77 Times Square & Thai Garde Restaurants
79 Pasta Paradiso
80 Left Bank Café
81 Le Graal
85 Kebab House

PUBS
1 Rabbitt's Bar
4 An Púcán
13 O'Flaherty's
21 McSwiggan's
44 Taaffes
47 King's Head
55 The Lisheen Bar
58 Seagán Ua Neachtain
68 Quays
83 Roisín Dubh
84 Taylor's Bar
86 Monroe's Tavern
88 The Blue Note
89 Claddagh Ring
90 Crane's Bar

OTHER
2 Cyberzone
3 American Express
8 Bank of Ireland
9 Browne's Doorway
10 Pádraic O'Conaire's Statue
12 Bus & Train Station
14 Island Ferries
16 Town Hall Theatre
18 Town Hall
19 Franciscan Abbey
20 Corrib & Apollo Taxis

23 Stephen Faller Jewellery Store
24 Eyre Square Centre Entrance & Bureau de Change
25 Bank of Ireland
27 Tourist Office
29 Celtic Cycles
31 Post Office
32 Bubbles Laundrette
36 Lynch's Castle & Allied Irish Bank
37 St Nicholas' Cathedral
38 Eason's Bookshop
39 Mulligan Records
40 Augustinian Church
41 Lynch Memorial Window
42 Collegiate Church of St Nicholas of Myra
43 Nora Barnacle's Home
46 The Galway Theatre (Irish Language)
48 Hawkins House Bookshop
49 Malt House Shopping Arcade & Olde Malt Laundrette
50 Radar Stores
51 Galway Taxis
52 Kenny's Bookshop
53 Charlie Byrne's Bookshop
60 Druid Theatre
62 Mayoralty House
64 Design Concourse Ireland
74 Bridge Mills Shopping Centre
75 Garda Station
78 Spanish Arch & Galway City Museum
87 Jimmy Starlight's Internet Café
91 The Laundrette

Lynch's Castle has numerous fine stone features on its façade, including the coats of arms of Henry VII, the Lynches and the Fitzgeralds of Kildare, as well as gargoyles, which are unusual in Ireland.

THE SPANISH ARCH
A 1651 drawing of Galway clearly shows its extensive city walls. But since the visits of Cromwell in 1652 and William of Orange in 1691, and the subsequent centuries of neglect, the walls have almost completely disappeared. Located near the river to the east of Wolfe Tone Bridge, the Spanish Arch (1584) appears to have been an extension of the walls through which ships unloaded their goods – often wine and brandy from Spain.

The small, unremarkable **Galway City Museum** (☎ 567641), by the arch, opens 10 am to 1 pm and 2 to 5 pm Monday to Saturday. Admission costs £1/50p.

ST NICHOLAS' CATHEDRAL
From the Spanish Arch, a pleasant riverside path runs upriver and across the Salmon Weir Bridge to the second church in town dedicated to St Nicholas. The cathedral is a huge, imposing structure, dedicated by the late Cardinal Richard Cushing of Boston in 1965. Tasteful it's not, and critics vie for the most caustic descriptions of this monument to inelegance.

Inside things are a little less grandiose, but it's a mishmash of styles and intentions. Even the cathedral's proper name is a bit of

GALWAY

a mouthful: the Catholic Cathedral of Our Lady Assumed into Heaven and St Nicholas.

SALMON WEIR

Salmon Weir Bridge crosses the River Corrib just east of the cathedral. Upstream is the great weir where the waters of the Corrib cascade down one of their final descents before reaching the sea, 1km to the south. The weir controls the water levels above it, and when the salmon are running you can often see shoals of them waiting in the clear waters before making the rush upstream to spawn in Lough Corrib.

The earliest records of Galway include references to the de Burgo family owning the fisheries on the town's weirs. Today they're owned by the Central Fisheries Board. The salmon and sea trout seasons are usually February to September, but most fish pass through the weir during May and June. To obtain fishing permits you must write to The Manager, Galway Fisheries (☎ 562388), Nuns Island, Galway.

SALTHILL

Within walking distance of the city is Salthill (Bóthar na Trá), an old-fashioned seaside resort. The beaches are often packed in hot weather but are not particularly good. **Leisure World** (☎ 521455) in Salthill Park, with several covered pools and a giant waterslide, opens 8 am to 10 pm daily, year round. Admission costs £3.50/2.50 (students £2.50, families upwards of £9).

ORGANISED TOURS

The Spiddal-based O'Neachtain Tours (☎ 553188) runs day-long coach tours to Connemara or the Burren and Cliffs of Moher leaving the Galway tourist office at 9.45 am (9.55 am from the Salthill tourist office branch) and returning at 4.45 pm. Both tours cost £10/5 (students £8). Lally Coaches (☎ 562905), also in Spiddal, operates a similar tour of Connemara; the departure points, times and prices are the same as the O'Neachtain ones.

May to September, the *Corrib Princess*

(☎ 592447) operates daily cruises lasting one hour 30 minutes on the River Corrib and Lough Corrib. The boat departs at 2.30 and 4.30 pm (plus 12.30 pm in July and August) from Eglinton Pier, at the northern end of Waterside St, upriver from the Salmon Weir. Cruises cost £5/2.50. You can also book at the tourist office.

SPECIAL EVENTS

Galway has a busy calendar of festivals and other events. The well-established Jazz Festival takes place in February, and in April the Cúirt Poetry and Literature Festival (☎ 565886) grows in importance every year.

The Galway Film Fleadh (☎ 751655), in early July, is one of the biggest film festivals in the country. The city parties with a vengeance at the Galway Arts Festival (☎ 583800) in late July/early August; the whole town turns out for this two-week extravaganza of theatre, music, art, comedy and a parade.

The last week of July is Galway Race Week (☎ 753870), which is as much an event off the course as on it; the racecourse, 3km east of the city centre at Ballybrit, hosts a traditional Irish fair. The highlight of the late-September Galway International Oyster Festival (☎ 527282), which was established in 1954, is the world oyster-eating championships.

PLACES TO STAY

Galway has a huge variety of accommodation, but you may still have difficulty finding a bed in July and August. There's more accommodation in Salthill, a couple of kilometres to the south-west.

Camping

Hunter's Silver Strand Caravan and Camping Park (☎ 592040) is just west of Salthill on the coastal road (R336). Large/small tents cost £7/6 plus 50p per adult; the site opens Easter to September. *Spiddal Caravan and Camping Park* (☎ 553372) is 18km west of Galway on the R336. It is also signposted in Irish as Pairc Saoire an Spidéil. A car and tent costs £9; cyclists

Claddagh

If you ever go across the sea to Ireland
It may be at the closing of the day
You can sit and watch the moon rise over Claddagh
And watch the sun go down on Galway Bay

Arthur Colahan, 'Galway Bay', 1947

A romantic icon in the hearts and songs of Irish-Americans for generations, Claddagh village was once Galway's main commercial fishing centre – up to 3000 people and 300 boats were based here at one stage. Strictly speaking, the district begins at the southern end of Wolfe Tone Bridge. Among the boats were the traditional Galway sailing vessels with pitched black hulls and rust-coloured sails known as '*púcáin*' and '*gleoitoige*', today collectively called Galway hookers.

Claddagh used to have its own costume and dialect, as well as its own king. Although the traditional Claddagh of thatched roofs, Irish speakers and fishing boats disappeared in the 1930s, you'll still see many people wearing Claddagh rings. Those rings with a crowned heart nestling between two outstretched hands signify friendship (the hands), loyalty (the crown) and love (the heart). If the heart points towards the hand, the wearer is taken or married; towards the fingertip means that he or she is looking for a mate. It has been the wedding ring used throughout much of Connaught since the mid-18th century and is enjoying something of a renaissance today, judging from the well-stocked jewellery-shop windows.

NICKY CAVEN

A Galway hooker

and hikers pay £3.50. It opens year round. *Ballyloughane Caravan and Camping Park* (☎ 755338) is at Ballyloughane Beach on the Dublin road (N6), 5km east of Galway. For drivers, a site for a large/small tent costs £7/6; cyclists and hikers pay £4.

Hostels
There are legions of hostels in and around Galway. They open year round except for the An Óige and Mary Ryan hostels.

Several hostels are extremely central. At the large IHH *Great Western House* (☎ 561150, Frenchville Lane), adjacent to the bus and train station, dorm beds cost £9.50 (£12.50 in four-bedded rooms), 22 private rooms cost £16 per person, and

there's a sauna. The security-conscious IHO *Galway Hostel* (☎ 566959, Frenchville Lane) offers dorm beds costing £8 and six private rooms costing £9.50 per person. The modern 150-room *Kinlay House* (☎ 565244), on Merchants Rd opposite the tourist office, is well equipped and has a variety of rooms costing £8.50 to £12 per person (includes a light breakfast). The 15 private rooms here cost £13 to £20 per person. Round the corner, the less attractive IHO *Celtic Tourist Hostel* (☎ 566606, Queen St) offers dorm beds costing £8 and six doubles costing £13 per person.

The IHH *Barnacle's Quay Street House* (☎ 568644, 10 Quay St) has 109 dorm beds costing £8 to £13; doubles cost £26 to £32.

The IHO *Corrib Villa* (☎ 562892, 4 Water-side St), near the Salmon Weir Bridge, costs £8.50; there are no private rooms. The independent *Wood Quay Hostel* (☎ 562618, 23-24 Wood Quay), in St Anne's House just north of the city centre, costs £8 (£20 for one of two doubles) and has a decent kitchen and eating area but cramped wash-rooms and rickety bunks. Around the corner is the IHO *Salmon Weir Hostel* (☎ 561133, St Vincent's Ave), where dorm beds cost £8, and the three private doubles cost £20.

On the other side of the river, the independent *Arch View Hostel* (☎ 586661), with 60 dorm beds costing £6, is hidden away at the junction of Upper and Lower Dominick Sts, west of Wolfe Tone Bridge.

If you continue north-west from Upper Dominick St through the name changes of Henry St and St Helen's St, then turn left (south) onto St Mary's Rd, you'll come to An Óige's huge 200-bed *Galway International Youth Hostel* (☎ 527411). This hostel in St Mary's College opens June to August. Situated between central Galway and Salthill, it can be reached on bus No 1 from Eyre Square. Dorm beds cost £9, in-cluding a light breakfast; there are also fam-ily rooms.

The independent, friendly *Mary Ryan Hostel* (☎ 523303, 4 Beechmount Ave, Highfield Park) is past Salthill south-west of the centre. It's about a 20-minute walk, or you could take bus No 2 from Eyre Square to Taylor Hill Convent. The hostel has twin rooms only (£8.50 per person) and opens mid-June to mid-September. Ring first to make sure there are rooms available.

B&Bs

In summer you may have to travel to the suburbs. There aren't many B&Bs in the city centre, but it's worth trying Mrs Sex-ton's *St Martin's B&B* (☎ 568286, 2 Nuns Island Rd), delightfully situated right on the Corrib. The friendliness of the owners and proximity to the sights, restaurants and pubs in the centre put it above everything else in Galway. It costs £15 to £18 per person.

There are plenty of places less than 10 minutes' walk away from the centre on Newcastle Rd, which runs parallel to the river to the west in a north-south direction, becoming the N59 to Clifden. *Villa Nova* (☎ 524849, 40 Lower Newcastle Rd) starts at £22.50/40 for singles/doubles. North of the city Forster St becomes College Rd, again about 10 minutes' walk, where there are lots of B&Bs. *Copper Beech House* (☎ 569544) at No 26 is a large, modern guesthouse with well-equipped rooms, and chalets at the back. Singles/doubles start at £20/36.

Salthill and adjacent Renmore are good hunting grounds for B&Bs; Upper and Lower Salthill Rds are packed with places. Particularly good B&Bs include *Norman Villa* (☎ 521131, 86 Lower Salthill Rd) cost-ing £37/65. *Devondell* (☎ 523617, 47 Devon Park, Lower Salthill Rd) is down a cul-de-sac. Singles/doubles here cost £24.50/40. *Roncalli House* (☎ 584159, 24 Whitestrand Ave, Lower Salthill Rd) has been recom-mended by readers and costs £18 per person. It opens year round.

Along Upper Salthill Rd try *Mandalay by the Sea* (☎ 524177, 10 Gentian Hill), which starts at £22.50/36. Also in Gentian Hill is *Bay View House* (☎ 522116) in a cul-de-sac; it costs £24.50/36. *Clare Villa* (☎ 522520, 38 Threadneedle St), near the water, and Mrs Lally's *Bayview* (☎ 526008, 20 Seamount), off Threadneedle St, cost £25/37.

Hotels

Spanish Arch Hotel (☎/fax 569191, Quay St), with 20 singles/doubles, costs £80/99 and is charming. Just south overlooking the river and Wolfe Tone Bridge, the huge *Jury's Galway Inn* (☎ 566444, fax 568415, Quay St), with 128 rooms, has a flat room rate costing £45 to £99 (for up to three adults), depending on the season. The sumptuous 114-room *Great Southern Hotel* (☎ 564041), taking up the complete eastern side of Eyre Square, costs £91/138.

PLACES TO EAT
Restaurants
The Quay St area is awash with restaurants, but finding a quiet one can be difficult. *Sev'nth Heav'n*, beside the Druid Theatre

on the corner of Courthouse Lane and Flood St, is an excellent place for pasta (around £5.95) and good vegetarian dishes. *Fat Freddy's* in the Halls on Quay St also offers pasta (spaghetti bolognese with garlic bread costs £3.95) and is popular. The Italian-style *Brasserie Eleven (19 Middle St)* serves pizza and pasta main courses starting at £6.50 and great salads (£4.50).

McDonagh's (Quay St), a Galway fixture for years, is excellent for seafood (fish and chips costs £3.80); be sure to try the 'wild' local mussels. *Quay West (☎ 563015, 9 Quay St)*, diagonally opposite the hostel, is relatively trendy, as its name would imply, and serves a £16.75 set dinner. The popular French-style *Pierre's (☎ 566066, 8 Quay St)* offers a three-course dinner costing £11.90.

Brannagan's (☎ 565974, 36 Upper Abbeygate St) claims to serve 'Italian, French, Cajun, Mexican and Oriental food', with main courses starting at £7.95. It opens from 6 pm daily.

On the other side of the River Corrib *Le Graal (13 Lower Dominick St)* is a charming choice for lunch or dinner, with main courses costing £7.50 to £10.95, including nightly vegetarian and fish specials.

An Indian restaurant worth trying is the long-established *Shama (☎ 566696, Flood St)*, with tandoori and balti specialities starting at £7.50. For Chinese food there's the vegetarian-friendly *Times Square* near the Spanish Arch, on Spanish Parade just off Flood St, where meatless choices cost £6 to £6.50.

Thai Garden (☎ 567865, Spanish Parade) offers a wide variety of Thai dishes and a four-course dinner (£18.50).

Galway's most astonishing restaurant – in every sense – is *Kirwan's Lane Creative Cuisine (☎ 568266)* at the southern end of Kirwan's Lane, the oldest street in the city. It's a place that could happily sit in the most stylish areas of New York or London. Appetisers cost £4.95, main courses £7 to £8.50.

One of the best restaurants in the country is *Drimcong House (☎ 555115)*, 14km along the Clifden road (N59) past Moy-

cullen. It can't be recommended highly enough and has a very reasonable (for its price bracket) five-course set menu costing £27, including vegetarian choices. It opens for dinner 6.30 to 10.30 pm daily but closes late December to March. In summer you need to book well ahead.

Fast Food & Cafés
Hungry Grass (Upper Cross St) serves baguette sandwiches (£2.95) and lots of other wholefood possibilities, including salads costing less than £3.95. A few doors down, in the historic Slate House dating from 1615, *Busker Brownes* is a popular, almost 24-hour café-bar with excellent seafood; a crab-meat sandwich costs £4.95. *Food for Thought* is a wholefood (though it also serves chicken and fish) lunchtime possibility on Lower Abbeygate St, with sandwiches/main courses starting at £1.95/3. Another good choice is *Mocha Beans* on Lower Cross St, serving a variety of coffees and all-day breakfasts (£3.95).

Couch Potatoes (Upper Abbeygate St), next to Brannagan's restaurant, is a very appropriate place for a bite in this tuber-devouring land; spuds with various delicious fillings cost around £2 to £4.95. It opens noon to 9 or 10 pm daily. Nobody does fish and chips (starting at £4.80) better than *Conlon's Restaurant (Eglinton St)*.

Le Café de Paris is in the Cornstore on Middle St, while *Sails*, a popular self-service restaurant, is on the lower level in the Eyre Square Centre; seafood chowder at the latter costs £1.95.

The choice isn't so good on the other side of the river, but *Left Bank Café (Lower Dominick St)* is a good sandwich place and opens 8 am to 7 or 8 pm daily. Next door, the bright *Pasta Paradiso* serves pasta and pizzas starting at under £5. For late-night eats, *Kebab House*, farther along on Upper Dominick St, is a good bet.

ENTERTAINMENT
The *Galway Edge* includes listings of what's on in Galway and the surrounding area. Published on Thursday, it is available free from the tourist office and other venues

around town. Also check the *Galway Advertiser* on Thursday. The *List Galway* broadsheet, containing weekly news on events, music, theatre, pubs and clubs, is available free around town.

Pubs

There is always lots going on in Galway's pubs. The cosy, 100-year-old *Seaĝan Ua Neaĉhtain (17 Upper Cross St)* has a truly fabulous atmosphere and can attract a somewhat flamboyant crowd. Farther north, the *King's Head (High St)* has a sports bar and music most nights in summer. The enormously popular *Taaffes* is a music and sports bar almost next door. *McSwiggan's (Daly's Place)*, near the eastern end of Eyre St, is big and busy. The *Quays (Quay St)* is full of bric-a-brac and draws a great crowd at the weekend and in summer. *The Lisheen Bar (5 Bridge St)* is one of the better traditional-music venues on this side of the Corrib.

There are some flashier but less atmospheric pubs around Eyre Square, including *O'Flaherty's*, in the Great Southern Hotel on the square itself; *An Púcán (11 Forster St)*, just off the square, with music most nights; and the refurbished *Rabbitt's Bar (23 Forster St)*.

Across the river the choice spot for traditional music and ballads (and set dancing on Tuesday) is *Monroe's Tavern* on the corner of Upper Dominick and Fairhill Sts. The *Róisín Dubh ('Black Rose'; Upper Dominick St)*, opposite, is good for alternative music. *Taylor's Bar* next door and, round the corner on West William St and its extension Sea Rd, the *Claddagh Ring* and *Crane's Bar* all have music. *The Blue Note (3 West William St)* has live jazz and rock a few nights each week.

Theatre

Galway has three good theatres. The long-established *Druid Theatre (☎ 568617, Courthouse Lane)* is famed for its experimental works, while the new *Town Hall Theatre (☎ 569777, Courthouse Square)*, just off St Vincent's Ave, is more middle of the road. The most important theatre in Gal-

way – but not of much interest to most travellers – is *An Taibhdhearc na Gaillimhe (The Galway Theatre; ☎ 562024, Middle St)*, which stages plays in Irish.

SHOPPING

The purchase of choice for most visitors to Galway is a Claddagh ring in silver or gold (see the boxed text 'Claddagh' earlier in this chapter). Price them at one of the many jewellery shops in the town centre, such as Stephen Faller (☎ 561226) on Williamsgate St.

On Kirwan's Lane, the Design Concourse Ireland (☎ 566927) is a wonderful place to look around; it displays (and sells) the cutting edge in Irish design – from furniture and tableware to high fashion in Donegal tweed (no less) – from all 32 Irish counties.

If you're an aficionado of traditional Irish music go to Mulligan Records (☎ 564961), 5 Middle St; it does mail order. One of the better places for outdoor gear such as hiking boots and backpacks is Radar Stores (☎ 568810), 15 Mainguard St.

The big, modern Eyre Square Centre, to the south-east of Eyre Square, cunningly incorporates a reconstructed stretch of the old city wall. Other shopping centres are Bridge Mills, in an old mill building by the river at the western end of William O'Brien Bridge, and The Cornstore on Middle St.

Just outside town, the Royal Tara China factory (☎ 751301) at Mervue is worth a look. Take the N6 Dublin road then turn at the first left after Ryan's Hotel. The Galway Irish Crystal Heritage Centre (☎ 757311) at Merlin Park, a bit farther along the N6, will meet all your needs in the stemware department. If you're interested in how the local marble is worked, head for the factory and showroom of Connemara Marble Industries (☎ 555102) in Moycullen, 13km north-west of Galway on the N59.

GETTING THERE & AWAY
Air

Carnmore Airport (☎ 755569) is 10km east of the city near Inverin. There are two Aer Lingus flights daily to and from Dublin.

Bus

From the bus station (☎ 562000), behind the Great Southern Hotel on Eyre Square, there are regular Bus Éireann services to all major cities in the Republic and the North – and points in between. A lot of private companies are also represented. The one-way fare to Dublin (three hours 45 minutes) costs £8.

Feda Ódonaill Coaches (☎ 761656) runs a service between Crolly, County Donegal (five hours 30 minutes), and Galway via Donegal and Sligo twice daily (three on Friday and Sunday). The buses depart from in front of the cathedral, except the last bus on Sunday (8 pm), which leaves from Eyre Square.

Nestor Travel (☎ 797144) runs between four and seven buses daily to Dublin via Dublin Airport. The first bus leaves Forster St Bus Park at 7.15 am (7.55 am on Sunday), the last at 6 pm. The stop in Dublin is at the Tara St DART Station on George's Quay.

From June to September, Michael Nee Coaches (☎ 095-51082) runs up to four buses daily between Forster St and Clifden (one hour 25 minutes).

Edward Walsh Coach Operators (☎ 098-35165) runs a bus from Eyre Square to Westport (four hours) at 5.10 pm on Sunday. McNulty Coaches (☎ 097-81086) leave Eyre Square for Belmullet (five hours) via Westport and Newport at 4, 5.30 and 6 pm on Friday.

For details of buses to Rossaveal (for the Aran Islands) see Getting There & Away in the Aran Islands section later in this chapter.

Train

From Ceannt train station (☎ 564222), behind the Great Southern Hotel on Eyre Square, there are up to five trains daily to/from Dublin (one way £21, two hours 30 minutes). Connections with other train routes can be made at Athlone (one hour).

GETTING AROUND
To/From the Airport

A bus runs once daily Monday to Saturday between the airport and Galway bus station (£2.50). It leaves the airport at 1.25 pm, and leaves the bus station at 12.50 pm. A taxi to or from the airport costs about £10. If you're driving, take the main Dublin road to Oranmore and turn north, then watch out for the signs to the airport.

Bus

You can walk to almost everything in Galway and even out to Salthill, but there are regular buses from Eyre Square. Bus No 1 runs from Eyre Square to Salthill and sometimes on to Blackrock; bus No 2 goes from Knocknacarra and Blackrock through Eyre Square to Renmore; bus No 3 runs between Eyre Square and Castlepark; and bus No 4 goes to Newcastle.

Car

Drivers will need parking discs to park on the street; these are available from newsagents. The car park just over William O'Brien Bridge is next to the garda station, so it should be safe.

Bicycle

Most hostels, including Kinlay House and Salmon Weir, rent bikes. At Celtic Cycles (☎ 566606), on Queen St next to the Celtic Tourist Hostel, bikes cost £7/30 per day/week.

Taxi

Galway Taxis (☎ 561111) is on Mainguard St; Corrib & Apollo Taxis (☎ 564444) is on Eyre St north of Eglinton St. There are also a couple of big taxi ranks in the city centre on Eyre Square.

South of Galway City

Many visitors pass through the small part of County Galway south of the city on their way to or from the spectacular limestone Burren region in County Clare. But there are many places worth visiting in the area, including the tranquil monastic settlement and round tower at Kilmacduagh.

CLARINBRIDGE & KILCOLGAN
☎ 091

Some 16km south of Galway, Clarinbridge (Droichead an Chláirín) and Kilcolgan (Cill Choglán) are the focus for Galway's famous Clarinbridge Oyster Festival, which is held during the second weekend in September. The old-fashioned, thatched *Paddy Burke's Oyster Inn* (☎ 796107, Clarinbridge) is famous for its association with the festival. It opens for lunch and dinner until 10.30 pm daily; a dozen oysters florentine cost £15. A little farther south, signposted off the road in Kilcolgan near the post office, is *Moran's Oyster Cottage* (☎ 976113), a wonderful thatched pub and restaurant overlooking narrow Dunbulcaun Bay, where the famous Galway oysters are reared. During the festival, the world oyster-opening championships are held at Moran's.

Getting There & Away
Clarinbridge is on the main Galway to Gort, Ennis and Limerick road (N18) and is served by numerous Bus Éireann buses from Galway. Kilcolgan is also on the N18, and Moran's Oyster Cottage is about 1.5km to the west.

KINVARA & AROUND
☎ 091

Kinvara (Cinn Mhara) is a delightful village tucked away on the south-eastern corner of Galway Bay. A small stone harbour is home to a number of Galway hookers (traditional sailing boats). Kinvara is a quaint, relatively quiet spot and doesn't attract anything like the number of visitors that Ballyvaughan, 24km west, does. A few kilometres west of Kinvara, you reach County Clare and the start of the Burren limestone region.

Dunguaire Castle
Dunguaire Castle, north of Kinvara on the shore, was erected around 1520 by the O'Hynes. It later passed into the hands of Oliver St John Gogarty (1878–1957), poet, writer, surgeon, Irish Free State senator and 'the wildest wit in Dublin'. The castle is supposedly built on the site of the 6th-century royal palace of Guaire Aidhne, the king of Connaught.

The castle is in excellent condition, and the displays on each floor are dedicated to a particular period in its history, right down to the last mildly eccentric owner, who lived here during the 1960s. It has a gift shop and guided tours, as well as medieval banquets (☎ 637108, 061-360788 in Shannon), held at 5.30 and 8.45 pm daily, May to September. They're on a more intimate scale than the ones at Bunratty Castle near Shannon in County Clare and slightly cheaper at £29 per person.

Dunguaire Castle opens 9.30 am to 5.30 pm daily, mid-April to September. Admission costs £2.75/1.50.

Just south of Dunguaire is a bare **stone arch**, the only remains of an older castle.

Special Events
On the bank-holiday weekend in May, Kinvara hosts the Fleadh na gCuach (Cuckoo Festival), a music festival. In early August, the Cruinniú na mBáid (Gathering of the Boats) festival is a celebration of the Galway hookers.

Places to Stay
The IHH *Johnston's Hostel* (☎ 637164, Main St) opens July to August only. Dorm beds cost £7.50.

Six kilometres north-west, signposted off the main road to Ballyvaughan (N67), is the An Óige *Doorus House* (☎ 637512). The hostel building was once owned by a count called Floribund de Basterot, who entertained such notables as WB Yeats, Lady Augusta Gregory, Douglas Hyde and Guy de Maupassant here. Yeats and Lady Gregory are said to have first mooted the idea of the Abbey Theatre in Dublin while visiting Doorus House. It's a good base for exploring the Burren and opens year round. Beds cost £7/5.50.

Many B&Bs are scattered around the Doorus Peninsula, including *Burren View* (☎ 637142), 5km north-west of Kinvara, which costs £22.50/36 for singles/doubles and opens April to October. Three kilometres north of Kinvara *Clareview House*

(☎ 637170) costs £24/35 and is open the same months.

Places to Eat
The excellent little *Café on the Quay*, overlooking the harbour, serves snacks and light meals all day; Kinvara Bay mussels cost £5.25. *Rosaleen's (Main St)* serves dinner main courses costing £8 to £12; meals at lunchtime, such as spinach and mushroom lasagne (£3.95), are cheaper.

Getting There & Away
From late May to late September, Bus Éireann bus No 50 serves Galway, Kinvara, Ballyvaughan, Lisdoonvarna, Doolin, the Cliffs of Moher, Lahinch, Miltown Malbay, Doonbeg, Kilkee, Kilrush, Tralee and Cork. The bus runs three to four times daily Monday to Saturday, and twice on Sunday.

Bus No 423 serves the Burren coast once daily, running via Kinvara between Galway, Ballyvaughan, Black Head, Fanore, Lisdoonvarna and Doolin.

For more details contact Galway bus station (☎ 091-562000).

GORT & AROUND
☎ 091
In Gort, 37km south-east of Galway just off the N18, a 16th-century Norman tower known as **Thoor Ballylee** (☎ 631436) was the summer home of Yeats from 1922. The restored tower contains his furnishings and fittings and you can see an audiovisual presentation on his life. It opens 10 am to 6 pm daily, Easter to September. Admission costs £3/1.20.

About 5km north of Gort is the Dúchas-run **Coole Park** (Cúil; ☎ 631804), with direct access from the N18. It was the home of Lady Augusta Gregory, co-founder of the Abbey Theatre and patron of Yeats. An exhibition focuses on the literary importance of the house and the natural history of the surrounding reserve.

Coole Park opens 9.30 am to 6.30 pm daily, mid-June to August; and 10 am to 5 pm Tuesday to Sunday, mid-April to mid-June and in September. Admission costs £2/1.

Five kilometres south-west of Gort is the extensive monastic site of **Kilmacduagh**. Beside a small lake is a well-preserved round tower, the remains of a small 14th-century cathedral (Teampall Mór Mac-Duagh), an oratory dedicated to St John the Baptist, and various other little chapels. The original monastery is thought to have been founded by St Colman MacDuagh at the beginning of the 7th century. St MacDuagh founded the monastery under the patronage of King Guaire Aidhne of Connaught, who gave his name to Dunguaire Castle in Kinvara. Such was the monastery's importance that it became the focus for a new diocese in the 12th century. The round tower is 34m tall and leans some 60cm from the perpendicular. The doorway is 8m above ground level. There are fine views over the Burren from here. You can visit any time.

There are regular buses from Galway to Gort.

Connemara

Connemara (Conamara) is the wonderfully wild, barren region north-west of Galway city. It's a stunning patchwork of bogs, lonely valleys, pale grey mountains and small lakes that shimmer when the sun shines. Its devotees – Irish, French, Americans, Germans – buy up remote cottages as holiday homes or spend a small fortune on a week's holiday in a castle hotel during the salmon-fishing season.

Connemara isn't a distinct geographical region like the Burren. At its heart are the Maumturk Mountains and the grey, quartzite peaks of the Twelve Bens (or Pins), which offer some tremendous hill walking. They look south over a plain dotted with lakes and run southwards into the sea around Carna and Roundstone in a maze of rocky islands, tortuous inlets and sparkling white beaches. The coastal road west of Spiddal (R336) eventually enters this maze, and it's well worth losing yourself for a day or two around Carraroe; the Garumna, Lettermullen and Lettermore Islands; Roundstone; and Ballyconneely Bay.

Pink granite is the predominant rock in this lower country, while the mountains and northern part of the region are made of a mixture of quartzite, gneiss, schist and greenish marble.

However, the best scenery is in the middle of the region. The journey from Maam Cross north-west to Leenane (R336) or north-east to Cong (R345) takes you through Joyce country, a stunning mountainous region. The trip north along Lough Inagh Valley past the Twelve Bens and around Kylemore Lake would be difficult to surpass anywhere in the country.

One of the most important Gaeltachtaí in the country begins just west of Galway city around Barna and stretches westwards through Spiddal and Inverin, and along much of the coast as far as Cashel. Ireland's national Irish-language radio station, Radio na Gaeltachta, is based at Costello and does much to sustain the language. The Irish-language weekly newspaper *Foinse* (*Source*) is published in Spiddal.

Heading west from Galway you have two options: the coast road (R336) through Salthill, Barna and Spiddal, or the inland route (N59) through Oughterard, which leads directly to the heart of Connemara.

The excellent *Connemara: Introduction and Gazetteer* by Tim Robinson (Folding Landscape Maps, £12) is a must if you intend any detailed exploration. *Connemara: A Hill Walker's Guide* by Robinson and Joss Lynam is also invaluable.

GETTING THERE & AWAY

There are numerous Bus Éireann services running to most parts of Connemara. Many of them originate in Galway, so check with the bus station there (☎ 091-562000) for times and fares. Services can be sporadic, and many operate May to September only or July and August only.

Bus Nos 61 and 419 run between Galway, Oughterard, Maam Cross, Recess, Roundstone, Ballyconneely and on to Clifden five times daily (twice on Sunday), late June to August. Bus No 61 also continues from Clifden to Kylemore, Leenane and Westport; at other times of the year it runs

only once daily from Galway to Clifden via Maam Cross and Leenane, but doesn't make all the above stops.

Galway, Cong, Leenane and Clifden are connected by the infrequent bus No 420, Monday to Saturday. Bus No 424 runs between Galway, Spiddal, Inverin, Rossaveal, Carraroe and the Lettermore and Lettermullen Islands, five times daily (once on Sunday). Bus No 416 runs once daily Monday to Saturday, year round, between Galway, Oughterard, Maam Cross, Rosmuc, Recess, Glinsk, Carna and Moyrus.

Many roadsigns in this area are in Irish only. See the Place Names Appendix at the back of this book for their English-language equivalents.

SPIDDAL

☎ 091 • pop 300

Just 17km west of Galway, Spiddal (An Spidéal) is a lively little roadside settlement with some good pubs. Some of the houses are among the finest in Ireland, partly because of grants from the Irish government to encourage people to continue living in the area and to speak Gaelic. East of the village is the Irish-language **Coláiste Chonnacht** (Connaught College; ☎ 553383), founded in 1910, and **Standún** (☎ 553108), a massive craft shop that also operates a bureau de change (open 9.30 am to 6.30 pm Monday to Saturday, March to December) and tearoom. Nearby, in front of the large Ceardlann Craft Centre, is a good **beach**, which can get crowded during summer.

If you're looking for open landscapes and wild coastlines, leave Spiddal behind and head west towards Roundstone.

SPIDDAL TO ROUNDSTONE

West of Spiddal, the scenery gets more dramatic. Before Costello (Casla), you'll notice signs for Rossaveal (Ros a' Mhíl), the main departure point for ferries to the Aran Islands (see Getting There & Away in the Aran Islands section later in this chapter). Past Costello it's well worth turning west off the main road for **Carraroe** (An Cheathrú Rua) and into a maze of rugged islands, all connected to the mainland, and

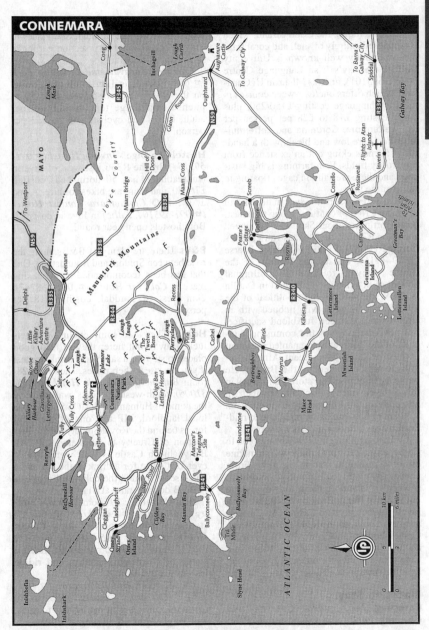

CONNEMARA

GALWAY

inlets. Carraroe is famous for its fine beaches, including the Coral Strand, which is composed entirely of shell and coral fragments. Equally well known is University College Galway's Irish Language Centre (☎ 091-595101), or Áras Mháirtín Uí Chadhain, which offers one/two-week courses in the Irish language costing £150/250, plus board costing £18 to £28 per person per day. Lettermore, Gorumna and Lettermullen Islands are low and bleak, with a handful of farmers eking out an existence from tiny, rocky fields. Fish farming is big business, and there are salmon cages floating in some of the bays.

From Screeb (Scriob) you can head north to Maam Cross or continue along the coast. Near Gortmore, about 5km west of Screeb along the R340, is the Dúchas-run Pearse's Cottage (☎ 091-574292). Pádraig Pearse (1879–1916), one of the leaders of the Gaelic revival, founded the bilingual School of St Enda (Scoil Éanna) in Dublin in 1908. He was the least political of the 1916 rebels, being heavily imbued with an almost religious need for blood sacrifice, but nevertheless was the commander-in-chief of the insurgents and named president of the provisional government. After the revolt he was executed by the British. He wrote some of his short stories and plays in this cottage, which is also called by its Irish name, Teach an Phiarsaigh. It opens from 9.30 am to 6.30 pm daily, mid-June to mid-September. Admission costs £1/40p.

Continuing along the R340 brings you to Carna, a small fishing village with a marine biology research station nearby. From Carna there are some good walks out to Mweenish Island or north to Moyrus and out to Mace Head. Back on the R340, it's a lovely journey north to Cashel (An Caiseal) and south again on the R341 to Roundstone. Cashel Equestrian Centre (☎ 095-31082), about 1.5km west of Cashel, has horses and Connemara ponies for hire and gives riding lessons (starting at £10 per hour).

Places to Stay
Camping The *Spiddal Caravan and Camping Park* (also signposted as Pairc

Saoire an Spidéil) is on the R336 coastal road 1.5km west of Spiddal. See Places to Stay in the Galway city section earlier in this chapter for details.

Carraroe Caravan and Camping Park (☎ 091-595266) is 1km south of Carraroe on the R343. It costs drivers £5/5.50 to pitch a small/large tent, plus £1.50 per adult; hikers and cyclists will pay £3 per person.

Hostels An Óige's *Inverin Hostel* (☎ 091-593154), by the R336 just west of Inverin (Indreabhán), has 50 dorm beds costing £7/5.50, and there are bikes for hire. A bed at the IHO *Connemara Tourist Hostel* (☎ 091-593104, Aillie) in Inverin costs £7. Both hostels open year round.

B&Bs There are plenty of B&Bs along the road between Spiddal and Roundstone. One that has been recommended as a relaxing place is *Col Mar House* (☎ 091-553247), 2km west of Spiddal, costing £18 per person.

Hotels There are some exclusive hotels tucked away out here; they're also good places to stop for a sandwich, drink or meal if you can rise to their prices. The lovely 28-room *Ballynahinch Castle Hotel* (☎ 095-31006), south-west of Recess, was formerly the home of Humanity Dick (1754–1834), a local landlord, MP and one of the chief forces behind the Royal Society for the Prevention of Cruelty to Animals (RSPCA). Ballynahinch Castle is well worth a visit even if it's just for a drink in the bar and a quick scout around the delightful grounds. A B&B double starts at £114.40.

Near Cashel, the 19-room *Zetland Country House Hotel* (☎ 095-31111) offers B&B starting at £55 per person, while *Cashel House Hotel* (☎ 095-31001), with 32 rooms, starts at £60.75 per person. It has a stable of Connemara ponies, and riding lessons are available.

The 22-room *Hotel Carraroe* (☎ 091-595116, Carraroe) – also called Óstán An Cheathrú Rua – is a bit more down to earth, with singles/doubles starting at £50/80.

ROUNDSTONE
☎ 095 • pop 280

The small fishing village of Roundstone (Cloch na Rón), 16km south-west of Recess on a western extension of Bertraghboy Bay, consists essentially of one main street of tall houses, shops and a couple of pubs overlooking the water. The small harbour is home to lobster boats and many a *cúrach* (currach), the featherweight rowing boat of black tar on hide or canvas laid over a wicker frame.

Just south of the centre is an Industrial Development Agency (IDA) **craft complex**, in Michael Killeen Park, with various small factory shops selling everything from teapots to sweaters. One of the more interesting shops is Roundstone Musical Instruments (☎ 35808), which makes and sells the *bodhrán*, the goatskin drum beloved of traditional Irish musicians, as well as tin whistles, harps and Irish flutes. It opens 9 am to 7 pm Monday to Saturday, year round, and has a branch open April to September in Clifden. Farther south and off the road to Ballyconneely (R341) are the magnificent **white beaches** of Gurteen (or Gorteen) Bay and Dog's Bay.

Looming behind the neat stone harbour is **Mt Errisbeg** (298m); it's the only significant hill along this section of coastline. There's a pleasant walk from Roundstone to the top: follow the small road past O'Dowd's pub in the centre of the village. From the summit there are wonderful views across the bay to the distant humps of the Twelve Bens.

Places to Stay
Gurteen Beach Caravan and Camping Park (☎ 35882), 2km west of town near the beach, costs £7 per person for hikers and cyclists. For B&B, Mrs Lowry's excellent *St Joseph's* (☎ 35865, Main St), overlooking the harbour, costs £25/36 for singles/doubles. It's almost worth coming to Roundstone just to stay at this friendly place; in summer it serves an excellent evening meal costing £12. *Roundstone House* (☎ 35864), a 13-room hotel on Main St, has good views over the bay to Connemara and costs £65 to £81 for doubles.

Places to Eat
Several pubs serve food. *O'Dowd's* (*Main St*) dishes up good food in the bar and in the restaurant, where half a dozen excellent fresh oysters cost £4.50. Nearby *Beola Restaurant* (☎ 35871) serves seafood costing £10 to £14. It opens for lunch and dinner. There's a small coffee shop in the *IDA craft complex* just outside the village, open all day.

WEST OF ROUNDSTONE
Some 12km west of Roundstone is **Ballyconneely**. If you detour south off the R341 towards the Connemara Golf Club, you pass the ruins of **Bunowen Castle** before reaching the shore at **Trá Mhóir** (Great Beach), a superb expanse of impossibly white sand.

OUGHTERARD
☎ 091 • pop 700

The small town of Oughterard (Uachtar Árd), 27km along the main road from Galway to Clifden, calls itself the 'Gateway to Connemara'. And sure enough, immediately west of town, the countryside opens to sweeping panoramas of lakes, mountain and bog that get more spectacular the farther west you travel.

Oughterard itself is a pleasant little town and one of Ireland's principal angling centres. It has a number of good cafés, pubs and restaurants as well as some fairly exclusive country-house establishments hidden in the surrounding countryside.

The focus of the anglers' attention is Lough Corrib (see the following section), just north of town. Nearby attractions include Aughanure Castle to the south-east and the lovely drive along the Glann Rd by Lough Corrib to a vantage point overlooking the Hill of Doon.

Information
The extremely helpful, locally run tourist office (☎ 552808) is on Main St. It opens from 9 am to 5.30 pm Monday to Saturday, and 10 am to 2 pm on Sunday, June; 9 am to 7 pm Monday to Saturday, and 10 am to 2 pm on Sunday, July and August; 9 am to

5.30 pm Monday to Saturday, September; and 9 am to 5.30 pm on weekdays, the rest of the year.

The Bank of Ireland, Main St, has an ATM and bureau de change. You can also change money at Fuschia Crafts, Main St, and Keogh & Sons Sweaters, Market Square. The post office is at the eastern end of Main St next to the Mace supermarket.

Aughanure Castle

Three kilometres east of Oughterard and off the main Galway road (N59) is the 16th-century O'Flaherty fortress, Aughanure Castle, built on the site of earlier structures. The clan controlled the region for hundreds of years after they fought off the Normans, and the 'fighting O'Flahertys' were constantly at odds with the forces of Galway. The six-storey tower house stands on a rocky outcrop overlooking Lough Corrib and has been extensively restored. Surrounding the castle are the remains of an unusual double bawn or perimeter fortification. Underneath the castle, the lake washes through a number of natural caverns and caves.

The Dúchas-run castle (☎ 552214) opens 9.30 am to 6.30 pm daily, mid-June to mid-September. Admission costs £2/1.

Places to Stay

Hostels The *Canrawer House Hostel* (☎ 552388) is at the Clifden end of town, just over 1km down a signposted turning. The bunk beds cost £9 (£9.50 with continental breakfast), five regular beds with their own bathroom cost £9.50, and the one double en suite room costs £20. *Camping* costs £5, which includes use of hostel facilities; the kitchen is big. You can also hire boats.

On Camp St is the IHH *Lough Corrib Hostel* (☎ 552866). From Market Square, turn north past the Lake Hotel, and it's about 200m along on the left. At the time of writing it was still operating but was up for sale.

B&Bs There are legions of B&Bs around Oughterard, but not many right in town.

One of the few is the *Jolly Lodger* (☎ 552682), in a stone house on Main St, where singles/doubles cost £20/32. B&B at *Woodlawn House* (☎ 550198), in Doon, Rosscahill, on the Galway side of Oughterard, starts at £23/32. Farther east of Oughterard and travelling towards Portacarron and the lake, you'll see plenty of signposts.

If you turn north at the main crossroads in Oughterard and travel 5km along Glann Rd towards the Hill of Doon, you come to the excellent *Glann House* (☎ 552127), starting at £20.50/32.

Hotels The *Corrib House Hotel* (☎ 552329, Bridge St) is a comfortable old hotel with 26 rooms costing £27.50 to £40 per person. *Currarevagh House* (☎ 552312) is a 19th-century mansion just outside Oughterard on the shore of Lough Corrib and is renowned for its exquisite evening meals (£20) and quality accommodation. Rooms cost £48.50 to £58 per person; it opens April to mid-October. It's difficult to think of a more romantic place anywhere.

Places to Eat

On Main St, *Village Restaurant* is an excellent low- to medium-priced restaurant with very good coffee, lunches and dinners (when main courses cost from £9 to £12). *O'Fatharta*, farther east on Main St, is another cosy coffee-shop-cum-restaurant. For good pub food and meals, try *Boat Inn* on Market Square; steak in the restaurant costs £13.95.

Keogh's Bar, on the square, also does reasonable pub food; bacon and cabbage costs £4.50. At the western end of Main St is the upmarket *Waterlily*, right on the river and near the bridge.

Nearby is the *Corrib House Hotel*, where roast chicken in the restaurant costs £7.95. Dinner main courses at the *Lake Hotel* (☎ 552794) cost £9 to £13.

Entertainment

Many of the pubs have music, including *Faherty's*, next to the Lake Hotel, and *Boat Inn* and *Keogh's Bar* on the square.

Walker's paradise: the ruggedly beautiful Maumturk Mountains, Connemara, County Galway

A cow contemplates the view in Connemara, County Galway.

Galway hookers (traditional boats) are a typical sight along the coast of Connemara.

A deserted cottage on Inishmór, one of the Aran Islands, where Irish is the native tongue

Rush hour on Inishmór, County Galway

Inishmaan, Aran Islands, County Galway

Getting There & Away

From Oughterard you can catch boats to Inchagoill Island (see the following section).

LOUGH CORRIB

The Republic's largest lake, Lough Corrib is over 48km long and covers some 200 sq km. It virtually cuts off western Galway from the rest of the country and has over 360 islands. On the largest one, Inchagoill, there's a monastic settlement that can be visited from Oughterard or Cong.

Lough Corrib is world famous for its salmon, sea trout and brown trout, and the area attracts legions of anglers from all over the world in season. The highlight of the **fishing** year is the mayfly season, when zillions of the small lacy bugs hatch over a few days (usually in May) and drive the fish and anglers into a feeding and fishing frenzy. The hooks are baited with live flies, which join their cousins dancing on the surface of the lake. The main run of salmon does not begin until June. The owner of Canrawer House Hostel in Oughterard is a good contact for information and boat hire. You can buy fishing supplies from Thomas Tuck (☎ 091-552335) on Main St in Oughterard.

Inchagoill Island

The largest island on Lough Corrib and some 7km north-west of Oughterard, Inchagoill is a lonely place hiding many ancient remains. Most fascinating is an obelisk called the **Lia Luguaedon Mac Menueh** (Stone of Luguaedon, Son of Menueh) marking a burial site. It stands some 75cm tall near the Saints' Church, and some people claim that the Latin writing on the stone is the oldest Christian inscription in Europe apart from those in the catacombs in Rome. It certainly is the oldest Latin inscription in Ireland.

Teampall Phádraig (St Patrick's Church) is a small oratory of a very early design with some later additions. The prettiest church is the Romanesque **Teampall na Naoimh** (Saints' Church), probably built in the 9th or 10th century. There are carvings around the arched doorway.

The island can be reached by boat from Oughterard (or Cong in County Mayo). April to October, Corrib Cruises (☎ 091-82644) sails from Oughterard to Inchagoill Island (£8/4) and on to Cong (£12/5). Departures are at 11 am and 2.45 and 5 pm.

MAAM CROSS TO LEENANE

West of Oughterard, **Maam Cross** (Crois Mám) is the first settlement along the Clifden road (N59). By the turn-off for Leenane, *Peacocke's* (☎ 091-552306) is a huge tourist complex complete with bar, shops, restaurant and petrol station. There's also a tacky model donkey and a replica Irish cottage from *The Quiet Man* film, where crafts can be bought. The trip to Leenane is lovely, but if you have only one run through the region it's better to stay on the Clifden road and turn north onto the R344 into the **Lough Inagh Valley** instead. It's also a pleasant journey south towards **Screeb** and the coast.

LEENANE

☎ 095 • pop 50

Leenane's name in Irish, An Líonán, means 'ravine', referring to the way the sea edges its way into narrow, fjord-like Killary Harbour. Leenane itself makes a convenient stopover on the way north, and the road north-west to Louisburgh via Delphi is startlingly beautiful. Like Cong in County Mayo, the village can boast a film connection, having been the location for *The Field*, which was shot in 1989. It is based on John B Keane's poignant play about a tenant farmer's ill-fated plans to pass on a rented piece of land to his son. The dance and pub scenes were filmed in the village and the church scene at nearby Aasleagh. The village's name has also made it on the literary map with the success in London and New York of young dramatist Martin McDonagh's play *The Beauty Queen of Leenane*. There's no bank but there is a post office with a bureau de change.

The **Sheep and Wool Museum** in the Leenane Cultural Centre (☎ 42323), over the bridge from the centre, focuses on the woollen industry and gives demonstrations of carding, spinning and weaving, with a 15-minute video every half-hour which sets the historical and social scene. Admission costs £2/1. Locally made woollen garments are on sale, and there's a coffee shop that serves dinner in the evening.

There are several excellent walks from Leenane, including one to **Aasleagh Waterfall** at the eastern end of Killary Harbour.

In the centre, *Village Grill* is a good choice for snacks; breakfast costs £4. Pub food is available at *Gaynor's* and *Hamilton's* in the centre or at the *Carraig Bar*, about 1km north-east of Leenane just before the Mayo border.

The turn-off to Delphi, in County Mayo (see the Counties Mayo & Sligo chapter), is to the left shortly after you cross over the county border.

RECESS & AROUND
☎ 095

Recess (Straith Salach), on the N59 between Clifden and Maam Cross, is nothing more than a few houses and Joyce's Craft Shop. Turning north about 2km west of here brings you onto the R344, which will take you through the wonderful Lough Inagh Valley. If you continue along the main road (N59) towards Clifden instead, there are some marvellous views over **Lough Derryclare** and **Pine Island**. The grassy lay-by overlooking the island is an excellent *place to camp*. About 1km west of here off the Clifden road is a dead-end road heading north into a great valley enclosed by a ring of six of the **Twelve Bens**. It's a beautiful drive up this road, and there's a challenging circuit hike of the six peaks.

Back on the main Clifden road and another 1km west is the An Óige *Ben Lettery Hostel* (☎ 51136). It's an excellent, popular base to explore the Twelve Bens and makes a good starting or finishing point for the walk mentioned previously. The hostel, 8km west of Recess, 13km east of Clifden, opens Easter to September. Beds cost £7/5.50.

Lough Inagh Valley
The journey north along the Lough Inagh Valley is one of the most scenic in the coun-

try. There are two fine approaches up valleys from the south, starting on either side of Recess, and the long sweep of Derryclare and Inagh Loughs accompanies you for most of the way. On the western side are the brooding Twelve Bens, while just beyond the valley on the northern side is the picturesque drive beside Kylemore Lake.

About 7km up the Inagh Valley is the atmospheric, Victorian *Lough Inagh Lodge* (☎ 34706), an upmarket country-house hotel where singles/doubles start at £87/124 (including breakfast) in high season. It's a worthwhile place to stop for a snack, particularly in good weather. The location is magnificent and there's a path in front of the lodge down to the lake.

Towards the northern end of the valley, a track leads off the road west up a blind valley, which is also well worth exploring.

Kylemore Abbey & Lake
About 17km north-east of Clifden and just outside the northern end of the beautiful Lough Inagh Valley is the almost equally scenic Kylemore Lake and its accompanying abbey. The road skirts the northern shore of the lake, winding through overhanging trees, with magnificent views across the silent lake. South of the lake are the Twelve Bens and Connemara National Park, while the mountains behind the abbey are Dúchruach (530m) and Binn Fhraoigh (545m).

The lake passes under the road and extends to the north, where you will see the castellated towers of the 19th-century neo-Gothic Kylemore Abbey among the trees. The abbey was built for a wealthy English businessman, Mitchell Henry, after he had spent his honeymoon in Connemara and had fallen in love with the region. During WWI, a group of Benedictine nuns left Ypres in Belgium and eventually set up in Kylemore, turning the place into an abbey.

Today, the nuns run an exclusive convent boarding school. Some sections are open to the public 9 am to 5 pm daily, March to October; and 10 am to 4 pm daily, November to February. There's also a craft shop and tearoom here.

You can walk up behind the abbey to a statue overlooking Kylemore Lake. A short walk beside the lake from the abbey is the restored neo-Gothic **Memorial Church** (1868).

CLIFDEN
☎ 095 • pop 800

Clifden (An Clochán), the capital of Connemara, is some 80km west of Galway at the head of narrow Clifden Bay. Astride the Owenglin River, the tightly packed houses and the needle-sharp spires of the town's churches are shadowed by the steep Twelve Bens to the east. A landlord, John D'Arcy, was the main force behind the establishment of the town around 1812, but the Famine ruined the family, and their estate along The Sky Road is now deserted.

Information

The tourist office (☎ 21163) is at the bottom of Market St. It opens 9.30 am to 5.30 pm Monday to Saturday, mid-April to September. At other times inquire at the Connemara Walking Centre (☎ 21379) at Island House on Market St closer to the square. There's a Bank of Ireland branch down from the square and an AIB branch on the square; both have ATMs. The post office is on Main St, just up from the square, where you'll also find a laundrette, the Shamrock Washeteria.

Activities

There are superb **cycling** possibilities. All you need to plan your tour of the area is Map 31 in the OS Discovery Series. Connemara Walking Centre (see Information earlier) runs guided **walking** trips to local geographical- and natural-interest sites. A day walk costs £15; longer walks are available. The centre also sells maps. See the following Around Clifden section for good local walks and cycle routes.

Errislannan Riding Centre (☎ 21134), about 3.5km south on the Ballyconneely road (R341), has Connemara ponies for hire (£15 per hour) for **riding** along the beach and up into the hills. Lessons are available.

Places to Stay
Camping & Hostels The IHH *Clifden Town Hostel* (☎ 21076) is in the centre of town on Market St and charges £9 for dorm beds and £10 per person in one of three private rooms.

Leo's Hostel (☎ 21429), belonging to both the IHH and IHO, is near the square. It charges £8 for dorm beds in high season, £20 for private rooms, and also has camping space. Both hostels open year round. The IHH/IHO *Brookside Hostel* (☎ 21812), down by the Owenglin River in a quiet location on Hulk St, costs £8 for dorm beds, £18 for private rooms. It opens March to October.

B&Bs & Hotels In town, *Kingstown House* (☎ 21470, Bridge St) costs £16 to £18 per person. Many B&Bs are to the south on the Ballyconneely road (R341). One kilometre from Clifden and signposted off the road is *Mallmore House* (☎ 21460), where B&B costs £20 per person. *Actons* (☎ 44339), at Claddaghduff to the north-east, has been warmly recommended. Singles/doubles start at £30/50.

Barry's Hotel (☎ 21287, Main St), with 18 rooms, costs £30 per person June to September, while B&B at the 19-room *Alcock & Brown Hotel* (☎ 21206), in the town centre, costs £37. A more upmarket choice is *Foyle's* (☎ 21801), also on Main St. From June to August its 28 rooms cost £50 per person; it closes November to March.

Places to Eat
EJ Kings, on the square, serves pub food year round, with the entrance to its more formal restaurant round the corner on Market St. The food is good and reasonably priced; Irish stew costs £8.50 in the restaurant. The *D'Arcy Inn* (*Main St*), opposite Barry's Hotel, serves similar fare, with the accent on seafood; bar meals cost under £7.

Salmon Leap Seafood Restaurant three doors away offers salmon main courses starting at £9.50. *O'Grady's Seafood Restaurant* (☎ 21450, Market St), a sister restaurant to the highly recommended Kirwan's Lane Creative Cuisine in Galway, is one of the best restaurants in western County Galway and opens for lunch and dinner until 10 pm Monday to Saturday. Fresh mussels at lunchtime cost £6.95. *Fogerty's (☎ 21427, Market St)* is also worth trying, especially for its set dinner (£19.50).

For snacks during the day try *Cullens (Market St)*, which becomes a more formal restaurant in the evening, when its chicken kiev costs £7.50.

Shopping
Makers of the *bodhrán*, Roundstone Musical Instruments (☎ 21516) has a branch next to the Salmon Leap restaurant on Main St. It opens April to September.

Getting There & Away
The bus stop is outside Cullen's on Market St. For information phone the bus station in Galway (☎ 091-562000). Buses run between Galway and Clifden and Westport via Oughterard and Maam Cross or via Cong and Leenane. For more details, see the introductory Getting There & Away entry to this Connemara section.

From June to September, Michael Nee Coaches (☎ 51082) runs between Clifden (from the square) and Galway up to three times daily. Three daily buses (at 11.15 am and 1.35 and 5.45 pm) also leave Clifden for Cleggan, from where the ferry sails to Inishbofin and Inishturk islands.

Getting Around
John Mannion (☎ 21160, 21155), on Railway View off Main St, is a Raleigh agent and hires out bicycles, as do the Clifden Town and Leo's Hostels.

AROUND CLIFDEN
The road south of Clifden (R341) passes the fine beach at **Mannin Bay** on its way to **Ballyconneely**. Heading directly west from Clifden, **The Sky Road** takes you on a loop out to a townland known as Kingston and back to Clifden through some rugged, stunningly beautiful coastal scenery. The round trip of about 12km can easily be walked or cycled.

The deeply indented coastline farther north brings you to the tiny village of **Claddaghduff**, which is signposted off the road to Cleggan. At Claddaghduff the clifftop *Acton's Restaurant (☎ 095-44339)* serves good food, and exhilarating views of the Atlantic are thrown in. It opens Tuesday to Sunday, late May to late September. Turning west here down by the Catholic church you come out on **Omey Strand**, and at low tide you can drive or walk across the sand to **Omey Island**, a low islet of rock, grass and sand with a few houses for the island's population of 20. During the summer horse races are held on Omey Strand.

CLEGGAN
☎ 095

Cleggan (An Cloiggean) is a small fishing village 16km north-west of Clifden. Many visitors pass through en route to Inishbofin Island. The village has a post office but no bank. If you need to stay here there are a few B&Bs in and around Cleggan, including *Harbour House (☎ 44702)*, where singles/doubles cost £24.50/36. The village has several pubs. *Oliver's* and *Joyce's* serve bar food, while *Newman's* dishes up music on Sunday.

Getting There & Away
See Clifden and the introductory Getting There & Away entry to this Connemara section for information on buses. Cleggan is the departure point for boats to Inishbofin Island (see the following entry). Boats also leave here for Inishturk Island; for more details see that section in the Mayo & Sligo chapter.

INISHBOFIN ISLAND
☎ 095 • pop 200

Inishbofin Island, some 9km out in the Atlantic from Cleggan, is a haven of tranquillity. It consists of some of the oldest rocks in Ireland, and the **birdlife** includes corncrake, chough, corn bunting and a variety of sea birds. It's compact – 6km long by 3km wide – and the highest point is a mere 86m above sea level. Good sheltered beaches, open grasslands, quiet lanes and a strong sense of isolation make Inishbofin special. Just off the northern beach is **Lough Bó Finne**, from which the island gets its name. '*Bó finne*' means 'white cow'

History

Inishbofin's main historical figure of note was St Colman, who at one stage was a bishop in England. He fell out with the English Church in 664 over its adoption of a new calendar, and exiled himself to Inishbofin, where he set up a monastery. Northeast of the harbour is a small 13th-century **church and hollowed stone**, or '*bullaun*', which are said to occupy the site of Colman's original monastery.

Grace O'Malley, the famous pirate queen who was based on Clare Island, used Inishbofin as a base in the 16th century.

Cromwell's forces captured Inishbofin in 1652 and built a star-shaped prison for priests and clerics. Many died or were killed, and one bishop was reputedly chained to Bishop's Rock near the harbour and drowned as the tide came in.

Information

Inishbofin's small post office has a grocery shop as well as a currency-exchange facility. Pubs and hotels will usually change travellers cheques. For walking tours of Inishbofin, contact Island House (☎ 21379) in Clifden.

Places to Stay & Eat

You can pitch a tent on most unfenced ground and near the beaches. The IHH **Inishbofin Island Hostel** (☎ 45855), a fine hostel 500m up from the harbour, opens April to October. Dorm beds cost £7 and doubles cost £20. *Camping* is also available.

For B&B try **Hybrazil** (☎ 45817), which has four singles/doubles with shared bathroom costing £20/34; it opens from May to October.

The modern, comfortable **Day's Hotel** (☎ 45803), open April to October, has turf fires and a dining room looking out over the sea. Rooms start at £30 per person. The food is creative, with excellent fresh fish;

Legend of Inishbofin Island

According to legend, Inishbofin Island was once permanently enveloped in a thick blanket of fog. Some fishermen came upon the island and lit a fire near the lake – and immediately the mist began to clear. Emerging from the mist was a woman with a long stick driving a white cow (*bó finne*) in front of her. She hit the white cow with the stick, turning it to stone. Irritated at such behaviour, the fishermen grabbed the stick and struck her, upon which she also turned to stone.

Until the late 19th century, two white stones stood by the lake: the 'remains' of the cow and its owner.

main courses cost £12 to £14. *Day's Pub*, next door, serves up bar food and a lively atmosphere. The family-run *Doonmore Hotel* (☎ 45804) offers B&B starting at £22 per person. Seafood is the speciality; dinner costs around £18.

Getting There & Away

The *Queen* leaves Cleggan for Inishbofin at 11.30 am and 6.45 pm, April to October, with an additional sailing at 2 pm, June to August. It departs Inishbofin at 9 am and 5 pm (plus an extra sailing at 1 pm, June to August). The fare is £12 return (bikes go free), and the trip takes 45 minutes. Ring ☎ 44642 for details.

You can also take the smaller, less comfortable but cheaper *Dun Aengus* mailboat; buy your ticket (£10 return) from the kiosk on the pier. Call ☎ 44750 or ☎ 45806 for details.

LETTERFRACK
☎ 095

Letterfrack (Leitir Fraic), founded by the Quakers in the mid-19th century, is some 15km north-east of Clifden on the N59. It lies at the head of Ballynakill Harbour, but the sea is visible only from west of the crossroads and from the entrance to Connemara National Park. The village is barely

GALWAY

more than a crossroads with a few pubs and B&Bs. *Veldon's* serves good bar food.

The small IHH *Old Monastery* hostel (☎ *41132*), open year round, is recommended because of its free breakfast, friendliness, and £7.50 optional vegetarian evening meal. There are also bikes for hire, and *camping* (£4) is possible, so it's worth considering as a base for visiting Connemara National Park, which is literally next door. Dorm beds cost £7.50; one of the four private rooms costs £10 per person.

In July and August, Bus Éireann (☎ 091-562000) buses run once daily Monday to Saturday from Clifden; the rest of the year they operate twice a week.

CONNEMARA NATIONAL PARK

Connemara National Park, which is managed by Dúchas, covers 2000 hectares of bog, mountain and heath south-east of Letterfrack. The headquarters and visitor centre (☎ 095-41054) are housed in pleasant old buildings just south of the crossroads in Letterfrack. The park remains open until dusk.

The park encloses a number of the **Twelve Bens**, including Bencullagh, Benbrack and Benbaun. The heart of the park is **Gleann Mór** (Big Glen), through which flows the River Polladirk. There's fine walking up the glen and over the surrounding mountains.

The **visitor centre** will give you an insight into the park's flora, fauna and geology, as well as showing maps and various trails. Bog biology and the video *Man and the Landscape* are interesting, so wandering around is not a waste of time. It has an indoor eating area and rudimentary kitchen facilities for walkers.

The centre opens 10 am to 5.30 pm daily, April, May and September; 10 am to 6.30 pm daily, June; and 9.30 am to 6.30 pm daily, July and August. Admission costs £2/1.

There are usually guided **nature walks** on Monday, Wednesday and Friday in July and August, leaving the centre at 10.30 am and taking two to three hours. Bring good boots ('knee-high ones', one reader recommended) and rainwear. There are also short, self-guided walks. If the Bens look too daunting, you can hike up Diamond Hill nearby.

NORTH OF LETTERFRACK

There's some fine scenery along the coast north of Letterfrack, especially from Tully Cross east to Lettergesh and Salruck, home to the Little Killary Adventure Centre.

North of Letterfrack you first come to **Tully Cross** (Tulna Croise), which has a line of neat, thatched holiday cottages for rent and some nice little pubs.

Just short of Salruck is **Glassillaun Beach**, a breathtaking expanse of pure white sand. There are other fine beaches, at Gurteen and at Lettergesh, where the beach horse-racing sequences for John Ford's 1952 film *The Quiet Man* were shot.

Things to See & Do

There are fine **walks** all along the coast and around Renvyle Point to Derryinver Bay. There's an excellent hill walk, which takes four to five hours each way, from the post office at Lettergesh up Binn Chuanna and Maolchnoc and then down to Lough Fee.

Focusing on the sea and marine life, **Oceans Alive** (☎ 095-43473) is an aquarium and museum complex on Derryinver Bay. It opens 10 am to 7.30 pm daily, May to August; and 10 am to 5 pm daily, the rest of the year. To get there from Letterfrack head north to Tully Cross and turn northwest for Renvyle. Oceans Alive is 2.5km beyond Renvyle.

For **sea trips or deep-sea angling** on the MV *Queen of Connemara*, contact John or Phil Mongan at Oceans Alive; for **horse trekking** contact Joe O'Neill (☎ 095-42269).

The **Little Killary Adventure Centre** (☎ 095-43411), in a valley near Salruck, is a well-run place offering B&B accommodation costing £13 per person, plus courses in canoeing, sea kayaking, sailing, rock climbing, and just about every other adventure sport you can think of. It's scheduled to move to a new site near Leenane, so call ahead. The Web site is www.killary.com.

On Glassillaun Beach to the north-east is **Scuba Dive West** (☎ 095-43922), offering courses and diving on the surrounding coast and islands.

Places to Stay
Camping The *Renvyle Beach Caravan and Camping* (☎ 095-43462), open mid-March to September, is west of Tully and costs £7 to £8 for tents or £3 per hiker or cyclist. East of Tully Cross near Lettergesh Beach is *Connemara Caravan and Camping Park* (☎ 095-43406). It costs £8 to pitch a two-person tent here (hikers £4), and each extra adult/child costs £4/1. The site opens May to September.

Hostels The An Óige *Killary Harbour Hostel* (☎ 095-43417), 13km north-east of Tully Cross on Rosroe Quay, 8km off the N59, costs £7/5.50 and opens March to September. The Austrian philosopher Ludwig Wittgenstein (1889–1951) stayed here for seven months in 1948. Some food and supplies are available at the hostel, but the nearest shop is 5km away in Lettergesh, so stock up in advance. There's a fine hike from the hostel along an old road by the fjord to Leenane.

Hotels The 56-room *Renvyle House Hotel* (☎ 095-43511) is a converted country house in Renvyle and was once owned by the poet Oliver St John Gogarty. It's the best place in the area to have a drink or snack or to relax after a walk, but staying here would destroy most travellers' budgets: singles/doubles cost £100/160, but there are special rates throughout the year.

Overlooking the ocean and open year round, the long-established *Sunnymeade* (☎ 095-43491) offers B&B at a much more down-to-earth £24.50/36.

Getting There & Away
Bus Éireann (☎ 091-562000) bus No 420 runs Monday to Saturday year round between Galway and Clifden, calling at Cong, Leenane, Salruck, Lettergesh, Tully Church, Kylemore, Letterfrack, Cleggan and Claddaghduff en route.

KILLARY HARBOUR & AROUND
Mussel rafts dot long, narrow Killary Harbour, which looks like a fjord but may not actually have been glaciated. It's 16km long and over 45m deep in the centre, and has a superb anchorage. **Mt Mweelrea** (819m) towers over its northern shores. From Leenane at the south-eastern end of the harbour, the road west for about 2km along the southern shore before veering inland. However, you can continue **walking** along the shore to Rosroe Quay on an old road.

County Mayo begins just north-east of Leenane, and there is magnificent scenery around the northern side of Killary Harbour and up the R335 to Delphi and into the Doolough Valley, one of the most scenic in the country.

Aran Islands

The same stretch of limestone that created County Clare's Burren region surfaces in the middle of Galway Bay to form the three Aran Islands (Oileáin Árainn): Inishmór, Inishmaan and Inisheer. The islands are like one long, undulating reef, with no significant hills or mountains – although, on the western side of Inishmór and Inishmaan, the land rises high enough to create some very dramatic cliffs over the Atlantic. As in the Burren, the limestone and, below that, the older bluestone create a spectacular moonscape: sheets of grey and grey-blue rock with flowers and grass bursting from the cracks.

Even the smallest patches of rocky land are bordered by stone walls. Over the centuries, tonnes of seaweed were brought up from the beaches, mixed with sand and laid out on the bare rock to start walls. The walls may be hundreds or even thousands of years old, so have respect for them and replace any stones you dislodge. On Inishmaan and Inisheer many of the walls are up to eye level, and it's a joy to walk for hours along the sandy lanes between them. The odd-looking seaweed you will see drying atop the stone walls on the islands is sea rod collected at low tide. It's sent to the mainland, where it's used in the production of certain cosmetics. A tonne of the slimy stuff earns the collector about £150.

The islands are major tourist attractions, with quick, convenient travel connections to the mainland, a plethora of B&B and hostel accommodation, and a veritable armada of bicycles to hire. Inishmór – the largest of the three – is exceedingly busy during the summer, with armies of day trippers and shuttle buses all over the island. At the busiest times, the 100 or so licensed vehicles on Inishmór get locked in traffic jams in the lanes!

If you have the time, try to get to the smaller islands, particularly Inishmaan – the least visited – and allow yourself a few days for exploration. Inisheer is the smallest and closest to land, just 8km from Doolin, in County Clare.

You can change money on the islands but banking facilities are limited and there are no ATMs.

HISTORY

The islands have some of the most ancient pre-Christian and Christian remains in Ireland. Farming was once much easier to pursue here than on the densely forested mainland. The most significant ruins on the islands are massive Iron Age stone forts, such as Dún Aengus on Inishmór and Dún Chonchúir on Inishmaan. Almost nothing is known about the people who built these structures, partly because their iron implements quickly rusted away. In folklore, the forts are said to have been built by the Firbolgs, a Celtic tribe who invaded Ireland from Europe in prehistoric times.

Christianity reached the islands remarkably quickly, and some of the earliest monastic settlements were founded by St Enda (Éanna) in the 5th century. Any remains you see today are later, from the 8th century onwards. Enda appears to have been an Irish chief who converted to Christianity and spent some time studying in Rome before seeking out a suitably remote spot for his monastery. Many great monks studied under him on Aran, including Colmcille (or Columba), who went on to found the monastery on Iona in Scotland.

From the 14th century on, control of the islands was disputed by two Gaelic families, the O'Briens and the O'Flahertys. During the reign of Elizabeth I, the English took control, and in Cromwell's times a garrison was stationed here.

As Galway's importance waned, so too did that of the islands. They became a quiet and windy backwater. The islands' isolation allowed Irish culture to survive when it had all but disappeared elsewhere. Irish is still very much the native tongue, and until around the 1930s people wore traditional Aran dress: bright-red skirts and black shawls for women, baggy woollen trousers and waistcoats with a colourful belt (or *crios*) for men. The classic white sweater knitted in complex patterns originated here. You may still see old people wearing some elements of traditional dress, particularly on Inishmaan. The other Aran trademark is the currach (a boat made of waterproofed hide or canvas).

BOOKS & MAPS

The elemental nature of life on the islands has always attracted writers and artists. The dramatist John Millington Synge (1871–1909) spent a lot of time on the islands, and his play *Riders to the Sea* (1905) is set on Inishmaan. His book *The Aran Islands* (1907) is the classic account of life here and is readily available in paperback. The American Robert Flaherty came to the islands in 1934 to shoot *Man of Aran*, a dramatic account of daily life. It became a classic and there are regular screenings of it in Kilronan on Inishmór. The islands have produced their own talent, particularly the writer Liam O'Flaherty (1896–1984) from Inishmór. O'Flaherty, who wandered around North and South America before returning to Ireland in 1921 and fighting in the Civil War, wrote several outstanding novels, including *Famine*.

The mapmaker Tim Robinson has written a wonderful, though not easily accessible, two-volume account of his explorations on Aran called *Stones of Aran: Pilgrimage* and

Stones of Aran: Labyrinthe (Penguin). His *The Aran Islands: A Map and Guide* (£5, or £10 with a Companion Guide) is superb. Two other excellent publications in paperback are *The Book of Aran*, edited by Anne Korf and published by Tír Eolas (£15.95), consisting of articles by 17 specialists covering diverse aspects of the islands' culture, and *Aran Reader* (Lilliput Press, £15.95), with essays on the islands' history, geography, culture, and so on, by various scholars.

GETTING THERE & AWAY
Air
If time is important or seasickness on the often rough Atlantic a concern, you can fly to the islands with Aer Árann (☎ 091-593034). The mainland departure point is Connemara regional airport at Minna, near Inverin, 38km west of Galway. A connecting bus from outside the Galway and Salthill tourist offices costs £2.50 one way. The return flight to the islands costs £35/29/20 for adults/students/children (aged 12 and under); for £29 you can fly one way and take the ferry the other. Flights operate to all three islands four times daily (hourly in summer) and take less than 10 minutes.

Boat
Only one big ferry line makes the run to the islands daily year round. Island Ferries' services from Rossaveal, 37km west of Galway, are popular because the crossing is quick (about 40 minutes) and there are frequent sailings. The ferries operate up to six times daily in summer (two or three times daily in winter), costing £15/8 (students £12) return. The return Galway to Rossaveal bus trip costs £4/3/2 and leaves the Island Ferries Galway office (☎ 091-568903) off Victoria Place opposite the tourist office one hour 30 minutes before the scheduled departure. If you have a car you can leave it free in the car park near the Island Ferries Rossaveal office (☎ 091-561767).

From June to September, Island Ferries also operates direct services from Galway to Inishmór costing £18/10 (students £15) return for the 46km trip (one hour 30

minutes). There are usually two daily sailings in July and August, and one daily in June and September.

O'Brien Shipping (☎ 091-567676) operates a cargo boat service that takes passengers to Inishmór daily year round and four times weekly to Inishmaan and Inisheer. The boat usually departs from the Galway docks at 10.30 am. O'Brien Shipping has a desk in the Galway tourist office in summer.

Doolin Ferries (☎ 065-74455) operates a service (April to September) from Doolin to Inisheer and (May to August) to Inishmór. It's only 8km to Inisheer, taking about 30 minutes and costing £15 return. See the Doolin section in the County Clare chapter for more details.

GETTING AROUND
The islands of Inisheer and Inishmaan are small enough to explore on foot, but to see larger Inishmór, bikes are the way to go. You can also arrange transport on Inishmór with any of the small tour vans or pony traps (see Getting Around in the Inishmór section later in this chapter).

Inter-island services are run by Island Ferries (☎ 091-561767). From May to September, according to demand, one to four Rossaveal to Inishmór boats daily continue to Inishmaan and Inisheer, but from October to March there are only about three weekly.

INISHMÓR
☎ 099 • pop 900
Inishmór (Big Island), or just Árainn in Irish, the largest of the three islands, slopes upwards from its comparatively sheltered northern shores to the southern edge, then plummets straight into the tumultuous Atlantic Ocean. After climbing the hill west of Kilronan, the island's capital, all you can see is rock, stone walls and boulders, scattered buildings and the odd patch of deepgreen grass and potato plants.

Orientation
Inishmór is 14.5km long and a maximum 4km wide, running north-west to south-east. All ferries and boats arrive and depart from

Kilronan (Cill Rónáin) on Cill Éinne Bay on the south-eastern side of the island. The airstrip is 2km farther south-east, on the other side of the bay, and faces Kilronan. One principal road runs the length of the island, with many smaller lanes and paths of packed dirt and stone leading off it.

Information

The small tourist office (☎ 61263), on the waterfront west of the ferry pier in Kilronan, opens 10 am to 5 pm daily, April to mid-September. At other times, the Inishmore Island Co-operative (☎ 61354) is your best bet for information. The Bank of Ireland north of the centre opens Wednesday only, but the post office nearby, the Ionad Árann (Aran Heritage Centre) and many shops change money.

Things to See

You'll get a better appreciation of your trip if you first visit Ionad Árann (☎ 61355), just off the main road leading out of Kilronan. It offers a useful introduction to the geology, wildlife, history and culture of the three islands. Robert O'Flaherty's 1934 film, *Man of Aran*, is screened here regularly (£2.50). The centre opens 10 am to 5 pm (7 pm June to August) daily, April to October. Admission costs £2.50/1.50. It also has a coffee shop.

Inishmór has three impressive stone forts, probably about 2000 years old. Two-thirds of the way down the island from Kilronan and perched on the edge of the sheer southern cliff, **Dún Aengus** is one of the most amazing archaeological sites in the country. It has a remarkable *chevaux de frise*, a defensive forest of sharp stone spikes around the exterior of the fort to help stop any would-be attackers.

Dún Aengus is a magical place and shouldn't be missed: you won't forget the sight and sound of wild swells pounding the cliff face. Try to go at a quieter time, such as late evening, when there are fewer visitors. Be *very* careful when approaching the cliffs. There are no guard rails and the winds can be strong; tourists have been blown off and killed on the rock shelf below.

Aengus, King of the Firbolgs

Folklore suggests that Aengus was a king of the Firbolgs, a legendary Celtic tribe from Europe who are said to have retreated to Aran and built the stone forts after falling out with the mainland chiefs. Other sources say that he was a 5th-century Irish chief and pupil of St Enda, the islands' most important saint.

Halfway between Kilronan and Dún Aengus is the smaller **Dún Eochla**, a perfectly circular ring fort. Directly south of Kilronan and dramatically perched on a promontory is **Dún Dúchathair**. It's surrounded on three sides by cliffs and is less visited than Dún Aengus.

The ruins of numerous stone churches trace the island's monastic history. The small **Teampall Chiaráin** (Church of St Kieran), with a high cross in the churchyard, is near Kilronan. To the south-east, near Cill Éinne Bay, is the early-Christian **Teampall Bheanáin** (Church of St Benen). Past Kilmurvey is the perfect **Clochán na Carraige**, an early-Christian stone hut which stands 2.5m tall, and the ruins of various small early-Christian remains known rather inaccurately as the **Na Seacht dTeampaill** (Seven Churches), consisting of a couple of ruined churches, monastic houses and some fragments of a high cross from the 8th or 9th century. To the south is **Dún Eoghanachta**, another circular fort. Near the airstrip are the sunken remains of a church said to be the site of **St Enda's Monastery** in the 5th century.

There's a fine beach at **Kilmurvey**, west of Kilronan, and it's pleasant to stay here away from the 'bustle' of Kilronan. Before the beach, in the sheltered little bay of **Port Chorrúch**, up to 50 grey seals make their home, sunning and feeding in the shallows.

Places to Stay

Camping The *Inishmór Camp Site* (☎ 61185) occupies a fine setting near the beach in Mainistir, almost 2km north-west

INISHMÓR

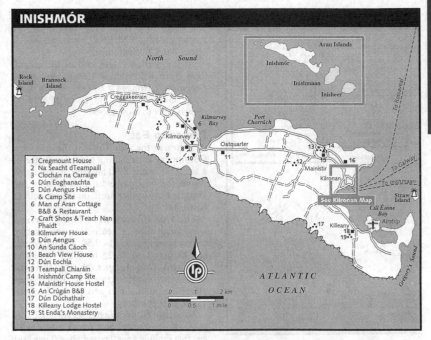

1 Cregmount House
2 Na Seacht dTeampaill
3 Clochán na Carraige
4 Dún Eoghanachta
5 Dún Aengus Hostel
  & Camp Site
6 Man of Aran Cottage
  B&B & Restaurant
7 Craft Shops & Teach Nan
  Phaidt
8 Kilmurvey House
9 Dún Aengus
10 An Sunda Cáoch
11 Beach View House
12 Dún Eochla
13 Teampall Chiaráin
14 Inishmór Camp Site
15 Mainistir House Hostel
16 An Crúgán B&B
17 Dún Dúchathair
18 Killeany Lodge Hostel
19 St Enda's Monastery

of Kilronan and about a 30-minute walk from the pier. Facilities are basic, and cost £2 per person. The *Dún Aengus Hostel* (☎ 61318) has a camp site costing £2.50 per person, which includes use of the hostel's facilities (see Hostels below).

Hostels Clean *Kilronan Hostel* (☎ 61255), only a short walk from the pier and above Tí Joe Mac's pub, offers beds in dorms (which are all en suite) costing £8 to £9. It provides bike hire, and residents can store their luggage here. *St Kevin's Hostel* (☎ 61484), between Tí Joe Mac's and the Spar supermarket, opens in summer only and costs £8 per bed.

The small and basic *Aharla Hostel* (☎ 61305), in Kilronan just off the road leading to Kilmurvey, has two rooms with four beds each that cost £7 per person.

North-west of Kilronan, at the IHO *Mainistir House Hostel* (☎ 61169) dorm beds cost £7.50 to £8.50 and doubles cost £24, including a breakfast of porridge and scones. The hostel runs a van to meet guests at the ferry pier.

Dún Aengus Hostel (☎ 61318) is near the beach on the western side of Kilmurvey Bay some 7km from Kilronan. This is a pleasant country house costing £7 per night, and there's free pick-up and delivery from/to the ferry.

South-east of Kilronan, the small IHO *Killeany Lodge Hostel* (☎ 61393) has 14 beds costing £5 per person. It opens March to October.

B&Bs The numerous B&Bs in and around Kilronan include the large, friendly *Dormer House* (☎ 61125) behind Tí Joe Mac's in Kilronan, where rooms cost upwards of £17 per person (£19 with en suite). It opens year round. *Bayview Guesthouse* (☎ 61260), open March to mid-November, enjoys an enviable position overlooking the harbour and starts at £18/34 for singles/doubles.

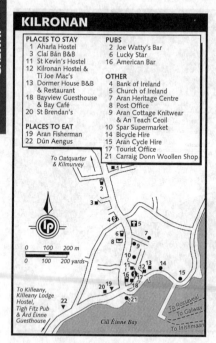

KILRONAN

PLACES TO STAY	PUBS
1 Aharla Hostel	2 Joe Watty's Bar
3 Claí Bán B&B	6 Lucky Star
11 St Kevin's Hostel	16 American Bar
12 Kilronan Hostel &	
Tí Joe Mac's	**OTHER**
13 Dormer House B&B	4 Bank of Ireland
& Restaurant	5 Church of Ireland
18 Bayview Guesthouse	7 Aran Heritage Centre
& Bay Café	8 Post Office
20 St Brendan's	9 Aran Cottage Knitwear
	& An Teach Ceoil
PLACES TO EAT	10 Spar Supermarket
19 Aran Fisherman	14 Bicycle Hire
22 Dún Aengus	15 Aran Cycle Hire
	17 Tourist Office
	21 Carraig Donn Woollen Shop

To Oatquarter & Kilmurvey

0   100   200 m
0   100   200 yards

To Killeany,
Killeany Lodge
Hostel,
Tigh Fitz Pub
& Árd Éinne
Guesthouse

Cill Éinne Bay

To Rossaveal
To Galway

To Inishmaan

Farther west is *St Brendan's* (☎ *61149*), in a charming old house on Cill Éinne Bay, where B&B costs £12 to £15 per person. It opens year round.

Árd Éinne Guesthouse (☎ *61126)* is farther west still and offers rooms costing £18 to £20 per person. It opens March to early November.

Along the road to Kilmurvey, *Claí Bán* (☎ *61111)* costs £25/30, or £30/34 with en suite bathroom. It opens year round. To the north is *An Crúgán* (☎ *61150)* costing £23/32. It opens March to November.

The appropriately named *Beach View House* (☎ *61141)* in Oatquarter some 5km north-west of Kilronan, charges £23/34. It opens May to September.

Overlooking Kilmurvey Bay, *Man of Aran Cottage* (☎ *61301)*, where some of the eponymous film was shot, offers B&B, March to October, starting at £25/36. *Kilmurvey House* (☎ *61218)*, in a lovely old

mansion on the path leading to Dún Aengus and close to a Blue Flag beach, has 12 rooms costing £20 to £25 per person. It opens April to September.

At the north-western end of the island, 9km from Kilronan in Creggakeerain, is *Cregmount House* (☎ *61139)*, which overlooks Galway Bay and costs £24/34. It opens April to November.

Places to Eat

In Kilronan the *Bay Café* at the Bayview Guesthouse is a relaxing place for coffee or a snack. It opens 8.30 am to 9.30 pm daily. About the best place for pub food is *Joe Watty's Bar*, farther north on the way out of Kilronan.

The *Aran Fisherman* (☎ *61104)* serves a wide range of meat, seafood and vegetarian dishes costing around £9.50, though pizzas and burgers cost £5.25 to £7.95. Its sister restaurant, *Dún Aengus* (☎ *61104)*, to the south-west overlooking Cill Éinne Bay, offers a similar menu and prices. It opens 11 am to 9 pm daily.

Mainistir House Hostel serves good, organic buffet dinners at 8 pm (7 pm in winter) that include vegetarian dishes. They cost £7 for residents and £8 for non-residents.

Man of Aran Cottage, in Kilmurvey, also serves organic food, including vegetarian options, in its teashop (sandwiches start at £2) and restaurant (dinner starts at £13).

Outside Kilronan, at the beginning of the path leading to Dún Aengus fort and near several craft shops, is the small, thatched *Teach Nan Phaidt* (☎ *61330)*, which offers sandwiches and seafood.

The larger *An Sunda Cáoch* ('The Blind Sound'; ☎ *61218)*, farther down the path, serves light meals costing under £5 and filling soups.

Entertainment

There's music in most Kilronan pubs at night. For Irish music and '*craic'* at its best, try *Joe Watty's Bar* or, west of the village, *Tigh Fitz*. *Tí Joe Mac's* in the centre is a bit basic but sometimes has music. The *American Bar* (An Américéan Béar) has better music and a friendly crowd. Another entertaining option is the *Lucky Star* between the bank and post office.

Shopping
A hand-knitted Aran sweater is on many people's shopping list when visiting the islands. In Kilronan, either Aran Cottage Knitwear (☎ 61117), on the road to Kilmurvey, or Carraig Donn Woollen Shop (☎ 61123), near the old pier, can accommodate. An Teach Ceoil (The Music House), next to Aran Cottage Knitwear, sells a good selection of traditional Irish music CDs and tapes.

Getting Around
Two places near the pier hire out bicycles. One of them is Aran Cycle Hire (☎ 61132), which has very good bikes costing £5 per day. You can also bring your own bicycle out on the ferry.

Numerous minibuses greet tourists as they disgorge from the ferry. They offer two hour 30 minutes tours of the island's principal sights at a cost of £5. However, walking and cycling will give you more of a sense of the place.

Pony traps with a driver are available for a trip from Kilronan to Dún Aengus costing around £20 (for up to four people).

INISHMAAN
☎ 099 • pop 300
Although Inishmaan (Inis Meáin, 'Middle Island') is the least visited of the Aran Islands, it's well worth the effort of getting there. Martin McDonagh's play *The Cripple of Inishmaan* may have put the island's name on the world map, but the locals aren't hell bent on attracting tourists, so visitor facilities are limited.

Inishmaan is roughly rhombus shaped, about 5km long by 3km wide. The fields are bordered by high stone walls, and it's a delight to wander along these boreens or along the cliffs to take in some of the tranquillity that attracted the playwright JM Synge and the nationalist Pádraig Pearse.

Orientation & Information
Inishmaan's main settlement is An Córa, whose buildings spread out along the road that runs east-west across the centre of the island. The principal boat landing stage is on the eastern side of the island, while the airstrip is in the north-eastern corner. In An Córa, the helpful Inishmaan Island Co-operative (☎ 73010), north-west of the pier and post office, dispenses tourist information.

Things to See
The chief archaeological site is **Dún Chonchúir**, a massive oval-shaped stone fort built on a high point and offering good views of the island on a fine day. It's similar to Dún Aengus on Inishmór, but is built inland overlooking a limestone valley. Chonchúir is said to have been a brother of Aengus. Dún Chonchúir's age is a bit of a puzzle: it's thought to have been built somewhere between the 1st and 7th centuries.

The **thatched cottage** on the road just before you head up to the fort is where JM Synge spent his summers between 1898 and 1902.

Cill Cheannannach is a rough 8th- or 9th-century church south of the pier. The well-preserved stone fort **Dún Fearbhaigh**, a short distance west, dates from about the same time.

Synge's Chair is at the west of the island near the end of a path that leads to a sheer cliff overlooking Gregory's Sound. It's a sheltered spot where the writer, JM Synge, spent much time in reflection.

In the east there's a safe beach, **Trá Leitreach**, north of the boat landing stage.

Places to Stay
One of the best B&Bs is Angela Uí Fátharta's *Créig Mór* (☎ 73012), about 500m north-west of the pier in Creigmore. It costs upwards of £14 per person and opens from March to December. *Máire Bu Uí Mhaoilchiaráin's* (☎ 73016), a good B&B on a corner south of the post office, is similarly priced. Another good one in An Córa is *Máirín Concannon's* B&B (☎ 73019), across the road from the island's only pub, costing £14 per person.

Máire Uí Fátharta's B&B (☎ 73027), in Ard Álainn past the road up to Dún

GALWAY

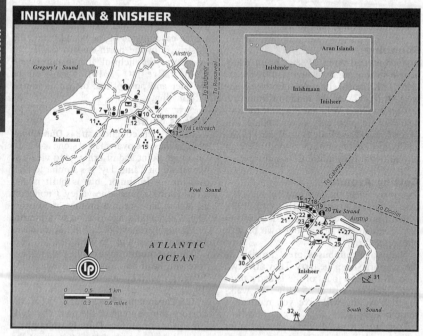

INISHMAAN & INISHEER

Chonchúir, opens Easter to September. Prices start at £14 per person with shared bathroom.

Places to Eat

Most B&Bs serve evening meals costing £10 to £12. There are only two restaurants, which open seasonally. *Tigh Chonghaille* (☎ 73085), just up to the right of the pier, serves mostly seafood, with lunchtime main courses costing £5. It also provides B&B.

An Dún (☎ 73068), opposite the entrance to Dún Chonchúir, offers reasonably priced omelettes, pasta for lunch (around £6) and dinner main courses costing £9 to £15.

The island has just one pub, *Teach Ósta Inis Meáin* (☎ 73003) in Baile an Mhothair, serving snacks, sandwiches, soups and seafood platters 11.30 am to 6 pm (7.30 pm in July and August). This terrific little bar hums with life on summer evenings.

Shopping

Inishmaan is home to Cniotáil Inis Meáin, a knitwear factory that exports fine woollen garments to some of the world's most exclusive shops, but sells them much cheaper here from its factory shop (☎ 73009).

INISHEER
☎ 099 • pop 300

Inisheer (Inis Oírr, 'Eastern Island') is the smallest of the three Aran Islands and only 8km off the coast from Doolin in County Clare. The view from the ferry is of a sheltered white beach backed by modern bungalows – few traditional thatched cottages and buildings survive – overlooked by a squat, stone 15th-century castle. To the south there's a maze of fields with barely a building in sight. The island has a timelessness about it, and a summer stroll through its sandy lanes is hard to beat. Despite a regular ferry service and proximity to the mainland, the absence of major archaeological

INISHMAAN & INISHEER

PLACES TO STAY
4   Créig Mór
6   Máire Uí Fátharta's
9   Máire Bu Uí
    Mhaoilchiaráin's
12 Máirín Concannon's
17 Mrs Bairbre Uí Chonghaile
    B&B & Fisherman's Cottage
    Restaurant
19 Brú Radharc
    Na Mara
22 Monica Chonghaile
24 Hotel Inisheer
    (Óstán Inis Oírr)
25 Inisheer Camp
    Site
29 Radharc an Chláir

PLACES TO EAT
7   An Dún
13 Tigh Chonghaille

PUBS
10 Teach Ósta Inis Meáin
18 Tigh Ned
23 Tigh Ruairí

OTHER
1   Inishmaan Island Co-operative
    (Tourist Information)
2   Cniotáil Inis Meáin Knitwear
    Factory
3   Post Office
5   Synge's Chair
8   Synge's Cottage

11 Dún Chonchúir
14 Cill Cheannannach
15 Dún Fearbhaigh
16 Inisheer Heritage House
    (Museum)
20 Tourist Information
21 Cill Ghobnait (Church of St
    Gobnait)
26 Dún Formna & O'Brien Castle
27 Teampall Chaoimháin
    (Church of St Kevin)
28 Post Office
30 Tobar Éinne
    (Well of St Enda)
31 Plassy Freighter
    Shipwreck
32 Inisheer Lighthouse

sites and tourist amenities keeps the number of visitors down, making Inisheer rather special.

Information

From June to September a small kiosk at the harbour provides tourist information 10 am to 6 pm daily. You can also contact the nearby Inisheer Island Co-operative (☎ 75008) for assistance. The post office, south of the pier, changes money.

Things to See & Do

Most sights are in the north of the island. The 15th-century **O'Brien Castle** (Caislea'n Uí Bhriain) overlooks the beach and harbour. It was built within the remains of a ring fort called Dún Formna dating from as early as the 1st century. Nearby is an 18th-century signal tower. On the Strand (An Trá) is the 10th-century **Teampall Chaoimháin** (Church of St Kevin), with some gravestones and shells from an ancient kitchen midden (dumping ground). **Inisheer Heritage House** (☎ 75021), west of the beach and pier, is a typical stone-built thatched cottage with some interesting old photographs. It has a craft shop and café.

Cill Ghobnait (Church of St Gobnait), south-west of Inisheer Heritage House, is a small 8th- or 9th-century church named after Gobnait, who fled here from Clare trying to escape an enemy who was pursuing

him. A 2km walk south-west of the church leads to the **Tobar Éinne** (Well of St Enda).

The best parts of Inisheer are uninhabited and the signposted 10.5km **Inisheer Way** is recommended. The eastern road to the lighthouse is more popular, but the coast around the western side is wilder. On the eastern shore is the rusting hulk of the *Plassy*, a freighter wrecked in 1960 and thrown high up onto the rocks. The uninhabited lighthouse (1857) on the island's southern tip, with its neat enclosure, is off limits.

Places to Stay & Eat

The basic *Inisheer Camp Site* (☎ 75008), overlooking the Strand, opens May to September and costs £2.50 per site including shower. Open year round, the clean IHH *Brú Radharc Na Mara* (☎ 75024), near the pier, charges £7.50 for dorm beds, and has two double rooms costing £22; continental or Irish breakfast is extra and dinner costs £10.

Radharc an Chláir (☎ 75019), a B&B near the castle, starts at £17/28 for singles/doubles, with dinner costing £11. It opens year round. Other B&Bs charge similar rates. In West Village try *Mrs Bairbre Uí Chonghaile* (☎ 75025) or *Monica Chonghaile* (☎ 75034).

Open April to September, modern *Hotel Inisheer* ('Óstán Inis Oírr'; ☎ 75020), just up from the Strand, offers B&B starting at £25/46 with bathroom. The hotel serves bar meals and its restaurant serves reasonable seafood, with dinner main courses starting at £10.

Fisherman's Cottage (☎ 75073), near the pier, serves organic food and very good seafood; vegetarian meals are also available. Lunchtime meals start at around £5, while most dinner main courses cost £9 to £13.

Entertainment

Inisheer's two pubs are *Tigh Ned*, just up from the Strand, and *Tigh Ruairí*, past the Hotel Inisheer in Baile Lurgan.

Getting Around

Bikes are available for hire from Brú Radharc Na Mara hostel and at Rothair Inis Oírr (☎ 75033) costing £5 per day.

Eastern Galway

Separated from the wild, bleak landscape of Connemara and the county's western coast by Lough Corrib, this region is markedly different. Eastern Galway is relatively flat, and its underlying limestone has given it a well-drained, fertile soil. This is the largest section of the county, but it lacks areas of significant interest. Country towns such as Ballinasloe, Loughrea and Tuam serve relatively prosperous farming regions.

GETTING THERE & AWAY

Several Bus Éireann (☎ 091-562000) express buses from Galway serve Ballinasloe and Loughrea; local bus No 427 connects Galway, Ballinasloe and Loughrea with Portumna.

BALLINASLOE & AROUND

☎ 0905 • pop 5790

The biggest town in eastern Galway, Ballinasloe (Béal Átha na Sluaighe) is on the main Dublin to Galway road (N6), with most traffic diverted south round the town centre. The town is pleasant enough, but there's no real reason to stay, except possibly over the eight days at the start of October when **Ballinasloe Horse Fair** attracts horse buyers, horse sellers and merrymakers.

Historically, Ballinasloe was a strategic crossing point over the River Suck. In the early 12th century, Turlough O'Connor, king of Connaught, built a castle to guard the river crossing, and this became the nucleus of the town's development.

Around 6km south-west of town on the N6, Aughrim was the site of a crucial victory by the Protestant William of Orange over the Catholic forces of James II in 1691, the bloodiest battle ever fought on Irish soil. The **Battle of Aughrim Interpretive Centre** helps put it in perspective (it was closed at the time of writing because of staffing difficulties but should be open by the time you read this). There are signposts from the interpretive centre indicating the actual battle site. At the IHH *Hyne's Hostel* (☎ 73734), close to the centre, dorm beds cost £7 to £8.50, private rooms £17.

CLONFERT CATHEDRAL

Around 21km south-east of Ballinasloe is the tiny 12th-century cathedral at Clonfert. The monastery is said to have been founded in 563 by St Brendan the Navigator and was ravaged by Vikings in 844 and 1179. The remarkable six-arched Romanesque doorway, with its human and animal heads, dates from the 1160s, but much of the limestone carvings were badly restored in the 19th century.

LOUGHREA & AROUND

☎ 091 • pop 3360

Loughrea (Baile Locha Riach) is a large, busy market town 26km south-east of Galway. It gets its name from the little lake at the southern end of town. **St Brendan's Catholic Cathedral** (1903) is renowned for its Celtic revival stained glass and furnishings. Loughrea has Ireland's only functioning medieval **moat**, which runs from the lake at Fair Green near the cathedral to the River Loughrea north of town.

Seven kilometres north of Loughrea near Bullaun is the remarkable **Turoe Stone**, a phallic standing stone covered in delicate

La Tène-style relief carvings. It dates from between 300 BC and AD 100. There are similarly carved stones in Brittany associated with La Tène Celts (late Iron Age). The stone wasn't set here originally, but was found at an Iron Age fort a few kilometres away.

PORTUMNA
☎ 0509 • pop 1000

In the south-eastern corner of the county, the lakeside town of Portumna is an attractive place and a popular base for boating and fishing on **Lough Derg**.

Dúchas-run **Portumna Castle** (☎ 41658) was built in 1618 by Richard de Burgo (or Burke) and boasts a formal, geometrically laid-out garden of some pretension. The castle opens 10 am to 5 pm Tuesday to Sunday, May to early June; and 9.30 am to 6.30 pm daily, early June to early October. Admission costs £1.50/60p.

Counties Mayo & Sligo

Despite the fact that Mayo and Sligo share a history of rural poverty and are equally remote and underpopulated, County Sligo – the smaller of the two – is better known to most travellers, thanks largely to the poetry of WB Yeats. However, the qualities of landscape and sense of place that inspired Yeats belong equally to both Mayo and Sligo. And, apart from a small number of towns such as Sligo, Westport and Cong, both counties are ideal for anyone wishing to escape the well-worn tourist trail. Mayo in particular is just waiting to be discovered by intrepid travellers.

County Mayo

Mayo (Maigh Eo) has an identity that distinguishes it from other parts of Ireland on several different levels: an introspective landscape, a Connaught accent with its own inflection, and a people who seem far removed from cosmopolitan Dublin or touristy Killarney. The relative poverty of the land meant that the invaders left it till last, but what delayed the English is what attracts today's visitors: lakes, mountains, boglands, and a low population density.

The county was particularly hard hit by the Famine, and the woeful refrain 'County Mayo, God help us!', still used among older Irish at home and abroad, probably dates from this sad time.

Mayo's more recent history has been marked by massive, ongoing emigration and, apart from the small industries that sustain Castlebar's relative prosperity, there's a chronic lack of employment opportunities.

CONG
☎ 092 • pop 300
Blink your eyes while passing through the small town of Cong (Conga) and you won't see much, but there's a great deal hidden behind that ordinary main street. In 1951

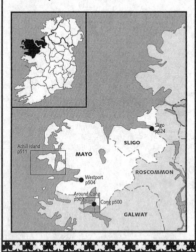

American director John Ford came here with John Wayne and Maureen O'Hara to film *The Quiet Man*, and there are still many reminders of that momentous event.

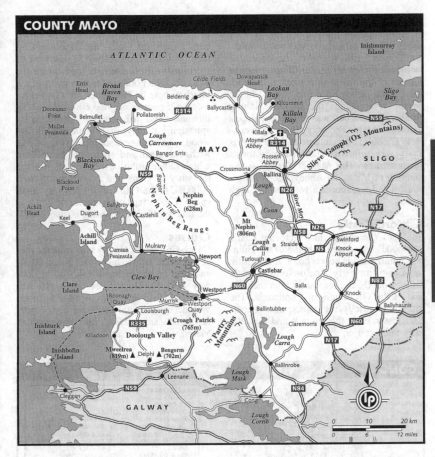

COUNTY MAYO

True fans of the film will want to buy *Complete Guide to the Quiet Man Locations* by Lisa Collins.

Cong is just east of the border with County Galway and 1km north of Lough Corrib.

Information

The tourist office (☎ 46542), in the old courthouse building opposite Cong Abbey along Abbey St, opens 10 am to 6 pm daily, April, May and September to mid-November; and 9.30 am to 8 pm, June to August. Get a copy of the *Heritage Trail* brochure to explore the town and discover the fascinating history of the 1123 Cong Cross, now in the National Museum in Dublin. The local booklets *The Glory of Cong* and *Cong: Walks, Sights, Stories* have more information. A self-guided tour using *The Quiet Man* map takes in locations from the film.

There are no banks in Cong, but you can change money at the post office and O'Connors craft shop, both on Main St.

Cong Abbey

This 12th-century Augustinian abbey, which was founded by Turlough Mór O'Connor, high king of Ireland and king of Connaught, in 1120, occupies the site of a 6th-century abbey. It has a carved doorway on the northern side and fine windows and decorated medieval stonework in the **Chapter House** – some of the finest such work in Ireland. West of the abbey on a small island in the nearby river stands the **Monk's Fishing House**, where a bell was rung every time a fish was caught. The ugly 1960s-style concrete Catholic church, beside the abbey, is an eyesore built with utter disregard for its surroundings. The **Market Cross**, at the junction of Main and Abbey Sts, is the reconstructed remains of a 14th-century high cross.

Ashford Castle

South of the town, this Victorian castle (☎ 46003) was once the home of the Guinness family and is now a hotel. It stands on the site of an early Anglo-Norman castle built by the De Burgos family after their defeat of the O'Connors of Connaught. The interior is strictly for guests, and it costs £3/1 just to enter the grounds and view the fairy-tale exterior.

Quiet Man Heritage Cottage

In a life-imitating-art exercise so twisted it begs a map, the Quiet Man Heritage Cottage (☎ 46089), on Abbey St just west of the tourist office, attempts to re-create the exact set John Ford used to film many of the interior shots of *The Quiet Man* in Hollywood. Of course, original cottages such as this one – and their interiors – were his inspiration but, hey, they want real Hollywood. The cottage also contains the **Cong Archaeological and Historical Exhibition**, which rather ambitiously attempts to trace the story of Cong and its surrounds from 7000 BC to the 19th century in a very small space. The cottage opens the same hours as the tourist office. Admission costs £2.50/1.

Cruises

Corrib Cruises (☎ 46029) sails from the pier at Ashford Castle to Inchagoill Island (£8/4) and then on to Oughterard in County Galway (£12/5). Departures are at 10 and 11 am and 2.45 and 5 pm, April to October. Weather permitting, there are also departures at 11 am and 2.45 pm, November to March.

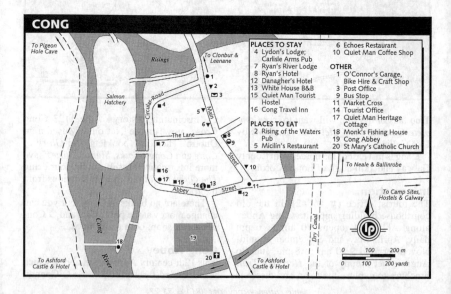

CONG

To Pigeon Hole Cave

Risings

To Clonbur & Leenane

Salmon Hatchery

Circular Road

The Lane

Cong River

To Ashford Castle & Hotel

Main Street

Abbey Street

Dry Canal

To Neale & Ballinrobe

To Camp Sites, Hostels & Galway

To Ashford Castle & Hotel

PLACES TO STAY		
4	Lydon's Lodge; Carlisle Arms Pub	
7	Ryan's River Lodge	
8	Ryan's Hotel	
12	Danagher's Hotel	
13	White House B&B	
15	Quiet Man Tourist Hostel	
16	Cong Travel Inn	

PLACES TO EAT	
2	Rising of the Waters Pub
5	Micilin's Restaurant
6	Echoes Restaurant
10	Quiet Man Coffee Shop

OTHER	
1	O'Connor's Garage, Bike Hire & Craft Shop
3	Post Office
9	Bus Stop
11	Market Cross
14	Tourist Office
17	Quiet Man Heritage Cottage
18	Monk's Fishing House
19	Cong Abbey
20	St Mary's Catholic Church

0   100   200 m
0   100   200 yards

MAYO & SLIGO

Places to Stay

Camping You can camp at *Cong Caravan and Camping Park* (☎ *46089, Lake Rd*), 2km east of town in Lisloughrey, off the Galway road (R346), for £6.50 (children £1); or at *Courtyard Hostel* (see Hostels, next) farther east at Cross. The sites open year round.

Hostels There are two hostels in the centre of Cong. *Cong Travel Inn* (☎ *46310*) provides excellent-value, modern, clean, en suite rooms with tea/coffee-making facilities costing £10 per person. Round the corner, *Quiet Man Tourist Hostel* (☎ *46089*) charges £7.50 for dorm beds, £18 for doubles.

The popular IHH *Cong Hostel* (☎ *46089*), next to the camp site in Lisloughrey, offers good facilities and charges £7.50 for dorm beds, £18 for doubles. It screens *The Quiet Man* and Yves Boisset's 1971 film, *Un Taxi Mauve*, also filmed in Ireland, every night. *Courtyard Hostel* (☎ *46203*), 3km farther east, in Cross, charges £8 for dorm beds, and the two doubles cost £16.

B&Bs Central B&Bs include *Lydon's Lodge* (☎ *46053*), at the start of the circular road, charging £25 per person for rooms with bath, and *White House* (☎ *46358*), across from the abbey on Abbey St, where singles/doubles go for £20/34. There are some B&Bs down The Lane heading towards the river, including *Ryan's River Lodge* (☎ *46057*), where rooms cost upwards of £18 per person. All three B&Bs open March to October.

Hotels At *Ryan's Hotel* (☎ *46243, Main St)* rooms cost from £27.50 to £35 per person, depending on the season. *Danagher's* (☎ *46028, Abbey St)*, near the town's main junction, is an old-style, 11-room hotel with rooms costing £25 per person. That's a positive giveaway compared with the room rates of £242 to £522 charged mid-May to September at *Ashford Castle* (☎ *46003*).

Places to Eat

Some eateries open from May to September or October only. The *Rising of the Waters* pub in Main St serves light meals, as does *Quiet Man Coffee Shop* at the southern end of the street. *Danagher's Hotel* has a fine old bar, a basic eating area and a fancier restaurant. Bar food costing £7 to £12 is available at *Ryan's Hotel*. Attached to Lydon's Lodge is the recommended *Carlisle Arms* pub-restaurant.

If your credit card won't accommodate the *Ashford Castle* restaurant, where dinner costs £38 per person, consider unleashing it at *Echoes* (☎ *46059, Main St)*, an award-winning restaurant that proves fine dining has arrived in rural Ireland. Starters cost about £4.50; main courses range from £12.95 to £15.80. A similarly priced alternative is *Micilín's Restaurant* (☎ *46655*), a few doors along, where starters cost upwards of £3.50, mains £11 to £15.

Getting There & Away

Bus Éireann (☎ 096-71800) bus No 51 between Galway and Ballina stops at Ashford Castle gates in the early afternoon Monday to Saturday, while bus No 420 from Galway to Clifden stops outside Ryan's Hotel in the early evening.

If you're travelling by car or bike farther into County Mayo, eschew the main N84 to Castlebar and take the longer, but much more attractive, route west to Leenane (starting with the R345) and north to Westport via Delphi.

Getting Around

There are enough interesting sites close to Cong to make a bike worth having. In summer they can be hired from O'Connor's (☎ 46008), on Main St. (O'Connor's is the combined Esso station, Spar supermarket and craft shop next to the Rising of the Waters pub.)

AROUND CONG

There's a surprising amount to see and do around Cong, including a collection of caves, a canal that never functioned, a stone circle and a curious folly. The limestone strata of the Cong area account for the numerous caves, for the failure of the canal and for the local phenomenon known as

MAYO & SLIGO

'the rising of the waters', where water from Lough Mask to the north percolates through the limestone and emerges from the ground at Cong before flowing down to Lough Corrib.

Caves

The Cong area is peppered with caves, many of them only a short walk from the village.

Pigeon Hole is about 1.5km west of Cong and can be reached by road or by the walking track from across the river. Stone steps lead down into the cave, which is sometimes very wet. There's a local legend about two fairy trout who dwell there.

From the Pigeon Hole, take the R345 west towards Clonbur, passing the Giant's Grave turn-off, and go on to a lane that turns south about 5km from Cong. A stream flows into the extensive **Ballymaglancy Cave**, which is off the road to the right. The

cave has stalactites and stalagmites and has been explored for about 500m.

Two other caves are north-east of Cong, near the road to Cross (R346). **Captain Webb's Hole** is just outside the village, a short distance beyond the dry canal and behind the school grounds. It's actually a deep, water-filled hole in the ground where, two centuries ago, a local villain is said to have hurled a succession of local women. Another 200m from Cong, a wide path leads to **Kelly's Cave**, which is usually locked up; the key is kept at the Quiet Man Coffee Shop, and a small deposit may be required. **The Lady** and **Horse's Discovery** are two other caves beside a road to the castle.

The Dry Canal

Lough Mask is about 10m higher than Lough Corrib, and in the mid-18th century it was decided to cut a canal between the two. The project started in 1848, using

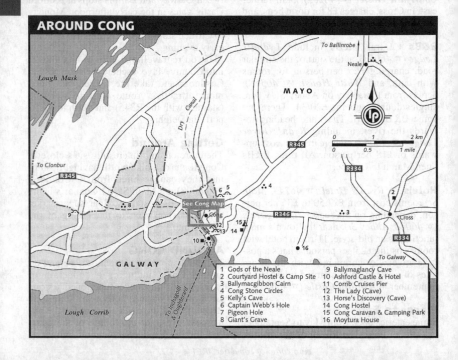

AROUND CONG

To Ballinrobe

Lough Mask

To Clonbur

MAYO

To Galway

GALWAY

Lough Corrib

To Leenaun & Oughterard

1 Gods of the Neale
2 Courtyard Hostel & Camp Site
3 Ballymacgibbon Cairn
4 Cong Stone Circles
5 Kelly's Cave
6 Captain Webb's Hole
7 Pigeon Hole
8 Giant's Grave
9 Ballymaglancy Cave
10 Ashford Castle & Hotel
11 Corrib Cruises Pier
12 The Lady (Cave)
13 Horse's Discovery (Cave)
14 Cong Hostel
15 Cong Caravan & Camping Park
16 Moytura House

labourers'who were desperate for work due to the deprivations of the Famine years. In 1854, when construction was nearing completion, the economic basis for the canal was already coming into question as railways rapidly spread across the country. Then a greater problem was discovered – the canal wasn't watertight. The porous limestone simply soaked up any water that flowed into the canal – like a plughole. Although various schemes for sealing the canal bed were considered, the whole expensive project was abandoned in 1858. The dry canal, complete with locks for raising and lowering the water level, runs north-south to the east of Cong.

Circles & Graves
The stone slabs of the megalithic burial chamber known as the **Giant's Grave** can be visited easily between the Pigeon Hole and Ballymaglancy Cave. A path leads into the forest south of the R345 road to Clonbur, about 3km from Cong. About 100m from the road take the turn-off to the left; the grave is off that path to the right.

There are several stone circles in the area, including the excellent **Cong Stone Circles** about 1.5km north-east of Cong just east off the Neale road (R345). About 3.5km east of Cong, north off the Cross road (R346), is **Ballymacgibbon Cairn**, supposedly the site of a legendary Celtic battle. **Moytura House**, near the shores of Lough Corrib, takes its name from this battle and was a childhood home of Oscar Wilde.

Neale
The village of Neale, 6km north-east of Cong, has some interesting sites. If you take the turn-off at the northern end of the village, the curious stone known as the **Gods of the Neale** is about 200m east of the main road, just inside the walls of Neale Park. The slab, originally found in a nearby cave, is carved with figures of a human, animal and reptile in low relief and is dated 1757.

Inchagoill Island
In the centre of Lough Corrib is the island of Inchagoill (see Lough Corrib in the Con-

nemara section of the County Galway chapter for details). The island can be reached by boat from the jetty next to Ashford Castle (see Cruises in the Cong section earlier in this chapter) and from Oughterard in County Galway.

WESTPORT
☎ 098 • pop 4500
Westport (Cathair na Mairt) is on the River Carrowbeg and the shores of Clew Bay in the southern half of County Mayo. It didn't acquire its postcard prettiness gradually, like many other small Irish towns – it was designed that way. The Mall, with the river running down the middle, is as picturesque a main street as you'll find anywhere. The present Westport House was built on the site of an O'Malley castle, which was once surrounded by about 60 hovels and the original settlement of Westport. These were moved when the house was planned, and the Brownes, who came here from Sussex during the reign of Elizabeth I, even had the course of the river altered to make the Mall a grand approach to the gates of the house. This wasn't entirely successful, as the Mall is still subject to occasional flooding.

Orientation & Information
Westport consists of two parts: the town proper and Westport Quay on the bay, just outside town on the road to Louisburgh (R335). The tourist office (☎ 25711), on the Mall, opens 9 am to 6 pm Monday to Saturday (plus Sunday in July and August), April to September; and 9 am to 12.45 pm and 2 to 5.15 pm on weekdays, the rest of the year.

For information about fishing, inquire at Hewetson (☎ 26018) on Bridge St.

The P Dunning pub, on the corner of The Octagon and James St, offers Internet access costing £3 per half-hour. The AIB, on Shop St, and the Bank of Ireland, on the North Mall near the post office, have ATMs and bureaux de change. The Bookshop on Bridge St has a good selection of OS maps, at the back, and books on Ireland.

Westport Washeteria, open from 9.30 am to 6 pm (1 pm on Wednesday) Monday to

MAYO & SLIGO

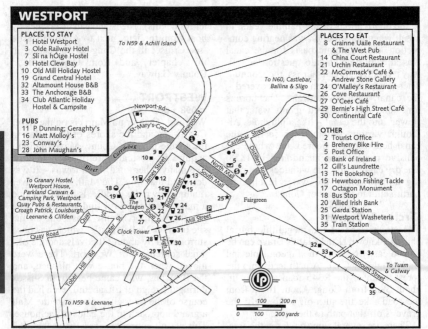

WESTPORT

PLACES TO STAY
1 Hotel Westport
3 Olde Railway Hotel
7 Slí na hOige Hostel
9 Hotel Clew Bay
10 Old Mill Holiday Hostel
19 Grand Central Hotel
32 Altamount House B&B
33 The Anchorage B&B
34 Club Atlantic Holiday
     Hostel & Campsite

PUBS
11 P Dunning; Geraghty's
16 Matt Molloy's
23 Conway's
28 John Maughan's

PLACES TO EAT
8 Grainne Uaile Restaurant
    & The West Pub
14 China Court Restaurant
21 Urchin Restaurant
22 McCormack's Café &
     Andrew Stone Gallery
24 O'Malley's Restaurant
26 Cove Restaurant
27 O'Cees Café
29 Bernie's High Street Café
30 Continental Café

OTHER
2 Tourist Office
4 Breheny Bike Hire
5 Post Office
6 Bank of Ireland
12 Gill's Laundrette
13 The Bookshop
15 Hewetson Fishing Tackle
17 Octagon Monument
18 Bus Stop
20 Allied Irish Bank
25 Garda Station
31 Westport Washeteria
35 Train Station

To N59 & Achill Island
To N60, Castlebar,
Ballina & Sligo
Newport Rd
St Mary's Cres
Newport St
Castlebar Street
Distillery Road
Carrowbeg
River
James Street
North Mall
South Mall
Bridge Street
To Granary Hostel,
Westport House,
Parkland Caravan &
Camping Park, Westport
Quay Pubs & Restaurants,
Croagh Patrick, Louisburgh,
Leenane & Clifden
The Octagon
Shop St
Mill Street
Fairgreen
Quay St
Peter St
Clock Tower
Quay Road
John's Row
Tober Hill Rd
High St
Altamount Street
To Tuam
& Galway
To N59 & Leenane
0 100 200 m
0 100 200 yards

Saturday, is on Mill St near the clock tower. Gill's Laundrette, on James St, is convenient to the Old Mill Holiday Hostel, but is not self-service.

Westport House

The present house (☎ 25430) dates from 1730. Commercialisation is pushed to the hilt here, from a hokey 'dungeon' to tacky souvenirs for sale in the 'Gifte Shoppe'. Admission to the grounds is free but to the house it's a pricey £6/3; if you visit the zoo as well, the cost rises to £9.50/5 (families £29). The house and zoo open 10.30 am to 6 pm Monday to Saturday, and 2 to 6 pm on Sunday, July to late August; 2 to 6 pm daily, June and late August; and 2 to 5 pm daily, May and early September. Consider a visit only if your itinerary doesn't include an Irish stately home elsewhere.

To reach Westport House, head out of town west on Quay Rd towards Croagh Patrick and Louisburgh. After about 1km,

just before you get to Westport Quay, there's a road to the right which leads to the entrance to the grounds.

The Octagon Monument

This memorial was erected in 1845 in honour of an eminently forgettable local banker, whose statue stood upon an octagonal podium at the top of the column. During the Civil War, troops decapitated the statue, and it was later removed. In 1990 a Roman-looking statue of St Patrick complete with serpent-entwined staff replaced the unfortunate capitalist.

Clew Bay Heritage Centre

The heritage centre (☎ 26852), in Westport Quay, has an interesting collection of local artefacts and documents, including the spinning wheel presented by the people of Ballina to Maud Gonne, the dynamic political rebel who was married briefly to Major John MacBride and was the object of Yeats' adoration. Also housed in this centre are the records of the trial of Patrick Egan, who commandeered Westport House during the 1798 Rising. The centre also provides a genealogical service. It opens 10 am to 5 pm on weekdays, and 3 to 5 pm on Sunday, July to September; and noon to 3pm on weekdays, the rest of the year. Admission costs £2.

Places to Stay
Camping The *Parkland Caravan and Camping Park* (☎ 27766), on the Westport House estate and accessible by the same road that leads to the house, charges a pricey £14.50 for a two-person tent with car; hikers and cyclists pay £12 per tent. Consider using the *Old Head Forest Caravan and Camping Park* 16km away near Louisburgh (see the Around Westport section later in this chapter).

Hostels In the centre, the well-equipped IHH *Old Mill Holiday Hostel* (☎ 27045, *Barrack Yard*), just off James St, costs £7 for dorm beds. Enter through the arch. There's one double room, four family rooms, and the hostel opens year round. The super An Óige *Club Atlantic Holiday Hostel* (☎ 26644, *Altamount St*), near the train station, has even better facilities. Dorm beds cost £6.50 to £8, singles £10 to £16, and doubles £16 to £28. Although there's an enormous eat-in kitchen, you can order breakfast costing £2. It has a games room, and a conservation area in the grounds at the back. It opens March to October.

The more simple IHO *Granary Hostel* (☎ 25903, *Quay Rd*) is in Westport Quay, near the Westport House entrance. Dorm beds in this former granary cost £6. There's a big garden at the back to hang out your washing and a conservatory. The hostel opens April to September.

Back in Westport itself, the small but comfortable *Slí na hÓige Hostel* (☎ 28751, *North Mall*) has dorm beds costing £7. It opens June to September.

B&Bs The tourist office books rooms in the town's plentiful supply of B&Bs but, if you should arrive late, Altamount St has a few

of the cheaper ones and they're close to the train station. Try *The Anchorage* (☎ 25448, *7A Altamount St*), where singles/doubles with shared bathroom cost £20/30. Nearby, *Altamount House* (☎ 25226) charges upwards of £22.50/32 and opens March to October.

Hotels The *Hotel Clew Bay* (☎ 25438, *James St*) has 29 rooms costing £32.50 to £40.50 per person, depending on the season. In the same category is *Grand Central Hotel* (☎ 25027, *The Octagon*), which was closed for total refurbishment at the time of writing.

The 15-room *Olde Railway Hotel* (☎ 25166), where Thackeray chose to stay on his tour around Ireland in the 19th century, is next to the tourist office. Singles/doubles in this Victorian showcase cost upwards of £65/90 from July to September. *Hotel Westport* (☎ 25122, *Newport St*) is functional by comparison but charges more during the same period: £85/130. Call to find out about any special deals.

Places to Eat
Bridge St has a fair selection of cafés, including *McCormack's*, upstairs in the Andrew Stone Gallery, where lunch costs around £7. *Cove Restaurant*, farther down, serves light meals during the day and is a mainly seafood restaurant at night. Another good choice for lunch or a snack is *Bernie's High Street Café*, south of the clock tower, where pasta costs £5.50 (closed Monday). *Continental Café*, almost opposite, offers good vegetarian food. On The Octagon, *O'Cee's* is a popular lunchtime cafeteria-style eatery open 9 am to 7 pm, Monday to Saturday; fish with vegetables costs £4.85.

Grainne Uaile, at The West pub on the corner of Bridge St and South Mall, opens for lunch and dinner to 10 pm daily; pasta main courses cost £7.50, seafood £8.50 to £10.50.

The immensely popular *O'Malley's*, upstairs on Bridge St, has a vast, varied menu culled from different cuisines, including Thai, Indian, Mexican and Italian; pastas cost around £8. Almost opposite is the

MAYO & SLIGO

charming *Urchin* restaurant, with *nouvelle* main courses costing £8.50 to £13. If you're in need of a fix of rice or noodles, you could do worse than *China Court* (☎ *28177, Market Lane*), off Bridge St, which offers a four-course lunch (£8) and opens daily.

At Westport Quay, just outside town on the road to Louisburgh (R335), there are several pubs and restaurants mostly specialising in seafood. Near the entrance to Westport House, *Quay Cottage* (☎ *26412*) serves evening meals costing £10 to £17, including a couple of vegetarian choices. On the quay itself *Asgard Tavern* offers a seafood platter costing £8.60. Nearby, *The Towers* pub serves fresh mussels in wine (£5.90) and has a beer garden. Farther out, the *Sheebeen* pub serves good lunches and dinners.

Entertainment

There are a number of excellent pubs in Westport, including those on Quay Rd, with music most weekends and throughout the week in summer. *Matt Molloy's (Bridge St)* is owned by Matt Molloy of the Chieftains; it is way overcrowded and sometimes there is an entry charge (£4 to £6) when it has 'name' Irish music sessions. *Conway's (Bridge St)* is a quieter, old-style place, and *John Maughan's*, near the clock tower, sometimes has music.

Two pubs rub shoulders and face The Octagon. *P Dunning* offers TV sports, while *Geraghty's* has music nightly. Both put tables out on the pavement on fine days.

The West, on the corner of Bridge St and South Mall, has music sessions on Sunday.

Getting There & Away

Bus Bus Éireann (☎ 096-71800) buses running Monday to Saturday to/from The Octagon in Westport include: two to Achill, up to five to Ballina (two on Sunday), one to Belfast (No 66), two to Cork (one on Sunday), up to six to Galway (one on Sunday), and two to Sligo (one on Sunday). For Shannon Airport and Limerick, change in Galway.

Train The train station (☎ 25253) is on Altamount St, 500m from Fairgreen, and

within easy walking distance of the town centre. There are three daily connections (four on Sunday) to Dublin (3½ hours) via Athlone.

Getting Around

You can call a taxi on ☎ 25539. Bicycles can be hired from Breheny Bike Hire (☎ 25020), on Castlebar St, just east of the Mall, costing £7/30 per day/week, or from Club Atlantic Holiday Hostel (see Places to Stay, earlier), which also provides a trilingual pamphlet with seven suggested itineraries.

AROUND WESTPORT
Croagh Patrick

Croagh Patrick (also known as 'the Reek') towers to the south-west of Westport. It was from the top of this mountain that St Patrick performed his snake-expulsion act – Ireland has been free of venomous serpents ever since. Climbing the 765m holy mountain is an act of penance for thousands of pilgrims on the last Sunday of July (Reek Sunday). The truly contrite make the trek along Tóchar Phádraig (Patrick's Causeway), the original 40km route from Ballintubber Abbey, and ascend the mountain barefoot.

The trail for less contrite folk begins beside Campbell's pub in the village of **Murrisk**, west of Westport. There's a sign (between the pub and the car park) pointing the way, and there's no mistaking the route. If the weather is clear, the two-hour climb gives fine views year round. Opposite the car park is the **National Famine Memorial**, a metal sculpture of a three-masted sailing ship covered in skeletons, commemorating the Potato Famine. Following the path down past the memorial brings you to the remains of **Murrisk Abbey**.

Louisburgh & Around
☎ 098

Louisburgh (Cluain Cearbán) got its name from the first marquess of Sligo, who laid it out and had a relative fighting against the French at the Battle of Louisburgh in Canada. The town is home to the **Granuaile Visitors Centre** (☎ 25711, 66341), dedicated to the life and times of Grace O'Malley (1530–1603), the pirate queen and the most famous of the O'Malley clan. The centre, in a disused church on Church St near the fire station, also includes an exhibition devoted to the Famine. It opens 10 am to 6 pm Monday to Saturday, June to September. Admission costs £2.50/1.50.

There are some excellent **beaches** in the vicinity; Old Head Beach (which has a Blue Flag) and the Silver Strand are particularly sandy and safe and are suitable for **surfing** and other water sports.

About 4km from Louisburgh and just off the main road to Westport is the *Old Head Forest Caravan and Camping Park* (☎ 66021). Large/small tents cost £8/6.50 plus 50p per person. The beach is only 300m away.

Bus Éireann (☎ 096-71800) bus No 450 links Westport and Louisburgh via Murrisk up to three times daily, Monday to Saturday.

Doolough Valley
There are two roads connecting Westport and Leenane (County Galway), but the one nearest the coast (the R335) via Louisburgh and Delphi travels through the stunning Doolough Valley. It's wildly beautiful, not least because of the lonely expanse of Doo Lough (Dark Lake) with the Mweelrea Mountains behind. At the southern end of the lake, Bengorm rises to 702m. The landscape changes from baize green and sparkling wet stone to a forbidding grey as shadows envelop everything when cloudbanks spread in from the Atlantic.

During the Potato Famine, the valley was the scene of tragedy when some 600 men, women and children walked from Louisburgh to Delphi Lodge in the hope that the landlord would offer them food. Help was flatly refused, and on the return journey around 400 perished through hunger and exposure. There's a memorial to the unfortunate souls along the road.

Killadoon
Killadoon is a small village on the coast reached by a narrow coastal road heading south from Louisburgh or by turning west off the R335 at Cregganbaun. The main

Grace O'Malley

Grace O'Malley (1530–1603), also called Granuaile and the daughter of a Connaught chief, established her own fleet and commanded her own army. From her Clare Island base she controlled the Clew Bay area and attacked the ships of those who had submitted to the English. In 1566 she married Richard Burke, a neighbouring clan chief (her first husband, Donal O'Flaherty, had died years earlier), and her power grew to such an extent that the merchants of Galway pleaded with the English governor to do something about her.

In 1574 her castle (Carrigahowley Castle, now called Rockfleet Castle, near Newport) was besieged, but she turned the siege into a rout of the English and sent them packing. In 1577 she was held in prison but, mysteriously, managed to get herself released on a promise of good behaviour. Over the next few years she craftily entered a number of alliances, both with and against the English.

In 1593 she travelled to London and was granted a pardon after meeting Elizabeth I, who offered to make her a countess. Grace declined, for she already considered herself the queen of Connaught.

Back in Ireland she appeared to be working for the English, but it seems likely that she was still fiercely independent. In the final recorded reference to her, in the English State Papers of 1601, an English captain tells of meeting one of her pirate ships, captained by one of her sons, on its way to plunder a merchant ship.

attractions here are the panoramic ocean views and the long sandy beaches.

On Thursday only, Bus Éireann (☎ 096-71800) bus No 450 from Westport and Louisburgh continues to Killadoon.

DELPHI
☎ 095

The Brownes of Westport were originally a Catholic family, but they converted to Protestantism in order to avoid the constraints of the penal laws. This allowed one of the family to be ennobled as the marquess of Sligo at the time of the Act of Union in 1801, and the second marquess gave the unlikely name of Delphi to his fishing lodge in Mayo. A friend of Byron, he had travelled in central Greece and returned home convinced that his fishing territory bore an uncanny resemblance to the area around Delphi.

The remote *Delphi Hostel and Adventure Centre* (☎ 42246, email delphigy@iol.ie) provides organised outdoor activities in July and August. Check out their Web site at www.delphiadventureholidays.com. Dorm beds cost upwards of £9, and private rooms go for £20/32 without/with bathroom. Meals and bicycle hire are also available.

At *Delphi Lodge* (☎ 42211), which caters mostly to anglers, permits are available for fishing in the local waters. It has B&B accommodation costing £30 to £60 per person.

CLARE ISLAND
☎ 098 • pop 150

Clare Island, at the mouth of Clew Bay, is 5km from the nearest mainland point, Roonagh Quay. Bay View Hotel (☎ 26307) has tourist information and attracts sea anglers, scuba divers and sailing folk.

The mountainous island rises up to **Mt Knockmore**, which, at 461m, is the highest point and dominates the landscape. The island has the ruins of the Cistercian **Clare Island Abbey** (circa 1460) and **Granuaile's Castle**, both associated with the piratical Grace O'Malley. The tower castle was her stronghold, although it was altered consid-

erably when the coastguard took it over in 1831. Grace is said to be buried in the small abbey, which contains a stone with her family motto: 'Invincible on land and sea'.

The island has safe, sandy beaches and is perfect for **walking** and **climbing** on a clear day. It is also one of the dwindling number of places where you can find **choughs**, which look like blackbirds but have red beaks.

Places to Stay & Eat

Of the B&Bs, one of the least expensive is *Ballytoughey Lodge* (☎ 25412), which costs £16 per person and also offers organised treks and residential study tours. Mary O'Malley's *Cois Abhainn* (☎ 26216) costs £18/32 for singles/doubles; it's 5km from the harbour but you can arrange a pick up. The more unusual *Clare Island Lighthouse* (☎ 45120), dating from 1806, has all the comforts one would expect for £55/90. *Bay View Hotel* (☎ 26307), beside the harbour, is the main place to stay. Singles/doubles cost upwards of £23/40, and it opens June to September.

If you're just going for the day, it's best to take your own food, though pub grub is available at the Bay View Hotel, and B&Bs do evening meals for residents and non-residents (upwards of £10).

Getting There & Away

Clare Island Ferries (☎ 28288, mobile 087-414853) and Ocean Star Ferry (☎ 25045, mobile 087-2321785) make the 25-minute trip from Roonagh Quay, 8km west of Louisburgh. There are five sailings daily in July and August, and from three to five daily in May, June and September. Return fares cost £10/5.

INISHTURK ISLAND
☎ 098 • pop 90

Inishturk Island lies about 12km off Mayo's western coast. Evidence of pre-Christian life has been found, but it's believed that the ancestors of many of today's inhabitants were driven here in Cromwell's time. The island doesn't receive many tourists, despite the two **sandy beaches** on its eastern side, wonderful **flora and fauna** and a rugged, hilly landscape ideal for **walking**.

B&B is available at a few places, including *Ocean View House* (☎ 45520, *Garranty*), which charges £18/34 for singles/doubles, and *Teach Abhainn* (☎ 45655), which charges £18/28. Both offer dinner (£12) and open year round.

Contact the island's tourist association (☎ 45510) for details of transport from Roonagh Quay (return £15/7.50). *Caher Star* (☎ 45541) sails from Cleggan Pier in County Galway to Inishturk via Inishbofin at 11.30 am on Wednesday, Thursday, Friday and Sunday in summer. It leaves Inishturk at 9.30 am. The return fare is £7.50/3.75.

NEWPORT
☎ 098 • pop 520

The small 18th-century town of Newport (Baile Uí Fhiacháin), on the River Newport about 12km north of Westport, is a popular base for **fishing** in the nearby loughs and Clew Bay.

The tourist office (☎ 41822), on Main St opposite the Angler's Rest pub, opens weekdays, June to September. The post office, with a bureau de change, is on the other side of the river. There are no banks.

From 1892 to 1936, the Great Western Railway ran a line from Westport to Achill Sound. It was later pedestrianised and now offers an interesting **walk** across the viaduct that dominates Newport, with views of the river. Newport is also at one end of the Bangor Trail (see the Bangor Erris section later in this chapter).

Places to Stay & Eat

In the centre is *Debille House* (☎ 41145), with singles/doubles costing £25/40, but it opens June to October only. *Reek View* (☎ 41202), on the Mulrany road (N59), charges £20/30 and opens year round. The poshest place in these parts is the genteel *Newport House* (☎ 41222), in the centre, which costs upwards of £78/126. Dinner here is a stiff £32, but the snug little bar is worth a visit any time.

Bridge Inn (*Main St*), next to the Newport House entrance, serves light food cost-

ing £4 to £8. *Debille House Café* costs about the same. Across the river on the road to Westport, *Black Oak Inn* serves bar food and has a small restaurant.

Getting There & Away

In July and August, Bus Éireann (☎ 096-71800) bus No 66 from Achill Sound to Belfast stops at Newport and goes on through Ballina, Sligo and Enniskillen. Year round, another service links Achill Sound and Westport via Newport once daily, Monday to Saturday. The bus stop is outside Debille House.

AROUND NEWPORT
Burrishoole Abbey

Founded in 1486 by the Dominicans, what remains of the abbey is a solid tower and the eastern window of the cloisters. It's beside the river that drains Lough Furnace into the sea. About 2.5km north-west of Newport on the Newport to Achill road, a sign points the way, and it's 1km down to the left.

Rockfleet Castle

Formerly known as Carrigahowley, this 15th-century castle has a strong association with Grace O'Malley (see the boxed text earlier in this chapter). The story goes that, after the death of her first husband, Grace got married a second time – to Richard Burke – on the condition that at the end of the first year either party could summarily dissolve the marriage. When the year was up she shut herself up in her fortified castle and announced the divorce as he approached.

Whether the story is true or not, the castle, at the head of the inlet, does look impregnable. Grace O'Malley is supposed to have lived out the rest of her years here, and in 1574 she successfully repulsed an English force besieging the castle.

To get there, turn south at the sign about 5km west of Newport on the road to Achill.

Mulrany

This small town (An Mhala Raithní, also called Mallaranny or Mulrany) stands on the isthmus between Clew Bay, with its (supposed) 365 islands, and Bellacagher Bay and boasts a **lovely big beach**. To get to it, either take the footpath opposite the defunct Mulrany Bay Hotel, a huge cream-and-chocolate pile on the N59, or continue a little way past the hotel and bear left following the Atlantic Drive sign, then left again where the sign points to Mallaranny Strand, another Blue Flag beach.

Mulrany Bay Hotel may reopen one day, and if it does the owners will hopefully retain the Lennon Suite, named after John Lennon, who came here for a visit and ended up purchasing one of the little islands in Clew Bay.

Places to Stay & Eat

The An Óige *Traenlaur Lodge* (☎ 098-41358), charging £7.50/5.50 for dorm beds, is on Lough Feeagh 8km from Newport and signposted on the road to Achill.

Achill seems the obvious destination if you're travelling from Newport, but the wild Curraun Peninsula, joined to Achill Island by a bridge, has a couple of B&Bs where you can get away from it all. *Curraun House* (☎ 098-45228), open June to September, is attached to the George Pub, which serves lunch and dinner, and offers B&B costing £13 per person. To get there, follow the beautiful Atlantic Drive road from Mulrany; Curraun House is on the south-western corner of the peninsula, just before a sign pointing up to Achill Sound. Shortly after you turn up towards Achill Sound you come to Mrs Cannon's *Teach Mweewillin* (☎ 098-45134), open April to September. It charges £22.50 for singles without bathroom and £18 per person in en suite doubles.

The beach at Mulrany has a field marked out for *camping*, and there are public toilets nearby.

ACHILL ISLAND

☎ 098 • pop 3500

Joined to the mainland (the Curraun Peninsula) by a bridge, Achill (An Caol) combines views, bogland and mountains on just one island – at 147 sq km, the largest off the Irish coast. For most of this century Achill was forgotten by tourists and, many of the islanders would assert, the Dublin government. The amount of arable land is limited, and there are few employment opportunities to keep young people around. Slievemore Deserted Village is the most dramatic evidence of the process of decay that affected remote rural Ireland. Things are changing, however, as the number of visitors increases.

The village of **Dooagh** is where Don Allum, the first person to row across the Atlantic Ocean in *both* directions, landed in September 1982 in his 6m-long plywood boat, the *QE3*, after 77 days at sea. The Pub (that's its name) has photos and other memorabilia of the feat, and there's a small memorial opposite.

The village of Keel is the island's main centre of activity.

Information

The helpful, locally run tourist office (☎ 47353), in a portable cabin beside the Esso service station on the road to Keel, opens 9 am to 5 pm on weekdays year round (with extended hours in July and August). Bord Fáilte (☎ 45384), in a cabin at the other side of the same service station, opens in July and August only.

Most of the villages have a post office. O'Malley's Spar supermarket in Keel doubles as a post office and will change money. There are no banks on the island but mobile banks visit the various villages; the tourist office's *A Visitor's Guide* has the times.

Slievemore Deserted Village

Different explanations have been given for the abandonment of Slievemore some time in the middle of the 19th century. The 'booley houses' here were the summer residences of cattle grazers. Years of famine may have forced them to seek a living nearer the sea: the inhabitants, it seems, moved permanently down to the coast at Dooagh. In modern times people have started moving back to the area and there is new housing near the village.

ACHILL ISLAND

MAYO & SLIGO

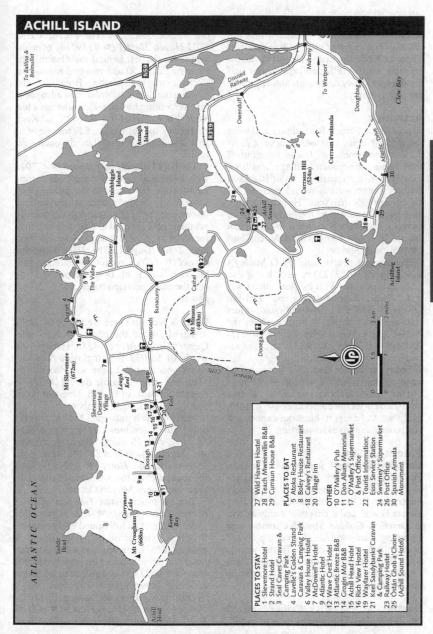

PLACES TO STAY
1 Slievemore Hotel
2 Strand Hotel
3 Seal Caves Caravan & Camping Park
4 Lavelle's Golden Strand Caravan & Camping Park
6 Valley House Hostel
7 McDowell's Hostel
9 Atlantic Hotel
12 Wave Crest Hotel
13 Atlantic Breeze B&B
14 Grogin Mór B&B
15 Achill Head Hotel
16 Rich View Hostel
19 Wayfarer Hostel
21 Keel Sandybanks Caravan & Camping Park
23 Railway Hostel
25 Óstán Ghob a'Choire (Achill Sound Hotel)
27 Wild Haven Hostel
28 Teach Mweewillin B&B
29 Curraun House B&B

PLACES TO EAT
5 Atoka Restaurant
8 Boley House Restaurant
18 Calvey's Restaurant
20 Village Inn

OTHER
10 O'Malley's Pub
11 Don Allum Memorial
17 O'Malley's Supermarket & Post Office
22 Tourist Information; Esso Service Station
24 Sweeney's Supermarket
26 Post Office
30 Spanish Armada Monument

MAYO & SLIGO

Beaches

Achill has some lovely beaches that are often all but deserted even in fine weather. Those at Keel, Keem and Dugort (Doogort on some maps) are Blue Flag beaches, and the ones at Dooega, Dooagh and Dooniver are just as sandy.

Activities

The island is perfect for walking and even the highest point (Mt Slievemore, 672m) presents no problems. It can be climbed from behind the deserted village, and from the top there are terrific views of Blacksod Bay. A longer climb would take in Mt Croaghaun (668m), Achill Head and a walk atop what are said to be the highest cliffs in Europe. The walk is covered in *New Irish Walks: West and North* (Gill & Macmillan) by Whilde & Simms.

Sea-angling gear is sold by O'Malley's Island Sports (☎ 43125) in Keel. It can also arrange boat hire. With its clear, clean waters Achill is a good diving spot. Dol-Fin Divers (☎ 45473), in Achill Sound, offers training and equipment hire, as does the Achill Island Scuba Dive Centre (☎ 087-234 9884), in Keel, which also arranges accommodation packages.

Other activities include windsurfing, hang-gliding from the top of Mt Minaun (403m), rock climbing and surfing. Richie O'Hara at McDowell's Hotel (☎ 43148), south-west of Dugort, hires out canoes and surfboards and gives instruction.

Places to Stay

Camping The *Keel Sandybanks Caravan and Camping Park* (☎ 43211) charges £6.50 for a tent site and opens June to early September. In the north, close to the Valley House Hostel and a beautiful sandy beach, is *Lavelle's Golden Strand Caravan and Camping Park* (☎ 47232), charging £6 and open mid-April to October. To the west is *Seal Caves Caravan and Camping Park* (☎ 43262), which also charges £6 (plus 50p per person).

Hostels At the IHO *Railway Hostel* (☎ 45187), on the eastern side of Achill

Sound bridge, dorm beds cost £6 and the one double costs £14. The excellent IHO *Wild Haven Hostel* (☎ 45392) is over the bridge on the left behind the church. The basic rate is £7.50 and two-bed rooms cost £2.50 extra per person. Breakfast and evening meals can be ordered in advance at this welcoming hostel, which also has a bar. *Rich View Hostel* (☎ 43462), in Keel, charges £7 for dorm beds, £20 for one of its five doubles. All three hostels open year round.

The IHO *Valley House Hostel* (☎ 47204), with a licensed bar and dorm beds costing £6.50, is in the north of the island, with some lovely sandy beaches within walking distance. It opens mid-March to October. To get there, take the road to Keel and turn right (north-east) at the Bunacurry junction signposted for Dugort. The IHH *Wayfarer Hostel* (☎ 43266), open mid-March to mid-October, is in Keel. Dorm beds cost £6.50 and the three private rooms cost £7.50 per person.

B&Bs & Hotels There are plenty of B&Bs scattered around the island. In Keel, Mrs Quinn's *Grogin Mór* (☎ 43385) charges upwards of £20/32 for singles/doubles and opens year round. To the west in Pollagh, Mary Sweeney's *Atlantic Breeze* (☎ 43189) charges upwards of £19/28, hires out bikes, and opens April to September.

Many of the hotels open May to October only, but *Slievemore Hotel* (☎ 43224, Dugort), with 18 rooms, opens year round and charges upwards of £27/36. Nearby, the 15-room *Strand Hotel* (☎ 43241), facing the sea and close to a small beach, costs the same and opens May to October.

The 36-room *Óstán Ghob a' Choire* (Achill Sound Hotel; ☎ 45245) is on the western side of Achill Sound bridge and the first hotel you come to on the island. It charges £25/45 in high season. Another hotel that opens most of the year is *Atlantic Hotel* (☎ 43113, Dooagh), which charges £30/48 in summer for its 10 rooms.

Other hotels that open seasonally are the 19-room *Achill Head Hotel* (☎ 43108, Keel), *McDowell's Hotel* (☎ 43148, Slieve-

more Rd) and the 12-room ***Wave Crest Hotel** (☎ 43115, Dooagh)*.

Places to Eat
If you're camping or hostelling, stock up at Sweeney's supermarket, which is just across the bridge as you enter Achill, or at O'Malley's Spar supermarket in Keel. Nearly all the hotels serve lunch or dinner to nonresidents, with dinner costing upwards of £14 at the ***Strand Hotel*** in Dugort, and up to £16.50 at the ***Atlantic Hotel*** in Dooagh.

At Dugort the cosy little ***Atoka Restaurant** (☎ 47229)* has a conventional menu of fish and meat dishes costing £8 to £11.50, and vegetarian pie costs £6.50. At Keel the most popular eating place is ***Boley House Restaurant** (☎ 43147)*. If that's full try farther down the road at the junction, where ***Calvey's Restaurant*** opens all day and serves breakfast. Also close by is ***Village Inn***, serving pub food and dinner.

Entertainment
From May to September most pubs and hotels have music. The best time of year for traditional Irish music and dance is the first two weeks of August, when the Scoil Acla Festival promotes Irish culture and music through a number of workshops. Most bands end up in the pubs at night.

Getting There & Away
In July and August Bus Éireann (☎ 096-71800) bus No 66 runs from Dooagh, outside O'Malley's, to Keel, Achill Sound, Westport, Sligo, Enniskillen and eventually Belfast. It leaves Dooagh at 7.30 am and Achill Sound 20 minutes later. Coming from Westport, the bus leaves at 5.45 pm.

Year round, Monday to Saturday, a bus runs across the island from Dooagh, taking in Keel, Dugort, Dooega and Achill Sound before crossing to Mulrany, Newport, Westport and finally Ballina. Check the schedule with the tourist office as it changes daily.

Getting Around
Bikes can be hired from the Railway Hostel, Achill Sound Hotel or O'Malley's Island Sports (☎ 43125), the Raleigh Rent-a-Bike agent, in Keel.

BANGOR ERRIS
☎ 097
The main reason for visiting this village is to begin or end the 48km **Bangor Trail**, which connects Bangor (Bain Gear), as its called, and Newport. This extraordinary walk takes you through the bleakest, most remote landscape found anywhere in Ireland. The useful *County Mayo: The Bangor Trail* (£6) by Joe McDermott & Robert Chapman is available in Keohane's Bookshop in Ballina and elsewhere. Unfortunately, you'll need more than one of the 1:50,000 OS maps to cover the trail.

Hillcrest House (☎ 83494, Main St) has B&B from £22.50/32 in singles/doubles and opens year round. Opposite, *Kitty's Tavern* (aka Kiltane Tavern) serves pub food all day and has fresh and smoked local wild salmon for sale.

See Getting There & Away in the following Mullet Peninsula section for bus transport information.

MULLET PENINSULA
☎ 097
Probably the least visited corner of Ireland, this strange, remote region has a population density of only 10 people per sq km. The flat peninsula, 30km in length, rarely rises more than 30m above sea level, and the boggy land offers a poor livelihood. The western side is exposed to the Atlantic, while its eastern coast forms part of the sheltered Blacksod Bay. The peninsula is Irish speaking and Belmullet is the main town.

Information
In Belmullet, Erris Tourist Information Centre (☎ 81500), Barrack St, opens 9.30 am to 5.30 pm Monday to Saturday, Easter to September. McIntyre's Travel (☎ 81147), an agency on Main St, has some local information, and there's a tourist-information board opposite the Anchor pub. The Ulster Bank (Banc Uladh) is on Main St, and the Bank of Ireland is at the roundabout to the

east; both have ATMs. The post office is at the western end of the same street, opposite the Údarás na Gaeltachta (Gaeltacht Authority; ☎ 82382) and library, which has a small exhibition on the peninsula.

Belmullet

Belmullet (Béal an Mhuirthead) was founded in 1825 by the local landlord, William Carter, and built on an unimaginative plan, with one main street and side roads at right angles. Carter also designed a canal joining Broad Haven Bay with Trawmore and Blacksod Bays to the south, and a bridge now crosses the narrow channel.

Blacksod Point & Around

The road south from Belmullet curves round the tip of the peninsula before rejoining itself at Aghleam. Near the point are the remains of an old church, and the view across the bay takes in the spot where *La Rata Santa Maria Encoronada*, part of the 1588 Spanish Armada, came in and was later burned by the captain. He then left to join two other Spanish ships that had found refuge farther north, in Elly Bay.

The road to Blacksod Point passes Elly Bay on the eastern coast, which has a decent beach and is a favourite haunt of birdwatchers. Farther south it passes sandy Mullaghroe Beach. In the early years of this century, a whaling station operated at Ardelly Point, just north of the beach.

Doonamo Point

This typical promontory fort is the main point of interest north of Belmullet. It's built on a spit of land and defended by water on three sides. There are other forts farther north near Erris Head, but this one is the most accessible.

Places to Stay & Eat

There's the usual run of bungalow B&Bs on the main road approaching Belmullet. Singles/doubles cost £17/30 at *Western Strands Hotel* (☎ 81096, Main St). If its 10 rooms are full, Mrs Gaughan's *Mill House* (☎ 81181, American St), nearby, has four rooms costing £17/28. It opens June to August.

Appetiser Café, at the top of Main St, serves soup, salads and sandwiches costing under £2, meals costing £3.

There is *Padden's Family Fare Restaurant* on the roundabout at the start of Main St. *Western Strands* serves snacks, and a set dinner in its rear dining room costs £15.

Getting There & Away

One Bus Éireann bus daily Monday to Saturday runs from Ballina to Bangor Erris (one hour) and Belmullet (1½ hours) then south to Blacksod Point. Contact Ballina bus station (☎ 096-71800) for the schedule. McNulty's Coaches (☎ 81086), with an office on Chapel St in Belmullet, runs a bus to Galway and Ennis in County Clare via Newport and Westport at 5.30 pm on Sunday. There's also a daily service to Castlebar via Newport departing at 8.15 am and leaving Castlebar at 5.30 pm. There's an additional service from Belmullet at 5.30 pm on Sunday.

Getting Around

In Belmullet, you can hire bikes from Walsh's Garage (☎ 82260), Chapel St, opposite the McNulty's Coaches office.

POLLATOMISH
☎ 097

At tiny Pollatomish (Poll an Tómais), also spelled Pullathomas, some 16km east of Belmullet, signposted on the road to Ballycastle (R314), there's a sandy beach and headland walks nearby. The excellent IHH *Kilcommon Lodge Hostel* (☎ 84621) has dorm beds costing £7.50 and opens year round.

BALLYCASTLE & AROUND
☎ 096

The Ballycastle (Baile an Chaisil) area boasts some of the oldest, most extensive Stone Age excavations in Europe, and some beautiful coastal scenery. The village itself consists of one sloping street. A small seasonal tourist office is near the church at the bottom of the main street, but is scheduled to move.

Céide Fields

Over 5000 years ago there was a wheat-and-barley-farming community with domesticated cattle and sheep at Céide Fields (Achaidh Chéide). The growth of the bog led to the decline and eventual end of the community, and their stone walls and farm buildings disappeared into the bog. Perhaps the farmers, gradually diminishing the soil's fertility, contributed to the growth of the bog, or maybe the wet climate made it inevitable. Whatever the cause, the farms lay buried for thousands of years, but have now been excavated and opened to the public as the oldest enclosed landscape in Europe and the most extensive Stone Age monument in the world.

The Interpretive Centre (☎ 43325), run by Dúchas in a modern glass pyramid overlooking the site, incorporates an exhibition court and audiovisual room detailing aspects of the site's architecture, botany and geology (a script of the exhibition is available in French and German). There's also a panoramic viewing platform and tearooms. It opens 9.30 am to 6.30 pm daily, June to September; 10 am to 5 pm daily, mid-March to May and October; and 10 am to 4.30 pm daily, November. Admission costs £2.50/1.

Céide Fields is 8km west of Ballycastle on the main R314 road.

Downpatrick Head

North-east of Ballycastle, Downpatrick Head has a fenced-off blowhole that occasionally shoots up plumes of water. The rock stack just off the shore is called Dun Briste.

Places to Stay & Eat

B&B is available from *Sunatrai* (☎ 43040), on the road to Downpatrick Head from Ballycastle, costing £20/32 for singles/doubles from mid-June to mid-August. The *Céide House* pub (☎ 43105) in town has similarly priced rooms.

Beyond Céide Fields at Belderrig, which has another prehistoric farm site, *The Hawthorns* (☎ 43148) offers B&B year round costing £22.50/32, while *Yellow Rose* (☎ 43125) is a little cheaper at £20/30.

Shanaghy (☎ 43305), 3km west of Ballycastle, has attractive holiday cottages available for £140 to £260 per week, depending on the size of the cottage and the season. There are special weekend rates.

In Ballycastle, the *Céide House* pub and the nearby *Katie Mac's*, which has a beer garden, serve food costing upwards of £5. At the bottom of the main street *Mary's Bakery and Tea Rooms* serves good sandwiches, cakes and apple tart.

Getting There & Away

Bus Éireann (☎ 71800) bus No 445 runs between Ballina and Ballycastle once or twice daily, Monday to Saturday, stopping outside Katie Mac's.

KILLALA & AROUND
☎ 096 • pop 710

It's claimed that St Patrick founded Killala (Cill Alaidh), and the 25m round tower is evidence of the role the town played in early Church history. The tower was struck by lightning in 1800 and the cap is a later reconstruction. The Church of Ireland cathedral is supposedly built on the site of the first Christian church, where St Patrick installed Muiredach as the town's first bishop.

It's the French connection that has really put Killala on the map, however. On 22 August 1798, over 1000 troops under the command of General Humbert landed in Killala Bay, the plan being that Irish peasants would rise in rebellion and help Napoleon in his war against the British. At first there were dramatic successes, with Killala, Ballina and Castlebar falling. On 8 September, however, Humbert was defeated by Cornwallis at Ballinamuck in County Longford. The best account of Humbert's arrival in Killala was written by the Protestant Bishop Stock. He was put under house arrest by the French, and his *Narrative* is available in some bookshops in Ballina and Castlebar.

Information

Tourist information is available 9.30 am to 5.30 pm daily, July to September, from the

Community Centre (☎ 32166) as you enter Killala on the Ballina road (R314). There are no banks, but there's a post office in the centre.

Rathfran Abbey
The Dominicans came here in 1274 and built a friary, but only some ruins remain. In 1590 the friary was closed down and burned by the English, but the monks stayed in the community until the 18th century.

Take the R314 road that heads north out of Killala and, after 5km and crossing the Cloonaghmore River, turn right. After another 2km turn right at the crossroads.

Breastagh Ogham Stone
The stone is 2.5m high, but the ogham script is not easy to read. It's in a field by the left side of the R314 just past the crossroads with the turning for Rathfran Abbey (not the earlier crossroads, which has a sign for both the stone and the abbey). Cross the ditch just where the sign points to the stone.

Kilcummin & Lackan Bay
Kilcummin, at the head of Killala Bay, is where General Humbert's army landed in 1798. A right turn off the main R314 is signposted for Kilcummin. On the R314 just after the turning to Lackan Bay a sculpture of a French revolutionary soldier helping a prostrate Irish peasant marks the place where the first French soldier died on Irish soil. Lackan Bay itself is wonderfully sandy and ideal for young children.

Places to Stay & Eat
The B&Bs are mostly outside Killala. *Beach View* (☎ 32023) is reached by turning right at the sign to the beach. Singles/doubles here cost £22.50/32. Nearby, *Chez Nous* (☎ 32056) charges £20/32. Both open year round.

On the Ballycastle road, *Anchor Inn* serves food, including cod and chips costing £5.50. Opposite, *Country Kitchen Restaurant*, one of the few restaurants around, is recommended; its mixed grill costs £7.75 and there are several vegetarian options costing £4.25.

Getting There & Away
The Ballina to Ballycastle bus, which runs once or twice daily Monday to Saturday, stops outside the hostel and McGregor's. Ring ☎ 71800 for details.

BALLINA & AROUND
☎ 096 • pop 8200
The largest town in the county, Ballina (Béal an Átha; pronounced 'balli-*nagh*') is renowned for its fishing and is a good base for exploring northern Mayo and the North Mayo Sculpture Trail. The tourist office has free maps of interesting walks near the town.

Ballina is a not-unattractive Connaught town, with some decent pubs and fine restaurants. Its most famous progeny is Mary Robinson, the much loved former president of Ireland.

Information
The tourist office (☎ 70848), across the River Moy from the centre, on Cathedral Rd near West Bridge, opens 10 am to 1 pm and 2 to 5.30 pm, Monday to Saturday, mid-April to September. There are several banks on Pearse St, including the Ulster Bank and Bank of Ireland, both with ATMs and bureaux de change. The post office is at the top of O'Rahilly St, the southern extension of Pearse St.

Keohane's Bookshop, Tone St, has a decent selection of maps and walking guides. Opposite is the Jiffy Cleaners laundrette, though it's not self-service.

Rosserk Abbey
Close to the River Rosserk, a tributary of the Moy, this Franciscan abbey dates from the mid-15th century. It's remarkably well preserved, and there's an interesting carved piscina (a perforated stone basin for carrying away the water used in rinsing the chalices) in the chancel. Like Rathfran Abbey near Killala, Rosserk was burned down by Richard Bingham, the English governor of Connaught, in the 16th century.

To get there, leave Ballina on the R314 for Killala and after 6.5km turn right at the sign and take the first left at the next crossroads. The loose sign at this junction may point in any direction but the right one. Continue for another kilometre, then turn right at the next sign for the abbey.

Moyne Abbey

This abbey was established by the Franciscans around the same time as Rosserk. It, too, was burned down by Richard Bingham in the 16th century. Perhaps he did a better job on this one, as it is in worse condition than its neighbour.

After leaving Rosserk Abbey go back to the main road and continue north for another 3km until you can see the abbey on the right across a field. After returning across the field, continue north-west for 1.5km until the main R314 is reached. Turn right for Killala or left for Ballina.

North Mayo Sculpture Trail

This trail of 15 outdoor sculptures essentially follows the R314 from Ballina (Point A, *Guest Space* by Peter Hynes) to Blacksod Point (Point O, *Deirble's Twist* by Michael Bulfin). The project was inaugurated to mark 5000 years of Mayo history, and leading sculptors from eight countries were commissioned to create works of art reflecting the beauty and wilderness of the northern Mayo countryside.

Fishing

The **River Moy** is one of the most prolific salmon rivers in Europe and a leaflet listing the fisheries and contacts for permits is available from the tourist office. You can see the scaly critters jumping in the Ridge (salmon pool), with otters and grey seals in famished pursuit. The season runs from February to September, but the best fishing is June to August.

Lough Conn, south-west of Ballina, is an important brown trout fishery, and there's no shortage of places with boats and ghillies available round the lake. Pontoon is a good base for trout fishing in both Lough Conn and **Lough Cullin** to the south, and again there are plenty of places hiring boats and dispensing advice. The daily rate for hiring a motor boat is £30.

Swimming

Ballina Swimming Pool (☎ 70506), up behind the tourist office off Cathedral Rd, opens daily and costs £2.20/1.10.

Special Events

The two-week Ballina Street Festival, one of the best outdoor parties in the country, takes place in July. Heritage Day is when shopfronts – and Ballina townsfolk – take on a 19th-century look during the festival.

Places to Stay

The well-equipped *Belleek Caravan and Camping Park* (☎ 71533) is 2.5km north of town off the road to Killala (R314). A tent costs £6, and there is a £1 charge per person. Hikers and cyclists pay £3.50, motorcyclists £4.

Ballina has plenty of B&Bs. *Adara House* (☎ 71112, Station Rd), south-west of the centre, stays open year round and charges £20 for singles without bathroom, £34 for en suite doubles.

Bartra House (☎ 22200) is an old-style hotel on Pearse St with 22 rooms costing £30 to £35 per person, depending on the season. Ballina's poshest hotel, complete with swimming pool, is the 50-room *Downhill Hotel* (☎ 21033), with rooms costing £45 to £54 per person. It's north of the centre on the Sligo road (N59). An equally posh guesthouse, *Mount Falcon Castle* (☎ 70811), 6.5km south of town on the Foxford road (N57), charges £35 to £60 per person.

Places to Eat

A good choice for a moderately priced meal is *Tullios (Pearse St)*. Meat and poultry main courses cost £6.50 to £12, pastas £5 to £8.

Salmon – poached, grilled, baked or smoked – is the speciality of Ballina and you could try it at the excellent *Old Bond Store (Dillon Terrace)*, off the northern end of Pearse St; salmon, poached or grilled, costs £8.50. You could also try some at *Murphy Bros*, a pub-restaurant on Clare St north of the tourist office, which offers a three-course dinner costing £20.

Cafolla's (Bridge St) is a café and take-away serving fish, grills and burgers. *Padraic's*, next to Keohane's Bookshop, has a wide selection of quick meals, with big portions costing upwards of £4.95. *The Junction*, on the corner of Pearse and Tone Sts, is similar (chicken costs £3.10) and opens till midnight. Lots of pubs on Pearse St serve lunch.

Entertainment

Ballina counts some 60 pubs, and many have traditional-music sessions on Wednesday and Friday evenings. Among the best are *Broken Jug*, at the top of O'Rahilly St, *Brogan's (Garden St)*, *Murphy Bros (Clare St)* and *An Bolg Buí* (The Yellow Belly) by the river on the corner of Bridge and Barrett Sts.

Getting There & Away

Bus From the bus station (☎ 71800), on Kevin Barry St south-west of the centre, Bus Éireann buses go west to Achill Island, east to Sligo, to the North (Belfast, Enniskillen, Derry) and south to Limerick, Shannon and Cork.

Two private bus companies run scheduled trips at cheaper rates, though they basically operate to transport pupils to and from school. Treacy Coaches (☎ 22563) runs a daily return service from outside Dunnes store on Pearse St to the Quay St car park in Sligo (50 minutes). Barton Transport (☎ 01-628 6026) has a daily return service between Ballina and Dublin (Cook St).

Train The train station (☎ 71800) is on Station Rd, the southern extension of Kevin Barry St.

The Westport to Dublin train stops at Ballina up to three times daily. Connections to other routes can be made at Athlone.

Getting Around

Bicycles can be hired from Gerry's Cycle Centre (☎ 70455), 6 Lord Edward St; turn right at the top of O'Rahilly St and it's about 500m on the left.

CROSSMOLINA & AROUND
☎ 096

The small undistinguished town of Crossmolina (Crois Mhaoiliona), 13km west of Ballina, sits near the northern shores of Lough Conn. There's a small seasonal tourist office off the main street, and a Bank of Ireland opposite Hiney's pub.

North Mayo Family History Research & Heritage Centre

If you have a family connection with northern Mayo, this is the place to contact (☎ 31809, email normayo@iol.ie). An initial assessment costs £50; if this looks promising your full family record is researched (£150, less the initial assessment fee).

The heritage centre houses a collection of old farm machinery and domestic implements. It opens 9 am to 4 pm on weekdays, and 2 to 6 pm at the weekend, June and September; and 9 am to 4 pm on weekdays, the rest of the year. The centre is about 3km south, in Castlehill on the Castlebar road.

Errew Abbey

The abbey is the remains of a house for Augustinian monks built around 1250 on the site of an earlier 7th-century church. As in other abbeys in Mayo, the monks wisely chose to live close to where they could fish, and the location of Errew Abbey is particularly picturesque.

To get there, take the Castlebar road south, and 1km past the heritage centre turn left at the sign and keep going for another 5km.

Activities

Crossmolina serves as a quiet retreat for anyone wishing to fish in Lough Conn or explore the lakes and scenery around Mt Nephin (806m). The mountain takes under two hours to climb and is described, along with other walks in Mayo, in *New Irish Walks: West and North* (Gill & Macmillan) by Whilde & Simms.

Places to Stay & Eat

Enniscoe House (☎ 31112), in Castlehill near the heritage centre, is a friendly 18th-century home offering B&B costing £62 to £152 per person; dinner costs £25. It opens April to mid-October. **Shalom House** (☎ 31230), at Gortnor Abbey, charges £16/28 for singles/doubles for B&B; dinner costs £12. It opens March to September.

Hiney's pub in the town centre, voted the best pub in Mayo in 1998, serves good bar food all day. Nearby, the inexpensive **Tea Rooms** has sandwiches costing upwards of £1.

Getting There & Away
There are regular Bus Éireann (☎ 71800) buses to Ballina and Castlebar. The bus stop is outside Hiney's pub.

CASTLEBAR & AROUND
☎ 094 • pop 7650
Castlebar (Caisleán an Bharraigh) has far less appeal to travellers than Westport or even Ballina. The old shops have been replaced by modern stores, and there's little to evoke its past, but the town does have a place in history.

Here in 1798 General Humbert's army of French revolutionary soldiers and dispossessed Irish peasants encountered the numerically stronger British forces under the command of General Lake. The defeat of the British and their ignominious cavalry retreat became known as the Castlebar Races.

The large, attractive village green, known as the Mall, was once the cricket ground of the Lucan family, who own a significant amount of property in the area. The notorious Lord Lucan disappeared after the murder of his children's nanny in London in 1974.

Information
The tourist office (☎ 21207), on Linenhall St near the Castlebar Shopping Centre, opens 9.30 am to 1 pm and 2 to 5.30 pm, mid-April to early September. To get there, turn left (west) at the northern end of Market St, the main thoroughfare.

The AIB, Market St, and Bank of Ireland, Ellison St (the northern extension of Market St), have ATMs and bureaux de change.

Una's Laundrette is on New Antrim St, round the corner from the tourist office and a short walk from Hughes House Holiday Hostel.

Turlough Round Tower
The 9th-century tower stands next to a ruined 18th-century church and a graveyard that is still in use. The tower is about 5km north-east of Castlebar on the N5 road.

Michael Davitt Memorial Museum
The museum in Straide (Strade on some maps) is attached to the church and houses a small collection of material relating to the life and times of Michael Davitt (1846–1906), a Fenian and founding member of the Irish National Land League, who is buried in the churchyard. The museum opens 2 to 6 pm, Tuesday to Saturday, April to October. Admission costs 50p.

Take the N5 east and turn left (north-east) onto the N58 to Straide. It's 16km from Castlebar.

Ballintubber Abbey
The only church in Ireland that was founded by an Irish king and is still in use, Ballintubber Abbey (☎ 30934) was set up in 1216 next to the site of an earlier church founded by St Patrick after he came down from Croagh Patrick. It's one of the most impressive church buildings in Ireland and well worth a visit.

Features of the church include the 15th-century western doorway and 13th-century windows on the right side of the nave. The nave roof was erected in 1965 and is an Irish-oak reproduction of the timber one burned down by Cromwell's soldiers in 1653.

Take the N84 heading south to Galway and after about 13km a signposted road on the left leads a farther 2km to the abbey.

Places to Stay
The immaculate IHH **Hughes House Holiday Hostel** (☎ 23877, Thomas St), which is round the corner from the tourist office, opens May to September and has dorm beds

MAYO & SLIGO

costing £8.50 and two private rooms costing £11 per person.

There are lots of B&Bs in and around Castlebar, but among the most central is *Ivy House* (*☎ 21527, Castle St*), just off Market St. Open year round, it has singles/doubles costing £25/36.

Places to Eat

Gavin's Bakery, on Market St, is a good spot for sandwiches, snacks and cakes. There's a reasonable café in the *Linenhall Arts Centre* next to the tourist office. Back on Market St, the *Oriental* Chinese restaurant serves main courses costing upwards of £5.80 and opens daily.

Two decent choices on New Antrim St are *Jay Dee's Restaurant and Coffee Shop* and the popular *Café Rua*, where soup and bread costs £2.85. The upmarket *Daly's Hotel* (*☎ 21961, The Mall*) has a varied bar menu; a vegetarian burrito costs £4.

Getting There & Away

Bus Numerous Bus Éireann (*☎ 096-71800*) buses connect Castlebar with the rest of the country. Express bus No 21 connecting Westport (20 minutes) and Dublin (four hours 30 minutes) stops outside Flannelly's pub on Market St three times daily (once on Sunday) in each direction. Bus No 51 runs south to Shannon and Cork and north to Ballina four times daily (twice on Sunday). Bus No 69 north-east to Sligo (two hours 15 minutes) and Derry (four hours 15 minutes) goes once daily, Monday to Saturday, July and August only.

McNulty's Coaches (*☎ 097-81086*), which is based in Belmullet, runs a daily service from Castlebar to Belmullet at 5.30 pm. It returns from Belmullet at 8.15 am.

Train The Westport to Dublin (three hours 15 minutes) train stops at Castlebar three times daily. The train station is out of town on the Galway road. For times call ☎ 098-25253.

Getting Around

Taxis can be hired by ringing Hughes Taxis (*☎ 088-601453*).

Bike World (*☎ 25220*), New Antrim St, and Tommy Robinson's service station (*☎ 21355*), Spencer St, rent bikes. The latter charges £8/35 per day/week and organises cycle tours of the area.

KNOCK
☎ 094 • pop 440

The once undistinguished village of Knock (Cnoc Mhuire), at the junction of the N17 and the R323, has been famous for over a century as the site of visions and miracles: Catholic Ireland's answer to Lourdes or Fatima.

The Knock Marian Shrine consists of several churches and shrines, including the modern basilica and the Church of the Apparition. North of the latter are shops, restaurants and the tourist office (*☎ 88193*), which opens 10 am to 6 pm daily, May to September. There's a Bank of Ireland nearby with an ATM, but it opens only 10.15 am to 12.15 pm on Monday and Thursday, May to October (Monday only the rest of the year).

Church of the Apparition

One wet evening in August 1879, two Knock women were apparently struck by the sight of Mary, Joseph and St John the Evangelist standing in light against the southern gable of the local church. Others were called to witness the apparition, and a Church investigation quickly confirmed the apparition as a bona fide miracle. Other miracles followed as the sick and disabled claimed amazing recoveries after visiting the church. Another Church commission upheld Knock's status in 1936. Today, the Knock industry continues, and dutiful worshippers are always found praying at the chapel built to enclose the scene of the apparition. Above the altar is a sculptural representation of what people saw. Near the church is the modern **Basilica of Our Lady, Queen of Ireland**, which can accommodate 12,000 people.

Accompanying the fervent, almost medieval piety of the pilgrims is a display of commercial exuberance that can seem unspeakably tacky. Wall thermometers, shake-up snow domes and plastic holy-water bottles shaped like the Virgin are easy to mock. But just remember that many people have spent much of their savings to come here and, for many of the Catholic faithful, Knock is as sacred a place as the Wailing Wall in Jerusalem is to Jews, Mecca to Muslims or the Ganges to Hindus. Knock was visited by Pope Paul VI in 1974, Pope John Paul II in 1979 (the centenary of the apparition) and Mother Teresa in 1993.

Knock Folk Museum

This small museum (☎ 88100) is one of the better ones of its type around and also serves as an ideal introduction to the Knock phenomenon. There's plenty of material on the apparition and subsequent Church commissions of inquiry, including photographs of the crutches left behind by grateful pilgrims. The museum also houses an extensive collection of craft tools, costumes and various artefacts relating to rural life in the west of Ireland. It is all attractively presented.

The museum is in a building near the basilica and opens 10 am to 6 pm (7 pm in July and August) daily, May to October. Admission costs £2/1.25.

Places to Stay

The *Knock Caravan and Camping Park* (☎ 88100), a five-minute walk south of the shrine, costs £7.50 (hikers and motorcyclists £5.50) and opens March to October. *Byrne Craft Shop* (☎ 88184), just behind the Church of the Apparition, offers B&B, as does *Aisling House* (☎ 88558), near the entrance to the shrine on the Ballyhaunis road (R323), costing £16.50 per person. The 10-room *Knock International Hotel* (☎ 88466, Main St), in the village, charges upwards of £25 per person.

Getting There & Away

There are daily flights from Dublin to Knock Airport (☎ 67222), 15km north by the N17 near Glentavraun. Bus Éireann (☎ 096-71800) bus No 21 connects Knock with Castlebar, Westport and Athlone three times daily (once on Sunday). There are also regular direct connections with Sligo, Galway, Dublin, Ballina and Cork.

County Sligo

Despite its small size, County Sligo (Sligeach) provides a rich variety of scenery and numerous prehistoric sites. Its closest association, however, is with the poet and dramatist William Butler Yeats (1865–1939). Though he was educated in Dublin and London, his poetry is inextricably linked with the county of his mother's family. He visited Sligo frequently, becoming a close friend of the Gore-Booths, who lived at Lissadell. There are many reminders of Yeats' presence in the county town of Sligo and in the rolling green hills around it.

SLIGO

☎ 071 • pop 18,000

In Sligo town, outside the Ulster Bank on Stephen St, is the interesting **sculptural portrayal of Yeats** that has his poetry inscribed all over it. Hard to find are two famous lines from 'Easter 1916':

> All changed, changed utterly:
> A terrible beauty is born...

The poem pays homage to the executed rebels of the Easter Rising, including John MacBride, who was married to Maud Gonne. Yeats' unrequited love for Maud Gonne underlies many of his greatest poems. Politics divided them: while she remained a rebel and a socialist all her life, Yeats ended up alarmingly close to fascism.

Information

The modern North-West Regional Tourism office (☎ 61201) is south of the centre on Temple St. It opens 9 am to 5 pm on weekdays, and 9 am to 1 pm on Saturday, April to June; 9 am to 8 pm on weekdays, and 9 am to 5 pm on Saturday, July and August; and 9 am to 5 or 6 pm on weekdays, the rest of the year. You can get a free photocopied map and sheet titled 'A Walking Tour of Sligo' here. In July and August, the local

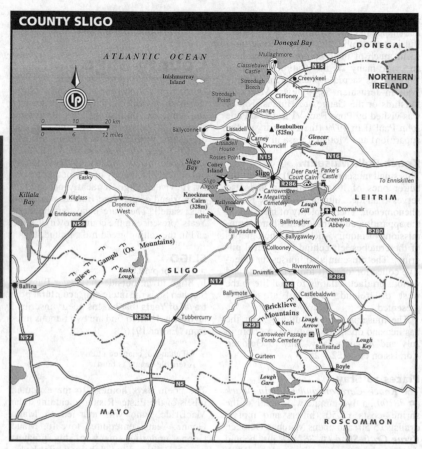

Chamber of Commerce has a tourist-information desk at the Quinsworth Shopping Centre.

Ulster Bank, the Bank of Ireland and the AIB, all with ATMs and bureaux de change, have branches on Stephen St.

The post office is on Wine St.

You can leave your laundry at Pam's Laundrette, Johnston Court, off O'Connell St, which opens 9 am to 7 pm Monday to Saturday.

Visit Keohane's Bookshop, Castle St, for maps and books by and about Yeats. The Winding Stair Bookshop, at the corner of Lower Knox St, has Irish-interest books and a café.

Sligo County Museum & Niland Gallery

Although there is other material here at the museum-gallery on Stephen St, the main appeal is the Yeats room, chock-a-block with manuscripts, photographs, letters and newspaper cuttings connected with the poet. The room also contains an apron dress worn by Countess Constance Markievicz (a member of the Gore-Booth family) while interned in Britain after the 1916 Rising.

The gallery upstairs has a good selection of paintings by Irish artists such as George Russell, Sean Keating and Jack B Yeats, brother of the poet, who said he never did a painting without putting a thought of Sligo into it.

The museum and gallery open 10.30 am to 12.30 pm and 2.30 to 4.30 pm Monday to Saturday, June to September; and 10.30 am to 12.30 pm Monday to Saturday, April, May and October. Admission is free.

Sligo Abbey

The town's founder, Maurice FitzGerald, established the abbey around 1250 for the Dominicans, but it burned down in the 15th century and was rebuilt. It was put to the torch once again in 1641, and ruins are all that remain.

The oldest parts of the abbey are the choir, the 15th-century eastern window and the altar.

The abbey (☎ 46406) is a Dúchas site and opens 9.30 am to 6.30 pm daily, June to September. If it's locked, a key is available from the caretaker, Mr Loughlin, at 6 Charlotte St. Admission costs £1.50/60p.

The Courthouse

The Victorian architecture of the courthouse on Teeling St is very unusual for Ireland, and it stands out as a reminder of the other power that once ruled this land. The exterior is extravagantly Gothic and modelled on the Law Courts in London. Inside, the building still functions as a working courthouse, and on a busy day the foyer takes the overspill from the small public gallery.

Yeats Building

On the corner of Lower Knox and O'Connell Sts, near Hyde Bridge, is the Yeats Building, the centre for the Yeats International Summer School (☎ 42693), an annual international gathering of scholars. The rest of the year it houses the Sligo Art Gallery (☎ 45847), with travelling exhibitions and paintings often up for sale. It opens 10 am to 5 pm on weekdays, and 10 am to 2 pm on Saturday.

Special Events

The 10-day Sligo Arts Festival (☎ 69802, email artsfestival@tinet.ie) takes place from late May to early June.

Places to Stay

Camping The closest camp site is *Gateway Caravan and Camping Park* (☎ 45618) in Ballinode, 3km north-east of Sligo on the N16. It costs £8.50 for tents, plus 50p per adult; hikers and cyclists pay £5. Farther afield, the *Strandhill Caravan and Camping Park* (☎ 68120), 8km west of Sligo and off the road to the airport (R292), charges £5.50 to £6.50 for a tent plus 50p per person. A third camp site close to Sligo is at Rosses Point (see the Around Sligo Town section later in this chapter).

Hostels In Marymount, the IHH *Eden Hill Holiday Hostel* (☎ 43204, Pearse Rd), about a 10-minute walk south-east from the centre on the Dublin road, costs £7 for dorm beds or £17 for one of two doubles. It opens year round. North of the centre the IHH *White House Hostel* (☎ 45160, Markievicz Rd) costs the same, but there are no private rooms. The smaller IHO *Yeats County Hostel* (☎ 46876, 12 Lord Edward St), opposite the bus/train station, costs £6.50. The modern, excellent IHO *Harbour House* (☎ 71547, Finisklin Rd), about 1km northwest of the centre, offers dorm beds costing £8 and private rooms costing £10 per person. It opens year round and offers bike hire.

B&Bs & Hotels The less expensive B&Bs are found on the various approach roads into town, including the smoke-free *Lissadell* (☎ 61937, Mail Coach Rd), with en suite doubles costing £20 per person.

Renaté House (☎ 62014, Upper John St), in the centre, is a traditional B&B costing upwards of £20/30 for singles/doubles.

Silver Swan (☎ 43231) is a comfortable and friendly hotel by the River Garavogue and close to the centre. It charges £28 to £40 per person. Also central and charging the same rates is the 11-room *Clarence Hotel* (☎ 42211, Wine St). The stately

MAYO & SLIGO

SLIGO

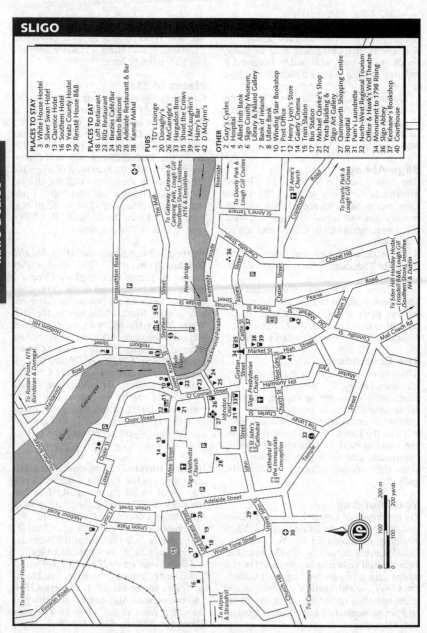

PLACES TO STAY
3 White House Hostel
9 Silver Swan Hotel
13 Clarence Hotel
16 Southern Hotel
19 Yeats County Hostel
29 Renaté House B&B

PLACES TO EAT
18 Loft Restaurant
23 Ritz Restaurant
24 Beezies Café/Bar
25 Bistro Bianconi
28 Adelaide Restaurant & Bar
38 Kamal Mahal

PUBS
1 TD's Lounge
20 Donaghy's
26 McCarrigle's
33 Hargadon Bros
35 Shoot the Crows
39 J McLaughlin's
41 Harry's Bar
42 D McLynn's

OTHER
2 Gary's Cycles
4 Hospital
5 Allied Irish Bank
6 Sligo County Museum,
   Library & Niland Gallery
7 Bank of Ireland
8 Ulster Bank
10 Winding Star Bookshop
11 Post Office
12 Henry Lyon's Store
14 Gaiety Cinema
15 Train Station
17 Bus Station
21 Michael Quirke's Shop
22 Yeats Building &
   Sligo Art Gallery
27 Quinsworth Shopping Centre
30 Hospital
31 Pam's Laundrette
32 North-West Regional Tourism
   Office & Hawk's Well Theatre
34 Monument to 1798 Rising
36 Sligo Abbey
37 Keohane's Bookshop
40 Courthouse

William Butler Yeats

The most celebrated of Irish poets, William Butler Yeats (1865–1939) was born in a suburb of Dublin. His mother was from Sligo, and Yeats spent a lot of time there as a child. At the age of nine he moved with his family to London, but six years later they returned to Ireland. His early interest in the occult led him to help found the Dublin Hermetic Society, and the budding poet became more and more interested in Irish mythology.

As his poetry became better known, he counted among his friends William Morris, George Bernard Shaw and Oscar Wilde. At the age of 37, he met the much younger James Joyce, who remarked that the meeting came too late for Joyce to help Yeats improve his writing! Yeats' most important encounter, though, was with Maud Gonne (1866–1953), whose nationalism and socialism provided a healthy balance to his predilection for mysticism and an ill-defined romanticism. The story of

NICKY CAVEN

their relationship has attracted a lot of speculation – especially about the sexual side – with Maud Gonne finally refusing to marry him. She took the title role in his one-act play *Cathleen Ni Houlihan* (1904), which has been credited as the catalyst for the 1916 Easter Rising.

Yeats became a senator of the Irish Free State in 1922 and the following year he received the Nobel Prize for Literature. In 1928 he moved to Italy, where, in the following years, his flirtation with fascism sat uneasily alongside his stature as a poet of world renown.

MAYO & SLIGO

Southern Hotel (☎ *62101*), with 68 rooms on Lord Edward St near the bus and train stations, charges upwards of £49/74.

Places to Eat

Good for lunch, snacks or coffee, *Ritz Restaurant (O'Connell St)* is a big place but likely to be crowded. *Bistro Bianconi (44 O'Connell St)* serves decent Italian dishes costing £11 to £14; salads and pizzas cost £8. *Beezies*, a flashy, modern café-bar, down the alleyway round the corner, serves soups, sandwiches and pasta (£4.50) from 12.30 to 6 pm daily.

In the Quinsworth Shopping Centre car park, *Adelaide Restaurant and Bar* is popular with townspeople; a mixed grill costs £4.25.

One of the better restaurants around is *Loft* (☎ *46770, 17-19 Lord Edward St)*, upstairs at MJ Carr's pub, with Mexican, fish

and chicken dishes costing £8 to £11. The burgers (£6.15) are especially good. For Indian food, try the licensed *Kamal Mahal*, where main courses such as *aloo gobi* (cauliflower and potatoes) cost £4.95.

Entertainment

Sligo has the usual bevy of pubs, some with traditional music on certain nights, including *D McLynn's (Old Market St)* on Tuesday, *J McLaughlin's (Market St)* on Wednesday, and *Donaghy's (Lord Edward St)* on Sunday. *TD's Lounge (Lynn's Place)*, near Hughes Bridge, has bands most nights of the week. *McGarrigle's (O'Connell St)* has a good 'alternative music' bar upstairs.

No place in Sligo can beat *Hargadon Bros (O'Connell St)* for atmosphere, however. While it doesn't have music, this old place with its dark wood interior is like a stage set, with snugs, nooks, crannies and 19th-century bar fixtures.

Shoot the Crows (Castle St), near Market Square, attracts a younger crowd. Serious drinking is best conducted at *Harry's Bar (High St)*, where there are lots of happy-hour offers and the cheapest pints in town.

Theatre & Cinemas *Hawk's Well Theatre (☎ 61526, Temple St)*, attached to the tourist office, is always worth checking out to see what's on. The four-screen *Gaiety Cinema (☎ 62651, Wine St)* has films at 6.30, 8.30, 8.45 and 11 pm daily.

Shopping
For contemporary wood sculptures visit Michael Quirke in a former butcher's shop on Wine St. Examples of his work, which depicts figures from Irish mythology, are displayed in the window, and during business hours he can be seen sculpting.

Getting There & Away
Air From Sligo Airport (☎ 68280) there are direct daily Aer Lingus flights to Dublin.

Bus Bus Éireann (☎ 60066) bus No 23 runs three times daily to Dublin (one way £8, four hours). Bus No 64 provides a Galway to Sligo to Derry service three times daily. The bus station is below the train station, west of the centre on Lord Edward St.

Feda Ódonaill Coaches (☎ 075-48114, 091-761656) runs a service between Crolly (County Donegal) and Galway via Donegal and Sligo up to three times daily. The buses arrive and depart from in front of Henry Lyon's Store on the corner of Wine and Quay Sts.

Train Trains leave the station (☎ 69888) three times daily (four on Friday) for Dublin via Boyle, Carrick-on-Shannon and Mullingar.

Getting Around
There's a bus service from the airport into town (£1.65), while a taxi costs about £9. Ace Cabs (☎ 44444) and Feehily's Taxis (☎ 43000) offer a 24-hour service. Bike hire

is available from Gary's Cycles (☎ 45418), Lower Quay St, costing £10/40 per day/week.

AROUND SLIGO TOWN
Rosses Point
The scene of a battle between two Irish warlords in 1257, Rosses Point (Ross Ceite) is a picturesque seaside resort with a lovely Blue Flag beach. It's easily reached on a Sligo town bus.

Places to Stay The *Greenlands Caravan and Camping Park (☎ 071-77113)* is next to the golf course near the beach. It opens at Easter and from late May to mid-September. It charges £8.50 for a tent plus 50p per person.

B&Bs aren't difficult to find, although they can fill up quickly in season. Try Mrs Gill's *Kilvarnet House (☎ 071-77202)*, with en suite singles/doubles costing £24.50/36, or, among the closest to the sea, Mrs Brady's *Coral Reef (☎ 071-77245)*, which charges £30/38.

The two hotels at Rosses Point are quite different in character: the larger 79-room *Yeats Country Hotel (☎ 071-77211)*, on the point, attracts families, while *Ballincar House (☎ 071-45361)*, with 25 rooms, is relaxed and peaceful and away from the beach. Rates at Yeats range from £25 to £75 per person, and at Ballincar from £37 to £59.50.

Places to Eat The *Nifty's Bunker* pub on the main road leading to the beach always serves pub food, and *Moorings Restaurant*, which serves mostly seafood (main courses costing £8 to £12), is close to the Yeats Country Hotel. Best of all, if your budget stretches to £25 per person, is the restaurant at *Ballincar House*.

Carrowmore Megalithic Cemetery
Carrowmore's megalithic cemetery has over 60 stone circles and passage tombs, making it one of the largest Stone Age cemeteries in Europe. Over the years, many of the stones have been removed – a survey

in 1839 noted 23 more sites than now exist – and a complicating factor is that some of the best stones are on private land.

The dolmens were the actual tombs and were probably covered with stones and earth, so it requires some imagination to picture what this 2.5km-wide area might once have looked like.

The Dúchas site centre (☎ 61534) opens 9.30 am to 6.30 pm daily, May to September. Admission costs £1.50/60p.

Two B&Bs close to the Carrowmore Dúchas centre are *Culbree House* (☎ 071-68189) and *Cillard* (☎ 071-68201), both with doubles costing £36.

To get there, leave town by Church Hill and carry on for 5km; the site is clearly signposted.

Knocknarea Cairn

About 2km north-west of Carrowmore is the hilltop cairn grave of Knocknarea. Around 1000 years younger than Carrowmore, the huge cairn (328m) is supposed to be the grave of the legendary Queen Maeve (Queen Mab in Welsh and English folk tales). The 40,000 tonnes of stone have never been excavated, despite speculation that a tomb on the scale of the one at Newgrange in County Meath lies buried below.

Mrs Carter's *Primrose Grange House* (☎ 071-62005), just along the road that leads to the Knocknarea car park, costs £25/38 for singles/doubles.

Leave Sligo as for Carrowmore and a sign shows the way to Knocknarea. If you're leaving from the Carrowmore Dúchas centre, continue down the road and turn right at the junction with a church. At the next crossroads (signposted Mescan Meadhbha Chambered Cairn) turn left, and leave your vehicle at the car park. From there it's a 30-minute walk to the summit and panoramic views.

Deer Park Court Cairn

This impressive court tomb (also called Magheraghanrush Court Cairn) stands on a wooded limestone hill with fine views of Lough Gill. The court area is in the centre of the tomb, with two burial chambers opening off at one end and another at the other end. The site has been dated to around 3000 BC.

Take the N16 east from Sligo and turn off on the R286 for Parke's Castle. Almost immediately after joining this road turn left at the Y-junction onto a minor road signposted for Manorhamilton. Continue for about 3km, park in the car park, then follow the trail through the trees.

Strandhill

☎ 071 • pop 650

The beaches at Strandhill are sandy, though not always safe for swimming, and at low tide you can walk across to Coney Island. The story goes that New York's own Coney Island was named by a man from Rosses Point. There's also a golf course. The three-star *Ocean View Hotel* (☎ 68115) offers B&B costing £32.50 to £45 per person, while *Dunes Tavern* provides bar food and music.

Getting There & Away

Apart from Bus Éireann (☎ 071-60066) bus No 473 from Sligo to Rosses Point, there's no public transport to the places of interest in the area. A bicycle hired in Sligo would be the best way of getting around. While it's possible to walk to both Carrowmore and Knocknarea from town, it's a long day's return trek.

SOUTH OF SLIGO TOWN
Collooney

☎ 071

Collooney is about 13km south of Sligo on the N4. The **Teeling Monument**, at the northern end of this village, commemorates the daring of Bartholomew Teeling. He was marching with Humbert's French-Irish army when it encountered stiff resistance from an English gunner. Teeling charged up to the gunner and killed him, thus allowing the army to march on to eventual defeat at the battle of Ballinamuck in Longford in September 1798.

Although the French were treated as prisoners of war, Teeling and 500 other Irishmen were executed.

MAYO & SLIGO

Near Collooney, **Markree Castle**, signposted off the main road on the left after leaving the village, has remained in the Cooper family since Cromwell's time. When Charles Kingsley stayed here in the 19th century he wrote that he cried over the misery inflicted on the local peasantry – while at the same time exalting in the excitement of fishing for salmon in the estate's river. And it's said that Mrs Alexander wrote the hymn 'All Things Bright and Beautiful' after her stay here.

Places to Stay & Eat The *Markree Castle* (☎ 67800) now functions as an 11-room hotel costing £52 to £58 per person. B&B is available at *Union Farm* (☎ 67136), 2km outside the village, costing £24.50/36 for singles/doubles with bathroom. Dinner costs £15.

Ballymote
☎ 071

Near this small town, 11km south of Collooney and off the tourist trail, is **Ballymote Castle**, on the Tubbercurry road. The early-14th-century castle, contested among Irish chiefs before succumbing to the English in 1577, is now crumbling in obscurity. From here O'Donnell marched to disaster at the Battle of Kinsale in 1601.

The **Protestant church** is worth a glance, if only to read the plaque saying that the clock was paid for by the tenants of Ballymote Estate as a mark of respect for Sir Robert Gore-Booth of Lissadell. Unlike many of these tributes this one was genuine: Robert Gore-Booth mortgaged Lissadell House during the Famine to raise money for food for the starving. Constance Markievicz, his daughter, received a minute-long ovation from the local peasants here after her release from a British jail in June 1917.

Places to Stay & Eat There are a few B&Bs here, including Mrs Mullin's *Millhouse* (☎ 83449), which costs £23.50/36 for singles/doubles, and Mrs McGettrick's *Hillcrest* (☎ 83398), with rooms costing £17 per person. The more upmarket *Temple House* (☎ 83329), an old Anglo-Irish home which gets its name from the Knights Templar, costs £45/80 with bathroom.

There are plenty of unpretentious pubs to choose from, and the *Old Stand Pub* serves reasonable bar food. *Stonepark Restaurant* upstairs is good for an evening meal; grilled rainbow trout costs £8.50. In front of the Stonepark Restaurant is *Corran's*, which has a café and takeaway service.

Carrowkeel Passage Tomb Cemetery

Situated on a hilltop in the Bricklieve Mountains overlooking Lough Arrow, this place is uplifting, with panoramic views on a clear day, and also a little spooky, given the 14 cairns, various dolmens and scattered remnants of other graves. The place has been dated to the late Stone Age (3000 to 2000 BC).

The site, west off the N4 road, is closer to Boyle in County Roscommon than Sligo town. If you're coming from the latter, turn right at the sign in the village of Castlebaldwin, then left at the fork as indicated. The site is about 2km uphill from the gateway. You can take an Athlone bus from Sligo and ask to be put off at Castlebaldwin.

Coopershill House (☎ 071-65108), in Riverstown, close to the Carrowkeel Passage Tomb Cemetery, halfway between Sligo and Boyle, is a handsome retreat for anyone wanting to relax in a Georgian family mansion. B&B costs upwards of £60/100 in singles/doubles, and there are facilities for boating and fishing. An Irish meal with good wine and open log fires costs £26.

Lough Arrow

The 8km-long Lough Arrow close to the Leitrim border is of interest to anglers, particularly for its brown trout (the season runs from May to September). Windsurfing and sailing are allowed on the lake.

The 10-room *Rock View Hotel* (☎ 079-66077), in Ballindoon on the lake shore, caters to anglers and offers B&B costing upwards of £20 per person. It opens March to October.

Tubbercurry

☎ 071

Quiet, off-the-beaten-track Tubbercurry, also spelled Tobercurry, comes alive around mid-July, when the week-long **South Sligo Summer School** (☎ 85010) of music and dance takes place. On the second Wednesday in August, the town's big **Fair Day** is held. Nearly all the pubs have music, and the first place to call in at is *Killoran's* (☎ *85111*), on Teeling St (the main street), which functions as a combined restaurant/pub/tourist office/takeaway/travel agent/off-licence.

Easky & Enniscrone

☎ 096

The main route west to Mayo is pleasant enough, but there's little to detain the visitor. The town of Easky (Eascaigh) has the ruins of a 15th-century castle, and the **surfing**, possible year round, is highly regarded. Easky Surfing and Information Centre (☎ 49020), open 10 am to 6 pm on weekdays, has details. Behind the centre is the *Atlantic 'n' Riverside Caravan and Camping Park* (☎ *49001*), where tent sites cost £3 plus £2 per adult.

The sandy Blue Flag beach known as the Hollow at Enniscrone (Innis Crabhann), farther west, is a popular holiday spot for families. Here, **Kilcullen's Seaweed Baths** (☎ 36238) opens 10 am to 9 pm (10 pm in July and August) daily, May to October; and 10 am to 8 pm at the weekend, November to April.

West Coast Cycles (☎ 36593) in Enniscrone rents bicycles costing £7/30 per day/week.

Getting There & Away

Bus The Bus Éireann (☎ 071-60066) Dublin to Sligo express bus No 23 and Galway to Derry express bus No 64 stop outside Quigley's in Collooney. Saturday only, Sligo to Castlerea bus No 460 stops at Collooney, Ballymote and Tubbercurry. Local bus No 475 runs from Sligo to Collooney, Monday to Saturday. Easky and Enniscrone are on the Sligo to Dooagh (Achill Island) and Sligo to Ballina bus routes.

Train The Dublin to Sligo train stops at Collooney and Ballymote three times daily (four times on Friday). Call Sligo station (☎ 071-69888) for times.

LOUGH GILL

A round trip of 48km would take in most of this lough south-east of Sligo as well as Parke's Castle, which, though in County Leitrim, is included in this section. There are legends associated with Lough Gill; one that can be tested easily is the story that a silver bell from the abbey in Sligo was thrown into the lough and only those free from sin can hear its pealing. We're all ears.

Dooney Rock

There are good views of the lough and its islands from the top of Dooney Rock. In 'The Fiddler of Dooney', Yeats immortalises the rock.

Leave Sligo south on the N4 and after 500m turn left at the sign to Lough Gill. Another left at the T-junction brings you onto the R287 and the Dooney Rock viewpoint.

Innisfree Island

If Yeats hadn't written 'The Lake Isle of Innisfree', this tiny island (Inis Fraoigh) near the south-eastern shore wouldn't attract so many visitors, and it would probably have kept the air of tranquillity that so moved the poet:

> I will arise and go now, and go to Innisfree,
> And a small cabin build there, of clay and wattles made;
> Nine bean rows will I have there, a hive for the honey bee,
> And live alone in the bee-loud glade.

From the Dooney Rock car park turn left at the crossroads and after 3km turn left again for another 3km. A small road leads down to the lake.

Creevelea Abbey (County Leitrim)

This was the last Franciscan friary founded in Ireland before the orders were suppressed. The columns in the cloister have

MAYO & SLIGO

some interesting carvings of St Francis, one displaying his stigmata and another one showing him in a pulpit with birds perched on a tree. The abbey was burned in 1590 by Richard Bingham, but restored by the monks before they were again ejected by Cromwell. They returned yet again and thatched the church roof, remaining here until the end of the 17th century.

From Innisfree, return to the R287 and continue east until you see the sign for the abbey in the village of Dromahair.

Parke's Castle (County Leitrim)

The placid setting of Parke's Castle, with swans drifting by on Lough Gill, belies the fact that the early Plantation architecture was created out of insecurity and fear by an unwelcome English landlord. The three-storey castle, which has been carefully restored, forms part of one of the five sides of the *'bawn'*, which also has two rounded turrets at the corners. This is a Dúchas site, so try to join one of the guided tours after viewing the 20-minute video *Stone by Stone*, which gives a general introduction to the antiquities of the area.

The castle (☎ 071-64149) opens 9.30 am to 6.30 pm daily, June to September; and 10 am to 5 pm Tuesday to Sunday, April, May and October. Admission costs £2/1.

From Creevelea Abbey, continue east along the R287. To return to Sligo from Parke's Castle turn west onto the R286.

Getting There & Away

Car & Bicycle Leave Sligo east via The Mall past the hospital, then turn right off the N16 onto the R286, which leads to the northern shore of Lough Gill and round to Innisfree. The southern route is less interesting until reaching Dooney Rock.

Boat *Wild Rose Water Bus* (☎ 071-64266) cruises Lough Gill twice daily, mid-June to September, from Doorly Park (a 30-minute walk east of Sligo town) and five times daily from Parke's Castle, and costs £6/2 (Sunday only in April, May and October). There's also a £4/2 tour around Innisfree, and one-way trips between Parke's Castle and Sligo.

NORTH OF SLIGO TOWN
Drumcliff & Benbulben

WB Yeats died in 1939 in Roquebrune, France, but his wishes were: 'If I die here, bury me up there on the mountain [the cemetery in Roquebrune], and then after a year or so, dig me up and bring me privately to Sligo'. True to his wishes, his body was interred in the churchyard at Drumcliff in 1948 – where his great-grandfather had been rector – although it was hardly a private affair, as the photographs in the Sligo County Museum make clear. **Yeats' grave** is on the left near the Protestant church, and alongside Yeats is buried Georgie Hyde-Lees, whom he married in 1917, when she was 15 and he was 52. The epitaph is from his poem 'Under Ben Bulben':

> Cast a cold eye
> On life, on death.
> Horseman, pass by!

Nearly 1300 years earlier, St Colmcille chose the same location for the foundation of a monastery (see the boxed text 'The Battle of the Book'), and you can still see the remains of the **round tower**, damaged by lightning in 1936. An 11th-century **high cross** is nearby. Its eastern face depicts Christ in Glory, Daniel in the lions' den, Adam and Eve, and Cain's murder of Abel. On the western side, the presentation in the temple and the crucifixion can be made out.

Look for the round tower on the N15 road from Sligo. Going by bus, take the 8.45 am bus from Sligo (arriving 9 am) because the next one is at 4.15 pm, which means you'll miss the two daily return buses that pass through Drumcliff at 12.45 and 4.53 pm (though there is a 3 pm bus from Sligo to Drumcliff on Saturday only).

The limestone plateau of Benbulben (525m), the most westerly of the Dartry Mountains, is about 2km north-east of Drumcliff and dominates the landscape.

Glencar Lough

Fishing apart, the attraction of the lake is the beautiful waterfall signposted from the car park. Yeats refers to this picturesque spot in 'The Stolen Child'. The surrounding countryside can be enjoyed best by walking east along the road and taking the steep trail that heads north to the valley.

From Drumcliff it's less than 5km to the lake, and there is also a bus service from Sligo. Ring ☎ 071-60066 for details.

Lissadell House

This is the ancestral home of the Gore-Booth family, among whose members was Constance Markievicz (1868–1927), a friend of Yeats and a participant in the 1916 Easter Rising. The death penalty she received for her involvement was later withdrawn and, in 1918, she became the first woman ever elected to the House of Commons. Like many Irish rebels since then, she refused to take her seat.

Constance's sister Eva was a poet, and Yeats' poem 'In Memory of Eva Gore-Booth and Con Markievicz' is inscribed on a sign at the entrance to the house.

> The light of evening, Lissadell,
> Great windows, open to the south,
> Two girls in silk kimonos...

Yeats was a frequent visitor to Lissadell and in 1894 he wrote of the interior: 'Great sitting room as high as a church and all things in good taste'.

Lissadell House (☎ 071-63150) opens 10.30 am to 12.30 pm and 2 to 4.30 pm Monday to Saturday, June to September. Admission costs £3/1.50, and the guided tour, which is informative and interesting, takes about 45 minutes.

To get there, follow the N15 north from Sligo and turn west at Drumcliff.

Mullaghmore

If you turn left at Cliffony, off the N15, the main road to Mullaghmore (An Mullach Mór) first passes **Streedagh Beach**, a grand stretch of sand that was the final resting place for many of the 1300 sailors who perished when three ships from the Spanish Armada were wrecked nearby.

The beach at Mullaghmore is also delightfully wide and safe. It was in this bay

The Battle of the Book

After Drumcliff, the first turn west goes to the village of Carney. Cooldrumman, just north of Carney, is where the Battle of the Book took place in the year 561. St Colmcille had borrowed a rare psalter from St Finian and made a pirate edition for his own use. When St Finian found out and demanded the copy, the resulting argument found its way to the high king of Ireland, who was asked to arbitrate. The delivered judgement was 'To every cow its calf and to every book its copy'. St Colmcille refused to accept the judgement, and in the battle that followed over 4000 people were slain. Struck with remorse and shame, St Colmcille built a monastery at Drumcliff before departing for ever into voluntary exile on the remote Scottish island of Iona.

that the IRA assassinated Lord Mountbatten and members of his family in 1979. On the way to the Mullaghmore headland you pass **Classiebawn Castle**, built for Lord Palmerston in 1856 and later the home of Lord Mountbatten. The castle isn't open to the public, but the neo-Gothic pile can be viewed from the N15 and the R279 as you approach Mullaghmore.

Inishmurray Island

If access were easier to arrange, a visit to this uninhabited island would be a must. It contains the remains of **three churches**, **beehive cells** and **open-air altars**. The old monastery is surrounded by a stone wall with five separate entrances to the central area, which contains the churches and altars. The monastery was founded in the early 6th century by St Molaise, and a wooden statue of the saint that once stood in the main church is now in the National Museum in Dublin.

The early monks on Inishmurray assembled some fascinating pagan relics. There's a collection of cursing stones; those who

MAYO & SLIGO

wanted to lay a curse did the Stations of the Cross in reverse, turning over the stones as they went along. There were also separate burial grounds for men and women and a strong belief that if a body was placed in the wrong ground it would move itself during the night.

Only 6km separates Inishmurray from the mainland, but there's no regular boat service and the lack of harbour makes landing subject to the weather. Trips can be arranged through Lomax Boats (☎ 071-66124) in Mullaghmore, from Streedagh Point through Joe McGowan (☎ 071-66267), or from Rosses Point through Tomas McCallion (☎ 071-42391). You need a group of at least six people to make it economical.

Creevykeel Goort Cairn
North of Cliffony on the N15 is a court tomb with a wide, high front tapering away to a narrow end. The unroofed court stands outside the front entrance. At some later stage, chambers were added to the western side of the cairn. It was constructed around 2500 BC.

Places to Stay
Celtic Farm Hostel (☎ 071-63337), 1km north of Grange, is a useful base for northern Sligo and opens year round. Dorm beds cost £7 and private rooms cost £10 per person. Connemara ponies can be hired for riding on the beaches nearby.

The *Shaddan Lodge* (☎ 071-63350), near Streedagh Beach, offers B&B costing £22.50/32 for singles/doubles and opens

from April to October. The German-owned *Horse Holiday Farm* (☎ 071-66152), at Mountemple 2km north of Grange, runs week-long trail-riding programmes including B&B and your own horse (upwards of £450).

At Drumcliff there are quite a few B&Bs, including Mrs Hennigan's *Benbulben Farm* (☎ 071-63211), in Barnaribbon, where you can get a single/double with bathroom for £24.50/36.

At Mullaghmore *Beach Hotel* (☎ 071-66108) has an indoor swimming pool and opens April to September. Rooms cost £27.50 to £37.50 per person, and fishing trips can be arranged.

Places to Eat
The popular *Yeats Tavern* restaurant on the main N15 road in Drumcliff opens until 10 pm daily. Lunch specials are good value; seafood costs £8.50 to £12. It's about 100m past Yeats' grave on the left of the main road. In Mullaghmore, *Fishes' Circle* restaurant at the Beach Hotel serves excellent seafood; crab sandwiches cost £6.25.

Getting There & Away
There are regular Bus Éireann (☎ 071-60066) buses between Sligo, Drumcliff, Grange and Cliffony, as most buses to Donegal and Derry go along the N15. In Drumcliff the bus stop is outside the creamery, in Grange it's outside Rooney's newsagents, and in Cliffony it's O'Donnell's Bar. The first bus stopping at all these places leaves Sligo at 8.45 am; the last bus from Cliffony is at 4.35 pm.

Central North

Someone once described Ireland as a dull picture with a wonderful frame. Indeed, most visitors are attracted by the frame – the coast – and rarely venture inland to explore the picture. There is good reason for this, at least in part: the six counties of the central north (Cavan, Monaghan, Roscommon, Leitrim, Longford and Westmeath) have long been considered Ireland's less appealing counties, with comparatively little to distract the visitor from the hue of grey that seems to envelop them. But while they may never lure the same hordes as the west or south, they do have a number of places of great interest, and the smaller number of visitors can make them that much more attractive.

Cavan, Monaghan and Donegal border Northern Ireland and, together with the six counties there, make up the province of Ulster. All border crossing points between the Republic and the North are now open, though you will occasionally have to pass through a garda checkpoint when crossing back into the Republic.

County Cavan

The low, undulating county of Cavan (An Cabhán) is barely a two-hour drive from Dublin and lies just south of the border with Northern Ireland. Cavan is dominated by lakes (it's said there is one for every day of the year), bogs and drumlins, which are small round hills deposited and shaped by retreating glaciers during the last Ice Age. In the far north-west of the county, the wild and barren Cuilcagh Mountains are the source of the River Shannon, at over 300km long the mightiest river in Ireland or Britain.

Cavan is famous for its potholed roads, which are often twisty and badly signposted. The roads seem to go over the drumlins, whereas in neighbouring Monaghan they go round them.

Cavan is in many ways a hard place, with

a no-nonsense attitude to life that is born out of the inclement weather, difficult economic circumstances and a people who have long been the butt of Irish humour as the most miserly in the country!

Cavan was the birthplace of Percy French, the late-19th-century songwriter responsible for 'The Mountains of Mourne'.

CENTRAL NORTH

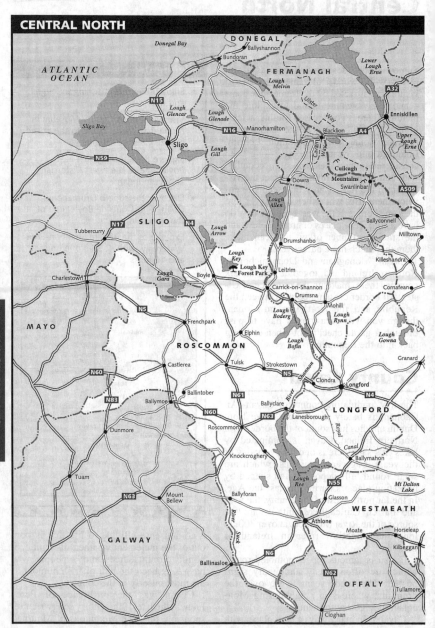

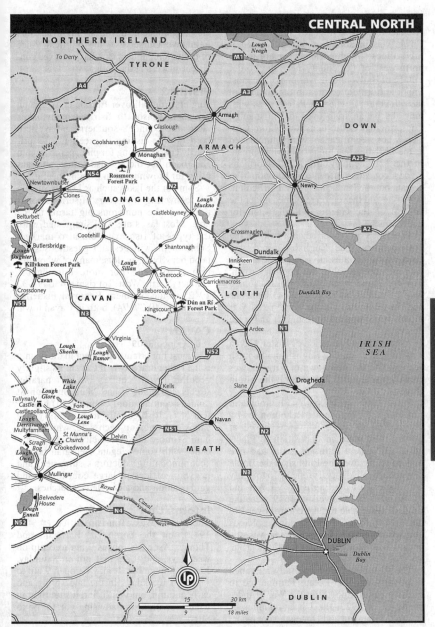

CENTRAL NORTH

HISTORY

Archaeological evidence suggests that Cavan was inhabited as far back as Neolithic times. Magh Sleacht, a plain in the north-west of the county near the border village of Ballyconnell, was one of the most important druidic centres in the country in the 5th century, when St Patrick was winning the pagan Irish over to Christianity. The principal Celtic deity was Crom Cruaich, whose significance swiftly diminished as the Christian teachings of Patrick spread. In the 12th century, the Anglo-Normans made a concerted effort to get a foothold in Cavan, but the landscape proved difficult to penetrate and the region remained under the control of the Gaelic O'Reilly clan for many years.

Their grip on power began to slip in the 16th century. The English 'shired' the county into baronies, dividing these among clan members loyal to the English Crown. The end came when the O'Reillys joined with the other Ulster lords – the O'Donnells and the O'Neills – in the Nine Years War (1594–1603) against the English and were defeated.

As part of the Plantation of Ulster, Cavan was divided up among English and Scottish settlers, and the new town of Virginia was created, named after Elizabeth I, the Virgin Queen.

In the 1640s, with Charles I in trouble in England, the Confederate Rebellion led by Owen Roe O'Neill, who was based at Cavan, took place in opposition to Plantation. O'Neill, a returned exile, had one major victory over the English at the Battle of Benburb in County Tyrone in 1646. Only with the end of the English Civil War and the arrival of Cromwell in 1649 were the English again able to take control over Ireland. Owen Roe O'Neill died in suspicious circumstances in 1649 – poisoning was suspected – in Cloughoughter Castle near the town of Cavan.

The Irish population generally remained in poverty and the Potato Famine led to massive emigration. After the War of Independence in 1922, the Ulster counties of Cavan, Monaghan and Donegal were incorporated into the South. With the border so close, republicanism is strong in Cavan: Sinn Féin (We Ourselves), the political voice of militant republicanism, has achieved consistent success at the polls.

FISHING

Anglers from all over Europe converge on Cavan in season to fish the many lakes along the county's southern and western borders. The fishing is excellent; it's primarily coarse fishing for pike, perch, bream and roach but there's also some game angling for brown trout in Lough Sheelin.

Some of the lakes such as Lough Sheelin are recovering after years of serious pollution from the numerous pig farms in the area. Most lakes are well signposted, with the types of fish available also marked. Some of the villages and guesthouses depend heavily on anglers, many of whom return every year. For more information, contact North West Tourism (☎ 049-433 1942) or the Northern Regional Fisheries Board (☎ 049-37174), both in Cavan town.

CAVAN

☎ 049 • pop 3509

The most important settlement in the county is the rather drab town of Cavan. Its slightly peculiar layout centres on two parallel streets, Farnham St and Main St. Main St (and its continuation, Connolly St) has the feel of an Irish country town, with typical shops and pubs on each side, while Farnham St more closely resembles a city avenue, with some elegant Georgian houses accommodating doctors' surgeries and lawyers' offices, a large courthouse and garda station and a couple of churches.

Information

The North West Tourism office (☎ 433 1942), on the corner of Farnham and Thomas Ashe Sts, opens 9 am to 5 pm on weekdays, and 9 am to 1 pm on Saturday, June to September. It may be open 9 am to 1 pm on weekdays in the late spring and early autumn, but you'll find it shut tight in winter – with a sign advising you to 'go to Sligo'.

You can change money at the ACC Bank, 91 Main St. The modern post office is on the corner of Main and Townhall Sts. You can leave your laundry at the Supaklene laundrette, on Farnham St about 100m from the bus station, or at the Laundry Basket, at the southern end of Connolly St. The latter opens 8.30 am to 6.30 pm Monday to Saturday. There's also a small genealogical office (☎ 436 1094) in Cana House, signposted up the hill from the Presbyterian church on Farnham St.

Things to See & Do

Cavan developed round a 13th-century Franciscan friary of which no traces remain. On the site of the friary in Abbey St is an 18th-century **Protestant church tower** which marks the grave of Owen Roe O'Neill, though it's not very impressive.

Lifeforce Mill (☎ 436 2722), on Bridge St along the little Kennypottle River, is a fully operational flour mill dating from 1846 that still uses the centuries-old 'cool' method of milling wheat. Visitors actually prepare a loaf of wholemeal brown bread on arrival and pick it up hot from the oven at the end of their 40-minute tour. The mill opens 10 am to 5 pm daily, May to September, and costs £2.50/1.50 (students £2, families £6).

Two kilometres south-east of the town centre on the Dublin road (N3) is the **Cavan Crystal Factory** (☎ 433 1800). It is Ireland's second-oldest crystal manufacturer and a real rival to the supremacy of Waterford Crystal in terms of quality and design. The showroom opens 9.30 am to 5.30 pm on weekdays, 10 am to 5 pm on Saturday, and 2 to 5 pm on Sunday. There are free factory tours (on the half-hour between 9.30 and 11.30 am on weekdays) in which you can see the crystal being blown and cut by hand. A visitor centre, glass museum, restaurant and coffee shop opened in 1998.

Courses in **canoeing** are given by local Irish Canoe Union instructors on the River Erne. Check out the notice board in Louis Blessing's pub. The large **County Cavan Swimming and Leisure Complex** (☎ 436 2888) in Drumalee north-east of town has a swimming pool (from £3.50/2) and a number of other sporting facilities. It opens 7.30 am to 10 pm on weekdays, and 11 am to 6 pm at the weekend.

Places to Stay

B&Bs There's very little choice in the town centre. The most central place with B&B-style accommodation is *Bridge Restaurant* (☎ 433 1538, 5 Coleman Rd), close to the bus station. It offers B&B in spacious rooms costing £20 per person, plus a £2 key deposit. *Oakdene* (☎ 433 1698, 29 Cathedral Rd), at the northern end of town, has four spotless rooms costing upwards of £24.50/36 for singles/doubles. *Halcyon* (☎ 31809), in Drumalee 600m north-east along the Cootehill road and then right by McDonald's shop, has five rooms at almost the same rates. *Rose's Brough House* (☎ 433 0311), 4km south-east on the Dublin road, has three rooms for £20/30 with separate bathroom.

There are some real gems farther out of town. *Lisnamandra Farmhouse* (☎ 433 7196) is 7km west along the Crossdoney road (R198) and well signposted on the left-hand side. B&B costs £24.50/37 with a shower, and a full dinner costs about £16. It opens from May to September and you should book ahead.

Hotels In the centre of town, almost opposite Market Square, you could try the very popular *Farnham Arms Hotel* (☎ 433 2577, Main St), charging £34/55 to £36/66 for singles/doubles, depending on the season. The recently refurbished *Kilmore Hotel* (☎ 433 2288), on the Dublin road just beyond the Cavan Crystal Factory, offers B&B costing upwards of £38/70 or £42/74.

Places to Eat

The town has fast-food places such as *Uncle Sam's* near the bus station on College St, or *Una's Takeaway* at the start of Connolly St opposite the small market. *Galligan's*, just off Main St on Bridge St, is good for inexpensive lunches and early dinners. The *Melbourne Bakery* is a small restaurant-cum-coffee-shop halfway up Main St. *Bridge Restaurant* is a good,

CENTRAL NORTH

reasonably priced place, with chicken dishes from £3 and fish from £3.95. It opens 9 am to 9 pm. For Chinese, try *Happy Valley Restaurant* where Main and Connolly Sts meet.

Farnham Arms Hotel has a comfortable lounge with reasonable food, and the restaurant at *Imperial Hotel* on Main St is popular with Cavanites.

The best place in town is *Olde Priory* (☎ 61898, *Main St*) in an old convent basement opposite the Melbourne Bakery. It serves pizzas costing upwards of £5 and also offers seafood, kebabs and vegetarian dishes. It has a bar and is closed Monday and at lunch on Sunday.

Entertainment

McGinty's Corner Bar (*College St*) has won a regional 'pub of the year' title and sometimes has music at the weekend. There are heaps of pubs on Main St. The *Black Horse Inn* is popular with young locals and has pool tables. You will occasionally find jazz in *Louis Blessing's* rustic pub in a small courtyard off Main St, while at the weekend the bar swings with the latest hits. *An Crúiscín Lán* (The Bumper) at the top of Main St has rock on Thursday night and Irish sessions on Friday. The most popular pub these days is the renovated *An Síbín* (The Speakeasy) on the corner of Townhall and Main Sts. There are DJs at the weekend and an Irish session midweek.

Getting There & Away

The small bus station (☎ 433 1353) is at the southern end of Farnham St near the bridge and roundabout. The ticket office opens 7.30 am to 8.30 pm daily (from 8.30 am on Sunday).

Cavan is on the Dublin to Donegal, Galway to Belfast and Athlone to Belfast bus routes. On weekdays there are five daily buses to Dublin (two hours), three buses to Belfast (three hours) and two to Galway (3¾ hours). Bus Éireann also has services running from Cavan through the county to Bawnboy, Ballyconnell, Belturbet, Virginia, Kells, Dunshaughlin, Navan and many other small towns, including Cootehill.

Wharton's (☎ 433 7114) runs private buses leaving the nearby Mallard's Hotel for Parnell Square in Dublin at 8 am Monday to Saturday. A one-way fare is £4.

Getting Around

Taxis can be ordered on ☎ 433 1172 or ☎ 433 2876.

AROUND CAVAN TOWN
Kilmore Cathedral

This modest Church of Ireland cathedral, built in 1860, is about 5km west on the R198 Crossdoney road to Killykeen Forest Park. On the western side of this relatively modern building is a fine 12th-century Romanesque doorway brought here from an Augustinian monastery on Trinity Island in Lough Oughter. If you look closely, you'll notice that some of the stones have not been replaced in the correct order. In the churchyard is the grave of Bishop William Bedell (1571–1642), who commissioned the first translation of the Old Testament into Irish; there's a copy of it on display in the chancel.

Killykeen Forest Park

This forest park (☎ 049-433 2541) is 12km north-west of Cavan on the shores of Lough Oughter. Lough Oughter has a tortuous outline, and the park has some fine walks, nature trails, fishing spots and good chalets for rent among its 243 hectares of trees and inlets. Many of the low wooded islands in the lake are likely to have been *crannógs* – fortified, artificial islands. Within the park to the north is the inaccessible **Clough Oughter Castle**, built in the 13th century by the O'Reillys on an island in the lake and the place where the rebel leader Owen Roe O'Neill died in 1649, reputedly from poisoning. The best way to get near it is from the south-east, along a narrow road running north from the village of Garthrattan.

Admission to the park costs £1.50 for a car, £3.50 for a family. There are self-catering chalets on the shores of Lough Oughter that sleep four/six and can be rented by the week for £180/212 (£350/465 June to August) or £145/170 at the weekend for three nights (£175/255 in summer).

Canadian-style **canoes** can be rented (☎ 049-32842) for a paddle on Lough Oughter or the Erne waterways, and there's coarse fishing and horse riding within the park.

Pighouse Folk Museum
From Crossdoney you'll see signposts for the Pighouse Folk Museum (☎ 049-433 7248) in Corr House, Cornafean. Its hodge-podge of artefacts dating from the 1700s are preserved in the original pighouse and barns. If you like rummaging through other people's attics, then you'll love this place. It's almost worth the trip just for the view the museum affords of the drumlins and valleys.

The museum opens by appointment, so phone ahead to see if Mrs Faris is going to be there. Unfortunately, it can only be reached by car. Admission costs £2.

Drumlane Monastic Site
One kilometre south of Milltown, north of Killeshandra on the R201 road to Belturbet, is Drumlane, a monastic site dating from the 6th century. (The small church and peculiar round tower just over 11m high were built later.) The monastery was founded by St Mogue, and the site's location between two small lakes – Drumlane and Derrybrick – and the surrounding hills is its most attractive feature.

Butlersbridge
☎ 049
Six kilometres north of Cavan is the pretty hamlet of Butlersbridge on the River Annalee. **Ballyhaise House** nearby was designed by Richard Castle (responsible for Dublin's Leinster House) and is worth a quick look for its fine brickwork. It's now an agricultural college.

Just near the river in Butlersbridge, *Ford House* (☎ 433 1427) has en suite singles/doubles costing £16/32; it opens May to October.

Derragarra Inn, a very attractive pub by the River Annalee, has good bar food available all day, a reasonably priced tourist menu and peat fires.

Belturbet & Around
☎ 049 • pop 1230
On the River Erne 16km north-west of Cavan on the N3, Belturbet is an angling centre with cruises available on Upper Lough Erne during summer. Turbet Tours (☎ 432 2360) has sailings on the Shannon-Erne Waterway between Belturbet and Ballyconnell from June to September aboard the *Erne Dawn*. The 2½ hour tour costs £6/3.50.

A very central choice for accommodation is *Erne View* (☎ 432 2289, 9 Bridge St) in the centre of town, with singles/doubles costing upwards of £16.50/33. *Hilltop Farm* (☎ 22114), in Kilduff 5km south on the road to Cavan, offers 10 rooms with B&B costing £24/37. Both places have facilities for anglers.

Bus Éireann (☎ 433 1353) stops here four times daily (three times on Sunday) in each direction on the route between Cavan and Donegal (2¼ hours). The bus stop is outside O'Reilly's Garage. You can rent bicycles – and seek advice about cycling routes – from Paddy Fitzpatrick's (☎ 432 2866) on Bridge St for £9 per day.

Lough Sheelin
Lough Sheelin, 24km south of Cavan, is noted for its game angling for brown trout, especially in May and June. The two main accommodation centres – at opposite ends of the 6km-long lough – are the villages of Finnea, just over the border in County Westmeath, and Mountnugent. There are several places in Mountnugent where you can stay and hire boats for fishing: *Sheelin Shamrock Hotel* (☎ 049-434 0387), with singles/doubles costing upwards of £25/40; *Ross House* (☎ 049-434 0218), from £23/34; and *Crover House Hotel* (☎ 049-434 0206), from £32.50/50 and open April to September.

WESTERN CAVAN
Sometimes known as the Panhandle because of its long, narrow shape, western Cavan is dominated by the starkly beautiful, but little-visited, Cuilcagh Mountains. To the south-west, Magh Sleacht, which is the area around Kilnavert and Killycluggin, is

CENTRAL NORTH

supposed to have been a druidic centre dedicated to the deity Crom Cruaich. In the far north-western corner of the county, the road runs parallel to the Northern Irish border before dividing. The left fork heads west to Dowra and Blacklion, a desolate area with some interesting ancient sites. The right fork heads north to Swanlinbar and the border.

Getting There & Away

There are few buses serving this remote part of the county. The express Donegal to Dublin buses pass through Ballyconnell, Bawnboy and Swanlinbar four times daily (three on Sunday). Swanlinbar is also on the Athlone to Derry route, which runs once daily Monday to Saturday. The Galway to Belfast bus stops in Blacklion twice daily (once on Sunday); the Sligo (from Westport in summer) to Belfast bus stops two or three times daily (once on Sunday). Contact Bus Éireann in Cavan (☎ 049-433 1353) for more information.

Ballyconnell
☎ 049

Ballyconnell, 29km north-west of Cavan and 7km west of Belturbet, is the gateway to the Cavan Panhandle. There's not a lot in the village itself, but it's a good base from which to explore. There are tours available on the Shannon-Erne Waterway (see the Belturbet & Around entry earlier in this chapter).

The county's only hostel, the IHH *Sandville House* (☎ 952 6297), is 3km south-east of Ballyconnell, signposted off the Belturbet road (R200), in a peaceful, rural two-hectare setting. Dorm beds cost £7, and there is an area to pitch a tent as well as a bike rental facility. The Dublin to Donegal bus stops at the Slieve Russell Hotel in Ballyconnell on request, and if you ring the hostel beforehand they can arrange to pick you up. It opens March to November.

Ballyconnell has lots of B&Bs. *Snugborough House* (☎ 952 6346) charges £25/36 for singles/doubles with bath. The *Angler's Rest* (☎ 952 6391) is a pub-cum-guesthouse which has en suite rooms costing £19/32.

The huge *Slieve Russell Hotel* (☎ 952 6444), 2km south-east of Ballyconnell, is something of a legend. Built by a local millionaire, it features marble, fountains, restaurants, bars, nightclubs, a swimming pool and an 18-hole golf course. B&B normally costs around £95/160 for singles/doubles, but there are frequent weekend and midweek specials.

Dowra & Black Pig's Dyke

Dowra is on the upper reaches of the River Shannon, and between the river and Mt Slievenakilla (545m) to the east is a 5km section of the mysterious Black Pig's Dyke, an earthworks that wriggles wormlike across much of the region. It's thought to have been built as a fortification and frontier of Ulster as early as the 3rd century. *Hi Way Inn* (☎ 078-43025) is the hamlet's only accommodation; singles/doubles cost £12/24.

Blacklion
☎ 072

Five kilometres south of Blacklion are the remains of a **cashel** (ring fort) with three large, circular embankments. Inside is a sweathouse, a stone hut that served as a type of Turkish bath or sauna and was used mostly in the 19th century. Between Dowra and Blacklion there are the remains of quite a number of these curiosities.

Lough MacNean House (☎ 53022, Main St) is one of the few B&Bs in or around Blacklion and costs upwards of £26/46 for singles/doubles. It also provides a much praised set dinner in the evening costing £25.

The Galway to Belfast and Sligo to Belfast buses stop in Blacklion twice daily (once on Sunday). In summer, the latter bus originates in Westport once daily and stops in Blacklion. The bus stop is in front of Maguire's.

The Cavan & Ulster Ways

Blacklion and Dowra are the ends of the 16km Cavan Way, and Blacklion is also on the Ulster Way. See Walking in the Activities chapter for details.

The Sweathouse

Sweathouses, built of stone and with a small opening or doorway, were used to ease aches and pains, some of them alcohol-inflicted. Readers of Leon Uris' epic novel *Trinity* will remember the well-used sweathouse in the fictional town of Ballyutogue.

A turf fire would be lit inside for several hours and when the sweathouse was sufficiently hot the fire was removed. The patient would then go inside and sit or lie on a pile of rushes or straw until they felt they had sweated enough. They would then emerge and take a dip in a nearby running stream.

EASTERN CAVAN

Heading east from the town of Cavan you move into the heart of drumlin country. The history of foreign settlement has left its mark on the fabric and layout of the main towns.

Getting There & Away

Four or five daily express Bus Éireann (☎ 049-433 1353) buses on the Donegal to Dublin route pass through Virginia (three on Sunday), and there are also three daily buses passing through between Cavan and Dublin. Cootehill is on a Dundalk to Cavan route, and two buses daily Monday to Saturday (four on Friday) link it with the county seat. There's a daily bus on weekdays during the school year (September to June) from Cootehill to Monaghan. A Dundalk to Cavan bus passes through Kingscourt on Tuesday only. There's also a Kingscourt to Navan to Dublin service which has two buses daily Monday to Saturday and one on Sunday.

Virginia

☎ 049

On the shores of Lough Ramor in the southeastern corner of the county, the origins of Virginia (Achadh Lir) go back to the Plantation of Ulster in the early 17th century. Like the US state first settled in 1607, it was named after Elizabeth I, the Virgin Queen. Six kilometres to the north-west is **Cuilcagh House**, home of the Sheridan family, where Jonathan Swift is said to have come up with the idea for *Gulliver's Travels* while visiting in 1726. Like the rest of Cavan, the accent can be quite difficult to decipher; locals pronounce the town name *Ver*-giny!

Places to Stay & Eat Five kilometres south of Virginia on the southern tip of Lough Ramor is the somewhat scruffy *Lough Ramor Camping and Caravan Park* (☎ 854 7447). It has only 13 tent sites, which cost £4.50 plus £1.50/50p per adult/child; motorcyclists pay £3.50 including tent, hikers and cyclists £3. It opens from mid-May to mid-September.

On the lake shore 1km from Virginia on the Dublin road, *St Kyran's B&B* (☎ 854 7087) opens April to September and costs upwards of £22/32 for singles/doubles without bathroom. Two kilometres south-west along the Oldcastle road (R395) is *White House* (☎ 854 7515), with four rooms costing £17 to £19 per person.

In the centre of town on Main St is the 15-room *Ramor Lodge* (☎ 47003), which has singles/doubles from £36/62. Just south-east of Virginia heading towards Dublin, *Park Hotel* (☎ 47235) is an 18th-century building overlooking a small lake, with 20 rooms at £80/145. It has a nine-hole golf course and good but pricey food (full dinner £27.50).

Sharkey's Hotel (Main St) offers teas, coffees and snacks all day and lunches in the bar.

Cootehill

☎ 049

Farther north, the small, neat market town of Cootehill (An Mhuinchille) is named after the Cootes, a Planter family who, after acquiring some confiscated land from the O'Reillys, were instrumental in founding the town in the 17th century. This colourful clan had many interesting members, including Sir Charles Coote, who was one of

CENTRAL NORTH

Cromwell's most ruthless and effective leaders, and Richard Coote (1636–1701), who first became governor of New York state, and then later New Hampshire and Massachusetts.

The Coote mansion, **Bellamont House** (1729), was designed by Edward Lovett Pearce (architect of the Bank of Ireland on College Green, Dublin) and is described as one of the best Palladian villas in Ireland. It opens in the afternoon and admission is free.

There are several dining and lodging options in the village.

Shercock
☎ 042

Shercock (Searcóg) is a pretty little village on the shores of Lough Sillan, 13km southeast of Cootehill. The lake is noted for its pike fishing. *Lakelands Caravan and Camping Park* (☎ 69488), about 1km west of the village in a tranquil setting beside the lake, charges £7 per tent plus 50p per person and opens Easter to mid-September. *Annesley Heights* (☎ 69667), a B&B south of town on the Carrickmacross road (R178), charges £20/36 for singles/doubles and opens year round.

Kingscourt
☎ 042

In the far east of County Cavan, Kingscourt (Dún an Rí) is a fairly drab village. **St Mary's Catholic Church** has some superb 1940s stained-glass windows by the artist Evie Hone. The church has views of the surrounding region, and just to the northwest is 225-hectare **Dún an Rí Forest Park** (☎ 67320), with wooded walks, picnic spots and a famous wishing well.

Mackin's Hotel (☎ 67208, Church St) is an ordinary country hotel with 15 rooms costing upwards of £21 per person. *Cabra Castle* (☎ 67030), 3km out of Kingscourt on the Carrickmacross road, is an imposing structure with 29 rooms and its own nine-hole golf course, but it isn't cheap. B&B costs £60/100 for singles/doubles, May to September. It's worth trying for a snack or meal at lunch or dinner (£21.95).

County Monaghan

Few visitors ever pass through Monaghan (Muineachán), a landscape of neat round hills, crisscrossed by unkempt hedgerows and scattered farms. The hills are drumlins, deposited by the glaciers of the last Ice Age in a belt stretching from Clew Bay in County Galway across the country to County Down. It's pleasant but never spectacular scenery. Walkers and cyclists may enjoy the many peaceful country lanes if the weather is cooperative. Monaghan has fewer lakes than neighbouring Cavan, though the fishing is still good.

Patrick Kavanagh (1905–67), one of Ireland's most respected poets, was born in this county, in Inniskeen. *The Great Hunger*, a long poem which he wrote in 1942, and *Tarry Flynn*, a novel written in 1948, evoke the atmosphere and frequently grim reality of life for the poor farming community.

The barren terrain has restricted the development of large-scale mechanised farming but, despite this, Monaghan's farming cooperatives are among the most active and forward-looking in the country. Monaghan is noted for its lace, and this eye-straining craft continues in Clones and Carrickmacross, the centres of the industry since the early 19th century.

HISTORY
The earliest traces of humans in this region date back to before the Bronze Age. None of the sites here measure up to the magnificent monuments of County Meath, though the Tullyrain Ring Fort close to Shantonagh in the south of the county is worth a look, as are Mannor Castle near Carrickmacross and the crannóg in Convent Lake in Monaghan, the county seat. Like Cavan, County Monaghan is lacking in religious remains despite its proximity to Armagh, the principal seat of St Patrick. The round tower and high cross in Clones in the west of the county are among the scant remains from this period of Irish history.

The Anglo-Normans were also less influential here than elsewhere. The county was controlled through the early Middle Ages by many Gaelic clans and septs, including the O'Carrolls, McKennas and MacMahons. Enemies for a long time of the O'Neills of Armagh, these families united with them on the losing side of the Nine Years War (1594–1603) against the English.

Unlike Cavan and much of Ulster, Monaghan was largely left alone during the Ulster Plantation. The transfer of Monaghan land to English hands came later – after the Cromwellian wars – and much of it was granted to soldiers and adventurers or bought by them from local chieftains (under pressure and often for a fraction of its true value). These new settlers levelled the forests and built numerous new towns and villages, each with their own Protestant church. The planning and architecture exemplified their tidy, no-frills approach to life. Disapproving of Irish pastoral farming methods, they introduced arable farming, and the linen industry later became very profitable.

Monaghan's historical ties with Ulster were severed by the partition of Ireland in 1922 and, though republicanism is quite strong, it's not as visible as you might expect. A number of towns have Sinn Féin bookshops and advice centres.

MONAGHAN
☎ 047 • pop 5628

The county town of Monaghan is 141km north-west of Dublin and just 8km south of the border with Northern Ireland. Though it has a population of less than 6000, it's the only town of any size in the county. Its design and buildings reflect the influence of the British newcomers of the 17th and 18th centuries and of the money generated by the linen industry in the 18th and 19th centuries. Compared to many Irish midland towns, Monaghan is a pleasant surprise: many of the town's important buildings are quite elegant limestone edifices.

History

Nothing remains of the ruling MacMahons' 1462 friary or their earlier forts, but in Convent Lake, just behind St Louis Convent, there is a small, overgrown crannóg that served as the headquarters for the family around the 14th century.

After the turbulent wars of the 16th and 17th centuries, the town was settled by Scottish Calvinists, who built a castle using the rubble of the old friary, some fragments of which can be seen near the Diamond. The 19th-century profits from the linen trade transformed the town and brought many sturdy new buildings.

Orientation & Information

The principal streets of Monaghan form a roughly continuous arc, broken up by the town's three main squares – Church Square, the Diamond (the Ulster name for town squares, despite their shape!) and Old Cross Square – where most of the sights and important buildings can be found. To the west of this arc at the top of Park St is Market Square. Here, the tourist office (☎ 81122), in the 1792 Market House, opens 9 am to 6 pm on weekdays, and 9 am to 1 pm on Saturday, March to October.

The post office is on Mill St, which runs between Hill St and North Rd. You can get your laundry done at Supreme Dry Cleaners on Park St just south of the tourist office on the left-hand side.

There are two small lakes, Peter's Lake to the north of the Diamond and Convent Lake with its crannóg at the south-western corner of town. A one-way traffic system operates through the centre of town.

Monaghan County Museum & Gallery

This excellent museum (☎ 82928) is just north-west of the tourist office at the start of Hill St and is one of the best regional museums in Ireland.

Taking up two Victorian houses, it includes exhibits from the Stone Age to modern times and has displays on local lace-making, the linen industries, the abandoned Ulster Canal (which runs just to the south of the town and is being renovated) and, of course, the border with the North. The museum's prized possession, though, is the **Cross of Clogher**, a bronze 13th- or 14th-century altar cross.

Local and national artists have exhibits in the Art Gallery wing. The museum opens 11 am to 5 pm Tuesday to Saturday (closed from 1 to 2 pm except June to September). Admission is free.

Other Things to See

At the top of Dawson St is **Church Square**, the first of the three squares, with an 1857 **obelisk** for one Colonel Dawson, who was killed in the Crimean War. Overlooking the square is a fine Doric 1830 **courthouse**, the former Hibernian Bank (1875) and the Gothic St Patrick's Church.

In the centre of town, the **Diamond** is the town's original marketplace, with a Victorian sandstone fountain presented to the town in 1875 in honour of the baron of Rossmore, a member of the area's former leading family. This spot was once occupied by the **Market Cross** (and sundial), which was moved to Old Cross Square at the end of Dublin St to accommodate the baron's memorial.

The birthplace of **Charles Gavan Duffy**, one of the leaders of the Young Ireland Movement and a founder of the *Nation* newspaper, is at 10 Dublin St. In the 1840s, the *Nation* set out to teach Irish people about their history and literature, as well as to present a non-sectarian view of Irish news. Later, Duffy moved to Australia, where he became a premier of Victoria. Nearby, the **Sinn Féin Advice Centre** has a display of republican literature.

South of the Ulster Canal on the Dublin road, the very imposing **St Macartan's Catholic Cathedral** with its slender spire was designed by JJ McCarthy (responsible for the College Chapel in Maynooth, County Kildare) and is said to be his finest building, though some feel it has been marred by the later addition of incongruous Carrara-marble statues. It has good views of the surrounding area.

Convent Lake with its crannóg is at the bottom of Park St, over the canal. **St Louis Convent Heritage Centre** (☎ 83529) has exhibits on the convent, crannóg and local history. It opens 10 am to noon and 2.30 to 4.30 pm, Monday, Tuesday, Thursday and Friday, and 2.30 to 4.30 pm at the weekend. Admission costs £1/50p.

Places to Stay

B&Bs Central *Ashleigh House* (☎ 81227, 37 Dublin St) has singles/doubles costing £20/36 with bath, £17/34 without. *Hilldene House* (☎ 83297, Canal St) charges £15/30 for rooms with shared bath.

On the Clones road south of the centre, *Cedars* (☎ 82783) has three rooms costing £21/34. *Lisdarragh House* (☎ 81473), 2km to the south on the Cootehill road (R188), charges £17 per person.

Hotels The fine, red-brick *Westenra Arms Hotel* (☎ 81517), in the Diamond in the centre of town, has 17 singles/doubles with bathroom costing £45/75. The Georgian *Lakeside Hotel* (☎ 835919, North Rd), beside Peter's Lake, is cheaper, with 10 rooms costing £35/60. The modern 40-room *Four Seasons Hotel* (☎ 81888), about 2km north on the Derry road in Coolshannagh, costs £56/95. On the Old Armagh Rd, superbly appointed *Hillgrove Hotel* (☎ 81288) costs upwards of £47/95.

Places to Eat

Pizza d'Or (Market Square), behind the tourist office, turns out good takeaway pizzas from £4.95 and opens from 5 pm until late. *Genoa (Dublin St)* is a popular fast-food place where the fish and chips are delicious. The 1st-floor *Flannery's (Church Square)* is great for cheap eats: nothing fancy, but tasty nonetheless. Just down from the Genoa is the attractive *Mediterraneo*, which serves pizzas (£5.95 or more), pasta (£6.95) and Italian main courses costing upwards of £8. *Dinkin's Coffee Shop and Restaurant (Church Square)*, next to the courthouse, serves solid fare such as hamburgers and chips downstairs and is busy at lunchtimes. The award-winning *Andy's Bar and Restaurant (12 Market St)*, facing the tourist office, is one of the better places in town for food or a quiet drink. Lunch costs about £5, a set dinner £16.95.

It's easy to see why WB Yeats found inspiration for much of his poetry in County Sligo.

Go for a paddle in County Sligo.

Letting life pass by in Westport, County Mayo

Fairy-tale Ashford Castle in Cong, County Mayo, was once the home of the Guinness dynasty.

It's worth any number of blisters for a view like this one in County Leitrim.

Jimmy Feeney asks himself why he didn't just buy roof tiles, County Cavan.

Lough Sheelin, County Cavan   Traditional shopfront in Ardagh, County Longford

There are two Chinese restaurants on Glaslough St, which runs north from the Diamond: *China Inn* and *Treasure House*. The latter is a favourite with the town's minuscule Chinese community (most of whom seem to own takeaway restaurants of their own).

Entertainment

Some of the best pubs are on Dublin St, including *McGinn's* and the popular *Shamrock Bar*, which has live music at the weekend. On Old Cross Square is *McConnon's Olde Cross Inn*. Another popular pub is *Terry's (Market St)*, near the museum. *Jimmy's (Mill St)*, across from the post office, is a quiet local. Just across from the tourist office, *Kavanagh's* is the place to go for traditional Irish music. *Hillgrove Hotel* has a nightclub where the latest chart hits are danced to on Friday and Saturday nights.

Garage Theatre (☎ 81597), north of town on the Derry road (N2) almost opposite the Four Seasons Hotel, hosts professional theatre companies as well as local amateur drama groups. *Diamond Screen* (☎ 84755) is a three-screen cinema beside the car park in the Diamond Centre shopping mall.

Getting There & Away

From the bus station (☎ 82377) on North Rd beside the former train station, there are numerous daily intercity services within the Republic and into the North. These include five or six daily (four on Sunday) to Dublin (two hours); four or five (two on Sunday) to Derry (two hours) via Omagh; and three (one on Sunday) to Belfast (two hours) and Armagh (40 minutes). There are also many daily local services to the nearby towns of Ardee, Castleblayney, Carrickmacross and Ballybay.

McConnon's private bus company (☎ 82020) runs two daily buses from Church Square to Dublin's Parnell Square, serving Carrickmacross, Castleblayney and Slane en route, and one daily bus to Clones.

Getting Around

Clerkin's Cycles, next to Pizza d'Or on Market Square behind the tourist office, rents out bikes in summer for £8 per day. Weekly rates can be negotiated. The closest other bike rental place is the local Raleigh dealer, Paddy McQuaid (☎ 88108) in Emyvale, about 12km north of Monaghan.

ROSSMORE FOREST PARK

This park (☎ 047-81968), 3km south-west of Monaghan on the Newbliss road (R189), was originally the home of the Rossmores, but only the buttresses to their castle's walls and the entrance stairway remain. Besides forest walks and picnic areas, the park has Californian sequoias, some of the tallest trees in Ireland. Other points of interest include the Rossmores' pet cemetery as well as Iron Age wedge and court tombs. A gold collar (or lunula) from 1800 BC was found here in the 1930s and taken to the National Museum in Dublin. Fishing in the lakes here is popular. Admission to the park is free for pedestrians and £2 if you bring in a car.

GLASLOUGH

☎ 047

Glaslough, 9km north-east of Monaghan, is a neat little village of cut-stone cottages set beside its namesake, Glaslough (Green Lake). To get there from Monaghan, take the N2 Omagh road north, turn east onto the N12 for about 2km then turn north onto the R185.

Beside the village is the 500-hectare demesne of **Castle Leslie** (☎ 88109), a magnificent 19th-century Italianate mansion overlooking the lake. The castle's attractions include a toilet used by Mick Jagger. Greystones Equestrian Centre (☎ 88100) has some fine hacks in the demesne, where there are 40km of trails.

The castle and gardens are open for tours only, at 3, 4 and 5 pm Monday to Thursday, June to August. Admission costs £3.50/2.

For the ultimate 'Victorian experience', you can stay in one of the castle's six bedrooms, all with original decor, for £78/116 for singles/doubles. Four-course dinners cost £27.50. For those whose budget is a bit more fragile, *Pillar House Hotel*

CENTRAL NORTH

(☎ 88125), at the entrance to the Castle Leslie estate, charges £20 per person.

CLONES & AROUND
☎ 047 • pop 1921

The border town of Clones (Cluain Eois), 19km south-west of Monaghan, was the site of an important 6th-century monastery that later became an Augustinian abbey. The bus stop, post office and banks, including a Bank of Ireland branch, are in the central Diamond, or square. The town is the birthplace and home of the Clones Cyclone, former world featherweight champion Barry McGuigan. Retired for nearly a decade, he recently came back into the limelight as a country-and-western singer!

Things to See & Do
Along with the scant remains of the **abbey** founded by St Tiernach on Abbey St, there is a truncated 22m-high **round tower** in the old cemetery south of town; the layout suggests it may be an early-9th-century example. There's also a fine **high cross** on the Diamond, with beautiful carvings depicting Adam and Eve, Daniel in the lion's den and, on the other side (north), the marriage at Cana and the miracle of the loaves and the fishes. Overlooking it is the Protestant **St Tiernach's Church**.

The Ulster Way in Northern Ireland runs through **Newtownbutler** in Fermanagh, 8km to the north-west of Clones. North of Newtownbutler, there is a **scenic drive** from Derrnawilt to Lisnaskea. South-east of Clones, the road from Newbliss to Cootehill is quite pretty and takes you to the edge of **Bellamont Forest**, which straddles the border with Cavan.

Places to Stay & Eat
The *Lennard Arms Hotel* (☎ 51075, *The Diamond*) charges £22/36 for B&B in singles/doubles with bathroom. *Creighton Hotel* (☎ 51284, *Fermanagh St*) is popular with anglers. It has 16 simple but comfortable rooms with bathroom at a reasonable £22 per person for B&B. This is also a nice place for a snack, lunch or full dinner (£10).

For a real treat, *Hilton Park* (☎ 56007) is an ideal place to forget the 20th century and blow any spare cash that may be weighing you down. Five kilometres south along the L45 then L44 to Scotshouse, this country house has its own estate and serves topclass food in regal surroundings. Many of the ingredients are grown on the estate's organic farm. B&B in six splendid rooms costs upwards of £67.50/115 for singles/doubles, and dinner costs £30 (without wine). The grounds of Hilton Park are open to visitors from May to September. Admission costs £2.50.

Getting There & Around
Bus Éireann (☎ 82377) runs buses from Clones through Monaghan and on to Castleblayney, Carrickmacross, Slane and Dublin three to four times daily (twice on Sunday). Buses stop in the Diamond. Ulsterbus (☎ 028-66 322633) has a number of daily buses on a route that takes in Monaghan, Clones, Enniskillen as well as Belfast. McConnon's (☎ 82020) runs a daily bus between Clones, Monaghan, Castleblayney, Carrickmacross, Slane and Dublin.

You can rent bikes in Clones at Canal Stores (☎ 52125) on Cara St.

CARRICKMACROSS & AROUND
☎ 042 • pop 1926

Carrickmacross (Carraig Mhachaire Rois), Monaghan's second-most-important town (after the eponymous county seat), was once a stronghold of the MacMahon clan. It owes its origins to the 3rd earl of Essex, who was a favourite of Elizabeth I and built a castle here in the 1630s. The site is now occupied by the Convent of St Louis. An extensive lace industry helped the early English and Scottish planters to develop this pleasant little town, which consists of one wide street with some lovely Georgian houses and an old Protestant church.

Things to See & Do
Carrickmacross Lace Gallery (☎ 966 2506) on Market Square, run by the local lace cooperative, has some fine displays and lace for sale. It opens 9.30 am to 12.30 pm and 1.30 to 5 pm Monday, Tuesday, Thursday

and Friday, and 9.30 am to 12.30 pm Wednesday and Saturday, May to October. Bustling **Main St** is replete with shops, pubs and some quite elegant Georgian houses, a testimony to the town's wealthier past.

There's **fishing** in many of the lakes around Carrickmacross, including Loughs Capragh, Spring, Monalty and Fea. Contact Jimmy McMahon at the Carrick Sports Centre (☎ 966 1714) for information on where to fish. Lough Fea has an adjacent 1827 mansion and a demesne with oak parkland. Five kilometres south-west along the R179 Kingscourt road is **Dún an Rí Forest Park** (☎ 67320) with trails and picnic spots.

Mannor Castle is an enormous and heavily overgrown motte and bailey, about 5km north-west of Carrickmacross in Donaghmoyne. This fortified Norman mound has fragments of a stone castle dating from the 12th century. Both structures were built by the Pipard family, who were given an estate here in 1186 by England's King John.

Places to Stay
Carrickmacross has lots of B&B accommodation. *Shirley Arms* pub (☎ 966 1209, Main St) offers reasonable singles/doubles costing £22/40 with bathroom. *Arradale House* (☎ 966 1941), a farmhouse on the Kingscourt road south of town, has eight rooms with bathroom costing £18/36. The sprawling *Nuremore Hotel and Country Club* (☎ 966 1438), on the outskirts of town, has every conceivable amenity, including an 18-hole championship-length golf course. Rooms cost upwards of £80/140.

Getting There & Away
Seven Bus Éireann (☎ 047-82377) buses daily (five on Sunday) to/from Dublin (1¼ hours) pass through Carrickmacross. There are at least three daily on a Letterkenny to Dublin route, two on a Coleraine to Dublin route and one between Clones and Dublin. Collins (☎ 966 1631), a private bus company, offers four departures daily to Dublin, three on Sunday. McConnon's (☎ 047-82020) service includes Carrickmacross on its Dublin to Monaghan and Clones route, which also passes through Castleblayney, with two daily buses Monday to Saturday.

The bus stop is outside O'Hanlon's shop on Main St.

INNISKEEN
☎ 042
The village of Inniskeen (Inis Caoin), birthplace of the poet Patrick Kavanagh, is 10km north-east of Carrickmacross. Kavanagh is buried in the local graveyard, where his cross reads: 'And pray for him who walked apart on the hills loving life's miracles'.

Patrick Kavanagh Rural and Literary Resource Centre (☎ 78560), housed in the village's plain chapel and focusing on the poet's life and work as well as local and folk history, opens 11 am to 5 pm on weekdays, year round, plus 2 to 6 pm on Saturday (June to September) and Sunday (mid-March to November). Nearby, the forlorn skeletal ruin of a **round tower** is all that is left of the 6th-century **St Daig monastery**.

CASTLEBLAYNEY
☎ 042 • pop 1884
Castleblayney (Baile na Lorgan), about halfway between Carrickmacross and Monaghan on the N2, is nicely situated near Lough Muckno, the county's most expansive and scenic lake. This small town takes its name from Sir Edward Blayney and his family, who built a castle by the lake in 1622 and were responsible for the construction of the plain Georgian courthouse and both the Protestant and former Catholic churches – an uncommon gesture by a landowner at the time.

Blayney's castle was sold in the last century to the Hope family and was renamed after them. In the demesne is the 365-hectare **Lough Muckno Leisure Park** (☎ 974 6356), which has lake-shore and woodland trails as well as golf, tennis, cycling, canoeing, sailing, water-skiing, fishing and horse riding.

Places to Stay
Lough Muckno Leisure Park (☎ 974 6356) has a 50-bed hostel costing £11.50 per

person. It opens April to October. *Connolly's Guesthouse* (☎ 974 5162) in Castleblayney has rooms with shared bathroom costing £14.50 per person and opens year round. The 27-room *Glencarn Hotel* (☎ 974 6666), on the Monaghan road, charges £35/70 for singles/doubles.

Getting There & Away

Castleblayney is on the main Monaghan to Dublin route, with seven buses daily in each direction. McConnon's (☎ 047-82020) private bus service also has a number of daily buses from Clones and Monaghan through Castleblayney and on to Dublin.

County Roscommon

County Roscommon (Ros Comáin), much longer than it is wide, is more a transit route than a destination in itself. But besides the sleepy county town (population 1432), there are places well worth visiting. Strokestown has one of the better-presented mansions in the country as well as the important Famine Museum. Just south of the Sligo boundary, the town of Boyle is also worth a stop, especially for the unique King House Interpretive Centre.

Much of Roscommon's western border follows the River Suck. About halfway down, a few kilometres inland from Ballyforan, is Dysart (Thomas St on some maps), ancestral stomping grounds of the illustrious Fallon sept. The remains of their castle are near the town, as is a recently renovated church, parts of which date from the 12th century, in the middle of an ancient cemetery. Roscommon's eastern border is formed by a number of loughs, including the large Lough Ree (or Rea), and the River Shannon, which flows between them. Naturally, fishing is a major draw.

STROKESTOWN & AROUND

☎ 078 • pop 572

Strokestown (Béal na mBuillí), on the N5 between the towns of Longford and Tulsk, is about 18km north-west of Roscommon. It owes its existence to the Mahon family, owners of Roscommon's second-most-important estate. Its incredibly wide main street was designed by one of the early Mahons, who took it upon himself to create Europe's widest street!

Strokestown Park House

At the end of Strokestown's main avenue are three Gothic arches, beyond which is this impressive stately home (☎ 33013), the seat of a 12,000-hectare estate granted to Nicholas Mahon by Charles II after the Restoration as a reward for supporting the House of Stuart in the English Civil War.

The original house, completed in 1697, was not considered imposing enough for Nicholas' grandson Thomas, who commissioned Richard Castle to build him a grand house in the Palladian style, as was the current taste. The only part of the original house to survive Castle's designs is the stillroom in the basement. Apart from some alterations made in the mid-19th century, the house has remained unchanged since Castle's day. The actual estate, however, decreased along with the family's fortunes, and when they eventually sold up to the local garage owner in 1979 the estate had been whittled down to 120 hectares. However, as the estate was never sold at auction, virtually all of the contents were kept intact.

In 1914 Olive Pakenham-Mahon married the heir to the Rockingham estate in Boyle, thus uniting the county's two biggest demesnes. The union lasted only a couple of months as Pakenham was killed in the early days of WWI. His widow maintained the estate until its sale.

David Thomson's *Woodbrook* (see Travel in the Books section of the Facts for the Visitor chapter) is the perfect book to read after your visit and is available here, and there are paintings by Woodbrook's (see Lough Key Forest Park in the Boyle & Around section later in this chapter) Phoebe Kirkwood adorning the walls of an upstairs bedroom.

Even children will enjoy the tour, which takes in a schoolroom and a child's bedroom, complete with 19th-century toys and fun-house mirrors. The 45-minute tour provides a fascinating glimpse into the Anglo-Irish Ascendancy and costs £3.25/1.50. The house opens 11 am to 5.30 pm daily, April to October.

In the old stable yards is the fascinating **Irish Famine Museum** (☎ 33013). The museum is an absolute must for anyone seeking to understand the devastating effects of the potato blight on Ireland. In a marked departure from the traditional silence about the disaster, the museum outlines in vivid detail the horrors of starvation and the irresponsibility of the government, which was too wrapped up in a *laissez faire* economic policy to intervene. One exhibit also draws parallels with world hunger and poverty today.

The museum keeps the same hours and charges the same admission fee as the house. A ticket combining the house and museum costs £6/3, while a ticket for the house, museum and gardens costs £8.50/4.

St John's Heritage & Genealogical Centre

North of the centre in a disused Protestant church, this attraction (☎ 33380) has local-history displays and one on Roscommon family names. There is an interesting exhibit called Ireland of the Heroes, with particular attention paid to the megalithic monuments at Rathcrogan and the *Táin Bó Cúailnge* (see the boxed text in the Counties Meath & Louth chapter). The centre also offers a family research service, with records dating back to the 1660s, for those whose families hail from County Roscommon. The initial charge is £25. The centre opens 9 am to 1 pm and 2 to 5 pm weekdays, May to September (though genealogical inquiries can be made throughout the year).

Elphin

Some 10km north-west of Strokestown, Elphin was an important bishopric from the time of St Patrick until 1961, when the seat was moved to Sligo. Ruins of the cathedral, parts of which date from about the 13th century, can be seen in the centre of town.

Places to Stay

Martin's (☎ 33247), in the centre of Strokestown not far from the heritage centre, charges £18 per person for B&B. *Church View House* (☎ 33047), 5km east of town, offers singles/doubles costing upwards of £22/36. It opens April to October. *Percy French Hotel* (☎ 33300) offers rooms costing £30/50.

Getting There & Away

The Bus Éireann (☎ 071-60066) express bus from Sligo to Athlone (via Roscommon and Boyle) stops in Strokestown once daily Monday to Saturday, mid-July to August, and once on Sunday year round. The Ballina to Dublin bus via Longford and Mullingar stops in Strokestown three times

CENTRAL NORTH

Famine, Suffering & Injustice

When the potato crop failed in the mid-1840s, Major Denis Mahon (landlord of Strokestown at the time) and his land agent simply evicted the hundreds of starving peasants who could no longer contribute to the estate's coffers and chartered ships to transport them away from Ireland. These overcrowded 'coffin ships', which carried emigrants to the USA and elsewhere, resulted in more suffering and deaths.

In 1847 Major Mahon was shot dead just outside the town, and one of the documents on display in the Irish Famine Museum in Strokestown is a newspaper account of how Patrick Hasty and Owen Beirne committed the deed. Their signed confession looks as suspicious as the ones that convicted the Birmingham Six – exonerated in 1991 – of terrorism in Britain in the 1970s.

---

daily (four on Sunday). The bus stop is outside Corcoran's on Main St.

BOYLE & AROUND
☎ 079 • pop 1690

Boyle (Mainistir na Búille) is a garrison town in the north-west of the county at the foot of the Curlew Mountains and on the River Boyle between Lough Key and Lough Gara. It has many attractions, including the fine Boyle Abbey, the renovated King House Interpretive Centre and the impressive Drumanone Dolmen just outside town. Maureen O'Sullivan, the American film actress and mother of Mia Farrow, was born in a house on Main St opposite the Bank of Ireland building in 1911. The long-suffering Mia visits Boyle regularly and stays *en famille* at her mother's childhood home – now a B&B – in Knockvicar to the north-east of Boyle near Lough Kee. Mention of actor-director Woody Allen, Mia's erstwhile partner, should be avoided at all costs in these parts.

History
Boyle grew up around the King-family estate at Rockingham, Roscommon's largest and most powerful demesne. Up to the early 1600s, there was little more than a settlement here. Connaught kings and chieftains such as the MacDermots and the O'Conors had engaged in a long-running battle to gain control over the area. In 1603, however, Staffordshire-born John King was granted land in Roscommon with a view to 'reducing the Irish to obedience' through the enforcement of the Penal Laws.

Over the next 150 years, his descendants proceeded to make their name and fortune, and by 1768 Edward King was made earl of Kingston. In 1730 the stately King House was built, but in 1780 the family moved to the grander Rockingham House, built in what is now Lough Key Forest Park. The majority of the estate was disbanded in the 19th century, leaving just the house, which was burned to the ground in 1957.

Information
The tourist office (☎ 62145), in King House

on the corner where Military Rd meets Main St, opens 10 am to 5 pm on weekdays, April to mid-September. At other times, seek assistance from the friendly staff at the interpretive centre or at the Úna Bhán Tourism Cooperative (see Organised Tours later in this section), both in King House, or from the tourism information board in front of the clock tower in the Crescent, the central square.

There's a National Irish Bank branch with an ATM on the corner of Bridge and Patrick Sts and a Bank of Ireland at the eastern end of Main St. The post office is on Carrick Rd, south of the river.

Boyle Abbey
Beside the N4, to the east of the town centre, is one of the finest Cistercian abbeys in Ireland, with remains dating back to the 12th century, when it was founded by monks from Mellifont in County Louth. In 1659 military forces occupied the abbey and turned it into a fort.

The interesting 13th-century nave in the northern part of the abbey has Gothic arches on one side that are narrower than the Romanesque arches on the other. The capitals are also distinctive. On the southern side of the abbey, once the refectory area, there is a fine stone chimney built after the monks left and the abbey became a fortified home. Edward King, whose death by drowning in 1637 inspired English poet John Milton to compose *Lycidas*, is buried here. The western side of the abbey was originally set aside for the monks' sleeping quarters. Later, the military forces had a dog kennel built into the left side of the gatehouse entrance.

The Dúchas-run abbey (☎ 62604) opens from 9.30 am to 6.30 pm daily, Easter to November. Admission costs £1/40p and guided tours are available on the hour until 5 pm.

King House Interpretive Centre
This interpretive centre (☎ 63242), which is certainly one of the most inspired in the country, is in a lovely mansion built by Henry King in 1730. It served as a military

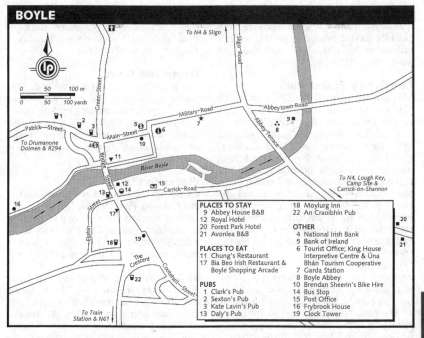

BOYLE

To N4 & Sligo

Sligo Road

Green Street

Military Road

Abbeytown Road

Patrick Street

Main Street

Bridge Street

Abbey Terrace

To Drumanone
Dolmen & R294

River Boyle

Elphin Street

Carrick Road

To N4, Lough Key,
Camp Site &
Carrick-on-Shannon

The Crescent

Costello Street

To Train
Station & N61

PLACES TO STAY
9 Abbey House B&B
12 Royal Hotel
20 Forest Park Hotel
21 Avonlea B&B

PLACES TO EAT
11 Chung's Restaurant
17 Bia Beo Irish Restaurant &
   Boyle Shopping Arcade

PUBS
1 Clark's Pub
2 Sexton's Pub
3 Kate Lavin's Pub
13 Daly's Pub

18 Moylurg Inn
22 An Craoibhín Pub

OTHER
4 National Irish Bank
5 Bank of Ireland
6 Tourist Office; King House
   Interpretive Centre & Úna
   Bhán Tourism Cooperative
7 Garda Station
8 Boyle Abbey
10 Brendan Sheerin's Bike Hire
14 Bus Stop
15 Post Office
16 Frybrook House
19 Clock Tower

CENTRAL NORTH

barracks for the fearsome Connaught Rangers (Wellington called them the 'Devil's Own') from 1788 until Irish independence in 1922, after which it sat derelict until the county council renovated it (1989–95) at a cost of £3 million. It contains audiovisual exhibits detailing the turbulent history of the Connaught kings, the chieftains, the town of Boyle and the King family, including a rather grim tale of tenant eviction during the Famine.

Kids will especially enjoy King House. It's very much a hands-on museum where they can try on ancient Irish cloaks, brooches and leather shoes, write with a quill 'pen' and even 'build' a vaulted ceiling – King House has four floors of them – from specially designed blocks. A tour of King House is an excellent precursor to one of the Famine Museum in Strokestown.

The centre opens 10 am to 6 pm daily, May to September; and 10 am to 6 pm at the weekend only, April and October. Admission costs £3/2.50/8 for adults/students/families.

Frybrook House

This rather magnificent Georgian mansion (☎ 63513) was built in 1750 for Henry Fry, who came to Boyle at the invitation of Lord Kingston. The drawing room contains some of the finest Georgian plasterwork anywhere and an Adams fireplace. The house was noted for its hospitality, and local lore has it that a bell was sounded every day at 5 pm inviting anyone who wished to come and dine. A tent was set up in the garden to cope with the overflow.

Frybrook House opens 2 to 6 pm daily, June to August. Admission costs £3/2/7 for adults/students/families.

Drumanone Dolmen

This superb dolmen is one of the largest in Ireland, measuring 4.5 by 3.3m, and was constructed before 2000 BC. To get there, follow Patrick St west out of town for 2km, then bear left at the junction sign for Lough Gara for another kilometre, passing under a railway arch. A sign indicates the path across the railway line.

Lough Key Forest Park

This 350-hectare park (☎ 62363), on the N4 3km east of Boyle, was part of the Rockingham estate, owned by the King family from the late 18th century until it was sold to the Land Commission in 1957. Rockingham House, designed by John Nash, was destroyed by a fire in the same year; all that remains are some stables and outbuildings and a tunnel leading from what was the house to the lake. The inexpensive café opens 12.30 to 6 pm and in summer a restaurant opens for lunch and dinner. The park opens daily year round and admission costs £1 (families £3).

Lough Key is at the northern limit for cruising on the Shannon. Rowing boats are available for a pricey £6 an hour, and fishing is a popular pursuit; a record-breaking 17.8kg pike was caught here in 1992. The ruins of a 12th-century abbey can be seen on tiny Trinity Island. On Castle Island, a 19th-century castle stands on the site of 16th-century MacDermot Castle.

Six kilometres from the park, on the N4 towards Carrick-on-Shannon, is **Woodbrook**, the demesne that is the setting for David Thomson's wonderful novel on the Anglo-Irish gentry. It is not open to the public, however.

Douglas Hyde Interpretive Centre

Frenchpark, some 12km south-west of Boyle on the R361, is home to the Douglas Hyde Interpretive Centre (☎ 0907-70016), in the former Protestant church where Hyde's father was rector. Hyde (1860–1949) was one of the founding members of the Gaelic League in 1893 and was later elected the first president of the Republic in 1937. This Renaissance man published many works of prose and poetry under the pen name An Craoibhín Aoibhinn (Delightful Little Branch), and he is buried in the

churchyard. The centre, also known as the Gairdín an Craoibhín (Garden of the Little Branch), opens 2 to 5 or 6 pm Tuesday to Sunday, May to September.

Organised Tours

Úna Bhán Tourism Cooperative (☎ 63033), whose office is in the grounds of King House, organises week-long cycling, horse-riding and fishing tours which include accommodation on a working farm. There's an excellent craft shop here open 10 am to 6 pm daily.

Places to Stay

Camping The *Lough Key Forest Caravan and Camping Park* (☎ 62212) is in the park: indicate your intention to camp to avoid the £1 admission charge. Camping costs £9 for a family tent, or £3.50 per hiker, cyclist or motorcyclist; electricity is an extra £1.50.

B&Bs Beside the abbey and the River Boyle, *Abbey House* (☎ 62385) charges £21.50/38 for singles/doubles with bath, and opens March to October. At *Avonlea* (☎ 62538), on the Carrick road (N4) just south-east of town and almost opposite the Forest Park Hotel, rates are £23/40 with bath. *Carnfree* (☎ 62516), almost next door to the hotel, charges upwards of £18 per person and opens year round.

About 1km farther on is the *Rosdarrig* (☎ 62040), charging £15 or £16 per person. Farther south on the N4, Mrs Kelly in *Forest Park House* (☎ 62227) offers B&B costing £22/37. *Riversdale House* (☎ 67012), in Knockvicar 12km north-east of Boyle on the R285, charges £27/40 and opens April to October.

Hotels In the town centre, the 18th-century *Royal Hotel* (☎ 62016) offers 16 rooms with bath for £42.50 per person, while the 12-room *Forest Park Hotel* (☎ 62229), just outside town on the N4, charges upwards of £40/80.

Places to Eat

The best place for a £3 or £4 pub lunch is *An Craoibhín (The Crescent)*, which is also the most popular pub in town. On Patrick St, reasonable pub food is available at *Sexton's*. For snacks and lunch the *coffee shop* in King House is a good bet. It opens 10 am to 6 pm daily.

Overlooking the river, *Chung's* serves passable Chinese food from 5 to 11.30 pm daily. Main courses range from £4.50 to £6.95. *Bia Beo* is a rare breed indeed – an Irish restaurant – upstairs in the Boyle Shopping Arcade on Bridge St. The *Royal* and *Forest Park* hotels do lunch and set dinners (£20.95 and £16.95 respectively).

Entertainment
Railway Bar near the station, *Clark's* and *Kate Lavin's* in Patrick St, and *Moylurg Inn*, opposite the clock tower in the Crescent, have music and a decent drop of Guinness.

Getting There & Away
From almost outside Royal Hotel (and opposite Daly's pub) on Bridge St, the Bus Éireann (☎ 071-60066) express bus leaves three times daily for Sligo (40 minutes) and Dublin (3¼ hours). From Boyle, a train goes three times daily (four on Friday) between Sligo (40 minutes) and Dublin (3¼ hours) via Mullingar.

Getting Around
You can order a taxi on ☎ 63344 or ☎ 62119. Bikes are available from Brendan Sheerin's cycle shop (☎ 62010) on Main St for £10 per day. It opens 9.30 am to 1 pm and 2 to 6 pm daily, except Wednesday and Sunday.

ROSCOMMON
☎ 0903 • pop 1432
The small county town of Roscommon (Ros Comáin), sitting at the crossroads of several major highways, has a few sights of interest that make it worth a stopover. The town gets its name from '*ros*' (wooded headland) and St Coman, who founded a monastery here in the 8th century.

The local tourist office (☎ 26342), in John Harrison Hall in Market Square, opens daily, late May to early September. The post office is next door, and there is a Bank of Ireland opposite Gleeson's Guesthouse on the square.

Things to See & Do
The Norman **Roscommon Castle** built in 1269 was almost immediately destroyed by Irish forces and rebuilt in 1280. The mullioned windows were added in the 16th century. The massive walls and round bastions give it an impressive look, standing alone in a field at the northern end of town off Castle St.

At the southern end of town off Circular Rd are the remains of a 13th-century **Dominican priory**, the most notable feature of which is an effigy of the founder, Felim O'Conor, carved around 1300. It's set in the north wall near where the altar once stood.

Roscommon County Museum (☎ 63856) is in John Harrison Hall on Market Square, a former Presbyterian church with an unusual window in the form of a Star of David supposedly representing the Trinity. The museum contains some vaguely interesting pieces, including an inscribed slab from St Coman's monastery and a sheila-na-gig from Rahara. The museum opens 10 am to 5.30 pm Monday to Saturday, April to October.

Market Square's Bank of Ireland used to be the **courthouse**. Opposite is the enormous **old jail**, where executions were carried out by 'Lady Betty' in the mid-18th century. She herself had been condemned to death after confessing to the murder of a lodger in her house – who turned out to be her own son. She escaped death by offering to take over as executioner.

Ask the tourist office for a map of the **Suck Valley Way**, a 75km walking trail. The river offers some of the best mixed fishing in Ireland, with rudd, tench, pike and perch in abundance.

Places to Stay
Gailey Bay Caravan and Camping Park (☎ 61058) is in Knockcroghery beside Lough Ree about 10km south-east of Roscommon on the N61 to Athlone; a sign points east just near the train station and it's

a couple of kilometres up the road. Pitching a tent costs £5 plus £1 per person; hikers or cyclists pay £3.50.

The 19-room *O'Gara's Royal Hotel* (☎ *26317, Castle St)*, in the centre of town, offers singles/doubles with shower and toilet costing upwards of £22.50/50.

A listed 19th-century house on Market Square has been tastefully restored and is now home to the *Gleeson's Guesthouse* (☎ *26954)*, which charges from £22.50 to £27.50 per person.

Regan's Guesthouse (☎ *25339)*, next door with 10 rooms, costs about the same but is not as nice. It does, however, have two new self-catering apartments.

The poshest place in town is the 25-room *Abbey Hotel* (☎ *26250)*, south-west of Market Square at the start of the Galway road. Singles/doubles cost £45/75 or £55/85, depending on the season.

Places to Eat
There are a number of cafés and fast-food places on Main St, including the *Alpine Grill*. *Gleeson's Restaurant*, in the guesthouse of the same name, on the square, serves a full Irish breakfast (£3.50) and lunch (from £3.95). It opens 8 am to 6 pm daily. *Regan's* next door has a standard dinner menu with the usual main courses (`with chips') from about £5. *China Palace* is a Chinese restaurant upstairs on Main St which opens 5 pm to 12.30 am Wednesday to Monday, and also from 1 pm for lunch on Sunday. *The Manse* restaurant in Gleeson's Guesthouse comes recommended by locals; all main courses cost about £9. *O'Gara's Royal Hotel* serves an excellent set dinner costing £17.

Entertainment
One of the best pubs in town is *Down the Hatch* on Church St. *Central Bar* and *JJ Hagerty's* on Market Square are also worth a look.

Getting There & Around
Bus Éireann (☎ 071-60066) express buses between Westport (2¼ hours) and Dublin (three hours) stop in Roscommon three times

daily (once on Sunday). Buses stop in front of Regan's Guesthouse on Market Square. Roscommon is also served by train three times daily (four on Friday) on the Dublin (two hours) to Westport (1½ hours) line.

You can order a taxi on ☎ 26096.

WESTERN ROSCOMMON
The village of Ballintober (Ballintubber on some maps; Baile an Tobair in Irish), about 15km north-west of Roscommon off the N60, is dominated by the 14th-century **Ballintober Castle**, built in the early 14th century and once home to the fierce O'Conors of Connaught. Cromwellian forces took the castle in 1652, but it was later restored to the O'Conors – only to be lost again after the defeat of the Catholics at the Battle of the Boyne in 1690. The large central courtyard has polygonal towers at each corner, and the whole edifice is a good example of an early Irish castle. Also in Ballintober is the **Old Schoolhouse Museum** (☎ 0907-55397), which re-creates a rural Irish classroom in the 1920s. It opens daily Easter to October. Admission costs £1.50/50p.

To the north-west past Castlerea on the N60, **Clonalis House** (☎ 0907-20014), built in 1878, opens to the public from 11 am to 5 pm Tuesday to Sunday, from June to mid-September. Admission costs £3.50/1.75. The house is rather cold and lacks atmosphere, but it does have the harp of Turlough O'Carolan (1630–1738), the great blind harpist and composer (see Around Carrick-on-Shannon later in this chapter) as well as a copy of the last Brehon Law (Irish common law dating back to pre-Christian times) judgement, which was handed down in 1580. Overnight guests are welcome at *Clonalis House* between mid-April and September. There are four bedrooms and singles/doubles cost £55/97.

County Leitrim

Leitrim (Liatroim) stretches 80km from the border with Longford to Donegal Bay in the north-west, with a short coastline of about 5km around Tullaghan. Lough Allen splits the county almost in two. The attractions in northern Leitrim, with its mountains and glens, are more accessible from Sligo and are covered in the Counties Mayo & Sligo chapter. Southern Leitrim's main interest is its lush scenery of lakes and drumlins but, while a walking or cycling tour of the area would be enjoyable, most visitors just speed through on their way north.

CARRICK-ON-SHANNON
☎ 078 • pop 1868

Carrick-on-Shannon (known simply as Carrick, or in Irish as Cora Droma Rúisc) straddles the border with Roscommon and is the main town in the county, marking the upper limit of navigation on the River Shannon. It is beautifully positioned over the river, and is a major centre for boating. In 1994 the last stretch of the **Shannon-Erne Waterway** was completed with the reopening of the Ballyconnell-Ballinamore Canal, completing 382km of navigable canals and loughs that begin in Limerick and end in Buleek on Upper Lough Erne. The canal has literally put Carrick-on-Shannon on the tourist map, and is the main reason for visiting the town (see Shannon-Erne Waterway later in this section).

Information

The tourist office (☎ 20170), on West Quay at the Marina beside Carrick Bridge, opens 9 am to 1 pm Monday to Thursday, and 9.30 am to 1 pm on Friday, May to September. A signposted walking tour takes in all the buildings and places of interest in town.

There's an Allied Irish Bank branch at the top of Main St. The post office is on Bridge St opposite Flynn's Corner House bar.

Costello Chapel

At the top of Bridge St, next to Flynn's Corner House, is the sombre little Costello Chapel. It measures only 5 by 3.6m and was built in 1877 by one distraught Edward Costello after the death of his wife. She is buried on the left side under a heavy slab of glass, and her husband was interred on the other side in 1891. The chapel was built on the site of the old courthouse, where 19 men were hanged in the 19th century.

Boating & Fishing

Michael Lynch (☎ 20034), based on the quay near the tourist office, has rowing boats for hire at £8 per hour, or between £25 and £35 per day for one with an engine. More upmarket launches are available through Tara Cruisers (☎ 20736), based at the Rosebank Marina on the Dublin road (N4). Moon River (☎ 21777) runs cruises in season from the Marina. Contact the tourist office or check the information board on the quay.

For information on fishing, contact the Carrick-on-Shannon Angling Association (☎ 20489).

Places to Stay

Camping is free on the river bank near the tourist office. Tokens for the showers at the nearby Marina office can be purchased from the Marina office.

The IHH *Town Clock Hostel* (☎ 20068), in the town centre at the junction of Main and Bridge Sts, offers dorm beds costing £6 to £7 and one private room costing £8.50 per person. The hostel opens from June to September.

Carrick has lots of B&Bs. On Station Rd, near the train station on the Roscommon side of the river, *Villa Flora* (☎ 20338), open April to October, charges upwards of £24/36 for singles/doubles (although visitors can get away with paying only £18 for a single), while *Ariadna* (☎ 20205), open year round, costs £17 per person. *Bush Hotel* (☎ 20114), in the centre of town, offers B&B with private bathroom costing upwards of £35/70.

Places to Eat

Flynn's is a fast-food joint on Main St next to the Corner House. *Coffey's Pastry Case* is a busy, inexpensive self-service coffee-shop-cum-bakery on the corner near the bridge and tourist office. Next door, *Cryan's Pub* serves a £3.25 lunch and has

CENTRAL NORTH

traditional-music sessions most nights. Next door *Buadh* (Victory) at the Oarsman Pub is a more expensive place with main courses (mostly seafood) costing £8 to £12.

Farther up Bridge St, *Mariner's Reach* serves lunch specials costing about £3.50, but even better is the four-course bar special available until 9.30 pm for £5. *Chung's (Main St)*, a branch of the Chinese restaurant in Boyle, County Roscommon, has dishes (with several vegetarian options) costing £4.50 to £6.50.

Getting There & Away
The bus stop is outside Coffey's Pastry Case on the corner near the bridge and tourist office. The Bus Éireann (☎ 071-60066) main express bus between Dublin (2¾ hours) and Sligo (one hour) stops there three times daily in each direction. There are also buses to Boyle, Longford and Athlone.

The train station (☎ 20036) is a 15-minute walk from the bridge on the Roscommon side of the river. Turn right over the bridge, then left at the service station. Carrick has three trains daily to Dublin (three hours) and Sligo (50 minutes), with an additional one on Friday.

Getting Around
You can hire bicycles from Geraghty's (☎ 21316) on Main St for £10 per day; it also rents out rods and tackle on a daily or weekly basis. The *Visitors' Guidebook* from the tourist office includes details of suggested cycling tours.

AROUND CARRICK-ON-SHANNON
The countryside around Carrick, with its quiet lanes and gently undulating landscape, is tailor-made for cycling.

Turlough O'Carolan Country
There are three places to visit in the area that are connected with the famous blind poet, composer and harpist Turlough O'Carolan (1670–1738). He spent most of his time in Mohill, where his patron, Mrs MacDermot Roe, resided, and a sculpture

on the main street of the town commemorates the association. To reach Mohill from Carrick-on-Shannon, follow the N4 to Dublin then turn east onto the R201 shortly after passing Drumsna.

O'Carolan is buried in Kilronan church, which preserves a 12th-century doorway, just over the border in County Roscommon. To reach the church, take the R280 north from Carrick-on-Shannon and at the village of Leitrim turn west on the R284 to Keadue (Keadew on some maps). In Keadue turn west on the R284 to Sligo.

Keadue was a coal-mining town at the foot of the Arigna Mountains until the 1980s and is now a spruced-up 'tidy-town competition' winner. It also has strong associations with the musician and hosts the annual O'Carolan Harp Festival during the first week of August.

Lough Rynn Estate
Lough Rynn, south of Mohill, was the home of the Clements family, the earls of Leitrim, and the various 19th-century buildings put up during the time of the 3rd earl are open to the public. Within the wooded estate (☎ 078-31427) there's a picnic site and restaurant, and guided tours of the principal buildings are available. It opens 10 am to 7 pm daily, late April to mid-September. Admission to the grounds costs £4 per car, £2 per person; the tour is another £1.50.

Drumshanbo
☎ 078 • pop 590
Drumshanbo (Droim Seanbhó), about 9km north of Carrick-on-Shannon on the southern shores of Lough Allen, is mainly a centre for coarse fishing. The Sliath an Iarainn Visitors Centre (☎ 41522) has an interesting audiovisual display (£1/50p) on the history and culture of the locality, and a non-functioning replica of an ancient Irish sweathouse not unlike a sauna. The visitor centre opens 10 am to 6 pm Monday to Saturday, and 2 to 6 pm on Sunday, April to September.

Mrs Mooney at *Drumshanbo Holiday Centre* (☎ 41013, 2 Carrick Rd), at the southern end of town, offers B&B costing

£16/32 for singles/doubles and provides local tourist information.

SHANNON-ERNE WATERWAY

The Shannon-Erne Waterway stretches from the River Shannon beside the village of Leitrim, 4km north of Carrick-on-Shannon, through north-western County Cavan to the southern shore of Upper Lough Erne, just over the Northern Ireland border in County Fermanagh.

The 382km-long waterway is a series of rivers and lakes linked by canals. The original canal, which was called the Ballyconnell-Ballinamore Canal, was completed in 1860, but soon fell into disuse with the coming of the railway. The canal was reopened in 1994 and, with its 34 stone bridges and 16 locks, is now busy with boats and pleasure cruisers.

Carrick Craft (☎ 20236) rents two-berth boats from £200/335 for three nights/one week, four-berth boats from £205/510, six-berth cruisers from £325/825, and eight-berth pleasure crafts from £498/1050. Emerald Star (☎ 078-20234 in Carrick-on-Shannon, 01-679 8166 in Dublin) has weekly rates of £675 for a three-berth, from £1030 to £1650 for a six-berth, and a large, very comfortable 10-berth for £1960.

Before you sail, rental companies show a video and give a one-hour lesson on how to manoeuvre a boat through the different locks. Before travelling, make sure you buy a chart of the waterway with depths and locations of locks; the chart is available in bookshops and costs £7. Pre-paid Smart Cards to operate the locks, showers, washing machines, chemical toilets and pumpouts at each mooring can also be purchased from Waterway Rangers and local shops along the Shannon-Erne.

The waterway is jointly operated by Dúchas, in the Republic, and the Department of Agriculture, in Northern Ireland.

LEITRIM WAY

The Leitrim Way begins in Drumshanbo and ends in Manorhamilton, a distance of 48km. See Walking in the Activities chapter for details.

County Longford

The history of County Longford (An Longfort) dates back to prehistoric times. St Patrick visited here and for centuries it was the centre of power of the O'Farrell family, who arrived in the 11th century. During the 1798 Rising, the British army under Lord Cornwallis defeated a combined Irish and French army at Ballinamuck, 16km north of Longford. The Potato Famine of the 1840s and 50s saw massive emigration; many Longford migrants went to Argentina, where one of their descendants, Edel Miro O'Farrell, became president in 1914.

Longford, the county town, is solidly agrarian and prosperous but of little interest to the tourist; many people pass through travelling between Dublin and Mayo or Sligo. **Carriglass Manor** (☎ 043-45165), 5km north-east, has been the home of the Huguenot Lefroy family since 1810. The manor has an interesting collection of furnishings and memorabilia, including Victorian costumes and handmade lace, and opens to the public June to September.

The 150km **Royal Canal** from Dublin passes through the county to meet the River Shannon near Clondra (or Cloondara) west of Longford. The canal's towpath provides an interesting walking route through the county.

The main attraction for most visitors to County Longford, however, is the fishing around Lough Ree and Lanesborough.

LANESBOROUGH

☎ 043 • pop 984

Also spelt Lanesboro in English (or, in Irish, Béal Átha Liag), this small town is the site of one of Ireland's first turf-fired generating stations, which dominates the skyline. It's close to the banks of the River Shannon and provides a flow of warm water into a channel. The river divides County Longford and County Roscommon, and Lanesborough is linked by bridge to Ballyclare on the Roscommon side.

There's an National Irish Bank branch on Main St a few doors down from MJS Motorcycles. The post office is farther east

CENTRAL NORTH

on Main St and opposite Samantha's Restaurant and Coffee Shop.

Fishing
When the mayfly appears in May, then again in August and September, this stretch of water becomes prime angling territory. Bream and tench are caught early in the morning and at night, while roach are available throughout the day. The water is only just over 1m deep. This isn't the only place to fish and inquiries should be made at Pricewyse tackle shop in the middle of Lanesborough.

You can hire boats for about £25 from the affable Mark Shields at MJS Motorcycles (☎ 21510) on Main St.

Places to Stay
B&B is available above *Samantha's Restaurant and Coffee Shop* (☎ 21558, Main St) for £17 per person. *Dunamase House* (☎ 21201, Rathcline Rd), south-east of the centre, charges from £21/32 for its singles/doubles and opens from April to September. The only hotel in town is the run-down *Sliabh Bán* (☎ 21790), which is also known as the Anchor, with B&B costing £19 per person. Some self-catering accommodation is available through the *Lough Ree Arms* pub (☎ 21145, Main St).

Places to Eat
Flagship, a restaurant in a converted barge on the Shannon, is a good, friendly place, open 8 am to 10 pm. Fish with salad and chips costs £7.50, and snacks are served as well. *Samantha's* is good for sandwiches and light lunches.

Lough Ree Arms and the thatched *Máirtín's Cottage Bar* attached to the Sliabh Bán Hotel serve reasonable pub food. Another decent pub is the *Shannon Princess* on a barge moored by the bridge.

Getting There & Around
Lanesborough is on the N63, halfway between the towns of Longford and Roscommon. The nearest bus and train stations are at these two towns, and there is a bus service to both from Lanesborough twice daily

Monday to Saturday. The Belfast to Galway express via Sligo and Longford stops in Lanesborough on Friday and Sunday only.

Harrison's Supermarket at the Statoil petrol station just over the bridge rents bicycles.

County Westmeath

Characterised by lakes and rich pasture land, Westmeath (An Iarmhí) is noted more for its beef than its scenic splendour or historic sites. An exception to the generally monotonous landscape is the area north of Athlone known as Goldsmith country, while the places of genuine interest in Westmeath – and there are a few – are mostly in the vicinity of Mullingar.

MULLINGAR
☎ 044 • pop 8040
Mullingar (An Muileann gCearr) is a prosperous market town – with a well-used commuter train service each morning and evening to and from Dublin – and much of the surrounding area is rather like the rich English countryside. There are some fine fishing loughs in the vicinity and a preserved bog that delights naturalists. The town itself is one of the few places outside Dublin that James Joyce visited.

The Royal Canal, linking Dublin with the River Shannon via Mullingar, was constructed in the 1790s as a rival to the Grand Canal. It never managed to compete successfully and, by the 1880s, passenger business had ceased. There was a slight revival during WWII with a turf trade to Dublin, but it finally closed in 1955. Restoration work west of Mullingar is in progress, with walkways and cycle trails under construction.

Information
Midlands-East Tourism (☎ 48650) is in Market House on the corner of Mount and Pearse Sts. It opens 9.30 am to 1 pm and 2 to 5.30 pm on weekdays year round; plus 10 am to 1 pm and 2 to 6 pm on Saturday, June to September. Next door is another tourist information centre (☎ 44044), oper-

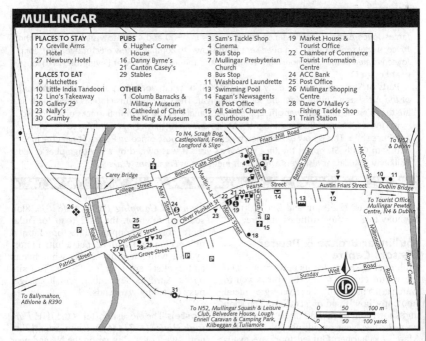

MULLINGAR

PLACES TO STAY	PUBS	3 Sam's Tackle Shop	19 Market House &
17 Greville Arms Hotel	6 Hughes' Corner House	4 Cinema	Tourist Office
27 Newbury Hotel	16 Danny Byrne's	5 Bus Stop	22 Chamber of Commerce
	21 Canton Casey's	7 Mullingar Presbyterian Church	Tourist Information Centre
PLACES TO EAT	29 Stables	8 Bus Stop	24 ACC Bank
9 Hatchettes		11 Washboard Laundrette	25 Post Office
10 Little India Tandoori	OTHER	13 Swimming Pool	26 Mullingar Shopping
12 Lino's Takeaway	1 Columb Barracks &	14 Fagan's Newsagents	Centre
20 Gallery 29	Military Museum	& Post Office	28 Dave O'Malley's
23 Nally's	2 Cathedral of Christ	15 All Saints' Church	Fishing Tackle Shop
30 Gramby	the King & Museum	18 Courthouse	31 Train Station

ated by the local chamber of commerce, but it does little more than distribute pamphlets and brochures. It opens 9.30 am to 5.30 pm on weekdays year round, plus on Saturday in summer.

There are a number of banks on the main street, which changes name five times, including an ACC Bank branch at the start of Oliver Plunkett St.

The post office is to the west on Dominick St.

The Washboard laundrette is on Austin Friars St, just before Dublin Bridge.

Cathedral & Ecclesiastical Museum

The Cathedral of Christ the King was built just before WWII and has large mosaics of St Anne and St Patrick by the Russian artist Boris Anrep.

There's a small museum of liturgical objects over the sacristy, entered from the side of the church, which contains vestments

worn by St Oliver Plunkett (see the boxed text 'A Moving Head' in the Meath & Louth chapter).

Guided tours (£1/50p) run between 3 and 4 pm on Wednesday, Saturday and Sunday, June to September. Otherwise call at the church house to the right of the cathedral inside the gates or phone ☎ 48338.

Columb Barracks & Military Museum

Mullingar's only visitor attraction of note is this small museum (☎ 48391) housed in the local army barracks. On display are all kinds of military paraphernalia, including weapons used in the War of Independence, Civil War and both World Wars. The display on what the Irish refer to as the 'old' IRA, which is those who fought for Irish independence (to distinguish them from their more modern and less palatable counterparts active in Northern Ireland since 1969), is the best part of the museum. The museum

The Joyce Connection

James Joyce came to Mullingar in his late teens in 1900 and 1901 to visit his father, John Joyce, a civil servant who had been sent to the town to compile a new electoral register. John Joyce worked in the courthouse on Mount St, and the Joyces stayed at Levington Park House near Lough Owel.

Parts of *Stephen Hero*, an early version (1904) of what would be published as *A Portrait of the Artist as a Young Man*, are set in Mullingar. The Greville Arms Hotel is mentioned, as are the *Westmeath Examiner* office, the Royal Canal and the Columb Barracks on Green Rd.

In *Ulysses*, Leopold Bloom's daughter, Millie, is working in Mullingar, employed in a photographer's shop. This is now Fagan's newsagent and sub-post-office on Pearse St near the junction with Castle St, but at the time of Joyce's visits it was owned by a photographer called Phil Shaw. Mullingar also gets a few brief mentions in *Finnegans Wake*.

opens 9 am to 12.30 pm and 2 to 4.30 pm Monday to Saturday. Admission is free.

Mullingar Bronze & Pewter Visitors Centre

Mullingar is known for its pewterware, and the visitor centre (☎ 44948) allows you to watch artisans turning the silvery-grey metal into cups, bowls and *objets d'art*. The shop and showroom open 9.30 or 10 am to 6 pm on weekdays year round; plus on Saturday, March to October. Guided tours are available from 9.30 am to 4 pm on weekdays (the last tour on Friday is at 12.30 pm). The centre is in The Downs, about 6km south-east of Mullingar on the Dublin road (N4).

Activities

The Mullingar Squash and Leisure Club (☎ 40949), Lynn Industrial Estate, offers squash, sauna, snooker and indoor bowls for £4. You can go swimming at the local swimming pool (☎ 40488) off Austin Friars St for £3. Mullingar Equestrian Centre (☎ 48331), south-west of Mullingar on the Athlone road (R390), offers riding packages.

Special Events

The Mullingar Festival (☎ 44044) is held in the second week of July. It's a low-key affair, the highlight of which is the election of the queen and the bachelor of the festival.

Places to Stay

Camping Camping at *Lough Ennell Car-* *avan and Camping Park* (☎ 48101), 8km south of town on the N52 road to Tullamore, costs a whopping £11/9 for a family/two-person tent and £2 per adult; motorcyclists with a tent pay £4.50, while hikers and cyclists are charged £3.50. The site opens April to September, and it can get busy on sunny weekends.

Hostels The closest hostel is the IHH *Farragh House* (☎ 71446) in Bunbrosna, 12km north-west of Mullingar on the N4 and near Lough Owel. It costs £8 to £9 for dorm beds, £10 per person for one of the two private rooms, and opens February to October (groups of 10 or more will be accommodated out of season). It rents boats and bicycles.

B&Bs Most B&Bs are on the approach roads from Dublin and Sligo. *Woodside* (☎ 41636) offers singles/doubles costing from £18/30, and *Moorland* (☎ 40905) charges £21/34 for rooms with bath. Both are on the Dublin road.

Hotels The friendly *Newbury Hotel* (☎ 42888, Dominick St) costs £28/42 for B&B in singles/doubles, or there's the more expensive *Greville Arms Hotel* (☎ 48563, Pearse St), which costs upwards of £50/90.

Places to Eat

The best takeaways in town are available from *Lino's (Austin Friars St)*. At *Nally's*

Restaurant (9 Oliver Plunkett St), main meals cost around £5 during the day, but the evening à la carte menu is a little more expensive; there is also a decent vegetarian selection. *Gallery 29 (29 Oliver Plunkett St)* is the nicest café in town. *Gramby Restaurant (Dominick St)* is a little more upmarket and opens 8 am to 10 pm (à la carte meals from 3 pm) daily. The bar food in *Greville Arms Hotel* is good, as it is in the hotel's *James Joyce Restaurant*, where dinner costs around £18.

Little India Tandoori (Austin Friars St) does reasonable takeaways, but main courses in the small restaurant are expensive at £7.50 to £10 (vegetarian dishes from £5.95). *Hatchettes (☎ 49755, 54 Austin Friars St)* serves starters costing upwards of £2.50, main courses from £9.50 and an excellent four-course dinner for £20. Hatchettes opens for lunch and dinner until 10.30 pm daily.

Entertainment

Hughes' Corner House, on the corner of Castle and Pearse Sts, has traditional music on Wednesday night and jazz on Thursday, while *Stables (Dominick St)* attracts blues bands. *Danny Byrne's (Pearse St)* has music on Thursday and Sunday nights and a wide selection of beers. *Greville Arms Hotel* (see Places to Stay earlier) has dancing on Sunday night, and country-and-western line dancing on Monday night. *Canton Casey's (Pearse St)* is a museum-quality old-style pub.

Getting There & Away

Bus Éireann (☎ 01-836 6111) runs two daily buses (one on Sunday) from Galway (three hours) to Dundalk (2¼ hours); three daily (four on Sunday) from Dublin (1½ hours) to Ballina (2¾ hours); three daily from Dublin to Sligo (2½ hours); and one daily Monday to Saturday from Dublin to Longford (one hour). All stop at Mullingar, and they arrive and depart from opposite the cinema in Castle St.

Trains stop at Mullingar (☎ 48274) three or four times daily in each direction on the Dublin (one hour) to Sligo (two hours) line.

AROUND MULLINGAR
Belvedere House & Gardens

Belvedere was the scene of a tale that finds its way into Joyce's *Ulysses*. Belvedere House was built around 1740 for the recently remarried Lord Belfield, 1st earl of Belvedere. He soon accused his young wife of adultery with his younger brother Arthur and imprisoned her here. She remained under house arrest for 31 years. When the earl's death finally released her, she was dressed in the fashion of three decades earlier. She died still protesting her innocence. Belvedere also sued his brother and had him jailed in London for the rest of his life.

Not far from the house, the **Jealous Wall** was deliberately built by the cantankerous Lord Belfield as a ready-made 'ruin' to block a view of the neighbouring house of a second brother, George, with whom he also fell out.

Belvedere House and Gardens (☎ 044-40861) are 5.5km south of Mullingar on the N52 road to Tullamore, just before Lough Ennell Caravan and Camping Park. The house itself, which is undergoing extensive renovations, is closed. The gardens open noon to 4.30 pm on weekdays, and noon to 6 pm at the weekend, May to October. Admission to the gardens costs £1.50/1.

Locke's Distillery

Some 16km south-west of Mullingar on the N52 road to Tullamore past Belvedere House and Gardens, Locke's Distillery (☎ 0506-32134), in the small town of Kilbeggan, still has a working mill wheel. The 35-minute tour of the distillery, which opens 9 am to 6 pm daily, April to October, and 10 am to 4 pm the rest of the year, costs £3/2. Lunch and snacks are served at the adjoining coffee shop, whiskey at the bar.

Crookedwood & Around

Crookedwood, about 5km north-east of Mullingar off the R394, is a small village on the shores of Lough Derravaragh. The lough is associated with the tragic legend of the children of Lir, who were transformed into swans by a jealous stepmother. Two ecclesiastical sites near Crookedwood are worth a visit. Three kilometres to the west is the **Multyfarnham Franciscan friary**. In the present church, the remains of a 15th-century church still stand, and there are outdoor stations of the Cross set beside a stream.

East of Crookedwood, a small road leads 2km to the ruins of **St Munna's Church**. It dates from the 15th century, replacing a 7th-century church founded by St Munna. This fortified church has a lovely location, and there is a grotesque figure over the north window. Keys to the church are available from the nearby bungalow.

Scragh Bog

Scragh Bog is a nature reserve and home to a rare wintergreen, *Pyrola rotundifolia*, which flowers around willow and beech trees in midsummer. Other, less rare, plants include members of the sedge family, orchids and sphagnum species, and there is a profusion of insects. This small bog is 7km north-west of Mullingar near Lough Owel on the N4 road to Longford. The Wildlife Service does not recommend unaccompanied visits, and waterproof boots are a necessity.

Tullynally Castle & Gardens

This seat of the Pakenham family and the earldom of Longford is another 'pretend' castle. The original fortress was converted into a house in the first half of the 18th century, and various additions were made over the next 150 years. The most notable feature is the extensive Gothic façade. The laundry is wonderfully preserved, and there are many workaday items that are worth examining.

The house opens 2 to 6 pm daily, mid-June to mid-August, with the first tour beginning at 2.30 pm. The cost is £4/2.75 and this includes admission to the 12 hectares of gardens and parkland, which open 2 to 6 pm daily, May to September (admission to the gardens only £2/1). It might be worth telephoning (☎ 044-61159) at other times.

To get there, take the N4 north-west out of Mullingar then follow the R394 north-east to Castlepollard. From there the castle

and gardens are signposted 2km to the north-west.

Fishing

Trout fishing is popular in the loughs around Mullingar, including Lough Owel, Lough Derravaragh, Lough Glore, White Lake, Lough Lene, Lough Sheelin, Mt Dalton Lake, Pallas Lake and Lough Ennell – where in 1894 an 11.9kg trout was landed, still the largest trout ever caught in Ireland. The fishing season runs from 1 March or 1 May (depending on the lake) to 12 October, and all the lakes except Lough Lene are controlled by the Shannon Regional Fisheries Board (☎ 044-48769).

For further information contact the Midlands-East Tourism office (☎ 044-48650); Dave O'Malley's (☎ 044-48300), 33 Dominick St; or Sam's Tackle Shop (☎ 044-40431), on Castle St. Sam's can provide boats on Lough Owel or Lough Ennell, plus ghillies and permits. For Lough Derravaragh contact Mr Newman (☎ 044-71206); for Lough Owel, Mrs Doolan (☎ 044-42085); for Lough Sheelin, Mr Reilly (☎ 043-81124); and for Lough Ennell, Mrs Hope (☎ 044-40807) or Mr Roache (☎ 044-40314).

Swimming

Swimming is possible in Loughs Lene, Ennell and Owel, but Derravaragh is very deep and has no shallows.

FORE VALLEY

Just outside the small village of Fore, in the north-east of the county near the shores of Lough Lene, are a group of early-Christian sites that date back to 630, when St Fechin founded a monastery here. There are no visible remains of this early settlement, but there are three later buildings still standing in the valley plain that are closely associated with a legend that Seven Wonders occurred here.

The Fore Valley is a great area to explore by bicycle or on foot. For a guided tour that takes in the early-Christian sites, see Loughcrew Cairns in the Counties Meath & Louth chapter.

The Seven Wonders of Fore

The oldest of the three buildings is **St Fechin's Church**, which may well mark the site of the original monastery. The chancel and baptismal font inside are early 13th century, and over the unusually large entrance there is a huge lintel stone carved with a Greek cross. It was supposed to have been put into place through the divine power of St Fechin's prayers and, as such, counts as one of the Seven Wonders.

A path runs up from the church to the attractive little **Anchorite cell**, which dates back to the 15th century and is another of the Seven Wonders. The Seven Wonders pub in the village holds the key to the hermit's cell.

Down on the plain, on the other side of the road, there are extensive remains of a 13th-century **Benedictine priory**, built on what was once bog (another Wonder). In the next century it was turned into a fortification; hence the castle-like square towers, each of which formed a separate residence, and loophole windows. The western tower is in a dangerous state – keep clear. Two other Wonders are a mill without a race and water that flows uphill. The mill site is marked, and legend has it that St Fechin caused water to flow uphill, towards the mill, by throwing his crozier against a rock near Lough Lene, about 1.5km away.

The last two Wonders are water that will not boil and a tree with only three branches that will not burn. Both are associated with St Fechin's well, which can be seen on the way to the priory from the road.

To get to the Fore Valley from Mullingar take the N4 north-west out of town and then follow the R394 road north-east to Castlepollard. From there the road to Fore is signposted.

ATHLONE

☎ 0902 • pop 7691

Despite its historical importance, due mainly to its strategic position midway on the River Shannon, the county town of Athlone (Baile Átha Luain) is an unattractive, rather unwelcoming garrison town; there's much more life and interest in Mullingar to the north-east. Although Athlone does have a few attractions, most of them are out of town. A visit to the castle is worth considering, and there are fishing and boat trips along the river to Lough Ree or to the Clonmacnoise monastic site in County Offaly.

Orientation & Information

Athlone is in the far south-west of County Westmeath on the border with Roscommon. It's on the main Dublin to Galway road (N6), and the River Shannon flows northwards through town into Lough Ree. The landmarks here are Athlone Castle and Sts Peter and Paul Cathedral, prominently located on the western bank of the river by the Town Bridge and overlooking Market Square. The castle houses the tourist office, a museum and a heritage centre.

The tourist office (☎ 94630) opens 9.30 am to 5.30 pm Monday to Saturday, May to mid-June and September to mid-October; and 9 am to 6 pm Monday to Saturday, mid-June to August. It has a *Tourist Trail* booklet that details three different walks. The local chamber of commerce has a good information office (☎ 73173) with brochures and pamphlets. Open year round, it's at the Jolly Mariner Marina in Coosan, north of the centre on the eastern bank of the Shannon beyond the railway bridge.

The Bank of Ireland is at the start of Northgate St, just up from Costume Place. The post office is on Barrack St beside the cathedral.

Athlone Castle & Museum

The Normans probably had an encampment by the ford over the river before they built a castle here in 1210. In 1690 the castle held out for James II, but the following year the bridge came under Protestant attack again, and this time the Jacobite city fell to the troops under William of Orange's Dutch commander, Ginkel. The Jacobites retreated to Aughrim and were decisively defeated there by Ginkel. Major alterations to the castle took place between the 17th and 19th centuries, and the ramp that forms the present entrance is a relatively recent addition.

CENTRAL NORTH

The oldest surviving part is the central keep, where the museum is now housed.

Athlone Museum (☎ 92912) has two floors: upstairs is the folk collection, and downstairs there are artefacts from prehistoric times. There's also an old gramophone that belonged to John McCormack (1884–1945), a native of Athlone and one of the greatest tenors of all time. It's still in working order, and there are records of his songs which you can ask to have played.

The museum opens 10 am to 4.30 pm Monday to Saturday, and noon to 4.30 pm on Sunday, May to September. Admission costs £2.60/80p (students £1.80, families £6).

The price includes a visit to the **heritage centre**, which has an audiovisual presentation on the town's history and flora and fauna.

Fishing

Just below the Church St end of Town Bridge on the eastern bank of the river opposite the castle, the Strand Tackle Shop (☎ 76729) is the place to go for information, boats and rods. A day's hire of boat and guide for mostly pike fishing will cost around £60. You can fish for free along the Strand.

River Cruises

Several companies offer cruises from Athlone.

Between July and September, Rossana Cruises (☎ 73383) offers a cruise on its Viking ship south to Clonmacnoise, an important early monastic site in County Offaly. It costs £10/4.50 (students £7) and departs at 10 am on Wednesday and Thursday.

Every day of the week there are cruises north to Lough Ree for £5/4. The boats usually depart from the Strand at 2.30 and 4.30 pm; a timetable is available from the tourist office.

The MV *Ross* (☎ 72892) has 90-minute cruises on Lough Ree costing £4.50/3 (families £13). The boats depart from the Strand at noon and 3.30 pm most weekdays in

summer, and from the Jolly Mariner Marina in Coosan at 3.30 pm on Sunday.

Places to Stay & Eat

Most B&Bs are to the east of Athlone on the Dublin road, including the *Auburn* (☎ 74323), with singles/doubles costing upwards of £22/34, which opens April to October. The 73-room *Prince of Wales Hotel* (☎ 72626, *Church St*) charges upwards of £45/78.

On the Crescent is the reasonably priced *Crescent Restaurant*.

Getting There & Away

The bus depot (☎ 73300) is beside the train station, and express buses stop there on many routes from the eastern to the western coast.

There are nine buses daily (eight on Sunday) to Dublin (two hours) and Galway (1¼ hours); three daily (one on Sunday) to Westport (2¾ hours); and two daily (one on Sunday) to Mullingar (one hour).

From Athlone train station (☎ 73300), there are three daily trains (four on Friday, two on Sunday) to Westport (2¼ hours) in County Mayo; five to seven daily (four on Sunday) to Galway (1¼ hours); and up to 11 daily (seven on Sunday) to Dublin (1½ hours).

The train station is on the eastern bank on Southern Station Rd. To get there, follow Northgate St up from Costume Place. Its extension, Coosan Point Rd, joins Southern Station Rd near St Vincent's Hospital.

Getting Around

You can order a taxi on ☎ 74400.

Bicycles can be hired for £7/30 per day/week from Hardiman's (☎ 78669), opposite the Athlone Shopping Centre on the Dublin road.

AROUND ATHLONE
Lough Ree

Just to the north of Athlone is Lough Ree, one of the three main lakes formed by the River Shannon.

The lake is celebrated for the early monas-

Goldsmith Country Cycling Tour

The following tour pretty much follows the one in *The Lough Ree Trail: A Signposted Tour* by Gearoid O'Brien and published by Midlands-East Tourism. It's available from the tourist offices in Athlone and Mullingar. The tour takes in places associated with 18th-century writer Oliver Goldsmith.

Five kilometres north-east of Athlone, the road comes to the village of Ballykeeran, to the west of which is the Lough Ree East Caravan and Camping Park. About 3km farther is the village of Glasson (or Glassan), which Swift called Auburn in his poem 'The Deserted Village'. Just north of the village a left turning goes to the Killinure Spur on the shore of Lough Ree. The turning is marked by No 8 on the Lough Ree Trail roadsign and it's 2.5km to a junction, marked as No 11 on the tourist trail roadsign. From there, another left goes down to the marina at Killinure, where you can rent boats.

Back at the No 11 junction, the road continues north for another 2.5km to a junction, No 14 on the tourist trail signs. Turning left leads to the Portlick Inn pub by the shore opposite Inchmore Island. Turning right at No 14 leads after 3km to the village of Tubberclair (or Tuberclare), which takes its name from a holy well, on the N55.

Continuing north, the road leads into Goldsmith country proper, with the reminders and remains of:

> The never-failing brook, the busy mill,
> The decent church that topt the neighbouring hill.

Nothing remains of the schoolhouse where the young Goldsmith and his fellow pupils wondered at the wisdom of their teacher:

> And still they gazed, and still the wonder grew
> That one small head could carry all he knew.

From Tubberclair northwards Goldsmith country extends into County Longford. From the site of the schoolhouse, it's about 15km back south to Athlone via the N55. The whole tour takes a couple of hours.

CENTRAL NORTH

tic ruins on its many islands and for some excellent trout fishing. The lough is also home to many migratory birds that come here to nest, particularly swans, plover, mallard ducks and curlew. Sailing is popular and the Lough Ree Lough Club (☎ 0902-75976), established around 1720, is one of the world's oldest yacht clubs. The Wineport Sailing Centre (☎ 0902-85466) has a dozen different boats for hire – from a 12m cruiser to dinghies – and offers sailing courses during the day and evening.

Goldsmith Country

From Athlone, the N55 north-west to County Longford runs close to the eastern side of Lough Ree and through Goldsmith country, so-called because of the area's associations with the 18th-century poet, playwright and novelist Oliver Goldsmith. The gentle aspect of the landscape makes it ideal for cycling.

Places to Stay Camping is possible at *Lough Ree East Caravan and Camping Park* (☎ 0902-78561) in Ballykeeran. Tent sites cost only 50p, though adults/children pay £2.50/1, and hikers and cyclists pay £2.50 including tent. *Portlick Inn* pub (☎ 0902-85204), near Killenmore, has a nearby guesthouse where B&B costs £14 to £19 per person. There are self-catering

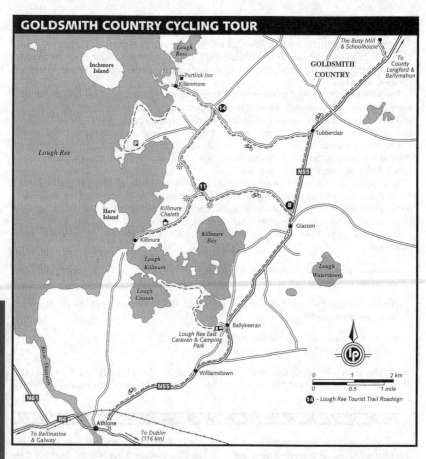

GOLDSMITH COUNTRY CYCLING TOUR

chalets available at Killinure, Glasson and Tubberclair; inquiries should be made at the tourist office in Athlone.

Moate
☎ 0902

The village of Moate, halfway between Athlone and Kilbeggan on the N6, about 40km south-west of Mullingar, gets its name from a nearby motte. **Dún na Sí Heri-** **tage Park** (Fairy Mound Castle; ☎ 81183) is a small folk museum with displays of 19th-century farm tools, kitchenware and the like; it also functions as a genealogical centre for those researching their Westmeath ancestors. The museum opens April to October and admission costs £1/50p. There's a traditional Irish session of music, dance and storytelling here at 9 pm on Friday, July and August.

County Donegal

County Donegal outdoes anywhere else in Ireland for bleakness, dramatic cliffs and hectares of peat bogs – all of which can be great if the weather isn't equally bleak, dramatic and, well, boggy. County Donegal extends farther north than Northern Ireland and is virtually separated from the rest of the Republic by the westwards projection of County Fermanagh.

Roughly one-third of Donegal lies in the Gaeltacht, where Irish is more widely spoken than English. You'll see signs pointing to offices of the Údarás na Gaeltachta, a government agency promoting the social, economic and cultural wellbeing of Irish-speaking areas. In the Gweedore region in particular, it has been instrumental in creating an industrial zone where hundreds of people are employed in the production of yarn, plastics, radiators and so on.

Tourism in County Donegal is extremely seasonal, and many attractions and most tourist offices open only June (interpreted pretty loosely here) to September – at the latest. Arrive in, say, March and you'll find much of the county shut down.

Although you can get around County Donegal by bus, it's a time-consuming endeavour, especially in winter. This is very much walking and cycling country. When driving, be prepared for switchback roads, suicidal sheep, directions only in Irish, signs hidden behind vegetation, signs pointing the wrong way or no signs at all.

Highlights

- Admire the view while walking or cycling over the Blue Stack Mountains near Lough Eske
- Go salmon fishing in the River Finn
- Visit the small, rugged island of Arranmore
- Get drenched in Glenveagh National Park
- View the dramatic Slieve League cliffs
- Walk the Bloody Foreland and Horn Head
- Check out the works of art at Glebe House and Gallery, then visit Tory Island, the inspiration for the artists
- Enjoy the view from Grianán of Aileách hilltop fort

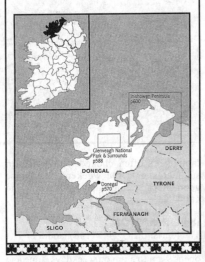

Donegal

☎ 073 • pop 3000

The town's name in Irish, Dún na nGall (Fort of the Foreigner), refers to the Vikings, who had a fort here in the 9th century. Donegal's later importance developed as it was the main seat of the O'Donnell family, which controlled this part of Ireland before the 17th century.

Donegal town, at the top of Donegal Bay, is the principal gateway for the rest of the county and is a pleasant, popular small place where it's well worth spending a little time. The triangular Diamond in the centre,

DONEGAL

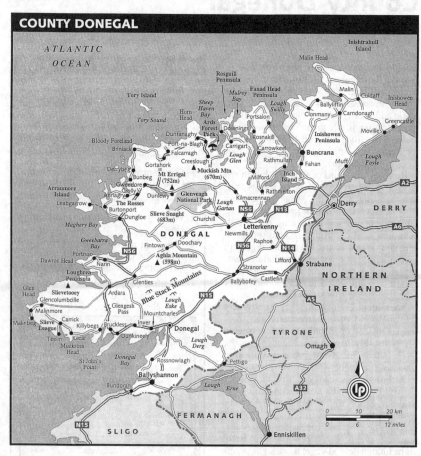

COUNTY DONEGAL

though it's often choked with traffic in summer and at the weekend, has some good shops selling quality souvenirs and garments.

INFORMATION

The tourist office (☎ 21148), south of The Diamond by the River Eske on the Quay, opens 9 am to 5 pm on weekdays, June and September; and 9 am to 8 pm on weekdays, July and August. Ask for *A Signposted Walking Tour of Donegal Town* to take in the sights. On The Diamond, the Bank of Ireland, AIB and Ulster Bank all have ATMs and bureaux de change. The post office is on Tirchonaill St north of The Diamond. The Four Masters Bookshop, on The Diamond, is the only one in town and has a small selection of maps. There's a laundrette in the Mill Court Shopping Mews, a small shopping centre off The Diamond.

DONEGAL CASTLE

Built on a rocky outcrop over the River Eske, what remains of this restored castle is impressive. It was built by the O'Donnells in the 15th century and may well have been burned down by Hugh Roe O'Donnell at the end of the 16th century rather than see it fall into the hands of the English. Sir Basil Brooke, the Englishman who took possession of the castle about 1623, rebuilt it in Jacobean style. Notice the floral decoration on the corner turret and the decorated fireplace on the 1st floor. Brooke also built the three-storey Jacobean manor house adjoining the castle.

Donegal Castle (☎ 22405), a Dúchas site, opens 9.30 am to 6.30 pm daily, March to October. Admission costs £2/1.

THE DIAMOND OBELISK

In 1474, Red Hugh O'Donnell and his wife, Nuala O'Brien, founded a Franciscan friary by the shore south of town. It was accidentally blown up in 1601 by Hugh Roe O'Donnell while laying siege to an English garrison, and little of it remains. What makes it famous is that four of its friars, fearing that the arrival of the English meant the end of Celtic culture, chronicled the whole of known Celtic history and mythology from 40 years before the Flood to AD 1618 in *The Annals of the Four Masters*. The annals remain an important source of early Irish history. The obelisk (1937) in The Diamond commemorates the work, copies of which are displayed in the National Library in Dublin.

DONEGAL RAILWAY HERITAGE CENTRE

The heritage centre (☎ 22655), in the former train station on Tirchonaill St northeast of the town centre, tells the history of the steam railway that ran from Ballyshannon to Derry until 1959. It opens 10 am to 5.30 pm Monday to Saturday, and 2 to 5 pm on Sunday, June to September; and 10 am to 4 pm on weekdays, October to May. Admission costs £1/50p.

FISHING

Permits are required for fishing in many of the local rivers. A permit for the River Eske, along with licences for salmon and sea trout, is available from Doherty's (☎ 21119) on Main St.

SPECIAL EVENTS

Donegal has a three-day Donegal Town Summer Festival in late June/early July, featuring song, dance and storytelling, with arts and crafts thrown in for good measure. The tourist office has details.

PLACES TO STAY
Hostels

The comfortable and friendly *Donegal Town Independent Hostel* (☎ 22805), registered with both the IHH and IHO, is 1km north-west of town on the Killybegs road (N56). Dorm beds cost £7, private rooms £8.50 per person. You can also *camp* in the grounds for £4 per person. The hostel is open year round. *Cliffview Holiday Hostel* (☎ 21684), also on the Killybegs road but closer to the centre, beside the Donegal Presbyterian Church, offers dorm beds costing £7 and private rooms costing £15 per person.

The An Óige *Ball Hill Hostel* (☎ 21174), in Ball Hill 5km south-west of Donegal, has an absolutely stunning setting at the end of a quiet road, right on the shores of Donegal Bay. The location is quite remote, so stock up on food before arriving. To get there, continue along the Killybegs road and look out for the signs on the left-hand side of the road about 5km out. Its 66 dorm beds cost £7/5.50 and it opens daily, Easter to September, and at the weekend only the rest of the year.

B&Bs

There are plenty of B&Bs within walking distance of the centre. *Drumcliffe House* (☎ 21200), off the Killybegs road (N56), is a pleasant old place with singles/doubles costing upwards of £20/30. Waterloo Place, north of the castle and beside the river, has a couple of guesthouses. *Riverside House* (☎ 21083) charges £17 per person, while at *Castle View House* (☎ 22100) singles/doubles cost £19/32.

On Main St *Atlantic Guesthouse* (☎ 21187) charges upwards of £20/30. *Tourist Lodge* (☎ 23060), opposite the tourist office on the Quay, has five triple rooms, which are good value at £18.50 per

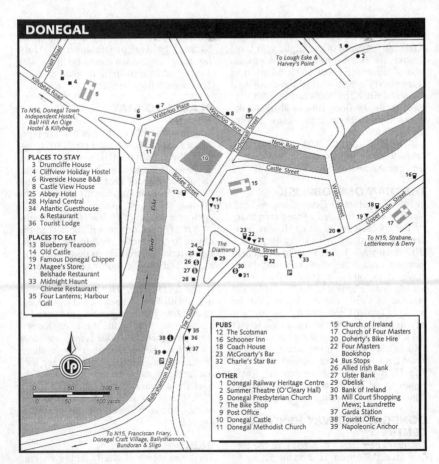

DONEGAL

To Lough Eske & Harvey's Point

To N56, Donegal Town
Independent Hostel,
Ball Hill An Óige
Hostel & Killybegs

PLACES TO STAY
3 Drumcliffe House
4 Cliffview Holiday Hostel
6 Riverside House B&B
8 Castle View House
25 Abbey Hotel
28 Hyland Central
34 Atlantic Guesthouse & Restaurant
36 Tourist Lodge

PLACES TO EAT
13 Blueberry Tearoom
14 Old Castle
19 Famous Donegal Chipper
21 Magee's Store; Belshade Restaurant
33 Midnight Haunt Chinese Restaurant
35 Four Lanterns; Harbour Grill

To N15, Strabane,
Letterkenny & Derry

PUBS
12 The Scotsman
16 Schooner Inn
18 Coach House
23 McGroarty's Bar
32 Charlie's Star Bar

OTHER
1 Donegal Railway Heritage Centre
2 Summer Theatre (O'Cleary Hall)
5 Donegal Presbyterian Church
7 The Bike Shop
9 Post Office
10 Donegal Castle
11 Donegal Methodist Church
15 Church of Ireland
17 Church of Four Masters
20 Doherty's Bike Hire
22 Four Masters Bookshop
24 Bus Stops
26 Allied Irish Bank
27 Ulster Bank
29 Obelisk
30 Bank of Ireland
31 Mill Court Shopping Mews; Laundrette
37 Garda Station
38 Tourist Office
39 Napoleonic Anchor

To N15, Franciscan Friary,
Donegal Craft Village, Ballyshannon,
Bundoran & Sligo

person. If these B&Bs are all full, there are plenty of others about town, including two on Ballyshannon Rd: *Hillcrest Country Home* (☎ 21837), charging upwards of £24.50/32, and *Ardlenagh View* (☎ 21646), costing £24.50/36.

Hotels
The 49-room *Abbey Hotel* (☎ 21014) and *Hyland Central* (☎ 21027), with almost twice as many rooms, are both on The Diamond; rooms at the former cost £35 to £40 per person, at the latter £35 to £50.

For something rural, try *Ardnamona House* (☎ 22650), a late-18th-century house with five singles/doubles costing upwards of £50/80, and a splendid garden, on the Lough Eske ring road.

Beautifully sited on the shores of Lough Eske and signposted from the Killybegs road is the 20-room *Harvey's Point Country Hotel* (☎ 22208), with rooms costing £35 to £50 per person.

PLACES TO EAT
There are at least half a dozen places to eat within 100m or so of The Diamond. *Deli Coffee House*, on The Diamond near the

Abbey Hotel, is one of the few places open early on Sunday; baguettes cost £2.50. *Atlantic Restaurant*, on Main St, is inexpensive, with meals such as haddock and chips costing under £4. *Famous Donegal Chipper* on Upper Main St provides a takeaway service. The small *Midnight Haunt* Chinese restaurant, upstairs on Main St, serves main courses costing around £7. On the northern side of The Diamond, *Belshade Restaurant*, on the 1st floor of Magee's store, serves breakfast (£4.50) and lunches with vegetarian choices. Nearby, *McGroarty's Bar* offers good snacks, sandwiches (starting at £2.25) and substantial pub lunches.

Round the corner is the *Old Castle* pub, one of the fancier places in town, with good-value lunches costing £6 to £10. Close by, the *Blueberry Tearoom* serves quiches, soups and sandwiches (£3.50).

Opposite the tourist office on the Quay there's *Four Lanterns* for fast food. *Harbour Grill* next door serves pizzas (£3.60 to £6.25), seafood and steak.

For a real treat, try the restaurant at *Harvey's Point Country Hotel* (see Places to Stay, earlier). A five-course dinner will cost £30. Reservations and dressy attire are required.

ENTERTAINMENT
Numerous music pubs can be found on Main and Upper Main Sts, within a stone's throw of The Diamond, including *Coach House*, at the western end of Upper Main St, and *Schooner Inn* just beyond it. *Scotsman* (*Bridge St*) attracts a friendly, local crowd ready to sing or strum at the drop of a pint. *Charlie's Star Bar* is another lively place, with more-modern music and a younger crowd.

In July and August, *Summer Theatre*, run by a local theatre group, presents plays by Donegal playwrights in O'Cleary Hall, opposite the Donegal Railway Heritage Centre, three times weekly at 9 pm.

SHOPPING
Well worth a browse is Magee's in The Diamond. It has its own garment factory and

sells its tweed rolls at £18 per metre. A mailing service is available. Tweed jackets cost around £150 and skirts £60. There are lots of Aran sweaters costing around £80. It opens 9.45 am to 6 pm on weekdays, and 9 am to 6.30 pm on Saturday.

Also worth visiting is Donegal Craft Village (☎ 22228), a complex of small art and craft workshops by the side of the N15 en route to Ballyshannon about 1.5km south of town. Pottery, crystal, batik, garments and jewellery are all made on the premises. It opens 9 am to 6 pm Monday to Saturday, year round; plus 11 am to 6 pm on Sunday, July and August.

GETTING THERE & AWAY
Frequent Bus Éireann (☎ 21101) buses connect Donegal with Derry, Enniskillen and Belfast in the North; Sligo, Galway and Killybegs to the west; Limerick and Cork in the south; and Dublin in the south-east. The bus stop is outside the Abbey Hotel.

Private coaches operated by Feda Ódonaill (☎ 075-48114, 091-761656) run to Galway daily, via Ballyshannon, Bundoran and Sligo. They leave from in front of the Donegal tourist office at 9.45 am and 5.15 pm daily and reach Galway Cathedral (or Eyre Square on Sunday evening) at 1.10 and 8.45 pm. There's an additional departure on Friday at 1.15 pm, and on Sunday they leave at 9.45 am and 4.15 and 8.15 pm. The fare for anywhere within County Donegal is £3 or £4.

It's also worth checking out McGeehan Coaches (☎ 075-46150), which does Donegal to Dublin (one way £11) three to four times daily (more in summer) and departs from outside the garda station across from the tourist office.

GETTING AROUND
Doherty's (☎ 21119), on the corner of Main and Water Sts, hires out bikes costing £6/30 per day/week. The superior Bike Shop (☎ 22515), across from the castle on Waterloo Place, also charges £6/30 per day/week. The owner of the Bike Shop is very friendly and knowledgeable and will help you plan a cycling itinerary.

DONEGAL

Around Donegal Town

LOUGH DERG

From June to mid-August this small lake due east of Donegal is alive with pilgrims who spend three days on the small **Station Island** in the middle of the lake where St Patrick is believed to have stayed and fasted. Anyone over the age of 14 is welcome, and some 30,000 turn up every year. But be warned: only genuine pilgrims are allowed on the island. The pilgrimage starts with a 24-hour vigil; one meal (of dry bread and black tea) a day is permitted; and everyone is expected to complete the Stations of the Cross in bare feet on the first day, having fasted from the preceding midnight. The pilgrims reach the island by boat, but outside the pilgrim season there's no regular service to the island. Further information is available from The Priory (☎ 072-61518, email lochderg@iol.ie), St Patrick's Purgatory, Pettigo.

Lough Derg Visitor Centre (☎ 072-61546), on Main St in Pettigo (Paiteagó), 7km south of the lake, details Lough Derg's Celtic past and recounts the story of St Patrick. It opens 10 am to 5 pm Monday to Saturday, and noon to 5 pm on Sunday, May to October. Admission costs £2/1.

Places to Stay

If you're making the pilgrimage to the island you don't need to book accommodation. In Pettigo, *Avondale* (☎ *072-61520*), on the Lough Derg road, offers B&B costing upwards of £16 per person. *Hilltop View* (☎ *072-61535*), at Billary just before Pettigo on the road from Donegal, charges upwards of £18/32 for singles/doubles.

Getting There & Away

Pettigo and Lough Derg are extremely remote, at the end of a road across the moors. During the pilgrim season (1 June to 15 August), a special Bus Éireann service (No 31) leaves Dublin's Busáras at 10 am daily, arriving at Lough Derg shore at 1.45 pm.

During the same period bus No 68 leaves Galway at 9 am, stopping at Sligo and Ballyshannon – but not Donegal – before reaching Lough Derg at 2.15 pm. The first boat leaves at 11 am, the last at 3 pm.

LOUGH ESKE

This picturesque area north-east of Donegal is good for **fishing**, or for **cycling** or **walking** over the Blue Stack Mountains, from which there are great views. If you're walking, consider using the guide *New Irish Walks: West and North* (Gill & Macmillan) or *Hill Walkers' Donegal* (Shanksmore Press) by David Herman, available from the Four Masters Bookshop in Donegal.

Getting There & Away

Leave Donegal from The Diamond on the N56 to Killybegs. About 300m past the bridge, turn right following the signs to Harvey's Point Country Hotel. The ring road eventually joins the N15 to the northeast of Donegal, so it makes a convenient cycling trip. If you hire a bike from the Bike Shop in Donegal, they'll give you a photocopied map.

ROSSNOWLAGH
☎ 072 • pop 50

If you want a beach holiday without the amusement arcades, Rossnowlagh (Ross Neamblach), south-west of Donegal, is the place to visit. The sandy Blue Flag beach is stunning, extends for nearly 5km and is good for **surfing**.

Ard-na-Mara (☎ *51141*) offers B&B costing £30/50 in singles/doubles and opens January to mid-November. *Sand House* (☎ *51777*) is a 45-room beach hotel charging £49.50 to £65 per person. The front rooms have magnificent sea views.

BALLYSHANNON
☎ 072 • pop 2400

This busy, hilly, small town is set above the River Erne with a small adjunct of shops and houses south of the river connected by a bridge. Ballyshannon (Béal Átha Seanaidh) could be more appealing than Bundoran as a base for exploring the coastline before heading up to Donegal. It's also convenient for trips into the North, with regular buses to Derry and Enniskillen.

Orientation & Information

The centre of Ballyshannon, north of the river, has two main streets converging below the distinctive clock tower of Gallogley Jewellers: Main St runs to the northwest and Market St to the north-east. There's an AIB branch (with an ATM) and a post office at the start of Market St a little up from Gallogley Jewellers. On the other side of Market St, just down from Seán Óg's Pub, is a laundrette.

Allingham's Grave

The poet William Allingham (1824–89), best remembered for 'The Fairies', which begins 'Up the airy mountains/Down the rushy glen', was born in Ballyshannon and is buried in the graveyard. It's signposted at the first left up Main St after Dorrian's Imperial hotel. The tombstone is on the left side of the churchyard.

Donegal Parian China Visitor Centre

Parian china is lighter and more translucent than bone china. All the pieces manufactured by Donegal Parian China are on display (and for sale) at the centre (☎ 51826), which is about 1.5km south-west of Ballyshannon on the Bundoran road (N15). Prices range from around £8 for small pieces to £250 for a full tea set. Free guided tours, a tea room, a bureau de change and mail-order service are all laid on. The centre opens 9 am to 6 pm Monday to Saturday, and 10 am to 6 pm on Sunday.

Water Wheels

Water Wheels (☎ 51580) is a heritage centre with an audiovisual display, craft shop and café in the restored mills of Assaroe Abbey, founded in the late 12th century by Cistercian monks from Boyle in County Roscommon. To get there, turn left off Main St onto Bridge St, past the Thatch Pub, and take the road to Rossnowlagh (R231). After about 2km, signs indicate Water Wheels

and Abbey Mill on the left. It opens 11 am to 7 pm daily, June to September; and 2.30 to 7 pm on Sunday only, the rest of the year. There are fine views of the Erne Estuary and Donegal Bay.

Places to Stay

The IHH *Duffy's Hostel* (☎ 51535), less than 1km north of town on the road to Donegal, has a dozen beds costing £6 each and opens April to September. You can *camp* in the garden for £3.50 per person, and the hostel has bikes for rent.

There are lots of B&Bs, including *Bri-Ter-An* (☎ 51490, Bundoran Rd), where singles/doubles cost upwards of £20/32. The best hotel in town is the grand *Dorrian's Imperial* (☎ 51147, Main St), with 26 rooms costing £30 to £45 per person.

Places to Eat

Kitchen Bake, on Main St near where it meets Market St, serves cakes and coffee. A great place for breakfast (£2.95) and sandwiches (from £2.25) is *Dead Poet's Café* just opposite.

Cúchulainn's pub, on the corner diagonally opposite Seán Óg's, does takeaways and has a restaurant upstairs. *Embers*, in Paddy Donagher's pub next to Seán Óg's, serves seafood, pasta and a few vegetarian options at lunch and dinner. The bar at *Dorrian's Imperial* hotel serves pub food at lunchtime and offers a set dinner costing £15.

There's a *coffee shop* in the Water Wheels heritage centre at Assaroe Abbey north-west of town.

Entertainment

Pubs have live music throughout the summer, but the ideal time to be entertained in Ballyshannon is during the August bank holiday weekend music festival, the first weekend in August. The pubs to check out are *Seán Óg's (Market St)* and the lovely little *Thatch Pub (Bridge St)*, just off the top of Main St as you turn towards Rossnowlagh. Across the River Erne are *Owen Roe's*, *Fergie's Pub* and *Commercial Bar*. *Abbey Centre* (☎ 51375), at the top of

DONEGAL

Market St on the corner of Tirchonaill St, has one cinema screen and stages occasional plays.

Getting There & Away

There are regular daily Bus Éireann (☎ 074-21309) buses to Bundoran, Derry, Sligo, Galway, Donegal and Dublin (via Enniskillen, Cavan and Navan). The bus station is between the bridge and the Gallogley Jewellers clock tower.

Feda Ódonaill buses (☎ 075-48114) depart from outside the Olde Distillery pub opposite the bus station for Donegal, Letterkenny, Dunfanaghy, Gweedore and Crolly at 12.45 and 6.35 pm Monday to Saturday (with extra departures at 4.10 and 8.30 pm on Friday), and at 5.45 and 11 pm on Sunday. It leaves for Sligo and Galway from in front of Maggie's Bar, south of the river near the roundabout, at 10 am and 5.30 pm Monday to Saturday (and also at 1.30 pm on Friday), and 10 am and 4.30 and 8.30 pm on Sunday.

BUNDORAN

☎ 072 • pop 1460

Bundoran (Bun Dobhráin) is one of Ireland's most popular summer seaside resorts, but the rest of the year it's generally passed by. It's not hard to see why: Main St – East End and West End – is a series of games arcades, including some real antique shove-ha'penny games, fish and chips shops, and tacky souvenir stands. The town is frequented mainly by Catholic Northerners, and at night the traditional music in the pubs favours the rebel over the folk song.

Information

The tourist office (☎ 41350), in a kiosk opposite the Holyrood Hotel, opens 9 am to 5 pm daily, June to mid-September; and 9 am to 5 pm Monday, Friday and Saturday, the rest of the year. The post office is near the tourist office, and the AIB on Main St has an ATM and bureau de change.

Activities

Just north of the town centre, **Tullan Strand** is a handsome Blue Flag beach with waves big enough to deter swimmers. The strange cliffside rock formations have whimsical names such as Fairy Bridges and Puffing Hole.

Children enjoy **Waterworld** (☎ 41787), where a slide pool, wave pool and restaurant pack them in by the hundred. The noise level in here probably breaks several EU standards. Tickets cost £3 for children aged under eight, £4 for those aged eight to 16, and £5 for wrinklies. It opens 10 am to 2 pm and 3 to 7 pm daily, Easter week and June to August; and 10 am to 2 pm and 3 to 7 pm at the weekend, April, May and September.

On Tullan Strand, the **Bundoran Equestrian Centre** (☎ 41288) organises riding sessions along the beach, as well as instructional courses.

Places to Stay

Should you decide to give Bundoran a whirl, there's the IHH *Homefield Hostel* (☎ 41288, Bayview Ave), with 30 dorm beds costing £10 to £12.50, and eight doubles costing up to £25. You're spoiled for choice when it comes to B&Bs, though few places stand out. *Ceol-Na-Mara* (☎ 41287, Tullan Strand) has singles/doubles costing £25/36 and opens March to October. Going upmarket, the 58-room *Holyrood Hotel* (☎ 41232, Main St) charges £57/84 for B&B in the high season. The modern *Grand Central Hotel* (☎ 42722), farther up Main St, charges £50/80 during the same period.

Places to Eat

There's no shortage of cafés and fast-food places along Main St. Try the cafeteria-style *Blazing Saddles*, near the Holyrood Hotel, where roast beef costs £4.75. In summer *Kitchen Bake*, halfway along the street in a converted 19th-century church, offers light meals in more imaginative surroundings; seafood chowder with bread costs £2.75. Despite its name there's nothing Sri Lankan about *Café Ceylon*, which offers burgers, fish and chips (£3.40) and the like.

Getting There & Away

Bus Éireann (☎ 074-21309) buses stop in Railway Yard; turn down beside the Railway Bar and Blazing Saddles restaurant to find it. There are direct daily services to Dublin, Derry, Sligo, Galway and Westport. Ulsterbus (☎ 028-90 333000) has three services daily (one on Sunday) to Belfast and Enniskillen. Feda Ódonaill (☎ 075-48114) buses from Crolly to Galway stop in Bundoran outside the Holyrood Hotel at 10.05 am and 5.35 pm Monday to Saturday (plus at 1.35 pm on Friday), and at 10.05 am and 4.30 and 8.30 pm on Sunday.

Getting Around
The Hire and Sell Centre (☎ 41526), at the Ballyshannon end of town, offers bikes costing £6 per day plus £20 deposit.

South-Western Donegal

MOUNTCHARLES TO BRUCKLESS
Apart from some pubs and cafés in Mountcharles and Dunkineely, there are few places to eat, so stock up before leaving Donegal or Killybegs.

Mountcharles
☎ 073
Mountcharles (Moin Séarbs) is the first town you'll hit travelling along the coastal road (N56) west of Donegal. It has a **safe, sandy beach**, and Michael O'Boyle's (☎ 35257) boat, the *Martin Óg*, is available for **deep-sea angling** from £15 per day, including rod and tackle. (The boat leaves from the Mountcharles pier; take the first turning on the left as you come into the village from the east.) Mountcharles is the birthplace of Seamus MacManus, a local poet and *seanchaí* (storyteller) who regaled locals with tales around the village pump in the 1940s and 1950s.

The road west to Bruckless passes through the village of **Inver**, which has its own small beach.

Places to Stay The *Coast Road* guesthouse (☎ 35018), on the main street, offers rooms costing £16 per person and opens

year round. Near the church, *Clybawn* (☎ 35076, Station Rd) has singles/doubles costing upwards of £22.50/32 and opens April to September.

Dunkineely
☎ 073
A little farther west at Dunkineely (Dún Cionnfhaolaidh or Dún Cionnaola), a minor road runs down the promontory to the beach at **St John's Point**. There's no sand here, but there are good coastal views, and the waters around the point are a prime **diving** site.

The IHO *Blue Moon Hostel* (☎ 37264, Main St) charges £6 for dorm beds or £6 per person in private rooms. It opens year round and *camping* is also available.

Bruckless
☎ 073
Bruckless (An Bhroclais) is about 2km west of Dunkineely. **Horse riding** and **pony trekking** are available at Deane's Open Farm (☎ 37160).

The clean, attractive IHH *Gallagher's Farm Hostel* (☎ 37057), with 18 beds in converted farm outbuildings, is halfway between Dunkineely and Bruckless on the N56. Dorm beds cost £7.50 plus £3.50 for breakfast. *Camping* is also possible here for £4 per person, with separate kitchen facilities from hostellers. The hostel supplies guests with a list of walks in the area. *Bruckless House* (☎ 37071), just past the hostel, is a cut above the usual B&B, and a night in this 18th-century home costs upwards of £25 per person.

Getting There & Away
Bus Éireann (☎ 21101) bus No 494 leaves Donegal for Killybegs three times daily (four in July and August) Monday to Saturday, stopping outside Mulhern's pub in Mountcharles, the Inver post office and Clerkin's Mace Foodstore in Dunkineely.

KILLYBEGS
☎ 073 • pop 1630
Killybegs (Ceala Beaga) is Ireland's most important fishing port, and some travellers may be put off by the smell created by the

DONEGAL

large fishmeal processing plant on the eastern outskirts. The town is also noted for its handmade carpets.

Information

The tourist information point – a board with maps – is in the car park by the harbour. The Bank of Ireland, on Main St, has an ATM and bureau de change. The post office is opposite the harbour.

Things to See & Do

A right turn in town up the steep hill brings you to St Catherine's Church, which contains the **tomb of Niall Mór MacSweeney**, who was head of the MacSweeney clan, one of Donegal's ruling families before the Flight of the Earls in 1607. The tombstone is carved with Celtic-style patterns and the figure of a gallowglass. Gallowglasses were Scottish mercenaries who first came to the north and west of Ireland in the late 13th century. At first they were only hired by the big chiefs, but by the late 15th century their descendants were being employed around the country as personal bodyguards and constables.

Several operators offer **fishing** trips with the opportunity to catch pollock, cod and whiting as well as other types of fish. Try Anthony Doherty (☎ 31079), who can arrange inclusive B&B and angling deals for groups of eight people or more, or Brian McGilloway (☎ 31144). The Harbour Store (☎ 31569), by the wharf, sells fishing gear.

The wild, secluded **Fintra Beach** (also spelled Fintragh), about 3km west, is fun to explore and the water is clean and safe for swimming.

Special Events

The town hosts a huge International Sea Angling Festival in July.

Places to Stay

If you decide to stay in Killybegs and don't like the smell of fish, pick a guesthouse along Fintra Rd on the western outskirts. There you'll find the clean and friendly *Oileán Roe House* (☎ 31192), where B&B costs upwards of £22.50/32 in singles/

doubles. It opens May to September. Alternatively, there's *Glenlee House* (☎ 31026), just across the road, charging £24.50/36 for en suite rooms. Other nearby places on Fintra Rd include *Bannagh House* (☎ 31108), charging £35 for doubles and open April to October, and the ambitiously named *Lismolin Country Home* (☎ 31053), a bungalow B&B open year round and charging £24.50/36.

Tullycullion House (☎ 31842), a lovely place 2km east of the centre, opens from March to November. Singles/doubles start at £22.50/32.

The 38-room *Bay View Hotel* (☎ 31950), in the centre of Killybegs, with a leisure centre and pool, charges £60/92 in the high season.

Places to Eat

You can pick up fish and chips opposite the car park at *Melly's Café*. A better place for seafood takeaway, though, is *Killybeg's Catch-West* (*Main St*) near the Sail Inn pub, where fish and chips costs £3.95. *Sail Inn* itself serves cheap pub grub and has a restaurant upstairs.

Cope House on Main St houses the *Ship's Inn* pub, with bar food and harbour views, and the *Peking Chef* restaurant (☎ 31894), with Asianesque specialities. *Harbour Bar*, facing the wharf, serves breakfast from 9.30 am daily and offers seafood lunches.

Bay View Hotel has a downstairs pub-brasserie and a lovely upstairs restaurant specialising, not surprisingly, in seafood, with mains costing £8.95 to £14.95. The excellent three-course set dinner costs £17.

Getting There & Away

Bus Éireann (☎ 074-21309) bus No 494 from Donegal to Killybegs runs three times daily (four times in July and August) Monday to Saturday. Bus No 492 runs to Portnoo via Ardara and Glenties twice daily Monday to Saturday in July and August (as far as Glenties only on Tuesday, Thursday and Friday, the rest of the year). Bus No 490 heads west to Kilcar and Glencolumbcille once daily Monday to Friday, twice on

EOIN CLARKE

Mountcharles, Donegal

TOM SMALLMAN

Donkeys in Clonmany, County Donegal, pull their photo faces.

GARETH McCORMACK

There's a shortage of beach umbrellas at Trabane Strand, near Malinbeg, County Donegal.

GARETH McCORMACK

You'll only have yourself for company if you climb Mt Errigal, County Donegal.

Ireland's first Cistercian monastery at Mellifont, County Louth

Loughcrew Cairn, Meath

The view of Carlingford Lough from Slieve Foye on the Cooley Peninsula, County Louth

Monasterboice, County Louth

Yellow Steeple, Trim, County Meath, a victim of Cromwell's army

Saturday. In July and August an extra bus runs daily Monday to Saturday, and buses continue to Malinmore twice daily, Monday to Saturday. The bus stop is outside Hegarty's shop.

McGeehan Coaches (☎ 075-46150) runs a service from Glencolumbcille to Dublin stopping at the Pier Bar by the harbour car park at 8.10 am daily, with additional buses at 5.40 pm on Friday and 3.45 pm on Sunday. Extra buses are laid on in summer.

KILCAR & AROUND
☎ 073 • pop 1300
Kilcar (Cill Chártha) and neighbouring Carrick (An Charraig) are good bases for exploring the magnificent indented coastline of south-western Donegal and the Slieve League cliffs. Kilcar is an important centre for the manufacture of Donegal tweed. Just outside Kilcar is a small, sandy beach.

Information
In July and August tourist information is available from the Craft Shop (☎ 38002) in Kilcar. There are no banks here or in Carrick. The post office in Kilcar is off Main St near the river.

Donegal Tweed
Beside the Craft Shop is a small tweed factory, Studio Donegal (☎ 38002), offering free guided tours on weekdays. In the Craft Shop itself, the tweed can be bought by the metre for about £10; you're unlikely to get better prices than this anywhere else in Donegal.

Slieve League
Carrick, 5km north-west of Kilcar, is where you turn off for Teelin and the Bunglas viewing point for Slieve League, a cliff face dropping some 300m straight into the sea. To drive to the cliff edge, be sure to take the turn-off signposted Bunglas from the Killybegs to Glencolumbcille road (R263) at Carrick, and continue beyond the narrow track signposted Slieve League to the one that's signposted Bunglas.

Walks
There are a number of local walks that take in many prehistoric sites. Three walks that start in Kilcar are collectively known as the **Kilcar Way**. From Teelin, experienced walkers can spend a day walking north via Bunglas and the somewhat terrifying One Man's Path to Malinbeg, near Glencolumbcille.

Special Events
In early August, Kilcar, like Killybegs, hosts an International Sea Angling Festival, followed almost immediately by the Kilcar Street Festival.

Places to Stay
On the western side of the village is the welcoming **Dún Ulún House** (☎ 38137, Coast Rd). It charges £9.50 to £12.50 for dorm beds and £16 for B&B; family rooms cost £20 to £35. Across the road it also has tiered **camp sites** on the hillside (with great views) costing £3 per person; a shower and toilet block is nearby. The equally friendly IHH **Derrylahan Hostel** (☎ 38079), some 3km west of the village, charges £6 in six-bed dorms and £16 for its two doubles; **camping** costs £3. There's a small shop, plentiful cooking facilities and a group house accommodating 46 people; a phone call from Kilcar village or Carrick will get you a lift to the hostel.

For B&B, **Kilcar Lodge** (☎ 38156, Main St) charges upwards of £20/30 for singles/doubles. It opens April to September.

Places to Eat
The thatched **Piper's Rest** pub (☎ 38205) in Kilcar serves good soup, snacks and seafood and has traditional-music sessions. **Restaurant Teach Barnaí** (☎ 38160, Main St) offers an international menu.

On the road between Kilcar and Killybegs is the panoramically situated and extremely popular **Blue Haven** (☎ 38090), with main courses costing around £7.

In Carrick, the **Slieveleague Bar** (☎ 39041) serves pub grub.

Getting There & Away
Bus Éireann (☎ 074-21309) bus No 490 connects Kilcar and Carrick with Killybegs

DONEGAL

and Glencolumbcille once daily Monday to Friday, twice on Saturday. In July and August an extra bus runs daily Monday to Saturday. McGeehan Coaches (☎ 075-46150) runs a service from Glencolumbcille to Dublin stopping at Carrick at 7.40 am daily, with additional buses at 5.10 pm on Friday and 3.15 pm on Sunday; they stop in Kilcar outside John Joe's pub about 10 minutes later. There are extra buses in summer.

GLENCOLUMBCILLE
☎ 073 • pop 260

The name in Irish of this collection of tiny settlements– Gleann Cholm Cille (Glen of Columba's Church) – suggests that the 6th-century St Colmcille (alias Columba) lived in the valley here, and the remains of his church can still be seen. Every year at midnight on 9 June – the saint's feast day – the village becomes the focal point of a penitential walkabout. Settlement of the area dates back 5000 years and Stone Age remains dot the landscape.

The village appears as Glencolmcille or Glencolmbkille on some maps.

Information
The Lace House (☎ 30116), Cashel St, dispenses information 10 am to 6 pm daily, June to August. There are no banks but the post office has a bureau de change.

Folk Village Museum
This heritage centre (☎ 30017), 3km west of the centre of Glencolumbcille, was established by Father James McDyer in 1967. It comprises several replicated thatched cottages as lived in by people in the 18th and 19th centuries, with genuine period fittings. The shebeen house sells unusual local wines (made from things such as seaweed

---

A Tale of Two Priests

While the sexual improprieties of the Catholic clergy in Ireland may grab the headlines, most of the faithful like to think of their priests and nuns as 'living saints' who perform corporal works of mercy and contribute to the development of the community. County Donegal can claim two of them.

When Father James McDyer came to Glencolumbcille from Tory Island in 1952, he was galvanised into action by seeing a community in decay with an emigration rate of 75%. He organised cooperatives and diversified farming practices as well as promoting tourism. By 1964 emigration had dropped to 20%. The Folk Village Museum he established in Glencolumbcille in 1967 – long before such heritage centres became trendy and there were substantial EU grants to help set them up – is the most tangible evidence of the work of a priest who played a remarkable role in the development of a community.

Another cleric who made his mark on a remote part of rural Donegal was Father Diarmuid Ó Péicín. When the then retired Jesuit missionary visited Tory Island for a day trip in 1980, he encountered a totally dispirited people. A severe storm in 1974 had cut the island off from the mainland and, after it subsided, a number of islanders migrated to the mainland.

By the time Father Ó Péicín arrived the remaining islanders were convinced that the government was going to abandon the island and move the population to the mainland. The 'lonely rock' they called home would thus go the way of the Blasket Islands (see the Kerry chapter), abandoned in the 1950s. Father Ó Péicín took up the fight and campaigned both in Ireland and abroad for an electrification and water scheme for Tory, proper sanitation, a regular ferry and a new harbour. Although he remained for only four years, his work and spirit encouraged the islanders to fend for themselves, and all of this was eventually achieved.

You can read about Father Ó Péicín's work in his autobiography, *Islanders: The True Story of One Man's Fight to Save a Way of Life* (Harper Collins).

and fuchsias) alongside marmalade and fudge. The old National School is also open to visitors, and there's a short nature trail up the hill behind.

The museum opens 10 am to 6 pm Monday to Saturday, and noon to 6 pm on Sunday, Easter to September. Admission costs £2/1.25 and includes a tour of the site's buildings.

Malinmore Outdoor Pursuits Centre

Overlooking Malin Bay, this sports centre (☎ 30123) offers scuba diving, canoeing, snorkelling, fishing, orienteering, boat trips and other activities. Accommodation packages are available.

Beaches

The beach opposite the folk village can be dangerous due to the undercurrents. It's worth making the short journey west of Glencolumbcille to Doonalt, where there are two sandy beaches. Another beach can be found at the end of the road to Malinbeg, where steps descend to a lovely sheltered cove.

Courses

From late March to October, **Oideas Gael** (☎ 30248, email oidsgael@iol.ie), at the Foras Cultúir Uladh (Ulster Cultural Foundation), 1km west of Glencolumbcille, offers a number of adult courses in the Irish language and in traditional culture – from Donegal dancing and marine painting to *bodhrán* (hand-held goatskin drum) playing and tapestry weaving. For the language courses (absolute beginners welcome) fees are £50/110 for a three-day-weekend/week-long course; cultural courses cost £70 to £90 and last a week.

Shared accommodation with other course participants costs £60 per person per week, and £125 with breakfast and dinner.

Places to Stay

The friendly *Dooey Hostel* (☎ 30130), the flagship property of the IHI, is about 1.5km beyond the village and offers everything from *camping* space (£3.50 per person) and

dorm beds (£6) to three private rooms (£8 per person) and a group house for 20 people with superb views out over Glen Bay. The hostel has six kitchens and, rather surprising for somewhere as remote as this, it offers wheelchair access. If you're driving, take the turn beside the Glenhead Tavern; if walking or cycling, take a short cut up the track beside the Folk Village.

A pleasant B&B next to the hostel with good views is Anne Ward's *Atlantic Scene* (☎ 30186), charging £13 per person and open May to September. At Malinmore, about 2km west of the Folk Village, *Ros Mór* (☎ 30083) is a pleasant place charging £18/30 for B&B in singles/doubles. Nearby is the renovated *Glencolumbcille Hotel* (☎ 30003), with 35 doubles costing £60 including breakfast.

Places to Eat

The restaurant and teashop above *Lace House* opens noon to 3.30 pm and 5 to 9 pm daily. Soups, sandwiches and burgers cost less than £2; meals cost under £4. The café at the *Folk Village* sells excellent Irish cakes, apple tart and bread. Probably the best place to eat is *An Chistin* (☎ 30213) at the Ulster Cultural Foundation. It specialises in seafood (smoked salmon costs £3.95) but also serves good cakes and pastries. It opens 9.30 am to 9.30 pm.

Shopping

Glencolumbcille Woollen Market (☎ 39377), 3km south-west of the village on the R263, is an outlet for Rossan knitwear and has a large array of Donegal tweed jackets, caps and ties alongside lambswool scarves and shawls. Also available are Aran sweaters and handwoven rugs. At Lace House, Rossan sells knitted garments, jackets and rugs.

Getting There & Away

Bus Éireann (☎ 074-21309) bus No 490 leaves for Killybegs at 8.30 am Monday to Saturday, plus 11.35 am on Saturday. There's another bus at 12.35 pm daily in July and August.

McGeehan Coaches (☎ 075-46150) leave daily from outside Biddy's Pub for Donegal and Dublin (Royal Dublin Hotel on O'Connell St). From Dublin the bus leaves at 6 pm (there are extra buses at 4.30 pm on Friday and at 10 am on Monday), arriving at Glencolumbcille at 11 pm. Departure from Glencolumbcille is at 7.30 am (with extra buses at 5 pm on Friday and at 3 pm on Sunday). McGeehan also runs to Letterkenny (two hours) via Killybegs, Ardara and Glenties, at 7.30 am Monday to Saturday. It leaves Letterkenny for Glencolumbcille at 4.45 pm.

ARDARA & AROUND
☎ 075 • pop 650

The scenically positioned, small heritage town of Ardara (Árd an Rátha) is an important centre for the manufacture of knitwear and handwoven tweed. Tourist information is available from Ardara Heritage Centre (see the following Things to See & Do section). On The Diamond there's an Ulster Bank with an ATM; the post office is opposite.

Things to See & Do
The road from Glencolumbcille to Ardara goes via the stunning **Glengesh Pass**, a glaciated valley that suddenly opens up before you, with long winding bends carrying the road down to the river. Before entering Ardara, a small road to the left runs down to the tiny village of **Maghera** and its attractive beach with caves that can be explored. Be careful as some of them flood when the tide comes in. The long, narrow **Loughros Peninsula** that extends from Ardara and separates Loughros More Bay from Loughros Beg Bay is also worth walking or cycling.

Ardara Heritage Centre (☎ 41704) tells the story of Donegal's role in the weaving industry and gives you the chance to watch a handloom weaver. An audiovisual presentation upstairs describes the surrounding area, and there's a small café. The centre opens 10 am to 6 pm Monday to Saturday, and 2 to 6 pm on Sunday, Easter to September. Admission is free.

Special Events
The Ardara Weavers Fair has its origins in the 18th century but went into decline early

in the 20th century. It was revived and now takes place over the first weekend in June.

Places to Stay
Drumbarron Hostel (☎ 41200), on The Diamond, charges £6 for dorm beds and £14 for its one double. It opens year round.

Drumbarron House (☎ 41200), next to the hostel, has four singles/doubles costing upwards of £17/28. It opens year round. ***Laburnum House*** (☎ 41146), also on The Diamond, on the corner of the Portnoo road, offers B&B costing £13.50 per person. On Front St, quiet ***Brae House*** (☎ 41296) has en suite rooms costing £16 per person and opens year round.

Places to Eat
The best place for snacks or a meal is ***Nancy's Bar*** down by the bridge. This small, dark place has lots of atmosphere and serves burgers, various seafood dishes (including garlic oysters) and a ploughman's lunch. ***Charlie's West End Café***, at the Killybegs end of Main St, can do you breakfast, as well as soups, sandwiches (starting at £1.10) and meals (£3.75).

Entertainment
Peter Oliver's Central Bar has live music at night at the weekend (nightly from June to September) and invites all musicians to join in. Another place to try is ***Corner Bar*** on The Diamond.

Shopping
Several shops specialise in locally made knitwear, and prices are competitive. Aran cardigans and sweaters cost around £50, scarves around £15, and tweed jackets around £140. Compare prices and styles at Kennedy's (☎ 41106) and Bonner & Son (☎ 41303), almost side by side on Front St, and John Molloy (☎ 41133), 1km out on the Killybegs road and open 9 am to 8 pm daily, May to September; and on weekdays only, the rest of the year.

Getting There & Away
The Bus Éireann (☎ 074-21309) express Dublin to Donegal bus No 30 extends to

Ardara on Friday; Sunday only, the bus leaves Ardara for Dublin at 4.30 pm. In July and August, bus No 492 from Killybegs stops twice daily Monday to Saturday, in each direction, outside O'Donnell's in Ardara. The rest of the year, these buses run on Tuesday, Thursday and Friday only.

McGeehan Coaches (☎ 46150) runs a service to Dublin at 8.30 am daily from the post office (with extra buses at 5.45 pm on Friday and 3.45 pm on Sunday). The Glencolumbcille to Letterkenny bus via Glenties stops in Ardara at 8.30 am Monday to Saturday.

Getting Around
Byrne's of Ardara (☎ 41156), east of the centre, is part of the Raleigh Rent-a-Bike scheme.

DAWROS HEAD
The two camping and caravan sites here are packed out every summer with holidaymakers from the North, so the area is busier than you might expect. The Blue Flag beach at **Narin** is a big crowd-puller, and at low tide you can walk out to **Iniskeel Island** to the remains of a monastery founded by St Connell, a cousin of St Colmcille.

Signposts off the road from Narin to Rosbeg lead 3km to a lake in the centre of which sits 2000-year-old **Doon Fort**, a fortified oval settlement. To reach it, you need to hire a rowing boat (£3 per hour).

In 1588 the *Duquesa Santa Ana*, part of the Spanish Armada, ran aground off **Tramore Beach**. The survivors temporarily occupied O'Boyle's Island in Kiltoorish Lake, but then marched south through Ardara to Killybegs, where they set sail again in the *Girona*. The *Girona* met a similar fate that year off the Antrim coast in Northern Ireland, with the loss of over 1000 crew.

Places to Stay
Dunmore Caravan and Camping Park (☎ 075-45121, Strand Rd, Portnoo) charges £6 for tents – call first to check whether there's a space available. It opens midMarch to November. *Tramore Beach Caravan and Camping Park* (☎ 075-51491, Rosbeg) charges £7/9 for a small/large tent.

Take the road from Ardara to Narin then turn left, following the signposts.

There are a few B&Bs at Narin and Portnoo that open for the season (generally April to September). *Roaninish* (☎ 075-45207) charges upwards of £25/36 for singles/ doubles, and *Hazelwood* (☎ 075-45151) costs upwards of £15 per person.

Getting There & Away
In July and August, Monday to Saturday, Bus Éireann (☎ 074-21309) bus No 492 departs Killybegs for Portnoo at 10 am and 5.05 pm. From Portnoo it returns at 12.15 and 6.15 pm.

GLENTIES
☎ 075 • pop 800
The small town of Glenties (Na Gleannta) is on the Owena River at the meeting of two valleys, with the Blue Stack Mountains to the south. The town was home to Patrick MacGill (1891–1963), the 'navvy poet', and a summer school in his honour takes place in mid-August. Glenties has won the coveted title of Ireland's Tidiest Town on numerous occasions. It's a popular **fishing** destination and there are several pleasant **walks** in the area.

On the main street there's a board with tourist information beside the garda station, a Bank of Ireland with an ATM and bureau de change, and a post office.

St Connell's Museum & Heritage Centre
The local-history museum (☎ 51227), beside the old courthouse off the western end of the main street, has a small collection of local artefacts. These include an impressive set of early-20th-century bathroom fixtures in the basement, and reminders of the old Glenties to Fintown railway. It opens 10 am to 12.30 pm and 2 to 4.30 pm on weekdays, and 10.30 am to 12.30 pm on Saturday, April to September. Admission costs £2/50p.

Places to Stay
Clean, spacious IHH *Campbell's Holiday Hostel* (☎ 51491) is on the left beside the

DONEGAL

museum as you enter from Ardara on the N56. Beds in a dorm with en suite facilities cost £8, and there are seven twin rooms costing £20. There's also a big kitchen-cum-common-room, with a welcoming fire.

Two B&Bs are along Glen Rd about 1km out of town: *Claradon Country House* (☎ *51113*) and *Avalon* (☎ *51292*) both charge upwards of £22.50/32 for singles/doubles. The 20-room *Highlands Hotel* (☎ *51111*), on the main street, charges upwards of £30/52.

Places to Eat
Highlands Hotel serves substantial meals even on a Sunday evening; roast turkey costs £6.90, vegetable curry £7.50. Otherwise, there are several fast-food places on the main street, such as *Jim's Café*, for soups and sandwiches, and *Nighthawks* for pizzas (£3.75).

Entertainment
A number of pubs along the main street offer music at night. On Saturday the region's largest disco takes place at the *Limelight*.

Getting There & Away
In July and August, Monday to Saturday, Bus Éireann (☎ 074-21309) bus No 492 from Killybegs to Portnoo stops outside the post office in Glenties at 10.45 am and 5.50 pm. Coming from Portnoo, the bus stops in Glenties at 12.40 and 6.40 pm. The rest of the year, the bus runs Tuesday, Thursday and Friday only. On Friday the 5.15 pm express Dublin to Donegal bus No 30 extends its service to Glenties, arriving at 10.20 pm; Sunday only, the bus leaves Glenties for Dublin at 4.15 pm.

McGeehan Coaches (☎ 46150) runs a service from Glencolumbcille (stopping outside Highlands Hotel at 8.15 am) to Dublin (there's an extra bus at 5.30 pm on Friday and 3.30 pm on Sunday). There's also a bus to Letterkenny at 8.40 am Monday to Saturday.

INLAND TO THE FINN VALLEY
This part of Donegal is not well travelled – a blessing if you want to get away on your own for some fishing, hill walking or cyc-

ling. The **River Finn** is a good salmon river, especially if there has been heavy rain before the middle of June.

There's good **hill walking** on the Blue Stack Mountains and along the Ulster Way, but you need to be equipped with maps and provisions. Finn Farm Hostel (see the following Places to Stay section) dispenses maps and advice and will even arrange a pick-up at the beginning or end of a walk. A long, one-day trek could start from the hostel and end at Campbell's Holiday Hostel in Glenties or the hostel in Fintown.

The main town is **Ballybofey** (pronounced 'bally-boh-fay'; Bealach Féich), which is linked to adjoining **Stranorlar** by an arched bridge over the River Finn. There's a small locally run tourist office in the Ballybofey Balor Theatre on the main street, open 9 am to 5 pm weekdays. In Ballybofey's Protestant church is the grave of Isaac Butt (1813–79), founder of the Irish Home Rule movement. Fishing gear is available from the sports department of McElhinney's Store (☎ 074-31217) or from Mr G's Discount Store.

Fintown, 30km north-west by Lough Finn, is a much smaller settlement – just a cluster of houses, a hostel, shop, post office, garage and pubs. Nevertheless, a renovated part of the narrow-gauge **Fintown Railway** (☎ 075-46280) between Fintown and Glenties runs excursions alongside Lough Finn on 5km of track. Trains leave the station 11 am to 5 pm on weekdays, and 11 am to 6 pm at the weekend, July to September; and 1 to 4 pm on weekdays, and 1 to 5 pm on Saturday, June. Fares are £2/1 (families £6).

Places to Stay
The IHO *Fintown Hostel* (☎ *075-46244*) charges £10 for dorm beds and is beautifully situated above Lough Finn, with the Finnian's Rainbow pub at the end of the drive. The hostel closes in December. The IHH/IHI *Finn Farm Hostel* (☎ *074-32261*) is 2km from Ballybofey. The left turn is signposted off the Glenties road (R253). We've received various reports of declining standards here. Dorm beds cost £7, the two

private rooms cost £9 per person, and camping costs £4. Finn Farm opens year round.

There are B&Bs in both Ballybofey and Stranorlar to the north. *Finn View House* (☎ 074-31351), on the Lifford road in Ballybofey, offers rooms costing upwards of £16 per person, while Maureen Fahey's *Ashburn* (☎ 074-31312), on the Letterkenny road in Stranorlar, charges upwards of £18/32 for singles/doubles. *Kee's Hotel* (☎ 074-31018), in Stranorlar, where the mail horses were changed on the Derry to Sligo run in the 19th century, charges £54/94 in the high season, including use of the leisure club's swimming pool and sauna. The renovated, 88-room *Jackson's Hotel* (☎ 074-31021) also has a leisure centre and charges £40 to £46 per person.

Places to Eat

U Drop Inn, off the main street in Ballybofey, serves good bar meals such as vegetable curry with chips (£4). The small *Caife na Locha*, in Fintown, is run by a women's cooperative and serves tea and light meals; it opens daily in the summer. The big hotels offer set dinners costing about £15 to £20.

Entertainment

There's the small *Balor Theatre* (☎ 074-31840) in Ballybofey, but you'll have more fun checking out the area's traditional-music outlets. *Finn Farm Hostel* is a centre for a community work scheme aimed at reviving dying musical traditions, so if you stay during the week you'll be able to hear the musicians practising between 10 am and 6 pm. They also practise in the two Ballybofey pubs – *Claddagh* and *Bonner's Bar* – on Wednesday and Thursday nights. In Fintown, *An Teach Ceoil* (The Music House) is the venue of choice. *Glen Tavern*, midway between Glenties and Fintown, is renowned for its traditional music on Saturday night.

Getting There & Away

Bus Éireann (☎ 074-21309) express bus No 64 from Galway to Derry via Sligo, Donegal and Letterkenny stops three times daily

beside the car park at McElhinney's Store in Ballybofey. Local buses connect Ballybofey with Killybegs and Letterkenny.

McGeehan Coaches (☎ 075-46150) runs a Glencolumbcille to Letterkenny bus Monday to Saturday that stops in front of the Fintown post office at 1.25 pm (at 5.55 pm heading for Glenties, Ardara, Killybegs, Kilcar and Glencolumbcille). There's also a McGeehan Coaches bus from Fintown to Ballybofey at 1.25 pm Monday to Saturday, mid-July to August. It stops in Ballybofey en route to Fintown, Killybegs and Glencolumbcille at 5 pm.

The Feda Ódonaill (☎ 075-48114) bus from Crolly to Galway stops in Ballybofey outside McElhinney's at 9.15 am and 4.45 pm from Monday to Saturday (also at 12.45 pm on Friday), and at 9.15 am and 3.45 and 7.45 pm on Sunday.

North-Western Donegal

The various monikers that are bestowed on Donegal's scenery – wild, spectacular, dramatic – are nowhere more applicable than in the north-west of the county. Despite the absence of large towns, you're rarely far from a village or pub, and the area around Gweedore claims to be one of the most densely populated rural regions in Western Europe.

The stretch of land between Dungloe and Crolly is a bleak and rocky Gaeltacht area known as the Rosses. It contains numerous tiny lakes. The main attraction is the island of Arranmore, reached by ferry from the village of Burtonport.

The other accessible island, Tory Island, farther to the north, is even more appealing. The coastal area between Bunbeg and Dunfanaghy is absolutely superb, and there are wonderful cycling tours around the Bloody Foreland and Horn Head.

DUNGLOE & AROUND
☎ 075 • pop 990
Dungloe (An Clochán Liath), the capital of

DONEGAL

The Corncrake Crisis

Once, nights in the Irish countryside were punctuated by the distinctive 'crek, crek' cry of the lovelorn male corncrake. However, due to modern intensive farming practices, in 1988 an all-Ireland survey found only 903 birds still calling, and by the mid-1990s this number had fallen to just 130. Today the corncrake is high on the list of Irish endangered species and survives only in northern Donegal, the Shannon Callows, Mayo and small areas of the western coast.

The corncrake, a dowdy, secretive bird, winters in south-eastern Africa before arriving in Ireland to breed in April. Like so many endangered species, it has habits that render it peculiarly vulnerable to modern life. After laying their eggs in long grass, females stay with their chicks even as a mowing tractor's blades descend on them. Even if they realise the danger, long centuries of programming make them reluctant to rush for the safety of open ground.

The Irish Wildbird Conservancy (IWC) offers grants to farmers who delay mowing until August, when the nesting season is over, or cut the grass in 'corncrake-friendly' fashion. There's a 24-hour Corncrake Hotline (☎ 074-65126 in County Donegal, 096-51326 in County Mayo) and you'll see notices in shop windows inviting people to ring in if they hear a corncrake. An IWC officer then visits the site and decides if a nest is in need of protection.

These efforts seem to have had some positive effect. In recent years birdwatchers have reported a rise in the number of singing males, but there's still a long way to go before the bird is removed from the endangered-species list.

NICKY CAVEN

The distinctive cry of the male corncrake is on the rise.

the Rosses, makes a good base for exploring the region.

The tourist office (☎ 21297), off Main St behind the Bridge Inn, opens 10 am to 1 pm and 2 to 6 pm Monday to Saturday, June to August. If it's closed the Ireland's Alive office (☎ 22299), Gweedore Rd, may be able to help. The Bank of Ireland, Main St, has an ATM and bureau de change and the post office is on a road off Main St leading down to the bay.

Fishing for salmon and trout is popular and you can get tackle and permits from Bonner's on Main St. The nearest good beach is 6km south-west of Dungloe at Maghery Bay.

Special Events

In late July/early August, Dungloe hosts the 10-day Mary of Dungloe Festival, named after a popular 1960s song. Thousands crowd into town for a series of events culminating in a contest to pick the year's 'Mary'. Supposedly, she's selected on the basis of personality, but only women aged 18 to 25 are eligible to enter! The festival is a big, raucous, boozy affair and, although it's sometimes graced by big names such as singers Christy Moore or 'boy-next-door' Daniel O'Donnell, some people might want to avoid Dungloe at this time. If you do want to attend, book a bed well ahead. For more details phone Anne Marie Doherty (☎ 22120).

Places to Stay

The well-run, IHH-affiliated *Greene's Hostel* (☎ 21021, Carnmore Rd), open March to December, charges £7 to £8 for dorm beds and £9 per person in private rooms. There's also *space for tents*: £6 if you're hitching or cycling. You can hire a bike here for £5 per day. The An Óige *Crohy Head Hostel* (☎ 21950), 8km south-west of Dungloe at scenic Crohy Head (An Cruach), charges £6.50/5 and opens Easter to September.

In the centre, 16-room *Delaney's Hotel* (☎ 21033, Main St) charges upwards of £24/46 for singles/doubles. At *Óstán na Rosann* (☎ 22444, Mill Rd), just north of town past the Statoil service station, the 48 en suite rooms cost £55/70. The hotel's leisure centre includes a heated pool.

Places to Eat
The *Bridge Inn* pub, in front of the tourist office, serves light snacks, or there's nearby *Courthouse Restaurant* for cheap seafood meals. For a quiet spot during the day, seek out the *Lite Lunch* in the otherwise uninspiring Dungloe Centre shopping mall. In the evening, for takeaway food there's *Three In One*, which offers tasty burgers, kebabs and pizzas, or the Chinese *Lucky Jackpot*, up the hill past the garda station (noodles and other main courses cost under £5). *Delaney's Hotel* serves dinner costing £17.50, and at nearby *Riverside Bistro* beef lasagne costs £5.95.

Getting There & Away
Dungloe is served by several private companies but not Bus Éireann. McGeehan Coaches (☎ 46150) runs a service from Glencolumbcille to Dublin stopping at Greene's Hostel at 7.45 am Monday to Saturday (plus at 5 pm on Friday and 3 pm on Sunday). From mid-July to August it also has a daily bus from Dungloe to Fintown at 11.50 am.

O'Donnell Buses (☎ 48356) run from Dungloe to Belfast (4½ hours) via Burtonport, Bunbeg, Dunfanaghy, Letterkenny and Derry. Buses leave from in front of Delaney's Hotel on Main St at 7.15 am Monday to Saturday and 4.30 pm on Sunday. Derry-based Lough Swilly (☎ 028-71 262017, 074-22863) run a Dungloe to Derry service via Bunbeg, Dunfanaghy and Letterkenny three times daily on weekdays.

Twice weekly, Feda Ódonaill (☎ 48114) runs from Annagry (Anagaire) to Killybegs via Burtonport, Dungloe (8.10 am on Mon-

day and 2.40 pm on Sunday), Glenties and Ardara. In the other direction it runs twice on Friday only, stopping in Dungloe at 8.15 am and 10 pm.

BURTONPORT
☎ 075 • pop 280
The otherwise ordinary port village of Burtonport (Ailt an Chorráin) is the embarkation point for Arranmore. Back in 1974, the Atlantis commune was established here by one Jenny James, who practised a form of primal therapy. Her followers became known as 'the Screamers'. Eventually the commune relocated to the Colombian jungle and another group arrived to take its place. The Silver Sisters chose to live a Victorian lifestyle, complete with Victorian dress, and soon bizarre stories were circulating about them. They, too, moved on, allowing Burtonport to sink back into anonymity.

For **fishing** trips contact Donal O'Sullivan (☎ 42077) at the shop by the pier.

From mid-July to August, McGeehan Coaches (☎ 46150) runs one bus daily, Monday to Saturday, to Burtonport.

ARRANMORE
☎ 075 • pop 600
The small island of Arranmore (Árainn Mhór), 14km by 5km, has some spectacular cliff scenery, sea caves and sandy beaches. It has been inhabited for thousands of years, and a prehistoric fort can be seen on the southern side. The western and northern parts are wild and rugged, with few houses to disturb the sense of isolation. The **Arranmore Way** circles the island (allow three to four hours) and off the south-western tip is **Green Island**, a bird sanctuary. There's good **fishing** in the waters surrounding Arranmore, and in Lough Shure you'll find plenty of rainbow trout.

Places to Stay & Eat
The 10-room *Glen Hotel* (☎ 20505) costs £18 per person. *Bonner's Ferryboat Restaurant* (☎ 20532), near the ferry pier, offers B&B costing £15 per person. Several pubs serve food, including *O'Donnell's*

Atlantic Bar in Aphort and *Phil Bàn's Bar* in Leabgarrow.

Entertainment

The island's pubs enjoy a 24-hour licence to cater for the local fishing community and they regularly provide traditional-music sessions.

Getting There & Away

The Arranmore Ferry (☎ 20532), run by Bonner's, plies the 1.5km from Burtonport to Leabgarrow (return £6, 25 minutes). In July and August, there are eight daily crossings (seven on Sunday), starting at 8.30 am from Burtonport (noon on Sunday). The rest of the year there are at least five sailings daily (three on Sunday).

GWEEDORE & AROUND
☎ 075

The remote Irish-speaking district of Gweedore (Gaoth Dobhair) has a rugged coastline with many beautiful beaches, while its bleak interior contains many small fishing lakes. Ferries depart from Bunbeg for Tory Island.

Settlements hug the coastline. Derrybeg (Doirí Beaga) and Bunbeg (Bun Beag) virtually run into each other along the R257; the village of Gweedore is a few kilometres east on the R258. On the main road in Bunbeg there's an AIB with an ATM and bureau de change and a tourist-information point in its car park. There's a post office in Derrybeg.

Places to Stay

Hostels The IHO *Backpackers Ireland Seaside Hostel* (☎ 32244), at Magheragallon near Derrybeg, offers dorm beds costing £7 and private rooms costing £8 per person. It opens mid-March to October. The beautifully remote and friendly IHO *Screag an Iolair* (*Eagle's Nest;* ☎ 48593) is signposted up in the hills above Crolly, southwest of Gweedore on the N56. It charges around £7 for dorm beds, has two private rooms (£8.50 per person) and offers a free pick-up service if you don't fancy the 5km walk from the main road.

B&Bs & Hotels Bunbeg has plenty of B&Bs, with *The Beach* (☎ 31550, Strand Rd), by the beach, offering en suite singles/doubles costing £20/32, and *An Teach Ban* (☎ 31569), beside the AIB, charging upwards of £15 per person.

There are a couple of prettier places beside picturesque Bunbeg harbour, including *Bunbeg House* (☎ 31305), charging £19/34. In summer, heavy traffic to the harbour might detract a bit from its charm. *Fernfield* (☎ 31258), at Middletown in Derrybeg, charges £18/32.

The 36-room *Óstán Gweedore* (☎ 31177), by Bunbeg beach, has the best facilities, including a leisure complex. B&B costs upwards of £44 per person. B&B at the cosier *Óstán Radharc na Mara* (☎ 31076), also in Bunbeg, costs upwards of £30 per person.

Places to Eat

There are several eateries in Bunbeg, including *An Chisteanach*, opposite the Hudí Beag pub, which serves soups (£1.20) and snacks. *Mooney's Restaurant*, on the main road opposite Óstán Radharc na Mara, opens on summer evenings only. Óstán Radharc na Mara itself has two restaurants: *Clady Grill Room*, for grills and steak meals, and the more upmarket *Westport Room*. *Bunbeg House*, by Bunbeg harbour, offers dinner costing £16 and serves afternoon tea.

Entertainment

For traditional pub music it's hard to beat the Monday-night sessions at *Tábhairne Hudí Beag* (☎ 31016) in Bunbeg near Óstán Radharc na Mara.

Getting There & Away

Feda Ódonaill (☎ 48114) runs a service from Gweedore to Letterkenny, Donegal, Sligo and Galway. Buses depart at 7.30 am and 2.55 pm Monday to Saturday (plus at 10.30 am on Friday), and at 7.30 am and 2 pm on Sunday. They leave Bunbeg from near the turn-off for the harbour. From Galway, buses leave St Nicholas Cathedral at 10 am and 4 pm daily (plus at 5.30 pm on

Friday), and at 3 and 8 pm on Sunday (from Eyre Square).

DUNLEWY
☎ 075

The hamlet of Dunlewy (Dún Lúiche) sits at the foot of Mt Errigal beside Lough Dunlewy. Here the **Lakeside Centre** (Ionad Cois Locha; ☎ 31699) reconstructs the home of Manus Ferry, the last of the local weavers, who died in 1975. Visitors can watch the stages of weaving in operation, then go outside to see assorted farm animals, walk along the lake shore, take a boat ride with a storyteller on board to fill them in on local history, geology and folklore, or go pony trekking. In summer there are traditional-music concerts. There's an excellent café with a turf fire and a big shop.

A ticket for the house and grounds or a boat trip costs £3/1.50; combined it's £5/2.50. (A combined family ticket is particularly good value at £12.50.) The centre opens 10.30 am to 6 pm at the weekend, April and May; and 10.30 am to 6 pm Monday to Saturday, and 11 am to 7 pm on Sunday, June to September.

MT ERRIGAL & THE POISONED GLEN

You don't need to be an experienced mountaineer to climb Mt Errigal (752m), Donegal's highest peak, but the going can be tough and you should be wary of damp, misty days when visibility may drop with little warning.

There are two paths to the summit: the easier tourist route, which covers 5km and takes roughly two hours to complete; and the more difficult 3.25km walk along the north-western ridge, which involves scrambling over scree for about 2½ hours. Details of both routes are available at Dunlewy's Lakeside Centre (see the previous Dunlewy section).

Stories abound about how the Poisoned Glen got its name. The more prosaic suggest that it's because poisonous Irish spurge once grew here or because the original name – An Gleann Neamhe (The Heavenly Glen) – became corrupted to An Gleann Nimhe (The Poisoned Glen). Another theory is that the British were once camped here, and Irish rebels poisoned the water to kill their horses.

More imaginative is the tale of the ancient, one-eyed giant, Balor, who was killed here by his exiled grandson, Lughaidh, whereupon the poison from his eye split the rock and poisoned the glen.

It's possible to walk through the glen, although some of the ground is rough and boggy. From the Lakeside Centre a return walk along the glen is about 12km and takes from two to three hours.

Places to Stay

The IHO *Backpackers Ireland Lakeside Hostel* (☎ 075-32133), at the old Dunlewy Hotel, charges £7 for dorm beds and opens mid-March to October. The An Óige *Errigal Hostel* (☎ 075-31180), at Errigal, is a simple place on the R251 about 2km west of Dunlewy. Beds cost £7/5.50 and it opens year round.

GLENVEAGH NATIONAL PARK

Dunlewy's Lakeside Centre is beside the 10,000-hectare Glenveagh National Park (Pairc Naísúnta Ghleann Bheatha), which is in a lake-filled valley overlooked by the Derryveagh Mountains. Much of the land comprising the park was once farmed by tenants, 244 of whom were evicted by landowner John George Adair in the winter of 1861. A plaque on a gable end at Ardaturr farm commemorates their fate. Adair was responsible for the building of Glenveagh Castle (1870). After the mysterious disappearance of the second owner, the land was bought in 1937 by American Henry McIlhenny, who eventually sold it to the state and later donated the castle and gardens.

Adair's wife, Cornelia, introduced two things that define the National Park's appearance: the herd of red deer and the rhododendrons. The latter, despite their beauty in blossom, are seen as a pest, preventing broad-leafed trees from seeding.

The park's features include a nature trail through woods of Scots pine and oak to a

DONEGAL

stretch of blanket bog, a viewing point that's a short walk behind the castle, and a number of lakes, the largest of which is Lough Beagh.

The cleverly designed **Glenveagh Visitor Centre** (☎ 074-37090) has a useful audiovisual display on the ecology of the park and the infamous Adair. There's also an imaginative toy-theatre representation of the story. The restaurant serves hot food and snacks, and the reception sells the necessary midge repellent, as vital in summer as walking boots and waterproofs are in winter.

The park opens year round. The visitor centre opens 10 am to 6.30 pm (7.30 pm on Sunday, June to early September) daily between mid-April and September; and 10 am to 6.30 pm, Saturday to Thursday, October to early November. Admission costs £2/1 (families £5) and last admission is 90 minutes before closing.

Camping isn't allowed in the park.

Glenveagh Castle

The castle, built by John George Adair in 1870, was modelled in miniature on Scotland's Balmoral. Henry McIlhenny made it a comfortable gentleman's home with lots of reminders of the deer hunting once so important to upper-class life.

A guided tour takes in a series of rooms that look as if McIlhenny just left them. Some of the nicer ones, including the tartan-draped music room and the guest room for female visitors, are in the round tower. The drawing room has a splendid 300-year-old Adams-style fireplace bought by McIlhenny from the Ards estate near Dunfanaghy.

On a dry day the gardens are spectacular. They were nurtured for decades and include a variety of features: a terrace, an Italian garden, a walled kitchen garden, and the Belgian Walk built by Belgian soldiers who stayed here during WWI.

The castle opens the same hours as the

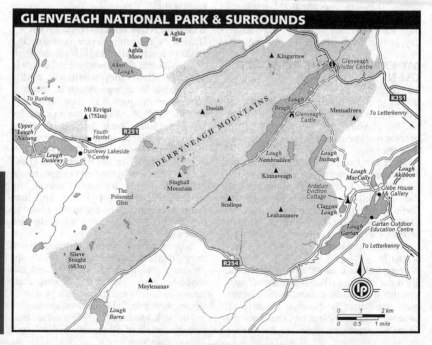

GLENVEAGH NATIONAL PARK & SURROUNDS

visitor centre, although the last guided tours leave about 45 minutes before closing time. Admission costs £2/1 (families £5) on top of the National Park admission charge. Free minibuses run from the visitor centre to the castle roughly every 15 minutes.

BLOODY FORELAND

Bloody Foreland (Cnoc Fola) gets its name from the red colour of the rocks at sunset, and the road to it is wonderfully remote, scenic and ideal for cycling. The small, 12-room hotel, *Foreland Heights* (☎ 075-31785), near the viewing point, opens April to September and costs £32/47 for singles/doubles in July and August.

TORY ISLAND

☎ 074 • pop 160

The remote, treeless Tory Island (Oileán Thóraigh), with its small Irish-speaking community, lies about 11km north of the mainland, exposed to the harsh elements of the Atlantic. There's just one pebbly beach, but the cliff walks and a visit to the island's pub or social club make a stay worthwhile. The island has two villages, West Town (An Baile Thiar), containing most of the island's facilities, and East Town (An Baile Thoir).

Things to See & Do

St Colmcille is said to have founded a monastery here in the 6th century. The only remains of this monastic era are near West Town: the **Tau Cross**, a small undecorated T-shaped cross on the pier, and a **round tower**, with a circumference of nearly 16m, built of rounded beach-stones and rough granite, with a round-headed doorway some distance above the ground.

The island is a good place for **birdwatch-ing**: the north-eastern side has cliffs where you can see colonies of puffin. The south-west is quite different – very flat but with some dangerous offshore rocks. It was here that the British gunboat *Wasp* was wrecked in 1884 while on a mission to collect taxes from the islanders. The independent-minded islanders still pay no taxes and elect their own 'king'.

Tory Island has an indigenous **school of painters**, whose work depicting island life has been exhibited around Europe. The most accomplished was James Dixon, who started painting in his 60s, when he was inspired by (or rather thought he could do better than) the English artist Derek Hill (see Glebe House & Gallery later in this chapter). He died in 1970. You can see and buy their work in the Dixon Gallery near the harbour.

Places to Stay & Eat

Radharc na Mara Hostel (☎ 65145), in West Town, opens April to October and charges £7 for dorm beds. The two villages have a few B&Bs, including *Grace Duffy's* (☎ 35136), in East Town, where singles/doubles cost upwards of £16/28 and dinner costs £8; it opens April to October. The 14-room *Óstán Thóraigh* (☎ 35920), in West Town, charges £40/60 in the high season.

In West Town, the small *Caife an Chreagáin* serves snacks, and you can get pub food or full meals (dinner £16) at *Óstán Thóraigh*.

Entertainment

Club Soisialta Thóraigh (*Tory Social Club;* ☎ 65121) has a bar and regular traditional-music sessions, as does *Óstán Thóraigh*.

Getting There & Away

Donegal Coastal Cruises (Turasmara Teo; ☎ 075-31340) operates a boat service from Bunbeg (☎ 075-31991) and Magheraroarty (☎ 074-35061), which is reached by turning off the N56 at the western end of Gortahork near Falcarragh. The road is signposted Coastal Route/Bloody Foreland. From June to September there's also a boat service from Port-na-Blagh near Dunfanaghy.

Boats leave from Bunbeg year round. Between June and October the boat leaves at 9 am daily and returns from Tory at 10.30 am (less frequently from November to May). The boat from Magheraroarty leaves at 11.30 am and 5 pm daily, June to September (plus 1.30 pm in July and August). On Wednesday, June to September, a boat also leaves Port-na-Blagh at 2 pm,

DONEGAL

returning at 6.30 pm. The fare is £15 return (bicycles free) but call ahead, as weather and tides can affect sailings.

Getting Around
Bike hire is available from Rothair ar Clós (☎ 65614) in West Town.

FALCARRAGH & AROUND
☎ 074 • pop 900

Falcarragh (An Fál Carrach) is a rather unremarkable resort village, but there's a good beach nearby. Together with neighbouring Gortahork (Gort an Choirce) it has a significant Irish-speaking community. The Bank of Ireland at the eastern end of Main St has an ATM and bureau de change, and the post office is across the road.

Things to See & Do
You can reach the **beach** (4km away) by following signs marked An Trá from either end of Main St. The beach is superb for walking, but swimming is unsafe because of the currents.

Muckish Mountain (670m) is a distinctive landmark that dominates the coast between Dunfanaghy and the Bloody Foreland. From the top, on a fine day, there are sweeping panoramic views. It can be climbed from south-east of Falcarragh by way of the inland road through Muckish Gap. Consult *New Irish Walks: West and North* (Gill & Macmillan) for details.

Places to Stay & Eat
The IHH-affiliated *Shamrock Lodge Hostel* (☎ 35192) has 14 beds in the village pub of the same name and charges £7 for dorm beds and £10 per person in private rooms. It's perfect for those who want a lively nightlife close by, but not if you want to sleep before 1 am. The huge *Baile Conaill* (☎ 35363), on the Ballyconnell Estate, some 10 minutes from the beach, has hostel accommodation costing £10, as well as B&B costing upwards of £16. It opens year round. *Cuan-na-Mara* (☎ 35327), 1km from Falcarragh in Ballyness, charges upwards of £22.50/32 for B&B in singles/doubles and opens May to October.

Gweedore Bar has a restaurant upstairs with fish costing £3, and *Coyle's Café* is almost next door. For fast food, try **Mighty Mac's Café** next to the post office.

Entertainment
In summer, pubs such as **Shamrock Lodge** and **Gweedore Bar** come alive at night, many with traditional music.

Getting There & Away
The Feda Ódonaill (☎ 075-48114) bus from Crolly to Galway stops in front of the phone box on Main St at 7.50 am and 3.15 pm Monday to Saturday (plus at 10.50 am on Friday), reaching Letterkenny about an hour later and Galway at 1.10 and 8.45 pm. On Sunday, buses leave at 7.50 am and 2.20 pm.

Anthony McGinley's (☎ 075-48167) bus leaves for Dublin at 7.25 am daily. Lough Swilly's (☎ 028-71 262017, 074-22863) Dungloe to Derry bus stops on Main St near the hostel at 10.35 am, noon and 5 pm on weekdays, plus noon on Saturday.

DUNFANAGHY & AROUND
☎ 074 • pop 280

Dunfanaghy (Dún Fionnachaidh) is a popular holiday resort in a small, discreet way. The vast sandy stretches of virtually empty beach are a big draw, and Dunfanaghy makes a good base for trips north to Horn Head, south to Letterkenny or west to Tory Island.

The AIB has a branch opposite the Carrig Rua Hotel, and the post office has a bureau de change open 9 am to 5.30 pm on weekdays.

Dunfanaghy Workhouse
After the passage of the Poor Law in 1838, workhouses were set up around Ireland to accommodate and employ the destitute in conditions deliberately intended to be uncomfortable. Men, women, children and the sick were separated from one other, and their lives were rigorously governed, with hard work the order of the day. Dunfanaghy's workhouse opened in 1845, just before the onset of the Famine, which

caused the number of residents to multiply. By 1847 it was expanded to accommodate some 600 people, double the number originally planned.

The workhouse, west of the centre up past the post office, is now a small heritage centre (☎ 36540) with information about its own and local history. It opens 10 am to 5 pm on weekdays, and noon to 5 pm at the weekend, Easter to October. Admission costs £2.50/1.25.

Dunfanaghy Gallery (☎ 36224), next door, started life as a fever hospital. Nowadays it houses art and crafts and opens 10 am to 7 pm Monday to Saturday.

Horn Head
Horn Head (Corrán Binne) has some of Donegal's most spectacular coastal scenery and plenty of birdlife. The towering, dramatic headland, with quartzite cliffs over 180m high, can be reached by continuing from the end of the walk described in the following entry, but the route can be perilous at times. Consult the guide *New Irish Walks: West and North* (Gill & Macmillan) or *Hill Walkers' Donegal* (Shanksmore Press) by David Herman.

An alternative route is to go by bike or car from the Falcarragh end of Dunfanaghy. The road circles the headland and offers tremendous views on a fine day: Tory, Inishbofin, Inishdooey and tiny Inishbeg Islands to the west; Sheep Haven Bay and the Rosguill Peninsula to the east; Malin Head to the north-east; and even the coast of Scotland.

Walking
You could easily spend a day walking this area. For an exhilarating walk, follow the road west towards Falcarragh for about 4km and turn right at the first track past the Corcreggan Mill Cottage Hostel. Continue along the track down to the dunes by first passing a farm, then crossing a field on a clearly indicated pathway.

The vast, lovely **Tramore Beach** opens up below the sand dunes. Turn right and follow the beach to the end, where you can find a way up onto a path that leads north to

Pollaguill Bay. From the bay you can continue to the cairn at the end of the bay and follow the coastline for a stupendous view of the 20m **Marble Arch**, carved out by the sea.

Organised walks are offered by Donegal Walking Holidays (☎ 36376), Sessiagh Cottage, Woodhill, Dunfanaghy.

Other Activities
Horse riding can be arranged through Arnold's Hotel (☎ 36208), which also offers birdwatching, painting and photography holidays. Pat Robinson (☎ 36280) organises sea-angling trips from nearby Port-na-Blagh on board the *Cricket*.

Places to Stay
Close to a large deserted beach, the IHH-affiliated *Corcreggan Mill Cottage Hostel* (☎ 36409), 4km from Dunfanaghy on the Falcarragh road (N56), offers accommodation in a converted railway car and former kiln house. Dorm beds cost £9 and the four private rooms cost £11 per person; *camping* is also possible costing £4 per person.

At both *Rosman House* (☎ 36273) and *Whins* (☎ 63481), B&B costs £24.50/36 for singles/doubles. The big, 32-room *Arnold's Hotel* (☎ 36208), overlooking Sheep Haven Bay, charges upwards of £39 to £47 per person. The 22-room *Carrig Rua Hotel* (☎ 36133) opposite charges £33 to £43.

Places to Eat
For coffee and cake, try the café attached to *Dunfanaghy Workhouse* on the N56. The restaurant at *Arnold's Hotel* has good views over the bay and serves hearty seafood and other meals costing £7.50 to £11.25. The menu at the *Carrig Rua Hotel* is much the same.

Danann's Seafood Restaurant (☎ 36150), next to McAuliffe's craft shop on the main street, is popular, with main courses starting at £11.50. It opens at 6 pm and reservations are often necessary. The reasonably priced *Danny Collins Restaurant* (☎ 36205), a few doors west, is also worth a visit and serves pastas costing upwards of £6.95.

DONEGAL

Getting There & Away

Anthony McGinley's (☎ 075-48167) bus for Letterkenny and Dublin leaves Annagry at 7 am daily and reaches Dunfanaghy at 7.35 am. Extra buses run at 3.55 pm on Sunday, Monday and Thursday and at 11.45 am and 3.55 pm on Friday. From Dublin, buses leave at 5.45 pm daily, with extra buses at 9.30 am Monday and Saturday, at 12.30 and 4.30 pm on Friday, and at 12.30 and 8.30 pm on Sunday.

Feda Ódonaill (☎ 075-48114) buses from Crolly to Galway stop in the square at 8 am and 3.25 pm Monday to Saturday, plus at 11 am on Friday. They leave at 8 am and 2.30 pm on Sunday.

Lough Swilly's (☎ 028-71 262017, 074-22863) Dungloe to Derry bus stops in the square at 10.55 am and 12.20 and 5.15 pm on weekdays, plus 12.20 pm on Saturday.

DUNFANAGHY TO CREESLOUGH
Ards Forest Park

The park, about 3km south-east of Dunfanaghy off the N56, has marked nature trails, varying in length from about 2km to 13km, and is also a wildfowl sanctuary. It covers the northern shore of the Ards Peninsula and there are walks to its clean beaches. In 1930 the southern part of the peninsula was taken over by Capuchin monks; the grounds of their friary buildings are open to the public. The park opens until 9 pm in summer and 4.30 pm in winter.

Doe Castle

The castle (Caisléan na dTuath) was once the stronghold of the Scottish MacSweeney family, who were employed by the O'Don-nells. Built in the early 16th century it was constantly fought over by the MacSweeney brothers. Early in the 17th century it passed into English hands and was repaired and in-habited until well into the 19th century. The curious slab that rests against the tower near the entrance is thought to be the tomb of one of the MacSweeneys. The castle is pic-turesquely sited on a low promontory with water on three sides and a moat hewn out of the rock on the landwards side. The best

view is from the Carrigart to Creeslough road. The castle can be viewed only from outside because of ongoing restoration work.

It's 5km from Creeslough on the Carri-gart road and is clearly signposted.

Creeslough

The small village of Creeslough (An Craos-lach), on the N56 near an inlet of Sheep Haven Bay, has an interesting modern church, best viewed against the outline of dis-tant **Muckish Mountain** (670m). The moun-tain can be climbed from here. A road turns off to the left 2km north-west of Creeslough, by a small derelict shop, on the N56; after 6km along here a rough track begins the as-cent. Consult *New Irish Walks: West and North* (Gill & Macmillan) for details.

Places to Stay

There are several B&Bs in the Creeslough area, including *Hillcrest* (☎ 074-38145), 2km north towards Ards, charging upwards of £18/30 for singles/doubles and open from April to September. *Loch na Toohey* (☎ 074-38061), in Ballyboes, has en suite rooms costing £24.50/40 and opens June to September. There are also some self-catering holiday cottages in the area. *Sarah McFadden* (☎ 074-38048) has a cottage that sleeps up to six people and costs £250 per week in July and August, £180 in May, June and September.

Places to Eat

You'll do better in Dunfanaghy or Let-terkenny than along the N56 that joins them. If you're hostelling or camping, there are supermarkets at Creeslough and Dunfanaghy.

At Port-na-Blagh, 1km east of Dun-fanaghy, is *Cove* (☎ 36300), a highly rec-ommended restaurant where reservations are usually necessary. Expect to pay about £25 per person.

In Creeslough, *Stonecutter's Rest* serves pub grub; sandwiches cost £1.20. Just south of Creeslough off the N56 is the inexpen-sive *Red Roof Restaurant*, open July and August.

DONEGAL

Letterkenny & Around

LETTERKENNY

☎ 074 • pop 10,000 (approx)

Letterkenny (Leitir Ceanainn) grew considerably after Derry, 34km north-east, was cut off from its hinterland by the partition of Ireland, and is now Donegal's largest town. There's not a great deal to detain a tourist, although it makes a pleasant enough stop en route to or from Derry. It's also an alternative base to smaller Dunfanaghy in the north or Dungloe in the west for exploring the surrounding areas.

Orientation & Information

Main St, said to be the longest high street in Ireland, runs from Dunnes Stores at one end to the courthouse at the other and divides into Upper and Lower Main Sts. At the top of Upper Main St there is a Y-junction: High Rd veers left, while Ramelton Rd goes right and down to the bus station and the road out to Derry and Dublin.

The tourist office (☎ 21160), on the Derry road about 1.5km north of town, is geared towards the motorist and can be accessed only via the southbound lane. You could walk there from the roundabout where the buses stop, but it wouldn't be an enjoyable experience. It opens 9 am to 8 pm Monday to Saturday, and 10 am to 2 pm on Sunday, July and August; and 9 am to 5 pm on weekdays, September to June. In the town centre on Ramelton Rd, the excellent Chamber of Commerce Visitor Information Centre (☎ 24866) has lots of free literature and advice. It also has the *Pleasant Walks in Letterkenny* booklet that'll help you focus on the highlights. It opens 9 am to 5 pm on weekdays.

Along Main St are branches of the AIB, Bank of Ireland and Ulster Bank, all with ATMs. The post office is on Upper Main St almost opposite the Central Bar. Browse-A-While is a newsagent-bookshop on Upper Main St with a small selection of maps.

Things to See & Do

The Gothic-style **St Eunan's Cathedral** (1901) sits west of the centre on Sentry Hill Rd (take Church Lane from Main St) and contains much intricate Celtic carving.

The small, modern **Donegal County Museum** (☎ 24613), on High Rd past Manse Hostel, has a collection of local archaeological finds, including some interesting Iron Age stone heads and early-Christian material, upstairs.

Downstairs there are temporary displays, often on the local tweed-making and weaving industries, and some telling photos about the realities of life in 19th-century rural Ireland to counterbalance the rather rosy version on display upstairs. The museum is open from 11 am to 12.30 pm and 1 to 4.30 pm Tuesday to Friday, and from 1 to 4.30 pm on Saturday. Admission is free.

Some **salmon and trout** rivers and lakes surround Letterkenny. The Letterkenny Anglers Association is open to visitors; membership and permits are available from Brian McCormick's Sports and Leisure (☎ 27833), 56 Upper Main St.

Letterkenny Leisure Centre (☎ 25251), opposite the Manse Hostel, offers swimming costing £3/1.50 (families £7), including use of the sauna and steam room before 3 pm. A ticket valid for all the facilities in the evening costs £3.50/2.50.

Special Events

The Letterkenny Festival (☎ 27856) is a four-day international festival of music and dance held at the end of August. It features a variety of music, from Celtic rock to folk and jazz, and includes a crafts day and competitions.

Places to Stay

Hostels The *Manse Hostel (☎ 25238)*, registered with both the IHH and IHO, is on High Rd at the top of Upper Main St and has dorm beds costing £7, private rooms costing £8. Family rooms are also available. It's friendly, with lots of info on what to see and do locally, and opens year round. The small IHO *Arch Hostel (☎ 57255, Upper*

DONEGAL

Corkey) has six dorm beds costing £7.50 and opens May to October.

B&Bs & Hotels For B&B try the secluded *Covehill House* (☎ *21038)*, set back from Ramelton Rd near the new theatre and likely to be quiet. Singles/doubles cost £20/30. Near the Manse Hostel, the functional *Carmel's* (☎ *21332)*, above a newsagent's on High Rd, is better than it looks from the outside and offers B&B costing £15 per person. The central, 27-room *Gallagher's Hotel* (☎ *22066, 110 Upper Main St)* charges £30/50. If everything's full, modern *Hotel Clanree* (☎ *24369)*, on the outskirts as you approach from Derry, charges £30/50.

Places to Eat

For dinner, *Gallagher's Hotel* serves bar food (£4 to £8) till 9 pm. *Taj Mahal* (☎ *27554)*, upstairs on Main St, serves tandoori and Pakistani food, with main courses costing £6 to £10.

The best place for a pizza or pasta (starting at £4.50) is *Pat's on the Square* in Market Square. *Pat's Too*, opposite the AIB on Main St, sells part-cooked pizzas to take away as well as kebabs and sandwiches. Close to Pat's Too is *Central Bar*, which serves pub food. *Bakersville*, in Church Lane off Main St, is small but pleasant enough for coffee and snacks, or there's the *Quiet Moment* tearoom in Upper Main St for baps, salads and meals; Cajun spiced chicken costs £4.25. *Yellow Pepper*, also on Main St, opens for breakfast and has excellent sandwiches; in the evening main courses cost £7 to £11 and include a selection of vegetarian dishes.

Inside Courtyard Shopping Centre, on Main St opposite Market Square, *Courtyard Café* is a good coffee shop open at 8.30 am. *Galfee's Restaurant*, in the basement, has a few tables outside looking onto a large painting, so you can appreciate Donegal's scenery even when it's raining outside. It serves snacks during the day and in the evening becomes a full-blown restaurant.

Four Lanterns, with branches on Lower Main St and Ramelton Rd, serves standard fast food.

Entertainment

One of the better pubs for music is *Central Bar* (*Upper Main St)*. The emerald-green *Cottage Bar*, across the road, has music sessions on Thursday night. *Pulse* is a big disco on Ramelton Rd, while *Downtown Pub* (*Upper Main St)* occasionally hosts a disco at the weekend.

On Ramelton Rd there's a four-screen *cinema* (☎ *21976)*. A new theatre is being built nearby.

Getting There & Away

Letterkenny is a major bus transport hub for north-western Ireland. The bus station (☎ *22863)* is by the roundabout at the junction of Ramelton Rd and the Derry road.

Bus Éireann's (☎ *21309)* express bus No 32 runs from Dublin four times daily (three on Sunday) to Letterkenny via Omagh and Monaghan. The Derry to Galway bus No 64 stops at Letterkenny three times daily (twice on Sunday) before travelling on to Donegal, Bundoran, Sligo, Knock and Galway. The Derry to Cork express bus No 52, via Letterkenny, Sligo, Galway and Limerick, runs twice daily (once on Sunday). The daily service (bus No 69) from Derry to Westport via Donegal, Sligo and Ballina also stops in Letterkenny.

Anthony McGinley (☎ *48167)* runs a daily service from Letterkenny to Dublin (three on Friday). Derry-based Lough Swilly (☎ *22863)* runs services regularly from Derry to Dungloe, via Letterkenny and Dunfanaghy, as well as directly to Letterkenny.

John McGinley (☎ *35201)* buses run daily from Annagry to Dublin through Letterkenny and Monaghan. The Feda Ódonaill (☎ *075-48114)* bus from Crolly to Galway through Letterkenny continues to Donegal, Bundoran, Sligo and Galway.

Monday to Saturday, McGeehan Coaches (☎ *075-46150)* runs a Letterkenny to Glencolumbcille service.

Getting Around

A taxi can be ordered from O'Donnell Cabs (☎ *22444)*. In summer, you can hire bikes from Church Street Cycles (☎ *26204)*, near the cathedral, which is part of the Raleigh Rent-a-Bike scheme. Bikes cost £10/40 per day/week.

AROUND LETTERKENNY
Newmills Corn & Flax Mills

In the village of Newmills, 6km south-west of Letterkenny, the restored mills are open to the public. The visitor centre explains the role of corn and flax and how they were produced. There's a riverside walk to a two-room 19th-century scutcher's cottage and a village forge. The Dúchas-run mills (☎ 074-25115) open 10 am to 6.30 pm (last tour 5.45 pm) daily, mid-June to late September. Admission costs £2/1 (families £5).

Colmcille Heritage Centre

Colmcille (also known as Columba) was born in Gartan, 17km north-west of Letterkenny, and the heritage centre (☎ 074-37306), on the shore of Lough Gartan, is devoted to his life and times, with a lavish display on the production of illuminated manuscripts.

Gartan clay is associated with the birth of Colmcille. The story is that Colmcille's mother, on the run from pagans, haemorrhaged during childbirth and her blood changed the soil's colour from brown to pure white. Ever since, the clay has been regarded as a charm. The clay is found only on townland belonging to the O'Friel family, whose oldest son is the only one allowed to dig it up. Ask nicely and the staff may produce some from under the counter.

The centre opens 10.30 am to 6.30 pm on weekdays, and 1 to 6.30 pm on Sunday, Easter and early May to early October. Admission costs £2/1.

On the way to the heritage centre you'll also see signs to the ruins of **Colmcille's Abbey** and to the site of the **saint's birthplace**, marked by a cross erected by Cornelia Adair in 1911.

To get to the heritage centre, leave Letterkenny on the R250 road to Glenties and Ardara. A few kilometres out of town, turn right on the R251 to the village of Churchill. Alternatively, from Kilmacrennan on the N56 turn west and follow the signs.

Glebe House & Gallery

The early-19th-century Glebe House, on the shore of Lough Gartan close to the Colmcille Heritage Centre, was once a rectory, then a hotel, and was bought by the artist Derek Hill in 1953 for £1000. Derek Hill was born in England in 1916 and worked in Germany before travelling to Russia. He visited Armenia with the intrepid explorer Freya Stark and became interested in Islamic art.

Glebe House is worth visiting for its works of art alone, and a fascinating guided tour of the house takes about 40 minutes. Landseer, Pasmore, Hokusai, Picasso, Augustus John, Jack B Yeats and Kokoschka are all represented. The kitchen is full of paintings by the Tory Island artists, including a bird's-eye view of West Town by James Dixon (see the Tory Island section earlier in this chapter). The kitchen is done up in a wonderfully folksy style and there's some original William Morris wallpaper in several rooms. Don't miss the unusual bathroom with the forwards-flushing toilet. The gardens are also wonderful.

The Dúchas-operated house (☎ 074-37071) opens 11 am to 6.30 pm Saturday to Thursday, Easter and late May to September. Admission costs £2/1 (families £5).

Doon Well & Rock of Doon

During penal times it was believed that wells had curative properties, and some people still believe this to be true of Doon Well (Tobar a' Duin), judging from the bits of cloth left hanging on the nearby bushes. There are good views from the top of the Rock of Doon (Carraig a' Doon), which is where the O'Donnell kings were inaugurated.

To get here the most straightforwards route is to take the signposted turn-off from the N56 just north of Kilmacrennan (the well and rock are about 1.5km north of the village).

Lurgyvale Thatched Cottage

The flagstone-floored cottage (☎ 074-39216), next to the road bridge on the N56 in the village of Kilmacrennan, is filled

DONEGAL

with rural artefacts. The cottage is easily spotted because of the large number of old farming implements scattered about. Staff at this early-19th-century cottage dispense tea and scones with homemade jam in the kitchen for around £2. It opens 10 am to 7 pm daily, Easter to September. Admission costs £1/50p.

On Thursday evening from 8.30 pm, traditional-music sessions are held with dancing and singing. In summer there are demonstrations of traditional crafts on the first Sunday of the month.

Gartan Outdoor Education Centre

The centre (☎ 074-37032), 18km north-west of Letterkenny, is set in its own 35-hectare estate on the shores of Lough Gartan. It conducts a variety of courses in summer, such as rock climbing, sea canoeing, windsurfing and hill climbing. Courses are run for both adults and children, groups and individuals, and full details are available on request. Including hostel accommodation, a weekend multi-skill course for adults costs upwards of £80.

Lifford & Around

☎ 074 • pop 1360

About 22km south-east of Letterkenny, along the N14, is the small town of Lifford (Leifear). It was once the judicial capital of County Donegal, a position now held by Letterkenny.

Lifford Old Courthouse Visitor Centre

This fine 18th-century courthouse has been converted into a heritage centre (☎ 41733), looking at both the historic role of Donegal's Gaelic chieftains and at some of the cases tried in the court and their verdicts.

For those who can't tell their O'Neills from their O'Donnells, some of the information provided in the Clans Room can be pretty heavy going. Descend into the courtroom, though, and the stories of 'Napper' Tandy, 'Half-hanged' McNaughten and other 'criminals' are riveting, and it's amazing how often they ended up being transported to Australia! Descend more stairs

and you end up in the chilly cells where there are models of some of the prisoners you've already heard about. Now you hear their side of the story.

The courthouse opens 10 am to 6 pm Monday to Saturday, and 2 to 6 pm on Sunday, Easter to September. Admission costs £2.50/1.

Cavanacor House At Rossgier, 3km north of Lifford off the N14, Cavanacor House (☎ 41143) is an attractive 18th-century building, once inhabited by Magdalen Tasker, who was the great-great-great-grandmother of James Knox Polk, 11th president of the USA from 1845 to 1849. King James II is said to have dined beneath a sycamore in the front garden during the Siege of Derry in 1689. Three rooms in the house are open to visitors, although the gallery at the back housing the paintings and sculptures created by its current owners is probably more interesting.

Cavanacor opens noon to 6 pm Tuesday to Saturday, and 2 to 6 pm on Sunday, Easter to September. Admission costs £2.50/1.50.

Places to Stay The *Haw Lodge* (☎ 41397, *Sligo Rd*) opens February to December and charges £21/32 for B&B in singles/doubles with shared bathroom, or £24.50/36 for en suite rooms. *Hall Greene* (☎ 41318) opens year round and offers en suite rooms costing £23/36.

Getting There & Away Bus Éireann's (☎ 21309) express bus No 32 from Dublin to Letterkenny stops in Lifford. Local buses connect Lifford with Letterkenny, Ballybofey and Strabane.

North-Eastern Donegal

ROSGUILL PENINSULA

From **Carrigart** (Carraic Airt) it's a 15km journey round this small, beautiful, scenic peninsula along a road marked Atlantic

Drive. Carrigart itself has a lovely beach, which is relatively deserted because the camp site at **Downings** to the north draws the crowds. The best beach for swimming is **Trá na Rossan**, and the An Óige hostel nearby is an added attraction. On no account should you go swimming in Boveeghter or Mulroy Bay – both are unsafe.

There's plenty of social life at night in the Downings pubs, which are often packed with holidaymakers from the North staying at Casey's Caravan Park.

Places to Stay

Casey's Caravan Park (☎ 074-55376), open from April to September, has limited camping space; it's best to ring first and check, though it doesn't take bookings. It costs £10 to pitch a family tent, £8 for a small tent.

The An Óige *Trá na Rosann Hostel* (☎ 074-55374), east of the beach, opens Easter to September and costs £6.50/5. It's 6km from Downings and hitching is the best bet if you're without wheels.

In Carrigart, *Sonas* (☎ 074-55401) offers B&B in en suite singles/doubles costing £24.50/36. Nearby in Dunmore, *Hill House* (☎ 074-55221) offers rooms with shared bathroom costing £15 per person and en suite singles/doubles costing £23/32.

There's a little more choice in Downings: *Baymont* (☎ 074-55395) and *An Crosóg* (☎ 074-55498) both offer B&B costing upwards of £16 per person. The 20-room *Beach Hotel* (☎ 074-55303) costs £18 to £24 per person and opens April to October.

Places to Eat

Carrigart is best for food. *Tasty Bite* opens 9 am to 6 pm and serves meals such as fish and chips (£4.95). *North Star* serves bar food, and *Weavers Restaurant and Wine Bar* (☎ 074-55204) offers meals costing around £6.

Getting There & Around

A local bus connects Carrigart and Downings, but it's of limited use for visitors from elsewhere. You really do need your own transport for this area.

FANAD HEAD PENINSULA

The Fanad Head Peninsula is north-east of Letterkenny. On the western side, **Carrowkeel** (Kerrykeel on some maps) has an attractive location overlooking Mulroy Bay. Nearby is 19th-century **Knockalla Fort**, built to warn of any approaching French ships. There's also the **Kildooney More portal tomb** to visit, but that's about it. The small villages of Milford and Rosnakill have little for visitors, and there are no particularly good beaches.

The eastern side of the peninsula is more interesting than the western side, and both Rathmelton (also spelled Ramelton) and Rathmullan make good bases for a quiet break. Accommodation is relatively limited, so it's wise to book ahead.

The Lough Swilly (☎ 074-22863) bus leaves Letterkenny at 10.05 am and 6.05 pm and reaches Milford an hour later. From Milford it takes a further 10 minutes to Carrowkeel and 35 minutes to Portsalon on the eastern side, handy for the camp site.

Rathmelton
☎ 074 • pop 920

On the eastern side, the first town you come to is pretty but somewhat rundown Rathmelton (Ráth Mealtain). It was founded in the early 17th century by William Stewart and boasts some fine Georgian houses and stone warehouses. When the railway was routed to Letterkenny instead of Rathmelton, a hush descended on the town.

The National Irish Bank, on the Mall by the river, has a bureau de change. The post office is off the Mall on Castle St.

In Back Lane the old Meeting House dating from around 1680 houses the **Donegal Ancestry Family Research Centre** (☎ 51266). It opens 9 am to 4.30 pm Monday to Thursday, and 9 am to 4 pm on Friday. Follow the sign for the post office, then turn right at Mary's Bar; the centre is about 150m on the right. The ruined **Tullyaughnish Church**, on the hill, is also worth a visit because of the Romanesque carvings in the eastern wall, which were taken from a far older church on nearby Aughnish Island, on the river that runs through town.

Places to Stay & Eat At the quiet north-ern end of Rathmelton is *Crammond House* (☎ 51055), where singles/doubles costing upwards of £22.50/32 come with a warm welcome. About 1.5km from the town cen-tre on the Milford road, *Clooney House* (☎ 51125) charges £23/34.

Fish House is attractively placed in an old stone building by the river and serves tea and light meals from 10 am to 7 pm. For something more substantial *Mirabeau Steak House* (☎ 51138), also by the river, cooks gigantic steaks (starting at £6.50) with homemade sauces. The fish dishes (starting at £4.95) are good, and there's a small vegetarian selection.

Bridge Bar, on the other side of the river, has a seafood restaurant with main courses costing £10 to £12.

Getting There & Away Lough Swilly (☎ 22863) buses connect Rathmelton with Letterkenny (25 minutes) three times daily.

Rathmullan
☎ 074 • pop 530

Like Rathmelton, quiet Rathmullan (Ráth Maoláin) feels as if it has been bypassed by the modern age, although in the 16th to 18th centuries it was the scene of momentous events.

In 1587, Hugh O'Donnell, the 15-year-old heir to the powerful O'Donnell clan, was tricked into boarding a ship at Rath-mullan and taken to Dublin as prisoner. He escaped four years later on Christmas Eve and, after unsuccessful attempts at re-venge, died in Spain, aged only 30. In 1607, despairing of fighting the English, Hugh O'Neill, the earl of Tyrone, and Rory O'Donnell, the earl of Tyrconnel, boarded a ship in Rathmullan harbour and left Ireland for good. This decisive act, known as the Flight of the Earls, marked the effective end of Gaelic Ireland. In the aftermath of the earls' departure, large-scale confiscation of their estates took place, preparing for the Plantation of Ulster with settlers from Britain.

Wolfe Tone was captured in Rathmullan following the 1798 Rising.

Rathmullan Heritage Centre This small heritage centre (☎ 58229) focuses on the Flight of the Earls and will mainly appeal to those with a deep interest in Irish history. It's housed in an early-19th-century fort built by the British when fearing Napo-leon's intentions. It opens 9 am to 5 pm Fri-day, 10 am to 5 pm on Saturday, and 10 am to 3 pm on Sunday, Easter to September. Admission costs £1.50/75p. In lieu of a tourist office, the heritage centre can help with inquiries about local accommodation, sights in the surrounding area and so on.

The sandy area near the pier outside the centre is the only clean part of the town's beach, but there's a strong smell of fish from the quayside warehouse.

Rathmullan Priory This Carmelite friary was founded around 1508 by the Mac-Sweeneys, and it was still in use in 1595 when an English commander, George Bing-ham, raided the place and took off with the communion plate and priestly vestments. The fact that it looks so well preserved is due to Bishop Knox's renovation in 1618; he wanted to use it as his own residence. The earls left Ireland for ever in 1607 from just outside the priory.

Places to Stay & Eat The IHO *Bunnaton Hostel* (☎ 50122), in Glenvar, north-west of Rathmullan, offers dorm beds costing £7 and three private rooms costing £9 per per-son. It opens February to October.

Eileen Gallagher (☎ 58177, Pier Rd) has a couple of rooms costing £16 per person. *Water's Edge Inn* (☎ 58182), just south of town, offers B&B costing £27 per person, and most of the rooms have fine views of Lough Swilly.

Rathmullan has three hotels, all quite dif-ferent in appearance and style. The 10-room *Pier Hotel* (☎ 58178), originally a 19th-century coaching inn, charges £15 to £25 per person and is very much a family es-tablishment. It does bar food as well as full à la carte meals and there are lovely lake views. About 2km north of town, *Rathmul-lan House* (☎ 58188) is a swanky 20-room country house with its own indoor heated swimming pool and sauna; rooms cost £49.50 to £55 per person. The 15-room *Fort Royal* (☎ *58100)* has its own private beach and organises sporting activities; rooms cost £35 to £55 per person. Dinner at the three hotels costs around £20.

Beachcomber Bar, just up from Pier Hotel, serves pub food.

Getting There & Away The Lough Swilly (☎ 22863) bus from Letterkenny arrives in Rathmullan at 10.45 am and 6.45 pm en route to Milford, Carrowkeel and Portsalon (morning bus only).

Portsalon & Fanad Head
Portsalon (Port an tSalainn), once a popular holiday resort with Northern Irish, has little to offer except a long, golden, sandy beach that's safe for swimming. Here *Knockalla Caravan and Camping Park* (☎ *074-59108)* has tent sites costing £7. It's another 8km to Fanad Head, the best part of which is the scenic drive there.

INISHOWEN PENINSULA
The Inishowen (Inis Eoghain) Peninsula, with Lough Foyle to the east and Lough Swilly to the west, reaches out into the Atlantic and extends to Ireland's northernmost point: Malin Head. The landscape is typically Donegal: rugged, desolate and mountainous. Ancient sites abound, but there are also some wonderful beaches and plenty of places where travellers can go off alone. Tourist offices in Donegal, Letterkenny and Derry have free leaflets about walks in the Inishowen area, complete with maps.

The peninsula has been designated a European Special Area of Conservation and is home to over 100 species of migrating and indigenous birdlife.

The route below follows the road out of Derry up the coast of Lough Foyle to Moville and then north-west to Malin Head before travelling down the western side to Buncrana. If you're coming from Donegal the peninsula could be approached from the Lough Swilly side by turning off for Buncrana on the N13 road from Letterkenny to Derry. Leaving from Derry, though, the first

village in the Republic is Muff. A scenic drive, the **Inis Eoghain 100**, is clearly signposted round the peninsula.

Muff to Moville
The tiny village of Muff (Mugh), only 8km north of Derry, has pubs offering food and music and a fair share of Northern visitors. North-east of Muff along the coast there are larger pubs catering to the same market. **Horse riding** is available at *Lenamore Stables* (☎ *077-84022)*, as are accommodation packages.

North of Muff at **Quigley's Point** (Rinn Mic Coigus) there are good views across Lough Foyle to County Derry

At **Redcastle**, south of Moville, there's a bunch of B&Bs and a hotel. Next to the village post office, *Fernbank* (☎ *077-83032)* offers B&B costing upwards of £16 per person. Overlooking Lough Foyle, the lovely 31-room *Redcastle Country Hotel* (☎ *077-82073)* has all the facilities of a big hotel, including a nine-hole golf course. Singles/doubles cost £65/110 in the high season. It serves substantial meals during the day and in the evening offers a four-course set dinner costing £14.

Getting There & Away Lough Swilly (☎ 028-71 262017, 074-22863) runs up to nine buses daily from Derry to Carndonagh via Muff, with almost as many buses to Shrove that also pass through Muff. There's no Sunday service on either route. Worth considering is Lough Swilly's eight-day Runabout unlimited-travel pass costing £18/9 (students £12).

Moville & Around
☎ 077 • pop 1390
Now a sleepy seaside town, Moville (Bun an Phobaill) was once a busy port where emigrants set sail for America. The **coastal walkway** from Moville to Greencastle takes in the stretch of coast where the steamers used to moor. Main St has several banks with ATMs and the post office.

Cooley Cross & Skull House By the gate of the Cooley gravehouse is a 3m-high

DONEGAL

INISHOWEN PENINSULA

cross, unusual because of the ringhole in its head through which the hands of negotiating parties are said to have clasped to seal an agreement. In the graveyard the small Skull House still contains some old bones. It may be associated with St Finian, the monk who accused Colmcille of plagiarising one of his manuscripts in the 6th century (see the boxed text 'The Battle of the Book' in the Counties Mayo & Sligo chapter). He lived in a monastery here that was founded by St Patrick and survived into the 12th century.

Approaching Moville from the south,

look out for a turning on the left (if you pass a church, you've gone too far) that has a sign on the corner for the Cooley Pitch and Putt. The graveyard is just over 1km up this road on the right.

Special Events The Foyle Oyster Festival is held in late September and its office (☎ 82042) is on Main St.

Places to Stay The IHH *Moville Holiday Hostel* (☎ *82378, Malin Rd*) charges £6.50 for dorm beds, £12 per person in private rooms. There are also a few B&Bs in and around Moville; for example, *Gulladuff House* (☎ *82378, Malin Rd*) charges upwards of £20/27 in singles/doubles, while *Barron's Café* (☎ *82472, Main St*) charges upwards of £14 per person. On the road out of town, *Iona House* (☎ *82173*) is a small, cosy place charging £20 per person. Off the bottom of Main St, the large 51-room *McNamara's Hotel* (☎ *82010*) charges £32 per person.

Places to Eat The *Barron's Café* and *McNamara's Hotel* are the best bets. Barron's Café serves an all-day breakfast costing £3.85, while set dinner at the latter costs £13. *Point* serves food until 11 pm (10 pm on Sunday).

Getting There & Away Lough Swilly (☎ 028-71 262017, 074-22863) runs up to four buses daily Monday to Saturday to Moville from Derry.

Greencastle
☎ 077 • pop 590
The popular resort village of Greencastle (An Cáisleán Nua), north of Moville, gets its name from the castle built in 1305 by Richard de Burgo, known as the Red Earl of Ulster because of his florid complexion. The Green Castle functioned as a supply base for English armies in Scotland and for this reason was attacked by the Scots under Robert Bruce in the 1320s. In 1555 the castle was demolished, and little of it survives.

Greencastle Fort (☎ *81279*) is inside a Napoleonic fort. Pub food is served all day in the Master Gunners' Bar, or you can dine in the Officers' Mess Bar, where a set dinner costs £18. *Kealy's Seafood Bar*, near the harbour, serves freshly caught seafood.

Five Lough Swilly (☎ 028-71 262017, 074-22863) buses travel daily, Monday to Saturday, between Derry and Shrove, passing through Greencastle.

Inishowen Head
A right turn outside Greencastle leads to Shrove; a sign indicating Inishowen Head is 1km along this road. It's possible to drive or cycle part of the way, but it's also an easy

walk to the headland, from where you can see the Antrim coast as far as the Giant's Causeway on a clear day. A more demanding walk continues to the sandy beach of **Kinnagoe Bay**. At Shrove, where the road left goes to the headland, a right turn goes to Dunagree Point and back to Greencastle, but this loop has little to recommend it.

Carndonagh
☎ 077 • pop 1600
Carndonagh (Cardomhnach), which is surrounded by hills on three sides, is a busy commercial centre serving the local farming community.

The Inishowen Tourism office (☎ 74933) is on Chapel St south-west of the main square at the top of Bridge St. It opens from 9.30 am to 5.30 pm on weekdays, September to May; and 9.30 am to 7 pm on weekdays, 10 am to 6 pm on Saturday, and noon to 6 pm on Sunday, June to August. It also sells fishing licences for all of Donegal. There are three banks on the main square and the AIB has an ATM; the post office is near the top of Bridge St.

Things to See On Bridge St in a small former Wesleyan chapel down from the post office, a collection of local folk items are displayed in the renovated **Inishowen Heritage Centre and Folk Museum**. It opens 1 to 5 pm Monday to Saturday, July and August.

At the Buncrana end of Carndonagh, the 7th-century **Donagh Cross** has been erected against the wall of an Anglican church. Next to the cross are two small pillars, one said to show a man with a sword and shield, possibly Goliath, next to David and his harp. In the graveyard there's a pillar with a carved marigold on a stem. On the other side of the stone there's a crucifixion scene.

Places to Stay & Eat The *Radharc na Coille* (☎ *74471*), at Teirnaleague, not far from the Donagh Cross, costs upwards of £15/28 for B&B in singles/doubles and opens April to October.

In the main square *Trawbreaga Bay House* is good for snacks and meals and

DONEGAL

serves an all-day breakfast costing £2.95. For an evening meal head down Malin Rd to *Corncrake Restaurant* (☎ 74534), where cod baked in a parmesan crust costs £10.50. *Quiet Lady* opposite serves excellent-value meals all day; pork chops with vegetables costs £2.95.

If you're off to Malin Head for the day or going on to the camp site at Clonmany, stock up with victuals at the Centra supermarket in Malin Rd.

Getting There & Away A Lough Swilly (☎ 028-71 262017, 074-22863) bus leaves Buncrana for Carndonagh at 8.40 am on weekdays, plus at 1 and 5.45 pm on Monday and Thursday and at 1.45 and 6.15 pm on Friday. On Saturday the buses go at 12.15, 2.15 and 6.15 pm. On weekdays they return from Carndonagh at 7.25 and 10 am and 4 pm. They also run a bus between Derry and Malin Head via Carndonagh three times weekly.

North West Busways (☎ 82619) operates a service between Letterkenny and Moville via Buncrana and Carndonagh.

Culdaff & Around
☎ 077

East of Carndonagh there are several ancient sites surrounding the secluded village of Culdaff (Cúil Dabhcha), which can be visited from the main Moville to Carndonagh road (R238). Culdaff itself has a beach that's good for **swimming** and is a popular **sea-angling** centre.

Clonca Church & Cross The carved lintel over the door of this 17th-century building is thought to come from an earlier church. In the north-eastern corner, the rather interesting tombstone was erected by one Magnus MacOrristin and has a sword and hurling stick carved on it. The remains of the cross show the miracle of the loaves and fishes on the eastern face and geometric designs on the sides.

Look for the turn-off to Culdaff, on the right if coming from Moville, on the left after about 6km if coming from Carndonagh. The Clonca Church and Cross are

1.5km on the right behind a couple of farm buildings.

Bocan Stone Circle There are better stone circles in Ireland than this one, which has only a few of some 30 original stones left, but the surrounding views help to conjure up the kind of significance the place must have held some 3000 years ago.

From Clonca Church, continue along the road until you reach a T-junction with a modern church and a cemetery facing you. Turn right here and after about half a kilometre turn left (no sign). The stone circle is inside the first heather-covered field on the left.

Carrowmore High Crosses Like the Bocan Stone Circle, these high crosses may prove a little disappointing to some. One is basically a decorated slab showing Christ and an angel, while on the other side of the road there is a taller cross with stumpy arms.

From Bocan Stone Circle and Clonca Church, retrace the route back to the main Carndonagh to Moville road and turn left, then almost immediately right. The sign to the crosses points in the wrong direction – ignore it.

Places to Stay & Eat Culdaff has a number of B&Bs, including *Ceecliff House* (☎ 79159), which opens year round and offers singles/doubles costing upwards of £22.50/32; dinner is an extra £12. The popular *McGrory's Bar* (☎ 79104) offers B&B costing upwards of £15 per person and serves good pub grub.

Entertainment At *McGrory's Bar* there are regular traditional-music sessions, and the attached *Mac's Backroom Bar* often attracts big-name musicians.

Malin Head

At the top of Inishowen Peninsula is Malin Head (Cionn Mhálanna), a familiar name to listeners of radio weather forecasts throughout the island. The northernmost point of Malin Head and of Ireland is called Banba's

Crown (Fíorcheann Éireann). The tower on the cliffs was built in 1805 by the British admiralty and later used as a Lloyds signal station. The ugly concrete huts were used by the Irish army in WWII as lookout posts.

Above **Ballyhillion Beach** nearby, the *Cottage* serves tea and snacks daily, June to September.

The pretty Plantation village of **Malin** (Málainn), 14km south of Malin Head, is centred on a triangular green. An interesting circular walk from the village green takes in a local hill with terrific views, as well as Lagg Presbyterian Church, the oldest church still in use on the peninsula. Children will love the massive sand dunes by the church.

Places to Stay There are two IHO hostels at Malin Head: the clean, friendly *Malin Head Hostel* (☎ 077-70309), open March to October, and the larger *Sandrock Holiday Hostel* (☎ 077-70289), open year round. Both charge £6.50 for dorm beds. Malin Head Hostel also has private rooms costing £8.50 per person.

There are also a few B&Bs, including Mrs Doyle's *Barraicin* (☎ 077-70184), charging upwards of £18/30 for singles/doubles.

In Malin, the small, 12-room *Malin Hotel* (☎ 077-70645) provides en suite rooms costing £25 to £35 per person.

Getting There & Away The best way to approach Malin Head is by the R238/242 from Carndonagh, rather than up the eastern side from Culdaff. Lough Swilly (☎ 028-7126 2017 in Derry, 074-22863 in Letterkenny) operates a bus which runs on Monday, Wednesday and Friday at 11 am between Derry and Malin Head via Carndonagh; on the same days a bus leaves Carndonagh at 3 pm for Malin Head. There are three buses from Derry to Malin Head on Saturday.

Ballyliffin & Clonmany
☎ 077

The small resort of Ballyliffin (Baile Lifin) attracts more Irish than overseas visitors. There's plenty of accommodation in the area. Both villages have post offices but no banks.

About 1km north of Ballyliffin is the lovely expanse of **Pollan Bay Beach**; unfortunately, it's not safe for swimming. A walk to the north of the beach brings you to the ruins of **Carrickbrackey Castle** (also spelt Carrickabraghy), dating from the 16th century. To reach the beach, turn down the road in Ballyliffin by the thatched cottage and Atlantic Ballroom. There's one sign on the road, but it's visible only from the Clonmany side.

The other beach is at **Tullagh Bay**, immediately behind the camp site. It's great for an exhilarating walk, but the current can be strong and swimming isn't recommended when the tide is going out.

Places to Stay & Eat The *Tullagh Bay Camping and Caravan Park* (☎ 76289) is near the beach at Tullagh Bay. There are legions of B&Bs on the 2km stretch of road between Ballyliffin and Clonmany, including *Ard Donn House* (☎ 76156), open year round and charging £20/36 for singles/doubles, and *Swilly View* (☎ 76137), open May to September and charging £13.50 per person.

The 13-room *Ballyliffin Hotel* (☎ 76101), near the post office, charges £35/60; bar food is available as well as a five-course gourmet dinner on Thursday costing £9 per person. The 12-room *Strand Hotel* (☎ 76017) costs £40/60, offers bar food and serves a special £18 dinner for two on Wednesday.

Entertainment Most pubs and hotels have music sessions in summer. In Clonmany, *McFeeley's* and *McCarron's Bar* are popular pubs, and *Mackey's Tavern*, in Tullagh Bay, has lively music sessions at the weekend.

Getting There & Away Lough Swilly (☎ 028-71 262017, 074-22863) buses run between Clonmany and Carndonagh: see the Carndonagh section earlier in this chapter for times – buses leave/reach Clonmany 20 minutes earlier/later.

DONEGAL

Clonmany to Buncrana

There are two routes from Clonmany to Buncrana: the scenic coastal road via the Gap of Mamore and Dunree Head, or the speedier inland road (R238). The **Gap of Mamore** (262m) descends dramatically between Mamore Hill and the Urris Hills into a valley where the road follows the River Owenerk most of the way to Dunree.

The main reason to pause in Dunree (An Dún Riabhach) is to visit the interesting **Fort Dunree Military Museum** (☎ 074-24613), on a windswept, rocky headland overlooking Lough Swilly. In 1798 Wolfe Tone, with the help of the French, planned to arrive at Lough Swilly and march on Derry. The British constructed six forts to guard the lough and the museum tells the whole story. The museum opens 10 am to 6 pm Monday to Saturday, and noon to 6 pm on Sunday, June to September. Admission costs £2/1. You can easily see fulmar nesting on the rocks below the fort.

Buncrana

☎ 077 • pop 3120

After Bundoran this must be the most popular resort in Donegal for holidaymakers from the North, but unlike Bundoran it contrives to suggest there's life beyond tourism. In fact, Fruit of the Loom has two knitting mills in Buncrana (Bun Cranncha), though they remain only because of Irish-government inducements offered after the company threatened to decamp to Asia. The resort has a long sandy beach on the shore of Lough Swilly that's safe for swimming, all the pubs you could hope for and several places of interest to while away your spare hours.

Ulster Bank, on Upper Main St, and the AIB and Bank of Ireland on Lower Main St, have ATMs and bureaux de change. The post office is on Upper Main St. Maginn Laundrette, on Maginn Ave off Main St, opens 8.30 am to 7 pm Monday to Saturday, but isn't self-service.

Tullyarvan Mill This community-run exhibition (☎ 61613), craft shop and café is about 1km north of town and well worth a visit. The exhibition is devoted to the restoration of the mill, local history, flora and fauna, and is attractively presented. The place is also worth visiting for its lively traditional-music evenings that take place regularly in summer.

The centre opens 10 am to 5 pm on weekdays, May to September. Admission to the exhibition is free.

To find the place, head north out of town on the R238 and follow the signs.

O'Docherty's Keep At the northern end of the seafront an early-18th-century, six-arched bridge leads to a tower house built by the O'Dochertys, the local chiefs, in 1430. It was burned by the English and then rebuilt for their own use. The big house nearby was built in 1718 by John Vaughan, who also constructed the bridge.

Places to Stay There's no shortage of B&Bs around town, but they can fill up quickly during August. The most central is *Town Clock Guest House* (☎ 62146, 6 Upper Main St), which is run separately from the downstairs restaurant. Clean, spacious, en suite rooms cost £18 per person. *Golan View* (☎ 62644), signposted about 450m east off Main St, charges £20/32 for singles/doubles.

Lake of Shadows Hotel (☎ 61902), in Grianán Park, costs £30/46 in the high season. To get there head down Church St from Main St towards the bay.

Places to Eat At the Clonmany end of town (turn right at the top of Main St), *Roadside Café* opens for lunch, and a takeaway service is also available. The café at the *Tullyarvan Mill* serves reasonably priced cakes and drinks. However, the best place in terms of choice is probably *Ubiquitous* (☎ 62530, 47 Upper Main St), a restaurant and bar complete with jukebox and main courses costing £9 to £12.

Across the road is *Wing Tai House* (40 Upper Main St), a Chinese restaurant that serves chips with almost everything. *Four Lanterns*, next door, dishes up fast food. *Town Clock* (6 Upper Main St) serves good meals all day; a three-course Sunday lunch costs £6.95.

Entertainment The main entertainment is found, unsurprisingly, in the town's many pubs along Main St. *Atlantic Bar* can be relied on for live music at the weekend, as can *Excelsior Bar*. *O'Flaherty's* has a large TV screen for watching sports. For somewhere quiet and relaxing there's *Cottage Bar* on Lower Main St. On Mary's Rd off the northern end of Main St there's a one-screen *cinema* (with bingo from 9 pm on Friday night).

Getting There & Around From Buncrana, Lough Swilly (☎ 028-71 262017, 074-22863) buses run daily from here to Derry and Carndonagh. Taxis are available from Roadside Café (☎ 61366) or Crana Taxis (☎ 62200), on Main St opposite Market Square.

South of Buncrana
Fahan A monastery was founded in Fahan by St Colmcille in the 6th century, and the **St Mura Cross** stone slab in the graveyard beside the Anglican church has been dated to the century after. Each face is decorated with a cross, and the Greek inscription, which isn't easily made out, is the only one known from this early-Christian period.

Grianán of Aileách This impressive stone fort atop Grianán Hill, 18km south of Buncrana and signposted off the N13, offers panoramic views of the surrounding countryside: Swilly and Foyle Loughs, Inch Island and distant Derry. The walls are 4m thick and enclose an area 23m in diameter. The fort may have existed at least 2000 years ago, but the site has pagan associations that go back much further. Between the 5th and 12th centuries it was the seat of the O'Neills before being demolished by Murtogh O'Brien, king of Munster. You

might be wondering how a fort that was demolished 800 years ago could look so complete – well, between 1874 and 1878 an amateur archaeologist from Derry reconstructed the fort, and this is mostly what you see today.

The attractive, circular **Burt Church** at the foot of the hill was modelled on the fort by Derry architect Liam McCormack and was built between 1965 and 1967.

Grianán of Aileách Visitor Centre The 19th-century church of Christchurch at Burt, on the N13 near the turn-off to the fort, houses displays on the hill fort and on the church's history. There's a life-size model of Muirchertach na gCochall Craicinn, a 10th-century ancestor of the O'Neills and king of Aileách from 938 to 943. In 942 he went on an extended tour of Ireland, recorded in verse by Cormacan Eigean. There are also models of members of Christchurch's Victorian congregation and information about the local flora and fauna. The centre (☎ 077-68512) opens from 10 am to 6 pm daily, June to August; and noon to 6 pm daily, September to May. Admission costs £2/1.10.

The restaurant here has a lot of character – the bar counter is created out of a Boer War memorial slab, for example – and stays open until 10 pm. It serves snacks during the day and has an à la carte menu in the evening with plenty of choices, including several vegetarian options.

Inch Island Few tourists make it to Inch Island, connected to the mainland by a causeway, but it does have plenty of **birdlife** in its western wetlands, an old **Napoleonic fort** open to the public, and **O'Dochartaigh Genealogy Centre** (☎ 077-60488) open 9 am to 6 pm on weekdays. *O'Doherty's* (☎ *077-60488*), to the right of the pier just past the sign to the beach, charges £16 per person for B&B and opens year round.

DONEGAL

Counties Meath & Louth

Heading north from Dublin along the coast takes you through Counties Meath and Louth before crossing the border with Northern Ireland into County Down. This low, coastal landscape is a contrast to the hilly country south of the capital, rising only slightly inland to the plain known in folklore as Murtheimne, where many events mentioned in the Iron Age saga *Táin Bó Cúailnge* (*Cattle Raid of Cooley*) took place. The epic's dramatic climax occurred on Louth's beautiful Cooley Peninsula, and many places there owe their names to the legendary heroes and battles of that time. And in Meath and Louth lie some of the most remarkable legacies of the ancient Irish people – the tombs of Newgrange and Loughcrew – as well as the fine monasteries at Monasterboice, Mellifont and Kells, built by early Irish Christians.

It would be wrong, however, to assume that the verdant, settled farmland of these two counties is firmly rooted in the past. Modern Meath is one of Ireland's best examples of the rural success of the Celtic Tige. Older farming traditions have blended well with a newer, more urbane outlook, which seeks to capitalise on opportunities in tourism and industry. Louth has two major industrial towns in Dundalk and Drogheda, and even in the smaller towns and villages a new thinking has emerged – one that pays homage to the more traditional past but is keen to get on with the future.

County Meath

Meath (An Mhí), Dublin's immediate neighbour to the north and north-west, has long been one of Ireland's leading farming counties, a plain of extremely rich soil stretching north to the lakes of Cavan and Monaghan and west before running into the bleak Bog of Allen. Among the huge fields are the solid houses of Meath's former settlers and today's prosperous farmers – many

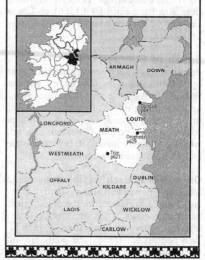

Highlights

- Discover the prehistoric remains at Newgrange and Knowth, older than the great pyramids of Egypt
- Track the remains of medieval Trim
- Explore the Hill of Tara, seat of power of the ancient high kings of Ireland
- Visit Mellifont Abbey and admire the high crosses at Monasterboice
- Circumnavigate the legend-soaked Cooley Peninsula
- Eat oysters in Carlingford

of whom are even wealthier since EU farming policies started offering subsidies for letting land lie fallow.

For a large county, Meath has surprisingly few major settlements. Navan, Trim and Kells are no more than medium-sized towns, while places such as Ashbourne, Dunshaughlin and Dunboyne on the southern fringe have become commuter suburbs

606

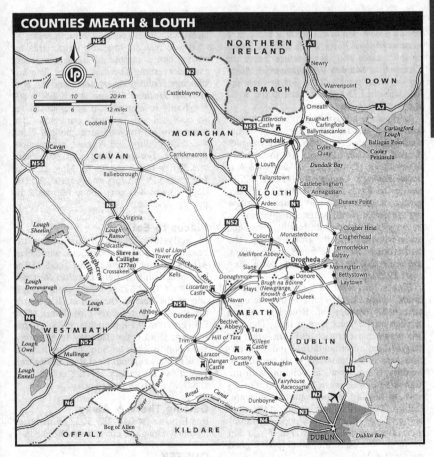

COUNTIES MEATH & LOUTH

of Dublin. The county's principal attractions are its ancient sites, and the isolated hills of Tara and Slane have immense historical significance. Also be sure to visit Butterstream Gardens in Trim, which are some of the finest in Ireland.

HISTORY

Meath's rich soil, laid down during the last Ice Age, attracted settlers as early as 8000 BC. They worked their way up the banks of the River Boyne transforming the landscape from forest to farmland. Brugh na Bóinne, an extensive prehistoric necropolis dating from around 3000 BC, lies on a meandering section of the Boyne between Drogheda and Slane. There's a group of smaller passage graves in the Loughcrew Hills near Oldcastle.

For 1000 years the Hill of Tara in Meath was the seat of power for Irish high kings, until the arrival of St Patrick in the 5th century. Later, Kells became one of the most important and creative monastic settlements in Ireland and lent its name to the famed *Book of Kells*, a 9th-century illuminated manuscript now displayed in Trinity College, Dublin.

THE COAST

Meath's mere 10km of coastline includes a number of small resorts with wide expanses of sand dunes and safe beaches. From the Elizabethan **Maiden Watchtower** in Mornington at the mouth of the Boyne there are fine views of Drogheda, 5km to the west, and the Boyne Estuary.

Laytown is a busy little place with golf, tennis and good windsurfing. It hosts annual horse races on the beach in mid-August. Outside Laytown, on the road to Julianstown (the R150), is **Sonairte National Ecology Centre** (☎ 041-982 7572), beside the River Nanny. It has an organic garden, a nature trail and exhibits displaying the use of wind, water and solar power. In the gift shop you can buy its own wine made from organically grown grapes. The centre opens 10 am to 5 pm on weekdays, and noon to 6 pm on Saturday. Admission costs £2/50p.

Barely 1km north of Laytown is **Bettystown**, whose claim to fame is that the magnificent 8th-century Tara Brooch was found in a box on the beach here in 1850. The only link between the brooch and Tara is that the magnificent ornamentation and the preciousness of its materials seem to indicate wealthy, if not royal, association with the high kings, who were based in Tara. It's now on display in the National Museum, Dublin. There is a long strand on the edge of the village which is very popular in summer, affording long walks and, if you can overcome the pollution, some pretty good swimming.

Both Laytown and Bettystown are popular holiday destinations for Dubliners and people from Drogheda and Dundalk.

Places to Stay

In Laytown, *Ardilaun* (☎ 041-982 7033, 41 Beach Park), near the beach, has singles/doubles costing £16.50/35, or £18.50/39 with bathroom. It opens April to September. *Tara Guesthouse* (☎ 041-982 7239) overlooks the beach and costs £15 per person. Breakfast is extra. It also serves dinner costing £10.

Hotel Neptune (☎ 041-982 7107) in Bettystown is an ordinary, medium-priced hotel with B&B costing £30 per person.

If you plan on lingering in the area for more than a couple of days you might consider renting a holiday cottage. The *Anchorage Holiday Apartments* and the *Bettystown Holiday Village* (☎ 01-660 1404 for both) in Bettystown have attractive, modern and well-equipped bungalows that sleep between five and seven people. For a weekend in July and August, a bungalow costs £200. For week-long stays, prices start at £200 from September to May, £250 in June, and £390 in July and August. A £100 deposit (which is part of the fee) must be paid in advance.

Places to Eat

In Bettystown, *Annabel Lee's* near the beach serves coffees and snacks, while *Fast Alfie's* nearby produces fast food of the burger-and-chips variety. *Bacchus Restaurant* (☎ 041-982 8251), on the main road, is one of the best in the region. It's beside the shore, and the early-bird dinner (6 to 7.30 pm) costs £14; thereafter it's à la carte. It opens from 6 pm Tuesday to Saturday, and noon to 7 pm on Sunday. You have to book at the weekend. Next door is *Tea and Talent*, an art gallery serving coffee, teas and light meals during the day.

Getting There & Away

Bus Éireann (☎ 041-983 5023) runs buses regularly along the coast from Drogheda.

DULEEK

☎ 041 • pop 1731

Duleek claims to have had Ireland's first stone church, and the town's name comes from *damh liag* (stone house). No trace of the church remains, however. The church's founder was the omnipresent St Patrick (wasn't he a busy man!), and it was built by his disciple St Ciarán sometime around 450. On its way to Armagh for interment, Brian Ború's body lay in state here after his death in 1014 at the Battle of Clontarf, where the Vikings were defeated. After the Battle of the Boyne in 1690, the defeated Jacobite forces retreated to Duleek while their

Battle of the Boyne

On 1 July 1690, the forces of the Catholic James II were defeated by those of the Protestant William III of Orange at the Battle of the Boyne. It was the decisive battle of the War of English Succession, confirming a Protestant monarch. The victory is still celebrated by Protestants in Northern Ireland as the Glorious Twelfth – the date having been adjusted in 1752 when the Gregorian calendar was adopted. (For more information see The Battle of the Boyne in the History section of the Facts about Ireland chapter.)

The battle site itself is just green fields. Nevertheless, a visit may give some understanding of the forces that shaped Ireland then and now. The site is near Oldbridge, 4km west of Drogheda, and is clearly marked by a huge orange billboard. A trail leads to a slight rise overlooking the battlefield. Before the battle, William's army camped just west of Oldbridge in what is now Townley Hall Demesne and Forest Park. The Jacobite camp was stretched out along the slopes of Donore Hill, 4km south of Oldbridge. James' command post was near the ruined church on the summit.

On 1 July, William's men crossed the river near Slane and Oldbridge and, despite the death of the able Marshal Schomberg in an Irish cavalry charge (an obelisk at the base of the bridge marks the spot), they outflanked James' forces and, in the face of brave resistance, routed them. The vanquished retreated to Donore and Duleek, where they spent the night, and then to the Shannon and Dublin.

James himself fled south to Dublin and then to Waterford, from where he crossed back to France and ignominious exile. Remnants of the Catholic forces regrouped and fought on for another year, but symbolically and politically the struggle was over.

NICKY CAVEN

William of Orange, victor of the Battle of the Boyne

leader, James, disappeared off to Dublin and then on to France.

St Mary's Priory and tower ruins date from the 12th century and contain a number of excellent effigies and tombstones, while outside there is a 10th-century high cross. The site was abandoned after Henry VIII's dissolution of the monasteries in 1537. The town square of Duleek has a **wayside cross**, erected in 1601 by Lady Jennet Dowdall in memory of her husband, William Bathe, and herself.

Annesbrook House (☎ 982 3293), open March to September, a comfortable country house surrounded by extensive wooded grounds 9km south of Duleek, offers rather expensive singles/doubles costing £35/55.

The house is a 17th-century building, but the Georgian additions date from a visit paid to Annesbrook by George IV in 1821: the owners felt the entrance wasn't grand enough and quickly added the portico.

There are a couple of pubs in the centre serving lunch, including *Greyhound Inn* on Main St.

BRUGH NA BÓINNE

There was extensive settlement along the Boyne Valley in prehistoric times, and the necropolis known as Brugh (or Brú) na Bóinne (Boyne Palace) was built in the area. This consists of many different sites, the three principal ones being Newgrange, Knowth and Dowth. They were the largest artificial structures in Ireland until the construction of the Anglo-Norman castles.

Over the centuries these tombs decayed, were covered by grass and trees and were plundered by everybody from Vikings to Victorian treasure hunters, whose carved initials can be seen on the great stones of Newgrange. The countryside around them is littered with countless other ancient mounds (or tumuli) and standing stones.

Newgrange

Newgrange is a huge, flattened, grass-covered mound about 80m in diameter and 13m high. The mound covers the finest Stone Age passage tomb in Ireland and is one of the most remarkable prehistoric sites in Europe. It dates from around 3200 BC, predating the great pyramids of Egypt by some six centuries. The purpose for which it was constructed remains uncertain. It may have been a burial place for kings or a centre for ritual – although the alignment with the sun at the time of the winter solstice might also suggest it was designed to act as a calendar.

The name derives from 'new granary' (the tomb did in fact serve as a repository for wheat and grain at one stage), although a belief more popular in the area is that it comes from the Irish for 'Cave of Gráinne', a reference to a Celtic myth taught to every Irish schoolchild: that of *The Pursuit of Diarmuid and Gráinne*, a story that tells of the illicit love between the wife of Fionn McCumhaill (or Finn McCool), leader of the Fianna, and one of his most trusted lieutenants. When Diarmuid was fatally wounded, his body was brought to Newgrange by the god Aengus in a vain attempt to save him, and the despairing Gráinne followed him into the cave, where she remained long after he died. This suspiciously Arthurian legend (for Diarmuid and Gráinne read Lancelot and Guenevere) is undoubtedly untrue, but it's still a pretty good story. Newgrange also played another role in Celtic mythology, serving as the site where the hero Cúchulainn was conceived.

Over the centuries, Newgrange, like Dowth and Knowth, deteriorated and was even quarried at one stage. There was a standing stone on the summit until the 17th century. The site was extensively restored in 1962 and again in 1975.

A superbly carved kerbstone with double and triple spirals guards the tomb's main entrance. The front façade has been reconstructed so that tourists don't have to clamber in over it. Above the entrance is a slit or roof box, which lets light in. Another beautifully decorated kerbstone stands at the exact opposite side of the mound. Some experts say that a ring of standing stones encircled the mound, forming a Great Circle about 100m in diameter, but only 12 of these stones remain – with traces of some others below ground level.

Holding the whole structure together are the 97 boulders of the kerb ring, designed to stop the mound from collapsing outwards. Eleven of these are decorated with motifs similar to those on the main entrance stone, although only three of these have extensive carvings.

The white quartzite was originally obtained from Wicklow, 80km to the south, and there is also some granite from the Mourne Mountains in Northern Ireland. Over 200,000 tonnes of earth and stone also went into the mound.

You can walk down the narrow 19m passage, lined with 43 stone uprights, some of them engraved, which leads into the tomb chamber, about one-third of the way into the colossal mound. The chamber has three recesses, and in these are large basin stones that held cremated human bones. Along with the remains would have been funeral offerings of beads and pendants, but these must have been stolen long before the archaeologists arrived.

Above, the massive stones support a 6m-high corbel-vaulted roof. A complex drainage system means that not a drop of water has penetrated the interior in 40 centuries.

At 8.20 am during the winter solstice (19 to 23 December), the rising sun's rays shine through the slit above the entrance, creep slowly down the long passage and illuminate the tomb chamber for 17 minutes.

There is little doubt that witnessing this is one of the country's most memorable, even mystical, experiences.

However, places to experience this annual event are booked up well into the next century, and the waiting list is now closed. However, for the legions of daily visitors – Newgrange is Ireland's most visited site – there is a simulated winter sunrise for every group taken into the mound.

A couple of things puzzled the archaeologists when studying the phenomenon. The light comes all the way down the passageway a few minutes after sunrise, not at the precise moment, and surprisingly it stops short of illuminating the centre of the back wall. Recent studies by cosmic physicists have found that the earth's position has shifted: when the mound was built, the sunlight would have illuminated the whole chamber precisely at sunrise. What is also puzzling is the fact that the tomb's builders were seemingly capable of complex mathematical calculations, and had instruments that, in effect, were more sophisticated than those available to the pioneers of mathematics, the Greeks. If this was the case, why then is there such scant evidence throughout the country of their brilliance?

In the past, visitors could go directly to Newgrange or Knowth for guided tours, but now they must assemble at **Brú na Bóinne Visitor Centre** (☎ 041-982 4488), south of the River Boyne and 2km west of Donore, from where they will cross the footbridge over the Boyne and be bused to the sites. Tours of Newgrange and the centre take place 9.30 am to 7 pm (6.30 pm in May) daily, May to mid-September; 10 am to 4.30 pm daily, mid-September to October; and 10 am to 5 pm daily, March and April. The last tours of the monuments leave 1½ hours before closing time, though you can enter the visitor centre 45 minutes before closing. Admission to the centre and Newgrange costs £3/1.25 (families £7.50, students £1.25), £2/1 (families £5, students £1) for just the centre, and £5/2.25 (families £12.50, students £2.25) for the centre, Newgrange and Knowth.

In summer, particularly at the weekend,

and during school holidays, Newgrange is very crowded and it's best to come during the week and/or first thing in the morning. Large groups must be booked in advance – because of this and the limited space inside the tomb, individual visitors may find themselves with a long wait at peak times.

There has been talk of closing the tomb to visitors altogether in order to protect the fragile carvings. If that happens, visitors will have to make do with a reproduction.

Knowth

The burial mound of Knowth (Cnóbha), north-west of Newgrange, was built around the same time and seems set to surpass its better-known neighbour, both in the extent and the importance of the discoveries made here. It has the greatest collection of passage-grave art ever uncovered in Western Europe, but it's still under excavation and the interior remains closed to visitors.

Modern excavations started at Knowth in 1962 and soon cleared a 34m passage to the central chamber, much longer than the one at Newgrange. In 1968 a second 40m passage was unearthed on the opposite side of the mound. Although the chambers are separate, they're close enough for archaeologists to hear each other at work. Also in the mound are the remains of six early-Christian souterrains (underground chambers) built into the side. Some 300 carved slabs and 17 satellite graves surround the main mound.

Human activity at Knowth continued for thousands of years after its construction and accounts for the site's complexity. The Beaker folk, so called because they buried their dead with drinking vessels, occupied the site in the Bronze Age (circa 1800 BC), as did the Celts in the Iron Age around 500 BC. Remnants of bronze and iron workings from these periods have been discovered. Around AD 800 to AD 900 it was turned into a *ráth* (earthen ring fort), a stronghold of the very powerful Uí Néill (O'Neill) clan. In 965, it was the seat of Cormac Mac-Maelmithic, later Ireland's high king for nine years. The Normans built a motte and bailey here in the 12th century. In about

1400 the site was finally abandoned. Excavations are likely to continue at least for the next decade.

Partly because of the archaeological work and partly because the later buildings on the site weakened the internal structures, making it difficult for anyone to walk along the passage, only the exterior opens for guided tours, which you must join at the Brú na Bóinne Visitor Centre (see the previous Newgrange entry). Knowth keeps the same hours as Newgrange but *only* from May to October. Admission to the visitor centre and the site costs £2/1 (families £5, students £1). See the Newgrange section for information on joint tickets.

Dowth

The circular mound at Dowth ('Dubhadh', meaning 'dark') is similar in size to Newgrange – about 63m in diameter – but is slightly taller at 14m high. It has suffered badly at the hands of everyone from road builders and treasure hunters to amateur archaeologists, who scooped out the centre of the tumulus in the 19th century. For a time, Dowth even had a teahouse ignobly perched on its summit. Relatively untouched by modern archaeologists, Dowth shows what Newgrange and Knowth looked like for most of their history. Because it's unsafe, Dowth is closed to visitors, though the mound can be viewed from the road. Excavations began in 1998 and will continue for years to come.

There are two entrance passages leading to separate chambers (both sealed), and a 24m early-Christian souterrain at either end which connect up with the western passage. This 8m-long passage leads into a small cruciform chamber, in which a recess acts as an entrance to an additional series of small compartments, a feature unique to Dowth. To the south-west is the entrance to a shorter passage and smaller chamber.

North of the tumulus are the ruins of **Dowth Castle** and 18th-century **Dowth House**.

A native of Dowth was one John Boyle O'Reilly (1844–90). For his part in the Irish Republican Brotherhood, O'Reilly was deported to a penal colony in Australia, from where he later escaped to the USA. As editor of the *Boston Pilot* newspaper he made an influential contribution to liberal opinion and supported the cause of minorities. The people of Boston erected a memorial to him in their city centre, while the locals did the same here in the churchyard beside the castle.

Newgrange Farm

A few hundred metres down the hill to the west of Newgrange tomb is a 135-hectare working farm (☎ 041-982 4119) with a large collection of animals on view, displays, a picnic area and a coffee shop. The farm opens for tours 10 am to 5.30 pm on weekdays, and 2 to 5.30 pm on Sunday (and Saturday in July and August), Easter Saturday to September. Admission costs £2.50 (families upwards of £9).

Organised Tours

Dublin-based Mary Gibbons Tours (☎ 01-283 9973) takes in Newgrange (or Knowth, according to demand) and parts of the Boyne Valley on Monday, Wednesday and Friday, leaving the Shelbourne Hotel on St Stephen's Green at 1.10 pm and the Dublin Tourism Centre on Suffolk St 10 minutes later. The £15 cost includes the admission fee. Bus Éireann's (☎ 01-836 6111) Newgrange and Boyne Valley tour departs Busáras in Dublin at 10 am, returning at 4.15 pm, Thursday and Saturday, February, March and November (£14/7); 10 am until 5.45 pm, Thursday and Saturday, April and October (£17/9); and 10 am until 5.45 pm Saturday to Thursday, May to September (£17/9).

Getting There & Away

Newgrange, Knowth and Dowth are all well signposted. Newgrange lies just north of the River Boyne, about 13km south-west of Drogheda and 5km south-east of Slane. Dowth is between Newgrange and Drogheda, while Knowth is about 1km north-west of Newgrange or almost 4km by road.

There are no direct buses to any of the sites. During most of the week the closest you'll get is Slane, which is served by up to six buses daily Monday to Saturday from Drogheda. On Saturday only the Drogheda to Slane bus stops at Donore, closer to the visitor centre, at 10.15 am and 2.10 pm.

SLANE
☎ 041 • pop 688

Built as a manorial village for an important castle, Slane (Baile Shláine) is a charming little place with stone houses and cottages and mature trees. Just south-west of the centre is the massive grey gate to the privately owned Slane Castle. Four identical houses face each other at the junction of the main roads. Local lore has it that they were built for four sisters who had taken an intense dislike to one another and kept watch from their individual residences.

Orientation & Information
Slane is perched on a hillside overlooking the River Boyne, at the junction of the N2 and N51, some 15km west of Drogheda. At the bottom of the hill to the south, the Boyne glides by under a narrow bridge.

The helpful community-run tourist office (☎ 982 4010), on Main St opposite the Conyngham Arms Hotel, opens 9 am to 6 pm daily, April to October; and 9.30 am to 5 pm on weekdays, the rest of the year.

The Hill of Slane
Just above the village, about 1km to the north, is the Hill of Slane. Tradition holds that St Patrick lit a paschal (Easter) fire here in 433 – just a year after his arrival in Ireland – to proclaim Christianity throughout the land. This act was in direct contravention of a decree issued by Laoghaire, the pagan high king of Ireland, that no flame should be lit within sight of the Hill of Tara. The king was furious but was restrained by his druids, who warned that 'the man who had kindled [the flame] would surpass kings and princes'. Instead, Laoghaire set out to meet Patrick and question him, and all but one of the king's attendants – a man called Erc – greeted him with scorn.

During the encounter, Patrick killed one of the king's guards and summoned an earthquake to subdue the rest. He then plucked a shamrock and used its three leaves to explain the paradox of the Trinity – the union of the Father, the Son and the Holy Spirit in one Godhead. The king made peace and, while he refused to be converted, allowed Patrick to continue his missionary work. Erc was baptised and later named as the first bishop of Slane. On Holy Saturday the local parish priest still lights a fire on the hill.

The Hill of Slane originally had a church associated with St Erc and, later, a round tower and monastery, but only an outline of the foundations remains. Later a motte and bailey was constructed and is still visible on the western side of the hill. A ruined church, tower and other buildings once formed part of an early-16th-century Franciscan friary. On a clear day, from the top of the tower, which is always open, you can see the Hill of Tara and the Boyne Valley, as well (it's said) as seven Irish counties.

St Erc is believed to have become a hermit in old age, and the ruins of a small Gothic church mark the spot where he is thought to have spent his last days, around 512 to 514. It's on the northern river bank, behind the Protestant church on the Navan road, and lies within the private Conyngham estate. It opens to the public only on 15 August.

Slane Castle
Slane Castle, the private residence of Lord Henry Conyngham, earl of Mountcharles, is west of the centre along the Navan road and is best known in Ireland as the setting for major outdoor rock concerts. Bruce Springsteen, Bob Dylan, the Rolling Stones and Guns 'n' Roses have appeared here, but events have dwindled of late due to local antipathy to hordes of young rock fans. There's usually only one concert each summer now.

Built in 1785 in Gothic Revival style by James Wyatt, the building was altered later by Francis Johnson for the visit of George IV to Lady Conyngham. She was allegedly his mistress, and it's said the road between Dublin and Slane was built especially straight and smooth to speed up the randy king's journeys.

Unfortunately, much of the castle, including some valuable furnishings, was destroyed by fire in 1991, whereupon it was discovered that the earl – a Lloyd's name – was underinsured. Money is now being raised for restoration. The castle and grounds are closed to the public.

Ledwidge Museum

Just about 1km east of the village on the Drogheda road is the Ledwidge Museum (☎ 982 4544). This labourer's cottage was the birthplace of Francis Ledwidge, a poet who died on the battlefield of Ypres in Belgium in 1917 just short of his 30th birthday. The cottage opens 9 am to 1 pm and 2 to 7 pm daily, April to September; and 9 am to 1 pm and 2 to 4.30 pm, the rest of the year. Admission costs £1.

Places to Stay

Hostels The nearest hostels are at Kells and Trim (summer only). See those sections, later in this chapter, for details.

B&Bs The lovely *Ye Old Post House* *(☎ 982 4090, Main St)*, a few doors east of the tourist office, charges upwards of £20 per person for its three en suite rooms. *Castle View House (☎ 982 4510)*, on the Navan road almost opposite the entrance to Slane Castle, costs upwards of £24/36 for singles/doubles, or £22/32 with shared bathroom. *Boyne View (☎ 982 4121)*, down by the river near the bridge, charges £28 to £32 for doubles.

Hotels The lovely old *Conyngham Arms Hotel (☎ 982 4155)* is near the crossroads in Slane village and has 15 singles/doubles costing £45/75 in summer (June to September). It has a reasonable restaurant, and you can get good snacks in the bar from 10.30 am to 7 pm.

Places to Eat

Ye Old Post House B&B is also a coffee shop and restaurant, with main courses (some of them vegetarian) costing upwards

of £3.95. It opens till about 9 pm. Pubs on Main St serving food include *Slane House* and *Knowth Tavern*.

Roadrunner Café is attached to a petrol station and shops about 1km north of the centre on the Derry road just beyond the turn to the Hill of Slane. It serves generous servings of straightforward food.

Mary McDonnell Craft Studio in Newgrange Mall on the Drogheda road has a nice coffee shop in summer where you can also get lunches. For a serious meal try *Conyngham Arms Hotel*, which has a menu costing £18.50.

Getting There & Away

Bus From Dublin, Slane is on the Letterkenny (three to five buses daily) and Armagh (up to six daily) routes as well as the less busy routes to Portrush (one or two daily) and Derry (two to four daily), which sometimes requires a change at Omagh. The stop is in front of the sweet shop on the Derry road. There's a bus service between Slane and Drogheda and Slane and Navan about six times daily. The stop is at Conlon's shop near the crossroads. For information ring Bus Éireann (☎ 01-836 6111) in Dublin.

Train Only the coast is served by the Dublin (Connolly Station) to Belfast line, with several stops daily between late May and early September at Mosney, a holiday centre 2km south of Laytown, which is itself just before Drogheda.

SLANE TO NAVAN

The 14km journey on the N51 south-west from Slane to Navan follows the Boyne Valley past a number of manor houses, ruined castles, round towers and churches; they're only of moderate interest compared to the fine sites elsewhere in County Meath, though.

Dunmoe Castle lies down a badly signposted cul-de-sac to the south 4km before reaching Navan. This D'Arcy family castle is a 16th-century ruin with good views of the countryside and of the impressive red-brick **Ardmulchan House** on the opposite side of the River Boyne. Cromwell is supposed to have fired at the castle from the riverbank in 1649, and local legend holds that a tunnel used to run from the castle vaults under the river. Near Dunmoe Castle is a small overgrown chapel and graveyard, with a crypt containing members of the D'Arcy family. Ardmulchan House, though somewhat dilapidated, is still used as a private residence.

You can't miss the fine 30m round tower and 13th-century church of **Donaghmore**, on the right 2km nearer Navan. The site has a profusion of modern gravestones, but the 10th-century tower with its crucifixion scene above the door is interesting, and there are carved faces near the windows and the remains of the church wall.

NAVAN
☎ 046 • pop 3447
The county town of Navan (An Uaimh) at the confluence of the Boyne and Blackwater Rivers is disfigured by the busy N3 Dublin to Cavan and N51 Drogheda to Westmeath roads, which cut off the rivers from the town. Navan was the birthplace of Sir Francis Beaufort of the British Navy, who in 1805 devised the internationally accepted scale for wind strengths. The town has a carpet factory, and Europe's largest lead and zinc mine, Tara, is 3km along the Kells road. Frankly, there is little here of any great interest.

Orientation & Information
Market Square is the town hub, with Ludlow, Watergate and Trimgate Sts leading off from it in the directions of the former town gates.

The local tourist office (☎ 21581) is in the town library on Railway St, about 500m south-west of Market Square. There's a map and information point in the town hall car park at the northern end of Watergate St.

The modern post office is past the big shopping centre on Kennedy Rd, which runs off Trimgate St, and there's an Allied Irish Bank branch on the corner of these two streets. The Bizzy Laundry is on Brews Hill, the continuation of Trimgate St.

Places to Stay
Hostels The nearest hostels are in Kells and Trim (summer only). See those sections, later in this chapter, for details.

B&Bs The *Lios na Gréine* (☎ 28092), almost 2km south of Navan on the R153 Kentstown road, has three doubles costing £36. *Highfield House* (☎ 27809), 3km from Navan in Balreask Old, offers singles/doubles costing upwards of £18/36; go 2km south along the N3 Dublin road until the Old Bridge Inn, then turn right and it's 1km along. *Swynnerton Lodge* (☎ 21371), 1km from Navan on the main road to Slane, is a 19th-century fishing lodge overlooking the Boyne and open April to September. It caters for fishing and shooting aficionados and charges upwards of £20/40. Dinner costs £15.

Hotels The *Ardboyne* (☎ 23119) is a first-class hotel on the Dublin road, charging £56/80 for B&B in singles/doubles.

In Kilmessan, 10km south of Navan and close to the Hill of Tara, the delightful little *Station House* (☎ 25239) costs £28/50.

Places to Eat
Restaurants One of the best places around is *The Loft* (26 Trimgate St), opposite O'Flaherty's, with 'funky food, art and music' every night until 11 pm and an early-bird special before 7 pm costing £6.95. More upmarket is the pan-Pacific *Hudson's Bistro* (☎ 29231, Railway St), with main courses costing upwards of £9.95. Hudson's opens for dinner from 6.30 to 11 pm Tuesday to Saturday.

Just across from Birmingham's Pub and next to the Palace Cinema is *Vivaldi's* (15 Ludlow St), offering a predictable menu of pasta dishes (starting at £5.95) and Italian main courses (starting at £8.95). On Brews Hill, the popular *China Garden* (☎ 23938) serves decent Chinese food, with main courses costing upwards of £7.50 and limited European food.

Light meals are available at lunchtimes at *Station House* (☎ 25239); its restaurant opens 6 to 9.30 pm Monday to Saturday.

The delicious – and filling – six-course dinner special (not available on Saturday) costs £12.95; quite a bargain.

Fast Food, Cafés & Pubs *Susie's Cookhouse* *(Watergate St)* serves good light lunches, as does *Valley Café* opposite, costing upwards of £3.70. *Pepper Pot* (full Irish breakfast £2.80), the cosy *Coffee Dock* and *Tasty Bites*, all in Trimgate St, are other good bets. The fast-food chain *Abrakebabra* has an outlet on Trimgate St.

For pub grub, try the comfortable *O'Flaherty's*, on the corner of Railway St and Brews Hill, or *Bernard Reilly's (Trimgate St)*. *Smyth's Flat House* at the roundabout opposite the tourist office/town library also serves good, solid food.

Entertainment

O'Flaherty's and *Bernard Reilly's* are popular, modern, comfortably furnished pubs on Trimgate St and its extension, Brews Hill. *Robbie O'Malley's* *(Watergate St)* is similar and has music on Monday.

The tiny *Birmingham's Pub* *(Ludlow St)* has an old wooden frontage and faded posters inside. They have music on Thursday. *Lantern Lounge* at the bottom of Watergate St has an Irish music night on Wednesday, as does *Henry Loughran's (Trimgate St)*. There's a nightclub in the Beechmount Hotel with line dancing at the weekend.

Palace Cinema (Ludlow St) still rakes up enough of an audience for its two screens.

Getting There & Away

Buses stop in front of the Mercy Convent on Railway St and in Market Square. Destinations and times are posted, or call Bus Éireann (☎ 01-836 6111) in Dublin for information. There are four or five daily buses (three on Sunday) to/from Dublin, and the same number to/from Donegal via Kells and Cavan. Other destinations include Galway, Drogheda, Trim and Slane.

Getting Around

You can order a taxi from Navan Cabs (☎ 23053), and there are ranks on Market Square and in front of the shopping centre on Kennedy Rd. Clarke's Sports (☎ 21130), in the back of the Navan Indoor Market at 39 Trimgate St, is the local Raleigh Rent-a-Bike dealer, with bikes costing £8 per day plus a deposit of £50. You'd have to negotiate a weekly rate.

AROUND NAVAN

There are some nice **walks** in the area, particularly the one following the towpath that runs along the old River Boyne Canal towards Slane and Drogheda. On the southern bank, you can go out about 7km as far as Stackallen and the Boyne bridge with ease, passing Ardmulchan House and, on the opposite bank, the ruins of Dunmoe Castle. (See the Slane to Navan section, earlier in this chapter, for details.) Going beyond the bridge towards Slane is trickier as the path is rough and in some places switches to the opposite side of the bank, with no bridge for you to cross over.

Just west of town is the **Motte of Navan**, a scrub-covered mound that tradition holds to be the burial site of Odhbha, the wife of a Celtic prince who had abandoned her for Tea (pronounced 'Tay-ah'), the lady who gave her name to Tara. Odhbha followed her husband to Navan and died of a broken heart. In reality, the 16m-high mound was probably formed naturally – a deposit of gravel from the Ice Age – and was then adapted by the Normans as a motte and bailey.

Two kilometres to the south-east of town are the impressive remains of **Athlumney House**, built by the Dowdall family in the 16th century with additions made 100 years later. This relatively intact castle was said to have been set alight in 1690 by Sir Lancelot Dowdall, after James' defeat at the Battle of the Boyne. Dowdall vowed that the conqueror, William of Orange, would never shelter or confiscate his home. He watched the blaze from the opposite bank of the river before leaving for France and then Italy.

Close to the Kells road (N3), 5km northwest of Navan, is the large ruin of a castle that once belonged to the Talbot family. **Liscartan Castle** is made up of two 15th-century square towers joined by a hall-like room.

TARA
The Hill of Tara has occupied a special place in Irish legend and folklore for millennia, although it's not known exactly when people first settled on this gently sloping hill with its commanding views over the plains of Meath. One of the many mounds on the hill was found to be a Stone Age passage grave from about 2500 BC, and during the Bronze Age people of high rank and status were certainly being buried here.

Much of the pagan significance of Tara (Teamhair) seems to have derived from its associations with the goddess Maeve (or Medbh) and the mythical powers of the druids or priest-rulers who reigned over part of the country from here. By the 2nd and 3rd centuries, Tara was the seat of the most powerful rulers in Ireland, a place where the *ard rí* (high king) and his royal court had their ceremonial residence, feasted and watched over the realm. While Tara's kings may have been more powerful than the others, they would by no means have held sway over all Ireland as there were countless other *rí tuaithe* (petty kings) controlling many smaller areas.

Tara's remains are not visually impressive. Only mounds and depressions in the grass mark where the Iron Age hill fort and surrounding ring forts once stood, but it remains an evocative, somewhat moving place, especially on a warm summer's evening.

As the focus of Irish political influence and a centre of pagan worship, Tara was targeted by the early Christians. A great pagan *feis* (festival) is thought to have been held around what is now Halloween. On Tara – if not on the Hill of Slane – St Patrick supposedly used the shamrock and its three leaves to explain the Christian Trinity. Hence the adoption of the shamrock as the Irish national symbol.

After the 6th century, once Christianity had taken hold and Tara's pagan significance had waned, the high kings began to desert Tara. The kings of Leinster continued to be based here until the 11th century, however.

In August 1843, Tara saw one of the greatest crowds ever to gather in Ireland. Daniel O'Connell, the 'Liberator' and leader of the opposition to union with Great Britain, held one of his 'monster rallies' at Tara, and up to 750,000 people came to hear him speak.

The Hill of Tara is an open site, accessible at any time, and is free.

Tara Visitor Centre
The former Protestant church (with a window by well-known artist Evie Hone) houses the Tara Visitor Centre (☎ 046-25903), where a 20-minute audiovisual presentation on the site called *Tara: Meeting Place of Heroes* is shown. During the summer the tour from here is a must, as the anecdotes really bring the mounds and relics to life. Admission to the centre and the tour costs £1.50/60p (families £4, students 60p). It opens – and tours are available – from 9.30 am to 6.30 pm daily, mid-June to mid-September; and 10 am to 5 pm daily, May to mid-June and mid-September to October. Last admission is 45 minutes before closing.

Ráth of the Synods
The names applied to Tara's various humps and mounds were adopted from ancient texts, and mythology and religion intertwine with the historical facts. The Protestant church grounds and graveyard spill onto the remains of the Ráth of the Synods, a triple-ringed fort supposedly where some of St Patrick's early meetings (or synods) took place. Excavations of the ráth suggest that it was used between AD 200 and AD 400 for burials, rituals and living quarters. Originally the ring fort would have contained wooden houses surrounded by timber palisades.

During a digging session in the graveyard in 1810, a boy found a pair of gold torcs (necklaces of twisted gold bands), now in the National Museum in Dublin. Later excavations brought a surprise when Roman glass, shards of pottery and seals were discovered, showing links with the Roman Empire, even though the Romans never extended their power into Ireland.

The poor state of the ráth is due in part to a group of British 'Israelites' who in the 1890s dug the place up looking for the Ark of the Covenant, much to the consternation of the local people. The Israelites' leader claimed to see a mysterious pillar on the ráth, but unfortunately it was invisible to everyone else. After they failed to uncover anything, the invisible pillar moved to the other side of the road but, before the adventurers had time to start work there, the locals chased them away.

The Royal Enclosure

To the south of the church, the Royal Enclosure (Ráth na Ríogh) is a large, oval Iron Age hill fort, 315m in diameter and surrounded by a bank and ditch cut through solid rock under the soil. Inside the Royal Enclosure are smaller sites.

Mound of the Hostages This bump (Dumha na nGiall) in the northern corner of the ráth is the most ancient known part of Tara and the most visible of the remains. Supposedly a prison cell for hostages of the 3rd-century King Cormac MacArt, it is in fact a small Stone Age passage grave dating from around 1800 BC and later used by Bronze Age people. The passage contains some carved stonework, but it's closed to the public.

The mound produced a treasure trove of artefacts, including some ancient Mediterranean beads of amber and faïence (glazed pottery). More than 35 Bronze Age burials were found here, as well as a mass of cremated remains from the Stone Age.

Cormac's House & Royal Seat Two other earthworks found inside the enclosure are Cormac's House (Teach Cormaic) and the Royal Seat (Forradh). Although they look similar, the Royal Seat is a ring fort with a house site in the centre, while Cormac's House is a barrow, or burial mound, in the side of the circular bank. Cormac's House commands the best views of the sur-

rounding lowlands of the Boyne and Blackwater Valleys.

Atop Cormac's House is the phallic **Stone of Destiny** (Lia Fáil), originally located near the Mound of the Hostages and representing the joining of the gods of the earth and the heavens. It's said to be the inauguration stone of the high kings of Tara. The would-be king stood on top of it and, if the stone let out three roars, he was crowned. The mass grave of 37 men who died in a skirmish on Tara during the 1798 Rising is next to the stone.

Enclosure of King Laoghaire

South of the Royal Enclosure is the Enclosure of King Laoghaire (Ráth Laoghaire), a large but worn ring fort where the king – a contemporary of St Patrick – is supposedly buried dressed in his armour and standing upright.

Banquet Hall

North of the churchyard is Tara's most unusual feature, the Banquet Hall, or Teach Miodhchuarta ('House of Meadcircling'; mead, which was a popular tipple, is fermented from honey). This rectangular earthwork measures 230 by 27m along a north-south axis. Tradition holds that it was built to cater for thousands of guests during feasts such as the feis. Much of this information about the hall comes from the 12th-century *Book of Leinster* and the *Yellow Book of Lecan*, which even includes drawings of it.

Opinions vary as to the site's real purpose. Its orientation suggests that it was a sunken entrance to Tara, leading directly to the Royal Enclosure. More recent research has uncovered graves within the compound, and it's possible that the banks are in fact the burial sites of some of the kings of Tara.

Gráinne's Fort

Gráinne's Fort (Ráth Gráinne) and the northern and southern Sloping Trenches (Claoin Fhearta) off to the north-west are burial mounds. Gráinne was the same daughter of King Cormac who was betrothed to Fionn McCumhaill (Finn Mc-

Fionn McCumhaill & the Salmon of Knowledge

Finnegan's wisdom was widely regarded throughout Ireland, and the young Fionn Mc-Cumhaill (Finn McCool) journeyed to his home on the banks of the Boyne to gain instruction. When he arrived, the master was engaged in trying to catch the Salmon of Knowledge, a fish that, despite Finnegan's great wisdom, had eluded him for many decades. When Fionn arrived, Finnegan felt a tug on his line and, sure enough, the great salmon was caught. He set the salmon on the fire and told Fionn to keep an eye on the fish and not eat any of it.

When he returned, Finnegan noticed something different about his new charge, and asked him if he had disobeyed his instruction. Fionn answered that he hadn't, but that when he was turning the fish he had burned his finger and sucked it to ease the pain. The old man then told Fionn to eat the rest of the fish as the knowledge was Fionn's already. From that day, whenever Fionn wanted to see into the future, all he had to do was suck his thumb.

Cool) but eloped with Diarmuid ÓDuibhne, one of the king's warriors, on her wedding night and became the subject of the epic *The Pursuit of Diarmuid and Gráinne*. See Newgrange earlier in this chapter for more information on the legend.

Organised Tours

From April to October, Bus Éireann sometimes includes the Hill of Tara in its day-long Newgrange and Boyne Valley Tour (£17/9). To check whether it will be included on a particular day call Bus Éireann (☎ 01-836 6111) in Dublin.

Getting There & Away

Tara is 10km south-east of Navan just off the N3 Dublin to Cavan road. Buses linking Dublin and Navan pass within 1km of the site; ask to be dropped off at Tara Cross, and then follow the signs.

AROUND TARA

Five kilometres south of Tara on the Dunshaughlin to Kilmessan road is **Dunsany Castle** (☎ 046-25198), the residence of the lords of Dunsany, former owners of the lands around Trim Castle. The Dunsanys are related to the Plunkett family, the most famous Plunkett being St Oliver, who was executed and whose head is kept in a church in Drogheda (see the boxed text 'A Moving Head' later in this chapter).

The present Lord Dunsany opens his house to visitors from 9 am to 1 pm Mon-

day to Saturday, June to August. Admission costs £3, and they prefer people to come as part of group tours organised by the Drogheda tourist office and the Irish Georgian Society. There's an impressive private art collection and many other treasures related to important figures in Irish history, such as Oliver Plunkett and Patrick Sarsfield, leader of the Irish Jacobite forces at the siege of Limerick in 1691.

Housed in the old kitchen and in part of the old domestic quarters is a new boutique that proudly sells the Dunsany Home Collection, featuring locally made table linen and accessories, as well as various articles for the home designed by Lord Dunsany himself, who is something of a well-known artist and designer. The boutique opens 10 am to 5pm daily, year round.

About 1.5km north-east of Dunsany is the ruined **Killeen Castle**, the seat of another line of the Plunkett family. The 1801 mansion was built around a Hugh de Lacy, lord of Meath, original dating from 1180. It comprises a neo-Gothic structure between two 12th-century towers.

According to local lore, the surrounding lands were divided at one point among the two Plunkett branches by a foot race. Starting at the castles, the wives had to run towards each other and a fence was placed where they met. Luckily for the Killeen womenfolk, their castle was on higher ground and they made considerable gains as they ran downhill towards their Dunsany counterparts.

Another 5km south-east on the Dublin road is the town of **Dunshaughlin** with Fairyhouse Racecourse 7km beyond. The Easter holiday races of 1916 attracted a large contingent of British officers from Dublin while the Easter Rising began.

TRIM
☎ 046 • pop 1740

Trim (Baile Átha Troim, 'Town at the Ford of the Elder Trees') is a rather sleepy little town on the River Boyne, with several interesting ruins. The medieval town was a jumble of streets and once had five gates. At one stage, there were also seven monasteries in the immediate area. In the past, few visitors have paused to inspect the impressive ruins of Trim Castle, Ireland's largest Anglo-Norman structure, but the castle is currently being restored with a view towards maximising its tourist potential. One plus is that it was a 'castle double' for York Castle in Mel Gibson's 1996 film *Braveheart*; when you see the ruins it looks as though the Scots actually did take the place!

According to local history, Elizabeth I considered Trim as a possible site for Trinity College, which eventually ended up in Dublin. The duke of Wellington went to school for a time in Talbot Castle/St Mary's Abbey, which served as a Protestant school in the 18th century. There's a local (and unlikely) belief that he was born in a stable south of the town, which probably arose from the duke's observation that being born in a stable didn't make one a horse, and thus his birth in Ireland didn't make him Irish! A Wellington column stands at the junction of Patrick and Emmet Sts. After defeating Napoleon at the Battle of Waterloo, the Iron Duke went on to become prime minister of Great Britain and in 1829 passed the Catholic Emancipation Act, which repealed the last of the repressive penal laws.

Trim was once home to the county jail, giving rise to the ditty: 'Kells for brogues, Navan for rogues and Trim for hanging people'.

Information

The tourist office (☎ 37111), on Mill St, opens 9.30 am to 6 pm daily, May to September; and 9.30 am to 5 pm Monday to Saturday, and noon to 4 pm on Sunday, the rest of the year. Among the brochures for sale is the handy little *Trim Tourist Trail* (70p) walking-tour booklet. The post office is at the junction of Emmet and Market Sts, where you'll also find an Allied Irish Bank branch.

In the same building as the tourist office on Mill St is Meath Heritage Centre (☎ 36633), with an extensive genealogical database for people trying to trace Meath ancestors. It opens 9 am to 1.30 pm and 2.30 to 5 pm on weekdays, and the minimum charge is £20. Noel French at the centre also runs group tours (from £2 per person per site) of Trim and other places of interest in Meath.

The Power & the Glory

Immediately next to the tourist office in Mill St is the informative **Trim Heritage Centre** (☎ 37227) with an exhibit known as The Power and the Glory, which outlines the medieval history of Trim in audiovisuals. It makes a good starting point for a tour of the town and opens 10 am to 6 pm daily, April to September. The 20-minute film is shown six times daily. Admission costs £2/1.25 (students £1.25).

Trim Castle

Hugh de Lacy founded Trim Castle in 1173, but Rory O'Connor, said to have been the last high king of Ireland, destroyed this motte and bailey within a year. De Lacy did not live to see the castle's replacement, and the building you see today was begun around 1200. It has hardly been modified since then.

Although King John visited Trim in 1210 to bring the de Lacy family into line – hence the building's alternative name of King John's Castle – he never actually slept in the castle. On the eve of his arrival, Walter de Lacy locked it up tight and left town, forcing the king to camp in the nearby meadow. De Lacy's grandson-in-law, Geoffrey de

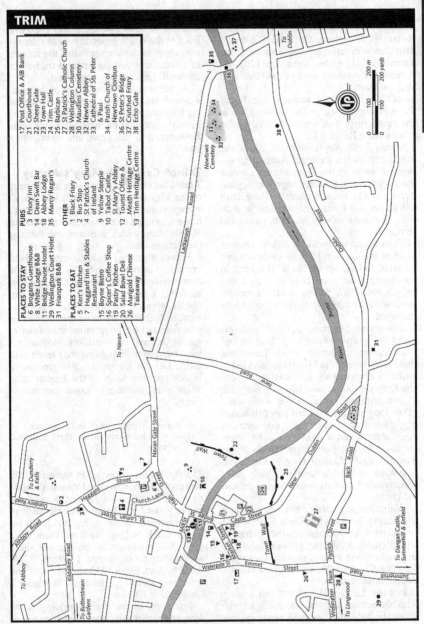

TRIM

PLACES TO STAY
6 Brogans Guesthouse
8 White Lodge B&B
11 Bridge House Hostel
29 Wellington Court Hotel
31 Friarspark B&B

PLACES TO EAT
5 Kerr's Kitchen
7 Haggard Inn & Stables Restaurant
15 Boyne Bistro
16 Spicer's Coffee Shop
19 Pastry Kitchen
20 Salad Bowl Deli
26 Marigold Chinese Takeaway

PUBS
3 Priory Inn
14 Dean Swift Bar
18 Abbey Lodge
35 Marcy Regan's

OTHER
1 Black Friary
2 Bus Stop
4 St Patrick's Church of Ireland
9 Yellow Steeple
10 Talbot Castle; St Mary's Abbey
12 Tourist Office & Meath Heritage Centre
13 Trim Heritage Centre
17 Post Office & AIB Bank
21 Courthouse
22 Sheep Gate
23 Town Hall
24 Trim Castle
25 Barbican
27 St Patrick's Catholic Church
28 Wellington Column
30 Maudlins Cemetery
32 Newton Abbey
33 Cathedral of Sts Peter & Paul
34 Parish Church of Newtown Clonbun
36 St Peter's Bridge
37 Crutched Friary
38 Echo Gate

Geneville, was responsible for the second stage of the keep's construction in the mid- to late 13th century. De Geneville was a crusader who later became a monk at the Dominican abbey he founded in 1263 just outside the northern wall of the town near Athboy Gate.

In 1399 Henry of Lancaster, later Henry IV, was imprisoned in the Dublin Gate at the southern part of the outer wall by his cousin King Richard II.

Throughout Anglo-Norman times the castle occupied a strategic position on the western edge of the Pale, the area where the Anglo-Normans ruled supreme; beyond Trim was the volatile country where Irish chieftains and lords vied and fought with their Norman rivals for position, power and terrain.

Trim was conquered by Silken Thomas in 1536 and again in 1647 by Catholic Confederate forces, opponents of the English parliamentarians. In 1649 it was taken by Cromwellian forces, and the castle, town walls and Yellow Steeple were badly damaged.

The grassy 2-hectare enclosure is dominated by a massive stone keep, 25m tall and mounted on a Norman motte. Inside are three lofty levels, the lowest one divided in two by a central wall. Just outside the central keep are the remains of an earlier wall.

The principal outer curtain wall, some 500m long and for the most part still standing, dates from around 1250 and includes eight towers and a gatehouse. The finest stretch of the outer wall runs from the River Boyne through Dublin Gate to Castle St. The outer wall has a number of sally gates from which defenders could exit to confront the enemy.

Within the northern corner was a church and, facing the river, the Royal Mint, which produced Irish coinage (called 'Patricks' and 'Irelands') into the 15th century. The Russian cannon in the car park is a trophy from the Crimean War and bears the tsarist double-headed eagle.

In 1465, Edward IV ordered that anyone who had robbed or 'who was going to rob' should be beheaded and their heads mount- ed on spikes and publicly displayed as a warning to other thieves. In 1971, excavations in the castle grounds near the depression south of the keep revealed the remains of 10 headless men, presumably the hapless criminals (or criminal wannabes).

At the time of writing, most of the castle was surrounded by an ugly wire fence and the keep overshadowed by a gigantic crane, as work continues on maintaining the ruins. However, it is still open, and admission is free.

Talbot Castle/St Mary's Abbey

Across the river from the castle are the ruins of the 12th-century Augustinian St Mary's Abbey, rebuilt after a fire in 1368 and once home to a miraculous wooden statue of the Virgin Mary which was destroyed during the Reformation.

Part of the abbey was converted in 1415 into a fine manor house by Sir John Talbot, then viceroy of Ireland. It came to be known as Talbot Castle. The Talbot coat of arms can be seen on the northern wall. Talbot went to war in France, where in 1429 he was defeated by none other than Joan of Arc at Orleans. He was taken prisoner, released and went on fighting the French until 1453. He was known as 'the scourge of France' or 'the whip of the French', and Shakespeare wrote of this notorious man in *Henry VI*:

> Is this the Talbot so much feared abroad
> That with his name the mothers still their babes?

Talbot Castle was owned in the early 18th century by Esther 'Stella' Johnson, the mistress of Jonathan Swift. She bought the manor house for £65 sterling and lived there for 18 months before selling it to Swift for a tidy £200 sterling. He lived there for a year. Swift was rector of Laracor, 3km south of Trim, from around 1700 until 1745, when he died. From 1713 he was also – and more significantly – dean of St Patrick's Cathedral in Dublin.

Just north of the abbey building is the 40m **Yellow Steeple**, once the bell tower of the abbey, dating from 1368 but damaged by Cromwell's soldiers in 1649. It takes its name from the colour of the stonework at dusk.

A part of the 14th-century town wall stands in the field to the east of the abbey, and includes the **Sheep Gate**, the lone survivor of the town's original five gates. It used to be closed daily between 9 pm and 4 am, and a toll was charged for sheep entering to be sold at market.

Newtown

About 1.5km east of town on Lackanash Rd, Newtown Cemetery contains an interesting group of ruins. What had been the **parish church of Newtown Clonbun** contains the late-16th-century tomb of Sir Luke Dillon, chief baron of the Exchequer during the reign of Elizabeth I, and his wife Lady Jane Bathe. The effigies are known locally as 'the jealous man and woman', perhaps because of the sword lying between them.

Rainwater that collects between the two figures is claimed to cure warts. Place a pin in the puddle and then jab your wart. When the pin becomes covered in rust your warts will vanish. Some say you should leave a pin on the statue as payment for the cure.

The other buildings here are Newtown's **Cathedral of Sts Peter and Paul** and the 18th-century **Newtown Abbey**, or Abbey of the Canons Regular of St Victor of Paris, to give it its full name. The cathedral was founded in 1206 and burned down two centuries later. Parts of the cathedral wall were flattened by a storm in January 1839, which also damaged sections of the Trim Castle wall. The abbey wall throws a superb echo back to **Echo Gate** across the river.

South-east of these ruins and just over the river is the **Crutched Friary**. There are ruins of a keep and traces of a watchtower and other buildings from a hospital set up after the crusades by the Knights of St John of Jerusalem, who wore a red crutch, or cross, on their cassocks. **St Peter's Bridge** beside the friary is said to be the second-oldest bridge in Ireland. *Marcy Regan's*, the small pub beside the bridge, claims to be Ireland's second-oldest pub.

Other Things to See

The site of the 13th-century Dominican **Black Friary** lies north of the town, near the junction of the Athboy and Dunderry roads. Only a few mounds remain.

At the other end of town, **Maudlins Cemetery** has a bronze statue of Our Lady of Trim, a later version of a wooden statue put in St Mary's Abbey after its 1368 restoration. The original statue, which was reputed to have miraculous powers, survived the abbey's suppression in 1540 and later came into the possession of a powerful local family. After the sacking of Drogheda in 1649, Cromwell's commander lodged in the house and the statue was burned as firewood.

On the western outskirts of Trim are the award-winning **Butterstream Gardens** (☎ 36017), signposted from the centre of town. They're open 11 am to 6 pm daily, April to September. Admission costs £3.

Places to Stay

Hostels The IHH *Bridge House Hostel* (☎ 31848), facing Bridge St, offers dorm beds costing £10 and two private rooms costing £12 per person. It opens April to September only.

B&Bs In the centre of Trim, *Brogans Guesthouse* (☎ 31237, High St) has an olde-worlde flavour and costs upwards of £25/40 for singles/doubles. It has an adjoining bar that serves lunch. *White Lodge* (☎ 36549) is 500m east of the centre at the northern end of New Road. B&B costs £25/36, or £22/32 without bathroom.

Linda O'Brien's *Friarspark* (☎ 31745), on the Dublin road, costs upwards of £17 per person. *Echo Lodge* (☎ 37945), also on the Dublin road, costs £25/36. Half a kilometre closer to Trim, *Bramley Townhouse* (☎ 31745) costs about the same. *Crannmór* (☎ 31635) is a converted farmhouse about 2km along the road to Dunderry, where singles/doubles with bathroom cost £24/36. It opens April to September only.

Tigh Cathairn (☎ 31996) is a country house surrounded by open fields, only 2km out of Trim on the road to Longwood. B&B costs £18/36.

Hotels Trim's only hotel is the 18-room *Wellington Court (☎ 31516, Summerhill Rd)*. Well-equipped singles/doubles cost upwards of £44/66.

Places to Eat

Emmet St has takeaway places, including *Marigold* for Chinese food. *Spicer's Coffee Shop (Market St)* is good for a snack. For a more substantial lunch, try *Salad Bowl Deli* or *Pastry Kitchen* next door on the same street. Both serve sandwiches and limited hot plates costing no more than £3. Almost opposite, *Boyne Bistro* also serves soups and sandwiches as well as more substantial lunches. *Dean Swift Bar (Bridge St)*, *Abbey Lodge (Market St)* and *Priory Inn (Haggard St)* are fine for bar food and lunches.

Stables (☎ 31110), the restaurant at the Haggard Inn on Haggard St, is one of the best places to eat in town and has a three-course menu costing around £14. Nearby is *Kerr's Kitchen*, where the cakes look fine.

Getting There & Away

Buses stop in front of Tobin's newsagent at the top end of Haggard St. Buses running between Dublin's Busáras (☎ 01-836 6111) and Granard pass through Trim four times daily (twice on Sunday) in each direction. Some of these buses continue on to Athboy and Navan. A same-day return to Dublin costs £5.

AROUND TRIM

Some 7.5km north-east of Trim on the way to Navan is **Bective Abbey**, founded in 1147 and the first Cistercian offspring of magnificent Mellifont Abbey in Louth. The remains seen today are 13th- and 15th-century additions and consist of the chapter house, church, ambulatory and cloister. After the suppression of the monasteries in 1543, it was used as a fortified house, and the tower was built.

In 1186, Hugh de Lacy, lord of Meath, began demolishing the abbey at Durrow in County Offaly in order to build a castle. A workman, known both as O'Miadaigh and O'Kearney, was offended by this desecration, lopped off de Lacy's head and fled. Although de Lacy's body was interred in Bective Abbey, his head went to St Thomas Abbey in Dublin. A dispute broke out over who should possess all the bodily remains, and it required the intervention of the pope to, well, pontificate on the matter, with a ruling in favour of St Thomas Abbey.

Some 12km north-west of Trim on the road to Athboy is **Rathcairn**, the smallest Gaeltacht (Irish-speaking) district in Ireland. Rathcairn's population is descended from a group of Connemara Irish speakers, who were settled on an estate here as part of a social experiment in the 1930s.

Six kilometres south of Trim on the road to Summerhill stands **Dangan Castle**, built by the Wellesley family and the boyhood home of the duke of Wellington. The castle is also supposed to have been the birthplace of Don Ambrosio O'Higgins (1720–1801), the Spanish viceroy of Peru and Chile at the end of the 18th century. His son Bernardo O'Higgins went on to become the liberator of Chile, and Santiago's main thoroughfare is named after him. The mansion's current state is the result of the efforts of Roger O'Conor, its last owner, who set it alight on a number of occasions between 1808 and 1809 for the insurance money.

Summerhill, another 5km farther south, is a pleasant, sleepy little village with a large, tidy green, but there's nothing much to do here except have lunch at *John Shaw's*, a pub-restaurant at the northern edge of the village. Jonathan Swift's connection with the area includes a curious folly in **Castlerichard**, a hamlet 10km west of Summerhill. By the church over the old bridge is a large stone pyramid inscribed with the word 'Swifte'.

Place to Stay

A farmhouse in the area makes for an interesting overnight option. *Cosy Gibbons Farmhouse (☎ 0405-57232)*, 8km south-east of Summerhill in the hamlet of Collegelands (on the road to Dublin), has four singles/doubles costing £22/36; it's next to the Forge pub (which is great for a drink!).

KELLS
☎ 046 • pop 2152

While almost every visitor to Ireland pays homage to the magnificent *Book of Kells* in Dublin's Trinity College, few come to see where it originated, and perhaps with good reason: present-day Kells (Ceanannus Mór) is a dreary place and little remains of the monastic site established here in the 6th century. Still, there are some fine high crosses in various states of preservation, a 1000-year-old round tower, the even older St Colmcille's House, and an interesting display in the gallery of the local church.

After establishing monasteries at Derry, Durrow and, in 559, Kells, St Colmcille (also known as St Columba) went into exile on the remote Scottish island of Iona. In 807, monks from the Iona monastery arrived here after 68 of their brethren were killed in a Viking raid. It's thought that they brought both the remains of their revered saint and an illuminated manuscript of the Gospels with them, bound in vellum and enclosed in a gold case. This extraordinary work of art consequently came to be known as the *Book of Kells*.

It was stolen two centuries later, but the thief was only after its gold case, and the manuscript was later found buried in a bog. Kells proved to be no safer than Scotland for the monks, however, as Viking raids soon spread to Ireland. Kells was plundered on no less than five different occasions between the 9th and 11th centuries. A century later, the Columbans moved their headquarters to Derry, and the monastery was abandoned.

Orientation & Information

The N3 from Dublin to Cavan almost bypasses the town. Turning south at Cross St brings you down to Farrell St, where you'll find most of the pubs and shops (including Maguire's, a newsagent and grocery with disposable mousetraps among other useful items!). The tourist office is in the heritage centre behind the town hall on Headfort Place. Kells Hostel is also helpful with queries. There's a Bank of Ireland branch on John St. The post office is on Farrell St.

Round Tower & High Crosses

The Protestant Church of St Columba west of the town centre stands in the grounds of the old monastic settlement. The church gallery has an exhibition on the settlement and its illuminated manuscript, with a facsimile on display. It opens 10 am to 5 pm on weekdays, and 10 am to 1 pm on Saturday.

A square belfry dating from the 15th century stands beside the church. Above the doorway is an inscription detailing the addition of the neo-Gothic spire in 1783 by the earl of Bective from a design by Thomas Cooley, the architect of Dublin's City Hall.

The churchyard has a 30m-high, 10th-century round tower on the southern side. It's now without its conical roof but is known to date back at least as far as 1076, when Muircheartach Maelsechnaill, the high king of Tara, was murdered in its confined apartments.

Inside the churchyard are four 9th-century high crosses in various states of repair. The West Cross, at the far end of the compound from the entrance, is the stump of a decorated shaft with scenes of the baptism of Jesus, the Fall of Adam and Eve, and the judgment of Solomon on the eastern face, and Noah's ark on the western face. All that is left of the North Cross is the bowl-shaped base stone.

Near the tower is the best preserved of the crosses, the Cross of Patrick and Columba, with its semi-legible inscription 'Patrici et Columbae Crux' on the eastern face of the base. Above it are scenes of Daniel in the lions' den, the fiery furnace, the Fall of Adam and Eve and a hunting scene. On the opposite side of the cross are the Last Judgment, the crucifixion, and riders with a chariot and a dog on the base. The council has plans to move this cross into the new heritage centre when completed to protect it from the elements.

The other surviving cross is the unfinished East Cross. On the eastern side is a carving of the crucifixion and a group of four figures on the right arm. The three blank, raised panels below these were prepared for carving, but the sculptor apparently never got round to the task.

St Colmcille's House

From the churchyard exit on Church St, St Colmcille's House is left up the hill, among the row of houses on the right side of Church Lane. It usually opens June to September; otherwise, pick up the keys from the brown-coloured house at No 1 Lower Church View as you ascend the hill.

This squat, solid structure is a survivor from the old monastic settlement. The original entrance to the 1000-year-old building was over 2m above ground level. Inside, a very long ladder leads to a low attic room under the roof line.

Market Cross

Until recently the Market Cross had stood for centuries in Cross St in the town centre, marking the farthest extent of the 10th-century monastery. It's said that it was moved here by Jonathan Swift, and in 1798 the British garrison executed rebels by hanging them from the crosspiece, one on each arm so the cross wouldn't fall over. Alas, in 1996 the cross met its ignoble fate – in a crass, modern manner. A motorist – local wags like to point out it was a woman driver – took a tight turn, reversed and toppled the 1000-year-old thing. It has now been repaired and will take pride of place in the new heritage centre. A replica will be placed in Cross St.

On the eastern side of the Market Cross are Abraham's sacrifice of Isaac, Cain and Abel, the Fall of Adam and Eve, guards at the tomb of Jesus, and a wonderfully executed procession of horsemen. On the western face, the crucifixion is the only discernible image. On the northern side is a panel of Jacob wrestling with the angel.

Places to Stay

The IHH *Kells Hostel* (☎ 49995) is next to Monaghan's pub on the Cavan road, 200m uphill from the bus stop. Dorm beds cost £6 to £7.50 depending on the season, and the two private rooms cost £7 to £9 per person. There's a full kitchen and other facilities. *Camping* in the garden costs £3 per person. You may have to check-in at Monaghan's pub.

Headfort Arms Hotel (☎ 40063, John St) offers 18 singles/doubles costing £30/58. Breakfast costs £6.50 extra. It has a nightclub and restaurant attached.

The wonderful 200-year-old *Lennoxbrook House* (☎ 45902) is in Carnaross, 5km north of Kells on the N3, and costs upwards of £18/36 for B&B. It opens year round.

Places to Eat

Penny's Place on Market St is an excellent café with homemade food; their brown bread has few equals. It opens until 6 pm, Monday to Saturday. *O'Shaughnessy's* pub farther west on Market St serves reasonable sandwiches and lunches. Next to the post office in Farrell St, *Round Tower* (☎ 40144) has a good restaurant and serves substantial pub lunches. On the same street, *McGee's*, on the corner opposite Maguire's, serves sandwiches, soups and afternoon teas. *Monaghan's* pub next to the hostel serves lunch costing around £5 and dinner with main courses costing upwards of £6.95.

Entertainment

O'Shaughnessy's features lots of rustic timber, while nearby *Blackwater Pub* has regular Irish music sessions. *Monaghan's* attracts a young crowd and often has music at the weekend.

Getting There & Away

Buses stop in front of the church on John St and near the hostel (request stop only). Times are posted at the stop or phone Bus Éireann (☎ 01-836 6111) in Dublin. Buses run from Dublin to Kells and Cavan and back almost hourly from 7 am to 10 pm. Two of the buses are express coaches on their way to and from Donegal. There are also regular services to Navan, Dunshaughlin and Drogheda.

AROUND KELLS
Hill of Lloyd Tower
The 30m tower on the Hill of Lloyd is visible from behind the hostel in Kells, and it's easy to see why it became known as the 'inland lighthouse'. Built in 1791 by the earl of Bective in memory of his father, it has been renovated and if it's open you can climb to the top for £1/50p, or picnic in the surrounding park. The tower is 3km north-west of Kells, off the Crossakeel road.

Crosses of Castlekeeran
Two kilometres farther down the Crossakeel road, signposted to the right, are the Crosses of Castlekeeran. Access is through a farmyard. Three plainly carved, early-9th-century crosses, one in the river, are surrounded by an overgrown cemetery, while at the ruined church in the centre are some early grave slabs and an ogham stone.

LOUGHCREW CAIRNS
North-west of Kells and near Oldcastle, the Loughcrew Hills – of which Slieve (or Sliabh) na Caillighe (277m) is the highest peak – give marvellous views east and south to the plains of Meath and north into the lake country of Cavan. On the summit of three of the hills – Slieve na Caillighe, Carnbane East and Carnbane West – are the remains of 30 Stone Age passage graves built around 3000 BC but used up to the Iron Age. In some cases, a large mound is surrounded by numerous, smaller satellite graves. As at Newgrange, larger stones in some of the graves are decorated with spiral patterns. Archaeologists have unearthed bone fragments and ashes, stone balls and beads. Some of the graves look like large piles of stones, while others are less obvious, the cairn having been removed.

To get there from Kells, head north-west on the R163. About 5km from Oldcastle you'll see a sign for Sliabh na Caillighe. Turn right, and at the first house on the right collect the keys to the cairn entrances from Basil Balfe (but ring ☎ 049-41256 first).

If anybody is there to collect it, a deposit of £5 (hikers can leave their backpacks as collateral!) is required, and a leaflet about the sites is available. A torch (flashlight) is useful on dull days. Coming from the east, the first group of hills – Patrickstown Cairns – is of little interest; the most interesting and intact remains are on the next two, Carnbane East and Carnbane West.

The owners of the Kells Hostel offer a guided tour, available between June and September, of the Slieve na Caillighe cairns which also takes in the Hill of Lloyd tower and the early-Christian sites at Fore Valley in County Westmeath. The tour costs £12 per person, with discounts for hostel residents. Raingear is provided, but you should wear suitable hiking shoes or boots.

Carnbane East
Carnbane East has a cluster of sites; Cairn T is the biggest at about 35m in diameter and has numerous carved stones. One of its outlying kerbstones is called the Hag's Chair and is covered in gouged holes, circles and other markings. You need the gate key to enter the passageway and a torch to see anything in detail. It takes about half an hour to climb Carnbane East from the car park. From the summit on a reasonably clear day, you should be able to see the Hill of Tara to the south-east, while the view north is into Cavan, with Lough Ramor to the north-east and Lough Sheelin and Oldcastle to the north-west.

Carnbane West
From the same car park, it takes about an hour to reach the summit of Carnbane West, where Cairn D and L are both some 60m in diameter. Cairn D has been disturbed in an unsuccessful search for a central chamber. Cairn L, north-east of Cairn D, is also in poor condition, though you can enter the passage and chamber, where there are numerous carved stones and a curved basin stone where human ashes were placed.

County Louth

Although the smallest county in Ireland (hence its nickname, the 'Wee County'),

Louth is home to the two principal towns of Ireland's north-eastern region.

Drogheda is the more pleasant town of the two, with a bustling town centre and some pretty interesting attractions; it also makes a good base for exploring the Boyne Valley, with its prehistoric sites to the west and the monastic relics to the north.

Dundalk is a border town to the north and a gateway to the lonely but scenic Cooley Peninsula. Its proximity to the border has meant that it has strong affiliations with republicanism, and has been a welcome haven for IRA activists on the run from the Northern authorities.

HISTORY

Humans have lived in this region since about 7000 BC, but Louth's Stone Age relics – like the Proleek dolmen and passage grave near Dundalk – pale in comparison with the Brugh na Bóinne relics in County Meath. Only with the coming of the Iron Age did Louth rival its neighbour.

Louth was part of the ancient kingdom of Oriel, which was the stage for many of the epic tales of Irish mythology. The north of the county and the Cooley Peninsula are the setting for legends of Cúchulainn, one of the most famous heroes of ancient Ireland, who was born and raised around Faughart, just north of Dundalk. Cúchulainn was the lead player in the story of the *Táin Bó Cúailnge* (*Cattle Raid of Cooley*), one of the great Celtic epic myths. See the boxed text later in this chapter. *The Táin* by Thomas Kinsella (Dolmen Press) is a modern version of this compelling and bloody tale.

St Patrick introduced Christianity in the 5th century, and numerous religious communities sprang up in the region. The monastery at Monasterboice and the later Cistercian abbey at Mellifont, both near Drogheda, are Louth's most interesting archaeological sites.

Irish society underwent a huge upheaval with the arrival of the Anglo-Normans in the 12th century. Hugh de Lacy's reward for his Irish conquests was the fertile land of Meath and Louth. Mottes, such as the one at Millmount in Drogheda, were first built around this time to defend Anglo-Normans against the hostile Irish.

The Normans' stone castles came later, and smaller satellite castles such as Termonfeckin, north-east of Drogheda, dot the countryside. The Norman invaders were responsible for the development of Dundalk, and for the two towns, on opposite banks of the Boyne, which united in 1412 to become what is now Drogheda.

These new settlers would become some of the staunchest defenders of Ireland in later centuries, particularly against the English parliamentarians. In 1649, Cromwell's forces massacred the native Irish and Anglo-Norman Catholic defenders of Drogheda for refusing to surrender.

Ireland succumbed to English control in 1690, after the Battle of the Boyne, where the Protestant William of Orange defeated his father-in-law, the English Catholic King James II. James had enlisted the help of the Irish in return for greater religious and political freedom, and his defeat resulted in a new influx of Protestant settlers.

DROGHEDA

☎ 041 • pop 24,460

The historic town of Drogheda hugs a bend on the River Boyne, 5km from the sea. It's a compact settlement, with a small village-like adjunct to the south of the river around Millmount. The town, which is pretty run-down in places, has undertaken a project of urban renewal which has brought new life to the place. The future looks bright for Drogheda, and plans to clean the Boyne (which is filthy around here) will go a long way towards making the town a very attractive spot.

Once fortified, Drogheda still has one town gate in fine condition, together with some interesting old buildings and the curious hump of Millmount, south of the river. The embalmed head of the Catholic martyr St Oliver Plunkett (1629–81) is housed in St Peter's Roman Catholic Church.

The town's name comes from Droichead Átha (Bridge of the Ford), after the bridge built by the Normans to link the two earlier Viking settlements.

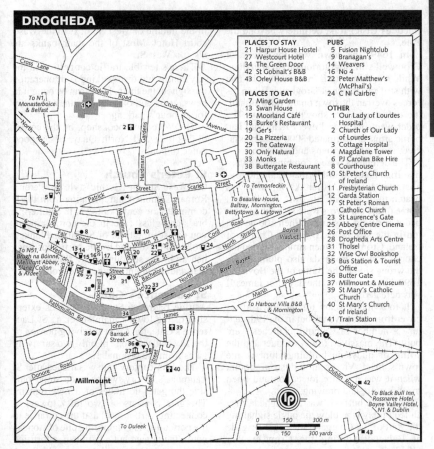

DROGHEDA

PLACES TO STAY
21 Harpur House Hostel
27 Westcourt Hotel
34 The Green Door
42 St Gobnait's B&B
43 Orley House B&B

PLACES TO EAT
7 Ming Garden
13 Swan House
15 Moorland Café
18 Burke's Restaurant
19 Ger's
20 La Pizzeria
29 The Gateway
30 Only Natural
33 Monks
38 Buttergate Restaurant

PUBS
5 Fusion Nightclub
9 Branagan's
14 Weavers
16 No 4
22 Peter Matthew's
   (McPhail's)
24 C Ní Cairbre

OTHER
1 Our Lady of Lourdes
   Hospital
2 Church of Our Lady
   of Lourdes
3 Cottage Hospital
4 Magdalene Tower
6 PJ Carolan Bike Hire
8 Courthouse
10 St Peter's Church
   of Ireland
11 Presbyterian Church
12 Garda Station
17 St Peter's Roman
   Catholic Church
23 St Laurence's Gate
25 Abbey Centre Cinema
26 Post Office
28 Drogheda Arts Centre
31 Tholsel
32 Wise Owl Bookshop
35 Bus Station & Tourist
   Office
36 Butter Gate
37 Millmount & Museum
39 St Mary's Catholic
   Church
40 St Mary's Church
   of Ireland
41 Train Station

History

There was probably a rough settlement here before the 10th century, but Drogheda really began to take shape around 910, when the Danes built defences to guard a strategic crossing point on the River Boyne. In the 12th century, the Normans built a bridge and expanded the two settlements forming on either side of the river. They also built a large defensive motte-and-bailey castle on the southern side at Millmount.

By the 15th century, Drogheda was one of Ireland's four major walled towns. Many Irish Parliament sessions were held here,

and Poyning's Law, passed here in 1494, is the most famous piece of legislation from Irish medieval times. It diminished prospects of home rule or independence for Ireland by granting the English Crown the right to veto any measures the Irish proposed to enact.

In 1465, the Irish Parliament conferred on Drogheda the right to a university, but the plan foundered in 1468, when the earl of Desmond was executed for treason. During the period of the Pale, when only a small portion of the country around Dublin was fully controlled by the English, Drogheda was a frontier town. Farther north were the fractious Ulster folk, definitely beyond the Pale.

In 1649, the town was the scene of Cromwell's most notorious Irish slaughter. While marching north from Dublin, he met with stiff resistance at Drogheda. When his forces overran the town on the third assault, the defenders were shown no mercy. The order went out to kill every man who had borne arms; an estimated 3000 were massacred, including civilians and children.

The defenders were a combination of native Irish and Anglo-Norman Catholic royalists led by Sir Arthur Aston, who was beaten to death with his own wooden leg. Some of the survivors were shipped to Barbados and sold as slaves. When 100 people hid in the steeple of St Peter's Church of Ireland, Cromwell's men simply burned the church down. Drogheda also plumped for the wrong side at the Battle of the Boyne in 1690, but surrendered the day after James II was defeated.

It took many years for the town to recover from these events, but in the 19th century a number of Catholic churches were built. The massive railway viaduct and the string of quayside buildings hint at the town's brief Victorian industrial boom, when it was a centre for cotton and linen manufacture, and brewing.

For trivia buffs, it was a Drogheda man called Finlay who blew the bugle signalling the start of the Charge of the Light Brigade at Balaclava during the Crimean War (1853–56).

Orientation & Information

Drogheda sits astride the River Boyne with the principal shopping area on the northern bank along the main street, called West St and Laurence St. The area south of the river is residential, dull and dominated by the mysterious Millmount mound. The main road to Belfast skirts round the town to the west.

The helpful tourist office (☎ 983 7070) is in an office at the bus station on the southern side of the river. It opens 9.30 am to 5.30 pm Monday to Saturday, and 11.45 am

to 5 pm on Sunday. The main post office is in the middle of West St, next to the Westcourt Hotel. Most of the main banks are also on West St.

There's terrible traffic congestion in the city centre and disc parking is in operation throughout the town. Discs can be bought in newsagents and other shops; they cost 30p for an hour's parking.

The Wise Owl bookshop, on the corner of Shop St and North Quay, has a good range of books.

St Peter's Church

On West St, the Gothic-style St Peter's Roman Catholic Church, dating from 1791, dominates the centre of town. In a glittering brass-and-glass case in the north transept you can see the head of St Oliver Plunkett (1629–81), executed by the perfidious English and now surrounded by flowers, candles and the attentions of the devout.

St Laurence's Gate

Astride Laurence St, the eastwards extension of the town's main street, is St Laurence's Gate, the finest surviving portion of the city walls and one of only two surviving gates from the original 11.

The 13th-century gate was named after St Laurence's Priory, which once stood outside the gate; no traces of it now remain. The gate consists of two lofty towers, a connecting curtain wall and the entrance to the portcullis. This imposing pile of stone is not in fact a gate but a barbican, a fortified structure used to defend the gate, which was farther behind it. When the walls were completed in the 13th century, they ran for 3km round the town, enclosing 52 hectares.

Millmount & Museum

Across the river from the town centre, in a village-like enclave amid a sea of dull suburbia, is Millmount, an artificial hill overlooking the town. Although it may have been a prehistoric burial mound along the lines of nearby Newgrange, it has never been excavated. There is a tale that it was the burial place of a warrior-poet who arrived in Ireland from Spain around 1500

A Moving Head

In the north transept of Drogheda's St Peter's Church, a relic lurks inside a soaring reliquary of solid brass and unbreakable glass. Closer inspection reveals the leathery head of St Oliver Plunkett, who was hanged in 1681 for his supposed part in the 'Popish Plot'.

Plunkett was born at Loughcrew, near Oldcastle, in 1629, a descendant of Brian Ború, who had defeated the Danes at Clontarf in 1014. In 1645 he was sent to Rome to complete his education and stayed in Italy for 25 years. Ordained in 1654, he became archbishop of Armagh and primate of all Ireland in 1670. Following his consecration, he returned to Ireland in 1670. In the first three years of his mission he confirmed 48,655 people, ordained many priests and set up what may have been the first integrated Roman Catholic and Protestant school in Drogheda.

But Plunkett lived during a time when the English were particularly paranoid about the supposed threat from Roman Catholicism, and in 1679 he was seized and imprisoned in Dublin, accused of involvement in the 'Popish Plot'. This was an entirely fabricated conspiracy dreamed up by Titus Oates, a ne'er-do-well with a long history of dubious dealings, who claimed in 1678 that he had uncovered a plot to kill Charles II and turn the country over to the Jesuits. Despite Oates' past, he was believed and about 35 men were put to death for supposed involvement. Plunkett was accused of planning the invasion of Ireland by foreign powers and in 1680 he was moved to London's Newgate Prison. Tried and convicted of treason, he was hanged at Tyburn on 1 July 1681. The very next day the plot was revealed as a sham. Oates himself was flogged, pilloried and imprisoned for perjury, only to be pardoned and granted a pension after the revolution of 1688.

At the time of Plunkett's execution, the custom was to quarter the body and then burn the parts. Plunkett's friends obtained permission to remove the body, but only just managed to snatch the head from the fire: scorch marks are still visible on the left cheek and the nose. The head and forearms were placed in tin boxes, and the rest of the body buried in St Giles Cemetery. Later it was exhumed and sent first to a Benedictine monastery in Germany, then to Downside in England. The head, meanwhile, was taken to Rome, then to Drogheda, where the Sisters of Sienna looked after it for the next 200 years.

In 1920 Plunkett was beatified and the head was given to the new parish church of St Peter's, 'the Oliver Plunkett Memorial Church'. Following a miraculous cure in a Naples hospital which was attributed to Plunkett's intervention, the pope canonised him in October 1975.

In 1990 the priest of St Peter's decided to have the head examined since it was showing signs of decay. At the same time a living descendant of the saint provided a blood sample so that Turin Shroud-style DNA tests could be carried out to verify its authenticity. The tests proved satisfactory and the saint's head was replaced in its reliquary inside an inner capsule containing silica gel, which would make it easier to maintain the correct humidity level. The reliquary was then enclosed in a pedestal shrine over 1m high and with a soaring 9m stone spire. Beside it is displayed the original certificate of authenticity, dated 1682.

BC. Throughout Irish history, poets have held a special place in society and have been both venerated and feared.

The Normans constructed a motte-and-bailey fort on top of this convenient command post overlooking the bridge. It was followed by a castle, which in turn was replaced by a Martello tower in 1808.

It was at Millmount that the defenders of Drogheda made their last stand before surrendering to Cromwell. Later, an 18th-century English barracks was built round the base, and today this has been converted to house craft shops, museums and a restaurant, though the courtyard retains the flavour of its former life.

The tower played a dramatic role in the 1922 Civil War, and the Millmount Museum has a colourful (and somewhat romanticised) painting of its bombardment. The top of the tower offers a fine view over the centre of Drogheda, on the opposite side of the river.

A section of the army barracks is now the Millmount Museum (☎ 983 3097), with interesting displays about the town and its history. Displays include three wonderful late-18th-century guild banners, perhaps the last in the country. There is also a room devoted to Cromwell's siege of Drogheda and the Battle of the Boyne. The pretty, cobbled basement is full of gadgets and kitchen utensils from bygone times, including a cast-iron pressure cooker and an early model of a sofa bed. There's an excellent example of a coracle, a tiny boat from earliest times. Across the courtyard, the **Governor's House** opens for temporary exhibitions.

The museum opens 10 am to 6 pm Monday to Saturday, and 2.30 to 5.30 pm on Sunday. Admission costs £2.50/1.50. You can drive up to the hilltop or climb Pitcher Hill via the steps from St Mary's Bridge.

Butter Gate The 13th-century Butter Gate, just north-west of Millmount, is the only genuine town gate to survive. This tower, with its arched passageway, predates the remains of St Laurence's Gate by about a century. St Mary's Churchyard to the southeast contains some of the original town wall and is reputedly where Cromwell breached the walls in 1649.

Other Buildings
On the corner of West and Shop Sts is the **Tholsel**, an 18th-century limestone town hall, now occupied by the Bank of Ireland. Off Hardmans Gardens is the rather charming and more recent **Church of Our Lady of Lourdes**.

North of the centre on William St is **St Peter's Church of Ireland**. This contains the tombstone of Oliver Goldsmith's uncle Isaac, as well as another on the wall depicting two skeletal figures in shrouds, dubiously linked to the Black Death. This is the church whose spire was burned by Cromwell's men, resulting in the death of 100 people seeking sanctuary inside. Today's church (1748) is the second replacement of the original destroyed by Cromwell. It stands in an attractive close approached through lovely wrought-iron gates. Note the old 'Blue School' of 1844 on one side.

On Fair St the modest 19th-century **Courthouse** is being renovated and is home to the sword and mace presented to the town council by William of Orange after the Battle of the Boyne.

Topping the hill behind the main part of town is the **Magdalene Tower**, dating from the 14th century, the belltower of a Dominican friary founded in 1224. Here, England's King Richard II, accompanied by a great army, accepted the submission of the Gaelic chiefs with suitable ceremony in 1395; but peace lasted only a few months and his return to Ireland led to his overthrow in 1399. The earl of Desmond was beheaded here in 1468 because of his treasonous connections with the Gaelic Irish. The tower is reputed to be haunted by a nun.

Organised Tours
The Drogheda Historical Society occasionally runs summer tours of the town; phone the Millmount Museum (☎ 983 3097) to check if anything is scheduled. Harpur House (☎ 983 2736) helps organise tours of Drogheda and the Boyne Valley. The tourist office runs walking tours of historical Drogheda. It also has a leaflet entitled *The Oriel Trail*, which outlines a 150km tour through the county beginning in town.

Places to Stay
Hostels The family-run *Harpur House* (☎ 983 2736, William St) is near the centre of town. Dorm beds cost £7 and double

rooms cost £10 per person. Breakfast costs an extra £3. A second hostel, **The Green Door** (☎ 983 4422, 47 John St), opened in June 1999 only 150m from the bus station. It has pleasant dorms with handcrafted wooden bunks costing £8 to £10, depending on the season; four-bed family rooms cost £13 per person.

B&Bs It's advisable to book ahead during the summer months.

South of the river, **Orley House** (☎ 983 6019), 100m off the main Dublin road in a housing estate, costs £28/40 in singles/doubles. Nearby, on the main Dublin road near the train station, is **St Gobnait's** (☎ 983 7844), costing £25/36 with bathroom.

Harbour Villa (☎ 983 7441) is 2km along the river towards the sea on the Mornington road. It overlooks the estuary and has small but pleasant rooms costing £22/40 with bathroom. Further up the scale is **Boyne Haven** (☎ 983 6700), on the Dublin road opposite the Rossnaree Hotel. Its three rooms all have showers and cost £30/40 with shared bathroom and £35/45 en suite.

Hotels The more upmarket **Westcourt Hotel** (☎ 983 0965, West St) is right in the town centre and normally costs £42/80 for singles/doubles, but it's worth asking about special weekend bargain breaks. Both Mary Robinson and Jack Charlton have visited here.

Boyne Valley Hotel (☎ 983 7737) is a 19th-century mansion set way back from the main Dublin road; it charges £45/85. Farther out on the same road you'll find the cheaper **Rossnaree Hotel** (☎ 983 7673), just over the border in Meath; it's good and costs £35/55.

Places to Eat

Restaurants Just opposite St Peter's on West St, **The Gateway** has a lunch-of-the-day special (£4.25) which is usually of the chicken-and-chips variety.

The excellent **Brasserie** at the Rossnaree Hotel serves an early-bird, three-course dinner from 6 to 7.30 pm costing £12.95; thereafter it's à la carte.

The rather cosy **Buttergate Restaurant** (☎ 983 4759), upstairs beside Millmount Museum, serves excellent food, with meals before 7 pm costing £8, and after costing £15 to £21. It opens for dinner Tuesday to Sunday and for lunch on Sunday.

Fast Food, Cafés & Pubs At the river end of Shop St, on the corner of North Quay, **Monks** (☎ 984 5630) is a new espresso bar and café. Grilled bruschettas cost upwards of £3.45, while open sandwiches start at £2.95. The coffees are good, and, strangely for Ireland, it is mostly smoke free. It is closed on Sunday. **Moorland Café** (West St) serves good coffee, snacks and light meals. A chicken burger with chips costs £2.95.

The busy, Italian-owned **La Pizzeria** (☎ 983 4208, St Peter's St) features pizzas costing under £6, from 6 to 11 pm. It also serves pasta dishes. Down an alley on the other side of the road, **Burke's Restaurant** serves soups costing £1.10 and main courses costing £3.50. **Ger's** is another possible lunch stop for coffee and sandwiches in St Peter's St.

The popular **Swan House** (☎ 983 5838, West St) is a Chinese restaurant; chicken dishes cost around £7 and it offers takeaways. **Ming Garden** (Trinity St) also serves Chinese food.

Only Natural (Stockwell Lane), on the corner with Dyer St, is the town's only health-food shop, dispensing the usual assortment of health foods.

The popular **Weavers** pub (☎ 983 2816, West St) serves some tasty pub food; lasagne with chips costs £3.95. **Branagan's** (☎ 983 5607, Magdalene St) is also popular, with a varied menu; main courses cost £6.50 to £12. About 1km along the Dublin road, **Black Bull Inn** (☎ 983 7139) was once winner of the regional Pub of the Year title, and gets the local vote. Most mains cost £7 to £12; Chinese-style duck costs £9.50.

Entertainment

Weavers (West St) always has a youngish crowd and has live music on Wednesday

MEATH & LOUTH

night, DJs at the weekend. *Bridie Macs*, attached to the Westcourt Hotel, also offers a wide range of musical possibilities on Thursday, Friday and Saturday. *Black Bull Inn*, about 1km along the Dublin road, has music at the weekend.

The traditional and old *C Ní Cairbre* (Carberry's) pub, on North Strand near Laurence St, is the town's best and most popular watering hole, though you might need infrared glasses because it is so dark inside! There are Irish music sessions on Tuesday night and Sunday afternoon. In theory it opens from 7.30 pm; in reality, opening hours vary depending on how the night is going. It gets busy on weekend nights and Sunday afternoon.

Peter Matthew's (aka McPhail's) on Laurence St is Drogheda's alternative to the older bars, attracting a younger crowd who prefer indie and dance music to the more traditional kind.

The *Earth* nightclub, downstairs in the Westcourt Hotel, is popular. Directly opposite, *No 4* is a pub that turns into a nightclub after 11 pm (free if you're there before, £5 if you arrive after 11 pm); it is a favourite of Drogheda's trendy young crowd. *Fusion* (12 George's St) is the town's other crowd puller, with a fairly animated disco from Thursday to Sunday nights with a mix of 60s, rock, funk and dance music. The Rossnaree and Boyne Valley Hotels on the Dublin road host *Place* and *Luciano's* nightclubs, respectively. Admission to all clubs costs about £5.

The two-screen *Abbey Centre Cinema* (☎ 983 0188) is at the back of the Abbey Shopping Centre off West St. In the municipal building on Stockwell Lane, *Drogheda Arts Centre* (☎ 983 3946) stages theatrical and musical events.

Shopping

The Millmount complex has a number of craft studios where you can buy all sorts of *objets d'art*. There's a jewellery studio (☎ 984 1960), a ceramic potter (☎ 984 6065), a decorative glassworks (☎ 984 5018) and a studio where you can buy hand-painted silks (☎ 984 1245). Call to arrange

a viewing of the work; some of it is of extremely high quality.

Otherwise, there are plenty of shops along West St, including an outlet of the Dublin based Flip, which specialises in 50s and 60s gear.

Getting There & Away

Bus Drogheda is only 48km north of Dublin, on the main N1 route to Belfast. The Bus Éireann station (☎ 983 5023), on the corner of John St and Donore Rd just south of the river, has numerous connections (6.15 am to 8.45 pm) with Dublin and Dundalk, as well as with Belfast and other centres. The one-way fare to Dublin is £4.50. There's a handy expressway service from Drogheda to Galway once each morning; you can get off at Athlone for connections to Limerick, Sligo and Donegal.

Cheaper is Capital Coaches (☎ 042-934 0025), which has a daily Dundalk to Dublin service through Drogheda; its one-way fare from Drogheda to Dublin is £3.

Train Drogheda train station (☎ 983 8749) is just south of the river and east of the town centre, off the Dublin road. Drogheda is on the main Belfast to Dublin line and there are five or six express trains (and many more slower ones) daily each way, with four on Sunday. This is the best line in Ireland, with excellent on-board service. The one-way, off-peak fare from Drogheda to Dublin is £8.50.

The train crosses the river just downstream from Drogheda on Sir John McNeill's mid-19th-century Boyne Viaduct, a fine piece of engineering which dominates the seaward view.

Getting Around

Drogheda itself is infinitely walkable, and many of the surrounding region's interesting sites are within easy cycling distance. PJ Carolan (☎ 983 8242), 77 Trinity St, is part of the Raleigh Rent-a-Bike scheme and offers good bikes costing £9 per day. Bridge Cycles (☎ 983 3742), on North Quay near the bridge, rents bikes costing £7 per day.

There's a small taxi rank (☎ 985 1839) on

Duke St, just off West St. There's a larger cab rank on Laurence St near St Laurence's Gate.

AROUND DROGHEDA

Drogheda makes an excellent base for exploring the Boyne Valley sites to the west – see Brugh Na Bóinne in the County Meath section earlier in this chapter for more details. In Louth itself, Mellifont and Monasterboice are two famous and picturesque monastic sites a few kilometres north of Drogheda. Travelling to or from Northern Ireland there's a coastal route, the faster and duller N1 main road route, and a more circuitous inland route via Collon and Ardee which can include Mellifont and Monasterboice.

Beaulieu House

Five kilometres east of Drogheda on the Baltray road is Beaulieu House, built between 1660 and 1666. The land, which had belonged to the Plunkett family since Anglo-Norman times, was confiscated under Cromwell. This lovely red-brick mansion, with distinctive steep roof and tall chimneys, is thought to have been designed by Sir Christopher Wren (architect of St Paul's Cathedral in London).

In 800 years the estate has been in the possession of only two families, first the Plunketts and then the ancestors of Lord Tichbourne. There's an impressive art collection, but it's a private residence, not open to the public.

Mellifont Abbey

Mellifont Abbey (☎ 041-982 6459), 8km north-west of Drogheda beside the River Mattock, was Ireland's first Cistercian monastery. The name comes from the Latin *mellifons* (honey fountain). In its prime, Mellifont was the Cistercians' most magnificent and important centre in the country but, while the remains are well worth seeing, they don't really match the site's former significance.

In 1142 St Malachy, bishop of Down, brought in a new troop of monks from Clairvaux in France to combat the corruption and lax behaviour of the Irish monastic orders. These strait-laced new monks were deliberately established at this remote location, far from any distracting influences. The French and Irish monks failed to get on, and the visitors soon returned to the Continent. However, within 10 years nine more Cistercian monasteries were established and Mellifont was eventually the mother house for 21 lesser monasteries. At one point, as many as 400 monks lived here.

Mellifont not only brought fresh ideas to the Irish religious scene, it also heralded a new style of architecture. For the first time in Ireland, monasteries were built with the formal layout and structure that was being used on the Continent. Only fragments of the original settlement remain, but the plan of the extensive monastery can easily be traced. Like many other Cistercian monasteries, the buildings clustered round an open cloister, or courtyard.

To the northern side of the cloister are the remains of a principally 13th-century cross-shaped church. To the south, the chapter house, probably used as a meeting hall by the monks, has been partially floored with medieval glazed tiles, originally found in the church. Here also would have been the refectory, or dining area, the kitchen and the warming room – the only place where the austere monks could enjoy the warmth of a fire. The eastern range would once have held the monks' sleeping quarters.

Mellifont's most recognisable building, and one of the finest pieces of Cistercian architecture in Ireland, is the *lavabo*, an octagonal washing house for the monks. It was built in the 13th century and used lead pipes to bring water from the river. A number of other buildings would have surrounded this main part of the abbey.

After the dissolution of the monasteries, a fortified Tudor manor house was built on the site in 1556 by Edward Moore, using materials scavenged from the demolition of many of the buildings. In 1603, this house was the scene of a poignant and crucial turning point in Irish history. After the disastrous Battle of Kinsale, the vanquished Hugh O'Neill, last of the great Irish chieftains, was given shelter here by Sir Garret Moore until he surrendered to the English Lord Deputy Mountjoy. After his surrender, O'Neill was pardoned but, despairing of his position, fled to the continent in 1607 with other old-Irish leaders in the Flight of the Earls. In 1727 the site was abandoned altogether.

The visitor centre next to the site describes monastic life in detail. Admission costs £1.50/60p. The grounds open 10 am to 5 pm daily, May to mid-June; 9.30 am to 6.30 pm daily, mid-June to mid-September; and 10 am to 5 pm daily, mid-September to October. A back road connects Mellifont with Monasterboice.

Monasterboice

Just off the N1 road to Belfast, about 10km north of Drogheda, is Monasterboice (Mainistir Bhuithe), an intriguing monastic site containing a cemetery, two ancient church ruins, one of the finest and tallest round towers in Ireland and two of the best high crosses. The site can be reached directly from Mellifont via a winding route along narrow country lanes.

Down a leafy country lane and set in sweeping farmland, Monasterboice has a special atmosphere, particularly at quiet times. The original monastic settlement at Monasterboice is said to have been founded by St Buithe, a follower of St Patrick, in the 4th or 5th century, although the site probably had pre-Christian significance. St Buithe's name somehow got converted to Boyne, and the river is named after him. It's said that he made a direct ascent to heaven via a ladder lowered from above. An invading Viking force took over the settlement in 968, only to be comprehensively expelled by Donal, the Irish high king of Tara, who killed at least 300 of the Vikings in the process.

Entrance to Monasterboice is free and there's a small gift shop outside the compound. There are no set hours but come early or late in the day to avoid the crowds.

High Crosses The high crosses of Monasterboice are superb examples of Celtic art. The crosses had an important didactic use, bringing the gospels alive for the uneducated – cartoons of the Scriptures, if you like. Like Greek statues, they were probably brightly painted, but all traces of colour have long disappeared.

Muiredach's Cross, the one nearest to the entrance, dates from the early 10th century. The inscription at the foot reads 'Or do Muiredach Lasndernad i Chros' (A prayer for Muiredach for whom the cross was made). Muiredach was abbot here until 922.

The subjects of the carvings have not been positively identified. On the eastern face, from the bottom up, are thought to be: on the first panel, the Fall of Adam and Eve and the murder of Abel; on the second, David and Goliath; on the third, Moses bringing forth water from the rock to the waiting Israelites; and on the fourth, the three wise men bearing gifts to Mary and Jesus. The Last Judgment is at the centre of the cross with the risen dead waiting for their verdict, and farther up is St Paul in the desert.

The western face relates more to the New Testament, and from the bottom depicts the arrest of Christ, Doubting Thomas, Christ giving a key to St Peter, the crucifixion in the centre, and Moses praying with Aaron and Hur. The cross is capped by a representation of a gabled-roof church.

The West Cross is near the round tower and stands 6.5m high, making it one of the tallest high crosses in Ireland. It's much more weathered, especially at the base, and only a dozen or so of its 50 panels are still legible.

The more distinguishable ones on the eastern face include David killing a lion and bear, the sacrifice of Isaac, David with Goliath's head, and David kneeling before Samuel. The western face shows the resurrection, the crowning with thorns, the crucifixion, the baptism of Christ, Peter cutting off the servant's ear in the garden of Gethsemane, and the kiss of Judas.

A third, simpler cross in the north-eastern corner of the compound is believed to have been smashed by Cromwell's forces and has only a few, straightforward carvings. Photographers should note that this cross makes a great evening silhouette picture, with the round tower in the background.

The **round tower**, minus its cap, stands in a corner of the complex. It's still over 30m tall but is closed to the public. In 1097, records suggest, the tower interior went up in flames, destroying many valuable manuscripts and other treasures. The church ruins are later and of less interest.

COLLON
☎ 041 • pop 308
Collon, a small village 10km north-west of Drogheda, was planned along English lines in the 18th century. It's now home to the newer Mellifont Cistercian Monastery, founded in 1958, which is housed in the former landlord's residence north of the village.

The highly recommended but expensive

Forge Gallery Restaurant (☎ *041-982 6272*), near the parish church, features meat, fish, game and some vegetarian dishes; a set dinner costs £24. It's in an old forge building and exhibits paintings by local artists. It opens Tuesday to Saturday.

ARDEE
☎ 041 • pop 3440
How many towns can claim to have two castles in their main street? The sleepy market town of Ardee (Baile Átha Fhirdhia) on the narrow River Dee is 10km north of Collon on the N2. Its long, tidy main street – divided into Bridge, Market and Irish Sts – is dominated by Ardee Castle to the south and Hatch's Castle to the north.

History
For a small town, Ardee has a colourful history. It takes its name from Áth Fhír Diadh

---

The Táin Bó Cúailnge (Cattle Raid of Cooley)

This remarkable tale of greed and war is one of the oldest stories in any European language and the closest thing Ireland has produced to the Greek epics. The story goes that Queen Maeve, the powerful ruler of Connaught, was jealous because she couldn't match the white bull owned by her husband, Ailill. She heard tales of the finest bull in Ireland, the brown bull of Cooley, and became determined to rectify the situation.

Maeve gathered her armies and headed for Ulster, where she conspired with her druids to place the Ulster armies under a spell. A deep sleep descended on them, leaving the province undefended. The only obstacle remaining was the boy warrior Cúchulainn, who tackled Maeve's soldiers as they tried to ford the river at Ardee in County Louth. Cúchulainn killed many of them and halted their advance. Maeve eventually persuaded Cúchulainn's half-brother and close friend, Ferdia, to take him on, but he was defeated after a momentous battle and died in Cúchulainn's arms.

The struggle continued across Louth and onto the Cooley Peninsula, where many place names echo the ensuing action. Sex rears its head regularly in the *Táin*, for Maeve was more interested in her chief warrior, Fergus, than in her husband. At various spots in the saga, they sneak off to make love, and in one instance Ailill steals the sword of the distracted Fergus, to shame him and show how careless he is.

While Maeve's soldiers were being despatched in all sorts of ways by Cúchulainn, Maeve had managed to capture the brown bull and spirit it away to Connaught. The wounded Cúchulainn defeated her armies, but the bull was gone. In the end, the brown bull killed Ailill's white bull and thundered around Ireland leaving bits of his victim all over the place. Finally, spent with rage, he died near Ulster at a place called Druim Tarb (Ridge of the Bull). Cúchulainn and Ulster then made peace with Maeve, and thus the saga ended.

(Fear Diadh's Ford), inspired by the well-known tale of the combat between Cúchulainn and his foster brother Fear Diadh, or Ferdia, as recorded by the ancient tale of the *Táin Bó Cúailnge*. After an almighty duel, Cúchulainn fatally wounded his beloved foster brother with the *gae bolga*, a weapon given to him by the demi-god Lug. Cúchulainn's grief was such that he never fully recovered. It is one of the most tragic and beautiful stories of the Cooley cycle.

In the 12th century, the area was turned into a barony and the town remained in English hands until being taken by the O'Neills in the 17th century. James II had his headquarters here for two months in 1689, prior to the Battle of the Boyne.

Things to See & Do
A square tower dating from the 13th century, **Ardee Castle** was an important outpost on the edge of the English Pale. It later became a courthouse and now houses a museum on the town's history, as well as a coffee shop and craft units. The smaller **Hatch's Castle** also dates from this time and it remained, from Cromwellian times until 1940, in the hands of the Hatch family. It's still a private residence.

The riverbank can be explored around the ford, where there's a well-tended **riverside walk** which has an impressive new bronze sculpture of Cúchulainn and Ferdia.

Places to Stay
Railway Bar (☎ 685 3279, Market St) offers B&B costing £17 per person. *Carraig Mor* (☎ 685 3513), 2km south of Ardee on the main Dublin to Donegal road, offers singles/doubles costing £22/36. *Gable's Restaurant* (☎ 685 3789, Dundalk Rd) offers rooms costing £24/40.

For a real treat, try the elegant Georgian *Red House* (☎ 685 3523), which stands in its own demesne. Take the Dundalk road past Gable's Restaurant and it's about 500m along on the left. B&B costs £47/70, or £55/90 with bathroom. Dinner costs another £25.

Four kilometres south of Ardee is *Smarmore Castle* (☎ 685 7167), a 14th-century

castle recently converted into a hotel. Rooms start at £100.

Places to Eat
Caffrey's bakery and coffee shop in the centre serves sandwiches, light meals and cakes. *Sizzlers Café* serves the full Irish breakfast all day costing £3.50. Chinese takeaways are available from *Chinese Palace* (☎ 685 3998) near the bridge. *Auberge*, farther along on Market St, is a restaurant and bar; mixed grill costs £7. Similar is *Brian Muldoon & Sons (Bridge St)*, where you can get a good steak. At the other end, on Irish St, a popular pub for meals is the *Lemon and Clove*.

At *Gable's Restaurant* (☎ 685 3789), a set dinner costs £22.50 (its desserts are particularly memorable), and opens Tuesday to Saturday. Bookings are advisable.

AROUND ARDEE
The Jumping Church of Kildemock
Three kilometres south-east of town are the remains of the area's oddly named landmark, the Jumping Church of Kildemock. On a thunderous night in February 1715, a storm caused a wall of St Catherine's Church to shift inwards from its foundations. However, rather than settle for this straightforward explanation, locals decided the church had miraculously jumped to exclude the remains of an excommunicated member of the flock who had been buried within its walls. Thus was born the Jumping Church.

Tallanstown
North of Ardee, the main road forks to Monaghan and Dundalk. The slightly more interesting route to Dundalk is via Tallanstown (Baile an Tallúnaigh), with nearby Louth Hall, once belonging to the Plunkett family, barons of Louth. Oliver Plunkett took shelter here among his relations in the 1670s. It's not open to the public.

Louth
North of Tallanstown (but the turn-off is just south of town), the county's namesake

is an insignificant little place with some mildly interesting remains. **St Mochta's** is a small 11th- or 12th-century church with an enclosure and stone roof. St Mochta, a British follower of St Patrick, founded a monastery here in the early 6th century. Nearby is the church of a 15th-century Dominican friary, sometimes called Louth Abbey.

Ardpatrick
To the east of Louth village are Ardpatrick and Ardpatrick House, home of Oliver Plunkett. There's a mound here where he is supposed to have illegally ordained priests. It was also a good vantage point to spot any advancing English soldiers.

THE COAST ROAD
While the most visually rewarding route between Drogheda and Dundalk is the minor inland road via Mellifont and Collon, the coastal route is also scenic. The latter heads off north under the railway viaduct, passes Baltray with its championship golf course, and continues on quiet country roads to Termonfeckin.

Termonfeckin
A 6th-century monastery was founded in Termonfeckin (Tearmann Féichín) by St Féichín of Cong, County Mayo. All that remains are some gravestones and a 10th-century **high cross**, on the left as you enter the churchyard.

There's also a 15th-century **castle** or tower house (you can get the key from across the road, 10 am to 6 pm) in a good state of preservation; it has two small corbel-vaulted alcoves and an anticlockwise spiral staircase (most go clockwise). From the village, follow the road to Seapoint Golf Club, take the first left, then first right.

Clogherhead
A couple of kilometres farther north is the busy seaside and fishing centre of Clogherhead (Ceann Chlochair), with a good, shallow Blue Flag beach. Around the town there are enjoyable walks along the coast

(partially marred by vistas of caravan parks) or out to **Port Oriel**, an attractive little harbour with views of the Cooley Peninsula and the Mourne Mountains farther north. During the summer, Port Oriel is home to a fleet of trawlers and smaller fishing boats.

On the southern side of the headland is **Red Man's Cave**. At low tide a reddish fungus becomes visible, covering the cave walls. According to folklore, a group of people fleeing from Cromwell hid in the cave. A barking dog then revealed the hideout and the people were slaughtered, their blood splashing on the walls, where it remains to this day. The cave is hard to find, so it's sensible to ask a local for directions, but even if you don't find it the walk is satisfying enough.

Annagassan
A minor road (R166), providing picturebook views, continues 12km north to Annagassan (Áth na gCasan), a town on the northern side of Dunany Point, at the junction of the Dee and Glyde Rivers. It's claimed locally that Annagassan is the site of the Vikings' first settlement in Ireland. Records suggest they sacked a monastery here in 842 and may have been responsible for the promontory fort, which is now a low mound overlooking the village.

Castlebellingham
North of Annagassan, the coast road joins the busy main N1 at Castlebellingham, only 12km from Dundalk. The village grew up around its 18th-century mansion, which is something of a disappointment after the imposing castellated entrance. The mansion is on the site of an earlier castle burned down by James II's troops; the owner, Thomas Bellingham, worked as a guide to William of Orange during his visit to Ireland between 1689 and 1690. The building is now a *hotel and restaurant* (☎ 042-987 2176), with singles/doubles costing upwards of £22/34.

Buried in the local graveyard is Dr Thomas Guither, a 17th-century physician supposed to have reintroduced frogs to

Ireland by releasing imported frog spawn into a pond in Trinity College, Dublin. Frogs, along with snakes and toads, had supposedly received their marching orders from St Patrick 1000 years earlier.

Places to Stay
The coast road doesn't have too many places to stay, but *Cross Garden* (☎ *041-22675)*, 1km south of Clogherhead on the Termonfeckin road, overlooks the sea and has very comfortable singles/doubles costing £20/30.

Places to Eat
The excellent *Triple House Restaurant* (☎ *041-982 2616)*, at the top of the hill in Termonfeckin, serves a lot of fish and some meat. There's a three-course menu from 6.30 to 7.30 pm costing £11.50; after that it's £17.50. It's closed Monday. For cheaper food, try the nearby *Waterside Inn*, which serves soup and sandwiches.

Clogherhead's pubs are pretty ordinary, but *Sail Inn* has a large restaurant with an open fire.

DUNDALK
☎ 042 • pop 25,762
Halfway between Dublin and Belfast, Louth's charmless county town of Dundalk takes its name from Dún Dealgan, a prehistoric fort which was reputedly the home of the hero Cúchulainn.

The town grew under the protection of a local estate controlled by the de Verdon family, who were granted lands here by King John in 1185. In the Middle Ages, Dundalk was at the northern limits of the English-controlled Pale, strategically located on one of the main highways heading north.

Dundalk is only 13km from the border and widely regarded as a republican stronghold. Indeed, a residential area of the town has been nicknamed 'Little Belfast' for the numbers of Northerners who have settled here in the past three decades, including what are (more than) rumoured to be IRA or INLA activists and sympathisers looking for a safe base from which to operate.

Orientation & Information
Northbound traffic sweeps round to the east of the town centre. The main commercial streets are Clanbrassil and Park Sts. The tourist office (☎ 933 5484) is on Jocelyn St next to Louth County Museum. It opens 9.30 am to 1 pm and 2 to 5.30 pm (6 pm in July and August) on weekdays (plus at the weekend in July and August), year round. At other times there are boards and maps with tourist information dotted around town. The main post office is on Clanbrassil St.

Things to See
The **Courthouse** on the corner of Crowe and Clanbrassil Sts is a fine neo-Gothic building with large Doric pillars which was designed by Richard Morrison, who also designed the courthouse in Carlow. In the front square is the stone **Maid of Éireann**, commemorating the Fenian Rising of 1798.

At the top of Church St, **St Nicholas' Church**, or the Green Church, is the burial site of Agnes Burns, elder sister of Robert, the Scottish poet. She married the local rector, and the monument was erected by the townspeople to honour them both. The 15th-century tower to the right of the church entrance is the oldest structure on the site.

The richly decorated **St Patrick's Cathedral** was modelled on King's College Chapel in Cambridge, England. In front of it on Jocelyn St is the **Kelly Monument**, in memory of a local captain drowned at sea in 1858. Also on Jocelyn St is the interesting **County Museum** (☎ 932 7056), with displays depicting the growth of industry in Louth since 1750. Two new floors opened in 1999 and are home to an exhibition on the area's Stone Age past. It opens 10.30 am to 5.30 pm Monday to Saturday, and 2 to 6 pm on Sunday. Admission costs £2/1.

At the eastern end of Jocelyn St is the Seatown area of Dundalk with its **castle** (really a Franciscan friary tower) and a derelict, sail-less **windmill**, the tallest in Ireland. If you arrive in Dundalk by train you pass the 1820 **garda station** on St Dominick's Place on the way into town. Its

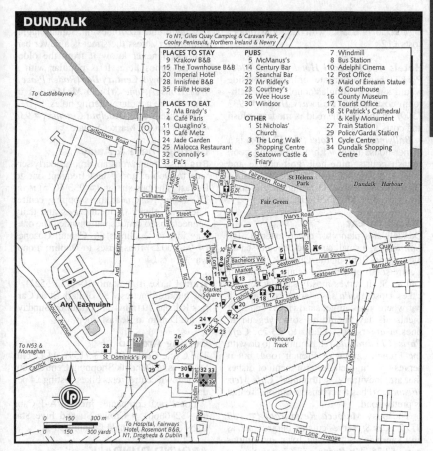

DUNDALK

To N1, Giles Quay Camping & Caravan Park,
Cooley Peninsula, Northern Ireland & Newry

PLACES TO STAY
9   Krakow B&B
15 The Townhouse B&B
20 Imperial Hotel
28 Innisfree B&B
35 Fáilte House

PLACES TO EAT
2   Ma Brady's
4   Café Paris
11 Quaglino's
19 Café Metz
24 Jade Garden
25 Malocca Restaurant
32 Connolly's
33 Pa's

PUBS
5   McManus's
14 Century Bar
21 Seanchaí Bar
22 Mr Ridley's
23 Courtney's
26 Wee House
30 Windsor

OTHER
1   St Nicholas'
    Church
3   The Long Walk
    Shopping Centre
6   Seatown Castle &
    Friary

7   Windmill
8   Bus Station
10 Adelphi Cinema
12 Post Office
13 Maid of Éireann Statue
    & Courthouse
16 County Museum
17 Tourist Office
18 St Patrick's Cathedral
    & Kelly Monument
27 Train Station
29 Police/Garda Station
31 Cycle Centre
34 Dundalk Shopping
    Centre

To Castleblayney

To Castletown Road

Fairgreen Road
St Helena Park
Dundalk Harbour

Culhaine Street
O'Hanlon Street
Legion Ave
Philip St
Bridge St
Church St
St Nicholas'
Fair Green
Marys Road
Castle Road

The Long Walk
Gardasse St
Bachelors Wk
Market St
Seatown
Mill Street
Quay St
Barrack Street

Easmuinn Road
Ard Road
Demesne Rd
Market Square
Crowe St
Francis St
Jocelyn St
Seatown Place

Ard Easmuinn
Mount Avenue

The Ramparts
Greyhound Track

To N53 &
Monaghan
Carrick Road
St Dominick's Pl
Anne St
Dublin Street
Patrick St

St Alphonsus Road

To Hospital, Fairways
Hotel, Rosemont B&B,
N1, Drogheda & Dublin
The Long Avenue

0   150   300 m
0   150   300 yards

---

first prisoner is believed to have been its architect, who misappropriated funds and was
arrested for non-payment of bills.

Places to Stay

Camping The nearest camping is at *Gyles
Quay Camping and Caravan Park* (☎ 987
6262), 16km west on the Cooley Peninsula.
It opens March to October, has excellent facilities and charges £8 per tent for up to two
people.

B&Bs An excellent B&B is *Fáilte House*
(☎ 933 5152), on the corner of Hill St and

The Long Ave, which charges upwards of
£17/32 for singles/doubles. Just as good is
Rosemont (☎ 933 5878), run by Mrs Meehan, near the Carroll's cigarette factory
about 2km south of town on the main
Dublin road. B&B costs £22.50/35, or
£26/40 with bathroom. *The Townhouse*
(☎ 932 9898, Jocelyn St) is an elegant B&B
charging £22/40.

Innisfree (☎ 933 4912, Carrick Rd),
close to the train station, is a pleasant, large
Victorian house with rooms costing £17/34,
or £20/40 including bathroom.

Krakow (☎ 933 7535, Ard Easmuinn St),

north of the train station, offers rooms costing £22/36, or £25/45 with bathroom; dinner costs £12.

Hotels The *Imperial Hotel* (☎ *933 2241, Park St)* has a better interior than the outside would suggest. Singles/doubles with bathroom cost £50/80. *Fairways Hotel* (☎ *932 1500)* on the Dublin road is modern, plush and costs £50/80.

Ballymascanlon Hotel (☎ *937 1124)* is a manor-house hotel with a swimming pool, squash courts, nine-hole golf course and other sporting facilities. It's 6km north of Dundalk on the way to Carlingford and costs upwards of £62/88 for B&B.

Places to Eat

Dundalk has plenty of cheap eateries. Try *Connolly's*, a small café and delicatessen on the ground floor of the Dundalk Shopping Centre south of the town centre and just off Dublin St. It serves mostly sandwiches and cakes. Upstairs, *Pa's* is a large restaurant and bar where you can get sandwiches and light meals all day, including some vegetarian ones. Burgers cost £2.50 to £3.75. *Café Paris (Clanbrassil St)* has nothing to do with the French capital or French food, but it serves up a high-cholesterol menu of dishes that are, inevitably, 'with chips'. *Café Metz (Francis St)* has an entensive bill of fare that is pretty good.

The busy *Malocca Restaurant* (☎ *933 4175, Park St)* serves curries, burgers, pizzas and sandwiches. Braised liver and onions costs £2.75. *Ma Brady's (7 Church St)* is a homely place where a substantial dinner costs £5 to £10; sirloin costs £8.50. The *Windsor* pub *(Dublin St)* serves light meals all day.

More upmarket places in town include *Quaglino's* (☎ *933 8567)*, an Italian restaurant near the post office where a five-course dinner costs £22. Back on Park St, *Jade Garden* (☎ *933 0378)* is an excellent Chinese restaurant with dinners costing £8.95 to £15.

Entertainment

Several good pubs are found around Park St. *Mr Ridley's* has pop/rock most nights,

while *Seanchaí Bar* has Irish music on Tuesday night and jazz/blues on Sunday night. *Courtney's* across the street is a newer bar, but you'd never know it from the olde-worlde atmosphere. It is popular with a younger crowd. *Century Bar (Roden Place)*, *Wee House (Anne St)* and *McManus's* in Seatown are popular watering holes.

The three-screen *Adelphi Cinema* (☎ *933 4843)* is just off Market Square.

Getting There & Away

Bus Bus Éireann runs an almost hourly service to Dublin and a less frequent one to Belfast. The bus station (☎ 933 4075) is on The Long Walk near the shopping centre. There are plenty of local buses and daily connections to centres nationwide. The one-way fare to Dublin is £6. Capital Coaches (☎ 934 0025) runs buses to Dublin; a one-way fare is £4.

Train Clarke train station (☎ 933 5521), a few hundred metres west of Park St on Carrick Rd, has 10 trains daily (four on Sunday) on the Dublin to Belfast line.

Getting Around

The Cycle Centre (☎ 933 7159), 44 Dublin St, opposite Dundalk Shopping Centre south of the town centre, rents bikes costing £4 per day.

Local taxi companies include A-1 Cabs (☎ 932 6666), 9 Crowe St, and Five Star Cabs (☎ 933 6000), 74 Clanbrassil St.

AROUND DUNDALK
Into Northern Ireland

If you're heading for Derry, take the N53 to the west of town, while for Belfast continue north on the main N1 route. If you're hiking or cycling and want to go directly to the Mourne Mountains, you can, June to September, get a ferry from Omeath to Warrenpoint in County Down.

The border is about 13km north of Dundalk. It's staffed by a garda and a British soldier (during the day anyway) but you probably won't be stopped. North of the border there are a couple of places where you can eat and change money.

Castleroche

Five kilometres north-west of Dundalk on the Castleblayney road, Baron de Verdon's 1230 Castleroche Castle is impressively situated on a pinnacle of rock. The triangular remnants of the building include a twin-towered entrance house and protective wall. One of the windows on the western side is called Fuinneóg an Mhurdair (Murder Window), because the baroness was said to have had the architect thrown from it to prevent similar castles ever being built.

Knockbridge

Five and a half kilometres south-west of Dundalk on the R171, in a field outside the village of Knockbridge, is the **Cloch a Farmore**, an upright stone against which the mortally wounded Cúchulainn is said to have tied himself to remain standing against his enemies. It was not until a cow alighted on his shoulder that they could be persuaded that he was dead and that it was safe to approach him!

In the village itself, the **parish church** has some fine examples of stained-glass windows designed by artisan Harry Clarke and a beautiful replica of the Clogher Cross.

Faughart

Faughart (Fochaird), about 4km north-east of Dundalk, has fine views and is reputed to be the birthplace of St Brigid, Ireland's most revered saint after St Patrick. She was the daughter of a local chieftain and settled in Kildare in the 6th century. The grotto and church here mark the spot of a monastery associated with her, and devotions are still carried out on 1 February, her feast day.

In the western corner of the graveyard is the grave of Edward Bruce, a king of Ireland who died in 1318. He was invited to Ireland from Scotland and crowned by the Ulster lords, who hoped he would create trouble for the English in Ireland. He accepted the job, hoping this would relieve English pressure at home on his brother, Robert Bruce of Scotland. The hero Cúchulainn is said to have been born near here.

Proleek Dolmen & Gallery Grave

Heading north from Dundalk, turn right after 3km towards Ballymascanlon Hotel, the start of the Cooley Peninsula ring route. In the grounds of the hotel, up by the 5th green of the golf course (there's a sign-posted trail for non-golfers), is the fine Giant's Load Proleek Dolmen and Gallery Grave.

Local legends say it's the grave of Para Buí Mór MhacSeóidín, a Scottish giant who came here to challenge Fionn McCumhaill, leader of the fabled Fianna warriors. It dates from 3000 BC, and the 47-tonne capstone sits precariously on three uprights. The pebbles on top are later additions and come from the belief that, if you can land a stone on top, any wish will be granted. Single women who achieve this are guaranteed marriage within a year.

COOLEY PENINSULA

East of Dundalk, the lonely moorlands of the Cooley Peninsula are the setting for a large part of Ireland's most famous fable, the *Táin Bó Cúailnge* (*Cattle Raid of Cooley*); see the boxed text earlier in this chapter. The low mountains are really a part of Northern Ireland's Mourne Mountains, but are cut off from them physically by the flooded valley of Carlingford Lough and politically by the border, which runs up the centre of the lough. The peninsula is a world of its own and has strong republican traditions.

The best way to explore the peninsula is by first circumnavigating it on the ring road, perhaps detouring closer to the sea at **Gyles Quay**, which has a safe beach, before arriving in Carlingford and Omeath. There's camping at *Gyles Quay Camping and Caravan Park* (☎ 042-987 6262), off the road to Greenore. Open March to October, it has excellent facilities and charges £8 per tent for up to two people.

Carlingford is probably the best base from which to venture inland over the peninsula's hilltops, soaked in the legends of the *Táin Bó Cúailnge*, through Windy Gap to the **Long Woman's Grave** and beyond to the picturesque country roads and forests which make the place a haven for walkers.

Carlingford

☎ 042 • pop 647

Near Carlingford (Cairlinn), the peninsula's mountains and views display themselves to dramatic effect. This pretty village, with its cluster of narrow streets and whitewashed houses, nestles on Carlingford Lough, beneath Slieve Foye (587m). After visiting in 1914, the Reverend Laurence Murray wrote of its 'medieval suggestiveness'; that suggestiveness survives today in the street plan and the crumbling walls and towers dotted around the village. Hard though it is to believe, not much of this was appreciated until the late 1980s, when the villagers got together to show what can be done to revive a dying community. The story of their efforts is vividly told in the heritage centre.

On a less pleasant note, the area around Carlingford has recently been excavated by the Irish authorities searching for IRA victims who 'disappeared' in the 1970s. After 20 years of silence, republican sources have begun locating hidden graves. So far, few bodies have turned up, largely due to inaccurate information about where the bodies are.

The Mourne Mountains are just a few kilometres north across the lough.

Information There's a small tourist office near the heritage centre. It opens 9 am to 5 pm on weekdays. At the weekend you can get information from the heritage centre itself. There's a small bank in the town, but it opens on Tuesday and Thursday only.

Holy Trinity Heritage Centre The heritage centre (☎ 937 3454) in Churchyard Rd is in the former Holy Trinity Church. The information boards are encased within closeable doors so that the centre can double as a concert hall outside visiting hours. A fine mural shows what the village looked like in its heyday, when the Mint and Taafe's Castle were right on the waterfront. A short video describes the village history and explains what has been done to give it new life in recent years.

The centre opens 11 am to 5 pm on weekdays, and noon to 5 pm at the weekend, year round. Admission costs £1/50p.

King John's Castle Carlingford was first settled by the Vikings, and in the Middle Ages became an English stronghold under the protection of the castle, which was built on a pinnacle in the 11th to 12th centuries to control the entrance to the lough. On the western side, the entrance gateway was constructed to allow only one horse and rider through at a time. King John's name stuck to a remarkable number of places in Ireland, given that he spent little time in or near any of them! In 1210 he spent a couple of days here en route to a nine-day battle with Hugh de Lacy at Carrickfergus Castle in Antrim. It's suggested that the first few pages of the Magna Carta, the world's first constitutional bill of rights, were drafted while he was here.

Other Things to See Near the disused station is **Taafe's Castle**, a 16th-century tower house which stood on the waterfront until the land in front was reclaimed to build the short-lived train line. The **Mint**, in front of the hostel near the square, is of a similar age. Although Edward IV is thought to have granted a charter to a mint in 1467, no coins were produced here. The building has some interesting Celtic carvings round the windows. Near it is the **Tholsel**, the only surviving gate to the original town, although much altered in the 19th century when its defensive edge was softened in the interests of letting traffic through.

West of the village centre are the remains of a **Dominican friary**, built around 1305 and used as a storehouse by oyster fishermen after 1539.

Carlingford is the birthplace of Thomas D'Arcy McGee (1825–68), one of Canada's founding fathers. A bust commemorating him stands opposite Taafe's Castle.

The Táin Trail Carlingford is the starting point for the 40km Táin Trail, making a circuit of the Cooley Peninsula, through the Cooley Mountains. The route is a mixture of surfaced roads, forest tracks and green paths. For more information contact the local tourist office or the office in Dundalk (☎ 933 5484).

Cruises Carlingford Pleasure Cruises (☎ 937 3239) runs one-hour cruises between May and September. The cost is £3/1.50 and there's no set time, as departure depends on the tides.

Special Events In mid-August the pubs are packed from morning to midnight when the village is overrun by 20,000 visitors to the Oyster Festival, with funfairs, live bands and buskers alongside the official oyster-opening competitions and tastings.

Almost every weekend from June to September, Carlingford goes event-crazy – there are summer schools, medieval festivals, leprechaun hunts and homecoming festivals.

Places to Stay Carlingford is a nicer place to stay than Dundalk and it has the bulk of accommodation on the peninsula, but options are limited and the village gets busy in summer, especially at the weekend.

The IHH *Carlingford Adventure Centre and Holiday Hostel (☎ 937 3100, Tholsel St)* is just off the main street. Dorm beds cost £8.50 to £9.50 in rooms for two to eight people, and bedding costs £1 extra. The adventure centre exists to teach rock climbing, orienteering, hill walking and windsurfing to groups, so it's a good idea to check whether any large and potentially noisy gaggles of school kids will be staying at the same time as you.

Carlingford's B&Bs are of a high standard, but there aren't many of them, so in summer and at the weekend it's wise to book ahead. *Viewpoint Guesthouse (☎ 937 3149)* overlooks the harbour in the village on the Omeath road. The motel-style singles/doubles cost £26/40, including an excellent breakfast.

Mourneview farmhouse (☎ 937 3551), 1km out of Carlingford in Belmont, costs £17/34. *Shalom (☎ 937 3151)* is along the

road towards the pier, and has rooms with bathroom costing £18 per person for B&B.

Two kilometres outside the village on the Dundalk road, *Ghan House (☎ 937 3682)* has comfortable albeit pricey rooms costing £30/60 for B&B. The breakfast is excellent.

McKevitt's Village Hotel (☎ 937 3116, Market Square) charges £28/56 for B&B and boasts a good bar and restaurant. *Jordan's (☎ 937 3223, Newry St)* has some comfortable, spacious rooms which cost £50/80 for B&B.

Places to Eat The *Carlingford Arms* serves hefty helpings of pub food; two people could manage perfectly well with one serving of fish and chips. A three-course dinner costs £13.50. *PJ's* pub, the rear extension of O'Hare's grocery store, serves half a dozen Carlingford Lough oysters with brown bread for £3.

Jordan's Restaurant (☎ 937 3223, Newry St) is a cosy place overlooking the water, and serves surprisingly sophisticated food. The menu ranges from oysters to unusual Irish dishes such as crubeens (pigs' trotters). There's a set dinner costing £23.50; for à la carte count on around £30 per person with drinks. It's a good idea to make reservations in summer.

Carlingford's newest eatery is *Magee's Bistro*, opposite Carlingford Arms; it is expensive but very good. Try the monkfish and black tiger prawns (£12.95). It closes on Tuesday.

When everything else in town is closed, *McKevitt's Village Hotel* may still be serving food; salmon costs £8.95. You can also get breakfast here costing £5.50, even if you're not staying.

Entertainment Popular pubs include *Carlingford Arms* and *Central Bar* opposite, which has Irish music at the weekend. *PJ's* pub, next door, is a traditional Irish bar with Irish music every Wednesday.

Getting There & Away Monday to Saturday, Bus Éireann (☎ 933 4075) runs buses five times daily to Dundalk, twice daily to Newry. There are no Sunday services.

MEATH & LOUTH

Omeath

☎ 042 • pop 315

Omeath (Ó Méith), smaller and less busy than Carlingford, lies across Carlingford Lough from County Down's Warrenpoint.

Facilities at the family-oriented *Táin Holiday Village* (☎ 937 5385), 2km south of Omeath on the Carlingford road, include a Jacuzzi and indoor pool; tent sites cost £17. Nearby is the An Óige *Omeath Hostel*, beside the Táin Trail.

Farther to the south of town is the friendly *Delamare House* (☎ 937 5101), opposite St Jude's Shrine. It's run by Eileen McGeown and B&B in the large, clean singles/doubles costs £22/32, or £25/40 with private bathroom.

Weather permitting, a passenger ferry (☎ 016937-72001) crosses the lough to Warrenpoint in County Down, 1 to 6 pm daily, May to September. A return ticket costs £2/1.

NORTHERN IRELAND

Northern Ireland

The prospect of permanent peace is likely to put Northern Ireland well and truly on the tourist map – and tourism, possibly more than any other industry, could bring enormous prosperity to a region that has suffered a quarter of a century of bad publicity.

It's worth remembering that, despite the apprehension caused by news of bombings and shootings, visitors to Northern Ireland have always faced more danger from erratic Irish drivers than from the Troubles.

In the North, you'll hear that the accent is distinctly different and notice that the currency is pounds sterling and distances are measured in miles, but otherwise things are very much the same north of the border. If anything, the Northern Irish are more friendly to foreign visitors than their compatriots in the South – perhaps to compensate for that bad publicity.

The rewards of a foray to the North are certainly worthwhile: the Antrim coast road follows an unbeatable stretch of coastline; there are some fascinating early-Christian remains around Lough Erne; Derry has one of the best-preserved old city walls in Europe, as well as vibrant nightlife; and Belfast, like Berlin, is a city in transformation.

Though some important issues remain unresolved and reminders of the Troubles abound, there is a feeling of tremendous optimism in Northern Ireland today – and visitors can't fail to be affected by it.

HISTORY

With the Industrial Revolution, Belfast and the surrounding counties became the industrial centre of the island, but the wealth generated by Belfast's industrial expansion went primarily to the Protestant community. In the late 19th and early 20th centuries, when Home Rule for Ireland became a possibility, the Protestant citizens of Belfast joined the Ulster Volunteer Force (UVF) in large numbers to resist any such move. The Catholic minority felt increasingly alienated and there were occasional sectarian attacks.

Partition

In the Government of Ireland Act of 1920 British Prime Minister Lloyd George split Ireland into two and allowed for Parliaments both north and south of the border. The division of the island was rough and ready. The Ulster Unionist leaders demanded only the six of Ulster's nine counties in which they were supported by half or more of the population. South of the dividing line, the country was overwhelmingly Catholic, with a small Protestant minority (5%). North of the border, the balance was very different, with a substantial Catholic minority (over 30%), and many areas, especially in South Armagh, where Catholics were actually in the majority.

The Anglo-Irish Treaty of 1921, which partitioned the country and granted southern Ireland its independence, was less than completely clear on the future of the North. A Boundary Commission was supposed to reconsider the borders and make adjustments as necessary – something it never did.

On 22 June 1921 the Northern Ireland Parliament came into being, with James Craig as the first prime minister. In 1923 the Civil War in the South ground to an exhausted halt with reluctant acceptance of Ireland's division. In the North, Catholic nationalists elected to the new Northern Ireland Parliament took up their seats with equal reluctance, but only in 1925, after the Boundary Commission had collapsed. The politics of the North became increasingly divided on religious grounds.

Protestant Dominance

The Northern Ireland Parliament sat from 1920 until 1972. During this time the Protestant majority made sure their rule was absolute by systematically excluding Catholics from power. The government at every level, from local councils to the Stormont Parliament, was Protestant dominated and consistently followed a 'jobs for the (Protestant) boys' approach. In the early 1970s, when Belfast's population was 25% Catholic, only 2.5% of Belfast Corporation jobs were held by Catholics. There was widespread discrimination against Catholics in housing, employment and social welfare.

The Protestant reluctance to share the country with Catholics was exacerbated by the shortage of things to share out anyway. The effects of the 1930s depression were even more severe in Northern Ireland than elsewhere in the UK, with unemployment averaging 25%. Per capita income was only about 60% of that in Britain, and indicators in every area from housing to public health were considerably worse than in Britain.

In 1922, the bitter struggle going on in the South spilled over the border and serious rioting broke out in Belfast. In 1935, 11 people died in further riots in Belfast. But in spite of all this, Northern Ireland remained relatively peaceful for many years after Partition.

In WWII, Belfast was heavily bombed, with many deaths and large areas of the city flattened. The first US army forces to land in Europe passed through Belfast on 26 January 1942. The strong support given to Britain's war effort further entrenched British backing of Northern Ireland's continued existence and independence. In 1949 the creation of the Republic of Ireland cut the South's final links, via the British Commonwealth, with the North. Even though the new Republic's constitution enshrined its eventual goal of regaining the North, this caused little stir. Not until the 1960s did Northern Ireland's basic instability begin to show itself.

Civil Rights

In the 1960s, the government under Prime Minister Terence O'Neill took the first tentative steps towards dealing with the problems of the North's Catholics. A meeting with the South's prime minister and a visit to a Catholic girls' school were hardly earth-shattering moves. But the reaction to these symbolic initiatives propelled Reverend Ian Paisley to front stage as the ranting personification of Protestant extremism. The next innocent addition to what was to become a messy stew was the creation of the Northern Ireland Civil Rights Association in 1967, to campaign for fairer representation for the North's Catholics.

It was in Derry (Londonderry) that Protestant political domination was at its most outrageous. In 1968 Derry's population was split approximately 60% Catholic to 40% Protestant, yet the city's council was consistently elected with exactly the reverse ratio. This was accomplished not only by a long-running gerrymander of the electoral boundaries, but also by handing out more votes to the Protestants via residency and home-ownership requirements. In October 1968 a civil rights march in Derry was violently broken up by the Royal Ulster Constabulary (RUC), and the Troubles, as they became euphemistically known, were under way.

In January 1969, People's Democracy, another civil rights movement, organised a Belfast to Derry march to demand a fairer division of jobs and housing and an end to unfair voting practices. Just outside Derry a Protestant mob attacked the marchers. The police stood to one side and then compounded the problem by a sweep through the predominantly Catholic Bogside area of Derry. Further marches and protests followed but, increasingly, exasperation on one side was met with violence from the other, and far from keeping the two sides apart the police were becoming part of the problem.

Finally, in August 1969, British troops were sent into Derry and, two days later, Belfast, to maintain law and order. Though the British army was initially welcomed by the Catholics, it soon came to be seen as a tool of the Protestant majority. The peaceful civil rights movement lost ground, and the Irish Republican Army (IRA), which had been hibernating, found itself with new and willing recruits for an armed struggle for independence from among the beleaguered

Catholic minority. Socialists such as Bernadette Devlin provided a brief flash of leadership, but it was 'the men with the guns' who soon called the tune.

The Troubles

For 25 years the story of the Troubles was one of lost opportunities, intransigence on both sides and fleeting moments of hope.

After 1971, suspected IRA sympathisers could be, and were, interned without trial. On Bloody Sunday (30 January 1972) 13 civilians were killed by British troops in Derry. An official inquiry into the circumstances surrounding the deaths was taking place at the time of writing. Northern Ireland's increasingly ineffective Parliament was abolished in 1972, although substantial progress had been made towards meeting the original civil rights demands. A new power-sharing arrangement was worked out in the 1973 Sunningdale Agreement, giving Catholics representation, but it was first rejected by the Protestants, then killed stone dead by the massive and overwhelmingly Protestant Ulster Workers' Strike of 1974.

While continuing to target people in Northern Ireland, the IRA moved their campaign of violence and terror to mainland Britain, bombing pubs and shops and killing many civilians. Their activities were increasingly criticised by citizens on all sides of the political spectrum, and by all mainstream political parties in Britain and the Republic. Meanwhile, Loyalist paramilitaries were running a sectarian murder campaign against Catholics. The Troubles rolled back and forth throughout the 1970s. Passions reached fever pitch in 1981 when Republican prisoners in the North went on a hunger strike, demanding the right to be recognised as political prisoners. Ten of them fasted to death, the best known being an elected MP, Bobby Sands.

The waters were further muddied by an incredible variety of parties, groups, splinter groups and even splinters of splinter groups, each with its own agenda. The IRA split into 'official' and 'provisional' wings, from which sprang even more extreme republican organisations such as the Irish National Liberation Army (INLA). Protestant loyalist paramilitary organisations sprang up in opposition to the IRA, and violence was frequently met with violence, indiscriminate outrage with indiscriminate outrage. The Royal Ulster Constabulary (RUC) was reorganised and retrained.

In 1985 the Anglo-Irish Agreement gave the Dublin government an official consultative role in Northern Ireland affairs for the first time. The idea was to make Northern nationalists feel that someone was looking out for their interests. However, Unionist politicians were outraged by what they saw as meddling by the Republic and protested against and boycotted anything to do with the agreement. From 1985 onwards there was a steady increase in the level and professionalism of violence from the loyalist side of the divide.

It's easy to line up the 'if only's when it comes to the problems of Ireland. If only the Home Rule movement hadn't encountered such violent opposition to Irish independence in the early part of this century, Ireland might be one country today and the problem would be simply not exist. Northern fears might have been reduced if only the Republic hadn't pandered to them by allowing the Catholic Church's prejudices (on sex, marriage, censorship and the position of the Church) to insinuate themselves into so many corners of the country.

Northern Catholics' antipathy to Northern Protestants might have been less if only they had been treated with some fairness between the 1920s and 1970s. Northern fears of Southern impoverishment might have been lower if only the Republic's government had not pursued its vision of a rural Arcadia for longer than was sensible. The British army's unpopularity might have been far less if only it hadn't overreacted so extremely to IRA provocation. And the North's unwillingness to countenance any agreement with the South might have been less if only the IRA hadn't been so callously indiscriminate in its violence or, equally frequently, so callously inept.

In 1970 the British home secretary, the hapless Reginald Maudling, was castigated for observing that the best hope for Northern Ireland was to achieve 'an acceptable level of violence'. Twenty years later that was precisely what had been achieved.

The Nineties

However, in the 1990s some external circumstances started to alter the picture. Membership of the EU had reduced the differences between North and South, while economic progress in Ireland shrunk the disparity between Northern and Southern standards of living. The importance of the Catholic Church in the South had also diminished.

In 1991, the various factions met for talks under Peter Brooke, the British government's representative in Northern Ireland. Further talks were held in 1992. On the surface nothing much seemed to come of all this, but behind the scenes individuals, and particularly the Social Democratic and Labour Party (SDLP; a mostly Catholic party) leader, John Hume, continued to beaver away, trying to persuade the mouthpieces of the main groups that something had to give.

In December 1993 the Downing Street Declaration was signed by British Prime Minister John Major and the Irish Prime Minister Albert Reynolds. It was a crucial element in the peace process, stating that Britain had no 'selfish, strategic or economic interest in Northern Ireland' and enshrining the principle of majority consent at the heart of any talks about constitutional change.

Then, seemingly out of the blue, on 31 August 1994 the Sinn Féin leader, Gerry Adams, announced a 'cessation of violence' on behalf of the IRA. In October 1994 the Combined Loyalist Military Command also announced a ceasefire. Most British troops were then withdrawn to barracks, and roadblocks were removed. There followed an edgy peace while all the parties restated their agendas.

In 1995 the British and Irish governments published two Framework documents intended to act as a basis for discussion on the way forwards. The first, *A Framework for Accountable Government in Northern Ireland*, set out the British government's proposals for restoring democracy through a new 90-member Assembly to be elected by proportional representation and with 'substantial legislative and administrative powers'. In the second, *A New Framework for Agreement*, the British and Irish governments put forward their joint proposals for relationships within the island and between the two different governments.

Although it was stressed that these were discussion documents and that nothing would be imposed on anyone without a referendum first, both sides dug in their heels. The main sticking point was the issue of 'decommissioning' – the requirement by Unionists that the IRA show good faith on a final peace settlement by surrendering its weapons before talks begin. For their part Sinn Féin and the IRA argued that no arms could be given up until British troops withdrew and political prisoners were freed, and that decommissioning should be part of the final settlement. With the peace process stalled, the IRA declared the ceasefire over when it exploded bombs in Canary Wharf in London on 9 February 1996, killing two people and injuring many more.

John Major's government, with a small majority in the House of Commons, had depended on the support of Unionist MPs. But in the British general election of May 1997, Tony Blair's Labour Party won a landslide victory enabling it to act with a much freer hand. In the same election, Sinn Féin's Gerry Adams and Martin McGuinness won two of Northern Ireland's seats in Westminster. In June, in the Irish Republic's general election, Fianna Fáil's Bertie Ahern, who had declared that he would be willing to talk to Sinn Féin about a new ceasefire, was elected as taoiseach.

In the same month, British officials, led by the then Northern Ireland Secretary Dr Mo Mowlam, promised to admit Sinn Féin to all-party talks in Stormont Castle following any new ceasefire. In the meantime the British and Irish governments had accepted the proposal by George Mitchell, the former US senator brokering the talks, on how to get round the decommissioning impasse. Talks on the future of Northern Ireland would take place parallel with the talks on decommissioning.

Encouraged by this, and by the decision of Ulster's Loyal Orange lodges to reroute or cancel some potentially violent 12 July marches celebrating the Battle of the Boyne, the IRA declared another ceasefire from 20 July 1997. Six weeks later Sinn Féin joined the peace talks and all sides sat down to negotiate for the first time in 25 years.

On 10 April 1998 an intensive series of negotiations culminated in the historic Good Friday Agreement, which put forward a new framework for British-Irish relationships. The agreement, which states that the political future of Northern Ireland depends on the consent of the majority of the people of Northern Ireland, was overwhelmingly endorsed by simultaneous referendums held in Northern Ireland and the Republic on 22 May 1998. Just over 71% of people in Northern Ireland voted to accept that Northern Ireland must be governed according to the democratic will, while the 94% Yes vote in the Republic signalled the end of Dublin's territorial claim over the six Northern counties. The South now aspires to a single united Ireland – with the people of the North having the final say at the ballot box.

The Good Friday Agreement included provision for the establishment of a 108-member Assembly to take over departments run by the British government's Northern Ireland ministers (see the following Government & Politics section), the terms of reference for an independent commission on the future of policing in Northern Ireland, plans for the release of most paramilitary prisoners within two years, the removal of security installations and a major reduction in the RUC.

The year of the peace agreement was also one of extreme violence. On 30 June 1998, despite a ban by the Parades Commission, the Orange Order announced that they would march down the Catholic Garvaghy Rd on their annual parade from Drumcree

Church to their lodge in Portadown, County Armagh. Loyalists opposed to the Good Friday Agreement wanted to both assert their right to march and damage the agreement. Escalating Protestant violence across the North culminated in a petrol bomb attack which burned to death three young boys on the morning of 12 July. The standing of the Orange Order took a serious battering when hardline Orangemen seemed more concerned with maintaining their political posturing than with condemning the murder of innocent children. Many members resigned and the order remains deeply divided over the issue of Drumcree and the Good Friday Agreement.

Then on 15 August 1998 came the single worst atrocity in the entire history of the Troubles: the bombing of the quiet market town of Omagh in County Tyrone by the Real IRA, a breakaway republican group opposed to the Good Friday Agreement. The 650kg bomb killed 29 people and injured 200. Confused telephone warnings caused the RUC to evacuate people to the very area where the bomb exploded. Swift action by politicians, including a statement by Gerry Adams condemning the bombing, prevented a loyalist backlash. Shortly afterwards the British and Irish governments passed strong new antiterrorist laws, and ceasefires were declared by the Real IRA, the INLA and the Loyalist Volunteer Force (LVF).

The peace process staggered on and in September 1998 David Trimble, leader of the Ulster Unionists, met Gerry Adams for the first time. Later in the year both David Trimble and John Hume, leader of the SDLP, were awarded the Nobel Peace Prize for their efforts in working towards peace in Northern Ireland.

The issue of paramilitary decommissioning has dogged the peace process throughout, with David Trimble refusing to allow Sinn Féin to take up their two ministerial seats in the Assembly before the decommissioning of IRA weapons, and Sinn Féin constantly reiterating that decommissioning was not a precondition to the implementation of the agreement. The exhaustive negotiations of the first half of 1999 ended in farce when the Ulster Unionists boycotted the Northern Ireland Assembly (see the following Government & Politics section) on the very day (15 July 1999) power was supposed to be devolved to Belfast.

Former US Senator George Mitchell, who brokered the peace talks of 1998, returned to Northern Ireland in September 1999 to lead an attempt to resolve the deadlock between the parties. At the time of writing, Mitchell's review was still under way.

Just a few days after the opening of Mitchell's review, the Independent Commission on Policing for Northern Ireland, chaired by former Governor of Hong Kong Chris Patten, published its report. The 128-page report, entitled *A New Beginning*, set out 175 recommendations aimed at transforming the Royal Ulster Constabulary (RUC), which has been disproportionately Protestant and unionist since it was first established in 1922.

The commission wants to see the proportion of Catholics in the force raised from 8 to 30% within 10 years (Catholics make up 42% of the population). The report also recommended that the RUC be renamed the Northern Ireland Police Service; that its badge, a harp and crown, be replaced; that the union flag no longer fly from police stations; that the current police authority be replaced; and that police numbers drop from 13,000 to 7,500. The report advised that an international commissioner be appointed to oversee the changes over the next five years. Implementation of the proposed recommendations depends very much on the outcome of George Mitchell's review.

On 12 October 1999, in a further move to push the peace process forwards, the UK Prime Minister Tony Blair appointed the hard-headed Peter Mandelson as Northern Ireland secretary. Mo Mowlam had been appointed to the position following Labour's election victory in May 1997. Mowlam was the first woman to hold the post, and many believe that it was her efforts that made the Good Friday Agreement possible.

NICKY CAVEN

**Social Democratic and Labour Party leader
John Hume**

GOVERNMENT & POLITICS

The new Northern Ireland Assembly was established as part of the Good Friday Agreement of 10 April 1998. Following a referendum which resulted in the majority voting in favour of the agreement, the Assembly was constituted under the Northern Ireland (Elections) Act 1998. Under the agreement, the Assembly will have full legislative and executive authority over six Northern Ireland government departments: agriculture, economic development, education, environment, finance and personnel, and health and social services.

On 25 June 1998, 108 members were elected to the Assembly by proportional representation (single transferable vote). The Ulster Unionist Party (UUP), led by David Trimble, won 28 seats; the Social Democratic and Labour Party (SDLP), led by John Hume, won 24; the Democratic Unionist Party (DUP), led by the Reverend Ian Paisley, won 20; Sinn Féin won 18; the Alliance party won six seats; the UK Unionist Party won five (four members have since resigned and formed the Northern Ireland Unionist Party); the Northern Ireland Women's Coalition won two seats; the Progressive Unionist Party won two seats; and independents won three (they have since formed the United Unionist Assembly Party).

The new Assembly met for the first time on 1 July 1998. David Trimble was elected as first minister (designate) and Seamus Mallon of the SDLP was elected deputy first minister (designate). The Assembly met on 15 July 1999 to nominate ministers to the executive committee but, because the meeting was boycotted by the UUP and the only parties to nominate were the SDLP and Sinn Féin, the nomination procedure could not go ahead. During the meeting Seamus Mallon resigned as deputy first minister and gave a speech highly critical of the Unionists.

At the time of writing the government of Northern Ireland had returned to the regime under the Anglo-Irish Agreement, which gave the Republic of Ireland a consultative role in the government of Northern Ireland.

NICKY CAVEN

Ulster Unionist Party leader
David Trimble

ECONOMY

During the 19th century, Northern Ireland was at the forefront of the Industrial Revolution and one of the most prosperous regions of Europe. The decline of traditional industries, such as shipbuilding, textiles and rope making, coupled with the economic dislocation caused by the Troubles and one of the highest birth rates in Europe, has meant an economy increasingly

characterised by high unemployment, low incomes and emigration. As a consequence, the region has been heavily subsidised by Britain, the European Union and the International Fund for Ireland (IFI), to which the US has been one of the largest contributors. In addition security operations have involved high levels of expenditure and employment on defence matters. Political and economic improvements have seen the high level of subsidy diminish, although it remains significant.

Northern Ireland's unemployment rate has fallen to under 7%, from a high of 17% in the early 1980s. While this has been aided by the large amounts of money that have been poured into Northern Ireland since the late 1970s, it also reflects a marked improvement in the performance of the local economy since the late 1980s. This has seen a reversal of the traditional pattern of emigration to one of immigration during the 1990s. The unemployment rate among the Catholic community has declined significantly and the economic gap between the Protestant and Catholic communities has narrowed in recent years.

However, the employment structure of the province still reflects the economic and political legacy of Northern Ireland's recent history. Just under 30% of the workforce is employed directly by the public sector and many more jobs are supported indirectly through continued high levels of public expenditure. Agriculture makes up around 6% of employment – three times the UK average – while manufacturing and construction account for a further 23%. The dependence on traditional sectors such as textiles and food remains higher than in the UK.

While the performance of the economy had already shown a significant improvement, the first ceasefire in 1994 brought an almost instant dividend in the shape of a 20% boom in tourism, especially from Britain and the Republic. After the collapse of the ceasefires in 1996, tourism figures dropped by approximately 30%. It was not until 1998 that an improvement was seen, with a 4% increase in visitors. Current predictions are that tourism has the potential to create 20,000 new jobs in Northern Ireland and increase its contribution to gross domestic product (GDP) by another 4%. This would bring tourism closer to Republic of Ireland levels, where tourism accounts for 6% of GDP.

The underlying growth of the economy has remained strong throughout the 1990s. The 1997 ceasefire is continuing to bring about positive economic developments. Foreign investment in 1997 to 1998 was a record £522 million, with an increasing share coming from high-tech sectors such as computer software. The major British retailers, such as Sainsbury's and Tesco, have expanded into Northern Ireland. The hospitality sector has shown a dramatic improvement, with a sharp rise in hotel space – including a Hilton hotel – and major investment in bars, restaurants and conference facilities, especially in the centre of Belfast.

With continued peace and an end to political uncertainty, these developments should continue well into the future.

Belfast

pop 279,240

Like Berlin and Beirut, Belfast is a city that is fast rebuilding and reinventing itself. Massive investment during the past few years combined with the optimism engendered by the peace process has transformed Belfast into something of a boom town.

A string of upmarket hotels, including the Belfast Hilton, opened in the late 1990s, along with dozens of smart restaurants, bars and cafés. The government-initiated Laganside project has cleaned up the much neglected River Lagan and is responsible for the regeneration of inner-city areas such as the trendified Cathedral Quarter, the development of spanking new riverside apartments, the 2000-capacity Waterfront Hall as well as a £91 million sporting and cultural complex, which is due to open in November 2001.

Step into a contemporary bar or restaurant and it's difficult to avoid picking up a sense of excitement, a general feeling and buzz that, maybe just maybe, after 30 years of war Belfast is about to join the rest of the world.

The city is home to about half a million people (about 30% of the population of Northern Ireland) and is compact and easy to get around, with most points of interest within easy walking distance of each other. Like any city worth its salt, Belfast contains some architectural and cultural gems, such as the impressive City Hall and the excellent Linen Hall Library. There are dozens of splendid Victorian pubs to explore and, for a city of its size, Belfast boasts a pretty good nightlife (much of it geared to the student population). It's also pleasantly situated: the Belfast Hills are visible to the west, the rocks and green slopes of Cave Hill loom over the city to the north, and the sweep of Belfast Lough cuts into the city centre from the north-east.

There are, of course, plenty of reminders of the Troubles to be seen, and the deep conflict and passions that have torn North-

Highlights

- Take a black-cab tour of the murals of West Belfast
- Eat out along the buzzing Golden Mile
- Sample the nightlife in the university area
- Hike up Cave Hill for great views
- Enjoy traditional music in fabulous pubs

ern Ireland apart over the decades are perhaps more acute in Belfast than anywhere else. But this shouldn't put anyone off visiting. Statistically Belfast is a much safer city for a visitor than even the most touristically inclined US metropolises. And although the so-called Peace Line still divides the Catholic and Protestant communities of Belfast, these days the gates remain open.

HISTORY

Compared with many other cities, Belfast is relatively new, and has few reminders of its pre-19th-century existence. The city's name comes from Beál Feirste (Mouth of the Sandy Ford), a reference to the River Farset, which used to flow through the town centre but is now contained inside an underground pipe. In 1177, the Norman John de Courcy built a castle by the River Lagan, and a small settlement grew up around it. Both were destroyed 20 years later, and the region was controlled for a long time afterwards by the Irish O'Neill family. The city began to develop in earnest in 1611 when Baron Arthur Chichester built a castle and promoted the growth of the settlement.

The first significant wave of foreign settlers were Scottish and English Planters brought in by James I in the early 17th century. They were followed by an influx of Huguenots in the late 17th century. These French Protestants, fleeing from persecution in France, laid the foundations for a thriving linen industry. More Scottish and English settlers arrived, and other industries such as rope making, tobacco, engineering and shipbuilding were developed.

Antagonism between Protestants and Catholics only really developed during the 19th century. Prior to this, Belfast had produced many Protestant supporters of an independent Ireland and a fairer society. The United Irishmen, who pushed for increasing independence from England, were founded in Belfast in 1791, and the struggle for fairer trading terms enjoyed Protestant and Catholic support.

During the 18th and 19th centuries Belfast was the one city in Ireland that really experienced the Industrial Revolution. Sturdy rows of brick terraced houses were built for the factory and shipyard workers. A population of around 20,000 people in 1800 grew steadily to around 400,000 at the start of WWI, by which time Belfast had nearly overtaken Dublin in size.

Queen Victoria visited Belfast in 1849 and her brief foray into the city has been immortalised by a large number of streets and monuments named after her. Belfast was granted city status by Victoria in 1888.

The division of Ireland after WWI and independence in the South gave Belfast a new role as the capital of Northern Ireland. It also marked the end of the city's industrial growth, although the decline didn't really set in until after WWII. Since the initial outbreak of rioting in 1969, Belfast has seen more than its fair share of violence and bloodshed, and shocking pictures of extremist bombings and killings, often mirrored by security-force brutality, have made Belfast a household name around the world. The mayhem reached its peak in the 1970s, and through the 1980s and into the 1990s the sectarian violence of Belfast appeared to have simmered down. The ceasefire in 1994 briefly raised hope that things might at last improve, but after the bombing of Canary Wharf in London in 1996 there was a return to the tit-for-tat killings.

Although the 1997 ceasefire has been met with greater caution, it has proved to be more enduring. Economically Belfast is reaping the rewards: unemployment is at an all-time low, house prices have been rising faster than in any other UK city and tourism is booming. There's never been a better time to visit.

ORIENTATION

The city centre is compact, with the imposing City Hall in Donegall Square as a convenient central landmark. Belfast's principal shopping district is north of the square along and off Donegall Place/Royal Ave. The pedestrianised streets around here are in part a by-product of the Troubles. At their height in the 1970s, terrorist activities turned the centre into a heavily militarised zone, but the security presence is very low-key now.

A little farther north the once run-down area around Donegall St and St Anne's Cathedral, the Cathedral Quarter, is being rapidly redeveloped, with trendy restaurants, bars and clubs springing up among the red-brick warehouses and fortified pubs.

Reminders of the Victorian era can be found in the stately buildings surrounding City Hall, in the narrow alleys known as the Entries off Ann and High Sts, and in the ornate Grand Opera House and Crown Liquor Saloon on Great Victoria St.

BELFAST

Heading south from Donegall Square, Great Victoria St and Dublin Rd lead to University Rd, where you'll find Queen's University, the Botanic Gardens and the Ulster Museum. There are dozens of restaurants and bars in this area – it's called the Golden Mile – and at night it's the most energetic and cheerful area of a generally hard-working city. Most of the city's accommodation options, including several hostels, are also south of the centre around the university area.

The Europa Bus Centre is behind the Europa Hotel, in Glengall St, along with the Great Victoria St train station. The Laganside Bus Centre is east of the Albert Memorial Clocktower opposite Queen Elizabeth Bridge.

A cross-harbour train link, the Dargan Bridge, runs alongside the Lagan Bridge north of Queen Elizabeth Bridge.

To the east of Donegall Square is Chichester St, which runs down to Oxford St, where you'll find the Royal Courts of Justice, St George's Market, the new Belfast Hilton and the Waterfront Hall, a large conference and concert centre. East of the river are Samson and Goliath, the giant cranes dominating the Harland & Wolff shipyards.

West of the centre, the Westlink Motorway divides the city from West Belfast. The (Protestant) Shankill Rd and the (Catholic) Falls Rd run west into West Belfast. The Peace Line built between the two was intended as a safety measure to discourage extremists of either ilk from creating mayhem then scuttling quickly back to their side of the tracks. It's now possible to cross from one side to the other.

Maps
The Northern Ireland Tourist Board (NITB) produces a good free map of the city centre. The *Collins Belfast Streetfinder* map (£2.99) is more detailed and includes a full index of street names.

INFORMATION
Tourist Offices
The NITB office (☎ 90 246609) is at St Anne's Court, 59 North St. In mid-2000 the office will move to 47 Donegall Place, near City Hall. Most of the year it opens 9 am to 5.15 pm Monday to Saturday. In June, July and August, it has extended opening hours which may vary depending on the number of visitors. In those months it usually opens 9 am to 7 pm on weekdays, 9 am to 5.15 pm on Saturday, and 10 am to 4 pm on Sunday. Outside these hours, a computerised database outside gives details of accommodation and so on. You can pick up information about the whole of Northern Ireland here, and book accommodation both within Northern Ireland and in Britain. There's also a bureau de change and souvenir shop.

There are tourist information offices in Belfast City and International Airports; the City Airport branch (☎ 90 457745) opens 5.30 am to 10 pm daily, while the International Airport branch (☎ 94 422888) opens 24 hours.

Bord Fáilte (Irish Tourist Board; ☎ 90 327888), 53 Castle St, opens 9 am to 5 pm on weekdays, 9 am to 12.30 pm on Saturday, March to September.

Money
There are branches of the major Northern Irish banks in the centre of Belfast. Most open 9.30 am to 5.30 pm on weekdays, and some open late on Thursday and on Saturday morning. There are plenty of ATMs around town; handy ones can be found along Donegall Place and south of the city centre on Shaftesbury Square.

The NITB has a bureau de change, as do the GPO on Castle Place and the post office in Shaftesbury Square.

There's a branch of Thomas Cook (☎ 90 550232) with exchange facilities at 11 Donegall Place, and another at the International Airport (☎ 94 422536) which opens 5 am to 10 pm Tuesday, Wednesday and Thursday, 5 am to midnight Friday, Saturday and Sunday, and 5 am to 11 pm on Monday.

Post & Communications
The GPO, on Castle Place at the junction of Donegall Place and Royal Ave, opens 9 am to 5.30 pm on weekdays, and 9 am to 7 pm

on Saturday. Other convenient post offices are in Shaftesbury Square and at the junction of University and Malone Rds.

There are plenty of public telephones, which are divided into coin only, phonecard only, and those that accept both. The local Mace convenience stores sell pre-paid phonecards.

You can log on to the Internet at Revelations Café (☎ 90 320337, email info@revelations.co.uk), 27 Shaftesbury Square. It opens 10 am to 10 pm on weekdays, 10 am to 8 pm on Saturday, and noon to 10 pm on Sunday. Access costs £5 per hour. Belfast Central Library offers Internet access for £2 per hour. See Libraries later in this section for opening hours.

Travel Agencies
The USIT/Belfast Student Travel office (☎ 90 324073) is at 13B Fountain Centre, College St. Queen's University Travel Centre (☎ 90 241830), in the Student Union Building on University Rd, is also run by USIT and opens to non-students too.

For more conventional travel information there's Thomas Cook (☎ 90 550232) at 11 Donegall Place.

Bookshops
Eason's (☎ 90 328566), 16 Ann St; Dillon's (☎ 90 240159), 42 Fountain St; and Waterstone's (☎ 90 247355), 8 Royal Ave, all have a good selection of books on Ireland. Queen's University Bookshop, at University Terrace opposite Queen's College, is also worth popping into if you're looking for books about the North.

Bookfinders Café (☎ 90 328269), 47 University Rd, is a second-hand bookshop and book-finding service with a gallery and popular café at the back.

The government-run Stationery Office Bookshop (☎ 90 235041), 16 Arthur St, has a selection of maps and guides. The Automobile Association (AA; ☎ 0990 500600), 108-110 Great Victoria St, sells maps and travel guides.

The Green Cross Art Shop (☎ 90 243371), 51-53 Falls Rd, has a range of books on Irish issues, mainly giving the republican perspective. The Irish language and arts centre Cultúrlann MacAdam ÓFiaich (☎ 90 245255), 216 Falls Rd, has some interesting titles on Irish culture, local history and politics.

Libraries
Belfast Central Library (☎ 90 243233), Royal Ave, opens 9.30 am to 8 pm Monday and Thursday, 9.30 am to 5.30 pm Tuesday, Wednesday and Friday, and 9.30 am to 1 pm on Saturday. See also the Linen Hall Library in the Around the Centre section later in this chapter.

Laundry
In the university area there's Mike's Laundrette and Agincourt Laundrette, 46 and 120 Agincourt Ave, and Cleanerette Laundrette, 160 Lisburn Rd. More fun is Duds 'n' Suds, 37 Botanic Ave, which incorporates a snack bar. It opens 8 am to 9 pm on weekdays, 8 am to 6 pm on Saturday, and noon to 6 pm on Sunday.

Medical Services
Accident and emergency services are available at the Royal Victoria Hospital (☎ 90 240503), on Grosvenor Rd west of the city centre; at the Mater Hospital (☎ 90 741211), on Crumlin Rd near the junction of Antrim Rd and Clifton St; and at the Ulster Hospital (☎ 90 484511), Upper Newtownards Rd, Dundonald, near Stormont Castle.

For prescriptions, travel vaccinations and so on, you should consult a GP as a temporary resident. All hostels and hotels should have lists of local practitioners.

Unlike in England, Scotland and Wales, the Abortion Act 1967 does not apply in Northern Ireland, so it is illegal. A local GP, however, should be able to give initial advice and guidance in the case of an unwanted pregnancy.

Emergency
For national emergency phone numbers see Telephone in the Post & Communications section of the Facts for the Visitor chapter. Other emergency numbers are the Rape

euro currency converter IR£1 = €1.27

BELFAST

BELFAST

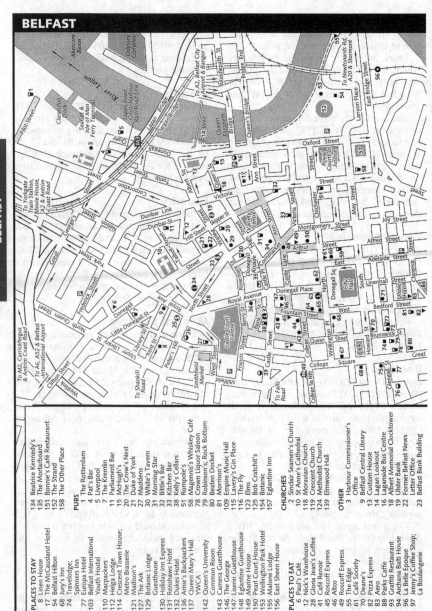

PLACES TO STAY
8   Linen House
17   The McCausland Hotel
54   Belfast Hilton
68   Jury's Inn
74   Travelodge;
     Spinners Inn
77   Europa Hotel
103   Belfast International
      Youth Hostel
110   Macpackers
112   Helga Lodge
114   Crescent Town House;
      Metro Brasserie
121   Madison's
127   The Ark
129   Botanic Lodge
      Guesthouse
130   Holiday Inn Express
131   Renshaws Hotel
132   Dukes Hotel
136   Arnie's Backpackers
137   Queen Mary's Hall
      YWCA
142   Queen's University
      Common Room
143   Camera Guesthouse
146   The George
147   Liserin Guesthouse
148   Eglantine Guesthouse
149   Marine House
150   Pearl Court House
153   Wellington Park Hotel
155   Malone Lodge
156   East Sheen House

PLACES TO EAT
6   Paul's Café
12   Nick's Warehouse
28   Gloria Jean's Coffee
41   Café Renoir
45   Roscoff Express
46   Altos
49   Roscoff Express
55   The Edge
61   Café Society
70   Deane's
82   Pizza Express
83   Aero
88   Parks Caffe
93   Graffiti Restaurant
94   Archana Balti House
96   La Belle Epoque
97   Jenny's Coffee Shop;
      La Boulangerie

134   Beatrice Kennedy's
135   The Mortarboard
151   Bonnie's Café Restaurant
152   The Strand
158   The Other Place

PUBS
1   The Rotterdam
4   Pat's Bar
5   Liverpool
7   The Kremlin
11   Parliament Bar
15   McHugh's
20   The Crow's Nest
21   Duke of York
27   Maddens
30   White's Tavern
31   Morning Star
32   Bittle's Bar
33   Kitchen Bar
38   Kelly's Cellars
51   Rumpole's
58   Magennis's Whiskey Café
78   Crown Liquor Saloon
79   Robinson's; Rock Bottom
80   Beaten Docket
81   Morrison's
109   Empire Music Hall
115   Lavery's Gin Place
116   The Fly
123   Elms
125   Bob Cratchit's
154   Botanic
157   Eglantine Inn

CHURCHES
2   Sinclair Seamen's Church
10   St Anne's Cathedral
118   Moravian Church
119   Crescent Church
124   Methodist Church
139   Elmwood Hall

OTHER
3   Harbour Commissioner's
    Office
9   Belfast Central Library
13   Custom House
14   Lagan Lookout
16   Laganside Bus Centre
18   Albert Memorial Clocktower
19   Ulster Bank
22   Former Belfast News
    Letter Office
23   Belfast Bank Building

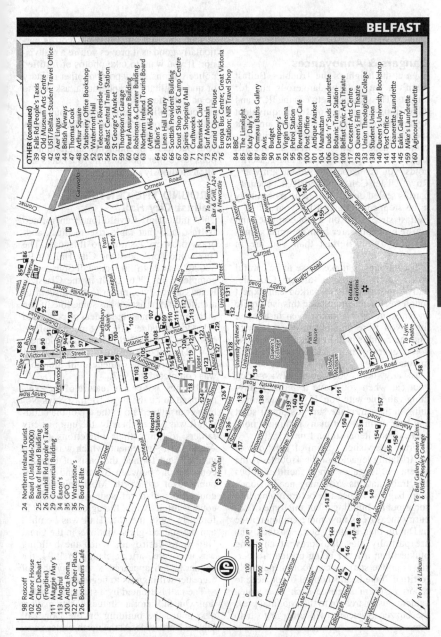

BELFAST

OTHER (continued)
39 Falls Rd People's Taxis
40 Old Museum Arts Centre
42 USIT/Belfast Student Travel Office
43 Aer Lingus
44 British Airways
47 Thomas Cook
48 Arthur Square
50 Stationery Office Bookshop
52 Waterfront Hall
53 Telecom's Riverside Tower
56 Belfast Central Train Station
57 St George's Market
59 Thompson's Garage
60 Pearl Assurance Building
62 Robinson & Cleaver Building
63 Northern Ireland Tourist Board
   (After Mid-2000)
64 Dillon's
65 Linen Hall Library
66 Scottish Provident Building
67 Scout Shop Ski & Camp Centre
69 Spires Shopping Mall
71 Craftworks
72 Brunswick Club
73 Surf Mountain
75 Grand Opera House
76 Europa Bus Centre; Great Victoria
   St Station; NIR Travel Shop
84 BBC
85 The Limelight
86 Katy Daly's
87 Ormeau Baths Gallery
89 Avis
90 Budget
91 Dempsey's
92 Virgin Cinema
95 Petrol Station
99 Revelations Café
100 Post Office
101 Antique Market
104 Manhattan
106 Duds 'n' Suds Laundrette
107 Botanic Train Station
108 Belfast Civic Arts Theatre
117 Crescent Arts Centre
128 Queen's Film Theatre
133 Union Theological College
138 Student Union
140 Queen's University Bookshop
141 Post Office
144 Cleanerette Laundrette
145 Eakin Gallery
159 Mike's Laundrette
160 Agincourt Laundrette

98 Roscoff
102 Manor House
105 Chez Delbart
    (Frogities)
111 Maggie May's
113 Moghul
120 Antica Roma
122 The Other Place
126 Bookfinders Café

24 Northern Ireland Tourist
   Board (Until Mid-2000)
25 Bank of Ireland Building
26 Shankill Rd People's Taxis
29 Commercial Building
34 Eason's
35 GPO
36 Waterstone's
37 Bord Fáilte

Crisis Centre (☎ 90 326803) and the Samaritans (☎ 90 664422, 0845 7909090).

Dangers & Annoyances
Even at the height of the Troubles, Belfast wasn't a particularly dangerous city for tourists. The violence between the IRA (and its various offspring) and the equivalent loyalist paramilitaries was usually aimed at specific people. Nevertheless, security precautions used to affect tourists as much as anyone. If the peace process and ceasefire holds, you can expect to see the army and Royal Ulster Constabulary (RUC) security patrols scaled down. You're no more likely to be stopped and asked for your ID on a Belfast street than on a London one, and you're probably safer from 'normal' criminal activity in Belfast than you are in London.

It continues to make sense to be careful where you park your car, though. Cars illegally (or suspiciously) parked can expect rough treatment. In practice this isn't quite as fearsome as it sounds: even in the bad times you were unlikely to come back to find the bomb squad in action just because you'd overstayed a parking meter for 10 minutes!

As anywhere, you should always lock your car when you leave it and take anything valuable with you. If you leave something in the car, make sure it's out of sight and bear in mind that many insurance policies exclude items stolen from cars.

From the visitor's point of view one of the irritating legacies of the Troubles is the absence of luggage storage facilities at bus and train stations. You may need to open your bag for inspection before going into some public buildings, but this type of security measure is now more commonplace in Dublin than Belfast! Some postbox slits are partially closed to prevent anything bulkier than a letter being posted. To outsiders police stations can look offputtingly fortified. Take heart, though: if you need to report a 'normal' crime such as a stolen camera, just march up to the door and press the buzzer. Someone will emerge to help you.

It's still a good idea to carry some form of identification on you: a passport is particularly good as it proves you're a real visitor. If you want to take photos of fortified police stations, army posts or other military or quasi-military paraphernalia, ask first to be on the safe side.

You're unlikely to get into furious political or religious arguments in Belfast pubs because both topics are usually avoided with outsiders. In staunchly single-minded pubs of either persuasion, outsiders are often studiously avoided!

AROUND THE CENTRE
Belfast City Hall
The Industrial Revolution transformed Belfast, and that rapid rise to muck-and-brass prosperity shows to this day. The fine white Portland-stone City Hall (☎ 90 320202, ext 2346) in Donegall Square was completed in 1906. Built in the Classical Renaissance style, much to the disdain of architectural purists, it has some fine Italian marble inside and a great deal of pomp and splendour outside. The first meeting of the Northern Ireland Parliament was held here in 1921, but it subsequently met at the Union Theological College until Stormont was completed in 1932.

The most noticeable feature of the exterior used to be the huge 'Belfast Says No' banner displayed along the top of the building. It was placed there by the unionist city fathers to show their objections to the Anglo-Irish Agreement, which was signed in 1985 and formed the basis of ongoing consultations between Britain and the Republic over the North. Most unionist city councillors also refused to take part in council affairs while the agreement was in force. In 1988 the City Hall was bombed and the stained-glass windows in the Great Hall were destroyed. When the building was uncovered after cleaning in 1994, the banner had disappeared, a small symbol of a greater willingness to negotiate.

The hall is fronted by a statue of a rather dour Queen Victoria. Statues of city mayors also guard the building on the Donegall Square North side. At the north-eastern corner of the City Hall grounds is a statue of Sir Edward Harland, the Yorkshire-born marine engineer who founded the Harland & Wolff shipyards. In its prime, the shipyard was one of Belfast's biggest businesses, and it still survives, if in much quieter form. The yard's most famous construction was the ill-fated *Titanic*, which sank in 1912 after colliding with an iceberg on its maiden voyage to America. A memorial to its victims stands on the eastern side of the City Hall.

The Marquess of Dufferin (1826–1902), whose career included postings as ambassador to Constantinople in Ottoman Turkey, St Petersburg in Tsarist Russia, Paris and Rome, and as governor-general to Canada and viceroy to India, has an extremely ornate temple-like memorial on the western side of the City Hall. He was responsible for adding Burma to the British Empire in 1886. Look out, too, for monuments to the United States of America Expeditionary Force, which arrived in Belfast in January 1942, and to the Boer War.

Free one-hour tours of the City Hall take place at 10.30 and 11.30 am and 2.30 pm on weekdays, and at 2.30 pm on Saturday, June to September; and at 2.30 pm Monday to Saturday, the rest of the year. Among other things, you get to see the Council Chamber with its red and blue flashing lights to tell councillors when they've overtalked their allotted 10 minutes; a painting of the proclamation of Edward VII outside City Hall (slashed by a visitor in 1991 and now behind glass); and some highly fanciful images in the grey and white marble of the hall.

Linen Hall Library

Opposite City Hall on Donegall Square North is the wonderful Linen Hall Library (☎ 90 321707, email info@linenhall.com), which was established in 1788 to 'improve the mind and excite a spirit of general inquiry'. The library houses some 260,000 books, more than half of which are part of its important Irish and local-studies collection. The political collection consists of pretty much everything that was ever written (some 135,000 publications) about Northern Irish politics since 1966. There's also an extensive performing-arts collection covering Irish theatre and actors, and an important historical collection of early Belfast and Ulster printing.

There's non-member research access to all collections and there's a comprehensive computer-based catalogue. Recent refurbishment (expected to be completed in August 2000) has seen the creation of a new reading room, a separate performance/lecture space and complete access for disabled visitors. The library has a small café and all the daily newspapers.

Thomas Russell, the first librarian, was a founding member of the United Irishmen and a close friend of Wolfe Tone – a reminder that this movement for independence from Britain had its origins in Belfast. Russell was hanged in 1803 after Robert Emmet's abortive rebellion. For over a century the library was in the White

BELFAST

The Red Hand of Ulster

The symbol of the province of Ulster is a striking red hand which you'll see displayed on coats of arms, in stained-glass windows and, vividly, above the entrance to the Linen Hall Library on Donegall Square North. The story goes that way back in the Middle Ages, when Viking raids were a regular occurrence, a group of Vikings had already settled the land and looked on in horror as another raiding vessel approached. The chief announced that the land would belong to whoever put their hand on it first, whereupon he sliced off his own hand and threw it forwards, thus beating the raiders to it. The O'Neill clan later adopted the red hand as their emblem, and it went on to become the symbol of Ulster.

Linen Hall, which was built from 1784 but demolished to make way for the City Hall. The entrance doorway to the present library is draped with stone linen and topped by the Red Hand of Ulster.

The library opens 9.30 am to 5.30 pm on weekdays, and 9.30 am to 4 pm on Saturday.

Other Donegall Square Buildings

Donegall Square, with the City Hall sat squarely in the middle, is undoubtedly the centre of Belfast. If you come into town by local bus you're likely to be dropped here, as most local bus services arrive and depart from around the square.

It has a number of interesting buildings, but easily the most magnificent is the wonderfully ornate **Scottish Provident Building**, built from 1897 to 1902, overlooking the City Hall from Donegall Square West. It's decorated with a veritable riot of fascinating statuary, including several allusions to the industries that assured Victorian Belfast's prosperity, as well as sphinxes, dolphins and a variety of lions' heads.

The building was the work of the architectural partnership of Young & MacKenzie, who counterbalanced it in 1902 with the **Pearl Assurance Building** on the Donegall Square East corner. Between these two examples of turn-of-the-century extravagance is the equally fine **Robinson & Cleaver Building**, once the Royal Irish Linen Warehouse and then Belfast's finest department store.

The Entries

The area immediately north of High St was the oldest part of Belfast but it suffered considerable damage during WWII bombing. The narrow alleyways known as the Entries run off High St and Ann St in the pedestrianised shopping centre. At one time they were bustling commercial and residential centres: Pottinger's Entry had 34 houses in 1822. Today pubs are just about all that survive down these hideaways. The **Morning Star** on **Pottinger's Entry** is one of the most attractive of these wonderful old Belfast bars, and it's recommended for food, too.

Joy's Entry is named after the Joy family. In 1737 Francis Joy founded the *Belfast News Letter*, the first daily newspaper in Britain. It's still in business today. One of his grandsons, Henry Joy McCracken, was executed for supporting the 1798 United Irishmen's revolt.

The United Irishmen were founded in 1791 by Wolfe Tone in Peggy Barclay's tavern in **Crown Entry**. They used to meet in **Kelly's Cellars** (1720) on Bank St off Royal Ave. **White's Tavern** (1630) on **Wine Cellar Entry** is the oldest pub in the city and is still a popular lunchtime meeting spot.

At the end of Ann St is **Arthur Square**, where five pedestrianised streets meet with a bandstand, buskers, preachers, hawkers and all sorts of other activities. This was once the central traffic junction in the city but the traffic has long been diverted. It was also the site of the Abercorn, a popular café before the Troubles, until one crowded Saturday lunchtime in 1972 when a terrorist bomb destroyed it; redevelopment has removed all trace of the place.

Crown Liquor Saloon

Across from the Europa Hotel on Great Victoria St, the Crown Liquor Saloon was built by Patrick Flanagan in 1885 and displays Victorian architectural flamboyance at its most extravagant. Owned by the National Trust and operated by Bass Ireland, this pub is on every visitor's itinerary: you need to get there early to have any hope of standing space, let alone a seat. The exterior is decorated with myriad different coloured and shaped tiles, while the interior has a mass of stained and cut glass, marble, mosaic and mahogany furniture. 'Gas' mantles provide atmospheric lighting.

A long, highly decorated bar dominates one side of the pub, while on the other is a row of ornate wooden snugs topped by stirring mottoes. The snugs come equipped with brass plates for striking matches and with bells which were once connected to the bell board behind the bar, enabling drinkers to demand top-ups without leaving their seats. You can no longer do that, but you can have yourself and your pint beamed to audiences around the world via the Crown's live Internet site.

The Crown was lucky to survive the 1993 bomb which devastated the Opera House and destroyed Robinson's, a couple of doors away. Above the Crown is **Flannigan's**, which displays memorabilia from the *Titanic*.

Grand Opera House

One of Belfast's great landmarks is the Grand Opera House (☎ 90 241919), across the road from the Crown Liquor Saloon on Great Victoria St. Opened in 1895, the Opera House was closed for a considerable part of the 1970s before a restoration project completely refurbished both the interior and the red-brick exterior.

It has suffered grievously at the hands of the IRA. A 450kg truck bomb caused extensive damage in December 1991, and a multi-million-pound reconstruction had barely been completed before another well-loaded truck was parked outside on 20 May 1993. The interior has been restored to over-the-top Victoriana, with purple satin in abundance and swirling wood and plasterwork. It's constantly busy with music shows, operas, plays and ballets.

Albert Memorial Clocktower & Around

WJ Barre's 1867 Albert Memorial Clocktower, located in Queen's Square at the junction of High and Victoria Sts, is not so dramatically out of kilter as the famous tower in Pisa, but it is, nevertheless, a leaning tower.

Looking across the River Lagan from the clocktower, eastern Belfast is dominated by the huge cranes of the Harland & Wolff shipyards. The modern Queen Elizabeth Bridge crosses the Lagan just to the south, but immediately south again is **Queen's Bridge** with its ornate lamps. Completed in 1843, this was Sir Charles Lanyon's (the pre-eminent architect of Belfast in its prime) first important Belfast construction.

Many of the buildings around the clocktower are the work of Lanyon. The white stone building immediately north of the clocktower was completed in 1852 by Lanyon as a head office for the **Northern Bank**. Farther north stands **Clifton House**, built in 1774 by Robert Joy (Henry Joy McCracken's uncle) as a poorhouse and the finest surviving 18th-century building in Belfast. East towards the river is the renovated **Custom House**, built by Lanyon in Italianate style between 1854 and 1857. On the waterfront side the pediment carries sculpted portrayals of Britannia, Neptune and Mercury.

Follow the waterfront round to the Sea-Cat and Isle of Man ferry terminal beside the **Harbour Commissioner's Office**. The interior of the office features striking marble and stained glass as well as art and sculpture inspired by Belfast's maritime history. The captain's table built for the *Titanic* lives unassumingly here, too. It was completed behind schedule and never made it on board. Guided tours of the office (☎ 90 554422) are available during the Belfast City Summer Fest (see Special Events later in this chapter). The office is also open during European Heritage Weekend, which takes place in October or November.

Sinclair Seamen's Church, next to the Harbour Commissioner's Office, was built by Charles Lanyon in 1857 and was intended to meet the spiritual needs of sailors coming into the port of Belfast. Part church, part maritime museum, it has a pulpit made from a ship's prow and an organ which sports starboard and port lights. The church opens during services from 2 to 5 pm on Wednesday, and at 11.30 am and 7 pm on Sunday.

Back along Donegall Quay is the venerable **Liverpool** pub, which so far has been spared any sort of olde-worlde renovation or trendification.

Ulster Bank & Around

The grandiose 1860 Ulster Bank survived the wartime bombing which obliterated much of this area. The imposing building has iron railings decorated with the Red Hand of Ulster, cast-iron lamp standards, soaring columns and sculpted figures depicting Britannia, Justice and Commerce.

BELFAST

The rooftop figures were by Thomas Fitz-patrick, who was also responsible for the carvings on the nearby Custom House. Inside the building's even more impressive, with cute blue cherubs playing instruments to customers queuing to access their bank accounts.

At the junction of Waring St with Donegall St is the deserted 1822 **Commercial Building**, easily identified by the prominent name of the Northern Whig Printing Company. Opposite is the **Belfast Bank Building**, now occupied by the Northern Bank and the oldest public building in the city (although bearing little relationship to its original design). The building started life as a single-storey market house in 1769, became the Assembly Rooms, with the addition of an upper storey, in 1777, and in 1845 was remodelled by Charles Lanyon to become the bank buildings.

The **former home of the Belfast News Letter,** 59 Donegall St, is an 1873 building decorated with bas-relief portraits of literary figures. The imposing **St Anne's Cathedral** was built from 1899 but has little of interest inside apart from the grave of Edward Carson (see the boxed text in the History section of the Facts about Ireland chapter). The **Bank of Ireland Building**, a fine example of 1920s Art Deco, is elegantly placed at the junction of North St and Royal Ave.

Lagan Weir & Lookout

Completed in 1994 at a cost of £14 million, the Lagan Weir was the first stage of Belfast's government-initiated Laganside Development Project, an ambitious scheme now in full swing which involves the regeneration of docklands and other riverside areas as well as sites within the newly named Cathedral Quarter, around St Anne's Cathedral (for more details see the following Laganside section).

Years of neglect and industrial decline had turned the River Lagan, the original lifeblood of the city, into smelly, unsightly mudflats. The weir (lit up in electric blue at night), along with a programme of dredging and aeration, has improved the water qual-ity and increased the depth of the river, so much so in fact that salmon, eels and sea trout are now migrating up the river in increasing numbers. Fishing stands have even been built along the Annadale Embankment, south-east of the university.

The Lagan Lookout Visitor Centre (☎ 90 315444) offers a state-of-the-art explanation of how the weir works and why it was needed, with interactive computers to bring things to life. The centre also has displays on the progress of the entire Laganside Project. A one-hour cruise on board *The Joyce* takes you upstream to Stranmillis, passing many of the new developments on the way. Beginning at 10 am, tours depart every hour daily from Lagan Weir and cost £3/2.

The Lagan Lookout opens 11 am to 5 pm on weekdays, noon to 5 pm on Saturday, and 2 to 5 pm on Sunday, April to September; and 11 am to 3.30 pm Tuesday to Friday, 1 to 4.30 pm on Saturday, and 2 to 4.30 pm on Sunday, October to March. Admission costs £1.50/75p.

Laganside

The second stage of Belfast's ambitious Laganside Project (also see the previous section) saw the development of Lanyon Place with the construction of the 2000-capacity Waterfront Hall, British Telecom's Riverside Tower and the 'jewel in the crown' of the city, the Belfast Hilton, which opened in September 1998. Projects completed since then include several clusters of Nineties-style riverside apartments (almost all sold before completion) and the restoration of listed buildings such as McHugh's bar and restaurant on Queen's Square and the ornate Victorian warehouses now housing the McCausland Hotel on Victoria St.

St George's Market (see the following section) has been refurbished, and the former gasworks, immediately to the east of Donegall Pass, is under development. New parks and public spaces linking all these areas are being established, and pathways along both banks of the river are under way. Footbridges linking Lanyon Place to East Bridge St and across to the eastern bank are also planned. Another project will see

Honey Pudding

For a comfort-laden steamed pudding from Ulster.

Bring 1½ cups of milk to the boil, sprinkle in 170g of porridge oats, and cook, while stirring, for five minutes. Add 56g of caster sugar, 2 tablespoons of clear honey, 28g of softened butter, the finely grated rind of 1 lemon, ½ teaspoon of cinnamon and mix well. Remove mixture from heat and beat in 3 egg yolks. Whisk the egg whites until they form soft peaks and fold into the mixture. Pour mixture into a buttered 1L pudding basin, cover with buttered greaseproof paper and seal with kitchen foil.

Place the basin in a steamer and steam over a saucepan of boiling water for 2 to 2½ hours. Serve with warm honey and cream. Comforts four to six people

Belfast's six bridges transformed by 'futuristic blue and white lights'.

Expected to open in November 2001, the Odyssey Complex is a £91 million sporting and cultural complex being built at Abercorn Basin on the eastern side of the river across from Clarendon Dock. Laid out as The People's Pleasure Park in the 1850s, the area was taken over by the shipping industry in the 1870s. Among other things, the complex will feature a science centre, a sports and entertainment arena and an IMAX cinema.

St George's Market

The elegant St George's Market, on the corner of Oxford and May Sts, was built in 1896 for the sale of fruit, butter, eggs and poultry and is the oldest continually operated market in Ireland. Restored at a cost of £3.5 million in 1999, the market now has additional retail and exhibition space. Market days (fresh flowers, fruit, vegetables and fish, plus general household and second-hand goods) are held on Tuesday and Friday, but there are plans to open on other days as well. Look out, too, for special craft and design fairs (the tourist office should have details).

SOUTH OF THE CENTRE
University Rd

Heading down University Rd from Bradbury Place, on the right is the 1887 **Moravian Church**. A left turn takes you into Lower Crescent, beside the 1887 **Crescent Church**, with its instantly recognisable

skeleton-like bell tower. The green behind the church is enclosed by Lower Crescent, Crescent Gardens and Upper Crescent. Walking round the green takes you past mid-19th-century neoclassical terraces, built by Robert Corry, a local entrepreneur, and possibly designed by Charles Lanyon. Across University Rd, WJ Barre's **Methodist Church** of 1865 completes the happy trio of University Rd churches. Continuing along University Rd the next street left is Mt Charles, with a group of stylish **villas** dating from 1842.

Across University Rd from the college building is the modern **Student's Union**, a stark contrast to the exotic **Elmwood Hall**. Built by John Corry, the architect son of Robert Corry, the Italian-inspired church building is now used as a university concert hall.

Ulster Museum

The Ulster Museum (☎ 90 383000) is set in the grounds of the Botanic Gardens near the university. As well as galleries on early and early-medieval Ireland, there are good displays on dinosaurs, steam and industrial machines, natural history and Irish painting. There's also a section on Irish linen, an interesting glass collection and several galleries devoted to changing exhibitions.

Items from the 1588 wreck of the *Girona*, a Spanish Armada vessel, are a highlight. The sumptuous gold jewellery found on board includes a ruby-encrusted salamander (these were mythical creatures who could survive fire, a very real hazard

BELFAST

on board a wooden fighting ship) and an inscribed gold ring. Up to 20 Armada ships were wrecked along the coast of Ireland after being caught in severe autumn storms as they attempted to return to Spain.

The museum was designed in 1911 but not completed until late in the 1920s. An extension was added in 1971, and the complex includes a shop and the Collections Café, overlooking the Botanic Gardens. The museum also runs a programme of weekend activities, lectures, poetry readings, films and talks. The museum opens from 10 am to 5 pm on weekdays, 1 to 5 pm on Saturday, and 2 to 5 pm on Sunday. Admission is free. Bus Nos 69 or 71 will get you there from the centre.

Queen's University

Just over 1km south of Donegall Square and the City Hall is the muted red-and-yellow-brick Queen's College building of Queen's University, Northern Ireland's most prestigious university. It caters for around 8000 students and has a particularly strong reputation in medicine, engineering and law. Although the plan of the college building is based on Magdalen College in Oxford, once again Charles Lanyon was responsible for the design. Queen Victoria was present for the laying of the foundation stone in 1845, and the building was completed in 1849.

The lofty entrance hall leads into the quadrangle. On the southern side a chimney has brickwork spelling out VR 1848 (Victoria Regina). Beyond the college building is the Old Library, designed by Lanyon's assistant WH Lynn and built in 1864.

Surrounding the university are quiet tree-lined streets with small cafés full of students. **University Square**, on the northern side of the campus, dates from 1848 to 1853 and is one of the finest terraced streets in Ireland. It was once known as the Harley St of Belfast, and is now owned by the university. Behind the Queen's College building, across Botanic Ave, is the colonnaded **Union Theological College**, originally the Presbyterian College. It opened in 1853 and it too was a Lanyon design. From the partition of Ireland it served as the Northern Ire-

land Parliament until 1932, when Stormont Castle took over for the next 40 years.

Botanic Gardens

The well-tended Botanic Gardens are a pleasant oasis just a stroll away from the university and the busy Golden Mile area. Once privately owned, the gardens date from 1827. Their centrepiece is the fine Palm House with its cast-iron and curvilinear glass construction, built between 1839 and 1852 and housing palms and other hot-house flora. Even though Belfast's pre-eminent architect, Charles Lanyon, played a part in its creation, the Palm House was essentially the work of Richard Turner of Dublin, who also built glasshouses in the Dublin Botanic Gardens and at Kew Gardens in London, and worked on the 1851 Crystal Palace in London.

Also in the Botanic Gardens is the unique enclosed Tropical Ravine, which was designed by the garden's curator Charles McKimm and completed in 1889. A raised balcony overlooks a jungle of tropical plants (including ferns, orchids, lilies, bananas and cinnamon) growing in a sunken glen. There's also a pool chock full of terrapins.

Just inside the gardens at the Stranmillis Rd gate is a statue of Belfast-born Lord Kelvin, who invented the Kelvin scale which measures temperatures from absolute zero ($-273°C$ or $0°K$).

The gardens open 8 am to sunset daily. The Palm House and Tropical Ravine open 10 am to noon and 1 to 5 pm (4 pm in the winter) on weekdays, and 1 to 5 pm on Saturday, Sunday and bank holidays.

Belfast has a number of other parks and gardens in and around the city, all of which are mentioned in the booklet *Parks of Belfast*, available from the tourist office. See also Cave Hill Country Park and Sir Thomas & Lady Dixon Park in the Outside the Centre section later in this chapter.

Sandy Row

Just a block west of Great Victoria St is the curving Sandy Row. This used to be the main road south out of the city, and it's still a working-class Protestant enclave, wedged in beside the wealthier Golden Mile area. Around here you'll find red-white-and-blue kerbstones and unionist murals, just like on Shankill Rd in West Belfast. Van Morrison fans may remember that he wandered 'up and down the Sandy Row' in his 1968 album *Astral Weeks*.

ART GALLERIES

Belfast's principal modern-art gallery is the well-designed **Ormeau Baths Gallery** (☎ 90 321402), near the BBC building on Ormeau Ave. The spacious galleries show contemporary Irish and international work. The gallery opens 9 am to 5 pm Tuesday to Saturday.

Old Museum Arts Centre (☎ 90 233332), 7 College Square North, a fine building dating back to 1831, houses temporary exhibitions of modern art as well as hosting theatre and dance performances, arts workshops and storytelling and poetry events. It opens 10 am to 5.30 pm on weekdays.

Smaller galleries include the Fenderesky Gallery at the **Crescent Arts Centre** (☎ 90 242338), 2 University Rd; **Bell Gallery** (☎ 90 662998), 13 Adelaide Park, southwest of the university; and **Eakin Gallery** (☎ 90 668522), 237 Lisburn Rd. Also see Malone House in the Outside the Centre section later in this chapter.

WEST BELFAST

The Catholic Falls Rd and the Protestant Shankill Rd in West Belfast have been battlefronts for the Troubles. Although the gates in the Peace Line dividing the communities now stand open (at least during the daytime), the scars of the past 30 years are readily visible: a youth centre and preschool so heavily fortified with concrete and barbed wire that they resemble bunkers, pubs with metal cages and cameras over the doors, black flags and plaques marking places where residents have been killed.

Despite the reminders of conflict, the area is quite safe for visitors. The old Victorian slums and the bulk of the 1960s tower blocks have been replaced by greatly improved public housing. New homes have

even appeared in areas close to the wall where not so long ago petrol bombs constantly flew.

The main reason for venturing into West Belfast is to see the powerful murals which chart the history of the Troubles as well as the political passions of the moment. The mural tradition in the loyalist camp began in 1908, with the appearance of exultant little King Billys celebrating victory at the 1690 Battle of the Boyne, and has continued on the whole to follow a militaristic trend. A typical image would be of cartoon-like masked Ulster Volunteer Force (UVF) paramilitaries clutching AK47s and vowing never to surrender. Images often incorporate traditional symbols of power such as the Unionist flag or the Red Hand of Ulster. You'll find loyalist murals on and around Shankill Rd, nearby on Crumlin Rd (A52), around Newtownards Rd in the east and in Sandy Row and Donegall Pass in the south.

Republican murals began appearing in support of the republican prisoners who went on hunger strike in 1981 to protest the loss of their political-prisoner status. One of the most famous of these murals is that of Bobby Sands near the Sinn Féin offices on the Falls Rd. Though military themes and the armed struggle figure largely in republican murals too, over the years their subject matter has broadened to cover wider political issues, Irish legends and historical events. The mural off the Falls Rd commemorating the 150th anniversary of the Potato Famine is particularly powerful; another is the mural celebrating women, children and workers on Ormeau Rd. Elaborate, very colourful images from Celtic mythology feature in several by well-known muralist Gerry Kelly, who learned his craft in Long Kesh, the political prison just to the south of Lisburn and also known as the Maze. Look for murals on Falls Rd as well as the area around Beechmount Ave, Donegall Rd and Shaw's Rd in West Belfast, and on New Lodge Rd in the north.

West Belfast grew up around the linen mills which propelled the city into its Industrial Revolution prosperity. It was an area of low-cost working-class housing, and even in the Victorian era was divided along religious lines. The advent of the Troubles in 1968 solidified the sectarian division, and the construction of the Westlink Motorway neatly divided the area – and its problems – from central Belfast. Since the start of the Troubles, working-class religious segregation has grown steadily and West Belfast is now almost wholly Catholic. Although Shankill Rd is the Protestant flip side of the Catholic Falls Rd, it's actually in retreat. Were it not for its strong symbolic importance, the shrinking proportion of Protestants in West Belfast would undoubtedly seem even smaller.

Getting There & Away

A recommended way to see the Falls and Shankill Rds is by an organised black-taxi tour (see Organised Tours later in this chapter). The cabs visit most of the more spectacular murals in and around West Belfast as well as taking in the Peace Line (where you can write a message on the wall) and other significant sites, such as the new Sinn Féin headquarters. It's also a good way of getting a colourful rundown on the history of the area.

Though there's nothing to stop you visiting under your own steam (taking the sorts of precautions you would in the rough end of any city), you can also travel along the Falls and Shankill Rds by People's Taxis. These recycled London cabs were set up by the Catholic and Protestant communities as alternative bus services when the ordinary services stopped running in the area at the height of the Troubles. Like buses, the taxis pick up and drop passengers as they go. Fares are 50p to 90p. Shankill Rd taxis (with orange licence discs) go from North St, Falls Rd taxis (with green licence discs) from Castle St, both sites close to the modern Castle Court Shopping Centre. Taxis stick to their own roads, but there is a changeover spot on both roads so that passengers can pick up a cab going to the other road.

Alternatively, bus Nos 12, 13, 14 or 15 will take you down the Falls Rd; bus Nos 39, 55, 63 or 73 go down the Shankill.

Falls Rd

Separated from the city centre by the Westlink Motorway, but actually a very short distance west of the centre, the ugly and infamous **Divis Flats** take their name from Divis Mountain, the highest summit in the hills that surround Belfast. They were constructed in the late 1960s during the worldwide mania for high-rise public housing, and as elsewhere in the world they quickly became 'vertical slums'. During their planning and construction they were actually welcomed by local residents as both an alternative to substandard housing and as a way of retaining the local community. Fearful of losing their congregations, the Catholic churches in the vicinity were particularly enthusiastic backers.

The Troubles quickly turned the flats into the scene of many confrontations between residents and the army. Today most of the flats have been replaced with modern housing but Divis Tower, a single block of high-rise flats, still stands. At the start of the Troubles the Irish Republican Socialist Party colonised its roof, winning it the nickname 'The Planet of the IRPS'. When the British army took their place, this was changed, predictably, to 'The Planet of the Apes'. The top storeys remain occupied by the British army, who come and go by helicopter.

Across Divis St a huge blue-and-white **mural of the Madonna and Child** decorates what was once the Brickfields Barracks, the first purpose-built police barracks in Belfast, now a refuge for homeless men.

From Divis Tower, Divis St runs west, becoming the Falls Rd, which runs in a south-westerly direction through the area known as the Lower Falls. On the right are a swimming pool and the former Sinn Féin offices – the massive boulders outside were placed there to deter car bombers. The new Sinn Féin offices are round the corner, inside the revamped **Conway Mill** building.

If you turn right (north) off the Falls Rd into the side streets you'll quickly come up against the **Peace Line**, a rough corrugated-iron wall set up in September 1969 as a 'temporary' barrier to separate Catholics from their Protestant neighbours. In places you could almost lean out of a back window and touch it. There are several gates in the wall, overlooked by cameras, which remain open until late afternoon during the working week.

On the other side of the Falls Rd in the Lower Falls, the old slums which stood here before the Troubles have been replaced with neat rows of houses, a reminder of the huge sums that have been spent on public housing over the past three decades. The Falls Rd passes the Royal Victoria Hospital, which developed a well-earned reputation for dealing with medical emergencies at the height of the Troubles in the 1970s.

Situated in a former Presbyterian church, a block or so past the hospital, is the Irish language and cultural centre **Cultúrlann MacAdam ÓFiaich** (☎ 90 245255), 216 Falls Rd. It's a cosy, welcoming place with a wide selection of books (see Bookshops in the Information section earlier in this chapter), Irish music tapes and CDs, and an excellent café (see Outside the Centre in the Places to Eat section later in this chapter). The centre also runs monthly music and poetry events and is a good place to find out what's going on around town, especially in West Belfast.

The area's famous murals are found along the Falls and in adjacent streets. It's a constantly changing art show, with new murals appearing over old, and demolition and reconstruction removing and replacing the canvases. Beyond the Lower Falls the road is less interesting until it reaches the **Milltown Cemetery**, the main site for republican burials, housing the graves of numerous noted republicans who have died in the hunger strikes, shoot-outs and other events of the Troubles.

The junction of Glen and Andersonstown Rds marks the end of the Falls Rd with a strongly fortified army base looking down the Falls from its position in the fork. It's one of four 'forts' in West Belfast. Andersonstown (Andytown) is about 3km from the centre and beyond here is Twinbrook, another staunchly republican suburb and the former home of Bobby Sands, the first 1981

hunger striker to die. In the development where he lived, one end of a block has been turned into a memorial. More murals, slogans and graffiti can be found in the Ballymurphy area by taking Whiterock Rd or Springfield Rd, north of the Falls, but these are thoroughly impoverished areas where a stranger will be very noticeable.

Shankill Rd

Shankill Rd begins not far west of St Anne's Cathedral and runs north-west towards the Crumlin Rd. Although the Shankill has been given less media and tourist attention than the Falls, it's also of interest. The street's name comes from *sean chill* (old church), and once again the brightly painted murals, including some of the Derry apprentice boys slamming the city gates in 1689, are the central attraction. Here the villains and heroes have switched roles, and the hooded and menacing paramilitaries are members of the Ulster Defence Organisation (UDA) and other similar Protestant groups, instead of the IRA or Irish National Liberation Army (INLA).

At the far end of Shankill Rd, look out for **St Matthew's**, a church built in a shamrock shape in 1872.

Beyond Shankill Rd, at the end of Glencairn Rd, is **Fernhill House: The People's Museum** (☎ 90 715599). Set up as a 1930s Shankill house, the museum has exhibitions detailing the Home Rule crisis and the two World Wars. It opens 10 am to 4 pm Monday to Saturday, and 1 to 4 pm on Sunday. Admission costs £2. Bus No 63 from City Hall goes close by.

OUTSIDE THE CENTRE
Harland & Wolff Shipyards

Although you can't easily visit the Harland & Wolff shipyards, they certainly dominate eastern Belfast, separated from the city centre by the River Lagan. The giant cranes known as **Samson and Goliath**, one of them over 100m high and 140m long, straddle a 550m-long shipbuilding dock, one of the biggest in the world and capable of handling ships of up to 200,000 tonnes. The shipyard was founded in 1833 but it was

BELFAST

under the Yorkshire engineer Edward Harland, who recruited the German marine draughtsman Gustav Wolff in 1858, that it assumed its leading role in Victorian shipbuilding. There's a statue of Sir Edward Harland by the City Hall. The *Titanic* was built here and more recent constructions have included oil tankers and passenger vessels, including the *Canberra* in 1960.

With substantial British government support the shipyard managed to continue through the 1970s and 1980s, when most European shipbuilding crumbled before Asian competition. Current employment is at a fraction of its former levels: in its heyday 60,000 people worked here; by the early 1990s workers numbered less than 2000. Work at the yards today is primarily maintenance and repair rather than new construction.

Stormont Castle

Situated 8km east of the centre, on Upper Newtownards Rd off the A20, Stormont Castle (☎ 90 760556) is home to the new Northern Ireland Assembly elected in June 1998. The lavishly restored neoclassical mansion stands at the end of an imposing avenue in the middle of 120 hectares of parkland. Built in 1932, this is where the Northern Ireland Parliament met until 1972, when power was transferred to London.

You can walk in the extensive grounds, but visits to the Parliament buildings must be arranged in advance. Citybus Nos 16, 17

and 20 run directly to Stormont from Donegall Square West in the city centre.

Cave Hill Country Park

Cave Hill Country Park (☎ 90 776925) covers 300 hectares of northern Belfast on the shores of Belfast Lough. Walks through the grounds are waymarked and it's a pleasant stroll to the zoo or Belfast Castle. Cave Hill itself is 355m high; from the top there are panoramic views over Belfast, Belfast Lough, and even parts of Scotland on a clear day.

The park contains evidence of prehistoric occupation in the form of several *ráths* and a *crannóg*. On top of Cave Hill one such ringfort is known as McArt's Fort, a prominent spot from which members of the United Irishmen, including Wolfe Tone, looked down over the city in 1795 and pledged to struggle for the independence of Ireland.

The peak was originally named after a 9th-century Ulster king, Matudhain, a name that gradually corrupted to Ben Madigan. One look at its profile, which dominates the Belfast skyline, and you'll understand why it's known as 'Napoleon's Nose' in popular parlance. In previous centuries Cave Hill was a popular site for lighting Halloween bonfires and for rolling hand-painted eggs downhill at Easter. To the north of McArt's Fort are five man-made caves, some of them accessible. To the south side there's a disused limestone quarry.

NICKY CAVEN

Neoclassical Stormont Castle, home of the new Northern Ireland Assembly

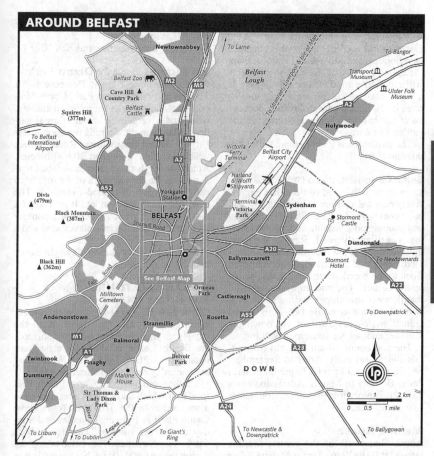

AROUND BELFAST

Map labels:

Newtownabbey
To Larne
To Bangor
Belfast Lough
Belfast Zoo
Transport Museum
Cave Hill Country Park
M2
M5
Ulster Folk Museum
Squires Hill (377m)
Belfast Castle
To Belfast International Airport
A6
M2
Holywood
A2
Victoria Ferry Terminal
Belfast City Airport
A52
Yorkgate Station
Harland & Wolff Shipyards
Divis (479m)
BELFAST
Terminal
Sydenham
Black Mountain (387m)
Shankill Road
Victoria Park
Stormont Castle
Black Hill (362m)
Falls Road
See Belfast Map
Ballymacarrett
A20
Dundonald
Stormont Hotel
To Newtownards
Milltown Cemetery
Ormeau Park
Castlereagh
A22
Andersonstown
Stranmillis
Rosetta
A55
To Downpatrick
M1
Balmoral
A23
Twinbrook
A1
Belvoir Park
DOWN
Finaghy
Dunmurry
Malone House
Sir Thomas & Lady Dixon Park
River Lagan
A24
To Lisburn
To Dublin
To Giant's Ring
To Newcastle & Downpatrick
To Ballygowan

0   1   2 km
0 0.5 1 mile

The country park encompasses two nature reserves, at Ballyaghagan and Hazelwood. There are five park entrances: beside Belfast Castle and the zoo; at Carr's Glen Linear Park, Ballysillan Rd; at Upper Cave Hill Rd; and in the Upper Hightown Rd.

To get there take Citybus Nos 8-10 or 45-51 from Donegall Square West.

Belfast Castle On the slopes of Cave Hill stands Belfast Castle (☎ 90 776925). There has been a 'Belfast Castle' since the late 12th century, but this particular model was only built, in the then fashionable Scottish Baronial style, in 1870. The castle was presented to the City of Belfast in 1934 and became a fashionable venue for weddings after WWII.

Though the council undertook extensive renovation of the castle between 1978 and 1988, the interior is modern and comfortable rather than inspired. Upstairs is the small Cave Hill Heritage Centre with details of the folklore, history, archaeology and natural history of the area (there's also a rooftop camera you can play with which is similar to those that look down from RUC guardposts) and the Ben Madigan restaurant (open for

Sunday lunch only). Downstairs is the Cellar Restaurant (see Outside the Centre in the Places to Eat section later in this chapter), an adjoining bar and a small antique shop.

Legend has it that the castle's residents will experience good fortune only as long as a white cat lives there, a tale commemorated in the formal gardens by nine portrayals of cats in mosaic, painting, sculpture and garden furniture.

The castle opens 9 am to 6 pm daily. Admission is free.

Belfast Zoo Belfast Zoo (☎ 90 776277) is an exceptionally good one and has aggressively pursued a policy of building new and large enclosures for its exhibits. The sealion and penguin pool with its underwater viewing is particularly good. Some of the more unusual animals include tamarins, spectacled bears and red pandas, but children flock to the meerkats and to the ring-tailed lemur colony. The zoo enjoys a splendid location on the slopes below Cave Hill with views out over Belfast Lough. The animal enclosures are laid out down the hillside, making for strenuous walking.

The zoo opens 10 am to 6 pm (last admission 5 pm) daily, April to September; and 10 am to 3.30 pm (2.30 pm on Friday) daily, October to March. Admission costs £5/2.60. Senior citizens and children under four get in free.

Malone House
About 5km south of the centre, Malone House (☎ 90 681246), Upper Malone Rd, is a late-Georgian mansion set in the grounds of Barnett Demesne, formerly a private estate and now part of the Lagan Valley Regional Park. Built in the 1820s for local merchant William Legge, the house is used for receptions and lectures but also houses a very good restaurant and the Higgin Gallery, which hosts painting exhibitions. The house opens 9.30 am to 5.30 pm Monday to Saturday.

The surrounding gardens are planted with azaleas and rhododendrons. Some of the paths criss-crossing the 41-hectare estate lead down to the recently reopened Lagan

Towpath, which follows the river all the way to Lisburn.

To get to the house take bus Nos 70 or 71.

Sir Thomas & Lady Dixon Park
Almost adjoining Barnett Demesne is Sir Thomas and Lady Dixon Park, Upper Malone Rd, which consists of rolling meadows, woodland, riverside fields and formal gardens. The main drawcard is the spectacular City of Belfast International Rose Garden, which contains more than 20,000 blooms. Among other displays, a spiral-shaped garden traces the development of the rose from early shrub roses up to modern hybrids. The roses are in bloom from late July. The park also contains a walled garden, a Japanese-style garden, a children's playground and a café.

The park opens during daylight hours daily.

ORGANISED TOURS
Bus & Taxi Tours
Citybus (☎ 90 458484) runs a three-hour Belfast City Tour which takes in all the city sights, including Stormont, the shiyards and Belfast Castle. It begins at Castle Place outside the GPO at 1 pm every Wednesday and Saturday during the summer.

Citybus also offers a 2½ hour Living History Tour which takes in the sites and areas associated with the Troubles. Tours leave Castle Place at 1 pm on Thursday and Sunday during the summer. Tickets for both Citybus tours cost £8. Tours also take place during the rest of the year, but are subject to demand.

Black-taxi tours that focus on West Belfast and the sectarian murals as well as taking in some of the major city sights are being offered by an increasing number of local cabbies. These tours are likely to vary a bit in quality and content, but in general they're an intimate (cabs take between four and seven people) and entertaining way to see the city and can easily be tailor-made to encompass what people want to see. Tours cost upwards of £6 per person and are best organised through the NITB or any of the city's independent hostels. The tours run by

Michael Johnson (☎ 90 642264) have been highly recommended.

Belfast International Youth Hostel runs its own two-hour tour (in a minibus rather than a cab) of West Belfast which has been recommended by several readers. Tours cost £7.50 per person and leave at 10.30 am daily from 22 Donegall Rd. Call ☎ 90 324733 to book.

Walking Tours
Following the original ramparts of the city, **The Old Town of 1660-1685** (☎ 90 246609) tour includes a visit to the Lagan Lookout. The 1½ hour tour departs from the NITB at 2 pm every Saturday and costs £4.

Bailey's Historical Pub Tours (☎ 92 683665) take in six of the city's historic pubs, including the fabulous Crown Liquor Saloon. Tours cost £5 and depart from Flannigan's (upstairs in the Crown Liquor Saloon on Great Victoria St) at 5.30 pm on Friday, at 4 pm on Saturday (April to October), and at 7 pm on Tuesday (June to August).

Belfast City Centre and Laganside Walk (☎ 90 491469) combines the Victorian city centre with views of Laganside. The two-hour tour costs £3.50 and departs from the front gates of City Hall at 2 pm on Friday, June to September.

Belfast City Walk (☎ 90 491469) takes in sights south of the centre, including the leafy university area. Tours leave from the Wellington Park Hotel on Malone Rd at 10.30 am on Saturday, June to September. The tour costs £3.50 and lasts for two hours.

Blackstaff Way (☎ 90 292631) is a fascinating tour leading through the heart of the city along the route of the Blackstaff River, which was channelled underground in 1881 after becoming so polluted that it was generally referred to as 'The Nuisance'. The one-hour tour costs £2 and leaves at 11 am on Saturday, June to September, from the Travelodge on Brunswick St.

Boat Tours
See the Lagan Weir & Lookout section earlier in this chapter for details of daily boat tours on the River Lagan.

SPECIAL EVENTS
See also the Public Holidays & Special Events section of the Facts for the Visitor chapter.

Belfast City Summer Fest (☎ 90 320202) takes place during May (the exact dates vary from year to year) and includes everything from classical and traditional music concerts to community events and the Lord Mayor's Show. Several buildings usually closed to the public open for guided tours.

Belfast Folk Festival (☎ 90 746021), featuring local, national and international performers, takes place on selected weekends throughout the summer and includes music workshops and ceilídhs.

Féile an Phobail (☎ 90 313440) takes place in West Belfast during the first week of August. Said to be the largest community festival in Ireland, events include an opening carnival parade, street parties, theatre performances, concerts, discussions and Irish-language events.

Belfast Festival at Queen's (☎ 90 667687), the second-largest arts festival in the UK, after Edinburgh, is an extravaganza of theatre, music, dance, comedy and visual art which all takes place in and around Queen's University during three weeks in November.

PLACES TO STAY
Accommodation options in Belfast have increased substantially over the past couple of years and there are plenty of new developments yet to come. At the top end, the Belfast Hilton offers 195 shiny new rooms, while budget travellers now have five central hostels to choose from. City B&Bs haven't multiplied as much and so tend to be expensive – £20 per person is the best you're likely to find. There are no cheap hotels as such but most offer good reductions for weekend stays. Book ahead in summer or during busy festival times.

Camping
Camping possibilities are limited: the only two sites close to Belfast are small and intended only for caravans or campervans. Tent sites can be found along the coast

beyond Bangor in the direction of Porta-ferry in County Down.

Jordanstown Lough Shore Park (☎ *90 868751*) is 8km north of central Belfast on Shore Rd in Newtownabbey. Although this is a well-equipped site, costing £7 per night and mainly intended for caravans (with only one tent site), it's very small and there's a maximum stay of two consecutive nights.

Hostels

Around the Centre The most established hostel in Belfast is *Arnie's Backpackers* (☎ *90 242867, 63 Fitzwilliam St*), centrally located in the university area. Dorm beds cost £7.50. There are decent laundry and cooking facilities and plenty of lively bars and restaurants nearby.

The Ark (☎ *90 329626, 18 University St*) charges £7.50 for beds in comfortable dorms. There's a small sitting room, kitchen and laundry facilities. Internet access is available, too. *Macpackers* (☎ *90 220485, 1 Cameron St*), opposite the Empire Music Hall, charges £7.50 for dorm beds (fifth night free) with breakfast included (cereal, toast, tea/coffee). There are two kitchens and laundry facilities.

The YHANI *Belfast International Youth Hostel* (☎ *90 315435, 22-32 Donegall Rd*), between Shaftesbury Square and Sandy Row, charges £8 or £9 for dorm beds, and £15/20 for singles/doubles. Breakfast costs £2. The hostel offers tours of West Belfast (see Bus & Taxi Tours in the Organised Tours section earlier in this chapter) and can organise cheap train tickets to Dublin. There's a laundry, the Backpackers Coffee House and plans for a kitchen and more beds.

You can get to all the above hostels by train to Botanic Station or by bus Nos 69-71 from Donegall Square.

The newest independent hostel in town is *The Linen House* (☎/*fax 90 586400, 18 Kent St*). Housed in a large former linen factory in the rapidly developing Cathedral Quarter, not far from the bottom of Shankill Rd, the hostel is spacious with comfortable beds and excellent showers. Beds cost £6.50 in an 18-bed dorm, £7.50 in an eight-bed dorm, or

£8.50 in a dorm with private bathroom. Singles/doubles cost £12/20. There's a kitchen, laundry and sinks in all the rooms. Internet access is available.

In theory, *Queen Mary's Hall YWCA* (☎ *90 240439, 70 Fitzwilliam St*) offers single and double rooms costing £15 per person including breakfast, but in practice it's usually full of long-term-resident students.

Outside the Centre From 26 June to 12 September *Queen's Elms* (☎ *90 381608, 78 Malone Rd*), run by the university, offers excellent accommodation. The rooms cost £8 for UK students, £9.40 for international students and £11.75 for non-students. Doubles cost £50. Rates include bed linen but not towels and there are cooking and laundry facilities. Rooms may also be available for short periods over Christmas and Easter.

Off Malone Rd is *Ulster People's College* (☎ *90 665161, 30 Adelaide Park*), which does bed and continental breakfast for £14, bed and cooked breakfast for £16.

B&Bs

The tourist office makes B&B reservations in return for a minimal booking fee. Credit card bookings can be made on freefone number ☎ 0800 317153.

Around the Centre Many B&Bs are in the university area with prices from £20 per person upwards. This area is close to the centre, and has always been safe and well stocked with restaurants and pubs. Botanic Ave, Malone Rd, Wellington Park and Eglantine Ave are good hunting grounds.

Botanic Ave near Queen's University is a pleasant residential street. The large and very comfortable *Helga Lodge* (☎ *90 324820, 7 Cromwell Rd*), just off Botanic Ave, costs upwards of £22/40 to £27/50 for singles/doubles. Note the colourful orange frontage. Most rooms have their own bathroom, TV and phone. Nearby is the handsome *Botanic Lodge Guesthouse* (☎ *90 327682, 87 Botanic Ave*), where the rooms all have TV and cost £22/40. Bus Nos 83, 85 or 86 from Donegall Square will get you to these two.

Also in this popular university area, **Queen's University Common Room** (☎ 90 665938, 1 College Gardens) offers B&B costing £36.50/58.

The George (☎ 90 683212, 9 Eglantine Ave) charges £20/38. At No 17 is **Liserin Guesthouse** (☎ 90 660769), costing £20/38. **Eglantine Guesthouse** (☎ 90 667585), at No 21, offers B&B for £20/38. At No 30 is **Marine House** (☎ 90 662828), which charges £22/40. **East Sheen House** (☎ 90 667149), at No 81, charges £19.50 per person.

Near Queen's University, B&B at **Pearl Court House** (☎ 90 666145, 11 Malone Rd) cost £23.50 per person. More expensive options include the **Camera Guesthouse** (☎ 90 660026, 44 Wellington Park), an Edwardian place where B&B costs £35/48 for singles/doubles.

Outside the Centre Along the Antrim Rd, good cheapies include **Drumragh House** (☎ 90 773063) at No 647. It's 3km north of the city centre, close to the zoo and costs £20/36 for singles/doubles. Also out here is **Aisling House** (☎ 90 771529, 7 Taunton Ave), off the Antrim Rd in a quiet residential area, with B&B costing £19 per person; the breakfasts come highly recommended.

The lovingly restored **Cottage** (☎ 91 878189, 377 Comber Rd, Dundonald) is about 8km east of the city; B&B costs £21/38.

Hotels

There's no shortage of hotel beds in Belfast, but prices are comparatively high, except at the weekend, when business travellers go home and prices drop accordingly. Most of the established hotels are south of the centre in the university area, with newer places springing up quickly in the regenerated riverside area.

Around the Centre Good value (especially for couples and families) given its location so close to the university is **Holiday Inn Express** (☎ 90 205000, 106A University St), which charges £59.95 per person (all rooms are double or twin) including

continental breakfast. The weekend rate is £50 per person including full breakfast. Internet access is available.

Madison's (☎ 90 330040, fax 90 328007, 59-63 Botanic Ave) has large, well-designed rooms complete with hair dryer and trouser press, and there's a swanky bar-restaurant downstairs. Rates are £65/75 for singles/doubles including full breakfast.

The stylish **Crescent Town House** (☎ 90 323349, fax 90 320646, 13 Lower Crescent), opposite the Empire Music Hall on the corner of Botanic Ave, charges £70/90 (£50/65 at the weekend) including full breakfast. The Metro Brasserie (see Restaurants in the Places to Eat section later in this chapter) is downstairs.

Wellington Park Hotel (☎ 90 381111, 21 Malone Rd) is another smaller hotel close to the Ulster Museum and Queen's University. Rooms cost £95/120 (£60/80 at the weekend) including full breakfast. The recently refurbished **Malone Lodge** (☎ 90 382409, 60 Eglantine Ave) charges £40/69 for B&B. In University St, **Renshaws Hotel** (☎ 90 333366), at No 75, charges £44/49 (£39/45 at the weekend), which includes continental breakfast. **Dukes Hotel** (☎ 90 236666), at No 65, is pricier at £95/110 (£52/72 at the weekend).

Travelodge (☎ 90 333555, 15 Brunswick St) is conveniently situated behind the Crown Liquor Saloon. Rooms here (single or double) cost £49.95 including breakfast. **Jury's Inn** (☎ 90 533500), close to City Hall in College Square opposite Spires Shopping Mall, is also good value. The three-star hotel has 190 rooms that can sleep up to three adults or two adults and two children. Rooms cost £63 (full breakfast is an extra £6).

The much bombed **Europa Hotel** (☎ 90 327000) is a Belfast landmark – many city directions begin with 'Do you know the Europa?' Now part of the Hastings Group, it's one of the city's best hotels. B&B costs £105/150 for singles/doubles during the week, dropping to £60/80 at the weekend.

Part of the Laganside redevelopment scheme, the new and elegant **McCausland Hotel** (☎/fax 90 220200, 34-38 Victoria St)

BELFAST

opened in January 1999 in two beautifully restored Italianate warehouses originally built for rival firms in the 1850s. Aimed at business travellers, the 60-room 'luxury boutique' hotel has single/doubles, with all the accoutrements, which cost upwards of £130/150. The hotel has a restaurant and a European-style café-bar.

Taking pride of place in Belfast is the 195-room *Belfast Hilton* (☎ *90 277000, fax 90 277277, 4 Lanyon Place*). Singles/doubles cost upwards of £160/178, while the presidential suite costs £500. An Irish breakfast costs £14.50 (presumably you get the works). The hotel has a top-end restaurant and an extraordinary bar which looks like a set for *Happy Days* on acid.

Outside the Centre Immediately opposite the terminal at the Belfast International Airport, in Aldergrove, *Aldergrove Airport Hotel* (☎ *94 422033*) has excellent rooms and facilities costing £75 per room during the week and £64/75 for singles/doubles at the weekend.

Off the main road to Carrickfergus is the pleasant *Glenavna House Hotel* (☎ *90 864461, 588 Shore Rd, Newtownabbey*), standing in quiet parkland, with rooms costing £70/85 (£45/60 at the weekend).

The glossy four-star *Stormont Hotel* (☎ *90 658621*), directly across from the Stormont Parliament building, on Upper Newtownards Rd east of the centre, charges £102/135 (£55/70 at the weekend). Everyone gets a rubber duck to float in the bathtub (must have something to do with Parliament).

PLACES TO EAT

Belfast has a surprising number and variety of restaurants, including a couple of the best in all Ireland. More than one journalist has noted that the Troubles seem to have given the citizens of Belfast a positive passion for eating out! Although there are plenty of new cafés and restaurants opening in central Belfast, the biggest choice is still to be found south of the city centre along the Golden Mile, the busy area that stretches from the Crown Liquor Saloon down Great

Victoria St and Dublin Rd all the way through the university area into the Lisburn, Malone and Stranmillis Rds.

Golden Mile

Restaurants On Bedford St, *Pizza Express* (☎ *90 329050*) is pleasant, with decent pizzas costing upwards of £6 and a good wine list. *Graffiti Italiano* (☎ *90 249269, 50 Dublin Rd*) serves excellent, filling pasta and fish dishes (seafood spaghetti, steamed mussels) costing upwards of £7. It opens 6 to 11 pm Monday to Saturday and 5 to 10 pm on Sunday.

There are quite a few Indian and Chinese restaurants around. *Archana Balti House* (☎ *90 323713*), upstairs at 53 Dublin Rd, offers balti curries costing £5 to £8. *Moghul*, on Botanic Ave, is a more traditional Indian restaurant offering tandoori dishes costing £8.95 and a good selection of vegetarian dishes costing £5.95. There's a £3.99 buffet from noon to 2 pm on weekdays. *Manor House* (☎ *90 238755, 47 Donegall Pass*) offers excellent Cantonese dishes costing upwards of £6.50.

Chez Delbart (also known as Frogities; ☎ *90 238020, 10 Bradbury Place*) is a fairly cheap-and-cheerful French place where you can get good savoury and sweet crêpes for £4.95.

Swish *Metro Brasserie* (☎ *90 323349*), in the Crescent Town House hotel on Botanic Ave, has a tempting menu with main courses (slow-roast loin of pork with Chinese cabbage, shitake mushrooms, bacon and scallion dressing) costing upwards of £7.50. Between 6 and 7 pm Monday to Saturday you can choose between two- and three-course Metro Rush Hour menus costing £9.95 and £12.50. Tapas are served between noon and 5 pm on Sunday.

The stylish *Antica Roma* (☎ *90 311121, 67 Botanic Ave*) serves pasta costing £7 to £8 and is open for lunch and dinner. *Madison's Bistro* (*59-63 Botanic Ave*), in the hotel, offers dishes such as tom yum soup with tiger prawns (£2.95) and linguini with curried lentils, coriander and yoghurt (£6.95). There's a good selection of coffee and wine. It opens daily for lunch and dinner.

Beatrice Kennedy's (☎ 90 202290, 44 University Rd) offers a varied and hearty dinner menu (game terrine; potato salad and pesto), with main courses costing upwards of £8. It opens 5 to 10.30 pm daily.

The Strand (☎ 90 682266, 12 Stranmillis Rd) offers dishes such as baked stuffed aubergine and Irish lamb noisettes. A three-course meal costs around £12. It opens from noon until late daily and also for breakfast from 10 am to 12.30 pm on Saturday and Sunday.

Aero (☎ 90 244844, 44 Bedford St) is a smart new restaurant and bar with an interesting menu and clever view of the attractive red-brick Victoriana outside on Bedford St. Main courses at lunch (gnocchi, goats cheese and baby tomato salad; cod and leek gratin with a tempura of oysters) start at £5.25. In the evening (until 7 pm) you can order a two-course pre-theatre menu costing £8.95. It opens from noon to 2.30 pm on weekdays and 5.30 to 10.30 pm Monday to Saturday.

French cuisine can be sampled in *La Belle Epoque* (☎ 90 323244, 61 Dublin Rd), Belfast's most authentic French restaurant. Fillet of beef with seed mustard cream costs £11.50. There are two-course set lunch menus costing £5.95 and £10.95. It's closed on Sunday.

Behind an anonymous frosted-glass façade, the Michelin-starred *Roscoff* (☎ 90 331532, 7 Lesley House, Shaftesbury Square) serves superb food in modern surroundings. The chef, Paul Rankin, has a tremendous reputation (and his own TV programme). There are two- and three-course set lunch menus costing £14.50 and £17.50, and from Monday to Thursday a three-course dinner menu costing £25.50. It opens for lunch and dinner on weekdays, and for dinner only on Saturday.

Fast Food, Cafés & Pubs The *Parks Caffe* (68 Great Victoria St), not far from the Ormeau Baths Gallery, offers a selection of coffees and light snacks – ciabatta, Italian cheese, salamis – and opens 9 am to 6.30 pm Monday to Saturday and 1 to 5 pm on Sunday.

Jenny's Coffee Shop (81 Dublin Rd) is a pleasant little café-cum-sandwich-bar with snacks such as lasagne costing £2.75. Next door at *La Boulangerie* you can get an after-lunch pastry.

Light meals, cakes and decent coffee are available from *Revelations Café* (27 Shaftesbury Square), all day between Monday and Saturday, and from noon on Sunday.

Bradbury Place and Botanic Ave are prime hunting grounds for cheap meals, and many of the cafés and restaurants are crammed with students from Queen's. *Maggie May's* (50 Botanic Ave) is very popular with students for cheap, healthy food and a great atmosphere. Vegetarian cottage pie costs £3.50. It opens daily for breakfast until late.

The extremely popular *The Other Place* (79 Botanic Ave) serves burgers and chips costing £3.95, with an accompaniment of popular music tracks and lots of student jollity. It also serves more substantial meals costing around £7, and you can bring your own wine. There's an equally popular branch on Stranmillis Rd.

Bookfinders Café (47 University Rd), at the back of the bookshop, is an excellent place for a quick lunch. *The Mortarboard* (3 Fitzwilliam St) serves good coffee and snacks until late.

Bonnie's Café Restaurant (☎ 90 664914, 11A Stranmillis Rd) is perfect for a light meal (fisherman's pie, baguettes) after visiting the Ulster Museum opposite.

Empire Music Hall (42 Botanic Ave) serves pizza and wine costing £5 from noon to 8 pm Monday to Saturday. An extensive pub menu includes burgers and roast of the day.

For down-to-earth food in fabulous surroundings you can't beat the *Crown Liquor Saloon* (☎ 90 249476, 46 Great Victoria St). Tuck into Irish stew, champ (potato mashed with spring onions) or Strangford oysters (£1 each) while admiring the Victorian décor. Main courses cost from £4.95 to £12. Food is served from noon to 8.45 pm between Monday and Saturday.

City Centre

Investment in central Belfast has seen dozens of new restaurants and cafés opening up over the past couple of years. The centre still quietens down considerably after the shops have closed, but during the day it's lively, with a distinct buzz of change and excitement in the air. All the pubs, cafés and restaurants in the centre do a roaring trade at lunchtime.

Restaurants If you feel like treating yourself to a grown-up meal while you're in Belfast, book a table at *Deane's* (☎ 90 560000, 38 Howard St), the city's newest Michelin-starred restaurant. You'll need to book well ahead (two to three weeks for a weekend night) for the restaurant upstairs, but you should be able to get a table in the brasserie downstairs. The food, wine, service and ambience are all excellent. In the brasserie expect to pay around £20 for a two-course evening meal (lamb medallions with creamed cabbage and cheese mash followed by rhubarb crumble and vanilla ice cream) with wine and coffee. The brasserie opens noon to 2.30 pm and 5.30 to 10.30 pm Monday to Saturday. The restaurant (£27 for a two-course set menu) opens 7 to 9.30 pm Tuesday to Saturday.

Another new place is *Nick's Warehouse* (☎ 90 439690, 35 Hill St), an enormous blond-wood and red-brick bar-restaurant buzzing with happy Belfastians. There's a good wine list and a fresh menu featuring salads and seafood (halibut with langoustine and sweet peppers). Expect to pay around £8 for a main course plus wine. It opens noon to 3 pm on weekdays, and 6 to 10 pm Tuesday to Saturday.

The Edge (☎ 90 322000), a well-designed and stylish café-bar and restaurant overlooking the river near the Hilton, opened its doors in June 1999. Main courses at dinner (fillet of pork with sage and caramelised apple with creamy calvados sauce) start at around £11. Lunchtime specials (lasagne verdi, stir-fried chicken) cost £5.95. Farther down the river the restored *McHugh's* (☎ 90 247830), Queen's Square, is similar, with pub food downstairs

and fancier dishes (grilled salmon, Barbary duck) available in the restaurant upstairs.

Fast Food, Cafés & Pubs For a good coffee-and-pastry breakfast, plus news papers and a great plate-glass street view, head for *Gloria Jean's Coffee* on the corner of Royal Ave and North St. If you're staying at the Linen House hostel and fancy a fry-up rather than a bowl of cornflakes, try *Paul's Café (187 Donegall St)*.

Café Society (3 Donegall Square East) is a pleasant spot for lunch right by City Hall. They have reasonably priced fresh pasta, pan-fried chicken and vegetarian dishes. *Café Renoir (5 Queen St)* serves decent baguettes and a range of filling vegetarian and wholefood dishes.

On pedestrianised Arthur St is the successful offspring of Roscoff (see Restaurants in the previous Golden Mile section), *Roscoff Express* (☎ 90 310108), which opened in 1998. A second one has since appeared on Fountain St. Choose from focaccia pizza (£5.50), asparagus ravioli (small £3.95, large £6.50) and rib-eye steak with red-wine butter and grilled tomatoes (£10.50). You can also order excellent sandwiches and salads and a selection of Irish cheeses. The café has a good wine list and a takeaway section. Both cafés open from 7.30 am for breakfast and from 11 am for lunch Monday to Saturday, and 6 to 9 pm on Thursday.

Altos (☎ 90 323087), on Fountain St, is a new café-bar-deli that produces excellent lunchtime food: chorizo sausages in French bread with harissa, french fries and salad; simple Italian dishes; good coffee and wine. Dishes cost upwards of £3.50; tapas and beer costs £5.90.

Belfast is full of congenial pubs, many of which offer hearty traditional food. Keeping a low profile on the corner of Victoria St near the Royal Courts of Justice, *Rumpole's* (☎ 90 232840, 81 Chichester St) is good for steak-type lunches. A block farther north, *Bittle's Bar* (☎ 90 311088, 70 Upper Church Lane) is a small pub in a rather interesting triangular building decorated with gilded shamrocks. It specialises in traditional dishes such as sausages and champ and Irish stew. The historic *White's Tavern* (☎ 90 243080), on Wine Cellar Entry between Rosemary and High Sts, serves down-to-earth pub food such as baked potatoes and chicken-and-broccoli bake.

Duke of York (☎ 90 241062) is another oldie, popular with journalists from the nearby local papers and stuffed with printing memorabilia. It serves sandwiches and excellent solid lunches costing around £5. **Kitchen Bar** (☎ 90 324901, 16 Victoria Square) is a great place for real ale, home-made soups and stews and the house speciality – Paddy's pizza created on a toasted soda-bread base. The Australian-run restaurant upstairs at the *Morning Star* (☎ 90 235986, 17 Pottinger's Entry) has a good reputation. The menu features traditional Irish dishes as well as more unusual things such as kangaroo and crocodile steaks.

Outside the Centre

South of the centre, *Mercury Bar and Grill* (☎ 90 649017, 451 Ormeau Rd) is another new spacious bar-restaurant that is trying hard and succeeding very well. It offers all-day brunch (grilled bacon, sausage, tomato, mushrooms, egg, pancakes, orange juice and endless tea or coffee £3.75; hot apple crêpes £2.75), a selection of light meals (steamed mussels, tempura of field mushrooms), substantial main courses costing upwards of £4.75 and an excellent wine list. There's live jazz at brunch on Sunday. It opens noon to 3 pm and 5 to 8.45 pm Monday to Thursday, noon to 9 pm Friday and Saturday, and noon to 8 pm on Sunday.

Upstairs in Belfast Castle, *Ben Madigan Restaurant* (☎ 90 776925) offers Sunday roast (£16) overlooking Belfast and Belfast Lough. You'll need to book a couple of days ahead. Lunch is served between noon and 2.30 pm on Sunday. *Cellar Restaurant*, downstairs at the castle, opens for morning coffee, afternoon tea and lunch and dinner Monday to Saturday. Lunch main courses cost upwards of £5.95, dinner mains upwards of £10.45. The adjoining bar serves bar snacks.

If you're exploring West Belfast, you

may like to drop into *Cultúrlann Mac-Adam ÓFiaich* (☎ 90 245255, 216 Falls Rd), the Irish language and arts centre, for a browse in the bookshop and some good home-cooked food (stews, soups, pizza, baked potatoes, fresh pastries with real maple syrup). The café opens 9 am to 5 pm Monday to Friday.

ENTERTAINMENT

Belfast's nightlife has never been buzzier – sleek new bars are opening practically daily, the club scene is booming and top-class live music is to be found in dozens of great venues around town. The breaking down of old barriers in Northern Ireland is being reflected in a resurgence of the arts in general – from a growth in community and Irish-language-based events to a flourishing visual-arts movement.

The entertainment-listings situation remains a bit of a moveable feast at the moment, with a comprehensive guide yet to emerge. The free *Big List*, published on Wednesday, is reasonable (venue phone numbers would be a good idea); the Metro section in *The Irish News* on Friday covers everything from music to art exhibitions and special events; and the music listing in Friday's *Mirror* is worth picking up.

Pubs

There's no shortage of pubs to explore in Belfast. Most offer music of one sort or another – after all, having an entertainment licence means you can stay open until 1.30 am. Licensing hours were relaxed following the ceasefires and it seems it'll take a while for the novelty to wear off. Many of the city-centre pubs are crammed to overflowing at lunchtime as well as in the evening (but there's always room for more) and some of the trendier bars have dress codes (usually no runners and no jeans).

Traditional Belfast has some fabulous pubs which are as much museums as drinking places. No-one should miss the *Crown Liquor Saloon*, opposite the Opera House, with its wonderfully ornate Victorian interior (see Crown Liquor Saloon in the

BELFAST

Around the Centre section earlier in this chapter).

The narrow alleys known as the Entries shelter a plethora of older pubs. Good ones to sample include the atmospheric *Morning Star* on Pottinger's Entry, the historic *White's Tavern* on Wine Cellar Entry (jazz on Thursday night, traditional Irish music on Friday and Saturday nights), and *Globe Tavern* on Joy's Entry.

Other older pubs in the centre include *Kelly's Cellars* on Bank St, which features folk and blues bands on Friday and Saturday nights, and *Duke of York*, hidden away down Commercial Court near St Anne's Cathedral. *Kitchen Bar*, on Victoria Square, is a great spot for real ales, home-cooked food and traditional-music sessions.

Maddens (*74 Smithfield*) is a down-to-earth establishment noted for its lively traditional-music sessions. Also excellent for atmosphere and unmissable for live music are three pubs situated over in the Clarendon Dock area: *Liverpool* (*44 Donegall Quay*), *The Rotterdam* (*54 Pilot St*) and *Pat's Bar* (*Prince's Dock St*). The Rotterdam hosts outdoor music gigs in the summer.

Trendy Built in the 1700s, *McHugh's*, not far from the river on Queen's Square, is the oldest building in Belfast. Restored at a cost of £2 million, it reopened in October 1998 and is now a very popular bar-restaurant with live music (mostly rock and cover bands) Thursday to Sunday nights.

Elms (*36 University Rd*) is a popular student pub with a disco and live music at the weekend. Farther south, *Eglantine Inn* (*32 Malone Rd*) and *Botanic* (*23 Malone Rd*) are institutions, packed at the weekend with students. Known as the Egg and Bott, they both feature music of one sort or another every weekend.

Empire Music Hall is a splendid Victorian building on Botanic Ave which hosts a variety of different evenings – revealing comedy on Tuesday, traditional Irish music on Thursday, salsa on Friday (with a class at 9 pm), and bands on Wednesday, Saturday and Sunday.

The Fly, on Lower Crescent near the Empire, is a stylish (provided you don't suffer from arachnophobia) new bar for young things. Huge metal spiders hunch on the walls behind the bar and dangle from the stairwell. The cocktails (£2.95) are called things like Fly-by-Night and Flyagra. There's a DJ on the middle floor every night and an Absolut Vodka Bar with comfy chairs on the top floor. Can this really be Belfast?

Robinson's, next door to the Crown on Victoria St, is a theme pub on four floors with music – from traditional to the latest young bands – most nights. In the basement is *Rock Bottom*, where Belfast's beautiful bikers and their molls hang out.

Beaten Docket (*48 Great Victoria St*) is a popular late-night weekend venue for 60s and 70s disco. *Bob Cratchit's* (*38 Lisburn Rd*) plays similar dance music and usually has a cover charge.

Lavery's Gin Palace (*14 Bradbury Place*) is popular with an extraordinary range of clients, from students to bikers to hardened drinkers. There's mixed dance music on most nights.

Morrison's (*21 Bedford St*) is the place to head to for soul, hip-hop, R&B and ragga. Keep an eye out for excellent live indie bands and late-night club events at *Magennis's Whiskey Café*, near St George's Market. *O'Neill's*, on Joy's Entry, is popular for hip-hop and R&B.

Nightclubs
See also pubs with late-night club events in the previous Pubs section.

Brunswick Club, on Brunswick St, offers hardhouse and techno. *Katy Daly's* (*Ormeau Ave*) offers live music as well as club nights.

The Limelight (*17 Ormeau Ave*) is a popular venue for dance music, and The Loft at *Dempsey's*, on Dublin Rd, draws a big crowd on Sunday night.

The trendy *Madison's* (*59-63 Botanic Ave*) plays mixed dance music at the weekend and live music in the Bistro on Thursday and Sunday evenings. *Manhattan*, on Bradbury Place, plays popular commercial

Gay & Lesbian Nightspots

Parliament Bar (2 Dunbar St), not far from St Anne's Cathedral, is Belfast's oldest gay venue. There's a mixture of live bands and club nights throughout the week, and on Tuesday a pop-trivia quiz followed by a late-night disco.

The Crow's Nest (26 Skipper St) has live music on Saturday afternoon, karaoke on Saturday night, a quiz night on Tuesday, a purportedly excellent bingo night on Wednesday, Club Adonis on Thursday and a disco on Friday.

The Kremlin, tucked away on Little Donegall St near the Central Library, is the city's newest gay venue. From 'cabaret' to cover bands, there's something on every night of the week. Revolution is the big club night on Saturday (4 pm to 3 am) and Monday is movie night (5 pm to 1 am).

dance music. *Thompson's Garage*, tucked away on Patterson's Place, hosts international DJs and is one of the most popular club venues in town.

Concerts

Belfast's largest concert venue is the impressive circular *Waterfront Hall* (☎ 90 334455, Lanyon Place). It hosts local, national and international performers from pop-music artists to symphony orchestras.

Northern Ireland's excellent Ulster Orchestra often plays in *Ulster Hall* (☎ 90 323900), on Bedford St. This is also the venue for larger rock-music events (and for lunchtime organ recitals and even boxing bouts).

King's Hall (☎ 90 665225) at Balmoral is another centre for big rock events. Get there by bus down Lisburn Rd or by train to Balmoral Station.

Performances also take place at *Elmwood Hall*, the church building now used as a concert hall on University Rd directly opposite Queen's College. *Crescent Arts Centre* (☎ 90 242338, 2 University Rd) hosts some excellent music concerts (from New York jazz to top-rate Irish music).

Cinemas

Belfast's biggest cinema complex, the 10-screen *Virgin Cinema* (☎ 0541 555176), is at the northern end of Dublin Rd, just south of the city centre. *Movie House* (☎ 90 755000), with five screens, is north of the centre in the Yorkgate Shopping Centre.

Queen's Film Theatre (☎ 90 244857), on University Square Mews near the university, is a two-screen arthouse cinema.

Theatre

The *Grand Opera House* (☎ 90 241919) on Great Victoria St is host to a mixture of good theatre, opera and music shows. The booking office (☎ 90 241919, 17 Wellington Place) opens 9.45 am to 5.30 pm Monday to Saturday. *Belfast Civic Arts Theatre* (☎ 90 316900, 41 Botanic Ave) chiefly puts on popular plays or comedies.

Farther out from the centre, *Lyric Theatre* (☎ 90 381081, 55 Ridgeway St) has a more serious bent and includes Irish plays in its repertory. Performances also take place at *Whitla Hall* in Queen's University. *Group Theatre* (☎ 90 329685), next door to Ulster Hall, stages work by local playwrights.

Both *Factory* (☎ 90 244000, 52 Hill St) and *The Old Museum Arts Centre* (☎ 90 235053), on College Square North, host theatre performances and comedy.

SPECTATOR SPORTS

Rugby, soccer, Gaelic football and hockey are played through the winter, cricket and hurling through the summer. International rugby and soccer matches take place at Windsor Park (☎ 90 244198), south of the centre off Lisburn Rd (bus Nos 58 and 59 go that way). You can see Gaelic football and hurling at Roger Casement Park (☎ 90 613661), Andersonstown Rd (bus Nos 14,

BELFAST

15 and 90). The Sports Council (☎ 90 381222) provides information on a range of sporting activities.

SHOPPING

Items particular to Northern Ireland that you may like to look out for include fine Belleek china, linen (antique and new) and Tyrone crystal.

The Wicker Man (☎ 90 243550), 14 Donegall Arcade, off Castle Place, sells a wide range of contemporary Irish crafts and gifts, including silver jewellery, glassware and knitwear.

Craftworks (☎ 90 244465), on Bedford St near the Ulster Hall, specialises in top quality work by craftspeople from all over Ulster. You'll find beautifully made designer knitwear, linen shirts, leather-wear, ceramics, bodhráns (traditional goatskin drums), textiles and jewellery.

For a selection of Irish music, try the Vintage Record Store (☎ 90 314888), 54 Howard St, or Cultúrlann MacAdam ÓFiaich (☎ 90 245255), 216 Falls Rd.

The newly restored St George's Market, May St, sells fresh fruit, vegetables, flowers and fish as well as a variety of other goods on Tuesday and Friday morning (from 8 am). There are plans to open on other days as well – check with the NITB. There's an antique market upstairs at 126-128 Donegall Pass from 9.30 am to 5 pm on Saturday.

For general shopping needs you'll find everything from Tesco Metro supermarket to Boots the Chemist in the compact central shopping area north of City Hall.

For camping gas cylinders, other camping equipment or for surfing gear, Surf Mountain (☎ 90 248877), 12 Brunswick St, in the centre, is excellent. There's also the Scout Shop Ski and Camp Centre (☎ 90 320580), 12-14 College Square East near Wellington Place.

GETTING THERE & AWAY
Air
There are flights from some regional airports in Britain, including Gatwick, to the convenient Belfast City Airport (☎ 90 457745), Airport Rd, but everything else

(flights from the Republic, Britain, Amsterdam, Brussels and New York) goes to Belfast International Airport (☎ 94 422888), 30km north of the city in Aldergrove by the M2. For details of flights and fares see Air in the introductory Getting There & Away chapter. Airline offices in Belfast include:

Aer Lingus
  (☎ 0645 737747) 46-48 Castle St
British Airways
  (☎ 0845 222111) 1 Fountain Centre, College St
British Midland
  (☎ 90 241188) Suite 2, Fountain Centre, College St

Bus
Belfast has two modern bus stations. The smaller of the two is the Laganside Bus Centre on Oxford St near the river, with bus connections to County Antrim, eastern Down and the Cookstown area.

Buses to everywhere else in Northern Ireland, the Republic, the International Airport and the Larne ferries leave from the bigger Europa Bus Centre on Glengall St, behind the Europa Hotel. Buses to Larne town, as opposed to the harbour, leave from the Laganside Bus Centre.

Pick up regional bus timetables at the bus stations or phone ☎ 90 333000 for timetable information. Ulsterbus produces an excellent free *Exploring Ulster* booklet with information on bus services and fares to major attractions accessible by bus from Belfast. For connections to Derry and Donegal contact the Lough Swilly Bus Company (☎ 71 262017) in Derry.

For security reasons there are no left-luggage facilities at Belfast bus stations.

Students are eligible for 15% reductions on Ulsterbus fares of more than £1.15 on production of their ISIC card.

For information on bus fares, durations and frequencies throughout Ireland see Bus in the introductory Getting Around chapter.

Train
Trains to all destinations, including Larne, Derry, Dublin, Newry, Portadown and

Bangor arrive and depart from Belfast Central. Trains also leave Great Victoria St Station for Portadown, Lisburn, Bangor, Larne Harbour and Derry. Great Victoria St is the most central station, while Belfast Central is east of the city centre on East Bridge St.

For tickets and information the NIR Travel Shop (☎ 90 230671) is at Great Victoria St Station next to the Europa Bus Centre. It opens from 9 am to 5 pm on weekdays, and 9 am to noon on Saturday. Information about local trains is also available from Belfast Central Station (☎ 90 899411).

There are at least six trains a day between Belfast and Derry. The trip takes just under 2½ hours and a one-way ticket costs £6.70. Dublin to Belfast trains run up to eight times a day (four on Sunday) and take about two hours at a cost of £17 one way.

On Sunday you can buy a £3 (before 3 pm) go-as-you-please ticket, allowing you to travel all over the Northern Irish train network.

For security reasons there are no left-luggage facilities at Belfast train stations.

For more information on the train network in Ireland see Train in the introductory Getting Around chapter.

Boat

Both the Isle of Man Steam Packet Company (☎ 90 351009) and SeaCat (☎ 0990 523523) dock in Donegall Quay, a short distance from the city centre. Isle of Man services run between Belfast and the Isle of Man during summer only. SeaCat operates huge catamaran car ferries between Belfast and Stranraer in Scotland.

Conventional ferries to and from Scotland dock at Larne, 30km up the coast from Belfast (see Larne in the Counties Derry & Antrim chapter).

Norse Irish Ferries (☎ 90 779090) runs a service between Belfast and Liverpool, and operates from the Victoria terminal, 5km north of town.

For more information on ferry routes, companies and prices, see the Sea section in the Getting There & Away chapter.

GETTING AROUND

Belfast has that rare thing – an integrated public transport system, with buses and trains linking both airports to the central train and bus stations, and to the ferries.

To/From the Airports

For information on facilities at the airports see Tourist Offices and Money in the Information section earlier in this chapter.

Belfast International Airport (☎ 94 422888) is 30km north of the city. Buses connect it with the Europa Bus Centre for £5/10 one-way/return. There are two services an hour, 19 daily even on Sunday. A taxi costs about £20.

The more convenient Belfast City Airport (☎ 90 457745) is only 6km from the centre, and you can cross the road from the terminal to the Sydenham Halt Station, from which a train to Botanic Station, which is in the popular university area, costs 90p. Citybus No 21 runs between Belfast City Airport and the centre for 80p. Bus services run roughly every half-hour on weekdays, less frequently at the weekend. A taxi fare to the city centre is about £5.

To/From the Ferry Terminals

Donegall Quay is a short bus ride or walk from the city centre. Trains for Larne Harbour depart from Great Victoria St Station, while buses leave from the Europa Bus Centre.

Bus

Citybus (☎ 90 246485) operates the bus system in Belfast, which is divided into zones. Very short trips in the centre cost just 50p, but in general around the city the standard bus fare is 90p, which gets you all the way to Cave Hill or Belfast Zoo. A multi-journey ticket costs £3 and gives you four rides at slightly lower cost and much greater convenience.

A Day Ticket gives you unlimited travel within the City Zone from 9.30 am on weekdays or all day at the weekend for £2.60. A seven-day bus pass costs £11.50.

Most local bus services depart Donegall Square, near City Hall. Timetables are available from the kiosk on Donegall Square West. Single tickets are bought from the driver, but multiple tickets need to be purchased in advance from kiosks on Castle Place or Donegall Square West.

Belfast has a good system of night buses on Friday and Saturday to enable people to join in the nightlife. Most buses leave from Shaftesbury Square at 1 and 2 am. You buy tickets (£2.50) in advance from a mobile ticket booth between 9 pm and 1.50 am. For night-bus information call ☎ 90 233933.

Train

A local train connects Great Victoria St Station and Belfast Central Station. Trains run frequently between Belfast Central and Botanic Stations until around 11 pm.

Car & Motorcycle

If you're driving, be fastidious about where you park. Although the Troubles have eased you still shouldn't park within the well-marked Control Zones. There are plenty of car parks in Belfast; it's wise to use them (see Dangers & Annoyances in the Information section earlier in this chapter).

Rental Rates change frequently so ring around (see also Rental in the Car & Motorcycle section of the Getting Around chapter). Car rental agencies in Belfast include:

Avis
  (☎ 90 240404) 69-71 Great Victoria St
  (☎ 90 452017) City Airport
  (☎ 94 422333) International Airport

Budget
  (☎ 90 230700) 96-102 Great Victoria St
  (☎ 90 451111) City Airport
CC Economy Car Hire
  (☎ 90 840366) 2 Ballyduff Rd
Europcar
  (☎ 90 313500) 6-24 Agincourt Ave
  (☎ 90 450904) City Airport
  (☎ 94 423444) International Airport
Hertz
  (☎ 90 732451) City Airport
  (☎ 94 422533) International Airport
McCausland Car Hire
  (☎ 90 333777) 21-31 Grosvenor Rd
  (☎ 90 454141) City Airport
  (☎ 94 422022) International Airport

Taxi

For information on People's Taxis in West Belfast see Getting There & Away in the West Belfast section earlier in this chapter. The regular black taxis that travel throughout the city have yellow plates back and front (£2 minimum fare) and are the only cabs that can be hailed in the street. Minicabs are cheaper and there are plenty around. Companies to call include Stranmillis Taxis (☎ 90 200400) and Sure Cabs (☎ 90 766666).

Bicycle

McConvey Cycles (☎ 90 491163), 467 Ormeau Rd, rents bicycles for £7/40 per day/week. A deposit of £30 is required. Re-Cycle (☎ 90 313113), 1 Albert Square, rents bicycles for £6.50/30 per day/week. The NITB has a leaflet outlining cycle routes in Northern Ireland.

Counties Down & Armagh

County Down

County Down is Northern Ireland's sunny south-east, being relatively dry. Neighbouring Belfast delivers hordes of day-trippers to the many seaside resorts on the coast, from Bangor to Newcastle and beyond. The shoreline runs from the flat Ards Peninsula, encompassing the drowned drumlins and nature reserves of Strangford Lough, to the Mourne Mountains, which coax the traveller farther south. In the famous lyrics by Percy French, the Mournes 'sweep down to the sea'; they're the highlight of Down. The interior of the county is well past its booming Industrial Revolution heyday but Hillsborough retains much of its Georgian splendour. The main Belfast to Dublin road crosses into the Republic just south of Newry.

HISTORY

The history of Down goes back 7000 years. The county has its fair share of early monuments: the Giant's Ring near Belfast and the Legananny Dolmen near Ballynahinch are two of the best examples.

St Patrick arrived in Strangford Lough in 432, and died in the area in 461. The whereabouts of his remains is disputed, though Downpatrick Cathedral is the favoured site.

By the time of St Patrick's death, the crusade he had started in Ulster had made Ireland Christian and turned him into one of the few genuinely national heroes. After St Patrick's death, Irish monasteries flourished, surviving repeated Viking attacks.

They were finally to lose out to the Normans, who ousted the Irish monks and built Grey Abbey on the Ards Peninsula and Inch Abbey near Downpatrick. Castles were their main priority, however, and many along the coast survive today.

The Scottish and English settlers who arrived with the Plantation were given large tracts of land previously occupied by the native Irish. They built towns and roads, and were responsible for the development of the linen industry in the 17th and 18th centuries.

Highlights

- Hike in the brooding Mourne Mountains
- Wander in the exquisite gardens of Mount Stewart
- Follow in the footsteps of St Patrick around Downpatrick
- Travel the beautiful coast roads of the Ards and Lecale Peninsulas
- Visit spooky Armagh Gaol in Armagh town
- Enjoy traditional singing in South Armagh

DOWN & ARMAGH

BELFAST TO BANGOR

Belfast creeps north-eastwards along the southern shores of Belfast Lough towards the Irish Sea. The A2 road out of Belfast

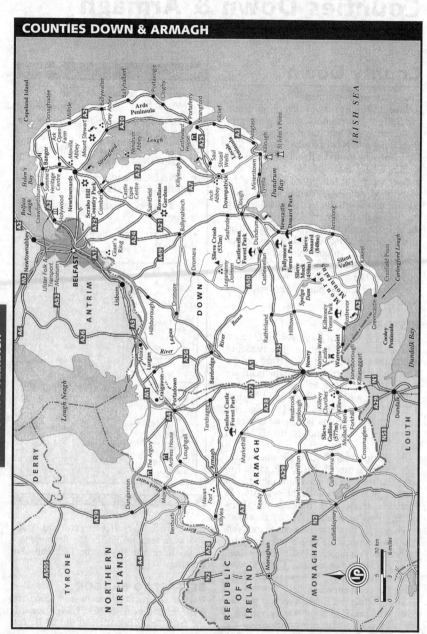

COUNTIES DOWN & ARMAGH

follows the railway line and is a pleasant route to the Ards Peninsula.

Ulster Folk & Transport Museum

This is one of the finest museums in Ireland, 11km north-east of Belfast, near Holywood. Farmhouses, forges, churches and mills (almost 30 buildings in all) have been very carefully reconstructed on the wooded 60-hectare site, with plenty of human and animal extras combining to give strong impressions of Irish life over the past few hundred years. From industrial times, there are complete terraces of 19th-century Belfast and Dromore houses. During the summer, activities such as thatching and horse ploughing are demonstrated for visitors.

On the opposite side of the road the transport museum is a sort of automotive zoo. The Dalchoolin Transport Galleries display horse carts, donkey *creels* (baskets), carriages, bicycles and one of the prototypes for a VTOL – a vertical take-off and landing aircraft. Particularly popular is the section that records the sinking of the Belfast-built *Titanic* in 1912.

Included in the large automobile collection is a gull-wing stainless-steel car, built in Belfast after former American General Motors whiz kid John de Lorean persuaded the British government that to invest £80 million in manufacturing a flash new car would help reduce Northern Ireland's horrifyingly high unemployment figures. Unfortunately the new car was launched into a market suffering from recession and much of the development money simply vanished into numbered Swiss bank accounts.

The park and museum (☎ 90 428428) opens 10.30 am to 6 pm Monday to Saturday, and noon to 6 pm on Sunday, July and August; 9.30 am to 5 pm on weekdays, 10.30 am to 6 pm on Saturday, and noon to 6 pm on Sunday, April to June and September; and 9.30 am to 4 pm on weekdays, and 12.30 to 4.30 pm at the weekend, October to March. Admission costs £4/2.50 (families £9).

Trains and buses to Bangor stop nearby; get off the train at Cultra Station. Bear in mind, though, that the site has been designed for drivers; it's hilly and spread out and you'll need a good half-day to do it justice.

There's a fine **coastal walk** of some 6km from Holywood to Helen's Bay, with more pleasant seashore trails continuing north-east to Grey Point.

Crawfordsburn Country Park

Just over 3km west of Bangor, off the B20 at Helen's Bay, this country park has a number of wooded and coastal walks, and a 20th-century gun emplacement. The large-calibre artillery have been trained on Belfast Lough since before WWI, though a shot has never been fired in anger. The command post and lookout station also remain.

The park opens 9 am to dusk year round and admission is free. Phone the visitor centre (☎ 91 853621) for details of occasional free guided walks; it opens 10 am to 5 pm daily, October to March; and 10 am to 6 pm daily, April to September. The park is accessible on Belfast to Bangor bus No 2 or also by train to Crawfordsburn (unstaffed) or Helen's Bay Station, the latter a wonderful little Victorian train station dating from 1865 and built by the marquess of Dufferin, who owned the surrounding estate.

The 17th-century *Old Inn* (☎ 91 853255, *15 Main St*) in the pretty black and white village of Crawfordsburn has bags of character but isn't cheap: B&B costs £90 for a single or double. It also serves dinner costing around £20.

BANGOR

pop 52,440

It's 21km from Belfast to Bangor (Beannchar), a seaside resort and dormitory town for Belfast commuters. The Belfast to Bangor train line was built in the late 19th century to connect the capital with what was then a flourishing resort. The opening of a 500-berth **marina** in 1995 seems to have lifted the fortunes of Bangor again, with new restaurants opening and hotels smartening themselves up. The **Pickie Fun Park**, with mute-swan pedaloes, continues the more kitsch tradition of British seaside resorts.

History

The town dates back to the 6th century, when the Abbey of St Comgall made Bangor one of the great centres of the early Church. St Comgall was a teacher and friend of St Columbanus and St Colmcille, two of Ireland's most famous saints. Because Bangor was close to the sea and so often the first landfall after their journey from Scandinavia, the Vikings repeatedly attacked Bangor Abbey, which was abandoned by the 10th century; only one wall remains today. The one priceless surviving relic – *The Antiphonary of Bangor*, a small 7th-century prayer book, the oldest surviving Irish manuscript – is now housed in Milan's Ambrosian Library.

Orientation & Information

Unusually, Bangor has a Main St and a High St, both busy commercial centres. The bus and train stations are side by side on Abbey St, at the top of Main St, near the post office. At the bottom of Main St is the marina, with B&Bs clustered to the east and west on Queen's Parade and Seacliff Rd.

For information on Bangor and the North Down region, call in to the helpful Tower House Tourist Office (☎ 91 270069), on Quay St, housed in a tower originally built as a fortified customs post in 1637. It opens 9 am to 5 pm on weekdays, 10.30 am to 4.30 pm on Saturday, and 1 to 5 pm on Sunday, September to June; and 9 am to 7 pm on weekdays, 10 am to 7 pm on Saturday, and noon to 6 pm on Sunday, July and August.

North Down Heritage Centre

Surrounded by Castle Park, this small museum (☎ 91 271200) is in the converted laundry, stables and stores of Bangor Castle in Castle Park Ave. It contains an early-9th-century handbell, some ancient swords, a milepost with distances in Irish miles, and a facsimile of *The Antiphonary of Bangor*, as well as details of the North Down Coastal Path. It opens 10.30 am to 4.30 pm (5.30 pm in July and August) Tuesday to Saturday, and 2 to 4.30 pm (5.30 pm in July and August) on Sunday. Admission is free.

Castle Garden Restaurant serves light meals.

Places to Stay

Accommodation can be hard to find even outside the busy summer months, so it's wise to book ahead.

B&Bs A cluster of virtually identical guesthouses lining Seacliff Rd offer B&B costing £14 to £18 a head. Among the cheapest are *Bayview* (☎ 91 464545, 140 Seacliff Rd), *Pierview* (☎ 91 463381, 28 Seacliff Rd) and *Snug Harbour* (☎ 91 454238, 144 Seacliff Rd).

More guesthouses are grouped along Queen's Parade overlooking the marina: *Battersea Guesthouse* (☎ 91 461643, 47 Queen's Parade) offers singles/doubles costing £25/37, while *Ashley House* (☎ 91 473918, 50 Queen's Parade) has rooms, some with en suite bathroom, costing £18/44.

A little farther out and likely to have a room when others don't is *Kildara Guesthouse* (☎ 91 461245, 51 Prospect Rd), between Main St and Hamilton Rd, which has rooms with shared bathroom costing £16 per person. There's another group of B&Bs on Princetown Rd, past Queen's Parade.

Hotels Formerly Sands Hotel, the recently refurbished *Bangor Bay Inn* (☎ 91 270696, 10 Seacliff Rd), overlooking the marina, has comfortable singles/doubles costing £60/85 (£45/65 at the weekend), including breakfast, and a pleasant restaurant serving reasonably priced pub food. *Marine Court Hotel* (☎ 91 451100, 18-20 Quay St) offers B&B (all rooms with bathroom) costing £80/90. *Royal Hotel* (☎ 91 271866, 26 Quay St) offers B&B costing £75/90.

Places to Eat

Heatherlea Tea Rooms (94 Main St), at the rear of a home bakery, serves terrific quiches, pies, salads and cakes. It opens 9 am to 5.30 pm Monday to Saturday. The popular *Vesuvio* (1st Floor, 8 Quay St) offers marina views and cheap pizzas and pasta dishes. It's closed on Monday.

The stylish **Café Brazilia** *(13 Bridge St)* serves filled baguettes (starting at £2.60), decent coffee and cakes to kill for. It opens 9 am to 6 pm Monday to Saturday.

Knuttel's *(☎ 91 274955, 7 Gray's Hill)*, opposite the marina, serves mainly seafood and traditional meat dishes (grilled sirloin steak; pork in sherry sauce). A three-course menu is available costing £13.75. It opens from 6.30 pm Tuesday to Thursday and from 6 pm Friday and Saturday; last orders are at 9.30 pm.

Grainger's *(☎ 91 467747, 9 Gray's Hill)* is a bright new place offering interesting lunch (rib-eye of beef with grilled potatoes and citrus salad £7.75) and dinner (suckling pig with fondant potatoes and charred pear £12.95) dishes. It opens for lunch and dinner Monday to Saturday, and lunch on Sunday.

Quay's Restaurant at the Royal Hotel (see Places to Stay, earlier) is also recommended. Main courses at lunchtime cost around £5; a four-course Sunday lunch costs £11.95. Mains at dinner (fillet of beef with scallion mash, pac choy, roast shallots and celeriac) start at around £10, with a three-course menu available costing £15.

The Michelin-starred **Shanks** *(☎ 91 853313)*, at the Blackwood Golf Club on Crawfordsburn Rd, has an interior designed by Terence Conran and a mouth-watering menu made for gourmets (venison with caramelised apples; local scallops with smoked chilli and basil risotto). Expect to pay around £25 for a three-course meal. It opens for lunch and dinner Tuesday to Saturday, and for lunch Sunday and Monday. Booking is essential.

Entertainment
The **Boom Boom Rooms** *(☎ 91 468830)* is a popular dance-music venue featuring house on Friday and funk and disco on Saturday. Cover charges are from £3 to £6. For traditional music, try **Calico Jack's** *(Quay St)*. The **Boardwalk** pub *(Gray's Hill)*, opposite the marina, has live music, too.

Getting There & Away
Bus Ulsterbus Nos 1 and 2 from Belfast de-part from the Laganside Bus Centre (☎ 90 320011) for Bangor. There's a bus each way every 20 minutes or so on weekdays, and every 30 minutes at the weekend, and the one-way fare is £2. From Bangor, bus No 6 heads for Newtownards, while bus Nos 3 and 7 travel across the north of the Ards Peninsula to Donaghadee and Millisle. These services run roughly hourly. For timetable details ring ☎ 91 271143.

Train There's a regular half-hourly service to Bangor (and the Ulster Folk and Transport Museum) from Belfast Central Station (☎ 90 899400). Bangor Station (☎ 91 474143) is on Abbey St.

NEWTOWNARDS & AROUND
Founded as a 6th-century ecclesiastical centre, Newtownards (Baile Nua na hArda) these days is a pretty quiet and ordinary market-garden town (many of Belfast's fresh vegetables come from the area). The tourist office (☎ 91 826846), 31 Regent St, next to the bus station, opens 9.15 am to 5 pm on weekdays, and 9.30 am to 5 pm on Saturday. The post office is also on Regent St, whose western and eastern extensions are Church St and Frances St respectively.

Scrabo Hill Country Park
The park (☎ 91 811491), 2km south-west of town, was once the site of extensive prehistoric earthworks, but these were largely removed during construction of the 1857 Memorial Tower in honour of the 3rd marquess of Londonderry. The summit (after 122 steps) of the 41m tower offers some expansive views of Strangford Lough. The park opens year round, while the tower opens 11 am to 6.30 pm Saturday to Thursday, June to September. Admission to both is free.

Somme Heritage Centre
Just over 3km north of town on the A21 is the Somme Heritage Centre (☎ 91 823202), which relates the circumstances leading up to the WWI Somme campaign of 1916 from the perspective of men of the 10th (Irish), 16th (Irish) and 36th (Ulster) divisions. It's

DOWN & ARMAGH

a high-tech show, with short films, a talking model of a wandering preacher and costumed interpreters to explain everything on a 25-minute guided tour. There's nothing at all celebratory about the displays, intended as a memorial to the men who died.

It opens 10 am to 5 pm on weekdays, and noon to 5 pm at the weekend, July and August; 10 am to 4 pm Monday to Thursday, and noon to 4 pm at the weekend, April to June and September; and 10 am to 4 pm Monday to Thursday, and noon to 4 pm on Saturday, the rest of the year. Admission costs £3.50/2.50. Bus No 6, between Bangor and Newtownards, passes the entrance, but you have to dash across a busy dual carriageway. There's ample parking space outside.

Ark Open Farm
Opposite the Somme Heritage Centre, on the other side of the dual carriageway, is the Ark (☎ 91 820445), an open farm with displays of rare breeds of sheep, cattle and poultry, alongside a few llamas and a donkey or two. It opens 10 am to 6 pm Monday to Saturday, and 2 to 6 pm on Sunday, year round. Admission costs £2.30/1.70.

Other Things to See
There's a ruined 13th-century **Dominican friary**, on Court St, and the scant remains of **Movilla Abbey** and its 13th-century church 1.5km to the east. There's some fine 18th- and 19th-century architecture in town, especially along Church St. Most striking is the 18th-century **Market House** on High St which once housed the town's prison, but is now the local arts centre. A lively **market** takes place in Conway Square in front of it every Saturday. A traditional harvest fair is held here in September. The **Market Cross** on High St dates back to the 17th century.

Places to Stay
There's no budget accommodation in central Newtownards. The attractive modern **Cuan Chalet** (☎ 91 812302, 41 Milecross Rd), west of town, offers B&B costing £16 per person, and opens year round. At **Greenacres** guesthouse (☎ 91 816193, 5

Manse Rd), in lovely gardens overlooked by the Memorial Tower, B&B costs £22/36 in singles/doubles with bathroom.

The neat, three-star **Strangford Arms Hotel** (☎ 91 814141, 92 Church St) offers B&B costing £70/80. The hotel restaurant offers a respectable à la carte menu.

Places to Eat
Knott's Cake and Coffee Shop (45 High St) offers light meals and a range of pastries and home-baked goodies. **Cafolla's** (15 Conway Square) has been serving decent fish and chips for ever. The best bet in town for a decent sit-down meal is probably **Roma's** (4 Regent St), a busy pub which serves food all day. Lunch specials cost £4.75.

Getting There & Away
The Ulsterbus station is on Regent St. There are buses about every half-hour to Bangor and Belfast (one way £1.50), and fewer services along the eastern and western sides of the Ards Peninsula.

STRANGFORD LOUGH
Cut off from the sea by the Ards Peninsula (see the following section), except for a 1km-wide strait (The Narrows) at Portaferry, Strangford Lough (Loch Cuan) is almost a lake. It's 25km long, about 6km wide on average and up to 45m deep. Large colonies of grey seals live in and around the lough, particularly at the southern tip of the peninsula, where the exit channel widens out into the sea. Birds abound on the shores and mudflats, including brent geese wintering from Arctic Canada, eider ducks and many species of wader.

Underwater the muddy lough has a diverse marine biology, which can be studied at closer quarters at Exploris in Portaferry (see Things to See & Do in the Portaferry section later in this chapter). Killer whales have occasionally come into the lough, spent a few days there, and caused a sensation. Strangford Lough oysters are a local speciality.

The lough is a great leisure resource, with boats and yachts plying their way up and down its sheltered waters. At Portaferry, however, 400,000 tonnes of tidal water surge through the strait four times daily; you can get some idea of the current's remarkable strength just by watching the Portaferry to Strangford ferry being whipped sideways by the riptide. There are boat trips around the lough; see Portaferry in the Ards Peninsula section later in this chapter.

The western side of Strangford Lough isn't as scenic or interesting as the eastern side (see the following Ards Peninsula section), although it's the route followed by the Ulster Way walking trail.

Western Shore

Castle Espie Centre Two kilometres southeast of Comber, the Wildfowl and Wetlands Centre at Castle Espie (☎ 91 874146) is a haven for fledgling ornithologists and for a large gathering of geese, ducks and swans. Many of the birds are so tame they'll take food from your hand. The centre opens 10.30 am to 5 pm Monday to Saturday, and 11.30 am to 6 pm on Sunday, March to October; and 11.30 am to 4 pm Monday to Saturday, and 11.30 am to 5 pm on Sunday, November to February. Admission costs £3/1.80. The best time to visit is May/June, when the grounds are overrun with goslings, ducklings and cygnets.

Trench Farm (☎ 91 872558) is almost 4km from Comber on the Ringcreevy Rd, with B&B costing £17.50 per person. Comber's *Old School House Inn* (☎ 97 541182), near the turning to Castle Espie, is the area's best-known restaurant. It concentrates on seafood, serves fresh oysters from its own oyster farm, has game in winter and a set dinner costing £17.95. It also offers B&B costing £45/65 in singles/doubles.

Nendrum Monastic Site The site is on Mahee Island, connected to the lough's western shore by a causeway; the remains of 15th-century Mahee Castle guard the causeway. Nendrum is earlier than Grey Abbey on the opposite shore; it was built in the 5th century under the guidance of St Mochaoi (St Mahee). The scant remains provide a clear outline of its early plan.

Foundations exist from a number of churches, a round tower, beehive cells and other buildings, as well as three concentric stone ramparts and a monks' cemetery, all in a wonderful country setting. A particularly interesting relic is the vertical stone sundial, which has been reconstructed with some of the original pieces. The ruins were uncovered only in 1844, even though the island has long been inhabited.

Access to the site is free, although there's a small visitor centre which charges 75/40p. An excellent video compares Nendrum to Grey Abbey, and there's some interesting material about the concept of time and how we measure it, presented in child-friendly fashion. The centre opens 10 am to 7 pm Tuesday to Saturday, and 2 to 5 pm on Sunday, April to September.

In Killinchy, *Burren Cottage* (☎ 97 541475, 19 Main St) charges £18 per person for B&B. *Barnageeha* (☎ 97 541011, 90 Ardmillan Rd) charges £25/45 for singles/doubles with bathroom; dinner costs £15. Near Killinchy, *Tides Reach* in Whiterock Bay, on the lough shore, is a small restaurant serving mostly seafood. It opens for lunch and dinner daily.

Killyleagh The A22 continues south to Killyleagh (Cill O Laoch), an old fishing village dominated by the impressive **castle** of the Hamilton family. Built originally by the Norman John de Courcy in the 12th century, this partly 14th- and 17th-century structure sits on the original motte and bailey and was heavily restored in 1850. Outside the gatehouse a plaque commemorates Sir Hans Sloane, the naturalist born in Killyleagh in 1660, whose collection was the basis for the founding of the British Museum. The parish church has the tombs of members of the Dufferin family, some of whom lost their lives in the battles of Trafalgar and Waterloo.

Killyleagh Castle (☎ 44 546527) has three gatehouse towers (complete with spiral staircases and roof terraces) available for rent of upwards of £200 per week. The two smaller towers sleep four and the larger sleeps five.

DOWN & ARMAGH

Dufferin Arms (☎ 44 828229, 35 High St), near the castle, provides luxurious B&B costing upwards of £32.50 per person. It also has an excellent restaurant and regular live-music nights.

ARDS PENINSULA

The Ards Peninsula (An Aird) slots in between the eastern side of Strangford Lough and the Irish Sea, with Newtownards and Donaghadee acting as gateways. From Newtownards the A20 heads south, following the lough shore, passing Mt Stewart House and Garden and Grey Abbey, before arriving at Portaferry, linked by ferry across The Narrows to Strangford on the western shore of the lough. The A2 heads back north along the peninsula's seawards side, passing through the fishing port of Portavogie to Millisle and Donaghadee. Relatively flat, the peninsula is about 6km wide and 35km long, with some good beaches. Dotted the length of the peninsula are the remains of tower houses, built after Henry VI offered a £10 subsidy to anyone constructing a tower to protect the coast in 1429; most date from the 16th century.

Nowadays the Ards is an agricultural region where farmers have diversified into ostrich rearing and daffodil-bulb cultivation. It's a world away from the tensions of Belfast, but you'll still spot red, white and blue kerbstones testifying to strong sectarian feeling. Watch out for dried *dulse*, Ards' edible seaweed, on sale in greengrocers; it tastes much as you'd expect – strong, salty – and is very much an acquired taste.

Due to the shortage of accommodation in Newtownards, Portaferry and Donaghadee, it may be best to explore the Ards using Bangor as a base for day trips.

Mount Stewart House & Gardens

Eight kilometres south of Newtownards, on the A20, is Mount Stewart. The magnificent 18th-century house and gardens were the home of the marquess of Londonderry, though much of the landscaping was carried out early this century by Lady Edith, wife of the 7th marquess, for the benefit of her children. The 35 hectares form one of the finest gardens in Ireland or Britain and are now in the charge of the National Trust.

The gardens are a cosmopolitan affair, with formal gardens, woodlands and lakes, elegantly populated by a vast collection of plants and statues. On the Dodo Terrace unusual creatures from history (dinosaurs and dodos) and myth (griffins and mermaids) join forces with giant frogs and duck-billed platypuses. The 18th-century owners constructed the Temple of the Winds, a folly in the classical Greek style built on a high point above the lough.

The classical house still has lavish plasterwork, marble nudes and valuable paintings (including a portrait of the racehorse Hambletonian by George Stubbs). Kings have stayed here in bedrooms dedicated to the great European cities. Viscount Castlereagh was born here; he went on to become British foreign secretary and was responsible for the passing of the Act of Union in 1801, dissolving the Dublin Parliament and making Ireland legally a part of Britain. Another member of the family was a general under the duke of Wellington.

The gardens open 10.30 am to 6 pm daily, April to September; 10.30 am to 6 pm at the weekend, October; and 2 to 5 pm on Sunday, March. The house (☎ 42 788387) opens 10.30 am to 6 pm Wednesday to Monday, May to September; and 1 to 6 pm at the weekend, April and October. The Temple of the Winds opens the same days as the house but only 2 to 5 pm. There's a tearoom for hot drinks, sandwiches and cakes. Admission to the gardens, house and temple costs £3.50/1.75. Bus Nos 9 and 10, from Belfast's Laganside Bus Centre and Newtownards, pass the gate Monday to Saturday.

Places to Stay About 7km south-east of Newtownards, off the A20, near Mount Stewart Gardens, is the idyllically situated *Ballycastle House* (☎ 42 788357), an 18th-century farmhouse. B&B costs £23/40 in singles/doubles with full facilities and top-class breakfasts. It also has a *self-catering cottage*. Take the first turning left after you pass the Newtownards Sailing Club.

Grey Abbey
pop 697

In the village of Grey Abbey, 3km southeast of Mount Stewart, are the fine ruins of a Cistercian abbey founded in 1193 by Affreca, wife of the Norman John de Courcy. The abbey was a daughter house of Holm Cultram Abbey in Cumbria and was used for worship as late as the 18th century. What remains is a characteristic 12th-century Cistercian ground plan, consisting of a large cruciform church, two chapels and parts of a refectory, chapter house and rest rooms.

The church was built in early Gothic style even though Romanesque still reigned supreme elsewhere in Ireland. At the far end of the church is a carved tomb possibly depicting Affreca; her husband may be represented by the effigy in the north transept. The grounds, overlooked by 18th-century Rosemount House, are awash with trees and flowers on spreading lawns, making this an ideal picnic spot. A sweet-smelling physic (herb) garden has been replanted, and there's a small visitor centre.

The grounds open 10 am to 7 pm Tuesday to Saturday, and 2 to 7 pm on Sunday, April to September. Admission costs £1/50p.

The small village of Grey Abbey has a cluster of **antique shops** tucked away in Hoops Courtyard off Main St (open 11 am to 5 pm Wednesday, Friday and Saturday) and half a dozen others on Main St itself.

Places to Stay & Eat The *Mervue* (☎ 42 788619, 28 Portaferry Rd) offers B&B costing £16.50/33 in singles/doubles with bathroom. *Brimar* (☎ 42 788681, 4 Cardy Rd) offers B&B costing £25 per person in en suite rooms. *Hoops* (☎ 42 788541, Hoops Courtyard) serves stupendous lunch dishes (excellent roast beef with the works £3.95), wicked cakes and tea in antique silver teapots. It opens 10 am to 5 pm Wednesday to Saturday.

Getting There & Away Ulsterbus Nos 9 and 10 go to Grey Abbey, Portaferry and Ballywalter from Belfast or Newtownards every hour or so.

Portaferry
pop 2324

Portaferry (Port an Pheire), a neat huddle of streets, is the most substantial settlement on the Ards Peninsula. It was originally called Ballyphilip; its new, duller name relates to its position as the terminus for the short ferry ride across the lough to Strangford. The renowned marine biology station on the waterfront uses the lough as an outdoor laboratory. The town itself is a sleepy place that feels like the end of the road, which of course it is. In good weather, you can sit outside the pubs on the waterfront and watch the lough and the ferry go by.

The tourist office (☎ 42 729882), on Castle St, near the tower house, opens 10 am to 5 pm (5.30 pm in summer) Monday to Saturday, and 2 to 6 pm on Sunday.

Things to See & Do You can take a look at the small 16th-century **tower house** on Castle Lane which together with the tower house in Strangford used to control water traffic between the shores of the lough and through The Narrows. Next to the tower house is the state-of-the-art aquarium, **Exploris** (☎ 42 728062), concentrating on marine life from Strangford Lough and the Irish Sea. Touch tanks allow visitors to stroke and hold rays, starfish, sea anemones and other sea creatures. Exploris opens 10 am to 6 pm on weekdays, 11 am to 6 pm on Saturday, and 1 to 6 pm on Sunday, March to August. The rest of the year it closes at 5 pm. Admission costs £3.85/2.70. It's likely to be very busy during school holidays.

Diving, fishing and **birdwatching** are all popular pastimes around the lough. Des Rogers (☎ 42 728297) takes out dive charters and the youth hostel has a compressor and special drying room. John Murray (☎ 42 728414) organises fishing and birdwatching trips as well as cruises on the lough.

Places to Stay At the YHANI-affiliated *Barholm Hostel* (☎ 42 729598, 11 The Strand), opposite the ferry slipway, beds cost £10.95. There's no curfew and food can be provided if you book in advance. It's a roomy place with 45 beds, an excellent kitchen, a big conservatory for breakfast and laundry facilities.

On the square, in the centre of the village, Mrs Adair's modest signless and nameless *guesthouse* (☎ *42 728412*), at No 22, offers B&B costing £16/30 in singles/doubles. At *Lough Cowey Lodge* (☎ *42 728263, 9 Lough Cowey Rd*), a few minutes out of Portaferry, B&B costs £20/35. The three-star seafront *Portaferry Hotel* (☎ *42 728231, 10 The Strand*) offers B&B costing £55/90. *The Narrows* (☎ *42 728148, 8 Shore Rd*), a very comfortable guesthouse a few steps farther along the seafront, costs £39 per person for B&B; all rooms have a view of the lough.

Places to Eat Across from the tower house, *The Cornstore* (☎ *42 729779, 2 Castle St*) specialises in local seafood (starters costing upwards of £2.50, main courses from £6) and opens for lunch and dinner Wednesday to Sunday.

The Narrows (see Places to Stay, earlier) offers superb food and wine together with excellent service and brilliant views of the lough. Expect to pay around £20 for an evening meal. It opens for lunch Tuesday to Sunday and for dinner (last orders 9 pm) Thursday to Saturday. *Portaferry Hotel* serves delicious seafood (stuffed mussels; fried oysters) as well as bar lunches, and opens daily.

Getting There & Away Ulsterbus Nos 9 and 10 go to Portaferry, Grey Abbey and Ballywalter from Belfast or Newtownards every hour or so. You can pick up buses for around the peninsula in Newtownards.

The ferry (☎ *44 881637*) sails every half-hour from Portaferry to Strangford and back between 7.45 am and 10.45 pm on weekdays, 8.15 am to 11.15 pm on Saturday, and 9.45 am to 10.45 pm on Sunday. The journey time is only around five minutes. The fare is £4 for a car and driver, £2.50 for motorcyclists and their bikes, and 80/40p for car passengers and those on foot.

Millisle & Around

Below the high street in Millisle (Oileán an Mhuilinn) lies a pretty shoreline, with a stone wall running out to sea, handy for watching the eider ducks and brent geese bobbing offshore. About 1.5km north-west along Moss Rd (the B172 to Newtownards) is **Ballycopeland Windmill** (☎ *91 861413*), an 18th-century tower mill which was in commercial use until 1915. It's been restored to working order, and has an adjacent visitor centre. It opens 10 am to 7 pm Tuesday to Saturday, and 2 to 7 pm on Sunday, April to September. Admission costs £1/50p. Bus No 7 from Donaghadee passes the entrance.

Places to Stay The *Ballywhiskin Caravan and Camping Park* (☎ *91 862262, 216 Ballywalter Rd*) has 20 pitches costing £5 per night and is open year round.

Mount Erin House (☎ *91 861979, 46 Ballywalter Rd*) offers B&B costing £15 per person. *Seaspray* (☎ *91 862389, 221 Ballywalter Rd*) charges £20/36 for B&B in singles/doubles.

Donaghadee
pop 4799

Donaghadee (Domhnach Daoi) is a pretty, small port, encircled by harbour walls designed by John Rennie in 1819 and completed by his son, Sir John Rennie, who designed several of London's bridges. In summer it's possible to get a boat out to the **Copeland Islands**, which were abandoned to the birds at the turn of the century; inquire at the Harbour Office at the southern end of the harbour towards the lighthouse.

In the village, **Grace Neill's** dates from 1611 and claims to be Ireland's oldest pub. Among its 17th-century guests were Peter the Great, tsar and later emperor of Russia, who popped by for lunch in 1697 on his grand tour of Europe. In the 19th century, John Keats found the place 'charming and clean' but was 'treated to ridicule, scorn and violent abuse by the local people... [who] objected to my mode of dress and thought I was some strange foreigner'.

Places to Stay & Eat The *Donaghadee Caravan Park* (☎ *91 882369, 183 Millisle*

Rd) has 10 tent and 10 campervan sites costing £6 per night.

There are a handful of B&Bs around, all charging between £15 and £20 per person. *Bridge House* (☎ 91 883348, 93 Windmill Rd), 3km from Donaghadee, has a couple of singles/doubles costing £15/28. *Lakeview* (☎ 91 883900, 92A Windmill Rd), next door, offers B&B costing £17/32. *Deans* (☎ 91 882204, 52 Northfield Rd) has beds for £19/34. *Waterside Shanaghan* has four rooms costing £20 per person.

The bright and pleasant bistro in *Grace Neill's (33 High St)* serves delicious lunch and dinner dishes (pork and leek sausages with champ and red-onion marmalade £5.75; fillet of wild duck with braised kale and pickled red cabbage £9.75). There's a 17th-century bar and beer garden. It opens Monday to Saturday.

Dunallen Hotel (27 Shore St) offers lunches with views of the bay. Farther round, *The Captain's Table (6 The Parade)* serves fish and chips, and is open for lunch and dinner daily.

LECALE PENINSULA

East of Downpatrick at the southern end of Strangford Lough is the Lecale Peninsula. From Clough, the A2 follows the coast east then north to Strangford, from where you have the option of taking the ferry across to Portaferry and the Ards Peninsula. St John's Point, the southern tip of the Lecale Peninsula, is surmounted by an automatic lighthouse. It's a wonder that St John managed to get a mention around this part of the world, because the Lecale Peninsula is unequivocally St Patrick's territory.

St Patrick (as you'll probably know by now) was originally kidnapped from Britain by Irish pirates and spent six years tending sheep on Slemish Mountain in County Antrim before escaping back to Britain. After religious training, he returned to Ireland to preach the faith in 432 and is said to have landed on Strangford Lough near Saul. Patrick's first church was in a sheep shelter near Saul, to the north-east of Downpatrick. Using Saul as his base, he made forays out into the country, returning to Saul after some 30 years of evangelising. He's buried nearby, or so the locals believe.

Strangford
pop 548

The small, quaint fishing village of Strangford (Baile Loch Cuan) is 16km north-east of Downpatrick. The Vikings sailed into the lough and noted the strong tidal currents through the strait – hence the name meaning 'strong fjord'. Most of the village is in a conservation area dominated by **Strangford Castle**, another 16th-century tower house; the keys are available from Mr Seed, 39 Castle St, 10 am to 7 pm daily. Steps at the end of Castle St (opposite the castle) lead to a network of paths and a fine view of the lough. There's a large and noisy colony of nesting terns on Swan Island, just off the slipway.

See Portaferry in the Ards Peninsula section earlier in this chapter for details of boat cruises on the lough and the car ferry between Strangford and Portaferry.

Places to Stay & Eat Accommodation is rather scarce in Strangford. *Strangford Caravan Park* (☎ 44 881888, 87 Shore Rd) has 30 tent and 30 campervan sites costing £5. There's also a camp site at Castle Ward (see the following entry). Otherwise, there's *Strangford Cottage* (☎ 44 881208, 41 Castle St) with B&B in singles/doubles costing £42.50/75.

Lobster Pot (☎ 44 881288) is a bar and restaurant on the square serving excellent seafood (half a lobster £14.95) and bar snacks. The nearby *Cuan Bar and Restaurant* (☎ 44 881222) also offers good food. A four-course Sunday lunch costs £10.95.

Castle Ward

Run by the National Trust, the 280-hectare Castle Ward Estate (☎ 44 881204) stretches away from the inlet to the west, with the house 2km along the Downpatrick road. It was built in the 1760s by Lord and Lady Bangor – Bernard Ward and his wife, Anne – who were quite a pair. Their tastes started poles apart, and diverging all the time. The result was Castleward House (and a

DOWN & ARMAGH

subsequent divorce). Bernard favoured the neoclassical Palladian approach, and was victorious in the design of the front façade and the classical staircase. Anne had leanings towards the Strawberry Hill Gothic style, which she implemented on the back façade and in her Gothic boudoir with its incredible fan vaulting. The rest of this great house is a mixture of their different aesthetic tastes.

Around the grounds are some decent walks with a Greek folly, a fine 16th-century Plantation tower house, Castle Audley by the lough, a Victorian laundry museum, vistas of the lough, and tearooms (open the same hours as the house), which also serve light lunches.

In summer Castle Ward hosts a series of open-air operas. The house opens 1 to 6 pm Friday to Wednesday, May to August; and 1 to 6 pm at the weekend, April, September and October. Admission to the house costs £2.60/1.30. The grounds open until dusk year round and admission costs £3.50 per car.

Castle Ward Estate has a *camp site* (☎ 44 881680) for caravans and tents costing £6 per night; the entrance is separate from the main entrance and closer to Strangford. Otherwise, accommodation in the area is scarce and you're better off heading for Portaferry or even Newcastle.

Strangford to Dundrum

A string of castles stretches from Strangford to Dundrum along the A2 road. The majority of them are large and in good condition.

Kilclief Castle Only 4km south of Strangford, Kilclief Castle guards the seawards mouth of the strait. This is the oldest tower house in the county, built in the 15th century by the adulterous bishop of Down. It has some elaborate details and is viewed as the prototype for other castles in the region. It opens 10 am to 7 pm Tuesday to Saturday, and 2 to 7 pm on Sunday, April to September. Admission costs £1/50p.

Ardglass Thirteen kilometres south of Strangford is Ardglass (Ard Ghlais), a fishing village with no less than seven castles or fortified houses from the 14th to 16th centuries. Ardglass Castle (now the clubhouse for the local golf club), and Gowd Castle adjoining it, has Horn and Margaret Castle towers nearby, while King's and Queen's Castles reside on a hilltop above the village. The only one open to the public is **Jordan's Castle** on Low Rd, a four-storey tower near the harbour. Like the others this was built by wealthy merchants at the dawn of economic development in Ulster. The castle now houses a local museum and a collection of antiques gathered together by its last owner. It opens 10 am to 7 pm Tuesday to Saturday, and 2 to 7 pm on Sunday, July and August. Admission costs 75/40p.

On the hill north of the village is a 19th-century **folly** built by Aubrey de Vere Beauclerc as a gazebo for his disabled daughter.

Just outside Ardglass on the Killough Rd is *Coney Island Park* (☎ 44 841210) with 50 tent pitches (£4 per night) and 30 campervan spaces (£8 per night). It opens 2 April to 24 November. On the B1 road from Ardglass to Downpatrick is *Strand Farm* (☎ 44 841446), a small B&B with three rooms costing £16 per person. At *Aldo's* (☎ 44 841315, Castle Place) in Ardglass, seafood or à la carte dinners cost less than £10 from 5 to 10 pm Tuesday to Sunday.

Killough Four kilometres west of Ardglass is the seaside village of Killough, planned by Castle Ward's Lord Bangor, who constructed the road that runs dead straight from here to his estate 12km to the north. The harbour has long silted up but the village still has a picturesque, vaguely continental feel, the tree-lined streets and buildings around Palatine St and Palatine Square exemplifying this. The Palatines were 17th-century German refugees escaping the Thirty Years War (1618–48).

A worthwhile **walk** is south to the 10th-century church ruins and nearby lighthouse of St John's Point, a return trip of about 4km. From the point, the path heads northwest to Minerstown and Tyrella Strand. The 7km stretch of firm sand along here is privately owned and you must pay to use it.

Clough This small town lies at the northern end of a long and narrow inlet, at the crossroads of eastern and southern Down, and is home to the ruins of yet another castle. **Clough Castle**, at the junction of the A24 and A25, is a good example of a 13th-century Norman motte and bailey with a small stone keep.

About 2km north of Clough on the A24, in the village of Seaforde, is the **Seaforde Tropical Butterfly House** (☎ 44 811225), which is set in a large walled garden. The butterfly house has hundreds of free-flying tropical butterflies and many safely caged tropical insects and reptiles. It might make a good place to break a journey south to Newcastle. It opens 10 am to 5 pm, Monday to Saturday, and 2 to 6 pm on Sunday, Easter to September. Admission costs £2.20/1.30.

Dundrum The final castle on this trip is 4km south of Clough on the shore of Dundrum (Dún Droma) Bay. **Dundrum Castle** was built in 1177 by de Courcy on the site of an earlier Irish fortification. The extensive ruins, a rugged fortress on a rocky outcrop amid the trees, dominate the village. De Courcy's castle was made of wood, and his successor, de Lacy, was probably responsible for most of the walls in the first years of the 13th century. King John confiscated the castle in 1210 and added the donjon at the highest point, its thick walls still containing the accessible stairway to the top. After a few changes in ownership it was captured from the Magennises by Cromwell, who blew it up in 1652.

You can walk up to the castle from the village centre or there's a car park just before it. It opens 10 am to 7 pm Tuesday to Saturday, and 2 to 7 pm on Sunday, April to October. Admission costs 75/40p.

At *Mourne View House* (☎ 43 751457, 16 Main St), B&B costs £15/26 in singles/doubles. It overlooks the quay and entry is off the street. There's pub food in places such as *Murlough Tavern* or *Road House Inn*. The *Buck's Head Restaurant* (☎ 43 751868) is the best place to eat and serves good seafood lunches and dinners; it offers a popular £11.50 three-course Sunday lunch.

DOWNPATRICK
pop 10,260

Downpatrick's name (Dún Pádraig) comes from Ireland's patron saint, who is associated with numerous places in this corner of Down. From Saul and Downpatrick Cathedral, he developed the island into a 'land of saints and scholars'. St Patrick had tried to land in Wicklow but was blown ashore at Strangford Lough near Saul.

Downpatrick is the county's administrative centre and capital, 32km south of Belfast. It was settled long before the saint's arrival, his first church here being constructed inside the dún, or fort, of Rath Celtchair, an earthwork still visible to the south-west of the cathedral. The place later became known as Dún Pádraig, anglicised to Downpatrick in the 17th century.

In the 11th century, St Malachy moved the diocesan seat to Bangor, but the transfer was short-lived. In 1176 the Norman John de Courcy claimed to have brought the relics of St Colmcille and St Brigid to Downpatrick to rest with the remains of St Patrick. This may have been a ploy to protect the churches of the town from the native Irish, who were disgruntled because the Irish clergy had been removed and replaced with Benedictines and Cistercians. Later the town declined along with the cathedral until the 17th and 18th centuries, when the Southwell family developed it into more like what we see today. Much of the Georgian work is centred on English, Irish and Scotch Sts, which radiate from the town centre, although the best is in the Mall leading up to the cathedral.

Information

The tourist office (☎ 44 612233) is in Market St opposite the bus station. It opens 9 am to 6 pm Monday to Saturday, and 2 to 6 pm on Sunday, mid-June to September; and 9 am to 5 pm on weekdays, and 9 am to 1 pm and 2 to 5 pm on Saturday, the rest of the year.

Down Cathedral

Over the past 1600 years a cathedral has been created that is a conglomerate of reconstructions. Repeated attacks by Vikings wiped away all trace of the earliest churches and monasteries here, then the Irish Augustinians produced little before being evicted by the Norman Benedictines. The Norman cathedral and settlements were destroyed by Edward Bruce in 1315. The rubble of those times was used in the 15th-century construction, which was finished in 1512 and lasted until 1538. After the dissolution of the monasteries it fell into ruins. Today's structure is an 18th- and 19th-century reconstruction with a few additions. Down Cathedral is also called the Cathedral of the Holy and Undivided Trinity.

In the grounds are a 9th-century high cross in poor condition and, to the south, a turn-of-the-century monolith with the inscription 'Patric'. It has been believed since de Courcy's time that the saint is buried somewhere nearby. The legend goes that Patrick died in Saul, where his followers were told by angels to place his body on an ox-cart and that the angels would guide the cart to the spot where the saint was to be buried. They supposedly halted at the church on the hill of Down, now the site of the cathedral. The interior (open 9 am to 5 pm daily) reveals a bygone era of churchgoing. The private pews are the last of their kind still in use in Ireland. Note the pillar capitals, the eastern window representing the Apostles, and the fine 18th-century church organ.

There's a memorial to an Oliver Cromwell, though not 'the' Cromwell. All the treasured relics of St Patrick wouldn't save a church in Ireland from destruction if it housed that man's body!

Inch Abbey

This abbey, built by de Courcy for the Cistercians in 1180 over an earlier Irish monastic site, is visible across the river from the cathedral. The Cistercians arrived from Lancashire in England with a strict policy of non-admittance to Irishmen and managed this for nearly 400 years before closing in 1541. Much of the remains consists of foundations and low walls only; the groomed setting in the marshes of the River Quoile is its most memorable feature.

The grounds open year round. The abbey opens 10 am to 7 pm (4 pm October to March) Tuesday to Saturday, and 2 to 7 pm (4 pm October to March) on Sunday, year round. Admission costs 75/40p. To get here head out of town for about 1.5km on the Belfast road, then turn left just before the Abbey Lodge Hotel.

Down County Museum

Down the Mall from the cathedral is the county museum (☎ 44 615218), housed in an extensive 18th-century jail complex. The gatehouse contains exhibits on the life of St Patrick, while the main buildings deal with the history of the county. In the cell block at the back are models of some of the prisoners incarcerated here. Perhaps the biggest exhibit of all is outside – a short signposted trail from here leads to the **Mound of Down**, a good example of a Norman motte and bailey.

The museum opens 11 am to 5 pm on weekdays, and 2 to 5 pm at the weekend, mid-June to mid-September; and 10 am to 5 pm Tuesday to Friday, and 11 am to 5 pm on Saturday, the rest of the year. Admission is free.

The Mall itself is the most picturesque street in Downpatrick, with some marvellous 18th-century architecture, including Soundwell School built in 1733 and a courthouse with a finely decorated pediment.

Quoile Countryside Centre

Signposted off Strangford Rd is the small Quoile Countryside Centre (☎ 44 615520), an educational centre with lots of info on the local flora and fauna. It's beside the ruins of **Quoile Castle**, a 17th-century tower house which stood on the shores of the River Quoile when it was first built. Access to the lower floors is via the Countryside Centre, which opens free 11 am to 5 pm on weekdays, and 1 to 5 pm at the weekend, April to September.

Places to Stay

Accommodation in Downpatrick is fairly thin on the ground. *Hillside* (*☎ 44 613134, 62 Scotch St*) is the most central B&B, with three rooms costing £16 per person. *Hill-crest* (☎ *44 612583, 157 Strangford Rd*) charges £17/36 in singles/doubles.

Farther afield is 200-year-old *Havine Farm* (☎ *44 851242, 51 Ballydonnell Rd*), about 7km south-west of Downpatrick and 3km north of Tyrella in Ballykilbeg. It has three bedrooms and B&B costs £16.50 per person in a truly rural environment.

Near Inch Abbey, the one-star *Abbey Lodge Hotel* (☎ *44 614511, 38 Belfast Rd*) has 21 rooms costing £45/60 including breakfast.

Places to Eat

By far the best place to eat is in the *Arts Café* in the Down Arts Centre. It's a fine red-brick Victorian building with a clock-tower, hard to miss at the centre of town, at the junction of English, Irish and Scotch Sts. It opens 10 am to 4.30 pm Monday to Saturday.

Harry Afrika's (*102 Market St*), immediately opposite the bus station, is a popular diner-style restaurant offering reasonably priced breakfasts, grills and daily specials. *Denvir's Pub* (*14 English St*) serves good wholesome dishes (Irish stew; fresh mussels) featuring fresh organic vegetables. It opens for lunch and snacks from noon to 2.30 pm and for dinner from 5.30 to 9 pm. *Abbey Lodge Hotel* has a good seafood-oriented restaurant with a £13 set dinner.

Getting There & Away

Ulsterbus Nos 15 and 215 depart regularly from the Europa Bus Centre in Belfast for Downpatrick bus station (☎ 44 612384), Market St, every half-hour or so (less frequently on Sunday).

AROUND DOWNPATRICK
Saul

Saul (Sabhal) is 3km north-east of Downpatrick off the A2 Strangford road. Upon landing near here in 432, St Patrick made his first convert, Díchú, the local chieftain, who gave St Patrick a sheep barn (*sabhal*) from which to preach. This was the saint's favourite spot and he returned here regularly. West of the village is the supposed site

of the barn, with a mock 10th-century church and round tower built in 1932 to mark the 1500th anniversary of his arrival. Beside the church is the surviving wall of a medieval abbey where St Patrick is said to have died. Also in 1932, a massive 10m-high statue was erected on nearby Slieve Patrick, with Stations of the Cross along its ascent.

Struell Wells

Two kilometres east of Downpatrick, on a back road behind the hospital, is the final pilgrimage site associated with St Patrick. Since the Middle Ages, the waters from these wells, which were referred to in early stories of St Patrick, have been popular cures for all ills, with one well specially set aside for eye ailments. The site's popularity was at its peak in the 17th century, and the men's and women's bath houses date from this time.

CENTRAL COUNTY DOWN

South of Belfast is pastoral countryside, with towns such as Craigavon, Lurgan, Saintfield, Ballynahinch, Hillsborough, Moira and Banbridge servicing the region. Hillsborough is a particularly attractive little town, but Moira too has a quiet charm. Craigavon is an ugly sprawl, best avoided, although many bus services connect here. Only Slieve Croob, south-west of Ballynahinch, breaks the flatness of the terrain. Down's greatest megalithic monuments are in this region, including the Giant's Ring and the Legananny Dolmen.

Giant's Ring

This earthwork is within easy reach of Belfast, only 8km south of the city centre, west of the A24 in Ballynahatty. The ring is a huge prehistoric enclosure nearly 200m in diameter, enclosing nearly 3 hectares. In the centre is the **Druid's Altar**, a dolmen from around 4000 BC. Prehistoric rings were commonly believed to be the home of fairies, and consequently treated with respect, but this one was commandeered in the last century as a racetrack. The 4m-high embankment was a natural grandstand and course barrier.

Rowallane Gardens

Rowallane Gardens (☎ 97 510131), signposted off the A7, 2km south of Saintfield, are renowned for spectacular displays of rhododendrons and azaleas in the spring (summer and autumn are brilliant seasons to visit, too). Rowallane House (now the headquarters of the National Trust in Northern Ireland) was inherited in 1903 by Hugh Armitage Moore, a distinguished gardener who spent 25 years developing the 21-hectare garden.

The magnificent massed plantings of rhododendrons thrive in the light acid soil, gentle rain and even temperature of the gardens, which are encircled by a windbreak of Australian laurels, hollies, pines and beech trees. The walled gardens feature rare primulas, blue Himalayan poppies, plantain lilies, roses, magnolias and autumn crocuses.

The tearoom serves hearty lunches, sandwiches, cakes and scones. The gardens open 10.30 am to 6 pm on weekdays, and 2 to 6 pm at the weekend, April to October; and 10.30 am to 5 pm on weekdays, November to March. Admission costs £2.50/1.25.

Saintfield
pop 2168

It's difficult to imagine, but the small, quiet town of Saintfield was the scene of the first of two County Down battles in the 1798 Rebellion. The local Presbyterian minister, the Reverend TL Birch, was active in the United Irishmen and had established a branch here in 1791. The rebels managed to hold the town for a few days but were defeated at Ballynahinch soon afterwards. The graveyard of the Presbyterian church on Main St contains a memorial plaque and the headstones of those killed in battle.

There are half a dozen or so **antique shops** along Main St well worth browsing in.

March Hare (Main St) serves excellent homemade soups, light meals and cakes. It opens 10 am to 5 pm Wednesday to Sunday. *White Horse Inn (49 Main St)* offers more substantial meat and fish dishes. It opens for lunch and dinner Monday to Saturday.

Legananny Dolmen

This is perhaps Ulster's most famous Stone Age monument, and features extensively in tourist literature. Situated just west of Slieve Croob (532m), the tripod dolmen is less bulky than most, and its elevated position gives it the great backdrop of the Mourne Mountains to the south. The source of Belfast's River Lagan is on **Slieve Croob**, and the mountain is crowned with the remains of a court cairn. Farther up, the summit presents a much wider panorama of the county.

To reach the mountain, head west from Ballynahinch along the B7 to Dromara, from where there are roads leading southeast across the slopes.

Hillsborough
pop 2407

The gracious small town of Hillsborough (Cromghlinn), 15km south-west of Belfast, was founded in the 1640s by Colonel Arthur Hill, who built a fort here to quell Irish insurgents. Fine Georgian architecture rings the square and runs down Main St.

The tourist office (☎ 92 689717) is in the Georgian courthouse in the centre of the village. It opens 9 am to 5 pm Monday to Saturday, May to September; and 11 am to 3.30 pm Tuesday to Saturday, October to April.

Things to See At the top of Main St, the most notable building is **Hillsborough Castle**, a rambling two-storey late-Georgian mansion built in 1797 and extensively remodelled in the 1830s and 1840s. From 1924 to 1973 it was the residence of the governor of Northern Ireland and is now the official residence of the secretary of state for Northern Ireland (the British government's main representative). The most notable exterior feature is the elaborate wrought-iron gates, dating from 1745, which were designed for Richhill Castle near Armagh and brought here when the house was restored after a fire.

The castle grounds and state rooms open Saturday morning, 17 April to 4 September (except 12 June). Admission costs £5/3.50 (families £12.50).

Leprechauns & Banshees

Now you see him, now you don't. The leprechaun is a little man no more than 150cm tall with a jaunty feather sticking out of his green cap. Of course he's at pains to hide from you because, as everyone knows, the leprechaun carries a crock of gold. Catch him and you can force him to give it to you. Take your eyes off him for a second and he'll vanish into thin air.

That's the blarney that has spawned many an Irish tea towel. In reality, scholars believe the leprechaun is a reminder of the days when the early Christians neutralised the power of the pagan gods by turning them into 'little people'.

Another mythical figure of Irish folklore is the banshee, from the Gaelic *bean sídhe* (woman of the fairy mound). She is a spirit whose wailing warns of the impending death of a family member, but it's believed by some that she warns families of pure Irish descent only.

NICKY CAVEN

Nearby is the Georgian **Market House** and at the bottom of Main St **St Malachy's Parish Church**, one of Northern Ireland's most splendid churches, with twin towers at the ends of its transepts and a graceful spire at the western end. Originally dedicated in 1663, St Malachy's was restored and improved in 1774 by the 1st marquess of Downshire, who was also responsible for its fine Snetzler organ. Inside, the nave and transepts are filled with box pews and there are some impressive 18th- and 19th-century wall tablets as well as a 17th-century copy of the Bible in Irish.

Beside the church are the ruins of **Hillsborough Fort** constructed by Colonel Hill in 1650 and remodelled into a Gothic-style tower house in 1758. The fort commanded the strategic pass of Kilwarlin and was used by William of Orange in 1690 on his way south to the Battle of the Boyne.

The fort opens 10 am to 7 pm Monday to Saturday, and 2 to 7 pm on Sunday, April to September; and 10 am to 4 pm Tuesday to Saturday, and 2 to 4 pm on Sunday, October to March. Admission is free.

Places to Stay & Eat There are a handful of B&Bs around, including *Avoca Lodge* (☎ 92 682343, 53 Dromore Rd), which has

one room costing £18.50 per person, and *Ballykeel House* (☎ 92 638423, 32 Ballykeel Rd), which has two rooms costing £20 per person. The two-star *White Gables Hotel* (☎ 92 682755, 14 Dromore Rd) offers B&B costing £79.50/100 in singles/doubles and has a decent restaurant open for lunch and dinner.

Plough Inn (3 The Square), which has been offering 'beer and banter' since 1758, serves excellent food for lunch and dinner. *Hillside* (☎ 92 682765, 21 Main St) serves good bar food at lunchtime and also has a top-class restaurant (three-course meals starting at £20) open for dinner Tuesday to Saturday.

Red Fox (6 Main St) is a pleasant teashop offering light meals and all sorts of baked goodies. It opens 10.15 am to 2 pm and 2.45 to 5 pm, Tuesday to Saturday.

Getting There & Away There are frequent daily services on bus Nos 38 and 238 to Belfast's Europa Bus Centre. Bus No 38 also runs back and forth to Lisburn.

Banbridge & Around

Fifteen kilometres south-west of Hillsborough is Banbridge (Droíchead na Banna), another Industrial Revolution town. The

DERRY & ANTRIM

Gateway Tourist Information Centre (☎ 40 623322), 200 Newry Rd, is out of the town centre at the roundabout. It opens 9 am to 5 pm (7 pm July and August) Monday to Saturday, and 2 to 6 pm on Sunday, Easter to October; and 9 am to 5 pm Monday to Saturday, the rest of the year.

Things to See & Do Near the centre at the bottom of the hill is the **statue of Captain Francis Crozier**, complete with polar bears which look like no other polar bears you're likely to encounter. A native of Banbridge, Captain Crozier was commander of HMS *Terror* in the 1840s, and explored the uncharted Antarctic continent. Later he went with Sir John Franklin in search of the elusive Northwest Passage. Franklin died on that voyage in 1847, and Crozier and his crew starved to death a year later, their bodies remaining lost in the Arctic for 10 years. Crozier lived in the fine blue and grey Georgian house across the road from the statue.

Banbridge is the start of a **Brontë Homeland Drive**, which travels the River Bann valley to Rathfriland 12km to the southeast. Patrick Brontë, father of the famous literary sisters, was born here and taught in a local school. The locals like to think that her father's tales of the Mourne Mountains inspired the bleak setting for Emily's *Wuthering Heights*. Milking this tenuous connection for all it's worth is the **Brontë Homeland Interpretive Centre** (☎ 40 631152) in what was Drumballyroney Church, 13km south-east of Banbridge. It opens 11 am to 5 pm Tuesday to Friday, and 2 to 6 pm at the weekend, March to October. Admission costs £1/50p.

If you don't want to do the entire Irish Linen Tour (see the following paragraph), you might want to pop into the **Ferguson Linen Centre** (☎ 40 623491), west of town on Scarva Rd. The only manufacturers of double damask linen in the world, the factory has been in operation since 1854. Tours (adults £2) run at 11 am and 3 pm Monday to Thursday, and at 11 am on Friday.

The tourist office is the 'gateway' for the so-called Linen Homelands (Banbridge,

Craigavon and Lisburn) and arranges the **Irish Linen Tour**. You can join tours of the linen towns on Wednesday, May to September (except the last three weeks in July). Tours begin at 10 am and take in the Irish Linen Centre in Lisburn, a flax farm in Dromore and a linen factory still in production, returning to Banbridge around 4 pm. The charge is £10/8.50, and advance booking (☎ 40 623322) is essential.

Places to Stay & Eat The *Mourne View* B&B (☎ *40 626270, 32 Drumnascamph Rd*), 4km west of town, has four singles/doubles with bathroom costing £20/34. *Fresh Winds* (☎ *40 622943, 30 Ringsend Rd*) offers B&B costing £20 per person.

Harry's Bar (*7 Dromore St*) serves good-value meals and bar snacks and opens for lunch and dinner Tuesday to Saturday, and for lunch on Sunday.

Getting There & Away Bus Nos 38 and 238 run regularly from Belfast's Europa Bus Centre via Dromore, Hillsborough and Lisburn; bus No 238 also runs to Newry.

SOUTHERN DOWN & MOURNE MOUNTAINS

The relatively compact yet rather impressive Mourne Mountains have long resisted human settlement. Today they are surrounded on all sides by towns and villages, but are crossed only by the B27 road between Kilkeel and Hilltown. The reservoirs of the Silent Valley and Spelga are among the few intrusions on nature. The steep and craggy granite peaks have suffered less from glaciation than other similar ranges. There are no low polished hills here.

The highest, most accessible peak is Slieve Donard (848m). In its shadow, the town of Newcastle is the best base for exploring this or other peaks, as the Mourne Heritage Trust here provides detailed information. The less adventurous can visit the numerous forest parks around Newcastle. For walkers, Newry and Downpatrick tourist offices stock *St Patrick's Vale: The Land of Legend*, which describes 31 walks. The Silent Valley Park plunges into the

Get cosy in a snug amid the flamboyant Victoriana of the Crown Liquor Saloon, Belfast.

The first meeting of the Northern Ireland Parliament was held at imposing Belfast City Hall in 1921.

See a show at Belfast's Victorian Grand Opera House.

Mural, Falls Rd, Belfast

DORINDA TALBOT

One of the many striking republican murals in the feisty city of Derry/Londonderry

PAT YALE

A statue symbolises hope for a peaceful future, Derry/Londonderry.

range's heart, surrounded by most of the peaks. Ben Crom, Slieve Muck and Slievelamagan are good for strenuous hiking. Westwards is the B27 road, which passes Spelga Dam, a picturesque drive in the evening when the sun goes down behind Eagle Mountain and Pigeon Rock Mountain. There's good rock climbing in this area.

As in Connemara, the farmers here have produced the characteristic patchwork of small fields with dry-stone walls out of the boulder-strewn landscape. The biggest of the walls, the Mourne Wall, is a different kettle of fish: it was built early this century to provide employment and to enclose the catchment area of the Silent Valley Reservoir. The wall stretches for 35km over numerous peaks.

Newcastle
pop 7214

All along the coast from the north of the county the Mournes beckon. If you stick to the coastline you'll eventually end up in Newcastle (An Caisleán Nua), 46km from Belfast. The town itself is unremarkable but it boasts a dramatic setting, with Slieve Donard stretching up behind the town and an attractive 5km crescent of beach.

Information The tourist office (☎ 43 722222), 10-14 Central Promenade, opens 10 am to 5 pm Monday to Saturday, and 2 to 6 pm on Sunday, with longer hours in summer. As well as the usual selection of brochures and maps, the office stocks an interesting range of traditional and contemporary crafts.

For more details on the Mournes, drop into the Mourne Heritage Trust (☎ 43 724059), 91 Central Promenade, beside the Avoca Hotel. The trust has a selection of books and brochures on the area and maps of suggested walks. It opens 9 am to 5 pm on weekdays. Guided walks (£5) of varying distances (four to 14km) into the mountains leave from the centre at 10 am at the weekend (but ring to double-check first).

Things to See & Do If you can't resist fast cars and shiny fenders, stop by the

Route 66 American Car Museum (☎ 43 725223), 94 Dundrum Rd. The result of a hobby that got out of hand, the museum displays 15 cars dating from the 1930s to the 1980s. The *pièce de résistance* is a 1959 white cadillac which features the biggest fins of all time. The museum opens from 10.30 am to 6 pm daily, Easter to September; and 2 to 6 pm at the weekend, the rest of the year.

Tropicana (☎ 43 725034), on Central Promenade next to the tourist office, is a family entertainment 'paradise' complete with outdoor heated fun pools, giant slides and the inevitable adventure playground and bouncy castle. It opens 10 am to 6 pm Monday to Saturday, and 2 to 6 pm on Sunday, June to August.

Places to Stay The central YHANI *Newcastle Youth Hostel* (☎ 43 722133, 30 Downs Rd), near the bus station and Slieve Donard Hotel, has 42 beds and charges £8.25 including bed linen. Facilities include a kitchen, laundry and TV room.

There are plenty of B&Bs in and around Newcastle. Central ones include *Arundel Guesthouse* (☎ 43 722232, 23 Bryansford Rd), which has four rooms costing £16 per person, and *Beach House* (☎ 43 722345, 22 Downs Rd), right in town opposite the beach, with singles/doubles costing £30/50. South of town by the harbour is *Harbour House Inn* (☎ 40 623445, 4 South Promenade), a guesthouse with four en suite rooms costing £25/40.

Glenside Farmhouse (☎ 43 722628, Tullybrannigan Rd), about 1km from Tollymore Forest Park, charges £12/22 for B&B. *Briers Country House* (☎ 43 724347, 39 Middle Tollymore Rd), almost 1km from Newcastle, has a lovely garden and nine very comfortable rooms costing £35/50.

Brook Cottage Hotel (☎ 43 722204, 58 Bryansford Rd) charges £45/70 for B&B in pleasant rooms, including breakfast. The turreted four-star *Slieve Donard Hotel* (☎ 43 723681, fax 43 724830, Downs Rd), beside the beach, offers rooms with all the trimmings costing £82/120, including breakfast. *Burrendale Hotel and Country*

Club (☎ *43 722599, 51 Castlewellan Rd)* is another upmarket place with similar prices.

Places to Eat The *Pavilion* (☎ *43 726239, 36 Downs Rd)*, down by the beach opposite the entrance to the Slieve Donard Hotel, is a good bet. Lunch specials (grilled swordfish steak with grapefruit and tequila salsa) cost £5.95 and there's a £3.50 children's menu. It opens for lunch and dinner Monday to Saturday, and for lunch on Sunday.

Seasalt (☎ *43 725027, 51 Central Promenade)* is a sunny new deli and café offering everything from organic soups to homemade beef-and-Guinness pie. It's a great stop for picnic food, too. It's also open for dinner (three courses £14.50) on Friday evening. *Maple Leaf Cottage (149 Bryansford Rd)* is a good tea-and-scone venue.

Burrendale Hotel has a high-quality restaurant open for lunch and dinner daily. Bar snacks and restaurant meals are available in *Brook Cottage Hotel*. *Oak Restaurant* at the Slieve Donard Hotel isn't bad either, with four-course dinner specials costing £20.

Getting There & Away The bus station (☎ 43 722296) is on Railway St and there's an hourly service from Belfast (return £7.90, 1¼ hours) on Ulsterbus Nos 18 and 20 through Ballynahinch. Alternatively, you can go from Belfast to Downpatrick and from there take Ulsterbus No 17 to Newcastle (20 minutes).

Getting Around Wiki Wiki Wheels (☎ 43 723973), 10B Donard St, near the main roundabout, rents bikes, as does Ross Cycles (☎ 43 778029), on Clarkhill Rd in nearby Castlewellan. Bikes cost £10/40 per day/week.

Around Newcastle

Newcastle is an ideal base from which to explore the Mourne Mountains, and there are three forest parks close by, for walks, hikes and pony treks. **Donard Park** at the southern edge of town is the best place from which to ascend **Slieve Donard**. On a good day the three-hour effort is well rewarded,

with Down's patchwork of fields, Scotland, Wales and the Isle of Man all on show. Two cairns near the summit were long believed to have been cells of St Donard, who retreated here to pray in early Christian times.

The 500-hectare **Tollymore Forest Park** (☎ 43 722428), 3km north-east of town, runs lengthy walks along the Shimna River and the northern slopes of the Mournes. The park opens 10 am to sunset daily, and admission costs £3 per car, £1.50 per motorcycle. The visitor centre is in a 19th-century barn, designed to look like a church, and displays the single plaster plaque that survives from Tollymore House as well as info on the flora, fauna and history of the park. It opens noon to 5 pm daily, June to August; and noon to 5 pm at the weekend, the rest of the year. Guided walks leave from outside at 2 pm on summer weekends.

Part of the park but with a separate entrance, **Tollymore Outdoor Centre** (☎ 43 722158) runs group courses on hill walking, rock climbing and canoeing; call to see what's offered when.

Farther north-east is the slightly smaller **Castlewellan Forest Park** (☎ 43 778664) and its lovely lake. Trout fishing is allowed (daily permit £8) and there's also boat hire. The internationally known **Arboretum** is well established, dating from 1740, with a wide variety of fine shrubs and trees. It opens 10 am to dusk, and admission costs £3 per car, £1.50 per motorcycle. The park entrance is off the main street in the village of Castlewellan and you could leave your vehicle there and walk in.

Outside the park is **Mount Pleasant Horse Trekking Centre** (☎ 43 778651), which caters to the experienced rider and the beginner, with various treks into the park costing upwards of £8 per hour inclusive of guide.

Places to Stay There are plenty of camp sites on offer, though they can fill up at the height of summer. Both *Castlewellan* and *Tollymore* parks have spaces for tents costing £6 to £10 depending on the season. There are several caravan parks (none with tent sites) along the coastal Dundrum Rd, including *Woodcroft Caravan Park* (☎ 40 622284, 104 Dundrum Rd) about 1km north-east of town.

Mournes Coast Road

The coastal drive along the A2 south and around the sweeping Mourne slopes is the most memorable journey in Down. Annalong, Kilkeel, Rostrevor and Warrenpoint offer convenient stopping points, from which you can detour into the mountains. If you take the Head Rd, following the sign for the Silent Valley 1km north of Annalong, you go through the beautiful stone-wall countryside, past the Silent Valley, and back to Kilkeel.

Annalong The busy little tourist spot of Annalong (Áth na Long), with its shingle beach, is 12km south of Newcastle. Overlooking the harbour is the nicely preserved **Annalong Corn Mill**, an 1830 watermill which still mills flour. The mill opens 11 am to 5 pm Tuesday to Saturday, February to November. There's a small admission charge.

B&B costing around £18 per person is available at *Four Winds* (☎ 43 768345, 237 Kilkeel Rd) and *Kamara* (☎ 43 768072, 106A Kilkeel Rd). Annalong's *Glassdrumman Lodge* (☎ 43 768451) is an expensive guesthouse, costing £95/135 for singles/ doubles, which also serves very good food (dinner £35). More down to earth is *Harbour Inn* by Annalong's waterfront, serving up fish, steaks and pub food daily.

Kilkeel Nine kilometres farther south is Kilkeel (Cill Chaoil), bigger than Annalong and with a quayside fish market stocked by Northern Ireland's largest fishing fleet. From Kilkeel the B27 ventures north into the mountains. The friendly tourist office (☎ 41 762525), on Newcastle St, the main street, is open 9 am to 5.30 pm Monday to Saturday, year round.

Chestnutt Caravan Park (☎ 41 762653), beside a Blue Flag beach, is good, with pitches costing £10 per night. B&Bs charging around £16 per person include *Mourne Abbey* (☎ 41 762426, 16 Greencastle Rd),

south of town, and *Sharon Farm House* (☎ 41 762521, 6 Ballykeel Rd), about 5km north-west in Ballymartin. Mourne Abbey opens April to September. *Hill View House* (☎ 41 764269), 6km north of Kilkeel, just off the B27, opens year round and offers B&B costing £21/34 in singles/doubles. The homely *Kilmorey Arms Hotel* (☎ 41 762220, 41 Greencastle Rd) costs £36.50/62. It also offers a medium-priced menu of familiar à la carte dishes.

Silent Valley Just east of Kilkeel is the Head Rd, which leads to the beautiful Silent Valley 6km north. In the valley the Kilkeel River has been dammed to provide water for Belfast. The dry-stone **Mourne Wall** surrounds the valley and climbs over the summits of 15 of the nearby peaks. Two metres high and over 35km long, it was built between 1910 and 1922 and outlines the watershed of the springs that feed the two dams.

At the southern end of the valley is the Silent Valley Information Centre (☎ 90 746581), behind the grey stone building. From near the car park (admission £3 per car, £1.50 per motorcycle, £1.50/50p per pedestrian) there's a bus up the valley to the top of Ben Crom. This operates daily in July and August, but in May, June and September it runs at the weekend only. Otherwise, it's a fine walk. The centre opens 10 am to 6 pm daily.

During July and August, Ulsterbus No 34A (the Mourne Rambler) runs from Newcastle to Silent Valley and the Spelga Dam, with four buses on weekdays, three on Saturday.

Greencastle Greencastle (Caisleán na hOireanaí), on the tip of a promontory across Carlingford Lough, is 6km south-west of Kilkeel. The first **castle** was built in 1261 as a companion to Carlingford Castle on the opposite side of the lough in County Louth. However, the square, turreted remains date from the 14th century. Once the property of the earls of Kildare, it was seized by the Crown and given to the Bagenal family of Newry in the 1550s. They

DOWN & ARMAGH

maintained it as a royal garrison until it was destroyed by Cromwell's forces in 1652. The rooftop provides a good vantage point west up the lough. The interior opens 10 am to 7 pm Tuesday to Saturday, and 2 to 7 pm on Sunday, April to September. Admission costs 75/40p.

Rostrevor From Kilkeel the journey is westwards along Carlingford Lough. Thirteen kilometres to the west, Rostrevor (Caislean Ruairi) is a pretty Victorian seaside resort of a couple of streets at the base of Slievemartin.

Just before entering the town from the north, the road passes a large **obelisk** to Major General Ross. A British commander in the American War of 1812, Ross's achievement was the capture of Washington DC and the burning of the White House. Up until then the presidential residence had been stone grey, but was painted white to cover the smoke and scorch marks left by Ross's men.

To the north-east of the town is **Kilbroney Forest Park** (☎ 41 738134) on the northern shores of Carlingford Lough. There's a forest drive and then a footpath to the top of Slievemartin, or a strenuous trek up the steepest side of the mountain. *Kilbroney Forest Park Camp Site (Shore Rd)* costs £6 per night.

Near Rostrevor, 2km inland by the Fairy Glen riverside walk, is the attractive early-18th-century *Forestbrook House* (☎ 41 738105, Forestbrook Rd). It charges £18 per person for B&B. There are several bright and welcoming pubs in town all offering decent pub food.

Warrenpoint & Around At the head of Carlingford Lough, on the way to Newry, is Warrenpoint (An Pointe), another spacious and picturesque resort. It's one of the livelier towns around, with an active nightlife in the pubs and halls.

The tourist office (☎ 41 752256), in the Church St town hall, opens 9 am to 5 pm on weekdays, year round, plus the weekend in summer.

Just over 3km west of Warrenpoint is the small **Burren Heritage Centre**, which has information about the court tombs and crannógs of the area, along with a collection of embroidery, tools and bits and pieces rescued from local churches. It has a craft shop and teashop attached. It opens 10 am to 6 pm Tuesday to Saturday, and 2 to 6 pm on Sunday, April to September; and 10 am to 5 pm on weekdays, the rest of the year.

On the main road from Warrenpoint to Newry you'll see **Narrow Water Castle**, a medieval tower house, standing on the shores of the lough, and the round tower of **Clonallan** monastic settlement on the opposite shore.

For somewhere to stay you could try *Fernhill House* (☎ 41 772677, 90 Clonallon Rd), where B&B costs £18.50 per person, or *Mariann's Place* (☎ 41 752085, 18 Upper Dromore Rd), which has rooms costing £20.

For food, *Bennett's (Church St)* offers local seafood, steaks and traditional pies. *Victoria (The Diamond)* has a tandoori Indian restaurant upstairs. Alternatively, *Diamonds* nearby has an extensive menu with something to suit most tastes, including vegetarians.

Weather permitting, a passenger ferry (☎ 41 772001) crosses the lough to Omeath in County Louth between 1 and 6 pm daily, May to September. It costs £2/1 return.

Newry
pop 22,975

Newry (An tlúr) has long been a frontier town, guardian of the Gap of the North, which lies between the Mourne Mountains to the east and Slieve Gullion to the southwest. Its name derives from a yew tree planted here by St Patrick in an early monastery, of which nothing remains.

A stone castle was first built in the town in 1180 by de Courcy, but it was repeatedly attacked. Cistercian monks came to shelter near the castle, until their abbey was taken over by Nicholas Bagenal in the 1570s. As grand marshal of all English forces in Ireland, the powerful Bagenal attracted the attention of some of the local rulers. One, Seán 'the Proud' O'Neill, completely destroyed the castle and house in 1566. In 1575 Bagenal used the rubble to construct the first Protestant church built in Ireland since the Reformation. He is buried in the grounds of St Patrick's Church of Ireland on Stream St.

Newry Canal, built in 1740, preceded the English network which led that country into the Industrial Revolution. The canal brought trade, and later its demise led to the decline of the town.

Always too close to the border to be popular with tourists, Newry is starting to find its feet. Its location makes it a good base from which to explore the Mourne Mountains, Slieve Gullion Forest Park and the Cooley Peninsula. Its position on the main Dublin to Belfast road (the A1/M1) also makes it a magnet for shoppers, in particular for Southerners who come for the cheaper merchandise, especially around Christmas. But traffic congestion is a year-round problem.

Information There's a small, helpful tourist office (☎ 30 268877) inside the town hall. It opens 9 am to 5 pm on weekdays, and 10 am to 4 pm on Saturday, June to September; and 9 am to 1 pm and 2 to 5 pm on weekdays, the rest of the year.

Newry Museum The small Newry Museum (☎ 30 266232), in the Arts Centre on Bank Parade, presents a detailed historical account of the town, and has some intriguing exhibits, including Admiral Nelson's cabin table from HMS *Victory*. This piece sits near the base of the entrance stairs, its glass case bearing only a small plaque naming the benefactor. The museum opens 9 am to 5 pm on weekdays, and 10 am to 1 pm on Saturday. Admission is free.

Town Hall The red-brick town hall was built in 1893 on the border of Counties Down and Armagh. So fierce was the rivalry between the two counties that it was erected right on the border, which meant building it on a three-arched bridge over Clanrye River. The cannon outside was captured during the Crimean War (1853–6) and given to the town in memory of the men who volunteered to fight in the war.

Newry Canal You can hardly miss Newry Canal in the centre of town where it parallels Clanrye River, separated from it by a narrow strip of land. It runs 29km north to Lough Neagh, and 9.5km south to Carlingford Lough. Victoria Lock, south of the town centre, has been restored for visitors as part of the long-term Newry Canal Restoration Project to restore the whole canal and reopen it to leisure traffic.

Places to Stay & Eat The *Ashton House* (☎ 30 262120) is on Fathom Line on Omeath Rd, close to town. It charges £20/36 for B&B in singles/doubles with bathroom. The modern *Hillside* (☎ 30 265484, 1 Rock Rd) is 8km north of Newry off the Belfast road and charges £17/34 for B&B. More central, *Millvale House* (☎ 30 263789, 8 Millvale Rd) charges £18/36 with shared bathroom. The new three-star *Canal Court Hotel* (☎ 30 251234, Merchants Quay) charges £60 per person including breakfast.

The best place to eat in town is the *Brass Monkey* (1 Sandy St), a bar and grill offering everything from seafood to steak. It opens daily for lunch and dinner. *Snaubs Coffee Shop* (15 Monaghan St) has a range of vegetarian options and freshly baked bread and cakes.

Getting There & Away From Belfast's Europa Bus Centre bus Nos 38, 45 and 238 run regularly to Newry bus station (☎ 30 263531) on Edward St. From the Mall in Newry, bus No 39 leaves once or twice an hour for Kilkeel, passing through Rostrevor and Warrenpoint.

Trains between Dublin and Belfast stop at Newry; the station (☎ 30 269271) is a fair way from the centre but there are bus connections.

County Armagh

County Armagh could be – should be – a major tourist attraction. Quite apart from

DOWN & ARMAGH

the venerable town of Armagh, there are some wonderful prehistoric sites, and more-modern sights, in the surrounding country-side. You could easily spend a week or more here. Unfortunately, modern history came very close to rendering the county a no-go area. Apart from small Protestant outposts such as Bessbrook, County Armagh is strongly Catholic and its national-ist identity is keenly felt. The resolve of its people to refuse incorporation into the UK has been steadfastly maintained.

ARMAGH
pop 14,640

Armagh (Ard Macha), one of the towns most worth visiting in the North, has suffered badly from the social and political unrest, but here, as elsewhere, there's cautious optimism that the peace process will continue and bring a tourism dividend. The St Patrick's Trian and Navan Fort developments are in-dicative of an effort to turn things round.

History

This compact little city lays claim to being one of Ireland's oldest settlements. Legend has it that the hill now home to the Church of Ireland cathedral was once the power base of Queen Macha, wife of Nevry, some time during the first millennium BC. She gave her name to the city, whose Irish form, Ard Macha, means 'Macha's height'. St Patrick set up the first Christian church in Ireland here, on a site at the base of the hill. Later the local chieftain, a convert to the new religion, gave Patrick the hilltop, and a church of some kind has stood on that spot for over 15 centuries, predating Canterbury as a Christ-ian religious site. By the 8th century Armagh was one of Europe's best-known centres of religion, learning and craftwork.

However, its fame was its undoing, as the Vikings raided the city 10 times between 831 and 1013, taking slaves and valuables, and leaving many dead in their wake. Brian Ború, who died in 1014 near Dublin during the last great battle to defeat the Vi-kings, was buried on the northern side of the cathedral.

With the Vikings gone, the Irish clans

fought each other for the city, and the Nor-man settlement in the 12th and 13th cen-turies saw more attacks. But the religious life continued, with the conversion from Celtic Christianity to Catholic customs in the 12th century and the establishment of a Franciscan friary in 1263. What the Vikings and Normans hadn't managed, the Refor-mation did. The monasteries and educa-tional establishments were destroyed by either English or Irish forces fighting yet again for control of the city. By the 17th century little was left of a once flourishing city.

During the Plantation, Irish landowners were thrown off their lands, and settlers from England and Scotland took their place. Today's Armagh is a largely Georgian con-struct and owes its distinctive architecture to Richard Robinson, a Church of Ireland primate. By the time of his arrival in 1765 the town had recovered, economically at least, from the many invasions and had a flourishing linen industry. In 1995 its old city status was restored again.

Information

The helpful tourist office (☎ 37 521800), 40 English St, inside the building housing St Patrick's Trian, opens 9 am to 5 pm Mon-day to Saturday, and 2 to 5 pm (1 to 5.30 pm in summer) on Sunday, year round. If you're intending to spend just one day here don't do it on Sunday, when, like the rest of Northern Ireland, Armagh more or less closes down.

St Patrick's Church of Ireland Cathedral

The core of the building dates right back to medieval times, while the rather dull sand-stone-clad exterior is the result of a 19th-century restoration by Primate Beresford. Around the exterior are a series of carved heads, and inside, along with the chilly wooden pews of established religion, are some interesting plaques and an 11th-century Celtic cross. The chapter house has assorted paraphernalia from the ancient city. Every time anyone has knocked down a house or rebuilt a wall and found some

ARMAGH

PLACES TO STAY
1 Dean's Hill
5 Desart House
6 Padua Guesthouse
17 Charlemont Arms Hotel
20 De Averell House
25 Armagh City Hostel

PLACES TO EAT
8 Our Ma's Café
18 Fat Sam's
19 Take Away Food Shops
31 Archway Coffee Lounge
33 Café Papa
34 Cottage Restaurant
35 Jodie's Restaurant

PUBS
9 Shambles Bar
11 The Station Bar
16 McQs
37 Calvert's Tavern

OTHER
2 Armagh Planetarium
3 Armagh Observatory
4 St Patrick's Roman
  Catholic Cathedral
7 Shambles Market
12 Bus Station
13 The Royal School
14 Sovereign's House
  & Fusiliers Museum
15 Courthouse
18 Fire Station
21 Charlemont Place
23 Post Office
  Tourist Office &
  St Patrick's Trian
24 Armagh Public Library
  (Robinson's Library)
26 Vicar's Hill
27 St Patrick's Church
  of Ireland Cathedral
28 Arts Centre
29 Cinema & Basement Café
30 Armagh County Museum
32 Sainsbury's
36 Brown's Bike Hire
38 Armagh Gaol
39 Franciscan Friary

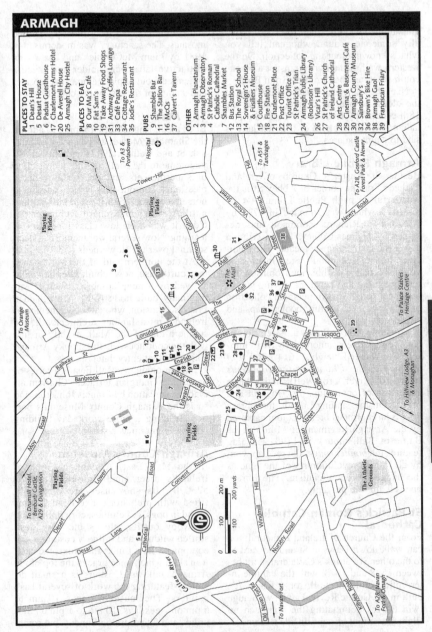

DOWN & ARMAGH

ancient object, it has been deposited here, unexamined and unexplained. There's usually someone around who can tell you what's known about the collection. On the western wall of the north transept a plaque commemorates the burial of Brian Ború.

Near the cathedral, **Vicar's Hill** is one of the oldest terraces in Ireland, built in the 18th century by Richard Castle in the Palladian style. The ghost of a green lady is said to haunt the area.

Armagh Public Library

Beside St Patrick's Church of Ireland Cathedral on the corner of Abbey St is the wonderful Armagh Public Library (☎ 37 523142), which was founded in 1771 by Archbishop Richard Robinson and designed by Thomas Cooley. The inscription above the main entrance means 'The medicine shop of the mind'. Step inside and you'd swear that Archbishop Robinson had just swept out another door leaving you to browse among his own personal collection of 17th- and 18th-century books, maps and engravings.

The collection includes a 1st edition of *Gulliver's Travels*, annotated by Swift himself, Sir Walter Raleigh's 1614 *History of the World*, the *Claims of the Innocents* (pleas to Oliver Cromwell), and a large collection of engravings by Hogarth and others. On the landing outside the library door is an enormous French colour captured by the Armagh Regiment of Militia at the Battle of Ballinamuck in 1798. The flag features the *bonnet rouge*, the red cap worn by all French revolutionists of the time as the badge of republicanism. The library opens 9 am to 5 pm daily.

St Patrick's Roman Catholic Cathedral

From the Church of Ireland cathedral you can walk down Dawson St and Edward St to the other St Patrick's Cathedral, built between 1838 and 1873, with the Famine interrupting building work for a while. It's built in the Gothic Revival style, with huge twin towers dominating the approach up flight after flight of steps. Inside it seems al-

most Byzantine, with every piece of wall and ceiling covered in brilliantly coloured mosaics. The sanctuary was modernised in 1981 by Liam McCormick and has a very distinctive tabernacle holder and crucifix which seem out of place among the mosaics and statues of the rest of the church.

The Mall

Back along English St (stopping to admire the **Shambles Market** at the corner of English St and Cathedral Rd) and Russell St, you come to the Mall. It's not a collection of supermarkets and dress shops but a pleasantly laid-out park which once held horse races, cock fighting and bull baiting, until Archbishop Richard Robinson decided it was a bit low class for a city of learning. Now several war memorials stand sentinel over the flowerbeds.

At the northern end of the Mall stands the **courthouse**, now rebuilt after being destroyed by a huge bomb in 1993. It was originally built in 1809 by Armagh man Francis Johnston, who later became one of Ireland's most famous architects. At the southern end of the Mall, exactly in line with the courthouse, is the spooky Armagh Gaol (see that entry, later).

Farther along the Mall East is a series of handsome Georgian terraces. **Charlemont Place** is a creation by Francis Johnston, and so is the Armagh County Museum's portico, fronting a more workaday building originally put up as a school.

Armagh County Museum

In the Mall East, Armagh has one of Ireland's nicer small museums (☎ 37 523070). Its showcases are pleasantly filled with prehistoric axe heads, items found in bogs, old clothes, corn dollies and strawboy outfits, plus some very dead stuffed wildlife, and military costumes and equipment. Don't miss the gruesome cast-iron skull which once graced the top of the Armagh gallows. Upstairs is a small art gallery featuring the work of several Irish painters. The museum opens 10 am to 5 pm on weekdays, 10 am to 1 pm on Saturday, and 2 to 5 pm on Sunday, but sometimes closes on bank holidays. Admission is free.

Royal Irish Fusiliers Museum

The museum (☎ 37 522911), which is in the old Sovereign's House near the courthouse, consists of much paraphernalia of war: polished silver and brass, medals and the little personal items that survived from the many battles the fusiliers fought. The museum opens 10 am to 5 pm on weekdays. Admission costs £1.50/75p.

Armagh Gaol

The rather forbidding Armagh Gaol, built in 1780 to the design of Thomas Cooley, stands directly opposite the courthouse at the southern end of the Mall. In use until 1988, it's now owned by Armagh City and District Council and at the time of writing was awaiting its fate. In the meantime, however, the building is open for tours and is pretty much as it was when the last prisoners left (though it's unlikely to stay that way for long!).

The building was substantially extended in 1819, possibly by Francis Johnston, who designed the General Post Office in Dublin. In 1846 the gaol was extended again. The following year, at the height of the Famine, there were 339 prisoners in the gaol with up to 21 inmates crammed into one cell. At this time the gaol also held dozens of children who had deliberately stolen food in order to escape the appalling conditions of the workhouse.

Public executions took place in front of the gaol up until 1866; after that prisoners were hanged out of public view in the Hanging Square. Some are buried in the grounds – reputedly under the enormous rhubarb patch.

In the 1920s it became a women's prison and in the 1970s C wing was added to house female political prisoners, in particular the Price sisters – Dolores and Marion – who were serving life sentences for a series of London car bombings.

The gaol is open for tours at the weekend and on bank-holiday Mondays from May to June. Admission costs £1/50p. Contact the tourist office for further information.

Armagh Observatory & Planetarium

A healthy walk up College Hill from the Mall brings you first to the 200-year-old observatory, which still contributes to astronomical research. It isn't open to the public but you can walk around the grounds 9.30 am to 4.30 pm on weekdays.

Farther up the hill, Armagh Planetarium (☎ 37 523689) has the interesting Hall of Astronomy displaying astronomical instruments, with lots of hands-on stuff, and an Eartharium Gallery designed to give visitors 'a global view of our home'. Both stand in Astropark, laid out to show the relationships of the different planets to each other.

The planetarium opens 10 am to 4.45 pm on weekdays (with shows at 3 pm), and 1.15 to 4.45 pm at the weekend (with shows at 2, 3 and 4 pm), year round; there are hourly shows on weekdays in July and August. Admission to everything costs £3.75/2.75.

Palace Stables Heritage Centre

The heritage centre (☎ 37 529629), 10 minutes' walk out of town off Friary Rd, stands in the grounds of the Palace Demesne, built by Archbishop Robinson when he was appointed primate of Ireland in 1769. As you turn into the demesne, you'll see the ruins of the Franciscan friary dating back to the 13th century. Much of its stonework was taken to build the demesne walls.

The stables house a set of tableaux meant to illustrate how a guest was entertained in the days of Richard Robinson, but as there are no real artefacts except in the coachman's kitchen downstairs it's of fairly limited interest. There's a nice coffee shop, craft shop and a children's playroom. The centre opens 10 am to 5.30 pm Monday to Saturday, and 1 to 6 pm on Sunday, April to August; and 10 am to 5 pm Monday to Saturday, and 2 to 5 pm on Sunday, the rest of the year. You have to go round with a guide. Admission and tour cost £3/1.90.

The palace itself houses council offices, but the ground floor lobby retains some of the grandeur of earlier days, with fine portraits of George III and his wife.

DOWN & ARMAGH

The Orange Order

Officially called the Loyal Orange Institution, the Orange Order is a secretive Protestant organisation committed to retaining Northern Ireland's political links with Britain. Estimated to have around 10,000 members (mostly men), the order was founded in 1795 in memory of King William III of Orange, who defeated Catholic King James II at the Battle of the Boyne on 12 July 1690. Since then the Orange Order has flourished, bearing much responsibility for strengthening the resistance to the granting of Home Rule in 1912 and objecting to almost any proposal that didn't leave Protestants politically dominant in the North. In the past, membership of the Orange Order was a necessity for anyone wanting to rise in Unionist politics. Between 1921 and 1969, all but three of the 54 ministers appointed to the Stormont government were members of the Orange Order.

The Orange Order celebrates the victory of William of Orange every year with a series of processions held between March and 12 July. The summer marching season has frequently precipitated violent clashes between Protestants and Catholics and in recent years the annual Drumcree Church Parade in Portadown has become a rallying point for hardline Orangemen, many of whom don't want to see the implementation of the Good Friday Peace Agreement. The standing of the Orange Order was seriously shaken during the 1998 marching season when widespread Protestant violence culminated in a petrol-bomb attack which killed three young brothers in Ballymoney, County Antrim. Despite fears of similar violence, the 1999 marching season turned out to be relatively peaceful.

National Trust property Ardress House (☎ 38 851236) which started life as a farmhouse and was upgraded to a manor house in 1760. Much of the original neoclassical interior remains and the farmyard still functions, with a piggery and smithy. The walled garden has recently been planted with a selection of old apple varieties and there's a small rose garden featuring old Irish roses. There are pleasant walks around the wooded grounds. It opens 2 to 6 pm at the weekend and on bank holidays, April, May and September; and 2 to 6 pm Wednesday to Monday, June to August. Admission costs £2.40/1.20 (families £6).

The Argory

A fine country house in 130 hectares of woodland above the River Blackwater, The Argory (☎ 87 784753) retains most of its 1824 fittings; some rooms are lit by acetylene gas from the house's private plant. There are two formal gardens featuring roses, Victorian clipped-yew arbours and a lime walk by the river. The house and grounds are open the same hours as Ardress

House and admission costs £2.60/1.30 (families £6.50). It's on Derrycaw Rd off the B28, 3.5km north-west of Moy.

Benburb Valley Park

The park straddles the River Blackwater, which is popular for salmon fishing and canoeing. In the park is **Benburb Castle**, founded by Shane O'Neill, who had a stronghold here long before the English arrived, though nothing remains of it. In 1611 Sir Richard Wingfield added a barn which does still stand. In the 19th century, floors were raised and a private house was incorporated into the building. During WWII, US troops used the place as a hospital and the towers were altered to allow access to the roofs. The castle has been restored along 17th-century lines. About 800m from the castle is **Benburb Valley Heritage Centre** in a restored linen mill. The centre and castle open 10 am to 5 pm Monday to Saturday, April to September. Admission costs £1.50.

The village of Benburb in County Tyrone is 11km north-west of Armagh; take the

A29 and then turn left onto the B128. The centre is on the left and clearly marked, and the castle is a short distance farther along.

Gosford Castle Forest Park

At this relaxing picnic spot children will enjoy the weird and wonderful poultry on display. Nature trails work their way around the park and through the trees. In the middle of it all is a vast mock-Norman castle that isn't open to the public. Admission to the park (☎ 37 551277) costs £2.50 per car, £1/50p per pedestrian. The park is beside the A28, south-east of Armagh near Markethill. Buses to Markethill stop outside.

SOUTH ARMAGH

The notoriety of south Armagh earned it the forbidding epithet of Bandit Country. The intensity of the armed conflict between the IRA and the British army was nowhere more evident or dramatic. At the height of the Troubles many small towns were effectively sealed off by the British military, and army helicopters buzzed overhead. Even now wreaths by the roadside bear silent homage to the many victims of the fighting.

Having said that, however, there's nothing to stop you visiting what is a lovely part of Ireland, steeped in legend and with some fascinating archaeological and ecclesiastical places to see. Most of the sights are around the Ring of Gullion, a ring dyke of rugged hills which encircles 577m Slieve Gullion (Sliabh gCuilinn), the mountain where the Celtic warrior Cúchulainn took his name after killing the dog (cú) belonging to the smith Culainn. Most places worth seeing could be taken in on a half-day trip by car from Armagh city or Newry. On a bicycle give yourself a couple of days at least.

Bessbrook

pop 3147

The small town of Bessbrook (An Sruthán) was founded in the mid-19th century by Quaker linen manufacturer John Grubb Richardson to house the workers of his flax mill. The layout of the houses and shops gave the Cadbury family the idea of building Bournville near Birmingham in England. Most buildings are made from local granite and arranged round two squares, each with a green in the middle.

Derrymore House

Just outside the village of Bessbrook is Derrymore House (☎ 30 830353), an elegant thatched cottage built in 1776 for Isaac Corry, who represented Newry in the Irish House of Commons for 30 years. The Act of Union was drafted in the drawing room of the house in 1800. The surrounding parkland was laid out by John Sutherland (1745–1826), one of the most celebrated disciples of Capability Brown. The house opens 2 to 5.30 pm Thursday to Saturday, Easter and May to August. Admission costs £1.80/90p (families £4.50).

Killevy Churches

Surrounded by beech trees, these ruined Siamese-twin churches were built on the site of a 5th-century nunnery founded by St Monenna and plundered by the Vikings in 923. During the Middle Ages a convent of Augustinian nuns was founded, but it was dissolved in 1542. The eastern church dates from the 15th century, the western one from the 12th century. The massive lintel on the western door with the granite jambs may be 200 years older still. Originally, the two churches were nearly a metre apart but became joined at an unknown date.

To the north, the traditional site of St Monenna's grave is marked by a granite slab, and a signed walkway leads to a holy well. Heading west out of Camlough, turn left at the crossroads, keeping the lough on the right. A junction on the road points right to the churches and left to Bernish Rock Viewpoint. The churches are 5km from Camlough and can be visited at any time.

Slieve Gullion Forest Park

The coniferous forest, on the B113 about 8km south-east of Armagh, covers the lower slopes of Slieve Gullion (577m), and a gorgeous 13km drive takes in a walk to a lake. The drive emerges from the trees to picturesque views of the Ring of Gullion, a circle of small hills round Slieve Gullion.

Next to the palace, the Primate's Chapel, designed by Thomas Cooley with a little help from Francis Johnston, is now deconsecrated. Inside are fine oak carvings, an elaborate coffered ceiling and stained-glass windows. Beside it, steps lead down to a tunnel. Archbishop Robinson didn't like the smell of cooking, so the kitchen was in an outside building connected to the palace by a tunnel. There's also an interesting ice house which would have once been filled with ice, which didn't melt as long as it wasn't exposed to outside air.

St Patrick's Trian

The old Presbyterian church behind the tourist office has been turned into a heritage centre (☎ 37 521801), focusing on the theme of faith. For children there's also a Land of Lilliput exhibition with a rather wonderful model of Gulliver tied down on the ground while the Lilliputians climb all over him. The story of his adventures in Lilliput is then retold by a gigantic, seemingly real, model of Jonathan Swift's famous creation.

It opens 10 am to 5 pm Monday to Saturday, and 2 to 5 pm on Sunday, September to June; and 10 am to 5.30 pm Monday to Saturday, and 1 to 6 pm on Sunday, July and August. Admission costs £3.75/2 (families £9.50).

Places to Stay

Camping You can camp at *Gosford Forest Park* (☎ 37 551277), about 11km south of town on the A28 near Markethill, for £6 to £9 per night.

Hostel The new YHANI *Armagh City Hostel* (☎ 37 511800, 36 Abbey St), near St Patrick's Church of Ireland Cathedral, is more like a small luxury hotel than a youth hostel. Comfortable twin rooms (£12.25 per person) come complete with en suite bathroom, TV and tea- and coffee-making facilities. There are also 12 small dorm rooms (upwards of £10.75 per person), a well-equipped kitchen, laundry, lounge, reading room and secure car park. From April to September the hostel is open all day, from

October to March it's closed between 11 am and 5 pm.

B&Bs Beyond the cathedral is *Padua Guesthouse* (☎ 37 522039, 63 Cathedral Rd), with two rooms costing £12 per person. *Desart House* (☎ 37 522387, 99 Cathedral Rd) has three rooms costing £15 per person. The handsome *Dean's Hill* (☎ 37 524923), up past the Planetarium on College Hill, offers B&B costing £25 per person. The sitting room has an open fire. *Hillview Lodge* (☎ 37 522000, 33 Newtownhamilton Rd) is a modern place just south of town offering B&B for £25/40 in singles/doubles.

Hotels The *Charlemont Arms Hotel* (☎ 37 522028, 63 English St) charges £30/50 for singles/doubles with bathroom. The three-star Georgian *De Averell House* (☎ 37 511213, 47 English St) has comfortable rooms costing £27.50/50. It also has a *self-catering apartment*. The small *Drumsill Hotel* (☎ 37 522009, Moy Rd) charges £30 per person. All three places have their own restaurant and rates include breakfast.

Places to Eat

There are a few places to get snacks or lunch but evening meals are more of a problem. *Pilgrim's Table Restaurant*, in St Patrick's Trian, is a pleasant and popular place for lunch, offering good-value soups, hotpots and vegetarian dishes. The *Shambles Bar* (9 English St) serves a good range of pub grub at lunchtime.

Archway Coffee Lounge (5 Hartford Place), off the Mall near the museum, is the place for pastries and delicious homemade cakes and pies. It opens 10 am to 5 pm Tuesday to Saturday. *Café Papa* (15 Thomas St) serves decent coffee and gourmet sandwiches.

Basement Café (Market St), below the cinema, opens until 7 pm Monday to Saturday for steak sandwiches and light meals. *Fat Sam's* (7 English St) serves tasty jacket potatoes starting at £2.25. *Cottage Restaurant* (Gazette Arcade), off Thomas St, looks nothing like a cottage but has a good selection of cheap lunches.

The basement restaurant at *De Averell House* (see Places to Stay, earlier) is recommended for dinner or Sunday lunch. Main courses cost around £8. It opens 6 to 10 pm Thursday, Friday and Saturday, and noon to 3 pm and 5 to 9.30 pm on Sunday. *Jodie's (☎ 37 527577, 37 Scotch St)* has a reasonable à la carte menu, too. It opens for lunch Monday to Saturday, for dinner Wednesday to Saturday, and 5.30 to 8.30 pm on Sunday.

If you're in Armagh on a Sunday morning and in desparate need of food, *Our Ma's Café*, on the corner of English St and Cathedral Rd, is open for a fry-up.

Spectator Sports
You may be lucky enough to catch a game of road bowls, a traditional game now only played in Armagh and Cork (see the boxed text 'Road Bowling' in the West Cork section of the County Cork chapter). Contestants hurl small metal bowls along quiet country lanes to see who can make it to the finishing line with the least number of throws. Games usually take place on Sunday afternoon, with championships held in May.

Getting There & Away
The bus terminal (☎ 37 522266) is in Mall West. There are daily connections with Belfast (roughly hourly) and to Enniskillen (Monday to Saturday), and a service to Dublin that involves a change of bus at Slane. The Belfast to Galway bus No 270 also stops in Armagh. A return fare to Belfast is £8.40. Bus Nos 40 and 44 run frequently (no Sunday service) to Newry.

Getting Around
Bikes can be hired from Brown's Bikes (☎ 37 522782), 21A Scotch St, for £4/24 per day/week.

AROUND ARMAGH
Navan Fort
A little over 3km west of Armagh is Navan Fort (Emain Macha), an Irish Camelot and the principal archaeological site in Ulster. The Egyptian geographer Ptolemy marked this site on his map of the known world in the 2nd century, naming it Isamnium.

Legend has it that a pregnant woman called Macha was forced to race against the king's horses here; at the end of the race she died giving birth to twins, and the name Emain Macha means 'Twins of Macha'. Another legend says that it was the great Queen Macha who began this place, marking out the area with her brooch.

Whatever its origins, the hill was the site for homes and a huge temple during both the Iron and Bronze Ages. At one stage an enormous timber structure was filled with lime and deliberately burned, suggesting that it was sent on its way to heaven rather than sacked by its enemies. Close by is a Bronze Age pond now called the King's Stables where remains of bronze castings have been found.

An impressive visitor centre (☎ 37 525550), in the shape of a Bronze Age building, details the excavation of the site and retells the legends associated with it. It's just a 10-minute walk behind the centre to the site itself, which offers magnificent views on a clear day.

The centre opens 10 am to 7 pm Monday to Saturday, and 11 am to 7 pm on Sunday, July and August; and 10 am to 5 pm (6 pm April to June and September) on weekdays, 11 am to 5 pm on Saturday, and noon to 5 pm on Sunday, the rest of the year. Admission costs £3.95/2.25 (families £7). It's just about walkable from Armagh, or you can take bus No 73 from Mall West.

Orange Order Museum
This Orange Order Museum, 10km north of Armagh in the village of Loughgall, was created in 1961 on the premises of what was then a pub. It opens on request during office hours; inquire in the building next door. It contains sashes and banners, and weapons from the 1795 Battle of the Diamond between the Protestant Peep o' Day Boys and the Catholic Defenders. This took place at Diamond Hill 5km north-east of the village and led to the founding of the Orange Order.

Ardress House
About 14km north-east of Armagh is the

Slieve Gullion can be climbed from the south or north. The south approach has a forest road for the first part of the journey, while the north approach is made a little easier because of a rough path all the way. On the summit there are two early-Bronze Age cairns.

The visitor centre (☎ 30 848084) and park open 10 am to dusk daily, Easter to September. Admission costs £2.50 per car.

Thí Chulainn Cultural Centre

In the village of Mullach Ban, just west of Slieve Gullion, is Thí Chulainn (☎ 30 888828), a cultural activities centre which runs an interesting programme of traditional music, arts and heritage events. The **Stray Leaf Folk Club** in Mullach Ban hosts regular folk-music sessions on Saturday night. The nearby village of **Forkhill** offers regular traditional-music sessions in the local pubs and in October hosts a festival of traditional Irish singing.

Crossmaglen

pop 1586

Crossmaglen (Crois Mhic Lionnáin) is a small town with a fierce reputation – more than 20 soldiers have been killed in the town square alone. The square is dominated by a sprawling, ugly army-cum-police post built right against the houses. Despite this, Crossmaglen is a friendly place with a reputation for excellent music sessions. The large market square here is the venue for a horse-trading fair in September.

The small tourist office (☎ 30 868900) on the square opens 9 am to 5 pm (6 pm in summer) on weekdays.

Places to Stay & Eat

In Crossmaglen, *Murtagh's Bar* (☎ 30 861378, 13 North St) offers B&B costing £15/30 in singles/doubles, plus dinner costing £8. On the B30 towards Newry, just after the junction with the A29, *Lima Country House* (☎ 30 861944, 16 Drumalt Rd, Silverbridge) charges £18 per person. The restaurant here opens for dinner Monday to Saturday.

There are a few places to eat in Crossmaglen, including *Chums (46 The Square)*, which opens for meaty lunches, and *Cartwheel (20 The Square)*, which serves pub food in the evening.

Getting There & Away

Bus No 42 runs regularly Monday to Saturday between Newry and Crossmaglen via Camlough.

Counties Derry & Antrim

Ireland isn't short of fine stretches of coast, but the Causeway Coast from Portstewart in County Derry to Ballycastle in County Antrim, and the Antrim coast from Ballycastle to Belfast, are as magnificent as you could ask for. Most spectacular of all is the surreal landscape of the Giant's Causeway. It's familiar from many a postcard and calendar, and looks like some weird image from a Magritte painting.

County Derry

The chief attraction of the county is the feisty and historic city of Derry (Doire) itself, nestled poetically by the wide sweep of the River Foyle. The city, and the entire north-west of Ireland, is now more accessible than ever with the recent announcement of cheap direct flights from London. Northeast along the coast there's good surf to be had at Portstewart and Portrush, and a fabulous 9km stretch of lonely beach to enjoy between Castlerock and Magilligan Point. From Portrush the 214km north-western section of the Ulster Way heads over the gently rounded Sperrin Mountains, which straddle the border of Counties Derry and Tyrone. Also within easy reach of Derry is the wild, alluring terrain of County Donegal.

DERRY
pop 72,330
The handsome city of Derry, the fourth largest in Ireland, comes as a pleasant surprise to many visitors. Though reminders of its troubled past abound – the huge murals in Bogside commemorating the civil rights movement and Bloody Sunday, the bristling army post inside the 17th-century walls – the overwhelming feeling is of tremendous optimism and renewal. More spirited than Belfast – or Dublin – Derry has a well-founded reputation for musical excellence. These days the pubs stay open late and

Highlights

- Discover the feisty city of Derry
- Travel the spectacular Causeway Coast
- Totter across Carrick-a-rede Rope Bridge west of Ballycastle
- Knock back some whiskey at Bushmills Distillery
- Journey to wild Rathlin Island

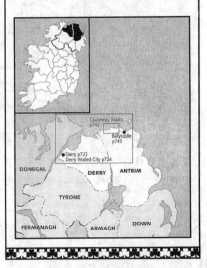

there's great music – from traditional to cutting-edge contemporary – to be had pretty much every night of the week. Add to this the resurgence of the arts in general, the dismantling of border posts, a rapidly improving economy and the energy and down-to-earth humour of the city's inhabitants and you have an unbeatable recipe for celebration.

There's a great deal of fascinating history to absorb in Derry, too. A leisurely circuit of the 17th-century city walls is a must, as is a visit to the award-winning Tower

COUNTY DERRY

COUNTIES DERRY & ANTRIM

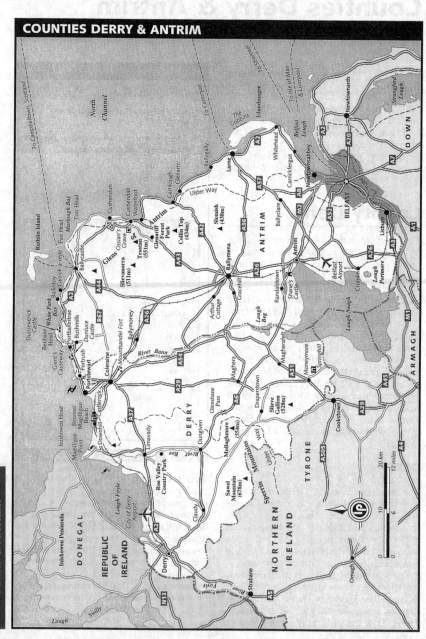

Museum, which charts the history of the city from it's monastic beginnings to the civil rights movement of the 70s. And just 6km over the border in Donegal is the Grianán of Aileách, a spectacular stone fort which dates back to 1700 BC.

History

Although you sometimes get the feeling that Derry's history started in 1688 with the seige, in fact there has been a settlement on the site since the 6th century, when St Colmcille (also known as St Columba) founded a monastic community on the hillside, probably where the Church of Ireland Chapel of St Augustine stands today. In the Middle Ages, Derry seems to have escaped the worst of the Viking raids and had a burst of independent prosperity in the 12th and 13th centuries under the Mac Lochlainn dynasty.

In the late 16th century Elizabeth I became determined to conquer troublesome Ulster, and an English garrison arrived in Derry in 1566. In 1600 a second, more last-ingly successful attempt to secure the town was made during the Nine Years War (1594–1603) against the O'Neills and O'Donnells.

In 1603 an English trading colony was established and given city status. Sir Cahir O'Doherty attacked this settlement in 1608 and virtually wiped it out, but in 1609 James I, determined to settle matters for good, granted land to English and Scottish settlers. The wealthy London trade guilds were put in charge of 'Planting' Derry and were responsible for the present layout of the walled city and for the walls themselves.

In 1688 the gates of Derry were slammed shut by 13 apprentice boys before the Catholic forces of James II, and some months later the great Siege of Derry began. For 105 days the Protestant citizens of Derry withstood bombardment, disease and starvation. Rejecting proffered peace terms, they declared that they would eat the Catholics first, then each other, before surrendering. By the time a relief ship burst

What's in a Name?

Derry's original name was Daire Calgaigh (Oak Grove of Calgach). In the 10th century it was renamed Doire Colmcille (Oak Grove of St Colmcille), in remembrance of the 6th-century saint who had established the first monastic settlement on the site. However, in 1609, when the English government decided to 'Plant' Derry properly, it signed an agreement with the Corporation of London to provide the necessary settlers. To commemorate this fact the city's name was lengthened to Londonderry.

Until the Troubles, people readily abbreviated the town's name to 'Derry'. At that point, however, what anyone called it suddenly became a touchstone for their political views, with Protestant unionists dogmatically asserting the full Londonderry and Catholic republicans equally firmly shortening it to Derry. Although the city is still officially called Londonderry, in 1984 the city council was renamed Derry City Council.

The naming controversy persists today, turning the normally straightforward business of buying a bus ticket into a political minefield. You can easily judge someone's position on the conflict by noting whether they react to your Derry with an emphatic *London*derry or vice versa. All over the country, but especially in the border areas, you'll see the word 'London' scratched off offending signposts.

On the radio, to avoid offending anyone, you may hear announcers say both names together – 'DerrystrokeLondonderry' – almost as one word.

Luckily, not everyone takes the Derry/Londonderry controversy too seriously. In Belfast, for example, wags have dropped both possibilities, opting instead for the simple 'Stroke City'!

through the boom on the River Foyle and broke the siege, an estimated quarter of the city's 30,000 inhabitants had died. It wasn't the final victory for the Protestant forces, but the long distraction gave King William time to increase his army's strength, and thus played an important role in his victory at the Battle of the Boyne on 12 July 1690.

In the 19th century Derry was one of the main ports from which the Irish emigrated to the USA, a fact commemorated by the sculptures of a departing family standing in Waterloo Place. It also played a vital role in the transatlantic trade in shirts and collars; supposedly, local factories provided uniforms for both sides in the American Civil War. To this day Derry still supplies the US president with 12 free shirts every year.

More recently, Derry has been a flashpoint for the Troubles. Resentment at the long-running domination and gerrymandering of the council by Protestants boiled over in the civil rights marches of 1968. Simultaneously, attacks on the Catholic Bogside district began, but by the time of the 12 July celebrations in 1969 the people there were prepared. Confrontation between Catholics and Protestants led to a veritable siege of the Bogside, and for over two days the community withdrew behind barricades. It was as if the Bogside had seceded from the UK, and even the government in the South talked of Ireland's duty to protect its own. It seemed that open warfare and disintegration could be prevented only by military intervention, and on 14 August 1968 British troops entered Derry.

In January 1972, Bloody Sunday saw the deaths of 13 unarmed Catholic civil rights marchers at the hands of the army.

Today, the old Bogside estate has been rebuilt, giving a curiously modern, neat feel to what was once a violent ghetto. After a 1981 survey discovered that almost 30% of the inner city was bombed out, abandoned or derelict, the Inner City Trust began work to make good the damage – work that is still continuing. Consequently, much of what you see inside the city walls now is fairly recently restored.

Major developments that reflect confidence in the future include the big Foyleside, Quayside and Richmond Shopping Centres and the Millennium Complex, an entertainment and retail centre currently under construction inside the city walls.

Orientation

The old centre of Derry is the small walled city on the western bank of the River Foyle. At its heart is the square called The Diamond, with Shipquay, Ferryquay, Butcher and Bishop Sts converging on it. The train station is on the eastern side of the River Foyle, while buses stop on the western bank, just outside the walled city. The Craigavon Bridge and farther downstream the Foyle Bridge link the two banks of the river. The Catholic Bogside area is below the walls to the west, while to the south is a Protestant estate known as The Fountain.

Information

Tourist Offices The tourist office, outside the city walls near the river at 44 Foyle St, houses both the Northern Ireland Tourist Board (NITB; ☎ 71 267284) and Bord Fáilte (☎ 71 369501). It opens 9 am to 7 pm on weekdays, 10 am to 6 pm on Saturday, and 10 am to 5 pm on Sunday, July to September; and 9 am to 5.15 pm (5 pm on Friday) on weekdays (plus 10 am to 5 pm on Saturday, Easter to June), the rest of the year.

Money The banks change punts into pounds and vice versa. The Bank of Ireland and the First Trust Bank on Shipquay St both have ATMs. There's a branch of Thomas Cook (☎ 71 374174) with exchange facilities in the Quayside Shopping Centre, and a bureau de change in the tourist office.

Post & Communications The main post office is on Custom House St, just north of the city walls. It opens 8.30 am to 5.30 pm on Monday, 9 am to 5.30 pm Tuesday to Friday, and 9 am to noon on Saturday. There's a convenient post office inside the city walls on Bishop St Within, south of The Diamond.

Internet Resources Internet access is available at the Central Library (see the Libraries entry, later) for £2.50 per hour; you'll probably need to book a terminal in advance. Steve's Backpacker's hostel, 4 Asylum Rd, provides Internet access for £3 per hour.

Travel Agencies The USIT travel office (☎ 71 371888), 33 Ferryquay St, opens 9.30 am to 5.30 pm on weekdays, and 10 am to 1 pm on Saturday.

Bookshops The Bookworm (☎ 71 261616), 16-18 Bishop St, is good for material on the Troubles, Derry and Ireland generally. Foyle Books (☎ 71 372530), 12 Magazine St, stocks a good selection of second-hand books. There's also Shipquay Books and News (☎ 71 371747), 10 Shipquay St, and a branch of Eason's (☎ 71 377133) in the Foyleside Shopping Centre.

Libraries Derry's Central Library (☎ 71 272300), just outside the city walls at 35 Foyle St, opens 9.15 am to 5.30 pm (8 pm on Monday and Thursday) on weekdays, and 9.15 am to 5 pm on Saturday.

Laundry Oakgrove Manor hostel has a laundry room downstairs. Alternatively, visit Duds 'n' Suds, 141 Strand Rd, which is about as glamorous as a laundrette can get – it has a pool table, electronic games and a snack bar! It opens 8 am to 9 pm on weekdays, and 8 am to 8 pm on Saturday. A wash, dry and fold costs £6.

City Walls

Until the mid-1990s, the presence of the army and protective iron gates made Derry's magnificent city walls hard to appreciate and impossible to walk round. The gates are still there, but now they're open and it's possible to walk all the way round the walls, taking in an extraordinary pop-up history tour as you go. Plaques round the walls provide visitors with some historical background.

Built between 1613 and 1618, the walls were the last complete set of city walls to

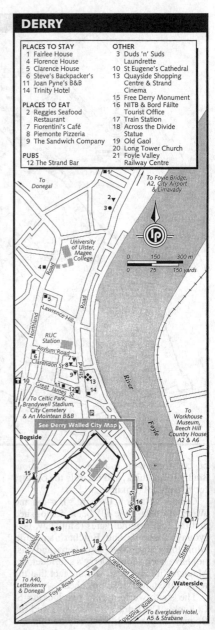

DERRY

PLACES TO STAY	OTHER
1 Fairlee House	3 Duds 'n' Suds
4 Florence House	Laundrette
5 Clarence House	10 St Eugene's Cathedral
6 Steve's Backpacker's	13 Quayside Shopping
11 Joan Pyne's B&B	Centre & Strand
14 Trinity Hotel	Cinema
	15 Free Derry Monument
PLACES TO EAT	16 NITB & Bord Fáilte
2 Reggies Seafood	Tourist Office
Restaurant	17 Train Station
7 Fiorentini's Café	18 Across the Divide
8 Piemonte Pizzeria	Statue
9 The Sandwich Company	19 Old Gaol
	20 Long Tower Church
PUBS	21 Foyle Valley
12 The Strand Bar	Railway Centre

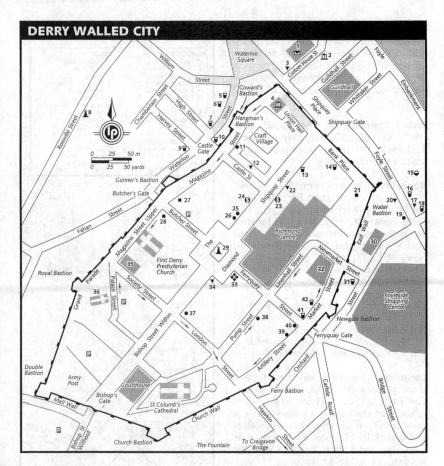

DERRY WALLED CITY

be constructed in Europe. They're about 8m high, 9m thick, and encircle the old city for a length of 1.5km.

Gunner's Bastion, Coward's Bastion and Water Bastion have all been demolished and the four original gates (Shipquay, Ferryquay, Bishop's and Butcher's) rebuilt, while three new gates (New, Ferry and Castle) have been added. Derry's sobriquet, the Maiden City, derives from the fact that the walls have never been breached.

The south-western end, overlooking St Columb's Cathedral on the inside and the Bogside to the north-west, is wired up and

provides an army lookout point for the Bogside. Behind the wall that runs beside the cathedral is an area called The Fountain, a predominantly working-class Protestant area where you can see a number of loyalist murals. The community here is the last significant Protestant enclave on the western bank of the river, the vast majority of Derry's Protestants having moved across the river to the Waterside area or even farther afield.

Outside Bishop's Gate on Bishop St Without is the one remaining turret of the Old Gaol, which was built in 1791.

DERRY WALLED CITY

PLACES TO STAY
27 Oakgrove Manor Hostel

PLACES TO EAT
 3 Rhubarb & Custard
12 Boston Tea Party
17 Café Nosh
20 Cappuccino's
22 Indigo Café-Bar-Restaurant
34 The Sandwich Company

PUBS
 5 Peadar O'Donnell's
 6 Gweedore Bar
 7 Dungloe Bar
 9 Bound for Boston
10 Castle Bar

13 The Townsman
14 Metro Bar
16 J&T McGinley's
18 Sandino's
31 Badger's
41 Anchor Inn
42 Linenhall Bar

OTHER
 1 General Post Office
 2 Harbour Museum
 4 Tower Museum
 8 Bloody Sunday Memorial
11 Foyle Books
15 Bus Station
19 Central Library
21 Millennium Complex

23 First Trust Bank (ATM)
24 Bank of Ireland (ATM)
25 Shipquay Books & News
26 Donegal Shop
28 Calgach Centre (Fifth Province
       & Genealogy Centre)
29 War Memorial
30 St Columb's Hall & Orchard
       Gallery
32 Rialto Entertainment Centre
33 Austin's Department Store
35 Apprentice Boys' Hall
36 Chapel of St Augustine Church
37 Bookworm Bookshop
38 Antique Market
39 The Playhouse
40 USIT Travel Office

Theobald Wolfe Tone, the founder of the United Irishmen, spent some time here following his capture after the failed rebellion of 1798. On the other side of the road, recent excavations have unearthed artefacts and fortifications dating back to the great siege.

An excellent overview of the Bogside and its defiant murals can be had by going up on to the city walls between Butcher's Gate and the army post. There you'll also see behind you in Society St the Apprentice Boys' Hall. Cannons, given by the London livery companies and reminders of the siege of 1689, still point out over the Bogside.

An empty plinth, once topped by a statue of the Reverend George Walker, the governor of Derry during the siege, stands on Royal Bastion. The 2.7m statue of Walker, seen by many as a symbol of unionist domination, was blown off by the IRA in 1973. The restored statue stands in the memorial garden beside the Apprentice Boys' Hall.

Tower Museum

Just inside Coward's Bastion, the modern O'Doherty's Tower houses the excellent Tower Museum (☎ 71 372411), which has won both Irish and British Museum of the Year awards. Very well-designed exhibits and audiovisuals tell the story of Derry from the days of St Colmcille to the present. Items on display include an incredibly well-

preserved dug-out log boat which has been carbon dated to around the time of St Colmcille's birth in the 520s.

Later there's a wonderful eyewitness account of Shane O'Neill and his soldiers arriving at the court of Elizabeth I to pledge allegiance to the Crown in 1562 (he later reneged):

...armed with hatchets, all bare-headed, their hair flowing in locks on their shoulders, on which were yellow surplices dyed with saffron, or stained with urine, with long sleeves, short coats and thrum jackets, which caused as much staring and gaping among the English people as if they had come from China or America.

There's also a lovely photograph of Amelia Earhart and her plane – after flying solo across the Atlantic in 1932 she mistook the city of Derry for Paris and landed in a field at Ballyarnett – surrounded by beaming locals.

Allow a good two hours to do the museum justice. It opens 10 am to 5 pm Monday to Saturday, and 2 to 5 pm on Sunday, July and August; and 10 am to 5 pm Tuesday to Saturday and on bank holidays, September to June. Admission costs £3.25/1.

Art Galleries

There are a couple of interesting galleries in Derry where you can catch contemporary

DERRY & ANTRIM

Irish and international work. **Orchard Gallery** (☎ 71 269675), Orchard St, opens 10 am to 6 pm Tuesday to Saturday. **Context Gallery** (☎ 71 373538), 5 Artillery St, opens 10 am to 5.30 pm Tuesday to Friday, and 10 am to 4.30 pm on Saturday.

McGilloway Gallery (☎ 71 366011), 6 Shipquay St, also shows modern Irish paintings and opens 10 am to 5.30 pm Monday to Saturday.

The Fifth Province

The Fifth Province (☎ 71 373177), at the Calgach Centre on Butcher St, takes you on a rather extraordinary multimedia trip through the mists of time with hunky Celtic warrior Calgach. Your senses will be bombarded, says the literature, and they are. The first part is a rather-too-long introduction to the history of Derry narrated by Richard Harris; in the second section (the best bit) you sit in a moving 'time chariot' and listen to the handsome Calgach tell tales of Celtic Ireland; finally there's an over-the-top celebration of Irish culture that has you convinced that everyone who ever emigrated from Northern Ireland ended up as an astronaut or president of the United States.

It opens 10 am to 6 pm daily, May to September. The journey takes one hour and costs £3/1.50.

The Calgach Centre also houses the **Genealogy Centre**, which has computerised records dating back to the early 17th century. It opens 9 am to 5 pm on weekdays for anyone wishing to trace their ancestors.

St Columb's Cathedral

Standing within the walls of the old city, St Columb's Cathedral (☎ 71 267313), built between 1618 and 1633, was the first Protestant church built in Britain or Ireland after the Reformation. Designed in a style known as Planter's Gothic, it shares the austerity of many Church of Ireland cathedrals, with dark, carved wooden pews, an open-timbered roof resting on the carved heads of past bishops and deans, and a gruesome skull-and-crossbones wall tablet in the northern aisle. Beside the pulpit is a cross of nails donated by Coventry Cathedral. Un-

usually, the bishop's throne is placed in the nave; the 18th-century mahogany chair inside the canopy is a beautifully carved example of what is known as Chinese Chippendale. The organ case over the western door is by the celebrated wood carver Grinling Gibbons.

In the porch is a mortar shell lobbed into the city during the siege by the Jacobites – it carried the terms of surrender. The Chapter House, now designated a museum, contains some drums, paintings, old photos and huge padlocks used to close the city gates in the 17th century.

It opens 9 am to 5 pm Monday to Saturday, April to October; and 9 am to 4 pm Monday to Saturday, November to March. Visitors are asked to donate £1 towards its upkeep.

Other Churches

The Church of Ireland **Chapel of St Augustine**, inside the city walls by Royal Bastion, is thought to have been the site of St Colmcille's 6th-century monastery.

Off Bishop St, outside the city walls, is St Colmcille's **Long Tower Church**, Derry's first post-Reformation Catholic church. Built in 1784 in brilliant neo-Renaissance style, it stands on the site of the medieval Tempull Mor (Great Church), which was constructed in 1164. Long Tower was built with the support of the Anglican bishop of the time, Frederick Augustus Harvey, who presented the capitals for the four corinthian columns which frame the ornate high altar.

The Catholic **St Eugene's Cathedral** in Great James St was begun in 1851 as a Catholic response to the end of the Great Famine. Dedicated to St Eugene in 1873 by Bishop Keely, the handsome eastern window is a memorial to the bishop. The bells of St Eugene's still ring every night at 9 pm as a reminder of the penal times when Catholics were forbidden to attend mass and were subject to a 9 pm curfew.

Guildhall

Just outside the city walls, the red-brick Guildhall (☎ 71 377335) was originally built in 1890 and rebuilt after a fire in 1908.

As the seat of the old Londonderry Corporation, which institutionalised the policy of discriminating against Catholics over housing and jobs, it incurred the wrath of nationalists and was bombed twice by the IRA in 1972. The Guildhall is noted for its fine stained-glass windows, including one of George V's coronation upstairs; others on the stairs commemorate the various London livery companies that played so divisive a role in the city's development. It opens 9 am to 5.30 pm on weekdays. Free guided tours take place during July and August.

Bogside & the Free Derry Monument

As you step out of Butcher's Gate, the Bogside comes into view, and down on the left is the famous 'You Are Now Entering Free Derry' monument. This was once the end wall of a row of old houses, but the area was rebuilt with low-level flats, and it now stands in the centre of a dual carriageway. During the early 1970s, until the army's Operation Motorman smashed the barricades in July 1972, this was a no-go area as far as the military authorities were concerned. It took 5000 soldiers with Chieftain tanks to bring down the barriers. The monument, with its much repainted slogan, remains as a defiant response to the army watchtower that continues to look down from the walled city on the Bogside.

There are a number of stunning republican murals in the area, many of which commemorate events from the civil rights movement and the battle of the Bogside – one shows a young Bernadette Devlin (see the boxed text 'Like Mother, Like Daughter' in the Counties Tyrone & Fermanagh chapter) speaking at a rally, another is taken from a famous photograph of a young boy wearing a gas mask and holding a petrol bomb, and another of Bloody Sunday shows a local priest holding aloft a white handkerchief in an effort to lead some of the injured to safety.

Bloody Sunday Memorial

On Sunday 30 January 1972, some 20,000 civilians marched through Derry in protest at the policy of internment without trial. It now seems clear that the 1st Battalion of the Parachute Regiment opened fire on the unarmed marchers. By the end of the day 13 unarmed people were dead, some shot through the back, and a 14th subsequently died of his injuries. None of those who fired the 108 bullets, or those who gave the order to fire, have been brought to trial or even disciplined. A new inquiry (the original Widgery Commission failed to find anyone responsible) was announced in 1998 and at the time of writing was still under way.

To reach the monument, leave the walled city by Butcher's Gate; it's a little to the right down near the roadside. The actual incident happened in the enclosed square across the road.

Craigavon Bridge

The double-decker bridge spanning the River Foyle was erected in 1933 and is named after the first prime minister of Northern Ireland, Lord Craigavon, who notoriously described Northern Ireland as 'a Protestant state for a Protestant people'. The bridge used to carry trains on the lower deck and cars on the upper, but since the railways were pruned back in 1965 it has carried cars on both decks.

Foyle Valley Railway Centre

Just outside the walled city by Craigavon Bridge, the centre (☎ 71 265234) stands on what was once the junction of four train lines. Exhibits inside tell the story of the railways, and you can take a 20-minute, 4km excursion on a train with diesel engine. The museum opens 10 am to 4.30 pm Tuesday to Saturday. Admission is free but the excursion, at 2.30 pm each day, costs £2.50/1.25.

Harbour Museum

A small, old-fashioned maritime museum (☎ 71 377331), with models of ships and the bossomy figurehead of the *Minnehaha*, takes up two rooms of the old Londonderry Port Building on Guildhall St. It opens 10 am to 1 pm and 2 to 4.30 pm on weekdays. Admission is free.

DERRY & ANTRIM

Workhouse Museum

Across the river in the Waterside area is the new Workhouse Museum (☎ 71 318328), 23 Glendermott Rd, housed in Derry's original workhouse, which operated from 1840 to 1946. The workhouse was capable of housing up to 800 people, and daily life was designed to encourage inmates to want to leave as soon as possible. One of the few exhibits on display is the grisly horsedrawn hearse which was used to transport the workhouse dead to outlying cemeteries.

There are also displays detailing the Potato Famine, and downstairs the excellent Atlantic Memorial exhibition tells the story of the WWII battle of the Atlantic and the major role that Derry played.

Organised Tours

In July and August walking tours of the inner city depart at 10.30 am and 2.30 pm on weekdays from the tourist office (☎ 71 267284). They cost £3/1.75 and last about 1½ hours.

From June to October, Northern Tours (☎ 71 309051) runs daily Essential Walking Tours of Historic Derry, departing from the Guildhall at 10 am, noon and 2 and 4 pm. The tours last 1¼ hours and cost £2.50/2. McNamara Tours (☎ 71 345335) runs 1½ hour walking tours at 10 am and 1.30 and 4 pm Monday to Saturday, June to September. Tours depart from the tourist office and cost £3/2.

Every Tuesday during July and August, Ulsterbus (☎ 71 262261) runs its 1½ hour Foyle Civic Tour of the city, departing from the bus station at 2 pm; it costs £3.20/2.20.

Special Events

Derry hosts a surprising number of festivals, including the week-long Foyle Film Festival in April; the Southern Comfort Jazz and Blues Festival in May; the Gasyard Wall Féile in July, which features concerts, theatre and Irish-language events; and the Féile na Samhna, the annual Halloween carnival which has the entire city dressing up and partying in the streets.

Places to Stay

Accommodation options in Derry are still fairly limited, so booking ahead is advisable, especially in July, when an annual gathering of O'Dohertys from around the world puts even greater strain on the accommodation supply.

Hostels The YHANI hostel is in the renovated *Oakgrove Manor (☎ 71 284100, 4-6 Magazine St)*, inside the city walls near Butcher's Gate, just 150m from the bus station. Dorm beds cost £6.50, or £8.50/7.50 with bathroom; singles/doubles cost £15 per person including breakfast. Cooking, laundry and currency exchange facilities are available.

Steve's Backpacker's (☎ 71 377989, 4 Asylum Rd), a short walk north of the walled city, is a small, friendly independent hostel offering beds costing £7.50 per night (fifth night free), including breakfast. Internet access is available for £3 per hour.

From mid-June to mid-September the University of Ulster's *Magee College (☎ 71 371371, 26 Northland Rd)* offers rooms costing £14.20 per person.

B&Bs Within walking distance of the bus station, the friendly *Joan Pyne (☎ 71 269691, 36 Great James St)* offers a bed and big breakfast costing £18 to £20 per person in a lovely 19th-century Victorian house. Farther to the north, *Clarence House (☎ 71 265342, 15 Northland Rd)* charges £25/40 for singles/doubles. Farther along, *Florence House (☎ 71 268093, 16 Northland Rd)* charges £17 per person. Farther north again, *Fairlee House (☎ 71 374551, 86 Duncreggan Rd)* has rooms costing £17. You can get to these places on bus No D6 or by shared black taxi from Foyle St.

An Mointean (☎ 71 287128, 245 Lone Moor Rd), south-west of the walled city near the Brandywell football ground, has two rooms with bathroom costing £18 per person and bicycles to rent for £7 per day. Cycle tours around Inishowen in Donegal are planned. Bus No D4 will take you down Lone Moor Rd.

Farmhouse accommodation costs about the same as B&B and there are quite a few places out at Eglinton on the A2 to Li-

The Derry Skeleton

As you wander around town, you'll soon spot the Derry skeleton, a mournful figure usually with his skull leaned to one side, adorning the city's coat of arms. There are several stories to explain how he came to be there. One suggests that he's associated with the 1689 Siege of Derry; another that he represents Sir Cahir O'Doherty, who had sacked Derry in 1608 to avenge an insult. Neither explanation is likely to be right, though, because the skeleton was already gracing the arms in 1600 when the first Plantation of Derry took place.

MATT KING

The most convincing suggestion is that the skeleton represents Walter de Burgo, an Anglo-Norman knight and nephew of the Red Earl, Richard de Burgo. He's said to have fallen out with his cousin William de Burgo, the earl of Ulster, who had him imprisoned in a dungeon in Greencastle in County Donegal. There, he eventually starved to death in 1332. If this story is true, the castle also shown on the coat of arms would probably be Greencastle. In 1311 Edward II granted the Inishowen Peninsula and the island of Derry to Richard de Burgo, thus explaining how his nephew ended up immortalised on the city's coat of arms.

---

mavady. For example, *Longfield Farm* (☎ 71 810210, 122 Clooney Rd) charges £20/36, and *Greenan Farm* (☎ 71 810422, 25 Carmoney Rd) charges £16 per person. Rates at both include breakfast.

Hotels The smart three-star *Trinity Hotel* (☎ 71 271271, fax 71 271277, 22-24 Strand Rd), just north of the city centre, offers singles/doubles costing £65/85 including breakfast. Special weekend packages (£79 per person for two nights' accommodation and one evening meal) are available year round.

At the time of writing, the Inner City Trust was constructing a 96-room hotel on Magazine St next to the YHANI hostel.

South of the city and on the eastern side of the river, *Everglades Hotel* (☎ 71 346722, fax 71 349200, Prehen Rd) charges £82/98. It's just off the A5 (Victoria Rd); from the city turn right after crossing Craigavon Bridge.

There are three other hotels on the eastern side of the river but north of the city. *Broomhill Hotel* (☎ 71 347995, fax 71 349304, Limavady Rd) is easy to find and costs £45/60. A little farther out, *White*

Horse Hotel (☎ 71 860606, fax 71 860371, 68 Clooney Rd) costs £50/60. Nearby and beside the Caw Roundabout, the circular *Waterfoot Hotel and Country Club* (☎ 71 345500, fax 71 311006, 14 Clooney Rd) has views of the River Foyle and the Donegal Mountains. Rooms cost £70/75. The hotel restaurant has a very good reputation.

East of the river, out towards Dungiven, the elegant 18th-century *Beech Hill Country House* (☎ 71 349279, fax 71 345366, 32 Ardmore Rd) has rooms costing £70.50/90 and an outstanding restaurant.

Places to Eat

For breakfast, *Cappuccino's (Foyle St)* does a decent fry-up costing £3.75 and has lunch specials starting at £2.95. It opens 8 am to 5.30 pm Monday to Saturday, and 9 am to 1 pm on Sunday.

Porter's Café Bar in the Trinity Hotel is a very popular and thoroughly pleasant place for lunch. Carvery meals cost £3.95; sandwiches and snacks (potato wedges with bacon and melted cheese) start at £2.50. The Trinity's main restaurant, *Nolan's Bistro* (☎ 71 271271), offers a varied dinner menu (£7.50 for a salmon fillet), which

DERRY & ANTRIM

features a couple of interesting vegetarian options.

Nearly all the pubs in town offer reasonably priced pub food and bar snacks. *Badger's (16 Orchard St)* is recommended for grills and steaks, and *Brown's Bar and Brasserie (1 Bonds Hill)* across the river has a very good reputation. *Linenhall Bar (3 Market St)* and *Metro (3 Bank Place)* are both decent places for a feed, too.

Café Nosh (☎ 71 308273, Foyle St), adjoining J&T McGinley's pub, is an excellent choice for dinner (pan-seared seabass on celeriac purée with spiced lentils and a tomato-and-basil sauce costs £8.75). It opens 5.30 to 10.30 pm Monday to Saturday, and 6 to 9 pm on Sunday.

Indigo (☎ 71 271011, Shipquay St) is a bright new café-bar-restaurant within the city walls serving light meals costing upwards of £3.50 and main courses from £5.95. It opens 11 am to 11 pm daily.

Boston Tea Party, in the craft village off Shipquay St, serves pies, soups and sandwiches from 9 am to 5.30 pm Monday to Saturday.

Piemonte Pizzeria (☎ 71 266828, 2 Clarendon St), close to Steve's Backpacker's, is a cheap-and-cheerful place offering pizzas starting at £3.90 and pasta dishes from £5. It has a BYO licence. Nearby, *Fiorentini's (47 Strand Rd)* opens daily for grills, fish and chips and ice cream.

Reggie's Seafood Restaurant (☎ 71 262050, 145 Strand Rd) serves everything from cockles and mussels to seafood chowder and opens for lunch and dinner Monday to Saturday. *The Sandwich Company (☎ 71 266771, 61 Strand Rd)* serves fresh sandwiches and salads in the daytime and turns into a Mexican restaurant in the evening. Another branch on The Diamond has a good selection of sandwiches and cakes.

The restaurants at *Beech Hill Country House* and *Waterfoot Hotel* are both very well regarded. (See Places to Stay, earlier.)

Entertainment

Pubs & Clubs Whatever you do in Derry, don't miss an evening in the lively pubs around town. They're friendly, full of atmosphere, open until late, within easy walking distance of each other (there are seven within spitting distance on Waterloo St) and jumping with excellent music pretty much every night of the week.

There's always live music (traditional and contemporary) to be found in the *Gweedore Bar* and *Peadar O'Donnell's*, next door to each other on Waterloo St. There are regular thumping club nights upstairs at the Gweedore, too. *Sandino's*, off Foyle St (named after Nicaraguan guerilla leader Augusto Sandino), is a popular venue for up-and-coming local bands as well as visiting musicians. *J&T McGinley's (Foyle St)* has live music most nights, and *Mullan's Bar (13 Little James St)* features jazz, blues and traditional sessions.

Popular club nights (mainly house and 70s and 80s dance music) take place at *Lava Lounge (113 Strand Rd)*, *Squires Nightclub (33 Shipquay St)* and *Fusion (Waterloo Place)*. *Dungloe Bar (41 Waterloo St)* has a funk and soul night on Friday.

Concerts & Theatre Classical concerts are held throughout the year at the University of Ulster's *Magee College* and the *Guildhall*. The tourist office has details.

Playhouse Community Arts Centre (☎ 71 268027, 5 Artillery St) is a venue for dance and theatre. *Rialto Entertainment Centre (☎ 71 260516, 5 Market St)* hosts exhibitions, concerts and drama. Theatre and dance can also be seen at *St Columb's Hall (☎ 71 262880, Orchard St)*.

The *Millennium Complex*, in the city walls by Bank Place, will have an auditorium for dance, drama and music.

Cinemas You can see films at *Orchard Hall Cinema (☎ 71 262845, Orchard St)* and *Strand Multiplex (☎ 71 373900, Quayside Shopping Centre)*.

Spectator Sports

Derry City Football Club play soccer at Brandywell Stadium (☎ 71 281333), Lone Moor Rd, south of the walled city. Gaelic football and hurling matches take place at Celtic Park (☎ 71 267142), Lone Moor Rd.

Shopping

Derry Craft Village (☎ 71 260329), tucked away off Shipquay St in the walled city, contains a number of craft shops selling Derry crystal (with a mail service), hand-woven cloth, ceramics, jewellery and other items crafted by local people. Most shops open 9.30 am to 5.30 pm Monday to Saturday, and some open on Sunday in summer.

There's a small antiques market on Pump St from 11 am to 5 pm Saturday.

If you're interested in traditional music, Soundsaround (☎ 71 374511), 22A Waterloo St, has an excellent selection.

Close to The Diamond is the Donegal Shop (☎ 71 266928), Shipquay St, selling garments, tweeds and souvenirs.

The two main shopping centres are the Richmond Centre, within the city walls, and the enormous Foyleside Shopping Centre, just outside. If you're staying north of the walled city, there's a handy Tesco in the Quayside Shopping Centre on Strand Rd.

Austin's, on The Diamond, is Ireland's oldest department store.

Getting There & Away

Air About 13km east of Derry along the A2 past Eglinton is City of Derry Airport (☎ 71 810784). Ryanair flies twice daily to London's Stansted Airport, and British Airways flies to Glasgow and Manchester. For more information see The UK in the Air section of the Getting There & Away chapter.

Bus The Ulsterbus station (☎ 71 262261) is just outside the city walls, on Foyle St near the Guildhall.

There are frequent services between Belfast and Derry. Bus No 212, the Maiden City Flyer, is the fastest (1 hour 40 minutes), followed by bus No 273, which goes via Omagh; a one-way ticket costs £6.80. A bus to Portstewart and Portrush leaves at 2.15 pm on Thursday and Sunday during most of June, and on Thursday, Friday and Saturday during most of July and August. Each day at 9 am a bus leaves Derry for Cork, arriving at 7.15 pm. The bus from Cork leaves at 9.15 am and arrives in Derry at 7.30 pm.

Bus Éireann operates a Derry to Galway service three times daily, via Donegal and Sligo. A single to Galway costs £14, although midweek you can get a return for the same price.

Lough Swilly (☎ 71 262017) has an office upstairs at the Ulsterbus station, and connects with Buncrana, Dunfanaghy, Dungloe, Letterkenny and Malin Head in County Donegal, across the border.

Feda Ódonaill (☎ 00-353-75-48114 in Éire, 0141-631 3696 in Glasgow) include a service from Letterkenny to Glasgow via Derry. It leaves the bus station at 8.45 am, reaching Glasgow around 4 pm. The coach from Glasgow leaves at 8 am from the Citizens' Theatre in Gorbals St and reaches Derry around 3 pm. Services run daily in July and August, four times weekly the rest of the year. The return fare is £60.

Train From the Northern Ireland Railways station (NIR; ☎ 71 342228), on the eastern side of the River Foyle, there are frequent Derry to Belfast services taking about three hours. The earliest train for Portrush departs at 6.10 am (11.10 am on Sunday), the last one at 7.10 pm. With a valid train ticket there's a free Linkline bus into the town centre from outside the station.

Getting Around

Bus No 143 to Limavady stops near the airport; otherwise a taxi to/from the airport costs about £10.

Local buses leave from Foyle St in front of the bus station, where there are also shareable black cabs to outlying suburbs such as Shantallow. Auto Cabs (☎ 71 345100) and Foyle Taxis (☎ 71 263905) operate from the city centre and go to all areas.

There are street-level car parks on Butcher St, behind the Richmond Centre and beside the station, and a multistorey one beside Foyleside Shopping Centre.

LIMAVADY & AROUND

Lying in the fertile valley of the River Roe, Limavady (Léim an Mhadaidh) was granted to Sir Thomas Phillips by James I in 1612 after the last ruling chief, Sir Donnell Ballagh O'Cahan, was found guilty of rebellion. The original Gaelic name means 'Leap of the Dog' and refers to one of the O'Cahans' dogs who jumped a gorge across the River Roe to bring warning of an unexpected enemy attack.

Today it's a quiet, prosperous small town whose main claim to fame is that one Jane Ross (1810–79) heard a travelling fiddler playing 'Londonderry Air' – aka 'Danny Boy', probably the most famous Irish song of all – and noted it down; a blue plaque on the wall of 51 Main St where she lived commemorates the fact.

It's well worth stopping at the Roe Valley Country Park, just south of town, for a wander along the picturesque river. There's also an excellent restaurant (The Lime Tree; see Places to Eat, later) in town.

Information
The tourist office (☎ 77 722226), in the council building at 7 Connell St, opens 9 am to 5.45 pm on weekdays, and 9.30 am to 5.30 pm on Saturday, April to September; and 9 am to 5 pm on weekdays, October to March.

Roe Valley Country Park
About 3km south of Limavady, this lovely park stretches for 5km either side of the River Roe, and is a world-renowned spot for trout and salmon fishing. The area is associated with the O'Cahans, who ruled the valley until the Plantations. The 17th-century settlers saw the flax-growing potential of the damp river valley and the area became an important linen-manufacturing centre.

In the visitor centre (☎ 77 722074), there are some excellent old photographs of the flax industry, and around the park are relics of that time. The weaving shed near the main entrance houses a small museum. The scutch mill, where the flax was pounded, is a 45-minute walk away, along the river, past two watchtowers built to guard the linen when it was spread out in the fields for bleaching.

The park also contains Ulster's first domestic hydroelectric power station, opened in 1896. It opens on request at the visitor centre next door.

The park itself is always accessible and the visitor centre opens 9 am to 5 pm daily, year round. The café opens 10 am to 6 pm on weekdays, and 10 am to 8.30 pm at the weekend. The park is clearly marked off the B192 road between Limavady and Dungiven. Bus No 146 from Limavady to Dungiven will drop you on the main road, but there's no weekend service.

Benone/Magilligan Beach
Some 9km in length and hundreds of metres wide at low tide, this huge Blue Flag beach – called both Benone and Magilligan – is worth a visit. Bordered by sand dunes and dramatic sea cliffs, the beach sweeps out to Magilligan Point, where a Martello tower stands and from where sailplanes and hanggliders can be seen riding the wind.

Downhill & Mussenden Temple
The eccentric Anglican bishop of Derry, and 4th earl of Bristol, Frederick Augustus Hervey, built a palatial home at Downhill in 1774. It was burned down in 1851, rebuilt between 1873 and 1876 and abandoned after WWII. The roof was removed for its scrap value and the remains of the small castellated building now stand forlornly on the clifftop.

The major attraction, a short walk from the house, is the curious little Mussenden Temple, built by the energetic bishop to house either his library or his mistress – opinions differ! He conducted an affair with the mistress of Frederick William II of Prussia well into his old age. Due to erosion the temple is now perched right on the cliff edge. To prevent it tumbling into the sea, in 1998 the National Trust inserted 'anchors', reinforced cables up to 15m long, into the cliffs below the temple to stabilise the area.

It's a pleasant walk to the temple and the reward is some fine views of the beach at Portstewart and also Benone/Magilligan, the train line below and the hills of Done-

The Flax about Linen

The manufacture of linen, probably the earliest textile made from plants, was once of vital significance to the Ulster economy. Linen was made in ancient Egypt and introduced into Britain by the Romans. The real boost to linen making in Ulster, though, came with the arrival of Huguenot weavers seeking sanctuary in the late 17th century.

The flax plant was sown in the north of Ireland from March to May and harvested in mid-August. The first stage in the harvesting was the pulling of the flax plants and bundling them into stacks for open-air drying. The seeds were removed and crushed for linseed oil or kept for the following year's planting. The second stage was a messy and smelly one, entailing the soaking of the bundles of flax in freshwater ponds, or 'lint holes', for up to two weeks. This process of 'retting' softened the outer stem and the 'scutching' could begin.

Scutching separated the dried flax stem; with the introduction of water wheels in the 18th century, large wooden blades pounded and loosened the flax. The fibres were then ready for spinning on a wheel before being woven into lengths of cloth. Some of this unbleached linen was sold as 'brown linen', hence the number of Brown Linen Halls that used to exist.

The next stage was the bleaching, carried out in the open air after the cloth had been soaked in water for hours. Huge lengths were stretched out across fields and left in the sunlight. The moisture in the material reacted with the sunlight to produce hydrogen peroxide, which bleached the cloth. The final stage involved the hammering of the cloth by wooden hammers, or beetles, which smoothed out the material and made it ready for selling to the public. Bleached linen was sold through the many White Linen Halls.

At its height the linen industry was so important that Belfast was sometimes referred to as 'Linenopolis'. Flax growing died out in the north towards the end of the 19th century but was reborn during WWI with the demand for parachute material. There was a similar resurgence during WWII, but most of the linen now purchased is made in Scandinavia with the aid of chemicals. In recent years there has been an attempt to reintroduce flax growing in Ulster, and you may spot the occasional field of blue flax.

You can visit a beetling mill at Wellbrook outside Cookstown in County Tyrone. For a complete picture of the linen industry and its history, visit the impressive Irish Linen Centre in Lisburn, County Antrim, near Belfast.

MATT KING

gal across the water. The beach immediately below is where the bishop set his own clergy to race on horseback, rewarding the winners by appointing them to the more lucrative parishes. In the distance shadowy outlines of the Scottish mountains are visible. The bishop inscribed a quotation from Lucretius on a frieze:

It is pleasant to see from the safe shore
The pitching of ships and hear the storm's roar.

The inscription is thoroughly appropriate on a windy day. The site is about 15km north-east of Limavady. It's owned by the National Trust but there's no admission charge. The temple opens noon to 6 pm daily, July and August; and noon to 6 pm at

DERRY & ANTRIM

the weekend and on bank holidays, April to June and September.

The original demesne created by the bishop covered some 160 hectares, much of which now forms part of **Downhill Forest** on the other side of the road. The beautiful landscaped gardens below the ruins of the house are the work of celebrated gardener Jan Eccles, who became custodian at Downhill at the age of 60 and created the garden over a period of 30 years. She died in 1997 at the age of 94.

Immediately past Downhill Inn, Bishop's Rd forks up to the left, leading over the mountains to Limavady, with terrific views from **Gortmore** picnic area.

Hezlett House, Castlerock

This house (☎ 70 848567) was built in the late 17th century. It is a single-storey thatched cottage noted for its cruck-truss roof gables of stone and turf strengthened with wooden crucks, or crutches. The interior decoration is Victorian. The house is owned by the National Trust and opens noon to 5 pm Wednesday to Monday, June to August; and noon to 5 pm at the weekend and on bank holidays, April, May and September. Admission costs £1.80/90p and there's a car park across the road. The house is 8km west of Coleraine at Liffock on the A2.

Places to Stay

Benone Tourist Complex (☎ 77 750555), adjacent to Benone Beach, charges £5.50 for tents and £9 for campervans. There's an outdoor heated pool, children's pool and bowling green. It opens April to September. **Castlerock Holiday Park** (☎ 70 848381, 24 Sea Rd) has tent and campervan sites. It charges £10 per night and opens March to October.

On the edge of the beach at Downhill, tucked beneath the sea cliffs, is the **Downhill Hostel** (☎ 70 849077), a beautifully restored 100-year-old house. It offers very comfortable accommodation in three dorms (£7 per night) or four double rooms (£12 to £18 per person, upwards of £22 for families). There's a well-stocked kitchen (including a comprehensive spice shelf),

laundry facilities and a big lounge with an open fire and a view of the sea. There are no shops in Downhill so it's a good idea to bring supplies with you.

Across from the beach, the small **Downhill Hotel** (☎ 70 848090) offers B&B costing £20 per person, although the future of the hotel was uncertain at the time of writing.

In Limavady, the one-star **Gorteen House Hotel** (☎ 77 722333, 187 Roe Mill Rd) charges £28/42 for B&B in singles/doubles. If you're coming in from Derry on the A2 turn right just after crossing the bridge and follow Roe Mill Rd down until it turns to the left past a cemetery; the hotel is off to the right. Otherwise, the pistachio-coloured 19th-century **Alexander Arms** (☎ 77 763443, 34 Main St) offers B&B costing £18 per person.

Places to Eat

The Lime Tree (☎ 77 764300, 30 Catherne St, Limavady) serves excellent meals with an emphasis on seafood. Starters (crab-and-prawn filo parcels with chilli-oil dressing) start at £2.25, main courses (hot wood-smoked salmon with lemon-braised fennel) start at £9.25. Light lunches cost upwards of £3.95. It opens noon to 2 pm and 6 to 9.30 pm Wednesday to Sunday.

Alexander Arms (Main St, Limavady) serves bar food and opens until 10.30 pm Monday to Saturday. The **Downhill Hotel** serves pub food.

Getting There & Away

Bus From Limavady, Bus No 134 travels to Downhill, Castlerock and Coleraine. No 234 travels to Coleraine. No 146 goes to Dungiven. Bus No 143 runs between Derry and Limavady almost hourly. There's no direct bus to Belfast from Limavady but connections can be made at Coleraine or Dungiven.

Train Castlerock is on the Derry to Coleraine train line. Ring ☎ 90 333000 for details. From the train station at Castlerock it's a very pleasant 40-minute walk through the Black Glen to Downhill – from the station head towards the sea, take the first left on Main St, continue past the caravan park and follow the signs for Bishop's Gate.

COLERAINE
pop 20,720

Although it stands on the banks of the River Bann, Coleraine (Cúil Raithin) isn't particularly attractive, and the pedestrianised town centre could be any British shopping area. But Coleraine is an important transport hub for County Derry and you could well find yourself waiting here for a bus or train connection. There are plenty of shops catering to the largely Protestant population, who first arrived in 1613 when the land was given by James I to loyal Londoners. The University of Ulster was established just north of town in 1968, much to the chagrin of Derry, which had lobbied hard to win it.

Information

The tourist office (☎ 70 344723), near the train station on Railway Rd and next to Coleraine Leisure Centre, opens 9 am to 5 pm (6 pm on Friday and Saturday in summer) Monday to Saturday.

Mountsandel Mount

Over 1km south of town, on the eastern bank of the river, is Mountsandel Mount, a mysterious mound that may have been an early-Christian stronghold or a later Anglo-Norman fortification. Just to the north-east of the mound, a Mesolithic site dating back to the 7th millennium BC has been excavated; post-holes, hearths and pits bear testimony to the early inhabitants of the area. The site is signposted from the Lodge Rd roundabout.

Places to Stay

Lodge Hotel (☎ 70 344848, Lodge Rd) charges £46/57 for singles/doubles, including breakfast. The *Town House* (☎ 70 344869, 45 Millburn Rd) charges £20/35 for B&B, while *Coolbeg* (☎ 70 344961, 2E Grange Rd), on the outskirts of town, charges £25/44.

All the other B&Bs are out of town; the tourist office has a complete list. The 17th-century *Camus House* (☎ 70 342982, 27 Curragh Rd), off the A54, 5km south of town, is worth the £25/45 it charges. *Tullan's Farm* (☎ 70 342309, 46 Newmills Rd) is a working farm just 2.5km from Coleraine; B&B costs £17/34.

Places to Eat

The *Little Tea Shop* in Diamond Arcade opens Monday to Saturday for set lunches and afternoon tea. *Pizza Pomodoro* (☎ 70 344444, 4 The Waterside) is popular with the local students. It opens 4.30 to 11.30 pm Monday to Sunday and has a BYO licence. *Water Margin at the Boathouse* (☎ 70 342222, Hanover Place) offers seafood, vegetarian and Chinese dishes. It opens every evening and for lunch on Sunday.

Getting There & Away

Bus The Ulsterbus No 218 travels express between Portrush, Portstewart and Belfast via Coleraine and Antrim. Bus No 234 takes an hour to reach Derry (£4.20).

The Antrim Coaster – bus No 252 – operates between Belfast and Coleraine twice daily, Monday to Saturday, from late May to late September. It leaves Belfast at 9.10 am and 2 pm, and Coleraine at 9.50 am and 4.10 pm. The trip takes about four hours. The open-topped Bushmills Bus – No 177 – is a double-decker that runs (weather permitting) from the Giant's Causeway to Coleraine five times daily, July and August. The trip takes just over an hour. Both buses run via Portrush, Portballintrae, Bushmills and the Giant's Causeway.

Train The Belfast to Derry trains stop at Coleraine and there's a branch line to Portrush. Ring ☎ 90 333000 for details.

DUNGIVEN & AROUND

The small market town of Dungiven (Dún Geimhin) has a couple of ecclesiastical sites and an excellent independent hostel, which could make it a better base than Limavady if you're travelling between Belfast and Derry or if you want to explore the Sperrin moors. The Ulster Way passes nearby.

euro currency converter IR£1 = €1.27

DERRY & ANTRIM

Dungiven Priory

The remains of this Augustinian priory, signposted off the A6 road to Antrim, date back to the 12th century, when they replaced a pre-Norman monastery.

The church contains the ornate tomb of Cooey-na-Gal, a chieftain of the O'Cahans who died in 1385. On the front of the tomb are figures of six kilted gallowglasses, mercenaries from Scotland hired by Cooey O'Cahan as minders and earning him the nickname na-Gal (of the Foreigners). In the 17th century another foreigner, Sir Edward Doddington, who built the walls of Derry, remodelled the priory and an adjacent small castle built by the O'Cahans. He constructed a private dwelling of which only the foundations remain.

Nearby is a bullaun, a hollowed stone originally used by the monks for grinding grain but now collecting rainwater and used as a site of pilgrimage and prayer by people seeking cures for illnesses.

Maghera Old Church

The church site goes back to a 6th-century monastery that was plundered by the Vikings in 832. The present ruined nave is 10th century, while the Romanesque door on the western side is two centuries younger. There are interesting motifs on the door jambs, and the lintel carries a fine crucifixion scene that's as good as the carvings on the celebrated high crosses. In the churchyard there's an unmistakable pillar stone, carved with a ringed cross. It's said to mark the grave of the 6th-century founder, St Lurach.

The town of Maghera is just off the A6 Derry to Belfast road and the best approach is from Dungiven via the Glenshane Pass. Rising to 555m, the road through the Sperrin Mountains offers dramatic views. Bus No 116 runs regularly between Coleraine and Maghera, bus No 278 less frequently.

Places to Stay

Five kilometres north of Dungiven, *Flax Mill Hostel* (☎ 77 742655, *Mill Lane*) is an idyllic countryside retreat run by Marion and Herman Baurr, who mill their own

flour, grow their own veggies and generate their own electricity. The cottage, now bright and comfortable and with a delightful conservatory and garden, stood empty for 37 years before the Baurrs bought it 10 years ago. Beds, in three dorms and one double room, cost just £5.25, or an outrageous £7 with breakfast! *Camping* costs £3.25. The hostel is signposted off the Limavady road. If you're travelling by bus, Marion or Herman will pick you up from Dungiven.

There are a few B&Bs in Dungiven, including *Bradagh* (☎ 77 741346, *132 Main St*), which costs £13.50 per person with shared bathroom and large breakfast.

Places to Eat

Castle Inn (*Upper Main St*) is the best place for a pub feed. It opens every day for lunch and dinner. If you're travelling on to Maghera on the A6, *Ponderosa Bar and Restaurant* at the top of the Glenshane Pass serves steaks, chicken and seafood.

Entertainment

Murphy's has music at the weekend and *McRenold's* is the best pub for a pint.

Getting There & Away

Express bus No 212 between Derry and Belfast runs 10 times daily (five times on Sunday) and stops on Main St in Dungiven. Ulsterbus No 146 travels between Limavady and Dungiven.

PLANTATION TOWNS

The rest of inland Derry, to the south of Dungiven, is strong Protestant territory made up of towns planned and created by London companies with gracious thanks to William of Orange for the grants of land. In Draperstown, Magherafelt and Moneymore the kerbstones are often painted red, white and blue, and for weeks after 12 July, when the victory of King Billy over the Catholics is celebrated, flags and banners proclaim the die-hard patriotism of the locals.

Springhill

Springhill (☎ 86 748210), 1.5km south of

Make friends with the sheep on the Antrim coast.

White Park Bay, Antrim

Soak up the peace and quiet at Ballintoy Harbour, County Antrim.

The giant surveys his handiwork at the Giant's Causeway, County Antrim.

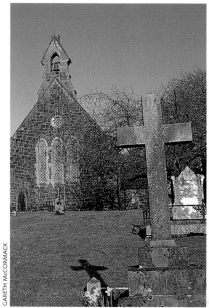

Find peace in County Tyrone.

Mt Sawel, Sperrin Mountains, County Tyrone

The Bronze Age Beaghmore Stone Circles, County Tyrone, are aligned with the sun, moon and stars.

Moneymore on the B18, is an interesting example of early Plantation architecture. The original house was built about 1695 by the Conynghams, who came here from Scotland after acquiring the 120-hectare Springhill Estate. It was built at the same time as Hezlett House near Castlerock but has little in common with that more humble abode. The central block has a high pitched roof, enlarged by the addition of the wings in the 18th century, which give a more solid air of Baroque assurance to the house. The barn is also late 17th century and was built to accommodate a warning bell. The Williamite war was over, but then, as now, a certain siege mentality remained. Inside the house is some old oak furniture, a library, a collection of weapons and many costumes.

The house opens 2 to 6 pm at the weekend, April to June and September; and 2 to 6 pm Friday to Wednesday, July and August. Admission costs £2.50/1.25.

PORTSTEWART
pop 6459

When the English novelist Thackeray visited Portstewart (Port Stíobhaird) in 1842, he noted the 'air of comfort and neatness'; nearly 160 years later this still rings true and the place has an air of superiority that distinguishes it from the more proletarian Portrush, 6km farther down the coast in County Antrim. A day could easily be passed visiting the excellent beaches in the vicinity (both Portstewart and Portrush have good surf), and the town makes a convenient base for the Giant's Causeway and other coastal attractions.

Orientation & Information

Portstewart consists of one long promenade. To the east it heads along the coast to Portrush and Ballycastle, and to the west to a fine beach, Portstewart Strand. The castle-like building perched at the end of the promenade is a Dominican school. Attractions west of town can only be reached by first going inland to Coleraine, then north again up the other side of a narrow inlet.

The tourist office (☎ 70 832286), in the

library in the lower level of the red-brick town hall at the western end of town, opens 10 am to 4 pm Monday to Saturday, July and August.

Things to See & Do

The wide, sweeping **Portstewart Strand** is about a 20-minute walk or a short bus ride west of town along Strand Rd. Despite the fact that the strand is a National Trust site, vehicles are allowed onto the firm sand, which can accommodate over 1000 cars. When someone is on duty (unlikely out of season or in the evening) there's a £2.50 charge to take cars on the beach.

In May the **North-West 200 motorcycle race** is run on a road circuit between Portrush, Portstewart and Coleraine. This classic race is one of the last to be run on closed public roads anywhere in Europe; most such events are now considered too dangerous. It attracts up to 70,000 spectators.

Places to Stay

Camping Camp sites are plentiful along the coast road. The council-run *Juniper Hill Caravan Park* (☎ 70 832023, 70 Ballyreagh Rd), 2.5km east, has a few tent sites costing £5. Inland towards Coleraine, *Portstewart Holiday Park* (☎ 70 833308) charges £8 for tent sites. For other nearby camp sites see Portrush, later in this chapter, and Limavady & Around, earlier.

Hostels The *Causeway Coast Hostel* (☎ 70 833789, 4 Victoria Terrace), at the eastern end of town, charges £6 per person in four-, six- or eight-bedded dorms, £7.50 in private rooms. It has its own kitchen and laundry, and welcoming fires in winter. Real baths also make a nice change from showers.

B&Bs There are a number of B&Bs at the eastern end of town at the junction of Victoria Terrace, Hillcrest and Atlantic Circle. The central *Craigmore* (☎ 70 832120, 26 The Promenade) costs £18.50 per person. *Mount Oriel* (☎ 70 832556, 74 The Promenade) charges £17 per person. *Akaroa*

(☎ 70 832067, 75 The Promenade) charges £20.

Hotels The two-star *Edgewater Hotel* (☎ 70 833314, 88 Strand Rd), overlooking Portstewart Strand, offers pleasant singles/doubles costing £58/95.

Self-Catering Describing themselves as 'exclusively adult', the cottages at *Rock Castle* (☎ 70 832271) overlook Portstewart Strand and vary from £190 per week for a one-bedroom unit in the low season to £485 for a two-bedroom unit in the high season.

Places to Eat
There's a well-stocked *health food shop* on The Promenade. For reasonably priced hot or cold lunches and early evening meals, try *Squires* (18 The Promenade). You can hardly miss neon-lit *Morelli's*, midway along The Promenade, which dispenses mouth-watering ice creams and good coffee. Next door, but part of the same complex, is *Nino's*, which serves hot meals as well as ice cream and usually has a vegetarian special costing around £3. Up some stairs and round the back, the *Outback*, yet another part of the same complex, serves steaks in the evenings.

The Anchorage, just off The Promenade, serves decent pub food. The lively bar here opens until late and there's usually live music at the weekend. *Edgewater Hotel* serves good food, too, and is the place to go for a sunset drink.

Ashiana (12 The Diamond) has a mixed menu of Indian and European dishes which includes a good vegetarian selection. Out of town towards Portrush, *Snappers* (21 Ballyreagh Rd) is a large seafood restaurant on the sea side of the coast road.

Getting There & Away
Bus Buses leave from The Promenade. Ulsterbus No 218 leaves Portstewart for Belfast eight times daily on weekdays, four times on Saturday and twice on Sunday, stopping at Coleraine, Ballymoney and Antrim. This is the express route and takes two hours. Bus No 218 also does the scenic

coastal route and takes four hours.

Bus No 234 leaves several times daily for Derry (once daily at the weekend) and takes an hour. Bus No 140 plies between Coleraine and Portstewart (17 minutes) roughly every half-hour (fewer on Sunday).

See Getting There & Away in the Coleraine section earlier in this chapter for information on the summertime Antrim Coaster and Bushmills Bus services.

Train The nearest station is at Portrush, with connections to the Derry to Belfast train at Coleraine. See Portrush, later in this chapter, for details.

County Antrim

Most visitors to Antrim pass along the coast, where there's little to remind one of the Troubles. The scenery is delightful and everyone is drawn towards the northern coastline, which bears the distinctive geological formation of the Giant's Causeway.

East of Ballycastle the distinctive cliffs of Fair Head mark the point where the coast turns southwards and the Antrim coast makes its way down to Larne and Belfast Lough. This coastal strip is known as the Glens of Antrim after the series of nine valleys which cut across the range of hills between Ballycastle and Larne. The A2 road runs along the coast for most of the way and it's an exciting route for cyclists. The short run between Waterfoot and Carnlough is particularly fine.

Inland, Antrim (Aontroim) is perhaps the least interesting part of Northern Ireland, and Antrim town has little to recommend it. To the south of Lisburn the infamous Long Kesh prison was the scene of the hunger strikes in 1981 which led to the deaths of 10 men who were campaigning for the right to be recognised as political prisoners.

PORTRUSH
pop 5703
The busy little resort of Portrush (Port Rois) bursts at the seams with holidaymakers

from all around the North in summer and on bank-holiday weekends. Not surprisingly, many of its attractions are unashamedly focused on families.

Information

The tourist office (☎ 70 823333) is in the Dunluce Centre on Sandhill Drive. It opens 9 am to 8 pm daily, mid-June to September; 9 am to 5 pm on weekdays, April to mid-June; and noon to 5 pm at the weekend, March and October.

Things to See & Do

In summer, **boat trips** depart regularly for cruising or fishing; contact the tourist office for a list of operators. For **pony trekking** contact the Maddybenny Riding Centre (☎ 70 823394) or Hillfarm Riding and Trekking Centre (☎ 70 848629), 47 Altikeragh Rd.

Portrush is carving out a name for itself as a **surfing** paradise. There are several surf shops, including the friendly Troggs (☎ 70 823923), 8 Bath St, which does board and wet-suit hire, surf reports and general advice.

Waterworld (☎ 70 822001), by the harbour, has pools, waterslides and spa baths for children to play in. The **Dunluce Centre** (☎ 70 824444) has a Turbo Tour, a hands-on nature trail with lots of buttons to press, and animated shows on local myths and legends. It opens 10 am to 8 pm daily, in summer; and 10 am to 5 pm daily, in winter. An inclusive ticket costs £4.50 March to September, £4 at other times.

Places to Stay

Camping The Bushmills Bus (No 177) runs to *Skerries Holiday Park* (☎ 70 822531, 126 Dunluce Rd), where a site costs £10. The smaller *Carrick Dhu Caravan Park* (☎ 70 823712, 12 Ballyreagh Rd) charges the same. *Golf Links Holiday Home Park* (☎ 70 823539, Bushmills Rd) offers sites costing £9.

Hostels A welcoming, independent hostel is *Macools* (☎ 70 824845, 5 Causeway View Terrace), with 20 beds in dorms with

sea views. Beds in single-sex dorms cost £7 (£8 in the one private room). There are laundry and cooking facilities; Internet access is available for £2 for the first 15 minutes; and there are bicycles to rent costing £5 per day.

B&Bs Places fill up quickly during summer and it's advisable to book in advance through the tourist office. Guesthouses with sea views include *Clarmont* (☎ 70 822397, 10 Landsdowne Crescent), *Alexandra* (☎ 70 822284, 11 Landsdowne Crescent) and *Belvedere* (☎ 70 822771, 15 Landsdowne Crescent). All charge from £20 for a double in the high season.

With more character, there's the *Old Manse* (☎ 70 824118, 3 Main St), which dates from 1850 and charges £21/40 for singles/doubles.

If you arrive late, there are also a few B&Bs immediately opposite the station in Eglinton St, including *Atlantic View* (☎ 70 823647), *Glenshane* (☎ 70 824839) and *An Uladh* (☎ 70 822221).

Hotels Singles/doubles at the three-star *Magherabuoy House* (☎ 70 823507, 41 Magherabuoy Rd) cost £60/100, while *Eglinton Hotel* (☎ 70 822371, 49 Eglinton St) charges £50/68; rates at both include breakfast.

Places to Eat

Libby's Coffee Shop, next to the post office on Main St, offers decent coffee and light meals.

Ramore (☎ 70 824313), next to Waterworld and overlooking the harbour, is Portrush's premier eating place. The wine bar downstairs opens for lunch from 12.15 to 2.15 pm (good-value lunch specials start at £4.95), and again from 5 pm, while the pricier restaurant upstairs opens from 6 pm. Main courses start at £11.95.

Donovan's (92 Main St), near the harbour, opens for pub food daily. *Don Giovanni's Ristorante* (Causeway St), near the junction with Eglinton and Main Sts, isn't as expensive as it looks. Pasta dishes cost £4.90 to £6.50.

Magherabuoy House has a good reputation for fresh seafood and local game. Generous helpings make the Sunday lunch particularly good value.

Entertainment
Harbour Bar, unsurprisingly located by the harbour, is immensely popular at night. *Rogues*, just across the road, has regular live-music sessions. About 1.5km out of town, *Kelly's* (☎ 70 822539) is a popular dance-music venue which regularly features DJs from London and Manchester. The owner keeps adding bars to the rambling complex – at last count there were about 13. A taxi will cost about £5 to get you there.

Getting There & Away
Bus The bus terminal is near the Dunluce Centre. Bus No 218 leaves several times daily from Portrush for Belfast, travelling inland via Portstewart, Coleraine, Ballymoney, Ballymena and Antrim. Bus Nos 139 and 140 run weekdays to Coleraine. In summer, bus No 278 runs daily to Dublin. Bus No 172 runs daily to Bushmills and Ballycastle.

See Getting There & Away in the Coleraine section earlier in this chapter for information on the summertime Antrim Coaster and Bushmills Bus services.

Train Portrush is served by train from Coleraine (12 minutes) roughly every hour. The earliest train leaves Coleraine at 8.02 am, the latest at 10.25 pm; from Portrush the times are 6.35 am and 8.20 pm respectively. At Coleraine connections can be made for Belfast or Derry. The journey to Dublin from Portrush, changing at Coleraine and Belfast, takes nearly five hours. Contact Portrush station (☎ 70 822395) for details.

Getting Around
For taxis call Andy Brown's (☎ 70 822223) or North West Taxis (☎ 70 824446). Both companies are near the red-brick town hall. A taxi to the Giant's Causeway costs about £10.

PORTBALLINTRAE
pop 756
Portballintrae (Port of the Town of Strand) is little more than a small harbour ringed with houses and a couple of seaside-style hotels. During WWI it was the only place in the UK to be shelled by a German submarine. Luckily, the result was no worse than a crater on the outskirts of town and the downing of the electric tram lines.

Dunluce Castle
The site, beside the A2 just west of Portballintrae, was used for defensive purposes long before a stone castle was constructed, as shown by the existence of a 1000-year-old souterrain. Parts of the castle date from the 14th century. In the 16th century it came into the hands of the Scottish Sorley Boy MacDonnell family, who extended the buildings and tried to strengthen its walls after a serious artillery attack by the English. In the 17th century a manor house with medieval floor plan and Renaissance embellishments was built inside the walls.

The southern wall, facing the mainland, has two openings cut into it which were made to hold cannons salvaged from the wreck of the *Girona*, a Spanish Armada vessel that foundered nearby. Perched 30m above the sea, the castle was of obvious military value, and there are extensive remains inside the walls, giving a good idea of life here.

The palatial hall needed two fireplaces, while the kitchen area has ovens, storage space and a drainage system all built into the stone. The lower yard retains the original cobbling and was surrounded by service rooms, some of which collapsed into the sea in 1639; servants and a night's dinner were lost.

The castle opens 10 am to 7 pm Monday to Saturday, and 11 am (2 pm from April to June) to 7 pm on Sunday, April to August; and 10 am to 7 pm Monday to Saturday, September; and 10 am to 4 pm Monday to Saturday, October to March. Admission costs £1.50/75p, which includes an audiovisual display telling the castle's history.

Places to Stay & Eat

The *Portballintrae Caravan Park* (☎ 20 731478, Ballaghmore Rd) has space for 16 tents costing £6 per night. The accommodating *Keeve-Na* (☎ 20 732184), beside the caravan park, offers B&B costing £17/32 in singles/doubles. At the sea-facing *Bayhead House* (☎ 20 731441, 8 Bayhead Rd), B&B costs £30/39. *Bayview Hotel* (☎ 20 731453, 2 Bayhead Rd) has an indoor heated swimming pool and costs £40/70, while *Beach House Hotel* (☎ 20 731214, 61 Beach Rd) charges £42/64.

Sallie's Coffee Shop (Seaport Ave) produces satisfying snacks during the day. Decent, substantial meals are available from *Beach House Hotel*.

Getting There & Away

Weekdays bus No 132 between Portrush and Ballymoney stops here twice daily. Bus No 138 runs regularly (except Sunday) to Coleraine and Portrush, while bus No 172 runs several times daily to Portrush and Ballycastle.

See Getting There & Away in the Coleraine section earlier in this chapter for information on the summertime Antrim Coaster and Bushmills Bus services.

BUSHMILLS
pop 1348

On the River Bush, Bushmills (Muileann na Buaise) is a small town off the A2 between Portrush and Ballycastle. At its centre is The Diamond, with a grim, grey circular clocktower and war memorial, from which Main St makes its way half a kilometre west to the famous Bushmills Distillery.

Bushmills Distillery

This is the only place in the world where Bushmills whiskey is distilled, and it is the world's oldest legal distillery. Whiskey was first officially distilled here in 1608, but records indicate that the activity was going on for hundreds of years before that. After a noisy tour of the industrial process (it's quieter at the weekend when production is halted), you're rewarded with a whiskey-tasting session in which you get to compare Bushmills whiskeys with other brands. These sessions take place in the 1608 Bar, where an exhibition area has been created in what were once malt kilns.

The distillery (☎ 20 731521) opens 9.30 am to 5.30 pm Monday to Saturday, and noon to 5.30 pm on Sunday (the last tour is at 4 pm), April to October; and 10 am to 5 pm on weekdays (the last tour is at 3.30 pm), November to March. Admission costs £3, children free.

Places to Stay & Eat

The spectacularly sited YHANI *White Park Bay Hostel* is 6km east of Bushmills (see the Giant's Causeway to Ballycastle section later in this chapter).

Ardeevin (☎ 20 731661, 145 Main St), on the way to the distillery, offers B&B costing £17 per person. The clean rooms have views of the weir at the back. At the pleasantly quiet *Bushmills Inn* (☎ 20 732339, Main St), single/double rooms cost £68/88. *Pineview* (☎ 20 741527, 111 Castlecatt Rd), a farmhouse 5km south of Bushmills, charges £16 per person.

Valerie's Pantry (125 Main St) opens in the daytime for grills and light meals. *Bushmills Inn* has an attractive restaurant serving everything from toasted sandwiches to full à la carte dinners. The cheaper brasserie opens only at the weekend.

Strangely, in a place synonymous with Irish whiskey, *Scotch House Tavern* on Main St boasts a wide range of Scotch whisky.

Getting There & Away

Bus No 172 connects Bushmills with Ballycastle, the Giant's Causeway and Portrush, as does bus No 254, which also goes to Coleraine, Larne and Belfast. Buses drop you off in The Diamond.

See Getting There & Away in the Coleraine section earlier in this chapter for information on the summertime Antrim Coaster and Bushmills Bus services.

GIANT'S CAUSEWAY

The chances are you've seen pictures of the Giant's Causeway (Clochán an Aifir), the

DERRY & ANTRIM

North's number-one tourist attraction, long before getting here. A bishop of Derry, who became interested in geology after seeing Vesuvius erupt, commissioned the paintings of the site that led to its fame. The hexagonal basalt columns are impressive and do look as if a giant might have playfully tipped out all 37,000 of them, if you count the ones under the water. According to legend the giant in question, Fionn Mc-Cumhaill (also known as Finn McCool), fancied a female giant on the Scottish island of Staffa and built some stepping stones to the island, where similar rock formations are found.

The modern, more prosaic explanation is that red-hot lava erupted from an underground fissure and crystallised some 60 million years ago into the shapes that we see today. The phenomenon is very clearly explained in the Causeway Visitor Centre (☎ 20 731855), alongside the surprising fact that the Causeway came to general notice as late as 1740. The audiovisual section, however, is more of an animated tourist brochure, debatably worth the charge of £1/50p. It costs nothing to make the pleasant 1.5km pilgrimage to the actual site.

From mid-March to the end of October minibuses with wheelchair access ply the route every 15 minutes (£1/50p return).

Different areas of the rock formations have their own names, most invented by the many Victorian guides who made a summer living escorting the tourists who arrived by tram from Coleraine. Past the main spill of columns, the pathway brings into view a formation that does deserve its own name. Chimney Tops was identified by ships of the Spanish Armada in 1588 as part of Dunluce Castle, and consequently fired upon.

Two well-established footpaths at different levels start from outside the visitor centre and form a circular walk. The less strenuous route is to follow the clifftop path out then down to the Causeway, then take the lower walk back to the visitor centre.

From the clifftop at Hamilton's Seat, there's one of the best views of the Causeway and headlands to the west, including Malin Head and Inishowen. If you want to go farther, the path continues round Benbane Head. The headlands become lower and lower until the path reaches the main road near Dunseverick Castle. The walk

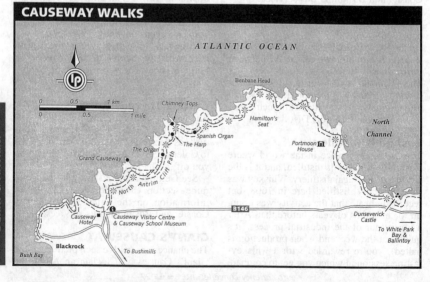

CAUSEWAY WALKS

from the visitor centre to the castle and back is 16km.

From below the remains of the castle a path winds up and round to the east, ending at Ballintoy. It crosses a number of small wooden bridges before reaching the beach at White Park Bay. There's a YHANI hostel here, so the whole 16km journey from the Giant's Causeway could be done in one day.

These walks follow the North Antrim Cliff Path, which actually begins west of the visitor centre at Blackrock, a short walk of about 2.5km. A useful map from the visitor centre details the walks, including the rock formations along the way.

The Giant's Causeway can be visited free of charge any time but the car park costs £2.50 (there's a free car park on Runkerry Rd a few minutes' walk from the visitor centre; turn left before the main car park). The visitor centre opens 10 am to 7 pm daily, July and August; 10 am to 5 pm daily, September to June. (It closes on Christmas Day and Boxing Day.) There's a National Trust shop and a café in the same building but they close earlier.

Next to the visitor centre, and mainly of interest to children, the **Causeway School Museum** opens 11 am to 5 pm daily, July and August. Admission costs 75/50p (families £2).

Places to Stay

See the following Giant's Causeway to Ballycastle section for information on the *hostels* at White Park Bay and Ballintoy. There are a handful of B&Bs around. *Lochaber* (☎ *20 731385, 107 Causeway Rd*), on the coast road, just 1.5km from the Causeway, charges £14 per person, while *Carnside Farmhouse* (☎ *20 731337, Causeway Rd*) costs £16 per person.

If you want to stay close to the Causeway, the two-star *Causeway Hotel* (☎ *20 731226, fax 20 732552*) is within spitting distance and charges £45/65 including breakfast. Otherwise, you could stay in Bushmills or Portballintrae, or even in Portrush or Ballycastle, and still visit the Causeway perfectly easily.

Places to Eat

The *Tea Room* in the Causeway Visitor Centre serves light meals. You can buy sandwiches and snacks in two small *shops* outside. More substantial meals are available at the nearby *Causeway Hotel*. Its restaurant is extremely popular, so it's wise to book in advance. Bar snacks are also available.

Getting There & Away

The B146 Causeway to Dunseverick road runs parallel to the A2 but closer to the coast and can be joined just east of Bushmills or near White Park Bay. Bus Nos 172 and 254 between Portrush and Ballycastle pass the site. It's only five minutes by bus from the Giant's Causeway to The Diamond in Bushmills and another five minutes to Portballintrae.

See Getting There & Away in the Coleraine section earlier in this chapter for information on the summertime Antrim Coaster and Bushmills Bus services.

GIANT'S CAUSEWAY TO BALLYCASTLE

Spectacularly sited by the side of the B146 (which is reached off the A2 coast road) is **Dunseverick Castle**, though unfortunately little remains of it. Older than Dunluce Castle nor Portballintrae, a castle on this site was once the home of Conal Cearnac, a famous wrestler and swordsman said to have been present at Christ's crucifixion; he reputedly moved the stone at Christ's sepulchre. St Patrick is also said to have visited the castle. A road was laid from here to Tara, the headquarters of the pagan high kings of Ireland.

Signposted off the A2 is **Portbradden**, a hamlet of half a dozen pretty harbourside houses. Tiny, blue-and-white St Gobban's church is said to be the smallest in Ireland, and it's easy to believe it.

Visible from Portbradden and accessible via the next road junction off the A2 is the spectacular **White Park Bay** with its wide, sweeping sandy beach. The modern YHANI *White Park Bay Hostel* (☎ *20 731745*) has a common room positioned to

DERRY & ANTRIM

soak up the view. Four-bed dorms cost £9.75/10.75 for members/non-members, and twins (complete with TV and tea- and coffee-making facilities) cost £11.75/12.75 per person. Rates include bed linen. The hostel has a bureau de change, and residents can hire bikes for £6 per day.

A few kilometres farther along is **Ballintoy** (Baile an Tuaighe), another picture-postcard village, set round a harbour. Look out for the idiosyncratically designed house on the right on the way down. About 200m past the harbour turn-off is *Sheep Island View* (☎ 20 762470, 42 Main St), an independent hostel offering beds in small en suite dorms costing £9 (children aged under 12 £6). There's a huge kitchen and laundry facilities. The hostel offers a pick-up service from the Giant's Causeway, Bushmills and Ballycastle. B&B is available at *Ballintoy House* (☎ 20 762317, 9 Main St) costing £16 per person. It opens year round. By the harbour, tiny *Roark's Kitchen* serves teas, coffees and light meals until 7 pm daily.

It's a scary traipse across the **Carrick-a-rede Rope Bridge** to a small island with a salmon fishery and hundreds of nesting fulmar and razorbill. Carrick-a-rede means 'rock in the road', and the 20m-long bridge sways some 25m above the rock-strewn water. It's especially frightening if it's windy, but there are secure handrails to help steady your nerves and your balance; stout footwear is advised and no more than two people should cross simultaneously. The bridge is put up every spring by workers at the fishery. Once on the island there are good views of Rathlin Island and Fair Head to the east. You can cross the bridge free, but the National Trust car park costs £2; it's a 1.25km walk from there to the bridge. The small National Trust Information Centre (☎ 20 731582) has a *café* and opens 10 am to 6 pm daily, April to August.

BALLYCASTLE
pop 4000

Ballycastle (Baile an Chaisil), where the Atlantic Ocean meets the Irish Sea, also marks the end of the Causeway Coast. It's a pretty, small town, with plenty of 18th- and 19th-century architecture, and its location makes it a natural base for exploring the coasts to the west or south. The beach itself may be nothing special but there's a seaside feel to the harbour area. The Giant's Causeway, Bushmills Distillery and Carrick-a-rede Rope Bridge are all less than 16km away, and the Glens of Antrim are due south.

Information
The tourist office (☎ 20 762024) is in the Moyle District Council Office on Mary St. It opens 9.30 am to 5 pm on weekdays, and 10 am to 4 pm on Saturday, Easter, June and September; and 9.30 am to 7 pm on weekdays, 10 am to 6 pm on Saturday, and 2 to 6 pm on Sunday, July and August. Pick up a free copy of the *Ballycastle Heritage Trail* leaflet here.

Things to See
The tiny **Ballycastle Museum**, in the town's 18th-century courthouse on Castle St, opens 2 to 6 pm Monday to Saturday, July and August. Admission is free. The **lookout** on North St has views of the harbour and the cliffs to the east, while down near the harbour is a **memorial** to Guglielmo Marconi (for details see the Rathlin Island section later in this chapter).

The remains of the Franciscan **Bonamargy Friary** are 1km east of town on the A2 to Cushendun, on the Ballycastle golf course. The friary was founded around 1500 and used for two centuries. South of the friary a vault contains the bodies of the MacDonnells, the earls of Antrim, including Sorley Boy MacDonnell from Dunluce Castle. Admission is free.

Special Events
In late May, the Northern Lights Festal is a three-day celebration of Ulster culture. Mid-June there's the three-day music and dance festival known as Fleadh Amhrán agus Rince.

The bigger Ould Lammas Fair, on the last Monday and Tuesday of August, is one of the oldest fairs in Ireland, dating back to 1606,

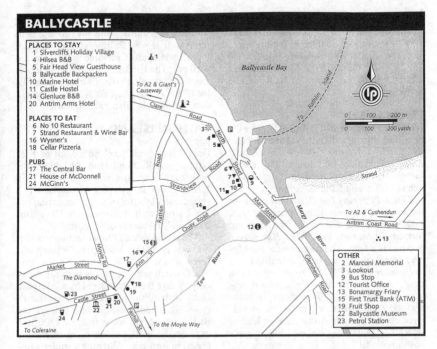

BALLYCASTLE

PLACES TO STAY
1 Silvercliffs Holiday Village
4 Hilsea B&B
5 Fair Head View Guesthouse
8 Ballycastle Backpackers
10 Marine Hotel
11 Castle Hostel
14 Glenluce B&B
20 Antrim Arms Hotel

PLACES TO EAT
6 No 10 Restaurant
7 Strand Restaurant & Wine Bar
16 Wysner's
18 Cellar Pizzeria

PUBS
17 The Central Bar
21 House of McDonnell
24 McGinn's

OTHER
2 Marconi Memorial
3 Lookout
9 Bus Stop
12 Tourist Office
13 Bonamargy Friary
15 First Trust Bank (ATM)
19 Fruit Shop
22 Ballycastle Museum
23 Petrol Station

and is associated with the sale of two traditional foods, yellowman and dulse. Yellowman is a hard chewy toffee, while dulse is a dried seaweed that's sold salted and ready to eat, although some people toast it. Always available during the Ould Lammas Fair, dulse is on sale generally June to September, while yellowman is available year round. The Fruit Shop on The Diamond often stocks both delicacies.

Places to Stay

Camping The *Silvercliffs Holiday Village* (☎ 20 762550, 21 Clare Rd) is a big caravan park and camp site, north-west of town and within walking distance. It costs £10 for tents or campervans. Facilities include a swimming pool, sauna and bar. On the A2 to Cushendun, 10km from Ballycastle, *Watertop Open Farm* (☎ 20 762576) has space for a few tents (£8.50 each) and is a good place for children, with pony trekking and farm tours.

Hostels The spacious and welcoming *Castle Hostel* (☎ 20 762337, 62 Quay Rd), just past the Marine Hotel, charges upwards of £6 per night.

Ballycastle Backpackers (☎ 20 763612, 4 North St), near the seafront and main bus stop, has accommodation in small dorms for £6; rooms in its private rooms cost £7.50.

B&Bs If you want to be close to the sea, *Fair Head View* (☎ 20 769376, 26 North St) is above the harbour; rooms cost £16.50 per person. Farther up is *Hilsea* (☎ 20 762385, 28 North St), with B&B costing £18 per person.

Glenluce (☎ 20 762914, 42 Quay Rd), painted white with blue trim, charges £20 per person. Other possibilities include *Fragens* (☎ 20 762168, 34 Quay Rd), *Ammiroy* (☎ 20 762621, 26 Quay Rd) and *Silversprings House* (☎ 20 762080, 20 Quay Rd), all charging £17 to £20 per person.

Hotels The *Marine Hotel (☎ 20 762222, 1 North St)* is right on the seafront and costs £60/70 for singles/doubles in the high season. The smaller *Antrim Arms Hotel (☎ 20 762284, 75 Castle St)*, inland, charges £22.50 per person. Rates at both include breakfast.

Places to Eat

Herold's Restaurant (22 Ann St) opens for breakfast, lunch and afternoon tea Monday to Saturday. *Wysner's (☎ 20 762372, 16 Ann St)* is the place for sausages and champ; there's also a restaurant upstairs which opens Friday and Saturday evenings.

Cellar Pizzeria (The Diamond) opens in the evening for reasonably priced pizzas, salads and pasta dishes. On the seafront, *Strand Restaurant and Wine Bar* serves pub meals all day. The restaurant at the *Marine Hotel* specialises in local seafood.

Number 10 (☎ 20 768110, North St) is a new restaurant offering excellent food, service and ambience. The menu features seafood (seared scallops on a bed of buttered chicory; grilled Arctic char) as well as interesting vegetarian dishes. Main courses cost around £12.

Entertainment

Marine Hotel has live music at the weekend during summer and a disco on Saturday night. There's more live music at the pubs *McGinn's (Castle St)* and the popular *House of McDonnell (Castle St)*, which has traditional-music sessions on Friday night. *The Central Bar (Ann St)* has regular traditional sessions, too.

Getting There & Away

Bus Nos 131 and 217 link Ballycastle with Belfast, and bus No 171 links the town with Coleraine, but there are no Sunday services on these routes. Bus No 172 provides daily connections with Bushmills and Portrush.

McGinns (☎ 20 763451), the local private bus company, runs to Belfast's Europa Bus Centre from The Diamond at 4 pm on Friday and at 8 pm on Sunday. It takes 1½ hours and costs £6/4 return.

The Antrim Coaster – No 252 – operates between Belfast and Coleraine twice daily, Monday to Saturday, late May to late September. It leaves Belfast at 9.10 am and 2 pm, and departs Coleraine at 9.50 am and 4.10 pm. The trip takes about four hours. It stops at Portrush, Portballintrae, Bushmills, the Giant's Causeway, Ballycastle, Cushendun, Carnlough, Glenarm and Larne.

RATHLIN ISLAND

pop 113

Only 22km from Scotland's Mull of Kintyre, rugged Rathlin Island (Reachlainn) is only 6km long and nowhere more than 1.5km across. It has a pub, a restaurant, two shops and a handful of accommodation options, along with approximately 100 inhabitants and thousands of seabirds.

The island, which Pliny mentions as Ricnia, was raided by Vikings in 795 and suffered again in 1595 when Sorley Boy MacDonnell sent his family here for safety only to have them massacred by the English along with all the inhabitants. The island's most illustrious visitor was Robert the Bruce, who spent some time in 1306 in a cave on the north-eastern point learning a lesson in fortitude. Watching a spider's resoluteness in repeatedly trying to spin a web gave him the courage to have another go at the English, whom he subsequently defeated at Bannockburn.

Another claim to fame is the fact that Rathlin Island was the first place to have a wireless. Marconi's assistant contacted Rathlin by radio from Ballycastle in 1898 to prove to Lloyds of London that the idea worked.

The birdlife at **Kebble Nature Reserve** at the western end of the island is the chief attraction. Guillemot, kittiwake, razorbill and puffin can be seen around West Lighthouse, but by late summer they're no longer nesting or rearing their young and are difficult to spot from the land. During summer a minibus takes you there from the ferry harbour. The service doesn't run to a timetable so check your return time.

The **Boathouse Centre** south of the harbour sells books and brochures and details the history, culture and ecology of the island. It opens daily from Easter to the end of October

Places to Stay

You can *camp* for free on the eastern side of Church Bay in a field not far from the harbour. *Soerneog View* (☎ 20 763954), south of the harbour overlooking Mill Bay, has six hostel beds costing £8 per person. *Richard Branson Activity Centre* (☎ 20 763915) offers dorm beds costing £10.

Rathlin Guesthouse (☎ 20 763917) by the harbour offers B&B costing £15 per person. Restored and run by the National Trust, *Manor House* (☎ 20 763964), also south of the harbour, offers B&B costing £26/30 in singles/doubles.

Getting There & Away

In theory a ferry service (☎ 20 769299) operates daily year round from Ballycastle, but boats may not sail when the weather is bad. It's wise to show up well in advance of the scheduled sailing time.

From June to September there are two morning and two afternoon crossings each way. Boats leave Ballycastle at 9.30 and 11.30 am and 4 and 6 pm. Boats leave Rathlin at 8.30 and 10.30 am and 3 and 5 pm. The trip takes 45 minutes and the return fare is £7.80.

MURLOUGH BAY

The scenic coast between Ballycastle and Cushendun is best covered by the Cushendun Scenic Route (to Torr Head) that takes in Murlough Bay. This is the most stupendous part of the Antrim coastline. The A2 goes inland between Cushendun and Ballycastle and cannot compete with the grandeur of the coastal route.

Leave your transport at the first car park – there are three altogether – where a map display sets out the walking possibilities. From the first car park walk No 1 is to Coolanlough, a 3.5km return trip. The views from Fair Head are magnificent. From a vantage point 186m above the sea, Rathlin Island is to the left, while out to sea the peaks of the Isle of Arran can be seen on a clear day beyond the Mull of Kintyre. The walk also takes in Lough na Cranagh, in the middle of which is an ancient crannóg.

The second walk begins from the second car park farther down the road; follow the clear pathway to the west. It leads to some abandoned coal mines, indicated only by arches in the rock, which are probably not safe to explore. By following the main road down past the second car park you come to a third parking area on the right. From there the road down becomes a green track and ends in a cul-de-sac by a small house.

Between the first and second car parks, the remains of a cross can be seen, a memorial to Roger Casement, whose family came from this area. Casement, who was hanged in London in 1916 for enlisting the aid of Germany in the nationalist struggle, made a last request to his cousin: `Take my body back with you and let it lie in the old churchyard in Murlough Bay'. It was 50 years before the British released the body.

CUSHENDUN

pop 347

Much of Cushendun (Bun Abhann Duinne) is owned by the National Trust, and any new buildings must match existing ones. The distinctive black and white houses at the southern end are the work of Clough Williams-Ellis, designer of Portmeirion in North Wales, who came here to work for Lord Cushendun.

The village, on a bay with a small beach, is on the **Ulster Way** (see Walking in the Activities chapter) and part of the walk can be undertaken from here. North from Cushendun the walk goes inland before heading down to Murlough Bay and then along the coast to Ballycastle. Going south the walk travels inland nearly all the way to Cushendall.

Places to Stay & Eat

Camping is available at *Cushendun Caravan Park* (☎ 21 761254, 14 Glendun Rd), run by the local council. Tent sites cost £4.90, campervans £8.30. The only hotel is the unclassified *Bay Hotel* (☎ 21 761267, 20 Strandview Park), with rooms starting at £18 per person. *Cushendun* (☎ 21 761266)

DERRY & ANTRIM

is a guesthouse offering B&B costing £20 per person. It opens August and September. North of the village, *Villa Farmhouse* (☎ *21 761252, 185 Torr Rd*) has a great view over the bay and offers B&B costing £20/36 in singles/doubles.

Self-catering houses and flats around Cushendun go for around £180 to £380 per week. One of the cheaper ones is *Strand House Annexe* (☎ *90 241100*), but it has only one unit. *Mullarts Apartments* (☎ *21 761221, 114 Tromra Rd*) are inside a converted church.

Cushendun Village Tearooms, on the corner near the bridge, serves hot snacks and salads. Bar food and evening meals are available at *Bay Hotel. Mary McBride's* (*Main St*) offers locally caught seafood and homemade steak-and-Guinness pie. It opens for lunch and dinner daily.

Getting There & Away

Ulsterbus Nos 120 and 150 link Cushendun with Ballymena, Monday to Saturday, from where a connection to Belfast can be made. Bus Nos 156 and 162 travel to Larne, stopping at towns along the way, five times daily on weekdays, three times daily at the weekend. From Larne it's a short hop to Belfast.

See Getting There & Away in the Ballycastle section earlier in this chapter for information on the summertime Antrim Coaster bus.

CUSHENDALL
pop 1399

The red sandstone tower at the crossroads of this picturesque little village was built in the early 19th century by Francis Turnly. From the village the B14 road runs inland to Glenariff Forest Park, in the loveliest of Antrim's nine glens, from where the A43 rejoins the A2 south of Cushendall (Bun Abhann Dalla) at Glenariff, also called Waterfoot. The bay that the village overlooks is known as the Moyle. On a clear day you can see across to the Mull of Kintyre and the Scottish mainland.

About 5000 years ago, stone from nearby Tievebulliagh Mountain was the basis of an important stone-axe industry.

Information

The tourist office (☎ 21 771180), 24 Mill St, is run by the Glens of Antrim Historical Society. It opens 10 am to 1 pm and 3 to 7.30 pm Monday to Saturday, and 2 to 4.30 pm on Sunday, July and August; and 10 am to 1 pm and 3 to 5 pm Tuesday to Friday, September to June.

Layde Old Church

About 1km north of the village, this magical ruined church and churchyard stand beside a fast-flowing stream that heads down to the sea. The church is believed to have been founded by Franciscans but was used as a parish church from the early 14th century until 1790. The tombstones in the graveyard include MacDonnell memorials, and there's a rather pagan-looking one with a hole through it, immediately on the left after you enter the grounds. You can walk to the church along a lovely clifftop coastal path, or take the steep coast road (not the A2) which goes north to Cushendun and passes the YHANI hostel. The church is signposted off the road to the right, but it's difficult to see.

Ossian's Grave

Romantically, but inaccurately, named after the legendary warrior-poet of the 3rd century, this Neolithic court tomb consists of a two-chambered burial ground once enclosed by an oval cairn. The site is signposted off the A2 outside Cushendall on the Cushendun side. You can park at the farm and walk up.

Glenariff Forest Park

Over 800 hectares of woodland make up the park, and the main attraction is Ess-na-Larach Waterfall, about half an hour's walk from the visitor centre. There are various other walks, not all clearly marked; the longest is a three-hour circular mountain trail. Views of the valley led the writer Thackeray to exclaim that it was a 'Switzerland in miniature'. There's a £2.50 charge for cars, £1.50 for motorcycles and £1/50p for pedestrians. If you park at the Manor Lodge restaurant, on the road to the forest park, you need to pay the pedestrian fee only.

Opposite the entrance to the park is the start of the **Moyle Way**, which leads 32km north to Ballycastle.

Places to Stay

Camping Camping is possible at *Glenariff Forest Park* (☎ *21 758232*), outside the forest park, while *Glenville Caravan Park* (☎ *21 771520*), on the Layde road, has a small camping area, charging £3 per tent. *Cushendall Caravan Park* (☎ *21 771699*), on the coast road and overlooking the Moyle, is bigger and pricier at £4.90 per tent.

Hostels The large and very peaceful YHANI *Cushendall Hostel* (☎ *21 771344*) costs £8.25 and is on the Layde road that leads from Cushendall village up to Layde Old Church. Breakfast is available and you can hire bicycles for £6 per day.

B&Bs & Hotels The *Thornlea Hotel* (☎ *21 771223, 6 Coast Rd*) has singles/doubles costing £30/48 including breakfast. Next door, *Tros-Ben-Villa* (☎ *21 771130, 8 Coast Rd*) charges £20/35 for B&B. Farther up, off Coast Rd, *Mountain View* (☎ *21 771246, 1 Kilnadore Rd*) is cheaper, with beds costing £14/28. In the centre is *Riverside Guest House* (☎ *21 771655, 14 Mill St*), charging £18/32.

Places to Eat

Gillans Coffee Shop (*6 Mill St*) serves a great Ulster fry and snacks all day. On weekdays, *Thornlea Hotel* offers set lunch, high tea and à la carte in the evening. *Harry's Restaurant* (☎ *21 772022, 10 Mill St*) is very popular, offering good-value meals for lunch and dinner. Glenariff Forest Park has its own *Glenariff Tea House*, open for snacks daily from Easter to September. On the road to the park *Manor Lodge* (☎ *21 758221, 120 Glen Rd*) serves steaks and seafood.

Entertainment

On Friday and Sunday nights, tiny *Joe McCollam's* bar, also known as Johnny Joe's, is the place to go for traditional Irish music.

Getting There & Away

The buses serving Cushendall are the same as for Cushendun; see that section earlier for details.

CARNLOUGH

pop 1493

The good beach attracts holidaymakers, and there are many buildings made of the fine local limestone, commissioned to be built by the marquess of Londonderry in 1854. The limestone quarries were in use until the early 1960s, with the white stone bridge across the village carrying trains that brought the stone down to the harbour to be loaded on to ships for export.

The tourist office (☎ 28 885236) is in McKillop's store on Harbour Rd.

Places to Stay

Both *Bay View Caravan Park* (☎ 28 885685, 89 Largy Rd) and *Ruby Hill Caravan Park* (☎ 28 885692, 46 Largy Rd) have limited camping space and charge £4 per night.

Prosperous, solid *Londonderry Arms Hotel* (☎ 28 885255, 20 Harbour Rd) was built as a coaching inn by the marchioness of Londonderry in 1848. It was eventually inherited by a distant relation of hers, William Churchill, who sold it to the present owners. Singles/doubles cost £48/80, but there are special deals worth inquiring about.

Places to Eat

Londonderry Arms Hotel serves up locally caught fish, including lobster and wild salmon. *Arkle Bar* in the hotel, named by loyal followers of the Irish horse that won 27 of its 35 races before being put down in 1970, is decorated with photographs of the famous horse. *Glencloy Inn*, at the junction of Harbour Rd and Bridge St, serves bar snacks. *Harbour House Tea Rooms*, by the harbour, serves all-day breakfasts, teas and light meals until 8.30 pm.

DERRY & ANTRIM

Getting There & Away

Bus No 128 travels to and from Ballymena five times daily Monday to Saturday, with connections to Belfast. Bus No 162 between Cushendun and Larne stops at Carnlough.

See Getting There & Away in the Ballycastle section earlier in this chapter for information on the summertime Antrim Coaster bus.

GLENARM

pop 603

Glenarm (Gleann Arma), the oldest village in the glens, is 5km south of Carnlough and the first one you come to if you're travelling north from Belfast or Larne. The pavements are made from attractive black and white pebbling and many of the buildings are coated white from the limestone dust of the local quarries. In the glen stands **Glenarm Castle** dating from the early 17th century; it was remodelled in the 19th century and is privately owned.

Places to Stay & Eat

If you're coming from Carnlough, turn right at the crossroads for *Margaret's House* (☎ 28 841307, 10 Altmore St), which offers B&B costing £14 per person. *Mrs Dempsey* (☎ 28 841640, 35 The Cloney) charges £17 per person for B&B. *Drumnagreagh Hotel* (☎ 28 841651, 408 Coast Rd), singles/doubles cost £40/60.

McGeown's (22 Main St) features local seafood and opens for lunch and dinner as well as offering bar snacks. You can get a meal at the *Drumnagreagh Hotel,* too.

Getting There & Away

Bus No 162 runs between Larne and Cushendun, stopping at towns along the way.

See Getting There & Away in the Ballycastle section earlier in this chapter for information on the summertime Antrim Coaster bus.

LARNE

pop 17,580

Arriving from Scotland, Larne (Lutharna) offers a poor introduction to the spectacular Antrim coast and the rest of Northern Ireland. Conversely, if you've travelled down the coast, you might almost have forgotten the Troubles until the sectarian graffiti around Larne brings it back again. There's not too much reason for you to linger in Larne.

Orientation & Information

It's about a 15-minute walk from the ferry terminal to the town centre; take Fleet St on the right as you leave the terminal, then turn right again along Curran Rd, which becomes Main St and runs through the centre of town.

Inside the ferry terminal there's a small tourist information office with a helpful list of B&B phone numbers beside the phone booths. The main tourist office (☎ 28 260088) is in Narrow Gauge Rd. It opens 9 am to 5 pm on weekdays, October to Easter; 9 am to 5 pm Monday to Saturday, Easter to June and September; and 9 am to 5 pm Monday to Wednesday, 9 am to 6.30 pm on Thursday and Friday, and 9 am to 6 pm on Saturday, July and August. As you leave Larne town station, it's in the car park on the far side of the roundabout.

Things to See

Crumbling away at the end of a row of terraced housing, **Olderfleet Castle** is a fairly uninspiring example of a ruined 16th-century tower house; to get there from the ferry terminal, take Olderfleet Rd along the seafront and turn right following the signpost at the roundabout. More imposing is the 19th-century round **Chaine Memorial Tower**, north of the ferry terminal in Chaine Memorial Rd. It was built to commemorate James Chaine, an MP from 1855 to 1874. Chaine played an important role in getting Larne Harbour expanded to handle traffic with North America.

Heading along Curran Rd into town you'll pass two other reminders of Larne's American links. A **statue of a family group** commemorates the 52 people who emigrated to Boston from Larne on the *Friend's Goodwill* in 1717, while a **plaque** commemorates the arrival of the first

Americans into Larne during WWII in 1942.

Places to Stay

Camping The most convenient camp site, if you're just off a ferry or you want to stay near the terminal, is *Curran Caravan Park* (☎ 28 273797), five minutes from the harbour, on the left of Curran Rd, and reached by following the sign to the town centre. It costs £4.50 per night. One of Ireland's better little camp sites is at *Carnfunnock Country Park* (☎ 28 270541), nearly 5km north of town off the A2. It's a modest place but well run and pleasantly situated. A tent site costs £6.

B&Bs Closest to the harbour are a couple of B&Bs: *Manor Guesthouse* (☎ 28 273305, *Olderfleet Rd*), with singles/doubles costing £20/35, and *Bellevue* (☎ 28 270233, 35 *Olderfleet Rd*), with beds costing £15 per person. Also within walking distance of the harbour is the very comfortable *Seaview Guest House* (☎ 28 272438, 156 *Curran Rd*), which has rooms costing £20/35.

Hotels The *Curran Court Hotel* (☎ 28 275505, 84 *Curran Rd*), near the harbour and just past the camp site, charges £40/60 for singles/doubles. *Magheramorne House Hotel* (☎ 28 279444, 59 *Shore Rd*) is a classy Victorian establishment on the A2 south of Larne; rooms cost £40/72. *Highways Hotel* (☎ 28 272272, *Donaghy's Lane*), 1.5km from town, has rooms costing £47.50/69.

Places to Eat

The cafeteria-style *Captain's Kitchen* in the ferry terminal is a good fallback for hot and cold food at odd hours. Inexpensive places are at the harbour end of Main St. *Rumbles* (116 *Main St*) serves seafood, steaks and pasta dishes. It has a BYO licence and opens for lunch and dinner Tuesday to Saturday and on Sunday evening. *Carriages* (105 *Main St*) serves reasonable pizzas and kebabs in the evening. More typically Irish meals – meat-dependent and substantial – are available at the hotels.

Getting There & Away

Bus Bus No 156 is the regular service to and from Belfast. The earliest bus leaves the bus station (☎ 28 272345) on Circular Rd, without calling at the harbour, at 7.15 am, and the last one goes at 7.20 pm. It takes just over an hour and there are only three buses on Sunday. Bus No 162 to Cushendun, stopping at towns along the way, usually operates only from the bus station; late May to late September, it also operates twice daily via the harbour.

See Getting There & Away in the Ballycastle section earlier in this chapter for information on the summertime Antrim Coaster bus.

Train Larne has two stations: the main Larne town station (☎ 28 260604) for the town centre and Larne Harbour (the end of the line) for the ferries. The journey from Belfast Central takes about 50 minutes.

Boat P&O European Ferries occupies Larne's ferry terminal, beside a train station and bus stop, and with car hire and bureau de change facilities inside. P&O European Ferries handles the route from Larne to Cairnryan in Scotland; crossings take just over two hours.

For details of sailings contact the P&O European Ferries Travel Centre (☎ 28 274321), Passenger Terminal, Larne Harbour, BT40 1AQ. For more information, including fares, see the Sea section in the Getting There & Away chapter.

ISLANDMAGEE

A day trip to Islandmagee (Oileán Mhic Aodha) makes a pleasant excursion. The name is deceptive in that this is an 11 by 3km peninsula, not an island – but you get there by ferry from Larne. Close to the ferry landing point is the **Ballylumford Dolmen** in the front garden of a private home. Also at this northern end of the peninsula is **Brown's Bay**, which has a sandy beach. Open April to September, *Brown's Bay Caravan Park* (☎ 28 260088) has tent sites costing £7.

Taking the picturesque eastern coast road

DERRY & ANTRIM

(B150) brings you to **The Gobbins**: more than 2.5km of basalt cliffs with a path cut into the rock. During the 1641 rebellion, the garrison at Carrickfergus, seeking to revenge their fellow Protestants, massacred the Catholic inhabitants of the peninsula, throwing live and dead bodies over the cliffs.

Getting There & Away
The first Islandmagee ferries leave Larne at 7.30, 8 and 8.30 am, then on the hour until 3 pm, and then every half-hour until 5.30 pm; contact Larne Harbour Office (☎ 28 279221) for more details.

CARRICKFERGUS & AROUND
Carrickfergus (Carraig Fhearghais) is a commuter suburb just north of Belfast, noted for its wonderfully situated castle, overlooking the harbour where William III landed on 14 June 1690. There's a commemorative blue plaque on the site and a statue of the king on the seawards side of the castle. The town centre has some attractive 18th-century houses, and you can still trace a good part of the 17th-century city walls.

Orientation & Information
The train station is at the northern end of North St. Turn left outside the station and pass under North Gate; the castle is a five-minute walk downhill to the seafront. Ulsterbuses stop on Joymount Parade behind the town hall on the seafront.

The tourist information centre (☎ 93 366455) is on Antrim St inside the Heritage Plaza. It opens 9 am to 5 pm on weekdays, and 10 am to 6 pm on Saturday, April to September; plus noon to 6 pm on Sunday, July and August.

Carrickfergus Castle
Theatrically sited on a rocky promontory, commanding the entrance to Belfast Lough, this fine castle was built by John de Courcy soon after his 1177 invasion of Ulster. Besieged by King John in 1210 and Edward Bruce in 1315, and briefly captured by the French in 1760, the castle also witnessed an

attack on a British vessel in 1778 by the American John Paul Jones in the *Ranger* (the Americans won). The oldest part of the castle, going back to its Anglo-Norman origins, is the inner ward, which is enclosed by a high wall. The keep houses a museum telling the castle's history, and the site is dotted with life-size figures illustrating the castle's history and adding colour to what is undoubtedly Ireland's finest (and first) Norman castle.

The castle (☎ 93 351273) opens 10 am (2 pm on Sunday) to 6 pm daily, April to September; and 10 am (2 pm on Sunday) to 4 pm daily, the rest of the year. Admission costs £2.70/1.35; a joint ticket covering the Knight Ride as well costs £4.85/2.40.

Knight Ride
Inside the glistening, glassy Heritage Plaza on Antrim St is a smells-and-all ride through Carrickfergus' past. Seated in a giant knight's helmet hanging beneath a monorail you swing out over the atrium and then run back through time, catching quick glimpses of Mary Dunbar's haunted house and the hanging corpses of members of the 18th-century O'Haughan gang.

The Knight Ride (☎ 93 366455) opens 10 am (noon on Sunday) to 6 pm daily, April to September; and 10 am (noon on Sunday) to 5 pm daily, the rest of the year. Admission costs £2.70/1.35 (£4.85/2.40 for a combined visit to the castle).

St Nicholas' Church
The pillars in the nave date back to the church's establishment immediately after de Courcy's invasion of Ulster. Most of the rest dates to 17th-century restoration work, a particularly fine example of which is the Chichester memorial in the transept known as the Donegal aisle. It's probably the work of an English master mason who was influenced by the Renaissance style of northern Europe. Stained glass in the southern side and the nave's western end is 16th-century Irish work.

To gain admission call at or telephone the church office (☎ 93 360061), 3 Market Place, between 9.30 am and noon.

Andrew Jackson Centre

The parents of the 7th US president left Carrickfergus in the second half of the 18th century, hence the Andrew Jackson Centre (☎ 93 366455), a reconstructed dwelling of that era complete with fireside crane and earthen floor. It has displays on the life of Jackson, the Jackson family in Ulster and Ulster's connection with the USA.

Also here is the **US Rangers Centre**, with a small exhibition on the first US rangers, who were trained during WWII in Carrickfergus before heading for Europe.

The centre opens 10 am to 1 pm and 2 to 4 pm on weekdays, and 2 to 4 pm at the weekend, April and May; and 10 am to 1 pm and 2 to 6 pm on weekdays, and 2 to 6 pm at the weekend, June to September. Admission costs £1.50/75p. The centre is in Boneybefore, 3km north of Carrickfergus; there's a signposted right turn to the centre in Donaldson's Ave. The actual site of the ancestral home is indicated by a blue plaque just down the road from the centre. On weekdays you can get a bus to Downshire Rd, from where it's a short walk.

Places to Stay & Eat

Langsgarden (☎ 93 366369, 70 Scottish Quarter) offers B&B costing £19.50 per person. *Tramway House* (☎ 93 355639, 95 Irish Quarter South) charges £17 per person. *Dobbin's Inn Hotel* (☎ 93 351905, 6-8 High St) has been around for over three centuries and has a priest's hole and the original 16th-century fireplace to prove it; singles/doubles cost £46/66.

Café No 10 (10 West St) serves coffee, snacks and grills. From Monday to Saturday, *Courtyard Coffee House (38 Scottish Quarter)* serves light lunches as well as rich cakes; it has a smaller branch inside Carrickfergus Castle. The restaurant at *Dobbin's Inn Hotel* serves bar meals plus a set lunch and dinner.

Getting There & Away

Ulsterbus No 165 takes 15 minutes to Belfast's Laganside Bus Centre; bus No 163 takes 30 minutes. There are also regular daily trains from Belfast Central/Botanic Stations.

ANTRIM

pop 20,880

Antrim (Aontroim) is no more interesting than the rest of inland County Antrim. In 1649 the town was burned by General Monro, and in 1798 it resisted an attack by the United Irishmen. Modern Antrim town is dominated by its shopping centre, but there are a few older buildings, including the fine courthouse, which dates back to 1762.

Belfast International Airport is handy, only 6km to the south.

Information

The very helpful tourist office (☎ 94 465156), 16 High St, opens 9.30 am to 6 pm Monday to Saturday, May to September, and provides a free heritage trail guide. The Boardwalk Café (see Places to Stay & Eat, later) offers Internet access.

Things to See

In **Pogue's Entry**, a narrow alley at the end of Church St, a blue plaque marks the tiny, mud-floored home of Alexander Irvine (1863–1941), missionary and writer. His *My Lady of the Chimney Corner* tells the story of his mother's brave struggle to rear nine children in grinding poverty.

Antrim Castle Gardens, behind the courthouse, alongside Sixmilewater River, were originally laid out in the 17th century. Antrim Castle burned down many years ago but the gardens are open to the public.

A 10th-century **round tower**, 27m high, in Steeple Park about 1.5km north of town, is all that remains of a monastery that once stood on the site. The walls are more than 1m thick and the 10th-century dating is strong evidence for linking this and other towers with the Viking raids. Follow the signs for Steeple Industrial Estate, then for the Antrim Borough Council offices.

Places to Stay & Eat

It's best to avoid having to stay a night in Antrim if possible. B&Bs include *Brograni* (☎ 94 462484, 2 Steeple Green), which has rooms costing £17.50 per person, and *The Stables* (☎ 94 466943, 96 Milltown Rd),

DERRY & ANTRIM

with en suite singles/doubles costing £25/40. More B&Bs are found in nearby Crumlin, which is convenient for early-morning flight departures. The tourist office has a complete list.

The one-star *Deerpark Hotel* (☎ 94 462480, 71 Dublin Rd) charges £30/50 including breakfast.

Antrim is hardly filled with gourmet restaurants but for a light lunch you could try *Top of the Town* (77 Fountain St) or the *Boardwalk Café* (12 Market Square), which also has Internet access. *Pogues Tavern* (88 Church St) has bar snacks and live music at the weekend.

Entertainment
Clotworthy Arts Centre (☎ 94 428111) in Antrim Castle Gardens has a small theatre and hosts changing exhibitions. The gallery opens 9.30 am to 4.30 pm on weekdays, 9.30 am to 1 pm on Saturday, and 9.30 am to 9.30 pm on Sunday. Admission is free.

Getting There & Away
Bus Bus No 120 from Ballymena to Belfast stops in Antrim. There's also bus No 109 to Belfast via Lisburn.

Train Antrim is on the Derry or Portrush to Belfast (☎ 90 230671) train line. Trains to Belfast run 10 times daily.

BALLYMENA & AROUND
The predominantly Protestant town of Ballymena (An Baile Meánach) is the home turf of Ian Paisley, founder leader of the Free Presbyterian Church and the stridently anti-Catholic Democratic Unionist Party. The town council was the first in the North to fall under control of the Democratic Unionist Party in 1977, and voted unanimously to remove all mention of Darwin's theory of evolution from religious education in Ballymena's schools, for, as the mayor explained, 'If you believe you come from a monkey you'll act like a monkey'. The town is also the birthplace of the actor Liam Neeson, of *Schindler's List* and *Michael Collins* fame.

While Ballymena is a pleasant enough town, there's not much reason to linger. The tourist office (☎ 25 653663), 17 Bridge St, opens Monday to Saturday during the summer only. At other times contact Ballymena Borough Council (☎ 25 644111).

Arthur Cottage
The ancestors of Chester Alan Arthur, the 21st president of the USA, lived in a simple cottage about 6km north-west of Ballymena, near the village of Cullybackey. It opens to visitors 10.30 am to 5 pm on weekdays, and 10.30 am to 4 pm on Saturday, May to September. Interpreters in traditional costume demonstrate baking and quilting throughout June, July (except on the 12th) and August; call the tourist office for dates and times. Admission costs £1.10/55p. Take bus Nos 113 or 115 from Ballymena.

Gracehill
pop 681
In the mid-18th century many Protestant Moravians fled their homeland to escape religious persecution, and some of them settled in Gracehill (Baile Uí Chinnéide), 2km west of Ballymena, in a country not itself renowned for religious toleration. The Georgian architecture of their elegant village square includes a church (on the right as you enter the square) with separate entrances for men and women worshippers. If you'd like to see inside, visitors are welcome to services at 11 am on Sunday. Even the graveyard at the back of the church is laid out for men on the left and women on the right, with the numbered tombstones lying flat either side of the walkway! Man and woman alike, they're rapidly vanishing beneath a coating of moss and grass.

Bus No 127 from Ballymena stops at Gracehill. If you're driving, take the A42 past Ballymena's bus and train station; look for a brown sign with a church marked on it and take the turning to the left.

Places to Eat
Just over 6km east of Ballymena (turn after the Gracehill roundabout), *Galgorm Manor* (☎ 25 881001, 136 Fenaghy Rd) has the

best menu on offer in the area (Dundrum oysters, Donegal salmon, steamed chocolate pudding). It opens for lunch and dinner Monday to Saturday, and for dinner only on Sunday.

Getting There & Away
Bus Bus Nos 120, 149, 219 and 220 run south to Belfast, while bus Nos 115, 175 and 143 head north to Derry.

Train Ballymena is on the Derry or Portrush to Belfast (☎ 90 230671) line. Trains to Belfast run seven times daily.

LISBURN & AROUND
The small town of Lisburn (Lios na gCearrbhach), 12km south-west of Belfast, is most noted as the home of the excellent Irish Linen Centre, as well as the location of Long Kesh (aka the Maze) prison.

In the early 1600s the Crown gave the Conways a lease to settle Lisburn. In 1627 they were also given permission to hold a Tuesday market, which continues to this day. A disastrous fire in 1707 destroyed much of Lisburn but the 17th-century Market House survived to become an assembly hall in the 18th century.

In the 18th and 19th centuries Lisburn grew rich on the proceeds of the linen industry. The modern post office in Linenhall St stands on the site of the old Brown Linen Hall, where unbleached linen used to be sold. In the 18th century John Wesley came here several times, preaching in 1789 at Lisburn's first Methodist church in Market St.

The town seems to be undergoing a mini-boom at the moment, with various commercial and tourism developments either under way or on the drawing board. A new leisure complex is about to open and there are plans for an arts and performance centre, boat moorings along the Largan River, new department stores and apartments.

Information
The tourist office (☎ 92 660038) is in the same building as the Lisburn Museum, on Market Square. It opens 9.30 am to 5.30 pm (5 pm October to March) Monday to Saturday, and 2 to 5.30 pm (5 pm October to March) on Sunday, year round. It has a bureau de change and books accommodation.

Irish Linen Centre & Lisburn Museum
The Irish Linen Centre, inside what was once a drapery shop, is beside Lisburn Museum, itself housed in the fine old Market House, where brown linen was sold in the 18th century.

The museum on the ground floor has displays and exhibitions on the cultural and historic heritage of the region, while upstairs the Linen Centre's award-winning permanent Flax to Fabric exhibition details the fascinating history of the linen industry in Northern Ireland – on the eve of WWI Ulster was the largest linen-producing region in the world, employing some 75,000 people.

There are plenty of audiovisual and hands-on exhibits – you can try your hand at spinning flax and see weavers working on Jacquard looms – and the costume section contains some lovely work, including beautiful examples of damask linen and miniature linen tablecloths made for Queen Mary's dolls house.

Admission to Lisburn Museum is free but it costs £2.75/1.75 for the Irish Linen Centre. Both open the same hours as the tourist office.

Other Things to See
Just over 1km north-east of Lisburn is **Hilden Brewery** (☎ 92 663863), Ireland's oldest independent brewery. Housed in the courtyard of a former linen baron's mansion, the brewery opens 10 am to 5 pm Tuesday to Saturday and offers tours at 11.30 am and 2.30 pm. There's plenty of opportunity to sample a glass or two of real ale, and you can even stay and have a meal in the *Tap Room Restaurant*.

With your own transport you could also visit **Ballance House** (☎ 92 648492), 118A Lisburn Rd, Glenavy, 8.5km north-west of Lisburn. It's the birthplace of former New Zealand Prime Minister John Ballance

DERRY & ANTRIM

(1839–93). The farmhouse has been restored to its assumed appearance in 1850 and opens in the afternoon Tuesday, Saturday and Sunday, April to September. Admission costs £2/50p.

Places to Stay & Eat

You can visit Lisburn easily from Belfast but, if you do want to stay, there are a few B&Bs around. *Strathearn House (☎ 92 601661, 19 Antrim Rd)* charges £25/45 for singles/doubles. *Overdale House (☎ 92 672275, 150 Belsize Rd)* charges £22/33.

Probably the best place to eat is *Café Crommelin* in Lisburn Museum. It serves sandwiches and baguettes costing upwards of £2.35 and a wonderful selection of filled pastries. *Cocos (21 Railway St)* has breakfast and lunch specials (bacon-and-tomato croissant; smoked-salmon salad) and a good selection of coffees and cakes.

Getting There & Away

Bus Bus Nos 38, 51, 109, 523 and 525 leave frequently from Belfast's Europa Bus Centre. From Lisburn you can catch onwards buses to Hillsborough, Banbridge and Newry. For more information contact the local Ulsterbus office (☎ 92 662091), 2A Smithfield Square.

Train Lisburn is on the Belfast (☎ 90 230671) to Dublin train line. Trains to Belfast run frequently daily.

Counties Tyrone & Fermanagh

While Tyrone is the larger of these two counties (in fact, it is the biggest county in Northern Ireland), Fermanagh attracts more visitors, with its lakes, rivers and medieval sites. In Tyrone the peaty Sperrin Mountains offer good hiking opportunities. No trains operate in this part of Ireland, but Ulsterbus has services to most towns and the larger villages.

County Tyrone

The attractions of County Tyrone – forest parks, prehistoric sites, the lonely Sperrin Mountains – are sprinkled among some less-than-interesting towns in a way that makes it difficult for visitors to get a feel for the county as a whole. But it's worth the effort of trying to get to know Tyrone, for the county has an illustrious history, and its unspoiled countryside is ideal for those wanting to 'get away from it all'.

For centuries County Tyrone had been the territory of the O'Neills, until March 1603, when Hugh O'Neill, earl of Tyrone, finally submitted to the English at Mellifont. This marked the end of Gaelic Ireland. The English and Scottish Planters moved in, introducing linen in the 18th century. Many local people subsequently migrated to America, and there are still strong links with the USA today. The huge Ulster-American Folk Park near Omagh, sufficient reason in itself for visiting Tyrone, tells the story.

OMAGH
pop 17,280

Sadly, for a long time to come the market town of Omagh (An Óghmagh) will be remembered for the devastating car bomb which exploded in a street crowded with shoppers on 15 August 1998, killing 28 people and injuring 200. Planted by the breakaway republican group calling itself the 'Real IRA', the bomb was the worst sin-

Highlights

- Visit the Ulster-American Folk Park, one of the best museums in Ireland
- Explore the lonely Sperrin Mountains
- Discover the magic of Celtic and early-Christian archaeological sites around Lough Erne
- Admire the stately homes of Florence Court and Castle Coole near Enniskillen
- Go trout fishing, or just soak up the view, on Lough Erne

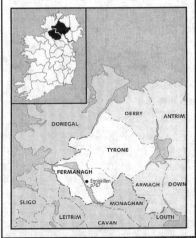

gle atrocity in the 30-year history of the Troubles. When Sinn Féin's president, Gerry Adams, denounced the bombing shortly afterwards and stated that 'the violence we have seen must be, for all of us now, a thing of the past, over, done with and gone', he was echoing the feelings of the vast majority. And the feeling of many is that the Omagh bomb has spelled the end of large-scale terrorist violence in Northern Ireland.

TYRONE & FERMANAGH

COUNTIES TYRONE & FERMANAGH

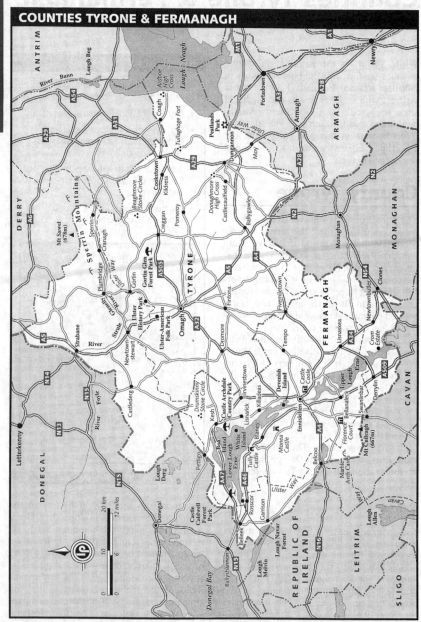

Situated at the confluence of the Cam-owen and Drumragh Rivers, which join to form the River Strule, Omagh serves as a useful base for the surrounding area. It also makes a good start or finish to a trip to the Sperrin Mountains or walking a section of the Ulster Way. There's a pleasantly rural independent hostel five minutes' drive out of town.

Information

From the confluence of the rivers, Market St and then High St lead west to the neoclassical 19th-century courthouse. The tourist office (☎ 82 247831) is in the Sperrin Centre at 1 Market St. It opens 9 am to 5 pm on weekdays and, from April to September, also on Saturday. There are several banks on High St, and the post office is next to the courthouse at No 7.

Places to Stay

Camping The closest camp site is at *Gortin Glen Caravan Park* (☎ 81 648108), 10km north-east of Omagh on the B48 Omagh to Gortin road. Tent sites cost £5; caravans cost £8. Bus Nos 92 and 213 (July and August only) stop nearby. The camp site is a few minutes from the Ulster Way, and campers get a discount at the Omagh Leisure Centre.

Hostels The spacious and welcoming IHH *Omagh Independent Hostel* (☎ 82 241973, 9A Waterworks Rd) is 4km north-east of town on the B48 to Gortin. From the bus station walk north on Mountjoy Rd, turn east at Killybrack Rd and follow the signs. The hostel is in a lovely rural setting and is awash with flowers in the summer. It has 28 beds (three of which are adapted for wheelchair users) and charges £6.50; the one private room costs the same per person. It rents bikes and opens year round. If you ring from the station, they'll come and pick you up.

B&Bs A standard B&B close to the centre and charging £16 per person is *Ardmore* (☎ 82 243381, 12 Tamlaght Rd). Go up High St from the tourist office, heading for

the courthouse at the top of the street, and take the left turn in front of the church into John St. Follow its continuation (James St) south and Tamlaght Rd is the second turning on the right.

Farther south is the *Four Winds* (☎ 82 243554, 63 Dromore Rd), which charges £18 per person for each of its three rooms. *Arleston House* (☎ 82 241719, 1 Arleston Park), off the Cookstown road to the east, has two rooms costing £18 per person.

Greenmount Lodge (☎ 82 841325, 58 Greenmount Rd) is a comfortable guesthouse with eight en suite singles/doubles costing £20/36. Dinner costs £13.

Hotels The only hotel in town is the two-star *Silverbirch Hotel* (☎ 82 242520, 5 Gortin Rd), which has 46 singles/doubles with bathroom costing £45/77 for B&B.

Places to Eat

Grant's of Omagh (29 George's St), round the corner from the courthouse, is recommended for reasonably priced meals and bar snacks. *McElroy's* (30 Castle St) is good for pub grub, too. *Restaurant Italiano* (☎ 82 259624, Campsie Rd) is a down-to-earth Italian-run place serving the real McCoy.

Carlton Coffee Lounge (31 High St), which is due to be revamped, serves excellent pastries, breads and decent coffee.

Out of town, on the A5 road to Newtownstewart about 1.5km from the Ulster-American Folk Park, *Mellon Country Inn* (☎ 81 661224, 134 Beltany Rd) has an excellent reputation. It opens Monday to Saturday and serves bar snacks, too.

Getting There & Away

Ulsterbus services connect Omagh with a number of towns in the North and in the Republic. Bus No 273 runs nine times daily (five on Sunday) to Belfast (1¾ hours) and seven times (five on Sunday) to Derry (1¼ hours). Bus No 274 runs seven times daily (four on Sunday) from Omagh to Dublin (three hours) via Monaghan (50 minutes) and Slane. A number of other buses leave Omagh for Dungannon (bus No 78) and

Enniskillen (bus No 94), where you change for Donegal, Killybegs and Glenties. Bus No 296 leaves Omagh for Cork (9¼ hours) once daily Monday to Saturday at 10.10 am and travels via Longford, Athlone and Cahir.

The bus station (☎ 82 242711), 3 Mountjoy Rd, is a short walk north of the town centre along Bridge St and across the River Strule.

Getting Around
Bicycles can be hired from the Omagh Independent Hostel (see Places to Stay earlier in this section) and from Conway Cycles (☎ 82 271258), 157 Lough Macrory Rd, 13.5km towards Cookstown, for £7/30 per day/week.

AROUND OMAGH
Ulster-American Folk Park
Situated 8km north-west of Omagh, the folk park (☎ 82 243292) is one of the best museums in Ireland and well worth a visit. Thousands of Ulster people left their country to forge a new life across the Atlantic in the 18th and 19th centuries; 200,000 emigrated in the 18th century alone. The American Declaration of Independence was signed by several Ulstermen, and the Exhibition Hall is able to offer many more examples of this transatlantic link.

The real appeal of the folk park, though, is the outdoor museum. The number of life-size exhibits is impressive: a forge, a weaver's cottage, a Presbyterian meeting house, a schoolhouse, a log cabin, a 19th-century Ulster street, an early street from western Pennsylvania, a typical one-room cottage dating from the period before the Potato Famine, and a ship and dockside gallery with reconstructed parts of an emigrants' ship.

Costumed guides and craftspeople are on hand to chat and explain the art of spinning, weaving, candle making and so on. There's almost too much to absorb in one visit, and at least half a day is needed to do the park justice.

It opens 11 am to 6.30 pm Monday to Saturday, and 11.30 am to 7 pm on Sunday

and public holidays, April to September; and 10.30 am to 5 pm on weekdays, the rest of the year. Admission costs £4/2.50 (families £10).

Bus No 97 to Strabane and Derry stops outside the park. On Tuesday and Thursday in July and August only, bus No 213 (the Sperrin Sprinter) leaves Omagh at 1.45 pm and stops at the park 20 minutes later, but you'd need to catch bus No 97 back.

Ulster History Park
The theme of this park is the story of settlements in Ireland from the Stone Age to the 17th-century Plantation. Full-scale models are on show of a Mesolithic encampment, Neolithic houses, a late-Bronze Age crannóg, a 12th-century church settlement complete with a stone round tower, and a Norman motte and bailey. There's also a reception building (☎ 81 648188) with a café, shop and audiovisual theatre and a model Plantation settlement from the 17th century. But the park is over-reliant on models and reconstructions, giving it a rather phoney feel.

It opens 10.30 am to 6.30 pm Monday to Saturday, and 11.30 am to 7 pm on Sunday, April to September; and 10.30 am to 5 pm on weekdays, the rest of the year. Admission costs £3.25/1.95 (families £10).

Ulster History Park is about 10km northeast of Omagh off the B48 road to Gortin. Bus No 92 between Omagh and Gortin stops outside Monday to Saturday.

Gortin Glen Forest Park
Over 400 hectares of Gortin Glen Forest form this park, mostly planted with conifers and containing a herd of Japanese sika deer as well as other wildlife. It's a park suited for cars and motorbikes, and a breathtaking 8km tarmac drive through the forest is the main way to get around. Near the main car park there are some wildlife enclosures, an indoor exhibit, a small nature trail and a café. An entry ticket costs £2.50 per car (£2 per motorbike) from the ranger on duty or from the ticket machine.

There's a manageable day's walk from Gortin Glen Forest Park to the Ulster-

American Folk Park along a section of the **Ulster Way**. The 16km trip is mostly over small roads, forest roads and tracks, and from the folk park bus No 97 can be caught back to Omagh. The last bus leaves the folk park at 7.30 pm. A leaflet and map entitled *The Ulster Way: North-West Section* is available from the Omagh tourist office.

Fishing
There is fishing along stretches of the three rivers around Omagh – mainly for brown and sea trout and salmon in season (April to mid-October). Permits, advice and information are available in Omagh from CA Anderson (☎ 82 242311), 64 Market St (the entrance is on Drumragh Ave).

SPERRIN MOUNTAINS
In the north-east of the county, the gentle contours of the Sperrin Mountains, some 64km from east to west, straddle the border with County Derry. The blanket bog and heather of the open moorland in the upper reaches contrast with the farmland and wooded valleys on the lower slopes. Wildlife is plentiful, and fishing for trout is a popular activity. The area is also littered with thousands of standing stones and chambered graves. The **Beaghmore Stone Circles**, on the south-eastern fringe of the mountains and signposted off the main A505 between Omagh and Cookstown, consist of seven stone circles (the stones are less than 1m high) and a dozen or so stone alignments and burial cairns.

The mountains reach their highest point at Mt Sawel (678m) just behind the **Sperrin Heritage Centre** (☎ 81 648142), 274 Glenelly Rd, Cranagh. In the centre, computer presentations and other displays are devoted to the historical, social and ecological aspects of the region. Gold has been found in the mountains, and part of the exhibition is devoted to it. You can even try your luck at prospecting in a nearby stream.

The centre opens 11 am to 6 pm on weekdays, 11.30 am to 6 pm on Saturday, and 2 to 7 pm on Sunday, March to October. There's a restaurant and café in the centre.

To get there from Omagh, follow the B48 north-east through Gortin to Plumbridge. From there it's about 13km east on the B47 to Cranagh. Buses from Omagh go only as far as Plumbridge.

While the Sperrin Heritage Centre can be easily reached from Cookstown via the B162 and B47, **An Creagán Visitor Centre** (☎ 80 761112) in Creggan is closer, about 20km to the west of Cookstown on the A505. It has an interpretive exhibition, rambling and cycling routes, bikes for rent and a licensed restaurant. The centre opens from 11 am to 6.30 pm daily, April to September; and 11 am to 4.30 pm on weekdays, the rest of the year.

If you're thinking of **walking** up Mt Sawel, inquire at the Sperrin Heritage Centre about the best route to take. The climb is easy, but some farmers are more accommodating than others when hikers cross their land. The Ulster Way comes in this direction, and it could be joined at Leagh's Bridge 6km away. This point is roughly halfway along the 55km Dungiven (County Derry) to Gortin section of the trail. Another outdoor trip through the Sperrins is on horseback. Edergole Riding Centre (☎ 86 762924), 70 Moneymore Rd, Cookstown, is a **horse-riding** school that organises three-day trekking trips through the mountains, or hourly hire costing about £8.

COOKSTOWN
pop 10,470
At one point Cookstown (An Chorr Chríochach) represented Northern Ireland at its most forbidding. The town, founded in 1609 by Planter Alan Cooke, has a wide, 2.5km-long main street with Catholics living at one end and Protestants at the other. Until recently, two heavily guarded checkpoints, nicknamed the 'daleks', stood at either end. Things have relaxed somewhat but the town remains a fairly uninspiring place (its great advantage, says the tourist literature, is convenient parking).

Information
The tourist office (☎ 86 766727), 48 Molesworth St, opens 9 am to 5 pm (6 pm on

TYRONE & FERMANAGH

Like Mother, Like Daughter

Bernadette Devlin was born at the Catholic end of Cookstown in 1947. As a student she became involved in the civil rights movement, and was elected from the Mid-Ulster constituency to Westminster in 1969 as the youngest ever MP.

She was imprisoned for her part in the 1969 Bogside confrontation in Derry, and after Bloody Sunday in 1972 her notoriety reached its peak when she physically attacked the British home secretary in the House of Commons.

After withdrawing from parliamentary politics, Bernadette McAliskey, as she became known, worked on issues of human rights and social justice.

When an IRA mortar bomb was defused outside Osnabruck barracks in Germany in June 1996, there were few clues to indicate who was responsible. Then later the same year the German police applied to extradite Roisin McAliskey to face charges.

The daughter of Bernadette McAliskey, Roisin was no stranger to controversy. Her staunchly nationalist family had been attacked in their Cookstown home by a Protestant assassination squad in 1981, an attack which left her mother partially disabled. Roisin herself had been filmed helping to carry the coffin of a leading republican.

At the time of her arrest Roisin was pregnant. Despite this she was held as a Category A prisoner in a jail designed for men. After determined protest, her security rating was eventually reduced and she was moved to Holloway and then into a prison hospital, where she gave birth to a daughter.

It remains to be seen whether the fingerprint evidence that the German police claim to have can justify the charges against McAliskey.

Tuesday and Thursday in July and August) on weekdays, and 10 am to 4 pm on Saturday, Easter to September; and 9 am to 5 pm on weekdays, the rest of the year.

Places to Stay & Eat

Drum Manor Forest Park (☎ 87 759664), a pleasant place 4km west of Cookstown on the A505 road, with a couple of lakes, a butterfly farm and arboretum, has 30 sites for caravans and campervans only (£6 to £9 per night).

Central Inn (☎ 86 762255, 27 William St) offers B&B costing £18 per person. **Edergole** (☎ 86 762924, 70 Moneymore Rd) costs £20 per person and has a horse-riding school. Both B&Bs are open year round.

The upmarket 53-room **Glenavon House Hotel** (☎ 86 764949, 52 Drum Rd) offers B&B costing £55/90 in singles/doubles. At the cheaper **Greenvale** (☎ 86 762243, 57 Drum Rd) nearby, rooms cost £35/55.

Gaslight (40 Loy St) is the best bet for pub food. **Red Rose Café** (86 Chapel St) serves decent steaks and salads in the evening and opens for Sunday lunch. A favourite lunch spot (chicken curry; vegetarian bakes) among locals is the **Courtyard** (56A William St). Lunch and dinner are available at the hotels mentioned above, too.

Getting There & Away

Bus No 110 connects Cookstown eight to nine times daily (three times on Sunday) with Belfast (1¾ hours) via Antrim. Bus No 278 runs once or twice daily Monday to Saturday to Dungannon (20 minutes), Armagh (50 minutes) and, in the Republic, Monaghan (1½ hours) and Dublin (four hours). Bus No 80 shuttles regularly between Cookstown and Dungannon, where you can connect with bus No 273 to Belfast, Omagh or Derry. Bus No 89 makes three to five daily trips to Coagh from Monday to Saturday.

The bus station (☎ 86 766440), on Molesworth St near the tourist office, opens from 9 to 11 am and 1.30 to 5.30 pm on weekdays.

AROUND COOKSTOWN

No public transport goes directly to the following sights, though buses do pass close by. For bus numbers, times and fares check with the bus station in Cookstown (☎ 86 766440).

Wellbrook Beetling Mill

Beetling, the final stage in the making of linen, is when the cloth is beaten with wooden hammers, or beetles, to give it a smooth sheen. There were once six such mills at Wellbrook. The hammers were driven by water, and one of the mills (☎ 86 751735) is maintained by the National Trust and can be seen in operation. It was literally deafening for those employed here.

The beetling mill opens 2 to 6 pm Wednesday to Monday, July and August; and 2 to 6 pm on Saturday, Sunday and bank holidays; April to June and September. Admission costs £1.80/1. Take the A505 Omagh road 5km west to Kildress and turn right at the church; it's about 1km from there.

Tullaghoge Fort

This hill fort was the burial ground of the O'Hagans, chief justices of early Ireland, and the coronation place of the O'Neills as kings of Ulster in the 11th century. A map dated 1601 marks the spot on the hillside to the south-east where the stone coronation chair stood. The following year the chair was destroyed by General Mountjoy while in pursuit of Hugh O'Neill, the last of the clan to be crowned.

To reach Tullaghoge, leave Cookstown on the A29 Dungannon road south then turn left onto the B520; the fort is 4km south-east of Cookstown.

Ardboe High Cross

The 10th-century Ardboe (Ard Bo; the 'd' is not pronounced) high cross stands 5.5m high in front of a 6th-century monastery site, now housing the ruins of a 17th-century church. With Lough Neagh – the largest lake in Ireland or Britain – in the background, it should be more dramatic than it is. The cross is one of the best preserved in Ulster, with the eastern face showing Old Testament scenes and the western side New Testament ones. On the eastern side try to make out Adam and Eve, the sacrifice of Isaac, Daniel and the lions, the Burning Fiery Furnace, a bishop with people around him, and Christ in glory. The New Testament side has the Magi, the miracle at Cana, the miracle of the loaves and fishes, the entry into Jerusalem, the arrest of Christ and the crucifixion. A lot easier to decipher are some of the 18th-century tombstones in the churchyard.

Ardboe is 16km east of Cookstown on the shore of Lough Neagh. To get there take the B73 through Coagh and turn south just before Newtown Trench.

DUNGANNON
pop 9420

Until 1602, when the castle and town were burned to prevent them falling into the hands of the English, Dungannon (Dún Geanainn) was one of the chief seats of the O'Neill family. Plantation of English and Scottish settlers took place in the 17th and 18th centuries.

In 1969 the town entered the history books when the Civil Rights Association, formed a year earlier to protest against the rampant social and political inequalities suffered by Catholics in Northern Ireland, organised its first march from Coalisland south-west to Dungannon. The crowd of 4000 was met by a police cordon outside the town and, although there was no serious violence, it was the beginning of a new era.

Information

The local tourist office – the so-called Killymaddy Tourist Amenity Centre (☎ 87 767259) – is inconveniently located some 10km south-west of Dungannon on the A4 Ballygawley road. It opens year round. In town you might be able to pick up a few brochures at the council office (☎ 87 725311) in Circular Rd next door to the large Dungannon Leisure Centre. The office opens from 9 am to 1 pm and 2 to 5 pm on weekdays.

The Heritage Centre (☎ 87 724187), 26 Market Square, holds records relating to Tyrone and Fermanagh.

You'll find several banks and the post office in the centre on Market Square.

Tyrone Crystal

At the Tyrone Crystal factory (☎ 87 725335), just north-east of town, tours cover the different stages in the production of crystal, starting with a visit to the furnace where the molten glass is prepared and then hand-blown. The glass pieces are then checked for faults, bevelled, marked, cut and polished.

The showroom contains examples of all the crystal, including slightly imperfect pieces that do not bear the Tyrone Crystal insignia but cost about 25% less.

The tour costs £2, which you get back if you buy something. The factory opens 9.30 am to 3.30 pm Monday to Saturday, April to October; and 9.30 am to 3.30 pm on weekdays, the rest of the year. To get there take the A45 towards Coalisland for about 2.5km – it is clearly signposted – or catch bus No 80 heading for Cookstown.

Places to Stay

Camping The *Killymaddy Tourist Amenity Centre* (see Information, earlier in this section) has a camp site with full facilities which costs £8/6 for caravans/tents. The entrance to Parkanaur Forest Park is about 3km from here.

Dungannon Park (☎ 87 727327, Moy Rd) is in a quiet location, has good facilities and costs the same. To get there, take the A29 south towards Armagh for 2.5km and turn left (west) at the signpost.

B&Bs & Hotels The *Mikora Lodge* (☎ 87 767171, 16 Thornhill Rd) offers B&B costing £18 per person. *Mrs Currie* (☎ 87 723156, 225 Ballynakelly Rd) has rooms costing £16 per person. *Grange Lodge* (☎ 87 784212, 7 Grange Rd), south-east of Dungannon towards Moy, is a guest-

house where B&B in singles/doubles costs £49/69.

The two-star *Inn on the Park* (☎ 87 255151, Moy Rd) is a small hotel with 13 en suite rooms costing £45/70.

Places to Eat

Just down from Market Square on the corner of Scotch and George Sts, the *Northland Arms* serves pub food and set meals, as does the *Fort (Scotch St)*. *Viscounts Great Food Hall (10 Northland Row)*, in a converted church, offers brunch, a carvery lunch and à la carte dinners. *Number 15 (15 Church St)*, a café-restaurant in Murray Richardson's bookshop, has a salad bar and lunches costing less than £5 as well as homemade scones and cakes. The restaurant at *Inn on the Park* serves decent steaks and fish.

Getting There & Away

Bus No 80 shuttles regularly between Dungannon and Cookstown (20 minutes) to the north. The No 278 service runs once or twice daily Monday to Saturday south to Armagh (30 minutes) and, in the Irish Republic, to Monaghan (one hour) and Dublin (3½ hours). The journey between Dungannon and Belfast (50 minutes) or Enniskillen (1½ hours) is possible on bus No 261 up to 10 times daily (five on Sunday). Bus No 273 links Dungannon with Belfast, Omagh and Derry up to eight times daily (four on Sunday).

The bus station (☎ 87 722251) is at the bottom of Scotch St, over the bridge and to the left.

AROUND DUNGANNON

See also the Around Armagh section in the Counties Down & Armagh chapter for details of local places of interest.

Peatlands Park

Peatlands Park Visitor Centre (☎ 38 851102) has an informative display about peat, aimed at a young audience. The bog garden is worth a visit if only to familiarise yourself with the sundew, one of two carnivorous plants indigenous to Ireland. It's a tiny thing, easily missed. Pitcher plants also thrive in the garden, but these were introduced into Ireland over a century ago from Canada. Also in the park are two lakes, a small forest and an orchard.

An open-top, narrow-gauge railway, once used for transporting peat, does a 15-minute circuit of the park for children. From Easter to the end of September trains run from 2 to 6 pm Saturday and Sunday (daily in July and August) for 70/30p. The visitor centre has the same hours.

To get to Peatlands Park, which is at The Birches some 13km south-east of Dungannon, take Exit 13 off the M1 motorway heading towards Belfast.

Donaghmore High Cross

The cross is a hybrid, being made of the base and shaft of one cross and the head and part of the shaft of another. The join is clearly visible. The carved biblical scenes are similar to those on the Ardboe Cross. On the eastern side are the angel and shepherds, the adoration of the Magi, the miracle at Cana, the miracle of the loaves and fishes, and the arrest of Christ and the crucifixion. On the western side are Adam and Eve, Cain and Abel, and Abraham and Isaac. The nearby heritage centre (☎ 87 767039), based in a converted 19th-century school, opens 9 am to 5 pm on weekdays, year round; plus 11 am to 4 pm on Saturday, May to August.

The cross is 8km north-west of Dungannon on the B43 road to Pomeroy, easily spotted at a road junction in the village of Donaghmore.

Castlecaulfield

Not a castle as such but the remains of what was once a substantial Jacobean house, Castlecaulfield was built in the early 17th century by Sir Toby Caulfield on the site of an earlier fort belonging to the O'Donnellys. Over the gatehouse, the Caulfield coat of arms can be made out, and this survived the O'Donnellys' act of revenge in 1641 when the house was burned down. The house was rebuilt and, in 1767, hosted a church service by John Wesley, the founder of Methodism.

To get to Castlecaulfield, take the A4 west out of Dungannon and after about 6km a small road is signposted to the right.

Parkanaur Forest Park

About 1.5km from Castlecaulfield, an oak forest is being developed on what was once the Burgess family estate. The Victorian dwelling is now used as a training centre for the disabled. The old farm buildings display farm and forest machinery, and there are some short nature trails. The park has four colour-coded walking trails.

The white fallow deer in the park are descended from the oldest deer herd in Ireland, going back to 1595, when a doe and a hart, a gift from Elizabeth I to her goddaughter, were raised at Mallow Castle. The park brought five deer from Mallow in 1978.

Grant Ancestral House

Ulysses S Grant led Union forces to victory in the American Civil War and was later elected the 18th US president for two terms (1869–77). The home of his mother's family has been restored in the style of a typical 19th-century Irish small farm. The furniture is not authentic, but the original field plan of this 4-hectare farm is still there, together with various old farming implements.

The visitor centre has an exhibition and café and opens noon to 5 pm Monday to Saturday, and 2 to 6 pm on Sunday, April to September. Admission costs £1/50p. The site is 20km west of Dungannon. Take the A4 west and turn left at the sign just before the village of Ballygawley.

County Fermanagh

The River Erne wends its way through County Fermanagh – one of the smallest counties in Ireland – into a lake that is 80km long. The point at which Lough Erne constricts is the town of Enniskillen, in the centre of Fermanagh and a good base for exploration. The town's efficient tourist office serves the whole county.

Lower Lough Erne, the more developed of the lake's 'halves', attracts people for varying reasons: the fishing is superb; there are good facilities for water sports outside Enniskillen; and Devenish and White Islands have fine ecclesiastical remains. A third island, Boa, has a cemetery with a unique stone statue dating back around 2000 years.

Early-Christian missionaries settled in Fermanagh, but the religion penetrated the local pagan culture slowly. Viking and Norman invaders couldn't subdue the region and even the Tudors were unable to do so until after 1600, when Enniskillen finally fell to the English. Planters then moved in and quickly established a series of castles around Lough Erne. The town of Enniskillen was transformed into a centre of colonial power, and its strategic importance to the British led to its unparalleled boast of possessing two royal regiments.

At the time of Partition, Fermanagh was reluctantly drawn into Northern Ireland – despite the fact that most of its people were Catholic – and its nationalist spirit has not diminished. British Parliament does not like to be reminded that one of its members was allowed to starve himself to death in an effort to establish political recognition for IRA prisoners. Bobby Sands was elected as MP for Fermanagh and South Tyrone in the spring of 1981, and he died 66 days after beginning his fast, without ever taking up his seat in Westminster.

ENNISKILLEN
pop 11,440

The town of Enniskillen (Inis Ceithleann) is a useful centre for activities on Upper and Lower Lough Erne and the antiquities around them. Oscar Wilde and Samuel Beckett were both pupils at the Portora Royal School north-west of the centre. The town is predominantly Catholic, close to the border, and lacks the dourness of some of the North's other towns.

In November 1987 an IRA bomb exploded at a Remembrance Day service in Enniskillen, killing 11 innocent people.

Orientation & Information

The town centre is on an island in the waterway connecting the upper and lower loughs. The main street changes name several times, but the clock tower marks the centre. The other principal thoroughfare through town is Wellington Rd, which runs south of and parallel to the main street.

The helpful, well-run Fermanagh Tourist Information Centre (☎ 66 323110), just south of Wellington Rd, opens 9 am to 5.30 pm (6.30 pm in July and August) on weekdays, 10 am to 6 pm on Saturday, and 11 am to 5 pm on Sunday, Easter to September; and 9 am to 5.30 pm on weekdays, the rest of the year.

The Bank of Ireland has a branch on Townhall St open 9.30 am to 4.30 pm on weekdays. You can also change money at the tourist office and at the post office, which is on East Bridge St and opens from 9.30 am to 5.30 pm on weekdays, and from 9.30 am to 12.30 pm on Saturday.

Enniskillen Castle & Museums

The Fermanagh History and Heritage Centre and the Regimental Museum of the Royal Inniskilling Fusiliers are both inside the castle (☎ 66 325000).

The heritage centre occupies the central keep and contains artefacts on local farming and manufacturing. The Regimental Museum, in the turreted building known as the **Watergate**, is crammed full of medals, guns and uniforms of both the fusiliers and the dragoon guards, Enniskillen's other regiment. The centre and museum open 10 am to 5 pm Tuesday to Friday, and 2 to 5 pm on Saturday and Monday (plus Sunday in July and August), May to September; and 2 to 5 pm on Monday, and 10 am to 5 pm Tuesday to Friday, the rest of the year. Admission costs £2/1 (students £1, families £5).

Cole's Monument

The monument, in Forthill Park at the eastern end of town, was named after the 1st earl of Enniskillen's son, Galbraith Lowry Cole (1772–1842), one of Wellington's generals. The 108 steps inside this Doric column can be climbed for rewarding views of

TYRONE & FERMANAGH

ENNISKILLEN

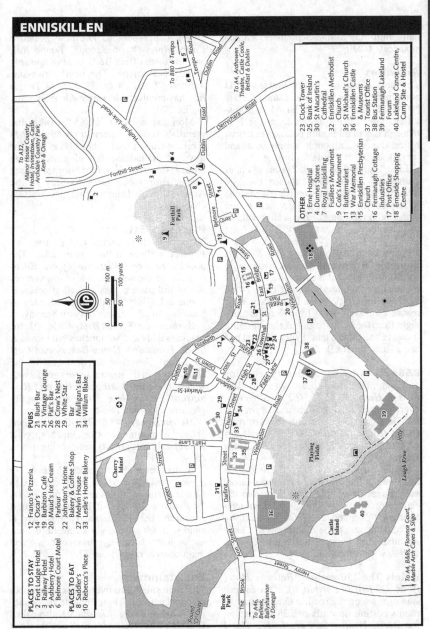

PLACES TO STAY
2 Fort Lodge Hotel
3 Railway Hotel
5 Ashberry Hotel
6 Belmore Court Motel

PLACES TO EAT
8 Saddler's
10 Rebecca's Place
12 Franco's Pizzeria
14 Oscar's
19 Barbizon Café
20 Maud's Ice Cream
22 Parlour's Home
   Bakery & Coffee Shop
27 Melvin House
33 Leslie's Home Bakery

PUBS
21 Bush Bar
24 Vintage Lounge
28 Pat's Bar
29 Crow's Nest
29 White Star
   Bar
31 Mulligan's Bar
34 William Blake

OTHER
1 Erne Hospital
4 Dunnes Stores
7 Royal Inniskilling
   Fusiliers Monument
9 Cole's Monument
11 Buttermarket
13 War Memorial
15 Enniskillen Presbyterian
   Church
16 Fermanagh Cottage
   Industries
17 Post Office
18 Erneside Shopping
   Centre
23 Clock Tower
25 Bank of Ireland
30 St Macartin's
   Cathedral
32 Enniskillen Methodist
   Church
35 St Michael's Church
36 Enniskillen Castle
   & Museums
37 Tourist Office
38 Bus Station
39 Fermanagh Lakeland
   Forum
40 Lakeland Canoe Centre,
   Camp Site & Hostel

the surrounding area. It opens 2 to 6 pm daily, mid-May to mid-September. Admission costs 60/30p.

Activities

The best place for hiring **water sports** equipment is the Lakeland Canoe Centre (☎ 66 324250) on Castle Island in Enniskillen. Free ferries depart from the Fermanagh Lakeland Forum behind the tourist office. Canoes, sailboards, sailing boats and jet skis are all available for hire.

Erne Tours (☎ 66 322882) runs 1¾ hour **cruises** of Lough Erne aboard the MV *Kestrel* with a stop at Devenish Island, June to September. For more information, see Cruising in the Lough Erne section later in this chapter.

Places to Stay

Camping & Hostels There's hostel-style accommodation and a camp site open year round at the *Lakeland Canoe Centre* (☎ 66 324250) on Castle Island, which can be reached by ferry (free) from 9 am to midnight from the Fermanagh Lakeland Forum. It costs £8 to pitch a tent, £9 for a hostel bed and £10.50 for B&B.

B&Bs Places can be found on the outskirts of town, west along the A4 (Sligo Rd). *Rossole House* (☎ 66 323462, 85 Sligo Rd), overlooking a small lake, costs £18 per person. Just a little farther out, the *Ashwood Guest House* (☎ 66 323019) is well appointed, spacious and charges £25/36 for singles/doubles.

At the other side of town B&Bs can be found along the B80 road to Tempo. *Lackaboy Farm* (☎ 66 322488), 1km from the centre, has rooms costing £30/52. *Drumcoo House* (☎ 66 326672, 32 Cherryville), by the roundabout on the road north to Castle Archdale and Omagh, has rooms costing £22/40 with bathroom.

Hotels The 150-year-old *Railway Hotel* (☎ 66 322084, 34 Forthill St), at the eastern side of town on the road to Omagh, has 19 rooms costing upwards of £28 per person for B&B. Nearby is *Fort Lodge Hotel* (☎ 66 323275, 72 Forthill St), where rooms cost £30 per person. The new *Belmore Court Motel* (☎ 66 326633, Tempo Rd), east of town, offers B&B costing upwards of £23 per person. The nearby two-star *Ashberry Hotel* (☎ 66 320333, 14 Tempo Rd) has comfortable singles/doubles costing £45/70.

More expensive at £62/85 for B&B, the grand, 44-room *Killyhevlin* (☎ 66 323481) is on the Dublin road. About 11km north of town in Killadeas, the elegant *Manor House Country Hotel* overlooks Lower Lough Erne (see Places to Stay in the Around Lough Erne section later in this chapter).

Places to Eat

For sandwiches, salads and pastries try *Rebecca's Place* in the Buttermarket. The popular *Franco's Pizzeria* (*Queen Elizabeth Rd*) on the northern side of town serves pizzas and pasta dishes as well as seafood. It opens for lunch and dinner Monday to Saturday and for dinner only on Sunday.

Barbizon Café (*East Bridge St*) is OK for snacks, salads and set lunches but closes at 6 pm. *Johnston's Home Bakery and Coffee Shop* (*Townhall St*), just east of the clock tower in the centre, serves good sandwiches and pies. *Mulligan's Bar and Restaurant* (*33 Darling St*) is a thoroughly pleasant spot for a bite to eat and a pint.

Melvin House (☎ 66 322040, 1 Townhall St) serves morning coffee, lunch specials (roast lamb; fresh trout) and evening meals, daily.

By the roundabout, *Saddler's* (*Belmore St*) is a steakhouse where meals cost £10 to £13; it opens daily. *Oscar's* (☎ 66 327037, 29 Belmore St), one of Enniskillen's best restaurants both for food and atmosphere, is nearby. It has quite a varied menu, including at least three vegetarian options, and main courses range from £7.95 to £12.95.

Entertainment

The main street through town has a number of popular pubs. These include the Victorian *William Blake* (*Church St*), also called Blake's of the Hollow, which has music at the weekend; *Crow's Nest (12 High St)*, which has music most evenings (traditional Irish sessions on Monday in summer); *Vintage Lounge (Townhall St)*; *Bush Bar (East Bridge St)*, with music (including Irish sessions) on Monday, Wednesday, Friday and Saturday; and *Pat's Bar*, next to Melvin House, which occasionally has music at night.

During the year just about every kind of performance takes place at the *Ardhowen Theatre (☎ 66 325440)*, about 2km south of the town centre on the Dublin road (A4). The programme includes concerts, local amateur and professional drama and musical productions, pantomime and films.

Shopping

The best place for shopping in Enniskillen is the Buttermarket (☎ 66 324499), off Queen Elizabeth Rd. The refurbished buildings of the old marketplace house a variety of craft shops making and selling their wares; ceramics and jewellery are the best buys. Another good outlet for crafts is Fermanagh Cottage Industries next to the Presbyterian church on East Bridge St. The Erneside Centre is a modern complex of shops, cafés and a supermarket across the waterway south of Wellington Rd.

Getting There & Away

Ulsterbus No 261 runs up to 10 times daily (five on Sunday) via Dungannon to Belfast (two hours). Bus No 296 runs to Derry (2½ hours) via Omagh (one hour) and, in the other direction, to Cork (8¼ hours) via Athlone (three hours). The No 262 service runs to Sligo (1½ hours), Ballina (1¼ hours) and Westport (4½ hours). There's also a service from Enniskillen to Bundoran via Belleek. Bus Éireann's bus No 30 between Dublin (three hours) and Donegal (1¼ hours) calls at Enniskillen four times daily (three times on Sunday).

The bus station (☎ 66 322633) is opposite the tourist office on Shore Rd.

Getting Around

Bicycles can be hired at the Lakeland Canoe Centre (☎ 66 324250) for £10 per day.

AROUND ENNISKILLEN
Sheelin Antique Lace Museum

Just over 6km south-west of Enniskillen in the village of Bellanaleck, the small Sheelin Antique Lace Museum (☎ 66 348052) houses a beautiful collection of Irish lace dating from 1850 to 1900. Lace-making was a particularly important industry in Fermanagh and the neighbouring counties both before and after the Famine. With trade and agriculture depressed, it was seen as a way of providing employment for women and of relieving poverty. Prior to WWI there were at least 10 lace schools in County Fermanagh. The museum has linen, lace and oil lamps for sale. Next to the museum, the 200-year-old thatched Sheelin Restaurant offers lunches, bar snacks and evening meals.

Castle Coole

This mansion (☎ 66 322690) designed by James Wyatt ranks as probably the purest expression of late-18th-century neoclassical architecture in Ireland. The house was completed in 1798. Over the following two centuries the Portland stone exterior absorbed water to the point that the walls started to crumble.

The National Trust embarked on an expensive rebuilding of the outside walls and an extensive redecoration of the interior. The result is that now the house displays the pristine elegance of its original conception. The austerity of the design borders on the sterile; the obsession with symmetry is almost neurotic; and the guided tour takes in many examples of form triumphing over substance: fake doors balancing real ones, hollow columns painted to resemble marble ones, keyhole covers on doors that have no keyholes.

The tour first visits the male sanctuary of the library where, as the guide points out, once locked the doors could be opened from the inside only. Most of the furniture is original, and the curtain rail is typical of the extravagance of the 2nd earl of Belmore, who decorated the house. The 1st earl spent so much money having the place built that he had nothing left for decorations.

TYRONE & FERMANAGH

The castle is in a 600-hectare landscaped demesne and its lake is home to a colony of greylag geese.

The castle opens 1 to 6 pm Friday to Wednesday, May to August; 1 to 6 pm at the weekend and on public holidays, April and September; and 1 to 6 pm daily, Easter. Admission costs £2.80/1.40 (families £7). Castle Coole is on the Dublin road (A4), 2.5km south-east of Enniskillen.

Florence Court

This Palladian mansion (☎ 66 348249) is named after the wife of John Cole, who settled in the area in the early 18th century. His son built the present central block and the wings were added by his grandson, although the architect is unknown. The house was acquired by the National Trust in the 1950s and partly rebuilt after a fire in 1955. It's said that every Irish yew tree has its origin from one in the garden of Florence Court.

Unlike Castle Coole, Florence Court has a lived-in feel to it, and despite the fire much of the original rococo plasterwork remains – the staircase is the best example of it.

In the grounds there is a walled garden and a forest park which has a number of walking trails; one of the trails leads to the top of Mt Cuilcagh (667m).

Florence Court opens 1 to 6 pm Wednesday to Monday, May to August; 1 to 6 pm at the weekend and on public holidays, April and September; and 1 to 6 pm daily, Easter. Admission costs £2.80/1.40 (families £7). The house is almost 13km southwest of Enniskillen; take the A4 Sligo road and turn left onto the A32 Swanlinbar road.

Marble Arch Caves

The extensive Marble Arch Caves (☎ 66 348855) are very popular and very commercialised; it's wise to phone ahead and book on the 1½ hour tour. The caves open from 10.30 am daily, mid-March to September; the last tour is at 4.30 pm. The cost is £6/3 (students £4, families £14) and the tour starts with a boat trip on the river running through the caves.

During the summer there are occasional free guided walks through the surrounding limestone hills conducted by the Department of the Environment. Inquire at the tourist office in Enniskillen or contact the Nature Reserve Office (☎ 68 621588) at Castle Archdale Country Park in Lisnarick.

The Marble Arch Caves are 16km southwest of Enniskillen near the border. They are reached via the A4 (Sligo road) and the A32 (Swanlinbar road). The site is well signposted.

LOUGH ERNE

Stretching for 80km, Lough Erne is made up of two sections: the Upper Lough in the south and the Lower Lough in the north. The loughs are joined by the River Erne, which begins its journey in County Cavan and flows out to Donegal Bay west of Ballyshannon. The lakes have numerous islands, many containing Celtic and early-Christian archaeological sites (see the Around Lough Erne section later in this chapter). Coarse and game fish are plentiful, and birdlife, especially on Upper Lough Erne, is abundant.

Fishing

The lakes of Fermanagh are renowned for coarse fishing, but trout are found in the northern part of Lower Lough Erne, close to Boa Island and Kesh Bay. (Lough Melvin, near the town of Garrison, is home to the Gillaroo trout.) The Lough Erne trout fishing season runs from the beginning of March to the end of September. Salmon fishing begins in June and also continues to the end of September. The mayfly season usually lasts a month from the second week in May. There's no closed season for bream, eel, pike, perch, roach or rudd.

A coarse-fishing licence or permit is required for Lough Erne and a game permit or licence for fishing in Lower Lough Erne other than from the shore. These can be purchased from the Fermanagh Tourist Information Centre (☎ 66 323110) in Enniskillen or the marina (☎ 68 628118) at Castle Archdale Country Park, which also hires day boats. Most of the rivers in County Fermanagh are privately owned, and information on those rivers where permission need not be sought is available from the tourist office in Enniskillen. It also has a list of ghillies available.

Cruising

The MV *Kestrel* (☎ 66 322882) is a 56-seater waterbus that cruises the lough for 1¾ hours, calling at Devenish Island along the way. It departs from the Round 'O' Quay at Brook Park, a short distance out of Enniskillen on the A46 to Belleek. Tours operate from Easter to September (call to check times) and cost £5/2.50.

The *Inishcruiser* (☎ 68 628550) offers two-hour cruises from the Inishclare restaurant complex at Killadeas 11km north of Enniskillen. Tours run from April to September and cost £7/3.50. You can also take a 90-minute trip (☎ 67 722122) aboard a Viking longboat replica from the Share Centre on the Derrylin road about 7km from Lisnaskea. Tours cost £4/3 (families £12).

There are about nine companies in Fermanagh that hire out cruisers on a weekly basis. The rates vary from about £400 for a four-berth to about £1100 for an eight-berth. Just as many companies also rent out day boats at Belleek, Enniskillen, Garrison, Kesh, Killadeas and Newtownbutler. Prices start at about £25 for a four-person rowing boat with outboard engine and £50 for six-seater with front cabin and diesel inboard engine. The tourist office in Enniskillen has a full list of the companies and costs.

AROUND LOUGH ERNE

There are a number of ancient religious sites and other antiquities around Lough Erne. In early Christian times the lough was an important highway providing a route from the Donegal coast to inland Leitrim. Churches and monasteries acted as staging posts, and in medieval times there was an important pilgrim route to Station Island in Donegal that went via Lough Erne.

The village of Belleek, famous for its chinaware, is just inside the Northern Irish border and easily reached from either side of the lough.

The places below are set out in an anti-clockwise tour north from Enniskillen.

Devenish Island

The most extensive of the ancient sites at Lough Erne is Devenish Island (Daimh Inis). A monastery here, founded by St Molaise in the 6th century, was sacked by Vikings in 837 in just one of the many incidents of its colourful history. There are church and abbey ruins, some fascinating old gravestones, an unusual 15th-century high cross, an excellent small museum and one of the best round towers in Ireland. The 25m-high tower dates from the 12th century and is in perfect condition.

A ferry runs across to the site from Trory Point landing, some 6.5km north of Enniskillen. To get there, take the A32 heading for Irvinestown and after 5km look for the sign on the left. It's just after a Burmah service station and before the junction where roads fork left to Kesh and right to Omagh. The ferry runs continuously from 10 am to 6.30 pm Tuesday to Saturday, and 2 to 7 pm on Sunday, April to September. The return fare is £2.25/1.20 and the crossing takes 10 minutes.

Killadeas Churchyard

Tucked away in a small graveyard stands the **Bishop's Stone**, a remarkable stone carving dating from between the 7th and 9th centuries that encapsulates the transition from Celtic Paganism to Christianity. The face that stares out from the front seems quite at odds with the side engraving of a bishop with bell and crozier.

Just after the turn-off for Devenish Island on the A32, follow the B82 along the shoreline towards Kesh and look for the sign to the Manor House Country Hotel. Continue past this sign for just over 1km and look for the small church on the left side of the road.

White Island

White Island, close to the eastern shore of the lough, has the remains of a small 12th-century **church** containing a line of eight statues thought to date from as early as the

TYRONE & FERMANAGH

6th century. Nothing remains of the earlier monastic settlement except the boundary bank that can still be made out on the far side of the church. The most impressive surviving part of the church is the Romanesque door on the southern side.

The eight **stone figures** are intriguing. The first resembles a sheila-na-gig, while the next is of someone reading a book or holding some object. Number three is obviously ecclesiastical. The next one has been identified as the young David, but the meaning of his hand pointing to his mouth has been lost. Number five is a curly-haired figure holding the necks of two griffin-like birds. Number six has a military appearance, number seven is unfinished and the last one is a single frowning face that resembles a death mask.

From April to September a ferry runs across to the island from the marina in Castle Archdale Country Park, which is 16km north of Enniskillen on the Kesh road (B82). The ferry operates every hour on the hour from 10 am to 7 pm daily and costs £3/2. The sailing takes 15 minutes.

Drumskinny Stone Circle & Alignment

This circle is made up of 39 stones with a small cairn and an alignment of two dozen stones and dates back to the Bronze Age. The circle is 7km north-east of Kesh and signposted just beyond the junction with the road to Boa Island.

Boa Island

At the northern end of the Lower Lough is narrow Boa Island, which is connected at both ends by bridges to the shore. The **Janus figure** (also known as the Lusty Man) in Caldragh graveyard could be 2000 years old, one of the oldest stone statues in Ireland and quite unparalleled. Another, more recent, stone figure stands beside it.

There's just a small sign to the cemetery, about 1km from the bridge at the western end of the island, 6km from the eastern-end bridge.

Castle Caldwell Forest Park

At the entrance to the park, the **Fiddler's Stone** is a memorial to a musician who fell off a boat in a drunken stupor and drowned in 1770. The castle itself was built between 1610 and 1619, but all that remains is a ruin. The park is a nature reserve full of birdlife and the main breeding ground of the common scoter duck. There are three colour-coded walks ranging from 1.5km to 4km. The park is about 5km west of Boa Island along the A47.

Sheila-na-Gig

The term sheila-na-gig is probably an anglicisation of Síle na Gcíoch (Sheila of the Teats). It refers to crude carvings of women displaying exaggerated genitalia on the outside of certain medieval churches and buildings. One theory traces their origin back to the exhibitionist figures found in French Romanesque churches that illustrated the ungodly powers threatening men.

Another theory is that they're representations of Celtic war goddesses. Early Irish sagas such as the epic *Táin Bó Cúailnge* (*Cattle Raid of Cooley*) refer to women using overt genital display as a weapon to subdue the hero Cúchulainn. This may have encouraged the belief that the Sheilas could ward off evil and hence explain their incorporation into early-Christian architecture.

Other theories are that they may have been connected with some sort of fertility cult or used as a fetish against the evil eye.

MATT KING

Belleek
pop 550

The main reason for stopping in the village of Belleek is to visit the world-famous Belleek **pottery works** (☎ 68 659300), which has been producng fine china since 1857.

There are regular tours every 20 minutes, from 9 am on weekdays, the last tour beginning at 4.30 pm (except on Friday, when the last one is at 3.30 pm). The small museum at the visitor centre, the showroom and café are open daily, April to October, and on weekdays, November to March.

Also in Belleek is the **ExplorErne Exhibition** (☎ 68 658866), which tells the story of the Fermanagh lakeland. It opens 10 am to 6 pm daily, mid-March to October.

Lough Navar Forest

In this coniferous forest, on the western shore of Lough Erne, an 11km scenic road leads up to a viewing point overlooking the lough and the mountains to the north. A section of the Ulster Way passes through the forest. An entry ticket costs £2 per car. The park is signposted off the A46.

Tully Castle

A signposted left turn off the A46 some 16km south-east of Belleek leads to Tully Castle. The castle was built in 1613 as a fortified home for a Scottish Planter's family, but it was captured and burned by Roderick Maguire in 1641. The bawn (cattle enclosure) has four corner towers and retains a lot of the original paving. The vaulted ground floor has a large fireplace with an equally large staircase leading to the 2nd floor and attics above that.

The castle opens 10 am to 7 pm Tuesday to Saturday, and 2 to 7 pm on Sunday, April to September.

Monea Castle

Continuing south on the A46 towards Enniskillen there is a signposted turn to the right to the B81 and Monea Castle. This was built as the best of Fermanagh's Plantation castles around the same time as Tully Castle. It too was captured in the 1641 rising but remained in use until the mid-18th century, when it was gutted by fire. The main entrance has two imposing circular towers topped with built-out squares in a style that can be found in contemporary Scottish castles. There's no charge for viewing the remains. A crannóg sits in the nearby lake.

Crom Estate

Situated on the shores of Upper Lough Erne, south-west of Newtownbutler, the National Trust's Crom Estate (☎ 67 738174) covers 760 hectares of woodland, parkland and wetlands. There are numerous walking trails and several ornamental buildings, including the ruins of old Crom Castle, a boathouse and an island folly. There are boats and bicycles for hire, seven cottages available as *self-catering accommodation* (upwards of £185 per week) and *camping* facilities. The estate is open from 10 am to 6 pm Monday to Saturday and noon to 6 pm on Sunday, between April and September.

Places to Stay

Camping The *Castle Archdale Caravan Park* (☎ 68 621333), 12km north-east of Enniskillen, is dominated by on-site caravans, but has good facilities. Tents cost £10, caravans £12. Outside Kesh, *Lakeland Caravan Park* (☎ 68 631578) also has caravan and tent sites.

On the other side of the lough at Blaney, on the A46 to Belleek and behind the Blaney service station, *Blaney Caravan Park* (☎ 68 641634) has tent/caravan sites costing £6/11. South of Enniskillen and about 2km north-west of Lisnaskea near Upper Lough Erne, camping is possible at *Mullynascarthy Caravan Park* (☎ 67 721040) costing £6/11, and *Share Holiday Village* (☎ 67 722122) in Shanaghy for £7/10.

Hostels There's an excellent and very peaceful YHANI hostel at *Castle Archdale Country Park* (☎ 68 628118) which is housed in converted 18th-century stables. Beds cost £8.25. It opens from March to

TYRONE & FERMANAGH

October. Ulsterbus No 194 from Enniskillen to Pettigo stops outside the park, from where the hostel is a 15-minute walk, but it runs only when school is in session. At other times take the bus to Lisnarrick Corner (four departures daily), which will drop you off about 1.5km from the park.

B&Bs There are plenty of B&Bs along the roads that skirt either side of Lough Erne. *Lakeview Farm* (☎ 68 641263) is on the A46 at Blaney, with singles/doubles costing £17/32. On the other side of the lough at Killadeas, *Beeches* (☎ 66 628527) has four rooms costing £20/25 and boats for hire. *Greenwood Lodge* (☎ 68 631366) in Ederney, east of Kesh, charges £20/35 for B&B. In Belleek itself, *The Fiddlestone* (☎ 66 658008, 15 Main St) is a friendly place with five rooms costing £18 per person and a lively bar downstairs.

Hotels The grandly situated *Manor House Country Hotel* (☎ 68 621561), overlooking Lough Erne about 11km from Enniskillen in Killadeas on the B82 to Kesh, has 46 rooms costing £70/90 for singles/doubles. At the 18-room *Mahon's Hotel* (☎ 68 621656, Mill St) in the centre of Irvinestown the rates are £37.50/70, and the bar is packed with local people at the weekend. *Drumshane Hotel* (☎ 68 621146), in Lisnarick due west of Irvinestown, is a good 10-room hotel with a restaurant, a grand piano in the bar and rooms costing £32.50/65. On the main street in Lisnaskea, *Ortine Hotel* (☎ 67 721206) has 18 rooms costing £28.50/47.

Places to Eat
Open daily, the restaurant at *Manor House Country Hotel* (see Places to Stay, earlier)

has à la carte and set dinners costing around £20 per person. There's traditional and country music at the weekend in summer. *Inishclare Complex* (☎ 68 628550), just north of Killadeas, has a good restaurant and bistro with great lough views.

In Irvinestown, 13km due north of Enniskillen, *Hollander* (☎ 68 621231, 5 Main St) is a family-run pub-restaurant with a reputation for good food at reasonable prices. Reservations are recommended. The restaurant opens for lunch and dinner daily. Across the road from Hollander, *Central Bar* serves food during the day and was a popular watering hole for US pilots.

North-west of Kesh on Boa Island, *Lusty Beg Island* (☎ 68 631342) serves everything from smoked Irish salmon to baked potatoes. It opens for lunch and dinner daily and there's a tearoom in the summer.

In Belleek, *Cleary's Corner Bar* (5 Main St) serves pub grub from noon Monday to Saturday and has traditional Irish music on Friday.

Getting There & Away
From Enniskillen, Ulsterbus No 64 runs on Tuesday, Thursday and Saturday to Belleek (1¼ hours) via Garrison on the western side of Lower Lough Erne. Bus No 99 also goes to Belleek, following the western shoreline through Blaney (15 minutes) past Tully Castle and Lough Navar Forest. On the eastern side bus No 194 runs daily to Irvinestown (35 minutes), Lisnarick (50 minutes) and Kesh (one hour).

Getting Around
Cycle-Ops (☎ 68 631850), Mantlin Rd, Kesh, hires bikes for £7.50 per day (half-day £5). It also has tandems, and child seats are available.

Language

In my cottage I have never heard a word of English from the women except when they are speaking to pigs or dogs.

JM Synge, *The Aran Islands*

Although English is the main language of Ireland, it's spoken with a peculiar Irish flavour and lilt. Indeed the Irish accent is one of the most pleasant varieties of English to be heard. Some of the peculiarly Irish sentence constructions in English are closely related to the Irish language. For instance, the usual word order in Irish sentences is verb, subject, object. The present participle is also used more frequently, in constructions such as 'Would you be wanting a room for the night, then?' Another peculiarity is the use of 'after' as in 'I'm after going to the shop', meaning 'I've just been to the shop'. The Irish also make good use of scatological references in their speech – the word *shite* often finds its way into everyday conversation.

English is spoken throughout Ireland, but there are parts of western and southern Ireland known as Gaeltacht areas where Irish is the native language – Kerry, Galway, Mayo, the Aran Islands, Donegal, and An Rinn in County Waterford (and there's also a small pocket in Meath). The number of native speakers is around 83,000. Irish is a Celtic language, probably first introduced to Ireland by the Celts in the last few centuries BC. Irish is similar to Scottish Gaelic, and has much in common with Welsh and Breton.

Officially the Republic of Ireland is bilingual, and many official documents and roadsigns are printed in both Irish and English. The reality, however, is a little bit more complex.

Until the time of the Plantation in the late 16th and early 17th centuries, successive invaders had been assimilated and had adopted the Irish language. From the time of the Plantation, Irish was seen as the language of the old Irish aristocracy, the poor and the dispossessed; strenuous efforts were consequently made by the English to wipe it out. Social advancement meant giving up Irish. When independence was achieved in 1921 efforts were made to revive the language, but progress has been slow.

Irish is compulsory in both primary and secondary schools in the Republic, and most colleges and universities require prospective students to pass the subject in their school-leaving exams. Despite this – partly because too much emphasis is placed on the complex grammar and too little on speaking the language – most Irish school leavers would be hard pressed to hold a simple conversation in Irish, despite having just completed 13 years of daily classes in it. Many complain that it's a waste of time studying a difficult language that's not in everyday use.

However, attitudes are changing and speaking Irish no longer carries a stigma. Even in Dublin there's a revival, with several Irish-medium infant and junior schools, and a local radio station broadcasting in Gaelic. The national Irish-language radio station, Radio na Gaeltachta, broadcasts from Connemara; Telefis na Ghaelige is the national Irish-language TV station; and RTE, the Republic's state-sponsored broadcaster, has daily news bulletins and programmes in Irish. An increasing number of people derive intense satisfaction from speaking and keeping alive an ancient aspect of Ireland's culture. Irish is also one of the official languages of the European Union.

Lonely Planet's *Western Europe phrasebook* devotes a chapter to the Irish language.

Pronunciation
There are three main varieties of pronunciation of Irish in the Gaeltacht areas. These are: Connaught Irish (Galway and northern Mayo), Munster Irish (Cork, Kerry, Waterford) and Ulster Irish (Donegal). The pronunciation guidelines given here (in italics) are an anglicised-spelling version of the 'standard' form, an amalgam of the three dialects.

775

Vowels

a	as in 'cat'
á	as in 'saw'
e	as in 'bet'
é	as in 'hey!'
i	as in 'sit'
í	as in 'fine'
o	as in 'son'
ó	as in 'cow'
u	as in 'but'
ú	as in 'put'

Consonants

c	as in 'cat'
ch	as the 'ch' in the Scottish 'loch'
d	as in 'do' when followed by 'o' or 'u'; as the 'j' in 'jug' when followed by 'e' or 'i'
dh	as the 'y' in 'young' when followed by 'e' or 'i'; as the 'g' in 'huge' when followed by 'o' or 'u'
t	as the 'ch' in 'church' when followed or preceded by 'e' or 'i'; as the 't' in 'toast' when followed or preceded by 'o' or 'u'
th	as the 'h' in 'house'; sometimes silent at the end of a word
s	as the 'sh' in 'shirt'

Greetings & Civilities

Hello.	Dia Dhuit. (lit: God be with you)
	dee-a-gwit
Goodbye.	Slán Agat.
	slawn aguth
Good night.	Oiche mhaith.
	eehah woh
Welcome.	Céad mhíle fáilte. (lit: 100,000 welcomes)
	kade meela fawltcha
Thank you.	Go raibh maith aguth.
	goh rev moh aguth
Thank you very much.	Gur a mhíle maith agat.
	gur a mila moh agut
Please.	Le do thoil.
	le do hull
Excuse me.	Gabh mo leiscéil.
	gamoh lesh scale
How are you?	Conas a tá tú?
	kunas a taw too?

I'm fine.	Táim go maith.
	thawm gohmoh
What's your name?	Cad is anim duit?
	cod is anim dit?
My name is (Sean).	(Sean) is anim dom.
	(Sean) iss anim duhm
Yes.	Tá/Sea.
	thaw/shah
No/It is not.	Níl/Ní hea.
	neel/nee hah
another/one more	ceann eile
	keown ella
good, fine, OK	go maith
	go moh
nice	go deas
	goh d'yass

Questions & Comments

Why?	Cén fáth?
	kane faw?
What is this?	Cad é seo?
	kod ay shoh?
What is that?	Cad é sin?
	kod ay shin?
How much/ How many?	Cé mhéid?
	kay vaid?
Where is...?	Cá bhfuil...?
	kaw will...?
Which way?	Cén slí?
	kane shlee?
I don't understand.	Ní thuigim.
	nee higgim
big/small	mór/beag
	moor/beeugh
expensive	ana dhaor (lit: very dear)
	ana gare
open/closed	oscailte/dúnta
	uskulta/doonta
slowly/quickly	go mall/go tapaidh
	guh mowl/guh topigg

Getting Around

I'd like to go to...	Ba mhaith liom dul go dtí...
	baw woh lum dull go dee ...
I'd like to buy...	Ba mhaith liom cheannach...
	bah woh luhm kyanok...

ticket	ticéid	
	tickaid	
boat/ship	bád/long	
	bawd/lung	
car/bus	gluaisteáin/bus	
	glooshtawn/bus	
here/there	anseo/ansin	
	anshuh/onshin	
stop/go	stad/ar aghaidh	
	stod/err eyeg	
town square	lár an baile	
	lawr an vollyeh	
street/road	sráid/bóthar	
	sroyed/bowher	
town/city	baile/cathair	
	bollyeh/kawher	
bank/shop	an banc/siopa	
	an bonk/shuppa	

Accommodation

one night	oíche amháin	
	eeheh a woin	
one person	aon duine	
	ayn dinna	
bed/room	leaba/seomra	
	leeabah/showmra	
hotel	óstán	
	oh stahn	
bed & breakfast	loístín oíche	
	leestin eeheh	

Time & Days

What time is it?	Cén tam é?	
	kane towm ay?	

Signs

TOILET	LEITHREAS
	lehrass
MEN	FIR
	fear
WOMEN	MNÁ
	m'naw
POLICE	GARDAI
	gardee
POST OFFICE	OIFIG AN PHOIST
	if-ig on pwisht
TELEPHONE	TELEFÓN
	tay lay foan
TOWN CENTRE	ANLÁR
	an laah

7 o'clock	seacht a chlog	
	shocked ah klug	
today/tomorrow	inniu/amárach	
	innyuv/amawrok	
hour/minute	huair/noiméid	
	oor/nomade	
week/month	seachtain/mí	
	shocktin/mee	

Monday	dé luan	*day loon*
Tuesday	dé máirt	*day mawrt*
Wednesday	dé céadaoin	*day kaydeen*
Thursday	déardaoin	*daredeen*
Friday	dé haoine	*day heena*
Saturday	dé sathairn	*day saheren*
Sunday	dé domhnaigh	*day downick*

Numbers

½	leath	*lah*
1	aon	*ayn*
2	dó	*doe*
3	trí	*three*
4	cathar	*kahirr*
5	cúig	*koo-ig*
6	sé	*shay*
7	seacht	*shocked*
8	ocht	*ukth*
9	naoi	*nay*
10	deich	*jeh*
11	aon deag	*ayen deeuct*
12	dó deag	*doe dayugg*
20	fiche	*feh-ha*
21	fiche aon	*feekh-ayn*
30	tríocha	*chree-okha*
40	daichead	*daykh-ayd*
50	caoga	*ka-uga*
60	seasca	*shay-ska*
70	seachtó	*shocked-ow*
80	ochtó	*ukth-ow*
90	nócha	*now-kha*
100	céad	*kade*
1000	míle	*meal-ah*

Glossary

AIB – Allied Irish Bank
An Óige – literally The Youth; Republic of Ireland Youth Hostel Association
An Taisce – National Trust for the Republic of Ireland
Anglo-Norman – Norman, English and Welsh peoples who invaded Ireland in the 12th century
ard – literally high; Irish place name
ard rí – Irish 'high king'

bailey – outer wall of a castle
banshee – female spirit whose wailing warns of impending death
bawn – area surrounded by walls outside the main castle, acting as a defence as well as a place to keep cattle in time of trouble
beehive hut – circular stone building shaped like an old-fashioned beehive
Black and Tans – British recruits to the Royal Irish Constabulary shortly after WWI, noted for their brutality
Blarney Stone – bending over backwards to kiss this sacred rock in Blarney Castle, County Cork, is said to bestow the gift of the gab, or allow you to 'gain the privilege of telling lies for seven years'
bodhrán – pronounced 'bore-run'; hand-held goatskin drum
Bord Fáilte – literally Welcome Board; Republic of Ireland Tourist Board
botharin – small lane or roadway; also known as boreen
Bronze Age – earliest metal-using period, around 2500 BC to 300 BC in Ireland, after the Stone Age and before the *Iron Age*
B-specials – Northern Irish auxiliary police force, disbanded in 1971
bullaun – stone with a depression, probably used as a mortar for grinding medicine or food and often found on monastic sites

CAC IRA – Continuity Army Council of the IRA, a breakaway group
caher – circular area enclosed by stone walls
cairn – mound of stones heaped over a prehistoric grave

cashel – stone-walled circular fort; see also *ráth*
cath – literally battle; Irish place name
ceilí – pronounced 'kay-lee'; session of traditional music and dancing
Celts – *Iron Age* warrior tribes which arrived in Ireland around 300 BC and controlled the country for 1000 years
chancel – eastern end of a church, where the altar is situated, reserved for the clergy and choir
cill – literally church; Irish place name; also known as kill
Claddagh ring – ring worn in much of Connaught since the mid-18th century, with a crowned heart nestling between two hands; if the heart points towards the hand then the wearer is taken or married, towards the fingertip means he or she is looking for a mate
clochán – dry-stone beehive hut from the early Christian period
control zone – area of a town centre, usually the main street, where parked cars must have at least one person inside
craic – conversation, gossip, fun, good times; also known as crack
crannóg – artificial island made in a lake to provide habitation in a good defensive position
creel – basket
crios – multicoloured woven woollen belt traditionally worn in the Aran Islands
cromlech – see *dolmen*
currach – rowing boat made of a framework of laths covered with tarred canvas; also known as cúrach

Dáil – lower house of the Republic of Ireland Parliament
dairtheach – oratory, a small room set aside for private prayer
DART – Dublin Area Rapid Transport train line
demesne – landed property close to a house or castle
diamond – town square

dolmen – tomb chamber or portal tomb made of vertical stones topped by a huge capstone, dating from around 2000 BC

drumlin – rounded hill formed by retreating glaciers

Dúchas – government department in charge of parks, monuments and gardens in the Republic; formerly known as the Office of Public Works

dún – fort, usually constructed of stone

DUP – Democratic Unionist Party, hardline Northern Irish Protestant loyalist party founded by Ian Paisley

Éire – the Irish name for the Republic of Ireland

esker – gravel ridge

Fianna – mythical band of warriors who feature in many tales of ancient Ireland

Fianna Fáil – literally Warriors of Ireland; major political party in the Republic of Ireland, originating from the *Sinn Féin* faction opposed to the 1921 treaty with Britain

Fine Gael – literally Tribe of the Gael; major political party in the Republic, originating from the *Sinn Féin* faction that favoured the 1921 treaty with Britain; formed the first government of independent Ireland but has subsequently gained power only as part of a coalition; see also *Fianna Fáil*

fir – literally men, singular 'fear; sign on men's toilets

fulacht fiadh – *Bronze Age* cooking place

Gaeltacht – Irish-speaking area

gallery grave – tunnel-shaped burial chamber

garda – Irish Republic police; plural gardaí

ghillie – fishing or hunting guide; also known as ghilly

gort – literally field; Irish place name

Gothic – style of architecture characterised by pointed arches, common in Ireland from the late 12th to the 16th century

Hibernia – literally the Land of Winter; Roman name for Ireland; the Romans had confused Ireland with Iceland

hill fort – usually dating from the Iron Age, hill forts are formed by a ditch that follows the contour of the hill to surround and fortify the summit

Iarnród Éireann – Republic of Ireland Railways

INLA – Irish National Liberation Army, extremist *IRA* splinter group

IRA – Irish Republican Army, dedicated to the removal of British troops from the North and the reunification of Ireland

IRB – Irish Republican Brotherhood, a secret society, founded in 1858 and revived in the early 20th century, that believed in independence through violence if necessary; precursor to the *IRA*; also known as the Fenians

Iron Age – in Ireland this lasted from the end of the *Bronze Age* around 300 BC (the arrival of the *Celts*) to the arrival of Christianity around the 5th century AD

jarvey – driver of a jaunting car

jaunting car – Killarney's traditional horse-drawn transport

keep – main tower of a castle

Lambeg drum – very large drum associated with Protestant loyalist marches

leprechaun – mischievous elf or sprite from Irish folklore

lough – lake, long narrow bay or arm of the sea

loyalist – person, usually a Northern Irish Protestant, insisting on the continuation of Northern Ireland's links with Britain

Mesolithic – (also known as Middle Stone Age) time of the first human settlers in Ireland, about 8000 BC to 4000 BC

mná – literally women; sign on women's toilets

motte – early Norman fortification consisting of a raised, flattened mound with a keep on top; when attached to a *bailey* it is known as a motte and bailey fort, many of which were built in Ireland until the early 13th century

naomh – holy or saint

nationalist – proponent of a united Ireland

Neolithic – (also known as New Stone Age) period characterised by settled agriculture and lasting from around 4000 BC to 2500 BC in Ireland; followed by the *Bronze Age*

NIR – Northern Ireland Railways

NITB – Northern Ireland Tourist Board

North, The – political entity of Northern Ireland, not the northernmost geographic part of Ireland

Ogham stone – Ogham (pronounced 'o-am') was the earliest form of writing in Ireland, using a variety of notched strokes placed above, below or across a keyline, usually on stone

Oireachtas – Parliament of the Republic, consisting of a lower and upper house, the *Dáil* and Senate

Orange Order – loyalist Protestant organisation in Northern Ireland that takes its name from William of Orange, the Protestant victor of the Battle of the Boyne; members are known as Orangemen and they meet in Orange Lodges

óstán – hotel

Palladian – style of architecture developed by Andrea Palladio (1508–80), based on ancient Roman architecture

Partition – division of Ireland in 1921

passage grave – Celtic tomb with a chamber reached by a narrow passage, typically buried in a mound

penal laws – laws passed in the 18th century forbidding Catholics to buy land, hold public office and so on

Plantation – settlement of Protestant migrants in Ireland in the 17th century

poteen – pronounced 'potcheen'; illegally brewed potato-based firewater

Prod – slang for Northern Irish Protestant

Provisionals – Provisional IRA, formed after a break with the official *IRA*, who are now largely inconsequential; named after the provisional government declared in 1916, they have been the main force combating the British army in the *North*

ráth – circular fort with earth banks round a timber wall

Republic of Ireland – the 26 counties of the *South*

republican – supporter of a united Ireland

ring fort – circular habitation area surrounded by banks and ditches, used from the *Bronze Age* right through to the Middle Ages, particularly in the early Christian period

Romanesque – style of architecture seen in 12th-century Irish churches and monasteries, superseded by *Gothic* in the late 12th century; characterised by rounded arches and vaulting

round tower – tall circular tower dating from around the 9th to 11th centuries, built as a lookout and sanctuary during the period when monasteries were frequently subject to Viking raids

RUC – Royal Ulster Constabulary, at the time of writing the name for the armed Northern Irish police force

SDLP – Social Democratic Labour Party of Northern Ireland, representing predominantly liberal, middle-class opinion opposed to violence; mostly Catholic

seisún – music session

sept – clan

shamrock – clover, a plant with three leaves said to have been used by St Patrick to illustrate the Holy Trinity

shebeen – from the Irish 'síbín'; illicit drinking place or speakeasy

sheila-na-gig – literally Sheila of the teats; female figure with exaggerated genitalia, carved in stone on the exteriors of some churches and castles; various explanations have been offered for the iconography, ranging from male clerics warning against the perils of sex to the idea that they represent Celtic war goddesses

shillelagh – stout club or cudgel, especially one made of oak or blackthorn

Sinn Féin – literally We Ourselves; political wing of the *IRA* formed in the early 20th century

Six Counties – the six out of nine counties of the old province of *Ulster* that form Northern Ireland

slí – hiking trail or *way*

snug – partitioned-off drinking area in a pub

souterrain – underground chamber usually associated with ring and hill forts; probably provided a hiding place or escape route in times of trouble and/or storage space for goods

South, The – Republic of Ireland

standing stone – upright stone set in the ground, common across Ireland and dating from a variety of periods; usually the purpose is obscure, though some are burial markers

tánaiste – Republic of Ireland deputy prime minister

taoiseach – pronounced 'teashock'; Republic of Ireland prime minister

TD – teachta Dála; member of the Republic of Ireland Parliament

teampall – church

Tinkers – derogatory term used to describe Irish gypsies, communities that roam the country; see also *Travellers*

trá – beach or strand

Travellers – the politically correct term used today to describe Ireland's itinerant communities

Treaty – Anglo-Irish Treaty of 1921, which divided Ireland and gave relative independence to the *South*; cause of the Civil War of 1922-3

Tricolour – green, white and orange Irish flag designed to symbolise the hoped-for union of the green Catholic Southern Irish with the orange Protestant Northern Irish

turlough – from the Irish 'turlach'; small lake that often disappears in dry summers

26 Counties – Republic of Ireland

UDA – Ulster Defence Association, loyalist Northern Irish paramilitary organisation

Ulster – one of the four ancient provinces of Ireland; a term sometimes used to describe the six counties of the *North*, despite the fact that Ulster also includes Cavan, Monaghan and Donegal in the Republic

unionist – person who wants to retain Northern Ireland's links with Britain

United Irishmen – organisation founded in 1791 aiming to reduce British power in Ireland; led a series of unsuccessful risings and invasions

UUP – Ulster Unionist Party, the principal Northern Irish Protestant political party, founded by Edward Carson

UVF – Ulster Volunteer Force, an illegal loyalist Northern Irish paramilitary organisation

Volunteers – offshoot of the *IRB* that came to be known as the *IRA*

way – long-distance trail

YHANI – Youth Hostel Association of Northern Ireland

Appendix – Place Names

Place	Irish Name	County
Achill	An Caol	Mayo
Adare	Áth Dara	Limerick
Adrigole	Eadargóil	Cork
Allihies	Na hAilichí	Cork
Annagry	Anagaire	Donegal
Annalong	Áth na Long	Down
Annascaul	Abhainn an Scáil	Kerry
Antrim	Aontroim	Antrim
Aran Islands	Oileáin Árainn	Galway
Ardara	Árd na Rátha	Donegal
Ardboe	Ard Bo	Tyrone
Ardee	Baile Átha Fhirdhia	Louth
Ardfert	Ard Fhearta	Kerry
Ardglass	Ard Ghlais	Down
Ardmore	Ard Mór	Waterford
Ards Peninsula	An Aird	Down
Arklow	An tInbhear Mór	Wicklow
Arlow	Eatharlach	Tipperary
Armagh	Ard Mhacha	Armagh
Arranmore	Árainn Mhór	Donegal
Athlone	Baile Átha Luain	Westmeath
Athy	Áth Í	Kildare
Avoca	Abhóca	Wicklow
Ballina	Béal an Átha	Mayo
Ballinasloe	Béal Átha na Sluaighe	Galway
Ballinspittle	Béal Átha an Spidéil	Cork
Ballintober	Bail an Tobair	Roscommon
Ballintoy	Baile an Tuaighe	Antrim
Ballybofey	Bealach Féich	Donegal
Ballybunion	Baile an Bhuinneánaigh	Kerry
Ballycastle	Baile an Chaisil	Antrim, Mayo
Ballyferriter	Baile an Fheirtearaigh	Kerry
Ballyheigue	Baile Uí Thaidg	Kerry
Ballyliffin	Baile Lifin	Donegal
Ballylongford	Bea Atha Longphuirb	Kerry
Ballymena	An Baile Meánach	Antrim
Ballynahinch	Baile na hInse	Down
Ballyshannon	Béal Átha Seanaidh	Donegal
Ballyvaughan	Baile Uí Bheacháin	Clare
Banbridge	Droíchead na Banna	Down
Bandon	Droichead na Banndan	Cork
Bangor	Beannchar	Down
Bansha	An Bháinseach	Tipperary
Bantry	Beanntrai	Cork
Belfast	Beál Feirste	Belfast
Bessbrook	An Sruthán	Armagh
Belmullet	Béal an Mhuirthead	Mayo
Birr	Biorra	Offaly
Blarney	An Bhlarna	Cork
Blasket Islands	Na Blascaodaí	Kerry

782

Place	Irish Name	County
Bloody Foreland	Cnoc Fola	Donegal
Boyle	Mainistir na Búille	Roscommon
Brandon	Cé Bhréannain	Kerry
Bruckless	An Bhroclais	Donegal
Bruree	Brú Rí	Limerick
Bunbeg	An Bun Beag	Donegal
Buncrana	Bun Cranncha	Donegal
Bundoran	Bun Dobhráin	Donegal
Bunratty	Bun Raite	Clare
Burren, The	Boireann	Clare
Burtonport	Ailt an Chórrain	Donegal
Bushmills	Muileann na Buaise	Antrim
Cahir	An Cathair	Tipperary
Carlingford	Cairlinn	Louth
Carlow	Ceatharlach	Carlow
Carndonagh	Cardomhnach	Donegal
Carraroe	An Cheathrú Rua	Galway
Carrick	An Charraig	Donegal
Carrickfergus	Carraig Fhearghais	Antrim
Carrickmacross	Carraig Mhachaire Rois	Monaghan
Carrick-on-Shannon	Cora Droma Rúisc	Leitrim
Carrigaholt	Carraig an Chabaltaigh	Clare
Cashel	Caiseal Mumhan	Tipperary
Castlebar	Caisleán an Bharraigh	Mayo
Castleblayney	Baile na Lorgan	Monaghan
Castlemaine	Caisleán na Mainge	Kerry
Castletownbere	Baile Chais Bhéara	Cork
Cavan	An Cabhán	Cavan
Céide Fields	Achaidh Chéide	Mayo
Charleville	Rath Luirc	Cork
Clare	An Clár	Clare
Clarinbridge	Droichead an Chláirin	Galway
Clear Island	Oileán Cléire	Cork
Cleggan	An Cloiggean	Galway
Clifden	An Clochán	Galway
Cloghane	An Clochán	Kerry
Clones	Cluain Eois	Monaghan
Clonmacnoise	Cluain Mhic Nóis	Offaly
Clonmel	Cluain Meala	Tipperary
Clontarf	Cluain Tarbh	Dublin
Cobh	An Cobh	Cork
Coleraine	Cúil Raithin	Derry
Cong	Conga	Mayo
Connemara	Conamara	Galway
Cookstown	An Chorr Chríochach	Tyrone
Cootehill	An Mhuinchille	Cavan
Cork	Corcaigh	Cork
Corofin	Cora Finne	Clare
Costello	Casla	Galway
Creeslough	An Craoslach	Donegal
Crossmaglen	Crois Mhic Lionnáin	Armagh
Crossmolina	Crois Mhaoiliona	Mayo
Culdaff	Cúil Dabhcha	Donegal
Cushendall	Bun Abhann Dalla	Antrim
Cushendun	Bun Abhann Duinne	Antrim

Place	Irish Name	County
Dalkey	Deilginis	Dublin
Derry/Londonderry	Doire	Derry
Derrybeg	Doirí Beaga	Donegal
Devenish Island	Daimh Inis	Fermanagh
Dingle	An Daingean	Kerry
Donaghadee	Domhnach Daoi	Down
Donegal	Dún na nGall	Donegal
Downpatrick	Dún Pádraig	Down
Dowth	Dubhadh	Meath
Drogheda	Droichead Átha	Louth
Drumshanbo	Droim Seanbhó	Leitrim
Dublin	Baile Átha Cliath	Dublin
Duleek	Damh Liag	Meath
Dundrum	Dún Droma	Down, Tipperary
Dunfanaghy	Dún Fionnachaidh	Donegal
Dungannon	Dún Geanainn	Tyrone
Dungarvan	Dún Garbhán	Waterford
Dungiven	Dún Geimhin	Derry
Dungloe	An Clochán Liath	Donegal
Dunkineely	Dún Cionnfhaolaidh	Donegal
Dunlewy	Dún Lúiche	Donegal
Dunquin	Dún Chaoin	Kerry
Dunree	An Dún Riabhach	Donegal
Easky	Eascaigh	Sligo
Ennis	Inis	Clare
Enniscorthy	Inis Coirthaidh	Wexford
Enniscrone	Innis Crabhann	Sligo
Enniskillen	Inis Ceithleann	Fermanagh
Ennistymon	Inis Díomáin	Clare
Falcarragh	An Fal Carrach	Donegal
Fanore	Fanóir	Clare
Fermoy	Mainistir Fhear Muighe	Cork
Galway	Gaillimh	Galway
Giant's Causeway, The	Clochán an Aifir	Antrim
Glandore	Cuan Dor	Cork
Glenarm	Gleann Arma	Antrim
Glenbeigh	Gleann Beithe	Kerry
Glencolumbcille	Gleann Cholm Cille	Donegal
Glendalough	Gleann dá Loch	Wicklow
Glengarriff	An Gleann Garbh	Cork
Glenties	Na Gleannta	Donegal
Glenveagh	Gleann Beatha	Donegal
Gortahork	Gort an Choirce	Donegal
Gracehill	Baile Uí Chinnéide	Antrim
Great Blasket Island	An Blascaod Mór	Kerry
Greencastle	An Cáisleán Nua	Donegal
Greencastle	Caisleán na hOireanaí	Down
Gweedore	Gaoth Dobhair	Donegal
Hillsborough	Cromghlinn	Down
Holy Island	Inis Cealtra	Clare
Howth	Binn Éadair	Dublin

Place	Irish Name	County
Inch	Inse	Kerry
Inisheer	Inis Oírr	Galway
Inishmaan	Inis Meáin	Galway
Inishmór	Inis Mór/Árainn	Galway
Inishowen	Inis Eoghain	Donegal
Innisfree	Inis Fraoigh	Sligo
Inniskeen	Inis Caoin	Monaghan
Inverin	Indreabhán	Galway
Islandmagee	Oileán Mhic Aodha	Antrim
Kells	Ceanannas Mór	Meath
Kenmare	Neidín	Kerry
Kilcar	Cill Chártha	Donegal
Kildare	Cill Dara	Kildare
Kilfenora	Cill Fhionnúrach	Clare
Kilkee	Cill Chaoi	Clare
Kilkeel	Cill Chaoil	Down
Kilkenny	Cill Chainnigh	Kilkenny
Killala	Cill Alaidh	Mayo
Killaloe	Cill Dalua	Clare
Killarney	Cill Airne	Kerry
Killybegs	Ceala Beaga	Donegal
Killyleagh	Cill O Laoch	Down
Kilmainham	Cill Mhaigneann	Dublin
Kilmallock	Cill Mocheallóg	Limerick
Kilronan	Cill Rónáin	Galway
Kilrush	Cill Rois	Clare
Kingscourt	Dún an Rí	Cavan
Kinsale	Cionn tSáile	Cork
Kinvara	Cinn Mhara	Galway
Knightstown	Baile An Ridire	Kerry
Knock	Cnoc Mhuire	Mayo
Knowth	Cnóbha	Meath
Lahinch	Leacht Uí Chonchubhair	Clare
Lanesborough	Béal Átha Liag	Longford
Larne	Lutharna	Antrim
Lauragh	Laith Reach	Kerry
Leenane	An Líonán	Galway
Leitrim	Liatroim	Leitrim
Letterfrack	Leitir Fraic	Galway
Letterkenny	Leitir Ceanainn	Donegal
Lifford	Leifear	Donegal
Limavady	Léim an Mhadaidh	Derry
Limerick	Luimneach	Limerick
Lisburn	Lios na gCearrbhach	Antrim
Liscannor	Lios Ceannúir	Clare
Lisdoonvarna	Lios Dún Bhearna	Clare
Lismore	Lios Mór	Waterford
Lispole	Lios Póil	Kerry
Listowel	Lios Tuathail	Kerry
Longford	An Longfort	Longford
Loop Head	Ceann Léime	Clare
Lough Neagh	Loch nEathach	Antrim
Loughrea	Baile Locha Riach	Galway
Louisburgh	Cluain Cearbán	Mayo

Place	Irish Name	County
Maam Cross	Crois Mám	Galway
Malahide	Mullach Ide	Dublin
Malin	Málainn	Donegal
Malin Head	Cionn Mhálanna	Donegal
Mallow	Mala	Cork
Maynooth	Maigh Nuad	Kildare
Mayo	Maigh Eo	Mayo
Meath	An Mhí	Meath
Millisle	Oileán an Mhuilinn	Down
Mitchelstown	Baile Mhistéala	Tipperary
Moira	Maigh Rath	Down
Monaghan	Muineachán	Monaghan
Monasterboice	Mainistir Bhuithe	Louth
Monasterevin	Mainistir Eimhín	Kildare
Mt Brandon	Cnoc Bhréannain	Kerry
Mountcharles	Moin Séarbs	Donegal
Mountshannon	Baile Uí Bheoláin	Clare
Moville	Bun an Phoball	Donegal
Muff	Mugh	Donegal
Mullaghmore	An Mullach Mór	Sligo
Mullingar	An Muileann gCearr	Westmeath
Mulrany	An Mhala Raithní	Mayo
Naas	An Nás	Kildare
Navan	An Uaimh	Meath
Nenagh	An tAonach	Tipperary
New Quay	Ceibh Nua	Clare
New Ross	Rhos Mhic Triúin	Wexford
Newbridge	Droichead Nua	Kildare
Newcastle	An Caisleán Nua	Down
Newport	Baile Uí Fhiacháin	Mayo
Newry	An tIúr	Down
Newtownards	Baile Nua na hArda	Down
Ogonnelloe	Tuath Ó gConnaille	Clare
Omagh	An Omaigh	Tyrone
Oughterard	Uachtar Árd	Galway
Pettigo	Paiteagó	Donegal
Pollotomish	Poll an Tómais	Mayo
Portaferry	Port an Pheire	Down
Portarlington	Cúil an tSúdaire	Laois
Portlaoise	Port Laoise	Laois
Portrush	Port Rois	Antrim
Portsalon	Port an tSalainn	Donegal
Portstewart	Port Stíobhaird	Derry
Quin	Chuinche	Clare
Randalstown	Baile Raghnaill	Antrim
Rathfarnham	Ráth Fearnáin	Dublin
Rathlin Island	Reachlainn	Antrim
Rathmelton	Ráth Mealtain	Donegal
Rathmullan	Ráth Maoláin	Donegal
Recess	Straith Salach	Galway
Roscommon	Ros Comáin	Roscommon

Place	Irish Name	County
Roscrea	Ros Cré	Tipperary
Rossaveal	Ros a' Mhíl	Galway
Rosscarbery	Ros O'gCairbre	Cork
Rosses Point	Ross Ceite	Sligo
Rosslare	Ros Láir	Wexford
Rossnowlagh	Ross Neamblach	Donegal
Rostrevor	Caislean Ruairi	Down
Roundstone	Cloch na Rón	Galway
Salthill	Bóthar na Trá	Galway
Scarriff	An Scairbh	Clare
Scattery Island	Inis Cathaigh	Clare
Screeb	Scriob	Galway
Shercock	Searcóg	Cavan
Skellig Islands	Oileáin na Scealaga	Kerry
Skibbereen	Sciobairín	Cork
Slane	Baile Shláine	Meath
Sligo	Sligeach	Sligo
Sneem	An tSnaidhm	Kerry
Spanish Point	Rinn na Spáinneach	Clare
Spiddal	An Spidéal	Galway
Strabane	An Srath Bán	Tyrone
Strangford	Baile Loch Cuan	Down
Strangford Lough	Loch Cuan	Down
Strokestown	Béal na mBuillí	Roscommon
Swords	Sord	Dublin
Tara	Teamhair	Meath
Thurles	Durlas	Tipperary
Tipperary	Tiobraid Árann	Tipperary
Tory Island	Oileán Thóraigh	Donegal
Tralee	Trá Lí	Kerry
Trim	Baile Átha Troim	Meath
Tuam	Tuaim	Galway
Tullamore	Tulach Mór	Offaly
Union Hall	Bréantrá	Cork
Valentia Island	Oileán Dairbhru	Kerry
Ventry	Ceann Trá	Kerry
Virginia	Achadh Lir	Cavan
Warrenpoint	An Pointe	Down
Waterford	Port Láirge	Waterford
Waterville	An Coireán	Kerry
Westmeath	An Iarmhí	Westmeath
Westport	Cathair na Mairt	Mayo
Wexford	Loch Garman	Wexford
Wicklow	Cill Mhantáin	Wicklow
Youghal	Eochaill	Cork

LONELY PLANET

Guides by Region

Lonely Planet is known worldwide for publishing practical, reliable and no-nonsense travel information in our guides and on our Web site. The Lonely Planet list covers just about every accessible part of the world. Currently there are thirteen series: travel guides, shoestring guides, walking guides, city guides, phrasebooks, audio packs, city maps, travel atlases, diving and snorkeling guides, restaurant guides, first-time travel guides, healthy travel and travel literature.

AFRICA Africa – the South • Africa on a shoestring • Arabic (Egyptian) phrasebook • Arabic (Moroccan) phrasebook • Cairo • Cape Town • Cape Town city map• Central Africa • East Africa • Egypt • Egypt travel atlas • Ethiopian (Amharic) phrasebook • The Gambia & Senegal • Healthy Travel Africa • Kenya • Kenya travel atlas • Malawi, Mozambique & Zambia • Morocco • North Africa • South Africa, Lesotho & Swaziland • South Africa, Lesotho & Swaziland travel atlas • Swahili phrasebook • Tanzania, Zanzibar & Pemba • Trekking in East Africa • Tunisia • West Africa • Zimbabwe, Botswana & Namibia • Zimbabwe, Botswana & Namibia travel atlas
Travel Literature: The Rainbird: A Central African Journey • Songs to an African Sunset: A Zimbabwean Story • Mali Blues: Traveling to an African Beat

AUSTRALIA & THE PACIFIC Auckland • Australia • Australian phrasebook • Bushwalking in Australia • Bushwalking in Papua New Guinea • Fiji • Fijian phrasebook • Islands of Australia's Great Barrier Reef • Melbourne • Melbourne city map • Micronesia • New Caledonia • New South Wales & the ACT • New Zealand • Northern Territory • Outback Australia • Out To Eat – Melbourne • Papua New Guinea • Papua New Guinea (Pidgin) phrasebook • Queensland • Rarotonga & the Cook Islands • Samoa • Solomon Islands • South Australia • South Pacific Languages phrasebook • Sydney • Sydney city map • Tahiti & French Polynesia • Tasmania • Tonga • Tramping in New Zealand • Vanuatu • Victoria • Western Australia
Travel Literature: Islands in the Clouds • Kiwi Tracks • Sean & David's Long Drive

CENTRAL AMERICA & THE CARIBBEAN Bahamas and Turks & Caicos • Bermuda • Central America on a shoestring • Costa Rica • Cuba • Dominican Republic & Haiti • Eastern Caribbean • Guatemala, Belize & Yucatán: La Ruta Maya • Jamaica • Mexico • Mexico City • Panama • Puerto Rico
Travel Literature: Green Dreams: Travels in Central America

EUROPE Amsterdam • Amsterdam city map • Andalucía • Austria • Baltic States phrasebook • Barcelona • Berlin • Berlin city map • Britain • British phrasebook • Brussels, Bruges & Antwerp • Budapest city map • Canary Islands • Central Europe • Central Europe phrasebook • Corsica • Croatia • Czech & Slovak Republics • Denmark • Dublin • Eastern Europe • Eastern Europe phrasebook • Edinburgh • Estonia, Latvia & Lithuania • Europe • Finland • France • French phrasebook • Germany • German phrasebook • Greece • Greek phrasebook • Hungary • Iceland, Greenland & the Faroe Islands • Ireland • Italian phrasebook • Italy • Lisbon • London • London city map • Mediterranean Europe • Mediterranean Europe phrasebook • Norway • Paris • Paris city map • Poland • Portugal • Portugal travel atlas • Prague • Prague city map • Provence & the Côte d'Azur • Romania & Moldova • Rome • Russia, Ukraine & Belarus • Russian phrasebook • Scandinavian & Baltic Europe • Scandinavian Europe phrasebook • Scotland • Slovenia • Spain • Spanish phrasebook • St Petersburg • Switzerland • Trekking in Spain • Ukrainian phrasebook • Vienna • Walking in Britain • Walking in Ireland • Walking in Italy • Walking in Switzerland • Western Europe • Western Europe phrasebook
Travel Literature: The Olive Grove: Travels in Greece

INDIAN SUBCONTINENT Bangladesh • Bengali phrasebook • Bhutan • Delhi • Goa • Hindi/Urdu phrasebook • India • India & Bangladesh travel atlas • Indian Himalaya • Karakoram Highway • Kerala • Mumbai • Nepal • Nepali phrasebook • Pakistan • Rajasthan • Read This First: Asia & India • South India • Sri Lanka • Sri Lanka phrasebook • Trekking in the Indian Himalaya • Trekking in the Karakoram & Hindukush • Trekking in the Nepal Himalaya
Travel Literature: In Rajasthan • Shopping for Buddhas

LONELY PLANET

Mail Order

Lonely Planet products are distributed worldwide. They are also available by mail order from Lonely Planet, so if you have difficulty finding a title please write to us. North and South American residents should write to 150 Linden St, Oakland, CA 94607, USA; European and African residents should write to 10a Spring Place, London NW5 3BH, UK; and residents of other countries to PO Box 617, Hawthorn, Victoria 3122, Australia.

ISLANDS OF THE INDIAN OCEAN Madagascar & Comoros • Maldives • Mauritius, Réunion & Seychelles

MIDDLE EAST & CENTRAL ASIA Arab Gulf States • Central Asia • Central Asia phrasebook • Hebrew phrasebook • Iran • Israel & the Palestinian Territories • Israel & the Palestinian Territories travel atlas • Istanbul • Istanbul to Cairo • Jerusalem • Jordan & Syria • Jordan, Syria & Lebanon travel atlas • Lebanon • Middle East on a shoestring • Syria • Turkey • Turkish phrasebook • Turkey travel atlas • Yemen
Travel Literature: The Gates of Damascus • Kingdom of the Film Stars: Journey into Jordan

NORTH AMERICA Alaska • Backpacking in Alaska • Baja California • California & Nevada • Canada • Chicago • Chicago city map • Deep South • Florida • Hawaii • Honolulu • Las Vegas • Los Angeles • Miami • New England • New Orleans • New York City • New York city map • New York, New Jersey & Pennsylvania • Pacific Northwest USA • Puerto Rico • Rocky Mountain States • San Francisco • San Francisco city map • Seattle • Southwest USA • Texas • USA • USA phrasebook • Vancouver • Washington, DC & the Capital Region • Washington DC city map
Travel Literature: Drive Thru America

NORTH-EAST ASIA Beijing • Cantonese phrasebook • China • Hong Kong • Hong Kong city map • Hong Kong, Macau & Guangzhou • Japan • Japanese phrasebook • Japanese audio pack • Korea • Korean phrasebook • Kyoto • Mandarin phrasebook • Mongolia • Mongolian phrasebook • North-East Asia on a shoestring • Seoul • South-West China • Taiwan • Tibet • Tibetan phrasebook • Tokyo
Travel Literature: Lost Japan

SOUTH AMERICA Argentina, Uruguay & Paraguay • Bolivia • Brazil • Brazilian phrasebook • Buenos Aires • Chile & Easter Island • Chile & Easter Island travel atlas • Colombia • Ecuador & the Galapagos Islands • Latin American Spanish phrasebook • Peru • Quechua phrasebook • Rio de Janeiro • Rio de Janeiro city map • South America on a shoestring • Trekking in the Patagonian Andes • Venezuela
Travel Literature: Full Circle: A South American Journey

SOUTH-EAST ASIA Bali & Lombok • Bangkok • Bangkok city map • Burmese phrasebook • Cambodia • Hanoi • Healthy Travel Asia & India • Hill Tribes phrasebook • Ho Chi Minh City • Indonesia • Indonesia's Eastern Islands • Indonesian phrasebook • Indonesian audio pack • Jakarta • Java • Laos • Lao phrasebook • Laos travel atlas • Malay phrasebook • Malaysia, Singapore & Brunei • Myanmar (Burma) • Philippines • Pilipino (Tagalog) phrasebook • Singapore • South-East Asia on a shoestring • South-East Asia phrasebook • Thailand • Thailand's Islands & Beaches • Thailand travel atlas • Thai phrasebook • Thai audio pack • Vietnam • Vietnamese phrasebook • Vietnam travel atlas

ALSO AVAILABLE: Antarctica • The Arctic • Brief Encounters: Stories of Love, Sex & Travel • Chasing Rickshaws • Lonely Planet Unpacked • Not the Only Planet: Travel Stories from Science Fiction • Sacred India • Travel with Children • Traveller's Tales

Index

Text

Bold indicates maps.

Contents – Text

COUNTY WICKLOW   214

COUNTIES WEXFORD & WATERFORD   234

COUNTY CORK   267

COUNTY KERRY   316